The 8th Air Force in World War II

There have been some great traditions
Through a thousand years of kings,
Long centuries of battles fought,
Crusades, campaigns and things
That gave to many regiments
Traditions tried and true,
Honors aged and multiplied,
As they fought decades through

The echo of the trumpeter
Whose repertoire at large,
Embraced but one great battle call:
'Forward! Bayonets! Charge!'
There's the spirit of the Alamo,
of courage unsurpassed;
Concord Bridge and San Juan Hill,
Verdun's 'They shall not pass!'

Such fighting makes tradition.
But today, unlike the past,
A fledgling code, without prelude
Becomes tradition fast.
The Air Force carved its heritage
On the highways of the skies,
Blazing there the fighting code
Of every man who flies.

Yet few know this tradition
The armadas built upstairs,
Where the bombers blazing fifties
Defy the flak and dare
The fighter packs, the rocket bombs
And shell blasts - to attack!
It's a mighty proud tradition
To have 'never been turned back!'

"Men of the 'Fortress,'" Corporal Ellsworth B. Laurence

On the Highways of the Skies

The 8th Air Force in World War II

Martin W. Bowman

Schiffer Military History
Atglen, PA

Book Design by Ian Robertson.

Library of Congress Control Number: 2008936225

Printed in China.
ISBN: 978-0-7643-3090-2

We are interested in hearing from authors with book ideas on related topics.

Published by Schiffer Publishing Ltd.
4880 Lower Valley Road
Atglen, PA 19310
Phone: (610) 593-1777
FAX: (610) 593-2002
E-mail: Info@schifferbooks.com.
Visit our web site at: www.schifferbooks.com
Please write for a free catalog.
This book may be purchased from the publisher.
Please include $5.00 postage.
Try your bookstore first.

In Europe, Schiffer books are distributed by:
Bushwood Books
6 Marksbury Avenue
Kew Gardens
Surrey TW9 4JF, England
Phone: 44 (0) 20 8392-8585
FAX: 44 (0) 20 8392-9876
E-mail: Info@bushwoodbooks.co.uk.
Visit our website at: www.bushwoodbooks.co.uk
Free postage in the UK. Europe: air mail at cost.
Try your bookstore first.

Contents

Acknowledgments

Norman K. Andrew; John Archer; Tom Allen, Walter Austin, William D. Allen, Carl L. Anderson, Mike Bailey; Lieutenant. Colonel Don Baldwin, Marvin Barnes, Ron and Carol Batley of the Thorpe Abbotts Memorial Museum; Lieutenant. Col. Tom Belovich; Jule F. Berndt; William A. Berry, Ray A. Betcher, Franklin L. Betz; Richard Bing; Rudolph Birsic, Bob Bishop, Ken Blakeborough; Theo Boiten; William A. Boutelle; General Harold W. Bowman, Thompson H. Boyd, Stan Brett; Cy Broman; Bob Browne, Eugene F. Britton; Charles L. Brown; Eberhard Burath; Vernon D. Burk, Historian, United States Third Air Force; John W. Butler; Waldo D. Butler, Bill Cameron, Robert Capaldi, Lieutenant Colonel Thomas Cardwell, Bill Carleton, Claude E. Campbell, Frederick L Carr; William L. Case; Ed Chalifoux, Tony Chardella; Donald V. Chase; Guy "Chuck" Chookoorian; Forrest S. Clark, Rougham Tower Assoc; Pete Clark, Ralph S. Cohen; George M. Collar; Howard "Pappy" Colby; Bob Collis; Henry C. Cordery, Coen Cornelissen; Frank Cotner; Walt Cranson; Hugh K. Crawford, Harry H. Crosby, Clyde Crowley; Curt Crouch, Arthur T Cullen; Charles E. Cupp; Tom Cushing; Roy G. Davidson; Philip C. Day; Cyrnik de Decker; Henry A. DeKeyser; Rob de Visser; Abel 'Abe' L. Dolim; Bill Donald; Colonel John Driscoll, Richmond Henre Dugger, General Ira C. Eaker, Georg-Peter Eder; Ralph Elliott, Ralph C. Ernst; Bill Espie; Stewart Evans; Patricia 'Pat' Everson; Sam N. Fain; Michael P. Faley; Robert L. Ferrell; Albert J. Filiponis, Reuben Fier, Thomas J. Fitton; Richard E. Fitzhugh, Robert M. Foose; John C. Ford, George P. Fory; Albert D. Franklin, Friends of the Eighth (FOTE), Norman E. Freidman; Kenneth H. French; Lieutenant. Col. Charles H. Freudenthal; "Hap" Galfunt; Gene Gaskins; Richard Gibson; Edward R. Glotfelty; Lieutenant Colonel Harry D. Gobrecht; Ken Godfrey, John Goldsmith; Larry Goldstein; Lee C. Gordon; Wayne T. Gotke; Chris Gotts, Steve Gotts; Dan Graham, Sol Greenberg, John E. Greenwood, Lee C. Gordon, Hank Gladys, Herman Hager, Alan Hague, Charles J. Halbert, Cliff and Wendy Hall; Frank Halm, Russ Harriman; Charles E. Harris; Cliff Hatcher, Ian Hawkins; Russ D. Hayes, Alan Healy, Henry Heckman; Andy Height; Vincent A. Hemmings; Pete Henry; Leonard W. Herman; Howard E. Hernan, Ed Hicks; John Hildebran, Derek Hills and the staff of the 2nd Air Division Library, Norwich; Harry Holmes; John A. Holden, Virgil R Huddleston; Robert L. 'Bob' Hughes, Ed Huntzinger, John Hurd, Fred Huston; The Imperial War Museum (Air Historical Branch), Glenn B. Infield, Bishop E. Ingraham; Ben C. Isgrig; Loren E. Jackson; Robert A. Jacobs; Joe F. Jones Jr., Dick Johnson; Ivan Johnson, Clifford D. Jones; Edwin O. Jones, Ken 'Deacon' Jones; Philip Kaplan; David Kibble-White; Walter J. Konantz; Jim Kotapish, John Knox, Jake D. Krause, James Kidder, Lieutenant. Gen. M. Keck, Colonel Myron H. Keilman, Friedrich J. Kowalke; Beirne Lay, Jr., Al La Chasse, General Curtis E. LeMay; Louis Lawrence; Alfred R. Lea, Richard E. Lewis, Rusty Lewis, Irving Lifson, Art Livingston, Harry W. Love; Will Lundy; General Lewis Lyle; Bob Maag, Floyd H. Mabee, Ron Mackay; Ped G. Magness, Brian H. Mahoney; James J. Mahoney, George Makin, Edward Matter; Roxy Marotta, George Matecko, Dave Mayor; George Mazzara; John W. McClane; Gerald "Bill" McClelland, Anthony J. McComiskey, Frank McGlinchey, Brian S. McGuire; Ian McLachlan, James Kemp McLaughlin, Newton L. McLaughlin, Duncan McTeer; Nigel McTeer; William B. Menzies, Abe Millar, Dwight N. Miller; John A. Miller, Gus Mencow, Raymond P. Miller, Francis S. Milligan; Ministry of Defence (Air); Werner Molge; Eric Mombeek; Paul Montague, A. F. Moore; Ralph J. Munn; Emmett J. Murphy, Art Nanas, Orlo G. Natvig, Grady Newsom, Don C. Neville, William Nicholls, Wiley S. Noble, Norfolk and Suffolk Aviation Society, Lieutenant. Col Harlan Oakes, Jim O' Brien; Walter Don O'Hearn; Don Olds, Merle C. Olmsted; Malcolm 'Ossie' Osborn, John Page, Ted Parker, George H. Parker, Simon Parry; Ralph K. Patton, Colonel Budd J. Peaslee; General Maurice Preston, Richard H. Perry; Nick G. Plackis; Cliff Pyle, Roy L. Rainwater, Pat Ramm; William C. Rawson; Ralph Reese; George B. Reeves; George Reynolds, Connie and Gordon Richards; Heinz Riediger; Bill Robertie, Wilbur Richardson; Rick Rokicki, William "Bill" Rose, George Rubin; William E. Ruck; Perry Rudd, Jack Rude; Bob Scalley; Ben Schohan; Marty Schreck, Ernst Schröder; Keith C. Schuyler; Robert W. Seelos; George Sesler; Bob Shaffer, Robert H. 'Bob' Sherwood; Francis X. Sheehan, Robert J. Shoens; Colonel Albert E. Shower, Graham and Anne Simons; Fred Sissenstein, Alvin D. Skaggs, Lloyd B. Slimp, Adolph J. Smetana, Judge Ben Smith, Jr.; Derek Smith; Edwin "Ted" Smith, Lloyd T. Smith, W. Griswold Smith, Bob Spangler, Otto Stammberger; Hans-Heri Stapfer; William Sterret, Eric Swain; Robert H. Sweatt, Malvern R. Sweet, William C. Stewart; Paul Surbaugh, Henry Tarcza, Robert H. Tays; Robert H.

Tennenberg; Leslie G. Thibodeau, Frank Thomas; Thorpe Abbotts Memorial Museum; Father G. Thuring, Paul W. Tibbets; Tibenham Aero Club, Ralph J. Tomek; James V. Tootell, Louis J. Torretta; Ralph Trout, United States Embassy; Horace Varian, William W. Varnedoe Jr.; John Vasco; Russell K. Wagner, Fred O. Walsh; Richard Walsh; Geoff Ward, Lowell S. Watts; Perry Watts; Gordon W. Weir; Hank Wentland, Lieutenant General Charles B. Westover, David M. Williams, Alan R. Willis, Dan Winston, Ellis B. Woodward; Lieutenant Colonel John H. Woolnough, Mike Wysoki, Joe Wroblewski, David M. Williams, Henry A. West, Richard J. Walsh, Robert "Peck" Wilcox, Karl Wendel, Peter Wood, Rougham Tower Assoc; Truett Woodall, Jr.; 'Dusty' Worthen, Ken Wright, Richard Wynn; Sam Young; and Earl Zimmerman.

Introduction

In the 1930s one of the main theories about strategic air power was that unescorted bombers could get through to a target if they were arranged properly and armed sufficiently. In America this theory was discussed and taught at the Army Air Corps Tactical School at Maxwell Field, Alabama. There a small, influential group of officers on the faculty, led by Major Harold L George, Major Donald Wilson, 1st Lieutenant Kenneth L Walker, and 2nd Lieutenant Haywood S. "Possum" Hansell, Jr., developed a set of concepts about air power. They believed that air power could directly influence the course of wars by having strategic air forces fly long range missions and destroy an enemy's industrial infrastructure. Further, they taught that these long-range bombers, if properly equipped with defensive armament and organized into massed formations, would be capable of penetrating an enemy's defenses – even in broad daylight - and striking directly at the enemy's will to resist.

As the decade of the 1930s progressed, these teachings developed into an unofficial doctrine of air power that became prominent in WWII. There were doubters. 2nd Lieutenant (later General) Curtis E. LeMay, who was at Selfridge Field in Michigan in the 1930s when the U.S. really did not have an air force, was of the opinion that generally he did not think many ever believed that was the way to do it. He felt they would have to do some unescorted missions if they were going to do any bombing at all. "It could be done, yes, but you paid a price for it. When war in Europe broke out in 1939 RAF Bomber Command certainly paid a price for it. Bombing in daytime in order to see and hit their targets and unescorted, they drifted into bombing mainly at night to keep their losses down to an 'acceptable' level. Then the *Luftwaffe* in the Battle of Britain in the summer of 1940 began to pay a price for it and also switched to bombing by night."

In June 1941 President Franklin D. Roosevelt had approved the plan for the formation of a new, autonomous army division: the Army Air Forces (AAF), although the Air Corps and Air Force Combat Command were to remain in being until 9 March 1942. Major General Henry H. "Hap" Arnold was given overall command of the new service. Arnold and his staff formulated a policy (AWPD/l) of relentless air attacks against Germany, strategic defense in the Pacific Theater, and air operations in the defense of the Western Hemisphere. First priority was given to Germany's electric power grid, followed in importance by its transportation system of rail, road, and canal, then its oil and petroleum industry. It was argued that strategic bombing of these targets, together with the neutralization of the *Luftwaffe* and submarine and naval facilities might render a land campaign unnecessary. The Boeing B-17 Flying Fortress and the Consolidated B-24 Liberator four-engined bombers were to be the prime weapons in the U.S. offensive in Europe, and the method would be daylight precision bombing.

The U.S. Army Air Corps started out bombing in daylight, with better equipment for the purpose (gyroscopically controlled bombsights to carry out precision bombing of specific German targets) and more and better armament than RAF Bomber Command. (Wellingtons, Whitleys, and Hampdens were armed with .30 caliber guns and were not as strong defensively as the B-17 Flying Fortress) In 1942 American and RAF air leaders disagreed on the best method for employing strategic air forces against Germany. Initially the AAF planned to carry out massed daylight strikes against specific targets in Germany, whereas the RAF, relying on the operational experiences learned the hard way in 1939-41, adopted a strategic bombing campaign based on a stream of bombers flying at night and striking "areas" rather than precise targets. The British wanted the USAAF to join RAF Bomber Command in its night bombing offensive. The USAAF, however, was not about to change its daylight precision bombing concept, which had been honed to perfection at ranges at Muroc Dry Lake, in California's Mojave Desert, in 1940 by the B-17B high altitude bombers of the 2nd and 7th Bomb Groups. By using the top secret Norden bombsight, experienced bombardiers found that they could place their practice bombs within yards of the target from as high as 20,000ft – which led to claims that bombs could be dropped in a pickle barrel from such heights. Precision bombing called for attacks in daylight, but the ideal conditions found in California were not often found in Europe, as VIIIth Bomber Command would soon find to its chagrin. Eventually the British, notably Winston Churchill, came to accept the American method of bombing, and it would grow into a formidable "round the clock" bombing strategy that would contribute decisively to the defeat of Germany.

1

The Eagle Spreads its Wings

"...To anyone who inquired, my buddies and I were ready for anything the Germans could throw at us. We were eager to get at them and get the war over. This was light years from the truth. I was about as eager as someone being prepared for radical surgery to his gonads...In desolation I spent my last day at home revisiting the familiar scenes of my youth. I borrowed my dad's car and drove out to Senior High and visited all of my former teachers. They seemed glad to see me and wished me luck. I drove by the tennis courts where I had spent most of my time in the summer playing tenniswith Billy Cromer and Red Henderson.[1] *The corner at Elliston's Drug Store, where the old gang had hung out, was now deserted. There was the Standpipe, long a Waycross landmark and a visual atrocity if ever there was one, but it loked like the Taj Mahal to me. My next stop was the old courthouse, which had always resembled a medieval castle complete with turrets, spires and a bell tower. As a little boy I had followed my dad to court and had seen many spectacular trials there. The town clock struck every hour in those days and it was a sound I dearly loved. I drove out the Savannah Highway and stopped for a beer at Riverside, the nightspot, which all the teenagers had frequented. I put a nickel in the jukebox and played 'Cherry' by Erskine Hawkins and then 'Summit Ridge Drive' by Artie Shaw, but there was no one to dance with. Memorial Bridge was my favorite place, on the beautiful Satilla River. As a child I had roamed its length and breadth, fishing and swimming, hunting and camping. Gazing out over the languid, wine-colored stream, I sat there on the sandbar a long time. I viewed all these scenes as one who was seeing them for the last time. These things were all I had. I was not leaving a wife or a girlfriend behind; I knew nothing of the manifold mysteries of adulthood; and I felt at that moment that I was very likely going to be cheated of all those things. Self- pity consumed me, in this case perhaps justified. I had no choice in the matter either; it was a man's place to go. I was only 20 years old. I did not wish to lay down my life for anyone or any cause; yet the idea that I could refuse to do so was beyond my comprehension."*

Ben Smith, *Chick's Crew*[2]

In the USAAF in 1942 there were thousands of young men eager to fly, and they were trained into accepting that daylight was the best time to fight the aerial war in Europe. The American High Command believed in its own mistaken prophecy that bombers, heavily armed so as not to need escort fighters, could, during daylight hours, penetrate even the strongest defenses and achieve "pickle barrel" bombing accuracy that bombardiers had performed in the clear skies of Texas and the southern states. Drawing upon their own bitter experience of the disastrous daylight bombing campaign of 1939-40, few in the RAF believed that the 8th Air Force in England could succeed where they and the *Luftwaffe* during the Battle of Britain had failed. Eventually the British, notably Winston Churchill, came to accept the American method of bombing, and it would grow into a formidable "round the clock" bombing strategy that would contribute decisively to the defeat of Germany.

Although the United States could not prevent the attack on Pearl Harbor, far-reaching decisions had been made in the event that America should become involved in the conflict with the Axis powers. Between 27 January and 27 March 1941, agreements between the United States and Great Britain were made for the provision of naval, ground, and air support for the campaign against Germany. As a result, a special U.S. Army Observer Group, headed by Major General James E. Chaney, was activated in London on 19 May 1941. One of Chaney's first tasks was to reconnoiter areas regarded as potential sites for U.S. Army Air Force (USAAF) installations. During late 1941 several tentative sites were explored, including Prestwick, near Ayr in Scotland, and Warton, near Liverpool (the proposed site for a repair depot). Others, like Polebrook, Grafton Underwood, Kimbolton, Molesworth, Chelveston, Podington, and Thurleigh, all in the Huntingdon area, would soon become familiar homes to B-17 Flying Fortress groups. On 2 January 1942 the order Major General Henry "Hap" Arnold, the Commanding General, Army Air Forces,[3] signed activated the 8th Air Force, and the headquarters was formed at Savannah, Georgia, 26 days later.[4] Arnold instructed Brigadier-General Ira C. Eaker to assist in the formation of a headquarters for the American air forces in Great Britain. Eaker was designated, as Commanding General of VIII Bomber Command, and his duties were to help prepare airfields and installations, and understudy the methods of RAF Bomber Command. The choice of Eaker for such tasks was ideal.[5] By February 1942 Eaker had appointed six staff officers who would fly with him to England and form the "advance detachment" of VIII Bomber Command. One of them was Beirne Lay, Jr.[6] He recalls:

"I had been a 'first John,' walking down the hall of the old WD Munitions building in Washington in December 1941, when Eaker stopped me. 'Want to come with me?' he asked. 'Yes Sir!' I answered, having no idea what he meant. He walked on. The next thing I knew I was packing for England. En route we golfed for 13 days in Bermuda waiting for good weather for the Pan Am clipper to Lisbon. Portuguese agents ransacked our luggage at the Hotel Metropole. On 20 February we left in civilian clothes and boarded a KLM DC-3 at 0700 at Cintro Land Airport for the one-hour flight to Porto where we were to refuel for the flight to England. I particularly remember Eaker at 'the gate.' The gate was down; no one in sight and our driver just sat. Eaker got out of the ear, strode determinedly to the gate and raised it for us. Typical. At Porto we changed into our uniforms. At 1220 hours we were at 10,000ft when we were nearly shot down by a Messerschmitt 110 in the Bay of Biscay, but his engine started smoking just before he intercepted us and he headed for the French coast. We landed at 3 am at Whitechurch aerodrome Bristol and then we were flown to Hendon in a Flamingo transport aircraft piloted by a group captain. A large party, including Air Vice Marshal Baldwin, met us at Hendon. In London we overnighted at the Strand Palace Hotel."

Initially, Eaker's headquarters was established at RAF Bomber Command Headquarters at High Wycombe on the green flanks of the rolling Buckinghamshire Chilterns. It was here on 22 February that VIII Bomber Command was formally activated. Prior to military use the headquarters had been a girls' school, but there was nothing second-hand about the Americans' future air bases proposed for the Huntingdon area. This flat Fenland stretch of countryside had originally been considered by the RAF for occupation by a new Bomber Command formation before this idea was discarded. The airfield construction program continued, and these bases would soon become the launching pad for the first American four-engined bomber in Europe: the B-17 Flying Fortress.

Although Eaker's brief was, for the most part, to establish a bombing force, many of his staff officers were, in one quarter at least, thought to be unsuitable for such a task. Major General Chaney had personally checked the background of the 19 staff officers supplied to Eaker and found that "in general they have had only pursuit training. Moreover, a large number have come direct from civil life without military background of any kind. Three served with bombardment units some years ago and their bombing experience must therefore be regarded as virtually negligible." Apart from Lieutenant Colonel Frank A. Armstrong, Jr., a regular officer who had been chosen first, the selection process for Eaker's other staff officers was unconventional to say the least. Beirne Lay Jr., one of Eaker's original "six," explains why there were so many "amateurs" (as he called them) on Eaker's staff:

> "'Hap' Arnold had told Eaker: 'You can train a smart civilian to be a soldier faster than a dumb staff officer.' I was a writer, hence billed for VIII Bomber Command's first historian. I also filled in first with the additional duties of Mess Officer and egg forager, PRO and aide and officially, also a member of A-3[7] and athletics officer. We had hotly contested bouts of volleyball, trying to ram Eaker's cigar down his throat - I got one direct hit. The four other originals were Major Peter Beasley, a successful businessman; Captain Fred A. Castle, a former Air Corps pilot, an executive of Sperry and well qualified for A-4[8]; Lieutenant Harris Hull, a crack PRO, A-2[9] and Lieutenant William Cowart, Jr., a 'gung-ho' young fighter pilot, Eaker' s first aide."

Almost six months were to elapse before the 8th mounted its first all-American bombing mission on German-held territory, so Eaker's "amateurs" had ample time in which to study RAF bombing methods and prepare to receive their own bombers. Between 31 March and 3 April 1942 Eaker and his staff officers made a more detailed reconnaissance of the Huntingdon area, and the seeds of the future American presence were thus sown. Meanwhile, in America, B-17 and B-24 heavy bombardment groups were activated for deployment to Britain.[10] On 3 February 1942 three B-17 groups—the 97th, 301st, and 303rd—were formally activated. It fell to these three groups, together with the 92nd (activated on 1 March 1942) and two Liberator groups, to establish the nucleus of the 8th's heavy bombardment force in England.

Lieutenant Colonel Cornelius W. Cousland had assumed command of the 97th Bomb Group upon its formal activation at McDill Field, Florida.[11] By April the group consisted of only 32 Fortresses, but on 12 May Colonel Cousland received his overseas orders. Aircraft and crews began flying out at once to San Antonio and Middletown, Pennsylvania, while the Headquarters Squadron returned to McDill Field. A week later the ground echelon entrained for Fort Dix, New Jersey, and on the night of 3 June was transported to Brooklyn docks, where in the dusk the men could see the charred hulk of the *Normandie* lying on her side. Ferry barges transported them the short distance to the Cunard liner-turned-troopship, *Queen Elizabeth*.[12] The liner made the journey safely without attacks from enemy aircraft or submarines and, on the morning of 9 June, dropped anchor in the Firth of Clyde. Lighters ferried the men ashore to Gourock where a train awaited them. As the train steamed southwards, the faces of many young Americans were pressed against the compartment windows, scanning the countryside and showing special interest in the bomb damage to the cities and towns.

Two days later, after a stopover at Carlisle, the men detrained at Oundle and the 97th Bomb Group divided, the 340th and 341st Squadrons traveling by bus to their new base at Polebrook, Northamptonshire, arriving at 0500 hours.[13] The 342nd and 414th Squadrons left the train at Kettering and traveled by bus to Grafton-Underwood.[14] On 1 July 1942 *Jarring Jenny* became the first VIII Bomber Command Fortress to land in the United Kingdom when she put down at Prestwick. Three days later the following entry was made at High Wycombe: "Arrival of aircraft: 1 B-17E. Total 1." Normally, the arrival of this first group would have been rapturously received by all and sundry. But the event was somewhat overshadowed by the decision, taken on 2 July, to dispatch six American crews of the 15th Bombardment Group (Light), together with six RAF crews, on a daylight sweep against four German airfields in Holland. It was the first time American airmen had flown in American-built bombers against a German target but, although it was important historically, the Independence Day raid was not an unqualified success. Two of the aircraft manned by Americans were shot down by what the RAF formation leader described as "the worst flak barrage he had encountered in over 60 operational missions."[15] Despite the disappointing effect the raid had, the press hailed it as the start of a "new and gigantic air offensive." All indications were that it would be, with the arrival early in August 1942 of two more heavy bombardment groups, the 92nd and the 301st. The 92nd, commanded by Colonel James S. Sutton, became the first heavy bombardment group to make a non-stop flight successfully from Newfoundland to Scotland. On 28 August 1942 the last of the four squadrons landed in the United Kingdom, and the 92nd set up home at Bovingdon, Hertfordshire. Meanwhile, the 301st Bomb Group, commanded by Colonel Ronald R. Walker, flew in to Chelveston and Podington in Northamptonshire.

If the press expected the gigantic new air offensive to begin at once they were disappointed. The fledgling 92nd, 97th, and 301st Bomb Groups, about to spread their wings in Europe, had been formed in the turbulent weeks following Pearl Harbor, and their training had been deficient in many respects. Some air gunners had little or no training in aerial gunnery, some radio operators could not send or receive Morse, and the pilots were not versed in high altitude and formation flying. Many crews, untrained as they were, had only just got to know one another when they were pitched headlong into an air war America thought she could wage in daylight without escort.

Meanwhile, at the end of July Eaker asked Colonel Frank A. Armstrong to take over command from Colonel Cornelius Cousland, who was sacked for running a "lackadaisical, loose-jointed, fun-loving, badly trained (especially in formation flying) outfit" which was "in no sense ready for combat." Armstrong was a cool, tough, no-nonsense North Carolinian who had been the only regular officer in Eaker's original contingent of 19 staff officers. His West Point training, erect bearing, and wind-tanned face—for the last 14 of his 39 years most of his time had been spent in the cockpits of military aircraft—commanded the respect of those who served with him. He had worked closely with his RAF counterparts during the early, formative days at High Wycombe. Once at Grafton-Underwood, Armstrong worked his new crews hard. Major Paul W. Tibbets, Group Flying Executive Officer of the 97th and charged with formulating tactics at Polebrook, recalls:

> "The seven weeks of training between our arrival in England and our first raid paid off handsomely. I shudder to think of the results had it not been for the intensive practice afforded during this period."

Colonel Armstrong, ably supported by men such as Major Paul Tibbets, took the group apart and put it back together again in a matter of little more than two weeks, and by mid-August he was able to report that 24 crews were available for combat missions. The night of 9 August found the loading list (crewmen assigned to Fly) on the operations bulletin board at Polebrook for the first time. Bombs were loaded into the bays, ammunition was checked out, equipment pre-flighted, and procedures checked, only to have the weather "scrub" the mission. Two days later it was responsible for the loss of a 97th Bomb Group Fortress in Wales, when all aboard were killed. The often atrocious English weather was the bane of all air operations in the United Kingdom for much of the 8th's stay in eastern England. Tension mounted again with this cancellation and the cynics spoke louder. The RAF made every conceivable effort to help the 8th get into the war as quickly as possible, but had remained skeptical about its ability to bomb in broad daylight. "I remember some of the discussions held by RAF officials who tried to dissuade us from daylight bombing," said Major Tibbets. "These centered on their belief that we would be 'shot out of the air' by fighters and flak. Consequently, most of us were apprehensive since it appeared we were up against 'supermen' and that our fate was in their hands." Critics of the American air forces were loud in their fault-finding, and the continual questioning by American newsmen as to when the first heavy bomber mission would be flown was irritating the crewmen, especially when they themselves did not know the answer.

The continual wrangle as to whether day bombing would be possible over the Continent became so tense that on 15 August Lieutenant General Dwight D. Eisenhower, commanding the American forces in Europe, denied that this argument was hindering American air action. On 16 August Peter Masefield, air correspondent, wrote in the *Sunday Times*: "American heavy bombers, the latest Fortresses and Liberators, are fine flying machines, but are not suited for bombing in Europe. Their bombs and bomb loads are too small, their armor and armament are low." He suggested that the Fortress was more suited for flying patrol missions over the Atlantic. But that night the loading list was posted again, and this time the weather held. The first Fortress strike of the war was scheduled for the following morning, Monday, 17 August. Major Tibbets and Frank Armstrong went to Grafton on 17 August to conduct the mission briefing:

> "We elected to take Butcher's aircraft because of its good crew and maintenance status. Frank Armstrong was not qualified in the B-17 so he elected to fly with me in the lead aircraft of the main group departing from Grafton Underwood. Twelve aircraft were designated as the main force to strike at the Rouen/Sotteville marshaling yards in northwestern France, and another six from Polebrook were to act as a diversionary force going to St. Omer."

One crewman later remarked that, on the morning of 17 August, the lights of the briefing room might have been glowing from the electricity in the air. Even the briefing officer showed the tension of the moment. Major General Carl "Tooey" Spaatz, the American air commander in Europe, and members of his staff were present.[16] Approximately 30 newspapermen added to the tension with their hurried scribbling as details of the historic mission were given out. Briefing over, crews prepared to take off. At Grafton-Underwood 12 B-17s were taxied out, and the crews were lined up for take-off in two flights of six. At 1526 hours Colonel Armstrong and Major Tibbets took off in *Butcher Shop*. Tibbets says:

> "*Butcher Shop* was not my regular aeroplane and I was not flying with my regular crew. My future missions would be flown in *Red Gremlin* with my regular crew, including navigator Dutch Van Kirk and bombardier Tom Ferebee, who would finish the war with me.[17]
>
> "It was just past mid-afternoon when we lifted off into sunny skies. All the planes were in the air at 1539 hours. We started our climb for altitude immediately and had reached 23,000ft, in attack formation; by the time we left the coast of England and headed south across the Channel. I wondered whether or not all aircraft would make it or whether there would be aborts. However, it was a banner day with no aborts. As we departed the English coast out over the Channel, the RAF escort of Spitfire Vs joined us. Group Captain [later Air Chief Marshal] Harry Broadhurst was leading the RAF escort fighters and it was an emotional, spine-tingling event—we were off to do battle for real and fighters were there to give us protection and comfort."

General Carl Spaatz had felt confident enough to allow Brigadier General Ira C. Eaker to fly on the mission. He joined the crew of *Yankee Doodle*, lead aircraft of the second flight of six. As the formation crossed the French coast the German radio proved as skeptical as the Allied critics by announcing that "12 Lancasters" were heading inland. When Lieutenant Levon L. Ray, lead navigator, hurriedly checking his flight plan, called over the interphone "Navigator to pilot, will you swing 220° please?" Colonel Armstrong replied, "Pilot to navigator: don't just ask me to turn 220°. If you want me to turn, you tell me to."

The turn from the target found flak awaiting them for the second time, and two Fortresses received minor damage. At Ypreville fighters began to make their appearance, and Sgt Adam R. Jenkins, the tail gunner aboard *Bat Outa Hell*—flying "tail-end Charlie"—had his hands full. He reported later:

> "There were eight of them in 'V' formation and the leader waggled his wings and came for us. When they were about 300 yards away I figured it was about time for me to do something. So I pulled the trigger and it looked like the ends of his wings came off. The other seven scattered."

One fighter was chased into the line of fire from Sgt Kent R. West, ball turret gunner aboard *Birmingham Blitzkrieg*, and was fired upon. West became the first American crewman to be credited with the destruction of a German aircraft. Altogether two German fighters were shot down, and five more claimed as "probables" for the loss of two Spitfires.

Ten minutes before the bomb run began Lieutenant Frank R. Beadle, the lead bombardier, exclaimed in a sing-song voice "I can see the target. I can see the target!" Crew members twisted and turned, probing the beautiful bright blue sky for signs of possible enemy fighter attacks; a movement which would soon be known as the "Messerschmitt twist." Crews were relieved that "here was the target at last," and the tension they had been feeling began to ease. As the Initial Point was reached and the bomb run begun, Beadle again moved to the center of the spotlight. As he manipulated the switch to open the bomb bay doors of *Butcher Shop* he could be heard singing over the intercom, "*I Don't Want To set the World On Fire!*"

Packed into the bomb bays of the twelve Fortresses were 36,900lb of British bombs in the form of 45 600-pounders and nine 1100-pounders. The heavy bombs (carried by three of the B-17s) were for the locomotive repair shops, and the 600lb bombs for the Buddicum rolling stock repair shops. Even if the bombs missed, RAF reconnaissance photos had revealed concentrations of more than 2000 freight cars at Sotteville. Any damage to what was the largest switching facility in northern France would make spectacular front-page news the following morning. Bombing was made from 23,000ft, and a few bombs hit a mile short of the target. One burst hit about a mile west in some woods, but the majority smashed into the assigned area. Major Tibbets says:

> "We caught the Germans by surprise. They hadn't expected a daytime attack, so we had clear sailing to the target. Visibility was unlimited and all 12 planes dropped their bomb loads. Our aim was reasonably good but you couldn't describe it as pinpoint bombing. We still had a lot to learn. At least half the bombs fell in the general target area. One of the aiming points took a direct hit and there were a number of bomb craters within a radius of 1500ft. Bombs intended for the other aiming point fell about 200ft to the south. While the results did not come up to our expectations, our accuracy was considerably better than that achieved by the RAF in its night attacks, or by German bombers in their raids on England. By the time we unloaded our bombs the enemy came to life. Anti-aircraft fire, erratic and spasmodic at first, zeroed in on our formations as we began the return flight. Two B-17s suffered slight damage from flak. Three Bf 109s moved in for the attack but the Spitfires that accompanied us quickly drove them off. The only German planes I saw were out of range and I got the impression that they were simply looking us over.
>
> "A feeling of elation took hold of us as we winged back across the Channel. All the tension was gone. We were no longer novices at this terrible game of war. We had braved the enemy in his own skies and were alive to tell people about it."

Shortly before 1900 hours anxious watchers on the Polebrook control tower began counting in the formation. Down below, equally anxious base personnel, fellow airmen, high-ranking American and RAF officers, and about 30 Allied pressmen gathered to witness the end to a historic mission. Specks were spotted in the distance, and a hurried count could locate only eleven Fortresses. As the landing pattern was formed cheers were heard, for in the distance came the straggler. Three of the B-17s, in complete disregard for air discipline, peeled out of formation and buzzed the control tower. Under the circumstances no one seemed to mind. In came *Baby Doll*, *Peggy D*, *Big Stuff*, *Butcher Shop*, *Yankee Doodle*, *Berlin Sleeper*, *Johnny Reb*, *Kissey-me-Kowboy*, *Birmingham Blitzkrieg*, and the rest. Tibbets concludes, "Once back at base we were debriefed and then there followed a 'victory celebration' at the club with some RAF fighter pilots in attendance." Interrogation proved almost farcical, as everyone seemed to want to talk at once. The crews were happy to learn that there were no losses, the most serious damage having occurred on the diversionary flight, when a pigeon smashed through the windshield of a B-17 and the fragments of Plexiglas left minor scars on a bombardier and navigator. The diversion, although not quite going according to plan, had proved successful. Three Fortresses in the 340th Bomb Squadron and three from the 341st had flown in separate elements. The latter had not been able to locate its fighter escort and, following instructions, had returned early.

General Eaker told the assembled reporters that the crewmembers on the bombing raid were enthusiastic and alert, but nonchalant to the point of being blasé. This attitude, the General felt, was good, for it meant that the men were confident, without being cocky. He added that additional drill in the use of oxygen was needed, and that air discipline would have to be improved, for a tighter formation would be necessary to enable the gunners to function as a team unit. General Spaatz, elated with the success of the mission, stated: "I think the crews behaved like veterans. Everything went according to plan." The youngest man aboard, Sgt Frank Christensen, who had not yet turned 18, remarked: "It's all in the day's work." The *New York Times* communiqué describing the mission was placed on the front page, along with the Peter Masefield story from the *Sunday Times*. Colonel Armstrong's remark upon his return, "We ruined Rouen," was without doubt an exaggeration, but the raid focused world attention on VIII Bomber Command. The first of the congratulatory messages to arrive came from Air Marshal Sir Arthur Harris, Chief of RAF Bomber Command:

> "Congratulations from all ranks of Bomber Command on the highly successful completion of the first all-American raid by the big fellows on German-occupied territory in Europe. Yankee Doodle certainly went to town and can stick yet another well-deserved feather in his cap."

When the news of the first bombing mission by VIII Bomber Command reached Washington, the Chief of Air Staff arranged for a memorandum (prepared for General Hap Arnold's signature) to be sent to General George C. Marshall, Chief of Staff, for the attention of Admirals Ernest J. King and William D. Leahy. This declared:

> "The attack on Rouen again verifies the soundness of our policy of the precision bombing of strategic objectives rather than the mass bombing of large, city-size areas."

Carl Spaatz and Ira Eaker had put their careers on the line by insisting on the policy of daylight precision bombing. Eaker had been a fighter pilot before General Arnold sent him to England to study RAF Bomber Command and assess the potential for bombing the enemy "around the clock." In spite of advice to the contrary from senior officers in the RAF, Eaker had concluded that daylight precision bombing was a gamble worth taking. It was his idea that Germany and its environs could be bombed to defeat with B-17s and B-24s pounding them in daylight and RAF bombers at night.[18] One week after the bombing of Rouen the Vichy Government issued a protest, claiming that 15 soldiers had died. The typewritten communiqué blamed "American" airmen, but this had been corrected in pencil to say "Anglo-Saxon aviators," with an additional correction that the dead soldiers were "German."

On 19 August the 97th Bomb Group despatched 24 B-17Es in support of the Allied landings at Dieppe. Their target was the airfield at Abbeville-Drucat in northern France, home of the infamous *Jagdgeschwader* 26, or "Abbeville Kids," whose yellow-nosed FW 190 pilots were among the *Luftwaffe* elite.[19] JG 26 and the American bombers would meet on many occasions in the coming months. Two of the B-17s aborted because of mechanical failures, but the rest of the Group plastered the airfield, destroying a hangar and severely cratering, or "postholing," the runways. Fortunately the *Luftwaffe* was heavily engaged over the Dieppe area and did not show. British High Command reported that 16 fighters were either destroyed or damaged as a result of the bombing strike, and the airfield itself was put out of action for a vital two hours. In addition, the controllers of the whole of the fighter area remained out of action until that evening. Air Marshal Sir Trafford Leigh-Mallory, Chief of RAF Fighter Command, added his congratulations: "The raid on Abbeville undoubtedly struck a heavy blow at the German fighter organisation at a very critical moment during the operations...." RAF fighter pilots reported the following day that the main area of the Drucat aerodrome appeared to have been "completely demolished." Yet despite these successes, JG 26 was in action over Dieppe all day.[20]

The morning of 20 August brought a hurried call from photo-reconnaissance informing Eaker that 1600 goods wagons and 17 locomotives were parked in the Longuneau marshaling yards in Amiens. Twelve Fortresses in the 340th and 342nd Bomb Squadrons were airborne, and eleven bombed through slight flak. Spitfires protected the formation, and a Belgian fighter pilot who witnessed the raid reported that the bombers scored at least 15 direct hits. The bomber crews were jubilant but senior staff officers were more reserved, well aware that so far they had flown only shallow penetration missions in predominantly fine weather. The case for daylight, high-altitude, precision bombing was, as yet, unproven. The indications were that the B-17s would not be able to flaunt themselves over enemy targets with impunity for very much longer.

In the early morning of 21 August 12 Fortresses were despatched to bomb the Wilton shipyards at Rotterdam, the most modern in all Holland. Crews still felt confident, knowing that the faithful RAF Spitfires would again be on hand to protect them. But the B-17s were slow to form up after leaving Grafton-Underwood. One Fortress was barely airborne when it was forced to abort and a replacement joined the formation. Three other B-17s suffered generator failures, which caused the gun turrets to become inoperative, and they returned to base. Sixteen minutes late for the escort, the remaining crews knew the fighters would not be able to escort them all the way to the target. The Dutch coast was in sight when the recall message came through and the Spitfires turned for home. They were immediately replaced by upwards of 25 German fighters in what became a prelude to a running fight that lasted for 25 minutes. The bombers' mass firepower was a little more than the *Luftwaffe* pilots could handle, and two fighters fell to the Fortresses' guns. Sgt Adam R. Jenkins, flying the tail turret aboard *Johnny Reb* this time, drew first blood. Sergeant Roy Allen, the top turret gunner, fired one burst and his guns jammed. John N. Hughes, one of the waist gunners, sucked a lump of ice into the mouth of his oxygen tube in the excitement and was forced to hold the mask with one hand and fire his gun with the other, while nearing collapse from lack of oxygen.

In the nose compartment Harold Spire, the navigator, had just fired at a crossing fighter when a burst of cannon fire tore through the windshield. Donald A. Walter, co-pilot, was raked from his legs to his chest and died instantly, and the splinters of Plexiglas seriously wounded Richard S. Starks, the pilot. While struggling for breath Starks managed to call for help, and Edward Sconiers, bombardier, and Sgt Allen came to the cockpit. Sconiers removed the dead co-pilot and took his place at the controls, hoping that what he had learned about piloting before washing out of flying school would be useful to him now. Holding on to the stick, the pilot began giving instructions to Sconiers while the tail and ball turret gunners continued to blaze away at their five pursuers. *Johnny Reb* lagged behind the rest of the formation with its Nos.3 and 4 engines hit. Despite this, Sconiers managed to nurse the ailing bomber back to England and land at Horsham St. Faith, near Norwich. During the remainder of the flight Sgt Franky Rebellow, top turret gunner in the lead ship piloted by Captain Rudolph Flack, had fired away with such abandon that he had run out of ammunition. He crawled to the cockpit, slapped Colonel Armstrong on the back, and screamed in his ear "Not a bullet left!"

The press enthusiastically credited the nine Fortresses with six fighters destroyed and praised them for beating off 25 Focke-Wulfs. Some RAF officers, however, remained skeptical, and it later transpired that only a handful of fighters had actually fired on the formation.

Eaker took advantage of the *Luftwaffe's* inexperience in dealing with American bomber formations, and on 24 August despatched a dozen 97th Bomb Group B-17s led by Major Paul Tibbets to the shipyard of the *Ateliers et Chantiers Maritime de la Seine et Le Trait*. Brigadier General Newton L. Longfellow, the new bomb wing commander, took his place aboard Tibbets' B-17 for his combat orientation flight.[21] Twelve of the 48 bombs fell within 500 yards of the aiming point, but no material damage seemed to have been done to the yards. One wayward bomb luckily hit and sank a U-boat tied to the docks, but overall it was the poorest bombing to date. Flak caused damage to the Fortresses, and two officers and three sergeants received slight wounds. On the way home the formation was jumped from above by yellow-nosed Bf 109s, which, during an overhead pass, fired 20mm cannon shells into Tibbets' cockpit, shattering the instrument panel and severely injuring Lieutenant Gene Lockhart, co-pilot, in the left hand. The top turret gunner was also seriously injured. Tibbets, who was also wounded, wrote later:

> "Newt panicked. He started grabbing for the throttles and we had a critical situation. I told him to quit. He didn't even hear me. The only thing I could do was hit him with my right elbow. I was able to catch him under the chin while he was leaning over and I knocked him flat on his fanny. He calmed down then and when he got back on his feet he spent the next half-hour ministering to the injured. Having done what he could for Lockhart's hand, he bandaged the head of the turret gunner who was lying on the floor unconscious. After lifting Lockhart out of his seat and making him as comfortable as possible on the floor, with a parachute pack for a pillow, Longfellow took over the co-pilot's duties to help me fly the plane. When you have wounded aboard, you fire a Verey pistol on final approach to the runway. Newt did that and as we rolled to a stop, ambulances moved in beside us to speed the injured men to the base hospital. All recovered in good time although there were some uneasy moments in the case of Lockhart, who had lost a large quantity of blood.
>
> "A ceremony was arranged soon after the mission so that General Spaatz could present the Purple Heart to those who were wounded. I was in that group but, quite frankly, I was embarrassed by all the fuss. My injuries consisted of a couple of punctures on my left wrist and several inside my left leg just above the knee. All were little more than skin-deep."

This event was as much for public relations as to honor the wounded, and General Eaker despatched Beirne Lay, now on the staff of General Spaatz as public relations officer, to cover the ceremony. First his assignment met with many difficulties, as Lay explains:

"I got nowhere for three days with Tib's subordinates because I couldn't get any okays to set things in motion. Tib was too busy to bother with me, snowed under as he was with more pressing demands. Finally, I got my dander up and accosted him in his office.

"'Major Tibbets,' I said hotly, 'can you give me just five minutes?'

"'I wish I had five minutes,' he growled.

"'General Spaatz sent me down here to do a job. I need your okay to work out the details with your adjutant.'

"'Stop right there,' he cut in. 'I'm dealing every day with matters of life and death and I can't spare a man from the squadron for frills.'

"'You may call this review ordered by Spaatz and Eaker a frill, but I should think you'd have enough interest in your squadron to give them their due.'

"He sprang up and advanced toward me, his face flushed, near breaking under the strain of fatigue. 'You have a lot of guts coming down here from your plush headquarters at 'Pinetree' and telling me I don't really care about my squadron, because I don't have time for a PRO show!' I immediately backed up, apologizing for my choice of words. He calmed down enough for me to explain how distasteful my job was to me and that I'd much prefer to change places with him. He called in his adjutant and gave the necessary orders."[22]

With the good weather continuing to hold, bombing missions were becoming almost everyday events at Grafton-Underwood and Polebrook. On 27 August nine Fortresses returned to the Wilton Shipyards at Rotterdam, which was once again working to full capacity. Although only seven of the B-17s bombed, hits were claimed on two ships and the center of the target was well covered. The following day the 97th Bomb Group despatched 14 B-17s to the Avions Potez factory at Meaulte, in northern France. Most of the bombs (from the eleven Fortresses that bombed) fell in open fields, although some "post-holed" the runways. The B-17s returned intact, but one Canadian-crewed Spitfire was missing. It was on this mission that American fighter pilots were also represented for the first time.

On 29 August, for the third day running, the 97th Bomb Group was airborne, and 12 of the 13 B-17s despatched bombed the German fighter base at Coutrai-Wevelgem, in Belgium. The results appeared good, and even the British press, which had at first been cautious of American claims, now openly praised them. However, Spaatz and Eaker refused to read too much into the Fortresses' success (claimed in some circles to have scored better than 70% in hits). It was early days yet, and moves were afoot to transfer the 97th and 301st Bomb Groups to the 12th Air Force, activated at Washington, DC, on 20 August. Although Eaker continued to use the two groups at every opportunity, it meant he would have to reorganize and plan for the future.

Eaker needed a Combat Crew Replacement and Training Center, but personnel and equipment were in such short supply that the 92nd Bomb Group, with its base at Bovingdon, was selected for the task. Bovingdon became known as the 11th Combat Crew Replacement Center and, for a few important months, provided many new combat crews that the 8th was to need so badly as operations increased. This meant that the group's latest B-17Fs were no longer needed for combat and, almost immediately upon their arrival at Bovingdon they were transferred to the 97th Bomb Group.[23] On 5 September the 97th Bomb Group despatched 25 of its newly acquired B-17Fs, together with 12 Fortresses of the 301st Bomb Group (flying its first combat mission of the war), to the marshaling yards at Rouen. Thirty-one B-17s bombed and six aborted owing to mechanical problems. Approximately only 20% of the bombs fell within the target area and some hit the city. Unconfirmed reports claimed that 140 civilians were killed and about 200 (mostly French) were wounded. One bomb, a dud, hit the city hospital and went through to the basement. Although aircrew had been badly wounded during the first nine Fortress missions, not one B-17 had been lost. It could not last.

On 6 September Eaker mounted his largest bombing mission so far, to the Avions Potez factory at Meaulte—using for the first time the 92nd Bomb Group, which scraped together 14 B-17Es and crews, filling in with ground personnel, some of them privates. They joined with 22 B-17Fs of the 97th in the main strike while the 301st Bomb Group flew a diversionary raid on St. Omer-Longuenesse airfield. Thirty Fortresses crossed Meaulte, but only six in the 92nd Bomb Group attacked the target. Focke Wulf 190s of II./JG 26 were encountered continuously from the French coast to the target, and the escorting four squadrons of Spitfire IXs failed to rendezvous with the bombers. JG 26 intercepted the Spitfires and shot down three. About 50 FW 190s and a handful of Bf 109s bounced the Fortresses. Lieutenant Clarence C. Lipsky's B-17 in the 97th Bomb Group was attacked by Hauptmann Conny Meyer, CO II./JG 26, and it went down northwest of Amiens at 1855 hours. It was the *Luftwaffe's* first American heavy bomber victory of the war. Four parachutes were seen to open.

Lieutenant Leigh E. Stewart in the 92nd Bomb Group, who was pursued by at least five FW 190s, flew the second B-17 lost on the mission. *Oberfeldwebel* Willi Roth of 4./JG 26 finally shot the B-17 down at 1906 hours, and Stewart crashed into the sea northwest of Le Treport. RAF Air-Sea Rescue launches searched the area but without success. The losses and wounded aboard the Forts[24] had a chastening effect on both groups, as Paul Tibbets recalls:

> "The blow came as a personal shock to me because Lieutenant Lipsky was one of my favorites.[25] Up to this time, the war had seemed a little more than a game in the sense that we flew out in the morning and came back a few hours later after dropping our bombs and eluding enemy flak and fighter fire... Now at last the war was a bloody reality for all of us."

2

Lighting the Torch

"We had reason to take pride in the fact that the mission eventually saved a considerable number of lives and played an important part in lighting the 'Torch.'"

Lieutenant Colonel Paul Tibbets

The 92nd Bomb Group had only flown the 6 September mission because the 8th was so desperately short of aircraft, spares, and personnel. This constant drain on its resources was a direct result of the need to supply the 12th Air Force, destined for the Mediterranean Theater. (Its future commander, Brigadier General James H. Doolittle, would not be appointed until 23 September.[26]) Unfortunately, few in the 8th were aware that the 12th Air Force was destined for Operation *Torch*, and therefore had top priority when it came to spares, personnel, B-17Fs, and even training. New groups had to be trained by the 8th for eventual transfer to the 12th Air Force, a task Eaker could well have done without at such a crucial time in the 8th's history. Crews in the 92nd Bomb Group were disappointed to learn from the General that they were to continue with their training program while other B-17 groups continued flying missions to France and the Low Countries.

On 7 September the 97th and 301st Bomb Groups were despatched to Holland to bomb the shipyards at Rotterdam again. A storm warning was flashed to the outbound Fortresses, with most of the crews receiving it and returning safely. However, seven Fortresses in the 97th Bomb Group formation continued to the target, where the *Luftwaffe* was waiting for them. The German fighter pilots hurled themselves into the fight, desperate for the kill. The lead ship of the flight, flown by Captain Aquilla Hughes, bore the brunt of the enemy attacks, and the ball turret gunner was killed and three other gunners were wounded. Two engines were put out of action, and the oil lines and hydraulic lines to the brakes were shot out. The radio began malfunctioning, and Hughes was forced to drop out of formation. Two flights of 12 fighters each attacked the stricken B-17, but her gunners fought back tenaciously and claimed three fighters destroyed, two in flames. Although badly damaged, the lead ship and all the other six B-17s managed to fight their way out of trouble and make it home safely.

Seven days later the 97th and 301st Bomb Groups were, on paper at least, assigned to the 12th Air Force, although they continued flying combat missions under the banner of VIII Bomber Command.[27] On 26 September three squadrons of Spitfires were assigned to escort 24 B-17s over the harbor at Brest. The American Eagle Squadron (133) had moved to Bolt Head, on the south coast of England, so that the fuel supply would permit the maximum time over the target. At briefing the bomber crews were told that the target would be covered by cloud and they would have a wind of 100mph from the south. The statement concerning the wind proved an unexplained and costly error, for the wind was out of the north, adding to their speed. Unable to see the coastline, the navigators in the bombers flew on dead reckoning, and when they were actually over their target their plotting charts had them still short of the target. Twenty-four Spitfires turned back with their assignment completed, leaving 133 Squadron, along with the B-17s. Unable to locate the target owing to the briefing error, the bombers turned north for their bases with the Spitfires staying with them and depending on them for proper navigation. Running short of fuel, the Spitfires were soon forced to leave the formation to seek their own bases. When they broke out of the clouds expecting to be over Cornwall, they were in fact over the heart of Brest. Enemy anti-aircraft fire opened up on them immediately and, lacking fuel, they were helpless. Eleven Spitfires were forced to land in France, and the 12th, nursing his fast dwindling fuel supply, attempted to glide back to England but crashed on the cliffs of the Lizard. The Fortresses were able to buck the headwind and return to base.

Although the 97th and 301st Bomb Groups were soon to join the 12th Air Force, the complete break up of VIII Bomber Command was avoided by the formation of four new groups (the 91st, 303rd, 305th, and 306th) which were undergoing training in America. The CO, 36-year old Lieutenant Colonel Curtis E. LeMay, directed the 305th Bomb Group's training program without compromise.[28] One of the officers who served under LeMay at Salt Lake City and Muroc Dry Lake, California, was Captain Clifton Pyle, who was assigned to the Group in April 1942.

> "I was designated one of the flight commanders in the 422nd Bomb Squadron, which was commanded by Major Thomas K. McGehee. The immediate mission of the Bomb Group was to train three cadres of primary flight crews, a pilot and engineer in each, for new groups that were being organized. Then we were to accept and train a new cadre of personnel, this time the whole crew and proceed overseas. Lieutenant Colonel LeMay demanded the best from each man. If the man did not 'produce,' he would fire him. Several examples were made in this regard and it took little time for the entire group to start stepping in line. He was a believer in exactness in flying, abiding by the book as far as possible but wanted the job done. He would not tolerate laziness of any type and he didn't want any 'unlucky' person on his team. He would fire a person for being 'unlucky' as quick as incompetent. All during the training period Colonel LeMay

was a strict disciplinarian. He explained it was for our benefit and the best chance of survival. Most of the crews thought he was a little too rough. Colonel LeMay was soon known to all as 'Ole Iron Ass' and he was referred to in public as 'Ole Iron Tail' or 'Ole Iron Pants.' Regardless of his persistent firmness, he soon gained our respect, admiration and full support. He was one who believed in flying with his crews and did so on numerous occasions."

Other groups training for eventual movement overseas were encountering similar problems to those experienced by the 305th Bomb Group. All crews had to be declared operational by the Preparation for Overseas Movement (POM) Inspectors before they could fly the hazardous Northern Ferry Route to England. Among the first groups declared operational was the 91st `Bomb Group, commanded by Colonel Stanley T. Wray, who had assumed command of the group on 15 May 1942 after serving with the 92nd Bomb Group as its Executive Officer. He would have to wait until early in October before the 91st had enough B-17s on strength, although one squadron began the flight to England late in September 1942. Two parent groups—the 303rd commanded by Colonel James H. Wallace and the 306th commanded by Colonel Charles "Chip" Overacker—departed for the United Kingdom during September also. The 8th Air Force desperately needed these "new" groups, but it would not be until November 1942 that it could call upon all four for combat operations. Four airfields had been made available for the "new" groups. All were located within a 12-mile radius of Bedford, about 40 miles north of London. The 91st was allocated Kimbolton, and the 303rd, 305th, and 306th—all of whose ground echelons began arriving in the United Kingdom throughout September, October, and early November 1942—were allocated Molesworth, Grafton-Underwood, and Thurleigh respectively.

Among those in the 306th Bomb Group who traveled to England was Al La Chasse, bombardier in Lieutenant John Olsen's crew:

> "On 1 September, after a good night's rest, we had taken off from Gander Bay, Newfoundland, in darkness, for a jump straight across the Atlantic to Prestwick. Previously, we had left Westover Field, Massachusetts, after weeks of preparation, shakedown, fuel consumption tests and submarine patrols. Our trip was a 'first' for a whole group to leave and arrive as one group. There were two plane losses and the loss of one crew."

After several days of waiting in Scotland, the 306th air echelon was green-lighted to go to Thurleigh. All this activity did not go unnoticed by the enemy, as La Chasse explains:

> "The day we brought *Snoozy II* in, the English tower master said on open radio, 'I say there, American aircraft, this is your field: you are cleared to land.' 'Lord Haw Haw' must have been listening for, that night on radio, he said: 'Welcome to England, 306th Group!'"[29]

Meanwhile, the ground echelon of the 305th Bomb Group, which arrived in the UK aboard the *Queen Mary* on 12 September, took over the vacated base. Then they awaited the arrival of the air echelon, which early in August had departed Muroc Dry Lake for Syracuse, New York, for six weeks' advanced flight training. At Syracuse the 305th received the balance of its B-17Fs, but they could not be flown to England until modifications had been made. Finally, amid fears of a move to the Pacific Theater minus its ground echelon, the 305th was on its way to England. On 19 October the air echelon departed for Gander. Cliff Pyle was among those who made the trip:

> "The day of departure was one day after my wife gave birth to a baby girl. It was nearly a year later before I had a chance to see her for the first time."

Many men would never see their loved ones again, and these thoughts were uppermost in the minds as they touched down at Gander for the flight to Scotland. One B-17 was forced to ditch off Nova Scotia in bad weather after losing a propeller, but the crew literally jumped off the aircraft on to the shore. One other B-17 lost two propellers but managed to land safely in Scotland, but not at Prestwick. Cliff Pyle was another who landed elsewhere. "Arriving over the Liverpool area, the group ran into some bad weather with low visibility and ceilings. This alone would not have deterred us from continuing to our destination, Grafton-Underwood, but there were numerous balloons tied to steel cables floating around in and out of the clouds. We were not briefed (to this situation). Instructions by radio advised us to land at a suitable airfield and report in by phone. My aircraft and three others landed at Pickapoo Park, just outside Liverpool. Three days later, after the weather cleared, we made it to Grafton-Underwood in good shape."

Grafton-Underwood offered some home comforts. The same could not be said for the bleak and underdeveloped bases at Kimbolton, Molesworth, and Thurleigh. Crews in the 306th Bomb Group were sent to other bases, as the hard top on the runways at Thurleigh had not hardened. Air Ministry workers and U.S. Engineers took care of expansion work and repaired the runways. The Group spent several days collecting its aircraft and flying them back to Thurleigh, where they continued to use the runways during the repair work.[30] Kimbolton airfield did not endear itself to the officers and men of the 91st Bomb Group commanded by Lieutenant Colonel Stanley T. Wray. They had arrived at the base on 1 October and soon their B-17s were breaking up the runways. The Nissen huts held damp, and the men felt cut off from civilization. It was not until early October that the 91st had enough B-17s to complete its aircraft complement. Meanwhile, crews used their time wisely before beginning operations as Squadron-Leader Phibbs, the RAF Liaison officer at Kimbolton, recalls. "Their Fortresses lacked sufficient protection in the cockpit so the more enterprising among their crews stole armor plating from some British armored cars which had been left on the airfield by the RAF Regiment for airfield defense!" On 13 October Wray visited Bassingbourn, in Cambridgeshire, a pre-war RAF station with permanent runways, solid brick buildings, and comfortable messes. Wray decided it would be ideal for the 91st, and the following day "Wray's Ragged Irregulars," as they were nicknamed, moved in and took up residence. At headquarters Brigadier-General Newton L. Longfellow was taken aback by the move, and remonstrated that no decision to move the 91st had yet been taken. Wray explained there was a decision and that they had made it. Eventually, headquarters came round to their way of thinking, and the group remained until the cessation of hostilities.

The first two B-24D Liberator groups (the 44th and 93rd) also arrived in England in September-October 1942.[31] On 5 September the B-24s of the 93rd began leaving Grenier Field on the long journey to Alconbury in England. However, the crews soon ran into bad weather and were forced to seek shelter for four days at Newfoundland. At 1830 hours on 9 September the weather cleared and Lieutenant John H. Murphy, in the 328th Bomb Squadron piloting *Shoot Luke*, led 17 Liberators into a flaming red sunset and across the inhospitable North Atlantic.[32] Shortly after dark they again encountered bad weather, but this time tried to climb above it. At 12,000ft ice began to form on the wings and propellers, only to be dislodged by the slipstream and hitting the fuselages with cracks that sounded like gunfire. Arch Rantala, navigator on *Shoot Luke*, became ill when his oxygen-supply failed, and to make matters worse the wind, which was stronger than anticipated, took the Liberators northwards and off course. Landfall at Prestwick was finally made 8 hours and 15 minutes after leaving Newfoundland. The air echelon then flew to Alconbury, their new home in Huntingdonshire. In October the 44th Group arrived in England to join them.[33]

2nd Lieutenant Bill Cameron, a co-pilot in the 44th, awaited his Squadron's deployment from Grenier Field to England:

> "I was assigned to the 67th Squadron and met my pilot, 1st Lieutenant Chester 'George' Phillips. Phillips called everyone 'George' so the name stuck. He was a typically rugged Texan and a fine pilot. At Grenier we had only four B-24s and about six 'first' pilots for the entire Group. We later received 27 new Liberators along with additional 'first' pilots. We made a shakedown flight to Florida and back in our new planes, and on 4 October flew off one by one for Gander, the first leg of the long trip to England. By the time we arrived over Gander the clouds were on the ground and there were no instrument landing systems. However we got down after several attempts. After a few days' waiting for good weather we took off again for England on 9 October in *Little Beaver*."

Another crewmember of the 67th Squadron who made the same crossing was 1st Lieutenant Bob Bishop, navigator on *Suzy Q*, flown by Howard "Pappy" Moore and named after his three-year-old daughter. A little older than most of his contemporaries, Moore was an exceptional pilot. Later at Shipdham he was to take bets on the number of times he could spin his wheels on the grass before landing on the concrete runway. Bishop and all the other navigators navigated the 2800-mile journey using celestial navigation because electrical storms ruled out the use of instruments. St. Elmo's fire lit up the instruments of *Suzy Q*, and the Northern Lights were also in evidence as, halfway across, Bishop navigated using the RAF method of predetermined star paths charted on graph paper so that only a single star shot would give some indication of the aircraft's position. The combined storm and overcast had ruled out celestial navigation. Although *Suzy* Q made its projected landfall at Prestwick, others were not so lucky. Lieutenant Cameron, in Phillips' B-24, veered off course and landed at Bally Herbert, in Northern Ireland, while Lieutenant John Long overflew Scotland, having been misdirected by a spurious German radio signal. Fortunately RAF Spitfires managed to intercept him and he turned back. On 11 October the 67th Squadron flew to Shipdham to rejoin the other B-24s that had flown in from Cheddington. At Shipdham the October winds had brought rain, turning the airfield into a sea of mud. One by one the Liberators touched down to the voice of "Axis Sally," or the "Berlin Bitch," as the Americans called her, welcoming the new arrivals over the German radio. One B-24 ran off the runway and became stuck fast.[34]

While the "new" groups got to grips with their English bases, the established groups carried the war to the enemy. On 2 October the 97th Bomb Group, now commanded by Colonel Joseph H. Atkinson (Colonel Armstrong having moved up to Bomber Command), was despatched, together with the 301st Bomb Group, to Meaulte. The target was the Potez factory at Meaulte again.[35] Lieutenant Charles W. Paine Jr, pilot of *Phyllis* in the 301st, was one who flew to Meaulte, and he recalled:

> "When the signal for the take-off came, I was so scared that I could hardly talk. Somehow though, I managed to make it. We were in vee of vees all the way to the target. Our ship was 'Tail-end Charlie,' the rearmost left-hand ship in the formation and hence the last to bomb. We hit scattered heavy flak on our way in, but it was slight and did no harm. We got well over our targets, in formation and unmolested, and the bombing part was easy. But that's when the enemy fighters started to pour it on. The Germans' strategy was obviously to pick on the last ship and shoot it down. All the gunners in the crew started calling through the interphones, 'Enemy aircraft at 3 o'clock, Lieutenant. At 5 o'clock... At 9 o'clock...' They were all around us.
>
> "The fighters were employing two tactics that were new to me. When they peeled out of their formation to attack, they came in so close together that by the time one snip had shot up and banked away, the next in line had his sights on us. The other dodge they used was to pretend to come in on one of the other ships and then do a 20° turn and shoot the hell out of us. Mostly they came from the rear, but at least one of them came up under us from in front, stalled, and as it fell off, raked us the length of the Fortresses' belly. I could feel his hits banging into us. As a matter of fact I could feel the effect of all their fire. It was rather like sitting in the boiler of a hot-water heater and being rolled down a steep hill. There was an explosion behind me as a 20mm cannon shell banged into us just behind the upper turret and exploded, and I kept thinking, 'What if it hit the flares?' If it hit the flares and ignited them, I knew we'd go up like a rocket. Then I looked out at the right wing and saw it was shot to hell. There were holes everywhere. A lot of them were 20mm cannon holes, and they could tear a hole in the skin big enough to shove a sheep through. The entire wing was just a Goddamn bunch of holes.
>
> "One of the waist gunners yelled through the interphone, 'Lieutenant, there's a bunch of control wires slapping me in the face,' which meant that the tail surface controls were being shot up. The right-hand outboard engine 'ran away,' and the engine controls were messed up so we couldn't shut it off. The left-hand inboard engine also quit, and the whole left oxygen system had gone out. I tried to get the ship down to 20,000ft to keep half my crew from passing out. One gunner passed out from lack of oxygen, and the radio operator, seeing him lying by his gun, abandoned his own oxygen supply and put the emergency mask of the walk-around bottle over the gunner's face. The gunner revived just in time to see the radio operator pass out. He in turn took the emergency mask off his own face and revived the radio operator with it.
>
> "The ship went into a steep climb which I couldn't control. There was something wrong with the controls. I motioned to the co-pilot to help me, and between the two of us we managed to get it forward and assume normal level flight. Then I started to think. The enemy fighters were still shooting us up. We had a long way to go to reach England and safety. We were minus two engines, and it took almost full left aileron to hold that damaged right wing up. It was time, I decided, to bale out of the aircraft. So I yelled into the interphone 'Prepare to abandon ship.' But just about that time the top gunner slid out of the top turret and fell between the co-pilot and me. His face was a mess. He was coughing blood. I thought he had been wounded in the chest. It later proved that he wasn't, but he was clearly in no condition to bale out of the airplane. I called for the bombardier and navigator to come up and help us with the top turret gunner and they did. Back in the waist one of our gunners was manning two guns despite a bad bullet wound in his leg. I don't know how many fighters we damaged or destroyed. There wasn't time to worry about that. We got over the Channel finally, and a flight of Spits came racing out to meet us. Brother, they looked mighty good. We nursed the Fort across and made a belly landing at Gatwick, the first airdrome we could find. We nicked a hangar on the way in but somehow we made it."[36]

The vast steel and locomotive works at the Compagnie de Fives, Chemin de Fer du Nord at Lille had long been earmarked as a target because of its importance to an enemy who was suffering an acute shortage of rail transport. Eaker also saw it as the ideal target to demonstrate high altitude precision bombing, but it was not until 9 October that VIII Bomber Command could assemble enough bombers to destroy the target. A few weeks before, the Command could muster only twelve aircraft. By including the B-24D Liberators of the 93rd Bomb Group at Alconbury and Fortresses of the 306th Bomb Group, both of whom were flying their maiden missions, Eaker could assemble an unprecedented 108 bombers for the raid. Furthermore, seven bombers would fly a diversionary sweep towards the Continent, and the main force would be escorted by a strong contingent of RAF and USAAF fighters.

At Alconbury Colonel Ted Timberlake addressed his crews at that first briefing. He said, "I know you Joes can do it." Briefing over, Timberlake boarded *Teggie Ann* and led 24 of the B-24D Liberators off to form up behind the force of B-17s. As the formation approached the French coast Lieutenant Edmund J. Janic, bombardier on *Shoot Luke*, reported over the intercom that the navigator had been taken ill, and that to proceed could prove fatal. The pilot turned back. One of the Group's B-24s was lost over France, and *Ball of Fire Junior* made the five-hour flight only to crash-land at another airfield on its return. In all only ten of the Group's Liberators bombed the target, and the results were considered generally poor.

For Henry A. West, a navigator with the 352nd Bomb Squadron in the 301st Bomb Group at Chelveston, the Lille raid would be his fourth operational mission:

> "The 301st were briefed to fly from Chelveston to Norwich, leaving the coast at Felixstowe and heading for Bray, France, to Mouscron, then to the target. We were to circle to the left and leave France via Gravelines and head for North Foreland and back to base. The secondary target was Coutrai aerodrome and the third target was St. Omer airfield. At the general briefing later we were told that we would meet about 100 FW 190s and moderate to heavy anti-aircraft fire. I went out to the plane at about 0645 and worked on my maps, plotting courses and making entries in the log and just generally getting everything in order, such as checking the guns and ammunition. We started engines on schedule but take-off was six minutes late and we finally got off at 0753. We circled the field, getting into formation, until we departed on course. Everything went according to schedule."

The same procedure was being enacted at the other B-17 bases in the region. At between 0800 and 0830 hours Colonel Charles "Chip" Overacker Jr led 23 crews off from Thurleigh in a 369th Squadron Fortress with Captain James A. Johnston and his crew. Each plane had a crew of nine, a second waist gunner not thought necessary. As the B-17s circled the airfield, 2nd Lieutenant Albert W. La Chasse, the bombardier in *Snoozy II* in the 367th Squadron, flown by Captain John Olsen, waved goodbye to his buddy, "Butterball" Jones:

> "His aircraft was grounded because we were using some of their parts to fly the mission. I never saw him again. He fell out of his ship's bomb bay on a mission to the sub-pens in France after his ship was forced into the water by enemy fighters."

The 306th joined with the 92nd, 97th, and the leading 301st, with the B-24Ds of the 93rd Bomb Group falling in behind the formation began crossing the coast of England at Felixstowe at 0912. At about the same time as the formation left the coast of England III./JG 26 *Kommandeur*, Hauptmann "Pips" Priller, was leading his pilots off from their airfield at Wevelgem. They headed north to intercept the bombers. It was almost inevitable that mistakes and mechanical problems would overshadow an operation of this size, mounted for the first time. Seven Fortresses in the 92nd Bomb Group formation returned early to Bovingdon, Two 306th Bomb Group B-17s aborted the mission before reaching the enemy coast, and other groups also lost some of their number. Henry West in Major Dean Byerly's Fortress in the 301st formation had no such problems:

> "We picked up our fighter escort at Felixstowe, about three squadrons of Spitfires and three squadrons of P-38s.[37] On the way to the target, as we were entering enemy territory, we had some inaccurate flak but generally we proceeded to Lille without incident. Colonel R. R. Walker, our CO, who was leading the entire mission, got fouled up somewhere and we just invited trouble by stooging around France for a while doing 180° turns. Finally, we found the target but, just as Arthur "Catman" Carlson, my bombardier, was sighting through his bombsight, a formation of B-17s cut in front of us and we were forced to bomb another target. This turned out to be the railway goods terminus."

Nearing the target flak enveloped the formation, and in the 306th, Colonel Overacker's Fortress was hit in the No.2 engine and he was forced to relinquish the lead. Al La Chasse recalls:

> "Some smoke and dust covered the target area. As we continued the run a line of B-24s out of position were coming across the target area from the east, heading towards England. Flak hit our right inboard engine and set it on fire. Norman Gates, the co-pilot, somehow extinguished it. Flak increased. I was surprised it came in so many colors. On the bomb run Captain Olsen trimmed the ship before turning the control over to me. I released the bomb load not knowing there would be several malfunctions causing bomb rack problems. The plane lifted, lightened by the bomb drop. The B-24s were now behind us. It was 0942, time over the target as per mission plan. For *Snoozy II* the war was about to begin and end. With only three engines pulling we began a silly 360° turn into enemy territory. Where were the P-38s? None!"

As the Thurleigh Group came off the target about 50 of the "Abbeville Kids" attacked from the rear and head-on. La Chasse continues:

> "At about 1000 yards at 3 o'clock there immediately appeared, in line astern, a gaggle of Me 109s stalking us with four years' war experience. 'Ass-end Charlie' was about to become a 'sitting duck'! The interphone came alive with voices.
>
> 'Top turret: Jerries climbing into the sun behind me.'
>
> 'Red lights flashing on the instrument panel; four bombs hung!'
>
> I couldn't bring the doors up with the armed bolts still there. One stray armor-piercing bullet in the right place and boom, no anything!
>
> 'Bandits were everywhere. Where are those Goddamn P-38s? Sounds like typing on loose paper indicated enemy shells were ripping into the ship's skin surfaces. *Snoozy II* began to lag behind the rest of the formation. 'Honest John' McKee's ship tried lagging back with us. Good old 'Honest John'. He tried.

'Tracers were coming and going in all directions. 'How can I toggle armed bombs in a canted ship?' I thought. They hadn't taught me that in cadet training. I thought, 'Salvo! That's it: dump the whole damn load, bombs, shackles and all.'

'Now we were headed west, towards the white cliffs of Dover. Then suddenly S/Sgt Bert E. Kaylor, tail gunner, screamed, 'Jerries at 6 o'clock!'

'I thought, 'Boy that's right up our butts.' Out of the sun the bastards came. I could feel each gunner's position as they fired. Tail, ball and waist gunners each took turns. Again, where are those -------- P-38s?

'Now only Truman C. Wilder, the ball turret gunner, was still firing. Oh, oh, a belly attack was coming. All at once a German fighter flew right by our nose with a dirty yellow belly and nose with a white prop' spinner and black-painted corkscrew lines like a top. I tried to contact anyone on intercom but there was no sound."

"Pips" Priller had singled out *Snoozy II* (he identified it as a Liberator!), and he pumped cannon and machine-gun fire into the B-17 leaving Olsen and Gates dead in their blood-spattered cockpit.[38] La Chasse wrote later:

"From behind came a hell of a thumping noise. We had taken a full burst of 20mm cannon into the flight deck. Shortly thereafter the sun went by the nose as the ship went into a flat spin. We were lucky: it could have been in a tight vertical spin. Bill Gise, our navigator, got caught in the centrifugal force of the spin. Everything loose flew through the air and plastered on the side of the ship. We finally made it back to the escape hatch to bale out into the 'wild blue yonder.' I followed Gise out after some trouble with the hatch. God must have opened it. The ride down was just like the book on parachutes said it would be, scary but nice. I was alive."

Three other bombers were lost. Two of them fell to JG 26. III./JG 26 engaged the four-engined American bombers in combat for the first time on this day. From the recollections of *Oberleutnant* Otto Stammberger, leading the 9th *Staffel*, it becomes clear that for both sides it was quite a novel experience:

"The *Staffel* had just landed under my command at Wevelgem, when around 0830 hours we were scrambled. We should climb into the direction of St. Omer. However, we didn't gather systematically as when we were flying at a height of 3500 to 4000 meters, we already spotted a quite large pile of formidable fat bluebottles, which were approaching from the direction of St. Omer. They were American bombers of the Boeing B-17 type. They were not flying in a tight formation, as they flew in three rows and all 'vics' obviously flew higgledy-piggledy. Up to a height of 6000 meters, vics of *Viermots* were cruising along and above these I saw the vapor trails of fighter aircraft. In the meantime, the bombers had flown just past the west of Lille. Until we arrived at the bombers, the stream had turned tightly to the left and to the south of Lille and at last I got into a firing position. We charged into the single vics with our fighters attacking in pairs. We came in from behind, throttled back and fired our guns. The things grew bigger and bigger and all our attacks were commenced and broken off much too early, as we were afraid of flying into the 'barn doors'. I was wondering why I didn't register any hits, until I thought about the size of the lumps: a wingspan of 40 meters! Therefore, charge in at much closer range and so fast that nothing would happen to us anyway. Then commence firing, starting with the engines in the left wing. At my third pass, both engines were on fire and I succeeded in hitting the right outer engine as well, which belched forth smoke and the '*Kahn*'[39] plunged down to the left and towards the ground in wide spirals. At a height of 2000 meters four or five men baled out and to the east of Vendeville and the '*Kasten*'[40] crashed. I watched this from above and then I decided to go after the others. Yet miraculously, the sky was empty! Anyway, I was out of ammo for my cannons so I backed out towards home."[41]

Hauptmann Klaus Mietusch, meanwhile, led his 7th *Staffel* in an attack on the American bombers (which he mistook for RAF Stirlings), and he despatched *Big Eagle* of the 93rd Bomb Group near Lille.[42] Mietusch then pursued a B-17. Return fire downed his wingman, *Unteroffizier* Viktor Hager, who baled out badly wounded, but he could not open his parachute and he fell to his death. Mietusch made a second pass and damaged a B-17.[43] Captain Alexander Simpson's B-24 in the 93rd Bomb Group was also missing in action.[44] Only 69 bombers hit their primary targets and many of the bombs failed to explode. The inexperienced 93rd and 306th had placed many of their bombs outside the target area, killing a number of French civilians. Traffic control was bad, and some of the bombardiers never got the target in their bombsights. During the post-mission interrogations crews revealed that they had made 242 encounters with *Luftwaffe* fighters and put in fighter claims for 48 destroyed, 18 probably destroyed, and four damaged.[45] At the time the figures did much to compensate for the largely inaccurate bombing.

The Lille mission placed the American bomber crews firmly in the public eye and focused attention, perhaps wrongly, on their ability to knock down fighters rather than carrying out their primary task; that of destroying important targets. The very name conjured up visions of vast aerial fleets bent on destroying the greatest possible number of enemy aircraft, but the destruction of the enemy's ability to make war was the first consideration. Lieutenant Colonel Paul Tibbets, when interviewed by DeWitt Mackenzie of the Associated Press about the Lille raid, said:

"We had it hammered into us constantly that in practice we must watch out for the folks beneath us. This reaction persisted during my first three raids. Finally, I got used to the idea but I am cautious. When I look at a 2000lb bomb in the bay of my ship, I know a lot of people may get hurt. My anxiety is for the women and kids. You see, I have a three-year-old boy of my own at home. I hate to think of him playing near a bombed factory. That makes me careful. Lille is the most heavily populated area we have attacked and our target was in the thick of it. As we came above a great circle with a church beside it, which was the guide for our target, it came over me that if we missed the target we would hurt a lot of people. I gave the bombardier a heap of mental support to get his target. We don't want to kill French people. We don't want to hit anything but our target."

Plans meanwhile were being laid for an Allied invasion of North-West Africa. Operation *Torch*, as it was code-named, would involve both the American and British military forces, which would land at Oran and Algiers. No one was certain how the French forces in Algeria would react. In response to a request from General Charles Mast, the French Commander in Algiers, Major General Mark Clark, Lieutenant General Eisenhower's deputy, and other high-ranking American officers were flown to Gibraltar on 19 October by Paul Tibbets and Wayne Connors in *The Red Gremlin* and *Boomerang*. Clark and his party then went by submarine to Algeria to confer with Mast. The mission was successful, and Tibbets wrote later:

"We had reason to take pride in the fact that the mission eventually saved a considerable number of lives and played an important part in lighting the 'Torch'"

Meanwhile, the U-boat pens on the French Atlantic coast had to be knocked out or crippled, so that the undersea raiders could not seriously affect the '*Torch*' convoys carrying men and materials to North Africa. RAF Bomber Command had not even dented the U-boat lairs in 1941, and in 1942, during a respite, the Germans had methodically reinforced the shelters with almost 16ft of concrete. In October that year shipping losses rose dramatically, and November was to be even worse.

On 20 October 1942 Brigadier General Asa N. Duncan, Chief of Air Staff, issued a revised set of objectives to be carried out by VIII Bomber Command. In part it stated: "…Until further orders, every effort of the VIII Bomber Command will be directed to obtaining the maximum destruction of the submarine bases in the Bay of Biscay..." Duncan's crews, however, did not share the General's need for hitting the pens. They believed they should strike at the submarine yards inside Germany. However, the limited number of B-17s and B-24s available to the 8th at this time meant they would have to strike at the turn-around ports on the French Atlantic coast.

The scene, then, was set, but the weather threatened to ruin any immediate relief to Allied shipping the raids on the pens might bring. Eleven missions scheduled for October 1942 were scrubbed, and only one mission, on 21 October, was flown when B-17s of the 97th, 301st, and 306th Bomb Groups and B-24s were despatched to the U-boat pens at Keroman, about 11 miles from Lorient.[46] The two forces flew a long over-water flight in the Bay of Biscay to reduce the threat of *Luftwaffe* interception. However, thick cloud at their prescribed bombing altitude of 22,000ft forced all except the 15 Fortresses of the 97th Bomb Group to return to England. Major Joseph A. Thomas, the 97th lead pilot and Colonel Atkinson, who occupied the co-pilot's seat, saw no reason to turn back, and descended through the cloud, breaking clear over the target at 17,500ft. The German defenders were caught napping, and before the alarm was sounded 2000lb bombs were exploding in the target area, 21 falling within 1000ft of the MPI. Five hit the central block of shelters, yet did not penetrate more than 5ft.[47] However, three general workshops and a pair of floating docks were destroyed, and two U-boats not in their pens were damaged. Just after re-crossing the French coast, the formation of 15 Fortresses was bounced by a swarm of yellow-nosed FW 190s, which attacked them in such a manner that the high tails of the B-17s shielded them from fire positions in the radio hatch and top turrets. The attacks were ferocious and incessant, and centered upon the rear of the formation. Three B-17s were shot down.[48] A further six received varying degrees of damage. The 97th Bomb Group gunners claimed 10-4-3, but morale sagged with the knowledge that the 97th now had the highest losses of any group to date.

It was unfortunate that the 97th had flown what was to be its last mission from England under such a depressing cloud. Now they and the 301st were to come under the control of the 12th Air Force for Operation *Torch*.[49] But before that happened Paul Tibbets was ordered to assemble a fleet of six B-17s for another airlift to Gibraltar. His passenger in *Red Gremlin* would be General Dwight D. Eisenhower, who was the supreme commander for the operation. Mark Clark would fly in *Boomerang* with Lieutenant Wayne Connors. On 2 November the six B-17s flew from Polebrook to Hurn airport, near Bournemouth, to rendezvous with the military leaders who had left London by special train. Bad weather prevented take-off until 5 November when, although it was still not completely clear, Eisenhower could delay no longer. (The first landings in North Africa were scheduled for early on 8 November). John C. Summers' B-17,[50] whose passengers included Brigadier General Jimmy Doolittle and Brigadier General Lyman L. "Lem" Lemnitzer, CO of the 34th AA Brigade, had hydraulic failure taxi-ing out for take-off from Hurn. Summers was forced to wait until next day to fly to Gibraltar. Not long after leaving the coast of England the B-17 was attacked by four Junkers 88s. Only the top turret, ball turret, and tail guns were installed, so Summers tried to outpace his attackers. General Lemnitzer, who had an Army Distinguished Marksman Medal, is reported to have "manned a machine gun and was credited with an assist in downing one of the enemy aircraft!" A 20mm shell exploded in the cockpit, wounding Thomas F. Lohr, co-pilot. Another shell knocked out the No. 3 engine. Only when the Ju 88s were running low on fuel did they break off the attack and Summers managed to escape. *Red Gremlin* and three others arrived at Gibraltar on 6 November. Summers' disabled Fortress arrived early the following day, just in time for the invasion, which began in the early hours of 8 November with U.S. paratroopers flown out from England in 47 AAF transports. Tibbets and the *Red Gremlin* remained at Gibraltar while three of the Fortresses returned to Predannack on 9 November, from where they later made their final departure for North Africa.[51]

The landings at Casablanca, Oran, and Algiers were a success. Tibbets was informed that Major General Mark Clark wanted to get his staff to Algiers, and once again *Red Gremlin* and *Boomerang* were used, together with an escort of 16 Spitfires. The B-17s landed at the Maison Blanche air base, right in the middle of an air attack on the city. A Ju 88 exploded and scattered the area with debris, and another dropped a stick of bombs only 100ft from *Red Gremlin*. Tibbets then expected to return to Gibraltar and fly Eisenhower in, but that task was allotted to another B-17 in the 97th Bomb Group. Tibbets could only reflect "My stint as a chauffeur for the top brass had ended. I could now go back to being a warrior."

3

Fall of the Forts

"Our plane had 62 holes in it and we got off better than anyone else did. We learned a lot about flying and we learned that you had to stick together for protection."

Captain Robert K. Morgan, pilot of the *Memphis Belle*

The 97th and 301st departed from England late in November 1942 for North Africa, and earned undying fame with raids from the desert and later from Italy.[52] The future now looked bleak for the remaining groups in England. They still had to prove that high-altitude missions in daylight, often without escort, could justify further B-17 and B-24 groups being sent to the ETO. Shallow penetration missions, or "milk-runs," as they began to be called, were not the answer but, for the time being, VIII Bomber Command could not flaunt itself in force over the Continent. "Tip and run" missions to the U-boat pens would remain the order of the day, as Eaker pulled out all the stops in an effort to help stem the tide of U-boats entering the Bay of Biscay. In the first bombing mission since 21 October VIII Bomber Command struck at the U-boat pens at Brest, on the French Atlantic coast, on 7 November. At Bassingbourn the 91st Bomb Group, led by the CO, Colonel Stanley T. Wray, were pitched into the fray for the group's inaugural mission as part of the force of 57 B-17s and eleven B-24 Liberators from the 93rd Bomb Group[53] that were despatched. Thirty-four of the bombers unleashed nearly 80 tons of bombs on the French Atlantic port. Captain Robert K. Morgan was flying the *Memphis Belle*, destined to become one of the most famous if not *the* most famous B-17s of the war, on the mission:[54]

> "It was very successful even though the weather wasn't at its best. We encountered quite a bit of flak; Brest at the time was one of the hottest flak areas. We were at 20,000ft, flying a formation we thought up ourselves – a pretty loose formation. There were some enemy fighters in the sky but the Groups just saw them. They made one or two feeble attacks at the end of the last group. We all came home with the idea that this was a snap."

The force returned without loss, although eleven B-17s in the 91st Bomb Group were damaged, and the 306th came under attack from fighters in the target area. Two fighters jumped Captain John Ryan's Fort, and gunners aboard Lieutenant George Buckey's aircraft fought off three FW 190s, one of which was claimed shot down. Three B-24 crewmen were wounded, and *Hellsadroppin*, piloted by Lieutenant Julian A. Harvey, crashed at Exeter after sustaining battle damage. The B-24 was damaged beyond repair.

"Chip" Overacker's group seemed to emerge from the encounter over Brest with renewed confidence. But for the next two consecutive days morale at Thurleigh took another dent. On 8 November 42 B-17s in the 301st and 306th Bomb Groups were sent to bomb Abbeville-Drucat airfield and the Ateliers d'Hellemmes locomotive and freight car works at Lille at a cost of eight Forts damaged and three crewmen injured. The 4th Fighter Group provided top cover, but no enemy fighters were engaged because they waited until the Spitfires, low on fuel, left. In half an hour 30 enemy fighters made at least 200 attacks on the five Fortresses in the 369th Squadron in the 306th Bomb Group, which chose to make a second run on the target. Incredibly, four of the bombers survived, but Captain Richard D. Adams' B-17, which suffered a flak hit in the left wing between the two engines, was easy prey for the fighters. Fuel sprayed out of the wing and one of the engines was on fire. Adams tried in vain to shut down the engine. The flight controls were inoperative, and the increasing bank angle was getting dangerously steep. The instruments and oxygen system were also out, and with the plane at 20,000ft Adams rang the alarm bell and called over the interphone for the crew to "abandon ship." Adams only pulled his ripcord at 2000ft, but the long delayed jump might have been the reason Adams was saved from being captured, a fate that befell four of his crew.[55] Eleven 91st Bomb Group B-17s, meanwhile, attacked Abbeville/Drucat airdrome at a cost of five aircraft damaged and five crewmen wounded.

The next mission, to St. Nazaire, on the southern coast of Brittany, where the Loire empties into the Atlantic, was to provide a much stiffer test for the "freshman" 91st Bomb Group. This port was the home of one of Germany's most notorious U-boat pens. Over 50 heavy anti-aircraft guns were situated at St. Nazaire, and more were in the process of being installed. Captain Robert K. Morgan recalls:

> "At St. Nazaire the Germans had two methods of defense: (1) tracking the formation and (2) setting up a barrage. When they set up a barrage they knocked the hell out of us. We went in, one Group behind the other on the same beading, usually at altitudes of 1000ft difference. The German fighters would meet us before we got to the IP and would fly at our level as we turned onto our IP and opened bomb bay doors. They would radio the ground our altitude and airspeed and course. When they did that, the ground crews would figure ground speed and bomb release line and then put up a barrage that was waiting right on the bomb release line. It knocked the hell

out of us. The British anti-aircraft told us the best thing to do was to get the Germans to go back to tracking. If you could make them track, you could use evasive action and fool them almost every time. We did get them to start using tracking again. Here is how. The next time we went down there [17 November] the Groups were just as close, but we traveled all the way through France at about 2000ft different altitude than that at which we would bomb and just at the IP we lost altitude and went in on the target. Not all the planes went in on the same heading. Each took a different one. That way, the bomb release line wouldn't be the same; the barrage wouldn't do a lot of good, probably hitting only one of the Groups. To avoid being hit on this tracking method, we would set our course, fly for a few minutes, change course about 5° and lose and gain 500 to 1000ft. We did this slowly. That made it hard for them to get an altitude on us by radar. By the time we got near the target they had more altitudes than they knew what to do with and by the time we turned in to the target it was hard for them to get us. In our plane we worked out a pretty good system, which was used by most of the boys. We were the lead ship in the majority of our formations."

Tail gunner Sgt Quinlan explains:

"We had a system of calling flak out by the numbers. 'Six o'clock' was the position straight from the end of the tail, '5 o'clock' was on the left side (the pilot's right) and '7 o'clock' was the ether side. So if I saw flak, at our altitude or above or below, I would call it out, such as 'Flak 6 o'clock' or 'Flak 6 o'clock up' or 'Flak 6 o'clock down.' If I saw it was coming directly toward us I would tell the pilot it was moving in. The pilot would throw the plane out of the position end the flak would burst right where we had been. I wouldn't call flak out if it were bursting all around in the sky; only if it was coming towards us. Flak can follow a ship. You see a burst here and you see another burst there and you can tell that it is following you. It doesn't follow in a straight line, but it will be drawing a head on the ship. I would wait until it seemed to be drawing a bead on our formation and then I would call it out. The pilot would divert his position and the flak would burst away from us. One time we were flying along and I said 'Flak burst at 6 o'clock,' but at the time we were on the bombing run. Then I called it out again and the pilot moved the ship just in time. The flak burst where we had been a moment before. I think that in this way we saved a lot."

Captain Morgan adds:

"We found that to be the case a lot of times. If you call out flak, if all the gunners on the ship call it out, the pilot is able to move the plane around in such a way that the flak many times goes right on by you in the position you were in a few seconds before. We found out that it took the Germans about 40 seconds to change their track and start shooting again. By that tine we would be somewhere else. Naturally, when you got on the bombing run, you can't do anything about it. The boys that led those raids kept those planes straight and level on the run even though the flak was pretty difficult. I saw only one plane knocked down by flak and that got a direct hit in the bomb bay. I saw many get hit and knocked out of formation by flak. I have been asked many times how active the German flak was. I have been at 29,000ft over Wilhelmshaven and that flak was right up there with us. The British had some Mosquitoes over Essen at 35,000 and the flak knocked eight Mosquitoes down. So it is pretty accurate. That was one lesson we learned at St. Nazaire. We learned that we could make the Germans track us and could keep them from hitting the whole formation with flak. That was pretty important."

On the face of it, St. Nazaire was hardly the setting for a bombing experiment, but bombing results had been so inconsistent on the early raids that Eaker decided to send the bombers in at much lower altitudes on 9 November. Instead of going in over the target at the usual 20,000ft the leading 91st Bomb Group formation would cross St. Nazaire at 10,000ft, and the last group, the 306th, would go in at 8000ft. Such was the need for pinpoint accuracy that one squadron would go in as low as 7000ft. At Thurleigh "Chip" Overacker was incredulous. He phoned HQ to seek clarification, and as soon as the bombing altitudes were confirmed he protested, but his words fell on deaf ears. The hard-pressed Colonel retorted, "*If my crews have to fly the mission, I'll lead them!*" He therefore chose to fly the mission in Captain Henry W. Terry's plane, who would fly the mission as his co-pilot with his normal crew. Overacker's four squadron commanders refused to send their men unless they were with them, and they would fly the mission too.

Twenty B-17s took off from Thurleigh but seven aborted, leaving 13 to continue to the target. The force of 31 B-17s and B-24s[56] swept out over the sea towards St. Nazaire at 500ft to avoid being tracked by enemy radar. Nearing the target, the groups climbed to their briefed altitudes and began their bomb runs. Light flak (20mm and 37mm) embraced the low-flying Fortress formations, but the Liberators, flying at 18,000ft, came through without any serious damage. The heavier dual-purpose 88mm anti-aircraft guns were responsible for the most damage, and the Fortresses bore the brunt. Three Fortresses were lost in rapid succession to the flak over St. Nazaire, and they all came from Overacker's Group. *Man O'War*, flown by Lieutenant James M. Stewart, went down with all of the crew killed. *Miss Swoose*, flown by Lieutenant John R. Barnett, was shot down after "Bombs Away." Lieutenant Loyal M. Felts' Fort was hit on the bomb run when the first flak bursts knocked the No.3 engine off its mounting. One of the bursts shot away the Plexiglas nose, knocking Lieutenant Andrew L. Graham Jr (bombardier) off his seat, back against Lieutenant Forrest D. Hartin (navigator), and the bulkhead at the back of the forward fuselage. Then the Fort tilted over into a dive, and Graham fell out. Fortunately, he was wearing a seat-type chute and he managed to pull the ripcord and land safely. Hartin was trapped for a time, but worked his way free, and he bailed out despite having been hit by flak while in the aircraft. Germans shot him while descending, and on landing he sprained both ankles.[57] Co-pilot Robert J. Jones was knocked out of the plane by the force of the explosion and survived. The seven other men in the crew died. The intense flak succeeded in breaking up the formations, and they flew back to England in disarray. At Thurleigh, an inspection by the engineering department revealed that Overacker's plane was severely damaged with hits on both wings, the No.2 and 3 engines, the bombardier's compartment, the left elevator, the bomb bay doors, and the propellers on Nos.1 and 2 engines.

Every B-17 but one in the leading 91st Bomb Group formation was peppered with flak, but all managed to return safely to base. Even so, it was a mission Captain Robert K. Morgan, flying the *Memphis Belle*, was sure "none of his crew would ever forget":

"The four groups weren't in sight of each other when we left England. We came down to France outside the water area, down low. We were almost on the deck. We came straight into St. Nazaire, then began to climb to 8500ft, made a run to the northwest and dropped back to the water. The main idea of the raid was to surprise the Germans. It did surprise the fighters, who never got up but it didn't surprise the flak guns. Our plane had 62 holes in it and we got off better than anyone else did. We learned a lot about flying and we learned that you had to stick together for protection."

The subsequent critique confirmed that the 8th could never again flaunt itself over such a heavily defended target at such low altitudes. Bombing had been better than on previous missions, but could not be justified on this kind of loss ratio. Losses would have been heavier if the *Luftwaffe* had intercepted and shot down the stragglers. From thenceforth St. Nazaire became known as "Flak City," and bomber crews would not venture below four miles high. Missions to the U-boat lairs became an almost established routine, and the Germans moved in more and more anti-aircraft guns, until by November there were 75 ringed around the city alone. Gradually, the number was increased until it passed 100. Soon flak was so accurate it was even dangerous well in excess of 20,000ft. The truth of the motto "The higher, the fewer" was established, as Captain Robert K. Morgan confirms:

"We went back to St. Nazaire four times but always at high altitude. Twice we went in over land, over the southern part, trying to fool the Germans and make them wonder whether we were going to St. Nazaire or Brest or Lorient. We would head for Lorient then change and go to St. Nazaire. Many times we would get almost to the target before we would see an enemy fighter because they didn't want to take a chance on outguessing us and sending ships one place only to find that we gone another. When they did hit us – and they did many times before we got to our IP – flak didn't seem to follow us, even though this was the hottest flak area in this stretch of France. The fighters would attack us right through the flak, right on the bombing run. My gunners said they had seen them shot down by their own flak. They didn't seem to mind though. We didn't try to bomb the submarine pens themselves because a 2000lb bomb bounces off them. We knocked out repair installations and the locks. And when they got them repaired, we knocked them out again. The theory was that this made the pens useless. The same with Lorient and Brest."

On 15 November the 305th Bomb Group was scheduled to fly a practice mission. However, there were many problems for the new group to overcome, as Cliff Pyle explains:

"We had been at Grafton-Underwood only a short time when the 97th Bomb Group was assigned our aircraft before they left for North Africa. We had very little time to flight-test our new aircraft before we were scheduled for combat missions. My aircraft had a peculiar problem of losing power as we gained altitude and the cause was difficult to locate. Consequently, we named our plane 'SNAFU' (Situation Normal, All Fouled Up). My crew and I were not too fond of this name and after a couple of missions we decided to change the name to '*We The People*.' The Gulf Oil Company, whose popular radio program had the same name, recommended this name to us.

"It was decided that we would fly a few diversion flights to the Channel and back. This would also provide a familiarization 'look-see' at the countryside. Our first flight on 15 November was cancelled when the Commander of the 1st Bomb Wing learned that we were about to take off without ammunition on board. We had not fully realized that we were now in the war zone where the enemy could strike at any time. Next day, the group was scheduled to fly toward Brest, go halfway across the Channel and return. I could not start my No.2 engine and aborted the mission. On 17 November we flew a diversion flight to within 30 miles of Brest and returned safely."

Thurleigh was fast becoming the home of an "unlucky" outfit, and was one of the Fortress groups that returned to the U-boat pens at St. Nazaire, on the coast of western France, on 17 November when the 303rd Bomb Group flew its maiden mission. Twenty-one aircraft took off from Molesworth at 0923 to join the other groups on the raid. Six aircraft aborted the mission, and the others returned to base with their bomb loads when the lead bomber failed to locate the target due to heavy cloud cover. Six 44th Bomb Group Liberators also failed to find the target. The 306th were scheduled to bring up the rear with twelve B-17s. Three planes returned early with supercharger and gun problems and only nine remained. All went well on the bomb run and the start of the return home, but twenty miles northwest of the target fifteen Fw 190s singled out the small formation at the rear as easy pickings. *Chennault's Pappy* flown by Captain Robert C. Williams, the slightly built 423rd Operations Officer in lieu of Lieutenant William H. Warner, who was ill, was badly shot up. The bomber was named by Lieutenant Raymond J. Check—an original pilot and a very popular member of the squadron—who thought that the large B-17s were fit to father the P-40s made famous in China by the Flying Tigers of Major General Claire Chennault.[58] Cannon fire tore away an elevator, and in the next fighter pass Williams and his co pilot, Lieutenant Warren George, Jr, had to use their combined strength on the controls to keep the nose level. George braced both legs against the control column to keep *Chennault's Pappy* in a reasonably normal flight attitude. Williams and George, and the gunners aboard the plane weathered the storm and force-landed at Exeter with a dead top turret gunner. Three other crewmen had to be hospitalized and the bomber never flew again. Lieutenant John M. Regan managed to land his badly damaged Fortress at Membury after taking a direct hit in the No.3 engine, which ripped off the cowling, and after some maintenance he took off for Thurleigh later on three engines. In all, 16 of the bombers on the mission were damaged and three crewmen were wounded. In the 93rd Bomb Group formation *Shoot Luke* shrugged off three flak shells that exploded under the port wing, almost turning the aircraft upside down. On the homeward flight Ju 88s attacked the formation for 45 minutes. *Shoot Luke* dispatched one of the fighter-bombers, which burst into flames and crashed into the sea. That night at Thurleigh General Eaker presented medals to men in the group.

On 18 November 65 bombers were despatched to U-boat ports in France again. Twenty-one B-17s in the 91st and 306th Bomb Groups raided La Pallice, but the 19 B-17s in the 303rd Bomb Group, which was flying its maiden mission this day, mistook St. Nazaire (more than 100 miles away) for La Pallice and dropped their bombs there. In a separate action 13 B-24Ds in the 93rd Bomb Group attacked Lorient. One Liberator was damaged beyond economical repair,[59] and three other B-24Ds were damaged. The 306th Bomb Group's run of ill luck continued also. *Floozy* was shot down by a combination of flak and fighters and crashed in the Bay of Biscay.[60] At Thurleigh respiratory ailments were rife, and the enlisted men grumbled about unsanitary conditions and the poor food on offer. Every army has its complainers and backsliders, but feeling sorry for one's self is not a condition that can be tolerated for long, especially if higher command identifies that the condition is widespread and constitutes a serious morale problem. (On 25 November the 306th Bomb Group were removed from the battle order, only resuming combat missions again on 12 December).

On 19 November VIII Bomber Command added the submarine yards at Bremen, Kiel, and Vegesack to its list of approved targets. These were the first USAAF targets in Germany. However, the VIII Bomber Command heavies were still having difficulty hitting the U-boat pens in France. No one knew this better than the 303rd Bomb Group, which was still smarting from its navigational error four days before. Now it was the turn of the 305th Bomb Group at Grafton Underwood to be blooded. (The group would fly their first seven missions from this muddy airfield near Kettering before moving to Chelveston). On 22 November Colonel LeMay gathered all his crews in one of the huts and told them that they "were on their own now." Cliff Pyle adds: "He further stated that he had done his best in training and he believed we would benefit from it. He said we would be face to face with the best of the German Air Force." Unfortunately for the 305th, LeMay's bombers (and those in the 91st, 93rd, and 306th Bomb Groups) failed to drop their bombs on the U-boat pens at Lorient because of solid cloud cover. Eleven bombers in the 303rd Bomb Group were the only B-17s to actually bomb the target.

On 23 November VIII Bomber Command returned to St. Nazaire for the fifth time in two weeks. Though the submarine shelters on the French Atlantic coast showed little permanent damage, Admiral Sir Dudley Pound, the Royal Navy's First Sea Lord, wrote to General Eaker praising the cumulative effects of U.S. bomber attacks on disorganizing the servicing schedule of the U-boat bases:

> "It is too early to say with certainty what effect these raids have had on the German U-boat campaign. The existing evidence suggests, however, that although the direct damage to the U-boats and their shelters may not have been very great, the raids have caused a dislocation of the ports and the delicate organization of the U-boat service, which is only just becoming apparent. If this is so, and I personally believe that it is, the U.S. aircraft will already have performed a valuable service and discovered one of the few chinks in the enemy's armour so far the U-boat campaign is concerned."

The problem was that, although on almost every mission the American bombs were hitting their targets, experience was proving that a single bomb or even a few bombs did not have enough destructive power on their own. Colonel LeMay was determined to alter this, and decided to try and achieve greater bombing accuracy by flying a straight course on the bomb run instead of zigzagging every ten seconds; a tactic which had been designed to spoil the aim of the German flak batteries. His plan was to cross the target faster, and therefore reduce the amount of time the German flak batteries had to fire on the formation. It was a big step for a group commander to take, and one that caused his crews great concern.

Altogether, 58 B-17s flew down to Davidstowe Moor, Cornwall, on 23 November to refuel before setting out for the Bay of Biscay and St. Nazaire. Bad weather and mechanical problems forced 13 B-17s to abort, and one 306th Bomb Group Fortress was shot down just before the target. By the time the target was reached, four out of the twenty B-17s in the 305th, five out of the ten 91st B-17s, and four out of the eight B-17s in the 306th had turned back early. Only 44 B-17s remained: the 91st and 306th Bomb Groups, together totaling only eight aircraft. Despite this, the groups pressed on to the target. The 305th Bomb Group carried out the longest and straightest bomb run yet seen over Europe, and strike photos later revealed that they had placed twice as many bombs on the target as any other outfit. LeMay said later:

> "I remember distinctly: it was seven minutes from the time we saw the target until the bombs fell off the shackles. Quite a long seven minutes for everybody concerned. Next thing I know I'm talking to my bombardier. 'How did you do? How was the run?'
>
> 'It was a good run and we got bombs on the target.'
>
> 'You sure of that?'
>
> 'He said. 'Yes, I am sure of it. It was a good run. But I could have done a little better if it hadn't been for those clouds; they kind of got in the way.' There wasn't a speck of cloud over the target in that hour. The clouds he was talking about were flak bursts. Just shows what complete tenderfeet we all were. This boy was looking down through the bombsight and he saw those big black clouds drifting by...no wonder it bothered him."

Despite his crews' worst fears, LeMay lost no crews to flak or fighters, although five other Forts were lost, 16 B-17s and one B-24 were damaged, three crewmen were killed, and 16 were wounded. German Fighter pilots employing a new tactic had more than made up for the lack of accurate flak. On previous missions the B-17s had been intercepted from the rear, where enough guns could be brought to bear on enemy fighters. However, *Luftwaffe* experiments had now proved that the frontal area of a B-17 offered very little in defensive firepower, and despite the dangers of very high closing speeds, was considered the best method of shooting them down.[61] *Hauptmann* Egon Mayer, *Kommandeur* III./JG 2, who led the attacking fighters this day, and *Oberleutnant* Georg-Peter "Schorch" Eder, *Staffelkapitän* 12./JG2,[62] are credited with developing the head-on attack, where the bomber armament was weakest. *Feldwebel* Fritz Ungar, fighter pilot with JG 54 and JG 26 between August 1943 and May 1945 (with three confirmed kills), tells of the head-on tactics:

> "During an attack from behind, we were under defensive fire from the bombers too long and at least three machine-gun positions fired at us from each aircraft. In addition, the escorting fighters had the task of keeping us away from the bombers. So, we had no option left but to attack from head-on. Everything went very quick in this tactic; every second brought us 220 meters closer together! And of course we didn't want to collide but pull away over the bomber. For this pulling up and over the bomber, one needed almost the whole last two seconds [= 400 meters]. Our guns were adjusted to 400 meters. Therefore, we had two options: to fire too early, already at a distance of 600 or 500 meters, or to pull up half a second later. A very dangerous business. We didn't have one second to fire our guns. It is incredible when one thinks of all the efforts that we had to make for just one second. One thing was absolutely necessary: aim very precisely for this short moment."

Determining whether an attack was exactly head-on or not when the targets were tiny dots in the distance was difficult, so Mayer and Eder refined their tactics. They tailed the bombers to determine their exact course, altitude, and speed before moving out to a safe distance on one flank and overtaking the bombers, reaching a point about two miles ahead, before turning for a head-on pass. The new tactic worked well. In one pass JG 2 knocked down four B-17s, three of them in the 91st Bomb Group formation. *Sad Sack*, piloted by Major Victor Zienowicz, CO of the 322nd Squadron, with Captain McCormick as co-pilot, went missing in action with all eleven crew. *Pandora's Box*, flown by Major Harold C. Smelser, CO of the 401st Squadron with Captain Duane L. Jones as co-pilot, crashed into the sea about thirty miles northwest of St. Nazaire with no survivors. The group navigator, bombardier, and gunnery officers were among the casualties. Badly shot up and with five of the crew dead, *The Shiftless Skonk* crashed near Leavesden, Hertfordshire. The 303rd Bomb Group's *Lady Fairweather*, flown by Captain Charles G. Miller, was shot down in flames near the target. In the 306th 1st Lieutenant Clay Isbell's B-17 was shot down on the bomb run. Isbell and seven of his crew were trapped when the Fortress exploded.

Eaker could not wait for B-17s with power-operated chin turrets and missions continued, weather and reorganization permitting.[63] Pinprick raids continued to be made on the U-boat pens with all available bombers. On 5 December Eaker telephoned Colonel Timberlake at Alconbury and ordered three squadrons (24 Liberators)[64] ready to be despatched to North Africa on 7 December to take part in ten days of disruptive raids against Axis ports and shipping.[65] The 67th Bomb Squadron in the 44th Bomb Group, at last receiving its full quota of B-24Ds, offset this loss to some degree. It enabled the Eightballs to fly its first full Group mission on Sunday, 6 December. (B-24 crews by now had flown so many diversionary missions for the B-17s that they had painted ducks on their B-24s' fuselages, each representing a decoy mission). Nineteen B-24Ds, including *Little Beaver* flying her first mission, took off from Shipdham and set off on a diversionary mission to the JG 26 base at Abbeville-Drucat airfield in Picardy, while 36 B-17s set out to attack the Atelier d'Hellemmes locomotive works at Lille. Sixteen squadrons of RAF Spitfires covered the attacking formations, but it did not deter the *Luftwaffe*, which attacked in some strength. Cliff Pyle recalls:

"The 305th was No.3 in the formation, stacked up. Major McGehee led the squadron but he had to turn back with aircraft problems and I took over the lead. Twelve FW 190s attacked our squadron and my tail-gunner claimed two shot down and the waist gunner, one. Ten minutes from the target, Lieutenant Prentice left the formation in flames and five parachutes were seen to open. We encountered very little flak in our position and there were no casualties among my crew."[66]

In the Liberator formation things began to go wrong shortly after take off when *Little Beaver* lost an engine when the supercharger controls were over-advanced during the climb to altitude. When the throttle was pulled back to slow down in formation the superchargers rammed in too much air and the engines were starved of fuel. The other B-24s continued to the target as *Little Beaver* returned to base. Nearing the French coast an abort signal was radioed to the Group after British radar tracked oncoming enemy aircraft. Only the 66th and 67th Squadrons received the signal, leaving six B-24s in the 68th Squadron to continue to the target alone. 6th *Staffel* JG 1 came to the rescue of the "Abbeville Kids," and *Oberfeldwebel* Hans Ehlers and *Unteroffizier* Wloschinski each claimed a bomber.[67] A 68th Squadron B-24D captained by 1st Lieutenant James D. Dubard, Jr, was attacked by upwards of 30 fighters in waves of two or three from 12 o'clock high, and very early in the battle Dubard lost his No.4 engine and had the No.3 damaged. Dubard and his co-pilot, 2nd Lieutenant Henry B. Kaitala, fought valiantly to keep in formation, but they could not maintain speed on the remaining engines and were picked off by the fighters. Although they must have known that they were doomed to a watery grave, none of the crew baled out, choosing instead to keep firing and take as many fighters with them as possible. For their bravery and gallant action each man was awarded a posthumous Silver Star.[68]

Following the Lille mission,[69] plans were formulated for an attack on Romilly-sur-Seine airfield 100 miles SE of Paris. The *Luftwaffe* was using it as a large repair base and stopping-off point for pilots going to North Africa to support Rommel's *Afrikakorps*. Its sprawling hangars offered an excellent target, and the risk in flying so deep into enemy territory was considered well worth taking. However, bad weather resulted in the cancellation of the mission on 10 December. On 12 December, when bad weather again prevented a large attack on Romilly-sur-Seine, 17 Fortresses attacked the marshaling yards at Rouen Sotteville,[70] and the Liberators went to Abbeville Drucat. Ninety bombers had already crossed the French coast before thick cloud resulted in a recall. The B-17 Groups sought the secondary target, the marshaling yards at Rouen. Cliff Pyle says:

"My plane was out of commission so I took Lieutenant Whitson's aircraft and crew with Whitson flying as co-pilot. We led the second flight in the 422nd Squadron at the bottom of the group, which was flying lead. This forced the enemy planes attacking head-on to hit our squadron first. We were hit again and again from the time we crossed the French coast until we returned over the English Channel. The enemy fighters were marked with yellow noses and consisted of Bf 109s and FW 190s. Just before reaching the target two yellow-nosed FW 190s attacked us simultaneously, shooting one of our engines out, bursting a cylinder and an oil line. They also put two holes through a prop' blade. The engine started smoking and we feathered the prop' but we couldn't stay in formation so we turned the engine back on. It was smoking furiously and consequently we drew more enemy fire than any other plane on the return trip. The targets, first and secondary, had 10/10ths' cloud cover, forcing us to return home with our bombs. Upon reaching the Channel, however, we salvoed the bombs, feathered the bad engine and landed without mishap. Our crew claimed three enemy aircraft shot down. No aircraft were missing out of the 305th. Other groups lost three bombers[71] and three Spitfires were missing. Nineteen enemy aircraft were claimed shot down - four by Spitfires and 15 by B-17s. This mission was claimed to be the hottest air battle fought so far."[72]

On 20 December missions resumed when VIII Bomber Command carried out its heaviest raid since Lille, sending 101 B-17s[73] to strike at Romilly-sur-Seine airfield. Twelve squadrons of fighters flew escort as far as Rouen. At this point II./JG 26, led by Major Gerhard "Gerd" Schöpfel, who had paralleled the American formation waiting for the escorts to leave, attacked the B-17s of the leading 91st from head-on.[74] For 15 minutes the B-17 crews came under fire from head-on attacks and two aircraft in the 91st Bomb Group were shot down. Lieutenant Robert S. English flew one of the two victims, both in the 401st Bomb Squadron.[75] Ralph J. Tomek, one of the waist gunners, and who was on only his fourth mission, recalls:

"Sixty fighters ripped through our formation and made decisive hits on one Fortress flying in the rear element.[76] The tail broke off and there was only one survivor. Salvador Dalteris, tail gunner, was fortunate enough to be in the part that broke off and managed to bale out. Later, he told me that his pilot had told everyone that day to wear their parachutes on the mission. If he hadn't he would never have made it. Our ship was the next to be picked off. The fighters made head-on attacks and put two engines out of action and killed my pilot, Bob English. Our B-17 nose-dived about 1000ft but by some miracle the top turret gunner, Sgt Mandell, scrambled out of his turret and managed to get the aircraft straightened out. The two engines were on fire and we were losing altitude rapidly. Near Paris, Mandell sounded the alarm to bale out."[77]

For an hour the enemy fighters attacked in relays, and JG 26 did not break off until the withdrawal escort appeared over the Channel. In the 91st Bomb Group formation *Chief Sly* was hit badly in the fighter attacks and limped back across the Channel. Lieutenant Bruce Barton crash-landed at Fletching, Sussex, with a seriously wounded navigator, Lieutenant Paul Burnett, who had received a bullet wound to his thigh. *Rose O' Day*,[78] piloted by Captain Ken Wallick, was hit badly by flak and fighters, but thanks to Barton and his gunners aboard *Chief Sly*, together they fended off the attacks and Wallick brought *Rose O'Day* home to Bassingbourn, where he landed safely. *Chief Sly*, though, was fit only for spare parts. S/Sgt Cecil H. Scott, the 27-year-old ball turret gunner on the *Memphis Belle*, recalls:

"About 300 fighters attacked in relays. The fight lasted a couple of hours, the longest one we had been in. they attacked us as soon as we crossed the coast and circled around us like Indians. Then they started attacking from all directions at once. I thought I got two but I didn't get credit for them. We kept plugging away at them and somehow got by. Practically all our ammunition was gone when we got back. As many times as they shot at us we didn't get a single bullet hole in the plane."

The 8 Ball in the 303rd was also hit badly and crash-landed at Bovingdon after eight of the crew had baled out over Maidstone. *Unteroffizier* Hubert Swoboda, a Bf 109G pilot of 11th *Staffel* JG 1, made a lone attack on a B-17, and he was hit by return defensive fire. His guns jammed and four P-47 Thunderbolts[79] arrived on the scene, so Swoboda approached the Fortress at speed from the right and rammed the Fort, striking the rudder and damaging the fin before it finally went down.[80]

At Thurleigh 18 Forts had taken off, but three—all from the 367th *Clay Pigeons* Squadron—were missing.[81] *Leutnant* Otto Stammberger, leading 9./JG 26 attacking with *Hauptmann* Egon Mayer's III./JG 2, saw a B-17 flip end-over-end before its tail section broke off and the Fortress fell away. Fighters raked the B-17,[82] which was flown by Lieutenant Danton J. Nygaard, a recent replacement pilot, with 20mm cannon fire shortly after the target, and shells exploded in the nose, cockpit, and throughout the fuselage. As the aircraft fell away from the formation it went into a flat spin and rolled over.[83] Stammberger meanwhile had picked out his own target. It was *Rose O'Day*,[84] flown by Lieutenant John R. McKee, one of the original nine pilots in the *Clay Pigeons* Squadron. As Stammberger started a second head-on pass McKee's crew began baling out at short intervals. Eventually there were nine chutes.[85] The third loss was *Terry And The Pirates*[86] piloted by Lieutenant Lewis McKesson, the former squadron operations officer.[87]

One of the airmen who flew on these early missions was Lee Gordon, a gunner with the 305th Bomb Group. He was nicknamed "Shorty" because of his 5ft 2inch frame, but what he lacked in height he made up for in guts and determination.[88] On 20 December Shorty Gordon filled in as ball turret gunner aboard *Cunningham's Coffin* (named after the pilot) for the raid on Romilly-sur-Seine, 150 miles southeast of Paris. He almost did not make the mission when one of his guns failed to work, but before they reached France he had both guns in working order. A dozen squadrons of RAF and USAAF Spitfires flew cover, but they were soon low on fuel and had to return to England just before the heavies reached Rouen. Yellow-nosed and black-nosed FW 190s met the B-17s at the coastline. Gordon recalls:

"The bombardier spotted two FW 190s coming in head-on and called out the direction of the attack. I turned my turret to the front and raised my guns. Cunningham pulled up the nose so I could get at them and there was a Focke Wulf about 100ft away. His wings looked like they were on fire because all his guns were going at once. I thought I was a gonner but I got in a quick burst and he flipped over as he went past. I tried to swing after him and get in another burst, but he was going too fast. He was only 50ft away and I gotta glimpse of the pilot in the cockpit. He was wearing goggles and had a leather mask over his face. He was looking at me and I was looking at him and that's all there is to it but I was damn scared at the time."

As the initial onslaught of FW 190s broke off to refuel, another fifty joined the running fight and continued making attacks until shortly before "bombs away." Cliff Pyle in *We The People* saw his squadron's bombs drop short of the target:

"We were using the tactics of squadron aircraft dropping on the lead squadron aircraft. However the target was hit by the mass with good results."

The *Luftwaffe* fighters, which had broken off to refuel appeared again on the homeward trip and made repeated attacks on the B-17 formations until the Spitfire escort showed up to cover the bomber's exit across the Channel. Captain Robert K. Morgan in the 91st Bomb Group recalls:

"We came in south of Paris and went on southward. German fighters picked us up. First one squadron hit us and stayed with us a way, then another and another. That kept up all the way to the target. We were shot at to the target, on the bombing run and off the run. By that time the first enemy planes had been down and refueled and picked up more ammunition. For one hour and 58 minutes they followed us. I never saw so many attacks in my life. We learned a particular lesson that day. That was to keep your eyes open for fighters. That was the only mission that German fighters slipped in on us without our seeing them. Two German fighters came in at 2 o'clock high and I still don't know where they came from. The first indication I had of them was that our top turret gunner was firing his guns; he didn't have time to call them out before he started firing. We were caught asleep and if they had been able to shoot straight we would have been shot down. This was a successful mission. We hit the hangars and the depot, we wrecked 100 airplanes on the ground and we hit the officers' club at lunchtime. We heard later that there was a cellar full of cognac, which we blew up."

The 303rd Bomb Group had despatched 20 B-17s from Molesworth. One of these was *Jersey Bounce Jnr*[89] piloted by 2nd Lieutenant John F. Henderson, which was badly damaged and the tail gunner seriously wounded. Two engines were knocked out and the aircraft rapidly lost altitude. T/Sgt Forrest L. Vosler, radio operator, had been wounded on his hands and feet when a 20mm shell exploded nearby; although badly injured he continued to fire his guns and send out distress signals. *Jersey Bounce Jnr* ran out of fuel and ditched just off the English coast, and a passing vessel picked up the crew.[90] After being returned to base Vosler was taken to a hospital in Northampton and then returned to the United States. Vosler was awarded the Medal of Honor for "conspicuous gallantry above and beyond the call of duty." President Franklin D. Roosevelt made the presentation at the White House.

The 21 B-24Ds in the 44th Bomb Group that set out for Romilly-sur-Seine on 20 December had not fared well. Nine of the Liberators aborted with troubles ranging from supercharger to oxygen and machine-gun failures. *Little Beaver* again experienced supercharger failure and was forced to abort after flying for three and three-quarter hours.[91] Twelve Liberators continued to the target where Spitfires from a Polish RAF squadron played a cat and mouse game with the *Luftwaffe*, boxing them in before shooting them down. Lieutenant Clyde Price crossed the target on his bombing run but the bombs failed to release. Captain Howard F. Adams, pilot of *Maisie* in the 66th Squadron, recorded in his diary:

"I was leading the second element of four planes while Colonel Taylor and 'Wild Bill' McCoy led the first element of the 66th. It was bitter cold - way below zero - but in a few minutes, we all forgot about that as we were attacked by some FW 190s. I closed in behind the first element until we almost touched wingtips, but all of a sudden a FW 190 came down in a screaming dive shooting at Major Key's ship just ahead of me and passing between him and my ship. This was my first sight of a German plane despite the fact that I have been in England almost three months now! He was so close that I could easily see the pilot and the beautiful yellow and silver markings of the plane. I watched him until he disappeared five or six thousand feet below us but it didn't take long as he was going close to 600mph. I was too busy to be scared but managed to call the crew on the interphone and told them to keep their eyes peeled for more fighters. My navigator had fired a quick burst on his .50 caliber nose gun at the first FW 190 to no avail. It took all my time and energy to keep in tight formation and so I did not see Paris as we passed almost over it. The Germans kept buzzing around us but I didn't see them. One of them dived on Major Key's ship just to my front and fired his 20mm which hit one of the gunners square in the head and that was the end of him.[92] Now and again I would hear a short burst from one of our guns and would look over at my tiny co-pilot, 2nd Lieutenant Stanley M. McLeod, huddled underneath his steel helmet. I returned his weak smile and went back to flying which was real work now as my fingers were like ice and my oxygen mask was full of water and ice. Every once in a while my plane would rock viciously and I knew that the flak was getting uncomfortably close. Being faster than the B-17s we flew back and forth over the top of them, finally working our way up so we were in the middle of the formation, which was lucky as the FW 190s were concentrating on the front and rear. We continued our running dogfight and after a wee bit I saw Paris spread out beneath us. The Eiffel Tower stood out like a sore thumb even from our altitude. It was not long before I saw several squadrons of RAF Spitfires cutting capers high above us. The white vapor trails against the blue sky were a beautiful and comfortable sight. *Maisie* roared along as faithful as ever, but I thought I never would reach the English Channel. We soon passed up the B-17s and headed for home feeling very happy and gay about our good luck. We chattered over the interphone like silly schoolboys though when our radio operator told us that there was a wounded man on Major Key's ship we sobered up some. I peeled off and landed very cold and tired. Food and sleep were all we could think about after our five-hour ordeal. So ended our first real raid!"

No Liberators were lost over the airpark. This time it was the Fortresses, flying slower and below the Liberators, who soaked up all the punishment. Altogether six B-17s, including four in the 306th, were lost and 29 damaged.[93] Acrimony developed between the B-24 and B-17 crews who had to run the gauntlet of the Liberators' bombs descending on them. Strong headwinds on the homeward journey made it a long crawl for the bombers. The raid achieved very little, but crews were told later that the German officers' mess had been hit at dinnertime and there had been many casualties. American gunners once again submitted high claims, and the initial score of 53 "kills" was reduced to 21, plus 31 "probably damaged." The true figure was three enemy fighters shot down and one damaged. In total 101 bombers were despatched to Romilly—the largest force despatched since the Lille raid on 9 October. Of these, 72 had bombed the target, but they had caused only minor damage to the German airfield. However, Romilly proved a turning point in the daylight aerial war in Europe. For the first time the B-17s had penetrated 100 miles into enemy territory and had successfully beaten off incessant fighter attacks without the aid of escorting fighters. It augured well for the embryonic bombing force in the months ahead.

Christmas 1942 was the bomber groups' first in the ETO. In an attempt to integrate the English and American communities, General Eisenhower instructed all units where possible to have Christmas dinner in English homes. If the winter had been long, cold, and monotonously dark, it was temporarily forgotten, as many an American airbase opened its doors to the British public. As the year drew to a close officers and men were still working on improving methods for bombing and aerial gunnery. The two problems were linked, and at Chelveston, where the 305th had decamped on 6 December, Colonel LeMay and his staff worked hard to find the best method of combating fighter attacks without compromising bombing accuracy and vice-versa. After trying "stacked up" formations of 18 aircraft, LeMay finally decided upon staggered three-plane elements within a squadron and staggered squadrons within a group. This would result in a complicated bombing procedure if each aircraft tried maneuvering for accurate aiming, so LeMay discarded individual bombing, which had been Standard Operating Procedure (SOP) from the outset. He replaced the technique with "lead crews" whose bombardier signaled to the rest of the formation when to bomb, so that all bombs were released simultaneously, no matter what position the aircraft were flying. This simple but brilliant idea could mean all bombs missing the target, but if all landed a short distance from the MPI, then a target could be successfully destroyed instead of damaged. The very best bombardiers were selected for the task and put into lead crews. LeMay's synthesis found support at Wing Headquarters, where first Brigadier General Lawrence S. "Larry" Kuter,[94] and later Brigadier General Hayward "Possum" Hansell lent encouragement, and so gradually lead crews, comprising highly trained pilots, bombardiers, and navigators, became SOP.[95]

Unfortunately, the new techniques could not entirely allow for the vagaries of the weather, and this was evident when the lead crew concept was attempted on 30 December over the U-boat pens at Lorient. The bomb run was made into the sun, and its glare gave the experienced *Luftwaffe* pilots a blind spot in which to attack the Fortresses. Making skilful head-on attacks, they succeeded in shooting down three B-17s, including a 91st Bomb Group ship that carried the 401st Bomb Squadron commander. Lieutenant Floyd E. Love pulled out of the 305th Bomb Group formation to assist a loner in the 306th Bomb Group and was promptly shot down.[96] On the return flight, the 305th formation thought it was over England when, due to a terrific headwind, it was still over France. The formation became lax, and the aircraft were spread out more than usual. Fighters seized upon the lapse and badly damaged Captain Everett E. Tribbett's Fortress *Boom Town*, piloted by Captain Clyde B. Walker, but they managed to make it to St. Eval with one dead and two wounded aboard.[97]

For the Americans' sixth raid on St. Nazaire on 3 January 1943, when the torpedo stores were the target, Eaker for the first time completely abandoned individual bombing in favor of group bombing. Each aircraft would release its bombs simultaneously with the lead ship. This method, if the aim was true, could produce the concentration of bombs needed to destroy the twelve feet of concrete protecting the U-boats. It was also planned to overfly the Brest Peninsula on the outward trip and to return by a different route. To avoid re-crossing France the bombers were to fly due south out over the Bay of Biscay and then swing wide right towards England. Altogether 107 bombers were dispatched, but mechanical failures accounted for many aircraft returning to base early, leaving only eight B-24s and 68 Fortresses to continue to the target, stacked upwards of 20,000 to 22,000ft. Visibility was unlimited, so an unusually long bomb run was ordered, but as the run was made into the wind the airspeed was reduced by more than half by a 115mph gale so fierce that the bomb run took twice as long as that briefed. The Liberators, flying 20mph faster than the Fortresses, started out behind the B-17s, but by the time they had reached the target they had caught up with the B-17s and were ready to bomb at a higher altitude. For ten minutes the bombers flew almost straight and level, so the enemy had ample time to concentrate their guns on the formation. The Germans put up a box barrage at the release-point, forcing the bombers to fly through intense flak and Colonel Robinson, seeing that the Fortresses were being decimated, was forced off the target, and the eight Liberators headed out to sea, jettisoning their bombs as they went. They made for home at a height of 200ft above sea level. Shorty Gordon, in *Cunningham's Coffin*, remembers:

"There was so much flak as we approached the target that all I could see was a great black cloud that hid the formation of Forts flying ahead. It was like a big thunderstorm, thick enough to walk on. We all agreed later that it was the largest and most accurate barrage ever thrown up at the Forts over Europe. The barrage was a swell sight but it never got on my nerves. When I heard 'bombs away' from the bombardier I tried to watch them. One couldn't follow them all the way down when flying at 25,000ft but I estimated their direction and the time they should hit. Some bombs were hitting the water near the target. One was closer, another hit the corner of the target and another two went right into the middle of it. There was a hell of an explosion and we found out later that we made a direct hit on a torpedo storage shed."

Captain Vincent B. Evans, a genial 23-year-old Texan and the bombardier on *Memphis Belle* in the 91st Bomb Group formation, recalls:

"It was a small target but very important and we were glad of the opportunity to lead the Eighth Bomber Command. As we turned to make a run on the target, which I knew by its relation to other buildings, we ran into a strong wind, which we hadn't anticipated. That caused the plane to go wide on the IP and we almost went over Nantes. It also caused our ground speed to drop to 85 or 90mph. There we were sitting up there like clay pigeons. I told Captain Morgan and Major C. E. Putnam, who was riding as co-pilot and wing leader, that it was going to be a long run. They said let's settle down on it. We were anxious to get it right. We had a 2½-minute run. The usual one was about 55 seconds. We were really sweating out the last few seconds of that run. The flak was terrific. I could see the flashes of the anti-aircraft fire through my bombsight and occasionally a fighter crossing underneath. I could hear flak slapping the side of the ship like kicking the door of a Model-T Ford. Later we discovered that we had a lot of holes in the ship and a tire was blown to hell. Captain Morgan asked me when the hell I was going to drop the bombs. I told him to take it easy. I put my cross hairs where I knew the target to be, although I couldn't make it out at that distance. The second I released the bombs; I knew they were going to be good. The bombardier can usually tell. They were squarely on the target."

Shorty Gordon continues:

"I could hear flak hitting the ship. I knew that if the flak hit me while I was looking down I'd get it in the face so I continued searching forward. About this time I heard someone on the interphone yell: 'I'm hit!' and then another say: 'I'm hit!' I thought this time we were going down in France. Everyone seemed to be shot up badly so I waited for the order to bale out. This was one mission I was wearing my 'chute. I was still searching forward when I saw the No.1 engine on fire. I stepped on the interphone button but it was dead. I wondered if I shouldn't get up into the ship and tell Cunningham. It was burning on the underside and he couldn't see it. I decided to stick in the turret because there might be more fighters coming. Finally, Cunningham saw the fire through a flak hole in the wing and pulled the fire extinguisher on the engine. That stopped the fire but the prop' was windmilling out of control and I was afraid it would tear off the engine.

"We were over the water on the way back when I suddenly remembered that I didn't have my Mae West and was trying to figure out how I could get ashore after hitting the water. But then I heard someone say that enemy fighters were approaching from 11 o'clock. I ran my guns to that position nearly straight ahead and waited. I could hear bullets hit our ship but I couldn't see the fighters. That was one of the worst things that could happen, hearing the other gunners fighting but not being able to help them.

"I heard the bombardier calling out: 'Two enemy aircraft coming in low from 3 o'clock!' I turned and saw them and gave the first one a long burst at 800 yards. They were FW 190s and one was following the other. I hit the first one. Both of them saw my tracers and started to break off. Then I gave the first one another good burst at about 600 yards and saw my tracers going into his engine. He caught fire and went into a dive. I followed him for about 5000ft then started searching for the other fighter. One of the waist gunners saw the first FW 190 splash into the water. It was easy to see because we were only at 15,000ft. The other fighter apparently turned back.

"My feet started to hurt pretty bad when we got down to 10,000ft because they began thawing out. I had to take off my helmet and tear at my hair to keep from feeling the pain. My electric shoes hadn't been working. That was the fifth time I froze my feet."

Of the 17 B-17s of the 303rd that flew the mission heavy flak and considerable fighter opposition resulted in the loss of four aircraft and 34 men.[98] The first two Fortress groups, due to strong headwinds and being somewhat off course, were forced to land at Talbenny, South Wales, with very little petrol remaining.[99] The weather over the target had been clear, but the return over the sea was made in thick fog. Crews could only see a few feet in front of them. When the Liberators neared the Brest Peninsula, however, it began to clear. Unfortunately the navigators' reports were ignored, and later the Isles of Scilly were mistaken for Brest. Consequently, the small formation flew further and further up the Irish Sea. It was only when the Irish coast and the very real threat of internment loomed before them that Colonel Robinson led the formation into a turn towards the Bristol Channel. Fuel in the tanks, which had been reduced before take off, was getting low, and had only allowed for landfall at Lizard Point. Crews, realizing that they had missed Lands End, searched for airfields in Wales. Lieutenant John B. Long, flying *Texan*, reached Talbenny airfield, which was occupied by a Czech squadron, only to have his last engine fail through fuel starvation as he made his approach and he crashed. The crew were uninjured. *Bat Out of Hell*, flown by 1st Lieutenant Roy B. Erwin, nose-dived into the ground from 600ft, and another B-24 with two engines out on one side flown by 1st Lieutenant Ray L. Hilliard crashed into some walls obscured by hedges. Hilliard's co-pilot died later in hospital. Erwin and two of his crew were killed, and three others were badly injured. *Little Beaver* put down safely at Talbenny and remained there for five days, buffeted by snowstorms.[100]

As the last of the B-17s touched down at their bases in the Midlands, intelligence officers began piecing together the results of the raid. Men waited with bated breath, none more so than at Chelveston, where LeMay and his senior officers eagerly sought confirmation that the new tactics had paid off. They had as far as the bombing went. Most of the 342,000lb of bombs had fallen smack on the pens, but seven bombers had been lost, 47 damaged, and two aircraft in the 305th Bomb Group were so badly shot up by flak that they were left at Talbenny. These were the heaviest losses VIII Bomber Command had suffered thus far. Two of the Forts lost came from the Thurleigh Group, whose navigators were now in such short supply that some of its B-17s flew without one.[101]

In the wake of the debacle in Wales Colonel Robinson was relieved of command of the 44th Bomb Group, and Colonel (later Major General) Leon W. Johnson replaced him at Shipdham.[102] On 4 January Eaker also relieved Colonel Overacker of command of the 306th Bomb Group and told Colonel Armstrong to take over.[103] On 15 January Armstrong transferred Lieutenant Colonel Delmar Wilson, the deputy commander, and brought in as operations officer 28-year-old Major Claude Putnam, who, like Armstrong, was a veteran of the 97th's early days in England. They began rebuilding the combat-decimated Group, and within a few days had begun to restore the fading morale, although Armstrong's stay would be short at just over a month.[104]

On 4 January the 92nd Bomb Group, less key personnel and all of the 326th Squadron, left Bovingdon and departed for Alconbury, five miles north of Huntingdon. Although Alconbury was ankle-deep in mud, morale was high because the move was generally interpreted to mean a resumption of combat missions. However, any personnel who believed this is to be true were soon disappointed. Crews were sent to the 91st and 303rd Bomb Groups as "temporary" replacements, and very few ever returned to the 92nd. Meanwhile, other groups continued flying combat missions, and on 13 January, a day beset by bad weather and German fighter opposition, VIII Bomber Command again set out for the locomotive works at Fives-Lille. The 44th Bomb Group flew a diversionary raid to the Dutch coast in an attempt to draw fighters away from the real raid. Howard Adams brought up the rear of the 17-ship formation. He wrote:

> "As the sun streamed into the cockpit a feeling of peace and serenity settled over me as I lazily shifted back and forth behind our leader, 'Wild Bill' McCoy. The German fighters and the bark of their guns were remote from my thoughts though the ever-present sense of danger kept us all on our toes."

For the B-17s, the contrast could not have been more different. The 305th Bomb Group again flew lead with Brigadier General "Possum" Hansell, Commander of the 1st Bomb Wing, flying in the lead ship, *Dry Martini & The Cocktail Kids*, normally flown by Captain Allen V. Martini. Martini missed the mission because of illness, and Major Thomas H. Taylor, CO of the 364th Bomb Squadron, took the pilot's seat. The Chelveston outfit was singled out for attack by upwards of 25 FW 190s of I and II./JG 26. They attacked in line astern, making their attacks from head-on at the same altitude as the Fortresses. *Unteroffizier* Erich Scheyda and *Oberfeldwebel* Heinz Kemethmüller claimed the B-17 flown by Lieutenant Conrad J. Hilbinger.[105]

Aboard *Dry Martini & The Cocktail Kids* the bombardier was able to get his bombs away accurately and on target in spite of the fighter attacks. Soon after the bomb run was completed, at about 1430 hours, a FW 190 came in weaving at 11 o'clock level. All guns on the Fortress that could be brought to bear on the fighter and others were firing. As the FW 190 kept boring in it kept up a steady fire and many shots found their mark. One of the cannon shells came in through the windshield and exploded. Major Tom Taylor, who was hit in the chest, was killed instantly. In the co-pilot's seat, 2nd Lieutenant Joseph J. Boyle was wounded in the explosion, and he thought at first that the engines were gone, but after pulling Taylor's body off the controls, he managed to pull back the stick and level off. *Dry Martini & The Cocktail Kids* was now out of position and came in for repeated fighter attacks. More hits pierced the nose, top turret, and ball turret. The top turret gunner, S/Sgt Bill Beach, and the radioman, S/Sgt O. E. Ballew, carried Taylor's body into the nose. In the meantime ball turret gunner S/Sgt J. F. Hill had been shot through the thigh and, although in great pain, continued to fire until he was pulled out of the turret by T/Sgt H. L. Mabry, right waist gunner. Beach returned to his turret while Ballew administered first aid to Hill. While all this was going on the B-17 was receiving hits in the nose, fuselage, cockpit, and tail. The radio was completely out except for interphone communication between co-pilot, tail gunner, and navigator. Cannon shells exploding in the nose blew the oxygen masks off the navigator and bombardier, who maintained continuous fire while they found new masks and put them on. In the meanwhile Boyle had managed to get the ship back into formation. Shrapnel hit Bill Beach in the leg a minute or two later, and he had his oxygen mask blown off also. He continued firing without his mask until Ballew, finishing the task of putting a splint on Hill's leg and assisted by Mabry, helped Beach down and administered first aid. In both cases aid was so efficiently rendered by Ballew that neither Hill nor Beach was permanently injured. Mabry then got into the pilot's seat and assisted Boyle in flying the aircraft. Sgt Hise meanwhile was firing his waist gun and Mabry's alternately. Sgt Willis, tail gunner, kept up his fire as each fighter dove away. He had the shoulder of his flying suit blown away by bullets, and the parachute on his back was riddled with shrapnel. Boyle, although in pain from a wound in his leg and shrapnel wounds to his face, skillfully continued to pilot back to base and landed with Mabry's assistance.

Captain Cliff Pyle was flying his seventh mission in the 305th Bomb Group this day:

> "The 422nd Squadron flew the fourth position (fill-in squadron). We flew in the 'tail-end Charlie' position; the lowest aeroplane in the group formation. On the way over we encountered very little flak at the coast of France but over the target we received many attacks from yellow- and black-nosed FW 190s, which we later learned were from Abbeville. These fighter pilots were experienced and daring. They would come straight in and at the last moment would start a rolling maneuver and dive downward, firing all the time. Some of our crews believed they had armor plate on the underside of their planes.
>
> "Everything went well until we reached the target area and then everything seemed to happen at once. Six Focke Wulfs attacked us simultaneously, head-on, concentrating their fire on the third and fourth squadrons, while others attacked the second squadron. During this burst the No.2 ship in the second element in the third squadron was shot down. Our ship received four cannon holes, two in the left wing, one in the right wing and the fourth went through the floor of the bomb compartment into the pilots' compartment, bursting the hydraulic lines. Hydraulic fluid spewed throughout the pilots' compartment, blinding Lieutenant Gilbert, my co-pilot and myself. Only moments later the windshield shattered inwardly. I believe this was caused by a hit on the side of the aircraft and was aggravated further by the top turret guns firing forward.
>
> "Gunfire from two other fighters entered the lower turret, wounding Sgt L. G. McCoy, the turret gunner. There were about 150 30-caliber holes in the wings along with the two cannon shots. There was a hole in the leading edge about the size of a bushel basket. A tracer bullet entered the radio compartment, setting fire to the upholstery. Luckily, I managed to stay in formation. The No.1 engine was misfiring and spewing black smoke and we feathered the props immediately. The No.4 engine was also smoking. We feathered it for a few moments at a time until we reached the coast. Then we began to lag behind but we arrived over Chelveston in time to land with other damaged aircraft first. We had to extend the landing gear by hand. The airfoil on the leading edge of the wing was destroyed and made the action of flying the aircraft very difficult. On the final approach

it required both of us to hold the plane steady. The crippled engine was unfeathered and used on the final approach. Knowing we had no brakes we lined up for a short landing. Touching down we discovered to our surprise, that both tires were flat and we landed far too short. This was lucky because we had no braking action. Realizing that we had to abandon the runway for other aircraft landing behind us, we blasted the engines with full power and managed to swing off and clear the runway. We ended up in the ditch and mud alongside the runway. Everybody had been 100% sold on the B-17 before this flight but afterwards we had nothing but pure admiration for it. After all the damage flak and flying bits of metal from the airplane wounded only three members of the crew. I suffered from minor frostbite after sitting in the draft of an open cockpit window with temperatures ranging from around 55° below zero."

If anyone needed proof that LeMay's tactics were right the raid had proved them beyond doubt. The bombing was so effective that VIII Bomber Command never had need to return to Fives-Lille.

The *Luftwaffe*, not satisfied with the relatively small numbers of bombers being shot down, revised its tactics on 23 January when the Americans attacked U-boat installations at Lorient, and they employed simultaneous fighter attacks instead of attacks in trail to good effect.[106] Captain Robert K. Morgan, piloting the *Memphis Belle* in the 91st Bomb Group formation, recalls:

> "Through the flak fighters were beginning to attack us. Because ours was the smallest of the four groups, they concentrated on us and for about 22 minutes they gave us hell. Most of the attacks were from the front. One Focke-Wulf 190, attacking straight in from 12 o'clock, was heading right into us. One of us would have to move. The usual procedure would be to dive. I couldn't do that because another group was below us, so I pulled her straight up. The shells that were intended for our nose got our tail. I didn't know what had happened until Sgt John Quinlan, my tail gunner started giving it to me play by play. 'Chief, the tail is hit, the whole back end is shot off!' I heard him say. 'Chief, it's blazing! The whole tail is leaving the plane!' There was a silence then. I asked for a report. Nothing happened. Finally, I heard Quinlan's voice again, 'Chief, it's still on fire! There goes another piece!' Another silence for a minute and then Quinlan said, 'Chief, the fire has gone out.' That was the sweetest music I had ever heard. I climbed up to look back and see what had happened. It looked like we had no tail at all. I got back in the cockpit and flew for two hours back to the base. It was tough flying and tougher than that to set her down. The elevators were damaged so badly that the controls jammed. But somehow we managed to get down safely. That was a close call."[107]

In England, meanwhile, there had long been talk suggesting that the small American force should be incorporated into the RAF night bombing campaign. Despite the value of daylight bombing, losses had continued to rise, and many senior officers in the RAF remained unconvinced as to its ultimate success. General "Hap" Arnold, Chief of the American Air Staff, was under pressure from various quarters by those who wanted to know why Eaker had been unable to mount more missions, and why it was French, rather than German targets that were being bombed. Once again the future of VIII Bomber Command as a separate bombing force was in question, and answers were desperately needed if it was to survive.

4

Trial by Combat

"Down in Ruhr Valley
Flying so low
Some chairborne bahstaad
Said I must go
Flak loves big bombers
Fighters do too!
P-47 Boys how I love you"
"*Down in Ruhr Valley*" to the tune of "*Birmingham Jail*"

On 14 January 1943 Ira C. Eaker, who since November 1942 had been acting Commanding-General of the 8th Air Force in the absence of General Carl Spaatz, received a cable from General "Hap" Arnold to meet him at the forthcoming Casablanca Conference in North Africa. Next day Captain Cliff Pyle and the crew of *We The People* were alerted to fly General Eaker to North Africa. The trip was conducted in the utmost secrecy:

> "We were instructed to get to a base on the west coast of Wales and await further instructions. Upon arriving at Milford Haven it was cold, wet and windy. We were told upon our departure from Chelveston that we were to fly Mitzie Mayfair and her dancing troupe to several Allied bases. At about 0300 we were awakened and taken to Base Operations where we were met, not Mitzie Mayfair, but General Eaker! He said we were to take off for Marrakech, North Africa, as soon as we were ready. Flight planning and checking over our aircraft took about two hours and we departed about 0500. General Eaker had a cold and asked that we did not fly too high. Our flight en-route to Marrakech was uneventful, flying in broken clouds all the way. However, one amusing incident occurred when we started test firing our guns. General Eaker's aide, Captain James Parton, jumped and his foot came down on the radio operator's table and broke the operator s watch. Landing at Marrakech we saw disabled Vichy French aircraft lying around all over the airfield. They had been shot up only a brief time before the invading Americans. General Eaker went by ear to the conference site and we waited at the airfield for further orders."

The conference of President Roosevelt, Prime Minister Winston Churchill, and the combined heads of staff took place at the Anfa Hotel on a hill overlooking the Atlantic just south of the town. Many of the villas in the vicinity had been taken over by senior officers, and General Eaker found himself billeted in one called *Le Paradou - The Paradox*! Only two months earlier the Anfa Hotel had been the venue of the German Armistice Commission, and the rooms still bore some of its furniture and fittings. Outside ran a barbed wire surround with cans containing small stones strung every few feet and armed sentries placed at short intervals. Arnold warned Eaker that Churchill and Roosevelt had agreed that the 8th Air Force would cease daylight bombing and join the RAF in night bombing. Eaker was shattered, but was determined to reverse the decision. He wrote his now famous memorandum, less than a page long, which summarized his reasons why the daylight bombing offensive should continue. Although not fully convinced, Churchill was impressed, particularly with Eaker's "round the clock" bombing strategy. The British Prime Minister agreed to extend the time Eaker needed to prove daylight bombing, and the conference approved additional aircraft for VIII Bomber Command.

Upon his return to England, Eaker decided his forces were now ready to attack Germany for the first time, and the target selected for 27 January was the U-boat construction yards at Vegesack, on the northwest German coast on the Weser.[108] RAF night bombers had heavily bombed the port throughout 1942, and it had long been earmarked as a possible target for the Americans. Though RAF Bomber Command had caused severe damage to the town and had destroyed a large naval ammunition dump, some of the U-boat slipways and dry-docks and shipyards had escaped damage. It was an ideal opportunity for Eaker to demonstrate that daylight precision bombing could triumph over RAF night bombing, though the raid would be more effective as a morale booster than simply an attack on the German war effort.[109] Colonel Frank A. Armstrong was selected by Eaker to lead the first American bombers over Germany, an event which would forever tag the 306th with the proud boast *First Over Germany*. Armstrong had earlier led the 97th on the first all-American bombing raid of the European war, and it was appropriate that he performed a similar role again. Flying with Armstrong as co pilot was Major Claude Putnam, group operations officer, with Robert Salitrnik, navigator, and Frank Yanussi, bombardier. Eighteen B-17s of the 306th headed five bomb groups making up 64 B-17s and Liberators that started the mission.

The bombers flew a dog leg route to confuse the enemy. As they climbed to altitude, the intense cold froze machine-guns and turret mechanisms and frosted over windscreens and bombsights. Despite their thick clothing, the men grew weak from cold and only kept their oxygen masks from freezing by rubbing them with salt. By the time the coast came into view only 55 Fortresses remained, and 53 of them dropped their bombs blindly from 25,000ft through a German smoke screen, which drifted lazily over the shipyards. The two others bombed Emden. Crews reported being attacked by about 50 fighters, including some twin-engined types. Nine bombers were claimed shot down[110] but the actual losses were three ships, one of them a 305th Bomb Group B-17 piloted by Lieutenant Vance W. Beckham.[111] The bombing was described as "fair," but the press was ready to fête the bomber crews, and the B-17s in particular. The B-17 was rapidly becoming the favorite of the American public, much to the chagrin of the Liberator crews who had failed to find their target. The "Eightballs" received barely a mention. The newspapers neglected the Liberators that had borne the brunt of the *Luftwaffe's* attack, allowing the Fortresses to slip through and drop their bombs. The 44th resented being used as bait while the Boeing boys captured the headlines. Conversely, the B-17 crews were becoming positively hostile to the B-24s dropping their bombs through their formations as they had done over Romilly-sur-Seine and St. Nazaire. The Fortress' popularity was given added impetus with the news that B-17 gunners had claimed 22 fighters shot down for the loss of two Liberators and one Fortress. Crews estimated that about 50 fighters, including some twin-engined fighters normally used on night interceptor missions, had attacked them. They did not press home their attacks and the American formation escaped lightly.[112]

Flushed with no small measure of success, Eaker decided to try to crack an even bigger nut. For years RAF crews had referred to the industrial German heartland of the Ruhr as "Happy Valley," and it was feared and respected for its lethal concentrations of heavy flak. Twice bad weather postponed the strike, and on 2 February the heavies actually got into the air only for the mission to be aborted because of worsening weather conditions. Finally, on 4 February 86 B-17s and B-24s took off and went all the way, flying a long, deceptive flight over the freezing gray waters of the North Sea before turning for Emden, Hamm, and Osnabrück. Captain Cliff Pyle, piloting *We The People*, was flying his 11th mission in the 305th:[113]

"We took off without an aircraft heater. It was minus 55° at 22,000ft and it was the coldest I had ever been. Four members of my crew had to be treated later for frozen limbs."

The weather grew worse, forcing the Fortresses to seek targets of opportunity at Emden and off the coast. The Fortress formation became strung out, and it became an open invitation to the *Luftwaffe*, as Cliff Pyle explains:

"Everything went well until we were about 100 miles inland. There about 50 enemy fighters met us. They attacked us continuously to the target and until we were 30 miles out to sea."

On board *Sunrise Serenader*[114] Shorty Gordon, the tail gunner, discovered to his dismay that his guns had frozen. It is doubtful he could have fired them anyway, because at 22,000ft and a temperature at minus 45°, he had taken off his electric gloves to work on the guns. Every time the moist surfaces of his fingers touched the barrels his skin welded to the steel surfaces. When he pulled his hands away the steel tore his skin an inch. He concentrated on calling out fighter positions over the intercom for his fellow gunners. As they bore in Shorty, who had been working on a supercharger inside the wing for most of the previous night, got so excited that he became unintelligible at times, and the gunners tried to tell him to "get the hell off the air!" But Shorty's intercom switch was locked in position and he continued with his roaring, graphic description throughout the 75-minute air battle. "I saw a Fortress drop out of formation with four FW 190s after it. The Fort took violent evasive action. It swung up and over into a complete barrel roll. Fighters did that, not Fortresses."

The battle reached fever pitch, and five Fortresses were brought down as the *Luftwaffe* single and twin-engined fighters tore into the depleted ranks of the formation. A hail of machine-gun fire stabbed the air as gunners, their frozen bodies temporarily forgotten in the heat of battle, peered in all directions, seeking out their foe. Although the Americans were not immediately aware, another change in *Luftwaffe* tactics saw the first use of night fighters of NJG 1 against them on 4 February. It was believed that the heavily armed Bf 110 night fighters would bolster the day fighter arm and prove effective against American day bombers. *Hauptmann* Hans-Joachim Jabs led eight Bf 110s of IV./NJG 1 into action against the B-17s.[115] Jabs, *Oberfeldwebel* Heinz Grimm, and *Unteroffizier* Alfred Naumann claimed three B-17s shot down in the ensuing combat, one of which was *El Lobo*, a 305th Bomb Group B-17 flown by Lieutenant Cornelius "Neil" A. Jenkins.[116] Naumann and Leutnant Karl Heinz Völlkopf attacked the formation head-on and shot a Fortress out of it, which dropped its undercarriage.[117] One engine smoked, the Boeing dropped back. Naumann turned back and renewed his attack from behind. As a result both went down in flames, but Naumann was able to ditch his aircraft on the northern shore of Ameland.[118] Grimm and *Feldwebel* Georg "Schorsch" Kraft, who was directed by [GCI][119] station *Eisbär* (Polar Bear), were the last of the 110 pilots to reach the formation at 7,000 meters, 20km west of Texel. *Feldwebel* Erich Handke, Kraft's *Bordfunker*,[120] recalled:

"Suddenly we spotted the 60 Boeings in a heap before us. I must admit that I had a slight twitch when I saw them! We felt so small and ugly compared to these 'flying fortresses.' We attacked from the side, with the section leader leading. But he turned in too soon so that we were not able to fire, passing behind the formation with everyone firing at us. We then attacked the last aircraft alternately from behind and above until we were both riddled. At Grimm's final attack a Boeing caught fire and crashed later on. All of Grimm's windows were shot to pieces, the radio operator, *Unteroffizier* Hans Meissner, wounded; the port engine had stopped. We also had to feather our port engine as it began to smoke. Both port tanks *and* the starboard rear one were shot through, the coolant and petrol pipes to the port engine and 'Schorsch' Kraft's bullet-proof windscreen were also gone. So both of us returned on one engine. As Grimm's starboard engine also failed he had to make a belly-landing."[121]

The 305th Bomb Group lost a second B-17 when a FW 190 slammed into *What's Cookin' Doc?* flown by Lieutenant William K. Davidson.[122] Shorty Gordon in *Sunrise Serenader* saw it:

"The Focke Wulf was starting to roll over and go into a usual dive away from our formation when his wing hit the wing of the Fortress in the element below us. The impact cut the wing off the fighter and knocked the wing off the Fortress just past its No.4 engine. The Fort started into a circle then went into a tight spin. It broke in two, right at the middle and the ball turret went spinning down looking like a baby's rattle. Then the wreckage exploded."

Returning across the North Sea, *Sunrise Serenader* dropped back to protect a crippled B-17 flying on three engines. A FW 190 approached and fired a burst of 20mm cannon into *Sunrise Serenader*, almost removing its wing. The gunners shot the fighter down and the B-17 limped home with part of one wing dangling.[123]

Bad weather grounded the 8th until 14 February when the B-17s flew an abortive strike against Hamm, while the B-24s, as usual, flew a diversionary feint. The 44th had flown so many diversion missions for the B-17s that the Liberators were scornfully referred to as the "2nd Bombardment Diversion." The mission on the afternoon of the 15th was to prove no exception. The B-24s—21 of them—were required to make a diversionary attack on Dunkirk. Their target was the *Togo*, a German Fighter Control ship. The 67th Squadron led by Major MacDonald headed the formation in *Betty Anne-Gallopin' Ghost*, which was piloted by Captain Art V. Cullen. *Little Beaver* flew on his left wing in the No.3 position in the lead element. Just beneath them were three B-24s of the second element, with six more to the right and six more to the left. The formation crossed the Channel to Le Havre. Aboard *Betty Anne-Gallopin' Ghost* MacDonald's navigator, Lieutenant "Ben" Franklin plotted a course to make the Germans believe that the Liberators were headed inland. However, they changed direction and flew straight and level up the coast of France to Dunkirk where, three years before, the Royal Navy and an armada of small boats had rescued the British Expeditionary Force from its beaches. But their long straight run had enabled the German gunners to determine their speed and height. From their high altitude the B-24s could release their bombs some distance out over the Channel and let their trajectory carry them in. MacDonald's bombardier, 2nd Lieutenant Paul D. Caldwell, cried out "target in view." Arthur Cullen flew P and I for a few seconds, changing direction a few degrees right. Flak enveloped the formation, and just as the bomb-release light came on at 1540 hours, their B-24 took a direct hit.

When Cullen had recovered from the shock the Liberator was in a dive with no other ships in sight. There was no roof on the cabin, just a windshield. The cowlings were blown off No.2 and 3 engines, which were smoking. He could not operate the rudder because his leg was broken. MacDonald, sitting in the co-pilot's seat, had a bad stomach gash but signaled to bale out. For a few moments the noseless bomber flew on, only to fall away to starboard with the port inboard engine aflame and the right inboard ripped from its mounting. Finally the starboard wing fell off and a huge explosion scattered debris among the formation. MacDonald baled out in extreme pain, Cullen helping him by pushing him through the hole where the roof had been. He then followed MacDonald, hitting the tailplane and breaking his arm, and then breaking his leg a second time. MacDonald died later in a German hospital, but Cullen was eventually repatriated in September 1944 after having broken his leg a third time.[124]

The following day Howard Moore assumed command of the 67th Squadron and led them to St. Nazaire.[125] Colonel Leon Johnson flew Group lead. Shortly after leaving the English coast, *SNAFU*, flown by Lieutenant Fred M. Billings, flying in front of Lieutenant John B. Long's *Texan II*, developed a fault and slowed down. Falling away to port it hit Long's port wing tip and locked there. Both aircraft were engulfed in the ensuing fire, and seconds after impact they exploded. Debris was scattered, some even reaching the Fortress formation flying below.[126] When the remaining Liberators arrived over the target it was shrouded by a smoke screen. 1st Lieutenant George Phillips lined up *Little Beaver* for a bomb run, but the bomb-bay doors refused to open. Lieutenant Bill "Bus" Hill, bombardier, leaped from the nose and scrambled into the bomb bay by way of the radio compartment. The doors still remaining closed, he decided to release the bombs anyhow. The bombs hit the doors with a splintering impact, leaving jagged edges flapping beneath the bomber, which threatened to break off and damage other B-24s. Bursts of flak jostled the B-24 and German fighters sparred for an opening. Phillips commenced violent evasive action. Tom Bartmess, the navigator, hunched over his tiny table in the nose and steadied himself against the bulkhead. Meanwhile, clinging precariously to the catwalk, Hill realized that the flapping doors must somehow be tethered, and as the gunners opened up on the German fighters he went to work with pieces of wire. For a time Hill hung in the bomb bay, 20,000ft above the earth. The remnants of the doors were eventually secured in what must have been the highest trapeze act of the war. On the homeward journey the formation escaped virtually unscathed, although they suffered further attacks by the *Luftwaffe*. Despite the intense flak over the target the "Eightballs" managed to hit the dock areas. The raid cost six Fortresses,[127] and most bombardiers missed the aiming point.[128] What was notable was that it was the first occasion in which the Eighth Air Force had bombed the enemy on two successive days, and the Liberators' effectiveness was at last noted.[129]

Another spell of bad weather prevented any missions being flown by the 8th Air Force until 26 February when Bremen was the target for 65 bombers. At Shipdham six B-24Ds in the 66th Squadron, 44th Bomb Group, including *Sad Sack*, flown by 1st Lieutenant Robert H. McPhillamey and 1st Lieutenant Wilbur E. Wockenfuss and *Maisie*, flown as usual by Howard Adams and Stanley McLeod, taxied out in somber mood.[130] McPhillamey and Adams had recently flown their B-24s to Langford Lodge, in Northern Ireland, for modifications, and while they waited had spent an enjoyable two days in Belfast "taking in a show and window shopping." As they taxied out at Shipdham, Adams' mascot, a little wooden doll of the same name, swung gently from the cabin windshield in front of him and his co-pilot. The crew had also found room for Robert Perkins Post, a *New York Times* war correspondent, the only one of seven in the "Writing 69th" who had asked to fly with the Eightballs on the mission.

At airfields on the Continent, *Luftwaffe* fighter pilots lay in wait for the Liberators and B-17 Flying Fortresses. Once again night fighter crews too were ordered to stand by. At Leeuwarden 30-year-old *Hauptmann* Ludwig Becker, *Staffelkapitän* 12/NJG 1, and a great night fighting tactician with 44 night victories, waited to fly his very first daylight sortie.[131] Shortly before take off he was informed of the award of the Oak Leaves to his Knight's Cross, which had been bestowed on him on 1 July 1942 after his 25th night victory, for his leading role in the development of the night fighter arm. Becker was part of a formation of 12 Bf 110s, again led by *Hauptmann* Hans-Joachim Jabs, which took off from Leeuwarden at 1135 hours in pursuit of the American daylight raiders. IV./JG 1 intercepted the B-17s and B-24s and they returned, claiming two shot down, but Becker's Bf 110 was missing. Completely at ease and master in the night battle against the British bombing offensive, Becker fell victim to the bomber gunners.

Meanwhile twelve Bf 109 pilots in I./JG 1, including 22-year old *Leutnant* Heinz Knoke, had taken off from Jever-Wangerooge airfield.[132] A heavy overcast had forced the B-17s to abort the primary target at Bremen and seek their secondary target at Wilhelmshaven. About 30 miles from the coast the B-17s were attacked by fighters so determined in their mission that they kept up their attacks all the way into the target. 1st Lieutenant George F. Stallman, one of twenty pilots in the 305th Bomb Group, piloted *Sad Sack*, the lowest Fortress[133] in the entire formation. About 15 minutes from Bremen he came under attack from two Bf 109s. They made several passes, and the bomber took hits in the right wing and No.4 engine, knocking the ship out of formation. All the gunners, including Shorty Gordon in the ball, returned fire. Lawrence C. Lovos, tail gunner, was wounded in the attack. *Arkie*, Captain Everett E. Tribbett's B-17,[134] and *Devil's Playmate*, Lieutenant Isaac D. Benson's aircraft,[135] were both brought down. Light flak also bracketed the formation, and aerial mines, slightly larger than shoeboxes, were fired into the air above the Fortresses by anti-aircraft guns. After each burst they fell slowly downward, suspended from small parachutes. An isolated flak gun hit *Sad Sack*'s right wing and the tail and put out the No.4 engine, knocking the plane out of formation. Stallman ordered the bombardier to salvo the bombs in order to try to catch up with the formation. The bombardier delayed a while, evidently looking for a good spot before he finally salvoed the bombs. On the run over the target *Sad Sack* received many more flak hits, which killed the top turret gunner and the co-pilot. Glass and flying fragments cut Shorty Gordon and blood ran down his face. Fortunately he was wearing his parachute, because Stallman gave the order to bale out. Gordon rolled out of the turret and almost immediately opened his backpack chute at about 24,000ft. He says:

> "The silk streamed out and I felt a terrific jerk. I had not bothered to adjust the straps. If I had not had some luck I might have slipped through my harness. The opening jolt jerked my boots right off my feet and I came down in my stockinged feet."[136]

Southern Comfort was lucky to make it home to Chelveston. Hugh Ashcraft, the pilot, recalled:

> "We had disposed of six of our bombs when the ship shivered and we knew we had been heavily hit. The bombardier sent away his four remaining bombs on the docks of Wilhelmshaven before turning to see if the explosion of a 20mm shell in the nose had killed the navigator. The navigator was alive and uninjured, although the shell had exploded only 3 inches away from his head and dented the steel helmet he was wearing. The explosion drove his head down on the navigator's table, which broke under the impact of the helmet. The only ill effect he suffered was that he could not calculate the course of the plane for about 20 minutes. During this time the bombardier handled the navigator's gun as well as his own. A moment later the right waist gunner phoned: 'Sir, No.3 engine has been hit and is throwing quite a bit of oil.' The oil had spread over the wing. A tongue of flame appeared. The co-pilot closed the cowl flaps and pulled the fire extinguishers. The fire went out. The propeller of the crippled engine was now windmilling and chewing away at bits of cowling. Sparks were bouncing off the oil-covered wing. At this point I noticed that the rudder did not respond. Presently we found that four square feet of it had been shot away. When the tail gunner reported the condition of the tail, or rather the lack of it, he also reported that still another shell had burst just in back of him inside the fuselage. There was no time to appraise the damage. *Southern Comfort* had lost air speed caused by the drag of the windmilling propeller and an attempt to rejoin several of the formations proved futile.
>
> "It was then that I realized that if we were to return to England we were going to have to do it alone, crippled and out of formation. The loss of the supporting guns of other aircraft in the formation was serious, but more serious was the choice of course. We flew due north, to put as much sea between the enemy fighters and us as possible. Meanwhile the No.3 engine was vibrating and the wild prop kept taking bites out of the cowling. We were out over the North Sea when I announced over the intercom: 'Those who want to, please pray!' Not long after that we sighted land. We weren't sure, but we thought it was England. As we neared our home base an inquisitive Mosquito spotted us and finally came so close that we could see the pilot shake his head at our battle-scarred condition. He waved his hand and left. Shortly afterward, we picked up our field."[137]

The Liberators too were set upon by I./JG 1. Captain (later Colonel) Bill Cameron, co-pilot *Little Beaver*, on 26 February recalled that "there were German fighters all over the place. They flew in so close to us that I could easily see the pilot and not only could I count their guns but I could pretty accurately judge their caliber. Fighters would fly alongside just out of range then turn in towards us. Our crew would fire like mad but just couldn't score a hit. I sat there feeling like a 'bulls eye' in a shooting gallery!" The German fighters had begun their attacks 30 miles off the coast, and they were so determined in their mission that the attacks would continue all the way into the target. *Night Raider*, also called *Heavenly Hideaway*, a 93rd Bomb Group B-24D flown by Captain Beattie H. "Bud" Fleenor, limped away from the target area with a supercharger out, flak holes in its fuselage, and a pair of useless tail guns that had frozen tight after only eight rounds. Fleenor's B-24 was attacked again and again. T/Sgt Lou Szabo, waist gunner, said later:

> "A FW 190 came towards us. His wings were pure red. I could almost see the lead coming point-blank. I froze on to the trigger. His left wing dropped off - he went hell-bent into the water. But he'd fired first and hit Jung [S/Sgt Robert P. Jungbluth, radio operator] and me. I knew Jung was hurt worse than I was. I looked up and saw part of his arm hanging above the window, looked around and saw his side intact. The 20mm blast had ripped Jung's arm from his body and the shrapnel had hit us both."

Szabo had over 80 pieces lodged in his body. Incredibly, *Night Raider* made it back to crash-land at Ludham, Norfolk, with a badly wounded crew, no hydraulic system, punctured tires, a 15-inch hole in the right tail flap, and 177 30 and 20mm cannon shell holes in the aircraft. One ground crew man said, "This one shouldn't have come back." Either *Unteroffizier* Heinz Hanke of 9./JG 1 in a FW 190 or *Unteroffizier* Hans Wennekers of 2./JG 1 in a Bf 109 had claimed the apparently doomed B-24 as their first victory.

Sad Sack, a 44th Bomb Group ship captained by Robert McPhillamey, was also shot down by one of these two pilots. McPhillamey wrote later:

> "They picked me off shortly before we reached the IP. Two engines were shot out and on fire. The oxygen was shot out and there was a fire in the bomb bay. Controls, elevators, wings etc., were also badly hit and the plane became inoperable." Wilbur Wockenfuss adds "We could see the coast of Sweden and opted to try for it but it soon became apparent to all of us that it was hopeless." Under these conditions McPhillamey gave the order to bale out. "At the time that all of this was happening we were flying near 30,000ft but couldn't go any higher to avoid the prop wash of the B-17s. 2nd Lieutenant Rexford W. Lippert, the navigator, was killed instantly in the plane by a 20mm shell, which decapitated him. S/Sgt Robert P. Gannon, waist gunner, was hit in the knee just as he baled out. Sergeant Alberto O. Salvo, belly gunner, was hit in the shoulder and chest and in several other places but he managed to bale out with the rest of us. He died in a hospital shortly thereafter. After the crew was out (I thought) I started to leave as well but our engineer, Sgt Eugene Rudiger, had passed out from lack of oxygen and was blocking the exit. I must have beaten and abused him very badly when trying to get past him. I finally made it and was about to jump when something stopped me. I thought, 'My God! I can't leave the engineer.' I reached back and grabbed him by the collar of his fur flying jacket and backed towards the bomb bay, falling out and dragging him with me. I saw him later on the ground and it looked like he had been through a meat grinder. I never did tell him that I had almost beaten him to death trying to get past him. I reasoned that he must have regained consciousness on the way down and pulled the ripcord."

Since the island of Texel the Liberators had come under attack. *Maisie* dropped behind, so 2nd Lieutenant Wayne Gotke, navigator, spent most of the time working with position reports trying to get short cuts filled into the flight to allow Howard Adams to gain and catch the rest of the formation. Gotke was to recall later:

"We fought off the planes with very minor damage until we almost reached rank to Oldenburg, then all hell broke loose. However, I am reasonably sure no one was injured up to this point. When we were almost to Oldenburg, fighters hit us from all sides."

Heinz Knoke drew closer:

"I must have opened the throttle subconsciously. I can distinguish the individual enemy aircraft now. Most of them are Liberators. They look as if their fat bellies were pregnant with bombs. I pick out my target. 'This is where I settle your hash, my friend,' I mutter. I shall make a frontal attack. The Yank is focused in my sights. He grows rapidly larger. I reach for the firing buttons on the stick. Tracers come whizzing past my head. They have opened fire on me!"

T/Sgt Robert K. Vogt, engineer-top turret gunner, had swiveled his turret into the line of Knoke's fighter and taken aim. From the nose Wayne Gotke and S/Sgt James W. Mifflin, assistant radioman, also let loose with their .5 calibers. Only Sgt William Welsh, belly gunner, who passed out from lack of oxygen was unable to open fire. Gotke thought that as far as he knew "he never regained his senses."

Knoke was unharmed by the return fire from *Maisie*. Now it was his turn:

"Fire! I press both buttons, but my aim is poor. I can see only a few hits register in the right wing. I almost scrape the fat belly as I dive past. Then I am caught in the slipstream, buffeted about so violently that for a second I wonder if my tailplane has been shot away. I climb up steeply and break away to the left. Tracers pursue me, unpleasantly close. Blast all this metal in the air! I come in for a second frontal attack, this time from a little below. I keep on firing until I have to swerve to avoid a collision. My salvos register this time. I drop away below. As I turn my head, flames are spreading along the bottom of the fuselage of my Liberator. It sheers away from the formation in a wide sweep to the right. Twice more I come in to attack; this time diving from above the tail. I am met by heavy defensive fire."

In the heat and turmoil of battle, confusion reigned aboard the devastated Liberator. Wayne Gotke claimed later that:

"Robert Vogt, engineer-top turret gunner shot down the first fighter (sic) and I shot down the next one (sic) but not until he had sent 20mms into the nose and cockpit. Sergeant Mifflin shot down the third (sic) from his waist position. At this point my left gun jammed and I know at least two planes made direct hits on our nose and flight deck. Someone, I am not sure who, was hurt on the flight deck and I was hit twice in the nose of the ship operating a jammed gun. 2nd Lieutenant Bill Hannan, bombardier was riding in the nose with me and was uninjured up to this point. He had passed out twice from lack of oxygen [crimped oxygen supply hose] and I had replaced his mask and straightened the hose to bring him back to normal. Engine Nos.3 and 4 had been hit and were on fire."

Knoke's shells had indeed found their mark, but the B-24 gunners had not hit the incoming fighter. The only shudders Knoke was experiencing were those caused by the recoil from his two cannons and 13mm guns. He watched his cannon shell bursts rake along the top of the fuselage and right wing of the doomed Liberator. He hung on to the stick with both hands. Knoke wrote:

"The fire spreads along the right wing. The inside engine stops. Suddenly, the wing breaks off altogether. The body of the stricken monster plunges vertically, spinning into the depths. A long black trail of smoke marks its descent. One of the crew attempts to bale out but his parachute is in flames. Poor devil! The body somersaults and falls to the ground like a stone. At an altitude of 3000ft there is a tremendous explosion, which causes the spinning fuselage to disintegrate..."

Wayne Gotke was working on his guns when, all at once, "it seemed as if someone pushed me from behind and all went black. I woke up falling through space and I pulled my ripcord, but with no results! So I reached back and tore the back off my chute and quickly pulled as much of the material out as possible until it all opened. My last look at our altimeter in the ship was at 26,000ft." Knoke recounts the events following the Liberator's crash:

"Fragments of blazing wreckage land on a farm 200 or 300 yards from the Zwischenahn airfield and the exploding fuel tanks set the farm buildings on fire. In a terrific power dive I follow my victim down and land on the runway below. I run over to the scene of the crash. A crowd of people are there, trying to fight the fire in the farmhouse. I join in the rescue work and bring out furniture, animals and machinery from the burning buildings. Smoke blinds and chokes me; my flying suit is scorched by the flames, as I drag a fat pig out by the hind legs, squealing like mad, from the pigsty, which is completely gutted by fire. The farmhouse and barns are saved. Strewn all over the cow field lies the wreckage of the Liberator. The explosion threw the crew out in mid-air. Their shattered bodies lie beside the smoking remains of the aircraft. One hundred yards away I find the captain's seat and the nose wheel. A little doll, evidently the mascot, sits undamaged between the shattered windows of the cabin.

"One hour later I land at Jever. My men carry me shoulder-high to the dispersal point. That was my fourth victory; on my 164th sortie ... I cannot help thinking about the bodies of the American crew. When will our turn come? Those men share, in common with us, the great adventure of flying. Separated for the moment by the barrier of war, we shall one day be reunited by death in the air."

Two men had survived from the doomed Liberator. Wayne Gotke was picked up after "dangling between two trees about 20ft in the air for about 25 minutes," afraid that if he unbuckled he would fall badly. "It was at the first-aid station that I saw S/Sgt Mifflin. Also there was Lieutenant Wockenfuss, the co-pilot of the other ship that was shot down." Wockenfuss had landed about a hundred yards from the main gate of a German Army camp, where he was met by dozens of excited soldiers. He had said "Hello" in his best German and one of the Germans responded, "Hello! For you the war is over!" He had lived in Cleveland, Ohio, for 17 years! The Germans told him that the enlisted men from the crew had landed safely and were being interned. McPhillamey landed near a small village close to Oldenburg and was captured immediately after a couple of shots were fired in his direction. He ran into Mooney, Wockenfuss, and two others of his crew at a police station in Oldenburg. Gotke continues:

"Wockenfuss said he had seen Captain Adams' leather jacket and it appeared the man had been killed. The Germans had obtained the ship's loading list from the jacket and asked me about a Robert Perkins Post, the *New York Times* correspondent who was flying with us. I gave them no information whatsoever as my orders were to say nothing in the hope that if men were at large their chances of getting home would be better. The Germans asked questions about Donald Bowie, one of the gunners and Hannan and from that I believe these two men could not be identified. I am under the impression that all the bodies were not found, or if found, could not be identified. Positive identification of the body of Robert Post was never made. His father, Waldron K. Post, continued to search for his son's grave or official verification as to the disposition of Robert long after the end of the war, but with no apparent success."

Bremen was the last mission of the month for the Eightballs. February had been a bad month for the 66th Squadron, which had lost three ships and their crews. Ironically, the hardest loss to come to terms with was McCoy's, who had perished in an accident, not at the hands of the *Luftwaffe*. Combat losses were to be expected and, although not liked, were accepted as part of the game of war.[138]

On 4 March the Fortresses were dispatched to the Hamm marshaling yards, the first U.S. raid on the Ruhr, while 14 B-24s flew a diversionary feint. Sixteen B-17s in the 91st Bomb Group led by Major Paul Fishburne in *Chief Sly II*[139] in the 322nd Bomb Squadron had taken off from Bassingbourn and should have formed part of a large force of 71 B-17s, which were bound for Hamm. But due to very bad visibility over East Anglia and the North Sea, the Groups did not find each other. Fishburne took the decision that the 91st would continue to Hamm alone.[140] His formation, having bombed Hamm whilst under fighter attack all the time were returning over Friesland Province, in northern Holland, when they were attacked by Bf 110s of IV./NJG 1 and III./NJG 1, which normally were engaged in nightfighting duties. The B-17 gunners put up stiff resistance in the face of overwhelming odds. *Hauptmann* Hans-Joachim Jabs of IV./NJG 1 and his three wingmen finished off a straggler, which had repulsed at least 30 attacks before finally going down. *Hauptmann* Herbert Lütje then claimed a B-17 at 1131 hours, and shortly after four Bf 110s finished off another.[141] The battle raged on for another ten minutes and *Excalibur*,[142] captained by Lieutenant Alan Brill, finally fell victim to a Bf 110, probably flown by Leutnant Oskar Köstler of IV./NJG 1. Brill ditched the heavily damaged bomber in very rough seas 40 miles west of Texel, and although it broke in two, the crew managed to get out safely and enter their dinghies. In a six-hour struggle with the high seas, three crew drowned before an ASR Walrus picked up the seven survivors. The 91st Bomb Group received a DUC for the action this day. Major Fishburne and Captain James Bullock, his navigator, were awarded the DFC for successfully leading and completing the mission. Lieutenants Brill and Lowry, who both drowned after ditching their B-17, were posthumously awarded the DFC.[143]

On the 4 March raid Colonel Leon Johnson, flying in 1st Lieutenant Jim O'Brien's B-24, a 24-year-old pilot in the 68th Bomb Squadron from Monongahela, Pennsylvania, had led the 44th Bomb Group to Brest. On 6 March the "Eightballs" flew their fiftieth mission when ten B-24s and five Liberators in the 93rd Bomb Group flew a diversionary raid on a bridge and U-boat facilities at Brest, while 71 Fortresses headed for the U-boat pens at Lorient. All the Liberators returned, but three B-17s were shot down by III./JG 2. On 8 March Brigadier General Hayward Hansell flew in the 305th Bomb Group formation for the raid on the marshaling yards at Rennes by 67 B-17s to see for himself if the success gained four days' earlier could be repeated. He was not disappointed. Fifty B-17s plastered the marshaling yards from end to end and effectively stopped any supplies reaching German bases in Brittany for up to four days.

Meanwhile, 16 B-24s in the 44th Bomb Group were dispatched to the marshaling yards at Rouen, in northern France. This was a diversionary mission to aid Fortresses attacking Rennes. Three squadrons of RAF Spitfires escorted the bombers, and for the first time the 4th Fighter Group's P-47C Thunderbolts flew interdiction strikes against airfields ahead of the bombers.[144] Captain Bob Bishop recalls that, "the sky was like a black cloud of fighters." Unfortunately, unknown to the bomber crews, the American fighters had encountered heavy opposition, leaving the B-24s to fend for themselves. However, some Liberators had their own problems. 1st Lieutenant James E. O'Brien led the "Eightballs" in *The Rugged Buggy* with Lieutenant Colonel James Posey, soon to take command of the 44th Bomb Group, aboard. O'Brien, however, was forced to return to base when one of the gunners passed out through lack of oxygen. Captain Clyde E. Price, flying *Miss Dianne* in the 67th Bomb Squadron, took over the Group lead, and 1st Lieutenant Robert "Bob" W. Blaine, who was flying *Emmy Lou*, moved up to the deputy lead. FW 190s of II./JG 26, led by *Oberleutnant* Wilhelm-Ferdinand "Wutz" Galland, brother of *Generalmajor* Adolf Galland, led fighters in a tight turn to go *von Schnauze auf Schnauze* (snout to snout). *Miss Dianne* and *Emmy Lou* both went down immediately. Only three gunners survived from Price's ship, which crashed in flames at Totes at 1404 hours with the bombs still in their racks. S/Sgt Kenneth L Erhart, gunner *Miss Dianne,* recalls:

> "We were hit by FW 190s as well as by flak, amidships. Needless to say, with oxygen and hydraulic lines damaged, fire was inevitable. The bale-out bell was sounded. The ship was well aflame. Due to the nose attack, the flight deck personnel did not make it out. I assisted Sgts Iris Wyer and Duane Devars out the right waist window and also checked on Sgt Fleshman, but he was already dead.[145] I baled out of the right waist window and, upon hitting the ground, saw Lieutenant Morton P. Gross, the bombardier, coming down. His whole abdomen was ripped open and he died in my arms with the German soldiers looking on. Gross told me to take his watch and give it to his mother, but the Germans took the watch away from me."

Unteroffizier Peter Crump had singled out *Emmy Lou*. He fired a long burst at Blaine's B-24 from long range, and the German could clearly see a number of hits in the cockpit area. Crump dived away in a split-S, then saw to his horror that he was immediately in the way of Blaine's jettisoned bombs. Crump managed to miss them in a tight turn, but lost sight of his target and could not say which of the falling aircraft was his kill.[146] He saw one of the doomed Liberators crash in a patch of trees north of the Seine, but without a witness Crump would not be awarded confirmation of his victory. Instead it went to *Oberfeldwebel* Willi Roth.[147] The Spitfire escort, which had had their hands full with Major (later *Oberst*) Josef "Pips" Priller's III./JG 26, finally showed up in time to prevent further losses. Even so, two Liberators barely made it back to Shipdham, and *Peg*, in the 93rd Bomb Group, which was attacked by *Oberleutnant* Johannes "Hans" Naumann of II./JG 26, limped back across the Channel and crashed at Bredhurst, Kent. At Shipdham, the ill-fated 67th Bomb Squadron was now reduced to only three original crews and aircraft.[148]

The 93rd's period of inactivity on its return to Norfolk from North Africa had been brief, and on 12 and 13 March some crews joined with the Eightballs on two diversionary missions to aid the Fortresses. Although the return of the 93rd met with some disfavor among the "Eightballs," most would have been quick to admit that their inclusion strengthened the Liberator's cause in the ETO. On the 12th Fortresses went to Rouen and on the 13th they were scheduled to hit Amiens. T/Sgt Harold P. Loch, the 23-year-old engineer-top turret gunner on the *Memphis Belle*, recalls that they had a "lot of excitement" on the Rouen raid:

> "We flew over the French coast, feinted and flew back across the Channel. We knew the Jerries would get wise some time and they did. Thirty or forty of them jumped us over the Channel. They

attacked from every position. Then, just after we dropped our bombs, more fighters came from out of nowhere. Our tail got hit. We weren't bothered much more until we got almost to the Channel. Then six of them jumped us, circled around our tail from 7 o'clock to 5 o'clock and went to work on us. Shells were bursting everywhere. Finally, the foremost fighter began to smoke. He turned away and the rest followed him."

Loch's pilot, Captain Robert K. Morgan, recalls the raid the following day:

"We had a raid on Abbeville airdrome, which was not scheduled. We were going to Amiens. The lead group was supposed to turn northeast of Dieppe but instead went over Dieppe. We got a little flak. I figured he had missed it and we turned back and found Amiens. There was just one little hole and it was closing over at that time. That crew made so many zigzags trying to find the target because they couldn't find a check that we never got on the bombing run. So we had to quit our run because we were afraid we would drop some bombs on one of the planes. We had fighter protection up in the vapor trail. We could see them occasionally and knew that they were up there. We had to make a decision – either to make another run on the target or to pick out another target. We knew we wouldn't be able to see it if we turned around. We knew the fighters were about out of gas and would go home any minute. And we knew there were a lot of enemy fighters in the area. While doing this concentrating we were make a left turn and we saw Abbeville airdrome. We made a bombing run on the dispersal area and hit a great deal of it. We found out later that we were lucky because we had just got to the French coast on the way home when 120 German fighters were screened just behind us. If we had made another run we would have had every one of these planes on us. When we checked with the other crews next morning, we found that almost everyone bombed a different target. They bombed all up and down in this section on the way home. We were the only ones that hit Abbeville. We learned a lesson about not turning to go back on a target again unless everyone goes back on the same target. Eighteen ships were not enough of a formation to fight German fighters."

On 18 March General Ira Eaker sent 73 Fortresses and 24 Liberators, the highest number of bombers so far, to attack the Bremer Vulkan Schiffbau shipbuilding yards at Vegesack, on the Weser, a few miles north of Bremen. The yards were ranked the fourth largest producer of U-boats in Germany. Near Heligoland the B-17s came under attack from the *Luftwaffe*, and the leading 303rd Bomb Group formation of 22 aircraft bore the brunt of most of the enemy fighters' venom. During the bomb run the group came in for some concentrated and accurate flak. Leading the 359th and lowest squadron was *The Duchess*, piloted by Captain Harold Stouse. Up front in the nose Lieutenant Jack Mathis, the lead bombardier, crouched over his bombsight and lined up the target below; as lead bombardier, Mathis was doing the aiming for all the other aircraft in the squadron using AFCE[149] for the first time. This equipment gave him lateral control of the aircraft through the Norden bombsight's connection to the autopilot.[150] Stouse took his hands off the control column, and the aircraft was literally in Mathis' hands until the bombs were gone. Mathis called out: "Bomb bay doors are open," and then instructed Stouse to climb a little more to their bombing altitude of 24,000ft. On the bomb run flak enveloped the 359th Squadron just seconds before the bomb-release point. One shell burst off to the right of *The Duchess* and just below her nose. It was near enough to send a large piece of flak hurtling through the side of the nose, shattering the Plexiglas and hurling Mathis and the navigator to the rear of the nose compartment. Mathis had his right arm almost severed above the elbow, and he had deep wounds in his side and stomach. Without any assistance from the navigator, Mathis crawled back to his bombsight and released the bombs. The navigator heard Mathis' voice falter after he had uttered: "Bombs..." Thinking Mathis' throat mike had been damaged by the explosion, the navigator went forward and finished the call: "Bombs away!" Without this confirmation Stouse would not begin evasive action, so essential after bomb release. Mathis reached over to push the bomb bay door handle to close the bomb doors, but as he did so he slumped backwards into the arms of the navigator. It was only then that the navigator realized that Mathis had been mortally wounded. Two bombers were lost on the raid, but *The Duchess* managed to bring Jack Mathis' dead body home to Molesworth. He was posthumously awarded the Medal of Honor for "conspicuous gallantry and intrepidity above and beyond the call of duty."

At Jever at 1412 hours operation orders for I./JG 1 arrived telling the Bf 109 pilots to intercept and attack a formation of heavy bombers approaching the coast of Germany. *Leutnant* Heinz Knoke and his comrades had been practising for a few days previously on bombing the tight formations of American bombers from above with 100Ib bombs.[151] However, the *Alarmstart* (scramble) on 18 March gave the pilots of 5./JG 1 too little time to arm their fighters with bombs, and so Knoke decided to attack with guns only on this occasion. At 25,000ft Knoke made contact with the American formation in the Heligoland area, and he led his flight in close formation in a head-on attack on the Liberators. He opened fire on a B-24 flying low right in the 93rd Bomb Group formation. It was *Hot Freight*, flown by 1st Lieutenant Howard E. "Tarzan" Kleinsteuber, which immediately caught fire and fell away to the right like a crippled beast. Knoke pursued it, attacking from the rear, then from head-on. Suddenly at 1514 hours *Hot Freight* exploded, hurling wreckage through the sky. Sergeant Louis A. Webb was the only survivor. Knoke hurled his FW 190 into a power dive to escape the flying engines and debris, and only just managed to miss the falling fuselage of the doomed Liberator.[152] In his diary Knoke says that his friend Dieter Gerhardt's first Liberator "went down a few minutes before."[153] Gerhardt was shot down moments later attacking a second *Viermot*. Though he managed to bale out he died of his wounds in his dinghy. Major John "The Jerk" Jerstad, who led the 93rd Bomb Group, reported that they were under attack from fighters for one hour and 45 minutes.

Lieutenant John H. Murphy flew *Shoot Luke* out of Hardwick with Lieutenant George Black in the co-pilot's seat, as Lieutenant Frank Lown now commanded his own B-24. Their trip was uneventful until the formation, flying 2000ft below the Fortresses, reached their bombing altitude 50 miles from the German coast. For almost one and three-quarter hours the Liberators came under constant fighter attack. However, the run into the target was good and the bombing successful. On the return leg the *Luftwaffe* stepped up its attacks, sometimes with as many as 30 fighters taking part. They engaged the nine-ship element of the 93rd and succeeded in hitting Frank Lown's No.4 engine and blowing a hole in his vertical stabilizer. Next it was the turn of the twin-engined Bf 110 and Ju 88s. Their attacks were more nerve-racking, taking longer to complete and break away. Just as the B-24 crews thought they were safe, the German pilots would fish tail their fighters and fire longer bursts. When at last the German fighters broke off their attacks the crew of *Shoot Luke* saw Lown's engine beginning to smoke and vibrate badly. The B-24 dropped from formation and Murphy and his crew decided to help Lown home. *Shoot Luke* broke formation and took up position off the stricken Liberator's wing. Unfortunately the stragglers attracted the attention of a lone FW 190. Its pilot surveyed the situation and made his attack from 9 o'clock with his four machine-guns and cannon blazing. Three bullets missed Frank Lown's head by less than 18 inches.

Shortly afterwards *Shoot Luke* bucked with a sudden explosion in the rear section. Although hit in the eye by fragments, S/Sgt Floyd H. Mabee in the waist remained at his gun and succeeded in shooting down the fighter. S/Sgt Paul B. Slankard, the tail gunner, was blasted through the top of his turret by a direct hit from a 20mm shell. Slankard flew for interminable minutes at 22,000ft with the upper part of his body protruding from his turret. His left foot, which had caught in the gun controls, was all that had prevented him from being shot, projectile fashion, through the turret roof. Floyd Mabee made his way to the bomber's tail, pulled Slankard back into the aircraft, and applied an oxygen-mask to his face; Lieutenant Edmund J. Janic, bombardier, crawled to the rear of the ship despite severe head wounds and applied sulfonamide to Slankard's wound. Janic and Mabee together dragged the severely wounded tail gunner to a hole in the fuselage where the frigid air entering the plane at a temperature of 45° below zero sealed the wound. The hypodermic needles had frozen, and no amount of warming in the crew's mouths could thaw them enough to enable drugs to be administered. Slankard remained in his precarious position for two and three-quarter hours while Mabee massaged his hands to maintain circulation. Janic returned to the flight deck and collapsed through loss of blood and shock. Lieutenant Arch Rantala successfully navigated the two bombers home. Frank Lown landed and thanked Murphy's crew, which completely filled an ambulance, for saving him and his crew from certain destruction. Paul B. Slankard, who had made medical history, eventually made a recovery from his terrible wounds.[154]

Vegesack was officially described as "extremely heavily damaged." The bombers had dropped 268 tons of HE smack on the target, and later photographic reconnaissance revealed that seven U-boat hulls had been severely damaged and two-thirds of the shipyards destroyed. British Prime Minister Winston Churchill and Sir Charles Portal, Chief of Air Staff, recognized the importance of the success achieved on the mission and sent congratulatory messages to Eaker. The next three missions did not go quite as well and eight bombers were lost.

On 22 March 84 Liberators and Fortresses attacked U-boat yards at Wilhelmshaven. Leutnant Heinz Knoke tried aerial bombing for the first time. He carried a 500lb bomb on the underbelly of his Bf 109G and he dropped it in the midst of a formation vic of Fortresses. Knoke observed a wing break off one of the B-17s. It was *Liberty Bell* of the 324th Bomb Squadron, 91st Bomb Group, piloted by Captain Hascall C. McClellan, and it scattered the two others. All eleven men in McClellan's crew perished when the B-17 crashed 18 miles off Heligoland. Colonel Ted Timberlake, who was leading the 93rd Bomb Group in *Teggie Ann*, narrowly escaped death when a 20mm shell entered the cockpit and missed him by only a few inches.[155] When the Liberator returned to Hardwick there were no less than 368 holes in the B-24D. 1st Lieutenant Jim O'Brien and Major Francis McDuff, the 68th Squadron Commander, led the Eightballs in *Rugged Buggy* behind five B-24s of the 93rd Bomb Group. Jim O'Brien described the mission as "hot as my first," and later counted 29 separate holes in *Rugged Buggy*. Despite a thorough going over by Bf 110s and FW 190s, it was flak rather than fighters that claimed the sixth original 67th Squadron crew. *Maggie*, Captain Gideon W. "Bucky" Warne's Liberator that was damaged by flak over the target area, and *Cactus*, a 506th Squadron replacement ship flown by 1st Lieutenant Virgil R. Fouts, whose crew were flying their first mission, both went down. This left *Little Beaver* and *Suzy Q* as the only remaining original Liberators in the 67th Bomb Squadron. Lieutenant Robert J. Walker, navigator aboard *Maggie*, was the sole survivor from the two B-24s.[156]

Shortly after noon on 28 March 103 B-17s and 24 B-24s set out to bomb the Rouen-Sotteville marshaling yards, but the Liberators were recalled early because of poor weather. The Spitfire escort at first failed to rendezvous with the Fortresses, and the B-17s flew a triangular course in mid-Channel, which allowed the *Luftwaffe* ample time to intercept them. When the Spitfires finally arrived they had to return low on fuel, leaving the B-17s to fly on alone to the target. IInd *Gruppe* JG 26 and 12./JG 2 tore into the unescorted B-17s. Though they damaged nine of the Fortresses, only one was shot down.[157]

Three days later, on 31 March 102 B-17s and B-24s took off to bomb the wharves and docks area at Rotterdam, but four of the six bomb groups which set out were recalled because of strong winds and thick cloud.[158] B-24D *Satan's Chariot* in the 409th Bomb Squadron, 93rd Bomb Group, flown by 1st Lieutenant William "Bill" F. Williams, was shot down by *Oberleutnant* Otto Stammberger of Fourth *Staffel*, II./JG 26, his fourth victory.[159] Thirty-three heavies hit the dock area. Many of the B-17s, blown off course by strong winds and bad visibility, missed their objectives completely and killed 326 Dutch civilians when their bombs hurtled down into the streets of Rotterdam. JG 1 intercepted the returning 305th Bomb Group formation over the sea and made one pass before their fuel was expended. *Unteroffizier* Peter Crump of 5./JG 26 attacked *Southern Comfort* flown by Lieutenant Hugh Ashcraft, and it caught fire between the No.1 and No.2 engines. During the latter stages of the fight the radio operator discovered the ship was on fire. "I was shooting my gun. I saw our rudder hit and then I looked down and saw the fire. At first it was behind the vents, inside the wing and then it started coming out." As the enemy attack slackened, Ashcraft turned out of formation and swung back toward the English coast. Solid overcast swallowed the plane. The fire, apparently feeding on oil and not gasoline, was now "very persistent in character." The rear gunner, who had been with *Southern Comfort* through all her troubles, recalled:

> "It didn't bother me so much this time, because I knew what it was. We had plenty of time to arrange everything and I just sat there waiting for the signal to leave. Most of the rest of the crew gathered into two groups, one around the navigator's escape hatch in the forward end of the ship and the other about the door at the rear of the fuselage."

> "We were in the clouds at about 15,000ft," reported Ashcraft, "dropping fast and on instruments. We couldn't see a thing, but the navigator said it was about time we were over the coast. He gave me a heading to fly, but the tail was a little shot up and I couldn't do much. I looked at the wing and could see the metal buckling and the flames getting around, so I decided all God's children ought to have wings."

As the alarm bell rang, the radio operator, who had been sending SOS signals, was waiting for an answer. He screwed his key down and prepared to jump with the rest. They were all out in less than a minute, each man instantly disappearing into the thick bank of clouds. Ashcraft waited until the last man had jumped—or until he thought the last man had jumped. Then he trimmed the ship so that it was flying level and followed the others overboard through the forward escape hatch. Later it was discovered that the left waist gunner, last man to leave by the door at the rear of the ship, had delayed to change his parachute. When he looked around he found himself in a pilotless and deserted airplane. He left immediately. Ashcraft remembers the long trip earthward:

> "It was like flying in a void. Just gray mist. You couldn't see anything. We weren't sure whether we were still out over the water or not. Somebody said there are no atheists in foxholes. Well, there

aren't any in parachutes, either. I guess it's the same whether you're down looking up, or up looking down."

The bombardier's main thought was to get back home before his roommates started dividing up his clothes:

"I could see one of them wearing my bathrobe. I finally hit a tree in an orchard. I looked down and there were a lot of firm-looking people waiting for me. They were all right, though, once they found out what side I was on."

Three of the gunners came down together, one of them with a five-foot rip in his parachute. The waist gunner reports:

"We had quite a trip down. Ball turret was a man who was always griping about something. Well, there he was, griping again about the holes in his chute. So I yelled to him: 'Listen, can you swim? Because if you can, you'd better get ready."

The three gunners came down just off the perimeter track of a British airdrome near the coast. The waist gunner, whose face was frozen and whose flying boots had been ripped off when he jumped, was dragged over some bushes and into a muddy creek. A group of workmen pulled him out. "It was just like a New York subway I didn't know what I was getting into." The bombardier and the other waist gunner landed in a swamp, the bombardier's chute pulling him along for 200 yards before it collapsed. "I don't know why I should have landed with my mouth open, but I did and it filled up with sewer water." The navigator and the radio operator came out of the clouds over a broad estuary and dropped into the water. At that moment a new ASR launch happened to be cruising the inlet on a test run. As the two Americans hit the water the launch came alongside the gunner and picked him up. A minute later they also had the navigator in the boat. They got a couple of cash customers on their first day out. "I didn't exactly cut a path when I hit, but I feel sorry for those poor surfboards and aquaplanes."

The only fatality among the crew was *Southern Comfort's* top turret gunner [S/Sgt Steve Gogoyla], who apparently slipped out of his parachute harness as he neared the ground. Three times the burning B-17 gracefully circled Wickham Bishops, a small village, and then crashed in a field; the last considerate act of a gallant lady.

Bad weather grounded the Eighth until 4 April, when 97 B-17s headed for the Renault works in the Billancourt district of Paris.[160] It took two hours for the four B-17 groups to complete assembly before a total of 97 Fortresses departed the rendezvous point at Beachy Head. However, when landfall was made at Dieppe, only 85 Fortresses remained, 12 having aborted through malfunctions. For once the sky was clear and blue, and many of the Spitfire escort fighters could be seen quite plainly. Others were simply vapor trails in the upper reaches of the atmosphere. From their altitude of 25,000ft, crews could see the black mass of Paris apparently cradled by the long curved arm of the River Seine, 95 miles in the distance. At 1414 hours the Fortresses were over their target and 251 tons of high explosive rained down on Paris. Flak was moderate and not too accurate, and crews were able to pick out the Renault works despite the industrial haze, which covered much of the city. Most of the 81 tons that landed square on the factory were released by 18 B-17s of the leading 305th Bomb Group formation, led by Major Thomas K. McGehee in *We The People*, flown by Captain Cliff Pyle. Before the last group had left the target a thick pall of smoke reaching to 4000ft blotted out the whole area. Unfortunately, the groups in the rear of the formation were not as accurate as the 305th had been, and many bombs fell outside the target area, causing a number of civilian casualties. North of Paris I./JG 2 and the operational *Staffel* of JG 105, both led by Spanish Civil War veteran Major Walter "Gulle" Oesau, *Kommodore* JG 2, made the first interception of the B-17s.[161] They made several head-on passes before the Fortresses reached the Rouen area, where 50-75 Bf 109G-4s and FW 190A-4s of JG 26 began attacks on the formation.[162] JG 26 made repeated frontal attacks, sometimes by four and six fighters at a time. Lieutenant T. Paxton Sherwood, co-pilot in H. J. Walker's crew, 305th Bomb Group, recalled:

"I saw the yellow-nosed fighters turn and fly on the bombers, particularly the low squadron, from 11, 12 and 1 o'clock high. They came through the squadron and rolled their armored bellies up for protection from our fire."

Dry Martini III, the lead plane in the 364th Bomb Squadron, 305th Bomb Group, was attacked by a swarm of enemy fighters. Cannon shells smashed through the windshield and Martini was temporarily blinded. His co-pilot, Lieutenant Boyle, was wounded and momentarily knocked unconscious. The B-17 dropped 1000ft before the two pilots could bring the Fortress under control. One engine was out and they were alone, easy prey for the fighters, or so JG 26 thought. They massed for the *coup de grace*, but although they riddled the airplane, and in particular the right wing and left aileron, they could not bring the aircraft down.[163] At 1433 the Spitfire escort reappeared to provide withdrawal support, but six of their number were shot down in a seven-minute battle without loss to the *Luftwaffe*. After the raid, photographs smuggled back to England by the French Resistance showed that the Renault works had been severely damaged. For its action this day, the 305th Bomb Group received a Distinguished Unit Citation.

On 5 April 79 B-17s and 25 B-24s were despatched to Belgium to bomb the ERLA VII aircraft and engine repair works at Mortsel, near Antwerp.[164] Eighteen B-17s in the 306th Bomb Group led the mission, with Lieutenant Colonel Jim Wilson and Captain John Regan in *Dark Horse* at the head of the formation. Brigadier-General Frank Armstrong, CO, 1st Bomb Wing, flew aboard this aircraft as an observer. The 368th Bomb Squadron flew Lead, the 423rd High, and the 367th "Clay Pigeons" Squadron flew Low. Twenty-one bombers returned early with mechanical problems, leaving 83 heavies to continue. The Thurleigh Group was the first to feel the weight of head-on attacks by FW 190A-4 and A-5s of JG 26 and II./JG 1, which continued all the way to the target. III./JG 26 had taken off to intercept the Fortresses in the Ghent area. Just before 1510 hours the *Kommandeur*, *Hauptmann* Fritz Geisshardt, and his *Stabs* Flight encountered the Forts. Geisshardt attacked a B-17, coming in from the right and to the side and from above. He went charging in again from the same direction but was hit in the abdomen by return fire from the B-17s.[165] At around the same time *L'il Abner*, flown by Lieutenant Clarence Fischer, was hit by flak over Ghent en route to the target and finished off by Major "Pips" Priller. The crew baled out before the Fortress exploded at Wilrijk.[166] Lieutenant Kelly Ross's aircraft was badly hit on the way into the target by cannon and machine-gun fire from *Hauptmann* "Wutz" Galland. After the No.2 engine was shot out Ross gave the order to bale out. All except the tail and waist gunners survived.[167]

The Fortress piloted by 1st Lieutenant William H. Parker was shot down at 1538 hours by *Oberfeldwebel* Adolf "Addi" Glunz of IV./JG 26, who claimed it as his 32nd of his eventual 71-victory tally.[168] At 1535 hours north of Antwerp *Oberleutnant* Otto Stammberger, *Staffelkapitän* 4./JG 26, found a faltering B-17 squarely in his sights. It was *Montana Power* flown by 2nd Lieutenant Robert W. Seelos in the 368th Bomb Squadron, which, after having lost its No.1 engine to flak, had dropped from formation during the bomb run. Stammberger raked the B-17 from head-on with a burst from his four cannon and two machine guns. Stammberger had to pull up quickly because the Fortress suddenly nosed downward. He watched the survivors bale out and saw the pilotless ship carry on for a short time before finally crashing at Kalmthout.[169] *Dark Horse* was hit by cannon fire from a FW 190 attacking head on during the bomb run. Lieutenant Colonel James Wilson, 306th Bomb Group CO, managed to bring the Fortress home safely to Thurleigh aided by Captain Robert Salitrnik, the lead navigator. Salitrnik had been critically wounded when he was hit in the leg by fragments from a can of .50 caliber ammunition, which exploded when hit by 20mm fire from a FW 190 during a head-on attack. (Salitrnik received four pints of plasma on arrival at Thurleigh and was out of shock the next day, but developed gas gangrene on 15 April and died the next day). Well-aimed bombing was not possible due to the persistent fighter attacks, which forced many bombers off course. This serious situation was aggravated by problems with the Norden bombsights in the 303rd (and 44th) Bomb Groups, and the 82 B-17s that got their bombs away consequently dropped most of them on Mortsel, where over 3000 houses were destroyed, killing 936 inhabitants and injuring 1342. Only four bombs hit the ERLA VII works, which killed 229 workers with another 78 missing. The ERLA Werke, however, suffered little damage, and within a few weeks aircraft and engine repairs were back to the normal level.

During the afternoon of 8 April a 4-plane flight in the 56th Fighter Group led by the CO, Colonel Hubert "Hub" Zemke, and four pilots in the 78th Fighter Group flew from their base at Horsham St. Faith, just outside Norwich, to the 4th Fighter Group base at Debden. They were to take part in a *Rodeo* set up by the RAF.[170] The combat-experienced Lieutenant Colonel Chesley G. Peterson, 4th Fighter Group Executive and Operations Officer,[171] led the combined force of 24 P-47Cs that took off from Debden and climbed to 30,000ft, and then swept over Dunkirk at full power. They penetrated 12 miles into enemy territory and returned after 90 minutes without seeing any enemy fighters. Colonel Zemke, Major Dave Schilling, and two flight commanders in the 62nd Squadron, Captains John C. McClure and Eugene O'Neill, stayed on at Debden to gain further operational experience. A few days of unsettled weather, however, kept them on the ground until the morning of 13 April when all three Fighter Groups flew a *Rodeo* to St. Omer, in the Pas de Calais, with the aim of luring the "Abbeville Kids" into combat. Again the *Luftwaffe* fighters failed to show. That same evening another sweep was laid on, and this time Loren G. "Mac" McCollom and Phil Tukey brought a flight each from Horsham St. Faith to rendezvous with Zemke's flight at Debden before they all set off to fly as the third squadron in the 4th Fighter Group formation. Zemke was forced to abort over southern England with a faulty oxygen supply. Dave Schilling took over the 56th lead and followed Chesley Peterson's 4th Fighter Group pilots to Le Touquet and out ten minutes later near Dunkirk, where they were greeted with a few bursts of flak. Captain Roger Dyar suffered a complete engine failure over Dunkirk, but from 31,000ft he was able to glide 25 miles across the Channel to belly-land near Deal. A burnt out ignition harness was found to be the cause of engine failure.

On the evening of 15 April, when the 4th put up 12 P-47s led by Major Don Blakeslee, and the 56th and 78th each put up 24 Thunderbolts for another sweep of the Pas de Calais, the two new groups met the *Luftwaffe* for the first time. When RAF Debden sector radioed a warning of enemy aircraft to the west of them and a swarm of fighters suddenly appeared from that direction, the P-47 pilots thought they were in for a fight, only to quickly discover it was another Thunderbolt group. By this time the 56th Fighter Group aircraft were scattered, and they made their own way back to Horsham St. Faith and a lecture on air discipline from Hub Zemke. The 4th Fighter Group did get into a fight on this occasion when they tussled with 15 FW 190A-4s of II./JG 1 over Ostend. Three FW 190s were claimed destroyed, and Major Don Blakeslee was credited with the first enemy aircraft shot down with a P-47. In fact, the German unit suffered no loss, although *Oberfeldwebel* Hutter of 5./JG 1 force-landed with battle damage at Woensdrecht. The 4th Fighter Group leader, Lieutenant Colonel Chesley G. Peterson, had to bale out into the Channel due to engine failure; he was picked up by ASR, wet but well. Two 334th Fighter Squadron, 4th Fighter Group P-47s and their pilots fell victim to *Oberfeldwebel* Ernst Heesen of 5./JG 1, his 26 27th victories.[172]

On 16 April newly arrived Lieutenant Claude W. Campbell's crew in the 303rd Bomb Group flew their first mission after flying four training flights, when 59 Fortresses bombed Lorient for the loss of a single B-17. Howard E. Hernan, the top turret gunner, recalled that "Claude Campbell was a good formation flyer and I guess they figured four training flights were all we needed." William A. Boutelle, Campbell's bombardier, wrote of the Lorient mission:

> "I'd heard plenty about these raids and, while a lot of the stories conflicted, knew a little of what to expect. As we approached the coast of France, though, my knees felt weak and the long time in which I had to set up my bombsight seemed to be flying by: I found myself rushing so fast that I made mistakes. I kept trying to look for the first flak and fighter and work my sight figures too. I settled down and set up my sight and looked up just in time to see the first fighters. There were two Focke Wulfs coming up at 11 o'clock low, so I reported and grabbed my gun, even though they were a mile out of range. They soon made an attack apiece from 12 o'clock with no results on either side. I did expend 15 rounds at one as he flashed by with his wings spouting 20mms like Roman Candles. About that time a formation of 10-15 fighters showed up and sat on our right wing, about 2000 yards away. Then they came barrel-essing in with a short burst for us and all they had for the group below. The tail gunner said it was 'Some show.'"

Howard Hernan continues:

> "A FW 190 came in at about 2 o'clock high. The pilot could not have had much experience firing at a B-17 because he fired from a long way off. I gave him a burst at about 1500 yards, a little further than I should have. About the same time he fired his 20mm cannon and they all went off at about 400 yards ahead of us. After he fired, he immediately flipped over on his back and down he went. It was the last I saw of him. We came through unscathed but the group lost two B-17s."

Eighteen Liberators meanwhile bombed Brest, The 44th Bomb Group had eight B-24s damaged, but the heaviest fighter attacks by JG 2 seemed to be aimed at the 93rd Bomb Group, which lost four B-24s to FW 190s attacking from the rear of their formation at the target. 1st Lieutenant Frank Hodges and his crew in *Liberty Lass* were the first to go down, followed by the crew of *Ball of Fire Jnr*, flown by Lieutenant Frank Lown.[173] Captain Bud Fleenor and crew (who had crashed at Ludham on 26 February) in *Missouri Sue* went down in the Channel after the bombardier had baled out over France. *Judith Lynn* was the fourth B-24 lost, and Lieutenant Packer nursed the crippled *Yardbird* back to England and crashed at St Eval.

On the morning of 17 April crews throughout eastern England were alerted for another strike, and a record 115 bombers were assembled for a raid on the Focke-Wulf plant at Bremen. For the first time two large-scale combat wings, with the 91st and 306th in the first wing and the 303rd and 305th Bomb Groups making up the second, were despatched. Each wing formation consisted of three group boxes of 18-21 aircraft, flown for mutual firepower and protection. Captain Robert K. Morgan, the pilot of the *Memphis Belle* in the 91st Bomb Group, explains:

> "The Germans had got pretty hot on the B-17s. They started coming in from nose of the ships and we had only two .50 caliber guns, which wouldn't go straight forward. We were working on the problem but hadn't solved it and hadn't put any more guns in. We found that by flying all four groups very close together we could get good fighter protection. This worked fine for a while. We would set one group at 22,000, one at 23,000, one at 24,000 and one at 25,000, always about 1000ft difference, on the same line with each other or behind each other. If the enemy attacked the middle Group the firepower of all the other Groups would be concentrated on the fighters. Trouble was, the Germans thought about things too. They worked out the best method of attacking our planes. They picked on the low front Group while all the back three Groups couldn't help out. We solved that by moving the second group up in front, the first Group behind them. In other words, the lead Group was higher than the second was.
>
> "The Bremen raid was about the most effective and successful raid we made from the standpoint of planning, efficiency, damage done and losses. We were briefed as well or better than for any other. The Germans had 178 flak guns to be turned on us. We went in from the southwest to the northeast on a heading so they could never get more than 72 guns on us. We found the plant and turned off to the right and made a complete turn and came out. That is the long and short way around but if we had come out the other way we would have had to run through the other 106 guns. We assembled over England below 5000ft and went out below 5000 until we got ready to turn and come in. we began to turn and climb and when we reached the German coast we had our altitude. We tried to make them think we were going to Wilhelmshaven and it seemed to work."

Eight bombers returned early with malfunctions, leaving the remaining 107 bombers to continue across the North Sea. The long over-water flight was uneventful and even monotonous. Some crewmen took advantage of the lull before the storm to catch up on some sleep or letters home. William Boutelle settled down to his note pad and began writing, 12,000ft above the North Sea:

> "As I write this I'm on my way to Bremen, one of the hottest spots in Germany. Yesterday we flew in the leading and highest group. In that position we had a very calm and, for the most part, boring flight. The lower and rear groups caught some hell from flak and fighters while we only saw a few puffs of ack-ack and about 20 fighters. Today promises to be a very different story. We're in the highest but last group and have a grandstand view of all the other ships, of which I can count over 100 right now. We should really see a show today. I'll see it all I hope."

Shortly after leaving the English coast, a German reconnaissance aircraft had spotted the mass of aircraft and the Americans' approach was radioed to fighter controllers along the enemy coastline. The German defenses did not know where the bombers were headed but, just after the B-17s passed the Friesian Islands, *Luftwaffe* fighters were vectored towards them. Captain Robert K. Morgan again:

> "The weather was pretty overcast below. It looked as though Wilhelmshaven was open and Bremen would be overcast, so I thought we might go back after Wilhelmshaven instead. But a few seconds later I found the target by flak. I looked over to the left and there was one black cloud sitting there and it was flak. I figured that must be Bremen. Sure enough, we could see Bremen when I turned. We went in from the southwest to the northeast. German fighters could be seen coming up from the ground and I have never seen so many at one time. I had to forget about the fighters because we started the run. We were the high Group. We made the run. The flak was pretty bad, bursting all around us. The boys in the low Group really caught hell from it. The Germans had set up the barrage and it worked well. When we turned off the target the fighters began to hit us. They had 109s, 110s, 190s and Ju 88s. But we found out that if you keep your Groups weaving, when the attacks come, you can nose down and turn into the attack and they won't hit you."

S/Sgt Casimer A. Nastal, a waist gunner and at 19 the youngest member of the crew of the *Memphis Belle* who before joining up had a job repairing washing machines, adds:

> "At the target the flak started. It was bursting outside the waist windows. I could have reached out and grabbed it. I kept thinking; 'Let's get the hell out of here.' The fighters came in bunches of 20 or 30. I saw two or three fighters hit by their own flak. It was so thick you could hardly see the ground. The Focke Wulfs were even bursting through our formation."

Howard Hernan recalls:

> "Of all the missions I would fly I never saw flak as had as on this mission. At briefing we had been told that there would be 496 batteries around Bremen. The Germans put up a box barrage. The 88s gave off black smoke when they fired and the 108s were gray. It was just like one black cloud. The windshield was broken out and flak holes appeared in the radio compartment. I tied a pillow into a hole in the window and Campbell flew on from the co-pilot's seat. We were flying No.2 off the lead ship on the right-hand side and so close were we that our wing tip was in the lead ship's waist window."

An estimated 105 enemy fighters of III./JG 54 and JG 11 were encountered on the bomb run, and they concentrated their attacks on the leading 91st and 306th formations. The 401st Squadron in the 91st Bomb Group lost all six aircraft flying as the low squadron in the 1st Combat Wing formation. Worst hit was the 306th, which lost ten bombers. The first to go down was Lieutenant Raymond W. Fortin's B-17, which suffered an engine fire and was finished off by fighters in the target area. *Banshee*, flown by Captain William J. "Wild Bill" Casey, was shot down, and all five crew in the back of the bomb bay were killed. Five others, including Casey, baled out and were made PoWs. Casey's right wingman, 1st Lieutenant Frank V. Watson, was hit by flak after bombs away and almost collided with *Banshee* before being finished off by Bf 109s firing 20mm cannon shells from their gun blisters beneath their wings. Captain Walter N. Smiley's B-17 was hit by fighters, but he made it across the target and out to sea before he realized they would not make it. Smiley turned back and ditched in the sea with no survivors. Lieutenant Robert C. Miller's B-17 was hit on the bomb run and severely damaged. He was unable to turn off the target with the formation and, flying straight ahead, he was quickly pounced on and finished off by fighters. Once the *Luftwaffe* fighters realized that Lieutenant Fred D. Gillogly's gunners were out of ammunition, and seeing that one engine was feathered, some Me 210s took up station alongside and shot out another engine. The B-17's wing caught fire, and over the North Sea Gillogly turned back towards land and the crew baled out.

Pride of "Kiarians" flown by Lieutenant Theodore A. Jankowski was badly hit in the nose, top turret, and the waist, and the No.3 engine was on fire and out of control. Flak at the target just after bombs away heavily damaged the tail. The plane lurched upwards and then went into an uncontrollable dive. Three men went down with the ship, and the radio operator was blown out when the bomber exploded. Fighters shot down *The Grim Reaper*, flown by Lieutenant Glenn J. Lally, after dropping his bombs. Lally and seven of his crew survived. *Unmentionable*, flown by Lieutenant Warren George Jr, went down before the target. To S/Sgt Donald J. Bevan, one of the gunners, "It was like firing into a feeding frenzy of sharks. Everyone was calm and stayed at his post until George finally told the crew over the intercom: 'All right, I guess we'd better bale out.'"[174] Captain Craig J. Harwood's Fortress, the last B-17 in the lead squadron, completed the bomb run, but flak holed the wings and set two engines on fire, and hydraulic fluid leaking into the bomb bay was also in flames. All the crew baled out, but three of them, including Harwood, who bled to death, died.[175]

The trailing groups did not suffer loss, although most aircraft had received some degree of fighter or flak damage. A gunner aboard *Queenie* in the 303rd Bomb Group wrote:

> "By this time the bombardier was on the bombsight and we were settling down on our bomb run. And then the flak began to come up at us. It came up so thick and fast that it looked as though we had run into a thundercloud… At the same time fighters coming head-on into us hit us. Just before our bombs went away our No.4 engine was hit and oil started pouring all over the place. Vibration caused by the windmilling propeller seemed to be about to shake the ship to pieces. When the bombs finally went, none of us felt them give the ship the jar they usually give it, as we were already bouncing around like a stovepipe hat in a March gale. The sky was literally swarming with fighters. The pilots made old *Queenie* hurl herself around the sky in evasive action dodging the oncoming pursuits until we must have looked like a small plane doing acrobatics. The pursuits came in so fast that at times the navigator and I had to be content with taking shots at every second or third plane making a pass at us. And the way we were thrown around in that nose from the evasive action made us feel like a pair of dice. All this time I was trying to navigate us out of that place by the fastest route possible. I'd get a checkpoint and then grab my gun and start spraying lead out like a hose. They had every kind of plane in the *Luftwaffe* up trying to knock us down. Bombing was excellent. As the English say, we really pranged the target. Not one of our bombs was off the target area."[176]

At Thurleigh, where ten ships were missing, the B-17 flown by Lieutenant Maxwell V. Judas was the only ship in the 368th Bomb Squadron to make it back. It was a "wing and a prayer" job on one and a half engines and flying all the way at 105 mph. *Old Faithful*, flown by Captain Pervis E. Youree, had made the bomb run with two engines feathered and the top turret shattered by gunfire from enemy fighters. Youree got the plane home by taking it down to the deck and flying for 200 miles at wave top height on one good engine. Lieutenant Leroy C. Sugg, the co-pilot, held the control cables for the No.3 engine together with his hands. Youree maintained 115 mph while the crew jettisoned everything they could, including the ball turret. Low on fuel, Youree put *Old Faithful* down at RAF Coltishall, Norfolk, on one wheel. "It's a kind of a mystery how we got back," Youree said later.[177] Lieutenant Kenneth A. Reecher returned to Thurleigh in formation with a 91st Bomb Group B-17. When he landed medics took away the dead body of his bombardier, who had been hit in the groin by a 20mm shell, which had severed a main artery. In all the 306th Bomb Group had lost 34 men killed in action, and morale was shattered, with the losses coming after five of the Group's B-17s had been shot down twelve days earlier. Major Thurman "Doc" Shuller said. "The Group tonight is stunned but not broken. We used to reel and rock with the loss of three planes in a raid but we didn't believe it possible to lose ten in one mission."[178]

The 14 B-17s that returned to Thurleigh had expended 98,000 rounds of ammunition. Claims were approved for eight fighters destroyed, two probable, and one damaged. In total, gunners put in claims for 63 fighters destroyed, but in reality only about ten fighters were actually shot down. Howard Hernan sums up the problem:

> "I know that gunners made many claims and probably a lot of us got credit her planes that were not actually shot down. I think this was true on both sides. In order to claim a fighter you had to have two other witnesses. Heaven knows how many men were shooting at the same plane. Intelligence would ask what was the exact location and it would sometimes take up to 45 minutes longer to sit in interrogation if you were claiming a fighter. By this time we were absolutely worn out, hungry, trying to get warm and it just wasn't worth the effort. After all, we weren't there to shoot down fighters. Our primary concern was the bombing of the targets. Eventually, intelligence told us that we were claiming too many fighters. From then on I never claimed another fighter, even if I knew I'd got it."

Captain Robert K. Morgan concludes:

> "We lost 16 bombers, all in the low Group. That was the greatest loss we had sustained to date. But the bombing was successful. There were three factories and two were completely destroyed and a third about 60% destroyed."

Albert Speer, the German armaments minister, had already issued instructions for dispersed fighter production six months previously. As for the high losses on the Bremen raid, General Hansell at First Wing Headquarters was in no doubt as to the cause. On 23 April he wrote in an Operation Report: "Most of our losses were the result of poor formation flying, which resulted in aircraft becoming separated and an easy prey to the fighters."

5

Gaining Strength

How well I remember that beautiful sight
Wispy contrails high in the heavens
And how we all welcomed the tail gunner's words
"Here come the P-47s"

During mid-April 1943, four new B-17 Groups (the 94th, 95th, 96th, and 351st) were despatched to Britain. All but the 351st were equipped with B-17Fs with long-range "Tokyo tanks" built into their wings and the tips to hold an additional 1080 gallons of fuel. However, the influx of new groups caused problems. Theater indoctrination was normally carried out at Bovingdon, but the facilities there were hopelessly inadequate for such a large influx of crews. As a result, the air echelon of the 95th Bomb Group joined the 92nd at Alconbury for combat training. They were to remain there for six weeks, during which time the ground forces of the 92nd found themselves responsible for up to 90 aircraft. The 95th flew practice missions every day, weather permitting, while the veteran crews in the 92nd found themselves in the role of instructors. Many of the experienced crews were quick to note the boyish enthusiasm displayed by the green crews. They knew they would learn the hard way, through experience, that there were no "milk runs" over Europe.[179]

Inexperience cost the 56th Fighter Group dearly on 29 April when 112 P-47s of the 4th, 56th, and 78th Fighter Groups flew another high altitude *Rodeo* over the enemy coastline, sweeping over the coast from Ostend to Woensdrecht. The 36 P-47s in the 56th Fighter Group, which were led on this occasion by Dave Schilling,[180] took off from Horsham St. Faith soon after midday. Climbing at around 700ft a minute, they headed for the enemy coast south of Flushing, where they were briefed to turn north and come out near The Hague. Once the group had passed 20,000ft Schilling discovered that his radio was faulty. Instead of turning back and handing over to one of the squadron leaders, he chose to continue in defiance of standard operating procedure. While still over the sea and about 15 miles from Blankenberge, the briefed point of landfall, FW 190s of the 6th and 8th *Staffeln* JG 26 dived down out of the sun from 24,000ft and attacked the leading 62nd Squadron from dead ahead. Schilling was unable to direct his squadrons or call for assistance, and as a result the 61st Squadron flying top cover was at first unaware of the battle. When it was it waited for the radio call that never came. The flights became scattered, and many pilots were unaware of what was happening and were at a loss to know what to do. Flying in pairs, the FW 190s swept in firing short, well-aimed bursts before diving away. *Unteroffizier* Wilhelm Mayer of the 6th *Staffel* claimed a P-47 30km north of Ostend, and *Oberleutnant* Hans Heitmann of the 8th *Staffel* destroyed a P-47 at Knokke. By the time the coast of England was regained fuel was so low that many Thunderbolt pilots in the 56th Fighter Group had to land at the first airfield they saw. Schilling's fighter was one of three that returned to Horsham St. Faith badly damaged. Colonel Zemke was in the tower, and from the radio talk realized that his group had seen action and that all was not well. He recalled:[181]

> "When Schilling landed I hopped in a jeep and drove over to where he had parked near a hangar. The P-47 had been shot up and the crew chief and mechanics were already trying to patch the holes. Schilling, in an agitated state, wanted to set up another mission to go out and seek revenge. I had to remind him that this could not be done without approval from higher authority and that he should settle down as this was going to be a long war. At the debriefing it became clear that two pilots were missing and that the mission had been a fiasco. Paramount among errors was the leader's failure to abort the mission when his radio was found inoperative. Without hesitation I took Schilling aside and admonished him for ignoring a golden rule. There was also some plain speaking to squadron and flight leaders who failed to communicate or respond in the situation. Two good men had been lost and two returning aircraft damaged—although happily the missing pilots survived as PoWs. We were a green outfit but this really was an ignominious combat debut.
>
> "A change in tactics following this mission involved the formations we flew. Hitherto individual flights had gone out in close finger-fours, each shifting into string trail behind its leader at the enemy coast. This flight battle formation, advised by the RAF in our stateside training days, placed the rearmost aircraft in a very vulnerable position. Other pilots were usually in no position to warn him of a surprise attack from the rear and in such an event the enemy was ideally placed to pick off the remaining planes ahead in the line. To improve matters, we staggered the two-plane elements in a flight and spread flights out in very loose formation. This gave better positioning for spotting attackers coming in from the rear and more flexibility in evading."

Eaker now scheduled another attack on harbor installations at St. Nazaire by 78 B-17s in two waves for May Day. At Thurleigh 18 Fortresses under the command of Lieutenant Colonel Claude Putnam, the CO, were off the ground at 0900 hours, joining the 91st Bomb Group over Bassingbourn to form the 101st Combat Wing. The two groups headed south to Portland Bill, where they met the 102nd Combat Wing comprising the 303rd, who were leading the mission, and the 305th. Several members of the newly arrived 351st Bomb Group at Polebrook accompanied 303rd Bomb Group crews on the mission to gain experience. The raid was a special one for Captain Cliff Pyle, who was flying his 25th and final mission in the 305th Bomb Group. Brest was the secondary target. Eleven planes aborted because of mechanical failures or personnel problems, 38 aircraft aborted because of weather and only 29 bombed St. Nazaire. Captain Robert K. Morgan, in the 91st Bomb Group formation, who was piloting the *Memphis Belle* on his 22nd mission, recalls:

> "We were supposed to go in by land and come out by water. The formation leader made a mistake and salvoed his bombs in the water. Everybody else did the same thing. We had been briefed to lot down on the deck as soon as we left St. Nazaire and come back as close to the water as we could. The lead Group let down to 8000ft. At 8000 there was an overcast and the lead Group stayed above it and came on out. The second Group did the same. Our Group, remembering what we were briefed, went down through the overcast and down on the deck. The fourth Group [306th] was in a predicament; they didn't know which Groups to follow. They decided to follow us down to the deck. We assembled and started back for England. Somehow the fourth Group, in getting through the overcast, had got ahead of our Group; next time we saw them they were up ahead, almost out of sight. We tried to catch them. Their navigator made a mistake and came back and hit France again. He thought he was in England. We saw the mistake soon enough for us, but we couldn't get in touch with them by radio because the lead ship's radio was out. They went on to Brest between 1500 and 2000ft. We went on and landed in England. [Bad weather forced the returning aircraft to be diverted to Exeter and Davidstowe Moor]. They landed there 30 minutes later, what was left of them. They had gone right over the Brest flak guns at 3500ft. The ones that got back were awful looking sights. The lead group didn't go on the water but we did."

Bombing on a 270° heading, Colonel Putnam led his Forts west and began letdown off the target. Thirty minutes later at 12,000ft the 306th turned to 320° and shortly thereafter made another smaller correction to the right. At 1313 the formation turned sharply to the right at 800ft towards what was assumed would be a landfall on southwestern England. There can have been no doubts in the lead ship that day, as new navigational procedure when position was at all in question was to fly 360° for 30 minutes and then turn to 45° and England would there. At 1340 the 306th B-17s made landfall at a harbor, and some men remarked later about noticing the "lights" blinking at them. Suddenly they were hit by flak fired from 88mm guns, heavy coastal artillery, and 8mm machine guns. By this time the Group were over the harbor of Brest, not over England. Frantically, the leaders began to turn the formation as quickly as they could. It demanded all the flying skills the pilots could muster to keep their planes in the air at low altitude; those on the inside of the turns struggled to keep from stalling, a maneuver that could easily have been fatal.[182] The aircraft flown by Lieutenant Edwin G. Pipp hit the water, the first of two—both in the 423rd Bomb Squadron—to go down in the harbor. S/Sgt Eli Rogers, his engineer, who had been wounded earlier by flak, recalled that the holes appearing in the top of the wing of their ship looked like "corn popping."[183] 1st Lieutenant Bart Wigginton's B-17 was also lost in the harbor and all his crew were killed. A 367th plane flown by 1st Lieutenant Owen Luby was ditched in the water outside Brest harbor was the third to go down and all the crew died. Lieutenant Einar H. Suomi's B-17 went down in the Bay of Biscay with all ten crew lost. Two other 306th Bomb Group B-17s were so badly damaged that they were left in Cornwall for salvage. One of them was a B-17E[184] in the 423rd Bomb Squadron flown by 1st Lieutenant Lewis P. Johnson Jr and his co-pilot, 2nd Lieutenant Robert "Bob" McCallum, an 11-day veteran and transfer from the RAF.

The B-17 was hit several times and caught fire in the radio compartment and in the tail area. S/Sgt Maynard H. "Snuffy" Smith, the ball turret gunner, who was on his first mission, hand cranked his turret to get it back into the aircraft. He climbed out and discovered that the waist gunners and the radio operator had baled out. He could have baled out himself, but the aircraft did not show any signs of leaving formation, so Smith assumed the pilots were still aboard, and he remained in the aircraft and fought the fire with a hand extinguisher. Then he jettisoned the oxygen bottles and ammunition in the radio compartment and manned the two waist guns during an attack by enemy fighters, stopping to dampen down the fires and treat Harris B. Goldberg, the badly wounded tail gunner. Johnson put down at Predannack, near Land's End, after Smith had thrown out all the equipment that was not nailed down. For his actions this day "Snuffy" Smith became the first enlisted man in the 8th Air Force to receive the Medal of Honor.[185]

Captain Robert K. Morgan, in the 91st Bomb Group, was scathing in his condemnation of the 306th Bomb Group's performance at St. Nazaire, "The leader of our Group never led another raid and never will." In his report to First Wing, Colonel Putnam wrote:

> "As usual, the navigation problem was made extremely difficult by having poor compass equipment. After the French Coast is crossed all radio aids, with the exception of the J Beams are useless, due to the fact that the enemy has beacons and stations set up to jam and meacon them. It is therefore necessary to rely wholly on the compass when flying under such poor conditions as those encountered on this mission. Compass installations at present are far too unreliable to put that much faith in them. There is a new heavy gyrocompass of exceptional reliability, of the remote reading type, which should be made immediately available to the operational groups." He added that "The leadership and navigation displayed by the lead Group of the 102nd Combat Wing was hardly exceptional."[186]

On 4 May VIII Bomber Command dispatched 79 B-17s on a five-hour round trip to the Ford and General Motors plants at Antwerp. They were escorted by twelve Allied fighter squadrons, including for the first time by six squadrons of P-47 Thunderbolts of the 4th and 56th Fighter Groups, who provided fighter escort up to 175 miles. More than 30 B-17s and B-24s that flew diversionary feints towards the French coast succeeded in drawing over 100 German fighters away from the main force, and they returned without loss after 65 bombers had got their bombs away on the factory. This day one of Hollywood's greatest stars flew with the 303rd Bomb Group formation, as Howard Hernan recalls:

> "We flew on Captain Calhoun's wing (CO of the squadron) and Clark Gable flew with him and handled the radio hatch gun. Claude Campbell, my pilot, could quite easily see the Hollywood film star grinning at him over enemy territory. Our crew had a theme song; *The Campbells Are Coming*. We would listen to it on the Armed Forces Network and when they signed off we would switch to 'Lord Haw Haw' who seemed to know more about us than people on our own base. He knew the theme song was being played and knew we were Campbell's crew so he would also play some music for us. He always added a little sarcasm but sometimes his music was better than that on the other radio networks. The Spitfires and Thunderbolts did a wonderful job of working the Focke-Wulfs over and it was a

very successful mission. One of our B-17s, piloted by Lieutenant Pence, was shot up by an FW 190 that jumped the group as we reached the English coast and the co-pilot got shot in the leg and never flew again; the radio operator got hit over the eye and in the leg. The Focke-Wulfs made a pass at us out of the sun. Every gunner had his gun out of his receiver because we thought we were safe. Never again did I take my guns out until I was on the ground. Next morning I looked over Pence's plane. It had nine holes in it and I measured them. The spread was 9ft, although they had been attacked from head-on. Captain Gable visited the co-pilot every evening at a nearby hospital to see how he was getting along."[187]

On 12 May the overall plan for the restructuring of VIII Bomber Command began to emerge. The 94th, 95th, and 96th Bomb Groups were to form a new 4th Bomb Wing in Essex and Suffolk under the command of Brigadier General Frederick L. Anderson, whose headquarters would be established at Marks Hall, near Colchester.[188] The three groups remained in 1st Bomb Wing "country" until their new bases were completed. The ground echelons of the 94th, 95th, and 96th Bomb Groups had only arrived in the United Kingdom on 10 May. On the night of the 12th orders arrived at Bassingbourn, Alconbury, and Grafton Underwood, respectively, calling for a maximum effort for a mission to St. Omer-Longuenesse airfield, starting at 1300 hours. Remarkably, the three new groups managed to put up 72 bombers for the mission to St. Omer, but at such short notice problems were bound to occur. The 96th failed to complete assembly and aborted the mission. One B-17 got into difficulties and ditched in the Channel where Air Sea Rescue rescued the crew. Thirty-one B-17s in the 94th and 95th Bomb Groups continued to the target, but they too were to experience difficulty. Captain Franklin "Pappy" Colby in the 94th Bomb Group, at 41 years of age the oldest combat pilot in the 8th Air Force, was on the mission:

"After many diversions and buzzing around over the North Sea to get the enemy fighters up and, hopefully, low on gas, we finally sallied across the Channel. As the weather was CAVU (Ceiling and Visibility Unlimited) we could see both shores plainly. From our height it looked like we could spit across the Straits of Dover. Major Louis Thorup led the High Squadron with me leading the second element of three ships behind him. It turned out to be a piece of cake. We saw no fighters and only three bursts of flak. However, the bombing smelled, as we completely missed the aerodrome and put the bombs out in fields with quite a few going into the town itself. It was a downwind bomb run and apparently our lead bombardier badly underestimated the force of the wind at 20,000ft."[189]

Losses were having an effect on morale at every bomb group, and they were perhaps more noticeable in the Liberator squadrons, whose numbers were fewer in comparison to the B-17 groups. The 44th Bomb Group at Shipdham had not received any replacement crews until late March or April, so Colonel Leon W. Johnson's Group had a limited number of crews, as he recalled:

"Every time we went out, while we might lose none, we might lose one or two. At dinner that night over at the club, there would be vacant seats. It was awfully hard. You didn't have to be very smart to figure out that if your force was going down all the time and you were doing the same number of missions and you were losing one and two and getting no replacements, your chances of surviving didn't look so good. As soon as the replacement crews started arriving, there were no problems at all. I don't mean to say that there were problems earlier, but you could see it in their eyes and their whole manner. Everybody did the calculations and they knew that their chances weren't very good. When the new crews came in, it changed completely."

It did not help either that the Fortress groups usually hogged the limelight when it came to publicity. To redress the balance Major John M. Redding and Captain Harold Leyshon paid a visit to Shipdham airfield, in the wilds of Norfolk, in the spring, where the crews of *Little Beaver* and *Suzy Q* in the 67th Squadron attracted their attention:[190]

"There is a clearly understood working agreement between crew and pilots that permits maximum effectiveness with the least expenditure of work, time and effort. Only crews that gain such ability survive long, for the Nazis are quick to take advantage of any slip. But how does food affect these things? Surely food alone doesn't make the difference between a lost crew and a safe one? No, not food alone. Yet it is a fact that the losses in a large group of men will be smaller if they are properly fed. And the phrase, properly fed, deals with more than cooking alone.

"The crews of the *Little Beaver* and the *Suzy Q* eat apart from the squadron mess. They have fostered a feeling of oneness among themselves to a point where they not only live together but they eat together, fight together and when the time comes, if it must, they will die together. Part of that feeling, that *esprit,* comes from their crew mess. The private mess they operate began because of the dislike of these men to 'foofaraw.' They didn't want to wear their blouses to dinner in the officers' mess. They came to England to fight a war.

"When they landed as part of the early contingents of 1st Wing, they were ready to fight their way into the country. They alighted from their planes at an air-transport base with guns loaded at ready in their holsters. Lieutenant Chester Lucius Phillips, who through the subtle alchemy of nicknames is called George, phrases it thus: 'We thought the war was right here in England instead of two hours flying time across the Channel.'

"These men wanted to grow beards and wear torn, comfortable uniforms like the men pictured at their posts in the Pacific. 'We didn't want to wear blouses and pinks and get all dolled up. To get away from that we just had to learn to cook, so we did,' Phillips explains it. In the Nissen hut where the crews of the *Little Beaver* and the *Suzy Q* await their dinner, there is a cheery odor of broiling pork. Through the pleasantly smoky atmosphere comes the crackle of spattering grease as the potatoes fry merrily on top of the little stove, behind the broiling meat. Coffee will be prepared later with Nescafe. The men are ready for their meal. And they are not wearing their blouses. It is important to them, this manner of eating."

When Group Staff decided to promote 2nd Lieutenant co-pilots to 1st Lieutenants and give them command of their own B-24s, "George" Phillips' co pilot, Bill Cameron, was among them. Cameron's new crew was made up of RAF transferees and five members of *Little Beaver's* ground crew. They were sent to gunnery school for two weeks. Bill Dabney and Tom Clifford joined the crew from the RAF as co-pilot and navigator, respectively. Gola Gibby and Roy Winters became the flight engineers, while Gerald "Sparky" Sparks, a "reject" from a B-17 unit, became the radio-operator. His guitar playing became a real morale-booster to the crew. "Gentleman" Jim DeVinney was the last to join the green crew, as bombardier. Before Bill Cameron's new crew became operational they were given a three-day leave, and Major Howard Moore went with them to London. There were still too few trained men available to fly the new Liberators. Lieutenant William Roach and his crew became the 67th Bomb Squadron's first replacements to arrive direct from the States and relieved the situation a little. In the 68th Bomb Squadron the CO, Major Francis McDuff, was rotated home, creating another vacancy. James E. O'Brien, who like the crews of *Little Beaver* and *Suzy Q* had been in England eight months, was promoted to major and given command of the Squadron. O'Brien returned to Shipdham, having been on detachment with RAF Coastal Command flying 300 miles out in the North Sea with a feathered prop on one engine while searching for German shipping.[191] The promotion came as quite a shock, as he recalls:

> "My only squadron experience other than flying, had been some additional duty as engineering officer at Barksdale Field during our training days in the States."

During off duty hours he and his buddies, Tom Cramer, Jim Dubard (who had been killed in December 1942), Bud Phillips, and Tom Landrum had a stack of records ranging from Brahm's concertos to *Who threw the Whiskey in the Well?* When the 44th flew its B-24Ds to England from Grenier Field, New Hampshire, in September 1942, the load had to be divided between aircraft because the breakable wax records were strictly non-regulation materials, and secondly, each B-24D was already seriously overloaded at take-off. O'Brien's crew, therefore, decided to carry the records over in *The Rugged Buggy*, while Lieutenant Tom Cramer's Liberator transported the phonograph. At Shipdham they discovered to their dismay that the 210 voltage in the Nissen huts only gave them about 10 rpm! But they had not brought the valued collection of records to England in vain—they played them with a finger assist in the middle of the turntable to obtain a wavering, variable quality between 10-17 rpm. One of Major O'Brien's favorite records was Maurice Ravel's *Bolero*, which featured as background music in the *Charge of the Light Brigade*, a movie he had seen in 1939. The *Bolero* theme resonated throughout the 68th Squadron area for weeks when it was played over and over again in the barracks at Shipdham. When in the second week of May the "Eightballs" were alerted for a mission to Kiel, Major O'Brien compared the mission's slow build up and shattering finale to the *Bolero* theme, although as it turned out, the *Charge of the Light Brigade* would have invoked a more appropriate comparison:

> "I had no sooner found out what a squadron commander was supposed to do, when word came on the calm night of Sunday 13 May recalling all the group maximum effort on the French port of Bordeaux. This would entail a long over-sea flight, a quick climb to drop bombs on the U-boat pens and then out again. Other than the hurry to install bomb-bay tanks, this didn't seem too much of an order. However, at 0200 hours the Field Order was changed to remove the bomb-bay tanks and load up with 4000lb of the new type incendiary clusters for a raid on Kiel, Germany. The obvious question was 'What good would incendiaries do at Kiel?' The explanation given at the briefing on the following morning at 0500 hours was that the B-17s were going to bomb the hell out of the U-boat pens, aircraft factories and seaport facilities and the B-24s were to kindle the fires. It was all very logical but it was a long trip without fighter escort."[192]

Following the change in orders Major O'Brien cancelled the recall of fellow crewmembers Lieutenants Tom Cramer and Bud Phillips that had been put out earlier. It was decided that the 68th Squadron could put up six B-24s without calling on either of them, provided that O'Brien flew with his usual co-pilot, "Mac" Howell, to check him out as first pilot for combat flying. "Mac" had been cheated out of many missions in his struggle to reach the magic 25 because senior officers had often ranked him out of the co-pilot's seat aboard O'Brien's ship, *The Rugged Buggy*. "Mac" never really wanted to be first pilot. Like countless others he just wanted to get back to the States to see his wife. O'Brien was single and not concerned about his own welfare in the same way that "Mac" was. The crew of *The Rugged Buggy* was short one radio operator, so T/Sgt Ralph C. Ernst filled in:[193]

> "The morning of Monday 14 May arrived (like most others)," recalls Jim O'Brien, "with the night orderly banging on my door and shouting, 'Mission briefing at 0500.' I had returned from a sortie 300 miles out to sea shadowing the German battleship, *Tirpitz* and had only got to sleep at 0400! After the ground crews under Captain Landrum and the armament crews under Lieutenant Thompson had worked all night taking out the bomb-bay tanks from the racks and reloading them with 100 pounders, we were briefed and ready for take off at about 0900 hours. The 44th was putting up 24 ships for the mission. I showed up not so much as the squadron commander but as co-pilot of *The Rugged Buggy* in a "tail-end Charlie" slot. What a glorious way to go!"

Crewmembers on three-day pass managed to get back to Shipdham before take off but were too late to be considered for the raid. Among them were Bill Cameron's new crew and Major Howard "Pappy" Moore, pilot of the *Suzy Q*, now one of the most famous Liberators in the group. The officers had arrived in Norwich on the London train at about 4 o'clock on the Monday morning, and they had met a GI trying to get back to Shipdham. He had word that the Group was to fly a mission that day. They all piled into a taxi and were back at Shipdham within an hour, in time for the briefing but too late to take part in the raid on Kiel. *Suzy Q* was undergoing maintenance in Northern Ireland, so Lieutenant Robert Brown, "Pappy" Moore's usual co-pilot, was re-assigned the pilot's seat aboard a new Liberator and *Miss Delores* or *Q for Queenie*, as it was known because of her call letter, that had sat at dispersal for some time. Lieutenant Hartley "Hap" Westbrook would fly co-pilot. Captain Bob Bishop, navigator, plus seven others, all from the *Suzy Q*, completed the scratch crew of *Miss Delores*. Gilbert "Gibby" Wandtke, the engineer, was not happy about the change in aircraft. He had been jilted by a Delores in the States, and claimed *Miss Delores* would probably take them over the target but would not bring them back! Lieutenant William Roach and his replacement crew would fly their first mission in the 67th Bomb Squadron in *Annie Oakley*. *Little Beaver*, Bill Cameron's former B-24, would as usual be piloted by Captain Chester "George" Phillips.

On previous missions the Liberators had bombed through the lower Fortress formations. To prevent this, higher headquarters decreed that on the mission to Kiel the Liberators would have to reduce their speed and fly behind the Fortresses. It was mooted that if the B-24s tried to slow down to the speed of the B-17s they (the B-24s) would "drop out of the sky." The B-24D's cruising speed was 180-185mph indicated, while the B-17s cruised at 160mph indicated airspeed. Not surprisingly, the news that the B-24s would fly to the target behind the Fortresses and the general rush in planning the mission caused a feeling of anxiety among the crew as they walked to their pre-flight huts. Jim O'Brien turned over his personal belongings to the clerk and received his usual claim check. He kept the sixpenny bit and good luck charm, which had brought him safely through his previous twenty missions, and put it with his small escape compass.

Bob Bishop and the others walked out to *Miss Delores* and climbed inside. Once inside they began checking the equipment and settled in for the long flight. O'Brien's crew clambered inside *The Rugged Buggy* and also began carrying out their pre-flight checks. Their ship was already a veteran of a score of missions over the continent, but this trip was something not previously attempted. As they taxied out behind Lieutenant George R. Jansen's ship, *Margaret Ann*, "Mac" Howell was saying, "If I get back from this trip, I'm going to get stinking drunk." ("A new experience for him," recalls O'Brien). Dick Castillo, the rear-gunner, commented, "Come on let's quit kidding, this will be just as tough as any we've ever flown." Jim O'Brien thought too about "Pappy" Moore's remark at briefing, "I wouldn't go on this mission if I were you."

At 0900 hours 21 Liberators began taxiing out at Shipdham for the mission to Kiel. The early morning fog and rain, which had cloaked the Norfolk countryside, did not hinder take off. For twenty minutes the heavily laden bombers circled the field and gained altitude before falling into formation. Assembly completed they headed out towards the small fishing port of Cromer, perched high on the Norfolk cliffs. Land fell quickly away until 50 miles out; the twin-tailed B-24s, flying as the low formation in the three-group 14th Wing, rendezvoused with over 100 B-17s stacked like pieces in a gigantic game of three-dimensional chess. Pilots in the B-24Ds tried to settle down to a constant cruising speed of 180mph while maintaining a height of only 500ft to avoid detection by enemy radar. The task was made that much more difficult because they had to continually zigzag twenty miles in one direction and 40 miles in the other in order to remain behind the slower Forts.

Despite this, O'Brien noted that the flight over the North Sea was made in "beautiful formation." He thought about the "Bolero" melody as the sea swept by beneath his speeding bomber:

> "This was the quiet beginning where the drums beat a soft rhythm and the flutes and piccolos spin their simple melody. About 200 miles out we started our climb to 21,000ft knowing that the Germans would have us tracked with radar from this point on. This was side two and three of the orchestrated rhythm; less subtle and more colorful and romantic."

The "Eightballs" should have avoided the Friesian Islands, but the constant zigzag course they had been forced to adopt caused them to stray off course, and they overflew the islands at 19,000ft. They were greeted with sporadic bursts of flak. "We responded," states O'Brien, "with the usual appreciation of poor marksmanship from ground batteries."

> "My attention was diverted momentarily to Tom Holmes' ship, which took a burst of flak and appeared to have flames coming out of the bomb bay. (He managed to maintain height and re-cross the sea to England.) I was overly concerned with Tom's welfare but suddenly two explosions rocked our ship. Side three of '*Bolero*' increased in volume out of nowhere. A real indication of trouble was the manifold pressure on the two left engines, which dropped to 15 psi and there was a sudden drag to the left, which Howell and I struggled to correct. I had thoughts of feathering the two left engines but that would have been a sure give-away to German fighters waiting to come in for the kill."[194]

The Rugged Buggy and the surviving Liberators continued to the target. Crews had been briefed to bomb from 21,000ft, but the constant zigzagging now brought them over Heligoland Bay at 18,000ft. As they turned into the strong wind for bombing they were down to 160mph—almost stalling speed.

> "The bomb bay doors opened," continues O'Brien, "and the 44th let go its clusters of matchstick incendiaries. These only created more confusion. The clusters did not hold together for more than 200ft before breaking up. As soon as they hit the slipstream they were all over the sky in a negative trajectory, flying back through the formation and bouncing off wings and propellers. Nothing worked better for the Germans at this point as the formation scattered to avoid these missiles. Meanwhile, we had dropped our own clusters of bombs and had plenty of trouble. The cockpit smelled of gasoline and our unspoken thoughts as Howell and I looked at each other were fire and explosion. We had now separated from the rest of the group after leaving the target and I noticed at least two other stragglers off to the right. One was Captain 'Swede' Swanson of the 506th Squadron. There was plenty of company joining us. Focke Wulf 190s were in formation on the left and Bf 109s off the right wing. 'Mac' McCabe in the top turret kept yelling through his oxygen mask to dip the wing so he could hit them with his .50s. Not knowing what else to do, Howell and I were just trying to keep the ship flying. We had been through this before and somehow fate had brought as through. In the past, we had outlasted German fighters until they turned back over the North Sea but now we were practically standing still in a 100mph headwind on a 285° heading with lots of German soil still underneath.
>
> "We had already turned to side four of *Bolero* and the noise and the increasing crescendo had mounted to a deafening roar. There must have been two Jerries sitting off our tail end pumping a steady flow of cannon and .30 caliber bullets into us. I heard several .30s zing into the cockpit and bounce off the armor-plated seats. Mixed in with these .30s were some incendiary bullets, which made a good mixture with the intense gasoline fumes and pretty soon we had a roaring furnace in the bomb bay. My first knowledge of fire was the intense heat all over the cockpit. I leaped out of my seat, breaking my oxygen hose in the process. I pulled open the top hatch directly in front of the top turret to get out, saw the whirling propellers and antenna wires and thought better of it. I stuck my head out of the hatch and my steel GI helmet, which we wore before the introduction of flak helmets[195], blew right off in the slipstream. If there was any time to take a second guess, it was then that I decided on some other exit."

Meanwhile Ralph Ernst, the radio operator, was trying very hard to extinguish the fire, using all the extinguishers he could lay his hands on:

> "I managed to put out the fire temporarily between extinguishers but I figured we would have to bale out as the plane would explode at any moment. I tried to open the bomb bay door to make an easy exit but there was no hydraulic pressure and it wouldn't open. The fire was really heavy now and I sat down on the catwalk and used my heel to open the bomb bay door. The fire must have weakened the corrugated metal but it was still difficult to free. However, I did manage to get it open far enough for us to jump out."[196]

Jim O'Brien also availed himself of the open bomb bay doors, but in his frenzied rush to escape the blazing bomber he snapped on a life raft dinghy instead of his parachute. "I threw the dinghy back to the floor," he recalls, "found my chest pack in time and got into the nice quiet atmosphere outside the plane. This final emotional crescendo ended the 'Bolero' with the crash of symbols, horns, tubas, gongs and trombones. One momentary musical note at the end was the pulling of the ripcord and the patient wait for a jerk. There was no jerk and I was sure the thing had failed, especially with the handle in my hands having a little 12-inch wire dangling from it. I was sure something had broken. This experience for every novice parachutist can take a few years from his life expectancy.

"Now all was peaceful and quiet as I looked up to see the secure strings of a parachute canopy lowering me to Mother Earth. The parachute training for 8th Air Force crews was nothing more than the usual instruction on bale out procedure: intercom verbal signals, one steady ring of the emergency bell or 'use your own judgement.' I'm sure that 99% of the 30,000 airmen PoWs never had time for bells or verbal signals. It was generally a spur of the moment decision reached when everything else had gone kaput. On the way down I decided that I should have my back to the wind. I experimented with the shroud lines, trying to turn the canopy so I was facing down-wing of my drift. All this did was make a violent swing that almost spilled the canopy. That experiment ended quickly. All kinds of debris were falling around me and a small piece of engine cowling narrowly missed me. I felt a sharp pain in his side and thought it might have been caused by a piece of shrapnel but it turned out to be nothing more than a stomach muscle strain caused by the exertions of the parachute descent. Shortly after I realized I had an open 'chute I looked up and saw another 'chute coming down beside me with one nylon panel torn open from top to bottom. I couldn't determine who it was. I landed in a Danish farmyard about 30 miles northwest of Kiel and was captured at about 1230 hours."

About an hour after the B-26s departed, the 1st Wing formation, flying without escort, was picked up, this time approaching the northwest coast of Germany. The German fighter controllers did not yet know where they were heading. At 1145 hours the formation turned south for the base of the Danish Peninsula. Five minutes later the German controllers scrambled their fighters when the Americans' destination became apparent.

Howard Hernan, top turret gunner in Lieutenant Campbell's crew in the 303rd Bomb Group formation, says that:

"The fighter opposition was intense and the flak heavy. We flew at 32,000ft in the high squadron, high group; the highest I had ever flown. Most of the 88mm flak was below us. The Germans did shoot up some '105s but these were inaccurate, some going off 2-3000ft above us. Captain Bales, Lieutenant Campbell's roommate, flying in *FDR's Potato Peeler Kids*, was shot down 20 miles offshore. With Captain Bales was Mark Mathis, whose brother Jack, had been killed over Vegesack. It was for this reason that Mark transferred from a B-26 outfit to his brother's group and he even flew in *The Duchess* where he used his brother's bombsight. Mark Mathis hated the Germans and was determined to avenge his brother and complete his 25 missions for him. The Kiel raid was his fourth mission. Nine 'chutes came out of the *Potato Peeler.* Bales appeared to have all his engines turning over although one or two could have been windmilling. He came around and made a water landing in the midst of all the 'chutes. We never heard anything from them again."

Kiel was bombed at 1205 hours with "good" results. At about the same time B-17s of the 96th and 351st Bomb Groups were approaching the airfield at Courtrai, in France. Just over 25 minutes later they returned east over Ypres to be met by *Luftwaffe* fighters, which became embroiled with the escorting fighters. Fifty Fortresses won through and bombed the hangars, dispersal areas, runways, and workshops at the airfield and put it out of action. The B-17s then flew north and headed for the coast between Ostend and Dunkirk. By 1255 hours most of the German fighters that took part in the first attack were forced to land and refuel. Five minutes later, German radar picked up the 94th and 95th Bomb Groups led by General Anderson near Ostend, heading for the Ford and General Motors plant at Antwerp. "Pappy" Colby reminisces:

"With no diversion at all we headed straight in to the target. At the IP we were supposed to meet our supporting fighters but we were twenty minutes late. Finally, we saw about 30 fighters at 2 o'clock and I heaved a sigh of relief, thinking our friends had waited for us. Suddenly, they attacked and at about the same time heavy flak started exploding dead ahead. We took violent evasive action and I was so busy for a few minutes that I didn't see much of what was happening. Then I discovered that the leading three-ship element of our low squadron had drifted left, out of the group formation and I had to decide quickly whether to stay with the group or follow him. I decided to stay with the group and it's lucky I did because flak started exploding right behind him where we should have been.

"It's nasty looking stuff- like an inverted mushroom of black smoke with a horizontal smoke ring which rises from the main burst and circles the stem. I heard our guns hammering and saw little white smoke puffs just ahead of the left wingman. For a moment I thought they were from his guns and then suddenly realized they were exploding cannon shells from German fighters.

"We dumped our load of five 1000lb bombs as carefully as possible and swung out over the coast for home. Flak followed us until we were out of range but the fighters eased up, probably because they were out of gas. Our own fighters finally joined us over the Channel, but at least one B-17 from another group was lost. My tail gunner saw him hit the ground and explode - no parachutes. Recce photos later showed a heavy bomb concentration on the Ford factory and the nearby canal locks and the west end of the General Motors plant also caught it."

The 44th's cargo of incendiaries had required a shorter trajectory and a two-mile longer bomb run than the B-17s. Flying a scattered formation, the B-24s were exposed to fighter attack. Altogether, five "Eightball" Liberators were lost, including three B-24Ds belonging to the 67th Squadron, which brought up the rear of the formation. The first to go down was Lieutenant William Roach and his replacement crew flying in *Annie Oakley*; there were only two survivors. *Miss Delores* was hit by flak over the target. One burst hit "Gibby" Wandtke, and he fell from the top turret with shrapnel wounds. John L. Susan, the radio operator, took over manning the turret. Unfortunately Susan's guns would not fire between the two vertical stabilizers and Roy L. Klingler, the tail-gunner, was dead. Six German fighters continued to fire at the ailing bomber from the rear. Two other gunners, George R. Millhausen and Richard Cate, were killed. Just after Haldon R. Hayward, the bombardier, dropped his bombs, Bob Bishop spotted a fighter boring in and shouted at Hayward to duck. A shell exploded on the Plexiglas nose and Hayward was struck in the face by fragments. Bishop had the paint stripped from his steel helmet by the blast. As *Miss Delores* fell behind the left wing started to burn. Brown gave the bale out order, but unknown to the crew the flak burst had also knocked out the intercom. Wandtke, although wounded, made his way aft via the open bomb bay at the height of the battle to warn the gunners to abandon ship.

The survivors proceeded to evacuate the aircraft. The time was just 1 o'clock. Bishop made his way to the nose wheel bay, where he looked out and saw a "red carpet of tracer." He paused for a moment until the German fighter ceased firing and then jumped. (Bishop knew the German pilot could not fire for long without his guns seizing up.) Feet up and head down in case the German should open fire on him, Bishop folded his arms into "wings," thinking it would aid his descent, but the reverse happened and he tumbled. Bishop quickly reverted to his former position and groped for the ripcord. He was horrified to discover it was not there! In his haste to leave the stricken Liberator Bishop had put his RAF type chest parachute on upside down! However, he located and pulled the ripcord after free falling to about 5000ft to avoid being fired upon by German fighters: "It was like standing on a motorbike doing 120mph, when suddenly, a little handkerchief came out. I thought it was rather small for a parachute—then the big parachute opened out and reduced my speed to practically nil in a split second." His flying boots went spinning off. Bishop decided to inflate his Mae West before he hit the water—a dangerous maneuver as the sudden force could have broken his ribs. Nevertheless, he hit the water safely and was hauled aboard a Danish trawler, where he collapsed on top of a bundle on the deck. The Danes shouted and gesticulated, and he found he was sitting on a wounded German fighter pilot who had been shot down in the same raid! After going underwater John L. Susan was pulled by his shroud lines from the sea by a fisherman. Brown, Westbrook, Hayward, Wandtke, and August Ullrich, the assistant radio operator gunner, were also rescued.

The third 67th Squadron Liberator lost was *Little Beaver*, piloted by Captain Chester "George" Phillips, which was shot down after leaving the target. Only four men from the eleven-man crew survived after three explosions rocked the ship. One of them was caused by a 20mm cannon shell, which exploded in the nose and ignited the hydraulic fluid accumulators. The flight deck became a mass of flames, and Philips and Everett W. Wilborn Jr, co-pilot, were killed. The aircraft went into a flat spin. Mike Denny, engineer, put on his parachute and then tried to extinguish the flames, but his efforts were in vain. He then had to save himself. Denny could not get the bomb bay doors open and was forced to crawl right through the bomb bay and bale out through one of the waist windows. William "Chubby" Hill, bombardier, was only saved by his steel helmet. Tom Bartmess, navigator, baled out of the aircraft, and about three minutes later Hill followed. The short delay was crucial. Bartmess landed in the water, but got caught in the shrouds of his parachute and drowned. Hill landed on dry land suffering from blows on the forehead caused by the opening of his parachute and the landing, a bruised back and shock. He joined Dale Glaubitz, the assistant engineer, and Charles Forehand, one of the waist gunners, as the only other survivors.

The fifth "Eightball" Liberator lost overall, and the only 506th Squadron aircraft lost was *Wicked Witch*, flown by Captain John W. "Swede" Swanson. Flak had damaged the No.2 engine before the target, but Swanson maintained formation and was able to salvo his bombs. As the group turned off the target *Wicked Witch* was finished off by enemy fighters making head on attacks. 2nd Lieutenant Richard L. Schiefelbusch, navigator, recalls:

> "Bombardier Sid Banks and I in the nose of the plane were aware at first of an order to bale out, which we did by going out through the nose door hatch. On the way down I saw two chutes, one on each side of me. The one between the coastline and me was Banks. I never knew who the other one was. I came down in the Baltic about ten miles from shore. Later, I found out that both Douglas B. Myers, co pilot and Swanson (the last one out) came down on land."

Scrappy, in the 66th Squadron piloted by 1st Lieutenant John Y. Reed, became the sixth and final 44th Bomb Group loss. Reed recalls:

> "We came under very heavy fighter attacks in the target area and were quite vulnerable because of our spread out bombing formation. Just prior to dropping our bombs, I saw a FW 190 peel off at us from about 1 o'clock and slightly high. As the puffs of bursting 20mm self-destroying ammo came toward us, it became apparent that the line of fire would put the successive bursts right into our cockpit. Purely reflex action alone caused me to hit the wheel in a dive to try to get below the line of fire, but unfortunately, the bursts did not quite clear the plane, but hit the top turret directly behind the cockpit. The resultant explosion tore the top turret canopy completely off and the shrapnel severely wounded T/Sgt Adam Wygonik about his head, neck and upper body. The inside of the turret and the gun barrels were pitted from the force of the shrapnel. Either the force of the explosion or Wygonik must have reflexively dumped his seat lever as he immediately fell out onto the flight deck. T/Sgt Alan Perry, radio operator, immediately sized up the situation, left his own oxygen supply and attempted some first aid at Wygonik, who was bleeding profusely from his head and body wounds - and no oxygen supply. Perry snapped Wygonik's chest pack onto his harness and put his hand around the ripcord ring, inasmuch as Perry intuitively concluded that Wygonik would die before we got back to England and medical attention. He intended to roll Wygonik out of the ship as we were still over the target area - and the possibility of immediate medical attention.
>
> "Perry was suffering from lack of oxygen and returned to his oxygen supply to keep from blacking out but when he was able to turn back to Wygonik, Adam was gone! Apparently, or intentionally or otherwise, Adam had rolled off the flight deck, onto the catwalk in the open bomb bay. The bay doors were still open as we were on the bomb run. No one could say for sure that Adam's chute had opened since all attention was on fighting off the attacking aircraft. We had no way of knowing whether Adam reached the ground dead or alive, though the odds seemed stacked against his survival due to the severity of his wounds and the resultant loss of blood and the fact that he was without oxygen even longer than Sgt Perry.
>
> "The plane, as we came away from the target, was severely damaged, with one engine smouldering, loss of top portions of one vertical stabilizer and rudder, multiple hits from 20mm fire including the blown-away top turret canopy. Unable to maintain position in our formation, I dove toward a group of B-17s that were ahead and below us in a shallow dive toward the coast and managed to hold position behind and below their rear flight. This protected our top with their bottom and rear turrets. After the fighter attacks broke off, we flew pretty much back to England."[197]

At the target the Germans methodically rounded up all the survivors and drove them away in police wagons. Jim O'Brien recalls:

> "We were held in prison for three hours. I found Norris Crisan, Bledsoe and McCabe but 'Mac' Howell didn't show up. A German medic brought in his dog tags and asked me, 'Do you know a little man in a yellow suit? He is *toten* (dead).' I kept hoping that the story was a bluff to get us to talk so we all acted as if we did not know 'Mac' and stuck to the 'name, rank and serial number routine' throughout all interrogations that followed. After extensive questioning by the English-speaking medic and some waiting around the town, eight of us were placed in a canvas-covered Renault diesel truck and proceeded to another town along dusty roads. We continued for about an hour to a point where we picked up some more prisoners including Ernst, Husselton, McCammand and Castillo. We carried on and after a few miles the truck stopped again. Sergeant Crisan was ordered to get out. He came back after viewing the wreckage of *The Rugged Buggy* and whispered that the radio set was intact after the crash and they simply wanted him to identify it. He didn't help them too much because he was the bombardier and loyal to the name rank and serial number" bit. Castillo was taken to hospital where his foot was later amputated. I never heard from him again except the rumor

that he was repatriated in a prisoner exchange in 1944. That night we arrived in an improvised military camp southwest of Kiel where we stayed overnight with the lights on and the guards over us."[198]

In four hours VIII Bomber Command had attacked four targets, losing 12 B-17s and B-24s and claiming 67 fighters shot down. RAF Spitfires and USAAF Thunderbolts had given excellent fighter cover on the Antwerp and Courtrai raids. Colonel Hub Zemke, flying LM-Z—now carrying the slogan *Moy Tovarish* (My Comrade)—led 34 P-47s of the 56th Fighter Group in support of the force of B-17s over Antwerp and shepherd them to the coast. The P-47s rendezvoused with the bombers over St. Nicholas at 1315 hours at about 30,000ft. It was a beautiful spring day and visibility was excellent. Over Antwerp at around his 2 o'clock position Zemke saw two FW 190s diving towards the B-17s. He made a 180° diving turn to pursue the enemy but they had disappeared, but shortly he noticed four aircraft about a mile to his left. They were FW 190s. Zemke called for a left turn and gradually got himself in a position behind them; they were flying a string formation, apparently oblivious to the P-47s' presence. Zemke singled out one of the FW 190s. His first burst missed, and his second burst produced a flash on top of his canopy. His fire on both passes was too high. The 190 immediately rolled over into a dive, but as he passed across his sight Zemke gave him a third burst and flashes appeared along his left wing root and fuselage before he disappeared from sight below. Zemke's exhilaration was short-lived, as his earphones rang with a warning that he was about to be attacked. He broke left into a climbing turn and saw three or four aircraft coming down head-on. As the leader got within range he fired a 3-second burst. He saw no hits or return fire before he was past and gone. His wingman, Lieutenant Justus Foster, had remained with him throughout, as did one other member of the flight. The No.4 man, Lieutenant Robert Johnson, was missing. The German fighters were now gone, and with fuel reserves low Zemke led the flight out over Flushing. His composure returned and was elated that he had scored his first "kill." Back at Horsham St. Faith Zemke found out that another flight in the 61st Squadron, which he had been leading, had attacked other FW 190s and made probable and damaged claims. Zemke was relieved to learn that all his P-47s had returned safely, Bob Johnson having returned home on his own. Expert evaluation of the 16mm gun camera film in the wing, which actuated automatically when the guns were fired to record bullet strikes, reduced his claim to "damaged." Later, the evaluation officer told him that he was lucky to even get that! His range estimation was way off, fire had been made at more like 1000 yards than 500 yards, and most of the 67 rounds he had fired had been sprayed harmlessly around the sky. Zemke had to wait until 13 June when he scored his first kills, downing two FW 190s near Cassel.

The 78th Fighter Group, with three squadrons of 16 P-47s each led by Colonel Arman Peterson, encountered more than 20 Focke-Wulf 190s and Me 109s at 20,000-24,000ft in the Antwerp area, and dogfights broke out all over the sky. Major James J. Stone, CO of the 83rd Squadron, claimed a FW 190 that was heading for the bombers. Captain Robert E. Adamina also claimed a FW 190, while Captain Jack J. Oberhansly and Captain Charles P. London got "probables." Colonel Peterson and four other pilots each damaged a 190. Adamina, Captain Elmer E. McTaggart, and Flight Officer S. R. Martinek were shot down.[199]

Not all the bombing was accurate—the Marauders returned safely, but missed their target at Ijmuiden completely—but for the first time Americans had shown that they were capable of mounting multiple attacks on a given day. The attack on Wevelgem airfield by the Fortresses had fared better. Bombs dropped by the 96th and 351st Bomb Groups so heavily damaged the airfield that III./JG 26 was forced to move to Lille-Nord. On the bombers' return east of Ypres they were attacked en masse by fighters.[200] Flak bracketed the 94th and 95th Bomb Groups at Antwerp, and the FW 190s and *Oberfeldwebel* Bach of II./JG 1 applied the *coup de grace* to a 95th Bomb Group B-17 captained by Lieutenant J. E. McKinley, which had already been badly shot up in an earlier fighter attack.[201]

On 15 May Eaker again diversified his forces, sending the 1st Wing to Wilhelmshaven, while 59 B-17s of the 4th Wing were allocated the naval base at Emden. Despite the unsuccessful attempt 24 hours earlier by Liberators using incendiaries at Kiel, B-17s of the 94th Bomb Group were each loaded with 500lb incendiary clusters for its raid on Emden. "Pappy" Colby was there:

"We climbed to 26,000ft over the North Sea, turned towards the German coast in a fake attack and then turned out again. The second time we turned in, the low squadron cadet in front of me missed the signal to turn and nearly tan into the lead squadron. The propellers were making heavy contrails that made visibility very bad. As we started to turn left, my left wingman, Lieutenant Eklund apparently didn't see us and started to slide into me. All that saved us from a collision is that, by the grace of God, his right wing suddenly cast a shadow on my left window. I looked up quickly to see what made the shadow and was horrified to see his wing almost on top of ours. I dumped the aircraft down desperately and his props missed us by barely 3ft. A second or two later and we'd both have had it.

"We regained formation but I stayed out to the left of the lead squadron to avoid any more fast turns. As we passed over some high clouds we saw a hole just beyond them and there, in plain sight, was our target. Everybody dumped the incendiaries but instead of the bundles dropping like bombs, they broke open and the 4lb sticks came fluttering back right through the formation, scaring the hell out of everybody. Heavy flak started bursting and for some reason the lead squadron turned right instead of left as we had been briefed and this left our low squadron out in the cold by itself Luckily, no fighters saw us and we hustled to get back into the protection of the group.

"As we crossed the German coast homeward bound, from behind us came about 25 enemy fighters. They passed us on our left as if we were standing still, pulled across in front of us and then dived head-on into our formation as all hell bust loose. They hit the lead squadron mostly and I saw at least ten or twelve 20mm cannon shells explode around our ships but everyone kept going. Our gunners were yelling, 'Attack 10 o'clock high; 1 o'clock high' and we were really busy. My right wingman, Lieutenant Jasper Moore, got jammed into the lead squadron again and had to fall back. Later, I found out he was hit by a 20mm in the tail, which almost severed his control cables.

"Suddenly, my bombardier, Bob Gamble, let out a wild yell and I discovered later that a shell had exploded under our nose, blowing out part of the Plexiglas window. Enough to scare anyone! Two Focke-Wulf 1 90s started a nose attack on us and all our gunners turned loose on them while they were still out 800 yards. The tracers flew like a garden hose in reverse and to my great surprise; they broke off the attack and turned away. We came home dog-tired and unhappy about the poor formation flying, which scared us as much as the enemy. One ship lost its tail gunner and we all had considerable flak damage."

Incredibly only one B-17, in the 95th Bomb Group, was lost on the Emden mission. Meanwhile, the 1st Wing had set a course for Wilhelmshaven. Thick cloud obscured the target, and the Fortresses were forced to seek alternative targets at Heligoland, Dune, and Wangerooge

Island. Heligoland was covered in only 4/10ths cloud and the flak was inaccurate. However, numerous enemy fighters put in an appearance and succeeded in shooting down five Fortresses.[202]

On 16 May VIII Bomber Command was stood down while maintenance was performed on the battle-scarred B-17s, blackened by two days' continuous combat. Bomber crews were glad of a respite, brief though it was. A fighter sweep by eleven P-47s of the 4th, 56th, and 78th Fighter Groups, however, was flown over northern Belgium. This resulted in combat action when they met 30 fighters of JG 1 in the Vlissingen area being led by the *Geschwader Kommodore*, Major Hans "Fips" Philipp, an ex-JG 54 *Experte*, who had assumed command of JG 1 on 1 April. Philipp claimed a P-47 as his 205th *Abschuss*[203] at 1312 hours, followed one minute later by another "Jug"[204] shot down by *Oberleutnant* Koch as his 16th kill.[205] Colonel Arman Peterson, 78th Fighter Group CO, destroyed one FW 190, and two more fell to the guns of his Group. There was only one victim, *Hauptmann* Dietrich Wickop, *Kommandeur* II./JG 1, who had 13 victories, including three B-17s.[206]

Meanwhile, the 322nd Bomb Group's new CO, Colonel Robert Stillman, had been called to a conference at HQ, Elveden Hall near Thetford. He was informed that reconnaissance photos of the P.E.N. electricity generating plant at Ijmuiden, on the Dutch coast, the target attacked by the Marauders on 14 May, had revealed no damage, and was still in full operation. Stillman was informed that VIIIth Bomber Command wanted the target to be attacked again on 17 May when Eaker once again intended to diversify his forces. (He would send the 1st Wing to Kiel and 55 Fortresses in the 4th Wing to the U-boat pens and the power station that served them at Lorient, while 39 B-24s, acting as an independent force for the first time, would go to Bordeaux). Colonel Stillman could not believe they were serious; stating that to attack the same target so soon could mean enemy defenses would be ready and waiting for them. General Newton L. Longfellow, who had replaced his old friend Eaker as commanding general of the VIIIth Bomber Command on 2 December 1942, was adamant that the attack should go ahead. Although he sympathized with Colonel Stillman's point of view, Longfellow threatened Stillman with the loss of his command if he refused to obey orders. Upset at the thought of sending his crews back to the same target so soon after their harrowing first mission (where they suffered a number of casualties and lost Lieutenant Howell and his crew in a crash near the base), Stillman returned to Rougham, near Bury St. Edmunds. The order for the mission arrived at 0036 hours on 17 May asking for a maximum effort raid, flying the same route as three days before. Lieutenant Colonel Alfred Von Kolnitz, the 322nd Bomb Group's Chief Intelligence Officer, was alarmed that the same route was to be flown, as he expected heavy enemy opposition. He wrote a memo to Colonel Stillman, ending it: "For God's sake - get fighter cover!"

The crews alerted for the mission were from the 450th and 452nd Squadrons, who with four exceptions had not flown the first mission. One of these was Colonel Stillman, who was determined to lead. The 322nd could field eleven B-26 Marauders for the mission, with the 452nd aircraft leading. Although the crews were confident of a second success, they all expected to meet stiff opposition, and many were convinced they would not return. Stillman was also convinced that the mission was going to be a disaster, but was determined to do his duty and ensure the target was knocked out this time. As he left the Intelligence Section after the mission briefing, Lieutenant Colonel Von Kolnitz said "Cheerio." Stillman answered, "No, it's goodbye." Trying to cheer him up, Von Kolnitz said, "I'll see you at 1 o'clock."

"It's goodbye," replied Stillman firmly.

At 1050 hours the Marauders began taking off. At 1147 hours and 33 miles off the coast of Holland Captain Stephens in the 452nd flight aborted due to power failure to the top turret and one engine not giving the correct boost. Off course, the remaining B-26s crossed the Dutch coast 25 miles from Noordwijk and headed toward Rozenburg Island, in the Maas River Estuary, the most heavily defended area in the Netherlands. They were showered by 20mm cannon shells. The lead aircraft took direct hits, which severed the flight controls and killed Lieutenant Resweber, Stillman's co-pilot. As a result of the loss of flying controls the Marauder snap rolled and Stillman saw the ground coming up to meet him. His plane crashed upside down, but amazingly Stillman, Sgt Freeman, and Sgt Willis were all pulled from the wreckage alive. The two sergeants survived the first mission and had now been lucky again.

The following flight, which was two miles to the south, also encountered heavy fire from the ground. Lieutenant Garrambone's aircraft was hit, he lost control, and the aircraft crashed into the Maas River. Garrambone and three of his crew survived. Believing that they were approaching the target area, pilots and navigators looked for the landmarks they had noted on the mission briefing. As they were way off course there were none, and they were flying somewhere between Delft and Rotterdam. Captain Converse now led the first flight and, taking evasive action to avoid flak, collided with Lieutenant Wolf's aircraft, which was leading the second element. Both B-26s went down, but four gunners survived from the two aircraft, one being Sgt Thompson, the fourth veteran of 14 May. Debris hit *Chickersaw Chief*, causing the pilot, Lieutenant Wurst, to crash-land the B-26 in a field near Mieje. Sergeant Heski, top turret gunner, lost a foot in the crash, and he was the only serious casualty. This left only Lieutenant F. H. Matthews and Lieutenant E. R. Norton of the third element of the lead flight in the air. Norton's co-pilot was his twin brother, J. A. Norton. These two aircraft joined the second flight to make a more effective force to bomb the target. Unfortunately, the second flight was as lost as the first and had no idea where the target lay. Forty-five miles into Holland the remaining aircraft decided to turn for home. Lieutenant Colonel Purinton, who was leading the second flight, asked his navigator, Lieutenant Jeffries, for a heading. Jeffries answered, "270°," followed by, "Hold it a minute, I think I see the target. Yes, there it is!" Bomb doors were opened, and Purinton's co-pilot, Lieutenant Kinney, sighted and dropped the bombs on what they thought was the target.[207] All aircraft dropped their bombs when Kinney dropped his, but they were heading directly towards the "real" target at Ijmuiden. There they encountered more heavy flak and Purinton's plane was hit, but he managed to ditch two miles offshore. Jeffries was killed in the crash, and a German patrol boat picked up the rest of the crew. Lieutenant Jones' aircraft was the next to be shot down and crashed. Lieutenant Aliamo was the only survivor. The Norton brothers, now flying at 250mph to try and make it home, were shot down west of Ijmuiden. Their tail gunner, Sgt Longworth, was the only survivor of their crew.

Only Lieutenant Matthews and Captain Jack Crane now remained, at some distance apart. They survived the coastal flak and raced for England. When the Marauders crossed the coast on their inbound flight, 26 FW 190s of II./JG 1 on a combat alert from Woensdrecht, southern Holland, were vectored to meet them. At 1218 they saw Matthews' and Crane's aircraft flying low and fast over the North Sea and they attacked. Crane told the top turret gunner and engineer, George Williams, *Come up front, George, there is something wrong with the rudder.* Williams checked the rudder cables and repaired a damaged section with some safety wire from the rear of the turret. As he returned to the turret the aircraft was peppered with bullets, and he saw the port engine in flames. He called to Crane but there was no reply. The plane started to lose altitude, leveled off, and then dived into the sea.[208] At Rougham, the estimated time for the Group's return was 1250 hours. On the control tower balcony, General Brady of VIIIth Bomber Command and other watchers were growing apprehensive. At 1305 hours a RAF listening post reported that it had intercepted a German radio transmission, which said that it had shot two bombers into the sea.

By 1330 hours it was decided that no aircraft were still airborne and that a disaster had occurred, with all ten B-26s being lost.[209]

The Fortresses and B-24s did not come through unscathed on 17 May either, although the *Memphis Belle* in the 324th Bomb Squadron, 91st Bomb Group at Bassingbourn, completed its 25th mission.[210] Six B-17s attacking Lorient failed to return, five of them being shot down by III./JG 2 from Vannes. "Pappy" Colby in the 94th Bomb Group relates:

> "As we came in off the sea about 30 fighters really gave us a going over. It turned out they were the famous yellow nose fighters who defended the St. Nazaire-Lorient area. To my amazement I saw one come right through the middle of the group formation in front of us. What a pilot! We made a fair bomb run and turn out but the fighters worked us over clear out over the sea. In the middle of the fight my entire left windshield suddenly showed a million cracks and I could barely see through it. A machine-gun bullet hit it, but luckily at an acute angle, so that while it shattered the inch-thick armor glass, it only put a small hole clear through. Lieutenant Winnesheik (our Indian Chief) lost an engine but made it back. I know we got at least one of their fighters because I saw the pilot parachute out of his burning aircraft. This was the roughest raid we had yet experienced."

Midnight, piloted by Ed Spevak, became the first 94th Bomb Group Fortress to fall victim to enemy action when it was knocked down by flak over the target. An engine caught fire and the aircraft fell out of formation. Fighters attacked and set another engine on fire. *Midnight* was engulfed in flame and smoke in the tail, and Spevak gave the order to bale out. "Pappy" Colby's crew counted eight parachutes. Walter Minor, *Midnight's* tail gunner, was hit just as he was leaving the burning aircraft. He floated down and saw a wing tear free from the fuselage and continue separately to earth. He and another crewmember were picked up by the French Underground and were returned to England via the Pyrenees, Spain, and Gibraltar. Ed Spevak and Don Nichols, co-pilot, also evaded capture and were returned to England.[211]

Next day (18 May) the CBO plan for round-the-clock bombing of the Reich from England by the RAF and 8th Air force was approved by CCS:[212] Ironically, the only 8th Air Force combat action involved another high-altitude *Rodeo* by the three American P-47 groups along the Dutch coast. Major Don Blakeslee in the 4th Fighter Group led his P-47s to Walcheren-Bruges-Nieuport. At 1655 hours three P-47s bounced four FW 190s 5000ft below, but the fighters got away. Seven minutes later a dozen Bf 109s approached the 4th Fighter Group at 9100 meters (30,000ft) after the P-47s had turned for England at Ostend. The 109s came in astern, and the P-47s broke around and dived on them. The 109s dived away in accordance with *Jagdwaffe* standard procedure, but this was a suicidal move, and the Thunderbolts turned into them with a vengeance. 1st Lieutenant Duane W. Beeson chased *Oberfeldwebel* Heinz Wefes of 4/JG 54 until the German baled out at 100ft for the first of the American's 17 victories of the war. Wefes' parachute failed to open and he was killed. 2nd Lieutenant Robert A. Boock in the 334th Fighter Squadron was shot down and KIA by Leutnant Melchior Kestel of the 9th *Staffel* JG 26 in the North Sea off the coast between Knocke and Blankenberghe at 1702 hours.[213] By the time Major "Pips" Priller and his FW 190s arrived on the scene the combats had ended and the Thunderbolts had regained altitude.[214]

On 19 May 102 Fortresses of the 1st Wing went to the turbine engine building at Kiel to finish off what had been missed five days previously, while further north, 64 B-17s in the 4th Wing attacked U-boat pens at Flensburg, on the Danish coast. A smaller force of B-17s flew a diversion. The Flensburg force returned without loss, but the Kiel force lost six Fortresses, three of which were ripped to pieces by bombs dropped from above by *Feldwebel* Jonny Fest,[215] *Feldwebel* Erich Führmann, and *Unteroffizier* Biermann of 5./JG 11. *Leutnant* Heinz Knoke's bomb failed to hit a *Viermot*, but at 1217 hours near Husum he brought down a B-17 using his cannon and machine guns.

Following this mission, fog and rain cloaked East Anglia and the Fens, preventing any missions being flown until 21 May when 98 B-17s in the 1st Wing were allocated Wilhelmshaven and 63 Fortresses in the 4th Wing bombed Emden. At Wilhelmshaven weather conditions hampered the formation, and it was further disrupted by constant head-on attacks by enemy fighters. The Emden force also encountered heavy fighter opposition despite diversionary ruses at the coast. Altogether, twelve B-17s were lost on the two raids. The 1st Wing came off worse with seven B-17s shot down, three of them from the 306th Bomb Group. The B-17 flown by 1st Lieutenant Maxwell V. Judas was shot down with the loss of three crew killed. A 20mm canon shell came through the cockpit and badly wounded Judas and his co pilot, but both men managed to bale out and they were captured. 1st Lieutenant Floyd J. Fields' B-17 was set on fire and Fields ditched in the North Sea. Fields and five of his crew drowned. A German seaplane picked up the five who survived after seven hours adrift in a dinghy. Flak and fighters hit *Dearly Beloved* of the 423rd Bomb Squadron, flown by Lieutenant Robert H. Smith, and gunners claimed a new record of eleven fighters before the B-17 was forced to ditch 60 miles off the coast of Germany. One of the fighters was claimed by 2nd Lieutenant Bob McCallum, who had taken over the vacated top turret, and earned a place in 8th Air Force history as the only co pilot to shoot down a German fighter. The crew spent thirty hours adrift in the North Sea in two dinghies until they were picked up by a Royal Navy minesweeper, and they later returned to Thurleigh before being sent to rest homes.

One of the German fighter pilots airborne on 21 May was *Oberleutnant* Eberhard Burath, *Gruppen* Adjutant I./JG 1:

> "21 May was a great and also difficult day. At 1030 we were directed against a 4-mot) formation, but did not find it and landed at 1113 at Schiphol. At 1221 we took off again against the returning formation. This time the directions were correct. We caught them about 100 km north of Ameland as they were heading in a northwesterly direction for home. I was wingman to Hauptmann Emil-Rudolf Schnoor. We drew past them and attacked from ahead. From too low, I got the B 17 flying on the outside right into my sights at an impossible angle. Leading by three lengths, I pressed all the firing buttons; no effect observed. After landing I was incredulous as Hauptmann Schnoor congratulated me for my first *Abschuss*. At this time I had been thinking of something entirely different. On breaking off from the enemy formation I had observed a FW 190 crashing into the sea and a parachute above it. I had started my stopwatch, noted the course and where this would have crossed the coast. Oberleutnant Munz, my old roommate from Mönchengladbach, was missing. I wanted to search for him. I took off as soon as my aircraft was ready. First to the noted place on the coast, then the reverse of the course I had noted and starting the stopwatch. When the time had elapsed I scanned the sea to right and left. Then I saw something yellow, a rubber dingy, but to my horror empty and bouncing about on the rough sea. Low over the water I searched around the dinghy in tight circles. Only white spumes, no other colors. 'Man, Hans, where are you?' Nothing. The red warning light urged me back. 68 minutes. A rescue seaplane was called and the position given. I took off once more and met with the rescue-Wal at the old position. We

searched until I had to return. 73 minutes. It had got dark and the seaplane also had to abandon the search. This loss hit me hard. Had he seen us during the search? What despair when we turned away! Six weeks later he was found on the beach at Sylt - 'a better man I never knew.'"[216]

With the increase in attacks on the north German coast, on 23 May III./JG 26 flew to Cuxhaven-Nordholz to reinforce JG 1, 2./JG 27, III./JG 54, and JG 11 against the American attacks. That same day in East Anglia the 94th Bomb Group began moving from Thurleigh to Earls Colne, in Essex, and the 96th Bomb Group began leaving Grafton Underwood for Andrews Field, six miles from Earls Colne. Grafton Underwood was taken over by the 384th Bomb Group, commanded by Colonel Budd J. Peaslee, which arrived in England during late May. The 1st Bomb Wing was strengthened by the arrival of the 381st Bomb Group, commanded by Colonel Joe J. Nazzaro, which flew into Ridgewell on 31 May, and the 379th Bomb Group, commanded by Colonel Maurice "Mo" Preston, which took over a new base at Kimbolton.[217] Bad weather throughout the latter part of May restricted deep penetration missions[218] and delayed the introduction of new groups like the 379th. Preston's group finally "got its feet wet" on 29 May when the target for 1st Bomb Wing crews was St. Nazaire. One could be forgiven for thinking that there was little left in the French seaports to bomb. Admiral Karl Doenitz said that, "No dog or cat is left in these towns." Heavy cloud moving across Western Europe resulted in several stop-go decisions before the B-17s finally got the green light. Colonel Preston remembers the 379th Bomb Group's debut well:[219]

"The powers-that-be were a little concerned and skeptical about sending a new, untried unit out on its first mission to a relatively tough target like St. Nazaire. So, I suppose in order to salve their consciences somewhat, they put us in what promised to be the safest position in the task force; the high group position in the last combat wing. They figured that we should sail through scot-free in that position but they underestimated the effect of their own tactics. A diversionary force had been sent out in an effort to induce the German fighters to take off early, thus forcing them to run out of gas as, or before, the main force arrived. Well, the tactic worked perfectly. The *Abbeville Kids* committed themselves early and soon ran out of gas. But they got back up in time to intercept us at the tail end of the bomber column just as we passed the IP. The fighters attacked us with a vengeance then drew off to hit us again as we departed the target and before we were able to reassemble in wing formation. We lost three aircraft and 30 crewmembers, including John Hall, a squadron commander. Swede Carlson, another squadron commander, lost two engines near the target and suffered damage to a third, causing his aircraft to be lost later when he had to land in a Brussels sprout patch in England.

"I saw flak for the first time in my life on the mission. Although it came from a little battery on Guernsey it was nonetheless real and it gave me my first big scare of the war. I was never quite as scared of flak again but that first view of something shot up there to kill me really got to me. The mission didn't go smoothly in all respects. There were planning errors revealed. There were personal errors. There were screw-ups and there were goofs. All of which made it clear to one young Lieutenant Colonel, out for his first exposure to the war, that we GIs didn't have our methods and procedures for fighting it down pat yet. There was room for improvement it seemed. And maybe there was still an opportunity for some of us Johnny-Come-Latelys to make a contribution or two to the winning of the war. I was forced to wonder, at the same time, how long we'd be around to make that contribution."

The inexperience associated with any new group continued, on occasions, to manifest itself among the elder groups, such as the 94th, which was briefed for Rennes this day. Problems occurred during assembly in bad weather and elements became disoriented. "Pappy" Colby, flying *Thundermug*, says that things were "SNAFU":[220]

"We noted the high squadron had no second element of three ships. They didn't catch up until we hit the French coast. Then, just before starting the bomb run, our leader ran us in behind another group and we all got shaken up by the prop' wash. We should have been 1000ft higher. As the bomb run started the lead squadron made a little right turn and the high squadron, instead of turning with him, came sailing right on top of us with their bomb bays open. I took one horrified look and pulled out to the left to get out from under them and then we scrambled to get back in place when the high squadron finally woke up. But the bombing stunk and his group leader never did release his bombs. The lack of training in formation flying displayed by some of the groups was appalling and was the cause of many of our problems.

"Right after leaving the target, the fighters came in thick but they mostly picked on the low squadron. We lost three crews and a fourth barely made it home on two engines, with a dead ball gunner and missing one man who fell out. There were two attacks by fighters dropping aerial bombs, who dove right through the formation from above. One came through between the second element of the lead squadron and us - a space of less than 100ft - and nearly took our wing off. Patrick, our radio gunner, hit the second fighter and a big piece of his wing flew off. Potts, our waist gunner, saw the pilot parachute out, so we claimed our third fighter kill. However, in knocking down the fighter, Patrick somehow put four .50 caliber bullets through the top of our rudder, breaking the top hinge and scaring hell out of Chris Thalman and myself when we felt the shock on our rudder pedals. Luckily, the middle and bottom hinges held and we got home safely.

"Since our trusty ship *Thundermug* now had a busted rudder, this meant we would fall behind the other crews in missions flown, as there were no spare ships. So I sold the Group Maintenance Officer on the idea of letting my crew swap rudders with a B-17 that was under repair waiting for parts - a 'hangar queen.' He wasn't happy about it but agreed finally and we made the swap with help from one of his mechanics who adjusted the cables. Thus we were able to get *Thundermug* and its crew back in business even though we bent a few regulations.

"General Eaker visited us and gave us a fine talk: telling us that if we finished 25 missions we would be through with combat and assigned to staff jobs. He estimated that 75% or more would return to the States for re-assignment. (I thought it would be nearer to 98%.) On 5 June Brigadier General Frederick L. Anderson, CO the 4th Bombardment Wing, visited us. He awarded us the Air Medal and I was the first man in the 94th to receive it, much to my gratification. All of my crew also received the medal."

In June 1943 General Ira Eaker was able to send the 1st and 4th Wings on two-pronged attacks against north German targets at Emden, Kiel, Bremen, Wilhelmshaven, and Cuxhaven on a single day. On the morning of 10 June, about 30 lead pilots, navigators, and bombardiers in the 94th Bomb Group at Earls Colne were briefed for a raid the following morning. "Pappy" Colby remembers that it was "very, very secret where we were going. But by 1030 hours the next morning the word was all over the Enlisted Men's Mess that we were going to Bremen. Security—ha, what a laugh! They briefed us at noon and we finally got going at 1500 hours."

Cloud and haze still filled the sky as 252 bombers headed for the target. Major Thorup led the 94th Bomb Group with the 333rd Bomb Squadron, and "Pappy" Colby led the second element behind him:

> "We came in too close to the north coast of Germany and ran into high cirro-cumulus clouds as we turned for Bremen. The target was covered with a solid layer of low cumulus clouds down to about 5000ft, which also partially covered Wilhelmshaven, our secondary target, so we made a 270° turn to the left and bombed Cuxhaven on the north coast of Germany. We hit it good and were on our way out when about twenty fighters caught up and attacked the lower groups behind us. A piece of flak flew in the open waist window on our left side and smacked against the machine-gun mount at the opposite window but luckily neither gunner was hit and no damage was caused to the mount (although it was hard on the gunners' kidneys)."[221]

The 1st Wing, meanwhile, discovering the primary target at Bremen to be obscured, turned for the secondary at Wilhelmshaven. During the bomb run the leading 303rd Bomb Group formation was bracketed by a severe flak barrage. The CO, Colonel Chuck Marion, lost two engines, and following aircraft had to maneuver violently and reduce speed dramatically to avoid a collision. Just at that moment the *Luftwaffe* took advantage of the now scattered formation and made repeated head-on attacks, during which one B-17 was rammed by a FW 190 that failed to pull out in time.[222] The 379th Bomb Group, flying only its second mission, bore the brunt of the attacks, as Colonel Preston well remembers:

> "The enemy fighters, as expected, first appeared as the lead wing of B-17s approached the shoreline just north of the target. The fighters came in large numbers; probably several hundred. As expected, they climbed to the bombers' altitude and then a little higher as they pulled on out to the right front of the bomber column a mile or so. Then they broke off in groups of four to six and swung around in a diving turn to deliver their attack from the front. They concentrated on the low group of those at the head of the column that, as it happened, was the 379th Group. The fighters approached upright until they reached a point about half a mile to the front, when they rolled on their backs, fired their guns and rockets and dived toward the earth. The little puffs of 20mm shells exploding were clearly visible as the fighters approached from up front. As soon as one bunch made its pass and disappeared earthward, another bunch would roll in for its run at the B-17s. And they kept coming and coming, on and on. They attacked all during the bomb run and the subsequent re-assembly and continued the attack until we crossed the coastline. Then the attacks stopped, probably because all their ammo was spent. A very typical engagement, although perhaps untypical in its severity and an effective one. The 379th lost six or one-third of its strength. Our gunners claimed many dozens of fighters destroyed. A strange thing: we always claimed to inflict great losses on the enemy in the tally sheets back in the 8th Air Force headquarters. I'm sure we destroyed the Luftwaffe many times over. Yet, in my personal experience, whereas I saw many B-17s shot down by enemy fighters - perhaps a score or more - and occasionally enemy fighters destroyed by friendly escort fighters, I never once saw a fighter destroyed by a B-17 gunner - not once. I am personally convinced that bombardment gunnery was a very ineffective weapon. It was certainly no match for the fighter."[223]

On Sunday, 13 June, 102 B-17s of the 1st Wing were assigned Bremen, while the 4th Wing went to Kiel for another raid on the U-boat yards. The 94th, 95th, and 96th Bomb Groups would take off from their bases at Earls Colne, Framlingham, and Andrews Field for the last time. Heavy losses in the Marauder groups prompted their transfer further south to the three B-17 bases so that fighter cover for them could be improved. When the B-17 groups returned from the raid they would touch down at the former B-26 bases at Bury St. Edmunds (Rougham), Horham, and Snetterton Heath, respectively. One of the aircrew in the 332nd Squadron, 94th Bomb Group, was Sgt Richard "Dick" Lewis from Chicago, the right waist gunner aboard *Mr. Five-by-Five*, flown by Captain Kee Harrison of Lombard, Illinois. Lewis recalls:

> "Our training, supervised by Captain Harrison, had been thorough and strict. I remember him as a warm but serious skipper who was a stickler for discipline and for attendance at ground school training. He was short and stocky and we named our ship in his honor. I owe my life to his total knowledge of the flight capabilities of our ship and to his combat flying skills. I was glad to be assigned to the Flying Fortress. The name alone gave me a special feeling of security. Having a pilot like Captain Harrison was certainly another large plus. Our ship and crew had been very fortunate on our early missions. Our first had been to St. Omer out of Bassingbourn, where we were temporarily based with the 91st Bomb Group. It had already established a solid combat record in the Eighth Air Force. Now we also were a unit of the 'Eighth.'[224] I remember the Kiel raid particularly. Cover from the short-range English Spitfires ended as we flew northeast over the North Sea. As we approached the German coast, swarms of German fighters rose to defend Kiel. It seemed that most of the Luftwaffe was gathered there. The action was intense and I saw many ships, both German and 8th Air Force, going down in flames or exploding in mid-air."

During the morning and afternoon of the 13th the short-ranged P-47s were used on two diversionary sweeps off the Belgian coast. In the morning the 56th Fighter Group (which had claimed its first victory the day before[225]) came upon 10./JG 26. Over Dixmuide Colonel Hubert "Hub" Zemke, the CO, claimed two of the FW 190s and one damaged, as he recalled in his combat report:

> "As flying wing commander of the 56th Fighter Group on this mission, I had decided that I would lead the 61st Fighter Squadron as bouncing squadron. The 62nd Fighter Squadron was to be close escort at the same altitude and slightly to the rear. The 63rd Fighter Squadron was to be high cover for the other two squadrons with a superiority of 1000-2000ft more or less to the inside of the course and slightly ahead where I could direct their direction and disposition. 'Take-off and climb of the squadrons was normal in that nothing of importance can be mentioned. The squadrons positioned themselves on the climb so that the 63rd was to the left and the 62nd was on the right. From Felixstowe to Gravelines the course was 174° through a thin layer of about 6/10 cirrus clouds. This gave me considerable anxiety, as the 56th Group was to give high support to the 4th Fighter Group. The layer being at 26,000ft, at this time, which was about 0930 plus hours, contrails were reported ahead going into France and were believed to be the 4th Fighter Group. Shortly thereafter, the Ground Operations reported bandits in the vicinity of Ostend heading west along the coast. Since the group had not reached France and were trying to give support to the 4th Group, who were only in visual contact by their occasional condensation trails ahead, it was decided to continue on plan.

"At about 0935 hours, while still over water, the Ground Operations reported that 20-plus bandits were in the Lille area, heading to the northwest (in our direction), altitude unknown. When the coast was reached at 0937 hours, a slight turn left was made placing the 63rd slightly ahead and well to the left, they having gained 2000ft of altitude over remainder of the group. Again Ground Operations gave me instructions that twenty-plus bandits were flying northwest at 20,000ft in the vicinity of Ypres, this being due ahead of us on course. A split second later I looked ahead at 11 o'clock and down slightly toward a very large hole in the cirrus clouds and saw 15 or 20 spots climbing in our direction. Some of these spots were leaving distinct vapor trails. They must have been 15 or 20 miles away at the time. They, as well as us, never altered course but closed at a very rapid rate. When a distance of two or three miles between forces had been reached, I saw that they were flying in three groups of approximately six each in what would be called a company front formation. They were then below 3 or 4000ft and well to my left. The altitude of my squadron was 27,000 at that time.

"The squadrons were told that I was taking the first section of eight of the 61st Fighter Squadron in a left diving attack. It may be noted that I forgot to touch my throttle and it remained at 31 inches Hg manifold pressure and 2550 rpm for the entire combat.

"At first I dove to attack the lower lead unit but changed my mind and continued down to attack a group who were slightly to the rear and above the lead unit. As the attacking dive commenced, the lead E/A group began turning to the right and the remainder to do likewise. This fact plus the fact that they never flew more than two or three lengths apart, leads me to believe that I was never seen but that all eyes were on the 63rd Fighter Squadron, which was well to my left and directly over the hole in the overcast.

"As I approached the last of the four enemy aircraft, directly astern, I noticed that the tail end aircraft had white stripes around the horizontal stabilizer and elevators. This made me hesitate for I thought these aircraft might have been P-47s coming out of France. Perhaps this hesitation helped me for I closed to 150 to 200 yards before firing. There was no doubt in my mind then. To destroy this aircraft was a mere matter of putting the dot on the fuselage and pulling the trigger. A split second after firing, the fuselage burst into flames and pieces of the right wing came off. I immediately went down to the right leaving the No.3 plane of the four aircraft string just ahead.

"This plane for some reason must have been weaving so that I had to give it some deflection. The deflection proved to be a bit excessive and I noticed strikes out on the right wingtip. The plane being in a right bank went down placing me directly in back of the No.2 plane of the string, which sat in the gunsight, as one would imagine for the ideal shot. Again, when the trigger was pulled this aircraft exploded with a long sheet of flame and smoke.

"Unfortunately the No.1 man of the flight of FW 190s must have become aware of the unhealthy situation and left the scene of battle in a dive so I didn't see him go.

"Each gun fired an average of 50 rounds in the three bursts mentioned above. Recovery was thereafter made due ahead to 26,000ft where a slight turn to the left revealed that Dunkirk was directly down to the left. On looking over the sky again, everything was well broken up and miles away. Only two other P-47s were with me out of the 16 first taken out. Combats were noted at great distances away so I ordered an assembly over Dunkirk. This was exceedingly difficult, as the R/T was as nearly jammed with pilots reporting each other as E/A as can be imagined.

"The assembly point was moved out over the sea from Dunkirk as quite heavy anti-aircraft was put up over the area. The squadrons were then ordered home, since the E/A had gone to the deck and it was believed all organizations were disorganized. In reality the 62nd and 63rd Fighter Squadrons never entered battle. I had failed to call them down until too late...The group continued on to home base with the two above mentioned squadrons giving support and picking up my stragglers. I claim two FW 190s destroyed and one FW 190 damaged."[226]

As it turned out, the 94th, 95th, and 96th Bomb Groups' last mission flown from bases in Essex was a disaster. It had been hoped that another two-pronged attack on the coast would split the German fighter force. But it turned out to be a total failure, with almost all the enemy fighters forsaking the 1st Wing (which lost four B-17s) to concentrate on the 4th Wing's 76 B-17s heading for Kiel in four combat boxes. On the approach to the target the fight started. Riding in the co-pilot's seat of the command aircraft flown by Captain Harry A Stirwalt in the 95th Bomb Group at the head of the Wing was Brigadier General Nathan Bedford Forrest III from 402nd Combat Bomb Wing (P) Headquarters. Forrest was the grandson of a very famous Confederate cavalry general in the American Civil War, whose motto had been *To win – git there fustest with the mostest*. On Forrest's instigation the 17 B-17s of the 95th Bomb Group's main formation (seven more flew in the Composite Group formation) were flying a hitherto untried "flat" formation, wingtip to wingtip, supposedly to be able to concentrate firepower ahead, below, above, and to the rear more effectively.

The other 4th Wing groups also came in for repeated attacks but not of the same intensity, which had decimated the 95th. Among the attackers were 6./JG 11, which claimed five *Abschüsse* and 32 Bf 109Gs and FW 190A-5s[227] at Nordholz led by *Hauptmann* Kurt Ruppert, adjutant of III./JG 26. The Bf 109Gs and FW 190s attacked the Fortresses just after the bomb run. Many of the Fortress gunners were unable to return fire as their guns, which were lubricated with a new type of oil recommended by Forrest, had frozen. A massive diving frontal attack raked the lead aircraft with cannon fire from one end to the other, and Stirwalt's ship fell out of formation and spiraled down.[228] Ruppert's *Gruppe* singled out the six B-17s of the low squadron of the leading 95th Bomb Group and made a rear pass, shooting down four Fortresses at a stroke. Ruppert's FW 190 was hit by return fire, and he was forced to bale out. He tried to open his parachute too quickly, and the speed of his descent ripped his old hemp harness, throwing Ruppert to his death.[229] Two more 95th Bomb Group B-17s were lost from the High Squadron, and three more from the Composite Group formation brought the group's losses to ten (an 11th crashed in England). The 94th Bomb Group was also hard hit. It seemed as if all the fighters (150) had ignored the two full groups in front, and had singled out the 94th and composite boxes because of their small numbers, as "Pappy" Colby recalls:

"By this time our low squadron only had four ships, as Sabella had aborted just before the target, leaving Bill Dauth in *Wolfpack* flying left wing on Major Thorup with me in trail all by myself. Just before the target a fighter came directly at Bill from 11 o'clock and knocked out one or more of his engines. He dropped back and some think he exploded. All ten men baled out in time and survived. Kiel was covered with clouds again (the second straight day the weatherman missed) so we bombed an industrial town southwest of it. Then, because the briefed flight plan called for it, we made a 60° right turn downwind, followed by a 270° left turn into the wind and across the Danish Peninsula. This right turn was a tragic mistake as it kept us an extra 15 minutes under heavy attack. Ships were going down all around us and the composite group behind us had completely broken up, with the survivors now trying to join us. Rawlinson was gone and just as we crossed the coast over Heligoland; three fighters made a rear attack on me, so I took fast evasive action. When they quit and I got back into position I couldn't find Thorup so I fell in on the left wing of somebody else. A little later we were starting to lose altitude. I suddenly discovered the ship I was flying with had left the others and we were three B-17s out in the cold all by ourselves. I immediately signaled him and the other wingman to follow me. The leader kept on for a little while and then decided he'd better follow us. About that time a Bf 109 came out of nowhere and made a pass at him but missed.

"I followed in loose formation behind the bunch I had joined (about ten ships) which turned out to be the combined remains of the 94th and the composite group. We were now down to about 3000ft over the sea and all relaxed, when four more Bf 109s suddenly attacked us. They got Hendershot, setting his wing on fire and he spun in. Another ship, *Shackeroo,* ahead of us had an engine burning so we went over to give him extra protection and discovered it was Thorup. Before we could get close they hit him again, blowing the entire left horizontal fin clear off the tail and knocking out both left engines. He managed to stagger along about ten feet off the water for a good 30 miles before his power failed and he pancaked into the sea. We flew back and forth above him to give him protection as all the rest had left. Although we saw one fighter in the distance, he didn't attack us. We tried to drop our spare life raft and also our portable radio but neither inflated when they hit the water and sunk before they could be recovered. So we climbed up to where we could radio England and sent a SOS and a position fix on them. When we got home, we passed all our information on to the British ASR. One of their aircraft sighted Thorup at 2230 hours and signaled a nearby MTB who came over and rescued the boys. They picked them up after eleven hours in the water and brought them in to Lowestoft."

Sergeant Richard "Dick" Lewis will never know how *Mr. Five-by-Five* came through unscathed:

"It seemed like a miracle. Returning, we were flying at low level over the North Sea. German fighters passed to the side of us at very high speed and out of gun range. Several miles ahead of us, they turned and came at us head on. Lieutenant Hendershot's plane [*Visiting Fireman*] was on our left wing. I saw cannon fire hit the leading edge of his wing. A section peeled off. Suddenly, the ship nosed up, did a complete loop and dove into the sea. It all happened in a few seconds. It was there and then it was gone. The entire crew of ten was lost. The shock of witnessing the agonies of those planes, followed by the fate of Hendershot's Fort is still an indelible memory. The B-17 was not invincible."

The 4th Wing groups put down at their new bases in somber mood. Captain John Miller, 412th Bomb Squadron Operations Officer in the 95th Bomb Group and pilot of the severely damaged Fortress *T'Ain't A Bird*, recalls that the news that 102 flight crewmembers were MIA had a stunning impact on his group commander. "Following a thoroughly depressing and sad briefing during which he listened to the accounts of the surviving crews in silence, Colonel Kessler, his eyes brimming with tears and very obviously distressed, could only murmur, to no one in particular, 'What's happened to my boys? What's happened to my boys?'" Sergeant Arlie Arneson, one of the waist gunners aboard *T'Ain't A Bird*, noted. "We had taken a beating, a heavy beating. Before the debriefing we received a drink or two of Scotch whiskey instead of coffee and a Spam sandwich. This was a first. All I wanted to do was to go off somewhere quiet to cry or get drunk. I did both."

All told, the 4th Bomb Wing lost 22 B-17s. Eaker referred to the Kiel mission as a great battle, and said he was satisfied with the results obtained. Brigadier General Frederick L Anderson, CO 4th Bomb Wing, said "It was a privilege to lead such men, who but yesterday were kids in school. They flew their Forts in the face of great opposition like veterans." In the wake of the Kiel battle the new 4th Wing CO, Colonel (later Brigadier General) Curtis E. LeMay, visited the 94th Bomb Group at Bury St. Edmunds. "He gave us the usual welcome talk," said "Pappy" Colby, "and he left the impression of being a bit hard-nosed about things but he had flown a lot of rough ones and had a good record. And he was trying to improve the poor formation, which had been so troublesome."

The exchange of bases heralded a new era for the 4th Wing, whose HQ was established at Elveden Hall, near Thetford, formerly the home of the 3rd Bomb Wing. The arrival of the 100th Bomb Group early that month (first to Podington, then to Thorpe Abbotts, Suffolk) and the imminent arrival of two more, the 385th and 388th, would increase the 4th Wing to six groups. Meanwhile, new commanders were posted to the 94th and 95th Bomb Groups. Colonel John "Dinty" Moore, CO of the 94th, and Colonel Alfred A. Kessler, CO of the 95th, were moved out, and Colonel Fred Castle and Colonel John Gerhart, respectively, took over. Gerhart had been one of the 8th's original staff officers at its activation in January 1942. Castle had been one of the original officers Eaker had brought to England in February 1942. Both Castle and Gerhart had spent a year helping shape the 8th Air Force, but both men, and Castle, in particular, had yearned for combat. Their experience would be needed now, as they set about lifting crews who resented the loss of their established commanders.

If anyone needed confirmation of the need to attack the *Luftwaffe* where it would hurt most, the Kiel debacle had proved it beyond doubt. Decisions taken at the Casablanca Conference led to the publication of operation "Pointblank," an intermediate priority objective aimed at the German fighter strength. The primary objectives listed were the "German submarine yards and hoses, the remainder of the German aircraft industry, ball bearings and oil..." Secondary objectives were "synthetic rubber and tires and military motor transport vehicles." The objective concluded: "It is emphasized that the reduction of the German fighter force is of primary importance: any delay in its prosecution will make the task progressively more difficult."

6

Battles with the *Luftwaffe*

Many a bomber knocked out of the fight
Forever their praises will sing
For while limping home through treacherous sky
They had "white noses" under each wing

Eaker now decided to send his bombers on the first really deep penetration of Germany on 22 June 1943 to the I. G. Farben Industrie Chemische Werke at Hüls, near Recklinghausen, on the edge of the Ruhr. The chemical and synthetic rubber plant, which had been almost untouched by war since 1942 when it was last bombed by the RAF, was essential to the German war effort, since their rubber supply in the Far East had been cut off by the Allied blockade.[230] Hüls accounted for approximately 29% of Germany's synthetic rubber and 18% of its total rubber supply. Every month it was turning out 3900 tons of synthetic rubber, much of it going to the Buna tire factory nearby. Most of the route would be flown without escort. Three diversionary raids were therefore planned to pull off most of the fighters from the main attacking force, which would still have its work cut out coping with the numerous flak guns that made Hüls the most heavily defended target in the Reich at this time.

Throughout East Anglia, on the morning of 22 June, crews were awakened and ushered into briefing rooms to hear about the part they would play in the Hüls mission. The Hüls force assembled over England and flew a dogleg course over the North Sea to a point off the West Friesian Islands, where it turned southwest for the target. Unfortunately, an intended diversion by a formation of 21 B-17s in the 100th Bomb Group (making its theater debut this day) was delayed because of ground mists and other problems, and played no major part in the proceedings.[231] Also, the 381st and 384th Bomb Groups, which were flying their maiden missions, were behind schedule and failed to make contact with the Spitfires and Thunderbolts, which were to escort them to the Ford and General Motors plant at Antwerp, and this lapse placed the 41 B-17s at the mercy of FW 190s of JG 26, which had refueled after an earlier raid by RAF medium bombers and Bf 109s of II./JG 1 and the ERLA factory protection *Schwarm*. Head-on attacks succeeded in shooting down four B-17s while three hardly damaged survivors flew their own formation, hugging the waves all the way back to England.

Major Pips Priller, leading his *Geschwader*, led the first JG 26 attack from the front before the Fortresses reached the target. The FW 190s made one pass through the bomber ranks in flights of six to eight and shot three B-17s of the 381st Bomb Group out of formation. Priller's victim was *Iron Gut Gert* flown by 2nd Lieutenant Earl R. Horr,[232] which was claimed shot down between Yerseke and Krabbendijke by both *Feldwebel* Adolf "Addi" Glunz of JG 26 and by *Unteroffizier* Niki Mortl of the ERLA *Schwarm*. The B-17,[233] flown by Lieutenant Martin L. Shenk, had suffered a runaway propeller on No.2 engine staggered across the target, and although badly shot up, he managed to make it back to crash land at Framlingham. 2nd Lieutenant John J. Martin's B-17[234] went down pursued by *Oberfeldwebel* Johann Edmann in the *Stabsschwarm*, who was hit by return fire from the Fortress, and he crash-landed near Woensdrecht with severe injuries. Only one man survived aboard Martin's B-17. *Hauptmann* "Wutz" Galland and the IInd *Gruppe* reached the Fortresses as they were leaving the target and they attacked from the rear. They made repeated attacks and were out of ammunition when the P-47s of the 4th and 78th Fighter Groups finally arrived to provide withdrawal support. The Thunderbolts claimed seven FW 190s and a Bf 109 for no loss, but JG 26 lost no further FW 190s, although two pilots were wounded. II *Gruppe* claimed four B-17s and was credited with three.[235] What follows is Colonel Hubert Zemke's personal report on the *Ramrod* flown on the morning of 22 June. The encounter with a FW 190 took place from 28,000ft down to 5000ft with thin cirrus at very high altitude and a few low alto-cumulus. Visibility was 15 to 20 miles:

> "I was leading the Group. On this operation the fighters of the USAAF were late to their rendezvous with the bombers through no fault of their own. Each Wing Commander knew this, so the original plan of a column of squadrons for each individual group was disregarded. As a result all ran into each other in the vicinity of the bombers, causing a complex situation of identification and battle. As leader of the first squadron, I headed for a formation of unidentified fighters close to the rear of the bombers and prepared for action. This attack was head-on through a group of P-47s of another Group, not enemy aircraft and as a result split my lead squadron up into pairs and flights. After two more attacks on planes, which were later identified as P-47s, I saw an aircraft below and at least five miles away, which was pressing an attack on the rear of the bomber formation. An attack was pressed on this aircraft, but because of the distance the rate of closure did not enable me to spring a surprise attack. The enemy aircraft recovered by rolling upwards just as I launched my attack from above. At this point each of us identified the other. The enemy broke in a left circle just as I was closing on him, causing me to give

a 30° deflection shot for three seconds. My added speed enabled me to gain a bit more altitude then he, although my circle was much wider.

"The next attack was about 45° from the front and as we closed the enemy aircraft went into an aileron roll of about two turns straight down. I followed, but on recovery, I found that both the enemy aircraft and myself were recovering at an angle of 45°, each endeavoring to gain an altitude advantage over the other. As was the ease, he finally leveled off with an altitude advantage of about 2000ft. The enemy aircraft position was then at 8 o'clock to me. My only alternative was to turn into him in a chandelle. His attack on me, therefore, was a dive, which carried him past me. As he went past I reversed direction to follow his dive but due to my slow acceleration - whereas he was diving - I could only give a burst with long range deflection.

"We again circled and recovered altitude, with the enemy aircraft on top by 2000 or 3000ft going in the same direction and out to the side, the altitude by now being close to 10,000ft. Again my only choice was to bear in on a head-on attack in order to shake him as much as possible. He continued on through the head-on and as he passed me I would let a burst go and then torn and try to follow him down. This last dive carried us to 5000ft, where he began a very slight climbing turn. My ammunition ran out as I fired at a range of 400 yards with a deflection of a ring-and-a-half.

"The engagement was immediately broken off and I turned away from him to go into a shallow dive towards home, passing out of enemy occupied territory between Schowen and Walcheren Island. On looking back I noticed that the enemy aircraft was in a similar dive going towards Flushing and was not endeavoring to press home an attack. Both of us were probably out of ammunition and were satisfied that we had had all the combat we wanted for one day. Points that were learned on my part were that the FW 190's recovery and climb were superior to mine from the time I lost my initial altitude advantage. His ability to gain altitude in a circle was definite and the only alternative when he dived was to come as close as possible to ramming him head-on before he circles too many times and got on my tail. The entire combat was extremely interesting and makes me a confirmed dive-and-recovery artist in the future, especially at low altitudes."

The failure of the diversionary forces had grave implications for the Hüls force, as "Pappy" Colby, leading the high squadron of six ships in the *Thundermug*, describes:

"What we didn't know was that they had actually alerted the fighters to our force: so we got the works. They hit us at the Dutch coast and it got progressively worse. Colonel Castle rode behind me on the campstool and took notes all through the thick of it, cool as a cucumber. When we were just short of the IP. Buck Steele, who was leading the 94th, was apparently hit and dropped rubber away leaving the group leaderless as the deputy leader had been hit earlier. This really put me in a bind since it didn't look as though there was time for anybody else to take over the lead squadron and the group lead. We had been briefed to drop our bombs on the leader so I made a fast decision to do our aiming and dropping and told Bob Gamble, our bombardier, to do his best. The ground was half covered with low clouds but just about this time something big exploded on the ground, sending up a tremendous column of black smoke. Gamble hollered, 'I can see it. I can see it!' and so I target turned on the autopilot so he could guide us in. We made a beautiful 55-second run and dropped our pattern square on the buildings alongside of the burning tank, which had exploded. We were eight ships in all, as some of the others had joined us.

"Flak, which had not bothered us up to now, suddenly became very heavy, indicating that we had caught them by surprise somehow. After dropping we made the standard left turn but when I looked for the lead squadron there was nothing but two or three scattered airplanes in sight, so we speeded up and joined a group ahead of us for mutual protection. The remains of the lead and low squadrons strung along with us and we caught up with the 95th Bomb Group. At Rotterdam the Spitfires met us and chased off the German fighters, but it was a rough mission and we were beginning to wonder about the invincibility of the 'Flying Fortress.' We lost two of our aircraft in the 333rd and the group lost quite a few more."

By the time the trailing groups had completed their bombing and made their 180° turns to the left, the smoke was as high as 17,000ft. Bombing had been highly successful and the Hüls plant was put out of action for a month. Full production was not resumed for another five months after that. Sixteen B-17s, including a YB-40, which flew with the 303rd Bomb Group, were lost. Fighters and flak had claimed most of the victims although the loss of the YB-40 was something of a mystery, as Howard E. Hernan, top turret gunner in *The Old Squaw* in the 303rd formation, relates:

"We were flying No.5 position in the low squadron. Two YB-40s flew on the lead ship's wings and another YB-40 flew in the No.6 slot. Just before the IP the YB-40 in front of us in the No.2 position suddenly went down. I couldn't understand how come he went down when there was no flak. Fighters had not then attacked us so it wasn't a fighter. I would think he had an engine malfunction and just couldn't keep up. The last I saw of him was after he dropped below us and made a big sweeping left turn to the path that we were to take when we came off the target. He probably thought we could catch up with him after we had completed our bomb run."[236]

Sergeant Richard "Dick" Lewis, right waist gunner aboard *Mr. Five-by-Five*, flown by Captain Kee Harrison in the 94th Bomb Group, recalls:

"Inbound to the Continent we lost an outboard engine. I don't think it was hit by enemy air or ground fire. It simply quit. With the prop feathered, we were unable to keep formation and became a sitting duck. Captain Harrison came on the intercom, informing us that he intended to try to escape by lowering the landing gear in sign of surrender and then diving the ship. We were told to hold our fire. Enemy fighters closed in to escort us to a landing. Suddenly, the dive began! This maneuver had never been covered in my flight training. It was a wild ride and I wondered if the ship would hold together. It did! Captain Harrison pulled her out at about a thousand feet and then dove again to treetop level, frustrating the enemy fighters, who broke off the action and left. He began zig zagging the plane back to England. We took a hit from a ground battery and Lieutenant Schaefer, our navigator, was wounded in the leg. Despite his injury, he stuck to his post, changing course every few minutes. And I'll never forget the sight of Dutch farmers standing in their fields, waving their arms and making the 'V' for victory sign as we roared overhead. I breathed a sigh of relief as the Channel appeared ahead of us and that mission came safely to a close. The inside of the ship was drenched with condensation from the rapid descent, -40F to +75F. The entire crew was grounded for several missions, recovering from related ear problems. *'Mr. Five-by-Five'* went into Repair Depot for replacement of several wing spars weakened or bent from pulling out of the dive. I never saw our plane again. Lieutenant Schaefer received the Distinguished Flying Cross for his extraordinary feat of navigation over unknown territory while wounded. I marvelled at Captain Harrison's skill and daring. That day ended as we went on the 94th sick call instead of into a German stockade - or worse."

"*Mr. Five-by-Five*" was not the only bomber needing overhaul. About 170 bombers received varying degrees of damage, and repair crews were kept busy for two days or more. On 25 June 275 B-17s were despatched to bomb targets in northwestern Germany. Cloud hampered bombing at Hamburg, the main objective, and split up the formations and scattered some of the groups in the sky—an open invitation to fighter attack. The 1st Bomb Wing lost 15 Fortresses, including six in the 379th Bomb Group, four of which were credited to I/JG 26 at Rheine, which intercepted the 1st Bomb Wing south of Emden. Three B-17s of the 4th Wing also failed to return.[237]

Cloud interfered on the 26th also when the heavies attacked an aircraft factory at Villacoublay, in the Paris area, and airfields at Triqueville, on the Seine Estuary and at Le Mans. Late that same afternoon, diversion raids were flown by RAF Typhoons against Bernay and Douglas Bostons, who attacked Abbeville-Drucat airfield, and German fighters were sent to intercept these attacks, but when it was realized that the heavies were on the way they were ordered to land again. In the early evening 42 B-17s in the 1st Bomb Wing bombed Triqueville airfield, and the close escort of Spitfires ensured that no German fighters could intervene. They did, however, attack the B-17s heading for Villacoublay, and concentrated their attacks on the 384th Bomb Group, which was flying the vulnerable low position in the leading wing. Four B-17s in the 384th Bomb Group were shot down by fighters.

Meanwhile, other fighters of JG 26, JG 27, and JG 2 had headed for the French coast to intercept a large formation off Le Touquet. When spotted in the vicinity of Forges at 25,000ft they turned out to be 47 P-47s.[238] They were from the 56th Fighter Group, led by the Flying Executive Major Loren G. McCollom, which had taken off from Manston, Kent, at 1812 hours to provide withdrawal escort for the B-17s that had bombed Villacoublay. *Jagdfliegerführer 2*[239] apparently ordered the fighters to ignore the fighters and seek out bomber targets. Major "Pips" Priller, *Kommodore* of JG 26, and his formation headed west, and at 1852 hours Priller shot down a 384th Bomb Group Fortress between Dieppe and Le Treport. P-47s in the 4th Fighter Group led by Major Don Blakeslee on a *Ramrod* to Gisors from Thorney Island were halfway across the Channel when Blakeslee was informed that the withdrawing bombers were early. After a gradual port turn on the rendezvous point the 4th Fighter Group spotted the bombers northwest of Le Tréport with enemy aircraft diving away. As the P-47s arrived six Bf 109Gs of Priller's 13th *Staffel* dived under the 334th Squadron and a combat developed 10 miles off Dieppe. Two 334th Fighter Squadron pilots Lieutenant Raymond C. Care and Lieutenant Duane W. Beeson each claimed a Bf 109 over the Channel at 1859 hours.[240]

The formation of 56th Fighter Group P-47s, meantime, had proved too much of a temptation for *Hauptmann* Wilhelm-Ferdinand "Wutz" Galland and his IInd *Gruppe* who were heading west when they spotted the Thunderbolts far out to sea, and which had just reached the bombers. Galland led his fighters down out of the evening sun from 23,000-26,000ft, and concentrating attacks on the 61st Fighter Squadron flying at 24,000ft, completely surprised the P-47 pilots from behind. Before they knew what had hit them Galland fired on one P-47 to the left of the formation and observed cannon strikes. He fired a second burst from the side and behind at about 50 meters and the Thunderbolt exploded. Parts of the wing, fuselage, and tail flew off, and the fighter dived away out of control and burst into flames. Galland did not observe the crash because he believed its destruction was certain, and he attacked a second Thunderbolt. In all, five P-47s were shot down without loss and a sixth came down in the sea off Scratby.[241] Lieutenant Robert S. Johnson in the 61st Fighter Squadron flying *All Hell* had a fortunate escape when a FW 190, which pursued him and pumped 20mm shells into his Thunderbolt, was forced to break off out of ammunition. With a wave and a shake of the head, the German pilot rocked his wings in salute and broke off, perhaps thinking that the stricken P-47 would never make England anyway. Johnson, however, managed to put down safely at Manston. Captain Gerald W. Johnson's claim for one enemy aircraft destroyed (the first of his 16½ victories) was confirmed. Interrogation revealed a confused situation with lack of co-ordination between squadrons. Once again air discipline left much to be desired. As combats had taken place near the same level as the bombers, many of the group's pilots had been forced into slow turning and climbing actions. It was clear the P-47 was no match for the Bf 109 or FW 190 in such circumstances, and Zemke complained to his superiors that having a fighter with such a poor rate of climb hampered the group's combat effectiveness. Slow to accelerate, the P-47 could gain on both the Bf 109 and FW 190 in a long dive, and an accurately aimed short burst from its eight 0.50-caliber guns had a devastating effect on the enemy. The momentum of the dive could be used to zoom-climb back to higher altitude. Slow turning fights were a no go in a combat situation when high speed must be maintained. Zemke's leadership became more severe, which did not endear him to many of his pilots. New formations and tactics were experimented with during the operations of early July, but it was clear that altitude advantage was the key to success with the Thunderbolt.

The 4th Wing at St. Nazaire directed the main bombing effort on 26 June. "Pappy" Colby recalls:

> "There was much speculation at the briefing because only ships with the 'Tokyo' extra range tanks were going. Our target was some kind of new lock at the sub pens. I led the 333rd Squadron with the job of filling in aborts from the 96th Bomb Group. We had a hell of a time trying to pick out the 96th from all the others in the sky because they didn't answer our flare recognition signals for a long time. We finally located them, late as usual and then had trouble following them as their formation was lousy and they were only doing 145mph. We filled in several aborts and, as we approached the IP, I tacked on to the lead element of their high squadron. They made a beautiful bomb run and each ship unloaded two 2000lb bombs on the target. Very heavy flak came up and a 6-inch piece of shell came up through the floor of the radio room and smacked Patrick on the fanny. Luckily, its force was pretty well spent and all he got was a big black and blue spot. It was a long way home and we were down to 300 gallons in the main gas tanks when we turned on our new 'Tokyo' tanks. They brought us home with plenty to spare.
>
> "That night after supper I was told to report to Colonel Castle at his quarters. I quickly cleaned up and wondered what had been said to put me in the doghouse again. To my great surprise, he asked me if I could take over command of the 410th Squadron and build it up to where it could become combat operational again. The squadron had lost nine out of its ten original crews and the replacements hadn't had a chance to really learn what combat operations were all about. It had lost both its COs and Ops Officer and had been withdrawn from operations as a squadron, with the new crews being used to fill in aborts. This put their people behind the rest of the group in acquiring the necessary 25 raids to complete their tours and made them very unhappy. I told him I would do my very best and the job

certainly boosted my morale. Next morning I took command of the 410th and Wally Barker, the Assistant Operations Officer, was sure glad to see me. He was a big help in briefing me on their problems. That afternoon, who should show up unexpectedly but the Bob Hope Special Services Show with Frances Langford, Jerry Colonna and Jack Pepper, their guitarist. They put on a terrific show that did us all a world of good. Unfortunately, the group had gone on a raid to Le Mans and didn't get to see the show. But when the tired crews from the raid came into the mess hall for debriefing, who was standing just inside the door shaking hands with each one, but Bob Hope and his entire cast. Some of the lads were so overwhelmed they had tears in their eyes and, personally, I'll never forget it."

On 28 June 191 B-17s in the 1st and 4th Bomb Wings (the latter using long range tanks for the first time) journeyed to St. Nazaire, and a smaller force of 50 B-17s in the 303rd, 379th, and 384th Bomb Groups headed for Beaumont Le Roger airfield further inland.[242] Units of JG 26 at Vendeville and Vitry took off to intercept, but soon landed when the bomber formations passed out of range. The German controllers waited until the Spitfire escort had turned back and then sent III./JG 2 into the fray. *Hauptmann* Egon Mayer's *Gruppe* claimed nine Fortresses for the loss of one FW 190 and its pilot. Four of the bomber losses were from the 351st Bomb Group, one was from the 91st, and the 95th Bomb Group lost three. Claude Campbell, who flew in the 303rd Bomb Group formation, which came through unscathed:

> "An excellent mission. Spitfires escorted us and we met no opposition. Since we flew at 28,000 to 30,000ft the enemy couldn't have seen us unless we were giving off vapor trails. Bombing was perfect. We hit the ammunition dumps and blew the whole works to hell. The aiming point was a cemetery just south of the ammunition dump. The best crack I heard about this raid was, 'the dead will rise tonight.'"

Eaker temporarily lost his three 201st (Provisional) Wing B-24 Groups at the end of June when they were needed in North Africa to swell the numbers of 9th Bomber Command Liberators in raids on Sicily and Italy, and the Ploesti oilfields in Rumania.[243] During 11-25 June the 389th Bomb Group, the third B-24 group to join the 2nd Bomb Division, flew into its base at Hethel, Norfolk. Colonel Jack W. Wood, the CO, was immediately put under pressure to get the group operational, and a temporary ground echelon was brought in, pending the arrival on 6 July of the regular ground personnel. Though crews did not know it, they would have just two weeks training in Norfolk before being thrust into a new kind of war. After a five-day orientation course the crews in the 44th Flying Eightballs, the 93rd Traveling Circus, and the 389th began flying low-level practice missions over East Anglia. They flew at less than 150ft en route to their target range over the Wash. Rumor and speculation increased as ground crews sweated to remove the Norden bombsights and replace them with low-level sights. Heavier nose armament and additional fuel tanks in the bomb bays gave the men clues as to their new role. At Hardwick, Colonel Addison Baker led his Liberators flying wingtip to wingtip at 150ft over the hangar line on the base, which served as a target. On some days the 44th and the 389th joined the 93rd in flights over the base in waves of three aircraft. They had been trained in the art of high-altitude precision bombing and were quite unused to low-level flying. On 25 June a mid-air collision involving two 389th Liberators occurred. One B-24 made it back to Hethel, but the other crash-landed. Eight men were killed and one died later.

On 30 June 124 B-24Ds in the three groups began their flight to North Africa via Portreath, in Cornwall, for the North African bases.[244] After taking part in raids on Italy on 20 July all five Liberator groups were withdrawn from the campaign, and 12 days' training for *"Tidal Wave"* (the code name for Ploesti) began, with practice flights against a mock-up target in the desert.[245] During the night of 31 July 177 crews in the 8th and 9th Air Force B-24 groups were briefed for the momentous raid, which went ahead when it was barely daylight on the morning of Sunday, 1 August 1943.[246]

Meanwhile in England, during July, in an attempt to bring more firepower to bear on the B-24 and B-17 formations, both the FW 190A and Bf 109G had their armament increased substantially. The Bf 109G-6/R6 now carried three MG 151 cannon in addition to its two MG 151 13mm machine guns, and the FW 190 now carried two Rheinmetall MG FF-M-20 cannons in addition to its two MG 15s. During July also, the FW 190A-6, equipped with two MG 151 20mm cannon in place of the MG-FF-M, became operational in the *Jagdgruppen*.

On 4 July neither the weather nor the Independence Day celebrations stopped the Fortresses from making a triple attack on targets in France. Altogether, 192 Fortresses of the 1st Wing were assigned the Gnome and Rhône Aero engine factory at Le Mans and an aircraft factory at Nantes, while 83 of the longer range B-17s of the 4th Wing went to the U-boat pens at La Pallice. Shortly after noon the two 1st Wing formations, flying parallel courses, crossed the French coast just east of the Cherbourg Peninsula, while the B-17s of the 4th Wing headed for La Pallice on the Bay of Biscay coast. At 1230 hours the 1st Wing formations crossed Laval, 80 miles inland, then split into two formations, one heading for Nantes and the other, Le Mans. The Nantes force was attacked by hordes of German fighters all the way from the IP, which did not break off until 35 miles after the target. The 92nd Bomb Group formation of 16 B-17s and three YB-40s came under heavy attack, and Lieutenant John J. Campbell's B-17 was believed to have hit the sea and burned. Six parachutes were seen to open and another partially opened.

This raid marked the return of the 326th Bomb Squadron to bomber operations, and it came in for repeated attacks by the enemy fighters. After bombing the target *Ruthie*, named by Lieutenant Robert L. Campbell in honor of his wife, was hit by cannon fire that punctured two fuel lines and destroyed the hydraulic system and flaps. Another 20mm shell penetrated the belly between the waist gun positions and exploded, wrecking the radio equipment. One shell also hit the ball turret and seriously wounded Richard O. Gettys in the face, chest, and groin. Despite his wounds he continued firing from the still serviceable turret until he passed out. Gettys was awarded the DSC for his action. John C. Ford, the tail gunner, was also slightly injured in the leg. Campbell nursed *Ruthie* home to Alconbury and landed with a flat tire. He succeeded in keeping the badly damaged B-17 on the runway for as long as possible, then whirled the aircraft around in front of the control tower and came to a halt. Campbell's proud lady was only fit for scrap after that, but he promptly named its replacement *Ruthie II*.

The Le Mans force encountered intense fighter opposition 15 minutes from the target, but the B-17s were able to pick up their fighter escort at Argentan and reach safety. For once the multiplicity of bomber attacks seemed to break up the *Luftwaffe* concentrations, and they were able to account for only three percent of the attacking force.

On 10 July 185 B-17s of the 1st Bomb Wing headed for airfields at Caen and Abbeville, while 101 B-17s of the 4th Bomb Wing went to Le Bourget airfield. Eighteen squadrons of Spitfires and eight squadrons of P-47s provided fighter cover. Bombing by the 1st Bomb Wing was largely ineffective, while none of the 4th Bomb Wing B-17s found their target because of cloud. Three B-17s were lost on the return. Two of these were from the Le Bourget attack force. *Exterminator*, a 412th Bomb Squadron, 95th Bomb Group Fortress flown by Lieutenant James R. Sarchet, was shot down by *Leutnant* Helmut Hoppe, CO 4th *Staffel*, JG 26 near Fecamp, west of Rouen, in his first pass.[247] Wutz Galland's IInd *Gruppe* continued to attack the bombers for ten more minutes until low fuel forced them to break off.

The weather continued cloudy, and VIII Bomber Command flew several more missions to France in the hope of spotting its targets. On 14 July, Bastille Day, groups appropriately attacked targets in the vicinity of Paris. The Focke-Wulf repair sub-depot of *Luftflotte* 3 at Villacoublay was well hit, with the result that the hangars were destroyed and 70 FW 190s were wrecked. Amiens/Glisy aerodrome and Le Bourget airport were also bombed. Le Bourget had seen the successful conclusion of Charles Lindbergh's record breaking Trans-Atlantic flight in 1927, and the raid therefore had a special significance for the new breed of American aviators. On 14 July Sgt Richard H. Lewis[248] recalls:

> "It was mid-morning. Our formation was approaching Paris to bomb nearby Le Bourget airfield. Each 'Fort,' including ours[249] carried 16 300lb bombs. At my fight waist gun position, I felt the ship take a forward hit. Smoke filtered back to the rear. 'What the hell is going on up front?' I yelled to Earl Porath, back-to-back with me at his left waist gun position. Through my own open gun port, I could see German fighters continuing the attack on the front of the ship, diving from above or zooming up from below like a swarm of angry hornets. The ship began to fall out of formation. I squeezed off a couple of ineffective bursts from my .50 caliber Browning machine gun as the fighters flashed by at such speed that it was nearly impossible to track them through my gunsight for more than a fraction of a second. Those German pilots were smart veterans. I could hear and feel Porath's .50 firing behind and Jeff Polk's twin .50s blazing away from his ball turret below. In the tail of the ship, Ossie Asiala's guns added to the racket but I couldn't hear firing from any of our forward guns.[250]
>
> "The smoke was getting heavier. The ship went into an abrupt dive, then leveled again and seemed to move erratically as if the pilot were taking evasive action. I realized that the German fighter attack had ended. I listened on the intercom for some word from the cockpit. Silence! We were in deep trouble. A horrible thought came to me. Had they all been killed up front? The ship went into a shallow dive and it was hard for me to hold my footing. Porath yelled, 'Here they come, Looie!'
>
> "German fighters were closing on us, not head on or diving but rather parallel to us, as if in escort. I could even see the pilot of one fighter looking at us. I was amazed by this tactic but didn't stop to think about it. My enemy was out there at practically point blank range. Instinct took over and I began firing. So did Porath, Polk and Asiala. Parallel to us, with their fixed wing guns at right angles to us they were totally defenseless. I saw two fighters in flames and one of them exploded as it fell. Others may have been hit but I wasn't sure.
>
> "Then all hell broke loose! Other German fighters raked the ship. Wires and control cables dangled like spaghetti. I listened for the bale-out order. Silence - again. She went into a steep dive. I was torn loose from my gun and flipped against the bulkhead. Porath slammed against me. Polk had gotten out of the ball turret and then he too, fell against the bulkhead. As I lay pinned there, I couldn't see out of the ship and thought, 'Oh my God, we're going straight into the ground.' I lost all hope. 'This is it,' I said to myself. Unbelievably, the steep dive angle was lessening and I dimly wondered if the ship was still airworthy and who was at the controls. Captain Harrison, I hoped. She began to pull out and leveled off. We staggered to our feet, heading for the door to jump. I struggled to hook my chute buckles as I got to the door. Porath was shaking his head 'No!' and pointing out the window. The ground was rushing up to meet us. We braced ourselves. We were going in! She nosed up gently as she bellied into a wheat field. The tail touched first and we heard a tearing, crunching sound. Someone yelled, 'The bombs!' We looked toward the bulkhead. The ball turret had torn loose and was pushed up through the floor. It seemed an eternity before we slid to a halt. There was no fire. Almost no sound. We had ridden her in! We forced the door open, jumped into the wheat field and everyone scattered. Ossie and I paired up. We saw Porath and Jim Curtis, the engineer/top turret gunner running together toward a wooded area. Polk and Charlie McNemar, our radio operator/gunner, ran together in the opposite direction. They all appeared in good shape. I don't remember seeing Captain Harrison and our co-pilot, Lieutenant David Turner, or our bombardier and navigator. I would wonder about their fate for many months. It was Bastille Day, 14 July 1943 in German occupied France. Ossie and I were alone in a French wheat field, belly-landed behind enemy lines - with a full bomb load."[251]

Staffelkapitän Georg-Peter Eder, 7./JG 2, said in his combat report of 14 July 1943:

> "We were doing about 450 km/h now and were coming down slightly, aiming for the noses of the B-17s. There were about 200 of us attacking the 200 bombers but there was also the fighter escort above them. We were going for the bombers. When we made our move, the P-47s began to dive on us and it was a race to get to the bombers before being intercepted. I was already close and about 600ft above and coming straight on: I opened fire with the twenties at 500 yards. At 300 yards I opened fire with the thirties. It was a short burst, maybe ten shells from each cannon, but I saw the bomber explode and begin to burn. I flashed over him at about 50ft and then did a chandelle. When I had turned around I was about a thousand feet above and behind them and was suddenly mixed in with American fighters.
>
> "Straight in front was a Thunderbolt, as I completed the turn and I opened fire on him immediately and hit his propwash. My fire was so heavy his left wing came off almost at once and I watched him go down…We flew south, ahead for a few seconds, preparing for another strike at the bombers and then, coming from above, I saw them. I called a warning: 'Indianer über uns!' and as they came in behind us we banked hard left. There were ten P-47s and four of us and we were all turning as hard as we could, as in a Lufbery.[252] I was able to turn tighter and was gaining. I pulled within 80 yards of the P-47 ahead of me and opened fire. I hit him quickly and two of the others got one each, so that in a minute and a half three of the P-47s went down…"[253]

The Amiens force had also come in for heavy fighter attack by 3/JG 27, II/JG 2, and JG 26, who took on the Thunderbolts of the 4th, 56th, and 78th Fighter Groups.[254] The Thunderbolts had rendezvoused with the B-17s at 0730 hours, and at about the same time Major "Wutz" Galland's formation had caught sight of the escorts. Over the radio Galland gave the rallying cry, "What are you waiting for," and three formations of German fighters attacked. They tore into the Fortresses for 20 minutes before the Thunderbolts were able to fend them off, inflicting heavy damage to 34 of the bombers, while one B-17 fell to the guns of a Bf 109 of 3/JG 27. Two more badly damaged Forts limped home to crash land in England. 3/JG 27 and II/JG 2 had been ordered to land as soon as the P-47s had intervened, and they put down at Poix to refuel and rearm. After a record turnaround time of 12 minutes they were airborne again, and they headed for the Villacoublay force, but without apparent success. Meanwhile, FW 190s of I/JG 2 and Bf 109s of II/JG 2 took on the 4th Fighter Group P-47s to the west of the Somme, near Le Treport, while Major "Wutz" Galland and his pilots battled with the P-47s of the 78th Fighter Group near Hesdin. Major Harry Dayhuff had led his group to Hornoy, where they had made rendezvous with B-17s bombing Amiens. Near Montrciul, as he led the 82nd and the 84th Squadrons into a large group of FW 190s heading for the bombers at Lelouget, more enemy aircraft joined the fight. 1st Lieutenant Donald Jackson was killed when he was struck by gunfire from the B-17s in the chase.

In the ensuing air battle "Wutz" Galland claimed a 78th Fighter Group P-47 over the north bank of the Somme Estuary northwest of Hesdin, and he claimed another 10-15 km west of Etaples. 2nd Lieutenant August V. DeGenaro, in the 82nd Squadron, flew the first of these P-47s. He had the right side of his canopy and instrument panel shot out causing shell splinter wounds in his hands, ankles, and right knee. At first he thought he was going to die, but he quickly recovered and got "damned mad," diving to 2000ft into a swarm of FWs, where he shot one down from 100 yards, probably destroyed another, and damaged a third.[255] Then he headed for the Channel, ducking into low clouds to evade three more FWs that followed him almost to the coast. All this time DeGenaro was flying his plane with no instruments and controlling it with his forearms only. The right aileron was gone, and the right wing and tail were badly damaged. A crash landing was out of the question, because he had unhooked his safety belt in combat and he could not re-hook it. DeGenero recalled:

"I headed out to sea again to bale out because I was afraid that if I baled out over land the plane would crash into one of the towns along the coast. I knew I was over England, because I saw the cliffs of Dover. I saw a fishing boat just off shore and decided to bale out near it.[256] The canopy of my plane had jammed and would not open, but since some of the glass had been shot away, I was able to punch and force my way through the canopy, bale out and open my chute. The fishing boat picked me up at once. If it had not, I would have drowned, because I was unable to undo my parachute harness and was getting weak from loss of blood."[257]

Despite the rising losses, new groups swelled Eaker's forces, and on 17 July a record 332 bombers were dispatched to Hanover. This figure was made possible by the introduction of both the 385th and 388th Bomb Groups, which were flying their first missions as part of the 4th Wing. Their debuts were somewhat subdued, because the mission was recalled due to bad weather after the bombers had crossed the Dutch coast, and on the return leg enemy fighters hit the B-17s. Meanwhile, the 385th had moved to Great Ashfield, Suffolk, during the first week of July, and the 388th landed at nearby Knettishall. The seventh and final group to join the 4th Wing, the 390th, flew south from Prestwick to its permanent base at Parham, near Framlingham, in pastoral Suffolk. The 8th now had the means to launch an all-out air offensive. All the commanders needed was a week of fine weather for "Blitz Week" to succeed.

7

Blitz Week and Beyond

Prom Bremen to Bordeaux
From Berlin to Oslo
Wherever those heavies go.

On 23 July General Eaker was informed that clear skies could be expected over Europe for a few days; long enough to mount the long-awaited succession of attacks, later called "Blitz Week." The momentous week began in the early hours of 24 July when it was revealed that the 1st Wing would bomb the nitrate plant of Nordisk Lettmetal at Heroya. Meanwhile, a smaller force of B-17s in the 4th Wing equipped with "Tokyo" tanks would bomb the harbor installations at Bergen and Trondheim. Although the latter mission would involve a 2000-mile round trip, the longest American mission over Europe thus far, the two missions were considered to be milk runs because the targets were lightly defended. Crews were warned of the need to conserve fuel, and for this reason there was no assembly; leaders simply took off and went on course at once, flying on low power settings to enable the formations to take up position over the North Sea. Well off the coast of northern Denmark the 1st Wing flew northeast up the Skagerrak and climbed to a bombing altitude of 16,000ft. The 4th Wing continued up the west coast of Norway to Bergen and Trondheim, not far south of the Arctic Circle. Cloud obscured the target at Heroya, but Colonel William M. Reid, CO of the 92nd Bomb Group, who flew as air commander, was awarded the Silver Star for setting up a new bomb run after Heroya had been cancelled out by the weather. The target was devastated and Colonel Budd J. Peaslee, CO of the 384th Bomb Group, wrote later "The mission to Heroya is considered by many authorities to be one of the outstanding missions of the war." Only one B-17, *Georgia Rebel* in the 351st Bomb Group, was lost on the raid. It was hit by flak, but the crew put down safely in neutral Sweden.

Altogether 167 bombers bombed Heroya, while 41 B-17s in the 4th Wing bombed Trondheim from 20,000ft. Testimony to their accuracy was provided later by a RAF photo-reconnaissance Spitfire that brought back photos of a sunken U-boat, a damaged destroyer, and gutted workshops in the harbor area. The other 4th Wing groups crossed Bergen harbor at 16,000ft, but the target was completely covered with clouds, and 84 aircraft had to return to England and land with full bomb loads—something crews were never happy about. About 15 Junkers 88s put in an appearance on the return leg but caused no damage to the B-17 formations.

Next day, 25 July, 218 bombers were sent to bomb the Blohm and Voss shipyards in Hamburg after the city was devastated the night before in the great RAF Bomber Command fire raid. One combat wing in the 1st Bomb Wing was dispatched to Kiel. Cloud cover and a towering 15,000ft column of smoke from the still burning fires at Hamburg caused 59 B-17s of the 92nd, 305th, and 306th Bomb Groups to abandon their strike altogether. Crews in the first elements managed to bomb before thick cloud added to the smoke and the shipyards were well hit. The Hamburg force was intercepted by III./JG 26 as the leading B-17s approached the Elbe estuary, and three Fortresses were shot down. Over Hamburg and beyond JG 11 took over, and finally, over the North Sea, the stragglers were attacked by II. and III./JG 1 from Rheine and Leeuwarden. II *Gruppe* shot down two B-17s and III *Gruppe* destroyed another. Major Karl-Heinz Leesmann, *Gruppen Kommandeur* III./JG 1, crashed into the sea after an attack on a B-17. His body was washed ashore on 16 August. Altogether 15 B-17s—seven of them in the 384th Bomb Group—were shot down, and 67 returned battle damaged. The Kiel force lost four B-17s and 50 returned damaged, two of which crashed on landing. JG 1 and 11 accounted for most of the 19 bombers that failed to return with 15 *Abschüsse*.

Meanwhile, 4th Bomb Wing Fortresses headed for Warnemünde, on the north German coast. Clouds obscured the target, and they were forced to head for the submarine construction yards at Kiel. The 94th Bomb Group was attacked near the target by about 30 fighters, and Lieutenant John P. Keelan's B-17, *Happy Daze*,[258] was seen to ditch about sixty miles off the coast returning from the raid on Kiel after being attacked by *Unteroffizier* Fritz Haspel of III *Gruppe*, JG 1. Keelan recalled:

> "When the fighters hit us, the wing swelled up like a balloon and then burst into flames and we went into a dive. I didn't give the order to bale out because I thought I might pull out of it. I got it under control only 150ft above the water, just in time to ditch. We tied our dinghies together and then started worrying. We were a long way from home and closer to Germany than any other land. We were afraid the Germans might pick us up. We not only watched Kiel burn that night but we actually sat out there in the water and had a grandstand view of the RAF bombing the German coast. We could see the flak bursting and the fires started by the RAF blockbusters. About noon the next day a British plane spotted us. He dropped three big dinghies and then hung around to protect us from possible attack by a Ju 88 that hovered in the distance. Soon another RAF plane joined him and then three more and then three Forts joined up. It looked like the combined Allied air force above us. One of the RAF planes dropped a launch by parachute. It was a sight to see that boat come parachuting down, settling right beside us. It was all closed,

with the hatches sealed. We opened it up and there were sleeping bags, food, water, gasoline and directions for running the thing. I had an idea I might get the boys to head for New York...."[259]

On 26 July more than 300 heavies were dispatched to Hanover and Hamburg. Thick cloud over East Anglia hampered assembly and, despite the recent innovation of "splasher" beacons for forming up, many groups became scattered and they were recalled. Only two combat wings won through to their targets, and 92 heavies bombed rubber factories at Hanover and 54 others attacked shipbuilding yards at Hamburg. Shortly before reaching the enemy coast the 17 Fortresses and two YB-40s in the 92nd Bomb Group came under frontal attack by FW 190s. *Yo' Brother*, 1st Lieutenant Alan E. Hermance's B-17, was seen to hit the water about ten minutes from the island of Nordeney with one engine on fire and the tail badly damaged. All ten crew perished. Captain Blair G. Belongia's B-17 came under attack from seven FW 190s, and two of his engines were put out of action. Belongia nursed the ailing bomber back across the sea and ditched about two miles off Sheringham, where the crew was rescued by a fishing boat after an hour in the water.[260] Other 92nd Bomb Group aircraft also suffered in the attack. One of these was *Ruthie II*, piloted by 1st Lieutenant Robert L. Campbell, who had brought the first *Ruthie* home from Nantes on 4 July, and his co-pilot, Flight Officer John C. Morgan, a 6ft, red-haired Texan. He had flown with the RCAF for seven months before transferring to the 8th Air Force. The navigator, Keith J. Koske, wrote later:

> "We were on our way into the enemy coast when we were attacked by a group of FW 190s. On their first pass I felt sure they had got us for there was a terrific explosion overhead and the ship rocked badly. A second later the top turret gunner, S/Sgt Tyre C. Weaver, fell through the hatch and slumped to the floor at the rear of my nose compartment. When I got to him I saw his left arm had been blown off at the shoulder and he was a mass of blood. I first tried to inject some morphine but the needle was bent and I could not get it in.
>
> "As things turned out it was best I didn't give him any morphine. My first thought was to try and stop his loss of blood. I tried to apply a tourniquet but it was impossible as the arm was off too close to the shoulder. I knew he had to have the right kind of medical treatment as soon as possible and we had almost four hours flying time ahead of us, so there was no alternative. I opened the escape hatch, adjusted his 'chute for him and placed the ripcord ring firmly in his right hand. He must have become excited and pulled the cord, opening the pilot 'chute in the up draft. I managed to gather it together and tuck it under his right arm, got him into a crouched position with legs through the hatch, made certain again that his good arm was holding the 'chute folds together and toppled him out into space. I learned somewhat later from our ball turret gunner, James L. Ford, that the 'chute opened OK. We were at 24,500ft and 25 miles due west of Hanover and our only hope was that he was found and given medical attention immediately.
>
> "The bombardier, Asa J. Irwin, had been busy with the nose guns and when I got back up in the nose he was getting ready to toggle his bombs. The target area was one mass of smoke and we added our contribution. After we dropped our bombs we were kept busy with the nose guns. However, all our attacks were from the tail and we could do very little good. I had tried to use my intercom several times, but could get no answer. The last I remember hearing over it was shortly after the first attack when someone was complaining about not getting oxygen. Except for what I thought to be some violent evasive action we seemed to be flying OK.
>
> "It was two hours later when we were 15 minutes out from the enemy coast that I decided to go up and check with the pilot and have a look around. I found Lieutenant Campbell slumped down in his seat, a mass of blood and the back of his head blown off. This had happened two hours before, on the first attack. A shell had entered from the right side, crossed in front of John Morgan and had hit Campbell in the head. Morgan was flying the plane with one hand, holding the half-dead pilot off with the other hand, 'and he had been doing it for over two hours!' It was no mean feat; Campbell was a six-footer and weighed 185lb. Morgan told me we had to get Campbell out of his seat, as the plane couldn't be landed from the co-pilot's seat since the glass on that side was shattered so badly you could barely see out. We struggled for 30 minutes getting the fatally injured pilot out of his seat and down into the rear of the navigator's compartment, where the bombardier held him from slipping out of the open hatch. Morgan was operating the controls with one hand and helping me handle the pilot with the other."

The radio operator and waist and tail gunners were unable to lend assistance because they were unconscious through lack of oxygen, the lines having been shattered several hours earlier. Morgan's action was nothing short of miraculous. Not only had he flown the aircraft to the target and out again with no radio, no intercom, and no hydraulic fluid, he had maintained formation the whole time. It was an incredible feat for a pilot flying one-handed. Morgan brought *Ruthie II* in to land at RAF Foulsham, a few miles inland of the Norfolk coast, and put down safely. Campbell died an hour and a half later. The other crewmembers survived, including Weaver, who was put in a PoW camp after hospitalization. On 18 December 1943, listeners to the BBC's evening news heard that Flight Officer (later 1st Lieutenant) John C. Morgan (now with the 482nd Bomb Group) had received the Medal of Honor from Lieutenant General Ira C. Eaker in a special ceremony at 8th Air Force Headquarters.[261]

On 26 July 92 heavies bombed rubber factories at Hanover and 54 others attacked shipbuilding yards at Hamburg. Twenty-four aircraft were lost, mostly to JG 1 and II.[262] *Leutnant* Eberhard Burath of I./JG1 recalled:

> "I caught, after my 54th scramble without enemy contact, having been separated from my own bunch, a straggling B 17 with the last of my fuel in the tank. There was not enough left for overtaking and an attack from ahead. Flying at the same level, I did a steep turn to starboard and fired a well-aimed burst at him from the cockpit right through to the tail. I would not liked to have been at the receiving end. Then I saw two Me 109s who must have given him the rest. I got myself an emergency bearing from Borkum. Everyone was shouting for bearings - and 'with God's help and my brakes' I managed to stop my 190 at the field's edge on the perimeter track. That's how I imagined a landing on an aircraft carrier. The take-off afterwards was equally hair-raising, just clearing the hangar roofs with the tail wheel almost touching the tops. It got more hairy as the week went on."

After stand down on 27 July the forecasters waited for the weather to improve over Europe. "Blitz Week" was resumed again on the morning of 28 July when aircraft factories were the targets for 182 B-17s in the 1st and 120 Forts in the 4th Wing. The 1st Wing were given the Fieseler aircraft works at Kassel, while the 4th Wing had the dubious honor of flying the deepest penetration so far, to the FW 190 factory at Oschersleben. P-47C Thunderbolts in the 4th Fighter Group led by Major Halsey would venture into Germany for the first time on a mission thanks to new 200-gallon unpressurized belly-tanks, or "Babies," as they came to be called.[263] The

4th Fighter Group was tasked to provide withdrawal support for the 1st Bomb Wing to Emmerich.

The Oschersleben raid was led by the 94th Bomb Group with the Group CO, Colonel Fred Castle, flying in the lead ship *Sour Puss*, flown by Captain "Pappy" Colby. He recalled that:

"On my map Oschersleben was a little over 90 miles southwest of Berlin but even with the new 'Tokyo' tanks it looked a hell of a long way. The plan called for the usual diversion thrust off the Friesian Islands with a 180° turn back towards England and then the real attack, crossing the coast near Emden and onto the target. Things began to go wrong early in the plan. The weather was supposed to be clear but instead we were flying between layers of stratus clouds as we started the diversion. Then the navigation went wrong because, instead of turning back 60 or 70 miles west of the Friesian Islands we went clear down on top of them and stirred up a hornet's nest of fighters based on Heligoland. They worked us over heavily, darting in and out of the clouds and one group lost three ships from a fighter who hid in the clouds above the formation, then swooped down and dropped an aerial bomb which exploded in their midst. The cloud layers were so thick we had a very hard time making the turn back towards England, with the result that everybody got lost and instead of leading a wing into the target, we only had 28 ships.[264] Colonel Castle was much upset, as orders were not to go in with less than 30 aircraft. He was unhappy about my turning in towards the target, but I conned him into going, saying I could see three more of our planes in the distance (I was not about to go back after all the hell we had just been through). We just started in over the coast without asking anybody and the other 27 planes followed me. The fighters followed us for about 100 miles but as we were now in tight formation they didn't attack."

Instead they concentrated their attacks on the groups that had aborted. *Leutnant* Eberhard Burath of 1./JG 1 recalls:

"The commander wanted to observe from a distance how an attack from ahead should really be carried out and I took his place as leader. We overtook a formation [B-17s in the 95th Bomb Group] entering the north of Holland, then Hauptmann Schnoor sheered off to get a good view from above. Now it was my turn. Far enough ahead, about 3 km, then right wing down to give the signal and a 180° turn to face the center of the formation. Good. So far and I am approaching from dead ahead. A glance to the side - and I am struck dumb - way ahead of the others, I am hurtling all alone at the *4-mots*. Now good night! Instead of spreading the defensive fire evenly to all, the Yanks concentrate on the lone cheeky one and the tracer comes flying at my breast. I make myself very small, get the B-17 I was aiming for briefly into my sights and press the trigger. Then it rattled into the kite like at a fireworks. 'Curtains and exit!'

"'Smoke!' Sheer off. The prop stopped but fortunately no fire. Handy that the Dutch have such nice fields. I selected a convenient one and approached, somewhat too fast, the kite refused to sit down. I passed the end of the field, a pity that the Dutch have so many canals. I passed over them with the nose into the opposite bank, tail up and ready for a somersault. But then my guardian angel gave the port wing a tiny nudge; my kite turned 180° on its nose and slapped neatly down. Potatoes rained down on the fuselage and then a wonderful calm after the storm. I thanked my guardian angel and crawl out of the cockpit into the potatoes. The machine looked quite sound, only 20cm shorter at the nose. I was soon collected from the nearby village of Buitenpost. I did not even get a rebuke. My comrades had taken too wide a turn; only later on, when the escorting fighters were there. Everyone thrust ahead in an attack, as it was none too healthy at the rear. So ended my role as *Gruppen* commander."[265]

Pappy Colby, meanwhile, "sailed down towards the IP," which was covered with about 7/10ths cloud:

"The navigator picked the wrong town. I don't blame him in the least, as the stupid staff people had picked the central town in a row of three all on the same railroad and all about the same size. So we turned on the bomb run and suddenly found that the target, instead of being dead ahead was off to our left 30 miles away. Nobody had any suggestions so I told the bombardier to keep the target in sight while we made a 180° left turn to bomb it on a westerly heading. We made a good bomb run and the photos showed later we did a good job hitting it in spite of the problems. Actually, the cloud cover was between 7/10ths and 5/10ths but from 26,000ft it's extremely hard to pick out landmarks. Despite the press story we had no fighters over the target but heavy flak crossing the coast on the way home. We did evasive action and gut home with no losses out of the 94th."[266]

The 182 B-17s that went to Kassel were limited in their bombing because of cloud that obscured the target, and only 49 claimed to have bombed the Fieseler aircraft works. JG 1 and II shot down the majority of the 22 bombers lost. I./JG 26 claimed a 92nd Bomb Group B-17 shot out of formation near Dordrecht by *Feldwebel* Erich Ahrens of 3./JG 26.[267] Bomber losses would have been higher if it weren't for the 4th Fighter Group. In spite of the new tanks being only half filled due to technical problems, the P-47s in the 4th Fighter Group caught the *Luftwaffe* by surprise. As the Debden Eagles arrived over Emmerich they found no bombers, but passing Leerdam they spotted a different gaggle of Forts under attack by 45 to 60 enemy fighters. The 335th Squadron passed over and in front of the B-17s, while the 336th Squadron went left and the 335th went to starboard to get at them. In a roaring dogfight lasting from 1155 to 1220 hours from Germany back into Holland, the 4th Fighter Group claimed three 109s and six FW 190s.[268] Nearing the end of the combat at around 1220 hours, and west of Rotterdam, Lieutenant Henry I. Ayers Jr in the 336th Fighter Squadron[269] was shot down by *Hauptmann* Rolf Hermichen of I./JG 26. Other Jug pilots heard his mayday call before he baled out to become a PoW.

On 29 July the 8th set out for the fourth time in five days, with the 1st Wing bombing the U-boat yards at Kiel, and 81 Fortresses in the 4th Wing the Heinkel assembly plant at Warnemünde, which had escaped the attention of the B-17s four days before.[270] The strain was beginning to tell, and the 385th Bomb Group lost three B-17s in a mid-air collision during assembly at only 2000ft, two miles from the English coast. Only six parachutes were seen to leave the three aircraft. However, the bombing of the Heinkel plant was described as "excellent," and FW 190 production was severely curtailed. Altogether, the 4th Bomb Wing lost four Fortresses and the 1st Bomb Wing lost six B-17s. Four of the 1st Wing's losses came from the 306th Bomb Group, whose crews had had little or no sleep at all since flying to Kassel the day before. They were intercepted by III./JG 26 from Nordholz. Thanks to radar, the *Luftwaffe* unit had an hour's warning of the bombers' approach, and they were able to mass and make contact with them at Heligoland Island. The 3rd *Gruppe* attacked the unlucky 13 B-17s of the Thurleigh Group (five had aborted) all the way across Schleswig-Holstein to the target. Newly promoted Captain George E. Paris Jr, in the 369th Bomb Squadron, which had now flown 42 consecutive missions without loss, was leading the Group. Just before the target, the first of more than 100 attacking aircraft hit the small formation in a vicious head-on pass. 1st Lieutenant Keith Conley, a 22-mission veteran, was probably the first to go down. *Oberleutnant* Paul Schauder, 9th *Staffel* CO, was credited with the kill.[271] Next was 1st Lieutenant Donald R. Winter's crew in the same low squadron. A wing came off and four of the crew were killed.[272] A few minutes later, Flight Officer Carl D. Brown's B-17 in the 376th Bomb Squadron exploded with the loss of all ten crew, and from the same squadron *Big Jack*, flown by Flight Officer Berryman H. Brown, went down after losing two engines.[273]

At Duxford on 30 July, as the 78th Fighter Group Thunderbolt pilots went into briefing at about 0800 hours, they knew it was going to be an unusual mission. The ground crews realized that recently arrived drop tanks denoted a long haul[274] and the big briefing map confirmed it. It was to be withdrawal support for 186 B-17s in the 1st and 4th Wings going to Kassel, a round trip of 600 miles, when Bomber Command brought down the curtain on "Blitz Week" with take off at 0854 hours.[275] The weather was fine, and the new tanks meant that the P-47s could escort the heavies almost to the target and back again. Without the P-47s losses would have been on an alarming scale, because the Fortress formations were hit by a ferocious onslaught of enemy fighters as Howard E. Hernan, flying as top turret gunner aboard *The Old Squaw* in the 303rd formation, remembers:

> "We were hit by more enemy fighters than ever before. The estimate was well in excess of 300. At one time I counted 157 flying off to our right. A fighter came down through our formation and then a whole *Gruppe* of them got ahead of us and started making pass after pass. Most of them we fought off and turned away at 7-800 yards. They would flip over on their backs and down they would go to get more latitude and then they would try again. Of course, the Luftwaffe painted their aircraft various colors and some were quite pretty. A snow-white Bf 109 dived on us. He had a beautiful Iron Cross painted on the wings and fuselage. He was coming so fast, with a strong tail wind behind him, that he came right through the formation and began making a turn to the right. So help me God he came between us and our wing man on the left, upside down, went between our wings and never touched either of us!"

The B-17 crews flew four of the six-hour round trip on oxygen, and over enemy territory Hernan's supply ran out. Arthur W. Miller, the co-pilot, had to feed him oxygen from walk-around bottles while he tried to shoot at incoming fighters. Hernan and Quick were each credited with one fighter apiece. On the way to the target the Fortresses had been aided by a strong wind, which had given them 160mph indicated airspeed. Now, on the homeward trip, they had to buck this wind. Howard Hernan picked out a landmark and looked down on it. Ten minutes later it was still there![276]

The bombers' route took them over Woensdrecht airfield, home for part of II./JG 1 and the scene of an ineffective attack by eleven B-26 Marauders that morning.[277] Parts of I./JG 26 took off from Woensdrecht and intercepted the bombers. *Leutnant* Göhringer of *Stab* I./JG 26 shot down two B-17s.[278] The Fortresses carried on to the target, where 134 bombed. Waiting for them on their return were the fighters from all four of the *Jagdflieger* defensive zones. Near Apeldoorn II./JG 26 attacked, sending two B-17s down in flames for the loss of three FW 190s. One of the B-17s[279] was flown by Lieutenant Guerdon W. Humason, with Major Robert F. Post, 532nd Bomb Squadron CO, 381st Bomb Group aboard, which came under attack from five FW 190s. The B-17's final destruction was credited to Major Wolfgang-Ferdinand "Wutz" Galland, II *Gruppe* CO.[280] *Hauptmann* Johannes "Hans" Naumann, 6th *Staffel* CO, was credited with the destruction of a 91st Bomb Group B-17.[281] *Unteroffizier* Gerhard Wiegand's claim of a 379th Bomb Group B-17 west of Eupen was upheld.[282] *Flieger* Hans-Walter Sander claimed a 96th Bomb Group B-17 at St. Trond, most likely *Dry Run II*, flown by 2nd Lieutenant Andrew Miracle, also in the 338th Bomb Squadron.[283]

Meanwhile, as the 78th Fighter Group approached the enemy coast, the new belly tanks were dropped 15 miles offshore of the Hook of Holland. The P-47s then climbed to penetration altitude as they flew on over Rotterdam and Nijmegen and entered Germany near Kleve before heading for the Rendezvous Point at Haltern. Nearing the rendezvous, the bombers were sighted at 11 o'clock 20 miles north, and the 78th turned left at 28,000ft, 4000ft above their charges, and began to take up station. Shortly after the turn, the 78th lost its second Group commander in less than a month (Colonel Arman Peterson having being KIA on 1 July), when Lieutenant Colonel Melvin F. McNickle's oxygen system failed and he lost consciousness. McNickle collided with his wingman, 1st Lieutenant James Byers, near Winterswijk, Netherlands. Byers baled out, but he also died. When McNickle regained consciousness, he was still strapped in his cockpit in the wreckage of his inverted crashed P-47 with the Dutch Underground trying to extricate him. McNickle had two broken shoulders and other serious wounds.[284]

The intervention by just over 100 P-47s in the 4th, 56th, and 78th Fighter Groups prevented further bomber losses. They claimed 24 enemy fighters shot down, the 78th Fighter Group claiming seven Bf 109s and nine FW 190s, including three, the first triple victory in the ETO, by Major Eugene P. Roberts in the 84th Fighter Squadron, who was flying *Spokane Chief*:

> "When we sighted the bombers off to our left we made a 90° turn and picked them up near Winterswijk. One straggling bomber was observed flying below the main formation in a dive, trailing black smoke and being attacked by about five E/A. I peeled my flight down and to the rear of the straggler. This would be about 1000ft below the main formation at about 21,000ft. All E/A sighted us and took evasive action to the extent that I was unable to close, although I did fire a burst with improper deflection. The E/A was in a diving attack from the rear on this straggler. I initiated my attack from the port side rear of the fighters, swinging in behind them to the right and broke sharply downward to the rear. I followed them in the climb, attempting to get a deflection shot. When he broke downward I found I was directly beneath the bombers and saw a number of ball turret gunners firing at my flight. I broke down and to the rear and pulled up to starboard side of the bombers about 1000 yards out and at about their level.
>
> "Looking up, I observed six E/A flying parallel to the bombers and about 1000ft directly above me. They failed to see us and did not take any action, so after they passed I made a climbing turn to the left to come up to their level and behind them. At this point I missed my second element and found myself alone with my wingman. In our pull up we missed the original six E/A sighted but sighted a single E/A ahead on same level at about 1500 yards. I dived slightly below, opened full throttle and closed to about 400 yards. I pulled up directly behind the E/A and opened fire. Several strikes were observed on E/A, his wheels dropped and he spun down trailing a large volume of dark smoke and flame.
>
> "I continued parallel to the bombers and sighted two more E/A about 2000 yards ahead. I used the same tactics, closing to 400 yards astern, pulled up and opened fire on port aircraft. I observed strike reports and E/A billowed smoke and flame, rolled over and went down. I was closing so fast that I had to pull up to avoid hitting him. I observed my wingman, Flight Officer Koontz, firing at the second aircraft but did not see the results. Both of these aircraft were FW 190s. After this second engagement, we were about two miles ahead

of the bombers still well out to their starboard side. About this time I observed a Me 109 peeled to starboard to attack the bombers head-on and I followed, closing to 500 yards before opening fire. Two bursts were behind but the third burst caught him and he spun down, trailing smoke and flame, 1500 yards ahead of the bombers."[285]

For fighting off superior numbers of enemy fighters in getting his triple, Major Eugene P. Roberts won the group's second Distinguished Service Cross within a month.

About 100 enemy aircraft were attacking the B-17s from the front and the rear. The rear attackers were firing their new rockets into the bombers as the 84th Fighter Squadron, 78th Fighter Group came diving in behind and up sun. Deputy Group CO Lieutenant Colonel James Stone eased in behind a Bf 109 and exploded him, as his wingman; Lieutenant Maxwell flew through the debris. Captain Jack Price destroyed a FW 190, and then he and his wingman, Lieutenant John Bertrand, each shot down another Focke Wulf in a second attack. Major John Irvin claimed two Bf 109s in formation abreast far behind the bombers. Flight Officer Peter Pompetti made another attack on three 109s. The right one dived away, and the leader took hits and just floated along on his back as Pompetti turned to the left 109, pulling in behind at 50 yards and firing with the few guns he had still working. Smoke poured out of the Messerschmitt and pieces fell off. The pilot was probably dead as Pompetti pulled up to avoid a collision and he lost sight of the disabled aircraft.

Major Harry Dayhuff found a Bf 109 making side attacks on the bombers and destroyed the fighter. 1st Lieutenant Arthur Richie dived after a FW 190 and fired all his ammunition into him, leaving the enemy aircraft belching smoke in a dive. Captain Charles P. London became the first American "ace" in the ETO when he shot down a FW 190 at 26,000ft and a Bf 109, both aircraft blowing up.[286] 1st Lieutenant William Madole caused an enemy aircraft to dive away with his first attack. Climbing back up in a vertical bank, he saw a FW 190 on a P-47's tail and, rolling, he raked the FW 190 with hits, nose to tail. Pulling up and going into his second attack on the enemy aircraft Madole witnessed the pilot take to his parachute. Running low on fuel by this time, the Group was forced to break off escort and head for home from near Tiel, Netherlands. Lieutenant Quince L. Brown in the 84th Squadron was chased to the deck by two FW 190s, which he soon out-distanced. Following the rail lines near Leiden, he saw a freight train and he shot it, probably becoming the first American pilot to strafe a ground target in the ETO in the process. Crossing the coast, Brown dropped so low to the sea to avoid the shore batteries that he hit the water with two of his prop blades, bending their tips, but still making it home. 1st Lieutenant Paul Lehman was on his way to the Channel when flak struck his engine, but it held together long enough for him to get out over the sea and bale out. A Walrus of ASR arrived about an hour and a half later and flew Lehman back to Duxford. 1st Lieutenant William Julian was forced to belly-land his damaged P-47 at West Wickham successfully. 2nd Lieutenant Warren Graff was shot down in the air battle and evaded capture to return in September.

Major Halsey led the 4th Fighter Group's second belly tank mission, a *Ramrod* withdrawal support for B-17s to Emmerich from 0856 to 1135 hours. As the Group passed Grosbeak two groups of bombers were spotted to the north. Halsey dispatched the 335th Fighter Squadron under Roy Evans to cover them. Out of everywhere 150 to 200 enemy aircraft attacked as the squadron pulled in. The 335th Fighter Squadron claimed five FW 190s from 1030 to 1040, losing one pilot as the fight ranged over the Netherlands. After the combat, the squadron remained with the bombers until the Dutch coast, breaking off for home at 1053. The other two squadrons continued on to the Rhine, rendezvousing with more Fortresses at 1015, flying at 27,000ft. They left the Big Friends at the coast at 1100. The 4th Fighter Group claimed a Box Score of 5 destroyed[287] for one P-47 lost.[288] Altogether 12 Fortresses were lost, including some that were so badly damaged that they never flew again. *Patches*, in the 384th Bomb Group, crash-landed at the fighter airfield at Boxted, and her parts were used later for other B-17s in the group. Six fighters were also lost.[289]

Next day, 31 July, VIIIth Bomber Command announced a three-day stand down from combat after a week of exhausting raids, which had cost about 100 aircraft and 90 combat crews. This reduced its combat strength to fewer than 200 heavies ready for combat. Crews had flown themselves almost to a standstill and were glad of the rest. Losses in men and machines were soon made good, and on 12 August the 390th Bomb Group at Framlingham helped swell the ranks of 243 heavy bombers despatched unescorted to targets in the Ruhr. Once again, the weather was to dog the mission and cause many groups to seek targets of opportunity. Groups became strung out, and the *Luftwaffe* seized the opportunity to strike at the widely dispersed formations. They hit groups time and again and inflicted heavy losses, particularly among the 92nd and 384th, which lost four and five aircraft, respectively. The anti-aircraft guns also found their mark, as Howard Hernan relates:

"The flak was terrific and at no time had we encountered more attacks from fighters. I sweated out the whole trip. We lost No.2 supercharger before reaching enemy territory and then No.1 engine began throwing gas and oil badly from the oil cooler vent. No 4 also began running roughly. Campbell had to feather the No.1 engine to prevent it from burning out. We lost oxygen on the right-hand side and had flak holes in several places. We were leading the second flight of the 303rd, which was leading the 1st Wing this day. *Old Ironsides,* our hutmates' aircraft piloted by Lieutenant Arthur H. Pentz[290] was off our left wing. When we were this close together I could see my friend John A. Dougherty in his top turret and we would help one another. I was basically patrolling forward before we got to the target. There was quite a bit of flak around, as there always seemed to be over the Ruhr Valley. I turned my turret around and looked over at Pentz's ship. It looked as though it was on fire from wingtip to wingtip. I just could hardly believe what I was seeing. I was actually yelling at them to bale out but they were still flying along as if nothing had happened. Pentz's ship had all colors of smoke coming out of it. Although there were a few fighters on us at the time, it was flak that had got them. They flew along momentarily beside us and then dropped out of formation. I called one of the waist gunners who always had a pair of field glasses and he followed it as far as he could. The last time he saw it, it was still on fire.[291]

"About a minute later another B-17, flying about 200 yards away and level with us at 10 o'clock, started to make snap rolls. It would snap over, level out momentarily and then make another flip. They were all to the right. I counted each one and he made 21! Each time he flipped over every gun position fired and the tracers would come flying out. The plane looked like a porcupine, Of course, this was because of centrifugal force: as the gunners tried to hold on they would press down on their triggers. I just could not believe that this plane was still holding together. After its 21st flip it leveled out and started to go down in a great big sweeping turn to the left. I often try to figure out what was wrong with this plane as there hadn't been any fighters homing in on him and he was a little too high for flak. I can only think the pilot was trying to set up the automatic pilot for the bombardier and somehow or other it had malfunctioned. It was certainly an empty feeling to look over the empty bunks that night. I vowed there and then that whatever crew replaced Pentz's, I was not going to make friends. I would be sociable and as pleasant as I could, but it was too hard when you lost them. Even to this day I cannot remember who moved into the hut or even what they looked like."[292]

Over 300 bombers were sent to attack targets in Holland and France on 15 August as part of the *Starkey* deception plan. This was created to make the Germans believe that an invasion of the French coast was imminent to relieve some of the pressure on Russia and halt troop movements to Italy. Strikes against enemy airfields in France and the Low Countries continued on 16 August.[293] Early that evening base operation staff throughout eastern England waited for their orders for the morrow and the anniversary mission of the 8th Air Force. Throughout the east of England staff waited in anticipation, none more so than at Grafton Underwood, where Budd Peaslee's 384th had a special interest. Speculation had been rife on the base ever since late in July when the group had received an order from higher headquarters. Colonel Peaslee explains:

"It said 'Select one of the best of your lead crews, stand them down. Send them to headquarters, VIII Bomber Command for special briefing, thereafter they will not leave the base nor communicate with other crews. They will fly practice flights daily and practice high-altitude bombing on the Irish Sea bombing range whenever possible."

Crews knew something special would be in the offing for the anniversary mission, but what? They had laid bets that the subterfuge was part of the preparations for the first-ever American air raid on Berlin; for others, an attack on Hitler's mountain retreat at Berchetsgaden was thought likely. In fact, Eaker and his planners had conceived a most ambitious and daring plan to attack, simultaneously, the ball bearing factories at Schweinfurt[294] and aircraft plants at Regensburg. The selection of Regensburg and Schweinfurt as the targets for the anniversary mission of VIII Bomber Command came at a time when the *Luftwaffe's* operational fighter strength on the Western Front was showing a significant increase. Regensburg was the second largest aircraft plant of its kind in Europe—the largest was at Wiener Neustadt near Vienna—and it was estimated that the total destruction of the plant would entail a nine-month delay in production. Immediate results would be felt in operational strength, it was hoped, between one and a half to two months.[295]

Not enough 1st Wing Fortresses were equipped with "Tokyo tanks," and could not make the 725-mile trip, but now preparations were almost complete for the daring double strike. Such was the importance that the "top brass" would lead the heavies deep into southern Germany. Even the loss of an eye in a bombing raid while he watched the Battle of Britain as an American observer was not enough to deter Brigadier-General Robert Williams, commander of the 1st Wing. He would lead his force to Schweinfurt, while Colonel Curtis E. LeMay led the 4th Wing to Regensburg.

To minimize attacks from enemy fighters it was decided that LeMay's B-17s would fly on to North Africa after the target. The 1st Wing, meanwhile, would fly a parallel course to Schweinfurt to confuse further the enemy defenses and return to England after the raid. Despite this crews remained skeptical, as Howard E. Hernan, in the 303rd Bomb Group at Molesworth, explains:

"We had been briefed for this one three weeks before, so naturally the Germans knew we were coming. Since the previous mission had been scrubbed we were called in every day and told not to mention the target area. Intelligence seemed to think there were a lot of spies in Great Britain."

Crews realized the risks better than anyone and were made aware how important the targets were. Claude Campbell, Hernan's pilot on the mission, wrote:

"Our target was the ball-bearing factory, or rather I should say the elimination of Schweinfurt and all its inhabitants. It is predicted that this is the strike that will break Hitler's back. We were told that within three months from this date Hitler would feel the blow so acutely that he will throw in the towel."

Despite the planning, Eaker and his subordinates were under no illusions. They knew the B-17 crews would have a running fight on their hands, but hoped that the four P-47 fighter groups detailed to fly two escort missions would keep losses down.

At Thorpe Abbotts, home of the 100th Bomb Group—part of the 4th Wing strike force—officers and men sat through the briefing. Among them was Lieutenant Colonel Beirne Lay Jr., who as a captain had been one of Eaker's original "seven" senior officers who had flown to England with the general in 1942. Lay had spent the early part of the war "flying a desk," but had clamored for action and had now got his wish. Lay would fly with the Hundredth as a special observer. His account, "*I Saw Regensburg Destroyed*," first published in the *Saturday Evening Post*, is one of the classical passages in the history of air warfare:

"In the briefing room, the intelligence officer pulled a cloth screen away from a huge wall map. Each of the 240 sleepy-eyed combat crewmembers in the crowded room leaned forward. There were low whistles. I felt a sting of anticipation as I stared at the red string on the map that stretched from our base in England to a pinpoint deep in southern Germany; then south across the Alps, through the Brenner Pass to the coast of Italy, past Corsica and Sardinia and south over the Mediterranean to a desert airdrome in North Africa. You could have heard an oxygen mask drop. 'Your primary', said the intelligence officer, 'is Regensburg. Your aiming point is the center of the Messerschmitt 109 aircraft and assembly shops. This is the most vital target we've ever gone after. If you destroy it, you destroy 30% of the Luftwaffe's single-engine fighter production. You fellows know what that means to you personally.' There were a few hollow laughs.

"After the briefing, I climbed aboard a jeep bound for the operations office to check up on my Fortress assignment. The stars were dimly visible through the chilly mist that covered our blacked-out bomber station but the weather forecast for a deep penetration over the Continent was good.[296] In the office I looked at the crew sheet, where the line-up of the lead, low and high squadrons of the group is plotted for each mission. I was listed for a co-pilot's seat. While I stood there and on the chance suggestion of one of the squadron commanders who was looking over the list, the operations officer erased my name and shifted me to the high squadron as co-pilot in the crew of a steady Irishman named Lieutenant Murphy, with whom I had flown before.[297] Neither of us knew it but that operations officer saved my life right there with a piece of rubber on the end of a pencil.

"At 0530 hours, 15 minutes before taxi time, a jeep drove around the 5-mile perimeter track in the semi-darkness, pausing at each dispersal point long enough to notify the waiting crews that poor local visibility would postpone the take-off for an hour and a half. I was sitting with Murphy and the rest of our crew near the *Piccadilly Lily*. She looked sinister and complacent squatting on her fat tires with scarcely a hole in her skin to show for the 12 raids behind her. The postponement tightened, rather than relaxed, the tension. Once more I checked over my life vest, oxygen mask and parachute, not perfunctorily, but the way you check something you're going to have to use. I made sure my escape kit was pinned securely in the knee pocket of my flying suit where it couldn't fall out in a scramble to abandon ship. I slid a hunting knife between my shoe and my flying boot as I looked again through my extra equipment for this mission; water canteen, mess kit blankets and English pounds for use in the Algerian desert where we would sleep on the ground and might be on our own from a forced landing. Murphy restlessly gave the *Piccadilly Lily* another once over, inspecting ammunition belts, bomb bay, tires and oxygen pressure at each crew station. Especially the oxygen. It's human fuel, as important as gasoline up where we operate. Gunners field-stripped their .50 calibers again and oiled the bolts. Our top turret gunner lay in the grass with his head on his parachute, feigning sleep, sweating out this 13th start.

"We shared a common knowledge, which grimly enhanced the normal excitement before a mission. Of approximately 150 Fortresses who were hitting Regensburg, our group was the last and lowest at a base altitude of 17,000ft. That's well within the range of accuracy for heavy flak. Our course would take us over plenty of it. It was a cinch also that our group would be the softest touch for the enemy fighters, being last man through the gauntlet. Furthermore, the *Piccadilly Lily* was leading the last three ships of the high squadron - the tip of the tail end of the whole shebang. We didn't relish it much. Who wants a Purple Heart?

"The minute hand of my wristwatch dragged. I caught myself thinking about the day, exactly one year ago, on 17 August 1942, when I watched a pitifully small force of 12 B-17s take-off on the first raid of the 8th Air Force to make a shallow penetration mission against Rouen. On that day it was our maximum effort. Today, on our first anniversary, we were putting 30 times that number of heavies in the air - half the force on Regensburg and half the force on Schweinfurt, both situated inside the interior of the German Reich. For a year and a half as a staff officer, I had watched the 8th Air Force grow under Major General Ira C. Eaker. That's a long time to watch from behind a desk. Only ten days ago I had asked for and received orders to combat duty. Those ten days had been full of the swift action of participating in four combat missions and checking out for the first time as a four-engine pilot. Now I knew that it was easier to be shot at than to be telephoned at. Staff officers at an Air Force headquarters are the unsung heroes of this war. And yet I found myself reminiscing just a little affectionately about that desk, wondering if there wasn't a touch of suicide in store for our group. One thing was sure; headquarters had dreamed up the biggest air operation to date to celebrate its birthday in the biggest league of aerial warfare."

The 147 bombers of the 4th Wing could not be delayed for more than 90 minutes if they were to reach North Africa in daylight, and for a time it looked as if their participation was at an end. Thankfully, the mist diminished slightly, and the roar of over 500 Wright-Cyclones was heard throughout East Anglia as the Fortresses thundered into the overcast. That they got off at all was due entirely to the fact that Curtis LeMay's groups had been practicing take-offs on instruments for the past few weeks. Colonel LeMay, flying in *Fertile Myrtle III!* flown by Captain Tom Kenny, took off from Snetterton Heath at the head of the 96th Bomb Group formation, which would lead the mission. Behind came the 388th and 390th Bomb Groups in the low and high positions, followed by the 94th and 385th making up the 2nd Combat Wing. Bringing up the rear of the formation were the 95th and 100th Bomb Groups, flying lead and low respectively, each carrying 250lb incendiaries to stoke up the fires created by the leading groups. Beirne Lay continues:

"At 0730 hours we broke out of the cloud tops into the glare of the rising sun. Beneath our B-17 lay English fields, still blanketed in the thick mist from which we had just emerged. We continued to climb slowly, our broad wings shouldering a heavy load of incendiary bombs in the belly and a burden of fuel in the main and wing tip 'Tokyo tanks' that would keep the Fortress afloat in the thin upper altitudes for eleven hours. From my co-pilot's seat on the right-hand-side, I watched the white surface of the overcast, where B-17s in clusters of six to the squadron were puncturing the cloud deck all about us, rising clear of the mist with their glass noses slanted upwards for the long climb to base altitude. We tacked on to one of these clutches of six. Now the sky over England was heavy with the weight of thousands of tons of bombs, fuel and men being lifted four miles straight up on a giant aerial hoist to the western terminus of a 20,000ft, elevated highway that led east to Regensburg. At intervals I saw the arc of a spluttering red, green or yellow flare being fired from the cabin roof of a group leader's airplane to identify the lead squadron to the high and low squadrons of each group. Assembly takes longer when you come up through overcast. For nearly an hour, still over southern England we climbed, nursing the straining Cyclone engines in a 300ft-per-minute ascent forming three squadrons gradually into compact group stagger formations, low squadron down to the left and high squadron up to the right of the lead squadron, groups assembling into looser combat wings of two to three groups each along the combat wing assembly line, homing over predetermined points with radio compass and finally cruising along the divisional assembly line to allow the combat wings to fall into place in trail behind the lead group of the air division.

"Formed at last each flanking group in position 1000ft above or below its lead group, our 15-mile parade moved east towards Lowestoft - point of departure from the friendly coast - unwieldy but dangerous to fool with. From my perch in the high squadron in the last element of the whole procession, the air division looked like huge, anvil-shaped swarms of locusts. Not on dress parade like the bombers of the Luftwaffe that died like flies over Britain in 1940 but deployed to uncover every gun and permit maneuverability. Our formation was basically that worked out for the Air Corps by Brigadier-General Hugh Knerr 20 years ago with 85mph bombers, plus refinements devised by Colonel LeMay from experience in the European Theater of war. The English Channel and the North Sea glittered bright in the clear visibility as we left the bulge of East Anglia behind us. Up ahead we knew that we were already registering on the German RDF screen and that the sector controllers of the Luftwaffe's fighter belt in Western Europe were busy alerting their *Staffeln* of Focke Wulfs and Messerschmitts.[298] I stole a last look back at cloud-covered England, where I could see a dozen spare B-17s, who had accompanied us to fill in for any abortives from mechanical failure in the hard climb, gliding disappointedly home to base.

"I fastened my oxygen mask a little tighter and looked at the little ball in a glass tube on the instrument panel that indicates proper oxygen flow. It was moving up and down, like a visual heartbeat as I breathed, registering normal.

"Already the gunners were searching. Occasionally the ship shivered as guns were tested in short bursts. I could see puffs of blue smoke from the group close ahead and 1000ft above us, as each gunner satisfied himself that he had lead poisoning at his trigger tips. The coast of Holland appeared in sharp black outline. I drew a deep breath of oxygen. A few miles in front of us were German boys in single-seaters who were probably going to react to us in the same way our boys would react emotionally speaking, if German bombers were heading for the Pratt & Whitney engine factory at Hartford or the Liberator plant at Willow Run. In the making was a death struggle between the unstoppable object and the immovable defense, every possible defense at the disposal of the Reich, for this was a deadly penetration to a hitherto inaccessible and critically important arsenal of the 'Vaterland.'

"At 1008 hours we crossed the coast of Holland, south of the Hague, with our group of Fortresses tucked in tightly and within handy supporting distance of the group above us, at 18,000ft. But our long, loose-linked column looked too long and the gaps between the combat wings too wide. As I squinted into the sun, gauging the distance to the barely visible specks of the lead group, I had a recurrence of that sinking feeling before the take-off - the lonesome foreboding that might come to the last man about to run a gauntlet line with spiked clubs. The premonition was well-founded."

Four P-47 groups were scheduled to escort the Regensburg force, but only the two squadrons in the 353rd Fighter Group (later relieved by the 56th Fighter Group) rendezvoused with the bombers as scheduled.[299] But their task was impossible. The overburdened Thunderbolts could not possibly hope to protect all seven groups in the 4th Wing in a long straggling formation that stretched for 15 miles. Fortresses in the rear of the formation were left without protection at all, and the bomber crews' worst fears were about to be realized. The Ist *Gruppe* JG 26, waiting up-sun and slightly above the Fortresses, immediately bounced the second combat wing head-on. The P-47s were trying to cover the first combat wing, so the FW 190s were able to approach unseen. They swept around in a left turn and flew through the Fortresses, hitting the trailing wing before breaking away in all directions. *Hauptmann* Karl Borris picked out a 94th Bomb Group B-17, the last aircraft in the middle formation, and fired. The Fortress burst into flames, sheered from the formation, and went down. At about the same time *Feldwebel* Erich Aherns of the 3rd *Staffel* claimed a 385th Bomb Group B-17 NW of Antwerp. A few minutes later *Oberleutnant* Artur Beese, *StaffelKapitän* 1./JG 26, claimed a B-17 near Berendrecht. *Hauptmann* Rolf Hermichen claimed another.[300] *Feldwebel* Edgar Dorre of the 9th *Staffel* shot down a B-17 at Genk. At 1142 hours *Leutnant* Erich Burkert claimed a B-17 at Eindhoven. At 1145 hours *Feldwebel* Werner Kraft of the 9th *Staffel* shot up a 95th Bomb Group B-17 in the rear box. As he pulled alongside the crippled bomber to look it over the right waist gunner promptly shot him down. *Unteroffizier* Fritz Fritzlehner of the 12th *Staffel* was shot down and killed by return fire from either a 95th or 100th Bomb Group Fortress. *Oberleutnant* Hans-Georg Dippel of the 9th *Staffel* tried a rear attack on the lead group of the lead wing, but return fire hit his Bf 109G6 repeatedly, and the fighter cart-wheeled through the 385th Bomb Group's formation until he was able to bring his fighter under control and bale out. Remarkably he was uninjured. Minutes later Major Loren "Mac" McCollom of the 56th Fighter Group, who had been loaned to lead the 353rd Fighter Group, saw a formation of Bf 109s 2000ft below at 24,000ft. He dived on them unseen and fired a burst of .50 calibers at the rear aircraft flown by *Oberfeldwebel* Heinz Kemethmüller of the 7th *Staffel*, who minutes earlier had claimed two B-17s, but they were not upheld. McCollom scored many hits and saw "sheets of flame," and he was able to claim the 353rd Fighter Group's first victory.[301] Kemethmüller was saved by his armor plate, and his only injuries were to his hands when the control column was shot from them. He stayed with his 109 until he reached low altitude, when he baled out near Leopoldsburg.

Lieutenant Richard H. Perry, co-pilot aboard *Betty Boop The Pistol Packin' Mama*, flown by Lieutenant Jim Geary in the 390th Bomb Group, recalls:

"Just after we reached the Dutch coast we were attacked by several FW 190s. A .30mm caliber armor piercing shell entered the waist gun area and went right through the steel helmet of Sgt Leonard A. Baumgartner and struck him in the head. The shell also shattered a rudder control cable, which made our landing in North Africa very difficult later. I went to the back of the airplane to administer to him. Baumgartner took his last breath in my arms."[302]

At 1017 hours, near Woensdrecht, Lieutenant-Colonel Lay saw:

"the first flak blossom out in our vicinity, light and accurate. A few minutes later, at approximately 1025 hours, a gunner called, 'Fighters at 2 o'clock low.' I saw them, climbing above the horizon ahead of us to the right - a pair of them. For a moment I hoped they were P-47 Thunderbolts from the fighter escort that was supposed to be in our vicinity but I didn't hope long. The two FW 190s turned and whizzed through the formation ahead of us in a frontal attack, nicking two B-17s in the wings and breaking away in half rolls right over our group. By craning my neck and back, I glimpsed one of them through the roof glass in the cabin, flashing past at a 600mph rate of closure, his yellow nose smoking and small pieces flying off near the wing root. The guns of our group were in action. The pungent smell of burnt cordite filled the cockpit and the B-17 trembled to the recoil of nose and ball turret guns. Smoke immediately trailed from the hit B-17s but they held their stations. Here was early fighter reaction. The members of the crew sensed trouble. There was something desperate about the way those two fighters came in fast right out of their climb, without any preliminaries. Apparently, our own fighters were busy somewhere further up the procession. The interphone was active for a few seconds with brief admonitions: 'Lead 'em more...' 'Short bursts' 'Don't throw rounds away'; 'Bombardier to left waist gunner, don't yell. Talk slow.'

"Three minutes later the gunners reported fighters climbing up from all around the clock, singly and in pairs, both FW 190s and Me 109Gs. The fighters I could see on my side looked too many for sound health. No friendly Thunderbolts were visible. From now on we were in mortal danger. My mouth dried up and my buttocks pulled together. A co-coordinated attack began, with the head-on fighters coming in from slightly above, the 9 and 3 o'clock attackers approaching from about level and the rear attackers from slightly below. The guns from every B-17 in the group ahead were firing simultaneously, lashing the sky with ropes of orange tracers to match the chain-puff bursts squirting from the 20mm cannon muzzles in the wings of the Jerry single-seaters. I noted with alarm that a lot of our fire was falling astern of the target - particularly from our hand-held nose and waist guns. Nevertheless, both sides got hurt in this clash, with the entire second element of three B-17s from our low squadron and one B-17 from the 95th falling out of formation on fire, with crews baling out and several fighters heading for the deck in flames or with their pilots lingering behind under the dirty yellow canopies that distinguished some of their parachutes from ours. Major John Kidd, our 24-year-old group leader, flying only his third combat mission, pulled us up even closer to the 95th Group for mutual support.

"As we swung slightly outside with our squadron, in mild evasive action, I got a good look at that gap in the low squadron where three B-17s had been. Suddenly, I bit my lip hard. The lead ship [*Alice From Dallas*] of that element had pulled out on fire and exploded before anyone baled out. It was the ship to which I had originally been assigned.[303]

"I glanced over at Murphy. It was cold in the cockpit but sweat was running from his forehead and over his oxygen mask from the exertion of holding his element in tight formation and the strain of the warnings that hummed over the interphone and what he could see out of the corners of his eyes. He caught my glance and turned the controls over to me for a while. It was an enormous relief to concentrate on flying instead of sitting there watching fighters aiming between your eyes. Somehow the attacks from the rear, although I could see them through my ears via the interphone, didn't bother me. I guess it was because there was a slab of armor plate behind my back and I couldn't watch them anyway. I knew that we were in a lively fight. Every alarm bell in my brain and heart was ringing a high-pitched warning. But my nerves were steady and my brain working. The fear was unpleasant but it was bearable. I knew that I was going to die and so were a lot of others. What I didn't know was that the real fight, the 'Anschluss' of Luftwaffe 20mm cannon shells, hadn't really begun. The largest and most savage fighter resistance of any war in history was rising to stop us at any cost and our group was the most vulnerable target.

"We absorbed the first wave of a hailstorm of individual fighter attacks that were to engulf us clear to the target in such a blizzard of bullets and shells that a chronological account is difficult. It was 1041 hours, over Eupen, that I looked out of the windows after a minute's lull and saw two whole squadrons, twelve Me 109s and eleven FW 190s, climbing parallel to us as though they were on a steep escalator. The first squadron had reached our level and was pulling ahead to turn into us. The second was not far behind. Several thousand feet below us were many more fighters, their noses cocked up in maximum climb. Over the interphone came reports of an equal number of enemy aircraft deploying on the other side of the formation. For the first time I noticed a Me 110 sitting out of range on our level out to the right. He was to stay with us all the way to the target, apparently radioing our position and weak spots to fresh '*Staffeln*' waiting farther down the road. At the sight of all these fighters, I had the distinct feeling of being trapped - that the Hun had been tipped off or at least had guessed our destination and was set for us. We were already through the German fighter belt. Obviously, they had moved a lot of squadrons back in a fluid defense in depth and they must have been saving up some outfits for the inner defense that we didn't know about. The life expectancy of our group seemed definitely limited, since it had already appeared that the fighters, instead of wasting fuel trying to overhaul the preceding groups, were glad to take a cut at us.

"Swinging their yellow noses around in a wide U-turn, the 12-ship squadron of Me 109s came in from 12 to 2 o'clock in pairs. The main event was on. I fought an impulse to close my eyes and overcame it. A shining silver rectangle of metal sailed past over our right wing. I recognized it as a main exit door. Seconds later, a black lump came hurtling through the formation, barely missing several propellers. It was a man, clasping his knees to his head, revolving like a diver in a triple somersault shooting by us so close that I saw a piece of paper blow out of his leather jacket. He was evidently making a delayed jump, for I didn't see his parachute open.

"A B-17 [*The WAAC Hunter*] turned gradually out of the formation to the right maintaining altitude. In a split-second it completely vanished in a brilliant explosion, from which the only remains were four balls of fire, the fuel tanks, which were quickly consumed as they fell earthwards.[304]

"I saw red-, yellow- and aluminium-colored fighters. Their tactics were running fairly true to form, with frontal attacks hitting the low squadron and rear attackers going for the lead and high squadrons. Some of the Jerries shot at us with rockets and an attempt at air-to-air bombing was made with little black time-fuse sticks, dropped from above, which exploded in small gray puffs off to one side of the formation. Several of the FWs did some nice deflection shooting on side attacks from 500 yards at the high group, then raked the low group on the breakaway at closer range with their noses cocked in a side slip, to keep the formation in their sights longer in the turn. External tanks were visible under the bellies or wings of at least two squadrons, shedding uncomfortable light on the mystery of their ability to tail us so far from their bases. The manner of the assaults indicated the pilots knew where we were going and were inspired with a fanatical determination to stop us before we got there. Many pressed attacks home to 250 yards or less, or bolted right through the formation wide out, firing long, twenty-second bursts, often presenting point-blank targets on the breakaway. Some committed the fatal error of pulling up instead of going down and out. More experienced pilots came in on frontal attacks with a noticeably slower rate of closure, apparently throttled back, obtaining greater accuracy. But no tactics could halt the close-knit juggernauts of our Fortresses, or save the single-seaters from paying a terrible price.

"Our airplane was endangered by various debris. Emergency hatches, exit doors, prematurely opened parachutes; bodies and assorted fragments of B-17s and Hun fighters breezed past us in the slipstream. I watched two fighters explode not far beneath and disappear in sheets of orange flame; B-17s dropping out in every stage of distress, from engines on fire to controls shot away; friendly and enemy parachutes floating down and, on the green carpet far below us, funeral pyres of smoke from fallen fighters marking our trail.

"On we flew through the cluttered wake of a desperate air battle, where disintegrating aircraft were commonplace and the white dots of 60 parachutes in the air at one time were hardly worth a second look. The spectacle registering on my eyes became so fantastic that my brain turned numb to the actuality of death and destruction all around us. Had it not been for the squeezing in my stomach, which was trying to purge itself, I might easily have been watching an animated cartoon in a movie theater.

"The minutes dragged on into an hour and still the fighters came. Our gunners called coolly and briefly to one another, dividing up their targets, fighting for their lives and ours with every round of ammunition. The tail gunner called that he was out of ammunition. We sent another belt back to him. Here was a new hazard. We might run out of .50 caliber slugs before we reached the target. I looked to both sides of us. Our two wingmen were gone. So was the element in front of us - all three ships. We moved up into position behind the lead element of the high squadron. I looked out again on my side and saw a cripple, with one prop feathered, struggle up behind our right wing with his bad engine funneling smoke into the slipstream. He dropped back. Now our tail gunner had a clear view. There were no more B-17s behind us. We were the last men.

"I took the controls for a while. The first thing I saw when Murphy resumed flying was a B-17 [*Escape Kit*] turning slowly out to the right its cockpit a mass of flames. Richard Snyder, the co-pilot, crawled out of his window, held on with one hand, reached back for his parachute, buckled it on, let go and was whisked back into the horizontal stabilizer of the tail. I believe the impact killed him. His parachute didn't open.[305] I looked forward and almost ducked as I watched the tail gunner of a B-17 ahead of us take a bead right on our windshield and cut loose with a stream of tracers that missed us by a few feet as he fired on a fighter attacking us from 6 o'clock low. I almost ducked again when our own top turret gunner's twin muzzles pounded away a foot above my head in the full forward position, giving a realistic imitation of cannon shells exploding in the cockpit while I gave a better imitation of a man jumping six inches out of his seat.

"Still no let up. The fighters queued up like a breadline and let us have it. Each second of time had a cannon shell in it. The strain of being a clay duck in the wrong end of that aerial shooting gallery became almost intolerable. Our *Piccadilly Lily* shook steadily with the fire of its .50s and the air inside was wispy with smoke. I checked the engine instruments for the thousandth time. Normal. No injured crewmembers yet. Maybe we'd get to that target, even with our reduced firepower. Seven Fortresses from our group had already gone down and many of the rest of us were badly shot up and short-handed because of wounded crewmembers. Almost disinterestedly I observed a B-17 pull out from the preceding 95th Bomb Group and drop back to a position about 200ft from our right wing tip. His right 'Tokyo tanks' were on fire and had been for a half-hour. Now the smoke was thicker. Flames were licking through the blackened skin of the wing. While the pilot held her steady, I saw four crewmembers drop out the bomb bay and execute delayed jumps. Another baled out from the nose, opened his parachute prematurely and nearly fouled the tail. Another went out of the left waist gun opening, delaying his opening for a safe interval. The tail gunner dropped out of his hatch, apparently pulling the ripcord before he was clear of the ship. His parachute opened instantaneously, barely missing the tail and jerked him so hard that both his shoes came off. He hung limp in the harness whereas the others had shown immediate signs of life, shifting around in their harness. The Fortress dropped back in a medium spiral and I did not see the pilots leave. I saw the ship though, just before it trailed from view, belly to the sky, its wing a solid sheet of yellow flame.

"Now that we had been under constant attack for more than an hour, it appeared certain that our group was faced with extinction. The sky was still mottled with rising fighters. Target time was 35 minutes away. I doubt if a man in the group realized the possibility of our getting much farther without 100% loss. I know that I had long since mentally accepted the fact of death and that it was simply a question of the next second or minute. I learned first-hand that a man can resign himself to the certainty of death without becoming panicky. Our group firepower was reduced to 35% and ammunition was running low. Our tail guns had to be replenished from another gun station. Gunners were becoming exhausted and nerve-tortured from the nagging strain - the strain that sends gunners and pilots to the rest homes. There was an awareness on everybody's part that something must have gone wrong. We had been the aiming point for what looked like most of the Luftwaffe. It looked as though we might find the rest of it primed for us at the target.

"At this hopeless point a young squadron commander [Major Gale Cleven, flying with Captain Norman Scott in *Phartzac*] down in the low squadron, was living through his finest hour. The 350th Squadron had lost its second element of three B-17s early in the fight south of Antwerp. Yet he had constantly maintained his vulnerable and exposed position in the formation rigidly, in order to keep guns of his three remaining ships well uncovered to protect the belly of the formation. Now, nearing the target battle damage was catching up with him fast. A 20mm cannon shell penetrated the right side of his airplane and exploded beneath him, damaging the electrical system and cutting James Parks, the top turret gunner, in the leg. A second 20mm shell entered the radio compartment, killing Norman Smith, the radio operator, who bled to death with his legs severed above the knees. A third 20mm shell entered the left side of the nose, tearing a section about two feet square and tore away the right-hand nose gun installations, injuring Norris Norman, bombardier in the head and shoulder. A fourth 20mm shell penetrated the right wing into the fuselage and shattered the hydraulic system, releasing fluid all over the cockpit. A fifth 20mm shell punctured the cabin roof and severed the rudder cables to one side of the rudder. A sixth 20mm shell exploded in the No.3 engine, destroying all controls to the engine. The engine caught fire and lost its power, but eventually I saw the fire go out. Confronted with structural damage, partial loss of control, fire in the air and serious injuries to personnel and faced with fresh waves of fighters still rising to the attack, this commander was justified in abandoning ship. His crew, some of them comparatively inexperienced youngsters, were preparing to bale out. The co-pilot pleaded repeatedly with him to bale out. His reply at this critical juncture was blunt. His words were heard over the interphone and had a magical effect on the crew. They stuck to their guns. The B-17 kept on.[306]

"Fighter tactics were running fairly true to form. Frontal attacks hit the low and lead squadrons, while rear attackers went for the high. The manner of their attacks showed that some pilots were old-timers, some amateurs and that all knew pretty definitely where we were going and were inspired with a fanatical determination to stop us before we got there. The old-timers came in on frontal attacks with a noticeably slower rate of closure, apparently throttled back, obtaining greater accuracy than those that bolted through us wide open. They did some nice shooting at ranges of 500 or more yards and in many cases seemed able to time their thrusts to catch the top and ball turret gunners engaged with rear and side attacks. Less experienced pilots were pressing attacks home to 250 yards and less to get hits, offering point-blank targets on the break-away, firing long bursts of 20 seconds and in some cases actually pulling up instead of going down and out. Several Focke Wulf pilots pulled off some first-rate deflection shooting on side attacks against the high group, then raked the low group on the breakaway out of a sideslip, keeping the nose cocked up in the turn to prolong the period the formation was in their sights. I observed what I believe was an attempt at air-to-air bombing, although I didn't see the bombs dropped. A patch of 75 to a hundred gray-white bursts, smaller than flak bursts, appeared simultaneously at our level, off to one side.

"Near the Initial Point at 1150 hours, one hour and a half after the first of at least 200 individual fighter attacks, the pressure eased oft although hostiles were still in the vicinity. A curious sensation came over me. I was still alive. It was possible to think of the target. Of North Africa. Of returning to England. Almost idly, I watched a crippled B-17 pull over to the kerb and drop its wheels and open its bomb bay, jettisoning its bombs. Three Me 109s circled it closely but held their fire while the crew baled out. I remembered now that a little while back I had seen other Hun fighters hold their fire, even when being shot at by a B-17 from which the crew was baling. But I doubt if sportsmanship had anything to do with it. They hoped to get a B-17 down fairly intact. We turned at the IP at 1154 hours with 14 B-17s left, two of which were badly crippled. They dropped out after bombing and headed for Switzerland. The No.4 engine on one of them was afire but the plane was not out of control.[307] Major William Veal, leader of the high squadron [in *Torchy 2nd*] received a cannon shell in his No.3 engine just before the start of the bombing run but went into the target with the prop feathered."[308]

In the one and a half hours preceding the bomb run, 17 Fortresses were shot down. The 385th Bomb Group lost three bombers, while others, so badly shot up, would barely make it over the treacherous snow-covered Alps. Aubrey "Bart" Bartholomew, a young Canadian-born ball turret gunner in *Raunchy Wolf*, was almost blown out of his turret at 19,000ft after persistent attacks during the bomb run. Bart's turret door blew off as a result of an ill-fitting door hinge, and only the toe of his left flying boot hooked under the range pedal of his guns saved him from being sucked out. Oxygen and interphone cables were severed, and he lost contact with the rest of the crew. Somehow he managed to pull himself back into his turret and attract the attention of a crewman who cranked him back into the B-17. The bombing was extremely accurate, and might well have had something to do with the presence of Colonel LeMay, exponent of high-level bombing techniques, in the first wave.[309]

Beirne Lay continues:

"And then our weary, battered column, short of 24 bombers but still holding the close formation that had brought the remainder through by sheer air discipline and gunnery, turned in to the target. I knew our bombardiers were grim as death while they synchronized their sights on the great Me 109 shops lying below us in a curve of the winding blue Danube, close to the outskirts of Regensburg. Our B-17 gave a slight lift and a red light went out on the instrument panel. Our bombs were away. We turned from the target towards the snow-capped Alps. I looked back and saw a beautiful sight - a rectangular pillar of smoke from the Me 109 plant. Only one burst was over and into the town. Even from this great height I could see that we had smeared the objective. The price? Cheap. 200 airmen."

Six main workshops were hit, five being severely damaged. A hangar was partially destroyed, and storerooms and administrative buildings wrecked. Thirty-seven Me 109s at dispersal were at least damaged, if not wrecked, and all production at the plant came to an abrupt halt. Although unknown at the time, by way of a bonus, the bombing had destroyed the fuselage jigs for a secret jet fighter, the Me 262. *All Shot to Hell* and *Madie* in the 390th Group[310] had been shot down in the target area. Two more of the Framlingham Group's B-17s (*Blood Guts & Rust* and *Purgatory Pete*), out of fuel, ditched in the Mediterranean.[311] The surviving 128 B-17s, some flying on three engines and many trailing smoke, were attacked by a few fighters on the way to the Alps. LeMay circled his formation over Lake Garda, near Verona, to give the cripples a chance to rejoin the Wing. *Flak Happy*, in the 100th Bomb Group, piloted by Ronald Hollenbeck, which had been hit in the bomb bay shortly before the target and had jettisoned its bombs, tried to make for Switzerland with two engines out, but the crew were forced to bale out over Italy. In the 390th *Battle Queen "Peg of My Heart"* made it safely to Switzerland, and 2nd Licutenant Stephen P. Rapport landed the smoking B-17[312] at Utzenstorf.

Fighter attacks had disabled two of *High Life's* engines, and 1st Lieutenant Donald K. Oakes in the 351st Squadron, 100th Bomb Group, headed for Switzerland, about 40 miles distant. *Unteroffizier* Otto Fries, a Bf 110 night fighter pilot in 5./NJG 1,[313] who had taken off from St. Trond to intercept the Boeings,[314] spotted the lone bomber turning away to the south. Fries put his 110 into a steep turn to port and followed the ailing B-17. As he got closer he thought he could recognize holes in the rear turret and the fuselage, and the propeller of the starboard outer engine appeared to be turning only by the slipstream. Fries peeled off to port, aimed at the starboard inner engine, and pressed both firing button and lever, but only one of his cannons fired a short burst, and not all of the four machine guns fired. Fries dived below the Boeing and pulled up his machine in a steep turn to port. His cannons were empty, and only two of the machine guns were working. Angry, Fries made two further attacks at the starboard inner engine with the remaining machine guns. At the second attack only a couple of bullets stuttered out, then it was finished. He turned the switch for the guns off and on again and tried both triggers. Nothing happened; machine guns and cannon remained silent. Fries sheered off to one side, and they continued alongside the bomber for a short while to see whether the crew would give up after all, but *High Life* continued steadily onwards to Switzerland. Oakes and Flight Officer Joe Harper, co-pilot, landed the disabled Fortress wheels-up on a Swiss fighter strip at Dubendorf, a small town near Zurich. The crew, who were veterans of twelve previous combat missions over Germany, were interned.[315] The B-17 was the first Fortress to land in Switzerland.

Among the survivors in the 100th Bomb Group[316] who headed for North Africa was Beirne Lay:

"We approached the Mediterranean in a gradual descent, conserving fuel. Out over the water we flew at low altitude, unmolested by fighters from Sardinia or Corsica, waiting for hours through the long hot afternoon for the first sight of the North African coastline. The prospect of ditching, out of gasoline and the sight of other B-17s falling into the drink seemed trivial matters after the vicious nightmare of the long trail across southern Germany. We had walked through a high valley of the shadows of death, not expecting to see another sunset and now I could fear no evil. Eventually, at dusk, with red lights showing on all of the fuel tanks in my ship, the seven B-17s of the group still in formation circled over Bertoux and landed in the dust after eleven hours in the air. Our crew was unscratched. Sole damage to the airplane - a bit of ventilation round the tail from flak and 20mm shells. We slept on the hard ground under the wings of our B-17 but the good earth felt softer than a silk pillow and, waking occasionally, we stared up at the stars. My radio headset was back in the ship. And yet I could hear the deep chords of great music."[317]

Red lights were showing on all four fuel tanks in every ship, and it was a ragged collection of survivors that landed at intervals up to 50 miles along the North African coast. Among the 14 survivors in the 390th Bomb Group, which had set out from Framlingham with 20 B-17s, was *Rick 0' Shay*, piloted by Captain Gerald F. Ritcher and Winfred W. Alfred. After the target *Rick O'Shay* fought a running battle with the fighters, and a 20mm shell exploded in the tail position, severely wounding the gunner in the chest and arms. Ritcher nursed the ailing bomber over the Alps with his oxygen system shot out and headed for the Mediterranean. The crew were weary from lack of oxygen and beating off fighter attacks. The *Luftwaffe* had attacked their B-17 in tens and twenties until they couldn't count them anymore. Apart from a six-minute respite over the target, it seemed they had been under attack for the greater part of the 11-hour flight. Now the calm, blue waters of the Mediterranean were in sight. No pilot in the group was certain he would make Africa, and several aircraft commanders knew they would not. Ritcher wrote later:

> "One by one they started slipping out of formation and headed down to the water. I saw three splash in before I realized that we'd have to go too. The crew threw everything overboard to lighten the aircraft. Guns, tools, ammunition, helmets, camera and everything they could tear loose went over the side before we settled down to ditch."

Ritcher watched the waves, looking for a trough to set the B-17 in, when Alfred spotted the African coast straight ahead. Ritcher pulled up the nose, prayed a little, and gunned the engines. *Rick O'Shay* made it, landing on a dry lake bottom. The pilots turned to taxi off to the side and the engines quit—out of fuel!

The 4th Wing had encountered so many fighters en route because thick inland mists had delayed the 1st Wing for three-and-a-half hours after the 4th Wing had taken off, and this had effectively prevented a two-pronged assault, which might have split the opposing fighter force. The delay gave the *Luftwaffe* time to refuel and re-arm after dealing with the Regensburg force and deal now with the Schweinfurt force. The 91st Bomb Group at Bassingbourn led the 1st Wing to Schweinfurt with Lieutenant-Colonel Clemens L. Wurzbach, the CO, and Colonel Cross of Wing headquarters flying lead in *Oklahoma Oakie*. Brigadier General Robert B. Williams, the task force commander also flew in the 91st formation. The 381st Bomb Group at Ridgewell flew low group. Following close on their heels was the 103rd Provisional Combat Wing led by Colonel Maurice "Mo" Preston, CO of the 379th Bomb Group:

> "I was positioned towards the front of the column and the 303rd flew the low box. The top box was a composite furnished by the 303rd and the 379th. We provided the top element of six airplanes in this composite box. We began to encounter enemy fighters when we were about halfway to the target and had them most constantly with us from there until we left the target area on the way out. There was every indication that the Germans were throwing at us just about everything they had in their inventory. We saw everything we had ever seen among those identification models we had hanging up back in our briefing room and some we just couldn't identify. Certainly, there were FW 190s, Me 109s and 110s, Heinkels, Dorniers and at times I thought I saw even a Stuka or two. And the planes apparently came from many different branches of aviation. Probably they had interceptor units, tactical air (ground support) units and even training units. You name it; they were all there. Probably as a result of introducing units that were not combat-seasoned, the tactics employed were most unusual. The fighters queued up as usual out to the right front and up high but then instead of turn-diving down for attack on the lower elements, they turned in more sharply and delivered diving attacks on the topmost elements - woe be it to that 379th element in the composite box. That entire element of six aircraft was left in central Germany that day. This was the only time I ever saw the Germans employ such a technique and it may have been limited to the particular force that attacked my part of their formation. I don't know, but it was certainly unusual. Even so, it was effective, as our losses will attest. Here again I must say that although I had a box-seat for the whole show - riding up front where I was - I saw those bombers go down but I didn't witness the destruction of a single fighter."

The 303rd Bomb Group, flying in the low box, also had its problems as Howard Hernan, in *The Old Squaw* piloted by Claude Campbell, recalls:

> "On the way over we had two abortives from our squadron, leaving it under-strength. It looked bad. We had a P-47 escort part of the way in and they were to pick us up on the way back. By this time they were using belly tanks and pilots would tell crews over the intercom when the fighters were due to leave. Quite a long while before we reached the target there were a lot of Me 110s. The P-47s were supposed to leave us about ten minutes previously. Out on the right of us flying out about 2000 yards were six Me 110s, flying in a stacked-up formation with the lead ship low. Occasionally, there would be a German fighter calling out our altitude to the ground for the flak gunners, but I'm sure these were not doing that. All the time I was watching these Me 110s and then I suddenly saw the sun glint off four wings of planes above us. Right at that moment I couldn't identify them so I kept my eye on them. When they got above these Me 110s they dived down and I could see that they were four P-47s that were supposed to have been gone ten minutes before. Flying a finger-four to the right, they came down at a 70 or 80° angle, made one pass and got all six Me 110s. They were just sitting ducks. The rear gunner in the last Me 110 evidently spotted the P-47s commencing their dive and baled out!
>
> "Immediately afterwards three enemy fighters came in at us from about 1 o'clock. A FW 190 was in the lead and right behind him came two P-47s on his tail. The FW 190 was making his turn to attack us and all six turrets were pointed at him. I'm sorry to say we got the FW 190 and the first P-47. The other Thunderbolt peeled off and headed for home. We felt bad about it and I doubt whether the P-47 pilot realized he was so close to the bomber formation. There was little flak from the target, which was battered from the bombs of other B-17s. We loosed our incendiaries into the middle of the town and, as we left huge fires were burning. The trip out was a long one and fighters were many."

The 56th Fighter Group, who were flying their second mission of the day, relieved the 353rd on schedule after taking off from Halesworth at 1520 hours, and they met the B-17s returning from Schweinfurt near the Dutch border as briefed. Colonel Hub Zemke wanted to penetrate as deeply as he could safely go and, as with the morning raid, he deliberately chose to cross the enemy coast at around 20,000ft on a direct line from Halesworth. The "bathtubs" were dropped as the P-47s passed near Antwerp, and while they continued a steady climb. With the extended range provided by their auxiliary fuel tanks Zemke led his "Wolfpack" 15 miles beyond Eupen, reminding his wingmen to swivel their heads regularly to see that they were not jumped by the enemy fighters. Visibility was unlimited. At 27,000ft Zemke spotted black specks in the deep blue ahead "like a swarm of bees." They were Fortresses, and most of the enemy fighters were at the same level, and as usual they were orbiting a few miles ahead prior to making a 180° turn to attack the combat boxes head-on. This gave the Thunderbolt pilots the advantage of being able to make diving attacks on the enemy fighters before they reached the B-17s, especially since there did not appear to be any top cover for the Bf 109s and FW 190s ganging up on the Fortresses. Turning left, Philip E. Tukey Jr took the 63rd Squadron out over the lead B-17 box, while "Gabby" Gabreski positioned above the left flank of the trailing formations, and Zemke led the 8 P-47s of the 62nd Squadron to the northern flank at the rear. To his surprise, to the rear Zemke noticed a small formation of 8 Bf 110s apparently preparing an assault on the bombers. Even more surprising was that some appeared to be painted white. There was no time for speculation. Zemke led the 62nd in a wide sweeping 360° turn to get into a position to attack. The 110s had seen the P-47s coming down and they scattered. Zemke picked out a slate gray 110 pulling away, and he dropped down to position dead astern and slightly below, trying to keep his tailplane between his aircraft and the aim of the German rear gunner. At around 300 yards Zemke fired a short burst. The next instant a body came hurtling out of the 110 and passed under his Thunderbolt. Still closing, he put two more bursts into each engine, causing long trails of smoke to stream back. Zemke's victim was now diving straight down, so he broke away to recover altitude. "Looking round to check my tail, the other 110s were nowhere to be seen."

The initial P-47 bounce had completely surprised the FW 190 pilots, who were not expecting to be attacked from the rear. *Ritterkreuzträger* Major Wilhelm-Ferdinand "Wutz" Galland, *Kommandeur* II./JG 26, disappeared from the action.[318] His wingman, *Unteroffizier* Heinz Gomann, had shouted a warning before he too was hit. Gomann scrambled out of his FW 190A-5, but his parachute got hung up on the tail, and when he finally broke free he was just above the ground. Gomann was knocked unconscious, but amazingly he suffered only slight injuries.[319] In all, the 56th Fighter Group claimed seven FW 190s, four Bf 109s, and five twin-engine fighters shot down in the lengthy combat. 1st Lieutenant Glen D. Schiltz Jr and 25-year old Captain Gerald W. Johnson, flying "*JACKSON COUNTY MICHIGAN. FIGHTER*,"[320] were each credited with three victories.[321] North of Antwerp, fuel reserves were reaching the point for return, and the 353rd Fighter Group had arrived to take on the escort, so Zemke called for the Wolfpack to break off and withdraw. The Thunderbolts had been in action no more than seven minutes, and they headed home, carefully monitoring fuel gauges as they went. Three P-47s and their pilots were missing, with one of these falling to the guns of *Hauptmann* Johannes "Hans" Naumann.[322] Pips Priller claimed a B-17 north of Liège at 1740 hours.[323] *Oberfeldwebel* Adolf "Addi" Glunz, attacking "alone, head-on and with a P-47 on his ass," in the words of Edgar "Ed" C. Burford, a crewman in a nearby B-17, shot down *Patches* in the 305th Bomb Group northwest of Diest at 1745 hours.[324] *Feldwebel* Karl-Heinz Zeschke of the 6th *Staffel* JG 26 followed *Our Mom*, a straggling 381st Bomb Group B-17, towards the coast, and fired at it until he was convinced that it was a "gonner."[325]

The coast of England was a welcome sight for the survivors, but not all the Fortresses were able to land back at their home bases. Lieutenant David Williams, lead navigator in the 91st lead ship, *Oklahoma Oakie*, recalls:

> "Our group had lost ten aircraft and we were one of only two aircraft which were able to make it back to Bassingbourn without an intermediate landing. At that we had part of our left wing shot off from a 20mm frontal attack, which resulted in our left wingman being completely shot out of the air. We discovered after landing that we also had an unexploded 20mm in our left main wing tank. A bullet of unknown caliber (I hope it was not a .50) came through the top of the nose, passed through my British right-hand glove, through my left pant leg and British flying boot without so much as breaking the skin, then out through the floor. It paid to be skinny at the time!"

At bases throughout eastern England anxious watchers counted in the returning Fortresses. At the 379th Bomb Group base at Kimbolton Forrest J. Eherenman, the navigator in Lieutenant Corson's crew, arrived in time to watch the bedraggled survivors return to base. "The sight was appalling. Forts came in one by one, some weaving and bobbing. There was a belly landing, with lots of wounded aboard. I would remember the name 'Schweinfurt.'"

Eighteen had taken off from Grafton Underwood, but the watchers in the control tower had no need to count further than 13. At Molesworth things were a little different, as Claude Campbell explains:

> "For some unknown reason there were no losses in the 303rd. The lead bombardier was hit in the stomach 45 seconds from the target and the waist gunner was killed and the other wounded. It was the longest, most impressive, toughest and the most important raid of the war. We got a bullet hole through our left aileron and one through the fuselage, which went under Miller's [the co-pilot] seat and a fragment struck my hand. Following the raid the 8th got the biggest letdown of the war by the RAF. The British night bombers were to follow us and do most of the damage. Our job was merely to start fires so they could saturate the area with blockbusters. But they assumed the target was hit and enough damage done so they failed to follow. It was discovered later that Schweinfurt was not hit as terrifically as supposed. We sacrificed 600 men, 60 planes and many injured men to start those fires."

Colonel "Mo" Preston concludes:

> "The first Schweinfurt was a matching of excessive efforts. We, for our part put up a maximum all-out effort in an attempt to deal the Hun a telling blow and at the same time prove to one and all the decisive nature and the viability of the daylight program. The Germans, on the other hand, felt themselves pricked at their sensitive heartland with their major industries threatened and the morale of their population in the balance. So they put up everything they had to stop the Yankee thrust and make it so costly it would not be repeated. The result was a mixed bag. Our effort fell far short of expectations but nonetheless achieved some of its purposes. But the losses suffered were certainly unbearable and could not be borne by us on a sustained basis."

VIIIth Bomber Command lost 36 Fortresses on the Schweinfurt raid, with a further 24 being lost on the Regensburg strike, making 60 lost in combat (almost three times as high as the previous highest on 13 June, when 26 bombers were lost). Worst hit were the 381st and 91st Bomb Groups, which lost eleven and ten B-17s, respectively.[326] Third highest loss of the day went to the 100th Bomb Group in the 4th Wing, which lost nine Fortresses. Sixty Fortresses had to be left in North Africa pending repairs, so in the final analysis, the 8th had actually lost 147 bombers to all causes on 17 August. The almost nonexistent maintenance facilities in North Africa ruled out any further shuttle missions, but General LeMay and the 4th Wing earned the following accolade from General Frederick L. Anderson at Wing headquarters, Elveden Hall. "Congratulations on the completion of an epoch in aerial warfare. I am sure the 4th Bombardment Wing has continued to make history. The Hun now has no place to hide."

8

Knights of the Sky

As missions grew long through death laden skies
Our bombers had little to fear
We had the best escort acclaimed by us all
'T'was a squadron of Thunderbolts near

The heavies were stood down on 18 August while 54 B-26 Marauders of the 322nd and 386th Bomb Groups were despatched to targets in Belgium and Holland.[327] The Fortresses' stand down, though, was brief, for on 19 August 125 B-17s of the 1st Bomb Wing were despatched to bomb the airfields at Gilze-Rijen and Flushing, while 45 Fortresses of the 4th Bomb Wing were sent to bomb the airfield at Woensdrecht. None who were briefed to bomb Woensdrecht was able to bomb because of bad weather over the target, and one B-17 was lost.[328] However, 93 B-17s of the 1st Bomb Wing force were successful at their targets.[329] P-47s and Spitfires shot down three of JG 26's fighters, while one FW 190A-4 crashed out of fuel and two Bf 109Gs were shot down by return fire from B-17s attacking Gilze-Rijen and Flushing.[330] At 1900 hours *Oberst* "Pips" Priller, CO of the *Geschwader*, and his long time wingman, *Oberfeldwebel* Walter Grunlinger, each claimed a 305th Bomb Group B-17, but it is most probable that these were one and the same aircraft, as the Chelveston group lost one B-17 this day.[331] *Hauptmann* Klaus Mietusch, CO III./JG 26, was credited with a 303rd Bomb Group Fortress northwest of Breda.[332]

The Schweinfurt losses were still having a mighty effect on the B-17 groups, and for three days no Fortress missions were flown. Then, on 24 August 110 B-17s of the 1st Bomb Wing were sent to Villacoublay airfield, with a dozen more B-17s flying a diversion. The 4th Bomb Wing put up 42 B-17s for a raid on other airfields. Some 166 P-47s flew escort, and only one bomber was lost on the day's missions. The "Jugs" claimed six enemy fighters for no loss to themselves. The Fortresses were out again on 27 August, when 224 B-17s were sent out on the first of the raids against V-weapon sites, when 187 B-17s got their bombs away on Watten. The heavies were escorted by 173 Thunderbolts, one of which was lost, while they claimed eight enemy fighters shot down. Four B-17s were lost.[333] The successes had come too late for Major General Frank O'D "Monk" Hunter, who on 29 August relinquished command of VIII Fighter Command to Major General William E. Kepner. Time had finally run out for the flamboyant World War One ace who, despite mounting pressure from his superiors in Washington to adopt new fighter tactics, had continued with his ineffectual and discredited fighter-sweep policy (a tactic supported by Eaker). Monk, who had spent most of his career arguing the point-defense case for the U.S. Army's fighters, had proved more than satisfied to augment the RAF fighter plan of using powerful short-range fighters that could defend friendly air bases and attack nearby enemy ones. Kepner, formerly the head of the U.S.-based 4th Air Force, was a fighter pilot's fighter pilot. He was aggressive, and he was prepared to embrace the realities of the air war in northwestern Europe.[334]

Shallow penetration raids, however, remained the order of the day for the B-17 groups during September, as VIIIth Bomber Command was not yet strong enough to mount raids deep into the *Reich*. On 2 September five forces totaling 319 B-17s were dispatched to bomb airfields in northwestern France, but cloud conditions prevented most of the Fortresses from dropping their bombs.[335] Colonel Hubert Zemke, 56th Fighter Group CO, who was leading three 12-plane formations, decided to make one final turn and sweep behind the Fortresses. *Hauptmann* Johannes "Hans" Naumann, II./JG 26 CO, and his fighters, flying at 25,000ft in thick but broken cloud, spotted two of the Thunderbolt flights in a clear layer below. He got in behind the Thunderbolts and dived, and pulled up in their blind spot beneath. The first burst from Naumann's cannon caused Lieutenants Wilfred Van Abel and Walter Hannigan, in Zemke's second element, to fall away and crash. Van Abel baled out and was taken prisoner. Hannigan was killed. Zemke had his instrument panel shattered and took a 30mm strike in the wing root, which severed a trim control cable. Worse, his engine quit. Zemke dived away to a safer altitude, but just as he was preparing to bale out his engine started again.[336]

Leutnant Dietrich Kehl of 11 *Stab*/JG 26 got into a turning battle with 1st Lieutenant John W. Vogt Jr (63rd Fighter Squadron) and followed him from Lille to the coast before exhausting all his ammunition on the P-47 and turning for home. Vogt recalls:

> "I broke into the first attack but a deflection shot from one enemy aircraft hit me (20mm) and my airducts were punctured enabling me to pull only 35-inches boost at 20,000ft. The same hit also caused my guns to become inoperative and blew away my elevator and trim tab controls. Several attacks were made in rapid succession upon me, causing me to break several times more - always into the attacks which this time were coming from all directions. I finally half rolled to the deck, with one FW 190 right behind me. He fired all the way down and because of insufficient manifold pressure in my aircraft, kept with me easily. I evaded by violent sliding and supping. I hedge hopped from the point where I hit the deck approximately 10 miles southeast of Ghent) to just north of Dunkirk with the 190 about 100 yards behind me all the way. I managed to evade his 20mm until

his supply was exhausted. He then continued to fire the .30 calibers, which did no serious damage when they did hit. The enemy aircraft broke off the engagement and I crossed the French coast. Some fragments from one of his 20mms embedded themselves in my leg but they were removed at a hospital near Eastchurch airdrome where I finally set down. Landing was made after sunset (approximately 2005 hours) with no flaps (hydraulic system shot out) and with wheels down. The ship nosed up at the end of the field."[337]

On the morning of 3 September the Thunderbolts were aloft again when four P-47 groups escorted 233 B-17s who pounded Romilly-sur-Seine and other targets in France. JG 2 attacked the 4th Wing near Paris, and before the IP the two JG 26 *Gruppen* singled out the 1st Bomb Wing targeting Romilly. North of Paris *Leutnant* Helmut Hoppe, 4th *Staffel* CO, made a head-on attack against 2nd Lieutenant Ralph Bruce's Fortress in the 407th Bomb Squadron, 92nd Bomb Group B-17, which pulled away from the formation and went down.[338] The 1st Bomb Wing lost three more B-17s, with *Oberfeldwebel* Addi Glunz claiming one of them east of Paris and *Feldwebel* Wilhelm Mayer of 6./JG 26 claiming another near Melun airfield.[339] Then, on 6 September General Eaker switched his attention to the aircraft component factories at Stuttgart. In all, 338 B-17s were dispatched.[340] The raid was a complete "SNAFU" from the start. Cloud interfered with assembly over England and prevented accurate bombing at the target. The B-17 formations came under sporadic attack shortly after crossing the enemy coast; an indication that the bulk of the fighter force was massing further inland for a concentrated strike. Thick cloud was also building up inland, and the feeling among the B-17 crews was that the mission should be aborted. However, the force carried on. Brigadier General Robert B. Travis, who had assumed command of the 1st Wing from Major General Robert B. Williams (who was moving to command the 1st Bomb Division), circled Stuttgart for approximately 30 minutes in a vain attempt to find the target. Claude Campbell was flying in the 303rd Bomb Group formation behind Travis:

> "The plug and magneto factory we had been briefed to attack was covered in clouds so we flew around dodging flak, trying to find a hole in the overcast. Fighters were flying around as bewildered as we were. Eventually, we dropped our bombs on God knows where (they hit a wheat field) and began to fight our way home."

The 388th Bomb Group was flying its 19th mission, which would be one to remember. At the IP flak had claimed 2nd Lieutenant J. A. Roe's B-17 *Silver Dollar* in the 563rd Squadron, and shortly thereafter fighters shot down the squadron's five remaining aircraft.[341] In all, the group lost eleven Fortresses, the highest loss it had sustained on a raid since joining the 8th in June. Many Fortresses came off their targets with their bomb loads intact, and 233 bombers released their bombs on targets of opportunity en route to the enemy coast. By the time the B-17s were east of Paris red lights began to show on the fuel gauges, and many crews began to wonder if they would ever make England. Three B-17s in the 92nd Bomb Group went down over the Continent, and three more were forced to ditch in the sea, out of fuel. One, which was severely damaged by flak, was successfully ditched two miles off the English coast by Captain Blair G. Belongia. It was the second time Belongia had ditched, the first being on 26 July when the target had been Hanover. All three crews were rescued and returned to Alconbury. Altogether, 118 crewmen were rescued from the "drink" this day.

The following day the 8th bombed enemy airfields in France and the Low Countries.[342] This was the 92nd Bomb Group's last mission from Alconbury.[343] On 13 September VIII Bomber Command was officially divided into three bombardment divisions, with the nine groups in the 1st Bomb Wing forming the 1st Bomb Division. The Liberator force in Norfolk and Suffolk became the 2nd Bomb Division and continued to fly missions separate from the two Fortress divisions. The six B-17 groups that formed the 4th Bomb Wing now formed the 3rd Bomb Division.[344] Next day over 100 B-17s and B-24s were despatched to attack airfields at Woensdrecht and Lille-Nord, but they were forced to abort because of bad weather. On 15 September a few bombers flew a night mission with the RAF against the Montluçon Dunlop tire factory.[345] During the day almost 140 bombers attacked the Renault aero engine works and a ball bearing plant at Paris, while a comparable force attacked airfields at Chartres and Romilly-sur-Seine.[346] Crews could have been forgiven for thinking they were now engaged on nocturnal missions because their return was made in darkness. S/Sgt John W. Butler, a gunner in the 328th Bomb Squadron in the 93rd Bomb Group who was on his third mission, flying in Thomas W. Atkinson's crew in *Tarfu* to the airfield at St. Andre, France, recalls:

> "We took off at 1530 and headed into France. Bomb load was 9 500lbs. We ran into quite a lot of flak and it was pretty damn good. We hit our target and we really were on the beam. On the way back it was pretty dark and some fool started firing at a flak burst. To think I used to be afraid of the dark and I wouldn't even ride the roller coaster. But I can say with the truth that I'd rather face fighter than flak as fighters you can shoot back but flak you can't you have just ride through it and hope for the best. Then someone mistook a B-24 for a bandit and set his No.2 engine on fire. They all started to fire at the poor devil. Four chutes got out. [347] I really sweated it out as tracers were going all over hell. It was also the first night landing in the ETO. We landed back at Hardwick at 9.25 pm. There was an air raid on when we arrived back over England and the sky was really lit up with searchlights."[348]

During early September the 94th Bomb Group had practiced taking off in squadrons and assembling as a group at night. The reason became apparent on 16 September, when more than 130 heavies returned to the French Atlantic coast in what was then the longest trip planned by VIII Bomber Command. The 1st Bomb Division was assigned the port installations at Nantes, while the longer range B-17s in the 3rd Bomb Division flew further south to bomb an aircraft plant at Bordeaux, at the mouth of the Gironde. This involved a 1600-mile round trip lasting eleven hours, and meant that their return would be made in darkness. A third, much smaller formation of bombers would bomb Cognac/Châteaubernard airfield and act as a diversionary thrust for the two larger formations.

Claude Campbell went with the 303rd Bomb Group to Nantes:

> "It was our roughest raid yet. I never expected to get our ship back to England. I was leading the top squadron in our group that led the wing. FW 190s hit us hard after our P-47 escort left us but we evaded them. However, we encountered accurate flak over the target and the oil line to our No.3 engine was cut. We couldn't feather the propeller and the engine began to vibrate terrifically. It was so intense the bulbs in the instrument panel broke loose. Finally, the pistons seized and the propeller crankshaft broke and the prop' began to windmill at very high RPMs. We could not maintain more than 150mph without causing excessive vibration. I expected the prop' to come off at any minute and either cut me in two or wreck the plane."

The co-pilot told Howard Hernan, the top turret gunner, to look around for a good place to crash land:

"I took a look and if anywhere would be good it was one of the many wheat fields. But I wasn't on my 24th mission about to make a crash-landing. I was for trying to fight it back home. I told the pilots it didn't look good. With that Campbell said he was going to try and get us home. He put the nose down and dived for the deck from 28,000ft. But the rest of the squadron stayed with us because they didn't know we had an engine out. Ordinarily, it was a, 'no-no' as they were supposed to go back with the rest of the group. It was all that saved us."

Campbell continues:

"Over the Bay of Biscay six Me 110s jumped us as we skirted Brest and made one pass at the formation, missing me but hitting my right wingman, Lieutenant Manning and cutting his rudder cable in two. The next pass got my left wingman, Lieutenant Baker, cutting his oil lines but neither of the two ships was knocked down. By this time I had reached cloud cover which I took advantage of. The 110s knocked down one Fort, which was straggling along on our left, when they made another pass at us, which we avoided. We knocked down two of the Me 110s on their final pass and then shook the rest off in the clouds. We flew for over three-quarters of an hour with the prop' windmilling. Miraculously, the prop' stayed on and we landed at a RAF base at Exeter. Never did I welcome but the day's operation cost us 13 bombers and bombing results were poor."[349]

The third formation of B-17s, led by the 94th Bomb Group, headed for Cognac/Châteaubernard airfield. However, only 21 bombers from the Rougham Group managed to find and hit the target because of thick cloud. The formation made its way back to England in gathering darkness, but the 94th put down without difficulty thanks to its night practice mission a few days before. Groups in the force that attacked Bordeaux were not so fortunate. Just off the southwest coast of England the B-17s encountered heavy rainsqualls, and this and the impending darkness dispersed the formation. The storm front knocked radio altimeters about 1000ft out of calibration and many pilots got into difficulties.[350]

Earlier, in the morning of the 16th, crews at Hardwick, Hethel, and Shipdham were stunned by the announcement that they would be returning to North Africa, this time to support the seriously threatened Salerno landings. However, when the groups arrived in the Tunis and Massacault areas news came through that the beachhead had been established, and the Groups were switched to other targets in Italy. With the departure of the three Liberator Groups, the 392nd was forced to go it alone. Training was stepped up, and the Wendling outfit flew more diversionary flights over the North Sea to aid the Fortresses.[351]

On the morning of 24 September crews were alerted for a mission to Stuttgart again. "Pappy" Colby, who on 21 September became the oldest combat pilot in the 8th Air Force at the age of 42, says:

"It was one of those days we should have stayed in bed, as the saying goes. The night before we had been told 'No ball game tomorrow' but at 0730 hours we were told to hurry for a 0900 hours take-off, which was damn short notice. The 410th had been scheduled to lead the group, but at the last minute this was changed to filling in the aborts. Everybody taxied out and two minutes before take-off the raid was cancelled, creating a small traffic jam taxiing back to the hardstands."

Adverse weather had led to the cancellation, and crews at bases in the east of England retired once again to their sacks. It was almost noon when they were recalled and quickly briefed for a hurried practice mission. "Pappy" Colby continues:

"At 1130 they decided to have a wing formation practice mission, following a Pathfinder aircraft and bombing a simulated target in the North Sea. Take-off was set for 1330 hours, which meant changing the bomb loads, re-installing machine-guns, etc. Everybody rushed but only about one third of the ships got their guns in."

The same problems befell the 100th Bomb Group at Thorpe Abbotts. Lieutenant John G. Gossage and his crew, who had flown their first mission to Nantes the day before, headed for *Laden Maiden* and discovered it still laden with 500lb bombs. The unloading would not have allowed the crew time to make the mission, so they were reassigned *Damdjfino II*. There was no time to check out the ship completely, and its ten machine-guns lay in the nose compartment. The situation was chaotic, with many 100th B-17s carrying skeleton crews, but assembly and climb went off without a hitch, and the mission seemed to be settling into a routine training flight. The groups of the 3rd Division were to rendezvous with Thunderbolt escort fighters near The Wash, and when ten to 15 dots appeared heading towards 6 o'clock, crews naturally believed they were P-47s. "Pappy" Colby relates what happened next:

"Suddenly, we were hit by about 15 German fighters and, of course, we had no fighter cover. They shot down one ship in the group behind me. As it glided down one 'chute came out and then it blew up. Seven Bf 109s came on through and one started an attack on us, as I was the last plane. Luckily, our tail gunner had gotten his twin fifties installed. He fired a long burst and the fighter turned away. There had been a sleek silver B-17 with no guns flying out to the side watching our formation and our practice bombing and evidently loaded with high-ranking headquarters people. Four fighters went for him and he really put it into a fast dive into some lower clouds to get away."

In the 100th Bomb Group formation, *Damdifino II* came in for some particularly heavy attacks by fighters using the sun to excellent advantage. They raked the fuselage, and a 20mm shell started a fire in the oil tank behind the No.3 engine. Gossage's first thought was to ditch, but the wing was burning fiercely, and the fuel tanks might disintegrate when the aircraft hit the water. He opened the bomb bay and ordered the crew to bale out. Lieutenant Theodore J. Don, the bombardier, baled out at 1000ft and hit the sea almost the same instant he pulled his ripcord. All except Gossage managed to evacuate the burning Fortress. Gossage tried to skim the water and extinguish the fire, but the bomber hit the sea nose down and quickly began sinking. The rudder pedals trapped Gossage's foot, but he managed to extricate himself, crawl through the side window, and surface from 15ft of water. *Damdifino II* floated for five minutes and sank. Don was later rescued by a flotilla of MTBs en route to the Dutch coast, but the co-pilot and the navigator were dead when they were picked up. The two waist gunners and the ball turret gunner were never found.[352]

The *H_2S* radar trials carried out on 23 September proved so impressive that General Eaker instructed that similarly equipped Fortresses should accompany the force of 305 bombers to Emden on 27 September. This small port was handling about 500,000 tons of shipping a month as a result of damage inflicted on Hamburg. Emden was also chosen because of its proximity to water, which would show up reasonably well on the cathode ray tubes. The debut of the H_2S equipped Fortresses aroused much curiosity at Bassingbourn, home of the 91st Bomb Group. Orlo Natvig, the radio operator aboard *Local Girl*, piloted by 2nd Lieutenant William G. Peagram, recalls:

"We got out to the planes waiting to take-off. The weather was looking like rain and a little fog. About that time a plane came in which looked at first sight like an ordinary B-17 but when it got down on the taxi-strip and pulled up by the operations tower we had a bunch of MPs surround the Fortress. We looked from as near a vantage point as the MPs would let us and saw what seemed to be a bathtub underneath the nose. Of course, this aroused our curiosity and, as it turned out, we were told that we were going to be led by this particular B-17 on the first USAAF radar mission. We would be dropping on smoke bombs that were to be dropped by the pathfinder plane. We were quite enthused about this. It was going to be a short mission so we were quite happy about the whole affair. At briefing my tail gunner and I had made the remark to the briefing officer, 'Well, this looks like a milk run'. As it turned out, it could not have been further from the truth.

"We went through the take-off preparations and without any questions at all and were soon on our way over. Everything seemed like a routine mission. We made the usual approach to Germany by going out across the North Sea, leaving only 14 minutes over enemy territory. Observing the coastline we started running into fighters. There was solid overcast underneath us as we approached the target. As we were going on into the target our ball turret gunner passed out. The waist gunner and I got him into the radio room and fixed him to the oxygen system. After he seemed fully recovered we gave him a walk-around bottle and helped him back into the ball turret. We assumed he would hook up to his own system but soon afterwards he passed out again. This time we brought him up and laid him on the floor of the radio room. We decided we did not have enough time to bring him round so we just left him with the oxygen switched on. In any case, we had more serious trouble on our hands with the fighters coming in at us. We returned to our battle stations and returned fire.

"One of the fighters' first passes was made from the belly side. I suspect that the Bf 109 pilots were experienced and must have seen the twin fifties in the ball turret pointing straight down and therefore decided to hit us from this vantage point. It was not manned so they proceeded to climb at us from underneath. They hit us in the wing on one of the first passes and the second time through they came up again from below and scored hits in the gas tank, which caught fire. We also suffered a hit in my compartment. An explosive shell entered the outer skin and all I could remember was that things started flying about and the radio-transmitter behind me was pretty well destroyed. About that time the fire in the left wing started blazing pretty well. We began to realize that we were now in very deep trouble. Our intercom was not operating; I imagine because of some of the fragments from the shell, so we were unable to converse with each other.

"The attack continued from various angles but our predominant concern was the fire in the left wing. We continued for a while but unknown to us the majority of the crew in the forward section had already left the ship. Peagram was the only one up front. He had remained true to his word that in the event of an emergency he would remain at the controls long enough to give his crew sufficient time to bale out. When the fire in the wing got so bad that I could see through the structure, I knew it was time to leave. The other waist gunner, S/Sgt Hutchinson and I took the ball turret gunner and got a parachute on him. We put him through the waist door hatch, pulling the ripcord as he went. He fluttered down and landed safely. Just after we lost our left wing. Hutchinson and I found ourselves clear back down by the ball turret on our sides. The only way we could go then was to scramble up the ribs of the ship, using it like a ladder. Hutch' went on out and I grabbed the pants of our other waist gunner, Peters and tried to get him to come along but he would not move. I wasted no more time and went on up the ribs. When I got to the door I didn't hesitate. I just baled right on out. When I got down the Germans made me disrobe and then they searched us. I put my flight coveralls back on and when I ran my zipper up, it came right off by my neck. I discovered that a piece of shrapnel had come right on through my coverall and had taken my zipper out. I guess it was very fortunate for me that I wore a flak suit that day. I had never worn one before."[353]

The Fortresses, which had bombed with the aid of H_2S equipped B-17s, had done remarkably well.[354] The H_2S sets seemed to provide the answer to the 8th's bombing problems, and Eaker was anxious to use them again as soon as possible. A period of bad weather gave the technicians time in which to iron out some of the teething troubles before the bombers were dispatched to Emden again on Monday, 2 October, with two H_2S-equipped aircraft of the 482nd Bomb Group. Brigadier General Robert B. Travis led the mission, taking the co-pilot's seat aboard a 384th Bomb Group Fortress named *Little America*. This time the H_2S sets worked perfectly, although inexperience resulted in one pathfinder aircraft releasing its bombs too early, and many B-17s dropped their loads short of the target. Winds also carried away smoke markers and disrupted the aim of the following formations. Despite a strong P-47 escort the *Luftwaffe* was again up in force. *The Eightball*, piloted by Lieutenant Bill Cabral in the 390th Bomb Group, lost its No.3 engine to flak and began trailing smoke. Cabral lost altitude and made a solo run on the docks at Emden. When he turned for home the bomber was still alone, and therefore an easy target for preying *Luftwaffe* fighters. Lieutenant Richard H. Perry, the co-pilot, recalls:

"It looked like the whole Luftwaffe was waiting for us at the German coast. I started calling them and our boys went to work at the guns." Soon *The Eightball* had twenty fighters on its tail and Cabral was forced to dive as fast as he dared into cloud cover at 16,000ft below. A fighter dove in at 12 o'clock and the whole bomber shuddered with the recoil as Lloyd J. Wamble opened fire from his top turret. Wamble hit the fighter in the fuel tanks and it exploded, showering the sky with debris and smoke. For the next 20 minutes *The Eightball* came in for repeated enemy attacks and two more fighters were shot down. Finally, *The Eightball* entered cloud cover at 3000ft and Cabral asked the crew over the intercom if everyone was all right. Dean C. Ferris, bombardier, replied that he was but thought he had better mention that No.4 engine was on fire. Orange flame covered the wing and threatened to ignite the fuel tanks. By now *The Eightball* was over Holland and Cabral asked the crew if they wanted to bale out or keep going. All wanted to keep going."

Cabral steered the ailing bomber around the flak at Rotterdam and headed out across the North Sea towards England. *The Eightball* lost altitude rapidly, and soon the badly damaged bomber was so low over the sea that salt spray entered the waist windows and splashed the gunners. The engine fire threatened to engulf the No.3 engine, and Cabral ordered the crew to take up their ditching positions. He was about to ditch, when in the distance he saw a large rolling wave and decided to fly through it, gambling that it would extinguish the raging fire. He took the B-17 in as low as he dared, and the wave washed over the wing. Cabral and Perry threw the throttles forward and lifted *The Eightball* clear of the water. The fire was out! Cabral cancelled the SOS to ASR and flew on to the coast of England, where he brought *The Eightball* in for a smooth landing at an emergency base. As the aircraft hit the runway, the propeller of No.4 engine spun off and rolled some distance down the runway. After the raid General Travis told reporters:

> "The raid went off like a military drill. It's not often you come back from a mission in which everything went off to perfection. I was particularly impressed by the discipline of our men. Our bombs went down together over the target. It was a good show and I was very pleased with it."

Travis had good reason to be pleased with the results. Apart from the bombing, losses had been negligible during this and previous raids on Emden. This was due mainly because the raids were carried out within the range of P-47s fitted with larger capacity drop tanks. Also, the *Luftwaffe's* single-engined fighter pilots, ill trained for blind flying on instruments, had difficulty in making interceptions through overcast conditions.[355]

In the late afternoon of 3 October Lieutenant Thomas S. Seay's crew was alerted to take part in a raid that night. His squadron, the 422nd Bomb Squadron, 305th Bomb Group, had already done a few trips at night. The reason for the switch had been the heavy losses on the Schweinfurt mission and the need to conserve the crews while the whole strategy was reassessed. They were assigned ship 42-3091, as it had "Tokyo Tanks," and their own *Sam's Little Helper* did not. Sergeant Bernard Resnicoff recalls:

> "Our regular bombardier who was on pass, had been recalled for the mission but did not make it in time for the briefing at 1600 hours. Lieutenant Pierce was assigned in his place. Our regular ball turret gunner, S/Sgt Abbott had a cold and was replaced by S/Sgt McCoy. I could have been grounded with a bad back that I had hurt on the Munich raid two days before but as my crew were a few missions ahead of me, I said nothing. After this mission, we were due for some R & R, to which we were all looking forward. The target was to be Frankfurt, which the AAF had bombed that afternoon. The RAF officer briefed us on the Bomber Command times on target. We were to fly above them and bomb on their target indicators. Our load was 6 x 500lb HE, one photoflash for the camera shot and over a quarter of a million propaganda leaflets. There would be a diversionary attack near Frankfurt, which would hopefully draw off some of the night fighters. Our regular bombardier, Lieutenant Harkavy, arrived half way through the briefing. Our S-2 finished off with the usual weather, radio information and time check. We were scheduled to start engines at 1930 and take-off at 2000. It was decided to go with Lieutenant Pierce as bombardier. We had no time to go to the mess hall for a meal and had to make do with a crummy sandwich, not exactly the best meal before a mission. We watched the planes from the day's mission land and then got on board the truck and went out to a tent beside '091'. After the crew did all their pre-flight checks, we sat around waiting to start engines and talked of what we would do on our leave. Lieutenant Troph, the co-pilot handed us our escape kit, money, a Milky Way and a pack of gum.
>
> "Just as we were due to start engines, Lieutenant Seay decided to visit the toilet by the tent. It didn't take long but it was a delay we didn't need. I sat down on an empty ammo box while they started the engines. No.1 started OK but No.2 coughed and died. The ground crew swarmed all over it and we tried again. Two more attempts and then we were told to grab our gear and get over to '056' the stand-by ship. We piled on a jeep nearby and all you could see were 10 men who seemed to be riding on something. They were still working on a generator on No.1 engine but the crew chief said it would be fixed momentarily. I had a mad dash back to 091 for my oxygen mask and when I got back, I found that the 'stand-by' crew had not cleaned the guns. Ground crew offered to help but would only have got in the way. I wanted to do my own anyway as I recall that one armament had put in a gun for Williams, our left waist gunner and when he went to charge it, he found the breech block had been put in backwards. We were set to go when we were told that the generator could not be fixed and that our original machine was now fixed, so once more, we scampered back to '091'. Tempers were getting short and everyone felt that the mission was 'jinxed'.
>
> "All four engines started, given a fast warm-up and we were on our way, 30 minutes late. At the end of the runway, we got the green light. Full power, brakes off and we rolled down the runway with the lights flashing past. A couple of gentle bounces and were in the air. At 1000ft, we circled the field and set course over the tower, climbing out on course. I checked William's mask, he had just turned 18 and he checked mine. Lieutenant Troph called for check-in, Burney in the tail checked in first, then Williams and myself, McCoy in the ball, Cox in the radio room and finally Browser in the top turret. Williams and I charged our guns twice, making sure we had a round in the chamber.
>
> "We passed over London and could see the searchlights although the city was blacked out. There were intruder planes in the area but we saw none. We crossed the coast at Beachy Head and headed for France. We were at 10,000ft and had a partial moon. We crossed France between Calais and Dunkirk and Williams and I got to our feet in readiness. Troph had us check in every 15 minutes making sure we had not fallen asleep.
>
> "As we crossed into Germany Seay told the bombardier that we couldn't make 30,000ft and to set the sight for 27,000ft. After the turning point, Seay said, 'set the sight for 25,000ft'. As we hit the IP the best the ship would do was 24,500ft. Pierce opened the bomb doors and had Cox check that they had opened. This was 2230. Sarrat called the pilot and told him as soon as 'bombs away', turn left 90° and head north. I could see the target by slightly leaning out of the window. Different colored target indicators were going down and I could see the fires and the lights in the city. The ship lurched slightly upwards and Pierce called 'Bombs Away'. This was confirmed by Cox in the radio room. One box of pamphlets didn't fall which meant someone had to go into the bomb bay and manually release them. Thirty seconds later the searchlights picked us up. I had seen a beam come from '12 o'clock' and sweep towards us over the right wing and stabilizer and pass on. It swept back over us a couple of times, then stopped. Immediately, the rest of the beams joined it and we were 'coned'.
>
> "Seay called and had the bomb doors closed. Seay started evasive action and Williams and I were thrown around. Williams let go of his gun and put both hands above his head to hold on to the armor plating to prevent his head from hitting it. I had put my left hand above my head and held on to the gun with my right hand. It was bright enough in the plane to have read a book. Standing and floating half the time, I bent my knees to absorb shock as we pulled up from a dive and when we started a dive, my arm kept me from hitting the roof.

"Suddenly, it became inky black. The lights had gone out. Seay leveled off and I put my chute on the floor in front of me and put my foot on it to keep it from being thrown around. Standing up, I slipped off the 'safety'. I glanced at Williams and he was still holding on to the roof as if the ship was still doing evasive action. I grabbed his sleeve and pulled but he wouldn't let go. I was expecting an attack by fighters. I had been told when the lights left, to expect them. I pulled him again but having been knocked around must have dazed him.

"Then it happened. Fighter in the 6 o'clock (tail) position. Tracers and incendiaries in twin paths flicked under the right stabilizer and wing. I could hear the tail guns firing and then the ball turret opened up. Bowser in the top turret called Seay to say that there was a small finger of flame between No.3 and 4 engines. Seay dove the ship until the co-pilot and top turret said it had disappeared.

"I couldn't see our attacker but by following the tracers, I saw where they had come from and eventually saw him. He passed out of range but the ball turret was still firing at him. As he came in from under the stabilizer, I let go with my gun. I had a nice belly shot at him then. I blinked and he was gone. It was a Me 109.

"A gun started firing and Cox yelled, 'Who in hell is firing?'

"I couldn't see the attacker but some of his tracers were going past underneath my window. I didn't know it at the time but we had been hit below the cockpit where the oxygen bottles were. Sarrat grabbed a fire extinguisher and fought the fire. It swept up into the pilots' compartment and Dowser got out of his turret and fought the flames there. The attacker was at the 6 o'clock position and the tail and bale were firing again, but I couldn't see a damned thing. The whole fuselage from the rear part of the radio room to the tail was raked by 20mm canon fire. It sounded as if someone had tossed a handful of gravel on a tin roof. I saw sparks as the 20mms hit the metal and disintegrated in all directions near me. I felt a twinge, but no hurt in my right arm. I glanced at it and looked around at Williams. He was just standing there with a shocked expression on his face as if he couldn't believe what had just happened. A huge red splotch was forming across the stomach of his overalls. I can imagine what thoughts shot through his mind in that split second - Home, Mother, Father, Sister and Girls. What would they say? Who would tell them? He didn't fall down, but just stood there. I took it for granted he was just scratched.

"I still couldn't see the fighter and I heard Troph ask if anyone was hit. I tried to reply that Williams was. The tail and ball were still firing and I turned as Williams slid down against me, to the floor. I tried to help him but the firing stopped and the whole ship began bucking and floundering in the air. I was thrown across him and was wondering if this was it and what had happened. (Burney later told me that a FW 190 had attacked from 6 o'clock low and he had shot its tail off) It had come up underneath and sideswiped us just beneath the radio room.

"Then I heard Troph yell, 'The whole right wing is on fire! Better get out before she blows up'.

"Pierce asked casually, 'Do you want the bomb doors open?'

"Cox replied, 'Roger, that's the only way I can get out'.

"When I fell, my oxygen mask and throat mike had torn loose. Disregarding them, I scrambled around trying to find my chute. I tried to hook both hooks on at the same time standing up, but only got one strapped on and let it hang lopsided. The glare from the fire threw an eerie light into the waist. The whole ship was a mass of flames, shooting back as far as the stabilizer. I stumbled over Williams as I headed for the waist door. I realized that I should help him and I looked for his chute. I couldn't find it as I floundered around the reeling ship. I was beginning to feel weak and dizzy from lack of oxygen. My mind seemed hazy but I remember opening the door handle as instructed and giving the 'release' a hard jerk. I gave the door a kick and it disappeared in front of me. I was panting now and as I took one last look at Williams, it seemed to me as if his face, reflected in the red glare, was looking right at me and pleading, "Please don't leave me!" I'll never forget that. I ignored my thoughts and finally got the other hook snapped on. I fell forward in a half dive out the door with my hands folded over the chute to protect it from the flames."[356]

On 4 October 361 bombers were dispatched, but without PFF [Pathfinder, or Radar]; bombing was out of the question at all primary targets because of cloud. Twelve B-17s were shot down, and losses would have been higher had it not been for the strong P-47 escort.[357] The 392nd Bomb Group, meanwhile, flew its fourth diversion mission, making a feint towards Bremen to try and draw *Luftwaffe* fighters away from the stream of Fortresses aiming to attack Regensburg and Schweinfurt. Captain (later Colonel) Myron H. Keilman, Operations Officer of the 579th Bombardment Squadron, flew deputy group lead in a force comprising two formations of 18 Liberators each. Previously the *Luftwaffe* had refused to be drawn by the diversionary feints. This time, however, the astute German controllers were convinced of the Americans' destination. Over 30 German fighters bounced the Liberators and a terrific battle ensued. At one time it reached a peak with approximately 150 enemy fighters involved. When it was all over four Liberators of the 579th Squadron had been shot down. Among them was one with the Squadron Commander, Major Donald Apport, aboard. Many other bombers badly damaged in the attack limped back to Wendling. Eleven crewmembers were wounded. Captain Keilman, who was assigned Squadron Commander that evening, recalls the mission:

> "We sure surprised those Me 109s and FW 190s with our forward firepower. Those Groups before the 392nd really had it tough with only flexible mounted 0.50 calibers in the nose of their B-24Ds and B-24Es. Head-on passes were really scary. On later missions, the Luftwaffe sometimes only struck the leading Group. It seemed strange that, with a few exceptions, they made their most persistent strikes, as the formations were 'out-bound.'"[358]

Throughout the remaining months of 1943 the Liberator force, even with the introduction of four new groups, was still not strong enough to mount deep penetration raids without fighter escort. Two of these new Groups – the 445th and 446th – arrived in Norfolk during the first week of November.[359] Meanwhile, during the night of Thursday 7/Friday 8 October there was a red Alert on the East Anglian bases, as enemy aircraft bombed between Bungay and Norwich. Personnel at Thorpe Abbotts saw ack ack, and a dozen aircraft were reported shot down within a few miles of the airfield, several in flames. An early radio report announced that 175 enemy aircraft were over England. At 0500 hours the "Bloody Hundredth" was alerted again, this time to be briefed to lead the 13th Wing to Bremen with take-off set for 1145 hours. Captain Everett E. Blakely, a lead crew pilot, Lieutenant Harry H. Crosby, lead navigator, and Lieutenant James R. Douglass, lead bombardier, had received two days of pre-briefing during secret trips to Elveden Hall, and so they knew what was planned. Crosby recalled that the general idea was that, "many hundreds of planes of heavy bombardment were out to 'Hamburg' Bremen":[360]

> "The unusual thing on this trip was that we were to lead the 3rd Combat Wing. This meant additional strain and responsibility on the part of our crew was a load to which we were more accustomed after

having been in this position a few times previously. Major John B. Kidd, who had done such a creditable job leading the 100th Group on the important Regensburg raid, was the command pilot sharing the piloting duties [aboard the lead aircraft, *Just a Snappin'*] with Captain Everett E. Blakely, now commander of the 418th Squadron. Our co-pilot, Lieutenant Charles A. Via, would ride in the position of tail gunner serving the vital function of formation control officer. S/Sgt Lyle F. Nord would act as radio gunner and assistant to T/Sgt Edmond C. Forkner. We'd always known we had a good crew. Way back in 1942 when the 100th Bomb Group was first formed, the first crew, which served as the nucleus of the group, was Lieutenant Blakely's crew. It had been formed from selected material from three first phase schools. This condition caused the crew to suffer from the stigma of being called the 'model crew'. They held several engineering records such as flight for endurance and maximum performance, which lasted for 17 hours, which drew them commendations from a general in the 2nd Air Force. I personally was a recent addition to the crew, necessitated when their regular navigator was made group navigator. But with all of this aside, from being regular guys and devoted to duty and good at it, our gunners waited till this day to not only prove themselves but also to illustrate just how vitally important it was that all crewmembers must be tops at their jobs when the time came."

Major Gale W. "Bucky" Cleven, the 350th Squadron CO, decided to fly the mission in *Our Babe* with Captain Bernard A. "Benny" DeMarco's crew, which would be deputy lead. Squadron commanders were required to fly ten missions, but Cleven was on his 20th, and he had never bothered to call for his DSC awarded him for gallantry on the 17 August raid on Regensburg. Just before take-off the co-pilot, Flight Officer James "Skip" Thayer, had been instructed to proceed to London to receive his commission as a second lieutenant. After chatting to Cleven he was given a choice "fly or go get the commission." Thayer decided to fly the mission. "He'd get the commission tomorrow."[361]

Captain Thomas E. Murphy, who had flown the Regensburg mission with Colonel Lay, was flying *Piccadilly Lily* on what was his 24th mission with Captain Alvin L. Barker, the 351st Squadron Operations officer, taking co-pilot 2nd Lieutenant Marshall F. Lee's seat. Lee would go along as ball turret man to observe the formation. Murphy's radioman and right waist gunner had completed their tours four days earlier. T/Sgt Derrell C. Piel, whose regular crew had failed to return from the 3 September mission to Paris, and S/Sgt Elder D. Dickerson, whose regular crew had completed their tour on 16 September, were drafted in as their replacements.

For some reason *Our Babe*, the deputy lead ship, reached the end of the Thorpe Abbotts' runway at 1143 hours for take off first, and after take off *Just a Snappin'* would have to maneuver a little to retake the lead spot. At 30-second intervals the rest of the High Squadron followed. *Heaven Can Wait* followed *Our Babe* down the runway, and *Squawkin Hawk*, a scheduled spare aircraft, was the last to get airborne. Lieutenant Harry H. Crosby continues:

"Briefing, take-off and assembly of the group were as usual except that the group formed in the record time of 18 minutes. The group climbed to 9000ft and passed over Buncher 8 at Framlingham, about 40 seconds behind the briefed time of 1246. However, the 100th Group in the lead position was joined by the 390th and the 95th without difficulty. The 13th Combat Wing passed over Spalding in excellent defensive formation at the exact time as briefed, 1312. By essing slightly, our combat wing fell into position as the third combat wing as scheduled. At 1329 the Wing, in unquestionably the best formation flown during my experience, passed over the English Coast nine miles north of Splasher Beacon 4. The course flown was nearly as briefed but a few minutes were lost due to slight discrepancies in turns and metro data. The journey over water was made unnecessarily hazardous due to the fact that planes, which aborted instead of clearing the formation, persisted in attempting to fly through our combat wing formation. On one occasion an entire six-ship squadron in good formation flew between the 100th and 390th Groups. Six minutes later a flight in equally good formation threaded itself through our formation. Two minutes later a single ship with what appeared to be a 'T' marking on the tail repeated the process.

"Our combat wing started the turn onto land near the island of Borkonny. At this time we had twenty-one ships in our group formation and our other two groups were in total or nearly complete strength. We crossed the coast at 1456 on course. Although a slight haze and a two-tenths undercast of low stratus were present, it was possible to determine our exact position by pilotage (visually). Reception on *Gee* failed upon crossing the coast due partially to jamming and lack of strength on transmission of the 'A' marker.[362] We approached Groningen on course and turned toward the IP two miles to the left of course in an effort to clear the combat wing ahead of us. On the approach to the IP it was observed that Emden, apparently remembering the two previous trips (27 September, 2 October) of the 8th Air Force to that area, had sent up a dense smoke screen. Also it was noted by several members of the crew that FW 190s, instead of devoting all their efforts on the Fortresses, in a few cases turned on our escort, long-range P-47s and engaged them in combat. The escort apparently was ahead of us defending the lead combat wing of the air division. 'The IP was reached at 1521.'"[363]

2nd Lieutenant Frank P. McGlinchey, bombardier on 1st Lieutenant William H. "Bill" MacDonald's crew in *Salvo Sal* in the 100th Bomb Group formation, recalls:

"The P-47s had given us good support and things seemed rather quiet as we winged our way towards the target. Minutes passed and soon we were over the IP. With bomb bays open we turned on the target. The groups in front of us were enveloped in a large black cloud as they passed over the target and dropped their payloads. It was the most intensive flak I had ever seen."

The German flak defenses had already calculated the height and speed of the previous wing, and had no need to alter those calculations, as the 100th sailed over the target at much the same height and speed. Captain Everett F. Blakely and Major John B. Kidd in *Just a Snappin'* led the group through the ugly bursts of flak, so thick they formed one large oily cloud. Lieutenant Harry H. Crosby continues:

"By now much of the ground haze had cleared away. My calculations had been proving accurate in my dead reckoning. But all these opportunities to check my navigation were unnecessary. Everyone on the crew knew that the intense black cloud ahead of us marked the vicinity of our target, the town of Bremen. I have been exposed to flak before and hadn't been particularly perturbed by its presence. I remember that in all of those instances each little burst of *Flieger Abwehr Kanonen* was a distinct mean-looking little black ball. But now, over Bremen, each little ball had lost its individuality and the whole thing was blended into a huge angry cloud. Too late I realized that our combat wing had been briefed to fly at an altitude too similar to that of the previous wing, for we sailed right into the midst of that cloud. I could just visualize the gunners on the ground checking back on their computations and sending up volleys using the same data…At any rate, two minutes before we hit the target our plane was hit by the first burst of flak. Our ball turret operator, S/Sgt William F. McClelland, announced in a calm voice that his turret had been struck but not pierced, by a flak burst. From that time his turret operated in a jerky fashion."

Everett Blakely did not need maps or their dead reckoning to tell them they were getting close to the target, nor to tell them that their arrival was expected:

"We could look ahead and see an immense, black, smoke-cloud hiding most of the business area of Bremen. What was worse, we could see a tremendous carpet of flak coming up to greet us. Not a few individual shots and some small black balls but so much solid flak you could almost slice it like a cake…we figured about 300 anti-aircraft guns were firing at us…"

A few minutes before bombs away Blakely saw a FW 190 collide with *Marie Helena*, and he was left with a "very sobering feeling in the pit of the stomach."[364]

Harry Crosby continues:

"Thirty seconds before the bombs were dropped a burst of flak hit our nose compartment shattering the window to the right of the bombardier's head. One fragment struck the bombardier, James R. Douglass, in the left side. It tore through his clothing and ripped the cloth of his flak suit but did not touch his skin. Despite this distraction and I am certain that Douglass thought he had been injured by the expression on his face, he continued the manipulation of his bombsight and bombs were away at 1525. (Even accepting the fact that we had been hit by flak, annoyed by fighters and had been searching for a target obscured by the typical smoke screen, our own and PRU photographs showed that his bombs were dropped accurately and destructively). A mere matter of seconds later our No.4 engine was destroyed by flak. The control wires were shattered and the left elevator was ripped to shreds, plunging our plane into a sort of spinning dive, completely out of control. We were plunging down in a helpless, careening dive. Flames were blazing from our #4 engine. Our control surfaces were all cut and torn. (I might add, parenthetically, that the 95th Group reported later that we were seen to fall into a flat spin, on fire and that three parachutes were observed to open from our plane.) The normal reaction on the part of our pilots should have been to think of their own personal safety or in cases of extreme nobility of character perhaps they would have been thinking about the other members of the crew. But they did not, even in this crisis, forget for one minute that they were the leaders of a great formation. Their first thought was of the crews behind them. In unison, as we fell into our dive, the words came over the interphone to our tail gunner. 'Signal the deputy leader to take over.'

"I can't help but think that as they fought for their lives they might have been excused for being too busy to think of their command but such was not the case. By this signalling the remainder of the formation was notified immediately that we had been hit and were aborting. This act would have prevented any planes being pulled even a few feet out of position into danger from the enemy aircraft buzzing about. (It was the misfortune of the 100th Bomb Group that the deputy leader was destroyed at this time and so many of the flight leaders likewise, that the group was left to do its best by tacking onto the 390th Group.) Back in the radio compartment our young radio operator knew what was going on. He knew he was in imminent danger of his life. But he also had a duty to do. Consequently he still remained at his position and radioed in to Wing HQ that, 'the target was bombed at 1525'.

"For 3000ft Blakely and Kidd fought to get that plane under control. It was only because of the superior construction of our bomber and its perfect maintenance, plus the combination of two skilled pilots that we ever even recovered from that dive. If I were an expert on stress and strain analysis, or a mechanic, or even a pilot, I would dwell at length on the manner in which the plane was restored to normal flying attitude. As it is, the procedure defies my description but I am certain it was a very great accomplishment. Blakely's description was a simple comment, 'You can lose altitude awfully fast when one engine goes sour and your controls are chewed to ribbons.' We dropped for 3000ft before Major Kidd and I could regain control. Most of the crew not strapped to their seats were thrown to the floor, shaken severely - but at last the ground was once more back where it ought to be, instead of standing up on one ear. Once more we were in level flight and, at least temporarily, safe. At 19,000ft we were able to look out the windows and were temporarily assured to note that the ground was now in the right place. A hurried consultation was held over interphone to determine a plan for fighting our way back to England.

"The following facts had to be considered: We had lost all communication back of the top turret, so it was impossible to determine the extent of injury and damage. Our control wires were fraying as far back as the top turret operator could see. At least two of the crew had reported being hit immediately after we left target. One engine was in such bad condition that bits and finally the entire cowling, was blasted off. We were losing altitude so rapidly probably because of the condition of the elevator that any but the shortest way back was beyond contemplation. So we headed across the face of Germany for home."

The deputy lead ship had also started down, and *Our Baby*, *Marie Helena*, *Piccadilly Lily*, *War Eagle*, and *Phartzac* followed in quick succession. Of the 350th Bomb Squadron, only Blakely's ship and Bill MacDonald's *Salvo Sal* remained. Frank McGlinchey scanned the sky:

"I looked for our two wingmen but saw no one. Our whole squadron of nine ships had been knocked out. (I learned later that only the lead ship made it back to England.) Although out of formation and heading back to England by ourselves (just after the bomb bay doors had closed out ship jumped as we received a very bad hit to the rear of No.2 engine), we seemed to be doing all right until a flight of German fighters bounced us. Suddenly, the intercom was alive with reports of fighters bearing in from all directions. All of our guns, with the exception of the two nose guns, were knocked out in 15 minutes. Our waist gunner, Douglas Agee, was killed by a direct hit from a fighter about two minutes after the attack started. All our left controls were shattered and we had to put out several fires. Our radio too was gone. One engine was running away and two more were just about to go. We were losing altitude rapidly and it was apparent we would not make it back to England. Suddenly, fire shot out from the rear of the undercarriage and beneath the wings. With the Zuider Zee directly in front of us, Bill MacDonald gave the order to bale out."[365]

Lieutenant Harry H. Crosby aboard *Just a Snappin'* continues:

"As we plowed across Germany with Blakely and Kidd carefully nursing the loss of each precious foot of altitude and flying at 120mph, we were subjected to the threat of innumerable attacks from enemy fighters. I will say that there were other straggling Fortresses who received a lot harsher treatment than we did. And I will venture a reason for this fact. Ahead of us a lone B-17 was limping along. A flight of three Messerschmitts was harassing it, darting in and out but not attacking. Finally all three swooped in and fired for a long time at the bomber. The bomber didn't go down but neither did any of the fighters. And those three small planes kept attacking that plane receiving no damage to themselves till finally the B-17 caught on fire. It was with a helpless feeling that we saw our last ally turnover, spin slightly and then burst into a huge ball of flame. Now the victorious Germans turned to us. And now comes the reason that we were able to return. From that point on there wasn't one single attack upon us that at least one enemy fighter wasn't destroyed. I believe that T/Sgt Monroe B. Thornton got the first one.

"On this attack which came slightly from the right, Thornton started firing when the fighter was about 800 yards away. At about 300 yards the effect of his firing began to show and the propeller fell off. Douglass and I both saw the pilot jump. Thornton got a couple of others too. One of them was a Me 110. It came at us high and from the right side. Another plane was flying with it in a stacked, slightly echeloned, position. Thorny said that it was firing at us before he was able to get his sights on either of them. The right engine of the fighter caught on fire and pieces flew off the left engine or wing. Our left waist gunner saw two occupant's bale out and both chutes open. His (Thornton's) third came very near to the Dutch border.

"Douglass got a Ju 88 that flipped around a long time before it came in on us. It came in about 300 yards and ended up in a vertical bank with its belly towards us. I saw almost the whole tail assembly shatter off before it fell into a spin. Smoke was pouring from its rear as it went down. Three minutes later another Ju 88 came at us from 10 o'clock. I was positive that my shots were hitting the plane at its exposed belly but the plane did not go down. It made no more attacks. Back in the tail, waist and radio compartments, our gunners were paying a heavier price for their planes. About the time that we went over the target, Via had reported that he was hit. We didn't know whether he meant his compartment or himself. That hit was a serious flesh wound in his right leg. But this didn't stop his shooting. As nearly as we can tell from his and the waist gunner's reports he destroyed his first for that day soon after Thornton hit his No.1.

"Two Me 210s came in together after hovering for some time at 1000 yards. Via picked out the second one and the left waist gunner and the radio gunner say it disintegrated in mid air. His second claim was the partner of one that our top turret gunner destroyed. Thornton saw it blow up nearly 500 yards out. Credit must be given to Via's shooting but when another fact is considered, his performance can be called truly heroic. In between his first and second planes, Via had had a projectile pass from the fat of his hip through his pelvis, severing his sciatic nerve, opening several blood vessels and passing on out his hip. Yet, even with this horrible injury, Via stuck to his position and didn't come out till we had crossed the enemy coast. S/Sgt Lyle F. Nord was pretty busy scratching flak fragments out of his face, head, neck and clothing but he still managed to bring down a fighter from a difficult position. Two Me 210s came in stacked up from about 600 yards out. Nord took one of them and our left waist gunner the other. The plane sideslipped to the right and then blew up. Pieces of the fighter splattered against our plane.

"The waist gunners each got two but the price was infinitely great. S/Sgt Edward S. Yevich has a double compound fracture in his forearm and a deep gash in his leg. S/Sgt Lester W. Saunders fought a gallant fight against death but succumbed in a hospital bed one week after our return. Yevich had been seared across the back by flak fragments at the target so he had a grudge against the first fighter who approached from the left side. He got it going away and two members of the crew saw it explode in midair. Saunders, at the other waist window, had already knocked his first fighter down too. (It was a Me 210). Almost immediately after Yevich's first went down, a 20mm shell tore through the left waist window into the pit of Saunders' stomach and hurled him back against the other side of the plane. I believe it was the same shell, which hit Yevich's gun and ricocheted into his arm. Yet in this gravely wounded condition, both of these gunners actually retained their positions and each one of them knocked out another fighter.

"After his first remark, we hadn't heard much from S/Sgt William F. McClelland. It wasn't till shortly before our crash landing that I learned why. He had destroyed two aircraft with his damaged turret before he himself was hit. The first flak that hit him tore deep into his scalp. But he kept his position. Later another burst, or perhaps an exploding 20mm scraped his face and made shreds of his oxygen mask, headset and clothing. Some place along the line he received an injection of flak in his leg. When the last volley rendered his turret useless -the door was blown clear off - he climbed out into the radio compartment. As we crossed the Dutch coast another burst of flak hit the flak suit on which he was lying and threw him into a bloody heap.

"All this time the pilots had been pretty busy piloting and I was occupied with navigating. The terrain was distinctive so it wasn't hard staying on the course we had selected. I did try to use the *Gee* box and I am positive I would have had a fix at 8000ft over the German-Holland border but some sort of projectile came through the floor and shattered the cathode tube. The radio, along with most of the electrical equipment, was long since non-functional."

Meanwhile, the remnants of the 100th Bomb Group formation flew on in disarray. Major Robert O. Good, the 390th Bomb Group leader, flying in *Six Nights in Telergma*, piloted by Captain Hiram C. Skogmo, had a ringside seat in the disaster. Seeing the 100th Bomb Group being decimated before his very eyes, Good radioed the other group commanders that he was taking the twenty aircraft in his group into the lead slot. The 390th made its bomb run over the center of Bremen, and then headed for the crippled 100th formation ahead. A group above covered the 390th as it made its maneuver, which allowed the 100th an opportunity to slide into position behind the 390th as it passed by. The survivors in the 100th realized the plan and fell in tightly from the rear. Major Good then slowed the formation to give the stragglers a chance to form up. The maneuver prevented the loss of at least four more B-17s that might otherwise have been lost to fighters or flak. Good said later that it was a demonstration of the finest teamwork he had ever seen in the air.

Crosby again:

"We crossed Germany and Holland on a line 30 miles north of Lingen, Ommen and Zwolle. We evaded all known flak areas and large towns. I remember a feeling of futility I experienced when explosions burst in and around our compartment. I was so certain that I was safe from flak area, yet here it was all around us. I yelled out over the interphone for someone to tell me where the flak was coming from. The bombardier told me that those explosions were 20mm shells. I didn't feel any better. I remember another instance when the bombardier turned around and looked at me. Two holes appeared on each side of the compartment and cotton batting sifted down as a bullet went between us. I don't remember his looking back at me again.

"Finally at 1620 we hit the Zuider Zee. We realized our predicament was still acute but just the same that water looked good to all of us. To avoid known fighter fields we turned to a course of 340° to cross over the West Friesian Islands. I was uncomfortably aware that a few weeks ago enemy fighters at precisely that point attacked a big formation on a practice mission. I hadn't even considered the coastal batteries. At our usual altitude they didn't bother us at all but at 7000ft, flying at 120mph, even popguns would have been a menace. They threw everything at us. Whole acres of some sort of light guns flashed up at our ship. Tracers from machine guns laced all around us. In credit to their gunnery we can say that we were hit plenty. Our No.3 engine, revolving feebly at least, now was non-existent. The whole situation was a series of cracking noises much like the closing of a book as volley after volley hit their target. Blakely and Major Kidd were risking everything in some last evasive action. One of them would see flak on one side and jerk the plane on one heading. The other would spot some on his side and back we would go. Their efforts were effective though, because we got through their last defense.

"We had survived everything that the Germans could send up at us there was still one thing to consider - gravity. Crossing the coast had cost plenty and we were now at 3990ft and sinking rapidly. Major Kidd asked for a heading to the closest part of England and I gave it to him. My ETA ran out and then some. As I checked back over my figures I glanced at my airspeed indicator and thought it looked suspiciously immobile. I rapped on it with my fist and the needle dropped to zero. It was then that I learned from a consultation with the pilot that we were making only 120mph instead of 150, as I had believed. I hurriedly redid my calculations and gave a correction in our heading. Bull knew we were a long way from home.

"Ditching seemed the next answer. Douglass went back to make the preparations. Two minutes later he was back with the news that we couldn't ditch, that our crewmembers were in too bad a condition to endure the movements ditching would cause. Moreover, our dinghy compartment was in shreds and at least one of them was in ribbons. That was the first that we in the front had learned of the severity of the situations back in the rear of the plane. Our next thought was to lighten the load of the plane. We threw everything away. Our guns went first and all the ammunition with them. I threw away my flying equipment, my *Gee* box, radio, anything with even an ounce of weight. Now comes an amazing fact: Although our airspeed still remained at 115-120mph, a very small number of miles above the stalling speed of our plane, Blakely not only managed to keep the plane level but actually gained 300ft of altitude.

"England seemed so far away. The ship was listing in such an attitude that our floating aperiodic compasses stuck on the side. I figured the sun should hit the Plexiglas front of the plane and called the pilot to correct him every time he went someplace else. By now our gas problem was serious. The very first airfield sighted, at Ludham, seemed large enough and occupied so we prepared for a crash landing. Most of us ganged up in the radio compartment. Saunders walked unaided to the radio compartment and smiled at us as we bustled about. I didn't dream how seriously he was injured because he kept cheering us up with his motions (thumbs up and thumb and forefinger circled). When he noticed in his dazed condition the excitement was about, he thought we were again being attacked so he tried to crawl to his turret to help ward off the fighters he thought were present. It was almost impossible to stop him.

"Forkner had always seemed young and perhaps excitable but he was all there on this trip. He had completely stopped the flow of blood from all wounds; he had disinfected all injuries. He had calmed his patients with morphine. He had them all covered with blankets to lessen the shock of the approaching landing and the mental shock of their pain. He had encouraged them all during the crossing. Moreover, even though his key had been shot away he still managed to send out distress signals by pounding his finger on his throat mike! (Actually, Forkner sent messages by touching two exposed wires of the smashed radio.) Thornton cradled Via with his body in the waist since the latter's condition prevented his being moved. The rest of us cushioned ourselves as best we could for a landing we knew was going to be rough. And it was. The tail wheel hadn't come down. The brakes were gone. One elevator was useless. Nothing worked properly at all. Even the hydraulic system failed. And to add to it all, just as we hit the ground the frayed cables to the rudder snapped. From then on, even the pilots were just riding.

"On the entire field there were two big trees together and the plane now completely beyond control, veered toward them. The largest one was hit while the plane was going about 50mph. Luckily it passed between the No.2 engine and pilot's compartment so we were swung around instead of being jerked to a halt. Nevertheless, the nose compartment was completely destroyed. But we were on the ground. Even the triumph of this was negated when we learned that we had picked an unused field. The planes we had seen on the perimeters were dummies. And medical aid was still two hours away! We did everything we could. Aid was summoned immediately. The rockets we had fired had been seen from Coltishall so it wasn't long till some RAF medical officers arrived. We were extremely grateful to Flight Lieutenant Nolan of RAF Coltishall for his medical care. Two ambulances arrived and our four wounded men, all busily engaged in cheering each other up, were loaded into them and soon were under expert medical care at the Norfolk and Norwich Hospital."

When word reached Thorpe Abbotts that the crew of *Just A Snappin'* were still alive the sea of despondency which had descended on base operations was lifted. Everyone had thought that the crew were "done for," and that they were more casualties on a day of high losses. Though the crew of *Just A Snappin'* were not yet aware of it, the Bloody Hundredth had lost seven B-17s and 72 combat crewmen. At least 13 more were in hospital suffering from wounds. In all, the 8th lost 26 bombers, 14 of them from the 3rd Bomb Division.[366]

On 9 October 378 B-17s and B-24s were dispatched to three targets in East Prussia and Poland in the longest mission to date. A total of 115 aircraft in the 1st and 41st Combat Wings were dispatched to the Arado aircraft component plant at Anklam, near Peenemünde, as a diversion for 263 bombers attacking the port of Gdynia and the Focke-Wulf plant at Marienburg. For Howard F. Hernan and two other members of Campbell's crew in the 303rd Bomb Group at Molesworth, the Anklam raid was their 25th and final mission of the war. The night before Campbell had been told he would lead the Anklam raid with Major William Calhoun, the 359th Squadron CO, but on the morning of the mission Campbell discovered to his dismay that he would miss the trip altogether. Calhoun would fly *The Eightball* with General Travis, the 1st Bomb Division commander, taking the co-pilot's seat. Howard Hernan and the rest of Campbell's crew would make up the complement. The news that Campbell would not be coming with them was a bad blow, as Hernan explains:

> "I couldn't believe it and my morale dropped to rock bottom. It seemed so strange to fly 24 missions with this good man and all he had got us through to have his place taken by a general. When we finally got away from the crowded flight line we taxied *The Eightball* up to the end of the runway where the gas trucks met us. We topped off our tanks and took off. I was never so glad to get away. We circled the field until the entire group had formed up. It was not until 0930 hours before we finally left the coast and headed out over The Wash towards Denmark. Then we were supposed to fire a green flare to let everyone know that the mission was on. I looked at the dashboard and counted 17 green flares and two red. I said I didn't think it a good idea for all those flares to be there. If one got hit it might start a fire. I couldn't very well throw them out of the plane because they might hit one behind. General Travis said, 'Fire 'em off' I did and it caused uproar because the rest of the group didn't know what it meant!
>
> "We flew out over the North Sea at probably only 5000ft; my lowest ever raid. After we had used our gas in the bomb bay tank I disconnected the hoses and told the bombardier to open the bomb bay doors and try to salvo it. Momentarily it hung up, so I kicked it and off it went. There must have been 115 tanks washed up along the coast that day. We made landfall on the Danish coast and turned southeast to make a feint towards Berlin. By this time the enemy fighters had hit us en masse. They tried to hit us in the lead plane and I had plenty to shoot at. (Later, when I saw the general's notes, he recorded that we had been attacked 114 times, 102 of those at 12 o'clock level, no less than two planes in each attack and one time as high as 14.) The 14 came at us wingtip to wingtip, firing rockets. There wasn't really much we could do about them, but I started on the one on the left and raked the entire formation.
>
> "Just before we reached the target a Ju 88 followed us out to our left at 10 o'clock, probably calling out our altitude. The General asked if I couldn't get him out of there. I informed General Travis that he was approximately 2500 yards away and it probably wouldn't do any good to shoot at him. However, I did notice that once in a while we would make a 1° turn to the left and I asked him if he would tell me the next time he was going to turn. This Ju 88 would not immediately correct his course as it took him a moment to notice we were turning. Consequently, that would narrow the gap. I really didn't think I had a chance of hitting him, but I set up the sight for his fuselage length. The General told me he was turning and I watched the Ju 88. He didn't correct right away and I had my graticules on him and figured he was probably 1500 yards away. As my sight was pointed towards him, I looked at my guns and they were out to my right so I knew that the sight was computing. I began firing off short bursts of four or five rounds at a time. After about the third burst the Ju 88's right engine caught fire, black smoke poured out and down he went. I don't think he crashed but the General saw what happened and I got credit for the Ju 88.
>
> "On our approach to the target there was little flak, although there was a lot around Peenemünde. There did not appear to be many fighters either so I had an opportunity of watching the bombs drop. I very seldom did this but since we were only at 12,500ft I figured I could follow them all the way down and see them hit. Our first bomb landed on a railroad car between two warehouses, blowing it to pieces, while others on either side of it turned flip-flops through the air. We completely saturated the target and started making our left turns to head back over Denmark and the North Sea."[367]

The Gdynia force, led by Lieutenant Colonel Henry G. MacDonald, 40th Combat Wing Operations officer, had continued on its 1500-mile round trip to the dock area. Flak was heavy over the target area, and on the homeward trip the *Luftwaffe* was waiting. William B. "Bill" Rose in the 326th Bomb Squadron, who was flying his first mission in the 92nd Bomb Group as co-pilot with an experienced pilot, recalls:

> "We had no fighter attacks going in, but on the way back they were waiting over Denmark. This was my first taste of combat. It amazed me how the German pilots could fly through the hail of shells we were firing at them. Every fifth round was a tracer. I watched a German fighter come in, met by a wall of tracer bullets. He shot down Bill Whelan's Fortress[368] and escaped, seemingly unscathed. My attitude changed. This was a game for keeps. They were out to kill us and we were going to kill them. It was kill or be killed. I felt like a Roman Gladiator whose only hope of surviving was to be more cunning, more careful and more deadly than his opponent. We needed that seriousness for the battle that lay ahead."

The third force of B-17s, which bombed Marienburg, achieved the greatest success of the day. The normally unfortunate 385th Bomb Group led the raid and lost only two aircraft, one through engine trouble. Anti-aircraft defenses, thought unnecessary at a target so far from England, meant that the force could bomb from between 11,000 and 13,000ft. At such heights accuracy was almost guaranteed, and 60% of the bombs dropped by the 96 Fortresses exploded within 1000ft of the MPI, while 83% fell within 2000ft. Before the raid, the Marienburg plant had been turning out almost 50% of the *Luftwaffe's* FW 190 production. Results were devastating, and General Eaker called it, "A classic example of precision bombing."

When *The Eightball* arrived back at Molesworth, the crew was "welcomed by the same throng, possibly more, than had seen us off." According to Howard Hernan:

> "I was overwhelmed and, of course, my good pilot, Claude Campbell, was there to greet us. Every man in the squadron was anxious for me to complete my 25 missions so they could tear my filthy coveralls off me. Everyone, including General Travis, 6ft 2 and weighing 200lbs who grabbed hold of my shoulder and yanked me clear off the ground, had a lot of fun tearing those coveralls off. General Travis told Campbell. 'This is the best goddam crew I've ever flown with.'"

At Thorpe Abbotts, Major John C. "Bucky" Egan, CO of the 418th Squadron, had "sweated out" the mission to Marienburg. As soon as the 100th formation had landed Egan requested and received permission from the CO, Colonel Neil "Chick" Harding,[369] to lead the group the next day. He was determined to avenge the loss of his close friend, "Bucky" Cleven, at the earliest opportunity. Egan wrote:

> "The briefing was the same as usual, until the S-2, my good friend Miner Shaw, flashed the photo picture of the old walled city of Münster. Shaw's voice droned on that we were going to sock a residential district. At this point I found myself on my feet cheering.

> Others who had lost close friends in the past few raids joined in the cheering. It was a dream mission to avenge the death of a buddy. The mission had not been set up for me to kill the hated Hun but as a last resort to stop rail transportation in the Ruhr Valley. Practically all of the rail workers in the valley were being billeted in Münster. It was decided that a good big bomber raid could really mess up the very efficient German rail system by messing up its personnel."

Altogether, 274 B-17s set out on a direct course for Münster, with 39 Liberators flying a diversion. Bomber crews were told that a maximum of 245 single-engined and 290 twin-engined fighters could be expected to oppose the mission. However, they would be given a strong Thunderbolt escort.[370] Leading the 100th Bomb Group formation at the head of the 13th Wing, Captain John D. Brady was flying in the No.1 position for the first time with Egan in *Mlle Zig Zag*. Egan wrote:

> "The coast came up and Brady made the sign of the cross just as the first burst of flak went off…one of those close ones with pretty red centers. We were being covered by P-47s but the dive and zoom boys couldn't take us all the way to the target because they didn't have the range.[371] From here to the target things weren't dull and occasionally a large bird would leave to land in a place he hadn't signed clearance for. Just as we approached the IP, I called out to the group that our high cover was leaving, watched them go, looked straight ahead and said, 'Jesus Christ! Pursuits at 12 o'clock. Looks like they're onto us!'"

These were the last words Egan was to broadcast for many months. Flak had knocked out the No.2 engine, then Nos.1, 3, and 4 proceeded to run away. Brady and Egan knew the time had come to bale out. Brady fought the controls while Egan organized the exodus. The engineer checked the rear of the ship, while the bombardier made certain that those in the nose had gone. "Bucky" Egan and Brady scrambled to the bomb bay, and both stood on the catwalk, doing an "after you, no, after you" act for a few precious seconds. Brady wanted to be the last out of the aircraft because it was his ship and his crew. Egan wanted to be last out because he was the senior ranking pilot. Suddenly, .30 caliber shells ripped through the fuselage six inches apart in a neat row about six inches below their feet, and both men jumped without further ceremony! Egan finally landed in a wood and, after evading immediate capture, was ultimately caught and sent to PoW camp (as were the rest of the crew), where he was reunited with his old buddy, "Bucky" Cleven.

The 14 B-17s in the 100th Bomb Group had come under fire from flak batteries and upwards of 300 fighters. The German aircraft approached in *Gruppen,* and broke into battle formations of between three to six aircraft that flew straight and level to their quarry. The attacks, which lasted for 45 minutes, were made up to 50 yards range, and then the fighters turned, took violent evasive action, and returned for another attack. The 100th reeled under the incessant attacks, in which twelve of the group's aircraft were shot down before the target. Among them were *Stymie*, *Forever Yours*, *Sweater Girl*, *Shackrat*, *El P'sstoff*, and *Aw-r-go*. 1st Lieutenant John K. Justice's *Pasadena Nena* was shot down over Holland on the homeward leg.[372] Only Captain Keith Harris, in the 390th Bomb Group flying composite (one plane only with the 100th Bomb Group), and Lieutenant Robert Rosenthal, flying only his third mission, had survived. These two B-17s made up the entire high squadron of the 100th. Contrary to popular folklore, Robert Rosenthal was flying *Royal Flush* this day, and not *Rosie's Riveters* (Which was still under repair following *Rosie's* debut on the disastrous mission to Bremen. *Spot Remover*, Captain Harris' regular B-17F, was also undergoing repairs, and he was flying a borrowed B-17G). Two of *Royal Flush's* engines were shot out over Münster, and a rocket shell tore through the right wing, leaving a large hole. Despite this, Rosenthal completed the bomb run and instigated a series of near fatal maneuvers to throw the flak guns off the scent.

Next to feel the full impact of the *Luftwaffe* attacks were the 18 B-17s in the 390th Bomb Group formation. As the group neared the target a large formation of aircraft was spotted off to the right. At first it was thought they were B-17s, but the stepped-up specks materialized into single-engined *Luftwaffe* fighters. While Bf 109s and FW 190s ripped through the depleted Fortress formations, the twin-engined fighters stayed out of range and fired explosive cannon shells from 1200 to 1500 yards. Ju 88s attacked with rockets from 800 to 1000 yards, and for the first time Dornier bombers flew parallel to the Fortresses and fired rockets from about 1500 yards. In about 25 minutes the 390th lost eight of its bombers as the rockets exploded among them.[373]

Captain Robert D. Brown, pilot of *Cabin In The Sky*, asked his tail gunner how the rest of the squadron was doing. The tail gunner reported back that their bomber was the only aircraft left in the squadron formation! Five of the group's eight losses had gone down in as many minutes. A few seconds later Captain Brown saw 36 fighters just ahead. His gunners had virtually no ammunition left, and the ball turret gunner could only point his empty guns in the direction of the *Luftwaffe* attacks. But *Cabin In the Sky* came through the battle over Münster.

Captain Gordon-Forbes, in the 390th Bomb Group, adds:

> "We caught the brunt of the first attack. 2nd Lieutenant George Starnes was hit at the middle of his ship by a rocket and the plane started to break in half. It nosed up and crashed into another, just above in the formation. Both planes fell away and went down in a column of smoke. [374] A ship on our right blew up with a great red flash. I saw the right waist gunner come out of his window in a grotesque swan dive. His chest was shot away…All the weariness of battle seemed to drain every ounce of strength I had. I felt like yelling and praying at the same time."

Gus Mencow, lead navigator, 520th Bomb Squadron, 390th Bomb Group, recalled later:

> "This was the most frightening of all the missions I flew. I still get scared and have weird dreams about that day. We did not have complete air supremacy and our fighters did not yet have long-range belly tanks. They could not follow us on long-range missions. We lost eight out of 19 aircraft. The flak was unbelievable and the Luftwaffe must have had every one of their planes attacking us. The loss of so many friends was overwhelming. I got a 109 and it went down smoking and burning."

After disposing of a large part of the 390th formation, the *Luftwaffe* turned on the 95th Bomb Group. The fighters flew parallel to the formation, out of range in groups of between 20 and 40 aircraft, stacked up echelon-down for frontal attacks. They flew on ahead of the bombers and then peeled off, one or two at a time, attacking the lowest B-17s in the formation. Of the original 95th formation of 19 aircraft, *Brown's Mule*, *Fritz Blitz*, *Patsy Ann III*, *Miss Flower*, and a fifth, unnamed ship had been shot down. Four of them were from the low squadron. The survivors continued to the target, desperately fighting off the intense *Luftwaffe* attacks. In the 390th Bomb Group formation Dean C. Ferris, bombardier, and Lieutenant Gordon H. Wharton, navigator, in the nose of *The Eightball*, piloted by

Bill Cabral, were firing their guns constantly as the battle raged. A hot shell casing from one of their machine-guns landed on a fleece-lined flying jacket lying on the floor behind the two men and started a fire. Ferris pounced on the blaze and beat out the flames before returning to his gun, where he continued firing despite his badly burned hands.

A live rocket entered the waist window of *Norma J*, piloted by Bruce R. Riley, but it did not explode. George T. Rankin grabbed the smoldering projectile in a flak vest and threw it back out of the window.[375] Up front James H. Shields, one of the few non-commissioned bombardiers in the 8th Air Force, placed his bombs on the target. During the bomb run Lieutenant Burgess W. Murdock, co-pilot of *Miss Carry*, in the 390th formation, took over the controls. Before the IP a large piece of flak had torn a ragged hole in the thigh of the pilot, Lieutenant Paul W. Vance. Vance used the rubber extension cord from his intercom connection as a tourniquet and wrapped his white flying scarf around the wound. He managed to direct Murdock through the bombing run and helped him maintain formation during the withdrawal from the target area. *Miss Carry* was fortunate. During the bomb run four ships on her wing had fallen out of formation and had been lost. After the target *Tech Supply*, flown by Lieutenant John G. Winant, Jr, son of the U.S. Ambassador to Great Britain, was hit by a rocket and exploded. It was Winant's 13th mission. The crew of *The Eightball* saw several parachutes leave the bomber.[376] Shortly after *Tech Supply* went down, *The Eightball* was hit in the right wing by a rocket. Richard H. Perry, the co-pilot, says:

> "The rocket sheared a path through the top half of the right wing (about 15ft from the end). The wing tip flapped up and down in the windstream and caused us to lose the lift that we should have gotten from the wing."

The combined efforts of Perry and Cabral were not enough to keep the bomber from falling out of formation, so Ferris was called to the controls. He stood between Perry and Cabral and managed, despite his injuries, to put a hand on each of the control wheels and help the pilots keep *The Eightball* straight and level in formation.

It was a great relief to one and all when the white vapor trails of the Thunderbolt escort could be seen directly ahead. There were few B-17s for the "little friends" to protect. The 390th now comprised a pitiful ten bombers from the 18 that had set out, and even the survivors were not sure they would make England. *Rusty Lode*, flown by Lieutenant Robert W. Sabel, had over 750 holes in her fuselage, huge gaps in both wings, rudder, and left aileron, and both flaps shot away. The bomber had been hit badly before the target, but Sabel forced his way home through incessant fighter attacks. However, not all his crew believed that they would make it home. William L. Ellet, Sabel's ball gunner, saw three parachutes open below the aircraft. He knew they must have come from his aircraft, so he climbed out of the turret and saw both waist guns hanging limp with their gunners gone. The tail gunner had also left the aircraft. Ellet almost ran to the radio room, where he found the radio operator slumped over his gun with what looked like a 20mm cannon shell burst in his face. Ellet scrambled back to the waist door and saw a bloodstained flak suit on the floor. Then the two turret guns opened up, and he knew he was not alone after all! Sabel managed to land *Rusty Lode* at Thorpe Abbotts with only two minutes' fuel supply remaining. Engineering officers declared that the feat was nothing short of a miracle!

At Framlingham, *Miss Carry* landed on the third attempt in fog. Vance, his leg shattered by a cannon shell, remained in a propped-up position behind the pilot's seat, directing Murdock and the top turret gunner to the airfield.[377] Also at Framlingham, Lieutenant Riley brought *Norma J* in with two engines out and a wounded tail gunner, whose injuries had prevented the crew from baling out. Riley put down in thick fog in a "field or nothing try" and landed safely. Bill Cabral and Richard Perry arrived over Framlingham and decided to climb to 2000ft to give the crew of *The Eightball* a chance to bale out if the rapidly diminishing fuel supply cut out altogether. Framlingham was completely fogged in, so Cabral headed for Thorpe Abbotts, where the weather was better. He and Perry brought *The Eightball* in for a crash-landing without injury to the crew.

Despite the fog, all ten surviving aircraft in the 390th made it back to Suffolk. *Betty Boop - The Pistol Packin' Mama*, flown by Captain James R. Geary, *Rose Marie*, and *Shatzi*, flown by Harold Schuyler, all managed to put down safely. *Cabin In The Sky* also put down without incident, and Captain Robert Brown put in his gunners' claims of eleven fighters shot down. Lieutenant Robert Schneider, who was flying *Little Mike*[378] because his regular B-17, *Geronimo*, was undergoing repairs, crash-landed at RAF Wattisham in Suffolk.

Some idea of the intensity of the Münster battle can best be judged by the fighter claims submitted at debriefing. Of the 180 "kills" claimed by the 3rd Division, 105 came from the 13th Combat Wing. In return, the 390th had lost eight of its 18 aircraft dispatched, and the 95th five out of 20 dispatched. It had been a black day for the 13th Wing, which had lost 25 of the 30 B-17s shot down or written off in crashes this day. The 100th Bomb Group's loss of 12 bombers brought its total to 19 in three days, and added credence to its "Bloody Hundredth" tag.

New crews replaced those lost on the mission, and were subjected to the usual "flakking process" accorded all fresh crews at bases in the region. At Thorpe Abbotts the process was probably more poignant. A new crew arrived at the base from Diss railway station in a truck to hear, as they disembarked, shouts of "fresh meat" and "meat on the table" coming from the combat barracks. Their career with the "Bloody Hundredth" had just begun.

Pilots of 4th *Staffel*, *Jagdgeschwader* (JG) 1, at Woensdrecht in June 1942 trying to relax in deckchairs during *Bereitschaff* (readiness) alongside a FW 190A-5 of the *Staffel*, which has the unit's characteristic *Tatzelwurm* emblem on the engine cowling. *II. Gruppe* was based at the airfield in Holland beside the Belgian border from February 1942 until July 1943, and flew against the American formations almost daily, weather permitting. The four *Gruppes* in JG 1, like JG 2, JG 26, and the other fighter *Geschwaders* in the *Luftwaffe*, was generally split up, each *Gruppe* occupying different airfields in the area. In the summer of 1942 the 4th and 6th *Staffeln* were based at Woensdrecht. (via Eric Mombeek)

B-17E 41-9129, which arrived at Prestwick, Scotland, on 24 July 1942 after repairs to mend a broken tail wheel sustained in an accident at Bathurst, New Brunswick. This Fortress was assigned to the 359th Bomb Squadron, 303rd Bomb Group, forming the BOLERO weather flight, and went on to serve the 97th, 92nd, and 305th Bomb Groups in the 8th Air Force before leaving the 1st Wing in 1943. (USAF)

B-17E 41-9023 *Yankee Doodle* was first assigned to the 92nd Bomb Group at MacDill Field on 13 March 1942. On 1 May the aircraft was transferred to the 414th Bomb Squadron, 97th Bomb Group, and once in England it was one of 12 E-models that took part in the Eighth Air Force's first B-17 mission of the war, flown on 17 August 1942. Piloted by John Dowswell, it carried Brigadier General Ira C. Eaker to Rouen. Seven days later, 41-9023 returned to the 92nd Bomb Group, where it served until 31 March 1943, when it joined the Blind Approach Training Flight (BAT Flight) at Bassingbourn (Note the RAF-style camouflage). In August 41-9023 was transferred again, this time to the 322nd Bomb Squadron, 91st Bomb Group, and it ended its ETO service with the 324th Bomb Squadron as a target tow and general liaison aircraft. 41-9023 was finally salvaged on 26 July 1945. (USAF)

An American Red Cross Clubmobile (a converted British bus) serves refreshments to ground crews of the 92nd Bomb Group working on B-17E *Phyllis* 41-9020 at Bovingdon, from where it made several courier flights to North Africa late in 1942. Clubmobiles were first introduced in 1942, and were manned by Red Cross girls who dispensed cups of hot coffee, cigarettes, chewing gum, doughnuts, and newspapers free of charge. By the end of 1943 there were fifty in operation, each servicing detachments six miles or more from a club. Bicycles were an indispensable feature of base life, and they were used by air and ground crew alike to cover the vast distances between the Nissen accommodations scattered around the bases to the mess halls, briefing rooms, and dispersal sites like this one. The 97nd acted as a Combat Crew Replacement Centre for VIIIth Bomber Command and did not fly its first combat mission until 6 September 1943. *Phyllis* had previously served in the 97th Bomb Group, and on 1 May 1943 was assigned to the 303rd Bomb Group at Molesworth. Some 512 B-17Es were built before large-scale production of the famous Fortress really started with the B-17E, which could be distinguished from the B 17E by its molded Plexiglas nose. (USAF)

P-47C Thunderbolt *Leaky Joe* at Bassingbourn. At the end of 1942 the P-47 was the only readily available American produced high performance fighter. 200 were sent to Britain in December 1942 and January 1943. (USAF)

Colonel Beirne Lay, Jr. (USAF)

Lockheed P-38 Lightning. Range was not something that had influenced the equipment of fighter units destined for the ETO because it was thought that operations would be similar to those undertaken by RAF fighters, where high-altitude performance seemed to be the important factor. Early American fighters such as the P-40, P-39, and the early Allison-powered P-51 were not more appreciated in the ETO, where most combats took place at higher altitudes. Some pilots never understood why the Allisons were not retrofitted with two-stage blowers, or even turbo-superchargers, as was done with the P-38. But airspeed alone was not the deciding element that it has often been pictured to be. It was not long since "experts" had believed that high-performance fighters would consign "dog-fighting" to the history books, but the old adage, "It isn't the size of the dog in the fight that counts; it's the size of the fight in the dog" was as true as it ever was. The 1st and 14th Fighter Groups were originally assigned to VIIIth Fighter Command, but were reassigned to the 12th Air Force in September, while the 20th Fighter Group, which flew its first combat mission from King's Cliffe, Northamptonshire, on 28 December 1943 converted to P-51 Mustangs in July 1944. The 55th Fighter Group flew its first combat mission from Nuthampstead on 15 October 1943, also converting to the Mustang in July 1944. The 78th Fighter Group flew P-38Gs from December 1942 until February 1943, when it converted to P-47C Thunderbolts. (USAF)

The 4th Fighter Group at Debden dispatched its P-47C Thunderbolts on their first combat mission on 2 October 1942, and the 56th Fighter Group flew its first mission from King's Cliffe on 13 April 1943. (USAF)

Bombs exploding at La Pallice, one of the many U-boat lairs on the French Atlantic coast. (USAF)

General Ira C. Eaker, Commanding General, U.S. 8th Air Force. (USAF)

The crew of B-17F-10-BO 41-24444 *The Red Gremlin* in the 340th Bomb Squadron, 97th Bomb Group, face the camera for a group photograph on 9 September 1942. "Their" bomber had been delivered to the 97th Bomb Group on 2 July 1942, having been flown to England by Lieutenant Charles N. Austin. It was renamed *Superman* when it was assigned to the 92nd Bomb Group on 24 August. Seen in the back row, from left to right, are Major Paul W Tibbets, Ryan, Tom W Ferebee, "Dutch" Van Kirk, Hughes, and Splitt. In the front row, again from left to right, are Peach, Quate, Fitzgerald, Gowan, and Fittsworth. On 17 August 1942 Tibbets flew 41-2578 *Butcher Shop* with the men of Lieutenant Butcher's crew to lead the first Fortress raid of the war with his CO, Colonel Frank A. Armstrong, Jr. Three years later Tibbets, his bombardier Tom Ferebee, and navigator "Dutch" Van Kirk flew in the same positions in B-29 *Enola Gay* on the first atomic bomb drop on Hiroshima, Japan, on 6 August 1945. 41-24444 returned to the U.S. in July 1944, and it was salvaged on 19 June 1946. (Paul Tibbets Collection)

Josef "Pips" Priller, *Kommodore Jagdgeschwader 26.* *(Bundersarchiv)*

Enlisted members in Lieutenant John H. Murphy's crew in *Shoot Luke* in the 328th Bomb Squadron, 93rd Bomb Group, at Hardwick preparing to go on leave. (USAF)

Oberleutnant Otto Stammberger, *Kapitaen* of the 4th *Staffel, JG1* from 26 February 1943 until he was seriously wounded by 331 Royal Norwegian Squadron Spitfires on 13 May 1943. (via Eric Mombeek)

The crew of *Our Gang* in the 324th Bomb Squadron, 91st Bomb Group at Bassingbourn. Far left is Sgt Jake Levine of East Nassau, Long Island, the top turret gunner. B-17F30-BO 42-5069 *Our Gang* was lost with Lieutenant William H. Wheeler's crew on the 17 August 1943 mission to Schweinfurt. (USAF)

A crewmember puts the finishing touches to B-17F-10-BO 41-24486 *Man O'War* in the 306th Bomb Group, which was lost on 9 November 1942. (USAF)

Above left: Ordnancemen in the 328th Bomb Squadron, 93rd Bomb Group attending to 1000lb bombs next to B-24D-1-CO 41-23737 *Eager Beaver* at Alconbury late in 1942. This Liberator was transferred to the 446th Bomb Group on 24 February 1944, and it was renamed *Fearless Freddie*. (USAF) Above right: Captain Adrian Poletti, group Roman Catholic chaplain, leads the crew of 1st Lieutenant Edward J. Hennessy, Jr., in the 368th Bomb Squadron, 306th Bomb Group, in prayer in front of B-17F-25-BO 41-24560 *Little Audrey* at Thurleigh. Captain Hennessy finished his tour on 29 June 1943 when the 306th Bomb Group flew their 50th mission. *Little Audrey* transferred to the 544th Bomb Squadron, 384th Bomb Group on 5 September 1943 and returned to the ZOI in June 1944. (USAF)

Aircrew in the 306th Bomb Group returning after a mission. (USAF)

B-17F-20-BO 41-24539 *Jersey Bounce* in the 358th Bomb Squadron, 303rd Bomb Group at Molesworth after returning from Rouen-Sotteville with a cannon shell in the fuselage on 12 December 1942. Three months later, on 18 March 1943 *Jersey Bounce* had two engines and a tire shot out over Vegesack but still managed to return safely. The Fortress had been assigned overseas on 16 September 1942 passed to the CCRC at Bovingdon on 27 July 1943. (USAF)

Colonel (later General) Curtis E. LeMay, CO of the 305th Bomb Group from 4 June 1942-15 May 1943. (USAF)

1st Lieutenant Curtis Burgan's crew and B-17F-27-BO 41-24624 *Madame Betterfly* in the 366th Bomb Squadron, 305th Bomb Group at Chelveston on 22 November 1942. L-R Standing: 2nd Lieutenant Charles K. Woodworth, bombardier (MIA 19.5.43, Kiel with Charles D. Clark crew PoW); 2nd Lieutenant Roger F. Moran, navigator (25 missions, returned to USA 3.8.43); 2nd Lieutenant Lawrence I. Leach, co-pilot (KIA 16.4.43); 1st Lieutenant Curtis A. Burgan, pilot (25 missions, returned to USA). L-R Kneeling: S/Sgt John T. Kuntz, engineer (25 missions, returned to USA June 1943); S/Sgt Stanley L. Farnsworth, tail gunner; Corporal Robert Ames, gunner (KIA 7.1.43 with Vance W. Beckham crew); S/Sgt Darrel W. Coats, gunner (MIA 26.2.43 with Everett E. Tribbet crew PoW); T/Sgt Frank J. Brinski, radio (25 missions, returned to USA June 1943); S/Sgt William A. Ford, waist gunner (MIA 26.2.43 with Everett E. Tribbet crew. PoW) On 19 May 1943 Captain Charles D. Clark's crew ditched in the North Sea after *Madame Betterfly* was hit by flak on the mission to Kiel. Three men perished, and seven were picked up and taken prisoner. On 26 October 1942 Clark's crew had been forced to ditch B-17F-30-BO 42-5059 *Hell's Angels* in the Atlantic off Nova Scotia, when all ten crewmembers were rescued. B-17F-27-BO 41-24592 became the second *Madame Betterfly*, and on 6 September 1943 this Fortress and 2nd Lieutenant Floyd E. McSpadden's crew landed at Dubendorf, Switzerland, out of fuel following the mission to Stuttgart. (via Bill Donald)

B-17F-27-BO 41-24606 *Werewolf*, which was assigned overseas on 18 September 1942 and was allocated to the 358th Bomb Squadron, 303rd Bomb Group. The aircraft had three engines shot out over France on 13 January 1943, but Lieutenant G. J. Oxrider got the Fortress back to England, and the plane landed in a field near Dawlish. A repair unit replaced all four engines and built an emergency strip for the aircraft, and it was flown out. *Werewolf* was later transferred to the 401st Bomb Squadron, 91st Bomb Group and finished its wartime career in 43 CCRC. (USAF)

A line-up of three B-17Fs in the 423rd Bomb Squadron, 306th Bomb Group at Thurleigh. B-17F-5-VE 42-5717 (center), the first Lockheed Vega-built B-17E, was lost on the mission to St. Nazaire on 16 February 1943 when 1st Lieutenant William H. Warner's crew were shot down. B-17F-40-BO 42-5180 (left) was lost on the 25 June 1943 mission to a target of opportunity at Bremen, when Lieutenant Thomas E. Logan's crew failed to return. B-17F-10-BO 41-24460 was transferred to the 482nd Bomb Group on 22 September 1943. (Richards Collection)

Above left: B-17F *Dry Martini & The Cocktail Kids* in the 364th Bomb Squadron, 305th Bomb Group with Captain Allen V. Martini (left). Center is Ed Kursel, a guy with an infectious smile. This aircraft was the second *Dry Martini & The Cocktail Kids*, the first (42-5057) being lost with Lieutenant Ronald N. Dahley's crew on the mission to Stuttgart on 6 September 1943 when it was ditched in the Channel (1 KIA. 7 PoW). (via Bill Donald) Above right: Bombs hurtle down on Lorient. (via Bill Donald)

Left: Major (later Lieutenant Colonel) James T. Posey, a West Pointer from Henderson, Kentucky, who flew with 1st Lieutenant James E. O'Brien on the 8 March mission. Posey led 21 B-24Ds in the 44th Bomb Group on the low level mission against the Ploesti oilfields in Rumania on 1 August, and he assumed command of the Eightballs on 3 September 1943. (Bill Cameron Coll) Right: A tired and haggard Captain Harold Stouse in the 427th Bomb Squadron, 303rd Bomb Group, who piloted B-17F-27-BO 41-24635 *The Eightball* to Wilhelmshaven on 27 January 1943, the first time the 8th Air Force bombed a German target, fills out his flight report after the mission. On 18 March Stouse flew B-17F-25-BO 41-24561 *The Duchess* home to Molesworth with the body of 1st Lieutenant Jack Mathis, the lead bombardier, on board. Mathis was awarded a posthumous Medal of Honor (the first awarded to an 8th Air Force crewmember) for his actions this day on the mission to Vegesack. *The Duchess* was returned to the ZOI by 1BAD on 6 June 1944. (USAF)

Lieutenant Cornelius A. Jenkins and the crew of B-17F-27-BO 41-24593 *El Lobo* (Spanish for Mr. Wolf) in the 364th Bomb Squadron, 305th Bomb Group, which on 4 February 1943 was hit by a FW 190 and both aircraft crashed. Six of the Fortress crew were killed, and the four others survived—they were taken prisoner. Standing L-R: Vincent Cook, tail gunner (PoW); Glenn Shaljean, bombardier (PoW); Leigh Monson, navigator (KIA); Andy Kerr, co-pilot (KIA); and Lieutenant Cornelius "Neil" Jenkins, pilot (KIA). Front Row: Albert R. Moline, engineer (KIA); Charles F. Jackson, waist gunner (PoW); T/Sgt Coy D. Martin, radio operator (PoW); Morris L. Tauber, waist gunner (KIA); and Dominic de Matto, ball turret gunner (KIA). (via Bill Donald)

Above left: 1st Lieutenant Hugh Ashcraft and his crew in front of B-17F-27-BO 41-24617 *Southern Comfort* at Chelveston. Standing L-R: William "Bill" Lakey, co-pilot; Jim Moberly, navigator; Lieutenant Hugh Ashcraft, pilot; Bert Wells, bombardier; and T/Sgt James N. "Jim" Patterson, waist gunner. Kneeling: S/Sgt Steve L. Gogoyla, engineer-top turret gunner (Killed 31 March 1943); T/Sgt Douglas C. Glover, radio operator; S/Sgt Frank M. Hilsabeck, tail gunner; S/Sgt Ray W. Armstrong, ball turret; and S/Sgt Frank M. Corser, waist gunner (who later underwent pilot training and was killed in the PTO). On 28 March 1943 Ashcraft brought *Southern Comfort* home after it was badly damaged in a fighter attack by *Unteroffizier* Peter Crump of 5./JG 26, who set the plane on fire between No.1 and No.2 engines. The crew abandoned the Fortress, which crashed near the village of Wickham Bishops. The only fatality among the crew was the top turret gunner, who apparently slipped out of his parachute harness as he neared the ground. (via Bill Donald) Above right: Bombs going down over Rotterdam, which was bombed by the 8th on 4 and 31 March 1943. (via Bill Donald)

Left: *Oberfeldwebel* Adolf "Addi" Glunz of 4./JG 26. On 5 April 1943 the Fortress piloted by 1st Lieutenant William H. Parker in the 306th Bomb Group was shot down at 1538 hours by Glunz, who claimed it as his 32nd of his eventual 72 victory tally. On 17 August 1943 Glunz shot down B-17F-25-BO 41-24564 *Patches* and 2nd Lieutenant Douglas L. Mutchler's crew in the 365th Bomb Squadron, 305th Bomb Group NW of Diest. (via Bill Donald) Right: Bf 110 pilots of NJG 1 submitted claims for three B-17s destroyed NW of Ameland on 4 February 1943. *Hauptmann* Hans-Joachim Jabs, *Oberfeldwebel* Heinz Grimm (pictured), and *Unteroffizier* Alfred Naumann were the claimants. All seven Bf 110s participating were either shot down or heavily damaged by return fire. *Leutnant* Heinz Grimm of IV./NJG 1 died on 13 October 1943 from wounds sustained over Bremen from his own flak defenses. He was awarded the *RitterKreuz* (*RK*, or Knight's Cross) posthumously on 5 February 1944 for his 26 night kills and the B-17 on 4 February 1943. (Ab A. Jansen)

Below: The tail unit of B-17F-25-BO-25-BO 41-24569 *Memphis Tot* in the 427th Bomb Squadron, 303rd Bomb Group, which was shot down by fighters of IV/NJG 1 on 4 February 1943. The Fortress, which was flown by Captain Lloyd R. Cole, crashed 8km northeast of Den Helder in the Waddensee at 1117 hours. Four of the crew were killed, while six survived to be taken prisoner. (Rob de Visser Collection via Theo Boiten)

Bf 110 nightfighter of IV/NJG1 that crashed on the beach at Ameland on 4 February 1943. (Ab A. Jansen)

Hauptmann Hans-Joachim Jabs, a seasoned combat veteran who had his first taste of action during the Battles of France, and who quickly became one of Germany's leading fighter pilots. The first use of night fighters of NJG 1 against American formations took place on 4 February 1943 when Jabs led eight Bf 110s of IV./NJG 1 into action against the American combat boxes. Jabs survived the war with 50 (28 night and 22 day) victories. (via Theo Boiten)

The "Eightballs" taxi out from their muddy dispersals at Shipdham. B-24D-5-CO 41-23818 *Texan II* in the unlucky 67th Bomb Squadron was lost in a mid-air collision with B-24D-53-CO 42-40354 *SNAFU* flown by Lieutenant Fred M. Billings, Jr., shortly after leaving the coast of England on 16 February 1943 when the target was St. Nazaire. Both aircraft were engulfed in flames, and seconds after impact both exploded, scattering debris even as far as the Fortress formation flying below them. All ten men in Lieutenant John B. Long's crew were killed, while one man survived from Billings' aircraft. (USAF)

Unteroffizier Heinz Hanke (right) of 9./JG1 waits beside his Focke Wulf 190A-4 as a victory symbol is added for a Liberator he claimed shot down on 26 February 1943. In fact, his "victim" *Night Raider*, a 93rd Bomb Group Liberator flown by Captain Beattie H. "Bud" Fleenor, limped back to England to crash-land at Ludham, Norfolk, with a badly wounded crew. Hanke shot down *Ain't Mis Behavin'* in the Bloody Hundredth on 20 February 1944. (via Eric Mombeek)

B-17F-27-BO 41-24639 *The Careful Virgin*, which reached the 323rd Bomb Squadron, 91st Bomb Group at Bassingbourn on 29 January 1943 after a crash landing in the USA late in 1942 that had delayed its assignment overseas. The Bassingbourn group, affectionately known as "Wray's Wragged Irregulars" after its CO, Colonel Stanley T. Wray, had flown its first mission on 7 November 1942. *The Careful Virgin* later transferred to AFSC for *Aphrodite* drone missions on 7 May 1944, and it was destroyed on the *Aphrodite* mission of 4 August 1944 when it was aimed at a V-weapon site at Mimoyecques. (USAF)

On 15 February 1943 21 44th Bomb Group B-24D Liberators attacked Dunkirk. (The "Flying Eightballs" had arrived in Norfolk from Cheddington early in October 1942, and flew their first mission one month after the 93rd, on 7 November.) Their target was the *Togo*, a German fighter-control ship. Their long, straight run had enabled the German gunners to determine their speed and height. Flak enveloped the formation, and just as the bomb-release light came on, the lead aircraft, B-24D-5-CO 41-23783 *Betty Anne*, which was piloted by Captain Art V. Cullen with Major Donald W. MacDonald, 67th Squadron CO, took a direct hit. It knocked the roof off the cabin and blew the cowlings off No.2 and 3 engines, which were smoking. For a few moments the noseless bomber flew on, only to fall away to starboard with the port inboard engine aflame and the right inboard ripped from its mounting. Finally, the starboard wing fell off and a huge explosion scattered debris among the formation, hitting another Liberator whose pilot managed to recross the Channel and force-land at Sandwich. MacDonald died later in a German hospital and Cullen, who was captured, was repatriated in September 1944. (USAF)

22-year old *Leutnant* Heinz Knoke of I./JG1 at Jever-Wangerooge. By late 1944 he had scored 44 victories in the west. On 9 October 1944, while travelling by road convoy from Austria via Prague, Dresden, and Berlin to a new base at Anklam, in North Germany, his Volkswagen was blown up when it ran over a mine in the road in Czechoslovakia and his left knee and right pelvis were shattered. He only just managed to avoid having his leg amputated, but his career as a pilot was over. He was awarded the *Ritterkreuz* on 27 April 1945. (via Eric Mombeek)

Above left: *Hauptmann* Ludwig Becker, *Staffelkapitän* 12./NJG1, a great night fighting tactician and the top-scoring *Nachtjagd Experte*. It was believed that the heavily armed Bf 110 night fighters would bolster the day fighter arm and prove effective against American day bombers. Becker failed to return from a daylight sortie against American bombers on 26 February 1943. (Theo Boiten via Rob de Visser) Center: Captain Howard E. Adams, pilot of B-24D-5-CO 41-23777 *Maisie* in the 66th Bomb Squadron, 44th Bomb Group, was killed when his Liberator was shot down on 26 February 1943 by *Leutnant* Heinz Knoke of I./JG. Only two men survived aboard the Liberator. Among the dead was Robert Perkins Post, a *New York Times* war correspondent, the only one of seven in the "Writing 69th" who asked to fly with the 44th Bomb Group that day. (via Steve Adams/via Eric Mombeek) Above right: Robert Perkins Post, the *New York Times* war correspondent who was among those killed aboard B-24D-5-CO 41-23777 *Maisie* in the 66th Bomb Squadron, 44th Bomb Group, which was shot down on 26 February 1943. (Hamilton)

B-17F-40-BO 42-5225 *Stormy Weather* in the 323rd Bomb Squadron, 91st Bomb Group, survived an encounter with German fighters on 4 March 1943, but returned to Bassingbourn with one engine on fire and overshot the runway. The aircraft was repaired and flew again, being renamed *V-Packette* in July 1943, only to be lost on the first Schweinfurt raid on 17 August 1943, when it was flown by 2nd Lieutenant Don Van Der Heyde. (USAF)

Above left: B-17F-27-BO 41-24614 *We The People*, in the 422nd Bomb Squadron, 305th Bomb Group at Chelveston with the pilot, Captain Cliff Pyle, far right. Crew L-R: Sgt Harold J. Fedora, radio operator (PoW 14.7.43); S/Sgt Arthur Laskowski, tail gunner; T/Sgt Vernon D. Myrin, engineer; S/Sgt Edgar S. Nichols, ball turret; S/Sgt Henry J. Skoufols, right waist; S/Sgt Joseph F. Devine, left waist (KIA on *Windy City Challenger* 14.7.43); 2nd Lieutenant John B. Mulvana, navigator; 2nd Lieutenant Russell K. Weller, bombardier; 2nd Lieutenant Fred R. Gilbert, co-pilot; and 1st Lieutenant Cliff Pyle. In more than thirty missions it never carried exactly the same crew twice, and no crewman was ever wounded. On 8 September 1943 *We The People* led the first 8th Air Force night-bombing mission of the war. *We The People* returned to the ZOI on 31 May 1945. (Cliff Pyle) Above right: Immediately after taking off from Deelen airfield on 11 March 1943, *Leutnant* Eberhard Burath's FW 190A-4 145555 of IV./JG1 crashed, most probably as a result of sabotage to his aircraft, which suffered 60% damage. (Eberhard Burath via Rob de Visser)

The crew of B-17F-10-DL 42-3002 *The Old Squaw*, which joined the 359th Bomb Squadron, 303rd Bomb Group at Molesworth on 8 April 1943, the day that Lieutenant (later Captain) Claude W. Campbell's crew made their first training flight. Back Row L-R: Claude Campbell, Miller, Ririe, and William A. Boutelle, bombardier. Kneeling L-R: Howard E. Hernan, top turret gunner; Wilson; Quick; Kraft; and Backert. *The Old Squaw* was lost on 6 September 1943 when it was ditched in the North Sea. Lieutenant Robert J. Hullar and crew were rescued. (Howard Hernan)

Left: Lieutenant (later Captain) Claude W. Campbell, pilot of *The Old Squaw* in the 359th Bomb Squadron, 303rd Bomb Group at Molesworth. (Howard Hernan) Right: Traditional "smoking" of the ceiling of the 306th Bomb Group Officers' Club at Thurleigh with missions. Major Harry Holt, CO 367th Bomb Squadron until 4 March 1943 (left); Captain John L. Ryan (with candle); Captain John L. Lambert, 367th Bomb Squadron, later CO 423rd Bomb Squadron; and Captain George Buckey, 367th Bomb Squadron CO, 19 August 1943-2 May 1944, lend support. Ryan took command of the 367th on 5 March, and he was shot down the next day. He evaded and returned to England after 42 days. This scene was used later in the famous movie *Twelve O'Clock High*. The 367th Bomb Squadron, which suffered the heaviest losses in 8th Bomber Command during October 1942-August 1943, was nicknamed "The Clay Pigeons." (Richards Collection)

B-17F-20-BO 41-24504 *The Sad Sack*, one of the original Fortresses assigned to the 91st Bomb Group. Along with sister aircraft 41-24505 *Quitchurbitchin*, *Sad Sack* was the longest-serving of the Bassingbourn group's original Forts. Both were among the first ten 8th Bomber Command B-17Fs to be returned Stateside on 15 March 1943 for training duties. (USAF)

Lord Trenchard, the "Father of the RAF," looks over a 93rd Bomb Group B-24D at Hardwick on 6 April 1943. In the background is Colonel Ted Timberlake, the CO. (USAF)

B-24D-10-CO 41-23874 *Ball of Fire Jr* in the 328th Bomb Squadron, 93rd Bomb Group in North Africa. This aircraft and Lieutenant Franklin D. Lown's crew FTR on 16 April 1943 when it crashed at St. Revan, France. (Pieter Bergman)

Above left: Captain Pervis E. Youree, 423rd Bomb Squadron, 306th Bomb Group pilot. On the 17 April 1943 mission to the Focke Wulf plant at Bremen, when the 306th Bomb Group lost ten B-17s, Youree brought *Old Faithful* home 200 miles at wave top height after fighters put out two engines and shot the aircraft almost to pieces, and he crash-landed at RAF Coltishall, Norfolk. Youree completed his combat tour on 29 June 1943, the Thurleigh group's 50th mission. (Richards) Above right: *Oberleutnant* Rolf S'trohall (of Rumanian origin), T/Officer of *GruppenStab* I./JG 1 (formerly *IV. Gruppe*), relaxes on the wing of his FW 190A-5 at Deelen airfield in April 1943. The black and white stripes painted on the engine cowling (and a chevron and circle in front of the fuselage) were applied to the *Stab* Flight's FW 190s for a short period during the spring of 1943. (Eberhard Burath, via Rob de Visser)

Above left: Deelen airfield, April 1943. Left is the FW 190A-5 carrying the double chevron of *Hauptmann* Fritz Losigkeit, *Gruppenkommandeur* of I./JG 1. In the background is the Ops tent, which was erected near the aircraft on the orders of *Hauptmann* Hans Philipp when he took command of JG 1 on 1 April 1943. At the end of May 1943 Losigkeit handed over command to *Hauptmann* Schnoor. (Eberhard Burath via Rob de Visser) Above right: A *Schwarzemänner* fastens the engine cover of a FW 190A of 10./JG1 at Deelen airfield, probably in mid-1943. Note the IV./JG 1 emblem of a devil rising over the clouds, which was adopted by the *Gruppe* during spring 1943. (Haspel via Rob de Visser)

A USAAF pilot tries the cockpit of a P-47C Thunderbolt for size. (USAF)

Contrary to popular belief, *Memphis Belle* was not the first heavy bomber to complete an 8th Air Force tour of 25 missions. This honor went to B-17F-25-BO 41-24577 *Hell's Angels* in the 358th Bomb Squadron, 303rd Bomb Group, which completed 25 missions between 16 October 1942 and 14 May 1943. When, in 1942 Captain Irl E. Baldwin and his crew had picked up 41-24577,. a new Boeing built B-17F from the United Airlines modification center in Cheyenne, Wyoming, he had proposed the name Yakima Queen, after his hometown in Washington state. The crew were not enthusiastic about the name, and on or about their fourth mission Baldwin called the crew on the aircraft's intercom and asked, "How about Hell's Angels" (after the World War I movie)? Baldwin had been deeply impressed by the movie and "Lilac Time." The entire crew agreed. "Hell's Angels" and the crew must have had charmed lives. When they finished their 25 missions, the 303rd Bomb Group had only eight of the original 35 crews and B-17s left. In June 1943, when Baldwin was awaiting orders returning him to the USA, he was invited to a party at the Bovingdon Officers club. There he met Ben Lyons, who was assigned to the BBC in London. Lyons asked Baldwin how it was that he happened to name his plane "Hell's Angels." Baldwin relayed the story to him, at which point he said "did you know that I was the leading man in that picture?" Feeling somewhat embarrassed, Baldwin said, "I guess I was too young to remember." Ben Lyons then asked if he remembered the leading lady Jean Harlow? Baldwin said "I think I remember her." *Hell's Angels*, which completed 48 missions on 19 May 1943, all without an abort, was autographed by hundreds of members of the 303rd Bomb Group at Molesworth early in 1944 and flown Stateside. Once back home Captain Irl Baldwin joined the plane for a tour of industrial war plants. *Hell's Angels* was broken up for scrap at Searcey Field, Stillwater, Oklahoma, in August 1945. (USAF)

B-17F-35-VE 42-5910 was assigned overseas in June 1943, and as *Hell-Cat* it joined the 365th Bomb Squadron, 305th Bomb Group at Chelveston. *Hell-Cat* was badly damaged on the raid on Romilly on 15 September 1943 and crash-landed at RAF Hawkinge with no injuries to the crew. The aircraft was scrapped. (via Bill Donald)

Above left: Major General George E. Stratemeyer talks with 44th Bomb Group CO, Colonel Leon Johnson, a 39-year old West Pointer (center), and Major Howard "Pappy" Moore and Lieutenant Bob Brown in the 67th Bomb Squadron by the nose of B-24D-5-CO 41-23817 *Suzy Q* at Shipdham on 21 April 1943. In the background is B-24D-25-CO 41-24278 *Miss Delores*, which FTR with Lieutenant "Bob" Brown and his crew on the disastrous mission to Kiel on 14 May 1943. Brown was among the survivors who became PoWs. Johnson, who led the "Flying Eightballs" in *Suzy Q* on the low-level mission on 1 August 1943 to "White V" Columbia Aquila at Ploesti, was awarded the Medal of Honor for his leadership on the raid. The medal was presented to him in a ceremony at Shipdham on 22 November 1943, by which time he commanded the 14th Combat Bombardment Wing. (USAF) Above right: S/Sgt Maynard "Snuffy" Smith MoH, 306th Bomb Group, May 1943. On 1 May Lieutenant Lewis P. Johnson, Jr.'s aircraft was hit several times, and it caught fire in the radio compartment and in the tail area. Smith, the ball turret gunner, who was on his first mission, hand-cranked his turret to get it back into the aircraft. He climbed out and discovered that the waist gunners and the radio operator had baled out. Smith remained in the aircraft and fought the fire with a hand extinguisher. The Fortress did not show any signs of leaving formation, so Smith assumed the pilots were still on board and went to treat the badly wounded tail gunner. Then he jettisoned the oxygen bottles and ammunition in the radio compartment, and manned the waist guns during an attack by enemy fighters, stopping to dampen down the fires and treat the tail gunner. Johnson put the B-17 down at Predannack, near Land's End, after Smith had thrown out all expendable equipment. He was the first Enlisted man to receive the Medal of Honor. (USAF)

On 13 May 1943 Brigadier General Hayward "Possum" Hansell, the 1st Wing CO, flew with Captain Allen V. Martini's crew in *Dry Martini 4th & The Cocktail Kids* in the 364th Bomb Squadron, 305th Bomb Group to Meaulte, France. Waiting for them on their return was Colonel Curtis E. LeMay. (via Bill Donald)

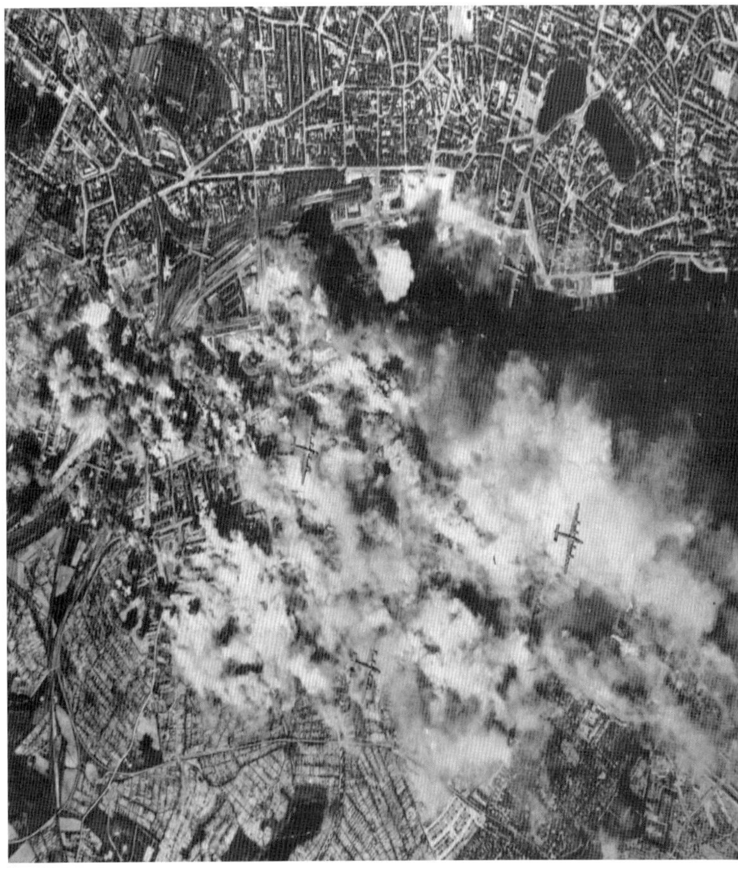

B-24Ds over Kiel, 14 May 1943. The B-l7 groups at last got their wish—they flew behind and above the B-24s for the first time in the European Theater of Operations. This resulted in heavy losses for the Liberators. The 44th's cargo of incendiaries had required a shorter trajectory and a two-mile longer bomb run than the B-17s. Flying a scattered formation, the B-24s were exposed to fighter attack. Altogether five Liberators were lost, including three in the 67th Bomb Squadron, which brought up the rear of the formation. The first to go down was Lieutenant William Roach and his replacement crew flying in B-24D-30-CO 42-40126 *Annie Oakley*. There were only two survivors. The 44th Bomb Group was awarded a Distinguished Unit Citation for its part in the Kiel raid, the first made to an 8th Air Force Group. (USAF)

Left: Captain Chester "George" Phillips (middle), a pilot in the 67th Bomb Squadron, 44th Bomb Group at Shipdham, died in one of three explosions which rocked B-24D-5-CO 41-23807 *Little Beaver* after leaving the target at Kiel on 14 May 1943. (Bill Cameron Collection)

Left: Major Jim O'Brien, 66th Bomb Squadron, 44th Bomb Group CO, who was shot down at Kiel on 14 May 1943 piloting B-24D-5-C0 41-23819 *The Rugged Buggy*. He spent the rest of the war as a PoW in *Stalag Luft III*. (O'Brien) Right: B-24D-25-CO 41-24278 *Miss Delores* in the 67th Bomb Squadron, 44th Bomb Group, which FTR with Lieutenant "Bob" Brown and his crew on the disastrous mission to Kiel on 14 May 1943. (Bill Cameron Coll)

B-24D-5-C0 41-23819 *The Rugged Buggy* in the 68th Bomb Squadron, 44th Bomb Group was one of six Liberators that FTR from the raid on Kiel. Lieutenant Mac Howell, the pilot, was killed. Sgt Van Owen was drowned in Kiel Bay despite wearing a Mae West. Major James E. O'Brien, the newly appointed squadron CO, and the surviving members of the crew were taken prisoners of war. After the raid there was serious talk of sending home all flying men who had completed 15 missions. However, their experience was considered vital, and they remained on active service. (USAF)

B-24D-5-CO 41-23807 *Little Beaver*. (Bill Cameron Collection)

Flak damage to B-24D 41-24009 *Margaret Ann* in the 68th Bomb Squadron, 44th Bomb Group, which Lieutenant George R. Jansen flew on the Kiel raid on 14 May 1943. The damage was repaired, and the Liberator was then transferred to the MTO on 15 October 1943. (Bill Cameron Coll)

Antwerp docks, which were bombed on 4 and 14 May 1943. (via Bill Donald)

Old Bill was the creation of British artist and *Stars and Stripes* cartoonist Bruce Bairnsfather (holding a brush for the benefit of the cameraman), who painted the nose of B-17F-65-BO 42-29673 in the 365th Bomb Squadron, 305th Bomb Group with a rendition of the World War I soldier. Bairnsfather was also responsible for several marvellous murals at Chelveston. (via Bill Donald)

B-17F *Turd Burd* in the 305th Bomb Group. (via Bill Donald)

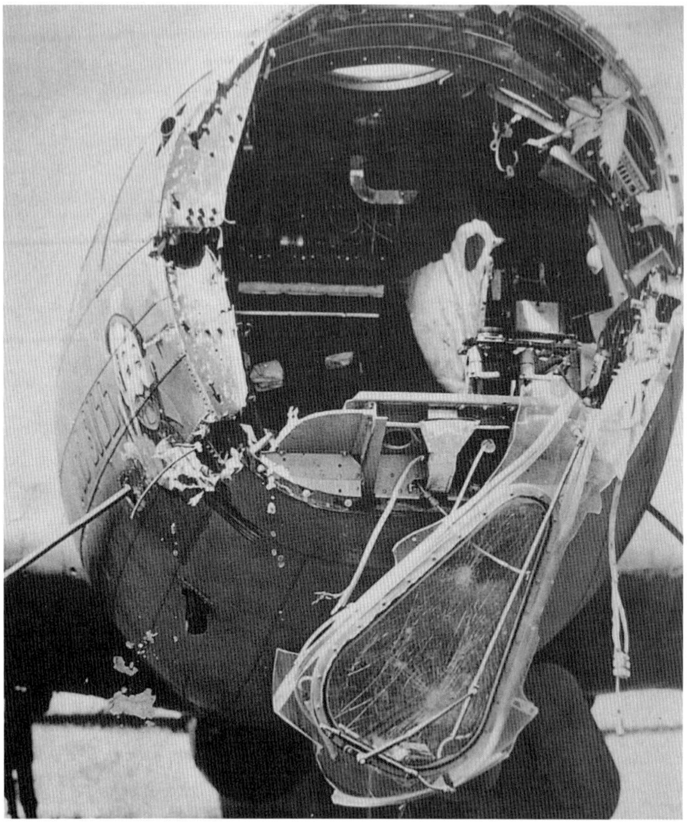

B-17F-65-BO 42-29673 *Old Bill* in the 365th Bomb Squadron, 305th Bomb Group in the aftermath of the raid of 15 May 1943 after pilot 1st Lieutenant William Whitson, helped by gunner Albert Haymon and bombardier 1st Lieutenant Robert W. Barrall, returned to Chelveston when 20mm cannon fire from fighters over Heligoland had riddled the Fortress and shot out the Plexiglas nose, killing navigator 2nd Lieutenant Douglas van Able and injuring Barrall. Whitson and Barrall were each awarded the DSC, and the rest of the eleven-man crew (which included a photographer) received eight Silver Stars and seven Purple Hearts. (via Bill Donald)

Hauptmann Dietrich Wickop, II.*Gruppe Kommandeur* JG 1, who was KIA on 16 May 1943 following combat with P-47 Thunderbolts. Wickop had thirteen victories, including three B-17s. (via Eric Mombeek)

Although B-17F-10-BO 41-24485 *Memphis Belle* in the 324th Bomb Squadron, 91st Bomb Group at Bassingbourn, was not the first Fortress in the ETO to achieve 25 missions, it nonetheless served Hollywood and the Army Air Forces' publicity machine well. After the *Belle's* 25th mission, to Lorient on 17 May 1943, she returned to the USA to begin a War Bond Tour. The movie made famous by the Fortress was first shown in April 1944. (USAF)

M/Sgt Joseph H. Giambrone paints the 25th bomb mission symbol on the nose of the *Memphis Belle* in the 324th Bomb Squadron, 91st Bomb Group at Bassingbourn after the *Belle's* 25th mission, to Lorient, on 17 May 1943. Although the *Belle* was not the first Fortress to achieve 25 missions, it nonetheless served Hollywood and the Army Air Forces' publicity machine well. Captain Robert K. Morgan, pilot of all 25 missions in this aircraft, is far right. His girlfriend, Miss Margaret Polk of Memphis, Tennessee, was the inspiration for the name. (USAF)

Pilots of 12./JG 1 at Mönchengladbach, October 1942. From left: *Unteroffizier* Anton-Rudolf "Toni" Piffer; *Hptfw* Werth; *Leutnant* Eberhard Burath; and *Leutnant* Hans Munz (KIA 21 May 1943). (Eberhard Burath via Rob de Visser)

B-17F-30-VE 42-5864 *Piccadilly Lily* in the 351st Bomb Squadron, 100th Bomb Group, which was flown to England in May-June 1943 by Lieutenant Thomas Murphy and his crew. *Piccadilly Lily* flew on the Group's first operational flight on 21 June when the Hundredth flew a diversionary mission. The ground crew later added a duck motif to denote the decoy mission, and the first combat mission followed on 25 June. Beirne Lay, Jr., flew in the co-pilot's seat aboard *Piccadilly Lily* beside Murphy on the Regensburg mission on 17 August 1943, and post-war Lay immortalised the aircraft in his book *Twelve o'Clock High*. (TAMM)

B-17F-1-BO 41-24341 was modified as an escort aircraft by Vega, and became known as the XB-40 (pictured at Burbank on the occasion of its first flight, 10 November 1942). XB-40s made their operational debut on 29 May 1943, when seven in the 92nd Bomb Group took part on a mission for the first time. Losses were not made good, although the YB-40s continued flying missions until the end of July 1943. Vega received no order for its proposed V-140 production version, and Douglas modified twenty Vega-built B-17Fs as YB-40s service-test models. (Boeing)

Left: *Leutnant* Eugen Wintergerst of 9th *Staffel* JG 1 is carried aloft in triumph after landing on 11 June 1943 when he shot down a B-17. Wintergerst was KIA in combat with Spitfires over Bergues, France, on 4 September 1943 when his Bf 109G-6 "Yellow 1" was shot down. (via Eric Mombeek) Right: B-17F-95-BO 42-30248 was assigned to the 410th Bomb Squadron, 94th Bomb Group on 2 June 1943, and was named *The Southern Queen*. In August this aircraft joined the 333rd Bomb Squadron and it was renamed *The Buzzard*, later becoming the *Prodigal Son* before finally becoming *Lassie Come Home*. 42-30248 and Lieutenant Robert C. Randall's crew FTR from the mission to Brunswick on 11 January 1944. Two of the crew were killed, and eight survived to be taken prisoner. (USAF via Geoff Ward)

Officers and enlisted men "sweating out the mission" at Snetterton Heath. The 96th Bomb Group were first stationed at the Norfolk B-17 base (since the war, a famous motor racing circuit) on 12 June 1943. The British vehicle in the foreground is an indication of the early help the 8th Air Force received from its British ally. Note the RAF liaison officer on the balcony of the control tower. (USAF)

Hollywood movie star Major Clark Gable poses with Lieutenant George Birdsong's crew of B-17F-30-BO 42-5077 *Delta Rebel No 2* in the 323rd Bomb Squadron, 91st Bomb Group at Bassingbourn, while shooting sequences for the documentary *Combat America*. Gable was also able to pass on hints and tips to aerial gunners on how to shoot down enemy aircraft, but when he saw the line of swastikas on the Fortress he said, "I guess I don't need to tell you guys anything more." *Delta Rebel No.2* and 2nd Lieutenant Robert W. Thompson's crew FTR on 12 August 1943 when it crashed at Bruninshausen, killing four crew. Six men were taken into captivity. (USAF)

Pilots in the 84th Fighter Squadron, 78th Fighter Group before the camera at Duxford in June 1943. Major Eugene Roberts (the CO) is second from right, front row. Gene Roberts commanded the 84th Fighter Squadron from August 1942 to 28 September 1943, and was then deputy CO of the Group until 17 December 1943. He flew 89 combat missions in the 78th Fighter Group, during which time he scored nine victories and one probable, all in P-47Cs like this one. All except two of his victories were achieved flying P-47C-5R-RE 41-6330 *Spokane Chief*. Lieutenant Colonel Roberts commanded the 364th Fighter Group, which was equipped with P-51D Mustangs, from 3 January to November 1945. (via Andy Height)

P-47C Thunderbolt 42-8626 UN-J in the 63rd Fighter Squadron, 56th Fighter Group flying off the starboard wing of a 100th Bomb Group B-17. (USAF)

Above left: B-17F-20-DL 42-3051 *Hell's Angels* in the 366th Bomb Squadron, 305th Bomb Group over the Hüls synthetic rubber plant, the most heavily defended target in the *Reich* at this time, near Recklinghausen, on the edge of the Ruhr, on 22 June 1943. B-17F30-BO 42-5059 was the first *Hell's Angels* in the 366th Bomb Squadron, but it had been ditched in the Atlantic off Nova Scotia on 26 October 1942. All ten of Captain Charles D. Clark's crew were rescued. (via Bill Donald) Above right: The Hüls force severely damaged the plant, and smoke rose as high as 17,000ft. Production was curtailed for a month, and full production was not resumed for five months after that. Sixteen B-17s were lost—ten of them shot down by 1st *Gruppe* JG 1, which also recorded eleven *Herausschusse*. Five FW 190s were damaged for no loss. *II.Gruppe* shot down one B-17. *III.Gruppe* shot down one B-17 and suffered one pilot WIA, while about ten Bf 109s were damaged in emergency landings after running out of fuel. (via Bill Donald)

B-17F-45-DL 42-3312 *Miss Sequatchiee*, which was assigned to the 570th Bomb Squadron, 390th Bomb Group on 14 June 1943. This Fortress and 2nd Lieutenant James A. Bonner's crew FTR from the mission to Huls on 22 June when it was hit by flak and crashed at Dreux, France. One crewman was KIA, and nine survived to be taken prisoner. (USAF)

B-17F-85-BO 42-30037 in the 546th Bomb Squadron, 384th Bomb Group, flown by 1st Lieutenant Lykes S. Henderson, is inspected by curious German officers after being shot down on 26 June 1943. This aircraft was an original Group B-17 assigned to the 384th in April 1943 at Sioux City, Iowa. (via Hans-Heiri Stapfer)

Right: Bombs going down on the U-boat pens at St. Nazaire on 28 June 1943 from 26,500ft. (USAF via Bill Donald)

Left: The wartime caption for this photo of Lieutenant Robert P. Bender in the 336th Bomb Squadron, 95th Bomb Group, reads: "He used up a million dollars worth of Fortresses [all named *Spook*, an unattractive girl in Bender's book] on 15 [sic] missions to German targets. Uncle Sam doesn't mind the expense because Bender has always bombed his targets, always brought his crew home alive and three times brought back enough of a B-17 to call it 'salvage.' On 12 May B-17F-65-BO 42-29704 *Spook* suffered bomb damage in the mission to Lorient but the Fortress made it back. On 17 May 1943 Bender crash-landed *Spook* at RAF Exeter returning from a mission to the U-boat pens in France and it was so badly shot up that it was salvaged. (B-17F-30-DL 42-3176 *Spook II*, which was assigned to the 336th Bomb Squadron on 21 May, joined the 527th Bomb Squadron, 379th Bomb Group at Kimbolton on 22 June and was re-named *Lady Astrid*. It went MIA with Lieutenant Johnson's crew on the 14 October 1943 mission to Schweinfurt. B-17F-30-VE 42-5882 *Spook III*, which was assigned to the 336th Bomb Squadron on 4 June 1943 was lost on 28 July with 2nd Lieutenant Francis J. Regan's crew when they ditched in the North Sea). On 28 June, low on fuel and with an engine shot out over St. Nazaire, 60 miles from England Bender ditched B-17F-95-BO 42-30286 *Spook IV* in the Channel. The crew were finally rescued by Air Sea Rescue 22 hours later. On a subsequent visit to a cinema the combat-fatigued pilot went berserk when a newsreel showed FW 190s attacking B-17s. Then on a test flight take-off in B-17F-90-BO 42-30226 *Spook #5*, Bender froze at the stick. Don Merton the co-pilot overpowered him and prevented a crash. Bender never flew #5 again (nor *Spook Six* (42-31063) that followed it in November 1943). Bender was hospitalized and returned to America, where he died of a heart attack at the age of 25. On 29 January 1944 *Spook #5* crashed on the mission on 29 January 1944 with the loss of five of 2nd Lieutenant James D. Higgins' crew. Five men survived to be taken prisoner." (USAF)

One of the most famous entertainers to visit England in wartime was undoubtedly Bob Hope, here with singer Frances Langford and Tony Romano with Sam Johnstone's crew in the 364th Bomb Squadron, 305th Bomb Group, and B-17F-95-BO 42-30242 *Pappy's Hellions* (formerly *Lal-lah-V III*) at Chelveston on 5 July 1943. L-R: Sam Johnstone, pilot; Ellsworth F. Kenyon, co-pilot; Martin Licursi, navigator; Arthur Englehardt, ball turret gunner; Frances Langford; Tony Romano (kneeling); Bob Hope; Donald Baer, engineer; Richard Lewis, waist gunner; and H. M. Bagby, tail gunner. R. L. Hutchinson, bombardier, was crawling around inside the B-17, giving "Bazooka" Bob Burns a guided tour of the aircraft. Kenyon took over his own crew, and they FTR from the mission to Schweinfurt on 14 October 1943. Radio operator Russell J. Algren was KIA. Kenyon and eight others survived to be made PoW. (USAF via Bill Donald)

Lieutenant John E. Perkins, Jr.'s crew and B-17F-20-DL 42-3049 *Windy City Challenger*, 422nd Bomb Squadron, 305th Bomb Group, after their return from the mission to Caen on 10 July 1943. The name referred to Chicago, where John Perkins and his original co-pilot, Harry Task, originated from. Originally, Perkins had been co-pilot on *Chuck Wagon*, and his two best friends were the pilot and bombardier before they finished their tour and returned Stateside. Jo Sippy, Perkins' girl in London and a former airline hostess, was a Red Cross girl at Rainbow Corner, who would accompany them on their visits to London. Perkins, whose father was English, was one of seven crew KIA on 14 July when *Windy City Challenger* was shot down. Crew, standing L-R: Lieutenant Thomas H. Seay, co-pilot (shot down and killed on a night mission 3.10.43); Charles H. Otis, navigator (PoW 14.7.43); Bernard Rensicoff, right waist gunner (pointing); Clarence W. Brauser (hands on hips, KIA 4.10.43), engineer top turret gunner; Joseph F. Devine, waist gunner (KIA 14.7.43); and Joseph C. Wendall, ball turret gunner (KIA 14.7.43). Kneeling L-R: George C. Carruthers, bombardier (PoW 14.7.43); John E. Perkins (KIA 14.7.43); Charles B. Cox, radio operator (KIA 14.7.43); George L. Friend, photographer (PoW 14.7.43); and Kenneth V. Myer, tail gunner (KIA 14.7.43). (USAF via Bill Donald)

Above left: The crew of *We The People*, 422nd Bomb Squadron, 305th Bomb Group, on their return from the mission to Caen on 10 July 1943. L-R standing: S/Sgt J. T. Strange, waist gunner; S/Sgt B. B. "Buster" Cop, waist gunner; T/Sgt Harold J. Fedora, radio operator (shot down flying on *Windy City Challenger* 14.7.43 - PoW); Major Jerald C. Price, co-pilot; 1st Lieutenant William A. Driscoll, bombardier; Captain Earl J. Aber, pilot (KIA 4.3.45); and S/Sgt James C. Millar, engineer. Front: 1st Lieutenant Arthur C. Lewis, tail gunner; S/Sgt J. W. Duntman, ball turret; and Clarence R. "Rusty" Webb, navigator. (USAF via Bill Donald) Above right: B-17F-20-DL 42-3049 *Windy City Challenger*, 422nd Bomb Squadron, 305th Bomb Group, goes down south of Paris on the mission to Villacoublay on 14 July 1943 after being raked by cannon fire from *Oberleutnant* Georg-Peter "Schorch" Eder, *Staffelkapitän*, 7./JG 2. In his combat report, 14 July 1943, Eder wrote: "We were doing about 450 km/h now and were coming down slightly, aiming for the noses of the B-17s. There were about 200 of us attacking the 200 bombers but there was also the fighter escort above them. We were going for the bombers.

Left: *Oberleutnant* Georg-Peter "Schorch" Eder, *Staffelkapitän* 12./JG 2. Eder had joined JG51 on the Channel coast in December 1940, but he did not achieve any kills. Transferred to the East for *Barbarossa*, he destroyed 10 Soviet aircraft before being badly wounded on 24 July 1941. In 1942 Eder returned to operations with 7./JG 2. Eder was shot down 17 times and wounded on 14 different occasions. On 15 March 1944, after leaving hospital after being wounded, he took command of 6./JG 1 and remained as its *Kommandeur* until 7 June 1944. Awarded the *Ritterkreuz* and transferred to JG 26, he finished the war with 78 victories, 36 of them *Viermots*. Twelve of his kills were gained flying the Me 262 jet fighter with *Kommando Nowotny* and JG 7. His war ended in hospital after being shot down by P-51 Mustangs. (Bill Donald) Right: The original crew of B-17F-65-BO 42-29717 *Mr Five By Five* in the 94th Bomb Group, some of whom were MIA in B-17F-35-DL 42-3190 when pilot Captain Kee Harrison crash-landed the aircraft in a French wheat field with its bomb load intact after being shot up on the Paris-Le Bourget mission of 14 July 1943. Standing, left to right: Staff Sergeants Jeff Davis Polk, Richard H. Lewis, Jim Curtis, Eino "Ossie" Asiala, Earl Porath, and Charlie McNemar, bombardier. Kneeling: Staff Sergeant Jack Amphlett, Captain Kee Harrison, Lieutenant Martin Stanford, and Lieutenant Robert Schaefer. Harrison was assisted by the French Underground, and barefoot, he later crossed the Pyrenees into Spain. Lewis and Ossie Asiala, also aided by the Underground, managed to evade capture until October, before being betrayed and sent to a PoW camp after some uncomfortable *Gestapo* interrogations. At *Stalag Luft VII* they were reunited with Curtis and Porath. Later, they heard that Lieutenant David H. Turner (their co-pilot), Polk, and Charlie McNemar had traveled with help from the Underground and had returned safely to England. *Mr Five By Five* was transferred to the 326th Bomb Squadron, 92nd Bomb Group on 1 August 1943, and then to the 544th Bomb Squadron, 384th Bomb Group on 13 August. *Mr Five By Five* was lost on the 25 February 1944 mission to Stuttgart when it was flown by Lieutenant Kack K. Larsen. All ten crew were taken prisoner. (Richard H. Lewis)

B-17F-35-DL 42-3190, 331st Bomb Squadron, 94th Bomb Group, which pilot Captain Kee Harrison crash-landed in a French wheat field with its bomb load intact after being shot up on the Paris-Le Bourget mission on 14 July 1943. Harrison and three others evaded and later returned safely to England. Four others were taken prisoner. (via Zden_k Hurt)

B-17F-35-DL 42-3190, 332nd Bomb Squadron, 94th Bomb Group, shot down by *Oberstleutnant* Egon Mayer, *Kommandeur* III./JG 2 on 14 July 1943. (Harry Holmes)

B-17F-65-BO 42-29670 *Thundermug*, formerly in the 333rd Bomb Squadron, 94th Bomb Group, was transferred to the 544th Bomb Squadron, 384th Bomb Group. It was one of seven in the Group that were lost on 25 July 1943 when it crashed at Hamburg. Two members of Lieutenant Kelmer J. Hall's crew were KIA, while eight were taken prisoner. (Richards)

B-17F-25-DL 42-3088 SU-G *Sugar Puss* in the 544th Bomb Squadron, 384th Bomb Group, which was one of seven lost by the Group on the mission to Hamburg on Sunday, 25 July 1943. Six of the losses were from the 544th Bomb Squadron. Four of Lieutenant Clarence R. Cristman's crew were KIA, and six survived to be taken prisoner. (USAF)

Lead navigator Lieutenant Kermit B. Cavedo in the 369th Bomb Squadron, 306th Bomb Group at Thurleigh liked the numerical connection between his Squadron and the "Fightin' 69th" Regiment of the First World War. Using a little literary lisence, he used the name "Fightin' Bitin," and applied it to the nose of B-17F-50-BO 42-5426. *Fightin' Bitin'* was one of four 306th Bomb Group B-17s lost during the raid on Kiel on 29 July 1943 when it carried 1st Lieutenant Donald R. Winter's crew, but both the name and the emblem, showing two insects sparring, were adopted by the 369th Bomb Squadron. Its sister squadron, the 367th, which had the heaviest losses in 8th Bomber Command during October 1942-August 1943, was nicknamed the "Clay Pigeons." (Richards Collection)

On 30 July 1943, near Apeldoorn, *II./JG26* attacked, sending two B-17s down in flames for the loss of three FW 190s. One of the victims was 42-3100 in the 381st Bomb Group, flown by Lieutenant Guerdon W. Humason, with Major Robert F. Post, 532nd Bomb Squadron CO, aboard, which came under attack from five FW 190s, and whose final destruction was credited to Major Wolfgang-Ferdinand Galland, II *Gruppe* CO. (USAF via Ron Mackay)

B-17F-55-BO 41-29508 *Southern Comfort Jr* in the 364th Bomb Squadron, 305th Bomb Group, which caught fire at Chelveston on 26 August 1943 during run up after an engine change, and was towed out of harm's way shortly after this picture was taken. The bomb load exploded and blew the Fortress to oblivion. (via Bill Donald)

B-17F-60-BO 42-29553 *Arkie II* in the 366th Bomb Squadron, 305th Bomb Group (which was named by Major Sydney R. Smith after his wife), was lost with 2nd Lieutenant Wright F. Gerke's crew on 12 August 1943. Eight men died and two were taken prisoner. The first *Arkie* was lost with Captain Everett E. Tribbett's crew on 26 February 1943 (via Bill Donald)

Above left: B-17F-20-BO 41-24524 *The Eagle's Wrath* in the 323rd Bomb Squadron, 91st Bomb Group at Bassingbourn, which was lost with Lieutenant Anthony G. Arcaro's crew on the 17 August 1943 mission to Schweinfurt. (USAF) Above right: Target photo of Schweinfurt under attack on 17 August 1943 taken from B-17F-75-BO 42-29870 *Big Moose* in the 305th Bomb Group flown by Don Moore. On 29 September *Big Moose* was transferred to the 545th Bomb Squadron, 384th Bomb Group, and was renamed *T.S.* Ironically, the aircraft was lost on the mission to Schweinfurt on 14 October 1943. All ten men in Lieutenant Giles F. Kauffman, Jr.'s crew survived and were taken prisoner. Ten days earlier they had been forced to ditch in the North Sea in *Ruthless*. (USAF via Bill Donald)

Above left: B-17F-30-VE 42-5867 *Alice From Dallas* in the 350th Bomb Squadron was lost with Lieutenant Roy F. Claytor's crew on the mission to Regensburg on 17 August 1943. Claytor, who was leading the second element of the low squadron, was shot down by flak bursts at 1020 hours while over eastern Belgium. The B-17 erupted in flames, and 8 men managed to bale out safely. Edward Musante's - the right waist gunner - parachute fouled the horizontal stabilizer, and he was killed when the aircraft exploded. The ball turret gunner was also killed after failing to get clear in time. For most of the crew it was only their tenth mission. . (via Michael P. Faley, 100th Bomb Group Historian) Above right: B-17F-85-BO 42-30066 *Mugwamp* in the 418th Bomb Squadron, 100th Bomb Group, seen here with Lieutenant Walter Moreno and his crew, which was flown on the Regensburg mission on 17 August 1943 by Charles Cruickshank and crew with Major John Egan in the co-pilot's seat. It survived the flight, but landed in North Africa so badly damaged that it was abandoned, but eventually it was repaired and returned to England, where it was reassigned to the 96th Bomb Group at Snetterton Heath, where it was renamed *Rum Boogie II*. It was withdrawn from combat status early in 1944 and was transferred to the 803rd (Provisional) Group at RAF Oulton, Norfolk, where it was fitted out with *Mandrel* and *Carpet* jamming equipment for use as a RCM aircraft. In July 1944 42-30066 was reassigned to Project *Aphrodite*, filled with Torpex high explosive, and on 30 October 1944 was flown from Fersfield, Norfolk, by 1st Lieutenant Barnes and his co-pilot, 1st Lieutenant McCauley, towards the U-boat pens at Heligoland. After the two pilots baled out a mother aircraft fitted with radio control guided the drone onto its target, but this aircraft and a second B-17 were destroyed, one being hit by flak before the target, and the other crashing to destruction in Sweden. (TAMM)

Below: B-17F-65-BO 42-29728 *El Rauncho*, which was assigned to the 332nd Bomb Squadron, 94th Bomb Group at Bassingbourn on 20 April 1943 before being transferred to the 544th Bomb Squadron, 384th Bomb Group on 12 July. It suffered battle damage on the Schweinfurt raid on 17 August 1943 and crash-landed at Grafton Underwood. (USAF)

B-17F-35-DL 42-3221/E *Whale Tail* in the 534th Bomb Squadron, 381st Bomb Group. This aircraft previously served in the 384th Bomb Group and put down at RAF Foulsham, Norfolk, on 25 June 1943. On 4 August 1943 *Whale Tail* crash-landed at Snetterton Heath and was salvaged. (USAF)

B-17F-20-DL 42-3051 *Hell's Angels* in the 366th Bomb Squadron, 305th Bomb Group, which ended up in a field at Chelveston on 31 August 1943 after overrunning the runway following the failure of the brakes. On 19 September *Hell's Angels* joined the 546th Bomb Squadron, 384th Bomb Group at Grafton Underwood, and it survived until the end of the war. It was broken up for scrap in August 1945. (via Bill Donald)

P-47C Thunderbolt 42-8001 in the 350th Fighter Squadron, 353rd Fighter Group. The 353rd Fighter Group flew its first combat mission on 12 August 1943. (USAF)

Above: B-17F-30-BO 42-5077 *Delta Rebel No 2* in the 323rd Bomb Squadron, 91st Bomb Group, is "awarded" the Air Medal. 41-24571 was the original *Delta Rebel*, being delivered on 8 August 1942 and assigned to Lieutenant George Birdsong's crew, but after diverting to Mitchel Field, New York, due to poor weather during a long training flight transient maintenance taxied the "*Reb*" into two other aircraft, badly damaging all three! Subsequently repaired, 41-24571 was renamed *Indianapolis War Bird* and issued to the 97th Bomb Group, and finally, the 49th Bomb Squadron, 2nd Bomb Group until 24 February 1943, when the entire squadron was wiped out at Steyr, Austria. *Delta Rebel No 2* carried on into 1943 until Birdsong went home to Mississippi. This aircraft and 2nd Lieutenant Robert W. Thompson's crew FTR from Gelsenkirchen on 12 August 1943 when 330 "heavies" hit targets in the Ruhr. (USAF) Right: Major (later Colonel, 67th Bomb Squadron, 44th Bomb Group CO) William "Bill" Cameron, pictured in front of B-24D-25-CO 41-24229 *Buzzin' Bear* at Shipdham. Bill flew many missions for the "Eightballs," including the low-level strike on the Columbia Aquila refinery at Ploesti on 1 August 1943 in *Buzzin Bear*, a reference to his home state of California. The *Bear* was one of eight Liberators in the 44th Bomb Group that FTR from a raid on Foggia, Italy, on 16 August when it carried 1st Lieutenant Leighton C. Smith and his crew. (Colonel William Cameron Collection)

B-17F-85-BO 42-30063 *Picklepuss*, piloted by Captain Robert Knox (front row, second left) in the lead squadron, was hit by fighters and knocked out of formation soon after crossing the River Moselle. A second attack inflicted more damage, and just south of Aachen the right wing was shot off in an attack by Messerschmitt Bf 110s. Three men, including Ernest Warsaw (front row, second from right), baled out safely, and a fourth was blown out in the explosion before the bomber hit the ground (Thorpe Abbotts Memorial Museum)

Captain Thomas H. Murphy (center kneeling), his crew, and ground crew in the 351st Bomb Squadron, 100th Bomb Group, face the camera in front of B-17F-30-VE 42-5864 *Piccadilly Lily*, which Murphy and Beirne Lay, Jr., flew on the 17 August 1943 mission to Regensburg. Two missions short of his 25th and final sortie Murphy volunteered to fly the 8 October 1943 mission to Münster. Thomas, four of his crew, and Captain Alvin L. Barker, 351st Bomb Squadron Operations Officer, who took 2nd Lieutenant Marshall F. Lee's seat with the co-pilot occupying the ball turret, were KIA. Five of the crew survived, and they were taken prisoner. Back Row L-R: Six ground crew followed by Albert C. Davis, waist gunner, and S/Sgt John J. Ehlen, top turret gunner (PoW). Front Row L-R: S/Sgt Aaron A. David, tail gunner (KIA); S/Sgt Gerald O. Robinson, gunner (PoW); 2nd Lieutenant Marshall F. Lee (KIA); Thomas Murphy (KIA 8.10.43); 1st Lieutenant Charles. C. Sarabun, navigator (PoW); 1st Lieutenant Floyd C. Peterson, bombardier (PoW); and Emmett H. Evans, radio operator. Davis and Evans had finished their tour and were replaced on the Bremen mission by S/Sgt Elder D. Dickerson and T/Sgt Derrell C. Piel respectively, both of whom were KIA. (TAMM)

B-17s in the 100th Bomb Group crossing the Alps on the mission to Regensburg. (USAF)

Strike photo of Regensburg on 17 August 1943 just after the 390th Bomb Group had passed over the target. (USAF)

Lieutenant Robert Wolff's B-17F-100-BO 42-30061 LD-Q *Wolf Pack* (center) in the 418th Bomb Squadron and three other 100th Bomb Group B-17Fs head for North Africa after the 17 August raid on Regensburg. Note the damage to Wolf's aircraft, which received 20mm cannon fire to the tail fin, and a life raft released hit the left tailplane. The top aircraft is B-17F-30-VE 42-5861 XR-J *Laden Maiden* flown by Lieutenant Owen D. "Cowboy" Roane in the 349th Bomb Squadron. Below this is B-17F-40-VE 42-5957 XR-D *Horny*. These three B-17Fs managed to reach North Africa; nine other 100th Bomb Group Fortresses did not. *Laden Maiden* FTR from a raid on 30 December 1943 with Lieutenant Marvin Leininger's crew. Only the bombardier and navigator survived, and they successfully evaded capture. The rest of the crew were KIA. *Horny* was salvaged on 9 May 1944. *Wolf Pack* returned to the ZOI on 12 July 1944 for War Bond publicity tours or for training duty before being declared surplus on 17 April 1945. (TAMM)

Back on the ground in North Africa, Fredric White (front row 2nd left), the bombardier in Lieutenant Robert Wolff's (smiling 2nd from right) crew, re-enacts their attack on Regensburg on 17 August 1943. Back Row L-R: Ira Bardman, radioman; A. M. Clark, gunner; W. J. Casebolt, gunner; J. D. Brady, engineer; A. H. Eccleston, assistant radioman; and W. F. Brown, assistant engineer. In the front row far left is Charles Stuart, co-pilot, and Lawrence McDonell, navigator, far right. (TAMM)

Young Arab children pose for the camera at the 100th Bomb Group's landing field in North Africa after the Regensburg mission. Maintenance facilities were "pitifully inadequate," and lack of replacement parts and equipment delayed many Fortresses' return to England for many weeks. The only detachments were a finance corps and some postal clerks, and as a result, 2780 gallons of kerosene were pumped into the wing tanks of Everett Blakely's B-17, and the crew spent many hours pumping it out again using a "hand apparatus." (TAMM)

Members of the crew of B-17F-100-BO 42-30359 in the 339th Bomb Squadron, 96th Bomb Group walking to operations in North Africa after the mission to Regensburg. 42-30359 and 2nd Lieutenant Linwood D. Langley's crew FTR on 29 November 1943. Eight crew were KIA, and two were taken prisoner. (USAF)

Crews in the 100th Bomb Group wearing Fez hats after the Regensburg mission on 17 August 1943. (TAMM)

Three 338th Bomb Squadron/96th Bomb Group B-17Fs in North Africa after the Regensburg mission. Right is B-17F-45-DL 42-3288 *Green Fury II*, which on 20 December 1943 was lost with 2nd Lieutenant Stanley P. Budleski's crew (6 KIA, 4 PoW). Next is 42-3442 *"Hell's" Chariot*, which was later renamed *Wacky Woody*. It was salvaged on 20 May 1944. (TAMM)

B-17F-100-BO 42-30358/X *Phartzac* in the 351st Bomb Squadron, 100th Bomb Group in North Africa after pilot Captain Norman Scott and his crew had flown the Regensburg mission with Major "Bucky" Cleven in the right hand seat. Cleven was recommended for the Medal of Honor for his actions on the mission, which resulted in *Phartzac* sustaining serious structural damage and the radioman killed in action. *Phartzac* was repaired and flew again, only to be lost on 8 October 1943 with Frank Meadows' crew when two bombs which had failed to release over the target at Bremen were hit by flak splinters and they exploded, blowing the ship to pieces. The navigator baled out, but his chute caught fire and he plummeted to his death. Only one waist gunner, who was blown through the side of the plane, survived, though he only regained consciousness ten days later. (TAMM)

Fries also claimed B-17F-85-BO 42-30080 *High Life* in the 350th Bomb Squadron, 100th Bomb Group, but the Fortress made it to Switzerland and crash-landed at Dubendorf. (TAMM)

Above left: *Unteroffizier* Otto Fries was a night fighter pilot in 5./NJG1 Bf 110 who scored 14 kills at night. In the daylight battle on 17 August 1943, when the 8th Air Force attacked Schweinfurt and Regensburg, he claimed two B-17s. Fries shot down B-17F-80-BO 42-30017 *All Shot To Hell* of the 568th Bomb Squadron, 390th Bomb Group, the exploded remains of which came down at Bringen, on the western banks of the River Rhine. All ten members of 2nd Lieutenant Ashbrooke W. Tyson's crew survived and they were taken prisoner. (via Theo Boiten) Above right: *Unteroffizier* Otto Fries and his *Bordfunker*, Fred Staffa. (via Theo Boiten)

B-17F-85-BO 42-30080 *High Life* in the 350th Bomb Squadron, 100th Bomb Group, piloted by 1st Lieutenant Donald K. Oakes and Flight Officer Joe Harper safely down in Switzerland on 17 August 1943 after the aerial battle with Otto Fries. (USAF)

B-17F-100-BO 42-30372 *Fertile Myrtle III* and B-17F-85-BO 42-30130 in the 96th Bomb Group crossing the Alps after bombing Regensburg on 17 August 1943. Brigadier General Curtis E. LeMay, who in July 1943 had been promoted 4th Wing CO, led the raid in Captain Tom Kenny's B-17F-100-BO 42-30366 *Fertile Myrtle III* in the 338th Bomb Squadron in the leading 96th Bomb Group. After the target the surviving 128 B-17s, some flying on three engines and many trailing smoke, were attacked by a few fighters on the way to the Alps. LeMay circled his formation over Lake Garda to try to give the cripples a chance to rejoin them. Although the Snetterton Heath group did not lose a single B-17, the 4th Wing lost 24 aircraft, while 60 Fortresses that made it to North Africa had to be left behind for repairs. *Fertile Myrtle III* was badly shot up over Bremen on 16 December 1943 and crashed at Taverham, near Norwich, after being abandoned by Kenney's crew. (via Geoff Ward)

Above left: Major Wilhelm-Ferdinand "Wutz" Galland, *Kommandeur* II./JG 26, wearing the *Ritterkreuz* he had been awarded in June 1943. (Achille Rely) Center: The wartime grave of Major Wilhelm-Ferdinand "Wutz" Galland, *Kommandeur* II./JG 26, who was killed in a surprise attack by Captain Walker "Bud" Mahurin in the 56th Fighter Group west of Maastricht on 17 August 1943. At the time of his death, "Wutz" had flown 186 combat sorties, during which he had accumulated 55 victories, including eight American *Viermots* and 37 Spitfires. (Otto H. Fries) Above right: *Unteroffizier* Bernhard Kunze of 1st *Staffel*, JG 1, beside his FW 190A-5 Werke Nr. 410055. The five victories include B-17s, the last two recorded for shoot downs on the "Day of the Fighters" on 17 August 1943. (via Eric Mombeek)

Unteroffizier Schönrock of 4th *Staffel*, JG 1, in front of his FW 190A-4 at Woensdrecht, who claimed two B-17s destroyed on 17 August 1943 (one of which was not upheld). (via Eric Mombeek)

B-17F-105-BO 42-30434 *Betty Boop The Pistol Packin' Mama* in the 570th Bomb Squadron, 390th Bomb Group, pictured in North Africa just after Lieutenant Jim Geary's crew had flown the Regensburg mission on 17 August 1943. This aircraft crashed at Laou, France, on 25 February 1944 with the loss of Lieutenant Robert B. Bowman's crew. Two of the crew were KIA and the rest were taken prisoner. (Gus Mencow Collection)

Distinguished guests and B-17F-35-VE 42-5910 *Hell-Cat* in the 365th Bomb Squadron, 305th Bomb Group at Chelveston on 17 August 1943. L-R: Lady Coombes; Major Lundquist; and far right, Bertram Cruger. *Hell-Cat* later transferred to the 422nd Bomb Squadron, and it was renamed *Homesick Angel*. It crash-landed on 15 September 1943 and was salvaged. (via Bill Donald)

56th Fighter Group pilots strike up a pose for the cameraman. Standing, left to right: Dave "The Silver Fox" Robinson, Intelligence Officer; Al Davis; and Handley Sayers. Front: Gordon Batdorf; Walt Moore; James Peppers; Ray Petly; Roger Dyar; Glen Schiltz; and John Vogt. Schiltz downed three FW 190s on 17 August 1943 and Vogt bagged one on 2 September 1943. (56th Fighter Group WWII Association via Alan Hague)

B-24Ds in the 93rd Bomb Group over Norfolk in late August 1943 after their return from North Africa where "Ted's Traveling Circus" were part of the Liberator force that bombed Ploesti and targets in Italy. Nearest aircraft is B-24D 41-24228 *Joisey Bounce* in the 328th Bomb Squadron. This aircraft was lost on 13 November 1943. The top aircraft is 41-23729 *Shoot Luke*, which was lost with Lieutenant Charles R. Hutchins' crew on 18 October 1943 and "C," the leading aircraft in the vic, is 41-23722 *Bomerang*, which returned to the ZOI in May 1944. (USAF)

B-17F-50-BO 42-5404 was assigned overseas in February 1943 and joined the 369th Bomb Squadron, 306th Bomb Group at Thurleigh. *Geezil* transferred to the 545th Bomb Squadron, 384th Bomb Group on 23 August 1943. The aircraft and 2nd Lieutenant Horace F. Writz's crew FTR on 30 January 1944 when it was hit by fighters and crashed at Himbergen, Germany, with the loss of seven men KIA and three PoW. (via Richards)

B-17F-27-BO 41-24587 *Bad Check* at dispersal beside a cornfield at Molesworth in August 1943. On 11 January 1944 *Bad Check* was one of ten B-17s the 303rd lost on the mission to Oschersleben when all the 1st Bomb Division groups were awarded a Distinguished Unit Citation. Four men in Lieutenant George S. McClellan's crew were KIA and six were taken into captivity. (USAF)

B-17F-60-BO 42-29557 *Yankee Gal* in the 366th Bomb Squadron, 305th Bomb Group at Chelveston on 22 August 1943. Note the extra pair of .50 caliber guns for frontal defense. This aircraft was transferred to the 384th Bomb Group at Grafton Underwood. On 10 October 1943 2nd Lieutenant William E. Kopf crash-landed at RAF Desford where *Yankee Gal* hit a hangar, and the Fortress had to be salvaged. (via Bill Donald)

9

Black Thursday

"Crew 37 hit the deck, briefing at 0500.' Black Thursday had begun."

Colonel Budd J. Peaslee

No bomber missions were flown 11-13 October. That afternoon Brigadier General Frederick L Anderson, Commanding General VIIIth Bomber Command, and his senior staff officers gathered at High Wycombe for the daily Operations Conference. The decision was taken to attack the ball bearing plant at Schweinfurt for the second time in three months to deliver a single, decisive blow against the German aircraft industry and stem the flow of fighters to the *Luftwaffe*.[379] Anderson and his senior staff officers were told that good weather was expected for the morrow. At once a warning order was sent out to all three bomb division headquarters with details of a mission (No.115) to Schweinfurt. The orders were then transmitted over Teletype machines to the various Combat Wing headquarters. Anderson hoped to launch 420 Fortresses and Liberators in a three-pronged attack on the city of Schweinfurt. The plan called for the 1st and 3rd Bomb Divisions to cross Holland 30 miles apart, while the third task force, composed of 60 Liberators of the 2nd Bomb Division, would fly to the south on a parallel course. The 923-mile trip would last just over seven hours, and meant that the B-17s of the 1st Division, which were not equipped with "Tokyo tanks," would have to be fitted with an additional fuel tank in the bomb bay. However, this meant a reduction in the amount of bombs they could carry. A -47 group would escort each division, while a third fighter group would provide withdrawal support from 60 miles inland to halfway across the Channel. Two squadrons of RAF Spitfire IXs were to provide cover for the stragglers five minutes after the main force had left the withdrawal area, and other RAF squadrons would be on standby for action if required. Despite these precautions, 370 miles of the route would be flown without fighter support. The plans then had been laid, but the success of the mission was in the lap of the gods. It needed fine weather and, above all, the fighters had to be on schedule.

During the early evening of 13 October and the early hours of 14 October, all the necessary information for the raid was teletyped to all Fortress and Liberator groups in eastern England. At 2315 hours Brigadier General Robert B. Williams, the commanding officer of the 1st Bombardment Division, received a message sent by General Anderson. It said:

'TO ALL LEADERS AND COMBAT CREWS. TO BE READ AT BRIEFING. THIS AIR OPERATION TODAY IS THE MOST IMPORATNT AIR OPERATION YET CONDUCTED IN THIS WAR. THE TARGET MUST BE DESTROYED. IT IS OF VITAL IMPORTANCE TO THE ENEMY. YOUR FRIENDS AND COMRADES THAT HAVE BEEN LOST AND THAT WILL BE LOST TODAY ARE DEPENDING ON YOU. THEIR SACRIFICE MUST NOT BE IN VAIN. GOOD LUCK. GOOD SHOOTING AND GOOD BOMBING. [SIGNED] Anderson."

The 96th Bomb Group would lead the 3rd Division with Colonel Archie Old, CO 45th Wing, in the lead ship, while the 92nd Bomb Group, at the head of the 40th Combat Wing, would lead the 1st Division with 21 Fortresses. Its commander would be Colonel Budd J. Peaslee, deputy commander to Colonel Howard "Slim" Turner of the 40th Combat Wing and formerly CO of the 384th Bomb Group. Budd Peaslee's pilot on the mission would be Captain James K. McLaughlin of the 92nd Bomb Group. He recalls:

"I shall never forget the many target briefings that Ed O'Grady, my bombardier, Harry Hughes, my navigator and I went through preparing for this famous raid. We had led our squadron [the 326th] on the first Schweinfurt raid on 17 August and, along with the others, did a pretty good job of missing the target too. We had all been apprehensive of the second raid because we'd been flying missions since we'd arrived in England in August 1942. And we had first-hand experience of how the Luftwaffe would punish us; particularly when we failed to knock out a target for the first time and attempted to go back."

Among the first of the 91st Bomb Group personnel to hear the news at Bassingbourn was David Williams, who in September had been promoted to captain and was appointed group navigator. Like McLaughlin, Williams had also been on the first Schweinfurt raid:

"I vividly recall the operations order when it came over the teletype in Group Operations during the wee hours of the morning of 14 October, as I had to do the navigational mission planning while the rest of the combat crews were still asleep. Thus we had already overcome the initial shock which we were to see on the faces of the crews somewhat later when the curtains were dramatically pulled back to reveal the scheduled second deep penetration to Schweinfurt."

At Kimbolton, Captain Edward Millson, or "Togglin' Ed," as he was known in the 379th Bomb Group, was his Group's lead bombardier. He recalled.

> "I was awakened at 0330 to go to Base Operations, where I found navigator captain Joe Wall hard at work on the flight plan and a map on the wall. A long line snaked its way across the map into the heart of Germany to Schweinfurt. That old feeling of excitement grew inside me."

At Polebrook 1st Lieutenant Jim Bradley, a lead bombardier in the 351st Bomb Group, really wanted to "get" Schweinfurt, since his original crew, without Walter Stockman and himself, went down on the first mission on 17 August:

> "When the order came during the night of 13 October I had already studied all approaches to the target and as confident that I knew it like my hometown. On the way to my barracks a couple of crewmen asked me where we were going on the 14th. I told them it was a real 'milk run.'"

Colonel Peaslee recalls:

> "From the beginning, mission No.115 was in doubt. A persistent low overcast had hung over the English bases for three days. Over the Continent the target areas were also blanketed by varying degrees of cloud coverage that had led to the enforced rest period granted the combat crews. The weather had permitted the maintenance crews to change many battle-damaged engines and patch up thousands of bullet- and flak-damaged bombers that had returned from the furious fights over north Germany and Poland. The night sky of 13 October showed no change, in fact there seemed to be some deterioration, as a damp mist fell silently from the dark windless sky. Nevertheless, those who might fly on the morrow must be prepared and at the bases the bars closed early."

In a hut at Snetterton Heath, S/Sgt Leo Rand, a replacement gunner who had arrived early that month and was awaiting his first mission on the morrow, was one of several who played Black Jack through the night. He won all the money in the pot, and one of the losers said jokingly, "I hope you get shot down tomorrow."

Crews slept in their beds piled high with blankets, uniforms, and anything else they could lay their hands on to keep out the freezing east wind, dreading the knock at the door that told them the mission was on. Colonel Peaslee continues;

> "The footsteps came in the early black hours of 14 October, as inevitably as the approaching day. The footsteps came to hundreds of crewmen over the English countryside and the doors rattled as they were yanked open and the darkness was ripped by the dazzling brightness of light bulbs. The voices of the runners were harsh, with a barely discernible note of comparison, as they sung out, 'Crew 37 hit the deck, briefing at 0500.' Black Thursday had begun."

The same scene was being replayed at all the bases in the east of England. At Thurleigh S/Sgt James E. Harris, a tail gunner in the 367th Bomb Squadron, 306th Bomb Group, recalled:

> "It was a cold, dreary, damp, typical English morning when the CQ (charge of quarters) came into our Nissen hut to waken the crews for a mission. We had heard the sounds of big engines being run up and pre-flighted on the hard stands around the perimeter of the airfield. As it was raining quite hard, I figured that the mission would be scrubbed. I was not feeling up to par so I remained in my warm sack while the others left for the mess hall. The CQ soon returned and told me to get to the briefing. I lost no time getting dressed and riding my bicycle on the shortest route to the flight line and the briefing."[380]

The sky was still dark and windless, and a heavy mist clung to the buildings and surrounding countryside as thousands of men cycled or trudged their way to the mess halls for unappetizing breakfasts of powdered eggs, toast, and hot coffee. At Chelveston, Sgt William C. Frierson, a spare ball turret gunner on 2nd Lieutenant Robert W. Holt's crew in *The Uncouth Bastard*, peered in the direction of the airfield and saw nothing. Even the runways were obscured. He was sure that the mission would be called off.[381]

Soon the crews were on their way again to the briefing halls to hear about the part they would play in the forthcoming mission. Colonel Budd J. Peaslee describes the briefing at Podington:

> "The briefing room filled rapidly as 210 crewmen and perhaps 25 briefing officers and key specialists, including flight surgeons, chaplains and unit commanders, completed the gathering. The senior officers, including the 92nd commander, Colonel William Reid of Augusta, Georgia, occupied the more comfortable seats near the stage in the front of the room. Ranged towards the rear on rows of hard chairs and benches were the crews...all these were present as the doors were closed and guarded against intrusion and prying eyes. A dignified middle-aged major opened the briefing. In civil life he had been a teacher in a small southern community. He had himself learned a thousand things never dreamed of when he volunteered to serve his country. Now he was an intelligence specialist and a good one. He opened the briefing in a calm and scholarly voice.
>
> "'Gentlemen, may I have your attention? This morning we have quite a show.' So saying, he drew back the curtains that had covered a large-scale map of Europe and the British Isles. In the hushed room all leaned forward intently to study the map with its heavy black yarn marking the routes over Britain, the Channel and across the occupied countries to a point deep in Germany. 'It's Schweinfurt again', said the major. For a moment there was dead silence as the major's words struck home with full impact on the minds of the men. Then a buzz of intelligible comment filled the room, punctuated by whistles, curses, moans and just plain vocal explosions. Above all came one remembered phrase that stood out in the tumult of vocal sound.
>
> "'Son-of-a-bitch and this is my 25th mission!'
>
> "Eyes turned towards the speaker and there were expressions of sympathy and condolence until a baby-faced pilot spoke. 'What the hell are you crying about? This is my first!'"

Bill Rose recalls:

> "When the briefing officer said 'Gentlemen, your target for today is Schweinfurt,' everyone groaned. The ball bearing plants would be heavily defended. We knew our third mission would be one Hell of a fight."

For the next half-hour the major and his aides spoke on the plan for the mission. Then it was the air commander's turn to say a few words to the crews he was to lead. Colonel Reid introduced Budd Peaslee to the expectant crews. Peaslee spared no punches. He told them straight out they were in for a fight. Their responsibility was to the group, not to the stragglers, and there was no room for useless heroics. He tried to think of something humorous to dispel the tension that had suddenly gripped the men, but he could think of nothing funny about the situation. Finally, he said:

> "If our bombing is good and we hit this ball-bearing city well, we are bound to scatter a lot of balls around on the streets of Schweinfurt. Tonight I expect the Germans will all feel like they are walking around on roller skates." "It was a weak effort," wrote Peaslee, "but they all laughed loudly, too loudly and the tension was reduced."

The news that Schweinfurt was their target brought mixed reactions from the men. At fog-shrouded and rain soaked bases throughout East Anglia, crews were weary from days of bitter combat and fitful sleep. There were few men on the bases who doubted it was an excursion into Hell, despite some officers' platitudes that it was going to be a "milk-run." At most briefing rooms the pulling of the curtain covering the wall map shocked the aircrews into silence. At Ridgewell the shock was probably felt the greatest. Crews were briefed at 0700 hours, and the mention of the word "Schweinfurt" brought back bitter memories of the 17th August raid when the 381st had lost eleven B-17s, the highest loss of all the groups. A medical detachment log earlier that month had concluded that the "mental attitude on morale of the crews is the lowest that has been yet observed." S-2, therefore, decided that at briefing it would perhaps be best not to mention that the entire *Luftwaffe* fighter force of 1100 aircraft was based within 65 miles of the bombers' route. As the medical officer went around to the crews to check equipment and pass out sandwiches and coffee he noticed that the crews were "scared and it was obvious that many doubted that they would return."[382]

Crewmen who had flown only a few missions noticed that even the veteran crews appeared to be in a state of shock. At Chelveston, as the curtain was jerked back and they all saw what the target was, there was instant whistling and nervous laughter and wise-cracking. Solemnly, one captain performed a ceremony that was reserved for tough targets: he took out a roll of toilet paper, tore off ten squares for each man, and passed them out. Lieutenant Edwin L. "Ted" Smith, co-pilot in Lieutenant Douglas L. Murdock's crew in *Sizzle*,[383] which would be #6 in the low squadron, recalls:

> "When we saw the tapes stretching that deep into Germany we all had misgivings. The gunners knew we were in for a fight and so they lugged extra ammo' boxes out to our aircraft."[384]

Eight men at the briefing had a special reason for wanting to complete the mission. Lieutenant Frederick E. Helmick was the bombardier on *Rigor Mortis*, flown by 1st Lieutenant Frederick B. "Barney" Farrell. S/Sgt Herman E. Molen was flying with 2nd Lieutenant Gerald B. Eakle's crew as toggelier. S/Sgt Thomas E. Therrien was right waist gunner on Flight Officer Verl D. Fisher's crew. All of these men were flying their 25th and final mission of their tour. So too were Lieutenant Raymond P. Bullock and Carl J. Brunswick, his engineer-top turret gunner, left waist gunner Harold E. Coyne, and tail gunner Alden B. Curtis, all aboard *Sundown Sal* (a brand new B-17G, which was named but never painted) in the 365th Squadron. Lieutenant Alden C. Kincaid, a pilot who had flown 21 missions and before that had flown Wellingtons on RAF night bombing operations, discovered that he would be the aircraft commander for Lieutenant Norman W. Smith's crew. Smith, who hailed from Hawaii, where his parents owned a pineapple plantation and had witnessed the Japanese bombing of Pearl Harbor on 7 December 1941, would move over to the co-pilot's seat.[385]

At the end of the briefing Lieutenant Joseph Pellegrini, lead bombardier in the B-17 flown by 2nd Lieutenant Joseph W. Kane, with Major Charles G. Y. Normand the Command Pilot, had a question for the CO, Lieutenant Colonel Donald K. Fargo. As the target was so important, could he take the 16 B-17s of the group over the target again if clouds obscured the aiming point? Fargo said, "Yes Pellegrini – you can go around a second time and a third and a fourth today. This is one target you must hit."[386] Pellegrini, one of 14 children born to Italian parents from South Philadelphia, was one of the few that did not have "butterflies" in his stomach.

Forrest J. Eherenman, the navigator in Lieutenant Corson's crew, who had arrived at Kimbolton on 17 August in time to watch the bedraggled survivors return from Schweinfurt, had not forgotten the word "Schweinfurt." "On 14 October," he recalls, "we heard that name again. Our crew in *Gay Caballeros* would be Tail End Charlie at the end of the low squadron. This would be our 10th mission."

Elmer Bendiner, a navigator who had flown the 17 August raid, recalled:[387]

> "Sitting on the wooden benches in the briefing room at Kimbolton at four that morning, we took the news that we were going back to Schweinfurt with only a few groans to indicate that we were alive to the problem. The neophytes among us were more boisterous. Actually in the group of eighteen crews slated to represent the 379th on that mission, only four had been in the Schweinfurt battle two months earlier when we were told we were going to write history and win the war. The spiel was more solemn this time. The message had not changed, but now the sacrifices of August recurred to mind like an insistent, muffled drumbeat beneath the text.
>
> "General Anderson sent us a personal message calling on us - not very tactfully, I fancied - to remember the blood and sacrifice of our comrades who had died on the same errand in August. We were to finish their job. Such high-toned dramatics usually read better than they play. For men like ourselves, the remnants of *Tondelayo's* crew,[388] the message from beyond the grave sounded particularly inappropriate. It was barely arguable that those who had died some seven weeks earlier at Schweinfurt or en route had a right to cry, like Hamlet's lugubrious father, 'Remember me.' But we – Bohn [E. Fawkes, Jr., the pilot], Bob [Hejny, bombardier], Larry, Duke and I - had flown with those nagging ghosts. We had gone through the fire with them and by luck had survived. Now they were using their exalted position to drive us into doing it all over again. It was easy for them to talk; they were safely dead and out of it all....
>
> "After the call to vengeance the briefing turned to the economic, political, social and psychological significance of ball bearings. The twice-told tale was intoned like a chant. This was again the day when the German machine was to be castrated.
>
> "Mo Preston would not say that our job was to be less difficult or less costly than it had been in August. He was an honest man. He would not fly with us that day and so wore his pinks, as if it were a holiday. Little Rip Rohr was in his flying suit, energetically waving his pointer like a sword. This would be his day."

At the briefing at Thurleigh S/Sgt James E. Harris, who had been on the first Schweinfurt, recalls that when the route map was uncovered and they saw that the "damned red line led to Schweinfurt; you could have heard a pin drop." George Roberts, radio operator in W. S. Kirk's crew, recalls:

"Our Group commander Colonel Robinson told the assembled crews that we would be bombing the most important target to date: the ball and roller bearing factories at Schweinfurt. The name had no meaning to me. The red string on the map told us we in for a long flight over heavily defended territory. The weather over England would remain marginal, but would be clear over the continent. We could expect serious fighter opposition, moderate to intense flak and a long cold ride. With this dire information we completed our pre-flight work and assembled for final instructions. Lieutenant Kirk said that this mission would be rough as the one to Bremen and an hour longer. We had from three to fifteen missions behind us. Kirk cautioned everyone to stay alert, conserve ammunition and guns by firing short bursts and be brief on the intercom."

Having flown the first Schweinfurt raid on 17 August, James E. Harris believed that:

"most secretly thought that this would be a one way trip. Schweinfurt again, deep into Germany, with a short-range escort. Was this trip necessary? Of course, we knew that it was. 'Theirs is not to reason why, theirs was but to do and die.' Oh, so true. W. N. Thomas, our regular pilot, was hospitalized and grounded and also that Joe Lukens, our regular bombardier was riding with a 'green' crew.[389] A combat crew that had trained together always had second thoughts whenever there was a replacement. A good crew could be compared to the precision of a fine watch or a good ball team, whose members know their plays and anticipate each other's moves and act accordingly; no mistakes. It was especially hard for a crew to accept a replacement pilot.[390] There were no reflections against the person, but our feelings were justified in situations like this."[391]

At Molesworth Lieutenant Robert Hullar, pilot of *Luscious Lady*, in the 427th Bomb Squadron, and his 24-year-old co-pilot, Wilbur Klint, learned that they would be in the second flight. Both men had flown the first Schweinfurt, and from that experience they knew that Mission 115 was destined to be "a shakey do," as Klint called it:

"The first Schweinfurt had been our second mission. This was mission No.11 for our crew. Colonel Stevens opened the briefing. 'Today's mission, if successful, can shorten the war by six months."

Briefing Officers spoke of routes where the flak was minimal, and of areas where fighters were not expected. They referred to the friendly fighter cover in glowing terms. But the majority of crews were not fooled, as 2nd Lieutenant Roy G. Davidson, one of the pilots in the 333rd Bomb Squadron at Bury St. Edmunds (Rougham), recalls:

"When the covers were drawn on the route map, it showed that the fighter escort only went a short way with us to the target. We would have a long way from France onwards without fighter cover and on the way back too. We knew that we were in for a pretty rough time but we had no idea just how rough it was going to be. We had not been on the first Schweinfurt raid and didn't realize how bad Schweinfurt was. Despite this I really looked forward to the mission because I thought the accomplishment would be great. It never crossed the minds of the crew that we would not complete our 25 missions. A telegram was read out telling us that this was one of the most important missions of the war. When we had knocked out the ball-bearing plants the war would come to a halt. We felt we were really going to contribute a lot towards winning the war.[392] I was flying in the low squadron as last man - the most vulnerable spot in the entire formation.[393] But we felt safe because even though we were the last 'plane in a string of over 200 bombers, there were going to be a whole lot of Liberators following right behind us. This would really put us right in the middle of the whole string, which seemed to be a pretty good spot to be in."[394]

Phillip R. Taylor, a waist gunner in the 91st Bomb Group at Bassingbourn, recalls:

"After the briefing my crew went back to our quarters and put on wool uniforms (ODs). Knowing what our target was, we expected to either end up in Heaven or a prisoner of war camp and we wanted to be properly dressed."

At Molesworth, Robert Voltz looked at the low clouds and wagered a £1 note with radio operator, Sgt Warren L. Harvie, that they would not leave the ground. However, the green flare was fired to signal "start engines," and a second flare was shot to start to taxi. They had three 1000lb bombs, plus an auxiliary fuel tank in the bomb bay. The auxiliary tank would be used for assembly and later jettisoned in the Channel. At Thurleigh, Jim Harris and the rest of Richard Butler's crew, and George Roberts and the others in Lieutenant W. S. Kirk's crew, donned their flying gear, checked out their parachutes, oxygen masks, escape kits, and the codes for the day. Then they boarded the trucks that took them to their hardstands. Kirk's crew had been assigned *Cavalier*, and Butler, 42-30175.

S/Sgt Leo Rand noticed that some of the veteran crews appeared to be in shock. The former steelworker from Youngstown, Ohio, did not scare easily, and Rand put it down to the fact that these men were tired and were probably overreacting. Then someone near him mumbled, "This is gonna be a tough day," and others agreed.

At Snetterton, Heath Eugene Sebeck, the engineer in 2nd Lieutenant Silas S. Nettles' crew in the 96th Bomb Group, had been called at 0430, but he had reasons to be happy. The night before he and two others on the crew had been the last shooters on the skeet range, and they decided to try a little hunting in the fields near the base. Within an hour they had rabbits and pheasants aplenty, and they took them to the Red Cross Club, where a lovely English lady had said she would fix them for one rabbit. That evening they had a feast fit for a king, which was quite a change from the usual menu of Spam and such. On returning to his Nissen hut Sebeck had found a letter on his bunk that looked good. He had applied for Aviation Cadet training in July, and this was a notification that he had been accepted, and would be called when an opening existed. He showed the letter to his pilot, who read it and said, "Well Sebeck, you won't be with us too much longer." How right he was. Sebeck put the letter in the pocket of his leather A2 that he always hung in the tail section of the plane. To make matters more tense, after the briefing Silas Nettles and his crew were sent by truck the 25 miles to Bury St. Edmunds to get a plane from the 94th Bomb Group. There they were given 42-23453 for this, their second mission. Their first had been to Bremen on 8 October when they had flown a new B-17 called *V Packet* (which was given to 2nd Lieutenant John J. Scarborough's crew, who shared their hut, to fly on the Schweinfurt mission). Nettles' crew had returned, somehow, with over 100 holes and one feathered engine. Jerry V. Lefors, the co-pilot, recalls:

"I had told the Crew Chief that all the engines would have to be replaced because we had flown for about 45 minutes on full RPM and maximum manifold pressure. (The rule was that an engine should be replaced if run under such conditions for 'several' minutes). The Maintenance Chief laughed and said that they would fire them up and if they ran, 'the plane goes up again'. There were few extra engines available. After the Bremen mission we felt like veterans because 'no mission could be rougher than that'. We scrounged the next day for armor plate and discussed carrying more ammunition. We were a green crew but united in our determination to complete our missions."[395]

At Thorpe Abbotts the 100th Bomb Group was still licking its wounds after the severe maulings of 8 October, when seven crews were lost, and 10 October, when 12 out of 13 crews failed to return. Despite these extremely serious losses and an unsuccessful appeal by Colonel "Chick" Harding, the CO, the "Bloody Hundredth" was still expected to make some contribution to the tonnage of bombs to be dropped on Schweinfurt. Lieutenant Robert L. "Bob" Hughes, pilot of *Nine Little Yanks and a Jerk*, says:

"The call came for the Hundredth to mount a maximum effort but there were only eight crews available. Some of the key positions, therefore, had to be taken by personnel from other groups."

The day before the mission Lieutenant William D. Allen, a bombardier in the 384th Bomb Group, was relaxing in the Officers Club at Grafton Underwood when a captain approached him, accompanied by the "biggest, toughest MP he had ever seen." Allen was ordered to report to Operations, where he was informed that he would be a fill-in lead bombardier in the 100th Bomb Group.[396] Hughes continues:

"The eight crews were broken down into flights. Four aircraft would be led by 'Cowboy' Roane, flying with the 390th Bomb Group, with four being led by myself flying with the 95th Bomb Group.[397] The mess hall seemed virtually empty as we had our usual breakfast of dried eggs, Spam, coffee, toast and good old orange marmalade with vast amounts of good American butter to go on that wonderful dark English bread."

For many it was to be their last breakfast on English soil. There was little hope for any man holding low rank who wished to take leave that was owing to them, either. It was a maximum effort and everyone was needed. At Framlingham, home of the 390th Bomb Group, Lieutenant Richard H. Perry had hoped to receive a short period of leave in London after his crash four days before:

"The squadron CO, Joe Gemmill, felt differently. His view was that the best way to get the 'butterflies out of our stomachs' was to participate in another mission immediately. We did fly the Schweinfurt mission, which was no 'milk-run' and I think in our case his approach worked fine. Later, when I became operations officer, I used this approach on many other crews that had rough missions."

As H-Hour approached the tension on the bases mounted. The weather in England was very bad, but at 0900 hours an American-crewed Mosquito in the 25th Bomb Group, 35,000ft over the Continent, radioed back the news to 8th Air Force headquarters that all of central Germany was in the clear.[398] An hour later the Fortresses began taking off. The weathermen had predicted overcast to only 2000ft, but the bombers were still flying around in cloud at heights of 6000ft and above, forcing the lead aircraft to circle for two hours. Flares were fired in a vain attempt to pull the formations together.[399]

Colonel Peaslee, the mission leader, and his pilot, Captain McLaughlin, sat waiting in the lead Fortress of the 92nd Bomb Group on the runway at Podington. Green flares shot skywards from the control tower, and the lead bomber moved to its take-off position. The time was 1012 hours. James McLaughlin released the brakes and throttled out towards the fading runway lights in the distance. Colonel Peaslee, sitting in the right-hand seat, listened intently as McLaughlin announced over intercom that he was taking off on instruments. He directed Peaslee to watch the runway, and if the B-17 should start to wander to one side or the other he was to overpower him on the rudder control and bring it back to safety on the runway. The lead bomber gathered speed, and at 100mph in the last hundred foot of runway it was airborne. Peaslee released the locks and pulled the "gear up" lever. They were followed by a further twenty bombers, and crews peered into the overcast for recognition points on the ground. In the dimness of the approaching day there was only a brief glimpse of the dark shadows of the woodland on either side of the runway clear zone, but this was almost instantly blotted out as the bombers entered the overcast.

The same procedure was happening at Thurleigh. George Roberts recalls that "shortly before start engine time at 0900 word came of a one-hour weather delay. It remained foggy with a 200ft cloud ceiling." 1st Lieutenant Harold K. McCaleb doubted that the raid would go ahead:

"Crews had been briefed at 0400 on the morning of 12 October for Schweinfurt. With rain and fog covering England, the mission was cancelled before the B-17 engines were started. Crews were again briefed for Schweinfurt on Wednesday and again, because of weather, the mission was cancelled. Now the end of the runway was not visible through the fog and rain. Most crews expected word that the mission had been canceled again."

Roberts continues:

"Promptly at ten the green flare was fired from the control tower and the engines came to life. We moved in line down the taxiway. Pilots did engine run-ups before moving onto the main runway. Under full throttle we began the dash down the concrete strip. Very near the end of the runway in felt the heavy plane leave the ground and ascend into the low hanging clouds. We would not break out of the overcast for another thirty minutes."

Aboard Butler's Fortress the engines were started. Kenneth McCaleb recalls:

"Unbelievably the command for take off was given for the bomb and gasoline loaded bombers to climb through the overcast with pilots wondering how they were going to land when the cancellation order was given."

Jim Harris continues:

"All secure, Butler waited for the signals to start engines and taxi to take-off position. It was a tense, anxious moment waiting for the flare, which signaled takeoff. I presumed that everybody involved, especially the flight crews, hoped for the word to scrub the mission. No such luck, so we proceeded to take off in the rain. It took quite a while to climb through the overcast. As we broke through the clouds, B-17s were popping up all around us. We were concerned about the instrument takeoff because we knew that the pilots, as good as they might be, had not had the opportunity to gain experience in instrument flying. Due to the weather, many groups failed to reach their predetermined assembly points. Many fighter groups could not take off in time to be of much help."

The Forts emerged from the overcast at several thousand feet, assembled in formation, and approached the enemy coast of Europe, and the clouds disappeared. Kenneth McCaleb observed that it was an "October Indian Summer day." George Roberts noted:

> "Our assembly and climb appeared normal, though other groups were having difficulty getting organized. We were in the high group of the 40th Combat Wing. Colonel Peaslee was leading the high group with the 92nd Bomb Group and the rest of the First Division. The 305th Group from Chelveston was flying the low element of the Wing. I listened on the radio for a possible recall, but all I heard was the steady call sign '7M' and the regular time check."[400]

At Molesworth, William C. Heller, who would soon take command of the 360th Bomb Squadron, taxied out for takeoff in heavy rain, which limited visibility:

> "Since we could not see the end of the runway, takeoff and climb were on instrument conditions from the start of the roll until break out in the bright sunshine at 7000ft."

At Kimbolton, after an exhaustive check Colonel "Rip" Rohr took *Rag'n Red* off at 1030 into what "Togglin' Ed" Millson, lead bombardier for the 379th Bomb Group, called "a sky already dotted with other Fortress formations." Twenty minutes later Lieutenant Corson took *Gay Caballeros* off and headed for the Tail End Charlie slot at the end of the low squadron. Forrest J. Eherenman, his navigator, recalls:

> "In an hour and a half we got assembled over the departure point (Splasher 6). A few minutes later we were committed to go to the target no matter what lie in wait over Germany."[401]

Peaslee and McLaughlin, meanwhile, had leveled out at 8000ft, and they began craning their necks to spot other aircraft. McLaughlin recalls:

> "After we were airborne and formed up, the first warning of what the day would be like came when we discovered that some of the groups and wings had not joined up in their proper sequences. The mission thus began in confusion because some group leaders could not find their wings."

The 92nd Bomb Group had cruised to the splasher beacon over Thurleigh and formed as a group, but at the second splasher, where the 40th Combat Wing was to assemble, the 305th Bomb Group failed to rendezvous.[402] Peaslee therefore decided to continue with just the 306th Bomb Group to the third assembly area at Daventry, in the Midlands, and fly on at 20,000ft to the English coast. Standing orders dictated that no air commander could send out a two-group combat wing; the risk of total annihilation of such a small defensive force was too great. However, Peaslee did not want to abort while he still had some options open to him. The 40th Combat Wing orbited according to procedure, and at 1220 hours led the 1st Division assembly line over the coast above Orford Ness. George Roberts, in the 306th Bomb Group, recalls:

> "We fired test rounds over the Channel and noted a few P-47 Thunderbolts as we crossed the French Coast. These 'Little Friends' did remain with us long."

Further south the 45th Combat Wing, with the 96th Bomb Group in the van, led the 3rd Division over the Naze and headed for the Belgian coast. With five other crews Silas Nettles, in the borrowed 94th ship, rendezvoused with the 96th Bomb Group, and they flew Tail End Charlie. By 1230 they were crossing the Channel at 23,000ft. Jerry Lefors says, "Flying Tail End Charlie was quite a job. We all knew what happened to stragglers so we tried to maintain a tight formation." Eugene Sebeck, the engineer, had his hands full. After take off he had never seen cloud conditions as bad, and he thought that they might run into another plane at any minute. They had finally got above the overcast and were on their way, but he had to maintain a watchful eye on the No.1 engine, which kept losing and then gaining about 100 RPM. Fuel consumption was high. Nettles requested his navigator, Robert O'Hearn, to calculate the rate of fuel use. They had barely enough to make it back if all went well. "Knowing we might have to bale out if we ran out of gas," says Jerry Lefors, "the crew elected to continue on." The crew test fired their guns over the Channel, and everything seemed OK. A short time later Sebeck swung his turret around towards the tail and watched their P-47 fighters leave after they had reached the limit of their fuel. Very soon he heard the message on interphone, "Enemy fighters coming." Things now started to get rough, and to add to their troubles the No.1 engine "ran away" after attempts to feather the prop failed. The only thing to do, says Sebeck:

> "was to cut power and fuel or it would tear itself apart. The windmilling prop dragged our airspeed down by 20 or more mph. Although the lead plane was flying at a steady speed, the slight variation in airspeed of the ships near the leader would parlay back through the formation. We were going from full RPMs to cutting back to near stall-out. This amounted to a lot of physical labor to handle the controls. We had learned we would flip onto our side and lose a thousand feet quickly by getting into wake turbulence created by the ships ahead."[403]

Behind the 45th Wing came the 4th Combat Wing, consisting of the 94th and 385th Bomb Groups, followed by the 13th Combat Wing made up of the 95th, 100th, and 390th Bomb Groups. Fifteen of the 164 aircraft in the 1st Division and 18 aircraft of the 160 aircraft in the 3rd Division either turned back with mechanical problems, or became lost in the cloudy conditions. The long and complicated assembly was also responsible for diminishing the Fortresses' vital fuel reserves, especially those carrying bombs externally to make up for the lack of internal tonnage taken up by the bomb bay fuel tanks. Many of these crews were forced to dump their wing-mounted bombs in the Channel or abort the mission. The 94th Bomb Group, part of the 4th Combat Wing, had difficulty in forming. Major Charles Birdsall led the 24 B-17s of the 94th off from Rougham and soon disappeared into cloud at only 2000ft. Crews cursed the weather forecasters, who had predicted cloud at 6500ft. Birdsall managed to get his B-17s into the correct slot in the wing formation, and they headed for the coast. Soon there was an opportunity for gunners to test-fire their .50 caliber machine-guns. In the waist section aboard Davidson's B-17, Claude Page and Arthur Howell fired off a few rounds. Page had asked Davidson to keep the $600 he had won at a crap game. He was afraid to go to bed with all this money. Page had promised himself "I'll send it home tomorrow."

The 3rd Bomb Division crossed the coast of Belgium near Knocke at 1255 hours, and proceeded on a converging course with the 1st Bomb

Division towards Aachen. The escorting P-47 Thunderbolts departed, and the Fortresses carried on alone to Schweinfurt. "Gus" Mencow, navigator of *Betty Boop, the Pistol Packing Mama*, in the 570th Bomb Squadron, 390th Bomb Group, piloted by Lieutenant Jim "Rally" Geary, recalls:

"We were leading the high squadron, with Bob Brown's crew of the 571st flying group lead. As our fighter escort left us everyone sensed that we were in for a tough mission. The German fighter attacks came sporadically, mostly in waves and it soon developed into a running battle extending for hundreds of miles across the skies of Europe. Although we were having it tough, it seemed that the 1st Bomb Division was really getting the brunt of the attacks in their formations well ahead of us."

Aborts had now reduced the 40th Combat Wing from 53 B-17s to 42, one third of a complete wing formation. Standing orders in the 8th prohibited bomber commanders to penetrate the enemy defenses with less than a complete wing formation. In this situation the wing would have to abort. However, Peaslee reasoned that the loss of 42 bombers would deprive the division of much needed firepower, and most importantly, additional bombs. He called for a report from the tail gunner, a regular lieutenant co-pilot for the lead crew who was acting as the eyes of the air commander by taking over the tail gun position. The lieutenant reported that the 1st Division was in excellent position and at full strength, except for the missing 305th Bomb Group. Peaslee decided to continue to the target, moving the 92nd and 306th formations into the high slot just above and to the left of the 91st. In effect this would give the 1st Wing five groups. Peaslee retained air command, but would relinquish the lead to Lieutenant Colonel Theodore Milton, CO of the 91st, flying at the head of the 1st Combat Wing in the *Bad Egg*, piloted by Captain Harry Lay (subsequently killed on a second tour in fighters). The air commander broke radio silence long enough to advise Milton of the plan, at the same time advising the new leader that the 40th Combat Wing would join his formation in close support, thus grouping nearly 100 bombers in a mutually protective mass. Milton must have had mixed feelings, because he had only taken off with eleven B-17s, now reduced to just seven because of aborts. Having the 305th along must have provided some relief. The news that the 91st was to take over the lead prompted Captain David Williams, the lead navigator flying with Milton, to think back to that fateful day on 17 August when the 91st had led the first Schweinfurt raid:

"Mission 115 was my 23rd combat mission and the second time that I would have the dubious honor of being in the very first B-17 over the target. It was an eerie feeling once more to be the vanguard, striking out across the Channel towards a target, which had dealt us so many devastating losses just a few months before. All the more so this time since four of our group had already aborted and we were setting course with just seven aircraft comprising the 91st effort. I kept thinking of the ten we had lost in August and somehow could not seem to reconcile the mathematics, which were going through my mind. The navigational chore ahead left little time for such speculation."

Bringing up the rear of the 1st Division bomber stream was the 41st Combat Wing, the third and final wing. In the lead was the 379th Bomb Group led by Lieutenant Colonel Louis W. "Rip" Rohr in *Rag'n Red*. The 303rd was in the high spot, and the 384th, low, in "Purple Heart Corner," led by Major George W. Harris, who had flown the first Schweinfurt mission, flying with Captain Philip Algar in *Windy City Avenger*. At mid-Channel the lieutenant tail gunner aboard Peaslee's ship reported, "Fighters at 7 o'clock climbing. They look like P-47s." The delay in forming up over England had put the Fortresses ten minutes behind schedule, and the 44 P-47s of the 353rd Fighter Group, which were on schedule, had met the bombers in mid-Channel. The 1st Bomb Division crossed the mouth of the Scheldt at 1225 hours, the same time as the 3rd Division was leaving the coast of England. Olds' force was only five minutes behind schedule, having avoided the bad weather problems that had dogged the 1st Division assembly. Aborts had reduced the numbers of Fortresses too.

In the 379th Bomb Group, *Ensign Mary*—named by the engineering officer, who was dating a Navy nurse—took the place of an abort at the French coast. S/Sgt Sam Mehaffey, the ball turret gunner, recalls:

"A flak barrage hit the group over France. The navigator called on interphone: 'The bombardier's hit, he's hit!' The pilot asked 'How bad?' 'Pretty bad' was the reply. (The bombardier had lost an arm) The pilot signaled to drop out and made a 180° turn."

Mehaffey swung his turret to the 6 o'clock position to watch the formation go on, and he saw their replacement become a black puff of smoke where they had been. It must have been a direct hit in the bomb bay. His friend, Francis S. Chard, from Minnesota, was on the unlucky ship that was blown out of the sky.[404] Up front in the 379th formation Captain Edwin Millson, the lead bombardier riding up front in *Rag'n Red*, recalls:

"At 1226 the tail gunner reported that the high and low formations in position as the English Coast slipped by below us. Overhead, waves of P-47 escort fighters appeared. Below was the icy Channel and ahead lay the long route yet to be covered. Light inaccurate flak to our right as we passed over the enemy coast indicated that Joe had us on course. The crew, alert and watchful, called out the presence of friendly fighters and we felt good with them around. Shortly after entering enemy territory near Aachen. They had to leave us. Their departure spelled trouble. We observed enemy 'Bandits' climbing. Little black dots grew into formations of Me 109 and FW 190 fighters, which began sweeping attacks on our formations. They came in fast from 11-1130 o'clock direction, rolling as they fired then split essed out of range. The interphone crackled: 'Fighters at one o'clock!' 'I smoked the Hell out of that one.' 'Fort down -six chutes!'"

Luscious Lady, in the 303rd Bomb Group, crossed the enemy coast at 1259 hours, flying at 24,000ft. Wilbur Klint recalls:

"From that minute until we left enemy territory at 1642 we were under almost constant attack by every type of plane the Krauts could coax up at our altitude. As on our first Schweinfurt raid, we encountered all the usual single and twin-engine fighters plus obsolete fighters and medium bombers. Intelligence had informed us that we would be within range of 1100 fighters. (Though subsequent reports estimated that only about half that number attacked, it seemed that 1100 struck our group alone). We were tucked away in the No.6 position of the lead squadron of the lead group. While this offered a definite advantage for protection from fighters, we were hemmed in on all sides by other B-17s. Everyone was using violent evasive action, which was an added hazard. With the Forts packed in a tight defensive formation, both Bob and I were at the controls almost all the time, trying to get the most evasive action possible without ramming one of our own planes."[405]

At 1305 hours 48 P-47s of the 56th Fighter Group rendezvoused with the 3rd Division. Of the 164 B-17s assigned to the 1st only 149 remained after mechanical failures resulted in 15 aborts, and the 3rd was reduced from 160 B-17s to 142 for the same reason. Over Walcheren Island more than 20 Me 109s and FW 190s, zooming in from over 34,000ft, attacked the 1st Division. The Thunderbolt pilots stood their ground and met the attacks at around 31,000ft, a height at which the Thunderbolt had the advantage over the enemy fighters. At 1330 hours, at a point between Aachen and Duren, the 353rd Fighter Group, at the limit of their range, was forced to break off and return to England. They had done their job well, beating off a succession of attacks and claiming ten fighters shot down and another five damaged or destroyed for the loss of one P-47 in combat, and another which crashed in England on the return leg.[406] As the 1st Division continued its southeasterly course, away from the heavily defended towns of Antwerp and Aachen, and as soon as the Thunderbolts had departed, the *Luftwaffe* sailed into the attack. Some 300 to 400 enemy fighters ripped through the unprotected Fortress formations amid fierce return fire from the bomber gunners.[407] Some of the enemy fighters were specially equipped to fire rockets and cannon shells into the wings and fuselages of the B-17s to blast and scatter the tightly packed formations, and make many of them easy prey for the fighters.

Captain McLaughlin recalls:

"The first big jolt came when my co-pilot riding in the tail called out. 'A large formation approaching at 5 o'clock', which we believed to be the 40th Combat Wing and which thereafter proved to be a large gaggle of twin-engined Messerschmitts passing us on the starboard side, positioning themselves for head-on passes and firing large rockets into the midst of our formations. With no fighter protection we soon became easy targets for the German rockets and as our damaged wingman fell behind we could see the FW 190s finishing them off with relative ease."

Crews had guessed before take-off that the *Luftwaffe* would be up in force, and after the "Little Friends" had departed the next fighters the 306th Bomb Group crews saw were Germans at 3 o'clock. The lead ship, piloted by Captain Charles Schoolfield and Captain Charles Flannagan, was one of many that carried an extra 12,000 rounds of ammunition. Three B-17s in the 306th Group had already turned back with mechanical problems, the last leaving at 1320 hours, just as the *Luftwaffe* were beginning their attack. The 15 remaining B-17s fought off the persistent attacks with as much firepower as they could muster. George Roberts, aboard *Cavalier*, recalls:

"The intense battle began with the Me 109s flying right between the Squadrons, ignoring the fire from the bombers. It was the most daring attack I had seen to date. The Germans were determined to stop the formations at any cost. The *Cavalier* was being raked with enemy fire. Quite suddenly, the plane shuddered from an explosion in the waist section. Sergeant Eugene Kelly called to say that a 20mm shell had hit his partner Sgt Robert Webber. I went back and noted Webber was bleeding from the upper right leg and the pelvic area. We moved him to the ledge near the ball turret. Kelly injected morphine, applied a sulfa pad and covered him with a blanket. As I was returning to my gun, an explosion in the radio room ruined my transmitter. At the same time my oxygen supply dropped to zero. I plugged into an emergency tank, which I turned on about once per minute. This fifteen minute supply was to last me for two hours.

"Ball turret gunner Robert Hill called on the interphone that he was out of ammunition and needed his guns reloaded. Kelly told him that he also was out of ammo in the waist and a little too busy to come to his aid. I told Hill that there was no spare ammo and no way that I could help him reload. He replied: 'Load lie up or I'm coming out of this tin can.' I said to stay in, move his guns around and pretend to be firing to discourage fighter attacks. His return words were, 'Like Hell, these guys are checked out and they are going to press the attack without fear of fire!' Lieutenant Kirk gave Hill permission to leave the ball and take over the waist gun left by the injured Webber. An Ammo check revealed that all gun positions were nearly out of bullets. Kirk told us to conserve our ammo and fire only short bursts and as the fighter got close and he would take evasive action when the fighter, coming from the rear, had lined up on us. Sergeant Cecil Poff in the tail and I in the radio room called each time we saw tracers coming from lined up fighters with the advice to: 'Kick it Sir.' This maneuver probably did more than anything to save us. I noted several planes with smoking engines and/or feathered propellers. As we approached the bomb run I saw seven chutes at 9 o'clock low and a B-17 in a slow spin."[408]

At 1400 hours 1st Lieutenant Douglas H. White, in the 367th Squadron, was the first to be shot out of formation by the German rocket-firing fighters after taking hits in the horizontal stabilizer. White's Fortress, a new B-17G, went down and exploded. Only the radio operator survived. 1st Lieutenant Willard H. Lockyear's B-17 was hit at about the same time by rockets and three engines were set on fire. The radio room also erupted in flames, and 2nd Lieutenant Paul N. Welton, the navigator, and 1st Lieutenant Albert J. Nagy, the bombardier, were killed in the nose of the aircraft. The stricken aircraft finally fell at Neuweld. The rest of the crew managed to bale out, but the ball turret gunner later died in hospital from internal injuries.

The fight reached a crescendo, and *Queen Jeannie*, flown by 2nd Lieutenant Robert "Bob" McCallum, was shot down.[409] 1st Lieutenant Vernon K. Cole's B-17 in the 423rd Squadron also went down, hit by a rocket-firing Ju 88, which set the bomb bay on fire.[410] The 306th gunners fought back. At 1410 hours S/Sgt William L. Threatt Jr, a waist gunner in 1st Lieutenant Virgil H. Jeffries' B-17, lead ship in the first element in the 423rd Squadron, shot down a FW 190 and damaged another. T/Sgt James S. Porter, the top turret gunner, aimed at a gaggle of four Ju 88s and scored hits on one of the attackers just as it fired off two rockets. The Ju 88's right engine appeared to leave its mounting, and the fighter spun away out of control. Porter himself was hit in the leg by a machine-gun bullet, but he stuck to his task and hit another fighter, which burst into flames. Henry C. Cordery, co-pilot, recalls:

"We were under constant attack. I don't know how long the first attacks lasted but there was a lull. I left my position to get more ammo' from the radio room. Passing through the waist I found the right waist gunner, Michele, severely wounded. His leg was off. The left waist gunner was also wounded. I called Lieutenant Moon, the bombardier. He came back and we both administered first aid. I took the protective covering off the needle of the morphine only to discover it was frozen. I must have had at least five uncovered and I put them all in my mouth to thaw them. I had considerable difficulty getting them out, as my hands were numb from the cold. Then I returned to my position and just about in time, as the attacks started again."

At 1415 hours a combination of flak and fighters shot down 1st Lieutenant John D. Jackson's B-17[411] over Friesburg. In the 369th Squadron, *The Wicked WAAC*,[412] flown by 1st Lieutenant George C. Bettinger, and

Piccadilly Commando, piloted by 1st Lieutenant Gustav S. Holmstrom, had also been lost.[413] In the 367th Squadron, 1st Lieutenant Richard Butler's B-17 was also in trouble, as Jim Harris, the tail gunner, recalls:[414]

"We had seen our Squadron and our Group picked off one by one. Problems began as we crossed the French Coast when flak practically tore off the right stabilizer. The tail section was vibrating badly. A few miles into France our rival crew in the 369th Squadron aborted for reasons unknown to us. Our navigator reported after an oxygen check that we had only enough oxygen to reach the target. We had just reasons to abort, but it would have taken more nerve to turn back than to continue on. This was a maximum effort mission, so we kept going. We had a few P-47 escorts, which had to turn back due to limited fuel. The German fighters hit us as soon as our escort left. I had never seen so many enemy fighters and planes of various types. The single engine FW 190s and Me 109s rolled through the bomb groups, twin engined planes beyond our range lobbed rockets at us, as bombers dropped aerial bombs from above into our formations. When we saw the fighters flying through their own flak, it was evident that they were going all out to stop us. The intercom was bedlam with crewmembers calling out fighter attacks. It got so bad that it didn't do any good to call them out. Our plane was shot up pretty bad, with three engines on fire. We were forced to bale out near the target."[415]

For a little over three hours, from 1333 to 1647 hours, exceptionally large numbers of enemy fighters attacked the 1st Division. The worst of these took place between Aachen and the Frankfurt area, and the out-of-position 305th Bomb Group suffered worst of all. Three B-17s in the Chelveston outfit had already turned back, one with a broken exhaust stack, one with an oxygen leak, and a third that lost its way during forming up. Fifteen remained, but any semblance to a group formation was nonexistent, and it was every squadron for itself![416] When the attacks began the high squadron was at 22,000ft and the low was at 21,400ft. Far ahead of these two units was Major Charles G. Y. Normand's four-ship lead squadron at 21,700ft. At first it was the low squadron that bore the brunt of the attacks, where none came in for rougher treatment than *Sizzle* and Lieutenant Douglas L. Murdock's crew in the "tail-end Charlie" slot in the Purple Heart Corner. Three FW 190s led by Major Johannes Seifert, II./JG 26 CO, which came in from the tail firing their 20mm cannons, hit *Sizzle* hard in the first pass. Ted Smith, co-pilot, recalls:

"An explosion occurred between the No.1 and 2 engines, stunning both Murdock and me. On coming to, we recovered control of the plane but realized both engines were out and that we were way out of formation. We also realized it was impossible to get back to the formation or to the deck in time to save the crew as six or eight FW 190s and Me 109s were chewing us up at close range. I ordered the crew out, flipped the auto-flight control on and baled out. Murdock was to follow but I never saw him again. The togglelier and the navigator[417] had already left when I checked their positions on the way past. Bill Menzies was the only crewmember I ever saw again."[418]

Seven minutes after the fighting commenced the 305th began to come apart. In just five minutes (from 1340 until 1345) four of the group's B-17s crashed west of the German border. Three went down in Holland and one in Belgium. 2nd Lieutenant Dennis J. McDarby[419] had been playing "catch up" since the mid-morning group assembly over England. Once again he was out of his #3 position behind the low squadron, with the low squadron still trailing Major Normand. McDarby was still struggling to recover from Normand's earlier, rapid acceleration that had left the high and low squadrons behind and far too spread out. The McDarby crew had become a straggler, and was a target for German fighters. The top turret gunner, T/Sgt Arthur E. Linrud, recalls:[420]

"From my position in the upper gun turret, I could see enemy planes in varying numbers high above us climbing to altitude to attack our bomber formations and all around us. Shortly, it became a matter of picking out one, getting it in the gun sight and squeezing off several bursts from the twin 50 caliber machine guns until it swept past, above or below, then repeating the action when another wave of fighters came in. Unless a plane blew up or smoked badly while in his sights, the gunner could not know if he damaged or shot one down. There wasn't time to look to check the results. One thing was for sure: an enemy caught in the gunner's sight was greeted with a hailstorm of bullets and red streamers of tracers as it came within range.[421]

"The attack continued unabated. FW 190s and Me 109s came diving at high speed, cannon and guns flashing along the leading edge of their wings. Occasionally, one dove through our formation, barely missing a bomber. Previously, the enemy was cautious, today was different. This was reckless and fierce last encounter for many airmen on both sides.

"As we moved deeper into enemy country, our bombers were damaged at an increasing rate. Unable to keep up, the damaged B-17s fell behind, then turned back, hoping to be lucky enough to make it to the Channel where Air Sea Rescue might get them out of the cold water. Going back with a damaged bomber meant probable attacks and a tense fight until one or the other went down. The more fortunate crewmembers were able to parachute to earth. Smoke poured from a bomber behind us and to our right. The next time I looked, it had pulled away from the formation and was in a dive, on fire and out of control. As I turned my turret to fire I could see that no part of the formation was escaping attack.

"Our plane shook violently from the impact and explosion of a cannon shell, or rocket, that smashed into the rear of the No.2 engine. It ripped a hole in the leading edge and left a smoking mass of ruin, just a few feet from my turret and the Pilot's position.

"Fortunately, McDarby was not injured and quickly got the plane under control. However, we were unable to stay in the formation. As we dropped down and fell back, McDarby checked the crewmembers, who were OK and reported that there was no way we could make it to the target with our bomb load. We would dump the bombs and go to low level and attempt to fight our way back to cloud cover to escape the fighters who were pressing the attack now that we were without the protection of the formation. As we descended, bullets hitting the fuselage had the sound of hailstones on a tin roof. The smoke from the No.2 engine turned into flames. Fanned by the slipstream, they reached the fuel tanks. Soon a huge ball of fire trailed past our tail section. A call on the interphone got me out of the turret. Lieutenant Donald Breeden, the co-pilot, motioned me to the cockpit. McDarby said, 'Remove the escape hatch cover. We'll never get this fire out now.' I snapped my parachute pack in place, climbed down, grabbed the emergency hatch release and gave the door a kick with my foot. It disappeared. As if by magic a hole cut out into the sky appeared. I was climbing back up to the cabin, when McDarby touched my head and said, 'Bale out, I've already given the order. The wing is going to break off. We're coming too.'

"I went back and sat with my feet hanging out the door. Glancing into the nose section, I saw navigator Lieutenant William Martin and bombardier Lieutenant Harvey Manley getting ready to follow me. With a quick departing wave, I gripped the 'D' ring and tumbled out into space. Onrushing air alerted me to give a firm pull on the 'D' ring. There was a sudden slap in my face from the chest parachute pack as it passed upward, then a jolt as the chute filled with air. Being suspended in the quietness was a contrast to the clatter and vibration of machine guns, tension of battle and the roar of engines. How quickly it had changed! The roar of a German plane passing overhead, too close for comfort, quickly brought me to reality. Several chutes were visible in the sky. Our plane, below and to one side, was falling out of control. The burning wing had broken off. The ground moved up to meet me. What before seemed like small dots were German civilians and soldiers moving to intercept landing airmen. I came down in a small field, landing on my feet but falling to the ground from the impact. After getting to my feet I heard that statement that would become familiar: 'For you the War is over,' spoken by a soldier with a pistol pointed at me."[422]

Next to go down was 2nd Lieutenant Gerald B. Eakle's B-17. S/Sgt Herman E. Molen, the toggelier, was cut on the neck by a piece of flying Plexiglas, and the navigator received wounds in both legs from shell fragments. An intercom check indicated that the waist area of the plane was "like a sieve." Alone and unable to keep up with the remainder of the 364th Squadron, Eakle did a diving 180° turn and headed for home, but they never made it. Further fighter attacks wrecked the aircraft, and Eakle gave the order to bale out. He and eight of the crew survived. Lieutenant Charles W. Willis Jr and five of his crew baled out over Holland four miles west of the German border after their B-17 was hit repeatedly by single and twin engined fighters firing shells and rockets into the formation. As the B-17s entered Germany *The Uncouth Bastard*, flown by 2nd Lieutenant Robert W. Holt, was shot down, and he and five crew were killed. Only Bill Frierson and three other gunners got out alive.

Lazy Baby, flown by 2nd Lieutenant Edward W. Dienhart, was knocked out of formation. The throttle controls for No. 1 and 2 engines were shot away. No.3 engine was dead, and a huge hole in the right wing fuel tank trailed a stream of gas that could ignite at any moment. A shell burst against the B-17's Plexiglas nose. It badly wounded bombardier Carl Johnson and navigator Lieutenant Donald F. Rowley, "a sunny optimistic golden boy from California…an athletic Los Angeles native with arms like oak branches who could do ten pushups at a clip [and who] never smoked, drank or swore...." The navigator, whose arms were nearly blown off in the explosion, plotted the B-17 crew's route to Switzerland even as he slowly bled to death. Another explosion had broken radioman Hurley "Smitty" Smith's left arm and riddled him with shrapnel. S/Sgt Bernie Segal, tail gunner, was anxious about the idea of baling out over Germany, as he was Jewish. Incredibly, *Lazy Baby* made it to neutral territory, and when Ed Dienhart belly-landed the badly ravaged B-17 in a sloping potato field at Reinach-Aesch, Donald Rowley ribbed his pilot that it was the best landing he had ever made. The young navigator, who the crew used to tease for being such a Boy Scout, but who they all secretly admired for it just the same, died from his wounds that same evening. He was buried four days later in Basle's Hornli cemetery.[423]

Approaching the Rhine, the B-17 flown by Flight Officer Verl D. Fisher, *Mary T*, flown by 2nd Lieutenant Robert S. Lang, *Lallah-V III*,[424] piloted by 2nd Lieutenant Ellsworth H. Kenyon, and 2nd Lieutenant Robert T. Skerry's B-17 were shot down.[425] Four men were killed aboard Fisher's B-17. One of them was Thomas Therrien, who before trying to exit the doomed plane helped the wounded radio operator and the other waist gunner out. Just as Therrien prepared to jump through the waist window a 20mm shell exploded next to him and killed him.

Luftgaukommando VI awarded the downing of Skerry's B-17 to six German flak units who had reported none of their fighters in the area. JG 26 "*Schlageter*," however, awarded the B-17 to *Oberfeldwebel* Willi Roth of 5./JG 26. When Skerry gave the order to bale out he had run out of options. The B-17 had two engines shut down and feathered—one was on fire—most of the tail surfaces were gone, and there was a large hole in the radio room. The Fortress was being shot to pieces from both ends, and flak was bursting all around the front of the ship while fighters were attacking from the rear. When it hit the ground the B-17 was 29 miles behind Normand's lead squadron.[426] By the time the 305th Bomb Group could see the city of Schweinfurt, 12 miles in the distance, it had lost ten aircraft, including all five in the low squadron and parts of the high and lead squadrons. Only five B-17s remained, and a Fortress from another group joined them.[427]

The 92nd was also badly hit, as Captain McLaughlin recalls:

"Under the pressure of continued heavy attacks our ranks were soon greatly decimated. After three hours, as we closed our formation for the target run, my group looked more like a squadron. We had but 12 airplanes left out of the 21 we took off with."

Bill Rose captained one of the 92nd crews that survived to the target:

"The Germans rose to meet us in full force. It was indescribable. This was the first time I had any thoughts that we were in for a fight. Fighters were everywhere. Rather than calling out when one was spotted, the gunners just shot. Everyone had his own target. I called Keith Kent my waist gunner to get the fighter on his side. He replied, 'Don't bother me, my gun's jammed. I'll get him in a minute.' He was so calm I thought we were back in gunnery school. I will always remember our tail gunner, Wally Eilers, reporting that we were going to get some protection from the rear by a group of Forts. We thought we weren't going to have the attacks on the tail like we had been getting on our last two missions. When they got close, he saw they were German multi-engine planes. Then, all of a sudden, 'Oh my God!' They fired a salvo of rockets into our formation. I was fortunate in that one went right past my window. The rocket landed right in the wing of the element leader right by a gas tank. I watched it burn and it wasn't long before the entire wing was on fire. The pilot dropped back and the stricken crew baled out. Eventually, the B-17 blew up. It was a terrible sight to see. I slid into his position and was the lone plane in the second element. The attacks continued. Our ball turret gunner pleaded for someone to help him get out. His guns were broken and the turret dammed. All he could see were planes going down out of control and in flames. He was trapped. No one could be spared from his guns. When he became emotional I told him, 'Get off the interphone, we will get to you as soon as possible.'"

Phillip R. Taylor, in the 91st Bomb Group, did not know what squadron his B-17 finally joined, but they ended up as a lead ship:

"We had our wing plane shot away three times. One scene remains as clear now as the day it happened. From the left waist position I watched one of the wing ships get hit and immediately start to burn. The pilot slipped the ship out of formation and held it steady so the crew could bale out. Within seconds she was really burning. The co-pilot looked up and saw me watching. He made no attempt to leave the ship or save himself. Instead, he waved at me. I waved back until she blew up a couple hundred yards out. There were only a couple of chutes out, one of which got tangled in the tail. That co-pilot, knowing he was about to die, did one of the coolest gestures I have ever seen."[428]

The 3rd Division encountered some fighter opposition, but it was not as intense as that experienced by the 1st Division. Only two Fortresses were shot down before the Thunderbolt escort withdrew. Bob Hughes, flying in the 100th Bomb Group formation, recalls:

"We were a little south of our course and about four minutes late. We could hear chatter on the radio from units and their escorts ahead of us, who seemed to be drawing enemy fighters. We seemed to be getting much less action than the 95th and 390th Bomb Groups in our wing."

It was still an unnerving experience, as Jerry Lefors recalls:

"As co-pilot without a gun to fire, you sit and watch. Three enemy fighters coming through our formation firing and being fired upon as they rolled upside down and peeled off below us fascinated me. About one out of three aircraft doing this maneuver went down in smoke. The intercom was busy at the beginning of the attacks: 'Fighters 1 o'clock high...' As the attacks gained in intensity - they were coming from all directions - the gunners were quieter, but I'm sure they weren't bored!"

The 3rd Division had proceeded on a converging course with the 1st Division towards Aachen. At 1410 hours the 1st Division, now flying an almost parallel course to the 3rd Division, arrived at a point 25 miles north of Frankfurt, where it was to change course and head south-southeast for the River Main. This was designed to deceive the German defenses into thinking that Augsburg or Munich was their destination. About ten miles south of the River Main, the 1st Division turned sharply onto a northeasterly heading for Schweinfurt.

By the time it entered the target area, the 1st Division had lost 36 bombers shot down and 20 had turned back, but the 3rd Division had come off surprisingly lightly, losing only two bombers to fighter attacks. This left a total of 224 Fortresses to win through to the target itself. Collectively, this seems a reasonable force, but most of the groups in the 1st Division had been torn to shreds by the intense fighter attacks, and some were barely skeleton formations. Of the 37 Fortresses in the 40th Combat Wing that had crossed the Channel, only 16 remained, and worse were to follow. Crewmembers recall the dozens of great red flashes in the flak columns as they turned on the IP. Many called out that the enemy was using red flak, not realizing that they were in fact witnessing the explosions of many B-17s in the groups ahead. The enemy pilots showed complete disregard for the tremendous flak barrage over the target, and made almost suicidal attacks on the bombers. For the moment the lead bombardier aboard the *Bad Egg* had to try and ignore the attacks as he set up the Automatic Flight Control Equipment (AFCE) that linked the aircraft's controls to the bombsight. The *Bad Egg* led the 91st over the city, and at 1439 hours they began unloading their deadly cargoes on the streets, houses, and factories of Schweinfurt. Budd J. Peaslee described it as "a city about to die."

The 91st was to claim the best overall bombing results for the 1st Division. However, the 351st Bomb Group was the most accurate, with Captain H. D. Wallace, squadron bombardier, in part of the group formation, placing all his bombs within 1000ft of the MPI. The composite group, led by Major John R. Blaylock, whose lead bombardier was 1st Lieutenant Jim Bradley, also did a commendable job on hitting the ball bearing factories at the target. After the mission, the crew would be ordered to report to the 8th Air Force Headquarters to receive a commendation for a job well done. Jim Bradley recalls:[429]

"We had great fighter protection to Aachen, Germany. When our Spits and P-47s left, the German Air Force was ready with a fighting welcome. The group to our rear was wiped out by the time we started the bomb run at Würzburg. When one Germans unit left, another took its place. I was a voluntary non-shooter, explaining to the crew that my hands were like those of a fine concert pianist and I could not get my bombing fingers tight from the recoil of the fifty caliber guns. Actually, I had grazed a couple of B-17s on a prior mission. For the good of the Eighth Air Force, I decided that I was too lousy in my shooting to risk the lives of the other crews. Major Blaylock was a perfect pilot, cool and poised. I had trained with him a number of times over the Irish Sea just to give me practice in turning a group or wing. Another group tried to cut in front of us on the bomb run, but we won in a game of 'Chicken' with them and didn't change course. I always took from five to seven minutes to set up the course and rate to drop the bombs. At the last second, the lights didn't come on, so I had to salvo six bombs and the bomb-bay gas tank. The cross hairs never moved after the bombsight clicked and the bombs were dropped. On the final run Paul Post lost an eye and the other waist gunner lost a leg. As we turned away from the target and headed back to England I went to the waist of the ship and closed the two side gun ports and tried to comfort the wounded. I feel badly that I wasn't a better medic who possibly could have saved Paul's eye. I couldn't tell him what was wrong with his eye, since there was no blood. The gunner's wound was in the upper groin area, so it was necessary to wrap it in telephone cable to stop the blood."[430]

Minutes from the IP Lieutenant Victor C. Maxwell's B-17 became the eleventh Fortress to be lost from the 305th Bomb Group formation when it came under heavy fighter attack and spun out of formation on fire. Maxwell and six of the crew died trapped in the bomber and only three gunners got out. 2nd Lieutenant Alden C. Kincaid on Major Normand's right wing had been wounded in the right arm by machine gun fire, and Lieutenant Norman W. Smith lay slumped in his seat. He had been dead for almost an hour. Four minutes intro the bomb run Kincaid's plane took a number of direct hits from 20mm cannon fire and two engines were put out of action. Kincaid ordered everyone out, and he and six of his crew made it. *Sundown Sal*, flown by Ray Bullock, was hit during the same attack that downed Kincaid's aircraft, and a 20mm cannon shell lodged in the fuel cell of the left wing and set it on fire. Bullock still had six minutes to fly before reaching the target, and *Sundown Sal* could blow up at any minute, but he told his crew that they could bale out if they liked, but he was going to complete the bomb run before leaving. All his crew agreed to stick with him until after bombs away. Bullock's burning B-17 and Barney Farrell's *Rigor Mortis* remained in formation with the lead ship, flown by 2nd Lieutenant Joseph W. Kane. Lieutenant Joe Pellegrini could see the target in his bombsight and knew he could hit it, but Normand did not think they could hold it on the run. Pellegrini, who had already set the cross hairs of the bombsight on the aiming point, begged Normand, "Major, please let me continue this run. Visibility is perfect; we can't miss!" But Normand decided to follow the 91st Bomb Group and ordered Pellegrini to bomb with them. Unfortunately, the 18 1000lb bombs dropped from the bomb bays of the three B-17s in the 305th Bomb Group fell in a civilian neighborhood. Immediately after "bombs away" *Sundown Sal* became the unlucky 13th and final victim in the 305th Bomb Group formation when it was abandoned by Bullock's crew, who all baled out successfully. Joe Kane's and Barney Farrell's B-17 turned away from the target and followed the lead group home.[431]

Then it was the turn of the 40th Combat Wing. McLaughlin and his bombardier, Edward T. O'Grady, conferred over the interphone, and as the bomber rolled out on a heading towards Schweinfurt they hooked up to the AFCE. Ahead of them was the daunting sight of the 1st Wing almost blotted from sight by the concentrated flak barrage. Captain McLaughlin recalls:

> "Looking back now I have to admire the courage of Harry Hughes as I listened to him on the aircraft interphone coolly directing Edward O'Grady to the target amidst the constant rock and roll of the exploding flak shells and fighter attacks. We had to calm down one of our leaders whose anxiety overcame him and he began to interrupt the interphone conversation during the bomb run by muttering to himself and damning the Germans!"

Flying in the No.5 slot in the 92nd Bomb Group formation directly beneath Peaslee and McLaughlin was Bill Rose:

> "I had positioned my plane directly under our squadron leader to give us protection from the top and both sides. When his bomb bay doors opened. I looked straight up when the bomb bay doors opened and I could see right into the bomb bay. If his bombs fell out prematurely they would fall on us so I told Mike [Erro A. Michelson, bombardier] to let me know one minute before 'bombs away' so I could cut the throttles and drop back. The bombs fell right in front of the nose of our plane. When all his bombs had gone and he had closed his bomb bay doors, I tucked back in as we headed for home. In my position the German pilots had a real hard time getting at us. The only way they could get to us was to come underneath. I think this was how we were able to survive; protected in every direction apart from underneath. We came home, the four of us, one right underneath another and one out on each side. The German attacks were less intense on our return over France. We ran out of ammunition. Our oxygen system was knocked out and we stayed in formation by using our "bale out" bottles of oxygen."

The 306th Bomb Group formation followed the 92nd Bomb Group. The fighters had left by now, and ahead and low George Roberts aboard *Cavalier* saw:

> "several white puffs of flak which became darker and more accurate as we approached the target. The barrage did not seem as heavy as that over Bremen, but I could feel the concussion and hear the 'Woof' and the peppering of the fuselage. When the bombardier called 'Bombs Away,' I checked the bomb bays to see that all bombs were out. The bomb-bay doors did not close, so Lieutenant William Pleasant the bombardier spent several minutes correcting the malfunction. Very few B-17s were left in our formation. I thought the fighters could easily finish us off. Luckily, we had only 13 minutes of new attacks, which were not as intense as before. Evidently, the German fighters had gone to attack the incoming bombers."

The 306th dropped its 1000lb bombs. Sixteen of them exploded within a 1920ft circle. About twenty minutes after the target flak scored direct hits on two engines of 1st Lieutenant William C. Bisson's B-17 in the 367th Bomb Squadron, while enemy fighters riddled the rear of the Fortress. Only the co-pilot and four of the crew in the rear of the aircraft baled out of the doomed B-17. En route to the target a Ju 88 firing rockets had knocked out the No.3 engine of the Fortress, flown by 1st Lieutenant Ralph T. Peters. The Fortress, which was also riddled with hundreds of flak fragments and 20mm bullet holes, managed to stay in formation until after bombs away, but when the 306th Bomb Group went into a climb from the 22,500ft bombing altitude, Peters was unable to stay with them. At 1520 hours, with the No.3 engine propeller running away, Peters gave the order to bale out. 1st Lieutenant James V. Vaughter, the bombardier, recalls:[432]

> "The plane exploded shortly after the last man dumped. It was normal operating procedure -for the bombardier to jettison the escape hatch and tumble out headfirst. The other crewmembers thought I was afraid to bale out, as I was so long at the escape hatch door. Actually, the door was dammed and I was working to get it loose. Our wing commander ordered the pilots to climb 4000ft in an attempt to avoid some flak and reduce enemy fighter abilities at the higher altitude. The climb put sufficient extra stress on our damaged engines to cause the runaway prop. We were 24,000ft when I tumbled out of the escape hatch. We had been briefed to free-fall when at high altitude for many reasons. This did not register with me, as I pulled the ripcord at the count of three. When German fighters were flying so close that I could see their faces quite clearly, I was wishing that I had been smarter. Crew members using chest chutes in lieu of seat chutes, were able to wear only the chute harness and hook the chute to the harness to bale out. This gave us more comfort and mobility, but also the dire possibility of not having a chance to hook on our chutes. I cannot remember hooking on my chest pack. I cried as I was floating down in the bright sunshine that October day some twenty miles south west of Schweinfurt. Tears came because I immediately thought about my mother, how she would worry, cry and pray about her baby boy. Crying was also the result of being frightened over the realization that I was helpless, was going to become a prisoner, was not going to make it back to Thurleigh and because I was so mad that the enemy had gotten the best of us. To this day, I don't consider myself a good loser; at times not even a good winner."[433]

As the 303rd Bomb Group turned and began the bomb run, Wilbur Klint in *Luscious Lady* saw three B-17s from the wing ahead:

> "completely disintegrate and fall earthward in flaming shreds. Not a chance that anyone got out of those bombers. This was our introduction to the recently developed German rocket launcher. The bomb run looked perfect. We were briefed to expect 56 heavy anti aircraft guns defending the target but they gave us little trouble compared to the hordes of fighters we met on the way in and who picked us up again before we were even out of the flak zone."

T/Sgt Leroy Mace, ball turret gunner in *Knock-Out Dropper* flown by Lieutenant John Manning, who was leading the low squadron in the 303rd Bomb Group formation, was glad that when they finally reached the target it was covered in a large amount of flak. Mace, who was on his 10th mission, believed that as long as they were in the flak, the fighters would leave them alone. But he was surprised when they flew right through the flak to get at them:

> "It was a good clear day for bombing. I watched our bombs hit the target; it was one of our best jobs ever. Then we were hit by a 20mm cannon shell that exploded and tore a terrific hole in the middle of our stabilizer. It knocked us out of formation. We dropped about 400 feet and found ourselves all alone. We had never seen so

many fighters! Lieutenant Manning was fighting to keep the nose of the ship down and told us to stand by to bale out, but to stand by our guns. I took off my electric heated clothing and stayed in the ball turret. One could see ships of all kinds going down. We expected to be knocked out at any time. There were 20mm shells passing all around us: We never can tell how they missed. There was a time when my guns, the tail guns and one upper turret gun were out. We finally got them all working again. Several planes that I shot at blew up. I think every gunner in the crew shot down at least two, but we did not claim them. The pilot called and said, 'Well, this looks like it!' He told us to stand by as we had an engine with a windmilling prop. We were waiting for the final word to bale out, but with God's help, we did not have to. I never left the ball. You never know what one goes through at times like this. Finally, the fighters left and we breathed a big sigh of relief. The sky was filled with parachutes, like flowers in the spring. I had never seen so many fighters in my life."

By the time Bill Heller's B-17 approached the target they were in trouble. His Fortress was carrying bomb-bay tanks with extra fuel, which proved to be a mixed blessing:

"After this extra fuel was used we found that due to a malfunction, we could not drop the tanks, even after a half hour of freezing activity by engineer Huston and bombardier DeSousa in the bomb bay at 25,000ft altitude. The crew realized that we would have to carry this additional hazard. An empty fuel tank, even on an automobile, can be a virtual bomb if hit by a red-hot bullet or shell. The crew did not relish this prospect of sudden death, but with typical dedication and courage, wanted to put the bombs on this target of special importance.

"As the formation proceeded into Germany, fighter attacks began that would continue in intensity for hours. The formation waded through literally clouds of flak. Fighters continued to harass the bombers. It became apparent that when two engines began losing power, we were unable to stay in formation. We could not continue under the present conditions of a heavy bomb load plus the extra gas tanks. The only chance of survival was to stay with the formation. I ordered the bombardier to salvo the tanks and bombs. We were then able to rejoin the formation. We flew over the target with open bomb-bay doors so as not to attract any more fighters than necessary. The bombs from the formation fell with good accuracy.

"Fighters and Forts were going down everywhere. The sky seemed full of chutes, some burning and some peacefully floating in the sky. I saw a Fort up ahead start to smoke; the next instant a sheet of flame. Then nothing! I saw a Fortress fly upside down in a very slow roll and then dive for terra firma. Ten chutes popped out from it on their start of a journey to a PoW camp. The flight continued with our crew calling out fighter attacks to be followed by that comforting shudder of the fifty caliber guns firing. The fighters included twin engine and single engine planes.

"Sometimes I wonder how we stayed in formation. My tail gunner S/Sgt Tony Laurinitis would yell through the interphone, 'Fighters coming in at 6 o'clock.' At the same time George Payne was yelling, 'Fighter coming in at 4 o'clock.' Then his guns would blaze. When gunners gave this information to the pilot, he flipped the Fortress in all attitudes to screw up the enemy's aim. Just as sure as I'd slip or dive the ship within the formation, shells would burst in clusters all about us, usually in the same spot where we were a second before. Wonderful cooperation between gunners and pilots. No wonder I loved them. It was a great moment when Tony yelled: 'I got him! There he goes!' Payne and Huston confirmed the kill as they saw the Me 110 go down and two chutes eject from it. We got two more that day; another Me 210 and a FW 190. Chutes were seen popping from both fighters.

"Our left waist gunner Leo Lanier, Jr., called on the interphone to say that the left horizontal stabilizer was badly shot up. Tail gunner Laurinitis added that the fabric was gone from the top of the flipper. There was a hole in the leading edge of the wing. Inches from my head, the windshield glass was shot out. I didn't notice the damage until sweat and the condensation from my oxygen mask started to freeze. The ball turret was inoperative, which the German's noticed and gave their full attention. Ball turret gunner S/Sgt Shultz found himself a sitting duck in a shooting gallery. I was used to doing evasive action on cue from the gunners, but was somewhat mystified by co-pilot Coppom's signals. I truly wondered, but seriously obeyed his motions. Any question in my mind was answered when just after following his motion to skid left, a great cluster of 20mm shells burst right where we had been; between Lieutenant Jokerts' Fort and mine. Jack Coppom was trained as a fighter pilot before being assigned as a B-17 co-pilot. Looking right into the sights of the fighters, he instinctively knew when they would fire. The technique worked every time."[434]

The 40th Combat Wing turned away from the target and headed in the direction of the 1st Combat Wing, now making for the French border. The withdrawal route, well away from the line of penetration, was devised by General Anderson to limit casualties, and took the bombers south of Paris and then north towards England. In the 306th Bomb Group formation Henry C. Cordery, the co-pilot in Lieutenant Jeffries' B-17, recalls:

"We came off the target and re-grouped. I looked around at the group and there wasn't much of us left. In my squadron we started with six ships in two three-ship elements and being in the lead ship I saw all five of them go down. Out of 18 aircraft we had six left. I remember someone, I believe it was Lieutenant Jeffries, saying, 'That's the government's half, now for ours.'"[435]

Captain McLaughlin spoke into his oxygen mask to his tired crew and Colonel Peaslee sitting beside him "We've flown this far for Uncle Sam, from here we fly for the U.S. - 'us.'"

The third and final wing, the 41st comprising the 379th and 384th Bomb Groups, added its bombs to the conflagration. Near the target Howard Stumpf, the radio operator-gunner aboard *Tallywhacker*, in the 384th Bomb Group, flown by Robert L. Robinson, counted 35 fighters flying parallel to them off their left wing "We flew tail end, high squadron of the low group. After abortions and shoot downs we became the only plane left in the 544th Squadron." Ball gunner Stanley Mozarka adds "We shot our way in and we shot our way out."

"Togglin' Ed" Millson in the 379th lead ship recalls:

"We wove our way through spotty opposition near Koblenz and Frankfurt. Joe Wall was successful in evading flak areas. We reached the initial point (IP) of the bomb run. I took control of the aircraft from Colonel Rohr. One glance took in the points we had spent weeks studying. Up ahead lay the target - Schweinfurt. Flak was uncomfortably close. One burst blotted my view for a long second. Rattle like hail on the roof announced another close call. I had the target lined up in the Norden bombsight. Smoke from hits on the other two factories was beginning to roll over our aiming point. As another burst rattled against *'Rag'n Red.'* I called 'Bombs Away. Doors closing. Let's get to Hell out of here!' As we turned off the target a formation of fifteen FW 190s ripped out of the sun in a vicious attack. Before anyone could open his mouth I heard the sharp crack of a bursting 20mm shell in back of me. I whirled around expecting to find Joe badly injured. Instead, I found him laughing and pointing at my chest chute, ripped and torn by the exploding shell. I was left without a chute, but it saved both of us from serious injury. The group lost three B-17s on that pass, one of which was rammed by an attacker. I think Jerry had every plane they owned in the sky. I saw three Forts in the wing ahead explode from rocket hits. The Germans were attacking from all directions around the clock. We saw several obsolete type aircraft, one of which was a Dornier 217. Forts from our group glided out of formation with feathered props or telltale damage. Frequently, the dark chutes of the German crews would be mingled with the white ones of the Americans."

At around 1450 the crew of the *Gay Caballeros*, in the Tail End Charlie slot in the 379th Bomb Group formation, started the bomb run through thick flak. Forrest J. Eherenman, navigator, who "shot down one Me 109 and possibly damaged another," recalls that "fighter attacks were too many to count." In his log he wrote: "Thousands of fighters attacking in squadrons."

"Later, I estimated that the number of enemy fighters at any one time to be around forty. In a single sweep our Group lost three B-17s, one of which was rammed by a German fighter. For two and half-hours I was too busy to make any more entries in my navigator's log. I ran out of ammunition again and again. I called for some more from the waist positions who didn't seem to be getting as many attacks as the frontal positions. In six hours of hell our oxygen was gone, our ammo was gone, our control cables gone and we had large holes in left wing, waist and stabilizer and the flaps were shot away and the hydraulic system was out. Fortunately, we were able to stay with the formation flying on three engines."

As the 41st Wing turned off the target in came the 3rd Bomb Division, flying six minutes behind, to take its turn. First over the target was the 96th Bomb Group at the head of the 45th Combat Wing. Amazingly, the Fortress piloted by Silas Nettles and Jerry Lefors was still holding formation despite the loss of their No.1 engine. Jerry Lefors says:

"As we neared the Initial Point of the bomb run we could see the familiar pattern of flak: a tri-dimensional checkerboard of deadly puffs of smoke. Through this we would reach the target. We were on the bomb run when the left inboard engine was hit. Nettles hit the feathering button and the prop slowed to a near stop but the system failed and the run away prop revved the engine up to about 3300 RPM. On bombardier Ed Jones' request, the crew elected to hang on and try to drop our bombs, since we had come this far. We dropped the bombs as the Group was making its turn to the right. We cut the turn short to try to catch up. Our screaming runaway prop was slowing us down to about 143 mph. I was nervously pushing against the knobs for every ounce of power from the three struggling engines. Cutting the corner still didn't catch our formation. Nettles and I communicated through sign language that we would join the next one. It's near certain doom to be alone with a crippled B-17. The Germans like the easy ones. We were being sprayed with bullets. We dove; hoping the prop would come off and give us that extra few mph we needed. The runaway prop was just as determined to hang on as we were. We joined the following group as they caught up to us. This Group was moving too fast for us, so we joined the last Group in the formation. Nettles tucked in level with the leader. This was our last hope, the last Group in Germany that day. There was a great expression of relief on the intercom. Someone said, 'Looks like I'll keep my date tonight.'

"Then we heard on the command channel: 'Group Leader, we're stalling out back here, can you speed up the formation?' Nettles broke in and said they would lose us if they went faster. For a short time we seemed to be holding our own, then the Group left us behind at about five miles per hour. Nettles and I were both perspiring freely, trying to keep the big bird flying. I had an odd feeling as the last group pulled away from us. I looked behind at the empty sky. We were certainly 'Tail End Charlie' now! The sight of black smoke pouring from the left outboard engine startled me. I thought, 'Oh God, I hope it's just oil smoke.' I strained to see if it was on fire, then noticed that Nettles was looking at the right wing. Our heads swung to opposite sides and we knew we had two engines burning."

Time was running out, as Eugene Sebeck recalls:

"We had been getting heavy flak and fighter attacks. All guns were busy. Without full power we were losing altitude and dropping back. As we passed our IP for the bomb run, thick black smoke poured out of No.1 engine. We were ordered to stand by to bale out. Not being able to wear my chute in the top turret, I had to step down to get it. My separate oxygen supply had been acting up so I hooked one side of my chute and hooked in to the main oxygen supply. When I got back into the turret I remember thinking, 'Boy I can see a lot better with that new oxygen', then I realized that while I was out of the turret it had been hit, but good! The gunsight, which would have been only a couple of inches from my face, was pulverized. Gears and pieces of the case were everywhere. Thinking that the turret was worthless, I got back out of the turret and was looking out the window near the cockpit when the pilots saw me. I heard those famous last words: 'Sebeck, get the hell back in that turret'. I got back in the turret. Then things *really* got rough. Our #4 engine was smoking and fighters were everywhere. Four FW 190s hit at once with the whole crew trying to keep them away. Three broke off the attack, but one was determined. He came in from 6 o'clock. I laid the '50s on him and let loose. It was like he ran into a stone wall and dropped like a rock. I can still hear the radio operator, Pat Putnam screaming in the intercom, 'Sebeck got him!'

"We were now in real bad shape. We had dropped our bombs on the target and were trying to get home. Our hopes were shattered when the #4 engine burst into flames, with the wing melting under the heat. Nettles said, 'Let's get outa here' and rang the bale out bell. I went to the bomb bay and tripped the doors, then opened the door to the radio room to see all the crew in the back leaving. I left through the bomb bay."

Lefors again:

"Nettles slapped my left arm and said, 'Let's get outa this thing LeFors.' I nodded. There was no doubt! Nettles had previously given the order to prepare to bale out. Now the final order: a bell signal and 'Bale Out!' According to our emergency plan I was to check that O'Hearn and Jones had heard the bale-out bell. The pitch of excitement had reached a peak. I'm sure we were all scared. I crawled down to the nose, my oxygen mask disconnected but still on my face. I looked at O'Hearn and pointed at the door, he nodded. I crawled and climbed back to the cockpit. We had our parachute harnesses on, but the chest pack chutes were behind our seats. I snapped on my chest pack and then I realized that I had not fastened my leg straps and panicked. There was no time to lose: Either engine could blow up the plane any second and the sound of German bullets penetrating the already riddled bomber added to the urgency of the moment. I struggled, reached over my chest pack, unbuckled my left leg strap from the side of the harness and with much strain, brought it between my legs and finally got it snapped.

"Meanwhile Nettles had set the automatic pilot, checked the rear of the plane and went to the bomb bay. While I struggled to get my straps fastened I think I signaled for him to go ahead. Just as I got the snaps together, I saw Nettles drop feet first out of the bomb bay. His parachute harness hooked on the bomb rack. I thought that as soon as I got my leg straps snapped I would get him loose. However, he shook himself free. As I stepped on the catwalk in the open bomb bay I knew that I was alone. Bullets were still tearing into the ship. A 500lb bomb remained in the nearby rack. I looked at the peaceful landscape four miles below and stepped into thin air. The loud blast of air at around 140 mph (the forward speed of the ship) surprised me. I was tumbling, trying not to pull the ripcord too soon. Finally, I found the ripcord handle with my left hand: I had snapped my chest chute on upside down in the excitement of the moment! There was a sudden jolt as the chute opened - then silence except for the whisper of the air passing through the silken canopy above. I watched our B-17 flying unmanned, until with a puff of smoke, the right wing blew off. I counted the other nine chutes floating earthward."[436]

The 96th Bomb Group's target was obscured by smoke from the preceding bomb runs, but crews had not flown this far to be thwarted by smoke from their own bombs and released them anyway. Waist gunner Leo Rand was standing ankle deep in spent shell casings after two hours of combat, and was thinking that all the good things that were supposed to happen, according to the morning's briefing, had not come about. He cursed to himself "All this briefing propaganda had to be a load of crap." A few miles from Würzburg an attacking Bf 109 was met by a burst of Leo's .50 caliber gun. The only effect he noticed was that the fighter's engine stopped. While he was concentrating on putting more lead into the attacker, the 109 pilot baled out into his line of fire and the .50 caliber slugs cut the unlucky German in two, leaving the indelible and gruesome sight of the upper part of a body hanging from a parachute. Rand became convinced that he had committed an unpardonable slaughter. He thought that if he lived through this mission, disgrace and probably a court martial would be his lot.

The second group in the wing was the 388th with 16 aircraft. The lead bombardier was unable to identify either the Kugelfischer ball-bearing works or the marshaling yards located to the south, so he set his sight on the bridge over the River Main and released his bombs slightly to the right of the ball-bearing plant. The bombs cascaded down into the southern half of Schweinfurt and the western end of the marshaling yards. The 13th Combat Wing was the last wing in the 3rd Division to cross Schweinfurt. "Gus" Mencow, in the 390th formation, recalls:

"As we neared the Initial Point the target came in to view and we started to peel off by groups to begin the bomb run. The sky over Schweinfurt was an awesome sight, with the black bursts of flak and here and there a ball of fire where a B-17 was hit. 'Mac' McCarthy, bombardier, looked back at me and from the look in his eyes over the oxygen mask I knew he was experiencing the same feeling of apprehension that I had. Suddenly, the look changed dramatically in his eyes and a twinkle appeared. I knew he was grinning under his mask. He reached for the microphone switch and said, 'Bombardier to pilot - Hey Geary, is there any way you can back up this crate? I think that would be our best way out of here!'

"'Will you shut up, McCarthy and get ready to drop your bombs,' said Geary.

"I could tell from the sound of his voice he was having difficulty to keep from laughing! God bless Mac. I knew then that if anything was going to happen over Schweinfurt at least we would all die in a happy mood."

Joey Poulin, the 19-year-old French-Canadian ball turret gunner on *The Eight Ball*, in the 390th Bomb Group, flown by Bill Cabral and Dick Perry, had a lucky escape when a piece of flak ripped off his turret door. Only his slender lifebelt prevented him from falling 25,000ft without a parachute (like almost all ball turret gunners, Poulin could not wear one in the close confines of his turret). Many gunners might have scrambled back into the belly of the aircraft, but if any *Luftwaffe* fighters spotted that the ball turret was out of action it would have been an open invitation to attack. Poulin chose to stick it out, praying all the time that the lifebelt would hold. Close on the heels of the 390th Bomb Group were the 95th and 100th Bomb Groups, their crews eager to release their bombs and head for home as quickly as possible. Lieutenant Bob Hughes, pilot of *Nine Little Yanks and a Jerk* in the latter group, recalls:

"We saw gas and oil fires dotting the countryside, attesting to the furiousness of the defense and the determination of the bomber crews to place their bombs squarely on the target and not be denied. From time to time, we had seen flak from a distance but as we neared the target area it took on a more personal feeling. Periodically, we could see the red hearts of the bursts of 'Big Stuff'. We could now see the target area. Lieutenant Richard F. Elliott our bombardier and I had attended a special briefing on the target even though we were scheduled to drop on the lead bombardier's release. This intense target study before take-off paid off handsomely because it allowed us to distinguish the target under the most unfavorable conditions. We had also been briefed about the smudgepots marking a dummy target area. Elliott and I recognized them for the dummies they were. They were smoking like the whole town was on fire.

"Suddenly, our attention was diverted. The leader of the 95th was struck by flak just as we approached the IP for the final turn to the target. He descended rapidly from formation. Flak was intense and my co-pilot Lieutenant Donald S. Davis, yelled 'Move Bob!' I had felt the 'whump' from the burst, which had lifted our wingman's plane and was sending it directly into us. Lieutenant Howard Keel temporarily lost control of the craft. The Good Lord kicked left rudder, down stick, left aileron, then back-stick and rolled out of a well-executed diving split 'S'. It allowed Keel to pass through the space, which we had occupied to execute a co-coordinated recovery. It also placed our ship on a direct course to the primary target. Dick Elliott picked up the target immediately and called 'Skipper, target dead ahead, set up and follow PDI!"

Nine Little Yanks and A Jerk was by now completely alone, so Hughes questioned Elliott:

"'Dick, I do not have the right to commit a man to this course of action against his will. It would have to be a 100% volunteer.' Dick called for a vote starting with the lowest ranking man. One by one all agreed and I said 'Gentlemen, we go!'

"We considered we had the element of surprise on our side and that we could maintain an appearance of a crippled aircraft by not opening our doors until just before 'bombs away'. We reinformed the crew that we were flying in a heavily defended area and the best information had it that the German planes would not penetrate the area. We also doubted that the flak guns would fire upon the one ship but would allow us to leave the area and become fighter bait. It was our best guess that they did not want to draw attention to the steam-plant and allied ball-bearing shops by firing on one ship. If we couldn't find it, they were not going to disclose it. Dick Elliott opened the doors just long enough to release the bombs. We already had our strike camera running. It was on intervolometer but our bombsight was not. Dick, knowing that he had the rate killed and the course was beautiful, set the selector switch on 'Salvo'. Bombs were away at 1454 hours. All fell in the MPI. The roar on the intercom was 'PICKLE BARREL!' *Nine Little Yanks and a Jerk* had just opened up the north segment of the target area and there were more bombs to follow. Our aircraft was strike photo aircraft for the 100th Bomb Group and we had picked up the 95th Bomb Group, which was still struggling, trying to get into formation. My wingmen joined me and we asked the new leader if we could be of assistance in re-forming the group, explaining that we had an experienced formation controller, Sgt Robert L. McKimmy, one of the finest formation critics in the business, riding the tail guns. The offer was graciously accepted. He lined them up for us in a hurry because we were running out of the defended area and in a very short time the 95th was formed and the 100th flight took its proper position in the high squadron. We rejoined the 390th Bomb Group and we were once again the 13th Combat Wing."

The 45th Combat Wing of the 3rd Division crossed Schweinfurt and dropped its bombs. The 4th Wing was the second wing to cross Schweinfurt' and they headed for the VKF plant. Roy Davidson recalls:

"My position in the group formation as 'tail end Charlie' really put us in the center of the whole shooting match. We went into the target amid very heavy flak and fighter attacks. The fighters continued to attack us right through to the target area. They even flew trough their own flak with no let up at all. But we were able to fight them off all the way to the target and out. Carl F. 'Hoot' Gibson, ball turret gunner, shot down a Bf 109 and the boys were really excited about this. But pretty soon the fighters came in thick and fast and everyone was getting to do a lot of shooting. By the time the fight was over I think most of the gunners aboard were out of ammunition. Fred Krueger, in the top turret, ran out and never did get to reload."

It was after the target that the 3rd Bomb Division met its stiffest opposition. Davidson recalls:

"We had gone into the target, dropped our bombs and had started back out, when the fighters made passes through the middle of the formation. They continued to attack the last group (385th) until they ran out of fuel and were forced to seek land. Maybe the fighters would make one pass at one group and then keep zigzagging through the formation until they got to the last group where they would continue attacking. We outfought the fighters but Richard Mungenast, the tail gunner, shouted that a Bf 110 behind us out of range was firing something at us and it was leaving a black stream of smoke. We didn't know what it was at the time but we discovered later that it was a rocket. We had never been told of the existence of such a device. The first shot burst way behind us. The Bf 110 pulled up closer and fired another one. It still burst short. Mungenast cried out, 'Here comes another black stream of smoke!' Right after that the missile exploded right under our plane. It felt as if we were on an elevator; it lifted us up and did all kinds of damage. The plane felt as it if was trying to turn a loop. Chochester and I had to apply full forward pressure with both hands and our knees on the wheels to keep the plane straight and level. Right after the explosion there was an awful lot of excitement on board. All the men in the back of the plane were wounded and screams of, 'I'm hit, I'm hit!' filled the intercom. I presume the explosion had also knocked off or damaged the flaps. The cable must have been broken because I could not adjust the trim tabs.[437]

"It wasn't long before we had a Bf 109 off each wing about 50 yards out. We had no ammunition left and anyway, three men had baled out and Mungenast was wounded. The only guns we had left were in the nose. The 109s were so close we could distinguish the pilots' facial features. I figured they were talking to each other to decide who would finish us off. They took it in turns to shoot at us, turning in directly from 3 o'clock. Whenever I saw his wings light up with cannon fire I took evasive action and turned towards him, like I was trying to ram him. Somehow or other, neither fighter succeeded in hitting us. I'll never know how in the world they missed us at such short range. We really gave it violent evasive action during each of their two or three passes and the maneuvering worked." (Eventually, Davidson's third engine cut out and he was forced to make a wheels-up landing in a cow pasture near the village of La Chappele-sur-Orbais. Guns protruding from the ball turret caused the B-17 to crack in the center, and bent the middle and tail sections upwards.)[438]

The city of Schweinfurt had soaked up over 483 tons of high explosives and incendiaries. The 3rd Division had dropped the most bombs on target, and the 390th was the most successful. Despite the lead ship experiencing difficulty, all 15 aircraft placed 50% of their bombs within 1000ft of the MPI. The Fortresses turned off the target and flew an almost complete 180° circle around Schweinfurt. A group of FW 190s headed for the 1st Division formation singled out the trailing 41st Combat Wing. The leading 379th Bomb Group lost three B-17s in the first pass, and another bomber also hurtled to earth after a collision with one of the fighters, which also went down. Both divisions headed for their respective rally points and began forming into combat wings again for the return over Germany and France. The surviving B-17s headed for the coast. "Togglin' Ed" Millson, in the 379th lead ship, recalls:

"Along the route home we could see smoking or flaming wreckage of bombers that had gone down during the aerial battle. After an eternity of bucking strong winds, which the German fighters utilized for head on attacks, friendly fighters appeared, swept in and dispersed our attackers. As the friendlies circled around us, one of the gunners was heard to utter, 'Thank God' voicing the sentiments of the entire formation. Soon, Joe announced that we had reached the cloud covered 'Tight Little Island' - England."

At 1640 hours the 1st Division crossed the Channel coast and was followed, just five minutes later, by the 3rd Division. Approaching the French coast, the two surviving aircraft in the 305th Bomb Group sighted the 92nd and 306th Bomb Groups for the first time on the mission. Luckily, the two B-17s had met little fighter opposition on the way home, for they had used almost all their ammunition before the target.

Incredibly, *Knock-Out Dropper*, in the 303rd Bomb Group, had made it this far, as Leroy Mace recalls:

"How glad we were to see England! The pilot said, 'Well men, we made it!' He called me and said I could get out of the turret, but to put on my parachute and stand by. I was glad to get out of that turret. Manning said it looked like we would have to leave the ship, as he didn't expect it to stay in the air long. He asked us how it looked in the back. We told him we thought it would hold but we could not be sure, it was a mess; the pilot said that anyone who wanted to could jump out. All the crew from the tail to the nose of the ship told him that if he stuck with it, we would too. If he was man enough to bring it in, we were men enough to stay with him. He waited a minute and said, 'OK. If that's the way it is, get ready for a crash landing. We are going in!' He made a perfect three-point landing. The ground crews were watching us; afraid we were going to crash. They said that in a few more minutes the whole stabilizer would have fallen off. There were a large number of holes all over the ship, but no one was hurt."

Robert Voltz was another in the "Hells Angels" Group who was "especially thankful to our Lord for being able to set foot on the good earth of England again." Bill Bergeron, first pilot with Colonel Kyle leading the 41st Combat Wing on his second trip to Schweinfurt, touched down at Molesworth after having to make three circles in order to give priority to the many badly damaged ships, several with wounded aboard. Bergeron recalled that "It looked like the Fourth of July fireworks so many flares were being shot off by the landing aircraft in distress." Lieutenant Robert Hullar and Wilbur Klint managed to get their badly damaged Fortress back, as Klint recalls:

"Our *Luscious Lady* suffered a broken wing spar, a shattered top-turret and a wide assortment of holes, which sent her off to the repair depot for a major overhaul. The *Lady* had to be patched up before she was flown to the depot. Many planes that made it back were out of commission for a week."[439]

The Fortresses' return to England was hampered by the same soupy weather that had dogged their departure. Captain McLaughlin recalls:

"This really topped it all off. Low ceilings and poor visibility loomed as an almost insurmountable problem because most of our remaining twelve aircraft were damaged and at least two had wounded on board who needed immediately attention.[440] Harry Hughes directed me to the landing end of our home runway at Podington, using for the first time an inter-setting 'Gee Box' line as an instrument approach system. With our wounded wingman - who as I recall was Lieutenant 'Smoke' McKennon - we tracked into a descending approach to the runway and when we had it in sight by pre-arrangement we pulled up and let him land. Then we led the other two remaining aircraft around and back to the final approach and landing… a long, tough, soul-searching day I'll not soon forget."

George Roberts, the radio operator aboard *Cavalier*, recalls:

"Clouds covered the Channel. Lieutenant Kirk, opting to return over the clouds, found the break he needed over England and circled the *Cavalier* to below the ceiling. I fired a flare as we approached the runway to signal the medics for the injured Webber. In bad weather, with a damaged plane in descending darkness, Kirk and Flight Officer Clyde Cosper made a good landing. Medics met us at the hardstand. Only five out of the eighteen planes of our group had reached the target. We were the only one from our 367th 'Clay Pigeon' Squadron. We had over 300 holes in the *Cavalier*, one of them large enough to fall through. Sergeant Webber, in serious condition, was taken to a regional hospital. It was his second Purple Heart in four raids. This was his last mission. One hundred of our friends did not return to Thurleigh. It was indeed a Black Thursday for those who had given their all on this 14th of October."[441]

Bill Rose recalls:

"On the order to 'Land any place you can,' Our squadron dispersed over the Channel. Out of the eighteen planes in the 92nd Bomb Group, which flew the mission, only four landed at our own base. Nine others landed at fields throughout England. One crash-landed and one burned after ground looping. Six were missing in action. When we spotted outer perimeter lights, I racked the plane around and tried to get in. The tower said that there was another B-17 on the same lights trying to land. We never saw one another and the tower could only hear us. I managed to land on the third try. There was a jeep at the end of the runway with a guide who stood in the rear to direct me to a parking spot. He didn't realize how fast I was coming. I saw his eyes get as big as saucers. He started beating the driver like a jockey hitting a racehorse to get in front while traveling backwards, ahead of us. I turned right at the end of the runway without ground looping, shut off the engines and turned into a parking stand off the taxiway. At debriefing, we learned that we were at Bovingdon, from where we had left the Combat Crew Replacement Center only three weeks before. Our de-briefing officer had survived the first Schweinfurt mission in August so he understood what we reported. We were served supper. Though we had not eaten since early that morning, none of us had an appetite. While we were picking at our food another crew came in. They had been in the traffic pattern with us, but had gone back up, headed for the Channel, turned on the autopilot and baled out."[442]

The *Gay Caballeros*, in the 379th Bomb Group, had managed to stay with the formation flying on three engines, but it lost another engine before reaching the English coast and began to lose altitude rapidly. Forrest Eherenman recalls:

"Lieutenant Corson made an emergency landing at a RAF base at Biggin Hill with much wiggling and ending up in a ground loop. Nobody was hurt and needless to say, the crew was thankful to be on the ground. We were overnight guests of the Royal Air Force. The RAF lived a bit better than American crews. Our plane never flew again. It was stripped and left to deteriorate in the English weather. Eleven out of seventeen 379th crews did not return to Kimbolton from the mission. Strike photos showed we had done a fine job on the target. We'd have other rough missions, including one to Berlin, but none like the October trip to Schweinfurt. Looking back, my 273 hours of combat seems like three hours of watching a movie. Your mind blots out things that are unpleasant and lets you remember more pleasant times."

The 388th Bomb Group did not lose a single plane on the Schweinfurt raid. Lieutenant Dan Sullivan put "*Susie Sagtits*" down at Biggin Hill with the gear up, having lost all hydraulic fluid from a flak hit, and with no brakes he still managed to avoid the Spitfires parked all around. The plane, whose name even by 8th Air Force standards was more than a little risqué, was showing red on all fuel tanks and had been through a lot, as Richard Donner explains:

"After bomb release we lost an engine and started to drop out of formation. Dan Sullivan took a poll as to whether we should go to Switzerland or try to get to France where the girls are prettier. France it was! Problems arose with enemy fighters after leaving the Group. After damaging two FW 190s our tail gunner was hit. We were able to hold altitude at 5000ft but the 'Abbeville Kids' were distracting us. Sullivan went down to some low clouds. The next poll was whether we should try to get across the Channel. We got in sight of the chalk cliffs and then unbelievably, the solid cloud cover over England opened up. Beneath was an airstrip. We had lost the hydraulic system along the way, so we cranked down the wheels."

"*Susie Sagtits*" made six or eight ground loops with no damage. The crew were able to get repairs and fly back to Knettishall after three days.

Bill Heller, in the 303rd, also put down at a RAF base as he recalls:

"With England a solid overcast ahead and not enough fuel to make an instrument let down, it was imperative that we leave the formation and try to find a hole through which we could descend. Twenty minutes before the fuel would have been exhausted a small hole appeared and we were able to spiral down at a rate of descent that frosted the instrument panel. We found a small RAF field just outside of London. The RAF recognized the emergency and immediately gave us a clear runway. A doctor and a chaplain met us as we taxied up to the line. We needed neither, thank God, but the thought that they were prepared for us again boosted our admiration for that organization. Three women mechanics (WAAF) repaired the battle damage temporarily and gave us enough fuel from their meager stores to get us back to our base at Molesworth. Our RAF hosts served us tea and dinner and provided beds for us. Before going to bed the gunners cleaned and oiled their guns. By 2100, after a good day's work, I went to bed with a word of thanks to Our Lord for our preservation."[443]

In all, the 1st Division had lost 45 Fortresses on the raid. At Chelveston, the ground staff and crews left behind were devastated to learn that theirs had been the highest loss of the day. Of the 18 B-17s that had taken off that morning, only Kane's and Barney Farrell's *Rigor Mortis* had returned to base. There was not even the consolation that some crews might have put down at other bases. Aboard Farrell's ship, Max Guber, the navigator, was removed unconscious from the plane, and it appeared at first that he had lost both eyes after being hit in the face and chest by an exploding shell. Guber owed his life to bombardier Fred Helmick, who though badly wounded in his shoulder and back had kept his oxygen supply going. While tending to the navigator Helmick noticed his own flying boots filling with blood. He was slowly bleeding to death, but somehow he survived the almost three and a half-hour flight back. Not only that, but he also navigated for his pilot too. Helmick needed 56 stitches to close the wounds. After hospitalization he was returned Stateside, having completed his 25th mission.

Second highest loss in the division went to the 306th Bomb Group with ten. "When we landed," recalls John E. Corcoran, the 19 year old ball turret gunner in William Tackmier's crew in the 367th "Clay Pigeons" Squadron:

"I think we were the first aircraft back. Our pilot, from Taft, California, was six foot three and 215lbs; age about 26 and a great guy. We were surrounded by 'brass' in jeeps. Major George Bucky and Major Ken Reechen asked where the others were. We told them that as far as we knew we were all that was left. I could see tears streaming down Buckey's face. He had sent us out and he had lost many friends. I have no idea how far we got into Germany but we did not reach the target. We were badly shot up and came home on the deck harassed by fighters and people shooting at us from the ground. I have no knowledge of where we bombed. With over eight hours flight time we got credit for the mission. We had led the high Group to Schweinfurt in August when, due to our position in the formation, we'd had rather an easier time of it. The guys behind us were pounded. On 14 October we were so far behind that we had no chance and the Germans had plenty of time to jump on us."

The 92nd Bomb Group had lost six, and a seventh was written off in a crash landing at Aldermaston. The 379th and 384th Bomb Groups had each lost six B-17s in combat, and three crews from the latter group had to abandon their aircraft over England, making nine in all.[444] *Windy City Avenger* was the only 384th Bomb Group B-17 to land back at Grafton Underwood; *Tallywhacker* and five others landed at other airfields. The 303rd Bomb Group lost two aircraft, including one that crash-landed after the crew had baled out near Riseley. The 91st, 351st, and 381st Bomb Groups each lost one B-17.

Stella, in the 384th Bomb Group, made it back to Grafton Underwood early after being forced to abort, as S/Sgt Don Gorham, the ball turret gunner, recalls:

"Not far out the lead ship developed trouble and aborted. As we were the only other lead crew in the squadron and flying the #4 slot, we took over the squadron lead. As we crossed the enemy coast No.2 engine gave out, but we continued on. We were having difficulty keeping up with the formation on three engines. 150 miles further into enemy territory No.3 engine gave out, forcing us to leave the formation. Perhaps it would have been better to continue, as we were now alone and open to enemy attacks. We lowered our wheels as a signal we were leaving formation and peeled off to our right. To abort so far inland was no picnic. Five minutes after we left a pair of determined FW 190s attacked us. The tail gunner called out the attack and Jake put *Stella* into a steep dive for evasive action. We dropped about 6000ft a minute and it was tough on our ears going down. The fighters still came in and opened up with 20mm cannon from 800 yards but missed. I guess we were hitting 250mph in the dive, really too much for a B-17 with a bomb load. However it was an emergency and Jake began to rock the ship. Both Compton and I had good shots, though they at first seemed out of range. The fighters stayed till we hit the coast where we finally sighted Spitfire escort fighters. We fired green flares signaling for protection. We salvoed the bombs in the Channel, as we couldn't climb with them aboard."[445]

Captain David Williams, in the 91st, concludes:

"Our crew in the *Bad Egg* was extremely fortunate on this trip for I do not recall any casualties and very little, if any, battle damage to the aircraft. Nonetheless, we had a grandstand view of the entire frightening battle, which once more was characterized by vicious frontal fighter attacks. They appeared to be concentrating their efforts on the low group rather than the lead group of aircraft. In any event we expended many thousands of rounds of .50 caliber ammo' against the attacking fighters on their way to the less fortunate Fortresses of our wing. Fortunately, the overcast had disappeared at the southern German border and the weather was absolutely clear for the remainder of the route to the target and withdrawal until just east of Paris. This provided us with an opportunity for precise navigation and excellent bombing but also provided a field day for the German fighters and anti-aircraft gunners. It was a long day, eight hours of logged air combat, 4% of complete a tour and one fifth of an Air Medal. We lost one aircraft from the 91st and we made it back. It was also good for some combat grog, but not quite yet for the lead crewmembers. Our day was not finished. We had to replot the mission track and write a report on the day's effort. All in all it was a very tiring day for those who had to plan it, brief it, fly it and report it. At least there was the satisfaction of having flown the mission as briefed."[446]

One by one the B-17s in the 379th Bomb Group landed back at Kimbolton and at other bases. Lieutenant Bohn Fawkes' B-17 made it back, but the pilot was not happy that Rip Rohr "had left his troops to flounder in the muck of an October fog."[447]

"Togglin' Ed" Millson concludes:

"At 1840 '*Rag'n Red's* wheels hit the runway. We had been in the air over eight hours. I knew our losses had been heavy but I felt the results of the bombing would help make the mission worthwhile. After de-briefing I rushed over to the photo lab where Captain Ted Rohr our Group photo interpreter was examining the wet prints. He answered the unasked question: 'You hit it. Brother you plastered it!' The Group that preceded us also had excellent results. This somewhat alleviated our losses."

Richard Simmons landed with two badly wounded waist gunners. James Foster, the right waist gunner, who was on his 13th mission, had looked at his watch as they were over the target, and consoled himself with the thought that the mission was half over. Ten minutes later two formations of Bf 109s attacked the 379th. Foster saw the lead B-17 in the element to his left go down, and then he saw the right wing ship and the last ship in the formation go down. The last thing he remembered of the battle was seeing a very bright yellow spinner on a Bf 109 and then "all hell broke loose." He was badly injured. Left waist gunner Ron Britten saved his life by holding an oxygen mask to his face. Britten was also injured, and he and Foster suffered severe frostbite before their journey ended when the ship staggered back to Kimbolton and landed. Jim Foster suffered numerous injuries, including a fractured skull, his left eye was gone, his right eye was badly damaged, and his right hand was broken. The medics were amazed that he still had some vision in his right eye when they took the bandages off.

Despite the "melange of planes in trouble - ours and theirs - parachutes, flak and fighters-fighters-fighters," Arvid Dahl landed *Dangerous Dan* at Kimbolton with just one hole in the left stabilizer:

"It was put there by my left waist gunner. There was so much to shoot at that he got carried away. To make a more difficult shot for the fighters who had us in their sights we would pull hard back on the control yoke, then back down. We got quite adept at 'jumpit' without losing our place in formation. The extra rounds we stole sure came in handy too! My crew usually fitted out a practice 'blue pickle' bomb and printed nasty sayings on it. We filled it from the product of the nearest outhouse. We rigged it with a fuse and small amount of explosive. In retrospect the Germans probably thanked us for the gift of fertilizer. It was our little special contribution to Schweinfurt. I wonder where it hit?"

Walter Bzibziak's B-17, in the 524th Bomb Squadron, made it back as William F. Barrett, co-pilot recalls:

"I remember vividly that for some reason the 303rd Group did not maintain its low group position, but moved into a double high group position to our left which may account for its low loss record that day. This left us somewhat unprotected from below. Most attacks were four abreast from head on. During one such attack my navigator or top turret gunner made a direct hit on the cockpit of an FW 190. The 190 then collided with the left wing of Lieutenant Zack's B-17 and both airplanes went down. Zack's crew and mine were roommates.[448] We suffered minor damage to our airplane; that is fourteen holes. We lost all radio communications and were running low on fuel. I recorded 8 hours and 20 minutes' flight time that day. When we arrived back in England there were only three planes in our group: Bill Hawkins', on his 25th raid, the first 379th Bomb Group crew to complete 25 missions; Colonel Rohr and our crew. It was solid undercast and with low fuel and no radio, we were sweating a landing place. Finally, a hole opened in the clouds and an airfield was visible. Colonel Rohr gave us a hand signal for peel-off and we followed the other two planes through this opening. We landed immediately, with out the conventional wing-waggle past the tower and the green biscuit-gun light. We found that we were at Little Staughton, a repair depot ten miles from our base at Kimbolton. Colonel Rohr and Bill Hawkins, knowing where they were, went on to land at Kimbolton. After calling our base, we were unsanctimoniously delivered home in the back of a GI truck about four hours later."[449]

The 3rd Division had lost 15 aircraft. The 96th had lost seven, including *Dottie J III*, flown by 2nd Lieutenant Raymond F. Bye, which made a wheels up landing in France,[450] but the losses could have been higher. *Dry Run IV*, Lieutenant Bill Burdick's B-17, was attacked by four Bf 109s, and the Fortress slid out of formation. One of the fighters dived from ahead and showed no sign of veering off. Burdick thought that the pilot was dead and tried to avoid a collision, but the fighter tore through the vertical stabilizer. At the same time another three fighters closed in. Burdick recalled:

"Our navigator shot down one at about 200 yards and the waist gunner got another which exploded off to our right. The plane that struck our rudder went into a dive. The fourth 109 beat it for home. After this attack the Fortress went into a spin and plunged from 23,000ft to about 5000ft. Two engines were out and things looked very glum indeed. With the automatic pilot we pulled out at 1800ft. Over occupied territory this is too close for comfort. We did make it back to England and landed at Hornchurch."

In the 413th Bomb Squadron, *Paper Doll*, piloted by Lieutenant Robert H. Bolick, had come through the hell over Germany unscathed, and the crew, who were on their 7th mission, were feeling relieved that the worst was over when 20 miles from the French coast their luck ran out. Flak suddenly exploded around them, hitting the right wing. Bolick went into violent evasive action; it was only a matter of seconds before a direct hit could be expected. The maneuvers and the flak put them out of the formation. Suddenly they were alone, the formation far in the distance. Two fighters came out of the sun firing shells and rockets, while a third attacked from below, making a row of holes in the belly of the plane. When a rocket exploded against the right side of the cockpit canopy shrapnel showered the pilots, and the ship was out of control. A moment later a 20mm shell missed the co-pilot Fred Downs and almost blew Bolick to pieces. He had bad wounds in his face, neck, and legs. More cannon shells exploded in the bomb bay, the rudder, and the #1 engine. *Paper Doll* skidded to the left, dropped a wing, and was going down. With the interphone system out, H. Miles McFann, the navigator, climbed up to the cockpit to check the situation and found a gory sight. Bolick was slumped over the wheel. Badly wounded, he sat up and leveled off the B-17 from her dive, then went down again, unable to move. Downs said, "See what you can do for Bolick." Downs needed help himself. He was hit in the right arm, right side, right leg, and multiple bleeding wounds in his face. McFann had some pilot training in light aircraft before the war and had flown the B-17 in a straight and level attitude on a couple of occasions, but now he was to learn more very quickly. Downs kept passing out and recovering briefly. The crew removed Bolick to the nose, and McFann climbed into the pilot's seat. He knew he was in real trouble. By now he didn't know his exact location. Downs would come to and try to give Miles advice on flying the Fortress. McFann got the radio operator to transmit "Mayday." This brought a pair of RAF Spitfires, which led them to an airfield with a long runway. Downs came to, and with his badly ripped arm, put his hands on the controls to help McFann. He'd shake his head as a signal to retard the throttle and nod as a signal for more power. Two thirds of the runway was used and they still hadn't settled. When he saw Downs trying to pull the wheel, McFann jerked it back into his stomach, kicked right rudder and got it straightened out. It veered slightly but stopped safely. Robert Bolick died before they landed, but the crew went on to finish 25 missions.[451]

Leo Rand's Fortress touched down at Snetterton Heath, and at debriefing his mind was occupied by the macabre experience of cleaving the German fighter pilot in two. At the first opportunity he sought out the Interrogation Colonel, James L. Travis, and blurted out that he had killed a man in a parachute. He was asked, "You didn't do it on purpose did you?" Rand replied that he had not. The colonel put his arm around the distraught ex-steelworker's shoulders and said not to worry.

The 94th lost six Fortresses, and the 95th and 390th each lost one B-17. Gus Mencow, lead navigator, 520th Bomb Squadron, 390th Bomb Group, recalled later:

> "We got 15 planes over Schweinfurt. One was lost to a combination of flak and fighters. Other groups did not fare so well. The flak was extremely thick but fortunately the Luftwaffe concentrated on other groups. When we got back to base and learned of the high losses it turned out to be a sad day. The week was just too much for all of us and Schweinfurt put the finishing touch. We felt convinced that getting through the war was impossible but somehow we carried on."

The 100th, 385th, and 388th Bomb Groups suffered no loss, although few aircraft if any escaped scot-free. Of the bombers that returned to England, 142 in both divisions were blackened and charred by fighter attacks and holed by flak. Bob Hughes, pilot of *Nine Little Yanks and a Jerk*, which put down safely at Thorpe Abbotts, concludes:

> "After our strike photographs had been developed and the damage assessed by local intelligence, the results were called into division. Dick Elliott and I had been summoned to observe the strike photos. Later in the evening word was received that General LeMay wanted me to attend the critique the next day. This was to be an experience for me. I had never seen so many 'Eagles' in one room. I had never even been to a critique. In fact I had never been out of formation over a target before. When all the representatives from all the groups were assembled the critique was called to order and we had just been seated when General LeMay asked. 'Will Lieutenant Hughes from the 100th Bomb Group come forward.' When I stepped up onto the stage he said. 'Will you tell this group what you did yesterday?'
>
> "I related how we had been forced to dive for our lives and that when we recovered, the target lay dead ahead; how all the men volunteered, that we had a perfect bomb run and that Elliott had 'pickle-barreled' the target. General LeMay asked how I knew we had 'pickle-barreled' the target. I informed him that I had studied the strike photos and that *Nine Little Yanks and a Jerk* was a designated strike photo aircraft for the 100th Bomb Group. He responded.
>
> "'That's right gentlemen, ten bombs MPI'.
>
> "Stepping up to the strike map he pulled the butcher paper away to reveal an enlarged strike photo showing the strike. His next comment was. 'The lieutenant should have a commendation.' To which the reply from the back of the room, in clearly enunciated words, was 'The S.O.B. should be court-martialed for breaking formation!' Those words were spoken by my now good friend, Colonel Budd J. Peaslee. Having reached the age of 25 I had watched enough cards to know that in poker this is called a 'push'. If I didn't ask for a commendation, Colonel Peaslee wouldn't offer a court martial!"[452]

Sixty Fortresses and 600 men were missing.[453] A further five B-17s had crashed in England as a result of their battle-damaged condition, and 12 more were destroyed in crash landings, or so badly damaged that they had to be written-off. Of the returning bombers, 121 required repairs, and another five fatal casualties and 43 wounded crewmen were removed from the aircraft. The losses were softened by Press proclamations that 104 enemy fighters had been shot down. The actual figure was something like 35, but both the Press and the planners alike were carried away on a tidal wave of optimism. Even the British Chief of the Air Staff, Air Marshal Sir Charles Portal, said. "The Schweinfurt raid may well go down in history as one of the decisive air actions of the war and it may prove to have saved countless lives by depriving the enemy of a great part of his means of resistance." Later, Brigadier-General Orvil A. Anderson, Chairman of the Combined Operational Planning Committee, publicly stated that, "The entire works are now inactive. It may be possible for the Germans eventually to restore 25% of normal capacity, but even that will require some time."[454] Four days after the raid General "Hap" Arnold confidently told gathered pressmen. "Now we have got Schweinfurt!" However, VIII Bomber Command had to return to Schweinfurt again and again before the end of hostilities.[455]

Four days after the raid Arnold told the press. "Regardless of our losses, I'm ready to send replacements of planes and crews and continue building up our strength. The opposition isn't nearly what it was and we are wearing them down. The loss of 60 American bombers in the Schweinfurt raid was incidental." This statement could hardly have endeared the general to his crews. Many had lost buddies on the raid, and for those who survived, life would never be the same again. Bill Rose recalls:

"My crew and I were now ten nervous wrecks and we didn't sleep much that night. In fact we slept fitfully for about the next year. Nightmares continued most nights until 1945. The battle has affected everyone; myself included, morally and in other ways, for the rest of our lives. Like the terrible battles of World War I, when 24,000 men could be and were, lost on a single day. The nightmare would not and never will go away."

The day after the second Schweinfurt mission, all heavy bomb groups were stood down to lick their wounds. At Bovingdon, Bill Rose went out to his bullet-riddled B-17 to see for himself how much damage had been caused:

"We had two of our machine-guns hit and bent back 90°. I thought, 'now we could shoot around corners.' The skin of our ship had holes all through it and was so badly damaged it became a 'hangar queen.'

"In the afternoon a bomber came down to pick us up and we got back to Alconbury to find only three planes on the field. The officer's mess was completely empty. The story was the same at every base."

"Pappy" Colby returned to Bury St. Edmunds after a 48-hour pass and looked over the damaged B-17s in the 94th Bomb Group:

"Most of our aeroplanes were spattered with flak holes and the Lockheed boys were busy patching them up. Eight replacement crews were sent in but due to heavier losses in some of the other groups five of them were re-assigned and we only kept three."

The losses and a spell of bad weather restricted VIIIth Bomber Command to just two more missions in October. On one of these, on 20 October, when 212 B-17s bombed Duren and Woensdrecht airfield, nine B-17s were lost.[456]

Eaker knew that his deep penetration missions were finished without a proven long-range escort fighter. "At this point nothing was more critical than the early arrival of the P-38s and P-51s," he said. (After the war General "Hap" Arnold frankly admitted that it had been "the USAAF's own fault" that the Mustang had not been employed operationally very much earlier.) The P-38 Lightning was not the total solution for long-range fighter escort duties. That would only come with the introduction of the P-51B Mustang, but when this magnificent fighter finally entered combat, on 1 December 1943, it was as a tactical fighter with the 354th Fighter Group, 9th Air Force, who flew a sweep over Belgium.[457] The first 8th Air Force group to receive the Mustang was the 357th Fighter Group at Raydon, Essex.[458] They flew their first escort mission on 11 February 1944, and in March that year P-51Bs would fly to Berlin and back for the first time. The Mustang was the straw that would break the back of the *Jagdgruppen* (the twin-engined fighters of the *Zerstörergruppen* in particular were no match for the P-51), but for the time being the bomber crews were, for the most part, still very much on their own against the *Luftwaffe*.

10

Four Miles High

"Many of the young gladiators of the air didn't make it through the war... Nothing can detract from their heroism in the face of impending combat. Even their drinking had a noble quality to it, like youthful gods who died young, sampling the divine nectar, living and loving deeply and above all, loving each other."

S/Sgt Forrest S. Clark, radio operator-gunner, 44th Bomb Group

The losses sustained on the Schweinfurt mission were gradually made good, and on 3 November the 8th dispatched over 500 bombers for the first time, when 566 B-17s and B-24s and H_2X ships of the 482nd Bomb Group were dispatched to the port of Wilhelmshaven.[459] Some groups carried incendiaries and, in the words of Captain Claude Campbell, flying his 24th mission in the 303rd Bomb Group in *The Eightball*, "intended to burn up the city." Cliff Hatcher was a recent replacement co-pilot in a new crew captained by Johnny Pyles:

"We took off in *Lil' Butch* and flew in 'Purple Heart Corner.' A new crew always flew in the tail-end of the formation. 'Purple Heart Corner' was on the left wing of the second element leader of the low squadron. We were the lowest 'plane in the formation. The opposite was tail-end-Charlie, which was in the top position off the right wing of the second element leader in the high squadron.

"During the mission a German fighter passed under our left wing less than 15ft below us. He was so close I could make out the features on the pilot's face and could see that he was wearing a light colored scarf. His guns were blazing and the black swastika stuck out sharply on the tail. Flying was in my blood. My father had been a pilot in World War I but had joined the Air Service towards the tail-end and had not seen combat. After the war he had his own aircraft. I remember Eddie Rickenbacker, Colonel Elliot Springs, Mike O'Leary and other aces. That camaraderie of World War One was still there when the German fighter came by. I was right in combat like Captain Elliot and the others. I sat there like a kid. This feeling persisted for two or three missions until I realized what I was into. Then I wasn't a kid any longer.

"A Bf 109 hit us and knocked out our No.2 engine. There were lots of contrails and we hid in them, flying behind our group. It proved successful and we got home although later out ground crew chief at Bury St. Edmunds told us he found a .50 caliber bullet in the inverter beneath my seat! Obviously one of our boys in the 94th thought we were a German fighter! The group lost only one aircraft, *Margie,* Lieutenant William L. Brunson in the 332nd Squadron being set on fire by a combination of flak and fighters. One to six 'chutes were reported."

The P-38 escort all the way to the target kept losses to a minimum, and crews were quick to praise their "little friends." Claude Campbell says, "I saw about 25 enemy fighters, but our boys kept them at bay. They came in real close and gave good protection to the stragglers. My hat's off to them and I hoped we could get more of them over to England. Clouds covered the target and bombing results could not be determined. There were no casualties in our group and I thought, 'Bring on the next one (my 25th and final mission).'"[460]

S/Sgt John W. Butler, in the 328th Bomb Squadron in the 93rd Bomb Group, was on his fifth mission, and he flew left waist in *Tennessee Rambler*, flown by T. U. Collins:

"We took off at 1015. We had P 47s as escorts. Boy, did they look good. Before we got to the target we had to feather No.4 engine on account of an oil leak. Four FW 190s attacked our formation and the right waist gunner fired some rounds. They then barrel rolled right through our formation. I saw a B-17 go into a spin and explode. No chutes. We had to fall back so ship No.10 fell back with us to help us in case of a fighter attack. Flak was pretty good and there was plenty of it. They had our range but not our deflection. It was minus 40 and pretty damn cold. The weather was very clear-and the fighter looked very pretty as they left their vapor trails in the sky. I also received the Air Medal so I was pretty happy over it as I certainly sweated it out long enough combat. Wouldn't be too bad if you could get a mission a week. That way you get in the habit and it would be just routine. Combat, especially the money was pretty good if you made it back but raids were very tiresome as the oxygen and the cold temperature really tired you out. A lot of my good friends went down. At first it bothered you, but later I didn't mind it so much. When you don't make it back the fellows divide up anything they wouldn't send home to your next of kin."

Two days later, on 5 November 374 Fortresses were dispatched to the iron foundry works and marshaling yards at Gelsenkirchen led by five *Oboe*-equipped pathfinders.[461] John W. Butler, meanwhile, flew as T.

U. Collins' left waist gunner again in *Q For Queenie*, when 104 B-24s headed for Münster—the scene of such devastation a month previously. Butler recalls:

"We took off at 1040 am to bomb a very important target. The Jerries did their damnedest to keep us from hitting it. Our bombload was 10 incendiary clusters of 500lbs each. Our job was to burn the town and transportation system. We had P-47 and P-38s for escorts and they sure did their job well. Visibility was damn good and the weather was 37 below. We ran into heavy flak three or four places along the way. There was plenty of it. Our supercharger on No.3 engine was broken so we had to drop back. Three Me 109s came up and Haggerty, the right waist gunner, fired a short burst at them. They threw their bellies up and dove downward. A Me 110 came in at 9 o'clock. I gave him a short burst and he lobbed a rocket into the formation ahead of us. I then gave him another burst of about twenty rounds and he started to smoke. He then peeled off and came in at 7 o'clock where I got in another short burst. A P-38 then jumped his tail and he started down when I lost sight of them."

For S/Sgt Forrest S. Clark, a B-24 radio operator-gunner, and Lieutenant Rockford C. Griffith's crew in the 67th Squadron, 44th Bomb Group at Shipdham, it was their first mission:

'The dawn came up early in that latitude. A sergeant in our barracks, 'Alabama' Gilbert, would always wake us up on mission days. He was the one who got us going, got us to briefings and to the dispersal areas. He was the one who sounded the call to duty at the first faint hints of dawn, a duty that some of us were fearful to answer. I was always up when the first light struck the long ribbon of runways. I took the convoy truck from the mess hall to the briefing shack with the others huddled against the morning cold. Not a word was spoken. Near the plane I pulled on my heated suit, a blue head-to-foot coverall.[462] Over it I drew my flight jacket and flak vest and then my Mae West life jacket. By then the runways were alive in the yellow dawn and I struggled to load my 50 caliber guns on the weapons truck. Bright sparkles of sunlight spangled the grass around the dispersal area. Sergeant Harold 'Jack' Harmon, waist gunner and armorer went off to one side in a ditch to smoke a cigarette to calm his nerves. I cautioned him about getting too close to the aircraft. My feet felt heavy in the wool flight boots as I walked to the rear of the plane, listening in the dawn quiet for any sound. And then I heard it. The sound of a morning lark in the hedgerows. Jack Harmon joined me. 'If we make it back,' I said, 'I hope we can hear that sound again.' Jack was checking his guns to see if they would fire. I know he said a prayer but I tried to be real macho and tough it out. A typical New Englander from Gorham, Maine, complete with accent, Jack was an amateur boxer and athlete in his high school days and an accomplished outdoorsman, hunter and fisherman. Harmon was regarded as being the 'pappy' or father figure because of his age (a few years older than other crewmembers). But he was the life and soul of the party when on leave.

"We called our pilot 'Grif' or 'Rocky'. He said he was from Coody's Bluff, Oklahoma. A quiet man with curly blond hair and a natural skill as a pilot, he had come up through the ranks and was well respected by enlisted men and officers alike.

"Abe Sofferman was the crew's radio operator and I became his assistant as well as tail gunner. Radio operators had no gun position but when there was no flight engineer they took the top turret gun. Most of the time we sat in a cramped space near the front of the plane behind the cockpit. Abe took his job seriously. He was the typical street-smart kid of the inner cities of America but he was much deeper than that in character and sensibility. Sofferman was always carrying sandwiches, which we suspected were from the mess hall and would secret them in his flight suit. He also stuck paperback books in his flight suit and would read them in flight. He would read voraciously about history and the lives of Alexander Hamilton, Abraham Lincoln and Benjamin Franklin. He was studious, deep and profound in his thinking and actually the only scholar on the crew. Although he had the manner of a quiet thoughtful man, under it all was an adventurous spirit and a quest or life in all its complexities. He and Bob Weatherwax, our cheerful, outgoing navigator, formed a close bond.

"We took off from the slick runway and formed up with the other bombers over the sea. We passed over the Dutch coast. I had never seen the sky so steely blue and such good visibility. I was flying in the tail gun turret and could see for many miles to the rear. We were in one of the lead groups and I could see spread out behind us most of the entire formations of the 8th Air Force. What a sight. What am I getting into? Wow. I never saw so many aircraft, I said to myself as I swiveled the turret about to coast as we passed over, a thin line edging a blue sea, the North Sea. We were bound for Germany and the target was the industrial city of Münster. It was an important war-production center and believed to be one of the key targets of the bomber offensive. The RAF had gone there a few weeks before and been severely attacked and suffered considerable losses. However, this day looked serene and deceptively beautiful. Below me the dykes of the Zuider Zee stood out clear and straight. I could see sunlight glinting off the surfaces of the bombers in the sky behind us, elements stacked up high and low, covering a large segment of sky. We were at bombing altitude by this time and I could see the small farms, little villages and canals of Holland below. It was getting cold in the turret and my feet were stuck so I worried if I could get out in time should there be a bale out. We were on oxygen, having exceeded the 10,000-12,000ft altitude. I could smell the rubber of the oxygen facemask and the faintly sweet odor of pure oxygen. It gave me a little high, a kind of euphoria of the heights. Had I remembered to check everything? Would the guns work when called on to do so if there were an attack? I checked the .50-caliber cartridge belts many times. The air was smooth and there was little or no turbulence. We were making our way inland over Nazi occupied Europe now and yet no enemy fighters were in sight. I thought this might be a milk run and began thinking of life back at the base.

"Next thing I saw were small clouds drifting by the tail section. I thought, 'that's strange, we must be getting into some cloud formations: perhaps a slight overcast.' I didn't think much about that at first but as these clouds continued and increased in numbers I thought it best to push on the intercom button and report to the pilot and co-pilot. Just as I was going to do so the voice of the co-pilot came over the intercom asking the tail gunner to report in. I had neglected to report as required of all crewmembers. I pushed the intercom button and said, 'Everything okay back here, except for a few small black clouds.'

"'Black clouds?' came back the voice at the other end of the intercom.

"'They look black to me,' I replied.

"'Damn it. That's flak!' shouted the co-pilot, Lieutenant Bill Tinsman. Bill was from Bucks County, Pennsylvania and a natural counterpart to Griffith - cool and collected under combat conditions, was a Rutgers man and I am sure he wanted to fly fighters. He was very neat in appearance and dress. Even when dressed for a mission he looked sharp and self-controlled.

"I looked out at the small clouds, closer now, fearing I was really in trouble with the pilot and co-pilot for not being more alert. I noticed now that the clouds were closer to us and each had in the heart of them, a red core, which flashed and then disappeared as the cloud drifted off to the rear 'They're shooting at us', I called out, not realizing I had the intercom button still depressed.

"'How did you know?' came the reply. 'Who do you think they're shooting at?' Just then a violent vibration shook the plane and it seemed to rear up in the front, dipping the tail section downward. 'We've been hit,' came the call over the intercom.

"'Check for damages. Any reports. All report in.' Again and again the plane rocked from side to side. From then on all hell broke loose. I saw planes going down, flaming wreckage as planes exploded and others spiraling down leaving a trail of smoke.

"Suddenly, I had more respect for the small black clouds. I realized that the war had begun for me and that the enemy was actually after us; after me! I began to sweat through my heated suit and nervously pressed the mask to my face. This was my baptism under fire, in a tiny, cramped turret 25,000ft over Germany on the way to Münster with a load of 500-pounders.

"Münster was a heavily defended city near the Ruhr. What they didn't tell us was that it was 'flak alley'. I had never seen flak before and did not report it at first. 'Get out and walk on it, boys,' came Bill Tinsman's voice on the intercom.

"'Land on it', sang back Sgt John Gibboney, the other waist gunner. 'Gib' came from Saxton, Pennsylvania and came to be well known for his wry wit and steadiness under combat conditions. He was a gunner but also, I thought, an assistant engineer. He became very familiar with the B-24 and later with the B-17. Gib often read scripture or church leaflets and was very close to his family.

"Gib and T/Sgt Earl Parrish worked together. Parish could not get much from reading the engineering manuals but Gib said he could do very well if shown the various parts of the aircraft. Parrish had a great memory once he tried something. I called Parrish a 'hard headed Hoosier' because he was from Freedom, Indiana. He never spoke much but he was quite responsive in flight conditions and was quick to learn the intricate mechanisms of the B-24.

"Out of the clear blue sky, Harmon said, 'look out there. Fighters - coming this way.'

"All I could see was endless blue sky. Sure enough within 45 seconds enemy fighters came in from the direction he had indicated. Sergeant William T. Kuban in the ball turret hanging there below us began firing away. Harmon and Gibboney let loose.

"Over Münster I heard the bombs going click, click, click as they left the bomb bays bound for our target. I saw them fishtail down into the clouds. But after a while I did not look anymore. There were sickening seconds or minutes when Dave Edmonds, our bombardier, held the bomber steady on the bomb run over the target. Edmonds was a congenial type who could converse about a number of subjects and was a frequenter of pubs. He was also a serious airman. He attended Valley Forge Military Academy before entering the Air Corps.

"We prayed that the flak gunners would not get our range.

"We were lucky and got back to the base. Bill Tinsman took me aside and said he was recommending I take a refresher aircraft identification course. 'After all,' he said, 'If I couldn't see flak, how could I see enemy fighters?' I decided, 'If I see anything with a wing and a propeller and it points its nose at us - I shoot!'[463]

"Our next missions were to Frankfurt, Zwickau and Solingen, among others. The greatest and happiest sound came when we heard the squeal of the landing wheels hitting the runway at home base. We knew then that we had survived. It was interrogation and back to the barracks to fall into our bunks to try to sleep for another dawn.

"The experience of flying missions has never been adequately told because no one has had the courage to tell it. There is fear - overwhelming and paralyzing fear-with every turn of the prop, every yard over enemy territory. A veteran pilot put it this way, "You know there are 127 ways to die on a mission and you never know when one of them will come your way. Even with the outside temperature at 20-30° below zero at altitude ("cold as a witch's tit," we used to say) I was sweating through my heated flight suit and sweat ran down my legs and into my flight boots. My hands got so sweaty I had trouble holding the guns or even putting the cartridge belts in. Prayer was never far away in our minds and we followed little safety measures like carrying an extra chute pack. We prayed at takeoff, we prayed at the RPs (Rendezvous Points), we prayed at altitude, we prayed over the target. And we sweated and prayed on final approach.

"Sometimes the connections to my electric heated suit would come loose. I panicked when I could not breathe and thought my oxygen had been cut off, until I cracked the hose connection to free up the flow again. Stupid things happened. Planes collided in forming up, at the RPs or coming back, or they crashed on takeoffs. Even though we did not know one another well in the beginning, some crewmen stood out. 'Red' was a mid-western kid with burning bright red hair, so innocent we believed him when he said he had never been with a woman. He grew up on a farm in Iowa far from the cities and from women, except for the girls he saw at a distance. On an early mission, Red was in the crew of a plane off our wing. The time came for the bomb run and the bomb bay doors opened. Then a shout went up over our intercom. "Damn!" The news came back that someone had dropped the bombs through one wing of Red's bomber and it went down. We doubted if they ever got their bombs away. Sometimes later I thought I could see Red's ghost on the airfield in the early morning mist. "Poor kid," a crewmate said. "He never had a chance." We were all kids. I was 21 when I started flying missions. In fact, the whole crew was very young, just out of high school or college."

For two weeks after the 5 November missions the weather grew worse and resulted in many abortive missions. It was not until 11 November that the 8th was in the air again, with a return to Münster.[464] Four B-17s, three of them in the 94th Bomb Group, which was flying as the low group led by Major "Pappy" Colby, and one in the 385th Bomb Group[465] were lost. Three were victims of FW 190s of the IInd *Gruppe* JG 26 at Epinoy that attacked the Fortresses repeatedly from 12 o'clock and 6 o'clock.[466] *Oberfeldwebel* "Addi Glunz" of the 5th *Staffel* claimed two B-17s southwest of Dordrecht, but he correctly received credit for only one. His second "victim" was *Lil' Operator*, which had the face of "Esky," the little man who appeared on the cover of *Esquire* magazine on its nose. Lieutenant Johnny Pyles, in the 410th Bomb Squadron, whose crew were on only their third mission, flew this Fortress. They occupied the tail-end-Charlie slot in the high squadron, which was reckoned to be the most dangerous position after "Purple Heart Corner." Everything was going well for the Fortress crew until shortly before bomb release. An explosion just forward of the engines on the left side rocked *Lil' Operator*. Oil began pouring out of No.2 engine and streaked back across the cowling and wing area. Pyles told Cliff Hatcher to keep an eye on the oil pressure and feather the No.2 propeller if necessary. Quickly the pressure dropped to nothing, and Hatcher punched the feathering button. *Lil' Operator* continued its bomb run, and Lieutenant Adolph J. Delzoppo, bombardier, released his bomb load over the target. The loss of one engine had considerably reduced their speed and they were now alone. "Bandits at 2 o'clock" crackled over the intercom, and Hatcher peered into the strong sun. Suddenly, out of nowhere appeared a Bf 109 that dived so close that for a moment the crew feared they were going to be rammed. Glunz opened fire, and several explosions occurred in the cockpit of the B-17, filling it with smoke. *Lil' Operator* fell off to the right, and disappeared into the undercast in a vertical dive at alarming speed. Glunz was sure it would not pull out.

Hatcher and Pyles opened their side windows to let out the smoke, and for the first time realized they were going down fast! Straining on their steering columns, they managed to right their bomber. Hatcher was sure No.3 engine was windmilling but three and four engine instruments had been shot out in the fighter attack. Pyles leveled off at 15,000ft and applied full left rudder to keep the bomber on course. Nos. 3 and 4 engine throttles were dead, so he decided to shut down No.3 engine. Then Ervin Smith, the ball turret gunner, called up on the intercom to say that the undercarriage was in the "down" position. Ross Andrews, the engineer, discovered a large hole in the right forward bulkhead of the bomb bay, which had been caused by two 20mm shells exploding in that area. It had cut off all the electrical supply to the right-hand side of the aircraft, and only the armored pilots' seats had saved Hatcher and Pyles from flying shrapnel. Amazingly, the top turret gunner had escaped injury after fragments had whistled around his legs. Pyles lost height and headed for some clouds. One and a half engines out and a lowered undercarriage were more than an open invitation to any enemy fighter pilots. It was certain death. Soon five fighters had ganged up on the crippled bomber. Harold Norris, the rail gunner, saw them first, approaching from the rear. *Lil' Operator* dodged in and out of cloud, and was soon down to just 500ft. Over towns and villages they flew, at rooftop height. Milburn Franklin passed up the temptation to strafe the streets, and instead the gunners took it out on the enemy fighters that continued to harass them until they were clear of the coast. Two enemy fighters were claimed destroyed.

At the coast Pyles eased up to 1000ft, and the crew began throwing out all excess equipment. As a result, the airspeed picked up a little and *Lil' Operator* flew on over the English Channel without getting her feet wet, thanks to the gentle manipulation of the No.1 throttle. As they approached the Bury St. Edmunds control tower, Cliff Hatcher tried calling, but the radios were dead. Luckily, the ADF was operating, and they were able to home in on the airfield. Pyles put the *Operator* down on the concrete runway, but No.4 engine resisted all Hatcher's attempts to kill it until the last minute. Both pilots hit their brakes hard, and the aircraft stopped just short of the end of the tarmac. Smoke and dust shot into the air, and the crew sat there for a few seconds until the very real threat of fire prompted them to evacuate the ship. Then came the distant scream of vehicles and the "blood wagons," with Colonel Castle at the helm. Castle made sure no wounded were on board and then demanded to know why Pyles had stopped on the runway. Other aircraft were about to land with wounded on board. Pyles explained their situation, and pointed out that they could not taxi away on one engine. Colonel Castle walked across to the *Operator*, rubbed his chin, and returned to the crew. He said, "You boys have had a trying day but you had better head for debriefing and then perhaps you can get some well deserved rest."

The next day Pyles' crew received a three-day pass to London, courtesy of the Colonel. At the end of their leave and while waiting for their train at Liverpool Street Station, the crew decided to drop into a small cinema nearby. Just after the lights went out a British newsreel feature appeared on the screen. It began, "American Flying Fortress Shot Down Over Münster." At debriefing Pyles had been told that his crew had been reported missing after being seen going straight down over the target. Now they sat there in the dimly lit London cinema watching a re-run of the *Operator* going down over Münster. As it reached the frame showing the large "Square A" and the lowered undercarriage the crew jumped out of their seats as one man, startling their fellow cinema goers with cries of, "Hey, that's us!" The manager finally persuaded the "rowdy," "drunken," and "obviously combat-fatigued Yanks" to leave his premises, and they never saw the movie again![467]

On 13 November 1943 272 B-17s and B-24s were directed to bomb targets at Bremen, but bad weather caused many in the 1st Bomb Division to abandon the mission during assembly, and only 143 of the heavies were successful. The mission cost 16 bombers, three of which were B-17s.[468] The 93rd Bomb Group suffered the day's highest loss, losing five B-24s. Next worst was the 392nd Bomb Group, which lost four Liberators.[469]

Throughout the first two weeks of November 1943 England was blanketed by thick wooly fog, and airfields were lashed with intermittent showers and high winds. When the bad weather front finally lifted on 16 November VIIIth Bomber Command struck at targets in Norway. *H_2X* and *Oboe* sets had been proving troublesome, and the break in the weather would enable crews to bomb visually. The 1st Bomb Division was assigned the molybdenum mines at Knaben, while the 3rd Bomb Division was to attack a generating plant at Vemark, in the Rjukan Valley. (Intelligence sources indicated that both targets were connected with the German heavy water experiments that would help give the Nazis the atomic bomb, although crews were not told this at the time.) At all 1st Bomb Division bases, Fortresses were rolled from their muddy dispersal sites and lined up for the green light at the end of the runways. At Molesworth the occasion was of special significance for the 303rd Bomb Group's *Knock-Out Dropper*, which was flying its 50th mission. If it completed the raid it would set a new 8th Air Force record for a B-17. *Knock-Out Dropper* was something of a "good luck" ship, but the same could not be said of *Shady Lady II*, a B-17 that had flown with the 351st Bomb Group at Polebrook on the group's first mission to Schweinfurt on 14 May 1943. Repairs to damage sustained on a recent mission had only just been completed, and the original crew refused to fly it anymore. It was decided, therefore, that it be assigned to a new crew, led by Lieutenant Joseph Wroblewski, who had won his pilot's wings at Altus, Oklahoma, in May 1943:

> "*Shady Lady II* was the first plane assigned to the 351st with a chin turret. This cut the airspeed by 10mph and made it a very clumsy and difficult aircraft to fly in formation. Knaben was my crew's first mission of the war. I didn't expect to go with them on this one. Normally, an inexperienced pilot performed duties as a co-pilot with another crew on his first mission. The plane was heavily loaded with 2500 gallons of gas and twelve 500 pounders, but she made take-off easily. After forming we headed for Knaben, almost 700 miles distant. Groups of formations were scattered around in every direction leaving vapor trails. All I could see of Norway were the mountains covered with snow. This mission was flown at 15,000ft and it was very cold. All but the co-pilot and myself wore heated suits."

Meanwhile, the 3rd Division struck at Rjukan, about 75 miles due west of Oslo. As the formation approached the target area there was no opposition, confirming the belief that the Germans would not be expecting a raid so far north. The 94th Bomb Group arrived ten minutes early and had to make a 360° turn. (Crews had been told to make certain that Norwegian workers were not on their shift when the bombs fell.) As the Fortresses crossed the target for the second time thick cloud obscured the plant from view, and the formation was forced to make another 360° turn in the hope it would clear. Reuben Fier, bombardier in Edward J. Sullivan's Fortress in the 94th formation, recalls:

> "While doing our 360° turns off the coast a B-17 in the 390th began doing slow gyrations in the sky without the benefit of anyone shooting at us. It felt like we were sitting in the balcony of a theater watching an actor perform before us, The B-17 finally sliced into the water in an inverted position. We did not see any parachutes nor could we understand what caused the unfortunate incident. Small ships were seen to head out towards the crash site but we were unable to see survivors or what happened when the boats arrived on the scene.
>
> "Our plane, momentarily attached to the 100th Bomb Group, began its run into the target behind other planes in formations before us but, due to the cloud, they were unable to drop their bombs. When the 100th approached the target the clouds drifted away and we dropped the first bombs on the target (which were what appeared to be large concrete buildings with flat roofs nestled in the mountains). As we later described to the *Stars and Stripes* reporter on our return to Bury; I could see the bombs mushroom into the flat roofs and after a short period of time, flames of many colors escaped through the roofs. By the time we turned off the target and began flying out to sea, parallel to the course we flew in, the target area was engulfed in black smoke rising to the sky. The following groups were seen to be dropping their bombs into the smoke and licks of flame were seen coming up from the target area. Little did we realize at the time that the heavy water was essential to the Germans in their early stages of nuclear research."[470]

The round trip to Knaben and Rjukan was slightly shorter than the 25 July 1943 1800-mile circuit to Trondheim and the 1600-mile round trip to Heroya. Lieutenant Joe Wroblewski returned to Polebrook at 1500 hours with 750 gallons of fuel remaining:

> "We were lucky to draw an easy mission first time out although the going was rough coming in to the English coast with rain, snow and low ceilings."[471]

Lieutenant John P. Manning successfully brought *Knock-Out Dropper* back to Molesworth to make it the first B-17 to complete 50 missions in the ETO. Crews told waiting newsmen that the only anti-aircraft fire they had encountered had come from a single flak ship in one of the fjords. Crews in the 3rd Division rejoiced over their accurate bombing of Rjukan, saying that the explosion had lifted their aircraft suddenly, "as if a giant hand was pulling them upwards. As it was we hit it right on the nose."

On 18 November, 127 heavies were dispatched to Gelsenkirchen again. However, the *Oboe* sets aboard the leading Fortresses gave trouble and directed the formation too far north of the target. After an unsuccessful battle with the elements, the B-17s were forced to return to England. The Liberator groups, meanwhile, had enjoyed good fortune in a return mission to Norway. One of the men at Shipdham who flew on the raid was S/Sgt Forrest S. Clark, the tail gunner on Lieutenant Rockford C. Griffith's crew in the 67th Bomb Squadron;

> "The night before the Oslo raid, 'Alabama' Gilbert got into a heated and lengthy blackjack game. Finally, he lost all his pay and threw down his wallet. 'I won't be needing that any more,' he said.
>
> "Next day 'Alabama' and the rest of our group took off from Shipdham to bomb the Ju 88 assembly plant at Oslo-Kjeller 18 miles east of Oslo. At about 100 hours our plane[472] was in a force of nearly 100 8th Air Force B-24s approaching the airbase from bases in England loaded with 500lb bombs. Bombing visibility was perfect. As we came up the Skagerrak and the Oslo Fjord I could see everything plainly etched in newly fallen snow. There had been a snowfall during the night and in the morning as we proceeded at 12,000 to 15,000ft I could see for miles from my position in the tail turret. The great city of Oslo lay before me, many buildings outlined in the snow. I saw the huge mountains of the spine of Norway reaching down from the far north, tiny villages and fishing vessels in the fjord. Going into Kjeller the formation passed over another German airbase, one situated on the coast. We saw enemy fighters off to the side as we went into the target area but they had not attacked us. 'They'll be back with their buddies, Sgt Harold 'Jack' Harmon, one of our waist gunners shouted over the intercom."[473]

At 12,000ft the 392nd lined up for the bomb run. The skilled navigator-bombardier team of Swangren and Good systematically checked off the course heading, landmarks, true airspeed, wind drift, and minutes to "bombs away." Myron Keilman, flying deputy lead, saw the target "standing out in the late morning sun" and thought that "it would be a shame to miss it." "Bombardier Joe Whittaker was following through with every essential detail of a bombing run," says Keilman:

> "Should anything have happened to the lead airplane and it had suddenly aborted the bomb run, Joe had his bombsight crosshairs on the aiming point of the assembly plant. If he had been given the command 'take over,' he could have successfully delivered the bombs."

Lieutenant McGregor in the lead aircraft held his B-24 precisely on altitude and airspeed, and he and the 20 bombers following released the 210 500-pounders on the target simultaneously.

On the return leg the same scattered to broken clouds lay across the Skagerrak beneath the formation. Suddenly the gunners spotted German fighters skimming across the cloud tops opposite the B-24s' line of flight. A dozen-plus Ju 88s climbed to make fast diving passes as they circled in behind the bombers. Liberator "outriders" moved into a tight formation, providing the mutual protection of concentrated firepower. Diving in pairs, the German twin-engined fighters lobbed rockets and 20mm explosive shells into the 392nd. Tail and top turrets responded with bursts of machine gun fire, and the ball turret gunners opened up below as the fighters broke off the attack. Sergeant T. E. Johnson, flying with Lieutenant Everhart, shot up one fighter so badly that it burst into flames and was last seen in an uncontrollable dive. Two Liberators were hit and began to lose power. They could not keep up with the rest of the formation, and as they fell behind the Ju 88s concentrated their fire on them. The B-24 pilots dived for cover and sheltered in the clouds. For a time they played hide and seek as the fighters circled, and eventually the bombers were lost from view. Wave after wave of enemy fighters pressed home their attacks, but in the 44th Bomb Group formation Forrest S. Clark succeeded in shooting down one Ju 88;

"Sitting in the tail position," he recalls, "I could look back and see a line of seven to ten fighters lining up to attack our rear. 'They're waiting in line to get at us,' I called over the intercom, pressing the mike to my throat. Suddenly they attacked from all sides. Two shells went through the turret directly over my head, missing me by inches. I followed one after the other as the Luftwaffe pilots zoomed in at our tail and then dove beneath us to come up in front, swing and line-up for another pass. One after another they came. Closer and closer. I tracked them with my twin .50-caliber guns, but could not get a good lead on any until they passed under us and then shot up again for the waist gunners to get shots at them. Finally, I fixed one in my sights as he leveled out and came in faster and faster. 'So close,' I said to myself. 'He's going to hit us: he's going to rain us.' I gripped the triggers of both guns, leveled them out and pressed down. I kept holding the triggers down, hoping they would not jam the belts. I could see my tracers going out in long lines right into his wing roots. Bright flashes of fire and traces kept boring into his wings until he came so close I could see the outline of the German pilot's head in the cockpit. Just as he slipped under us I saw a thin trail of smoke coming from the engine."

Clark was almost completely out of ammunition, and a 20mm shell hit Bill Kuban—the ball gunner, who was bringing him more rounds—in the head, knocking him unconscious and bleeding to the floor. Clark heard the bale-out bell, but at first he had difficulty in getting out of his shattered turret. Two men, John Gibboney and L. J. McAndrews, were getting ready to jump through the open camera hatch. Clark prayed, because he knew he would not survive long in the ice-cold sea if he jumped:

"I actually went down on my knees and prayed. Much to my surprise, just about that time the fighter attacks suddenly stopped and the Germans left us to what they must have thought was our death."

Lieutenant Joseph L. Houle's B-24,[474] which was severely damaged, tottered gallantly to within 50 miles of the English coast with safety in sight. But by now his fuel indicators were reading zero and he was forced to ditch. The aircraft seemed to break in two, and four minute figures were seen to slip into the icy waters of the North Sea. Griffith, himself flying on three faltering engines, circled over the scene while his radio-operator called ASR. With his own fuel supply running low, Griffith dipped his wing in salute to his fallen comrades and turned towards his base. ASR was unable to trace any of the crew or the aircraft. Griffith's Liberator spluttered on, just above the sea. Clark adds:

"More than once the call went out from the pilot to prepare to ditch but Kuban would surely have died if we ditched in the icy water. We limped on and more than once it seemed all engines quit and the 'plane stuttered as if in its death throes. But the 'plane would not die."[475]

Altogether, six B-24s were lost on the Oslo raid, including one each in the 93rd, 392nd, and 44th, which were forced to land in Sweden.[476] Forrest S. Clark concluded:

"Sixty-two 2nd Division men were lost. The bodies of Lieutenant Houle's crew were never found. 'Alabama' Gilbert was one of those who never returned. We cleaned out his clothes and found a dollar bill, it seemed the more we faced death, the more superstitious we became about everything, including what we said and thought and even the names and numbers of the planes. Even so the 18 November mission was the most successful of all the American missions on Norway during the war. It let the Norwegians know that the Allies had not forgotten them and it boosted their morale at a critical time. We challenged the German Air Force in Scandinavia at a time when it was strengthening its air defenses."[477]

Bad weather continued over the next few days, but did not prevent RAF Bomber Command bombing Berlin on the nights of 18/19 November and 22/23 November.[478] This led to rumors of an American follow-up raid being mounted on the capital the next day. Bill Rose was in the 92nd Bomb Group, which would lead the raid:

"We were on stand-down and consequently we stayed in the bar and drank more than we should have done. The bar closed at 12 o'clock and we hit the sack. Two hours later there came a guy waking us to go on a bombing mission! Of course we were in no physical shape to go but we managed to get through breakfast. Imagine our surprise and sobering effect when the curtain was pulled back to reveal the target. It was Berlin! We felt that, given such a target, even if we managed to survive the fighters and the flak on the run-in we would be lucky if there was anything left afterwards. There was not too much thought about being able to return so long as the bombing part of the mission could be completed. The Luftwaffe would certainly be waiting to finish off anyone coming back. As it turned out, the weather was as lousy as expected on the 23rd and you could hardly see. But we went out to the planes and started the engines before the red flare was fired canceling the mission. It proved one thing though, that security on the base was very poor, because it was well known that the target would be Berlin. We were very thankful the mission was scrubbed because we would certainly not have survived."

On Friday, 26 November, 633 bombers, the largest formation ever assembled by VIIIth Bomber Command, were directed against targets as far apart as Bremen and Paris. Two new B-17 groups, the 401st and 447th, had joined the 8th during November, and the 401st made its combat debut this day. Colonel Harold W. Bowman's outfit would swell the 1st Division stream to 505 bombers briefed for the port area of Bremen, while 128 B-17s of the 3rd Division would head for Paris, where skies were expected to be clear. For Lieutenant Joe Wroblewski, it was his second mission in the 351st Bomb Group at Polebrook:

"At 0550 we were awakened for our second mission. For breakfast it was lousy grapefruit juice, powdered eggs, hard crisp bacon, dried up toast and all this mixed with plenty of powdered milk. On top of this hot cakes with syrup that tasted like molasses. Then coffee for the short-winded crewmembers. We could even go back for seconds if you could get by the firsts. After briefing for our mission to Bremen, Germany on where to expect flak and enemy fighters we were off. We had a hard time keeping up in formation, being 'tail-end Charlie!' The chin turret on *Shady Lady II* helped to multiply our problem of trying to hang in formation in a clumsy sluggish way. As a result we used up a considerable amount of fuel changing power settings continuously. At 27,600ft the engines kept sputtering and gave us some trouble. Just about the time we reached enemy territory the tail-gunner (Scerrati) oxygen mask froze and he was without oxygen. Until another was brought back to him. The waist-gunner (Saxon) froze around his eyes and the ball-turret gunner (DeCresce) froze his fingers. We were at 27,600ft for 3 to 4 hours with a temperature of -55°C. Contrails were streaming behind each plane for a great distance. The black puffs of flak kept blossoming out on either side of us but not too close. They had our altitude figured very well. We had P-47 escort all the way and did not see any enemy fighters. Due to cloud coverage and a solid overcast the pathfinder was used to locate the target. After dropping our bomb load our gas gauges showed only a little over 100 gallons in each tank. We all began to sweat. But as we started our descent with low power settings our perspiration disappeared. We had fuel to burn. Physically I was bushed."

Claude Campbell was flying his 25th and final mission of his tour with the 303rd Bomb Group this day:

"Focke-Wulfs jumped us before we reached the enemy coast but I did evasive action and the boys shot 'em off. All kinds of enemy fighters were in the air, including old Stuka dive-bombers - a perfect illustration of Hitler's shortage of first-line fighters. We ran into a typically heavy barrage of flak over Bremen. The target was covered with clouds and bombing results could not be determined. P-47s picked us up and escorted us from the target so the enemy stayed away."[479]

Unfortunately, the weather forecasters were proved wrong, and the 3rd Division was forced to return with bomb loads intact. A 94th Bomb Group B-17 piloted by Lieutenant Johnny Pyles, who had brought *Lil' Operator* back to Bury on one engine two weeks before, was hit between the No.2 engine and the fuselage by a FW 190.[480]

At Chantilly, at 1040 hours *Oberfeldwebel* Adolf "Addi" Glunz claimed a 78th Fighter Group P-47.[481] The 78th Fighter Group had taken off from Duxford at 0927 hours and headed for mid-Channel, where they made rendezvous with 128 B-17s of the 3rd Bomb Division. After taking up escort above the bomber stream, the force flew the route of Dieppe-Montford-Evreaux to the target, a bearing industry at Montdidier, near Paris. As the Forts made their turn for the target east of Paris, about 30 German fighters went into attacks on the bomber's front and rear ranks. The 78th Fighter Group pilots quickly positioned themselves to meet the attack and went after the enemy. Major Jack Price started firing at a FW 190 from 550 yards to prevent it making a head-on pass at the bombers. He got good strikes all over the German, and closed to 100 yards before he had to break off to avoid running into the bombers. The FW 190 stalled and went down trailing smoke. Next Price caught a climbing Bf 109, came in astern at 300 yards, and exploded it in flames. Howard Askelson closed to 200 yards with an out-of-the-sun astern run at three Bf 109s near bomber level and sent one straight down in fire and lots of black smoke. The battle went on in a running fight until the force reached the Beauvais area, where 1st Lieutenant Warren M. Wesson took a long 600 yard shot at the line of flight of a FW 190 and held his trigger down as the German passed through his fire. Another pilot who saw the FW crash confirmed the victory. The 78th Fighter Group left the continent at Cayeux at 1120 hours and headed for England, where three of the Group's P-47s crash-landed at southeast coastal airfields.

At 1103 hours near Beauvais *Oberfeldwebel* Adolf "Addi" Glunz claimed his second kill of the battle when he despatched 42-31215 in the 349th Bomb Squadron, 100th Bomb Group. 2nd Lieutenant George W. Ford, whose crew were on their first mission, piloted the missing Fortress. An eyewitness reported that the Fortress was hit in the No.2 engine when two FW 190s attacked the low squadron at 1045 hours. It fell out of formation and dived for cloud cover. The fighters followed, but P-47 Thunderbolts went to the rescue. At 1048 hours one chute was seen to open, and at 1103 hours nine more chutes were seen. At 1105 hours it hit the ground and exploded. During its last few minutes in flight fire had spread over the entire left wing.[482]

One of the crewmen who fell into German hands on 26 November was Kenneth D. Williams, in the 508th Squadron. His capture was to have serious repercussions, because his A-2 jacket he was wearing when he baled out bore the words, *"Murder Inc"* on the back, as he recalls:

"Contrary to this I was not a Chicago gangster, being born in Charleston, North Carolina on 16 May 1922. We were assigned and our crew was given *'Murder Inc'*, an old veteran B-17 but we never flew any of our missions in her. An enlisted man entered our barracks one day and asked me if I wished the words *'Murder Inc'* painted on my jacket, to which I said 'Yes'. In fact no other crewmember had his jacket so decorated. On 16 November we had flown our first mission, to Knaben, in one of the first natural metal finish aircraft. Trouble with the fuel transfer system nearly forced us to divert to Sweden but the engineer cured the problem. On our second and final mission on 26 November I was given a parachute harness for a much larger man because my own was not available and I did not adjust the replacement equipment to my smaller frame. Engine malfunction on our assigned B-17 forced us to transfer to a 'spare' aircraft named *'Aristocrap'*. Changing aircraft cost us 15 minutes and resulted in our being unable after take-off to find our own formation, so we tacked onto an unidentified Group. Testing our guns over the Channel, I found the chin turret froze solid while under check and so we were left with only the two flexible guns for forward defense. Our promised fighter escort did not link up over its Dutch rendezvous and a P-38 pilot I later met in PoW camp said the escort was actually around but unable to find the bombers. Crossing into Germany I could see German fighters taking off: within minutes Me 109s and FW 190s were coming in through the formation. They ceased their attention only when flak was being directed at us.

"Just after bombs were released a chunk of flak hit the chin turret and a fragment barely missed me. In moving back to the flexible gun position I disconnected my earphones and microphone and lost touch with the rest of the crew. The Group now began a turn to the right while we flew straight on into Germany. I can only assume our controls were damaged, so preventing the pilots from following the other B-17s. All on our own we were attacked by numerous fighters. Six Me 109s linked up in one formation about 1000 yards out ahead. The first two came in, in echelon and blasted our nose and side areas. The remaining four also came in, in pairs and the first duo were back in position for a second assault by the time the last pair had cleared us! By this point I sensed something was wrong. Looking back through to the pilot's compartment I saw the first pilot banging on the nose escape hatch with an ammunition box, while a solid wall of flame rose behind him. It seemed the rest of our bomber was engulfed by fire. As I crawled back to assist the pilot he forced the hatch open with his foot, grabbed me by the waist and threw me out. As I fell my initial reaction was one of relief I had got away from the fire. Then I thought 'Did I put my 'chute on' and looking down at my chest saw - nothing!'

"Feeling something tugging at my shoulders I looked up and there a few feet overhead was my unopened 'chute securely hooked to the risers of my harness. Evidently I had clipped the parachute on my harness and the force of being ejected from the aircraft had ripped the risers loose: the 'chute was still firmly attached to the risers. As I was falling I saw the pilot pass me no more than 50ft away with a look of horror on his face. I thought when we landed I would kid him about how scared he had looked. I later discovered that both he and the co-pilot had baled out without their parachutes, which had evidently been burnt by the flames.

"I delayed opening my 'chute until well clear of the aircraft. I was unaware of the shock-effect of its opening and the too-large harness was forced up and tight around my neck. There I hung at 20,000ft over Germany unable to breathe. I grabbed the risers and gradually pulled myself up until my throat was not constricted and I could breathe again fully.

"A German fighter came straight at me but did not shoot, being content to circle my descent. I assumed he was radioing my position to ground personnel. I was drifting backward in a strong wind and the landing I made took me by surprise with its force - so violent was it that I did a complete backward somersault. My 'chute began to drag me and although I tried to rise in order to pull in the canopy I did not have the strength. Finally the base of the canopy snagged on a barbed wire fence and I was pulled up tight against it. The fighter buzzed me and the pilot saluted. My escape kit had been lost when the coverall pocket it was housed in was torn away. As I struggled free of the harness a sergeant and several soldiers came over a small hill. The sergeant said in a British accent, 'Are you hurt, boy?' I replied 'No' and he asked, 'What did you have for breakfast?' and I said, 'Bacon and Egg.'

"He said, 'I have not had bacon and egg for a long time' and he explained he had lived in London for over ten years and hoped to go back there after the war.

"He took me to his HQ, an anti-aircraft battery and after basic questioning he told me what my PoW treatment would entail, his description turning out to be quite accurate. He said I was his first 'capture' and asked if he could take my picture. This was done both front and back and these pictures were in fact the sole ones used by the Germans in their subsequent propaganda. Later that day I was removed to a Luftwaffe base where that evening a Luftwaffe pilot spoke to me. We did not speak each other's language but managed to get along all the same. There seemed to be a bond between us. We had both been 'up there' and knew what it was like more than anyone on the ground; it was as if the war was bigger than all of us and it was the war which was doing all the damage and was our real and mutual enemy. He said he has been a Stuka pilot over Malta where he was wounded in the leg. His leg was stiff and he had been grounded. Seeing my jacket insignia he recommended it be removed to save me future trouble. I sat up all night and picked off the paint with my thumbnail until by morning only a faint outline could be discerned. During the interrogation at Dulag Luft and my first few weeks at *Stalag Luft* I at Barth I heard no more about *'Murder Inc'*. However, things were to change later."[483]

Meanwhile, on 30 November, when 381 B-17s and B-24s were briefed to bomb Solingen, in the Ruhr, "Pappy" Colby, at Bury St. Edmunds, who had been waiting to fly his 25th and final mission of his tour, finally got his chance:

"At last I was started on my 25th and final raid, to a target about 20 miles east of Düsseldorf - right in 'Happy Valley' and hardly the milk-run thc 25th was supposed to be. We took off in rain and pitch darkness and climbed on instruments to 19,000ft before we got above the clouds. There were the usual problems coming up through the clouds and at assembly we only had 15 ships, while Blythe who led the A Group, had 20. The 385th leader and his deputy both aborted and they never did form up as a group. We got clear around to the Division assembly line and there was still nobody else in sight. About this time I suddenly noticed that the whole left side oxygen on my ship had apparently developed a leak, as it showed only 300lbs of pressure but should have been over 300lbs. What to do? Should I abort or try to keep going? I was leading the 94th and this was my 25th so I decided to keep going as long as possible. When we reached the Dutch coast our formation was down to nine ships as Keelan and several others had aborted. I decided to join the 95th Bomb Group for better protection and, as we sailed into Holland, we suddenly saw the entire 1st Division headed for home. Our formation now had four groups of good P-47 cover so I decided that if I could solve the oxygen problem we would keep going. I moved everybody off the leaking side but stayed on myself until it got down below 50lbs. Then I hooked into the right-side system that still had 275lbs and we stayed on it (at 28,000ft) all the way through to the target. When we finally started to descend on the way home we still had 110lbs but it was kind of nerve-wracking.

"There was a glimpse of Düsseldorf through the cloud layers but it's doubtful if we were on target when we unloaded the bombs. My little formation was down to seven ships over the target; two of which belonged to other groups. It was extremely lucky that there were no enemy fighters up, as they would have most certainly picked on our small formation. Apparently, bad weather at their fields kept them down. As long as I live I will never forget the first glimpse of the English coast, which told me I was coming home for good. I remember saying to myself, 'Pappy, with God's help you made it.' When we taxied into our hardstand, who should be there but Colonel Castle (with a bottle of Scotch), Lieutenant Colonel O'Connor, (the Group Operations Officer) and Major Birdsall, (322nd Squadron CO), to congratulate me on completing my tour. A big songfest at the Officers' Club that night and I wired my anxious wife that I had finished."[484]

On 1 December 299 heavies led by Colonel Budd J. Peaslee returned to Solingen and made a PFF attack. This time, the raid was more successful than the one the day before, and 281 sorties were deemed effective. Cloud cover forced the 3rd Bomb Division to abort the mission. The 1st Bomb Division lost 19 B-17s[485] and the 2nd Bomb Division five B-24s. S/Sgt John W. Butler, left waist gunner in *Tennessee Rambler* in the 93rd Bomb Group, wrote:

"We took off at 0830 and had to fly 15 minutes into France before we picked up our P-47 escorts. I was very glad to see those babies. Jerry attacked us and he really pressed his attacks. We were under attack for 45 minutes and I really sweated it out. There was also plenty of flak. We couldn't see the target, so we had to go around to the secondary. There was plenty of flak there too and *Iron Ass* on our wing had his wing shot off.[486] Red Carey, our right waist gunner, shot a Ju 88 down. Four yellow-nosed Bf 109s came diving down so close I could see the 'chute harness on Jerry. Carey fired at them, but no luck. I fired over 90 rounds at a Me 110; a Bf 109 and a Ju 88 but I really didn't get a good shot at them. I saw one bandit attack *Southwind* and it was in trouble. Three 'chutes came out, then five more bandits came down and they shot off the left wing. It went into a spin and burst into flames.[487] The weather was minus 37 and I really froze. This was T. U. Collins' 25th and final mission so he was very happy."[488]

On 5 December, 548 bombers set out to attack targets in France again, but bad weather completely disrupted the mission. Just over 200 Fortresses of the 1st Bomb Division were briefed to attack targets at La Rochelle and Paris, but thick cloud prevented any bombing, and none of the B-17s were effective. The same was true of the 2nd Bomb Division's attempt to bomb targets at Cognac-Châteaubernard and St. Nazaire, while the 3rd Bomb Division fared no better at Bordeaux-Merignac air depot. Only two B-24s in the 389th Bomb Group bombed the target, and just one B-17, in the 96th Bomb Group, was successful at Bordeaux. For this wasted effort eight heavies were lost. S/Sgt John W. Butler, in the 93rd Bomb Group, flew tail gunner in *O Carole N Chick*, piloted by J. V. Kemp:

"We took off at 0750 to bomb Cognac airfield in France. It was quite a long ways to the target area, which we reached with no mishaps. We were escorted by P-47s and P-38s. Temperature was minus 30. The weather over the target was 10/10 cloud cover so we couldn't drop our bombs. We were not allowed to drop our bombs just any place over occupied territory as we wanted to do as little damage as possible to the French people, except of course to a direct military target. I had just called the navigator over the interphone that it-would be nice if we could run into some flak so we could get credit for a mission, when all of a sudden I had all the flak I wanted. A ship in the 389th received a direct hit. He blew into a million pieces. Two chutes came out. The whole wing came off in one piece and it dropped by itself turning lazy circles. It was all on fire and it reminded me of a cartwheel from the Fourth of July."[489]

On 11 December the weather cleared sufficiently for the heavies to set out for Emden, their seventh trip to the city, and one of the most costly. S/Sgt John W. Butler flew his 9th mission, flying tail gunner in *Exterminator*, flown by J. A. Bogan. Butler recalled:

"We took off at 0830 to bomb the city of Emden, a pretty important shipping center. It was 39° below zero. My heated suit worked very good back in the tail. Being a tail gunner was nice as you had armor around you and all the bad stuff has gone by. We ran into a lot of flak at the target and it was pretty accurate. I heard a loud noise in the tail and I got out of turret to see where we were hit. The flak put a large hole in the vertical stabilizer. Then some fighters came in at 6 o'clock and in my hurry to get back in the turret I pulled my heated connection off on my right boot so my gloves and boots were not working. I checked all my circuits and even checked my fuses. I was beginning to become real cold. Then I happened to check my right boot. I put the plug back in and the heat came back to my feet and hands again. A Ju 88 came in on the tail but he was gone before I could get a shot in. I fired around 30 rounds at some Me 109s but no results. Flak also hit us in the waist. The tunnel gunner passed out from lack of oxygen. He fell forward on top of the camera hatch. Flak came through the side of the plane and passed the spot he was in, the lucky stiff. The Red Cross had hot cocoa waiting for us. It sure tasted good. Harry Fargo, flying tail gunner on *N-for-Nan* froze his hands and feet and they had to land at another field so they could him to a hospital. *Q-for-Queenie* made a crash landing on our home base but no one was hurt. My guns worked OK."[490]

Lieutenant Joe Wroblewski, in the 351st Bomb Group, recalled:

"We were up at 0400, ate breakfast, briefed and started engines on a flare signal. Another flare signal to start taxiing and we took off with a load of incendiaries to Emden, Weather was fine; temperature only -38° C and our engines ran smoothly. We encountered only light flak over the target. I only saw one enemy fighter. Other crewmembers said they saw five but they kept their distance. One tried to make some passes but was scared off by tracers from our gunners. They must have been young inexperienced enemy fighter pilots. We had an unidentified B-17 come into formation for a short while and then pull out again. It looked very suspicious."

Rocket-firing Bf 110s and Me 210s made persistent attacks on the bomber formations and 17 heavies were shot down, including *Six Nights in Telergma*, the lead ship piloted by Captain Hiram Skogmo, in the 390th Bomb Group. Captain Irving Lifson, one of the two navigators on board, recalls:

"We were feigning a raid on the Heligoland area, hoping to draw the enemy fighter planes up towards Denmark. Then we were to cut back on Emden. Shortly after turning back onto Emden eight Me 110s came through the formation, firing rockets. We were hit right away and set on fire. There were eleven of us on board and only Captain Donald Warren and myself the Group Navigator (who landed on the island of Nordeney) survived. German marines picked us up. Ernest Phillips, a gunner, landed in the North Sea and was picked up by a boat. Among those lost was Major Ralph V. Hansell, the 390th Operations Officer, the strike leader who was flying as co-pilot. I spent the rest of the war in *Stalag Luft I* Barth."

Captain Robert A. Lamb of Ridgewood, New Jersey, a P-47D pilot in the 61st Fighter Squadron, 56th Fighter Group, recalled:

"We were flying high when we rendezvoused with the bombers. I saw a group of Me 110s flying formation at the right of the bombers and dove on three of them at the right rear. I singled out a Me 110 on the left and started firing at 400 yards, closing to 50 yards. I saw strikes on the plane and pieces fly off. Suddenly the two men baled out and I broke off, almost running into a Ju 88, which came up from behind. I went under him and pulled up in front. He fired rockets, but they missed. Then I zoomed up in back of the bombers and saw six Me 110s. I came in from behind these as they made a left turn, so I closed on the third plane to the left and started firing. There were strikes on the fuselage and heavy strikes on the right wing, which collapsed. One of the men, probably the pilot, baled out. I headed for the next plane and registered a 'kill' without even firing at it because both the pilot and gunner baled out immediately."[491]

On 13 December, in a record flight, when 649 bombers hit the port areas of Bremen, Hamburg, and U-boat yards at Kiel, P-51s reached the limit of their escort range for the first time. This was also the first time in which more than 600 American bombers attacked targets in one day. The 2nd Bomb Division, which included 12 Liberators of the 445th Bomb Group at Tibenham for their first group mission, attacked the U-boat yards at Kiel. On 16 December 535 bombers, including Liberators of the 446th Bomb Group at Bungay (Flixton), making their bombing debut, flew a follow-up raid on Bremen. S/Sgt John W. Butler, in the 93rd Bomb Group, flew as J. A. Bogan's tail gunner in *Birmingham Express*[492] on his 10th mission of the war. Butler recalled:

"We took off at 0840 to bomb the city of Bremen. It was a very important target, as the world's biggest submarines were built there. The flak over the target was very good and Jerry wasted a lot of money trying to shoot us down. My right glove burnt out so I had to get out of the turret to get a new pair. Just when I was getting back in I heard our right gunner firing so I started firing at some yellow nosed Me 109s. I counted seven. I fired about 100 rounds but couldn't see any hits. Jerry would attack in pairs on a diving approach from 5 to 7 o'clock. Lieutenant A. A. Russ flew our plane today on his first mission and had the hell shot out of it. Two of his gunners went to the hospital, plus he had to land at another field [Tibenham]. I also received my first oak leaf cluster to my Air Medal."

On 20 December, during the third raid on Bremen in a week, bundles of *Chaff* were dropped to confuse enemy radar.[493] More than 470 bombers hit the port area, but 27 heavies were shot down. The 8th was stood down on 21 December, but the following day 439 B-17s and B-24s attacked marshaling yards at Osnabrück and Münster. The 2nd Bomb Division, its numbers increased by the addition of the 448th Bomb Group, was assigned Osnabrück. Sergeant Francis X. Sheehan, armorer-gunner in the crew of *Harmful Lil' Armful*, flown by Lieutenant Alvin D. Skaggs, recalls:

"Osnabrück turned out to be heavily defended. Although flak was minimal, the fighters were there in abundance, as we found out. My first encounter with combat commenced with black puffs of flak dotting the sky around us. It was something we never did get accustomed to. The effectiveness of this was shown when part of a ship began trailing smoke and parachutes. As we approached the target the aircraft to our immediate right dropped its entire bomb load on the left wing of a wingman that had drifted down and under him. Stunned, I watched the damaged aircraft fade left and over on its back. I prayed for 'chutes to appear, but none did. I was brought back to reality by the call over the intercom -'Fighters!' Twin-engined enemy aircraft were lobbing rockets into a formation of bombers to my right. At first they seemed oblivious to our presence. I fired at one of the fighters, who began trailing smoke and fire and went down through the clouds. I was later given credit for this."

S/Sgt John W. Butler, flying his 11th mission as left waist gunner in *Judith Lynn*,[494] in the 93rd Bomb Group formation flown by J. J. Collins, also had his hands full:

"We took off at 1115 to bomb the marshaling yards. The weather was very cold and I really felt it as it was minus 41. We were at 25,000ft. We lost one supercharger, as we crossed the enemy coast. We had P-38s and P-47s for escorts. Only saw a few bursts of flak but the enemy fighters pressed their attacks. A few planes were lost plus quite a few shot up. There was some Me 110s firing rockets into the formation behind us. One of the rockets hit one of our planes and put a large hole in the vertical stabilizer. Also, a B-24 had about 10ft of her wing shot off by fighters. She went into a spin and pulled out of it, then into a steep dive. There were no chutes. A B-24 was hit by fighters, went into an inside loop and started down in a dive. She broke into three pieces when she exploded. No chutes.[495] I fired around 80 rounds at silver painted Me 109. No results."

Altogether 13 Liberators were lost, including two each in the 446th, 448th, and 445th Bomb Groups. During its withdrawal support to Münster, the 4th Fighter Group found some rich pickings. Lieutenant Colonel Don Blakeslee was leading the group, and rendezvous was made with the B-17s at 1359 hours at 26,000 feet and 15 miles west of the target area. The 4th Fighter Group made a starboard and then a port turn over the target until 1415, and then followed the bombers out, breaking off at 1422. In the Enschede area of Holland four Bf 109G 5/6s of JG 26 were seen at 10/15,000ft. 1st Lieutenant John T. Godfrey, in the 336th Fighter Squadron, bounced two of the fighters, and Lieutenant Vasseure H. Wynn in the 334th Fighter Squadron joined him in the dive. A violent dogfight ensued, in which Godfrey's P-47 was severely damaged, but the two Thunderbolt pilots and a third claimed three 109s destroyed. In the event, Godfrey and Wynn were awarded a half share for one Bf 109, Wynn a half share with another pilot for a second 109, and Godfrey one with a half share in another. Their spirited action resulted in the deaths of *Unteroffizier* Günter Broda of the 9th *Staffel* and *Unteroffizier* Anton Jenner and *Fähnenjunker-Feldwebel*[496] Julius Richter of the 11th *Staffel*.[497]

The 8th was stood down on 23 December, but missions resumed on Christmas Eve when the B-17s were dispatched to mysterious targets in France, which went under the code-name *Noball*. It was rumored in the world's free press and in unofficial circles in Washington that the raids were part of a "pre-invasion" blitz. Crews speculated what the concrete sites were, and many dubbed them "rocket" installations, or Hitler's "secret weapons." British Intelligence revealed them to be sites for launching "V-weapons"—pilotless planes packed with a high explosive warhead in the nose and aimed at London. Sources revealed that 70 such sites were being constructed, and all-out raids were ordered at once.

To Lieutenant Joe Wroblewski in the 351st Bomb Group, it seemed as though, "every plane in Britain was up" on 24 December. The 447th Bomb Group at Rattlesden, which made its debut this day, further strengthened the Fortress formations. As it turned out, the 447th could not have had an easier debut. Joe Wroblewski confirmed as much when he wrote, "Our third raid in five days. We had no trouble at all. There was no flak and no fighters. How we loved this type of milk-run."

On Christmas Day the festivities got into full swing throughout the region. Americans dined with their English hosts, and deprived and orphaned children were invited to bases for Christmas dinner and afternoon parties. Unfortunately, the war was never very far away, and preparations were already being made for the next strike. It came on 30 December, when the 8th journeyed to the IG Farbenindustrie chemical works at Ludwigshafen, on the upper Rhine near the German-Swiss border. There was a solid undercast, but the clouds topped out at 10-12,000ft, and above them visibility was unlimited. The bombers maintained a tight formation, with their escorts able to keep them in sight while looking out for enemy fighters below. The route to the target had been planned so as to avoid flying across Holland and the Ruhr, where the German defenses were now very strong, and the bombers crossed the Seine Estuary into France, and then flew due east to Ludwigshafen.

Around mid-morning the route the bombers were taking confused the *Jafü* 4 controller, and he expected a raid on Paris, so he ordered II./JG 26 and the 4th *Staffel* I/JG 3 south. They soon intercepted the 1st Bomb Division formation. *Fähnenjunker-Feldwebel* Gerd Wiegand inadvertently led the 4th *Staffel* into the middle of a Thunderbolt formation. They were from the 353rd Fighter Group. South of Florennes, Belgium, at 1130 hours Wiegand got on the tail of one of the P-47s, which was being flown by 1st Lieutenant William "Dub" Odom, in the 350th Squadron, and shot him down. Odom was killed.[498] Half an hour later Wiegand and *Feldwebel* Robert Hager attacked a B-17G that was straggling. It was *Women's Home Companion* in the 303rd Bomb Group, piloted by Lieutenant William C. Osborn.[499] Wiegand left the "kill" to Hager, and this was his first victory.[500] The 353rd Fighter Group, meanwhile, broke up an attack by Bf 109s of I/JG 3 that had been sent south when an attack on Paris was expected. Two of the Bf 109s were shot down,[501] but the 353rd Fighter Group lost its second P-47 when an unseen enemy shot down 2nd Lieutenant Russell E. Moriarty in the 352nd Fighter Squadron. Moriarty baled out and was taken prisoner.

I./JG 26 intercepted the 3rd Bomb Division just as the 56th Fighter Group was breaking off, and the German fighter pilots were able to make a head-on attack that sent two B-17s down in flames before the next relay of Thunderbolts returned and scattered the Focke Wulfs. At 1343 hours near Soissons *Leutnant* Karl "Charlie" Willius, 2./JG 26 CO, shot down *Laden Maiden* in the 100th Bomb Group, piloted by 2nd Lieutenant Marvin L. Leininger and 2nd Lieutenant Albert W. Witmyer in the High Squadron. The Fortress was reported to fall behind and go down in flames after being followed by three FW 190s.[502] At the same time *Feldwebel* Heinrich "Jan" Schild, also of 2./JG 26, shot down B-17G *Sarah Jane*,[503] flown by 2nd Lieutenant Campbell C. Brigman Jr in the 571st Bomb Squadron, 390th Bomb Group, the bomber crashing near Vimy, in northern France.[504] The 100th Bomb Group lost a second B-17 when an enemy fighter attack damaged *Heaven Can Wait's* radio room with 20mm cannon fire that started a blaze, probably in the oxygen tanks.[505]

Cliff Hatcher, who flew with the 94th Bomb Group, recalls:

"We were attacked by Me 110s, Me 210s and FW 190s, which caused a lot of damage. The German fighters lined up wingtip to wingtip off to our right, out of range of our .50 calibers. About 18 of them were lined up like a row of battleships and when they fired simultaneously, it was like a naval broadside. They fired air-to-air rockets, one of which went right over our right wing by about 5ft. I felt sure it would hit the top turret but it missed us."

Fighters were not the only problem that the Third Division groups had to contend with. Leslie G. Thibodeau, flight-engineer/top turret gunner in *Pegasus Too* in the 388th Bomb Group, adds:

"Lieutenant Brown our navigator was hit pretty badly under the armpit as he was getting in some navigational reading. The bombardier, Lieutenant Kenneth Kelly and I had to remove our winter flying clothes to keep him warm. We gave him a shot of morphine and put a cigarette in his mouth once in a while. The flak hit an artery as the blood was about an inch thick all over his maps; of course, the blood was frozen."

In another B-17G in the 388th Bomb Group Lieutenant Art Carlsen's crew, on their seventh mission, were doing fine until tragedy struck *'Satan's Sister'*, as S/Sgt Robert E. "Bob" Scalley, the 6-foot tall, skinny, 18-year-old tail gunner, recalls:

"For the first time we were in the High Group flying at 25,000ft. At the IP another Group cut in front and we experienced severe prop wash. *Satan's Sister* initially tipped up 180° on her right wing, came back down, then went up and rolled over on her left wing (in other words - a slow roll with a full bomb bay!). The last report on the intercom was the pilot saying, 'We're going over'. Needless to say we went over and into a tailspin. At this point I assume that the pilot and Lieutenant Ben Scroggin, co-pilot were wrestling with the controls in a desperate attempt to recover from our dive and spin. *Satan's Sister* could not take the strain and she broke in two at the radio room. (Later, back at Knettishall returning crews reported that our ship had exploded on entering the clouds 5000ft below the formation). Danny Letter the radio operator was thrown out of the radio room without a parachute. Edgar Slintz, bombardier, was thrown through the Plexiglas nose without his parachute and into the No.2 propeller. His left arm was cut off and the lower half of his body was severed. John Bassler, navigator and the only married man in the crew, put his chute on and baled out through the nose. Carlsen, Harold Hawkins, engineer and Ben Scroggin, co-pilot had no chance at all to get out. After *Satan's Sister* broke in half the four crewmembers in the rear section were able to move around except Charles Parizo, left waist gunner, who was knocked unconscious. Jim Neal, right waist gunner, baled out through the radio room. Frank Brincat, ball gunner, baled out the waist door and I went out through my escape hatch. Charles Parizo died in the waist. Forty per cent of my crew survived. Seven was definitely not a lucky number for the crew of *'Satan's Sister'*."[506]

II./JG 26, meanwhile, had tracked the 2nd Bomb Division until the rear wing lost its fighter coverage when the 352nd Fighter Group's P-47s, which were scheduled to cover the withdrawal of the bombers, failed to show.[507] Things had begun to go wrong for the 352nd Fighter Group almost from the outset. Colonel Joe Mason, who was leading his Group, encountered a solid overcast, but he continued on course. Because of their contrails the Bomber withdrawal track could be seen a long way ahead, and Mason also saw that the first two boxes of B-24s were under P-47 escort. Mason turned his Group back along the bomber track and picked up two boxes of B-17s flying about 15 miles to the rear and 15 miles starboard of the first boxes seen. Nothing was seen to the rear of the bombers. Escort was given to these two boxes and several stragglers flying with them. The 352nd Fighter Group left them at 1400 hours and headed toward home base.[508]

As the 352nd continued on into France and approached Chalons, several pilots in the 328th Fighter Squadron noted a sharkmouthed Me-110 flying parallel to the bombers and attacked it. Within minutes the plane went down under the combined fire of Lieutenant Colonel Eugene "Pop" Clark and Lieutenants William Hendrian and Dave Zimms. A short time later, as they neared the port city of Calais, three FW 190s attacked the 487th Fighter Squadron, and this interception set in motion the events that cost the squadron three of its most experienced pilots. The 4th *Staffel* JG 26 had taken off from Wevelgem just after 1400 hours to look for stragglers near Dunkirk, and when they found a flight of three 352nd Fighter Group P-47s the Thunderbolts were too low on fuel to stay and fight.[509] *Fähnenjunker-Feldwebel* Gerd Wiegand chased Captain Don Dilling out to sea and later claimed to have shot him down, but out of fuel he belly landed in a field. Don Dilling recalls:

"We were letting down gradually from 30,000ft to 12 or 14,000 over Calais when three 190s bounced us. I looked at my gas gauges. The auxiliary tank was gone, of course and the peg on the main tank was right on zero. We had to cross over the Channel to get back to base. As I looked at my gauges one of the 190s made a pass at me and missed. As he went by at little more than wing's length I could see the pilot wearing a white silk scarf with his goggles pulled down over his eyes. With this fleeting look at the bandit I rolled over on my back and headed for the deck. My evasive action was so violent and fast that my compass was spinning as I entered the 'pea-soup' fog and you could not tell which way you were going but I headed out to what I thought was the Channel. Apparently I had crossed out near Calais and… I was flying parallel to it instead of crossing the Channel as I thought. After a few minutes flying in the soup I spotted land off to my right and thought I've got to get this thing down before I run out of gas. So I headed towards the land thinking I was in the Thames Estuary until they started letting me have it every kind of ground fire they had - small arms, tracer, 20mm and larger. I took a couple of hits in the tail section and headed back in over the land cursing those crazy sons of bitches thinking I was over England."[510]

Six of the B-17s in the 100th Bomb Group returned to Thorpe Abbotts with battle damage. 1st Lieutenant Dean Radkte's Fortress barely made it back after being hit by sustained flak in the target area, and was then attacked by two FW 190s southwest of Abbeville, where a number of 20mm shells riddled the left wing and nose. One shell entered the navigator's compartment and struck the co-pilot, Lieutenant Robert Digby, in the head, killing him instantly. Shell fragments struck Radkte, wounding him in the face, head, and neck beside his jugular vein. One fragment completely closed his right eye, and splinters from the instrument panel were driven into the muscles of his right leg, rendering it useless. The explosion also ripped the oxygen mask from his face and stunned the engineer, T/Sgt Van D. Pinner, who was hurled against the turret controls. Upon regaining his senses, Pinner thought first to escape, as he was certain that the plane had been blown apart. Through the smoke, he could see the pilot and co-pilot slumped over the controls. Blood was spattered over the shell-pitted compartment. The windows were shattered and broken. At this time, Radkte regained consciousness and saw Pinner about to leave. He yelled to him, and the engineer returned to his station. Radkte then called the rest of the crew and reassured them. Most of the crew were never aware that Digby had been killed, or that Radkte himself was severely wounded in the face, neck, and hands, and was almost blinded. 2nd Lieutenant William B. Agnetti, bombardier, was called up, and he moved the co-pilot's body to the navigator's compartment and then returned to assist Radkte. Due to the loss of one engine and severed control cables, the B-17 lagged behind the formation. Radkte doubted whether he could remain conscious long enough to bring the Fortress home, but with fingers useless because of severe cuts, he skillfully used the butts of his hands to manipulate the controls, and he fought his way back into position in the formation and he reached Thorpe Abbotts safely.[511]

Bombardier Harold Heyneman, who flew with Clement Cowan and his crew in the 100th Bomb Group, summed up the feeling at Thorpe Abbotts in December 1943. On reporting for duty, he was informed "Don't unpack your bags. Supply hates like Hell to pack them up again and you won't be here long...."

11

Bloody Battles

"One of the chutes failed to open because it was burned. The poor fellow landed on his feet, which were driven clear up to his stomach and burst his lungs. His entrails coming out of either side of his body beneath his armpits."

Earl Payne, 78th Fighter Group

On New Year's Eve VIIIth Bomber Command completed its second year in England with all-out raids on airfields in France. Missions of this nature were usually considered milk runs compared to the ones over stiffly defended targets in Germany. Bomber crews were quick to praise good fighter cover. T/Sgt Jack Kings, a B-17 waist gunner in the 388th Bomb Group, which went to Paris, wrote:

> "We were to do some of the first really pin point bombing if you could call it that. Hitting just and 'only' an airfield and nothing around it was touched. Due to spots of thick clouds scattered about, we as a group, had to circle the city several times to make certain the target was fully visible. Our fighter cover made sure no enemy aircraft would bother us. We really had deep respect for those fighter pilots."

Robert "Peck" Wilcox, a bombardier in Lieutenant Marvin H. Bender's crew in *Iron Ass*, in the 510th Bomb Squadron, the 351st Bomb Group at Polebrook, recalls;

> "I sat bolt upright in my bunk. The sergeant with his GI flashlight was awakening crews. He said, 'Lieutenant Wilcox, Lieutenant Freeman, breakfast is being served. Briefing at 0230 hours.' I shook my head, trying to clear the cobwebs and get awake. My gosh! I hadn't been in the sack very long. I had got back from Peterborough about midnight and had been on a mission over Germany the day before. I had hardly figured on another mission today but oh well! Get these missions over with and back to the States. I had qualified for the Air Medal the previous day so I only had 20 to go.
>
> "We met Bender and Grupp, our pilot and co-pilot, at the mess hall and had our bacon and eggs with plenty of coffee and not much talk. About everyone figured we would 'sir down' on this, the last day of the year and almost everyone was planning a New Year's Eve party. I know Andy, our engineer, Harold Long, the assistant engineer and I were looking forward to going back to Peterborough for a gala New Year's Eve. In the briefing room was another surprise. A lot of high brass were there in their flying clothes and the briefing officer told us, 'We're going on a milk-run to bomb the docks at Bordeaux. We'll be flying over water most of the way at 12,000ft. You won't have to wear oxygen masks all the time and you won't have to wear the heavy flying suits until we get ready to go in over the target area. If clouds should sock in the target, we'll come back and hit the secondary target, the airport at Cognac. Major John R. Blaylock of the 510th Squadron will lead the mission. Colonel Hatcher (the CO) will be in the lead plane.'
>
> "We were to fly No.2 right off Major Blaylock's wing. After briefing we caught our truck out to our plane, stopping en route to get our .50 caliber machine-guns. At the plane everything went well except that Plunkett, our ball turret gunner, wasn't with us. He had been grounded by the medics because of a bad cold. His replacement was Collins, who had several missions under his belt and both Andy and Long said he was OK.
>
> "The trip went well. It was good to do without flak so heavy you could get out and walk on it. We made our turn and went in over France and, sure enough, the Bordeaux area was covered with a thick cloud cover so we headed for Cognac. It wouldn't take too long to get there because Cognac is only about 75 to 80 miles from Bordeaux. The formation was in good shape and was pulled in close. There were some scattered clouds but no flak and no fighters. Up ahead I saw our target. Already the lead bombardier was sighting in on it and on we flew. I wondered why we weren't taking any evasive action. We were closing fast when, all of a sudden, all hell broke loose. The lead plane was the victim of a direct hit.[512] Our plane was hit; the air was turbulent. A big hole had been blasted in the nose. I dropped our bombs but no one had a chance to look down. Planes seemed to be going down all over. The formation was shot to pieces, I would say. We had an engine on fire and I remember Bender asking Collins about the damage and the fire. We made a circle all by ourselves and we were all alone. I mean all alone. What was left of the formation had headed for England but we were all of the opinion that we had lost several B-17s over the target area from some intense flak.[513]
>
> "Then it was Bender over the intercom, He said, 'We will be unable to make it back to England. We are too far from Switzerland

to go there and the plane may explode at any time.' So he gave the order to bale out. No one questioned it. I went out through the bomb bay after Freeman and Andy."

Andy Anderson walked out through Spain in one month, and Harold Freeman followed him out in three months. "Peck" Wilcox remained at large in France until September 1944, when he linked up with the Seventh Army during the liberation. The rest of the crew were made PoWs. After landing, the one regret "Peck" Wilcox had was "It was a long way from home and I wasn't going to be in Peterborough for any New Year's Eve party."

Twenty-four other bomber crews and four fighter pilots would not return to their bases to celebrate New Year's Eve either.[514]

Fog and rain grounded the bombers until 4 January 1944, when the 1st and 2nd Divisions went to Kiel. The 91st Bomb Group lifted off from Bassingbourn to become the first group in the 8th to reach 100 missions, although it had paid dearly for the privilege, losing more aircraft and crews on missions than any other group. At Molesworth, Russell F. Beach, an engineer-waist gunner in the 427th Bomb Squadron, 303rd Bomb Group, reported for the mission, having been returned to flying status by the medics after recovering from badly frozen feet, hands, and face he had suffered on his 13th mission. Flight operations, however, said that he was still on grounded status. Beach missed out as Lieutenant Fred C. Humpreys and his crew took off in *Sweet Anne*.

In the 93rd Bomb Group, S/Sgt John W. Butler was flying his 14th mission as left waist gunner in *On The Ball*, which carried 12-M-17 Incendiaries and was flown by J. J. Collins. Butler recalled:

"We took off at 0850. Kiel had 180 guns around the city. They reminded you of a neon sign. They'd go off four at a time. The temperature was minus 47. The slipstream was cold as hell. My oxygen mask kept freezing up. The vapor trails were very pretty, but they helped the Germans spot our formation. Jerry was really upset as he used a lot of ammunition trying to bring us down. Three planes behind us were knocked down. We lost a supercharger over the target so we were tail end Charlie again, as we had to drop back. We had P-38 and P-51 for escorts. The Mustangs were very good fighters. It was good to see them around. We were hit in the vertical stabilizer."[515]

Meanwhile, unescorted groups in the 3rd Division spearheaded an assault on enemy airfields in France. The 94th Bomb Group was assigned Bordeaux airfield, and for Cliff Hatcher, who was flying his tenth mission in *Belle of Maryland*, it was one of the toughest missions he had flown:

"For some reason the powers-that-be decided that the best route to Bordeaux was to fly straight in as if we were going to Germany, then turn due south and fly the whole length and breadth of France and out to sea, hitting the target as we went. We came under constant enemy attack from the time we hit France until we headed out to sea across the Bay of Biscay. Then we had to fly over the Normandy Peninsula and fighters hit us again. Three FW 190s queued up as we approached Bordeaux and the leader turned in towards our formation for a head-on attack. The two wingmen must have been trainees because they peeled off and headed for home. The leader was shot down but another three queued up, this time in front of us. They must have been veterans because they barreled in, straight at us. Trimble, the bombardier, shot at the three as they bore in and was credited with one 'kill' and with damaging the other. All three were burning. Our left waist gunner and our tail gunner each claimed a Bf 109. When we were over the Bay of Biscay I motioned Kacsuta, the pilot to take over but I couldn't take my hand off the throttles. I had my palm and fingers gripped over the top. My hand was literally frozen to the throttles (we had been under constant attack for maybe three hours). I finally had to take my other hand and use it to peel off each finger at a time. My hand hurt for days later. Over Normandy we ran low on ammo. Trimble had exhausted his in the chin turret and joined Ball, the navigator, in the nose. He began firing the flexible .50 caliber cheek gun while Ball fired the flexible .50 on the port side. Suddenly their guns jerked to a stop. They looked at them in disbelief only to discover that they had both been firing from the same ammo belt!"[516]

At Molesworth, Russell F. Beach waited for the Fortresses to return. *Sweet Anne* was missing after being hit by flak at Kiel, and it had gone down in the North Sea. Humphreys and his crew were never heard from again.

On 5 January a 331st Bomb Squadron, 94th Bomb Group crew led by pilot Lieutenant Glenn B. Johnson set out on a mission to a large German air base northeast of Bordeaux. The crew had no premonition of disaster as they boarded their B-17G, but Lieutenant Ralph K. Patton, the co-pilot, had a feeling that it was "going to be a rough one." Patton might have had cause for nerves, because the crew's usual ship, the *Horrible Hanks*, was out of commission with a cracked air intake. No crew liked flying a substitute aircraft—it was considered unlucky. Their replacement ship[517] was a relatively new aircraft, but it had been badly shot up, and had only just managed to make it back to England on a previous mission. Patton recalls:

"We had been briefed and it wasn't very reassuring, that we could expect heavy flak. There was also an operational training group of young fighter pilots about 60 miles south of Bordeaux and they had at least sixty fighters. Our fighter escort wouldn't be able to stay with us over the target because of fuel limitations. We could expect the 'schoolboys' to be there in force. About 15 minutes from the target, our fighters, already ten minutes over-extended, had to swing back and we were alone. We began our run, heading for pillars of smoke from the 'planes that had preceded us. Glenn Johnson, our 6ft 4in pilot, signaled he was taking over. Then I began the co-pilot's toughest job - sitting around with nothing to do but pray that the guns firing at us wouldn't find their mark. Just after we had dumped our bomb load a shock hit the 'plane. Johnson and I struggled to right it. Black anti-aircraft puffs were all around us. As we moved out of range the call came in over the intercom - 'Bandits 12 o'clock high!' Then they came in at 3 o'clock and one o'clock. Suddenly, five FW 190s in single file came in from 1 o'clock level. Orange puffs of 20mm shells could be seen on the leading edges of their wings. We headed west to get out over the water and limit the distance they could follow. On the second pass we knocked one of them down. On the third pass they fired four cannon shots in the tail before turning and heading back. Looking around we saw several empty spaces in the formations and a few cripples were limping away from the mainstream but we had our own problems. Suddenly, the tail assembly began shuddering and we had to reduce our speed to 150mph. Slowly the formation pulled ahead of us. When we reached the Breton coast the rest of the formation was almost eight to ten miles ahead of us. Suddenly, as anti-aircraft fire began to burst close to us and as we swerved to elude it, our gunners spotted two FW 190s hiding in the glare of the sun. Our tail-gunner called out, '*Here he comes!*' As he released his microphone switch I could hear his guns open fire. Those were the last words I heard him speak."

The Fortress was raked by 20mm cannon fire, and the tail-gunner was killed. Jim Stewart, the ball-turret gunner, was also killed. Johnson felt the control pressures go limp as the nose shot up violently. By the time Johnson gave the order to bale out, Patton was on his way to the escape hatch:

"Cannon shells were bursting in the waist, the radio room, the nose and the cockpit. There was a snap and the ship nosed straight up. We jammed the controls forward but there was no response. I was out of my seat and heading for the door when someone shouted, 'Bale-Out!' I jumped and held off as bog as I could before yanking the ripcord. I watched the folds of silk billow up in front of my face as it opened. Suddenly, it was quiet. I began counting other 'chutes: six of them. The throb of the FW 190's engine broke in and I saw one of the 'planes coming straight at me. I waited. I had heard stories about Luftwaffe pilots machine-gunning parachutists. But at about 50 yards he veered away. Out of ammunition? A nice guy perhaps? I don't know but he droned off into the distance and never returned.'(Sergeant William A. Munson, the waist-gunner, was killed on the way down.)

"I came in over a hedgerow, hit my heels and came down on the seat of my pants with a solid thud. I tried to collect my wits. My 'chute was draped in a large tree I had missed by a few feet. Forgetting all about concealing it, I left the 'chute hanging in the tree and ran to a group of peasants standing nearby. They seemed to be looking past me and turning, I saw Jack McGough, the bombardier. We shook hands and faced the peasants together. Some were frightened, some were amazed and a few were smiling warmly. Then the big figure of Glenn Johnson came lumbering across the field to join us and all three of us struck out along a winding pony trail. We soon stopped to figure out what had happened to the others while about 3/4 of a mile behind us, a pillar of black smoke marked the end of the bad luck '212.'"[518]

The 5 January missions were the last under the auspices of VIII Bomber Command. The 15th Air Force had now been established in Italy, and it was decided to embrace both the 8th and 15th in a new headquarters called U.S. Strategic Air Forces, Europe, at Bushey Park, Teddington, and Middlesex, previously Headquarters, 8th Air Force.[519] Two more B-17 groups arrived in East Anglia in January 1944. First to arrive was the 452nd Bomb Group, commanded by Lieutenant Colonel Herbert O. Wangeman, which was based at Deopham Green, ten miles southwest of Norwich. Close on its heels were the crews of the 457th Bomb Group, commanded by Colonel James R. Luper. By the end of the month all but two B-17s, which had crashed in Northern Ireland, had flown into their base at Glatton, Huntingdonshire. One by one the Fortresses flew in, circling Conington village and rattling the windows with the noise of their Wright Cyclone engines. In turn each B-l7 thumped down on to the concrete and rolled to a stop at its allotted dispersal point. The crews, stiff and tired, and a little deaf in the sudden silence of switched-off engines, were no doubt curious, and wondering what to expect as they climbed down from their aircraft. Some were anxious to get into action, while others were apprehensive about what was to come, but all were united in the general disapproval of the damp Fenland murk and mud that surrounded them that English January. Once arrived in England, the 457th was assigned to the 1st Bomb Division, joining the 351st at Polebrook and the 401st at Deenthorpe as part of the 94th Combat Wing. The 452nd, meanwhile, was assigned to the 3rd Bomb Division, joining the 96th and 388th Bomb Groups in the 45th Combat Wing. The two divisions now totaled 20 B-17 groups, and Doolittle had plans to increase this number.

The first mission under the auspices of the USSAFE was on 7 January, when 420 heavies caused heavy damage to war plants at Ludwigshafen and Mannheim. Major James M. Stewart, the famous Hollywood actor and CO of the 703rd Bomb Squadron, 445th Bomb Group, led 48 B-24s to the I. G. Farbenindustrie plant at Ludwigshafen.[520] As the bomb doors opened a shell burst directly under his wing, but Stewart managed to regain control and complete the bomb run. Beyond the target he joined the lone 389th, which had strayed off course. George Makin, bombardier in the deputy lead ship in the 389th Bomb Group flown by Norbert Gebhard, recalls:

"Stewart, a great individual who we all admired for his theater performances, saved my life and the lives of many other men in the 389th Bomb Group. I am referring to his skill, airmanship and discipline. The details of what happened on that 7 January can best be described by quoting a December 1945 '*Saturday Evening Post*' article and noting passages from the official Air Force Records, which state that, '...Slight enemy fighter action was met from the IP to the target. Those attacks were successfully repulsed. Not so, however on their return, as there were determined attacks of the FW 190s and the Me 109s south of Paris. The 389th led the 2nd Combat wing - Major K. Caldwell was the air commander. The wing formation after the rally point found the leader increasing air speed and taking up a course south of that as briefed. At first, the other aircraft thought the leader was making a dogleg to fall in behind the B-17s. But when it became evident that this departure from course was being adhered to, attempts were made to call the leader. The excessive air speed caused groups to string out. At 1308 hours the 389th found itself alone and unescorted south of Paris. About 35 FW 190s and Me 109s made vicious attacks. In the running battle, the leader, Captain David L. Wilhite with Major Caldwell, was shot down.[521]

"When the leader was shot from the sky, it was Jimmy Stewart who moved his entire group over the top of the new leader, Norbert Gebhard. It was this move that saved the 389th from annihilation because planes were spread out all over the sky and the aggressive yellow nosed fighters would surely have made their kill. I became a believer in the leadership abilities of Jimmy. He placed his aircraft over the new leader and the remaining planes of the 389th got back into tight formation for the trip back to England.

"When it was noted that the lead aircraft was off course, two alternatives were open to Stewart, both of them bad. He saw another formation leaving Ludwigshafen on course and knew he could easily switch over and tack-on behind it, this insuring the safety of his own group. But this would have meant abandoning to its lonely fate, the group that was blundering away from the main procession – an easy prey for fighters, which were sure to single it out in the way home. And yet, if he continued, for the sake of wing integrity, to follow a leader who was heading for disaster, he must accept the certainty of sharing concentrated fighter attacks and extensive flak damage. With a hollow feeling in his stomach, Jimmy told the new leader of the 389th that he was sticking with them, He closed the 445th Group in for support and the new leader changed course, came home safely with no more loss of aircraft or lives....to me, this was Jimmy Stewart's Finest Performance."[522]

A host of enemy fighters had attacked the returning bombers near the Biscay coast. S/Sgt John W. Butler, flying his 15th mission as tail gunner in *Texas Rambler*, piloted by Lieutenant L. D. Lange in the 93rd Bomb Group, wrote:

"We took off at 0840 to bomb the chemical works. It was like the DuPont in the United States. The temperature was minus 37. We ran into flak quite a number of times around the target area. It was really hot. We had P-47s for escorts and they sure looked good. The clouds were very thick and you couldn't see the ground. When we were about 200 miles in from the French coast the cloud cover was gone and we could see the ground very clearly. We passed over quite a few big cities. You could see trains and barges on the canals. Once in a while some German flak gunners would send up a few bursts to let us know that they still had ammunition. We were now without fighter cover. As we passed over two German airdromes you could see the German fighters taking off in pairs from the fields. We were in for a very hot welcome. These fighters were very good, as they were called the Abbeville kids. They shot down seven B-24s in our group including both planes that were flying on our wing. They really were very hot pilots and they didn't scare very easy. I noticed four Me 109s at about 1200 yards, at 7 o'clock. I had my guns set on them to see what they would do. They were just milling around. Then one peeled off and came into attack. I held my fire until he was about 500 yards. Then I opened up. I fired about 70 rounds. He was then in to about 200 yards. He started to burn and he peeled off toward 8 o'clock. He threw his belly up. I let loose about 30 rounds. He baled out and the plane started down and then exploded. My right waist gunner shot down a FW 190 and the pilot baled out as the plane exploded. I received my second oak leaf cluster to the Air Medal. Also, I was credited with one plane destroyed, so I also received another oak leaf cluster."

Leutnant Peter Spoden, a 22-year old nightfighter pilot in 5./NJG 5, was among those scrambled on 7 January to intercept a force of 502 bombers bound for Ludwigshafen:[523]

"This time we nightfighters arrived on the scene too late and all I could see were pieces of wreckage and between seven and ten American airmen in life jackets floating in the sea. They signaled towards us. They were in the sea between Bremen and Heligoland: we immediately alerted the German coast guard and stayed with the Americans, who kept waving towards us. And now the terrible thing happened; by the minute the movements of the men in the water became slower and in the end they didn't move any more at all. We could already see the German marine craft approaching and flew as low as we dared in an effort to keep the men awake. We were later told that no one survived and that all had died of hypothermia. From that day on I always flew with a one-man dinghy, which was firmly attached to my body, even on baling out."[524]

Lieutenant Colonel Don Blakeslee led the 4th Fighter Group in a Withdrawal Support to Ludwigshafen from 1140 to 1440 hours. After being vectored around over France the Group rendezvoused with the bomber stream over Lens at 23,000ft. Near Hesdin, a dozen FW 190s came down from above and up-sun in finger-fours to attack straggling B-17s in the lowest box. Blakeslee led the bounce, engaging the 190s in combat from 24,000 to 3000ft. With three Focke Wulfs on his tail pumping his Thunderbolt full of holes, Blakeslee claimed one shot down. Captain James A. Goodson and Captain Robert H. Wehrman came to the rescue, and Goodson downed two of the 190s.[525] *Unteroffizier* Gerhard Guttmann of 8th *Staffel* JG 26 received credit for destroying Blakeslee's Thunderbolt, but that evening 71 holes were counted in WD-C after a forced landing at Manston.[526]

On 11 January a maximum effort comprising all three bomb divisions, including 291 Fortresses, was mounted on aircraft factories at Waggum, Halberstadt, and Oschersleben in the Brunswick area, a city notorious for its flak and fighter defenses. Since the destruction of the FW 190 plant at Marienburg in October 1943, the Oschersleben plant at Brunswick had become the principal producer of this German fighter. All bombing was to be carried out using visual sightings, with the 3rd Division stoking up fires created by the 1st and 2nd Divisions, but if the weather intervened, crews were briefed to bomb the city of Brunswick using PFF techniques. Heavy rain pounded the bases in the east of England, and heavy cloud began drifting across the Channel, Holland, and into Germany. Command allowed the mission to proceed in the hope that the cloud would clear. For two hours the bombers assembled into their intricate formations, and then crews plowed on across the Channel, conscious that the fighter support would be severely restricted or abandoned altogether. The fighters did manage to take off, but they soon became lost in the cloud layers over England, and many were forced to abort the mission. The *Luftwaffe Gruppen* in eastern Germany were not affected by the cloudy conditions and were able to take off and mass for a concentrated attack, the strength of which had not been seen since the Schweinfurt battles of October 1943. With the American escort seriously depleted the order went out to the 2nd and 3rd Divisions to abandon the mission. The crew of *Dog Patch Raider*, in the 93rd Bomb Group formation, received credit for the mission because, as S/Sgt Butler recalled, "As we crossed the Dutch coast we ran into quite a heavy concentration of flak. It was my 16th mission and the temperature was minus 37°."[527] The 1st Division, which was about 100 miles from Brunswick, was allowed to continue. The 303rd Bomb Group was leading the 1st Division, and Brigadier General Robert Travis flew as Task Force Commander aboard *The Eightball*, piloted by Lieutenant Colonel Bill Calhoun, CO of the 359th Squadron. Just past Dummer Lake over 200 enemy fighters bounced the formation. General Travis was to tell newsmen later:

"The fighters ... in spite of our escort, came at us in bunches. Out first attack was from four FW 190s, the next from 30 FW 190s. Then twelve and they just kept coming. They attacked straight through the formation and from all angles without even rolling over. They seemed to let up just a little when we started out bombing run. There was a period of three minutes only, from the time the fighters first started to make their attack until they left us, when they were not around."

Lieutenant Joe Wroblewski flew in the lead position of the low squadron in the 351st Bomb Group at about 19,000ft:

"One wing was ahead of us and we were second with most of out fighter escort. Just ahead of us planes kept falling, spinning and exploding from somewhere up above. Our fighters and the enemy were dog fighting just prior to the recall message. Then our fighters left us. I saw one crippled B-17 going back below us escorted by two Bf 109s. The Fortress had its landing gear down as a signal that the crew was going to bale out. The German fighters were flying alongside to allow the crew to leave the aircraft before shooting it down. Any bomber that fell out of formation was a dead duck. I watched a B-17 off to our right by itself. A Me 110 got on its tail and really poured tracers into the bomber. It caught fire and, as the flames licked around the tail, I could see the tail gunner still firing back at the Jerry. Finally, the bomber climbed straight up and fell off into a spin, burning and breaking up. One yellow-nosed Bf 109 came in between our wingman and us with his guns blazing. He must have put a few holes in our tail but no one was hurt. Our waist gunner fell back away from his gun for a second when he saw this plane so close and when he did start shooting again he shot through our tail and through the B-17 flying next to us. The enemy fighters kept falling and exploding all around us but still they kept coming in without giving us a breathing spell. They tried real hard to break up our formation but we hung together for dear life. All I could hear over the intercom was, 'Fighter coming in at 5 o'clock, one at 7 o'clock, another at 9 o'clock low. Fighter coming in at 10 o'clock level!' It was almost useless to call them out. There were so many coming in from every direction.

"At about this time many thoughts began to go through my mind. My parachute was just behind my seat and the temptation to snap it on and get the hell out of it was very strong. But then I thought about the other crewmembers. I don't doubt that they were just as scared as I was but at least they could shoot back. I thought about the training that had led to our present situation and about how we had looked forward to being in combat. But that was before all this. Right then I would have settled for being just a potato peeler, mess cook, or whatever, washing kettles for the duration. Then Saxon said, 'Lead him Henkel, lead him a little more!' The tail gunner came in with, 'I got him! I got a Me 210! The pilot's baling out!' Somehow one of our P-51s got separated from his group so he tagged along with us. We were very grateful because he fought as long as his fuel permitted; chasing the enemy until his ammunition was gone. Then he just dived after the fighters to divert them from the B-17s. Watching this one fighter escort bolstered our confidence in survival and we all admired his guts. Later we learned his name was Major Howard. He got back to base safely. Our group got separated from the wing for just a short time while ready to bomb and in the mix-up we dropped out bombs on a small town. There were two holes in the railroad and three in the main highway. It was a great relief just to get rid of the bombs under the conditions."

Major James H. Howard, ex-Flying Tigers pilot in China and now CO of 356th Squadron, 354th Fighter Group, 9th Air Force, displayed "conspicuous gallantry and intrepidity above and beyond the call of duty" in action with the enemy near Oschersleben, when he came to the rescue of some Fortresses. The P-51 was still a well-kept secret, and the 354th was the pioneer Mustang group in the ETO. Howard was flying his usual mount *Ding Hao!* (Chinese for "very good") when the 354th provided support for a formation of B-17s on a long-range mission deep into enemy territory. As the P-51s met the bombers in the target area numerous rocket-firing Bf 110 *Zerstöreren* attacked the bomber force. The 354th engaged, and Howard destroyed one of the 110s, but in the fight lost contact with the rest of his group. He immediately returned to the level of the bomber formation and saw that German fighters were heavily attacking the B-17s in the 401st Bomb Group, and that no "little friends" were on hand. Howard dived into the formation of more than 30 German fighters and for 30 minutes single-handedly pressed home a series of determined attacks. He shot down three fighters and probably destroyed and damaged others. Toward the end of his action, Howard continued to fight on with one remaining machine-gun and his fuel supply dangerously low. Major Howard's brave single-handed action undoubtedly saved the formation. He was awarded the Medal of Honor.[528]

Meanwhile, the 94th Bomb Group, flying at the head of the 4th Combat Wing leading the 3rd Division, was only 25 miles from its objective at Waggum when the order to abort was given. However, Lieutenant Colonel Louis G. Thorup, in the lead ship, decided to press on to the target. Andy J. Caroles, a bombardier in the 331st Bomb Squadron, recalls:

"The weather over England was very bad when we took off and assembled. The mission was recalled about the time we left the English coast, but Colonel Thorup did not receive the message. As a result, our Wing and two others that did not receive the message apparently went on into the target, not knowing the mission had been scrubbed and the fighter escorts recalled. [529] It was a costly mix-up and cost us several good crews. The weather began clearing up as soon as we reached Germany and was perfectly clear in the area of the target. We made a 'dry run' and had to do a 360° turn and come in again."

Cliff Hatcher, flying *Belle of Maryland* in the No.7 position in the 94th Bomb Group formation, adds:

"It was a typical SNAFU mission and finished with some 94th aircraft flying in other group formations. Two of our crews flew with the 447th and we started off with another group. The target was clouded over and Thorup decided to do a 360° turn over the target. When he turned, the 385th and the 447th did not follow."[530]

Andy J. Caroles again:

"As we started our second bomb run the Me 110s began attacking us. The other two groups in our Wing had dropped their bombs on the first run and headed for home, leaving our group alone, We had a running battle for about an hour-the Me 110s attacking from 3 o'clock around to 9 o'clock with rockets and 20mms. One by one the ships around us would be knocked out of formation. The enemy fighters would then 'gang up' on these cripples and finish them off. Bloyd and Cox were doing violent evasive action all through these attacks and again and again I saw clouds of 20mm shells explode where we had been only a second before. It looked as if our group was going to be picked off one at a time. I was expecting our turn to come at any moment. About 90 miles from the coast six P-47s suddenly appeared and scared away the Jerries. Our formation was a sad sight - only 10 planes were left in it out of the original 21. Besides the ships from our group that went down, our formation lost three from the 447th Group,[531] which had tacked on to us. I saw one of the 447th ships go down. It was an all-silver B-17. The entire tail of this ship from the waist back was blazing fiercely and one Me 110 was sitting on his tail not more than 200 yards out, slugging it out with the tail gunner. The tail gunner finally hit the Me 110 and it peeled off and started down smoking heavily. I watched the flames eat their way forward on the ship as it flew on in formation for one or two minutes. Then, it suddenly nosed up, fell off on its back and went straight down. No chutes came out of it. It was a fascinating sight and one I'll never forget. Our ship came through the entire battle with one small flak hole. The Lord must have been watching over us and I'm thankful to be back from that raid in one piece."

En route home the *Luftwaffe* subjected the B-17s to continual aerial assaults, and few bombers escaped punishment. Cliff Hatcher continues:

"Before the battle was over the three aircraft in front of me were gone. Almost every type of German fighter attacked us and we lost seven of our bombers and one that was flying with the 447th. Our aircraft was involved in one hell of a fight on the way out. 20mm shells punched heck out of the nose section and how out navigator and bombardier survived, I'll never know. The shells started electrical fires and punched two gaping holes in the left side of the plane. Trimble observed that the tight side was in an even worse condition! We got back to Bury with an engine on fire and the ship was in such a badly damaged condition it never flew again. We counted over 1000 holes in the *Belle of Maryland,* not including the two big ones. The ship was cannibalized and made the group's losses nine in all."

For its action over Brunswick, the 94th received its second Presidential Unit Citation, as Hatcher recalls:

"We paid a hell of a price to get it. I knew I was lucky to be alive and the air war had changed for me. Shortly afterwards I was sent for a 'flak furlough' at Coombe House in southern England. We were in such bad shape 'Doc' Miller, our flight surgeon, went along with us. He too was getting 'flak happy' riding along with his boys!"

Other groups also paid a hell of a price. The 303rd lost ten bombers and the 351st seven, while the 91st lost five B-17s and the 381st eight. In all, 34 of the 174 Fortresses dispatched to Oschersleben were shot down, while two wings assigned the plant at nearby Halberstadt came through practically unscathed.[532] Reports were that the fighter opposition was the heaviest since the Schweinfurt mission of 14 October 1943. *Zerstören* of ZG 26 destroyed 20 *Viermots*, and III./JG 1 (operating from Volkel), II./JG 27 (from Eeldt), and probably elements of JG 11 were also successful against the combat boxes. JG 26, a constant thorn in the side of the B-17 crews, claimed 12 Fortresses. Three of the *Jagdesgeschwader's* claims were for a 482nd Bomb Group PFF Fortress and two 92nd Bomb Group B-17s. Twenty-two B-17s in the latter group had left Podington when, due to weather conditions, a recall had been sent out after the mission was despatched, but the message was not received. Continuing in alone, the 1st Bomb Division was jumped by over 200 enemy fighters just past Dummer Lake. Near Heerde, Holland, on the return the Fortress[533] piloted by 1st Lieutenant William B. Lock in the 326th Squadron went down with two of the crew dead. Three men evaded and five were taken captive. Also lost was the B-17 piloted by 2nd Lieutenant Joseph A Tryens in the 325th Bomb Squadron.[534] *Oberleutnant* Walter Matoni of 6./JG 26 and *Unteroffizier* Rudolf Georgi of 7./JG 26 were credited with these two kills.

The 306th Bomb Group put up 20 B-17s in the main group,[535] and the CO, Colonel George L. Robinson, led the 40th Combat Wing to Halberstadt. At just after 1320 hours FW 190s of I. and II./JG 26 came upon the 306th formation. *Oberleutnant* Artur Beese, *StaffelKapitän* 1./JG 26, went between Colonel Robinson's lead ship and the 482nd Bomb Group PFF ship flying on its wingtip and shot away the tail of the PFF Fortress.[536] 1st Lieutenant Willard D. Reed, an experienced 368th Bomb Squadron pilot, was lost off Robinson's left wing when his B-17F[537] was hit hard in the leading edge of a wing, and the extensive damage caused the bomber to go into a spin. A raging fire ensued, and the B-17 broke up in the air and went down at Nijverdal. Five of Reed's crew died. 2nd Lieutenant Donald W. Tattershall's B-17[538] in the 369th Bomb Squadron had the tail shot off, and was last seen near the Zuider Zee. It crashed at Diepenveen, Holland. Only the radio operator survived.

2nd Lieutenant Ross McCollom was on his second mission for the 367th Bomb Squadron, flying in the low squadron.[539] His right wing was struck by another B-17 in the formation, causing some damage. McCollom rang the bale-out alarm but regained control. Almost immediately, the B-17 was hit by three elements of FW 190s from head-on. Only the bombardier, 2nd Lieutenant Lloyd G. Crabtree, survived, the bomber crashing at Epe. *Arch Bishop*,[540] piloted by 1st Lieutenant George Campert, a veteran 367th Bomb Squadron pilot, was knocked out of formation during the fighter attack and was last seen flying beneath the formation. None of the crew survived when this aircraft crashed at Heten/Raalte, Holland. 2nd Lieutenant Perry Cavos and all of his crew[541] in the 368thBomb Squadron also went down at Heten/Raalte, probably after colliding with Campert's aircraft. From the five 306th Bomb Group B-17s to go down, 50 airmen were lost, of which, 43 were killed. Only one 4./JG 26 FW 190A-6 was lost during this one-sided air battle over central Holland; the pilot, *Unteroffizier* Heinz Voigt, baled out successfully.[542]

Lieutenant Kenneth F. Dowell's B-17, in the 369th Bomb Squadron, was hit by FW 190s who set fire to his No.3 engine. Dowell was unable to feather it and lost his electrical system, so that the alarm bell did not sound when he hit the bale out switch. Dowell put his B-17 into a dive to escape, with flames screaming out of the battered engine. It burned so furiously that it fell off the wing of the B-17. At 4000ft the Fortress became more manageable, the fire was out, and the pilot continued on toward England. While they were in the dive a Bf 110 flew along with them, spraying them with machine gun fire. Incredibly, Dowell got the B-17 home on three engines and crash-landed at RAF Great Saling. Lieutenant Charles J. Kinsey's B-17 was hit by a 20mm shell that hit the base of the pilot's window, wounding Kinsey in the leg and ending his combat flying. Kinsey still managed to put the badly shot up Fortress down at RAF Foulsham in Norfolk. Lieutenant Bill W. Casseday crash-landed his 369th Bomb Squadron B-17 at Horsham St. Faith, near Norwich, where it was declared a total loss.[543] In all, three of the Group's B-17s were damaged severely, eight seriously damaged, and four were classified as slightly damaged. Only eight Fortresses returned to Thurleigh unscathed.

Vast banks of stratocumulus clouds covering most of Germany prevented visual bombing of targets, so attacks on targets in France throughout the remainder of January and early February became the order of the day. When bad weather on 14 January prevented bombing in Germany the bombers were switched to V-weapon sites in northern France, when 527 B-17s and B-24s escorted by 645 P-38s, P-47s, and P-51s attacked 21 V-weapon sites in the Pas de Calais. The *Luftwaffe* was hard pressed to deal with the number of bombers – 844 tactical aircraft also hit targets in northern France this day – and the large number of Allied fighters on freelance sorties over northern France. Lieutenant Colonel Selden R. Edner, 4th Fighter Group Operations Officer,[544] led the Debden Thunderbolts on a *Freelance* to Magny-Soissons in the afternoon. During the mission 15 FW 190s were spotted 3000ft below. The 336th Fighter Squadron made the bounce, engaging the *Luftwaffe* from 18,000ft to the deck. Captain Don Gentile made a head-on run with two of them. They broke, and he chased and shot them both down, making him an ace. With two 190s still on his tail, he heard numerous strikes all over his Thunderbolt. He turned into them and promptly ran out of ammunition, watching one of the Focke Wulfs stick to him, flown by an experienced pilot. Fifty feet over the forest of Compiègne Gentile shouted over the R/T, "Help! Help! I'm being clobbered!" Other 4th Fighter Group pilots radioed back, but Gentile was too rattled to answer. All he could do was keep turning into the expert in the other cockpit. After 15 minutes of reversing turns and head-on attacks, the German pilot ran out of ammunition and both fighters turned for home. The Group reformed, and was vectored near Soissons, where twelve 190s were seen 2000ft below. The 334th Fighter Squadron made the attack, fighting all the way down to 2000ft. Near Cambrai another four FW 190s attacked Lieutenant Edmund D. "Gooney Bird" Whalen[545] and Lieutenant Alexander Rafalovich, but they shared in the destruction of one of the attackers. Having claimed eight enemy aircraft destroyed for no loss to themselves, the 4th Fighter Group headed for home and crossed out at 1528, flying at 25,000ft.[546]

Of the 29 missions flown during January and February 1944, 13 were to V-1 flying bomb sites.[517] On 21 January 795 B-17s and B-24s set out to bomb V-weapon sites and other targets in the Pas de Calais and at Cherbourg. Some of these aircraft bombed targets of opportunity, while some combat boxes remained in their target areas too long identifying targets. (One target reportedly required ten runs before the group dropped its bombs!) A total of 628 escorting fighters were to shepherd the bombers and protect them from *Luftwaffe* fighter attack. However, the delayed runs and constant circling of some of the groups meant that the escorting fighters became low on fuel and had to withdraw, leaving some of the attacking bombers vulnerable to fighter attack. Bombing was also hampered by the weather, which was poor, with heavy cloud over most of northern France, and fewer than half the bombers dropped their bomb loads on the assigned targets. The 44th Bomb Group was assigned two targets: the 66th and 68th Squadrons the V-1 site at Escalles-Sur-Buchy in the Pas de Calais, and the 67th and 506th Squadrons military installations at Agathe D'Aliermont. Normally the mission would have been regarded as a "milk run," as the targets were so close to the English Channel, but it proved costly for the "Flying Eightballs." V-1 sites were notoriously difficult to hit, and the bombing altitude for the attack was at 12,000ft. Conditions therefore favored the attackers. Once again, it was the "Abbeville Kids" of JG 26 that took off to meet the Liberators. At 1420 hours *Hauptmann* Karl Borris, CO of I./JG 26, and his 15 fighters took off from Florrenes to look for the "*Amis*." Over Poix Borris saw what he was hoping for—an unescorted *Pulk* (herd) of Liberators. He immediately gave orders for his fighters to attack from the rear, where the seven Liberators of the 68th Bomb Squadron were flying "tail-end Charlie" position in the formation. Here the JG 26 pilots had the richest pickings. Such was the speed and surgical method employed by the attackers that four pilots achieved all their five victories simultaneously at 1530 hours. All except one of the victims were from the 68th Bomb Squadron, which returned to Shipdham with only three Liberators.[548]

JG 26 also claimed a 56th Fighter Group Thunderbolt shot down, but it was not all one-sided. At 1440 hours, while flying at 17,000ft west of St. Quentin a flight of P-47s in the 353rd Fighter Group spotted four Bf 109s flying southeast just above the cloud tops. Major Walter Beckham and the rest of the flight opened their throttles and nosed down, closing easily. Beckham picked out the Bf 109G-6 flown by *Feldwebel* Hans Oeckel and fired at him from less than 200 yards astern, getting many strikes and setting the Messerschmitt on fire. Oeckel quickly baled out and landed safely east of Laon-Sissonne with facial burns and a slight concussion. It was Beckham's 12th victory, and his 13th soon followed. Beckham opened fire on another 109 to the right as he was breaking left. Range was so short that hits resulted in spite of the deflection. He followed this Bf 109 down in a series of maneuvers with throttle full back and turning so sharply that he was stalling most of the time. Beckham thought his quarry was also stalling. The electrical sight went out after the first burst at the second 109. Using the mechanical gunsight Beckham gave him a burst each time the 109 straightened out. His canopy and miscellaneous pieces came off, but Beckham did not think that the pilot got out before the fighter broke apart. The American ace watched one of his wings, with a piece of fuselage attached, spiraling down flaming. When it struck the ground it started a large circular area burning. Beckham's second victim was *Oberleutnant* Erich Burkert, an experienced pilot with two victories in 71 sorties, who had he lived would have been promoted to *Staffelführer*.[549]

S/Sgt John W. Butler flew his 17th mission this day when he flew as left waist gunner in *Naughty Nan*, flown by J. J. Collins. "The Traveling Circus" target was Bois Carre:

"We took off at 1210. The weather over the target was cloudy so we couldn't bomb it so we just cruised around to see if would clear. We came over Abbeville and they threw up a quite a lot of flak but it was way below so it didn't bother us. One plane received a direct hit there was nothing left of it. Those German flak gunners were getting pretty good. They were also shooting rockets up at us from the ground. They left quite a smoke trail behind them. Fighters knocked down some planes. So the whole mission didn't turn out to be a milk run as all the kids thought it would be."

The bombers were stood down for two days following the 21 January missions, but they were resumed again on 24 January when 857 bomber crews were briefed to attack aviation industry plants and marshaling yards at Frankfurt. Bad weather during assembly played havoc with assembly procedures. At Duxford, Earl Payne in the 78th Fighter Group watched the "Big fleets" of bombers taking off for Germany. He saw a B-17 flying near the field, which happened to blow up in mid-air before crashing into the hills beyond.[550] Payne counted six parachutes, and they seemed to take a long time to get down. Four landed out of sight, but two landed near the roundabout out of Whittlesford. One of the chutes failed to open because it was burned. "The poor fellow landed on his feet, which were driven clear up to his stomach and burst his lungs. His entrails coming out of either side of his body beneath his armpits."

Only 58 bombers completed the mission. The 2nd Bomb Division was recalled before being despatched, and at 1020 hours all groups were recalled due to worsening weather en route. All except the leading combat wing in the 3rd Bomb Division, which were at the German border and decided to select a target of opportunity, turned for home as instructed. Meanwhile, the 78th Fighter Group carried out an alternate diversionary patrol of the Malmedy-St. Vith area in Belgium. Southwest of Brussels the P-47s were bounced by FW 190s of the IIIrd *Gruppe* JG 26, who claimed two P-47s shot down. (One was subsequently changed to a "damaged.") Robert Knapp claimed one of the FW 190s, which was blindly following his wingman, Edward Downey, but JG 26 suffered no losses, and neither did the 78th Fighter Group. Two B-17s, however, were lost in action, and both were from the 335th Bomb Squadron in the 95th Bomb Group.[551]

The weather remained bad, and the next heavy bomber mission was not flown until 28 January when 54 B-24s were despatched to France. Forty-three Liberators bombed their targets, and all of the aircraft returned safely to their bases. The following day the bomber crews were assigned targets at Frankfurt. At Shipdham, Forrest S. Clark, in the 67th Bomb Squadron, was just recovering from a bout of sinusitis and had been in the base hospital. He and Abe Sofferman reported to the flight line for briefing. Radio operators were often called to fill out vacancies on crews. Sofferman volunteered for the Frankfurt mission with the crew of Lieutenant Harold Pinder, who was flying *Sky Queen*,[552] and Clark stood down. Of the 863 heavies despatched, 24 B-17s and five B-24s failed to return. Once again the *Luftwaffe* seized upon lapses in the bomber formations, which began to go awry soon after crossing the coast at Dunkirk, when navigational errors and radar problems caused several combat wings to fly most of the mission without fighter escort.[553] The FW 190s of the Ist and IInd *Gruppen* of JG 26 took off at 1010 and were vectored east to Namur, where they intercepted the B-24 formation. While some of the enemy fighters moved on to seek out B-17s in the 3rd Bomb Division formations, the 7th *Staffel* remained with the Liberators, and north and northeast of Trier they singled out the 44th Bomb Group formation. *Leutnant* Waldi Radener later claimed one of the Liberators, but this was not confirmed. *Unteroffizier* Kurt Stahnke singled out another Liberator – it was Pinder's – and the German scored hits near the bomber's right wing tip.[554] 1st Lieutenant Harold H. Pinder recalls:

"We were met on the coast and on in by both Me 109s and FW 190s. I had never seen them mixed before. At about 1102 hours we dropped out of control after about three separate enemy passes. We took 20mm hits under the flight deck that cut the control cables. I couldn't get the autopilot to take over control - probably a hopeless effort anyway. The aircraft dove out of control. I remember the wing afire and at least the #4 engine knocked out. Our B-24 began to lose altitude and fire was seen in the bomb bay. Co-pilot Larry Grono parachuted out and became a PoW. 2nd Lieutenant Alvan E. Stubbs, bombardier, died in the nose turret. Milas Green, the left waist gunner, was in shock from a 20mm hit through both lower legs. S/Sgt Jack C. Robison, the right waist gunner pushed Green out of the rear hatch and pulled his ripcord but he did not get out himself, possibly giving his chute to Green. Robison died in the plane, as did tail gunner Bill Paxton and ball turret gunner Robert L. Laucamp. Navigator Donald Boomer and Earl Hall the engineer also parachuted out."[555]

North of Ludwigshafen *Oberleutnant* Rudolf "Rudi" Leuschel *Staffelkapitän* 8./JG 26 shot down the Liberator[556] flown by 1st Lieutenant George H. Maynard in the 66th Squadron. S/Sgt Derise L. Nichols, tail gunner, recalls:

"We were over France and about an hour from the target, with all bombs on board, we were jumped by a flight of fighters and were hit immediately. Shells hit just behind me and made very large holes in the waist section. No.4 engine was hit and put out of action. So were the controls to the tail section. So the pilots could only control flight with the three remaining engines. With the possibility of getting back to England now so slight, the decision was made to head for Switzerland. The bombs were salvoed, but even then with the trouble of trying to steer with the engines, we continually lost altitude across France. We did finally cross the Swiss border but by then we were less than 1000ft. We were shot at and hit by (Swiss?) ground fire and No.2 engine was put out of commission as well. Not being able to gain altitude over the rising terrain of Switzerland, we had to circle back to abandon ship. Only the three of us got out – all from the rear – because we were so low by that time that the others did not have time to get out and open their chutes."[557]

Luckily for the "Flying Eightballs," P-38 Lightnings in the 20th Fighter Group appeared on the scene, and JG 26 was forced to break off their attacks and seek cover in the clouds. The Lightnings shot down three of the FW 190A-6s—killing all three pilots—while a fourth FW 190A-6 flown by *Leutnant* Klaus Kunze of 2nd *Staffel* JG 26 was shot down by a 20th Fighter Group P-38 or a P-47 from another Group.[558] Kunze, who was WIA, baled out safely south of Rheine.[559] The 20th Fighter Group lost two of their number to *Leutnant* Hans Hartigs of 2nd *Staffel* and *Gefreiter* Manfred Talkenburg of the 8th *Staffel*. Many of the IInd *Gruppe* pilots landed to refuel at Epinoy and Grevillers before taking off again to intercept more fighters, this time P-47s in the 355th Fighter Group. *Feldwebel* Wilhelm Mayer of the 7th *Staffel* was back in the air again at about 1220 hours, and ten minutes later he shot down a 355th Fighter Group P-47. Mayer landed, topped up his tanks, and rearmed before he took off again with his wingman to look for more stragglers. At 1320 hours he shot down a B-17. *Unteroffizier* Erich Lindner of the 8th *Staffel* had, meanwhile, claimed another 355th Fighter Group P-47 at 1230 hours 20km east of Marche.[560]

On 30 January the 8th returned to the aircraft factories at Brunswick, when a record 778 heavies were dispatched. Bombing was carried out by 701 of the bombers using PFF techniques for the loss of 20 aircraft. Next day 784 B-24s bombed V-1 sites being constructed at St. Pol/Siracourt, while 70 P-47s escorted by 87 Thunderbolts and 47 P-38s bombed Gilze-Rijen airfield. They encountered 84 enemy fighters, and in a fierce battle six P-38s were lost. The U.S. fighters claimed 13 enemy fighters destroyed. The bomb groups were stood down on 1 February, and missions resumed on the 2nd when 96 B-24s bombed V-1 sites in Northern France once more. On the 3rd 543 bombers bombed Wilhelmshaven, while 61 others bombed Emden and targets of opportunity. Bad weather caused more than 100 of the bombers to abort their mission.

On 4 February 433 bombers in 15 combat wings of B-17s and B-24s were dispatched to Frankfurt, on the Main River.[561] This presented a clear return on H_2S radar carried by PFF aircraft, and it was enough to allow the bombers to drop their loads through overcast with a fair degree of accuracy. However, H_2S failures and high crosswinds prevented accurate bombing, while several combat wings came under intense AA fire over the Ruhr. S/Sgt John W. Butler in the 93rd Bomb Group flew his 21st mission of his tour when he again flew left waist gunner in *Naughty Nan*, piloted by J. J. Collins. Butler recalled:

"We took off at 0915 to bomb the city of Frankfurt at 21,000ft. The temperature was minus 44, which is very cold. Before we passed the enemy coast my heated boots went out. So I went up on the flight deck and borrow the radio man's, as on the flight deck they have heat. I then went back to my waist gun position. We ran into heavy flak twice on the way to the target. Over the target it was pretty damn good. You should have seen Carey and I throwing the tin foil out. It is suppose the spoil the German radar equipment. We dropped our bombs and started for home. My heated suit went out for good. I had the ball-turret gunner came back in the waist to take my place as I then went up on the flight deck to try and keep warm. Our bombardier lost his oxygen supply so he came up on the flight deck also. My feet were frozen. The radioman fired a red flare as we came into land and the meat wagon followed us down the runway. We stopped and they took us off to the hospital. There were around twenty fellows in the hospital with frostbite. This was the worst mission I was on to have so many things go wrong."

Fortunately, the *Luftwaffe* was limited in its operations by the weather, though JG 26 claimed seven of the total of ten bombers shot down by the German fighters.[562] During combat with escorting P-47 Thunderbolts in the 352nd and 56th Fighter Groups, JG 26 lost one of its pilots and three others were wounded in action.[563] The Blue Nosed Bastards had rendezvoused with the bombers, which were far off course, in the vicinity of Aldenhoven. During the first 40 minutes of the escort all was quiet, but as the formation arrived in the vicinity of Brussels the 328th Squadron noticed two separate formations of bandits. One gaggle of FW 190s was at 26,000ft near Brussels, and the second was near Hasselt at 15,000ft. During the engagements that followed Lieutenants Francis Home and Fremont Miller each claimed a FW 190 destroyed.[564] Thus, the 328th Fighter Squadron in the 352nd Fighter Group was able to exact a measure of revenge for losses suffered the previous day.[565]

On the 5th 450 B-17s and B-24s attacked airfields at Châteauroux, Avord, Tours, Châtaudun, Orleans, and Villacoublay.[566] S/Sgt John W. Butler in the 93rd Bomb Group, which was given Tours as its target, flew his 22nd mission of his tour when he flew left waist gunner in 939-E[567] flown by R. R. Russ. Butler recalled:

"The CQ called me at 0630 to fly as a spare gunner. So by the time I made briefing room and out to the plane it was near takeoff time. They didn't pass any candy out today. I didn't have any breakfast either because everything was in a hurry. They had an oxygen leak in the tail turret so they had to replace the regular. We then had to take off 20 minutes late. We then headed for the rally point where we were finally able to pick our own group. The weather was nice and clear as we were only at 16,000ft so you could see the ground pretty good. Temperature was only minus 13. My heated suit worked real good. We had good fighter-protection as we had P-38s and P-47s. I saw one P-38 go down in flames but the pilot hit the silk. The plane broke in two and I watched it hit the ground. We got to the primary target and some ships dropped their bombs. We then went on to the secondary where we dropped our 12 500 pounders. I could see quite a few fires burning. Fighters shot down a B-24 in the 409th Squadron. Four chutes got out.[568] It was good mission as a whole. We received a large hole from flak in the de-icer boot."

On 6 February 206 bombers bombed more airfields in France and rocket launching installations at Eclimeux, although bad weather prevented more than 400 bombers completing their missions. It was a day of mixed fortunes for the American and German fighter pilots. The 61st Fighter Squadron, 56th Fighter Group claimed three Bf 109G-6s in JG 26 shot down northeast of the Paris area[569]—where the enemy pilots were about to pounce on the Fortresses. Two JG 26 pilots claimed a B-17 shot down at Melun[570] and a P-47 east of Paris.[571] South of the French capital a 56th Fighter Group P-47 shot down a FW 190A-6 flown by *Oberleutnant* Artur Beese, *StaffelKapitän* 1./JG 26. Beese, who had scored 22 victories in 285 combat sorties, tried to bale out, but he was killed when he struck the tail of his 190.

The Bomb Groups were stood down on the 7th. On the 8th 237 bombers attacked Frankfurt-Main using blind bombing techniques, and 127 heavies bombed V-weapon sites at Watten and Siracourt. Another 78 bombers blasted targets of opportunity. In all, 13 Fortresses were lost. JG 2 and 2./JG 26 combined to attack the B-17s in the 92nd Bomb Group, which had an unfortunate mission to Frankfurt. The lead ship failed to take off from Podington because of a mechanical malfunction and the deputy lead took over, but was then forced to abort shortly after entering the enemy coast. Some confusion resulted because the formation at the time was flying straight into the sun, and by the time the leader of the high squadron assumed group command, the 92nd were 30 miles off course and separated from the 40th Combat Wing. At this point "Fame's Favored Few" were attacked by 30 enemy fighters, and the group leader and wing aircraft were shot down.[572] The low squadron leader took over and, realizing the impossibility of joining the Combat Wing formation, he decided to abandon the mission.[573] JG 26 pilots also shot down six P-47s and P-51s in the 352nd and 354th Fighter Groups.[574] Immediately after rendezvous with the bombers, Red Flight of the 328th Squadron in the 352nd Fighter Group were en route to assist a straggling bomber being attacked by a FW 190 when they came under attack from *Hauptmann* Karl Borris and his 1st *Staffel* formation. The German pilots bounced them from out of the sun, and two P-47s went down immediately to the guns of Karl Borris and *Oberfeldwebel* Xaver Ellenrieder.[575] North of Laon *Leutnant* Waldemar "Waldi" Radener of the 7th *Staffel* claimed two more of the Group's P-47s. One of his victims crashed, but Lieutenant Raymond Phillips reached England and bellied his P-47 in on the coast. At Bodney the control tower operator recorded that Lieutenants John Walker, James Meager, and Harold Nussman had all been bounced while escorting a crippled B-17, and he added, "They didn't have a Chinaman's chance."[576]

S/Sgt John W. Butler flew his 23rd mission, flying as nose gunner in *Naughty Nan* in J. J. Collins' crew, when the 93rd Bomb Group went to Siracourt, as he recalls:

"We took off at 0715 to bomb the construction works at 15,000ft which we later learned were for the buzz bombs. The temperature was minus 30. I didn't go in the turret until we were at 14,000ft. You needed help getting in and out of the nose turret, as they had to close the turret door behind you. When you wanted to get out you had to call them on the interphone to let you out. Well, I threw my heated and heavy gloves up on the ammunition box and then I climbed in the turret. The navigator then closed the door for me. The four little windows were open and the guns were elevated so the wind was blowing in quite fast. It was very cold. I got my oxygen mask connected. I then tried to close the windows, but my hands were frozen. I couldn't reach my gloves because my guns were elevated. The main line was off and it had to be turned on from the outside. I plugged in my heated suit but I had no gloves on and they were beet red. I had no feeling in them. I finally got my throat mike on and I yelled over the interphone to get me the hell out of this turret. The navigator opened the door and pulled me out. I went up to the flight deck for heat. When my hands began to thaw out I really suffered. We shot a red flare as we came in for a landing. The pilot called for a meat wagon, which met us at end of the runway and took us to the hospital."

After another stand down on the 9th missions resumed again on 10 February, when 28 bombers hit the airfield at Gilze-Rijen, and Brunswick was the target for the 3rd Division. They were escorted by 466 Lightnings, Thunderbolts, and 9th Fighter Command Mustangs. The long-ranging P-51s could accompany the bombers to their targets and back again, but they were powerless to prevent German fighters causing carnage on a large scale. The enemy destroyed 29 of the 169 Fortresses despatched. Major Heinz "Pritzel" Bär, *Kommandeur* II/JG 1, shot down a Fortress and a Thunderbolt.[577] Once the B-17s had been picked up on German radar in sector "*Dora-Dora*" Heinz Knoke had been ordered to take off and climb to 25,000ft over Rheine. Over the Dümmersee he sighted Fortresses flying eastwards. He described the sight as "a truly awe-inspiring spectacle." Knoke picked out a group of Forts flying on the left flank of the main body and closed in for a frontal attack, but as he did so they altered course slightly and his attack was in vain. Swinging off to the right and round in a wide arc, he waited until his *Gustavs* were again flying ahead of the bombers, and then he came round for a second frontal attack. He wanted his 40 fighters to cut a swathe through the ranks of the Americans. By radio he urged his pilots to remain calm and make every shot count. The *Gustavs* kept close together. Knoke noticed Thunderbolts behind, but the American fighters were unable to intercept the 109s before they dived into the formation of bombers. *Unteroffizier* Raddatz held his *Gustav* flying almost wingtip to wingtip alongside Knoke's. Then suddenly there was a bright flash, and Raddatz immediately plummeted down vertically. Knoke continued closing in his Fortress, firing at the cockpit until he had to pull up sharply to avoid a mid-air collision. But his gunfire had its mark. The Fortress reared up on its tail, and others swerved out of its way. Then the left wing dropped, and the Fort went down out of control in its final death dive to disintegrate thousands of feet below. Though he was twice set upon, first by eight Mustangs and then by a pair of Thunderbolts, Knoke managed to shake them off, and he landed back at Wünsdorf, where he learned that Raddatz was dead.[578]

On Friday, 11 February, when the first P-51s joined VIII Fighter Command, 180 B-17s of the 1st Division attacked industrial targets at Frankfurt-Main and a V-weapon site at St. Pol/Siracourt, again while 130 heavies bombed Ludwigshafen and other targets of opportunity after the blind bombing equipment failed. The 3rd Division was rested, and the 2nd Division B-24s bombed targets in the Pas de Calais. At Hardwick, S/Sgt John W. Butler, now recovered from his ordeal on 8 February, flew as left waist gunner in *Willie's Worry* with J. J. Collins' crew when the 93rd Bomb Group returned to Siracourt to bomb the construction works again. It was Butler's 24th mission, and he recalled:

> "We took off at 0715. At 14,000ft it was 14 below zero. We met quite a lot of flak at the IP and those flak gunners were right on the beam as you could hear the flak bursting quite close. Turner's plane received a direct hit and then broke in half. The tail gunner fell out of his turret and hit the wing of the plane behind."[579]

The Fortresses bombed Frankfurt through 10/10th clouds in an attempt to hit the target that had been missed three days before. The bombers were protected by 15 groups of escorting fighters. At Duxford a number of P-47 Thunderbolts flew withdrawal support for the Fortresses returning from Frankfurt. One of the Jug pilots who took part was Grant Turley:

> "We escorted them out from North Central France. Just after rendezvousing with the bombers we ran into about 20 Me 109s. I was No.3 in Lieutenant Hockery's flight when we went into the middle of them. My wingman lost me (a bad habit my wingmen have had lately) but I bounced a 109, followed him through a cloud and got in a good burst. Saw strikes all over the cockpit and wing roots and a lot of smoke. He went straight down out of control. I am sure that the pilot was dead. I pulled back up through a cloud layer and went around and around with another one. This Jerry had one yellow stripe on his fuselage indicating that he was a squadron leader. He was plenty good. I only got a couple of 90° deflection shots at him. Came home on the deck. Shot down a Focke-Wulf 190 that was taking off. The flak and tracers were really buzzing around. I got lost and was sweating out my gas when I found that I had flown way out over the Brest Peninsula. I didn't know where I was until they started shooting flak at me over the Guernsey Islands. I really prayed to God coming across the water. I was at 2500ft. They shot flak all around me. I could hear it go 'whump' about ten different times. That's getting pretty close. I really kissed the ground at Warmwell, the base I landed at. I had only 17 and a half gallons of gas left. The weather was bad and my radio was dead but I started on to Duxford. I was forced down by the weather at Chettingford. Spent a bad night under wool blankets in a Quonset hut. It was rough and cold."[580]

The strong fighter escort helped keep bomber losses to a minimum, and five were lost on 11 February, three of the B-17s falling victim to JG 26. Flak and fighters had harried the 306th Bomb Group formation all the way from the coast to the target, which was bombed by 19 of the Group's planes. The B-17 flown by 1st Lieutenant Geno DiBetta and his crew in the 423rd Squadron was hit by flak at the IP, and the No.3 engine was put out of action. DiBetta and his co-pilot, 2nd Lieutenant Earl J. Wolf Jr, managed to keep in formation until bombs away, when they turned for home. Flak again hit the left wing, and DiBetta tried to reach a cloud bank below, but about six FW 190s caught up with the ailing Fortress, hitting the bomber on the first pass and then queuing up for head-on attacks, one after the other. Near Mons, Belgium, *Oberleutnant* Erich Scheyda of 3./JG 26 claimed the bomber's final destruction.[581] Northwest of Poix *Ain't It Gruesome*,[582] flown by Captain John P. Carson Jr in the 351st Bomb Group, was claimed shot down by *Oberfeldwebel* Adolf "Addi" Glunz, CO 5./JG26. Northeast of Beauvais *Tenabove*, in the 532nd Bomb Squadron, 381st Bomb Group,[583] fell victim to *Unteroffizier* Gerhard Guttmann.[584]

Next day, 12 February, 85 Liberators bombed V-weapon sites at St. Pol/Siracourt again. One of the crewmembers who flew on the raid was S/Sgt John W. Butler, who was right waist gunner in *Reddy Teddy*,[585] piloted by Lieutenant Glenn E. Tedford. Butler was flying his 25th and final mission of his tour in the 93rd Bomb Group. He wrote:

> "We took off at 0730 to bomb Siracourt from 18,000ft. Flak was pretty good, but none was close to us. It was minus 22. When I left the French coast behind I was very happy. I never wanted to see the French coast again except on a postcard or on a newsreel. It was a good mission to finish up on. I was a pretty happy guy when I landed."[586]

Next day the Chiefs of Staff accepted a revision of the CBO Plan when targets were reduced to a number that could be decisively attacked, and target lists were revised to keep up with the effort of the enemy to relocate vital industrial plants. Disruption of lines of communication and a reduction of the *Luftwaffe* fighter strength were now given high priority.

12

The Battles of Big Week

"Cold, distant stars flickered at us from a frosty sky as we entered the briefing building. In one respect, not yet apparent to us, this morning was different from the others. Our raid today was the beginning of a week which was to mark the biggest air battles of the European war, a week of 'all-out' conflict between the USAAF and the Luftwaffe. Before the next six days were past hundreds of American bodies would lie scattered across the continent; other hundreds would be in German prison camps and scores of our bombers would lie, bits of crumpled wreckage, in their own craters. But hundreds upon hundreds of Jerry fighters would drop from the flaming skies to rest in ruin as complete as that of many of the factories from which they came…."

Lieutenant Lowell H. Watts, pilot *Blitzin' Betsy*, 388th Bomb Group, 20 February 1944

Early in 1944 the *Luftwaffe* was still a force to be reckoned with, especially when one considers its day fighter *Geschwaders* of conventional fighters could, and did, shoot down dozens of B-17s and B-24s on a single mission. Despite a highly effective fighter shield of long-range P-51 Mustangs, which could accompany the bombers to their targets and back again, the USAAF was, on occasion, powerless to prevent German fighters causing carnage on a large scale, as the bombers flew even deeper and in greater numbers to the far flung targets of the *Third Reich*. Operation *Argument* was the first battle involving the mass use of bomb groups of the Strategic Air Forces (USSTAF). General Carl "Tooey" Spaatz and his subordinate commanders, Major General Jimmy Doolittle (8th Air Force) and Major General Nathan F. Twining (15th Air Force), planned to make a series of co-coordinated raids on the German aircraft industry, supported by RAF night bombing, at the earliest possible date. Good weather finally permitted "Operation *Argument*" to take place during the week 20-25 February, which quickly became known as "Big Week."

One of the airmen who participated was Myron Keilman:

> "The weather had been so bad that the 392nd had flown only 16 missions since 1 January. But by 20 February we had been both alerted and briefed and had taxied for take-off nearly every morning since General Doolittle took command. We waited for hours in the dense fog before the red flare fired from the control tower signaled, 'Mission cancelled'. Then back to the airplanes' dispersal pads; back to the dank Nissen huts; and back to the damp, ice-cold cots for needed sleep and tomorrow's alert. 'Damn the foggy weather, damn the war and damn General Doolittle too.' After those early-hour breakfasts the Mess Sergeant had to pick up the General's portrait from a face-downward position in the middle of the floor and rehang it in its respected place. Disrespect, yes, but who wants to be rousted out at 0300 hours day in day out just to sit in the fog? We couldn't win the war doing this and you didn't have to be a General to see that the weather was unfit to fly a bombing mission."[587]

Like so many mornings in England, the sky in the early hours of Sunday, 20 February, was clear, but a few stray clouds drifting in from the North Sea gave warning of an instrument assembly above 10/10ths cloud by take-off time. Some 1028 B-17s and B-24s and 832 fighters were assembled to attack twelve aircraft plants in Germany as the anticipated cloud scudded across eastern England, bringing with it snow squalls that threatened to disrupt the mission. The 1st and 2nd Divisions were briefed to hit the Messerschmitt plants at Leipzig, bombed only a few hours earlier by RAF Bomber Command.[588] The 3rd Division, meanwhile, would fly an equally long and arduous route to Posen, in Poland.[589]

Lieutenant Lowell H. Watts, pilot of *Blitzin' Betsy* in the 388th Bomb Group, who would be flying his 19th mission this day, viewed the map in the briefing room at Knettishall with a sense of foreboding:

> "The map was covered as always but there was an extension on the right-hand side of it. Out regular map, which reached from England to east of Berlin was too small for this raid! The cover was pulled away and there it was! The red tape ran out from England, over the North Sea to Denmark, across it, out over the Baltic Sea, then back in over eastern Germany and into Poland. Posen was our target. It lay almost 1000 miles away. 'Men,' Colonel William B. David (the CO) was saying. 'Your bomb load is 5000lb. Gas load, naturally, maximum. Don't start your engines before you have to. You'll need all the gas you have. Altitude is 11,000ft. Over the Baltic you'll climb to 17,000, which is your bombing altitude. If you lose an engine over or near to the target check your gas and, if you don't think you can make it, head for Sweden. Our wing is bombing Posen. The 13th Wing will go part of the way but are bombing about where you will hit the German coast, so you'll be alone all the way back. The rest of the 8th will be bombing targets all over central and southern Germany. You'll have no fighter escort so shoot at anything you see in the way of a fighter. Keep on the ball and good luck to all of you.'
>
> "I was very careful that morning to leave my personal belongings in the safe keeping of the PW room. Our chances of needing them that night seemed rather slim. Out at the plane we double-checked

everything with unusual care and threw in a couple of extra boxes of ammo. For the first time on a combat mission we noticed a box of 'K' rations in the ship. We'd need some food before we got home on a haul like this one. Just before taxi time we started the engines. We'd run them up while lining up for the take-off. There was no point using any gas we could save. We took off, climbed through the clouds and assembled. The rendezvous time was cut in half and we started out over the North Sea, tightening up the formation more as we went along and climbing to 11,000ft before levelling off. We used the lowest possible power setting and the lowest rpm possible and flew as smoothly as we could in an effort to make our gas last.

"Near Denmark the clouds began breaking up and, by the time we crossed the Danish coast, it was cleat as a bell beneath us. Something else met us besides good weather - Jerry fighters. Off on our left a group was under heavy fighter attack. Two bombers went down. Later, we saw ten 'chutes drop from another crippled plane but, pilotless as it was, this ship, slowly losing altitude, continued on eastwards and not until we were across the Danish peninsula did we lose sight of it. The FW 190s attacking us kept sweeping in until we were well out over the Baltic and the quaint red-roofed villages of Denmark had blended into the horizon behind us. We changed course to the southeast and climbed to 17,000ft. Clouds were piling up beneath us again and they covered the German coast. On and on we flew. We were almost to Poland now and Ju 88s, Me 110s and Me 210s had replaced the Focke-Wulfs, making steady, unrelenting diving attacks on our formation. Nowhere could we see a break in the overcast. There was a ruling that no target in an occupied country would be bombed except by contact bombing. Targets in Poland came under this category. So, after flying those hundreds of miles, many of them under fighter attack, we had to turn back, still carrying our bombs, tired, hungry, with the fighters still on us and a feeling of frustration in the knowledge that Posen's factories would still he turning out Focke-Wulfs on the morrow.

"We checked our gas tanks. They were less than half full and we were still lugging out bombs. The loss of only one engine would be enough to make us run out of gas. As it was, it would be nip and tuck. We should just make it but maybe we wouldn't. We were still at 17,000ft, using a lot more gas than we would have had we dropped our bombs and gone back down to 11,000. Sixteen of our 21 planes were still in formation. Our other two groups were a little better off. We had lost the left wing and the 'diamond' ships in our element, the second element of the low squadron. The VHF crackled to life. 'Wolfgang Yellow, Wolfgang Yellow, this is Wolfgang White calling. Open bomb bay doors. We're approaching our target.' Now over Germany, we were going to bomb a secondary target by PFF through clouds.

"Our bomb doors swung open as we fell in behind the 96th Bomb Group which contained the PFF ship. Suddenly, flak appeared - big, ugly mushrooming billows of black, blossoming out around the angry red flash of the shells' explosions. The flak became thicker and more accurate as we neared the point of bomb release. Our ship bounced as the sound of ripping metal brought a lump to our throats. A big jagged hole had made its appearance between our Nos.1 and 2 engines. The No.2 gas gauge still showed no indication of a leak. There were two tips in the No.2 cowling but the oil pressure was up and the engine was running smoothly. Ahead, two long streams of white arched down beneath the lead ship in the 96th formation. Those were the market bombs of the PFF ship. In a few seconds we were nearing those markers. As we passed them we dumped our bombs, happy to feel the plane leap upwards, free of its load. The flak pounded us for about a minute longer and then it began to disappear. At last we were heading home, free of out bombs and able to cut down on our power settings. Only a few Ju 88s were around. Now and then they would lob a rocket at us, careful to stay out of range of out 50s. One formation of the 88s lined up behind us and started pumping rockets at us. The projectiles sailed into the high squadron, bursting like flak. Fire broke out on the tight wing of one plane. It flew for a minute longer, then rolled up on one wing and started down. Suddenly, there was a flash; a huge billowy puff of smoke and jagged pieces of broken, twisted metal fluttered aimlessly earthwards.

"The hours dragged on. We'd been up almost eight hours now and we were crossing Denmark with the North Sea still separating us from England. Leaving the coast we let down to 10,000ft and loosened the formation as the fighters fell away. A glance at the gas gauges was anything but heartening. It would be a close one getting back today. We checked everything we might need if we should have to ditch. The sun was riding low in the west as we neared England. Every few minutes one of our planes would drop out of formation to save gas. A few we heard calling pitifully to Air Sea Rescue and soon, below us, one of the lone planes would glide with a splash into the sea, its gas exhausted. 'Pilot from navigator, we're over England. You can see a spot of coastline off to our right through that little hole in the clouds.'

"We watched the radio compass swing around, telling us we were passing over our field. Our squadron leader zoomed gently up and down. His left wing ship peeled off and was followed by the squadron lead ship, his tight wing ship and then our plane. The ships were letting down on a heading of 90°, disappearing one by one into the fluffy folds of white below us. Soon we were skimming the clouds and then we were in the soup, dark, lonely and uninviting. I was watching only the instruments now, heading 90°, flaps one-third down, wheels down, air speed 150, vertical speed 500ft per minute. Down, down, down we went, the gloom darkening each second. At 1000ft we were still on instruments. We were all dead tired but during the let-down we forgot it for the moment while eager eyes tried to pierce the murk for signs of the ground or other planes which might hit us. At 750ft we broke out. It was raining but visibility was fair. We turned almost 180° until the radio compass read '0' and flew on until landmarks became familiar. Finally, we saw flares up ahead and soon the runway became visible. A plane was on its approach. Another, too close to it, pulled up and went around again. We started our approach and let down with the fuel warning lights on and the gas gauges reading almost empty. We couldn't stay up much longer. Kennedy turned the turbos full on in case we should need the power if we had to go around again. Old *Blitzin' Betsy* settled down, floated a second and then touched the runway. We rolled to the end of the runway, another mission completed. Then we realized how tired we were."

The same tiredness prevailed on the 1st Division's effort at Leipzig. As the formation crossed into Germany it encountered single and twin-engined fighters of almost every type, including Stukas, He 111s, Dornier 17s, and Focke-Wulf 190s. The German pilots adopted American single-engined fighter tactics in an effort to gain favorable attacking positions. Lieutenant Joe Wroblewski was in the 351st Bomb Group formation:

"About 20 Bf 109s hit us just before the target and came in four at a time head-on. They flew right through out formation and slow-tolled beautifully while shooting. In the excitement some gunner from out own formation shot through one of our engines, cutting a gas balance line and mixture control cable. Besides having a few screwed up indicators on the panel and a worried mind, everything was okay."

In a last resort to deter the 1st Division, the Germans employed cable bombing methods. They did not work. The leading 401st Bomb Group, led by Colonel Harold W. Bowman, the CO, at the head of the 94th Wing flew on to the briefed point west of Brunswick and diverged to bomb the target. Despite a heavy flak barrage during the bomb run, which heavily damaged Bowman's aircraft, the formation bombed with excellent results. Colonel Bowman recalls:

> "Because the weather was uncertain we were provided with a PFF crew especially trained for instrument bombing. The weather en route was indeed bad and preparations were made for aiming by instrument means but as we approached the target area, the clouds opened up to 'scattered' and a visual sighting was made. The result was, for out group, 100% of our bombs within 1000ft of the aiming point."[590]

Over the target 42-38109 *Cabin In The Sky*, in the 364th Bomb Squadron, 305th Bomb Group, piloted by 1st Lieutenant William R. Lawley Jr, was hit by a 88mm flak shell, which did not explode when it went right through the left horizontal stabilizer and cut the control cable. Suddenly, *Cabin In The Sky* became very nose heavy. At "Bombs Away" the bombs refused to go, and Lawley tried to salvo them, but this failed. (The racks had moisture on them and they were frozen.) In the meantime, the rest of the formation had moved out because when they released their bombs their B-17s "jumped" a hundred feet or so. Lawley managed to get back into formation once, but he knew he could not get home like this, as he was pulling too much power. Enemy fighters singled him out, and on the first head-on pass they were hit all over. A shell came through the right windshield and hit Lieutenant Paul Murphy, co-pilot, in the face and exploded. He put his hands over his face and fell forward, hitting the control stick and knocking it out of Lawley's hands, forcing *Cabin In The Sky* into a steep spiral. Almost immediately, the B-17 dived from 28,000ft to 12,000ft. The left windshield was covered with blood, but Lawley's view was clear, and by looking out he realized that they were descending, and that the aircraft was in a turn. Lawley was able to correct it. He got the dead co-pilot off the controls with his right hand while bringing the aircraft out of its dive with his left. The group reported that they had spun in. Murphy's death slump had sent the B-17 spinning down, which the enemy fighter pilots must have thought was a fatal dive, because they passed up the stricken B-17 and did not attack again. By the time *Cabin In The Sky* had leveled out Lawley had already rung the alarm bell to signal the crew to get out, and then he received word that two gunners in the back were too critically wounded to bail out. Harry G. Mason, bombardier, came up and said, "Can we make this thing fly." Lawley replied, "I don't know. We'll try." All the crew agreed to ride out their luck. Two engines that had been set on fire were extinguished, and Harry Mason managed to salvo the bombs. There seemed a good chance they could make it safely to England. The bombardier later took over the controls when Lawley was on the verge of unconsciousness, but he recovered sufficiently to pilot the stricken bomber to England, where one engine died of fuel starvation. As Lawley made his approach to a Canadian airfield at Redhill—the first available airfield—another engine burst into flames. Despite this he belly-landed *Cabin In The Sky* safely on the one remaining engine, and all the crew were rescued. Lawley was awarded the Medal of Honor.

The 4th Fighter Group, led by Captain James A. "Goody" Goodson, led a Withdrawal Support to Kirkburg, Germany, from 1250 to 1625 hours. The Group rendezvoused with two combat bomb wings of B-24s and five combat bomb wings of B-17s at 1429 hours, flying at 23,000ft northeast of Koblenz. Five Bf 109s attacked with rockets and the 335th Fighter Squadron engaged them. Near Malmedy, eight FW 190A-6s tried to attack the first combat box of B-17s from the rear, but the 4th Fighter Group P-47s jumped them, and they had to break off. *Unteroffizier* Erwin Hell of the 6th *Staffel* was hit, and he baled out with minor injuries. Three more FW 190s were damaged. Captain Henry L. "Hank" Mills, Duane Beeson, and Lieutenant Pierce W. McKennon claimed a FW 190 apiece. 1st Lieutenant Richard I. Reed in the 335th Fighter Squadron shared a Bf 110 with Lieutenant Paul S. Riley before reed was shot down and killed NE of Koblenz by *Leutnant* Friedrich Lange of the 6th *Staffel*, JG 26, who 20 minutes earlier had shot down *Skunkface* in the 91st Bomb Group formation.[591]

Two other Medals of Honor were awarded for actions this day. During an attack by enemy fighters a cannon shell entered the cockpit of *Ten Horsepower*[592] in the 510th Bomb Squadron, 351st Bomb Group. Flight Officer Ronald E. Bartley, the co-pilot, was killed instantly. The right side of the pilot's face was torn off by splinters, rendering 2nd Lieutenant Clarence R. Nelson unconscious. Sergeant Joseph F. Rex, radio-operator, was also wounded in the attack, and the bomber suffered severe damage. 2nd Lieutenant Joseph R. Martin, bombardier, decided that *Ten Horsepower* was finished, and told the crew to bale out. Martin salvoed the bombs and then left the aircraft through the forward escape hatch. S/Sgt Archie Mathies (age 25), the Stonehouse, Scotland—born ball turret gunner—and Sgt Carl W. Moore, top turret gunner/engineer, decided to see what could be done for the pilot. They clambered into the cockpit. 2nd Lieutenant Walter E. Truemper, navigator, had also remained in the aircraft, and went up front to help Mathies. After much effort the body of Bartley was dragged out of his seat and placed in the nose.

The windshield was smashed, but Mathies, who had a couple of hours flying experience, took over the wheel. He believed he could fly the bomber back to England. Mathies and Truemper took it in turns to fly *Ten Horsepower* while the rest of the crew struggled to remove the dead co-pilot. His limp body forced both men to crouch on the floor between the seats, using only the elevators and ailerons to keep the B-17 airborne. Mathies had the greater knowledge of how to fly a B-17 and completed most of the route home. At times the cold, because of the smashed windshield, became so intense that Truemper and the others had to take turns at the controls. Mathies and Truemper did not know how to land a B-17 so, when they reached Polebrook, Mathies called up the control tower and told them of their predicament. The crew was told to bale out over the airfield, but because of the injured crew, Mathies and Truemper volunteered to remain aboard and try to bring the crippled bomber in for a crash-landing.

Colonel Eugene Romig, CO of the 351st Bomb Group, Colonel Elzia Ledoux, tower officer, and a flight engineer took off in *My Princess*[593] with the intention of flying alongside *Ten Horsepower* and assisting in the landing by radioing instructions to Mathies. Unfortunately radio contact could not be made between the two bombers, and visual directions were impossible, because *Ten Horsepower* was flying too erratically to allow Romig to get in close. Romig decided the only course of action was for Mathies to fly the bomber towards the sea and bale out. Mathies and Truemper still refused to leave their pilot and elected to try and land. The tower radioed a set of instructions, and the now crowded flight line waited as Mathies came in for the first approach. *Ten Horsepower* was too high and he had to abort. At this point five of the crew baled out, three of them sustaining broken legs. *Ten Horsepower* was by now far to the south of Polebrook and heading for Molesworth airfield. This second approach was also too high, so Romig and Ledoux, via the tower at Polebrook, instructed Mathies and Truemper to head north and try to land at their home base. However *Ten Horsepower* drifted northeast, passing Sawtry, the A1 road, and Glatton airfield. Here the B-17 veered off to the left in a sweeping, diving turn past the control tower. Believing the crew were attempting to land, ground staff fired off red flares. *Ten Horsepower* re-crossed the A1 and headed towards the village of Denton, seven miles from RAF Upwood.

From the actions of the errant B-17, which suddenly throttled back, it was obvious to Romig and Ledoux that Mathies and Truemper were going to attempt to put the B-17 down in a field (near Denton Hill). At 1700 hours, in a very large open field just south of Stilton *Ten Horsepower* touched down. Romig and Ledoux estimated that the aircraft was traveling at 200mph when it hit. The B-17 rolled for 50 yards or more before hitting a mound of earth, and then it cartwheeled before breaking into pieces. Mathies and Truemper died in the wreckage. Nelson was reportedly still alive when rescuers reached the wreckage, but he died later. Mathies and Truemper were posthumously awarded the Medal of Honor.

That night the crews in the 351st went to their barracks and caught up on some much needed sleep. Joe Wroblewski planned on taking a short catnap before dinner, but he was so exhausted after the mission it was not until the following evening that he awoke again.

There was no let-up in the campaign against the German aircraft industry, and next day, 21 February, 924 bombers[594] and 679 fighters fought their way through dense contrails and biting cold to their targets at Diepholz, Brunswick, Hanover, and Achmer. However, thick cloud obscured the objectives, and bombing had to be completed using PFF techniques. Many groups attacked targets of opportunity, and airfields and aircraft depots were heavily bombed. Heinz Knoke of 5./JG 1 had orders to draw off the escorting fighters "at any cost" and keep them engaged in combat while other *gruppen* attacked the bombers.[595] Five of the missing bombers were claimed destroyed by II./JG 1; three of them by Heinz Bär to take his score to 185 kills.[596] However, the *Gruppe* lost five pilots killed and four wounded. The 8th lost 19 bombers and five fighters, but 60 German fighters were claimed shot down.[597]

On 22 February the elements were responsible for collisions during assembly, and the 3rd Division was forced to abandon the mission completely. Overcast hampered the 2nd Bomb Division assembly over East Anglia, and eventually conditions became so bad that the Division had to be recalled while flying a scattered formation over the Low Countries. The 1st Division, led by Colonel "Mo" Preston, CO of the 379th Bomb Group, continued to the Junkers works at Oschersleben. Colonel Preston says;

> "There was pretty solid low undercast so as Strike Force Commander I directed strikes on targets of opportunity. Thereafter, the problem became one of finding our way home. The overcast extended indefinitely in all directions and we simply had no way of navigating except by dead reckoning and guesswork. Somewhere in out wanderings the wing in which I was flying suddenly came under fire - big black heavy intense flak. Inside the lead plane it seemed that we could feel every burst as it went off beneath us and bounced our plane around. Ahead and very close to us we could see not only the black cloud of each flak burst but also the flash of the explosion. This was unusual, for normally one doesn't see that much. We took evasive action and it may have helped but it didn't seem to get us out of the flak pattern. Meanwhile, my tail gunner was reporting planes going down - one of them at least, as a result of a direct hit, which exploded the plane. On this one there were no parachutes. Finally, we came out of it but not until we had lost four planes. This was the worst flak I ever saw and the heaviest loss to flak I ever experienced. I had already taken a piece of flak in my right foot from an isolated burst or two we had encountered on the way in to the target. Now I got another piece as a souvenir. It was about three inches long and an inch wide and hit me in the side, knocking the breath out of me but not penetrating the skin. Fortunately, it was spent when it got there. A Purple Heart for the piece in my foot but nothing for the piece in my hand. It was subsequently calculated that we got the flak from the guns at Cologne. I never wanted to go back to Cologne. I still flinch when I get near that place. A few terrible moments can leave an imprint on a fella."[598]

The 8th had also taken the precaution of flying a diversionary raid, sending some Fortresses to Aalborg, in northern Denmark. Bill Rose, who flew in the 92nd Bomb Group, was with them:

> "The lead pilot took the whole group into 10/10ths cloud, which went all the way up to about 20,000ft, instead of staying out in the clear and making a 180° turn to avoid them. All I could see was the wing of the man we were flying on. In cloud you lose complete orientation and I did not know whether we were up, down, sideways, or anything else. In all the years of flying this was the one and only time I suffered vertigo.
>
> "The sound indicated we were in a screaming dive but I believed in my instruments and rode it out. Eventually, we lost the man we were flying on. All we could do was make a 180 and come out. We broke out of the cloud and I found myself stretched way over in the seat but the plane was flying straight and level just as the instruments indicated. One plane coming out of the cloud flew straight into another plane going in and collided. It looked like a huge oil rank fire at 20,000ft with nothing but black smoke."

For the mission to the Junkers factory at Oschersleben the 303rd Bomb Group scheduled 38 aircraft for the raid. While the Group was assembling, *Hell's Angels II*[599] and 42-31516 in the 384th Bomb Group collided near Irthlingborough, Northamptonshire. The right waist gunner baled out and survived, but the rest of the crew were killed. The bombardier and navigator survived aboard the 384th aircraft. During the raid enemy fighters shot down four aircraft.[600] During this same raid S/Sgt William T. Werner, tail gunner on Lieutenant Estes' crew in *Luscious Lady*,[601] was awarded the DSC for extraordinary heroism. Badly wounded by a 20mm shell, he stayed at his post until all attacks were repelled. Further problems of aircraft colliding in mid-air when assembling after take-off occurred on 24 February. *Helen Highwater*[602] flew under 42-29823, piloted by 2nd Lieutenant J. H. Melton, and completely cut off the rudder and badly damaged the fin. Amazingly both aircraft landed safely at Molesworth with no injuries to either crew. This accident occurred during the form-up for the mission to Schweinfurt, where crews reported heavy flak concentrations. In all, 809 aircraft took part in this raid, the 303rd providing 27. Two B-17s were lost.[603]

On 23 February bad weather kept the 8th Air Force heavies on the ground, but 102 bombers in the 15th Air Force destroyed 20% of the ball-bearing works at Steyr, Austria. Next day 238 Fortresses of the 1st Bomb Division attacked Schweinfurt, losing eleven B-17s, while 295 B-17s of the 3rd Bomb Division struck at targets on the Baltic coast with the loss of five Fortresses.[604] The target for eight Liberator Groups of the 2nd Bomb Division was the Messerschmitt 110 aircraft works at Gotha, 420 miles due east of the White Cliffs of Dover.[605] Twenty-eight B-24s in the 445th [606] joined with the 389th and 453rd to form the leading 2nd Wing. The 14th Wing's 44th and 392nd Groups would fly behind the 2nd Wing, while the 20th Wing brought up the rear. Briefing for crews at Wendling took place at 0630 hours, and the briefing officer related the importance of the large plant to Germany's ability to carry on the air war. He also told crews that, "it was heavily defended by large 88mm and 110mm anti-aircraft batteries." They had already experienced this type of heavy artillery over Bremen, Kiel, and Wilhelmshaven. On this, the 392nd's 40th mission, the Liberators were almost certain to encounter heavy fighter opposition over enemy territory—400 miles there and 400 miles back. At 0810 hours the 392nd Liberators started up their engines, and five minutes later the lead ship taxied to take-off position. At 0830 hours the green flare from the control tower was fired to signal 'take-off." Jim McGregor, the lead crew pilot, revved his engines, checked his instruments, released his brakes, and rolled along the runway. Thirty-one Liberators followed behind at 30-second intervals. At 12,000ft, firing red-yellow identification flares into the clear sky, the Group formed up over Radio Beacon 21 into three Squadrons and flew the Wing triangular assembly pattern to King's Lynn. The 392nd led the 14th Wing, falling into No.2 position of the 2nd Bomb Division over Great Yarmouth. Gunners test-fired their guns as the DAL[607] headed east over the Channel, climbing to 18,000ft. At 1131 hours the force of 235 Liberators, each maintaining a speed of about 135mph, crossed the Dutch coast just north of Amsterdam and flew on over the Zuider Zee. Streaming vapor trails signaled the bombers' presence and their intent. By 1139 hours the leading 2nd Wing was flying ahead of schedule due to increased wind velocity and an unforeseen change in direction.

Flak was heavy over Lingen, and the Liberators encountered persistent attacks by the *Luftwaffe*. Even the arrival of three Thunderbolt Groups just after 1200 hours was unable to prevent five Liberators in the 445th being shot down in the space of six minutes. Over 150 enemy fighters ferociously attacked the formation all the way to the target despite close attention from escorting fighters. The Division beat off incessant attacks as it flew on over Dummer Lake, where it veered southeastwards to Osnabrück and the bombed-out airfields near Hanover. Three more 445th B-24s were shot down before the formation turned south near Gottingen at 1253 hours. Nine minutes later a 445th B-24 in the 703rd Squadron was shot down.

To the right, flying parallel to the Liberators' course, were the Fortress formations of the 1st Bomb Division heading for the ball bearing plants at Schweinfurt. Out over the North Sea B-17s of the 3rd Bomb Division were en route to their Baltic coast targets. P-47 Thunderbolts had escorted the Liberators to the vicinity of Hanover, and then the twin-boomed P-38 Lightnings and P-51 Mustangs orbited the formation as it proceeded to Gotha. Undaunted, FW 190s, Bf 110s, Me-210s, and Ju 88s raked the American formations with cannon and rocket-fire. Using the Liberators' thick vapor trails to excellent advantage, they often struck at any lagging bomber from below and behind. The *Luftwaffe* even attempted to disrupt the large and unwieldy combat wings.

At 1309 hours the Division changed course to the southeast with a feint towards Meinegen. Some confusion arose at the IP when the navigator in the 389th lead ship suffered oxygen failure and veered off course. The bombardier slumped over his sight and accidentally tripped the bombs. Altogether 25 Liberators bombed the secondary target at Eisenach. Before the small 445th formation reached the target its tenth and eleventh victims fell to the German guns. By now the 445th consisted of only 14 Liberators, three having aborted before entering Germany. Another 445th machine was shot down just after leaving Eisenach. The 13 remaining B-24s, realizing that they had veered off course, continued alone. They arrived over the target at 1325 hours and executed an eight-minute bomb run. Some 180 500-pounders dropped from 12,200ft inflicted considerable damage on the Gotha plant. Other 2nd Bombardment Division Groups, totaling 171 Liberators, dropped another 468 tons of assorted bombs from varying altitudes and directions. The 445th's 13th B-24 fell victim to the German defenses minutes after bombs away.

Myron Keilman was flying deputy lead to Lieutenant-Colonel Lorin J. Johnson, and recalled:

"Luftwaffe fighters made attempts to penetrate our formations but our 'little friends' kept them at a distance and, when the opportunity prevailed, dove in for a 'kill'. Using our thick vapor trails as a screen, the Germans often struck from below and from behind to shoot up any lagging bomber. Bending southeastward toward Gotha, the white, snowy earth looked cold and lifeless; only the large communities, rail lines and an autobahn stood out in relief. Fighter attacks became more persistent. By the time we reached our IP (Initial Point) to start our bomb run, the sky about our three squadrons was full of busy P-38s and P-51s fending off the Germans. They dove past the lead ship in pursuit of Messerschmitts and Focke-Wulfs making head-on attacks. Our gunners got in a lot of shooting, too. The staccato of the turrets' twin fifties vibrated throughout the airplane. It was real scary.

"The bombs were smack 'on target' but the battle wasn't over. No sooner had the wing left the flak than German fighters accosted us again. Strung out in trail and with some planes slowed down from flak damage, our three squadrons became vulnerable to vicious attacks. For the next hour and more Messerschmitt, Focke Wulf and Junker fighters worked us over until our fighters could fend them off. As deputy command pilot I frequently changed off flying formation with the airplane commander to keep occupied and not have to watch the Jerries press their blazing gun attacks. The interphone was alive with excited calls of enemy action. Head on passes and tail attacks; in singles and in 'gaggles'; rockets, 20mm cannon and even some cables were thrown at us. Seven of our B-24s were shot down. Many of us were shot up, but it was not all one-sided. The gunners of the 22 airplanes that returned accounted for 16 German fighters. The weather was very clear as we turned to the target. Red flares from the lead ship signaled 'bomb bay doors open'. The bombardier removed the heated cover blanket from the bombsight (they had heated blankets before the people did!). He checked his gyroscope's stabilization and all bombing switches 'on'. Our high and low squadrons fell in trail and all seemed great. Then pilotage navigator Kennedy, in the nose turret, observed the lead wing formations veering away from the target heading. A fast and anxious cross-check with lead crew navigator Swangren and a recheck of compass heading and reference points assured command pilot Lorin Johnson that the target was dead ahead. Within minutes Good, the lead bombardier called over the intercom 'I've got the target!' Lead pilot McGregor checked his flight instruments for precise 18,000ft altitude and 160mph indicated airspeed and carefully leveled the aircraft on autopilot. He then called back, 'On airspeed, on altitude. You've got the aircraft.' Making a final level of his bombsight, Good took over control of steering the aircraft with the bombsight.

"At 18,000ft it was 40° below zero but the bombardier never felt the cold as his fingers delicately operated the azimuth and range controls. He cross-checked all the bomb and camera switches to the 'on' position, especially the radio bomb-release signal switch that simultaneously releases all the bombs of the other aircraft in the formation.

"Maintaining perfect formation the 392nd fought its way through the German flak defenses and bombed the Gotha works with pinpoint accuracy. After Lieutenant Good had dropped the bomb load the camera recorded the impact of the bombs. Lieutenant McGregor took over and swung the formation to the outbound heading and the rallying point.

"Despite the now accurate flak the second and third squadron bombardiers Lieutenant Ziccarrilli and Lieutenant Jackson, steered their Squadrons to the precise bomb delivery points too. Of the 32 B-24s which took off that morning, 29 of them each delivered their 12 500-pounders precisely on target as briefed."[608]

But the 392nd paid dearly for its accuracy. Strung out in trail, and with some B-24s slowed down because of flak damage, the three Squadrons became vulnerable to vicious fighter attacks. For an hour after bombing the 392nd was subjected to head-on passes and tail attacks from singles and gaggles of *Luftwaffe* fighters. When the Group returned to Wendling at 1530 hours, seven hours after take-off, seven B-24s were missing, and another 13 landed with battle damage. Sixteen enemy fighters were confirmed destroyed by 392nd gunners.

The 13 surviving 445th Liberators, nine of them badly battle damaged, limped into Tibenham at about 1545 hours. Altogether the Group had lost 122 men on the bloody mission, including Major Evans, the 792nd Commanding Officer, and most of the Operations Staff. Captain Waldher, Operations Officer of the 700th Squadron, was also lost. The Group's gunners were credited with the destruction of 21 enemy fighters, plus two probables and two damaged. Six 389th Liberators were shot down in quick succession during the raid, while the survivors received further punishment on the homeward journey.[609]

The P-47 Groups had given a good account of themselves during the mission. The 4th Fighter Group, led by Lieutenant Colonel Edner, had provided a Withdrawal Support to north of Koblenz-Schweinfurt from 1225 to 1530 hours. The Group rendezvoused north of Koblenz with four combat bomb wings of Fortresses and one wing of Liberators at 25,000ft. As the P-47s pulled in, four FW 190s attacked the B-24s from head-on. The 4th Fighter Group's upper squadron drove them off when four more 190s and four 109s were engaged by the other two squadrons. One Focke Wulf was claimed shot down, but Lieutenant Joseph W. Sullivan was killed NW of Koblenz at 1420 hours.[610] Twenty miles from Dummer Lake, at Furstenau, the 78th Fighter Group bounced 20 to 25 enemy aircraft making head-on passes from above the bombers and chased them down to the deck. Near Dummer Lake, 1st Lieutenant Grant M. Turley saw a 359th Fighter Group P-47 600 yards above a Bf 109 firing at it, but not getting any closer or getting any hits on it. As the 359th Fighter Group P-47 finished firing, Turley closed to 150 yards and lit up the Bf 109's wing, canopy, and engine with hits. Pouring smoke, the 109 rolled over and the pilot baled out.[611] Lieutenant Max Juchheim followed two Bf 109s to the deck, hitting one steadily with a pair of two-second bursts at 200 yards. The 109's canopy came off and the fighter crashed in a field. Pulling up on the second one, Juchheim chased him over a little town where he streamed black smoke and, rolling inverted, crashed in a small wood. Lieutenant Robert Wise closed up astern of a FW 190 to 50 yards and exploded him with fuselage hits. Lieutenant Charles Peal hit another fighter in the fuselage and wing roots. His victim flattened out on the treetops with his prop windmilling and crashed and disintegrated into the ground. Lieutenant Walter Tonkin fired a long burst at a FW 190 at 50ft, and the fighter flashed, smoked, and hit the ground in flames. Tonkin's wingman, Lieutenant Randal Hathaway, saw three P-47s chasing a Bf 109 around a church steeple and he joined in the chase. Closing to 10° deflection, 50ft off the ground, Randal got heavy strikes in the 109's fuselage and wingroots, causing the fighter to hit hedges along the street and blow up in flames as it hit the ground.[612]

On 25 February the USSTAF brought the curtain down on "Big Week" when 1300 8th and 15th Air Force bombers and 1000 fighters were despatched on the deepest penetration into Germany thus far, to aircraft plants, ball bearing works, and components factories throughout the Reich. The 1st Bomb Division was assigned the Messerschmitt Me 410 experimental and assembly plants at Augsburg and the fighter plants at Stuttgart, while the 3rd Division returned to Regensburg for the first time since 17 August 1943 when the B-17s had suffered such devastating losses. The shadow of Schweinfurt and Regensburg was still uppermost in the minds of all the B-17 crews, and this time the 3rd Division would share the bombing role with the Italian-based 15th Air Force, which would bomb Regensburg an hour before the English-based force arrived over the city. The Germans had given top priority to the reconstruction of the Regensburg plant, and within six months had restored production to something like its previous output. Although most of the old buildings had been destroyed, several main buildings had been rebuilt, including a long assembly shop on a site where three had once stood.

News of the Regensburg strike came only hours after crews had logged 12 hours' flying time during a mission to the Baltic coast. It had not only been the longest raid they had flown so far, but also one of the toughest. Lowell Watts and the crew of *Blitzin' Betsy* at Knettishall were still very tired, as all crews were, when they were roused from their fitful sleep at 0300 hours, but the prospect of flying to Regensburg did not seem to sink in;

"Crews had arrived at that mental state," recalls Watts, "where one more extra long, extra tough raid, meant nothing to us. It was just another raid. As for myself, at least, I'd grown callused. The tougher the raid now, the better I liked it. Beautiful weather greeted us as we assembled over England and headed off across the Channel. We crossed the coast at 21,000ft, our formation assembled and everything was working OK. It was one of those rare days in the European theater when visibility was unlimited by fog, clouds or haze. Just as the enemy coast began passing beneath us, a murderous barrage of flak started coming up. We were supposed to cross the coast between Dieppe and Le Havre but we were evidently too close to Le Havre. We'd been through heavier flak before but the accuracy of this stuff was hard to beat. They had our altitude perfect. Then they began tracking us and in a matter of seconds those black puffs were riding tight along with us. The ship jerked a little to the sound of ripping metal. We'd been hit and hit hard. Our left wing showed a big, ragged hole. A few more bursts got in close enough to leave other hits showing in the nose and fuselage. Givens, flying our left wing, peeled off and headed for England. He'd probably make it back from out present position but he hadn't lasted long. Sweeney turned his ball turret to the front and looked over the bottom of our wing. 'Pilot from ball turret; there are a lot of holes in the wings, especially the left one, but I can't see any gas running out.'

"All four of our engines kept purring away and we were seemingly in pretty fair shape as we flew out of range of the flak. It was time now for our fighter covet to be showing up but they were nowhere in sight. For another 30 minutes we kept flying to the east and still found ourselves out there alone. Something had gone wrong with the timing. Then we began to see fighters but they weren't out own, they were Jerries. Focke-Wulf 190s, Ju 88s and Messerschmitt 109s were beginning to circle in ever increasing numbers and then they pulled up ahead of us and started their attacks. One B-17 dropped out of formation and lost altitude. 'Chutes appeared beneath it. As we watched him he started burning, leaving a long trail of black smoke behind. The crippled plane dropped fast then seemed to level out a little, sailed over the hills beneath and finally disappeared into a mass of flame and debris which scattered itself over almost half a mile as it hit and exploded. Another B-17 was hit and exploded, almost in the formation. A B-24 seemed to fall apart as the Jerries took on one of the B-24 formations.

"As time wore on we could see the FW 190s peel off from their attacks, dive almost straight down, levelling off just above the ground, make a brief half circle and land on the nearest field. They would taxi in; sit there for five to ten minutes and then we could see the dust behind them as they started up again. In another five minutes they would be back to the attack. It was sort of fascinating to watch that circle complete itself but at the same time very discomforting to realize that these fighters that were hitting us might follow us all the way in and out unless they were shot down. Of course, some of them were, but not enough. There was still no sign of out fighter cover.

"It was almost 1200 when we sighted a column of smoke rising almost to our altitude. It was dead ahead. If that was smoke from Regensburg, then the 15th Air Force had hit it and no question about it. The Alps were clearly discernible to the north of us now. They reminded me quite a little of our own Rockies. About then I was wishing they were the Rockies too. Upon reaching our IP we could easily see the 15th's target. All we had to do was follow that column of smoke down to the earth and there it was - what was left of it at least. We turned in for our bombing run and there above us was the most welcome sight I'd ever seen on a mission; a group of P-38s. At last, our fighters had found us!

"Up ahead the flak was getting thicker and thicker. One of our squadron leads was hit and peeled out of the formation so quickly that his whole squadron was scattered. Only half his planes got back into formation during the bombing run. Back behind us his second element of three ships was trying to catch up with us but they were too far behind. Then the flak got too heavy for us to worry about anyone but ourselves. We settled down on the last of the bomb run. The target was spread out beautifully below us in perfect visibility. A chance like this was a contact bombardier's dream come true. The bombs went out, we closed our bomb bay doors and turned away from the target. Behind us were those three planes, making a bomb run of their own. They looked so vulnerable and all alone back there but they made the run and pulled in with another formation without losing anyone.

"Below us our target was rapidly looking like the other one which had been hit by the 15th Air Force before we had arrived. Smoke was pouring upward, rising to about 20,000ft. The Jerries were still making things quite interesting but with our own fighters in the skies, a lot of their attacks were diverted. Now the strain began to tell. We'd done a lot of combat flying during the week and we were beginning to feel its effects. Kennedy and I began trading off on the flying. Both of us were so tired that after about 15 minutes we just couldn't hold formation, Never in all my missions had I reached the stage where I was absolutely too tired to fly, but I reached it on this raid. During a lull I looked around the formation. Several ships were missing and in three of the missing spots was a queer-looking sight. Three P-38s were flying formation with us. Each of them had lost an engine and had pulled into our formation for protection.

"Hours later we circled Knettishall and set *Blitzin' Betsy* down on good old terra-firma once again. Every man on the crew was completely fagged, sleepy, stiff, sore and just generally all-in. We taxied up to our hardstand and tumbled out. Those holes were even bigger and uglier-looking than we had realized. Quite obviously our wing was badly shot up. The gas tank had been hit in several places. Tired as I was, at that particular moment I could have taken my hat off to the engineers who had never seen combat but who had developed the bullet-proof gas tank. Our story of this particular day would have been quite different had those tanks never been designed."

The 8th lost 31 bombers, while the 15th Air Force lost 33 bombers. Thirteen of the B-17s lost by the 8th Air Force came from the 1st Bomb Division. The 306th Bomb Group were the low group in the 40th Combat Wing. At about 1210 hours on the way in, the Fortresses were bracketed by accurate and unexpected flak from Saarbrücken, which knocked a 92nd Bomb Group B-17 in the same wing out of the sky and split the 306th Bomb Group wide open to fighter attack.[613] Before the 306th could properly reform JG 26 made two diving attacks on the 368th Bomb Squadron formation. *Oberleutnant* Paul Schauder, 10th *Staffel* CO, and *Hauptmann* Klaus Mietusch, III *Gruppe* CO, shot down *Top Hat*, flown by Flight Officer James R. Coleman, and 1st Lieutenant Joseph M. Gay Jr's Fortress southwest and southeast of Charleville respectively.[614] Three FW 190s missed Coleman's B-17 with 20mm fire on the first pass, but coming from 3 o'clock on the second, put incendiary shells into the bomb bay and into the nose. Gay, who was a veteran of more than 20 missions, and three of his crew died in the plane. Of the six men who got out five of them survived to be taken prisoner. A third B-17[615] in the 368th Squadron flown by 1st Lieutenant Charles M. Bayless, who was being checked out as a first pilot on this mission, was hit by flak, which severed several of the control cables. The radio operator was killed when he was hit by flying shrapnel. All the other nine crew managed to bale out safely and they were taken prisoner.[616]

FW 190s of the 5th and 8th *Staffeln* JG 26 meanwhile had taken off from Laon-Athies as the Fortress formations passed overhead. *Staffelkapitän Hauptmann* Rudolf "Rudi" Leuschel, who was under orders to attack only unescorted combat wings, led his fighters off towards Saarbrücken after reports indicated that the American fighter escort was few in number. When Leuschel's Focke Wulfs reached their quarry they began making head on attacks on the 13th and 45th Combat Wing boxes.[617] *Oberfeldwebel* "Addi" Glunz, CO 5th *Staffel*, claimed *Liberty Belle-E* in the 570th Bomb Squadron, 390th Bomb Group flown by Lieutenant George Rains. 2nd Lieutenant Robert V. McCalmont, a bombardier in the 390th, witnessed the gallant Fortress pilot trying desperately to save his bomber:

> "I watched this guy do everything but a snap roll to shake off four Germans who were out with everything they had to get him. He dived, climbed and banked and one time went so close to the ground that plane and shadow seemed to converge [sic]. He headed back up again with one fighter still hugging his tail and leveled off below us. His last message came through our earphones: 'That's all brother, you're looking at my last engine!' The ship's nose pitched forward and a minute later it crashed and burned."[618]

The 96th Bomb Group lost four B-17s, and pilots of the 8th *Staffel* JG 26 claimed two of these. *Führer* (fighter leader) Waldemar Busch claimed the B-17 flown by Lieutenant Robert D. Lindstrom in the 339th Bomb Squadron at Alsbach, near St. Ingbert.[619] *Feldwebel* Josef Zirngible shot down *Wacky Woody* in the 339th Bomb Squadron being flown by 2nd Lieutenant William H. Lupole and his crew in the 452nd Bomb Group.[620] The 4th Fighter Group, led by the Executive Officer, Lieutenant Colonel Selden R. Edner,[621] were flying a Penetration Support to Sedan-Stuttgart. As the P-47s rendezvoused with the B-17s near Sedan they attacked and then bounced some of the Focke Wulfs. 1st Lieutenant Vermont Garrison was the first to shoot down one of the enemy fighters for his 6th victory.[622] Captain Don S. Gentile and Lieutenant Glenn A. Herter got two more, which also took Gentile's score to six. Then four more FW 190s were bounced, and Captain Duane W. Beeson and Lieutenant Pierce W.

McKennon got another two to take their scores to 12 and 3 respectively.[623] The Group broke away for Debden at 1302.

All three divisions of the 8th Air Force had exacted a heavy toll on the German aircraft plants. The 1st Bomb Division caused heavy damage to the Messerschmitt plants at Augsburg, and the ball bearing plants at Stuttgart were also bombed. The 2nd Bomb Division bombed the Messerschmitt Bf 110 components plant at Furth, and the 3rd Bomb Division and 176 bombers of the 15th Air Force caused very considerable damage to the Bf 109 plants at Regensburg. The latter hit the aircraft plants an hour before the England-based force arrived over the city. Output at both Augsburg and Regensburg was severely reduced for four months following the raids, which attacked the Me 410 assembly plant at Augsburg.

Thereafter, cloudbanks over the Continent brought a premature end to "Big Week," and enabled higher command time to weigh up the results and implications of their actions over the past five days. The intensity of the battles of "Big Week" can be judged by total losses of 226 bombers. Although the 8th had flown 3300 bomber sorties and had dropped 6000 tons of bombs during "Big Week," the destruction was not as great as at first thought. *Luftwaffe Gruppen* were certainly deprived of many replacement aircraft, and fighter production was halved the following month, but it had cost 400 bombers and 4000 casualties to achieve. Unfortunately, the small size high explosive bombs destroyed only the factories, leaving machine tools, lathes, and jigs virtually untouched beneath the wreckage. It was only a matter of time before this equipment was recovered from the wrecked plants and put into full production again. However, Doolittle and his staff officers believed the 8th had dealt the German aircraft industry a really severe blow, though losses were such that the bomb groups did not fly another mission until 28 February, when 181 B-17s and B-24s attacked V-weapon sites in the Pas de Calais. Half of the bombers dispatched were forced to return without getting their bombs away because of heavy cloud. Seven aircraft were lost mostly to flak.

Missions against the German aircraft industry were resumed on 29 February when 215 B-17s bombed production plants at Brunswick again, while 38 Liberators bombed V-weapon targets in France. Two days later, on 2 March the 8th Air Force returned to Frankfurt, sending 481 B-17s and B-24s to bomb the marshaling yards in the city. Only 137 heavies were able to bomb their briefed target because of failure of pathfinder equipment, and 133 heavies bombed targets of opportunity in southwestern Germany, including Mannheim/Ludwigshafen, Limburg, and Dürnbach. Some 84 heavies bombed the airfield at Chartres, in France. Near Koblenz, the IIIrd *Gruppe* JG 26 claimed two B-17s in head on attacks against the leading bombers in the formation. One of the victors was *Hauptmann* Hermann Staiger, CO 12th *Staffel*, whose Fortress went down west of Limburg. *Leutnant* Karl "Charlie" Willius, CO 2nd *Staffel*, claimed a B-17 at Wiesbaden, and *Oberfähnrich* Heinz Kemethmüller of 9th *Staffel* was credited with a B-17 damaged. JG 26 also tussled with P-47 Thunderbolts of the 365th Fighter Group in the 9th Air Force, who shot down three FW 190A-6/7s in the 6th *Staffel*. Two of the German pilots, including *Leutnant* Friedrich Lange, the *Staffelkapitän*, were killed, and the third was WIA. This same day *Oberstleutnant* Egon Mayer, the JG 2 *Kommodore*, who was flying his 353rd sortie, was shot down at Montmedy by a Thunderbolt in the 365th Fighter Group and killed.[624] JG 26 took off again a little after 1330 hours to attack the returning bombers. Northeast of Abbeville *Oberfeldwebel* Wilhelm Mayer of the 7th *Staffel* JG 26 attacked *Ole Basser*, a B-17[625] in the 570th Bomb Squadron, 390th Bomb Group, and shot it down while taking hits in the cockpit. Five of 2nd Lieutenant Everett J. Ferguson's crew were killed. The other five baled out and one evaded, but the others were captured.

Doolittle and his staff officers now felt confident to strike at "Big-B"—Berlin, the biggest prize in the *Third Reich*. A raid by the 8th Air Force on Berlin had been scheduled on 23 November the previous year, but had been postponed because of bad weather. RAF Bomber Command had been bombing the capital nightly for some time, but Berliners had never before been subjected to the round-the-clock bombing that had devastated so many other German cities.

"The very thought of making a raid on Berlin was almost terrifying," recalls Robert J. Shoens, a pilot in the 100th Bomb Group. "Rumors began flying thick and fast several weeks before the day arrived, adding to the apprehension and anxiety. Each day we would walk into the briefing sessions wondering if the tape on the wall map would stretch to 'Big-B' that morning. A great sigh of relief could be heard from the crews when the briefing officer pulled back the curtain and the tape went somewhere else. But sooner or later it was sure to come and it did."

13

Bomb Bays over Big B

"During the trip to the target, the most impressive sight was our glimpse of Berlin. As we passed by, we all vocally pitied the poor devils who drew it as their target for the day. There was the usual cloud of flak to wade through and there's no rougher job. We saw a few B-24s go down as their turn came."

Lieutenant Harry H. Crosby, 100th Bomb Group

The momentous day when the Eighth at last set out for Berlin arrived on the morning of 3 March. At bases throughout eastern England, briefing officers pulled back the curtains to reveal red tapes reaching like groping fingers all the way to Berlin, in the heart of *Nazi* Germany. Whistles and groans greeted the news. "What a birthday treat," thought Cliff Hatcher, as he sat through the briefing at Bury St. Edmunds. Only the day before he had celebrated his 21st birthday. Hatcher was one of 31 crews readied at Bury St. Edmunds for the raid, which was aimed at hitting Erkner, Germendorf, Annahof, and Berlin. The B-17s began taking off in marginal weather conditions. As crews flew on over the North Sea conditions grew worse. Eventually, the mission was "scrubbed," but not before a tragic accident occurred. Hatcher says:

> "We were midway in the stream in the vicinity of Kiel and kept trying to climb above the fog and cloud. It was hard trying to stay in formation. Unfortunately, we did not get the recall signal until after the groups in front of us and they turned before we did. Suddenly, I looked up and saw what looked like hundreds of B-17s heading straight for us. Lieutenant Donald L. Ahlwardt's ship[626] collided with an approaching B-17 and I flew right through the middle of a black cloud. I could feel the heat from the explosion. We bounced all over the sky and I thought we had had it but, incredibly, we survived and began heading back. We were maddened by the wasteful and needless collision."[627]

The 94th Bomb Group disrupted into chaos after the recall, and aircraft flew home in twos and threes, dropping their bombs en route. Hatcher dropped his bombs over Heligoland:

> "Coming back we ran into horrendous weather again. Half way across the North Sea we saw a front ahead of us. We were at 30,000ft. The temperature was about 60 or 70° below outside the aircraft so we decided to go over the front. We thought maybe we could find a hole between the thunderheads. We climbed and climbed and we still couldn't see the tops. We thought we'd have to go under it. We got down to about 15ft off the water but ice built up and we got slower and slower. All our de-icer boots had been taken off the B-17 when we had entered combat because they slowed the aircraft down. It was thought that the chances of icing up were negligible but this was one time they were wrong. We even used some flap to keep her airborne because we were so close to stalling. The only de-icing equipment we had was for the propellers. If we hadn't got that we wouldn't have made it. Eventually, we broke clear and just made it back. It was hell after the mission to have to fly like that. When we got back to Bury we looked the aircraft over and it was covered in burn marks. It was a miracle. How lucky could we get?"[628]

There was another shock in store for the returning crews:

> "Next day, Saturday 4 March, I walked into the Briefing Room at Rougham as scared as hell," says Hatcher. "'Big-B' was splashed all over the target map and I thought, 'I won't make it.'"

However, bad weather forced the B-24s to abort early, leaving 502 Fortresses and 770 fighters to continue to the target, and 219 B-17s hit targets of opportunity, while 31 B-17s in the 95th and 100th Bomb Groups defied the elements to drop the first American bombs on the Big City. They either did not receive the call signal or chose to ignore it and continued to the capital alone. Robert J. Shoens, in the 351st Bomb Squadron, 100th Bomb Group formation, recalls:

> "I was part of 'Fireball Yellow' and we received the recall and brought our bombs home. It wasn't until we landed that we learned that 'Fireball Orange' (the second group of aircraft in the wing) had not received the call and had somehow made their way to Berlin."

Fortunately, some of the Mustang escorts were still with the wayward bombers and provided support in the target area. There is no doubt that their appearance prevented a debacle. Fourteen minutes from the capital, German fighters attacked "Fireball Orange." The 95th bore the brunt of the attacks and lost four aircraft. However, the 100th lost only one: *Seaton's Sad Sack*,[629] piloted by 1st Lieutenant Stanley M. Seaton, who had been Shoens' best man at his wedding in May 1943. A short time later Shoens received news that Seaton [and 8 of his crew] was a PoW. Those aircraft that did get through to the capital claimed to have dropped the first American bombs on Berlin. The formation, led by the 95th Bomb Group, went for a visual run, but the clouds closed in again, and at 1342 hours the bombs were released under the direction of the leading 482nd Bomb Group PFF aircraft flown by Lieutenant William Owens, by which time flak had eased off. The return journey was "nothing short of a nightmare," and mostly was flown through "solid layers of clouds," as the formation was forced to descend because of "diminishing oxygen supplies." On landing at Horham and Thorpe Abbotts the exhausted B-17 crews were given a rapturous welcome by their ground crews, and within minutes all of them were enveloped by the triumphant ground staff and toasted with "a general issue of double scotches." The 95th Bomb Group was awarded its third Presidential Unit Citation, and the 100th was similarly awarded later.

On Sunday, 5 March, crews were briefed again for Berlin, but the mission was "scrubbed" because of bad weather, and the Liberators attacked targets in France instead, while some B-17 Groups went up and practiced bombing after the weather improved over east Anglia. It was but a stay of execution for many, because on Monday, 6 March, 730 B-17s and B-24s and 801 P-38, P-47, and P-51 escort fighters were despatched to targets in the suburbs of Berlin. Crews were well aware that the defenses in and around "Big B" had now been fully alerted, and a rough reception could be expected. The Germans knew only too well that any target that was not bombed because of a recall could be expected to be hit again at the earliest opportunity. The column, which stretched for 60 miles, was led by five heavily escorted Combat Wings in the 1st Division, which was assigned the ball-bearing plant at Erkner, a suburb of Berlin. Next in line were the 3rd Division, led by Brigadier General Russell Wilson, who flew in an H_2X equipped B-17, which was assigned the Robert Bosch Electrical Equipment factory. The Liberators in the 2nd Division again brought up the rear.

The bombers crossed the English coastline and the gunners tested their .50 calibers. The Channel passed beneath, then the Dutch coast dropped under the wings and fell away. *Jafü 4* directed some fighters against a formation of B-26 Marauders en route to Poix, but decided not to send any fighters to the north. Instead, *Jafü* had part of II./JG 26 fly east just in case the heavies turned for Frankfurt or targets in southern Germany. The bombers maintained their course, and so all three *Gruppen* were told to wait on their bases until the direction of the bombers' return flight could be determined. The bombers, meanwhile, sailed over the Zuider Zee and were almost over the German border when the storm broke. Over Dummer Lake the 1st Division was attacked by fighters, which concentrated on the leading groups, and the 91st, 92nd, and 381st were given a thorough going-over. The 457th Bomb Group was met by head-on attacks. One 109 that did not pull out in time crashed into 2nd Lieutenant Roy E. Graves' B-17, and the combined wreckage fell on 2nd Lieutenant Eugene H. Whalen's Fortress.[630] All three fell to earth.

Next it was the turn of the 3rd Division groups to feel the weight of the enemy attacks.[631] The unprotected 13th Combat Wing[632] caught the full venom of the enemy fighter attacks. It was another black day for the 100th in particular, as Robert J. Shoens, flying *Our Gal' Sal'* as part of "Fireball Yellow," again in the 351st Bomb Squadron, which flew lead, well remembers:

> "The group was going in with 20 planes - one short. It was a spectacular day, so clear it seemed we could almost see Berlin from over England. Somewhere over eastern France we suddenly realized that we hadn't seen our fighter escort for about 20 minutes, which meant that a relay had not caught up with us. (The German fighters had engaged them somewhere behind us, knowing it would leave us without fighter escort.) Ahead of us, probably 10 miles away, there appeared to be a swarm of bees - actually German fighters. Guesses ran to as much as 200. They were coming right at us and in a few seconds were going through us. On that pass they shot down the entire high squadron (350th) of ten planes."

The action took place over Haseluenne, a small German town 12 miles northeast of Lingen, and in about 60 seconds six of the high squadron were set on fire and began trailing long sheets of flame from their engines. As the fighters attacked again all six peeled away. Other B-17s were in obvious trouble. The B-17[633] leading the High Squadron caught fire after a head-on attack from a fighter that opened fire, killing pilot Captain David L. Miner and co-pilot George Kinsella. The nose was also shot away, and the bombardier slipped or was thrown from the nose without a chute. The ball turret gunner was also killed. The rest of the crew baled out and were taken prisoner.

The bomb load on *Sly Fox*[634] was thought to have exploded, killing all ten of 2nd Lieutenant Zeb Kendall's crew. The B-17[635] flown by 2nd Lieutenant Sherwin L. Barton, whose crew had only joined the Bloody Hundredth two weeks earlier, was knocked out of formation and set on fire. All ten men jumped safely and were captured on the ground. *Ronnie R*,[636] piloted by 1st Lieutenant Dean Radtke and co-pilot Gordon Devault, had two engines knocked out, and a fire started in the bomb bay. Nine men baled out and survived to be taken prisoner. The ball turret gunner was killed by a burst of 20mm fire that so badly damaged the turret that the crew were unable to get him into the aircraft. The plane crashed near Twistrigen. Fighters hit *Terry and the Pirates*,[637] piloted by Lieutenant William Terry and co-pilot William Peterson, soon after turning northeast near Dummer Lake, and it nosed over immediately into a spin. After falling many thousands of feet the wings came off and the fuselage twirled the rest of the way down. The tail broke off and the control cables snapped back, trapping the gunners. The engineer lost a leg below the calf to a 20mm shell and was thrown out just before the Fortress hit the ground. The remains of the Fortress came down near Quakenbrück, where the bombs exploded as the crew were being picked up by their captors. The tail section, containing the body of one of the gunners, was found some distance away.

Barricks Bag,[638] flown by Lieutenant Samuel L. Barrick and Ira Munn, had two engines knocked out and another damaged, and rapidly lost altitude. Unable to catch up, the bombs were jettisoned and they headed for neutral Sweden, where after crossing the coast they landed on the grass at Bulltofta airfield, near Malmo, where the left leg collapsed when it touched the ground.[639] The right wing and two engines of *Lucky Lee*[640] in the lead squadron caught fire, and Lieutenant George W. Brannan ordered his crew to bale out. Thomas Leslie, co-pilot, and Clyde Dale, navigator, were killed. The survivors were taken prisoner.[641] Six men aboard *Spirit of 44*,[642] flown by Lieutenant Merril T. Rish, baled out when the B-17 was suddenly engulfed in flames. Seconds later, the fuselage broke in two near the radio room and the plane exploded, throwing the top turret gunner and one of the waist gunners clear. The navigator, who was also blown out of the gaping hole, recovered to pull his ripcord.[643]

The Pride Of The Century,[644] flown by Lieutenant Coy I. Montgomery, who was leading the low squadron, crashed at Colnrade. Montgomery's crew had taken the plane when their own ship, a new B-17, was out of commission from their last raid to Berlin, when they returned on three engines. Montgomery was killed. The rest of the crew, including five replacements, baled out and were captured. *Going Jessie*,[645] flown by 2nd Lieutenant Robert C. Koper, was enveloped by fire, and only three crew were able to bale out before the B-17 exploded and crashed at Jump, near Oldenburg. All ten Fortresses formed part of the Low Box of the 13th

Combat Wing, B Formation, which originally consisted of 20 B-17s, until four aborted. Captain Jack Swartout, Ops Officer of the 351st, who flew with Lieutenant Frank Lauro and his crew in *Nelson King*, led the Box.[646] They barely escaped with their lives after colliding with a FW 190 in the initial attack. With only a spar securing what was left of the rudder—and this kept swinging from side to side—the plane peeled out and turned for home. Edward Handorf and his crew, who were flying Deputy Group lead in *Kind A Ruff*,[647] took their position.

The bomb bay of *Half and Half*,[648] flown by 1st Lieutenant John Lautenschlager, ignited following a fighter attack, and other shells crippled the oxygen system and knocked the nose and ball turret out. The bombs were immediately jettisoned, and the crew prepared to bale out. Lautenschlager was the last to leave, and as he cleared the tail *Half and Half* flared up and exploded to crash at Haltern, near Visbeck. John Stryjeski, radio operator, who bravely attempted to extinguish the flames, was killed when his parachute failed to open. The B-17[649] piloted by Lieutenant Albert F. Amiero was attacked by fighters over Haseluenne, and only left waist gunner Owen Stockton baled out. The other nine crew were killed when the aircraft exploded and crashed near Quakenbrück. *The BigassBird II*[650] plunged out of formation with its tail on fire and other damage. Lieutenant William E. Murray, pilot, was decapitated by a 20mm shell. The tail gunner, who was in the radio room having his head dressed by the radio operator, were both killed in the crash. The rest of the crew baled out and were taken prisoner.

As the Bloody Hundredth approached the outskirts of Berlin, the fighters knocked *Buffalo Gal* out of formation and badly damaged the oxygen system. Celesta Harper, pilot, daringly evaded the enemy planes by going into an almost vertical dive to 5000ft at 270mph and headed back to England. Lieutenant Mark Cope and co-pilot Martin Tashjian brought their ship back with a damaged engine, and as the fighters came in again, he jettisoned the bombs and put the plane into a dive and hid in the clouds. One of the waist gunners was wounded in the face, and the tail gunner was hit in both legs. Safely back at Thorpe Abbotts the crew claimed seven enemy fighters.

At 1312 hours, 73 minutes after the first attack, the outlines of Berlin appeared. By this time the Wing, led by Major "Bucky" Elton, had reformed. Moments after "bombs away" "*Rubber Check*,"[651] piloted by Lieutenant Frank A. Granack, was rocked by a heavy flak explosion near their right wing, and the No.4 engine was put out of action. Granack and Lieutenant Bob Dunham, the co-pilot, struggled to regain position in the flight, but he found it impossible to catch the faster moving formation. He informed Elton that if his air speed was reduced by about 5mph then he might be able to get back into the protection of the Group. Elton said that would be impossible, but he wished him "Good Luck." Gradually "*Rubber Check*" fell further and further behind and below the formation until they were all alone. Lieutenant Murray Geisler, navigator, informed Granack that he would give him a bearing for Sweden any time that it became necessary to head in that direction, but "*Rubber Check*" was not alone for long. "Fighters at 3 o'clock" crackled over the intercom. Bf 109s and FW 190s were attacking from several different directions, and they raked the length of the plane with heavy gunfire and a fierce running battle ensued. All the gunners fought back with all the 50-caliber power they could muster. The No.2 engine was having problems, and No.3 was damaged and out of commission, while 3 and 4 were smoking and threatening to catch fire. The intercom was shot out, and it was impossible to get a rapid assessment of the extent of the damage and casualties. The radio operator and one of the waist gunners were killed, and the other waist gunner was wounded in the leg. About this time the enemy fighter attacks slackened off for the moment, but the demise of "*Rubber Check*" was imminent. The survivors baled out as Granack held the controls for as long as he could. Finally, he let go and ran down the passageway to the bomb bay where he made a running, head first dive into space as he baled out.

At 1339 hours and after a lull the *Luftwaffe* returned, but the P-38s intervened, although sporadic attacks continued until the formation reached the North Sea. The last of the Group's planes to go down was "*Kind A Ruff*," which having survived the fighter attacks bombed the target and was en route home. At about 1420 hours near Diepholz a Bf 109 came in at 1 o'clock low and sprayed the front of the B-17 with 20mm cannon fire, which set the wing tanks on fire. Only two men in Lieutenant Edward Handorf's crew survived and they were captured.

The 100th Bomb Group lost 15 B-17s in all.[652] In 30 minutes the enemy shot down 23 Fortresses in the 13th Wing, or damaged them so badly that they were forced to ditch or crash-land on the continent.

Robert J. Shoens concluded:

> "When an airplane went down you had to shut out the fact that it took men with it. On this raid it became most difficult because so many were lost. One loss in particular was an example of this. The crew from our barracks were flying off the right wing of our plane. Suddenly, during one of the fighter passes, their entire wing was on fire. In the next instant there was nothing there. The fighters made two more passes and when it was over *Our Gal' Sal'* was all alone. The last airplane from the group that I had seen flying was Captain Jack Swartout in the 351st Squadron lead. [*Nelson King*] was struggling along with about 6ft missing from his vertical stabilizer and was the only other airplane from the squadron who came back with us. We saw another group ahead of us, so we caught up with it. The planes had an 'A' in a square on the tail so they were from the 94th. We flew on to Berlin with them and dropped our bombs. The flak was heavy but over Berlin the sky was black. The target was on the southeast side of the city. For reasons we couldn't figure out, the group we were with chose to turn to the left and go over Berlin. Since we were not part of the group we decided to turn to the right and get out of the flak. When we did that a German battery of four guns started tracking. They fired about 40 rounds before we got out of range. None of them came close because of the evasive action we had taken. Higher up and ahead of us we saw another group so we climbed and caught up with it. It was also from our wing, having a 'J' in a square on its aircraft's tails (390th). We flew the rest of the way home with them without further incident. It was still a beautiful day and with a chance to relax we began to wonder what had happened to our group. It couldn't be that we were the only survivors of 'Fireball Yellow.'"

The 452nd Bomb Group formation of six B-17s flying as the high squadron also suffered loss, as Hank Gladys, the bombardier aboard *Flakstop*, flown by Lieutenant Charles F. Wagner, recalls:

> "Flying back from the target we were about half-way through Germany when our fighter escort had to leave us as we were behind schedule because of our second pass over the target. Immediately the Germans came up after us. Later I learned that there were 33 of them after us. *Flakstop* was hit during a ferocious fighter attack. The first attack came from the rear, killing our tail gunner, Sgt G. L. James. Then the attack shifted to the front where they knocked out our left engine and damaged our wing on the right side."

Allan R. Willis, the co-pilot, says:

"The German fighters came like the proverbial swarm of bees. Six 109s and FW 190s took the 452nd as their quarry and the fun really began. Virtually all passes were made from 10 to 12 o'clock high. Our intercom was *kaput* and I could make no attempt at fire control. A second pass raked the fuselage from nose to tail. The third did the crucial damage. It must have hit the starboard side oil, electrical and fuel lines because both starboard engines, numbers three and four, began to splutter. The tachs immediately indicated nearly total loss of rpms. I hit the feathering switches but nothing happened. The props simply windmilled. The wide variation in rpms started *Flakstop* vibrating and we fell out of formation. Both Charlie Wagner and myself fought the vibrating control columns to try and maintain straight and level flight. There was no panic yet. We could see the Zuider Zee on the horizon. We didn't want to bale out over Germany because of the stories we had heard about the German treatment of downed fliers.

"I saw one of our gas caps fly off. The only explanation I could think of was that the intense vibration had loosened them. The airstream over the starboard wing must have set up a siphoning action and the gasoline and the hot oil might have come together. What I did know was that the entire starboard wing was, in a flash, a sheet of orange flame! In that single moment *Flakstop* gave up her role as a mighty Flying Fortress and became a flying coffin. It didn't take an aeronautical engineer to inform us that it was much safer outside than in. As I hit the bale-out bell (thank God that was working!) I glanced at the altimeter; 1400ft over Holland!"

Clyde J. Martin, the navigator, was first out of the front escape hatch:

"After I opened my 'chute a German fighter was still flying around us. I watched to see if his guns would fire on me but they did not. I landed in a pasture at about 0330 hours near the little Dutch town of Staphorst. I hid my 'chute and started walking."

Allan R. Willis continues:

"By the time I got down to the forward escape hatch, the engineer and the navigator had already jumped. Hank Gladys was about to go. He took one look at me, said, 'I've forgotten my cigarettes.' and went back into the nose. I swung out of the hatch (the wrong way!), got into the slipstream and nearly got cut in half by the bomb bay doors. After some frantic fiddling with a pilot 'chute that did not pop out, I finally felt the violent snap that tells you the 'chute has opened. When I hit the ground, Hank Gladys was there waiting for me!"

Gladys says:

"During all this, Lieutenant Wagner was trying to set the automatic pilot as he didn't know what the situation was in the other part of the plane. Right after I'd baled out, *Flakstop* went into a spin and crashed within my sight. Of the four remaining crewmembers in the back, three were killed and Sgt Lloyd Freeman, our ball turret gunner, was seriously wounded. He landed near Sgt Donald Potter, the flight engineer, who was advised by Dutch Underground workers to leave him, as the Germans were very near and searching for us. Porter and Martin were taken into the Dutch Underground and in September 1944 were liberated by the British Army. I never learned the fate of Sgt Freeman. The Dutch Underground said that one of our 'chutists was strafed and killed by one of the attacking FW 190s while floating down. Two other crewmembers' 'chutes failed to open after they baled out."[653]

After the heavies had dropped their bomb loads on the center of Berlin at about 1345 they reassembled and returned on the reciprocal of their outbound route. At 1330 hours *Jafü* 4 sent off all of JG 26's FW 190s from Florennes, Wevelgem, and Biblis, near Worms. Two *Gruppen* reached the strung-out bomber stream near Osnabrück at 1430 hours. The bombers were under the protection of the P-47s of the 356th Fighter Group, but the few P-38s now headed home after providing target escort. The Focke Wulf pilots had the advantage during their subsequent attacks, because the 2nd and 3rd Bomb Divisions were flying side-by-side, and this enabled the FW 190s to avoid the P-47s by flying in between the combat boxes. JG 26 claimed two 356th Fighter Group Thunderbolts and three bombers before starting on the stragglers. *Leutnant* Karl "Charlie" Willius, 2./JG 26 CO, destroyed a B-17 north of Koblenz. *Oberfeldwebel* Alfred Heckmann destroyed one of the Thunderbolts, and *Hauptmann* Karl Borris, CO of I./JG26, claimed a second, but this P-47, though seriously damaged, reached England safely. *Oberleutnant* Wolfgang Neu's victim was *Shack Rabbit*[654] in the 453rd Bomb Group, which he despatched south of Quakenbrück. Northwest of Quakenbrück, *Oberfeldwebel* Hans Heitmann of the 4th *Staffel* shot down *Lil' Opportunity* in the 410th Bomb Squadron, 94th Bomb Group, before he was shot down almost immediately after by a 356th Fighter Group Thunderbolt. Heitmann baled out with a badly injured right arm.[655] JG 26 finished their attacks by picking off two stragglers that had dropped from their formations after being damaged by the flak over "Big B." *Leutnant* Georg Kiefner destroyed a 458th Bomb Group B-24 at Almelo.[656] Near Julich *Oberleutnant* Walter Matoni shot down *Half Breed* in the 381st Bomb Group flown by 2nd Lieutenant Milton A. Fastrup.[657]

The first American air raid on Berlin had certainly flushed out the *Luftwaffe*, just as Doolittle had hoped it would. The Fortress gunners and the fighter pilots claimed over 170 German fighters destroyed,[658] but the Americans had suffered record losses. The 1st Division had lost 18 B-17s, the 2nd 16 B-24s,[659] and the 3rd 35 B-17s. Eleven fighters were also lost, while 102 bombers were seriously damaged.[660] The 69 bombers that failed to return to England represented the greatest loss so far at a loss rate of 10%. And 347 bombers were damaged, including 121 in the 3rd Division. Six were salvaged after landing. As for the results of the raid, the majority of the bombs fell on a 5-mile stretch of the suburbs, due mainly to overcast, creating huge fires and destroying the gas, power, and telephone services. Oslo Radio, which was German controlled, regarded it as "a catastrophe...." Even the Berlin News Agencies admitted that "several hundred bombers had reached the city, despite intensive flak and unceasing fighter attacks." Air Chief Marshal of the RAF Arthur Harris sent a message to his opposite number, Carl Spaatz, at High Wycombe:

"Heartiest congratulations on first US bombing of Berlin. It is more than a year since they were attacked in daylight, but now they have no safety there by day or night. All Germany learns the same lesson."

At Thorpe Abbotts, when it became clear that the Hundredth had suffered the highest loss of any group for the rest of the day, the crews "remained quiet and subdued." Few of the men wanted to talk, and if they did, it was in a low tone, or in a whisper. Some wandered off, wanting to be on their own, or rested on their beds, while others drank singly, or silently in small groups. Some, in their grief at losing their friends, openly cursed the desk-bound Generals for sending them to Berlin, when it was obvious the Germans knew they were coming. Even Colonel John Bennett, who within the last 24 hours had taken over as "Temporary Group CO,"[661] confessed, "We were a sad group of men that evening... I'm afraid I didn't appear too confident before my men...." On Tuesday the 7th the weather was bad, so there was no mission. Colonel Bennett said:

> "Thank God we had a day off to lick our wounds. I talked to the Division headquarters about some replacement crews, which were to arrive at the end of the week. We were alerted on Tuesday evening and at 10 o'clock I knew that the target was again Berlin. It's hard to describe the feeling that came over the few of us who knew the boys were going back over the same route which had cost us 50% of our forces on Monday."

On 8 March, when 623 bombers in ten combat wings were made ready for the third raid on "Big-B" that week, the 100th could only scrape together 15 Forts, and Colonel John Bennett led them.[662] The 3rd Division would lead the 8th to the VKF ball-hearing plant at Erkner, in the suburbs east of Berlin, escorted by 891 fighters, with the 1st Division flying in the middle and the 2nd again bringing up the rear. Lieutenant Franklin L. Betz, a navigator in the 379th Bomb Group at Kimbolton and part of the 1st Division force, was flying his first mission this day:

> "Promptly at 0915 hours the lead plane took off. Taxiing behind a line of Fortresses that one after the other soared into the gray sky, the pilot, Captain Douglas H. Buskey, swung our plane onto the runway as the B-17 before us started on its way into the 'wild blue yonder.' The four 1200 hp Wright Cyclone engines roared and our heavy bomb-laden plane shuddered as Buskey pushed the throttles forward. Bobbing gently, it rolled down the runway with increasing speed, the ride becoming smooth as the massive bulk lifted gracefully above the Huntingdonshire farmland.
>
> "Climbing steadily, one by one each of the 18 planes slipped into its designated place of the group formation; six in the lead squadron and six each in the high and low squadrons. Wide-eyed, my heart racing from excitement (or was it apprehension from the realization that I'd soon be departing the friendly shores of Britain), I was awed at the magnificent sight of the vast air armada stretching for miles in precise formations against the frosty blue sky. The palms of my hands were moist when we headed over the English Channel and I noted in my log, 'altitude, 20,000ft, time, 1106, ground speed, 170 knots.'
>
> "Scattered flak greeted us at the Dutch coast a few miles north of Ijmuiden. Happily though, the fighter planes we saw were identified as our 'little friends', P-51 Mustangs. On we droned, due east and the Dummer Lake in western Germany loomed ahead. Suddenly, black splotches darkened the sky around us a few miles north of the lake. Flak! The concussion from exploding shells rocked the plane. Fragments of flying steel tore through its aluminium skin. The oil line of No.1 engine was cut and, gushing like a geyser, the oil covered the cowling and adjoining wing surface, quickly congealing on the metal in the -30° temperature. Promptly, Buskey feathered No.1 engine as he called over the intercom, 'No.2 engine's only pulling half power.' We were flying on two and a half engines! Fortunately, none of the crew was hit. We learned upon our return to Kimbolton that flak had damaged the vital induction pipe of the turbo-supercharger, reducing the engine's thrust.
>
> "'Pilot to navigator, what's the estimated flying time to the target?'
>
> "Consulting my map and log I applied pertinent data to my E-6B computer and made a calculation.[663] 'Navigator to pilot,' I replied, 'It's approximately two hours flying time at our present ground speed'.
>
> "The plane rocked gently. 'Bandits at 2 o'clock high', the engineer called. Warily, I watched the two 109s, as yet out of gunfire range, while I manned the right nose gun. Flying high and ahead of us, suddenly they peeled off into a screaming dive, the front edge of their wings from which the tips of machine-gun barrels protruded, lighting up like firecrackers when they fired. In a flash they were way below us and out of range. Lucky! All the Fortresses in the formation continued droning determinedly toward Berlin. If any of them had been hit by the 109 gunfire, none had gotten it fatally this time.
>
> "'Pilot to crew. Despite the flak damage to two engines, the plane's flying well. We'll continue to the target in formation instead of dropping out and trying to get back to England alone. It could be tough going.'
>
> "Breathing heavily from the excitement of my first major encounter with flak and fighters, I slid onto the seat by the navigator's worktable to make entries in the log. Peering through the window over the worktable I saw twin-engined P-38s engaging enemy fighters, keeping them away from the bomber formations. A reassuring sight. High above the peaceful-looking German countryside we flew, in tight formation. Our course to the IP took us far enough south of Berlin to avoid the formidable anti-aircraft defenses. A lump rose in my throat when we turned onto the IP for the 13-mile run to the target. Five miles above the ball-bearing factory, the Germans had the sky enveloped in a murderous box barrage of flak and the air was filled with black puffs of exploding shells and unseen fragments of deadly steel.
>
> "The formation flew in a straight and unwavering line to the target. There was no turning back, no evasive action. The lead bombardiers were busily aiming their Norden bombsights on the target and the lethal loads of bombs would drop automatically from the bomb bays when the cross hairs in the exquisite bombsight centered on the buildings far below. At that moment, bombardiers in other planes of the group would release their bombs by flipping a toggle switch and the destructive explosives would hurtle toward the doomed factory. Ahead of us, planes in precise group formation entered the pall of smoke from bursting flak. Suddenly, a brilliant ball of orange lit up the sky. Hit by flak, a bomber exploded! No 'chutes were seen. Off to the right, one of the splendid aircraft, out of control, spun lazily to its destruction. It reminded me of a seedpod drifting from a tree. One, two, three 'chutes emerged from the plane, as it disappeared into a cottony cloud. Sweat from my brow trickled into my eyes.
>
> "The plane rocked from the concussion of bursting shells as we entered the envelope of fire. 'Bomb bay doors open,' the engineer called. 'Bombs Away!' cried the bombardier. The plane lifted perceptibly when the tons of bombs dropped from her belly. Ahead of us, bombers emerging from the flak barrage in ragged formation were attempting to close up for maximum protection against the Luftwaffe fighters circling above us. As we pulled away from the target area, the plane perforated by flak but the fliers unscathed, Buskey said, 'We've got to get the bomb bay doors closed quickly.

There's too much drag and with two and a half engines, I may not be able to keep up the formation.'

"Closing the massive bomb bay doors was no easy job. The engineer had to crank them shut since the electrical system, which powered the motor that normally closed them, was out. In a cramped space 25,000ft above Germany it was an interminable task. The temperature was way below freezing. He was wearing a weighty fleece-lined flight suit, gloves, flak vest and helmet, an oxygen mask with the hose dangling like an elephant's trunk and hooked into the life support system. There were wires from his throat mike and earphones to contend with plus a parachute strapped on his back.

"'Pilot to crew. Someone help the engineer close the doors.'

"'Yes Sir', the right waist gunner volunteered. This meant he had to disconnect from the plane's oxygen system and hook on to a walk-around bottle that provided about eight minutes of the life-giving element, a routine any time a crewman left his position to go elsewhere in the plane. The walk-around bottle was an aluminium cylinder six or eight inches in diameter and about 30 inches long. Really cumbersome. To get to the engineer and help him, in his bulky flight gear, the waist gunner had to shuffle through the radio operator's compartment, then into the bomb bay, balancing precariously on a narrow catwalk, squeeze between V-shaped bomb tacks, the bomb bay doors below him only partly closed, until he reached the engineer's station behind the cockpit.

"Buskey continued to do a magnificent job of flying the disabled aircraft and managed somehow to stay in formation. The engineer, Sgt George Thomas, was slowly and laboriously cranking the bomb bay doors closed. Those of us on the guns were warily watching the enemy fighters in the distance, who fortunately, didn't attack. Sergeant George Thomas said, 'Engineer to pilot. I see the waist gunner on the catwalk. He's stuck between the bomb racks. He can't move."

Sergeant Louis J. Kyler, the radio operator, closest to the helpless waist gunner, attempted to extricate him, but his oxygen bottle fell through the partly opened doors and he had to go back to his position and hook into the plane's oxygen system. Private Willis Volkeming, the left waist gunner, on his twelfth mission—the only experienced combat crewman aboard—came forward and tried unsuccessfully to rescue his buddy, who had fainted from lack of oxygen. Somehow he had freed himself, but unfortunately he had toppled off the catwalk and dropped part of the way through the bomb bay doors that were nearly closed.

The radio operator came back again and tried once more to save his pal but to no avail. He had to go back to his position for much needed oxygen:

> "Radio operator to pilot. We can't get the waist gunner out of the bomb bay. He's unconscious. You'll have to hit the deck if he's to live."
>
> "'Pilot to crew" Buskey called, his voice faltering. "'If I leave the formation and try to go it alone at 10,000ft or lower, where we don't need oxygen, we may not make it back to England. German fighters will jump us. It means losing one with the hope that the rest of us will get back."
>
> "The waning winter sun of late afternoon shone warmly through the transparent nose of the battle-scarred B-17 as we approached our airbase. The red flare fired from the plane by the engineer alerted the ground personnel that we had a casualty aboard and the tower gave the pilot priority to land."
>
> The plane dropped smoothly to the concrete runway, and the tires screeching on touchdown sounded like a whining protest against the terrible ordeal the plane and its crew had endured. Buskey taxied the splendid Fortress to its dispersal area. The medics removed the dead body of the right waist gunner and took him away.
>
> "I dropped to the ground from the plane's nose hatch, somber and weary after more than eight hours in the plane. I realized the hardening of a naive airman to combat in the crucible of war had begun."

The 352nd Fighter Group was one of the fighter groups that provided withdrawal support that afternoon for the bombers returning from "Big B." Cloud covered England as the Bluenosers took off from Bodney at 1345 hours, but before the mixed formation of seven P-51s and 16 Thunderbolts could clear the overcast, six of the P-47s in the 486th Squadron were involved in mid-air collisions.[664] The rest of the Group continued to the RP near Weitzen without seeing any enemy fighters.[665] By the time the 352nd arrived for withdrawal support the fighting had subsided, but near Dummer Lake Captain Edward J. "Pappy" Gignac, leading Purple Flight of the 486th Squadron in *Little Rebel*,[666] saw a straggling B-17 under attack by a Bf 109.[667] Gignac immediately called a bounce and started down. The 109 got several hits on the B-17 before Pappy could reach it. As he closed, he broke off his attack with a violent aileron roll and pulled up into a vertical climb. Gignac reefed it in violently and took a short burst, but his closing speed was so high that he could not follow him up. Even though his burst was short and at great deflection Pappy Gignac claimed destruction of the 109 because Lieutenant Ed Heller, flying Green 2, saw the pilot bale out just after he fired at him, and saw the aircraft hit the ground and explode. Gignac's victory was the first of many the 352nd Fighter Group would score in P-51 Mustangs.

About ten minutes later over Meppen, as the 487th was being relieved of escort duty by another unit, three Bf 109G-6s of JG 26 broke out of the sun.[668] Captain Virgil Kersh "Virg" Meroney, who was leading Blue Flight in *Sweet Louise*,[669] called out a warning to the Squadron, and then led his Flight in pursuit. Meroney, who had six outright victories and two half shares, was a natural pilot, an outstanding leader, and extremely aggressive in combat. When an enemy was in sight, he threw caution to the winds and went after him. He had all the qualities of a born hunter, with keen eyesight and quick reflexes, and he was entirely familiar with his equipment and its capabilities. Years of experience as a hunter and skeet shooter in Arkansas also helped. Meroney picked out the leader of the enemy formation. Two other Mustang pilots got on the tail of his wingman, *Unteroffizier* Emil Kempen of 9./JG26, who was shot down and killed at the Steinhuder Lake west of Hanover.[670] The leader tried to go to the aid of his wingman, but he was hit and damaged by Meroney with a burst of fire at high deflection. The German broke away, and Meroney followed his quarry down to treetop level and overtook him. As he pulled up on the Messerschmitt's right wing the pilot jettisoned his canopy. Meroney was sitting right on his wing and got a good look at him. Though he did not know it at the time, his victim was Major Klaus Mietusch, who was flying a Bf 109G-6.[671] Mietusch's parachute opened immediately and he landed safely, but his injuries were severe enough to keep him in hospital for a short spell.[672]

539 heavies got their bombs away over the German capital, which once again was heavily defended. The leading 3rd Bomb Division had encountered the fiercest fighter opposition on the raid, losing 23 Fortresses.[673] Worst hit group in the 3rd Division during the series of Berlin missions had been the 100th Bomb Group.[674] The 1st Bomb Division lost

five B-17s to fighter attacks and flak. Nine B-24s and 18 fighters were lost.

Despite the continued high losses, on the 9th 361 B-17s were despatched to bomb "Big B" again, but 10/10th's cloud prevented visual bombing, while 165 Liberators visited Hanover, Brunswick, and Nienburg. Weather conditions kept the *Luftwaffe* on the ground, and for once the enemy fighters were noticeable by their absence. The 800 escort fighters returned without claiming any enemy fighters, and the B-17 groups lost six of their number over Berlin, while the B-24 groups lost two, all to flak. Cliff Hatcher's crew in the 94th Bomb Group was relieved at the lack of opposition because it was their 25th and final mission. The crew of the *Grand Old Lady* had not been to "Big-B" before, having been forced to return early on 6 March. The 94th lost no aircraft, and Hatcher declared that he was "Happy as hell" to have completed his tour. He had made it, with the help of a little luck. He had missed the battles of "Big Week" and had survived the Berlin gauntlets, but he concluded, "I felt a nervous wreck after my last four missions."[675]

"Lady Luck" had also helped bring Bill Rose in the 92nd through 24 combat missions. On 8 March he had been flying *Black Magic* when he was forced to abort after all four superchargers failed. He jettisoned his bombs and returned to Podington, hugging the sea all the way. Luckily P-38s were in the vicinity and chased off any fighters in the area, then some P-51s escorted them back across the Channel. When the rest of the group returned Rose was in the officers' bar, and they told him he had been reported going down over Germany. But now the end was in sight.[676]

Smaller scale raids on targets in France and Germany followed the early March Berlin strikes. The 8th was stood down on 10 March, but next day PFF techniques were used by 121 B-17s to bomb Münster, and by 34 Liberators to attack a *Noball* site at Wizernes. V-1 targets were again bombed on 12-13 March. On the 15th 334 bombers were despatched to aircraft component factories at Brunswick. Some 157 of the attacking force were Liberators, 145 of which successfully bombed their targets. At Lille and Florennes, the 1st and 2nd *Gruppen* JG 26 were ordered to take off at 1100 hours and fly to Rheine to wait for the American bombers returning from Brunswick. Two FW 190A-6s collided on take off, and once airborne, the 7th *Staffel* was bounced by Spitfires of 401 Canadian Squadron, which were escorting some B-26 Marauders. *Leutnant* Wilhelm Hofmann, CO 8./JG 26, was credited with the destruction of a B-24 northwest of Gevelsburg.[677] In some fierce engagements the 56th Fighter Group claimed 24 for one. 1st Lieutenant Robert S. Johnson downed three to take his score to 22 and pass Captain Bud Mahurin who was on 19.

On 16 March 740 B-17s and B-24s went to factory and airfield targets in Germany, and 679 of the bombers bombed Augsburg, Ulm, Gessertshausen, and Friedrichshafen. Gunners claimed 68 enemy fighters. The *Luftwaffe* was up in force and 23 bombers were shot down. III/JG 2 and all three *Gruppen* JG 26 converged on the B-17s at Nancy-St. Dizier, where the 56th Fighter Group en route to support Fortresses on their way to Friedrichshafen also came on the scene. The Thunderbolt pilots claimed eleven victories, including three FW 190A-6s and a Bf 109G-6 of JG 26. All four pilots were killed. Gabby Gabreski was credited with two victories, as was Fred Christensen, who had joined the 62nd Squadron as a replacement in the late summer of 1943. Zemke's Wolfpack returned home with an 8 to 1 ratio of aerial victories to losses, by far the best in VIIIth Fighter Command.

Southwest of St. Dizier-Worms, *Hauptmann* Hermann Staiger, CO 12th *Staffel* JG 26, spotted a 445th Bomb Group Liberator—*Ballsafire*,[678] piloted by Lieutenant Richard A. Raroha, who had aborted the mission with mechanical malfunctions—and he shot it down.[679] The German fighters broke off to land and refuel at Chaumont, Laon, Reims, and Metz before they took off again under an hour and a half later in search of the withdrawing bombers. III/JG 26 found the unescorted B-24s in the 96th Wing over St. Dizier, and they attacked with all guns blazing. *Leutnant* Peter Reischer, CO 11th *Staffel*, shot a 458th Bomb Group Liberator out of formation at Vitry to claim a *Herausschuss*. *Unteroffizier* Heinz Gehrke of the 11th *Staffel*, who was flying a Bf 109G-6 on his first combat sortie, picked out a crippled 458th Bomb Group B-24 near Reims. It was *Downwind-Leg* in the 755th Bomb Squadron, flown by 2nd Lieutenant Neil A. J. Peters. Gehrke attacked *Downwind-Leg* three times before it finally went down. The Liberator finally crashed into the Channel with the loss of seven crew, and one of the survivors died later after ASR picked them up. Gehrke, meanwhile, was all alone, and he tried to join some fighters in the distance, but they turned out to be Thunderbolts of the 356th Fighter Group. The P-47s broke, and Gehrke made the fatal mistake of trying to out-dive the pursuing P-47s, and his Messerschmitt was ripped to shreds. He baled out, and was fortunate to suffer nothing worse than a strained back. His fellow pilots, meanwhile, had headed back to land at St. Dizier, but a flight of P-47s in the 84th Fighter Squadron, 78th Fighter Group, led by 1st Lieutenant Quince L. Brown, spotted the enemy fighters in the landing pattern. They were easy prey.

Brown led his flight down to the deck. Chopping throttle and skidding to slow down, he got behind a Bf 109 and at 50 yards he fired, scoring hits. The 109 flamed and crashed to the left of the runway. Brown then saw a parked Ju 88 ahead of him and torched it with a short burst. Climbing to 7000ft, Brown encountered two FW 190s coming at him from 9 o'clock. *Leutnant* Klaus Kunze of 1st *Staffel* piloted one of them. As Brown got into a left-hand Lufbery Circle with the two FW 190s, the wingman deserted his leader, who kept trying to outclimb and outturn the P-47, but Brown used water-injection and he caught up with Kunze, who dived through the clouds followed by the Thunderbolt. Keeping Kunze in his sights and firing at 350 yards, Brown watched the FW 190 roll on its back smoking and crash into a small creek. The German pilot was killed. With his wingman, Brown again climbed through the clouds and discovered two Bf 109s trying to tag them from behind. All the Messerschmitts went into a Lufbery turning battle, and again the German wingman split from his leader. The leader then tried to outrun the P-47s on top of the clouds, but the Thunderbolts stayed with him without resorting to water-injection. Brown cut him off from a hole in the clouds and scored hits. The leader was last seen going vertical into the clouds with heavy smoke streaming from his engine and wing roots. All three Bf 109s were shot down and their pilots injured.[680]

A mission to Frankfurt on 17 March was abandoned, but the heavies were out again on 18 March, when 738 B-17s and B-24s were despatched to an aircraft plant and airfield targets at Oberpfaffenhofen, Lechfeld, Landsberg, Memmingen, and Munich in southwest Germany, and the Dornier works at Friedrichshafen. Starting at 1000 hours, 28 Liberators began taking off from Wendling. Four returned early with mechanical problems, leaving the remaining aircraft to continue over France. 2nd Lieutenant Gerald M. Dalton's crew in *Amblin' Oakie*[681]—a Gotha veteran—got caught in prop wash and collided with *Late Date II*,[682] flown by 2nd Lieutenant Ellsworth F. Anderson, slicing off the tail and its turret. Both aircraft collided again as they went down and exploded in sheets of flame before crashing. As the bombers neared Friedrichshafen, the leading 44th Bomb Group at the head of the 14th Wing made an unscheduled 360° turn. The leading elements in the 392nd bombed the target, but the second block, disconcerted by the maneuvers ahead, chose to attack the rail yards at Stockach instead. The Liberators became strung out, and heavy flak dispersed the formation to such an extent that many B-24s flew over Swiss territory on the opposite side of Lake Constance and drew fire from the Swiss guns. The Liberators were running nine minutes late for their rendezvous with P-38 fighter escorts, which was missed, and the 14th

Wing was left to fend for itself against an estimated 75 single-engined enemy fighters. They attacked in line abreast, five and six at a time, and harried the Liberators for over 100 miles. Captain Myron Keilman in the 392nd formation recalls:

> "The lead ship had an engine shot out on the bomb run; then persistent fighter attacks worked the group over all the way to Strasbourg. A 20mm shell blinded the lead navigator."

Even when P-38s came to the rescue, the German pilots continued to press home their attacks. The 392nd was decimated, losing 15 Liberators, including *Old Glory*[683] in the 579th Bomb Squadron, flown by 1st Lieutenant Dallas O. Books, which was damaged by flak at the target. S/Sgt Chester C. Strickler, tail gunner, recalls:

> "The left waist, gunner, Norm Willig was laying on the floor and Robert Hampton in the ball, was not moving. Fire was streaming past the waist window. The right outboard engine was feathered. Another fire was between Daniel Jones in the nose turret and me in the tail turret. He was screaming, 'Help me Pappy, get me out Pappy.' Things were happening so fast, I was only reacting to the flames, when enemy fighters came in from all directions putting round after round into our ship. I screamed over the intercom to Lieutenant Dallas Books, 'Bank left and head for Switzerland!' His response, 'hang on, we'll be OK.' Again, the fighters came through what was left of the formation. The oxygen system failed and I became light headed. Our ship was streaming flames and slowing down, not able to keep up now, as more rounds came smashing through the ship. On the intercom I heard the co pilot, Captain John Slowik screaming and cursing the German fighters as more rounds came through *Old Glory*. The ship started to pitch and dive, then the oxygen tank next to my head exploded, blowing me out the waist window. I awoke to find myself' falling and instinctively pulled the ripcord. Pieces of the plane were falling around me, but I didn't see my ship, or my crew, or my friends, ever again."[684]

The 44th lost eight B-24s.[685] Colonel Joseph Miller, CO of the 453rd Bomb Group, was leading the 2nd Combat Wing on only his fourth mission. He was in the lead ship with Captain Joseph O'Reilly, the newly appointed Group Navigator, and Captain Stock, a pilot in the 733rd Squadron. Jim Kotapish, the co-pilot of *Reluctant Dragon*, flying below Stock's B-24, recalls:

> "Our astute group navigator had led the group over the harbor and everyone was waiting for us. The first flak burst hit the bomb bay of the lead ship and it immediately burst into flames. All I could think of was, "Please God, don't blow up right now or we'll get the whole 'plane in our nose. It didn't. It banked right in a low spiral and several men baled out of the plane, which was streaming flames from the bottom and the waist windows. The second burst hit our left wing. While I heeled over to follow the deputy leader out to sea, Ray Sears, pilot, was busying himself with No.2 engine, which had taken the brunt of the burst. I followed the flight of the lead 'plane as long as I could, but it fell behind."[686]

Next day the bombers carried out "milk runs" to V-1 sites in northern France, and 172 heavies unloaded their bombs over the *Noball* sites. On Monday, 20 March, bad weather and malfunction of blind-bombing equipment caused nearly 300 heavies to abandon the mission, and only 51 B-17s bombed industry and transportation targets at Frankfurt/Main, while 99 heavies attacked targets of opportunity. It was, however, a memorable day for the crew of *Smoky Liz* in the 731st Bomb Squadron in the 452nd Bomb Group at Deopham Green, who were flying their first mission, as Ralph Reese, the left waist gunner, recalls:

> "Target for today was a propeller factory at Frankfurt. We were awakened at 0130. Breakfast was at 0230 and briefing began at 0330. Takeoff was scheduled for 0715. Our bomb load was 39 demolition bombs. At 1155 hours we dropped 29 bombs. The nine remaining bombs were dropped in the English Channel as they failed to release over the target. Flak was very heavy over the target and we encountered flak over the French coast. The group became lost on the way out from the target and we headed for the French coast to follow back to England, as Norman Wright our navigator didn't have a map of the territory we were now over. We were being shot at all along the French coast and as we neared land we were running low on gas, Fred Whitlinger our pilot gave the signal to prepare for ditching and to lighten the ship. We started throwing out ammunition, guns and any equipment we could lay our hands on. We even threw out our parachute harnesses and even my pair of GI shoes, as we were a little excited. We spotted land and an English fighter base was near by so we made for it. It was a very small space to have to set a B-17 down in, but our pilot did it. As soon as the plane stopped rolling we jumped out and kissed the ground, as we never expected to see land that day. Our engineer checked the gas supply and found the tanks very dry. We had landed on the very most Southern tip of England and Bolt Head was the name of the Spitfire fighter base. We were housed at a nearby naval base. We remained there for two days and received excellent care. Finally, another ship from our Squadron came after us and we left *Smokey Liz* behind. It was later repaired and returned to base, where we continued to fly her. For being Mission No.1 it was a very exciting way to start our missions."

Marvin J. Byer, Ed Hartman's navigator in the 730th Squadron, adds:

> "We were flying deputy lead. At sometime during the bomb run, a bomb dropped through the nose of Jim Reynolds plane, also in the 730th, killing the bombardier. After we left the target, the lead navigator did not catch the drastic wind shift. Instead of going home, I knew we were heading southwest of Paris. We called the lead ship and Hartman relayed the information I was using. The wind had a drastic shift from our forecast and we were far off course. The Lead Command Pilot asked if we wanted to take the lead. I didn't want to take it away from the lead navigator. If he had the correct coordinates, he could get us home. We gave our coordinates in the open. After all, the Germans knew where we were; we didn't. Our route would have taken us to Bordeaux if we didn't change course and our group would never get home. The lead ship still did not change course. We called the Lead Command Pilot and he asked us to reconsider and take the lead. I am assuming his navigator didn't believe he could be 250 miles off course, particularly when no one else complained that we were off course. We took the lead and my options were to cut north across the Brest Peninsula or go west out over the water and then turn north to England. Hartman and I supposed our command pilot; decided we should do the latter. When we took the lead, Reynolds pulled underneath us into the #4 position and told Hartman he had confidence in us and let's get home. When we were abreast of Brest,

I used my drawing compass to find the closest beach in England. We made it to a RAF base in southern England. Reynolds landed at a different location."

On 21 March 56 B-24s bombed a V-weapon site at Watten, and about 650 B-17s and B-24s bombed the Berlin area. Twelve bombers were lost. Next day the heavies again sought the rich industrial targets of "Big B." Almost 800 B-17s and B-24s, including the 466th Bomb Group, which made its bombing debut, were dispatched, led by H_2X-equipped bombers flying their last mission under the control of the 482nd Bomb Group.[687] The 466th Bomb Group lost two B-24s in a mid-air collision.[688] For T/Sgt Donald V. Chase, a B-24 radio operator gunner in the 44th Bomb Group who had flown the Ploesti low level mission on 1 August 1943,[689] 22 March was his 20th mission. He recalls:

> "Six of our squadron aircraft participated in what was a mammoth raid, on Basdorf near Berlin but weather conditions forced the PFF system to be used, so Berlin was hit instead, with unobserved results. Take-off was at 0815 hours. It was a long day. Up hours before dawn; breakfast; briefing; pre-flight; 8½ hours in flight dodging our own aircraft on climb-out through the clouds (and on return, too); sucking in your breath as shards of 88s and 110s pierced our ship's thin, olive-drab skin; checking the configuration of fighters to determine if they were bandits or 'Little Friends'; hoping that the oil pressure of No.4 engine didn't drop any lower and possibly force your ship to be a straggler for E/A to prey on - all that kept the adrenaline surging. The flak over the city was intense and accurate of predictor-control fire and barrage fire type. Many of the group's aircraft received flak damage. Fighter support was excellent and no e/a were sighted. It was the duty of the radio operator to leave his regular position behind the co-pilot's seat, go to the belly of the B-24, straddle the narrow catwalk of the bomb bay and activate a push type lever which prevented the bomb doors from creeping, once the doors were opened preparatory to the bomb run. Secondly, he watched the bombs fall an, to the best of his visual acuity, assessed the bombing results after the bombardier activated the bomb release switch in concert with the lead or first aircraft in the squadron. It was on this mission that as I straddled the catwalk during the bomb run and pressed the bomb bay anti-creep lever, a chunk of shrapnel ripped through my bunny suit, nearly making an instant soprano out of me as it shorted out my suit. It was a cold flight home. All squadron aircraft returned at 1645 hours. The two-ounce shot of 86-proof was especially welcomed at the end of a difficult day. It hit my empty stomach like an exploding star."[690]

Altogether, the 8th dropped 4800 tons of high explosive on Berlin in five raids during March 1944. The raids cost the 8th scores of experienced crews and valuable aircraft, to say nothing of the mental scars on those who survived. Berlin would be indelibly printed on their minds for days, months, and even years to come.[691]

14

Flak and Fighters *Fortissimo*

"There was great competition among American fighter pilots to get their hands on the Mustang and Don Blakeslee pleaded with his general to exchange their old Thunderbolts for them. But a great daylight offensive was planned, the Normandy invasion would take place within three months and so the general answered that he did not see how Blakeslee's group could become non-operational for several weeks while they re-trained on to the new fighter. 'That's OK, General, sir,' replied Don. 'We can learn to fly them on the way to the target!'"

Air Vice Marshal J. E. "Johnnie" Johnson CBE DSO DFC
and the top scoring RAF fighter pilot in WWII

On 1 April the number of missions to complete a combat tour was increased from 25 to 30 missions. Thick cloud grounded the 1st Division, but the 438 B-17s and B-24s of the 2nd and 3rd Divisions continued on to the chemical works at Ludwigshafen. All 192 B-24s of the 3rd Division were forced to abandon the mission over France, leaving 54 B-24s to continue to the target, while 162 B-24s bombed targets of opportunity at Pforzheim, near Karlsruhe and Grafenhausen. *Unteroffizier* Albert "Adi" Boeckl of the 12th *Staffel* JG 26 and two pilots in JG 2 were credited with the destruction of B-24 *Judith Lynn*, flown by Lieutenant Joseph M. Soznoz in the 329th Bomb Squadron, 93rd Bomb Group, northwest of Reims at 1150 hours.[692] Return fire from the Liberators in the 20th Combat Wing hit *Unteroffizier* Kurt Hofer in the 3rd *Staffel* JG 26, and he died in the wreckage of his FW 190A-7 while trying to force land north of Reims-Pont Faverger.[693] One by one the remaining German fighters, low on fuel, landed to refuel and rearm and await the returning bombers, which could be expected later in the afternoon. En route to Ludwigshafen the 44th and 392nd Bomb Groups veered off course when the command pilot in the PFF lead ship, whose *Mickey* set had malfunctioned as the formations departed the English coast, decided to carry on to the target. Colonel Myron Keilman wrote:

> "Without visual reference with the terrain, the lead navigator[694] had to rely solely upon pre-briefed estimates of winds aloft to carry out his dead-reckoning type of navigation… There must have been quite a change in both the direction and velocity of the winds aloft [because] the formations were blown 120 miles to the right of course and 50 miles further in distance."[695]

On the return journey the 448th Bomb Group, which was flying unescorted after bombing Pforzheim, and those who dropped out of formation became easy prey for enemy fighters. *Leutnant* Peter Reischer and *Unteroffizier* Heinz Gehrke of the 11th *Staffel* JG 26 claimed two of the Seething Group's Liberators in the Reims-St. Pol area between 1330 and 1352 hours, but they had run almost out of fuel, and the crews had already decided to bale out.[696] At 1502 hours in the Pas de Calais JG 26 claimed a third 448th Bomb Group B-24 when *Oberfeldwebel* Erich Schwartz of the 4th *Staffel* picked out *Black Widow*,[697] being flown by Lieutenant Jack Black, and which was alone after flak damaged an engine over Roubaix, France. Schwartz knocked out the other three engines and was convinced he had destroyed the Liberator, but Jack Black flew *Black Widow* towards the Channel, where he ditched the aircraft in the sea 15 miles off Dunkirk. Black and his co-pilot, Joseph Pomfret, were badly injured in the ditching because 448th Bomb Group B-24s were not fitted with shoulder harnesses. Pomfret was in fact thrown out of his seat in the impact and badly injured. The others scrambled into the only life raft available. Pomfret, weakened by the cold, drowned before he could be taken aboard one of the life rafts. Sergeant Charles Nissen, who was injured and suffering from shock, died later. The eight survivors spent 44 hours adrift on the surface of the sea until they were spotted by Bert May, skipper of the *The Three Brothers* fishing boat. Miraculously, favorable winds blew the dinghies across the Channel to within 5 miles of the English coast and they were rescued. After this tragic loss of aircraft and crews the 448th did not return to full combat status until 8 April.

The weather in the first part of April was atrocious, and on the 8th the cloudy conditions abated, allowing the bombers to assemble in force and send 13 combat wings consisting of 644 heavies, including 192 bombers, which attacked Brunswick, along with aircraft depots throughout western Germany. Mustangs in the 4th Fighter Group were one of the fighter groups that supported the Brunswick force, and they attacked three separate gaggles of FW 190s and Bf 109s over a 30-mile area from 23,000ft to the deck. While leading the Group near Celle Major George Carpenter claimed two FW 190s destroyed. Carpenter recalls:

> "Lieutenant Piedler reported many a/c at 10 o'clock. They were flying close formation and looked like a box of bombers. We turned toward them, meeting them more or less head-on. They were 75 to 80 FW 190s and Me 109s. We attacked at once with all Squadrons but

were unable to prevent some of the e/a from attacking the bombers and knocking down four or five of them. I picked out a FW 190 and followed him down to about 6000ft where I got in a couple of good bursts with good results. The e/a went into a spin and I kept stalking him, thinking it was an evasive maneuver. However, the FW 190 did not recover and I saw it crash in a field with a great orange ball of flame. I then pulled up, saw another FW 190 and got behind him. I followed him through some rather violent actions down to the deck. I got a couple of good bursts into him, with several strikes in the cockpit area. He jettisoned his hood, but I did not see him bale out. I saw him crash three or four seconds later."

1st Lieutenant Pierce McKennon felt that he could not give a very coherent description because it was the first fight of this magnitude he had ever been in:

> "FW 190s were all over the place and every time I turned around I started shooting. I made attacks on about five different FW 190s: one of these I got strikes on. Looking over at one side of the fight there was a FW 190 and a P-51 going round and round, neither getting deflection on the other. I dove towards the FW 190 and clobbered him pretty good (about a 40° shot). He straightened out and I got in some more strikes on wing root and fuselage around the cockpit. He went into a sharp dive and then I overshot him. I turned sharply. Looking down, I saw him hit and litter a field with pieces. The fight started about 23,000ft and finally ended up on the deck. Boy! It sure was a honey. I claim one FW 190 Destroyed and one Damaged."[698]

A total of 34 heavies were shot down during the day's missions. Thirty of these were liberators, of which eleven were in the 44th Bomb Group and six were from the 466th Bomb Group.[699] The 361st Fighter Group, which was being led by the CO, Colonel Christian, was assigned to late withdrawal support along the B-24s' route home. The three squadrons of P-47s for the first time were carrying the 150-gallon belly tank, which allowed an added 50-mile combat radius. They arrived over Dummer Lake at the assigned time of 1430 hours and patrolled the area while awaiting the lead elements of returning bombers. At 1442 rendezvous was made with about 200 Liberators returning from attacks on aircraft plants near Brunswick. Within ten minutes, as the formations made their way steadily west, *Luftwaffe* fighters commenced attacks on the B-24s. Upon arriving on the bombers' left flank, 1st Lieutenant Alton B. Snyder, who was flying as Wabash Yellow Leader,[700] bounced a flight of four Bf 109s that had just made a pass. Snyder and his wingman, 1st Lieutenant Scott Naedele, chased the four Messerschmitts as they dove away, splitting into elements in the process. Singling out one of the enemy fighters, Snyder continued the chase down to 2000ft while repeatedly scoring hits on the 109 from 150 yards and the German spun in. Naedele, who had been covering Snyder's tail during the combat, suddenly spotted three more Bf 109s flying low on the deck and broke after them so rapidly that his leader failed to pick up on his move. Naedele looked back and saw that he was alone, but it was too late to break off the attack, as he was right in the middle of the three enemy aircraft. One of them, evidently their leader, was more aggressive than the other two and turned into him. Naedele and the German pilot soon found themselves in a tight circle in which neither pilot was able to get enough lead to shoot at the other. The other two Germans were apparently inexperienced pilots, as Naedele saw them "just stooging around watching and waiting for an opening." Eventually the German leader broke out of the circle, allowing Naedele a clear shot. The fighter, whose cowling was painted black and silver checkerboard, was hit repeatedly and crashed in a ball of fire. The remaining '109s gave a half-hearted chase, but Naedele applied maximum power and water injection to climb away at high speed. During the same engagement, Red Flight of the 375th Squadron watched as a single '109, painted black overall with black crosses on a white background on the wings, shot down a B-24 before they could get within range. The leader of Red Flight overshot the 109 during evasive action and 1st Lieutenant Eugene Cole had a clear shot. He closed from 500 yards to point-blank range and fired almost 1500 rounds of .50-caliber ammunition into the Messerschmitt, and the landing gear dropped and black smoke poured from the engine cowling. The 109 went into a vertical dive from 5000ft and crashed.[701]

Seven miles north of Zwolle Snyder attacked "Charlie" Willius. Snyder recalled:

> "I saw two FW 190s make a head on attack at the bombers. We immediately bounced the two e/a. Just after coming through the main box of bombers the two e/a bounced a straggler flying at 10,000ft and behind the main box. I observed strikes on the B-24 but he didn't go down.[702] The enemy aircraft immediately split-essed and we followed them down to 3000ft, opening fire at 300 yards. I observed many hits on the fuselage and wing roots. The enemy aircraft staggered momentarily and spun into the ground, bursting into flames."[703]

This was the "Yellowjackets'" most successful mission to date, with a total of nine aircraft claimed destroyed, two probables, and two damaged for the loss of one pilot. 1st Lieutenant Albert C. Duncan in the 375th Squadron disappeared during the combat, and a number of pilots reported seeing a yellow-nosed P-47 hit over Dummer Lake. Duncan's demise was awarded to *Oberleutnant* Erich Scheyda of 3./JG 26, who claimed a 361st Fighter Group P-47 at Lingen.[704] The use of the 150 gallon drop tank had boosted the 361st Fighter Group's combat endurance by a wide margin, but the P-47's capacity for burning fuel, especially in the high rpm settings necessary in a dogfight, was unsurpassed, and many pilots returned to Bottisham "on vapors."[705]

On Easter Sunday, 9 April, the 1st Division was assigned the FW 190 plant at Marienburg; the 3rd Division, Poznan; and the 2nd Bomb Division, the aircraft assembly plant at Tutow. The Marienburg plant had been the scene of a successful bombing attempt earlier in the war, but the component part of the plant had escaped bombing because a thick layer of cloud had obscured it from view. In all, 104 Liberators took off for Tutow. At 0900 a 392nd Bomb Group B-24 and *Might of the Eighth* in the 389th collided at 8000ft while forming up over north Norfolk.[706] At Horsham St. Faith 19 Liberators defied the elements and had taken off for Tutow, but bad weather caught up with them over the Continent and forced the majority to seek their secondary target at the airfield at Pachion. Bombing was ineffectual, and the Group lost four Liberators. Meanwhile, the 1st Division was en route to the FW 190 plant at Marienburg. Despite the loss of one combat wing and some combat boxes from another, 98 B-17s placed 71% of their bombs within 1000ft of the MPI. Leaving the target, the B-17s received radio orders to join 33 B-17s of the 3rd Division, which had bombed the FW 190 plant at Poznan, for mutual protection, but before they could rendezvous the 3rd Division came under heavy fighter attack. The leading 45th Wing bore the brunt of the attacks, but stout defense by the Fortress gunners kept losses down to just two aircraft. Meanwhile, a further 86 B-17s bombed the Heinkel plant at Warnemünde, while 40 B-17s bombed the airfield at Rahmel and 46 B-17s bombed airfields at Parchim and Rostock. Altogether, the 8th lost 30 bombers.

On 10 April 730 crews were "rewarded" with milk-run missions to airfield targets in France and the Low Countries. The 467th Bomb Group, which had been at Rackheath for just 29 days, flew its first mission to an aircraft assembly plant at Bourges airfield, in central France. The Group's state of readiness reflected the marvellous achievement of Colonel Albert J. Shower and his personnel. They had knuckled down to three weeks' intensive activity, and 52 B-24s were dispersed on the airfield.[707] Colonel Shower led 30 Liberators at 0600 hours in Lieutenant Kenneth Driscoll's B-24. The Group formation was split into two Squadrons, with Major Smith leading the second element in Lieutenant Richard Campbell's Liberator. A fair assembly was completed, and the 467th slipped into the 96th Wing formation, which joined the other Groups in the Divisional assembly line. Altogether the Eighth dispatched 730 heavies to pound aviation targets in the Low Countries and central France. Combat crews had studied flak positions, the position of target buildings as shown on the RAF night target charts, and target photographs during the pre-operational month at Rackheath. Bombardiers had paid particular attention to target photographs, from which they determined and pinpointed positions of the probable MPI. The mission went well. There was no flak at all at the enemy coast and no fighters appeared. It turned out to be a milk run. Good visibility over the target aided the 467th, which dropped its 1000lb GP bombs on the hangars and factory buildings. Other Groups too had bombed well, and a later reconnaissance revealed that the factory had been almost completely destroyed. The ground staff had been told of the 467th's estimated time of return, and had gathered in the warm sunshine by the briefing building. The expectant ranks cheered as the aircraft flew over the airfield in tight formation, and they were full of pride and relief as one by one all 30 Liberators peeled off and landed. Each one taxied along the perimeter track with the waist doors open. From inside and atop the aircraft, gunners and engineers waved to the waiting ground crews. Interrogation revealed that four aircraft had failed to bomb, but the other 26 had dropped 149,000lbs right on the target, although one squadron was slightly west of the MPI.

The 457th Bomb Group flew to Evre airfield, at Brussels, and the mission was so low-key that Perry Rudd even had time to take snaps of the city while he waited for "Bombs Away." Then things changed:

"We made three runs over the target despite the heavy flak. I was sitting in the camera well. Just after 'Bombs Away' sounded a piece of shrapnel, which had come through the bomb bay doors and through the radio room wall, hit me in the back about two inches above the bottom of my flak suit. The whole ship was shot up and we later counted more than 100 holes. No.3 and 4 gas tanks leaked and No.4 supercharger ran away coming home. The left horizontal stabilizer had a hole in it and another through the elevator. When we got back to Glatton the ship was sent to a sub-depot."

On Tuesday, 11 April, 830 bombers were dispatched in three separate forces to bomb aircraft production centers in eastern Germany. The German defenses were responsible for the loss of 64 B-17s and B-24s, one of the heaviest single-say losses of the war. Force 1 headed for Oschersleben, Bernberg, and Halberstadt, while Forces II and III were directed against targets at Sorau, Politz, Gulzow, Zarnglaff, and Rostock. Flying one of the 88 Fortresses in the 1st Division, which were assigned Cottbus and Sorau, was Lieutenant Joe Wroblewski in the 351st Bomb Group, who viewed the mission philosophically:

"The 11th of each month always seemed to be my day for missions. I was picked to fly with a new crew that had just arrived at Polebrook. It was usually standard procedure to take a new pilot and his crew on their first mission. We went to Arniswalde, Germany, which was our secondary target near the Polish border. We flew at 15,000ft, descending to 12,000ft at the target. That gave the anti-aircraft gunners a field day. They got their share of B-17s over Hanover. Bombers were blowing up, burning and falling out of control all around us. We all got scared as hell when a four-inch piece of flak came right through the nose and cut the oxygen line on the right side. The whooshing sound of the escaping oxygen under pressure made plenty of noise. The new pilot grabbed the controls from me and about pulled us out of formation in panic. I almost had to beat his hands off the yoke. I told him that if we did get out of formation by ourselves the enemy fighters would be on us like a pack of wolves. Some of our crewmembers had to use portable oxygen bottles after losing half our supply. Enemy fighters did not bother us although we could see other groups under heavy attack."

One of the groups, which came in for repeated attacks, was the 401st at Deenthorpe. Flying his 11th mission this day was John L. Hurd, the ball turret gunner aboard Lieutenant Francis L. Shaw's *Battlin' Betty*:

"My squadron was hit hard by flak and we lost four B-17s in this action. There were many flak bursts around our ship. From my position in the ball turret I was able to watch under the wings for fires. Immediately the No.3 and 4 engines started smoking and shortly afterwards my ball turret was hit and I was injured in the right butt! Our bombs were salvoed to guard against explosion just as one of our B-17s blew up. *Battlin' Betty* finally came clear of the flak and we slowed down and lost altitude. I was asked to leave the ball turret and have the radio operator look at my injury. He was unable to do anything as I had too many clothes on. About this time the pilot gave the order to bale out. I hooked on my chest-type parachute and placed my GI shoes inside my 'chute harness. We were over flat country and somewhere east of Hanover. I looked out of the bomb bay and then decided to jump out of the waist door. We were somewhere between 15,000 and 18,000ft. The two waist gunners and I were waiting to jump when I heard a loud crash. The ship started to rock to the left and knocked us against the left side of the ship. I thought to myself, 'It's now or never,' so I gave a big push and all three of us went out the door. It was very noisy as I left the ship and shortly after I pulled the ripcord. The 'chute opened and then the world was quiet."[708]

Meanwhile, other groups were suffering losses in the ferocious flak barrage, as Perry Rudd in the 457th Bomb Group formation recalls:

"We were knocked out of formation and fell a thousand feet before we recovered. We leveled out just in rime to witness a burning B-17 fall off its right wing directly over us. Lieutenant Matterell, the co-pilot, pulled our ship up on the left wing and we fell another 3000ft. The burning B-17 missed us by only a few feet. A piece of flak had entered the cockpit before exploding and had set the nose on fire. The flames spread through the open radio hatch of the doomed ship, leaving a trail of smoke as it spiraled down. Two men got out. The tail gunner went through a wing and a pilot banked his plane to let him by. Neither 'chute opened, if indeed either of them had them on."

At the target more flak bracketed the Fortresses. The lead bombardier in the 351st Bomb Group was hit in the arm, which had to be amputated later. Perry Rudd's B-17, meanwhile, had to salvo its bombs:

"The bomb doors would not close and we headed back to Belgium alone. We received about 20 flak hits on the homeward run. The right aileron was knocked out of position, the rudder was holed and the right flap was put out of commission. Lieutenant Hovey did a remarkable job of getting us back. We took our crash landing positions but it was a great landing at Glatton despite the damage, although the plane was later declared a sub-depot job."

The most remarkable feat of all was performed by 1st Lieutenant Edward S. Michael and 2nd Lieutenant Franklin Westberg in the 364th Bomb Squadron, 305th Bomb Group, who brought *Bertie Lee* home to England after it had been devastated by cannon fire and had plummeted into a 3000ft dive. An estimated 300 fighters filled the sky, attacking with suicidal ferocity. *Bertie Lee* began taking hits and was riddled from nose to tail. A 20mm shell entered the side of the cockpit, exploding on the instrument panel and wounding Michael in the thigh. Smoke filled the cockpit, and the windshield was smothered with hydraulic fluid. At the same time the B-17 went into a spin, and 3000 feet of altitude was lost before control could be regained. Wiping fluid off the windshield, Michael was informed by Ray Evans, the radio operator, that the bomb load of incendiaries was on fire and was "burning like hell." Michael told John Leiber, the bombardier, to press the bomb release button, but the bombs refused to budge. Fighters closed in for the kill and one made a head on pass, blasting Leiber into the navigator's position and scoring hits on the top turret. Michael gave the bale-out order. Those aft of the bomb bay, in the worst of the fire, prepared to leave. Michael felt a hand on his shoulder and turned around. The top turret gunner, Jewel Phillips, had a shell lodged in his shoulder, and one of his eyeballs had been blown out. Phillips, who had the eyeball cupped in his hand, calmly informed Michael about the status of the fire, but he needed urgent medical attention, and it was decided that his only chance of survival was to bale out and hope that the Germans would take care of him. Leiber placed Phillips' hand on his release ring, kicked open the nose escape hatch, and pushed Phillips out. (It was nine months before they learned that Phillips was alive and well in a PoW camp.) Ray Evans discovered that his parachute had been shredded by cannon fire. He shouted at his buddy, Arthur J. Kosino, waist gunner, "Don't leave me Art!" Kosino went back and prepared to clip their harnesses together in order to share a 'chute when he remembered that a spare was sometimes carried in the tail gun position. Kosino found it in a duffel bag and he gave it to Evans. They both jumped and the rest followed. They all survived and were taken prisoner.

A deafening gale was now roaring through the burning B-17, and Michael shouted at Leiber to bale out, but Leiber's parachute had also been shredded, and he showed it to Michael, saying it was useless. Michael could not leave Leiber to die. Westberg could not leave Michael, as he was too weak to fly alone, and Leiber was not about to accept someone else's parachute. Between them they decided to go together. Michael told Leiber to get rid of the bombs, which he did by operating a manual bomb release switch in the bomb bay. Returning to his station in the nose, he was just in time to score hits on a fighter making a head on pass. The fighter exploded and disintegrated just short of damaging the ship. Still under attack, and with the bomb bay doors frozen open, they managed to escape into a cloudbank and lose the fighters. Leiber began administering first aid to Michael, and moments later *Bertie Lee* took a hit from an anti-aircraft battery. Michael put the B-17 into a dive before levelling off at 75ft, and with 400 miles to England, kept *Bertie Lee* at between 50 and 75 feet the whole time. Flying on across France, German soldiers repeatedly took pot shots at them, and they could hear shells zinging through the ship. Leiber returned fire when he could. Mercifully, the guns in the flak towers could not bear down on them, as they were too low. Farmers in the fields kept pointing the way, and they battled on towards England. Over the English Channel a German fighter closed in to attack, and with nowhere to hide, the crew felt that 'this was it." However, the German fired a casual burst and then left, probably low on fuel. Some ships were sighted, and the crew considered ditching nearby, but Leiber pointed out that with the bomb bay doors open the ship would think they were under attack and start firing, so they flew on. Nearing land, they spotted Waltham airfield, near Grimsby. Michael circled the field and made an approach for a wheels-up landing on the grass. With the bomb bay doors open, no undercarriage, and no airspeed indicator or flaps, Michael nevertheless managed to get *Bertie Lee* down safely. Michael's feat earned the second Medal of Honor awarded to a member in the 364th Bomb Squadron, 305th Bomb Group.[709]

Bombing results were good, but enemy fighters outnumbered friendly ones, and the flak was accurate, varying from moderate to intense. Twenty aircraft out of the 28 dispatched by the 92nd Bomb Group, which were assigned the industrial area of Stettin, returned safely. However, savage and persistent fighter attacks and a concentrated flak barrage shot down six B-17s in the 325th Bomb Squadron, flying as the low squadron of the high group.[710] The entire mission was flown at an altitude of about 15,000ft and required 11 hours to complete. Crewmembers described it as one of the "roughest" in memory.

In the 45th Combat Wing in the Third Division the crew of *Smoky Liz*, in the 731st Bomb Squadron, 452nd Bomb Group, flown by Fred Whitlinger, flew their fifth mission when the target was the Junkers aircraft factory at Rostock. Ralph Reese, the left waist gunner, recalls:

> "We were awakened at 0230 and briefed at 0315. Breakfast was at 0345 with take off at 0625. Bomb load was 10-500lb demolition. We encountered Me 110s that stayed out of range of our guns and were shooting 20mm at a formation of Fortresses on our left. They knocked three Forts out of the formation. Then a FW 190 flew through our formation in front of our nose. He came through so fast that the bombardier didn't have time to call him out. All I saw of-him was a streak of tail The FW 190 shot up our No.1 engine, so that the pilot had to shut that engine off. We stayed in formation with the rest of the Group. I saw a Fortress go down on our right and saw five chutes come out. Then the FW-l90 took after the chutes. Whether he cut them we do not know. Flak was very heavy over the target and we received a number of hits. We saw eight Fortresses go down and a possible three enemy fighters shot down. Our escorts were P-47s and P-38s but they were not around when enemy fighters attacked us. We returned to Deopham Green at 1700. This was a very long mission and very tough all the way around. We had several.30 caliber holes in No.1 engine, two flak holes in the left wing and fuselage and a five-inch diameter flak hole in the right elevator. Target was bombed fairly well."

The fighters had some successes. The 352nd Fighter Group was split into two formations, one comprising the P-51 equipped 486th and 487th Fighter Squadrons to provide penetration support for the B-17s of the 1st Air Division, and the second comprising the 328th Fighter Squadron providing withdrawal support for the bombers. The Blue Nosed Bastards took off from Bodney at 0930 and joined with the bombers near Stendal at 1120 hours. The 40 minutes of escort was uneventful, but at 1200 hours, as the P-51s broke off escort, they were immediately presented with a number of ground targets. The 486th strafed two airfields near Torgau and claimed three aerial victories, seven more destroyed on the ground, two Ju-86s probably destroyed, and four others damaged in ground attacks. 1st Lieutenant Frank A. Cutler, who was leading Blue Flight in a Mustang called *Soldier's Vote*,[711] followed Yellow Flight down to strafe some planes on an airfield at Nehmsdorf, and he damaged a Ju 52 three-engined transport. Cutler then took his flight to a field a few miles to the west near Lonnewitz, where he saw a number of white Ju 88s, and he got good hits all over the wings and engines of one and left it burning. Leaving this field, Cutler was flying in a westerly direction when he saw a locomotive just leaving the bridge across the Elbe River at Torgau. Cutler made his pass at the engine and saw pieces of it thrown up in the cloud of steam from the boiler. He then flew over the town of Torgau on the rooftops heading west for a mile or two. He was keen to add to the two Bf 109s he had scored over Belgium on 20 February when he had been flying a P-47, and near Neiden-Torgau Cutler got his chance. When he looked to the left and behind he saw a Ju-52 and closed on him fast to about 200 yards before pulling the trigger. There were strikes on the landing gear and left wing root. As he passed over him Cutler flipped over and saw the left wing and engine in flames, and Lieutenant Anderson, his wingman, saw it hit the ground and burn. As he was on his back heading north and watching the Ju-52 go down Cutler saw two light blue FW 190s flying wingtip to wingtip directly below going west at about 1000ft. *Unteroffiziers* Heinz Voight and Karl Weiss of 4/JG 26 were flying them.[712] Cutler recalled:

"I headed for them and closed fast, firing on the plane on the right from about 100 yards. I saw strikes on the tail section, so I skidded left and fired at the second plane, which had not yet taken any evasive action. All my ammo was gone but the pilot must have been hit since the Focke Wulf whipped over to the left and exploded in the middle of the field. Then I noticed that the first FW 190 was burning in the next field a few hundred yards away. I was separated from my flight and the Group, so I climbed to 23,000ft and came home alone."[713]

Sergeant Louis J. Torretta, a tail gunner in the 447th Bomb Group in the 4th Wing, flew his 22nd mission this day:

"Wow, what a ride today. We took off at 0530. Our target was an oil plant near Poznan, Poland but again the weather was against us and we had to bomb the secondary target, which was an airfield at Airunwalde at Stettin. It was set out in the woods and we had a heck of a time finding it. When the Germans discovered what we were looking for they tried to hide it with a smoke screen and that just gave it away. We were able to see the target very clear and we had a good score. We ran into some enemy fighters and we sort of took a beating. They were Me 109s, about 12 of them. We lost Lieutenant [Howard S.] Pauling's crew #15. They were very good friends of mine. Later we heard they were headed for Sweden I hope they made it.[714] Temperature was 18 below zero. We landed at 1700. 11½ hours."

The 13th and 45th Combat Wings in the 3rd Bomb Division force were also confronted with bad weather in the Poznan area and were forced to bomb the secondary target at Rostock. Rocket-firing Me 410s and Ju 88s took advantage of a lapse in fighter cover and wreaked havoc among the leading groups. The 96th Bomb Group was worst hit, losing ten of the 25 bombers lost this day. Most of the crews who got back to England had been in the air for more than 11 hours, and tiredness had already begun to take effect during the last stages of the homeward leg. Lieutenant Bryce S. Moore, pilot of B-17 *Esky* (after the trademark character on the front of *Esquire* magazine) in the 551st or "Green" Squadron, 385th Bomb Group, returned from Stettin, his 26th and next to last mission, and longest at 10 hours and 30 minutes. He recalls:

"I was terribly distraught that the group lead radioed in the clear that because of weather we would bypass Stettin and bomb an alternate target. I knew the Germans monitored our frequencies and to alert their defenses of our eminent arrival seemed sheer stupidity at the moment, though I don't recall actually encountering any enemy fighter attacks or anti-aircraft fire over the target, whatever its name. On reflection I suspect that Colonel Vandevanter, the Command Pilot as well as Group Commander, was using a code name to mislead the enemy. If so, it worked. We were flying left wing (low) in the second element in the low squadron - not a good position because of the stratus clouds the group was struggling to climb over at about 28,000 or 30,000ft. Being the lowest ship in the group we were dragged through the tops of several cloud layers made worse by dense contrails from the planes ahead and above us and by other groups ahead of us whose contrails were sometimes at right angles to our heading as they climbed. This created a false sloping horizon and made us feel that we were in a turn when we weren't. Very uncomfortable, near-vertigo intermittently for a few seconds. To avoid running into other planes in the clouds I pulled to the left ten or 15 seconds then continued to climb straight ahead with all aboard keeping a lookout for other aircraft.

"Suddenly I noticed a small break in the cloud layer below us to my left and was surprised to see for perhaps two seconds a squadron of six twin-engine German fighter-bombers about 500ft below heading in the opposite direction. Apparently they were unaware of our presence, though of course I couldn't be certain. I called out their location to the crew and told the co-pilot that if the German squadron should attack our lone airplane we would dodge them by re-entering the cloud layer a few feet below. I then called the navigator and suggested he tune nearby Malmo, Sweden, on the radio compass in case we needed a safe haven from the German fighters since the clouds seemed thickest to our right (north). 'It's been tuned for five minutes!' was his quick reply. Happily, the Germans didn't attack and in a few minutes we were between cloud layers, sighted the group a short distance ahead, quickly caught up and proceeded to the new target. The trip home was uneventful till letdown when we broke up into squadrons and widened our disassembly pattern because of hazy conditions over East Anglia. Suddenly our squadron met another squadron head-on, with no time to maneuver. How we missed each other will forever be a mystery."

Lieutenant Joe Wroblewski in the 351st Bomb Group says:

"I kept seeing the English coast all the way back across the North Sea. It must have been a mirage. It seemed like we would never get back. I was dead tired when we eventually did get back and I passed out in the sack and slept like a log."[715]

Crews barely had time to catch up on some much needed sleep when 455 crews in East Anglia were told to prepare for another long mission on the 12th. Once again the targets were aircraft plants in central Germany. Men dragged themselves out of their beds and took off, but the weather intervened and the bombers turned back early. Although some crews came under fire, none were sorry the mission had been "scrubbed." It meant another day to live. Colonel (later General) Maurice "Mo" Preston, CO of the 379th Bomb Group, flying at the head of the leading 41st Wing, led the 1st Division to the ball-bearing plants at Schweinfurt, while the 3rd Division went to the Messerschmitt plant at Augsburg, in southern Germany. The 2nd Bomb Division was assigned German aircraft manufacturing installations near Munich. The 1st Division encountered strong fighter opposition, as Colonel Preston recalls:

"In all probability they made a direct head-on approach from a distance of 15-20 miles. The first we saw of them they were among us and already firing their guns. They made only a single pass and then went on through the lead wing, maintaining an upright position, thus abandoning, for at least this one time, their practice of attacking inverted and then pulling out in an earthward dive. The great majority of attacks were concentrated on a single box, a single element, of the wing formation. The high box[716] was chosen presumably because it was separated some distance from the remaining boxes. I made a determined effort via the radio to induce the element leader to get back into formation, but to no avail. He and his entire formation [8 aircraft] were shot down on a single pass made by the German fighters. I never saw such a thing happen before or since. One pass; scratch one entire formation! It was on this mission that we finally achieved a direct hit on the No.1 prime building, the elimination of which would do the greatest good. At least one 379th bomb went into that prime building. It probably didn't make a great difference to the war effort, but it's little successes like these that spice things up for the participants."

The 3rd Division was badly mauled by fighters and ten Fortresses were forced to head for Switzerland, with many others either shot down or badly damaged. The B-24s, which did not turn back until they had reached the German border, also came in for some rough treatment from three *Staffeln* of JG 26 and two of JG 2, which were assembled over Juvincourt by their ground controller. One of the B-24s in the 453rd Bomb Group carried the 2nd Combat Wing Leader, Major James M. Stewart, who on 31 March had joined the Old Buckenham Group as Operations Officer. Once the Liberators' route had been determined the German fighters were directed towards Luxembourg to meet them, and they were intercepted near Liège. The Liberators were being escorted by Thunderbolts of the 366th and 78th Fighter Groups, the latter now sporting black and white checkerboard nose cowlings following the 56th Fighter Group's varied success in fooling the Germans with colored nose paint. The distinctive markings also provided an easier form of recognition for trigger-happy bomber gunners and other escort fighters alike. Despite foul weather conditions, the 78th Fighter Group stuck with the 2nd Bomb Division until southeast of Aachen,, where the B-24s aborted, the last division to do so. The 445th Bomb Group B-24s lost sight of their P-47s when they entered a thin layer of stratus cloud, and *Oberleutnant* Walter Matoni, who was leading the JG 26 formation, saw the opportunity to attack from underneath. JG 2 joined them in the fight. The Focke Wulfs fired 20mm cannon shells into the B-24s with devastating effect. JG 26 claimed two of the Liberators and JG 2 three more before the P-47 pilots could see what was happening.[717] The Thunderbolts pitched into the fray and chased the Focke Wulfs in and out of the cloud layer, claiming six shot down. Four of the enemy pilots were killed, and the two others baled out safely.[718] At 1310 hours Quince Brown was leading the 84th Squadron near Duren when 30 plus FW 190s and Bf 109s emerged from above heavy clouds, flying in the opposite direction. Quince's formation turned and pursued the enemy fighters in a steep-climbing turn that overtook the German fighters, which scattered and dove for the deck. Brown picked out a FW 190 with a belly tank and at 5000ft raked the fighter from left wingtip to cockpit. The FW 190 exploded, and Quince flew safely through the flame and debris. Later near Malmedy, Belgium, Major Len Marshall, along with Karl Wagner, Robert Baker, and George Lundigan, chased several FW 190s to the deck. Marshall overshot his quarry, allowing Wagner to get in two long, wide angle deflection bursts, which caught the FW as it was belly landing. The FW's left wing broke off and it flipped on its back and exploded. As Wagner passed the FW's remains he saw the pilot lying off to the side where the explosion had thrown him.[719] Near Sedan, France, at about the same time a section of four 82nd Fighter Squadron pilots stumbled upon six Ju 87 Stukas beneath them milling around Ensheim airdrome, with another 50 plus parked on the field. The Thunderbolt pilots had difficulty trying to hang behind the dive-bombers long enough to take aim, but the outcome was never in doubt, as each man destroyed one before giving the airdrome a quick squirt.

Thereafter, the weather intervened once again and provided a much-needed respite for weary fighter pilots and bomber crews, ever conscious that soon they would be flying yet another mission, days, maybe even hours later. The waiting was agonizing for old and new crews alike. Lieutenant Abe Dolim, a Hawaiian B-17 navigator who, three years before, had witnessed at first hand the Japanese bombing of Pearl Harbor, was one of the officers in Joe Hamil's crew that arrived in Scotland aboard the *Queen Elizabeth* on 6 April. They were piped off the great Cunard liner at 1400 hours, and by 0300 they had arrived by train at Stoke on Trent.

"By midnight the next day" recalls Dolim, "we had learned to play darts and drink Guinness Irish beer. It's awful stuff but it's all they'd got. Learning about the God-awful British money system was another thing. However did they get screwed up with pounds, shillings and pence? We looked at a pound note the size of our dollar but it was worth four of our bucks. On the 11th we left Stoke at 1330 hours for the short trip to Bury St. Edmunds (Rougham) and the 94th Bomb Group."

On 13 April Abe Dolim was standing outside the ablutions building with another young officer who had graduated from the same navigation class in California, and who he had not met since phase training days. Dolim asked his friend about combat flying. The short, intense, dark-haired young man told him about the many losses of personnel, some of them mutual friends, about the deep penetrations into enemy territory, heavy flak concentrations, and fierce fighter attacks. As he spoke, his face revealed a deep down dread and fear of what tomorrow would bring. Dolim was aghast at what he saw and heard, and a thought flashed through his mind - "This man expects to die." Five days later, on Tuesday, 18 April, the 94th Bomb Group experienced the heaviest losses in months of combat. Ten of the crews (and nine in the 385th) failed to return from the mission to Berlin, and the intense young man was one of those listed as killed in action. Captain Lundak brought his B-17 back "shot to hell" and minus his tail gunner, who had baled out when the pilot dove his aircraft to the deck from 25,000ft. The crew had used up almost all their ammunition, and they could not maintain position with the group. Lieutenant Maurice Pearl, Lundak's navigator, told Dolim that about 60 FW 190s caught them outside the bomber stream. Bob Giles and Norman McComb were MIA. By the time Dolim flew his first mission (on 22 April) the 94th would have lost about 14 crews in combat or rotated home.

Most crews were fatalistic. Some missions were regarded with superstition. S/Sgt Forrest S. Clark, radio operator-gunner in the 44th Bomb Group, was superstitious, and feared flying a mission on 13 April;

"We had all nearly finished our missions and had some rough ones. The pilot, Lieutenant Rockford C. Griffith, had a particularly rough time in combat. By the time we went on the 13 April mission to Lechfeld we had cut in the roughest and most dangerous period of the 8th Air Force combat missions, the time when the Luftwaffe was very strong, the flak was heaviest and the losses were highest. The chances of surviving 25 or 20 missions were indeed slim. We had seen many of our friend's go down over Germany. We lost our bombardier, 2nd Lieutenant Dave Edmonds and Sgt Abe Sofferman, our first radio operator.[720] I had suffered frostbite, sinusitis, combat stress and injuries to my back and legs in combat flying but I was determined to go on. I had crashed, parachuted and narrowly missed being hit by enemy fighter fire. I would have preferred another date than 13 April but the crew and I had no choice. As we prepared for take-off I said, 'Why me on the 13th?' Anyway, it proved to be quite a mission among many I had flown to that date.[721]

"It was a long haul, a deep penetration, as they called it. I can still see that clear steely sky over Germany, the farmlands and the small villages shining in the sunlight, looking so peaceful, yet so deadly. We knew that to come down in that part of *Nazi* Germany would likely mean being beaten by a hostile civilian population because our officers at previous briefings had warned us of such incidents. The decisions we made that day shaped the rest of my life and my survival in WWII. We were at about 20,000ft over Lechfeld, a strategic Nazi airfield in southern Germany, when all hell broke loose. Flak came up at us from all sides and we scrambled to get out of the target area after 'bombs away.' I saw them go, fishtailing down on the runways and saw the *Nazi* planes parked on the dispersal areas, go up in a thousand splinters of steel and flames. Later, we learned the bomb pattern was 'excellent' and we had bombed what was a key German jet fighter base of the dreaded Me 262 and others of the once famous Luftwaffe. We found we were losing fuel at a rapid rate and falling inexorably behind the rest of our formation. It was impossible for us to maintain air speed. To try to make it over 600 miles or enemy territory in a shot up bomber losing fuel by the gallons would have been foolhardy and costly in manpower and in equipment. There is no question that we would not have made it and would have crashed or exploded in mid-air. The flight engineer, Sgt Earl Parrish checked the fuel gauges and found he had lost so much fuel we barely had enough fuel to make the Swiss border. We would have to either crash, a very risky business, or if successful, land and be taken prisoners of the Germans. The other possibility was to fall into the hands of a cruel crowd of pro-*Nazis*. Adding to our woes there suddenly appeared Me 109s following us as if waiting for the kill. We learned later that some of these aircraft were Swiss Air Force 109s.

"I fired off distress flares to alert the Swiss Air Force but we had to make an emergency landing at Dubendorf near Zurich. Our plane received four bursts of flak as we passed over the German-Swiss border. One of these flak bursts wounded Sgt Harold 'Jack' Harmon, one of our waist gunners. As soon as we got down a dozen armed soldiers surrounded our plane, one pointing a gun at my head. I thought we had come down in Germany. Our navigator, Lieutenant Ralph Jackson got out and the first thing he did was hang his parachute harness over the rifle of one of the soldiers. He said he was so disgusted because he had lost his original crew and had flown only three missions with us. The soldiers closed in around us and soon a Swiss colonel in full dress uniform stepped out of a car and told us we were in neutral Switzerland. This was our welcome to a neutral country in the midst of WWII, a not totally friendly welcome party. I had a sense of elation, yet sadness, because I had wished to finish my tour of duty and return to the US. Now my future was in doubt because no one knew then how long the war in Europe would last."[722]

Four days later, on 17 April, plans were drawn up for a raid the following day on Berlin. As usual, crews were alerted to fly the night before the mission. "Big-B" could never be described as an easy place to venture for crews who had been there before. It certainly was not the ideal target for new crews such as Lieutenant Anthony J. Cecchini's crew in the 360th Bomb Squadron, 303rd Bomb Group at Molesworth, who were waiting to begin their tour. Ben Smith Jr, the crew's radio operator, recalls:[723]

"We called Cecchini 'Chick'. He weighed over 200 pounds and had been a policeman in New York State. Italian to the core, he was red-haired and looked like a big Irish cop. He wore a perpetual grin and was quite a womanizer. The boy had a lot of charisma and personal charm. We adored him. Chick was a frustrated fighter pilot. He liked nothing better than to slip off with us and fly low-level with the B-17, buzzing farmhouses and tractors with the props almost touching the ground. This was hair-raising but somehow with him flying, we never worried. We had absolute confidence in him. There was not much discipline in the crew except in the air. Italians were notorious for evading military protocol and Chick was no exception. We tended to follow his lead. In training our crew was constantly being hailed before the Commandant of Crews. The officers and men all called one another by their first names. There was no sense of status and no saluting. Chick didn't care what we did and I don't remember his ever getting upset about anything, not even when we shot off the stabilizer. He was not impressed by brass, nor were we. Chick was our big brother, always coming up with a miracle just when we needed it and able to get us out of any kind of scrape. We believed he could fly rings around the rest of the pilots. Cecchini and Bachy, or Cliff Bachman, the flight engineer, flew several combat missions to get experience before the rest of us were allowed to go along. Bachy was the bravest of the brave. He would save our necks several times with his expertise. This kid was small in stature but a real knot. He once knocked a lieutenant cold at a nightclub in Grand Island, Nebraska and took off before the MPs could catch him. Bachy was from Grand Rapids, Minnesota and obviously of German descent. He was a superlative flight engineer and knew all there was to know about a B-17.

"Their first mission was a twelve-hour marathon to Marienburg, which ended in a crash landing. Chick had flown as co-pilot with Captain Bob Lynch, one of the veteran pilots.[724] Bachy's description of his initiation to the Big League dampened our enthusiasm considerably. He did not paint a pretty picture of what was in store for us. Shortly after arriving in England in early March I wrote my aunt advising that I was in a nice place and being treated well. I added, 'Haven't been in action yet, hope to start soon. It'll be a big show when we get started.' This was putting a brave face on things. The truth was I didn't hope to start soon. I hoped to start never! I would rather have been anywhere than where I was. I cursed myself for letting my pride get me into such a fix but I had come too far to back down now.

"That night as I looked up and down the row of bunks, there were many cigarettes glowing in the dark. There was not much sleeping going on. Chick's Crew were Catholic, Protestant and Jewish. We were descended from Irish, Italian, English, Scotch, Hungarian, Jewish and German immigrants, truly an all-American bunch. We were typical of the men who flew in the great bomber formations. We were a clannish bunch of fellows, closer than brothers, which was the format in all of the combat crews. Every one of us was a maverick in his own right. We had only two Southerners on the crew - Alvin and me. Alvin, the waist gunner, was Clarence Cogdell from Greenville, Tennessee. Lantern-jawed and of few words, he was a typical product of Appalachia. He and I had a mutual fondness for Blue Grass music. Of course, we changed his name to Alvin York (the hero of World War One) and thereafter called him nothing but Alvin. We teased the amiable Tennesseean constantly, but all we could provoke out of him was a good-natured grin. He was a gentle, sweet person.

"I was never referred to as anything but Snuffy or Houn' Dawg. I doubt seriously if anyone knew my real name. The navigator also had a sobriquet: Jasper, although his real name was Edward Veigel. He was also a Minnesotan, hailing from St. Paul. We called him Jasper because back in the States on our first cross-country flight, the pilot called up the navigator and asked him what was that town below. The navigator replied, "It's Jasper, Texas." Chick saw an airfield and called the tower below. It was the port of Beaumont. We were heading straight out to sea. Thereafter, the navigator was called Jasper, never anything else. He made few errors after that first monumental goof in training. Jasper was our mascot, the baby of the crew.

"Chunk, the other waist gunner, was Robert J. O'Hearn, an Irish kid from North Adams, Massachusetts. Chunk was my best friend and we were inseparable. Being Irish, naturally he liked to drink as well as I did. Bluff and hearty in manner, he was sentimental and tender hearted like most Celtics. Ward Hudson, the tail gunner, was from Chicago and in the kennel business. He and I didn't hit it off at first but many shared dangers caused us to be fast friends after awhile. He was a handsome, erect fellow, completely serious and more than a little bit aristocratic - not the usual tail gunner. Most of them were pee-wees. Ward was very proud of his Scotch ancestry and once on a trip to Scotland had his portrait made in the full Scottish regalia of Clan Graham. George Kepics, the ball-turret gunner, was of Hungarian descent and lived to gamble. He was from Trenton, New Jersey. We didn't like him much at first, because he was a wise guy. George was a typical Dead End Kid who knew all the answers. We tended to shun him and were inclined to be apologetic about him around the other crews. Our original estimate of him was completely erroneous; he was very courageous and dependable. He finally became one of us, the catalyst being the shared experience of aerial combat. Theodore McDevitt, the bombardier, was a dapper lad from Soledad, California, somewhat older than the rest of us. Mac was a jolly well-rounded person, easy-going and well liked. Sometimes there would be a malfunction in the toggling mechanism or the bombs would hang up in the bomb bay for some reason. When this happened, we gave Mac plenty of hell about it. It didn't faze him. We didn't care where he dropped the bombs just so he dropped them. It was always a relief to get the bombs away. After our disastrous eighth mission I seldom flew with Mac. We usually used a sergeant togglier.

"Our co-pilot, Stan Fisher was a handsome dark-eyed boy from Baltimore who was a little sensitive about his prominent nose. He possessed enormous good humor and was constantly exploding in laughter and giggles. Girls liked Fish and he was usually surrounded by a bevy of the soft creatures. He was a snazzy dresser, faultlessly groomed always. Fish was the first one of us to wear one of the sharp, new Eisenhower jackets, specially tailored for him. The airmen had been wearing these unofficial jackets long before Eisenhower decided to ape them. Fish also had a pair of English-style shoes with straps and buckles. He bought a beautiful fur parka at Goose Bay on our Trans-Atlantic crossing and always wore it when he was flying. We envied Fish mightily; as he was the closest thing to a playboy we had ever seen. We did not take him seriously for the simple reason that he seemed never to be serious. When Chick was wounded later, we didn't much want to fly with Fish, but we had no choice. I did not know that Fish knew this, but he has since reminded me of it in a letter. As so often happens, he got serious in a hurry when he had the entire responsibility for us. Fish was a little excitable but a good performer. He saved our necks a couple of times - no small thing.

"In the early hours of morning, the door flew open and this cheery soul named 'Fluke' [the CQ] came in, switched on the lights and started calling off the crews who were to fly the day's mission. He yelled, 'Cecchini's Crew' and my heart sank within me. I felt like a condemned man. Bachy was the first man up. He would head for Alvin's bunk, ripping the cover oft and say, '*Get up, Alvin. Ve haf to go fight der Fuhrer to-day!*' Alvin thought it was no time for levity and would flail away at Bachy with all his might, Bachy skipping just out of his reach. Flying a mission didn't seem to bother Bachy at all. The little fellow showed no outward signs of stress. He was still flying when I left the 303rd and went on to complete 52 combat missions, being decorated with the Silver Star and two Distinguished Flying Crosses.

"We donned our flying coveralls, heated suits and boots and headed to the mess hall down the road where the cooks were putting on a mission breakfast. The chefs were very solicitous, seemingly jovial. We could have pancakes, eggs sunny-side up or any way we wanted them. Sort of like, 'It's your last meal. You can have what you want.' To me it seemed a somewhat macabre occasion and I found their jollity very disquieting and out of place. I could eat none of the breakfast anyway. Even to this day I have butterflies before breakfast.

"All of the crews, officers and non-commissioned officers were briefed together. The radio operators were also given a separate briefing at which time they received a canvas packet with coded data called a 'flimsy.' In the main briefing hall the target remained covered until the Intelligence Officer came in. He was a dapper individual, sporting a mustache and quite hearty in manner for a good reason: he didn't have to go. These intelligence officers were non-flying personnel with some useful information and a lot that was useless. His first move was to peel back the cover from the map, an act, which was always met with a loud groan from the assembled crews. They were a lively bunch and time had to be allowed for them to get over the initial shock, sound-oft and 'cuss' a little while. After a time they subsided and he began. We could see that the red lines pinned on the map went deep into Germany. The target was the Heinkel plant at Oranienburg in the suburbs of Berlin. We were told that we could expect heavy fighter opposition, with flak at the target described as 'intense.' In other words, the target was heavily defended. We could see from the diagram that we were flying Tail-end Charlie in the high squadron. There would be a lead squadron, a low squadron and a high squadron.

"Catholic boys were receiving the Sacrament from the priest, Father Skoner. He was very popular with Protestants and Catholics alike, with none of the phony piety often found in clergymen, just one of the fellows.

"The briefing was over. We got up and started out. We climbed onto lorries and headed out for the hardstands where the Forts were parked. The ground crews swarmed over our B-17 getting it ready. The armorers were arming the bombs in the bomb bay. It was still pitch dark.

"We put our machine guns into their casings and attached the gun belts. When this was done, we went to the dispersal tent and lay down on the canvas cots, which were there for that purpose. We tried to log a little sack time before 'Start Engines;' the signal was a flare from the control tower.

"These quiet moments in the dispersal tent were always the worst part of the mission for me. I was always afflicted with an unbearable sadness at this time. I can still hear the clanking coughs of the aircraft engines as they struggled manfully in the damp mist and then caught up. We were on board and soon taxiing out in trail until we reached the end of the runway. Every 30 seconds a Fort would gun its engines and hurtle down the runway into the darkness. Finally, it was our time. We always sweated take-oft as we were heavily laden with gas and bombs.

"We climbed through the mist on a certain heading until we reached a predetermined altitude. At ten thousand feet Chick told us to go on oxygen. Thereafter, we had periodic oxygen checks with each position checking in. We learned the value of this on a later mission when the ball-turret gunner did not check in. We pulled him out of the turret unconscious and almost dead. His hose had become disconnected.

"At the appointed altitude the aircraft orbited around an assembly beacon, a ground installation emitting a signal. Each pilot knew his place in the formation from briefing. Take-off was in the same order. It remained only to locate the squadron leader or assembly ship. He would be firing a combination of flares like red-green. When the pilot saw his color, he joined up, tacking onto the leader in his proper slot while continuing to orbit. When all the aircraft were in the combat box, it headed out towards the North Sea or English Channel depending on where the mission was going. This is an oversimplification of the procedure, but it's basically how it was done.

"During all of this time there was complete radio silence, as the German interceptor stations were monitoring constantly. Looking back, I doubt if we ever fooled them. The planners would go to extreme lengths to conceal the mounting of a mission, but I doubt whether they could conceal something of that magnitude. I imagine the Germans had ample notice from their own agents in England of every mission we flew. I don't remember their ever being asleep when I visited Germany.

"So far I was fine. It was a bright, clear day marred only by the contrails of the bombers ahead of us in formation. I can recall a certain amount of exhilaration and pride. The great battle formations were something to see! As far as the eye could see there were B-17s, some of them olive drab F's; others, the new silver G's.

"The scene was innocuous enough. Nothing about it even hinted of danger. A formation of P-38's slanted overhead adding to my feeling of security. It seemed that we had been flying for hours without incident. We chatted a little on the intercom until Chick told us to shut up. I heard it before I saw it. Whomp-Whoosh. Simultaneously, the bombardier shouted, 'Flak, 12 o'clock. Christ, look at it!' By then we were at the IP and turning on the bomb run. A rush of cold air blasted the radio room as the bomb bay doors came open. The plane began to lurch and reel with the continuous explosions. Now I could see it. Oily, black bursts with crimson blossoms in the center. Everywhere. There were literally thousands of bursts as far as the eye could see. I was throwing *Chaff* out of the chute to confuse the German anti-aircraft radar and aiming devices. I couldn't see that it did any good at all. They had our range perfectly. It did keep me occupied, however.

"Just before Bombs Away a moving shadow caused me to look up through the open radio hatch. A bomber had moved directly above us. Horrified, I was looking directly into his bomb bay. I called the pilot and we slid over in the nick of time. The bomber lurched as the bombs went away. I stood up in the door of the bomb bay to see if the bombs had all gotten clear. As soon as I did, a jagged piece of shrapnel sliced the command radio set in two and struck me directly in the chest. I was wearing a metal flak vest, which was all that saved my life. It spun me around and stunned me momentarily. I saw that I was bleeding. A piece of spent metal had lodged in my neck and this was where the blood was coming from. I was not badly hurt and felt no pain at all, but I had had a close shave.

"A great column of smoke was coming up as we turned away from the target and headed for home. I felt that the worst was over, but we were in for some more excitement. The group strayed over Braunschweig, (Brunswick), which was not on our itinerary and got flakked again. This was not barrage flak. These gunners were really good and they were shooting at US. It was a chilling sight to see flak bursts directly ahead of us marching toward our bomber. At the last minute Chick would take violent evasive action and the last burst would explode beneath us. The formation was wallowing all over the sky. Not only were we dodging flak, but also we were trying desperately not to collide with other aircraft. We were finally out of their range and glad to be so.

"As a youngster I had stood on the edge of dove fields at daylight on frosty mornings and watched the doves coming to feed. They came in at great speed, dipping and darting and were laughingly called 'blue whistlers.' As soon as one was spotted, everyone had a go at him, but sometimes he made it through and flew on out of the field. It was a sad sight when one of those proud, beautiful birds crumpled up and pitched to earth. As the B-17s flew through the maelstrom of flak, I knew exactly how that poor dove must have felt. The guns were larger and so were the birds, but it was the "dove field" just the same. From this first mission on I never again had the feeling that we were out of danger until my feet were solidly placed on terra firma.

"Eventually we crossed the enemy coast and started letting down from altitude. It was a relief to take off the oxygen mask and relax a bit. I ate a Clark bar and felt better at once. We had been on oxygen for about eight hours. The hydraulic system was damaged; so we knew we were going to have some problems getting down. Fortunately, we were using the long runway. We touched down; and, after slowing a bit, Chick headed her off the runway onto the grass. We circled to the right, kept circling, slowing gradually; and finally she gave up the ghost and stopped. We got out and looked her over. It was unbelievable. We had taken a savage mauling and she was one more lacerated lady. That morning our bomber had been a lovely girl without blemish. The ground crews could do wonders with a shot-up B-17 but they had their work cut out for them with that one. Sometimes when one was shot up too badly, they made her a 'hangar queen' and cannibalized parts off her. I remember the ground crew laid some rueful looks on us.

"Lieutenant Holdcroft's crew did not return from the mission, the only casualty from our squadron. The mission would have wound up their tour of operations. We learned later that they were able to parachute safely and were interned as PoWs. Holdcroft wrote me later that they arrived at *Stalag Luft III* just after the Great Escape took place. The camp was in turmoil as the British prisoners were still at large.[725]

"The first thing we did after the mission was to go back for de-briefing or interrogation. Each of us was given a hefty shot of booze to take the edge off. Then the Intelligence Officer interviewed our crew, making inquiry about missing aircraft, whether parachutes were seen, the intensity of flak along the route and at the target, a description of enemy aircraft encountered and a welter of other subjects.

"The alcohol really got to us fast. I got a few extra shots from some of the others who did not drink. We had been on oxygen for a long time and were very susceptible. This caused us to exaggerate greatly but the IO dutifully wrote down everything we reported. At one of the de-briefings later, we reported some striped flak. It was duly noted.

"Well, I had made it - No.1! There was no panic. I had performed well, even coolly under fire and I had a wound to show for it. I had spent an entire year dreading this time with every fiber of my being. My fears had been imaginary. In a letter to the folks at home I had written about my baptism of fire. I told my mother that I had a slight wound, calling it a 'nice little memento,' and would probably get the Purple Heart. Mother was a great PR person. I was mortified at what happened next. The Waycross *Journal-Herald*, our local newspaper, came out with my senior class picture and a bold caption: War Hero Gets Purple Heart. What was worse, I didn't even get the Purple Heart.

"I was no longer worried about my performance. Now, I had a different kind of fear. I knew that we were in for some rough times. This was a bad scene and far worse than it had been represented to us. We were putting up 36 aircraft and losing one or two of them on almost every mission. Not allowing for those times when the group would have a really bad day, it didn't take a computer to figure what the odds of survival were for a combat crew - almost nil. It was not an encouraging prospect. Under our crew picture I wrote 'ETO champs'. I suppose everyone thought his crew was the best. They were a great bunch."

At Bassingbourn, on the night of 18 April 1st Lieutenant Sam Newton's crew in the 401st Bomb Squadron, 91st Bomb Group, waited to fly the first mission of their tour the next morning. They would fly *The Keystone Mama* to bomb Eschwege airdrome, in the Kassel area, the target for 53 B-17s in the 1st Bomb Division. Co-pilot Bert Stiles wrote:[726]

> "I was well established in the sack when a bunch of guys came in the room and turned the lights on. A bombardier and a navigator were putting their co-pilot to bed, but he'd broken away into my room.
>
> "He was pretty drunk, and he really had the bright stare of death in his eyes.
>
> "'So you made the team?' this co-pilot said.
>
> "I said, 'I guess so.' I was about half asleep.
>
> "All he did was laugh, just stand there and laugh, until the whole room was full of it, and shaking from it.
>
> "The bombardier and navigator got him under control then and took him away to bed. The bombardier came back after they put him away.
>
> "'That baby's got it bad,' he said. 'He won't last much longer. He's seen too many guys go down.'
>
> "When the lights were out again I lay there for a while, not ready to go to sleep.
>
> "...Nobody saw the fighters. They came out of the sun, and they only made one pass. One Fort blew up and one went down burning. La French was one of them and the drunken co-pilot that woke me up the night before was in the other.
>
> "'That poor bastard could see it coming,' somebody said.
>
> "'He knew it was his turn."
>
> "They were talking about that co-pilot.
>
> "But La French wasn't like that. He was all alive the last time I saw him. He rode that bike of his like it was Seabiscuit. And now he was just blood and little chunks of bones and meat, blown all over the sky. Or he was cooked, burned into nothing."[727]

Stiles said, "You don't remember much when the missions come fast." And they did. After the first two weeks it seemed to the co-pilot that he had been in the ETO "a hundred years, and all time before that was just a dream." Newton's crew were alerted eight days straight and they flew six missions, were called back once, and had an abortion in that time. On 20 April they flew a short mission in *Mary* to Croisette Beauvoir, near Calais, and then took *Cool Papa* to Erding, near Munich, on their third. *Cool Papa* was Sam Newton's name. In school everyone had called him "cool papa" because he was such a major operator. Stiles wanted to name the B-17 *The Witcherlybitcherly* or the *Nancy Moonshine*, and his mother wanted the crew to name it *Colorado Colleagues*, because they went to Colorado College. Most of the crew wanted to name it *Mary Helen* in honor of Newton's sister-in-law, who traveled from Omaha one night to visit them in Grand Island. Stiles had thought that she was "about the best-looking dame in the world." Newton's crew flew the *Cool Papa* to bomb Franscaty airfield, near Metz, on the 25th, and flew over the Zuider Zee again to Brunswick on the 26th. Two days later they flew *Cool Papa* to Avord to hit another airfield on their sixth. A short leave in London followed. When they got back to Bassingbourn the first thing they did was to sign in at the orderly room. One of the sergeants told them that *Cool Papa* had gone down at Troyes, France, with Lieutenant Albert F. McCardle's crew on 1 May. It had been hit by flak.[728] Stiles recalled that while they were in London *Cool Papa* was supposed to have her name painted on with a picture of "a dame with no clothes." It did not matter what the name meant. "The *Cool Papa* lived a short life."

Ben Smith's second mission, meanwhile, was a "so-called milk run to Cherbourg":

> "I did not consider any missions milk runs, since we frequently lost aircraft on these supposedly danger-free excursions. We opened the bomb bay doors before we reached the coast and during the bomb run we were exposed to some ferocious flak. On the next mission [Saturday, 22 April] we bombed marshaling yards at Hamm in the Münster-Essen area and put up a pretty good show. It had been a formidable target in the past. The mission started late because of bad weather; so we were after dark getting back."

The Hamm mission was the first flown by 2nd Lieutenant Charles D. Peritti's crew in the 68th Bomb Squadron, 44th Bomb Group.[729] The navigator was 2nd Lieutenant John W. McClane Jr., from Niagara Falls, New York, who though he turned 21 years old on 18 March 1944 looked more like 17. He had to get used to being asked by perfect strangers, "How old are you?" McClane recalled:

> "My pilots were ideally selected, as were our flight engineer, radioman and gunners. I had the one job that I was born to hold. I loved navigation and nothing was more enjoyable to me than my position. One could walk into a room full of air men and in a short time pick out with considerable accuracy who held what position just by observing the mannerisms of those present. Navigators were easy to sort out. Just look for a hypersensitive guy, someone who can't hold still one minute, an eager beaver asking questions unrelated to the interest of everyone else. It helped to be a little odd but I loved my job. The 'old man' of our crew was S/Sgt Paul M. Corlew at age 32 and the baby was S/Sgt Otho H. Freeman, age 19. 2nd Lieutenant John F. Warga our bombardier and our belly gunner, S/Sgt Charles J. Alexander (who we called 'Swoose' after the popular song of the day, 'Alexander the Swoose') were the whiskey drinkers in our crew. On our way over the South Atlantic while we were at Fortalaga in Brazil, Warga bought a 5-gallon wooden barrel of whiskey. But even

they could not drink the Brazilian rot-gut, as it was too strong. The only thing it was fit for was to start the coal fire in the pot belly stove in our hut at Shipdham; it must have been 500% proof, as it was as effective as gasoline. [730] Warga, who was as strong as an ox, not only could hold his liquor better than any one else in our crew (and perhaps the whole squadron) but the girls seemed to fall all over themselves about him. Every crew has to have someone who can be AWOL for three days and show up one minute before roll call. Anyone else, especially me, could be AWOL one minute and miss the same roll call. Warga often came to briefing with a severe hangover. He would stay awake long enough to get his bombing instructions and reach the flight line.

"At briefing I was told to look for 'light lines' the British had set up on the ground to lead us home. Each light had it's own code. Before take off I spread my navigation equipment out on the ground. While going over the maps, perhaps talking to the bombardier, I became cognizant of someone trying to get my attention. Just as I looked up, I caught a full slash of water in my face. It was the Group Chaplain asking God to look after us as we began our combat tour. Later I was to know why there are no atheists in combat. On many missions I had good reason myself to pray for God to spare us just this one more time. I will never understand why God answered this prayer for some and so many others were required to give their all."

Hamm was also the first mission for Lieutenant Abe Dolim who, with his pilot Lieutenant Joe Hamil and Sgt George Kelch made up the numbers in Lieutenant Scannell's crew. "This was typical of first mission assignments, mixing new replacements with seasoned crews" recalled Dolim:[731]

"We took off at 1400 hours in beautiful CAVU[732] weather topped with high cirrus clouds. On VHF I heard a weird chatter unfamiliar to me, code names like '*Fireball*', '*Vampire Violet*', '*Clambake Yellow*', '*Hotshot Red*' (our group code) and '*Rotate*' (our squadron code) badgered the radio waves. As we assembled over '*splashers*' and '*Bunchers*,' the sky became dotted with colored flares, singles and doubles, while hundreds of aircraft tacked on to flights, squadrons and groups. Finally, after more than an hour of forming, we took our place at the lead of the 4th Combat Wing and the entire Eighth Air Force, proceeding at 130mph indicated air speed.

"Our fighter escort of P-47s and P-38s picked us up just north of Ijmuiden on the Dutch coast. There were no reports or enemy fighters as we turned at the initial point (IP) and opened our bomb bay doors for the bomb run. From the IP onward, there was absolutely no evasive action. We saw the flak before we spotted the target. The 88mm explosions look like double black mushrooms as though the shell explodes in the middle and works itself out at both ends vertically. The railroad marshaling yard at Hamm, the checkpoint to 'Happy Valley' (The Ruhr) is 3½ miles long, the largest in Germany, so large that we bombed in combat wing formation - three groups abreast. Flak was not too accurate and we were lucky to be first over the target. Our bombs blanketed the yard; only a few appeared to go astray.

"Either the extreme cold at -40C or the tension caused me to pass water frequently. I discovered that no one used the relief tube in the bomb bay for two good reasons. First, the trip with an oxygen bottle is too much and second if one does use it but does not notify the ball turret gunner to rotate to 6 o'clock, his windscreen is very neatly frosted. We used empty bomb fuse containers with which we were very generously supplied by the armorer-gunners. The filled cans froze quickly and were stacked alongside a bulkhead until they were thrown out during the bomb run.

"As we turned off to the rally point, I looked toward 5 o'clock and saw a sky full of flak with two B-17s in trouble, one in a shallow dive afire and the other exploding after a short vertical dive. I watched several parachutes descend to German soil, then looked for my chest pack - it was not within reach. I made a note to stack it between my position and the emergency hatch against the bulkhead next to my navigation table. The trip back was uneventful, the 94th suffering no losses. My ears began to ring from the engine noise." [733]

2nd Lieutenant John W. McClane Jr. recalls:

"As navigator, it was not my duty to man a gun but I certainly did like the nose turret as it gave my navigation compartment much protection from frontal attack. On both take off and landing, I vacated my forward navigation compartment to stand behind the pilot. I would hold on to a steel protection plate at his back. This gave me an excellent view of take off and landing. If a crash situation were to develop, I was to sit on the floor with my back to the steel plate, my knees pulled up and my hands behind my head, which I would brace also against the steel bulkhead. Flak was moderate and fighters were few but the 68th Squadron did claim one. The thing that stands out was the return trip. As our formation approached the Channel, a single B-25 twin engined plane was flying about 10,000ft below us and on the same course. We were at 20,000ft. Smoke and flame were coming out of its port wing. I watched the crew bale out but the plane continued to fly on autopilot for several minutes before it exploded and a huge ball of orange flame and black smoke filled my sight. 'Poof', the plane was gone. This B-25 was the first of many planes I was to see on my tour of combat explode before my eyes.

"We crossed the sea as dark settled in. I soon began to pick up the 'light lines' and I had no problem whatsoever in navigating. We reached our field and Peritti landed using his wing lights. We had flown six hours. None of us thought this unusual until we saw what was happening. As we got out of the plane, we could see planes landing at nearby fields also using their wing lights but a number were exploding on the approach at their home bases east of us. At the time we could not imagine what was happening. The next day we were told that 15 Me 410 fighter planes had infiltrated our bomber stream as we crossed the Channel. They simply lined up their gun sights between the wing lights of a bomber on its approach to land and had a field day, like shooting fish in a barrel."

The eleven B-24 groups in the 2nd Bomb Division sped back to England as darkness descended, and were still over the North Sea at the official blackout time of 2138 hours. Unbeknownst to the crews, they were being chased by several Me 410A-1 *Hornisse* (Hornet) intruders of II./KG 51 *Edelweiss*. Led by their commander, Major Dietrich Puttfarken, KG 51 had taken off from Soesterberg, Holland, to infiltrate the returning bomber stream.[734] The attackers were aided in their approach by the American formation, which turned on their lights as darkness descended. It was so dark that the KG 51 fighter crews incorrectly identified their targets as RAF Halifaxes! One of the first victims was *Cee Gee II* in the 453rd Bomb Group, 735th Bomb Squadron at Old Buckenham, which was credited to *Leutnant* Nommining of II./KG 51, who blasted the Liberator 15 miles off the east coast. 1st Lieutenant James S. Munsey, whose B-24 was named in honor of his daughter Carole Geane, and his co-pilot Lieutenant Robert O. Crall sacrificed their lives so that their crew and companions might bale out from the flaming B-24. As *Cee Gee II* crossed the coast the fuel tanks exploded, blowing three crewmembers out, while five others were able to jump. Since the interphone system was gone, Munsey was unable to determine whether all his crew had jumped, and with complete disregard for his own safety, he remained at the controls until he no longer had sufficient height to bale out. Bob Crall, although ordered by Munsey to *get his butt* out of the airplane, said, *Well I'm staying with it too*. Munsey and Crall died together.[735]

In an instant, a 448th Bomb Group B-24 flown by 1st Lieutenant Cherry C. Pitts fireballed, plunged into the sea, and vanished beneath the waves with all ten crew. William E. Ruck, radio operator of *Ice Cold Katie*, piloted by James J. Bell, recalls:

"We didn't know that Me 410 night fighters had followed us back to England because it was full dark and they were apparently using clouds as cover. However, the English anti-aircraft batteries knew they were there because they showed up on radar. So a situation developed where English AA batteries were firing at the German night fighters who were firing at the American bombers who were firing at the German fighters. It was mass confusion on a grand scale and no one could say who caused damage to which planes. The first plane to attempt to land at Seething was *Peggy Jo* in the 714th Bomb Squadron. Following standard procedure, it turned on its landing lights as it approached Seething, which was the signal for the tower to turn on the runway lights. With its landing lights on the plane made an excellent target and the German fighters simply followed the runway lights and fired at a point between the two landing lights of the plane. The bomber's starboard engine was set afire, forcing the pilot[736] to pull up so the crew could bale out and the bomber crashed at Worlingham just beyond Seething. The second plane to come in was the *Vadie Raye* and she was on fire. Most of the crew had baled out but the pilots, Captain Alvin Skaggs and Captain William Blum, brought the plane down on the main runway, then swerved it off and into the field so it wouldn't block the landing of the following planes. The remainder of the crew got out and ran to safety just before the *Vadie Raye* exploded. The explosion and fire produced dense smoke, which blew across and greatly reduced visibility on the main runway."

Captain William G. Blum, who was also Command Pilot, wrote:

"Dusk fell as we were coming home from a raid on Hamm. It was almost impossible to see. Suddenly, I saw tracers shooting past from the rear. Our ship sort of shuddered as machine gun bursts hit us. I looked out and saw three black Junkers 88s peeling away from us. Our No.2 engine started to burn. Later, three crewmen baled out over England. As we came in flames were still shooting out of the engine and there was a big fire in the bomb bay. While we were still rolling 70 to 80mph three jumped out but no one was hurt. 1st Lieutenant Don Todt, navigator and two others went up through the top hatch and rolled out over the wing. It was a miracle they were not killed. The enemy fire had severed the gasoline line and it was dripping into the bomb bay, which already was burning like an inferno. Sergeant George Glevanik sat down on the catwalk and held the ends of the line together with his hands. That was all that kept us from blowing up."[737]

William E. Ruck continues:

"The third plane to come in [*The Ruth E.K. Allah Hassid*] landed safely, but was strafed as it rolled up the runway. The crew got the plane to the end of the runway, but because of the strafing, they abandoned it there and ran for the safety of a revetment. Our plane, *Ice Cold Katie*, was the fourth plane to land and as we came in on our final approach we could see the smoke from the *Vadie Raye* but, because of the smoke, we couldn't see the plane stopped at the end of the runway. We experienced some strafing as we rolled up the runway and it wasn't until we passed through the smoke from *Vadie Raye* that we were able to see the plane blocking the runway ahead. The pilots were able to stop *Ice Cold Katie* just short of that plane and, because of the strafing; we left the plane and ran for the relative safety of a revetment. The fifth plane to come in [*Tondelayo*] got down safely. But as it passed through the smoke from *Vadie Raye*, it found two planes blocking the end of the runway and was not able to stop before slamming into the tail of *Ice Cold Katie*, forcing it into the plane in front. When the pile up stopped the crew of this plane jumped out and ran for the revetment. One of the gunners somehow caught his parachute in something as he jumped out of the waist window and the ripcord was pulled. In the midst of the disaster and strafing we all had to laugh as we watched him run for safety with his parachute spilling out behind him. Now there were three planes blocking the end of the main runway and one on fire beside it, so the rest of the group had to land on the short runway. The strafing continued for what seemed like a long time, but it must have been just minutes, then the German fighters were gone from Seething."[738]

The B-17s generally avoided the intruder strikes, which were concentrated on B-24 bases in Norfolk and Suffolk. However, some 3rd Bomb Division bases in the vicinity also came under attack, as Bill Carleton, Engineering Officer at Thorpe Abbotts, remembers:

"At about 9 o'clock the planes of the B-24 base near us were late in returning from Hamm. As a result, it was necessary to turn on the runway lights. When those poor fellows started on their final approach they were shot down by the Jerries like sitting ducks. While all our planes were in, we were a little careless with our blackout and at least one German saw the lights near our Operations Building. He strafed the building as well as part of the field, but no one was hurt. Our perimeter defense threw themselves into action along with ninety percent of the base personnel, all of whom carried either a carbine rifle, a Browning automatic machine-gun or a Colt .45. A few minutes later a B-24 flew over and our perimeter defense opened up along with hundreds of other guns. Fortunately, they were all poor shots and the plane was not hit, but I quickly surmised it was getting pretty dangerous on the ground. Strafing was one thing, but to have 4000 'dingalings' shooting into the air was too much. I ran for cover in my newly-dug foxhole, tripped over the mound of dirt and fell into the hole on top of Sgt Spangler, the line chief, who had evidently taken refuge some time earlier!"

The wreckage, considerable at some bases, was cleared away and conditions returned to normal. Time was now fast approaching when the Allies could look ahead to the momentous day when the Allies would invade "Festung Europa."[739] The 8th Air Force was further strengthened, and preparations were begun immediately to get the new Groups operational in time for D-Day.[740] When that day was no one knew for certain. But it was imminent, and the three Bomb Divisions and fighter groups had to be prepared for a maximum effort when the fateful day finally arrived. During April, despite the obvious drawbacks in mixing two different types of heavy bomber—the B-17 and the B-24—six new B-24 groups joined the 3rd Bomb Division. Doolittle wanted to bring the 8th up to full strength using just B-17s, but there were simply not enough to go around. In contrast, by the late spring of 1944 five B-24 plants in America were producing more than enough Liberators. This uneasy marriage was to last only four months, by which time Doolittle had gone some way to achieving his all-B-17 force.[741]

On Monday, 24 April, 750 bombers were despatched to bomb aircraft plants in the Munich area, while in Italy another strong bomber force hit targets in the Balkans. Perry Rudd was in the 457th Bomb Group formation that struck at Erding, northwest of Munich:

> "There was no flak over the target but the fighters really gave us the works. I saw two B-17s go down. One had a direct hit on the vertical stabilizer and we could see right through it. There were lots of 109s that succeeded in breaking up a couple of our formations. Over Augsburg, Lechfeld and other towns nearby you couldn't pick out the formations for flak. One group struggled over Münster and had the heaviest concentration of flak I had ever seen. It blotted out the sky."

Ralph Reese, left waist gunner in *Smoky Liz* in the 452nd Bomb Group, recalls the mission, his 9th, to the Focke Wulf and Dornier plant:

> "We were awakened at 0330. Breakfast was at 0415. Briefing 0500. We took off at 0805 and departed the coast at 1110. Our 42 100lb incendiaries were away at 1315 from 24,000ft. Flak was very heavy over the target as our No.3 engine was hit, so our pilot tried to feather the prop but it failed. The prop kept windmilling and vibrating like a threshing machine. Finally the cowling and part of the prop hub flew off. Everyone grabbed his chute and was ready to jump upon the command. With the loss of one engine, we could not keep up with the formation, so became a straggler. Fortunately, we had fighter escort, as our No.1 engine had a two-inch flak hole and No.2 engine was leaking oil. We were in a tight situation, like 'Coming in On a Wing and A Prayer'. We were gradually losing speed and the fighter escort had to leave. Shortly, we saw fighter planes coming in on us 6 o'clock and we started firing away. The fighter planes tipped their wings to signal they were friendly instead of enemy. They turned out to be British fighters and they escorted home. We thought we would have to crash land but the pilot brought *Smoky Liz* in to a fine landing at 1715 hours. Battle damage was 101 flak holes, one large hole near my foot and two holes in the bombardier's dome."

The 41st Bomb Wing, which bombed the Dornier repair and assembly plant 15 miles south of Munich, bore the brunt of the attacks carried out by an estimated 200 enemy fighters. Of the wing's 15 losses, the 384th Bomb Group suffered the worst casualties, losing seven aircraft before the *Luftwaffe* turned its attention on the 40th Combat Wing. The 92nd Bomb Group, which achieved excellent results in the bombing of the Dornier assembly plant and repair works at Oberpfaffenhofen, 15 miles south of Munich, lost five bombers in the resulting aerial battle.[742] Thirteen B-17s landed in Switzerland this day from the total loss of 39 bombers.[743]

On 25 April almost 300 bombers blasted marshaling yards at Mannheim and airfields in France. The next day 292 heavies bombed Brunswick after thick cloud prevented bombing at primary targets. Nearly 50 more bombed targets of opportunity in the Hildesheim-Hanover areas. For the first time, on 27 April, when the 8th flew two bombing missions in one day and the following day, the heavies bombed targets chiefly in France. The 44th Bomb Group's afternoon mission was to the key marshaling yards at Chalons-Sur-Marne, south of Rheims, 60 miles east of Paris, one of the most vital marshaling centers between Paris and Germany. 2nd Lieutenant John McClane recalls:

> "We launched 25 planes as our part of almost 600 for the total of the day. (The morning effort was 20 planes to Moyenneville, France with the loss of one to enemy action.) A total of 72 aircraft attacked, from the 44th, 392nd and 445th Groups. Intelligence had reported a loaded ammunition train there. Our bomb load was 12 500lb bombs. Take off was after 1600 hours. The trip to the target was uneventful with no enemy aircraft attacks. The weather was beautiful and visibility unlimited. As we approached at 20,000ft the flak was moderately heavy but our bombardiers held us steady on course. Because the bombs fell in a large arc the bombardier released them some distance before we would fly over the target area. I heard 'Bombs Away', felt the plane lurch upwards as the load lightened and as one of my duties, pushed the salvo handle under my desk to release any bombs that might fail to fall or a result of water freezing the electronic latches.
>
> "I never failed to watch the bombs fall as I had the best view to see in all directions of any crewmember. My bubble windows on either side of my navigator compartment afforded full visibility straight down as well as forward, outward and to the rear. Just as our bombs began to walk across the assigned MPI, a most astonishing thing happened. I can't really describe what I saw but I'll try. Suddenly a blinding flash of light of brilliant silver, yellow and red exploded before my eyes. We were directly over an ammunition train when it blew to bits. Many locomotives and 600 railroad cars were disintegrated. A mile of track 200 yards wide was torn from the earth. I let out a yell and tried to describe to the rest of the crew what I was witnessing. I must have been very excited as my pilot asked me to calm down but I couldn't. As we left the target area, a huge mushrooming cloud began to rise. It was at 15,000ft in a few minutes and finally reached our flying altitude of 20,000 before we lost sight of it. No one else in the crew saw it explode - not even Warga our bombardier. For days I kept trying to tell the crew what I had seen until they all got fed up with my foolishness.[744] There were no incidents on the return to home base and we landed at 2100 hours after 5 hours and 40 minutes in the air. This was a bit late as the experience of 22 April had taught us."[745]

On 28 April the 100th Bomb Group bombed a *Noball* site at Sottevast, near Cherbourg. John A. Miller, right waist gunner in Lieutenant Larry Townsend's crew, was one of many at Thorpe Abbotts who could not believe his luck, as he explains:

> "A milk-run! The briefing officer described our mission and our route and it really sounded sweet. We would start our run over the water and only be over land a few minutes. 'There are only about eight guns there that will be able to reach you,' he said. Wow! This was really great! We wondered how the 'Bloody Hundredth' happened to get such a soft mission. Colonel Robert H. Kelly, fresh from the States, had just joined our group as CO on 19 April. At the morning's briefing he stood up and told us, 'There'll be no evasive action when we're on the bomb run.' Jack Swartout, a squadron CO, was to be the mission's air commander flying with Bill Lakin's crew but at the last moment Kelly bumped Swartout from Bill Lakin's crew and said he would fly as command pilot.[746] As we left the briefing room you could hear comments that 'Kelly sure picked a sweet milk-run for his first mission.'

"It was a beautiful day. We took off and soon we were starting on the bomb run. The flak was way below us as we made our run and there wasn't much of it. Then on the intercom I heard Townsend say that Kelly had called off the bomb drop and that we would have to go around again. We must have made the longest 360 in recorded history. Kelly took us far out over the water and it took forever. We came back in on the bomb run at the same speed, same altitude and the same course, flying in rigid formation as Kelly ordered. The Kraut flak guns got us good! The Kelly-Lakin lead B-17 received two direct hits, one between the No.2 engine and the cockpit and the second back toward the tail position. The plane disintegrated and fell to earth. Six of the eleven men aboard including Lakin and Colonel Kelly were killed.

"A second Fortress, flown by Lieutenant James W. McGuire, had its No.1 engine knocked from its mounting. The engine landed back on the left wing, setting it on fire. When it was directly in front of me at 3 o'clock there was a puff of smoke. I reported 'It's detonating'. As fast as I said that, it went puff, puff and blew to hell. As he dove out of formation the left wing snapped off and it cracked in two like an egg at the waist. The plane tumbled, a ball of fire, into the clouds below. A chute popped open in that fire. It burned immediately. The way that B-17 went down, the gyrations, how could a bombardier, of all people, get out and live to tell about it? But he did. John Jones, wherever you are, you're a walking miracle! (Six of the crew shared our hut with us in the 349th Squadron and all were KIA).

"The flak over Sottevast was unbelievably accurate! Every plane received hits and damage. Bernard Palmquist, the ball gunner on Ralph W. Wright's crew, was hit, the flak going through his shoulder. He told me later that he had never seen such flak. This was the only time he could actually smell it. [747]

"When we returned to Thorpe Abbotts we were one shook-up bunch of fliers. Major Elton was devastated at the loss of Bill Lakin, his friend and roommate. He was waiting at the hardstand with champagne to celebrate Lakin's last mission and Kelley's first lead. He also lost his line chief, S/Sgt 'Barney' Barnhart, who at forty had begged to fly.

"At interrogation we told our story about the milk-run Colonel Kelly had chosen for his first mission with us. The intelligence interrogators were awed and amazed. One was heard to say, 'Colonel Kelly hasn't even unpacked yet.'"

On Saturday, 29 April, 768 bomber crews throughout East Anglia were awakened early for briefing. At Great Ashfield, one of the 4th Combat Wing B-17 bases, 385th Bomb Group crewmen like Carlyle J. Hanson was one of those who made the mission. Hanson recalls:

"We got up at 0130 for target 'study'. The target was Berlin!"

The day was 2nd Lieutenant Charles D. Peritti's crew in the 68th Bomb Squadron, 44th Bomb Group at Shipdham, as the navigator, Lieutenant John W. McClane, recalls:

"The first two were not too rough and we were a little too complacent. After stumbling through the blackout to the breakfast that morning, the usual question was on everyone's lips, 'Where are we going today?' Was it going to be a 'milk run' over the coast of France or a deep penetration to the heart of Germany? As we filed into the large Nissen hut used for briefing, the men gathered together, as crews, sitting facing a stage with a huge map of Western Europe above it. However this map was securely covered with dark draw curtains. Suddenly the command, 'Attention' was sounded. In unison, all snapped to their feet and in walked the Commanding officer, Colonel John H. Gibson and his staff. The briefing officer stepped forward with a long pointer and the map curtains were quickly drawn open. At this movement we all knew what was our target for the day. The ribbons pinned to the map led straight to the heart of Hitler's Germany, the 'Big B' - Berlin. The howl and commotion could have been heard a block away.

"Finally, everyone settled down and the briefing officers proceeded to detail our objectives. The predicted weather, the expected fighter opposition and flak concentrations were outlined. The various pilots were assigned positions in each section of each squadron of the group. Some were to lead, others were to be wingmen, some were assigned high and others low positions in the formation. And of course, someone had to fly coffin corner, low left rear with the least protection from the guns of the fellow planes in the formation.

"The pilots, bombardiers, navigator, flight engineers, radio men and gunners all went to their own briefing for further details and instructions pertaining to their specific duties. The pilot was in command of the ship but the success of every mission depended upon close teamwork. No one man, crew, flight, squadron, group or Division did it all. In toto we were a powerful Air Force out to do battle with a determined enemy. Our objective was to do maximum damage to today's target. Theirs was to prevent us from reaching the target or to inflict such painful punishment that we would cease trying. The stage was set; the battle would soon begin. Hundreds of men would be either killed, wounded, or missing this day but nothing could stop the mission once it had been set in motion.

"Briefing over, we gathered as crews to be taken by truck out to our planes. Now began an extremely tense period. We would busy ourselves preparing for flight, each man checking what pertained to him. At the same time, we kept an eye on the tower because if the mission was aborted, a red flare would be sent aloft. If it were 'Go', a green flare was used. Today, the mission was 'Go'. The engines were started and we mounted the plane. The moment of truth was at hand. There was no option but to go and only God knew who would return."

At Rattlesden, 447th Bomb Group crewmen like Sgt Louis J. Torretta, a tail gunner, was among those who were flying. Torretta, who was on his 28th mission, recalled "We were awakened at 0230 and the weather looked very bad. But we flew anyway. Later the weather cleared a little." The target was the Friedrichstrasse Bahnhof, the center of the mainline and underground railway system in Berlin. Carlyle J. Hanson again:

"The assembly was rough because the overcast went up to 12,000ft. We were the lead ship in the high squadron of the lead group. After a messy wing assembly, the lead pathfinder went out in the middle of the Channel and the second one took over. It seemed like we got flak all the way in. Everything was covered with clouds. The navigator that was leading us screwed up and we were 25-miles off course and separated from the rest of the formations. We thought we were just going to have flak, which was very heavy, to watch out. We had an escort at the coast but being as we were off course the group that was supposed to relieve them could not find us and the ones that were with us had to leave, as they were getting low on gas. About five minutes later the co pilot called over the interphone and said it looked like a formation of Forts up ahead. Lieutenant Irwin, our bombardier, said, 'Hell, those aren't Forts; they are 109s and 190s.' And then they came in."

Part of the 4th Combat Wing had strayed off course, and near Magdeburg the enemy fighters wreaked havoc among the unprotected formation, shooting down or fatally damaging 18 Fortresses in 20 minutes. Seven of them came from the 385th Bomb Group.

T/Sgt Clarence L. Mossman, left waist gunner in *Worry Bird*, flown by 28-year-old Cleveland, Ohio, pilot Lieutenant Richard A. Spencer in the 549th Bomb Squadron, recalls:

"We were flying a tight formation and all the squadrons seemed to be in their right positions when the German fighters attacked. We did evasive action to help us from head-on attacks. We first spotted about 200 fighters about 12 o'clock high and in a few minutes they attacked us head-on, coming down out of the sun in waves of 40 and 60 at a time and doing barrel rolls right through the formations. They made three passes. Our left and also our right wingman went down. We had a lot of flak damage on our aircraft and also damage to our wing from 20mm shells fired by Me 109s that came down through our formation. All of the crew came through the mission without being wounded or killed."

Carlyle J. Hanson again:

"This undoubtedly was the worst day in my life to date. God answered my prayers for sure. After turning on the IP about 150 enemy fighters struck at us. They looked like a swarm of bees. They made three passes at us, knocking down seven out of our group. Flak was accurate and heavy. We didn't even get over Berlin, as the weather was too bad. It would have been twice as bad if we had of tried it. We dropped our bombs on a town about 30 miles southwest of Big B. I think we plowed up a field. Fred and Bob kept the plane going after #1 engine was knocked out and another was smoking. We got a little flak on the way home. 'One waist gunner was hit in the head by flak but wasn't too serious. A 20mm shell hit #1 engine. Flak flew all over the plane (it looks like a sieve). Knocking out the radio compass. I had my flak suit off and parachute on once and really thought I would be using it. One of the fellows in our barracks went down and it was his first mission. This was Fred's and Tony's 13th and my 14th. Now we sweat out Bob's 12B. It can't be any rougher. Our group lost more planes today than any other day other than their third mission last summer. Brandenburg was the place we hit. Humor for the day was when Jerry was coming in like bees. King hollers out, 'Flak at 3 o'clock!' we had been flying through flak for half an hour. We'd make seven trips to Berlin and they were all nasty."

Worst hit of all the Bomb Groups was the 447th. Sergeant Louis J. Torretta again:

"The first attack about 80 fighters came from 1 o'clock high. Their first pass at us they got Lieutenant [Warren D.] Donahue. He was flying #5 in our squadron. No.2 engine caught on fire and he went down in a steep dive. No chutes were seen.[748] (Every man on that crew would have been finished if they hadn't raised the quota). Then they made another pass and this one came from 10 and 11 o'clock high and low. This time they knocked Lieutenant [Hayden T.] Hughes out of the formation and he fell behind. And about ten of them jumped him and three were seen to bale out. Then he dove for the clouds. He was under control and that is the last we saw or heard of them.[749] The third attack came from 12 o'clock and 6 o'clock low and 9 and 3 o'clock level. This time they got [2nd] Lieutenant [Charles R.] Dowler.[750] Then a 20mm cannon shell hit and blew up in the tail about 16 inches behind me. I was wearing my flak suit and that is the only reason I am here to write this today. The force of the explosion and where it hit pushed me up against the armor plate with such force that it almost knocked me out. I heard the waist gunner call the pilot and say they knocked Torretta out of the tail. Then I could hear the pilot cussing. By this time I was getting my senses back and I tried to call the pilot and tell him I was still with them and that I was all right but my interphone had been hit and I could hear them but I couldn't answer. Finally the smoke cleared out of the tail and I motioned to the waist gunner that I was all right and that my interphone and oxygen was shot out. I switched over to my emergency supply. The waist gunner kept check on me and asked if I was hit. By this time I could feel the warm blood running down my back so I motioned to him that I was hit but I did not think it was serious. A few small fragments of the exploding shell had stuck in my back a little below where the flak suit ended. In all this we got one big hole about a yard in diameter in the tail. Also, a portion of our left wing was blown off and there were a number of small holes. I claimed one fighter destroyed as he blew up almost on top of me. (I am pretty sure he was the one that hit me). Irwin, our bombardier, Kouma our ball gunner, Simon our top turret and myself claimed four destroyed.

"Parachutes were seen all over the sky from our ships and from the Germans also. I had given up all hope of getting back because we were the only ship left in our formation, so I reached back and grabbed my parachute only to find it too was riddled. Then one lone fighter made another attack on us and I started to shoot and I discovered one of my guns was hit by one of the enemy bullets and it wouldn't work. This fighter fired a couple of times and quit I guess he ran out of ammunition. Thank God. That is the only thing that saved us if they would have had enough ammunition to make another attack we surely would have gone down. We had quite a bit of trouble with that left wing but good old Moe, our pilot, pulled us thru again. Boy what a pilot that guy is. I would fly thru anything with him at the controls. Our group put 21 ships up in the air today and eleven of them came back. I guess that is about all. Sure am glad to be back alive from this one."[751]

Perry Rudd, in the 457th Bomb Group formation, says:

"Germany announced the raid as soon as we hit the IP, 18 minutes at least from the target. There was little flak going in but plenty over the target. Their aiming point seemed to be in the lower boxes and we were in the higher box so we didn't get touched. The mission was planned for PFF but we could see the target quite clearly. Plans seemed to change at the last minute and we made a 360° turn near Berlin and went in 30 minutes late. We dropped three 1000lb demolition bombs and six 500lb incendiaries, which hit near a river bridge in the center of the capital. Each plane dropped three tons right on the target. The place must really have taken a beating: three divisions often wings bombed different sections and I saw only one plane go down, right over the target. It was in flames and broke up after a direct flak hit. There must have been 600 planes and even more fighters. I couldn't see how the city could be standing that night."

The 2nd Bomb Division, flying 30 minutes behind schedule, brought up the rear of the bomber stream, and was also met in strength by the *Luftwaffe*. After leaving Celle airspace the only protection afforded the B-24s was a solitary Mustang group, which was forced to retire just after the Liberators completed their bombing run. At the IP *Play Boy*, piloted by 2nd Lieutenant Franklin F. Cotner in the 466th Bomb Group, received a direct hit from an 88, which knocked out the No.3 engine. Cotner completed the bomb run, but *Play Boy* was attacked by fighters after the target and went down over Holland.[752] It was not until the Liberators reached the Dummer Lake on the homeward journey that P-47 Thunderbolt escorts reappeared. German ground controllers, however, seized upon the time lapse and directed over 100 fighters to the Hanover area to intercept. Lieutenant William Moore's B-24 in the 467th Bomb Group, which carried Major Robert Salzarulo, CO of the 788th Bomb Squadron, was shot down over Holland.[753]

2nd Lieutenant John W. McClane in the 44th Bomb Group formation, which sent 21 planes up this day with no aborts, continues:

> "According to '*Stars and Stripes*,' our ETO newspaper, this was the heaviest daylight assault in history on any one target. The Force was made up of 600 four motor bombers carrying almost 1500 tons of explosives and incendiaries. We were escorted by 814 fighters but the Germans were ready with some of the heaviest opposition encountered to date on daylight operations. One wing alone reported being attacked by at least 200 fighters. The resistance met by the various elements of the massive bomber fleet varied widely. Fortunately the 44th Bomb Group was well known by the Luftwaffe pilots as being a seasoned combat outfit and best left alone as long as there were less experienced groups that would be an easier target. A number of German interceptors did test us however, approximately 30 on the way to Berlin and 40 to 50 on the way out. My most vivid memory of the war was burned on my mind when we were approximately halfway to Berlin. Over my earphones came the voice of Paul Corlew, our engineer and top turret gunner, 'Fighters high at 1 o'clock'. I looked out of my astrodome and saw three German fighters circling. One could almost hear the lead pilot say, 'Watch me boys, I'll show you how it is done'. He peeled off into a wide arc so he was at an altitude headed straight for our formation. At this I switched positions so I could look out of my right bubble window, which afforded an excellent view forward, down and to the whole right of our line of flight. As he flew towards us he began to slow roll. I became very fearful as I was looking down his two 20mm wing cannons and with each burst, I saw the orange-red flash of the guns. He appeared to be aimed directly at me and I could not help but wonder where the shells were going. I fully expected the next one to explode in my navigation compartment. I was extremely fearful and yet spellbound at the same time. But what followed the next second or so really put fear into me. As the scoundrel slow rolled towards us, closing at rapid speed, I really became upset. It appeared to me that he was going to crash into our plane with a head on collision. I was petrified. Then suddenly Peritti lifted his wings in a vertical position so he could slice between our right wingtip and the left side of the plane on which we were flying wing. I jerked my head as he flashed by at which time I could easily see the German pilot at our wing tip; he just missed it by inches.
>
> "An awesome sight caught my attention. At the base of the wing of the adjacent plane, right at the inboard motor and fuselage, a large ball of orange flame exploded before my eyes. The whole left wing peeled off and to me, it seemed like an eternity that the plane stood there as if it were flying. It could have only been a few microseconds but the vision was burned in my memory like a still photograph. Then in a flash the plane flipped over on its back as the right wing was still flying. It was a violent motion that skewered the whole axis of flight. As the plane flipped, the force of the action catapulted the waist gunner on the right side out of the gun opening and towards our plane. The arc of his flight through the air put him towards our right wing and he fell between where I was standing at my bubble window and our right inboard motor. He wore only a harness with two nipples. Needless to say, this unfortunate waist gunner had no such opportunity to grab his parachute before he was thrown through the window. As he passed me, at most only a few feet away, he was kicking both feet and grabbing the air with his hands in desperation. Maybe he thought he could grasp our plane in some way to hold on.[754] I watched him plummet towards the ground until my attention went to the wreck of the one-winged B-24 falling through the sky. It was cartwheeling nose over tail over the one wing in a huge windmill spinning motion. All of the other nine men were trapped due to centrifugal force in the plane with no hope whatsoever of getting out, I thought. My eyes were glued to this action, as I watched the wreck tumble end over end for at least 10,000ft.[755]
>
> "I had lost all track of time or anything else that was going on around me when I heard on my helmet earphones, 'Second fighter coming in'. I looked up and saw a second enemy craft repeating what his leader had done. At this point my mind went blank. I was too absorbed in my own thoughts and fears. When I came back to reality we were approaching Berlin. The flak was intense. The defenders had 520 anti-aircraft guns trained in a 20-mile arc on us. The sky was one huge black cloud of exploding metal. The guns fired in batteries of four or so it seemed to me. When it was bursting at some altitude other than our own, we had little to fear but as soon as they zeroed in, trouble was at hand. I never did get over the fright of seeing a flak burst right in front of us. Then a second a little closer and a third even closer yet. With each burst, the plane would almost instantly fly through the black cloud. One could easily sense the cordite smell. At this point you knew the next burst would be inside your plane but with God's help, the burst would be directly behind the tail. This mission was the first time I prayed out loud for God to let me live through the battle. I asked him to let me survive the day. I promised I'd do anything he asked of me if only he would spare me.
>
> "Many planes went down. One slid off to the side in a rather steep dive. (I heard later that it was because they had lost their oxygen supply and had flown low level back to base). We did survive the flak barrage somehow and headed back to England but our troubles were not over by a long shot. We turned into a 100-knot headwind. Our indicated air speed was about 165mph and at 25,000ft and as cold as it was (-60° F) our true air speed was over 200mph. However with a headwind, our ground speed was something just over 100mph. Talk about eternity. This was it. We had 600 miles to go and it would take hours at the ground speed we were flying. Our fighter escort had turned back due to fuel consumption. Many planes were damaged and just would have made it home under the best of conditions but with the delay caused by this strong head wind some just could not make it. I don't know how many planes I saw go down that day on the way to target, over the city and on the way home! I know it was a great many. I saw some explode, others trailing smoke, others with wings on fire and many, many parachutes open as the crews baled out. But one sight stands out above all others on the way home. As we crossed the North Sea, I began to see planes ditching in the water. It was like watching a motion picture. I was so detached from the action! Some of the planes would glide to the gentlest stop and the men would climb onto the wings but others would hit a swell in the water and seem to dive nose first in a crumpled heap. It was obvious that almost no one could survive the shock. British PT boats were on hand to pick up survivors. This was one of the worst days ever for the Eighth Air Force.[756] When we reached base and landed at 1730 hours I actually bent over and kissed the ground, as I was so pleased to be

back. I had been in the air 8 hours and 15 minutes. Now I knew why we were told that if we flew 25 missions at an average of four losses per mission that we had a 100% chance of being shot down."[757]

The losses had a telling effect on those who returned. At Bury St. Edmunds Leo C. Riley, a co-pilot in the 94th Bomb Group, wrote:

"Things are pretty sad around the Nissen 91 today. We started on a raid to the heart of Berlin and had to turn back over Amsterdam. Chism and crew stood by but took off at last minute and have not been heard from since. There is no way to explain our feelings when men we knew and loved as brothers go down. Of course, there is a chance for them. There is always a chance, except for a direct hit and explosion. I never knew before how many times a day one could find time to pray, if one will try."[758]

May marked the beginning of all out raids on the enemy's railroad network in support of the *Pointblank* Directive, although raids also continued against V-1 sites in France. During the morning of 1 May more than 500 heavies were despatched to 23 *Noball* targets in the Pas de Calais, but most of the bombers were forced to abort because of bad weather. In the afternoon, 328 B-17s and B-24s bombing in individual combat wings attacked marshaling yards and railway centers in France and Belgium. It was John W. McClane's fourth mission:

"In the afternoon the 44th Bomb Group dispatched 15 aircraft, there were no aborts. Our target was the marshaling yards at Liège. We were part of the second wave of heavies to proceed over the continent that day. A total of 40 planes of the 2nd Bomb Division were effective over the target. All told 157 tons of bombs were dropped; our load was 8 1000lb bombs. Flak was moderate and the 44th Bomb Group encountered no enemy planes. The bombing accuracy was fair to good. All aircraft returned safely at 1845 hours after 5 hours in the air. The 8th Air Force sent out 328 heavy bombers for the day to seven different targets of which three were MIA along with the loss of three of our escort fighters.[759] This was the 17th straight day of the pre-invasion aerial offensive. General Doolittle announced that US heavies dropped more than 24,000 tons of bombs on German targets in April. There was considerable debate of using heavy bombers on rail targets. One school of thought said light bombers and fighter-bombers should be used in order to save the B-24s and B-17s for more strategic objectives. Also there were concerns for the civilian population in the occupied countries. In the light of 20/20 hindsight, we now know we followed the correct course. One change was made in the bomber formation, however, instead of large groups, a six-plane formation was used. Raids such as on my 2nd mission to Chalon-Sur-Marne, large numbers of planes were required but later such as my 28th mission to a road junction near Rouen it would have been utter folly to use more than six planes in any one formation.

"On 3 May the 2nd Division dispatched the only 8th Air Force planes for the day and then only by three Bomb Groups, the 44th 93rd and the 382nd. Take off was after the noon hour. The total number of planes was fewer than 50 all tolled of which 24 were 44th Bomb Group aircraft. Our particular target was a V-1 site near the railhead of Wizernes, 35 miles west of St. Omer. Bombing was by GH radar led by Pathfinders from the 93rd Bomb Group. There was no Luftwaffe opposition. However flak damaged 15 of our 24 planes but none so seriously that it could not be put back in action within 36 hours. No planes were lost by the 8th Air Force and only three airmen were wounded. Heavy cloud cover prevented an assessment of bombing results. We arrived back to base at 1715 hours after 4 hours and 30 minutes of flying."

Bad weather fronts over the continent halted deep-penetration missions like the one to Brunswick and Berlin on 4 May when 851 B-17s and B-24s were forced to abandon the mission over the Low Countries. John W. McClane recalls:

"Today was my first experience at flying through clouds so dense that we were forced to turn back when approximately half way to our intended target, an aircraft factory near Brunswick. Cirrus clouds up to 23,000ft so frustrated our navigation that the mission was recalled. Some groups encountered stiff enemy aircraft opposition but the 44th Bomb Group saw none nor did we have any flak damage. Our group of 14 planes, with Colonel John H. Gibson in command, led the 14th Combat Wing, which led the 2nd Bomb Division. Not one of 231 B-24s reached the target but 40 of 360 B-17s did bomb. No planes were lost but 16 were damaged with two airmen killed and one wounded. All told, this was a frustrating day. There was much confusion and the day seemed to me that we were in a dream world. The clouds were everywhere. we could not find an opening. The planes in our squadron weaved back and forth due to turbulence but there was a certain beauty due to the very dense contrails. We were credited with a sortie as we penetrated enemy territory for a considerable length of time. I was glad to get home after 4 hours and 45 minutes in the air."

The only raid on 5 May was mounted by 33 B-24s that bombed a V-1 site at Sottevast, and on 6 May 70 Liberators bombed another *Noball* site at Siracourt. Over 90 bombers were prevented from bombing other V-1 sites by thick overcast. It was hardly an inspiring debut for the 398th Bomb Group at Nuthampstead, who made their combat debut this day, just 31 days after leaving Rapid City, Dakota, and only 14 days after arriving in England.

During the morning of Sunday, 7 May, when 1000 American bombers were dispatched for the first time, the B-17s headed for Berlin. They were joined for the first time by B-24s of the 486th and 487th Bomb Groups.[760] Another 342 heavies bombed Osnabrück, Münster, and targets of opportunity. In the afternoon 28 B-24s bombed targets in Belgium. John W. McClane flew his 7th mission, to Osnabrück:

"The 44th Bomb Group dispatched 30 planes to the target, a marshaling yards and locomotive repair shops. Take off was 06:30 hours with no aborts. We carried 52 100lb oil bombs, A total of 165 B-24s carrying 146 tons of bombs reached the target of which one was lost and 23 damaged. The 44th suffered no losses although the flak was heavy over the target and one German fighter did pass through the formation. This was my second mission that was led by a PFF ship carrying *Mickey* H_2X radar. We never saw the target due to heavy cloud formation, which blanketed the area. Bombing altitude was 24,000ft and the temperature ranged at -42°F.

"We landed about 1400 hours after 7 hours and 30 minutes in the air but the day was not over yet. Not only did we have to go through debriefing and critique but Jerry gave us a little scare that night. 'Bed check Charlie,' as we called the German night bomber, paid us a visit about the time we had settled in our barracks for much needed rest. I ran for the air raid shelter, as did most everyone. We were tired after 4 missions in 7 days. Just this day alone in order to take off at 0630 hours, we had been awakened between 3:00 and 4:00 a.m. The orderly, who got us up, shone a flashlight in our eyes when he shook us. I never did get used to it and certainly did not relish it. (The old story goes he also woke up anyone else if he had a smile on his face.) The 8th Air Force also sent the 1st and 3rd Bomb Divisions to Berlin with about 600 B-17 Flying Fortresses. This force dropped 1344 tons of bombs on the Nazi capital losing only eight planes to enemy action. It was the eighth raid by the 8th Air Force on Berlin. All told, it was a good day for the 8th, sending out a grand total of 922 planes with 865 effective in deep penetration of the German homeland, losing only nine planes (1%). This day was special in another way for the 8th Air Force. It was the first time that over 900 heavy bombers were dispatched in one day. For some reason, the Luftwaffe chose not to oppose us as only nine enemy planes were sighted by all groups. 3500 planes of all types struck at the Nazi's from England and Africa inflicting severe punishment to the Axis."

The next day Berlin was again bombed in the morning—this time by 378 B-17s, while 287 B-24s and 49 B-17s hit aircraft factories in the Brunswick area and 29 other heavies attacked targets of opportunity.[761] For John W. McClane in the 44th Bomb Group, it was his first mission to the city of Brunswick, after they had been turned back by weather four days earlier, although, as he recalls:

"We were given credit for a sortie that day even though we never reached the city. Brunswick was an aircraft manufacturing center for the Luftwaffe, as well as a major rail center, 125 miles southwest of Berlin and with a population of 201,000 people. In spite of the Allied bombings, German fighter production was producing the planes they needed. The 44th Bomb Group dispatched 33 aircraft. Lift off was at 0600 hours. One plane turned back so 32 were effective over the target along with another 256 2nd Division Liberators. Our total load was 795 tons of bombs released from 23,000ft using PFF lead. Some reported 10/10ths cloud cover but visibility was at least 5/10ths. As we approached the target area between 150 to 200 enemy defenders made a strong defensive effort, 35 attacking us at one time. The 44th shot down a number of the flyers. Flak was always frightening at Brunswick and today was no exception. We had a good escort of P-38, P-47 and P-51 fighters from both the 8th and 9th Air Forces. The Germans were determined to defend the Reich's skies after their dismal showing the day before. Reports were made that some of the Luftwaffe planes tried to ram our bombers in deliberate collisions and a few succeeded. In all my missions, I never saw a fighter collide with one of our bombers but often I would deliberately not look at the battles going on around me as it frightened me and distracted my navigation. We wore steel flak helmets over our headgear. I would pull the front lip down so I could not see out but I was able to look to the ground to navigate. Peritti would wait until a fighter was lined up to fire at us, then at the last moment lift or drop our plane. The planes behind us would follow his lead in a wave motion. Only God knows where the cannon shells went that missed us. I do not know how many enemy fighters the gunners of our crew claimed but I'm sure we got our share of licks in. When we were in a battle and the guns were firing. I could smell the cordite. It was long after the war before the smell of gun smoke would not bring fear back to me. Also the excitement would make me sweat. I would have a cake of ice on my forehead where my perspiration was coming out from under my helmet. I pulled it off in little chunks.

"We returned to Shipdham about 1300 hours. Our actual flight time was 6 hours and 40 minutes. We were tired; as this was our 5th mission in only eight days but little did we know what was to come before we got any relief. The 44th Bomb Group lost one plane when it crashed at Halvergate, killing two of the crew. None were shot down in the air battles over Germany. All told eleven B-24s were lost, and the B-17s going to Berlin and other cities lost 25 more for a total of 36 for the day. Another 205 bombers were damaged, eight beyond repair. Men known KIA was eight, 15 wounded, and 373 missing. Our fighter losses were 13 in some very fierce dog fights. I would often watch these dogfights. They were usually off at a far distance and at a higher altitude. The contrails would show us the path of the planes as they maneuvered in violent arcs through the sky. Oh, what a beautiful sight to see our fighter escort catch up with us as we winged our way into enemy territory or pick us up on the way out. Sometimes they would fly over us or at our side. The fighter pilots were very cautious on how they would approach us however, never making a direct approach in case our trigger-happy gunner mistook them for the enemy. They would keep out of the range of our guns and rock their wings. The P-47 and FW 190 were very similar, as were the P-51 and Me 109. It was not until they were sure our gunners recognized their silhouette that they would approach our formation. On my 11th mission, I saw one of our P-47s shot down by our bomber force because he failed to observe this identification precaution. The sight that impressed me most was when a flight of P-38 twin tailed fighters would show up to escort us. The effect of this sight would send our internal communication system in a high pitch of approval and gratitude by all the crew. The P-38s were no better than the P-47 or P-51s and maybe not as effective but it was still a beautiful sight.[762]

"We were awakened early on Tuesday 9 May for our third combat mission in three days. This was the 15th straight day the heavies had hit the Third Reich. Fortunately for us, it was not going to be the deep penetration of Germany of our Osnabrück and Brunswick raids on Sunday and Monday. The target was an airfield 35 miles east of Brussels. The Germans had been using it to strike at the RAF with nightfighters. The 2nd Division sent out 290 B-24s with 101 going to St. Trond carrying a total bomb load of 227 tons. We were carrying 52 100lb bombs with instantaneous fuses. (This was the maximum we could carry as we only had 52 bomb shackles in the bomb bay; otherwise we would have had 6000 to 8000lbs of bombs of 500 to 2000lbs each).

"This was a straightforward mission. The sky was very clear with almost unlimited visibility. Our bombardier John Warga, as soon as we took off would curl up in the passageway between the forward compartment and the tunnel to the rear. The forward compartment is where the front gun turret, his bombsight and my navigation desk were located. When necessary, Warga manned the gun turret; otherwise he dozed at my feet. As we would gain altitude, the atmospheric pressure decreased until at 10,000ft we were required to put on our oxygen masks. In the meantime, he would supply us with all the gas we could stand. The fragrance would penetrate my navigation area and go up through the maze of pipes and wires separating my desk from the pilots and co-pilots feet and fill the pilot area and back into the radio and flight engineer's room. Needless to say, we were glad to breathe pure oxygen again. How Warga could be so relaxed as we approached the target area, I'll never know. When we were close to the IP, the initial point before the target where we would begin our bomb run, usually about 15 to 30 miles before bombs away, I would kick him with my left foot and say, 'Warga, wake up - we are coming to the IP.' At this he would become alive. He had to be one of the best bombardiers in the Air Force. He almost never missed. The flak would be exploding all around us and I'd be a nervous wreck but not Warga. He was completely calm. He stayed alert just long enough to see the bombs hit the target and promptly relax on the floor again. Planes could be burning and exploding all around us but who cared? Not Warga. The truth is that he was ideally suited for his job, certainly not navigator or pilot.

"As we were on the bomb run to the airfield at St. Trond, the flak was moderately heavy and at our altitude, which was bad news. This always 'scared me bad.' Why our bombs were set to explode as soon as they left our bomb racks, I do not know. All other times the bombs had a small propeller on the nose that would unscrew as it fell through the air thereby arming the bomb on it's way down. The sight of bombs leaving the nearby planes always fascinated me. We reached the drop point and the bombardiers released the bombs using an interverlometer, a device that let the bombs out one at a time. As they fell, it would appear the bombs were stacked one above the other suspended in space in a long stream, especially when they were stacked 52 high. I was looking directly at one plane when flak set off the bottom bomb. It exploded and set off the one above it which in turn set off the next higher and so on until the last exploded in or very close to the bomb bay. The plane fell out of formation and began to go down with the men baling out. I assumed then that the plane and all the crew were lost but the plane I saw explode was '*Northern Lass*' piloted by Lieutenant. J. P. Ferguson who did bring the badly damaged aircraft back to England and crash-landed at Attleborough. However five crewmembers baled out before the plane was brought under control. We landed before noon after being in the air 5 hours and 45 minutes. We still had to go through debriefing and critique, which took at least two more hours. I was pretty excited over what I had seen."

In all, 772 heavies were dispatched to enemy airfields and transportation targets on 9 May. The B-24s bombed airfields at Florennes, St. Trond, Nivelles, and Hody, as well as the marshaling yards. Major Ronald V. Kramer, 448th Bomb Group, was flying in the co-pilot's seat of Captain Robert T. Lambertson's B-24[763] when it was hit by flak and burst into flames just as they released their bombs on the marshaling yards at Liège, Belgium. All attempts to control the fire proved futile, and the crew were ordered to bale out. Kramer wrote:

"We were at 18,000ft. It looked a long way to the ground but I did not hesitate. I jumped and dropped several thousand feet on my back. There was a terrific jerk after pulling the ripcord. Everything seemed very quiet after the terrific noise a few minutes before. I saw the burning pieces of our aircraft falling and tremendous palls of fire and smoke coming from the target. It was a lonely feeling to see our bombers disappearing in the west when in another hour I knew they would be back at Seething."[764]

On the 11th 973 bombers were dispatched to marshaling yards in Germany and the Low Countries. The 44th Bomb Group "Flying Eightballs" were part of the bombing effort directed against the marshaling yards at Mulhouse, but the primary target was obscured by clouds, so several targets of opportunity were hit. The Liberator[765] flown by 2nd Lieutenant James H. Walsh Jr. was singled out northeast of Châteaudun by *Leutnant* Addi Glunz, CO 6./JG 26, who set the #1 engine afire. The B-24 left the formation "in difficulty" but still under control. Sergeant Joseph O. Peloquin, engineer, recalls:

"The time of day was very close to 1420. It's always been a habit of mine to look at watches when things occur - and I do recall that very well. We were shot down by Me 109s. Our position in the formation was Purple Heart Corner. It turned out to be just that! As an engineer, my position was the top turret and that is where I was just before it all started. Things were rather quiet and as we had a fighter escort, Lieutenant Walsh suggested that I go back and transfer my fuel. It would seem to be a good time as we had used enough from our main tanks to transfer in from the outer cells. And the fuel would be out of the way in case we ran into trouble later and couldn't spare the time. So I went back to the waist section and told Sgt Lawrence Richards to cover my position while I was doing my job of transferring the fuel. I could take his position if anything happened.

"Well, I had just had time to finish and was on my way back to the waist position when all hell broke loose. There was flak banging around us as well as fighters firing at us. One Me 109 hit us in the #2 engine, setting it on fire. Another shell exploded in front of us and blasted my headgear off just as I was scrambling to get my chest chute. Sergeant Puksta helped me to snap it on and that's when I could see that he had been hit also. I opened the escape hatch and told him to jump. He looked at me and said, 'You go first!' The plane was going down and he didn't look too good, so I told him to be damned sure to follow me. Puksta baled out, was captured and become a PoW.

"My experiences are ones that I still have nightmares about. When I jumped, I counted to about ten, - enough to clear the plane. We were at about 15,000ft at that time and I pulled my ripcord - and nothing happened. No chute came out! So I was falling free at 120mph and I tugged and pulled at the flaps on my chute - and finally pulled out a little of the silk or nylon. As I kept pulling, the pilot chute came out and it, in turn, released the main chute. All of this took so long that when it finally blossomed out, I was about 300ft from the ground! This is one of the reasons why the Germans did not spot me coming down. When I landed, I injured my left heel and I, too, had been hit by the shrapnel from that exploding shell that had hit Puksta. I had one in my arm above the elbow and several small ones in my face and another one in my neck, which just missed my jugular vein. This all took place near Patay, a little village about 20 miles from Orleans and known for its association with Joan D'Arc. I met up with Richards a couple of weeks or so after we baled out. To my surprise, we met on a bus, along with our Free French escorts, going to a farm camp in the Forest of Freteval, where the Germans had an ammunition dump and these men all hid out successfully, right under the German noses. When the camp was started, there were only about eight or ten of us, but things changed rapidly and soon there were several hundred of us evadees."[766]

JG 26 next turned their attention to the seventy Liberators of the 486th and 487th Bomb Groups of the 92nd CBW, which was on only its fourth mission. The formation had been briefed to bomb the marshaling yards at Chaumont, but the leading 487th Bomb Group had flown into a flak area near Châteaudun. Both the lead and deputy lead aircraft were shot down, and a third was crippled. Among the missing was the Group CO, Colonel Beirne Lay Jr. He recalled:

"I was riding in the co-pilot's seat and witnessed the explosion of my #3 man's B-24, busy at the time though I was with our own battle damage. The first burst was right in front of the nose… a blinding flash and flames where a B-24 had just been. My biggest worry while Walt Duer and I were evading capture for three weeks was falling into the clutches of the *Gestapo*. They were accountable to nobody and, I knew that they would never believe me when I told them that I, a Group Commander, did not know the date of D-Day (which we did not at that level) and that they would give me the works."[767]

The 303rd Bomb Group went to Saarbrücken to bomb railway marshaling yards. For Lieutenant Anthony J. "Chick" Cecchini's crew of B-17 *Sweet Melody* in the 360th Bomb Squadron, it was their eighth mission. As far as Ben Smith Jr, the radio-operator, was concerned, it was "an odyssey that should rightfully take its place in history alongside those of Ulysses, Jason and the Argonauts."[768] By now, after three missions under his belt, Ben Smith "was beginning to swagger a bit":

"I went out of my way to paint lurid pictures of aerial combat to the green crews coming in as replacements. Really there was no need to exaggerate. The empty beds in the huts were silent witnesses to that fact. I suppose veteran warriors from time immemorial have sought to frighten their novice companions. But none was more vocal than I in describing the maniacal fury of the German opposition. This bombastic euphoria was of short duration, however. It had been rumored in the squadron that we would be one of the lead crews after Captain Brinkley's crew finished their tour. This belief was reinforced when a bird colonel flew with us on one of our early missions, ostensibly to look us over. When we came off the target, it was my job to look in the bomb bay and see that all the bombs had cleared the racks. On this mission the flak was really coming up; so I hastily looked in the bomb bay, closed the door and yelled, 'Bomb bay clear.' I had seen no bombs. When we got down from altitude and were out over the Channel, I started through the catwalk and, to my horror, half of the bombs were in the bomb bay and still fully armed. Since we were nearing the English coast, Chick and the colonel decided to land with the bombs. They were too costly to jettison. We flew back to the 303rd and landed safely. Chick made a perfect landing. Thank God he did. I knew I was going to catch hell. For some reason the colonel did not chew me out, but I could see he was sore as hell. I had really blown it. We heard nothing more about 'lead crews' and my crewmembers blamed me for the fact that we were passed over. I had endangered the whole crew needlessly and I felt awful about it. I was completely deflated, a condition which became me more than my previous swaggering. When we were down, Chick looked at me and said, 'for Chris' sakes, Smitty,' but that's all he ever said.[769]

"For us, 11 May was a miraculous and incredible escape from the very maw of death. By the laws of probability, we shouldn't have made it. The trip into the target was uneventful, but we knew that it was heavily defended, as it was an important rail center. We were not deceived by the good beginning. The colonel who led the mission, a West Pointer, was a dauntless flier with an exalted reputation. The only trouble: these fearless career soldiers tended to share the opinion that combat crews were expendable; like in the 'Air Corps Song' it was our destiny to live in fame and go down in flames.

"We turned on the IP and opened the bomb-bay doors. We were getting punishing flak. Shrapnel cut off the navigator's oxygen supply and destroyed his radio compass, a crucial event as it turned out later. Unbelievably we were not dropping our bombs. The colonel was not satisfied. We left the target, made a wide circle and came around again for another bomb run. This time they really had our range. It was ferocious. All of the squadrons were badly chewed up by shrapnel. Many of the Forts were trailing smoke and had feathered engines. Some of them left the formation and headed to Switzerland.

"The bomb bay doors came open again and this time we dropped. Lieutenant Long's aircraft was burning. I could clearly see the waist gunners looking at us through the waist window. These fellows were our friends and lived in our barracks. They stayed in formation until Bombs Away and then started down out of control. Our tail gunner saw them blow up. This mission would have been their final one. Ironically, their regular radio operator had overstayed his leave in London and was not with them when they went down. He went to see the families of the dead airmen upon his arrival back in the United States. By way of consoling the widow of one of the gunners, he wooed and then married her.[770]

"Flak knocked out our two outboard engines and blew off one of our bomb-bay doors before we could get them closed. Smoke poured from the two disabled engines, which Chick had quickly feathered. We were strongly tempted to try for Switzerland but decided against it. We could not stay up with the formation, usually a fatal affliction. Slowly we lost altitude and forlornly watched our departing comrades in the bomber formation. We followed them until they were out of sight.

"Chick headed us in the general direction of home. When we were down to 11,000ft, we blundered over an enemy airfield. They began firing at point blank range and came within a hair of shooting us down. Chick put the ailing bomber into almost a vertical power dive to get away from the flak. We could not move because of the G factor and thought we had 'bought the farm' for sure. We could only stare at one another in mute terror. Chick and Fish pulled out just above the treetops. They ordered us to dump overboard everything that would come loose. It all went -ammunition, machine guns, radios and clothing - anything we could find that was not fastened down. At this point we were all in the radio room, my own post. I remember that we did something that seems melodramatic at this distance, but then it made sense. We all shook hands solemnly and bade each other good-bye.

"Everybody was ordered up into the nose to give us better balance (trim). I stayed back in the radio room to man the radio in case we made it out of Germany. We were now taking a scenic trip through Belgium, dodging church steeples and treetops. People were waving at us and terrorized farm animals were panicking and running away from our sound. After our spectacular dive, Chick had added full war-emergency power, which gave us about 140mph airspeed. It was too much. On full power the remaining two engines became overheated, turning cherry red and threatening to explode. Chick gradually reduced manifold pressure and RPMs, which allowed the red-hot engines to cool off and kept us airborne at 125mph, just slightly above stalling speed. We were right down on the deck with no room for mistakes and it was still a long shot as far as I was concerned. Later Chick referred to this as 'a piece of cake.' Ha!

"We had forgotten about the Channel defenses and, as we neared the coast, I began to see tracers streaking at us. At first I didn't realize what they were. We must have come out somewhere between Dunkirk and Ostend. Now all of the batteries of the coastal defenses started opening up on us with a vengeance. We could see the barbed wire and gun emplacements and I fancied I could see the coalscuttle helmets of the people who were firing at us. We could not shoot back. We had thrown away our guns. Shells were exploding inside the aircraft and once I leaned forward to see better through the acrid smoke. As I did, a machine gun bullet came through the floor and creased my scalp. I yelled, 'I'm hit!' I had seen a lot of war movies and I knew that was the appropriate response to the sight of my own blood.

"Explosions in the nose and cockpit wounded Chick, Jasper and Ward Hudson the tail gunner. A flak tower was trying to depress its guns to finish us off but Chick dived lower to prevent this. Chick continued to fly the plane, although he was in great pain. There was a three-inch piece of shrapnel sticking out of his thigh. We were jinking around a lot to spoil the enemy's aim. At last we saw with relief the coast pulling away from us and knew we were safe for the moment.

"I tuned in the distress frequency on the liaison set. The DF Station answered us immediately and started tracking us, as it looked likely we were going to come down in the water. We neared the English coast, sending 'darky-darky'; the military equivalent of 'may-day'. A fighter field either answered us, or we were directed to it by the DF station. Then an appalling realization came to light. We had no brakes or flaps; our hydraulic system was shot out; so we knew we were going to have to crash land. The fighter field was very small and had no runways. It was either a training field or a Spitfire base. Later we learned it was at Southend-on-Sea on the Thames Estuary.

"We came in very hot and had no room to go around again. After touch down we were quickly running out of field. The big bomber was rolling directly toward a concrete ammunition building. Quickly Chick unlocked the tail wheel, kicked the right rudder and gunned the left engine. We careened to the right and narrowly missed the ammo house. A thick barbed wire barrier surrounded the field. We cut a path through it as if it was ticker tape. The landing gear was washed out when we hit a stump or something and we started sliding on our belly. I was thrown violently around in the radio room. The bomber was completely out of control. We hit a ditch, slewed around and stopped. I jumped up and ran out of the plane.

"The rest of the fellows were getting the wounded out of the nose hatch and I helped. Chick was in great distress, but Jasper was still knocked out. The meat wagon and fire trucks came roaring up and in a matter of moments RAF chaps who were congratulating us on our stunning performance surrounded us. They took us to the Sergeant's Mess and began plying us with whiskey. We became hilarious. We were all wound up and talking a mile a minute. The Limeys were smiling at us indulgently. What sweet relief - we had made it!

"Somebody noticed my head was bleeding; so they took me to a hospital and cleaned me up. It was only a scalp wound, but I spent the night in the hospital. Next morning I had a pint of tea and a hearty breakfast and considered myself a very lucky boy. I knew I would get a Purple Heart this time. I didn't![771]

"We stayed at Southend for a few days. One night we borrowed RAF uniforms from our hosts and went into town to a dance. We looked very smart and military in them. The local girls were so surprised to find that we were all bloody Yanks. I visited Chick, Ward and Jasper in the hospital before we went back to the base. We didn't see them for a good while after that.[772] When we got back to Molesworth, everyone was surprised to see us. We were supposed to be dead. Friends had reported that we had gone down. Our stuff had already been divided among our comrades. It took us days to round up our bicycles, clothes and other property.

"We did not have to fly for a while. All of us were still 'shook up' considerably. Usually a combat crew was sent to the Flak House after such an experience, but for some reason they did not send us. The Flak House was an old English manor with lovely grounds and gardens and recreation facilities, where "flak happy" crews rested and recuperated. I never flew with Chick again.[773] When we were put back on operations, Stan Fisher became our first pilot. We were somewhat fearful although Chick had reassured us in the hospital, telling us that we were in good hands with 'Fish'. We knew they were a great team but we had not had much opportunity to see Fish perform as an aircraft commander since he had always been in the co-pilot's seat. He was from Baltimore, Jewish and quite a musician - a fantastic concert harmonica player. He had appeared with Fred Waring and some other big bands. Fish was an enthusiastic performer and wherever we were stationed he would be on variety shows. We basked in his celebrity status and because of him 'Chick's Crew' was a very popular one. Virtuosity with the harmonica, however, hardly qualified one to fly a four-engined bomber. We continued apprehensive through the first few missions with Fish as first pilot. It soon became apparent to us that Fish knew what he was doing and that he was a courageous and resourceful aircraft commander. When he got excited, he used to yell a lot, but he usually made the right decision when the chips were down. Fish was a survivor and at the time that was important to me. I always continued to think of him as the co-pilot even though I flew more missions with him as first pilot than I did with Chick. They were the best. Nobody could have brought '*Sweet Melody*' back to England but those two. It was an incredible piece of flying. As far as I knew, no four-engined bomber had ever before survived an 11,000ft-power dive. Chick was awarded the Silver Star for his heroic performance. The Congressional Medal of Honor was what he and Fish both deserved, but these were usually reserved for heroes who were no longer there to collect them. Chick also collected a Purple Heart, as did Jasper and Ward.

"My war was not over by any means. We were no longer a crew intact. In fact I was freelance now, as were the others, flying with this or that crew when a radio operator was needed. This freelancing made for a feeling of insecurity since there was some difference in the quality of pilots and crews. Having flown with Chick for so long, I immediately perceived the difference. He had been a superlative performer. We had been involved in many emergency situations, both in training and combat and he had been equal to all of them. I would not be writing this if that weren't true. An example of one of my experiences while flying with other crews involved a 'flak happy' pilot. Everybody in the squadron knew he had combat fatigue. He had been to the Flak House twice. He had no business flying and why somebody in authority couldn't recognize this fact, I don't know. I was posted to fly a mission with him along with others of my old crew. If that weren't bad enough, it was Berlin, the 'Big B.' We were somewhere back in the ass-end Charlie position when suddenly without warning this character left the formation and took us on a sightseeing tour all over Berlin, right by our lonesome. We all started yelling at him over the intercom to no avail. The air was full of hostiles. Why they didn't discover these 'easy pickins' I can't imagine. He rejoined the formation on the other side of town and we flew on back. Needless to say, he was grounded after that little piece of whimsy."

Four of Germany's five main oil plants were in the Leipzig area in central Germany. The big Leuna plant was at Merseburg, 18 miles west of Leipzig, while Lutzkendorf and Bohlen were in the same general area, and Zeitz was 25 miles southwest of Leipzig. A fifth oil plant was at Brux, 42 miles northwest of Prague. Russell A. Grantham, 836th Bomb Squadron Operations Officer in the 487th Bomb Group at Lavenham, recalls;

"During 1944, Leipzig was the most dreaded target in all of Germany. It was estimated that the Germans had amassed 2200 guns in the Leipzig area, mostly 88mm with some 105mm. This was completed with an estimated 600 guns protecting Berlin. Also, the Leipzig guns were in a rather concentrated area, while at Berlin the guns were in a large circle around the city, which you could fly through the ring and experience flak and then experience it again when you flew out of the ring. Also at Leipzig, the gunners adopted the tactic of determining your altitude and speed and setting up a box that you had to fly through. This allowed them to increase the number of shots and concentrate firepower."

On 12 May almost 900 B-17s and B-24s were dispatched with 980 escorting fighters in the first attack on the five main oil plants. This simultaneous attack on oil and aircraft was in keeping with Eisenhower's policy of pounding two of Germany's most valuable assets. Both had to be knocked out or crippled if the invasion of the Continent was to succeed. The bombers would fly a common course in trail to the Thuringen area, where the bomb divisions would peel off and attack their targets. Brux was the target for the 13th and 45th Wings of the 3rd Division. (This was the first time that the 8th had been assigned a target in Czechoslovakia.) The 1st Division sought the synthetic oil plants in the Leipzig area.[774] In the 2nd Bomb Division at Shipdham, T/Sgt Don Chase and John W. McClane were among those who sat through the briefing expectantly. Flight Office Metz' crew were minus a radio operator, so Chase flew his 25th mission (and his final three) with the crew. John W. McClane, who was on his tenth mission, recalls:

"When the briefing curtains were pulled back so we could see the large map of Europe, the ribbons indicated our target to be in the Leipzig area. For the first time, the 8th Air Force had set its goal to wipe out the synthetic oil plants so vital to the German war machine. This was a new kind of objective in the campaign to paralyze Hitler's Europe. There were three synthetic oil plants in the Leipzig area of which one was Zeitz, 20 miles to the southwest and our target for the day. Zeitz lay approximately 550 miles from our base at Shipdham but we flew many more miles than this as we never went straight to a target but took a 'Cook's Tour' of Europe zigzagging from France to Denmark in order to keep the Luftwaffe guessing where to concentrate their defenses. We would faint towards a potential target only to turn in another direction about the time the Germans had alerted their AA batteries and fighters. Sometimes the city we pointed towards would already be throwing up a flak barrage even though we had no intention of making this our target. Somehow this seemed to amuse us. To proceed, as the bird flies, to the target and back (about 1100 miles) would take less than six hours but we were in the air 8 hours and 20 minutes due to the assembly time and the evasive flight course.

"The 2nd Bomb Division dispatched 716 B-24s to Zeitz of which 19 planes were ours. Each carried 19 250lb bombs, however one of our planes had to abort and return to base making 18 over the target. Take off was approximately 0900 hours and we broke the English Coast about one and a half-hours later. We did not expect this to be an easy mission and we were not disappointed. The enemy fighters were out in great force but with over 1000 bombers to attack, they were spread pretty thin for which we were grateful. Flak was another thing. The Germans knew the importance of oil refineries so they set up an elaborate complex of anti-aircraft batteries. The refinery itself had sort of a trapezoidal shape and was set out in the middle of farm country. The visibility was extremely clear and even from more than 20,000ft the outline of buildings and oil storage tanks were clearly discernible. There were several villages within a mile of the refinery. The target stood out like a sore thumb with farms all around. The flak was intense; not one plane escaped damage. We were down to 18,000ft to achieve maximum accuracy. One of the 67th Squadron's planes was hit so badly that it had to drop out of formation where it became easy prey for the enemy fighters to pick off. This was the only 44th loss for the day.[775]

"When we departed the target area at Zeitz, the refinery was severely damaged and on fire. The great majority of all bombs dropped by the attacking 116 Liberators landed well within the strike zone. To me it appeared that we had destroyed the objective completely. 'So much for one synthetic oil plant', so I thought, but little did I know that the Germans had a fantastic ability to rebuild. We landed shortly after 1700 hours."

Fred Huston, a bombardier in a 337th Bomb Squadron, 96th Bomb Group crew who arrived in England in the early spring of 1944 ("having done what passed for phase training in Dyersburg, TN") recalls:

"My memory of some of the missions we flew are vivid in the extreme, others just names and how many hours it took to get there and back but the Merseburg-Lutzkendorf-Leuna missions still stand out, with a certain amount of terror included. It was the most screwed up of targets in all of Germany and every time we went there something happened to either cause us to miss the damned target or, I suspect, even to miss the European continent. Our first trip there I thought very little about it. It was just another place where the red string ended and the intelligence officer assured us was vital to the prosecution of the war. Of course, they said that about every target so we took it with a grain of salt. Some of them didn't seem all that important to a bunch of 20 year olds who were more concerned with the next pass to London than we were with saving the world. I am sure that I went to Merseburg something like four or five times. Merseburg was the first time I saw colored flak. I remember it as red, although there are those who remember it as pale blue. I still think it was red. Someone told us; probably someone who didn't know either, that it was to call in the fighters. Since we already had more fighters than Custer had Sioux, I thought that it was gilding the lily somewhat to call in something that we already had in abundance. But to me, one fighter was plenty for the day.

"I can also recall a sinking feeling in the pit of my stomach every time the string headed that way. The IO kept harping on the fact that this was an important target and we really should hit it someday, although I don't think that we ever did. At least no one said so if we tore the thing up. Every time we went something fouled up. I also remember that we always approached from the east and then screwed up. The last time we came in from the south and I doubt that we did any better.

"When the string reached Merseburg I had my usual cold chills. But off we went, this time with an IP south of Leuna. We were told that since Hamburg was no longer a target most of the guns had been moved to the Leipzig area and after the raid I believed them. The 1st Division led and they missed their IP and came across the target with a quartering head wind and only doing something like a 100mph ground speed across the target. They were getting the hell kicked out of them by both flak and fighters. The sky was filled with that peculiar gray green smoke that an exploding airplane left. This was not to say that they didn't have an abundance of guns left for us. We hit highly concentrated flak before we got to the IP, which wasn't the rule and was terribly unsporting of the flak crews. There was a lot of it and it was bouncing us around considerably and we lost a few airplanes before we got on the run properly.

"We made the bomb run with fewer than the 18 aircraft we started with and holes kept appearing in various parts of the airplane, like the wings and the bomb bay doors and the nose and everyplace else. Final count was something like 400 of them in the airplane. Just before bombs away one exploded just above the astrodome, removing it from the airplane and blowing a large and draughty hole in the nose. I knew I was hit because I had a bunch of blood running down my face and out of my glove. My navigator was deaf since a fragment had torn off the earflap of his flak helmet and split his right headset. We left the formation short No.4 engine and joined some other cripples after the run to get home. Mutual protection was the watchword... the more guns, the fewer Germans. I was resting on he base of the top turret when I stood up and my boot squashed and my leg gave out. That was the last of the battle damage. So yes, I remember Merseburg.

"Brux, the first time, we hit one hell of a front around the Flensburg Peninsula and everyone went on instruments and started edging away from the people nearest us. The fighters said that they couldn't top it out, so Air Force gave us a recall. Our command pilot that day was a West Pointer and he decided that the tough old 45th Combat Bombardment Wing would press on! But by the time we got through the front, even he could see the trouble. He didn't have very many airplanes left with him, what with people peeling off through vertigo and those who were just plain chicken. So we didn't go to Brux but got credit for a mission since we were past 6° east."

Altogether, 470 *Luftwaffe* fighters were sent up to oppose the American formations, and in one of the fiercest air battles of the war, 46 bombers (all except five were in the 3rd Bomb Division) were shot down, mainly over the Rheine-Main area.[776]

Abe Dolim, in the 94th Bomb Group, was among those who went to Zwickau:

"We took up the low position in a composite group with a 385th Group squadron leading and a 447th Group squadron in the high position. After crossing the enemy coast at Ostend we received reports that the Luftwaffe was up in force. Near Koblenz our escort of P-51s departed to chase bogies. Some minutes later, Lieutenant Maybank spotted a small formation of unidentified fighters at 3 o'clock level. I stood up to be close to my .50s and, as I squinted out toward 2 o'clock, I was shocked to see about six jet-black FW 190s flying right through the high squadron, attacking from 12 o'clock level. The group closed up - no one seemed to be hurt. About ten minutes later, ten more black FWs attacked the lead squadron from 12 o'clock level, some of them fish-tailing to rake their targets. Kelch, Long and I fired as they went by at 3 o'clock. One of the Focke-Wulfs rammed the No.6 aircraft in the lead squadron and both exploded. Two more B-17s dropped out of formation. One began a shallow trailing dive with all ten men baling our. The other maintained speed with the group about 500ft below the lead squadron and dropped its landing gear to communicate air surrender. After some minutes, it retracted its landing gear and rejoined the group, which was then about 20 miles southeast of Frankfurt.

"At our altitude of 19,000ft there were some stratus layers, ideal for the enemy and, as I scanned at 11 o'clock level, I spotted a large formation of fighters approaching from 2000 yards heading for our low squadron. I got on the intercom and notified the crew - Messerschmitt 109s, about 30 of them in three flights. We opened fire at about 1200 yards and I picked the far left 109 in the lead flight. Two of them were shot out of formation before they approached within 500 yards. A string of cannon shells, so close I heard their sharp cracks, exploded just in front of our nose. I fired about 60 rounds at the 109 until he passed by our No.1 engine forcing me to quit. He was closing fast from about 100 yards when I yelled at Wehtfrirz to get him. He poured .50s into the Messerschmitt at point-blank range. Apparently, the enemy pilot was not firing at this point or he would have raked us. His aircraft stalled after passing our tail gunner and us saw it go down and crash - the pilot did not bale out.

"The 332nd was lucky to be intact, having suffered no losses. The bomb run to the target was a question mark as preceding bombers created fires in the repair plant, forcing our lead bombardier to aim through the billowing smoke. Near Weimar, the low group to our right took a pass from 6 o'clock level by ten 109s with no apparent effect. The floor of our navigator-bombardier compartment was covered with empty .50 caliber casings and in moving about I felt 1 had roller skates on my fur-lined boots."[777]

The 13th Wing, comprising the 95th, 100th, and 390th Bomb Groups, and the 45th Wing, comprising the 96th, 388th, and 452nd Bomb Groups, meanwhile, carried out the long and grueling mission to the oil refinery complex at Brux.

Ralph J. Munn was the ball turret gunner of the *Lucky Lady*[778] in the 731st Bomb Squadron, 452nd Bomb Group, piloted by 1st Lieutenant Dick Noble. He recalls:

"The mission to Brux happened to be one of the days that I was with our own original crew. (I also flew spares for crews that were short ball gunners). The briefing at 0200 should have been the message we had been expecting for a week or ten days. When the map was pulled on the wall and an orderly started with the red ribbon to the target there was a hush over the entire room. The condition of the aircraft at Deopham Green was in no way airworthy or mechanically sound to make a trip of this distance. At best, even with extra fuel, it was the feeling of a no return."

Wilbur Richardson, a ball turret gunner in the 331st Bomb Squadron, 94th Bomb Group, was on his eighth mission. The pilot, John Moser, and the rest of the crew were unaware they would also be flying such a war weary B-17 until they taxied out at Bury St. Edmunds:

"'061, the 'F' we were assigned, had been shot up, repaired, crash-landed and repaired again. This queen had seen her best days. It just didn't fly that well. This all became apparent as we started our roll down the runway. We were at maximum load and 061 just barely got off. John Moser used up all of the runway and I saw green grass as we just lifted off in time. Close? Shades of Lindbergh. We were off for what was to prove an historic operation."

One by one the B-17s took off and completed their complicated group and wing assembly patterns. Manningtree was the final assembly point, and crews carried on over the Channel in a bomber stream. The bombers crossed the enemy coast between Dunkirk and Ostend near the French-Belgian border. Ralph Munn recalls:

"At daybreak we crossed over and went into Fortress Europe through Holland. There was the usual amount of flak but no fighters until we were quite deep into Germany. As usual, the enemy was reluctant to attack, until our P 47s and P 38 escorts made the turn for home base."

The 94th Bomb Group missed their rendezvous with the fighter escort. Wilbur Richardson explains the events that followed:

"We weren't long into Belgian airspace when all hell broke loose. The yellow-nosed 'Abbeville Kids' and the German Air Force rose to the occasion. Upward of 400 fighters attacked. In our area there were only six P-51s. Not much help with such odds. I watched as a '51 and a '109 collided head-on. We flew eastwards towards our target area, fighting all the way. The fighters came from all directions - the tail as well as the effective nose-on attacks. In some cases there were 25-30 abreast and even attempts at ramming by using a wing so the pilot could bale out, as we later learned. Attacks were made from 12 o'clock, circled and charged from 6 o'clock level so neither ball or top turret might get a line on them. As the upper and lower turrets could fire in all directions Bruton and I were kept busy twisting and turning constantly. The navigator, Les Ulvestad or the bombardier, Frank Sarno, called out 'Bandits 10 o'clock low' or 'Straight in at 12 o'clock'. If I weren't shooting to the rear, assisting the tail gunner, Gilbert Gabriel or some other direction, I'd swing forward ready to follow through coming from the nose. It was a busy time returning the fire of those fast-moving targets with winking flashes on the wings coming our way."

Clifford D. Jones, navigator in Lieutenant Lourie's crew, 96th Bomb Group, recalls:

"It was a beautiful clear day and the usual forming of groups into wings took place over England and then proceeding over the Channel to our various destinations. We picked up heavy flak near Koblenz but to my knowledge no planes were lost or delayed; however, for the 96th Bomb Group, this was just a harbinger of things to come. In no time at all we observed our fighter cover above us being drawn off to defend us against German fighters. Almost simultaneously, our crew was reporting attacks by enemy fighters from almost all points of the clock. With the exception of the tail gunner who wore a flat, back type parachute at all times; the remaining crewmembers had detachable chest type chutes. Obviously, attaching a chest chute on a buckle harness under a flak vest was extremely awkward. However, considering the pressing attacks on our group from the German fighters, in a brief lull, I decided to loosen my flak vest and put my chute on. Quite frankly, with all the bombers going down around us, I felt it was just a matter of time and if worse came too worse, I could, at least, make an immediate attempt to escape. It seems like a very short time thereafter, when tracking an Me-109 and firing my 50 caliber machine gun as he came in from 12 o'clock high and as he passed my line of vision there was a sudden jolt and shuddering of our aircraft. It seemed to stop in mid air and then fell off into an uncontrolled fall. As explained, with the exception of myself and my tail gunner, none of the other crewmembers would have had their chutes on and when our plane went down out of control, there would have been no chance, whatever, to recover any of the chutes. Through a miracle I escaped through the B-17's nose hatch and the tail gunner was blown out the rear. I personally believe the German fighter was out of control and had struck our B-17 amidships, as I do not recall any explosion."[779]

While some groups like the 94th were hit hard, others, like the 100th, escaped. Richard Wynn, the navigator in Lieutenant Alexander Kinder's crew in the 418th Bomb Squadron, which was on its 14th mission, recalls:

"Our Squadron was at the tail end of the 13th Combat Wing, which trailed the rest of the 8th. Our ship was the famed *Rosie's Riveters*, made famous by Robert Rosenthal, a legendary figure in the 100th. We inherited the ship from him when his crew finished its first tour. It was really either the second or third *Rosies*. There were fierce fighter attacks on the front end of the formation with heavy counter attacks from our fighter cover. We saw it but were not engaged with fighters the entire way to the target, which was an unusual experience for the 100th Bomb Group."

S/Sgt Sam N. Fain, ball turret gunner, *Lady Stardust II*, 452nd Bomb Group, flown by 2nd Lieutenant Milan "Mike" Maracek, recalled:

"Now I see the planes clearly – they are FW 190s and Me 109s; mean fighters to tangle with. They are making frontal attacks and coming in 15 at a time in a staircase formation. I pick up one in my sights and fire a five-second burst. They are firing cannon shells at us. I feel them hitting our ship and I am beginning to sweat now. I pick a FW 190 up in my sight track for one second and open fire. I follow him. He is going by off our left waist…got him. He explodes in a ball of fire. I swing my turret to 6 o'clock and I see five of our Forts going down on fire and explode, throwing flames around the sky. I see seven men bale out of a Fortress. An enemy plane circles them once and comes in firing at the chutes. They all catch fire and I can see the men falling to earth. I fire at the enemy ship for eight seconds. I see smoke trailing from his engine and sincerely hope that I got the rat. A man bales out of a ship in front of us and comes into our ship, breaking our Plexiglas nose, injuring our bombardier and navigator and throwing them into the catwalk of the ship. I look down at the ground and see many small fires and large ones burning. They are enemy fighters and our Forts. Another man bales out of a Fort in front of us. His chute hits our propeller blades. They cut the top out of his chute. I see him falling, looking back at his flapping shroud lines. I try to shoot him. He falls to the ground, still alive until he struck the earth. We limp over the target. There go our bombs. We made it…."[780]

T/Sgt Dwight N. Miller, radio operator *Lady Stardust II*, continues:

"I heard a sharp snap, something like flak. A parachute went over the right wing and also some stringy stuff was sliding back across my window. I opened the door and looked toward the cockpit. I was blinded by something plus a terrific wind. It was blood; a lot of it. I was covered from head to foot and it went on through the ship painting it red and freezing. The bomb bays were solid red and slippery. The nose was gone, because of the fellow that baled into it. That was what I saw on my window. The blood inside the ship came from Merle 'Uncle Dudly' Orcutt, engineer. The right side of his head was gone…We were going down, but I didn't know the altitude so I took an extra oxygen bottle and started up the catwalk. There was a hard wind coming from the front. I was holding the left rope when it broke. It was weakened by an exploding shell I guess. I fell on the right rope. It was OK, but I dropped my oxygen bottle and it went tumbling down. I spent some time trying to get the bomb bay doors up with my knife. The crank and extension were gone so I gave the job up. I took some wire from the bomb pins and fixed the rope back. I went up to the engineer. He didn't look like Dud. But from the feeling inside of me I had no doubt. He was dead.

"I went back to the waist gunners, got some first aid kits and hunted for the powder. There was none. The right waist gunner grabbed a bandage and put it on his head. The expression in his eyes reminded me of a patient taking his first look at the stub of his leg after an amputation. Red was still bleeding and as he would breathe, blood would come out the hole in his eye. I wiped the blood off his face. He returned the act and said, 'I thought you were a walking dead man.'

"...The tail gunner said something about strafing and then he yelled, 'Tail gunner hit'. From the way he said it, I knew there was a lot of pain. I grabbed the first aid kit and ran for him. After laying him down in the waist, I began slicing my way to his wound, which was centered in his back. It was a terrible hole and I hurried to get a bandage on so he wouldn't lose too much blood. After getting the bandage on, I gave him a shot of morphine...We were alone, flying just above the ground, like a coyote sneaking among bushes in fear of yelping hounds close behind. We passed over a fighter base and could see the Germans shooting at us. We could hear the machine guns rumble above the rumble and rattle of our own plane...Then came a call over the interphone that we loved to hear. 'There is the Channel ahead,'"[781]

Wilbur Richardson continues:

"We were hit in the No.1 engine. It lost a lot of oil and we had to feather it just prior to the target. It was a struggle to keep up with the group with bombs still aboard. The flak over the target was moderate, which incidentally, I almost welcomed because we had a brief respite from the fighters. We received some flak damage including the loss of some oxygen in my ball turret as well as some on the left side."

Ralph Reese, who was flying left waist gun position in *Smoky Liz* in the 452nd Bomb Group, recalls:

"Everything went smoothly until 15 minutes from the IP. Then we saw some planes on our wing go down in flames. To our delight, they were enemy planes being shot down by our P-47 fighter escorts. We saw one P-47 shoot down three enemy planes."

Ralph Munn continues:

"Until just short of target we had considerable action, mostly high level attacks down through the squadron. When we reached the IP the flak was a solid carpet. Up to this point we had not had a casualty outside of small to fist-size holes. I had always made it a practice to turn my turret to 12 o'clock when the bomb bay doors opened. Bruce dropped a salvo and at the same time Dick turned into the down wind leg. We were hardly off the target when we took a direct hit in the bomb bay area. In the meantime I had turned around to 6 o'clock to see what was happening. A fraction of a second later, there was another very bad jolt. This one knocked out my source of power, my electrical suit boots and gloves. I was hit in the back and the turret took considerable damage. My guns and intercom were out. It was slippery in the turret. I was then aware that I was isolated and had no control over what was to happen next. The second hit took out the left inboard engine and the ball turret. The engine out was an invitation for the remaining fighters to attack. I think that with the bomb bay doors down, they assumed we were damaged badly enough that they could work on a more active victim. I did not see another fighter until we reached the mountain foothills in eastern Belgium.

"By this time Moody and Brush had manually cranked me out of my turret. I was bleeding, but did not feel pain. About right here two fighters pulled up on our right wing very close. Dick called every one to hold their fire and prepare to jump. I later learned we were out of fuel and too much had been damaged to make it back to the Channel. One of the men in the waist pulled the emergency lever for the exit. The door was supposed to break away with the slipstream. Two men at a time took turns and had to beat it off with ammunition boxes. The frame never did give. We managed to beat the skin off enough that we could get through the opening with chutes on. I had made a fast trip up to the bomb bay to see if we could jump from there. No way. The keel girder was torn in several spots, complete in two. I could not see a hole large enough to get thru without being hung up. When I arrived back at the waist Moody came over and said, 'Dick just called and to get ready to bale out.' Within a matter of minutes we all evacuated the '*Not So Lucky Lady*.' Surprisingly it was a very orderly departure, no hesitations either. All of us had had enough for that day."[782]

Richard Wynn, in the 100th Bomb Group, continues:

"The IP was due south of Brux. Our bomb run was almost due north and we made a hard left at the RP and returned to an intersection with our inboard flight path and followed it home. The weather was ideal, with small cumulus clouds and virtually no wind over the target."

Ralph Reese, in the 452nd formation, describes the flak:

"It was very heavy over the target and beyond. We saw one B-17 shot down and I saw ten chutes open and glide towards the ground. The group behind us [100th] was attacked by Bf 109s, who stayed out of range and were able to reach our planes. We lost 14 ships out of our group."

Richard Wynn, in *Rosie's Riveters* in the 100th formation, was close behind the 452nd formation:

"Our wing hit the target in three waves. The first wave's target was the center of the installation and by the time we got there, heavy smoke had risen to well over 10,000ft. We encountered light flak over the target but observed some rocket-propelled anti-aircraft fire. We were hit in the No.3 engine and lost oil pressure before the prop could be feathered. Cockpit procedure was complicated by the fact that a faulty flare from the lead ship deposited a heavy film of 'guck' over the pilot's half of the windshield, putting the co-pilot in control of the ship. His visibility was also limited to some extent. With a windmilling prop and all of the drag it created, we were unable to keep up with the formation and became a single straggler on the way home with heavy fuel consumption on a very deep penetration. It is doubtful whether we could have made Britain. I did a fuel consumption problem after a while and had us running out of fuel about the time we would reach the Channel. It would have been interesting to see whether we could have made it or not. We expected fighter attacks and expected to get knocked down soon because Hollywood not withstanding, a single B-17 is mismatched against a flurry of fighters usually."[783]

Meanwhile, Wilbur Richardson's B-17F was fighting a grim survival battle:

"Soon after bombs away we endured the second half of the German fighter attacks. Twin-engined fighters joined the 109s and 190s. They sat out behind the bomber boxes in groups of 10-20 to fire rockets and cannon just out of effective range of our .50s. With the loss of oxygen we could not remain long in our group formation and we had to lose altitude relatively fast to make it with the oxygen we had left. Stragglers always attracted attention and on our way down 109s and 190s came at us and we received many hits. Bruton claimed one fighter and the tail and I claimed two apiece. As I was in the rear firing at one below, another fighter hit the top turret with cannon fire. I saw the Plexiglas and Jim Bruton's empty special leather flak helmet go over the right horizontal stabilizer. I thought he had had it. I later learned that he lost consciousness for a few moments and came to on the deck before Lieutenant Leo Riley, the co-pilot, could get to him. Jim wasn't hurt. Just highly put out and using four-letter words, as he couldn't vent his anger by returning their fire. The shells that knocked him out of the turret damaged both .50s and were beyond repair. He was very lucky. We also took cannon damage from the rear. One hit the right elevator severely limiting its travel. Moser used the trim tab while Riley exerted pressure on the yoke to maintain a little level flight. He locked his left arm around the control column and held on tightly to his left wrist with his right hand while he propped both feet against the instrument panel. The shell that damaged the elevator was followed immediately with another that went on through the elevator. The right waist window was hit and the left waist gun on the left side of the case and put the gun out of action. Ken Rasco was uninjured. We managed to join another group coming from another target until the fighter attacks let up. We couldn't get in too close because of the difficulty in flying level but we did get some help in covering the attacks. By the time we reached the coast we were somewhat behind and below our foster group. We kept losing altitude across the Channel and Moser thought we might need to land at the first opportunity. Riley felt he could hold on a little longer, as we seemed to have enough altitude to make just one attempt. Being alone and late we were able to make a straight in approach. This was fortunate because we lost No.3 engine through fuel starvation as the '17 was nosed down and lined up with the runway. For us, 11.45 hours in the air, according to John Moser. Because we were late and the crews at de-briefing had reported seeing us go down in trouble we were listed as MIA. We returned to our barracks just in time to stop our belongings from being picked up. '061 never flew again. It became a hangar queen to keep others in the air."

Lieutenant Leo Riley wrote:

"God has been good to us again today. It is 7:30 and we have just finished a mission that started out at 8:00 this morning. Once again, I am so tired I can hardly sit up. Wish I could write. After going through what I have today, I feel that I can't. Saw many big forts go down in flames. Our ship was shot to pieces plus a ship in our own squadron shot out our No.1 one motor. But God brought us back. Must be up again tomorrow. Too close."

Mike Wysocki, a lead bombardier in the 410th Squadron, 94th Bomb Group, who was flying his 26th mission this day, was angered by the ten-and-a-half hour round trip to Brux:

"General Doolittle had said missions were now getting shorter and easier! We were under constant fighter attack for four-and-a-half hours but we weren't so badly off as the Luftwaffe attacked us from the tail position. They would sit out of range of our gunners and lob rockets at out formation. I had a ringside seat of the 45th Wing who were right in front of us. B-17s, P-51s, 110s and 109s were going down all over the place. I heard that the 452nd really took a beating.[784] When we finally got back, after debriefing and cleaning up I went to the officers' club and proceeded to get gloriously drunk."

At Shipdham, Don Chase heard the news that Vance's aircraft had gone down. The young radio operator had also seen, off in the distance, about 2 o'clock level, a B-24 that had had its top turret plastic bubble shot completely away. Chase kept thinking, "Headless Horseman ... Headless Horseman...." The crippled ship had continued flying, but slowly fell behind the group formation. "As a straggler he was a prime E/A target. I hoped he made it":

"When a crew went down foot lockers were pried open and personal belongings minus any objectionable material or firearms, were collected and shipped to their next of kin. Their beds were stripped and the thin mattresses folded. Soon newly assigned young men would arrive and the beds would be made again.

"Next day I flew my 26th mission and the Group's seventh in a row. The top turret gunner got off several bursts, the empty casings clinking against one another as they fell onto the cabin deck. I crouched behind the armor plate that protected the co-pilot's back, only my helmet and eyes above the armor as I watched the action. Oh, how I wished I could shoot back...please don't let them strip my bed...."[785]

15

The Westwall

"We had no idea what we were bombing, as we had never heard of a buzz bomb. Generally these missions were thought of as 'Milk Runs' because of the short duration over enemy territory and with almost no aerial opposition but they could be rough from flak."

2nd Lieutenant John W. McClane, navigator, 44th Bomb Group

Long penetration missions were the order of the day in the month of May. On Saturday, 13 May, the 8th Air Force dispatched 749 bombers to targets in the Reich, the 1st Division going to Politz, on the Baltic coast, to bomb more oil refineries, while the 2nd was assigned Tutow, and the 3rd Division, the marshaling yards at Osnabrück. Perry Rudd, in the 457th Bomb Group, recalls the trip to Politz:

> "The clouds were 7 to 9/10ths so we headed for the secondary target at Stettin instead. The town center and the docks were hit and our 1000lb demolition bombs seemed to wreck the whole works. Flak over the target was light but they really knew how to use it. Every burst was just off our wing tips at exactly the right altitude. We came off the target with open bomb bay doors that we had to crank down. There were no escorts after the target but we could see Sweden off to out tight and it looked really peaceful. Coming back across Denmark there must have been some Danes on the guns because they fired at us plenty but a mile low and off to the left of us. Two or three guns opened up on a P-51 and gave him a really tough time. It was as if they were showing us they could do it is they wanted to but didn't."[786]

John W. McClane in the 44th Bomb Group adds:

> "For a second straight day we were assigned to fly deep into Germany. Our target was a FW 190 Fighter plane assembly plant one mile north of Tutow near the Baltic Coast about 60 miles northwest of Stettin and approximately 100 miles due north of Berlin. Take off was just after 1030 hours with a total of 17 44th Bomb Group planes. We took a southern route across Holland and Germany, feinting towards Berlin, which always aroused the Luftwaffe. The day before when our group went to Zeitz, the enemy fighter command had lost 150 planes defending their synthetic oil plants. Therefore they were licking their wounds and hesitated to throw their full remaining strength against us especially since we had over 700 of our own P-51, P-47 and P-38 fighter escorts protecting us. All told the 8th Air Force dispatched over 700 heavies of which 228 were B-24s reaching Tutow loaded with 572 tons of high explosives. Our fighters were very effective in keeping the interceptors away from us. I saw many dog fights going on at a distance however. Several enemy planes swept through our formation inflicting no serious harm to any of our planes. The 44th suffered no loss on this mission in spite of rather intense flak over the target and again on the way home.
>
> "I saw something on this mission I had never seen before and never saw again. It was the practice of our defending fighter at times to fly escort along side of us. Because of the great similarity of our P-47 and the enemy FW 190 and our P-51 and the Me 109 fighter planes, our escort pilots had to be very cautious on how they approached our bomber formations. Our gunners were a little trigger-happy so if a fighter pilot came in towards us without identifying his plane, it was assumed he was an enemy and fair game for our gunners. The method our friendly pilots used to identify themselves was to get out of reach of our .50 caliber machine guns and rock their wings so we could get a silhouette. Every airman, even myself who never manned a gun, was highly trained to recognize the subtle differences in shape between our planes and the enemy's but woe to one of our pilots who failed to make this maneuver. Once the pilot was sure we knew who he was, he would move towards us rocking his wings over and over just to be sure. Only then was it safe to get near us.
>
> "A group of about 20 Liberators were just ahead of the 44th, maybe less than a mile away, as we approached the IP and were ready to start the bomb run. I could see these planes very clearly and was watching them when a fighter plane swooped in towards their tail. Like the gunners of that group, I too thought it to be one of the enemy's, as the pilot attempted no recognition. Of course every tail gunner in the formation opened up. The fighter began to smoke and go into a spin. Not until then did I recognize it to be a P-47 Thunderbolt, one of our escort planes. The pilot baled out with his chute in full bloom. His plane continued to plummet towards earth until I lost sight of it. We were soon over the spot where all this had happened. I looked down where the pilot landed deep in Northern Germany and thought how mad this guy was about now. I don't know who he blamed but I firmly believe it was his own carelessness. This whole action was like watching a movie, as I was so detached. Every so often we were warned at briefing to be careful about who we shot

at. It seemed HQ had gotten messages from the Fighter Command that their planes were coming back to base with .50 caliber holes in them (no German aircraft used this size gun). Anyway, it made them a little angry and there were some valid threats that they would not protect certain groups if something were not done to stop it.

"Our bombs dropped squarely on target, AA fire was moderate. It was time to head home. It might be helpful if the reader were to look at a map of where the German, Danish, Baltic Sea and Swedish areas came together in order to get a better idea of our flight path back to England. We proceeded out over the Baltic Sea and turned westerly so we passed within view of the southern tip of Sweden then over the entire width of Denmark and finally to the North Sea where we took a south westerly course back to East Anglia, site of our home base.

"Neutral Sweden had Bulltofta airfield near its southernmost coast. Many times U.S. planes were forced to land there due to battle damage, with no hope of being able to reach England. Of course, the crews were interned for the duration of the war. We were briefed on how to reach this haven if the occasion arose, but were told that the U.S. had inspectors there to look over every plane as it came in. Any plane they judged to still be airworthy enough to have made it back, or if there was not sufficient evidence in their mind's eye for the pilot to have landed, he would be court-martialed when he was repatriated. Anyone could understand what a temptation it could be to cop out of the constant danger we faced day after day. With this background one can only guess what was in everyone's mind when I pointed out this emergency landing field as we passed by.

"The flight over Denmark, such a peaceful looking land to be occupied by the hated Nazis, was beautiful and uneventful. We broke the coast and when I felt it was safe I told everyone that they could remove their flak vests and helmets. We were out over the water and I had no reason to believe that anymore danger existed from anti-aircraft fire. I was wrong, about the time we pulled the straps that let these heavy protecting vests fall to the floor, wham bang, four very accurate flak burst went off close to us. It frightened the holy heck out of us. I looked down to the water to see where the AA was coming from and low and behold, the scoundrels had stationed a barge off the coast fitted with an AA battery. By the time we got our vests back on, it was too late. This taught me a lesson I never forgot; from then on I looked to be sure all was safe before announcing time to drop our vests. We still had 350 miles to go to get home. Total losses for the day was 12 bombers out of 691 to reach their various destinations. Of these one was from our force of 228 Liberators attacking Tutow. We landed shortly after 1800 hours having been in the air for 7 hours and 45 minutes. On this day I was awarded my first Air Medal."

On 14 May the weather grounded all three divisions and missions were scrubbed. At Molesworth, 2nd Lieutenant Richard R. "Dick" Johnson, co-pilot in 2nd Lieutenant Theodore R. "Bud" Beiser's *Buzz Blond* in the 427th Bomb Squadron, 303rd Bomb Group, waited to fly the first mission since the crew had arrived in England in April, and was bussed to Molesworth, as he recalls:

"It was the famous 303rd Bomb Group known as 'Hell's Angels.' As we drove past Molesworth and turned onto the base, which was a little over a mile from the village, we were greeted with some strange sights. There were so many B 17s that they couldn't be easily counted. The 427th Squadron to which we had been assigned was on the base, while the other three squadrons were just off the base. As we approached the barrack area of the 427th, some wag had hung a sign on the first billet area. The sign said, 'GIRLS WHO VISIT ON A WEEK END MUST BE OFF THE BASE BY TUESDAY.' Along the taxiway near the armament section row upon row of bombs were out in the open. Some of these larger bombs were fitted with wings and empennage to be used as glide bombs. After we got settled in and after hearing 'You'll be sorry' a few times we did the latest schooling and two short flights to familiarize us with the area. On 15 May we started earning our keep and learned why we had been trained so hard all these months. On our first mission I was to fly co-pilot for 1st Lieutenant Phillip W. O'Hare in 42-97391. He was almost finished with his tour and was to train me in all aspects of combat flying.[787]

"My first combat mission was to Mimoycques, near Calais to finish off a German project.[788] Our bombardier, Lieutenant Ed Cooper had the job of arming the six; 1000lb bombs after we were in the air. Each bomb had an 8-inch vane or propeller on the nose fuze, which was prevented from turning by a cotter pin through a hole. Each cotter pin had a bomb tag with warnings. As the pin was removed, a wire attached to the bomb bay was inserted through the cotter pin hole. When the bombs were dropped, they slid off the arming wire, which allowed the propeller to turn in the wind. After falling about 500ft, the propeller wound itself off the fuze, which was then armed and would explode the bomb upon contact. After he removed the bomb tags from the nose fuze, Cooper walked to the front of the airplane and gave each officer a tag to use as a souvenir. Charlie Latta did the same with the tail fuzes for the rest of the crew. I kept my mission diary on mine. On this first mission each B-17 carried 1700 gallons of gas and six 1000lb bombs. The bombs were fuzed at one tenth second at the nose and one fortieth second at the tail. One fortieth second would allow the bomb to penetrate a roof before exploding and the one-tenth second fuse would assure that the bomb would explode before deep penetration.

"This day's mission started with a 0400 wake-up call. Breakfast and briefing followed quickly and we were in our plane with the engines running by 0600. The lead plane took off at 0615 and all 20 B-17s were over the field and in formation, at 20,000ft at 0740. Our squadron, the 427th, was assigned the high position, behind and to the right of the lead squadron, the 358th. The 359th Squadron was low left. The 360th Squadron did not fly this mission. Each squadron furnished seven B 17s to the group formation, except the lead, which had six. Our squadron also furnished two spares that were to take up any position that might be left empty by an abort. They were to return to base before reaching enemy territory and if there was an abort later, the other B-17s moved into the empty slots, leaving the tail position empty. On this day there were no aborts and the spares returned to base. O'Hare's position in the squadron was No.7, 'Tail End Charlie.'[789] Just after 'Bombs away' from about 25,000ft we encountered some flak. However, it was light and inaccurate, the nearest burst being at least a quarter mile away. The German gunners may not have had their radar working and so were shooting at the noise of our engines. None of our aircraft sustained damage and all planes returned to base and landed before 1030. Total flight time was just over four hours. We were over enemy territory barely seven minutes."

John W. McClane, in the 44th Bomb Group, also flew a mission to France on 15 May. He recalls:

"After two deep penetrations of Hitler's Germany on the previous Friday and Saturday, what a relief to be informed that our mission on this Monday would be to the Pas de Calais area. No one jumped with joy however. We all knew that even though our course would carry our aerial task force over enemy held territory for a relatively short distance of only 109 miles, we could expect an intense and accurate flak barrage at most targets equal to many in Germany itself. Luftwaffe opposition was not a major worry as our fighter escorts were plentiful by this time but our gunners had to be constantly on the alert in case one or two enemy airplanes slipped past our 'little friends'. The Germans had been constructing launching sites for their V-1 'Buzz Bombs', which were soon to be sent against England and London in particular. We had no idea what we were bombing, as we had never heard of a buzz bomb. Generally these missions were thought of as 'Milk Runs' because of the short duration over enemy territory and with almost no aerial opposition but they could be rough from flak.[790]

"The 44th Bomb Group launched 17 planes, of which 16 joined 73 others of the 2nd Division to bomb a V-1 site under construction at Siracourt, two miles southwest of St. Pol and 45 miles due south of Dunkirk. All told we carried 352 tons of bombs. Our load was eight 1000 pounders. Our course took us due south from Shipdham to Clacton on the English coast, 50 miles east of London. From there we flew southeast to our famous entry point on the Belgian coast half way between Dunkirk in France and Ostend. Going south 36 miles put us 10 miles west of Lille. We took a southwesterly course for 28 miles to our IP. The bomb run was 12 miles northwest to the target. After unloading our bombs, we headed due west 33 miles where we broke the French Coast, went out over the Channel until we headed north again back to 'Jolly Old England'.

"If there ever were a 'Milk Run' this was it. We encountered no flak and the P-51 escort fighter spotted not one enemy plane. It was a most enjoyable trip. However we never saw the target due to a heavy cloud layer but this did not keep us from bombing. Usually the Germans jammed my *Gee* Box with spurious radio signals as soon as we crossed the enemy coast. This resulted in a multitude of blips on my screen to the point where I could not tell the true course from all this 'grass'. (It was called 'grass' as the phosphor on our cathode ray tube emitted a bright green color.) For some inexplicable reason, the Germans were not jamming our signals and my *Gee* Box was working perfectly. Warga had no idea where to drop the bombs. I asked him to calculate how far in advance of the bomb drop that would be required in order to hit the target from our 23,000ft altitude. He made this calculation which I plotted on my map. I then set the *Gee* Box controls to these coordinates. I watched the blips come closer and closer. When they got exactly one over the other I said, 'Bombs Away' at which time he released our load of explosives. Only 'Heaven Above' knows where those bombs went. Of course we reported this at debriefing at which time we got the impression that we had performed a 'job well done'. I often wondered over the years what the Germans thought when these bombs came out of nowhere. It's difficult to believe that we were in the air five hours. We landed approximately 1115 hours. I was sure proud of myself."

T/Sgt Don Chase, who was on his 27th and penultimate mission, agreed with McClane that "at last" it was "a *Noball* milk run aptly named." The radio operator hoped that "maybe, just maybe" his final mission might be another one like it. However:

"Weather-bound, the Group was stood down for the next four days. It was a trying time. I wanted to fly that final mission quickly. Yet I didn't want to fly it at all. I knew of at least one man (and I heard of others) who was killed on what was supposed to be his tour finale. After three days of rest, operations were resumed in a big way."

On Friday, 19 May, 888 B-17s and B-24s were despatched, the B-17s attacking targets at Berlin and Kiel, and the 300 Liberators, Brunswick. 2nd Lieutenant John W. McClane in the 44th Bomb Group recalls:

"It had been four days since our 'Milk Run' to St. Pol on Monday. This would be our 'thirteenth mission'. We could not hope for another easy one and when the curtains were drawn, we knew this was going to be another rough day. For the second time in eleven days, we were headed for Brunswick. Need anyone be reminded of the stiff fighter opposition we could expect and the accurate flak barrage over the city itself? Brunswick was known as the second 'Big B' - Berlin being the more noted. Lift off was 0900 hours with 28 of our planes, two of which were PFF. Our load was six 1000lb bombs. Ten other bomb groups and we made up the 272 B-24s of the 2nd Division to reach the objective. We hardly reached German airspace when the battle began. The Germans sent up two groups of fighters, one to distract our escort and the other to attack the 14th Combat Wing. We three groups flew together perhaps a half a mile apart. All hell broke loose when between 150 and 200 of the enemy planes swarmed all over us. Most of the enemy action was aimed at the 492nd Bomb Group.[791] Our 44th gunners were very busy; they shot down 13 of the attackers, four of which my 68th Squadron accounted for. No 44th plane was lost but what I saw happening to the 492nd Bomb Group was like watching a motion picture, as they were ahead of us within easy view. Enemy fighters in mass saturation swung in for the attack - some head on, others from up and into the rear of the formation. It looked like a massacre. One after the other of their bombers was shot out of the sky. I saw the whole thing and before it was over, the 492nd had lost eight of their number. Little could any of us know this was to be their lot as long as the Group remained in combat. They had inherited the Eightballs' jinx.

"We were still on the way to Brunswick. Our objective was the marshaling yards in order to disrupt traffic through this most important rail center. Being 125 miles west of Berlin, it was a vital junction for goods flowing from the east and north. Our B-24s all together had 700 tons of bombs and when we finally got there we delivered them on target with excellent results due to the fact that the cloud cover had dissipated so that our bombardiers were able to make a visual bomb run. But we were not there yet; we still had many miles to go when suddenly one of our motors began to smoke. Peritti feathered the prop and gave more power to the remaining three in order to keep in formation. We had apparently caught some enemy fire and were losing oil. This was bad news. Luftwaffe pilots just loved to see a plane fall out of formation. They were reluctant to come at us again as we had shot them up badly on their attack before but brother watch out for any bomber that left formation. Many times I saw one of our bombers leave formation and before long the enemy would be on the attack. They would swoop down on the crippled ship. It always seemed to me like a cat playing with a mouse. Most times I would watch our fellow airmen bale out before the plane made the final plunge to earth.

"We did not want to be one of these unfortunates so Peritti and I devised a plan. As I said before, we never flew in a straight line for long before we would alter course in order to not alert the Germans as to our final destination. Peritti ordered Warga to release our bombs to lighten our ship so we could keep up with the others. I was to plot a new course about ten minutes before the whole formation turned in order to 'cut the corner' and rejoin the group before the German pilots had a chance to get at us. In all my missions I never saw another plane do what we did that day. At every turn, to the target and on the way home, we cut the corner. It must have appeared odd to the rest of the squadron but they obviously could tell what we were doing and could see we had lost an engine. I feel it saved us from being shot down. Warga did release our bombs. If I lived to be a hundred years old, I'd still be able to close my eyes and see it again. He picked out a German farmhouse in the middle of nowhere. The bombs started walking across the barnyard, through the barn and into the house coming out the other side of the yard. No one on the ground could have survived this completely unexpected disaster. When questioned at interrogation why he picked this target, his reply was, 'What's the difference in destroying a farmhouse or a city house?' I never have had a bad conscious about it, as the Nazis had no qualms about sending V-2 rockets into England that plummeted out of the sky at 3000mph exploding with no warning whatsoever. This was war and we were just young boys playing the game.

"Finally we did reach the target and one can only imagine how helpless we felt going through the terrific flak barrage with no bombs to drop. We did not want to be exposed to this terrible danger but neither could we leave formation and as usual, we picked up our share of flak holes. With their bomb loads gone, the other planes in our formations now were able to fly faster than we were using only three motors. This put us in a tight spot. We continued to cut corners until we started to pass a nearby B-17 formation. Peritti left our Group and joined onto this Flying Fortress outfit. The B-24 could easily fly as fast with three motors as the B-17 with all four. We were told later that we really did look out of place with our square body, twin tailed Lib flying among the round bodied single tail Forts. We could have cared less; we needed the protection of a formation to keep the fighters off our backs.

"In spite of all that the Germans threw at us, the 44th lost not a plane or man this day but in turn we had punished them severely. We landed at 1600 hours having been in the air exactly 7 hours. To put the day in prospective for the whole 8th Air Force, 888 heavies were dispatched of which, 818 reached their targets. In the process 28 of our bombers and 19 of our fighters did not return. In the fierce aerial fighting, the Luftwaffe took a severe beating, as did the German cities."

No one at Shipdham was more relieved than T/Sgt Don Chase:

"We were lucky; others were not. The brunt of the E/A attacks was borne by the newly arrived 492nd Group. Attracted perhaps by the non-painted, silvery finish of the brand new planes that glinted in the sun, Me 109s and FW 190s evaded the cordon of American fighters and pounced on the fledgling Group, which was flying in tight formation off to our left and below us. I watched as E/A, lined up six or eight abreast, made a frontal attack that felled four, maybe five, bombers. I saw no return fire from the B-24 gunners who, possibly, held their fire thinking the oncoming fighters were friendlies. Few chutes were sighted as the 24s spun earthward in increasingly tight circles which caused an upward G-force that few men could overcome. Later, other B-24s fell but I looked away, feeling nauseous, as each began its fatal spiral. So, after 28 missions of varying intensity and the loss of many friends, I was through with combat.

"There had been no 'easy' missions, but some were much less difficult than others, especially when no enemy action occurred. Regardless of enemy activity many lives and ships were lost. Accidents plagued all operational Groups. Some crewmen were blown or fell out of aircraft. A couple of days prior to my 13th mission, a radio operator, seeking to obtain forgotten orders, left his A/C and walked into a whirling propeller, killing him instantly. Airmen died from oxygen starvation when icing conditions froze shut their masks' intake valves. Mid-air collisions claimed many lives and ships. When several hundred A/C climb through layered clouds, sometimes up to 20,000ft, a slight tracking error occasionally brought two ships together on a collision course. A few ships were knocked out of the sky when bombs from higher flying A/C ripped through the planes of a lower formation. Errant B-24 gunfire, too, added to our own toll. Several 24*s*, their IFF code (Identification Friend or Foe) inoperative, had been shot down by British A/A. There were no easy missions.

"And I wished that nobody, anywhere, ever had to go to war again."

Lieutenant Joseph Wroblewski at Polebrook, meanwhile, had embarked on his 30th and final mission in the 351st Bomb Group. The wait had been agonizing, as he recalled:

"After getting up at 1 and 2 o'clock in the morning for three straight days, each mission was scrubbed. All easy raids or 'milk runs'. Then at briefing I thought, 'Not again. To Berlin. My last mission.' I cussed the weathermen all the way. He said we would have overcast at the target with clouds coming up to 25,000ft. We went in at 27,000ft with a temperature of about -40°C. The clouds were nowhere to be seen except for a puff here and there. Visual bombing. Just before we got to Berlin about 50 Me 109s came up and made a pass at the group just ahead of us knocking down two bombers. I broke out in a sweat but was glad to get into the flak before they could make another pass. Flak was the lesser of two evils. It was heavy but not accurate. We only picked up a few small holes and one piece tore the tail gunner's shoe but no injury. Bombing was made visually. After 'bombs away' the trip back was uneventful. We got a good look at Berlin and saw bombs from the groups ahead exploding in the city. This being our last mission, we shot a green flare upon landing. It sort of upset our commander, Colonel Romig, because this was against orders. He threatened us but all we had to do was go on a practice mission two days later."

Dick Johnson, who flew with Bud Beiser on their second mission this day, recalls:

"The 427th Squadron was assigned lead and we flew in position #5. Berlin was the primary target; with Kiel as the secondary target in case Berlin was socked in.[792] Our route north over the English Channel was hampered by dense and persistent vapor trails of the preceding groups. Our cloud ceiling at take off was 2000ft, which altered our forming up a bit. However we departed the English coast with 18 aircraft plus two radar ships from another group. Soon, the lead ship of the low squadron aborted due to a supercharger problem. Our route to Berlin took us up the English Channel past Hamburg and across the Jutland peninsula to a southeasterly heading. This took us about midway between Hamburg and Kiel. Our escorting fighters were P-38 Lightnings and a few P-51 Mustangs. Their fuel range would not allow them to escort us all the way to Berlin and they dropped off just past Hamburg. Fortunately, we saw no enemy fighters close enough to identify and so our main problem was flak.

"As we approached the target, the flak was unbelievable. It was as if someone had painted a thin black line across the sky and it was exactly at our altitude of 26,000ft. As we approached Berlin, clouds covered over half the earth below us, which made the target difficult to see. Many of our aircraft dropped *Chaff*. This only helped during cloudy weather, as the German anti-aircraft gunners preferred visual sighting. Their 'Final Aimer' usually aimed for the left wing root of the lead plane. These 88mm cannons were all on turntables and all six guns turned in unison. The gunners were so good that they could fire a burst of six, every three seconds or so. While the aim was done from a control site, all six guns pointed parallel to each other and did not converge on the target. This allowed a wider pattern of bursts, which could cover an entire group of airplanes. The big disadvantage for the flak gunners was the necessity to lead the target by two or more kilometers. That was how much they had to allow for the interval of travel by the target until the explosive shell arrived. The gunners had to assume that the target would be at a given point when the explosive shell arrived. A slow turn by the target aircraft usually was enough to cause the flak to miss.[793]

"On this day, however, Lieutenant E. L. Roth and his crew of *Sky Duster*[794] in the No.3 position of the high squadron was hit by a direct burst shortly after bombs were dropped and went down. Only five parachutes were seen to emerge from the stricken aircraft. As co-pilot I was able to see this loss for a short while but our ball-turret gunner, Charles Lana and others got a first hand view. We had heard rumors that civilians had murdered some of our crewmembers that had baled out and this was confirmed after the war. After leaving the hell in the air, many were faced by an equal hell on the ground.

"Our Group Commander, Colonel Stevens was leading this mission against Berlin. He was flying with Lieutenant Bordelon of our squadron, which led the group that day. Of the 19 aircraft from our group, one was shot down by flak, three received major damage, eleven suffered less severe damage and only four B-17s came back unscathed. Our aircraft had several flak holes in the leading edges and a few in the sides. Ours was listed as 'major damage,' due to the fact that during the bomb drop, our B-17 was forced out of position by a neighboring aircraft. This put us directly behind the lead plane, so that when he dropped his bombs, his 'Sky Marker' bomb enveloped our plane with a white acid fog and flying home was difficult due to the milky looking windshield. Due to 6/10^{ths} cloud cover over Berlin, our bombing results were not very good. We felt let down, feeling that our effort was largely wasted after facing such battle conditions. Total flight time over 8 hours. Over enemy territory, 3 hours and a half. We reported 'Hot News' of a German naval convoy in the Hamburg Fjord on the way in, but couldn't see it on the way out, because of the ruined Plexiglas."

Fighter opposition was heavy, and 28 bombers failed to return. Three of them came from the 100th. Clarence F. Cherry, left waist gunner in *Rogers Raiders*, piloted by Julian Rogers, recalls:

"We left Thorpe Abbotts before daylight on 19 May. Our flight was to Berlin. We were hit with light to mild flak over the target. So we thought we had a good flight. On our way back over Denmark we were flying low squadron and 'tail-end Charlie' position when we were attacked by Me 109s and FW 190s. They made about six passes at our position before my left waist position gun was completely blown out and I was wounded in the head. They removed me to the radio room for aid. They began to throw out equipment to lighten the ship. Already, two engines were gone. Finally, the pilot, Julian P. Rogers, told our crew to prepare to ditch in the sea. We made a rough landing. They threw me out of the top window in the radio room and I came out on the wing and started to float away from our sinking Fortress. They pulled me into the life raft. It was shot with cannon holes. We were close to two islands off Denmark. We could hear the small engines on the boats in the harbor. Julian said to us. 'Row out to sea.' We were not going to be PoWs. I don't know how far we rowed. Later on a Fortress came low and made a fix on our position. Forty hours later a RAF ASR 'plane came over us and dropped a smoke flare on the water for wind drift. They dropped a wooden boat which had three parachutes attached to it. It dropped very close to us in the sea. We climbed aboard and started towards England. We ran into two Danish fishing boats and they interned us on their boat. They were going to take us back to Denmark as PoWs, but the British flying above us told them to stay put or be sunk. An ASR launch was on its way for us. We were taken to Great Yarmouth Hospital. All of my crew was saved. I stayed at Great Yarmouth hospital for a few days and then went back to flying and completed my tour."

On 19 May U.S. fighters claimed 70 enemy fighters for the loss of 19 of their own. *Oberleutnant* Georg-Peter Eder, II./JG 1, in his battle report of the downing of a B-24 at 6500 meters at Osnabrück-Rheine and further north at 1245 hours, reads:

"After being ready for the start. I commanded with the *Gruppe* at 1140 with the order to gather over Paderborn with the I./JG 1 and III./JG 1 at a height of 1000 meters and then proceed towards the Porta Westfalica at 7-8000 meters. The unit reached the commanded destination while climbing and received the order to fly at a course of 340°. After several changes of directions, the unit sighted the enemy and engaged in air battle with the battle group. The planned attack towards the battle unit was unsuccessful because the group became entangled in air battles with the fighter escorts. The unit turned away towards the east and prepared for a second unified attack. I attacked from the front and below a Liberator, which was flying as the second plane on the left in a closed Pulk. The Liberator burned immediately with a bright flare and separated from the *Pulk*. When it went down, I saw that the tail was separated from the plane and the Liberator exploded in the air. After this, more air battles with the enemy escort planes developed, which reached as far as the areas of Minden. After I tumbled around with several Thunderbolts in a height of up to 800 meters my plane lost its balance during a steep curve, when I saw under me a FW, which was pursued by two Thunderbolts. I balanced my plane again and shot from above and behind a long fire burst from a distance of up to 30 meters whereupon the two Thunderbolts exploded in the air."[795]

Also on 19 May, Lieutenant Moser's crew in the 94th Bomb Group returned to combat status, as Wilbur Richardson recalls:

"This was our crew's first trip to Berlin.[796] What made the 19 May trip memorable was that on the bomb run the ship above us [*Trudy*, flown by Lieutenant John Winslett] missed us with his bomb load. One of the 1000-pounders fell behind No.3 engine (I saw this one go by my ball turret). I quickly followed it down only to see it hit the left stabilizer of *Miss Donna Mae*, which was out of position below us. Apparently, it jammed the elevator in a down position. It lost altitude rapidly and began a steep dive. I watched in vain for 'chutes. None appeared.[797] Others indicated that the Fort started to break up although I didn't see it. The flak was heavy and some fighters were in the area but Brux had been much worse."

Abe Dolim was flying his 11th mission; his fourth to Berlin, flying with Lieutenant McMakin's crew, and also saw *Miss Donna Mae* go down:

"At bombs away over the target, our group leader began his right turn to the rally point while we were still dropping bombs. As we lagged in the second flight, the high squadron leader banked into our overhead airspace and a 1000lb bomb clipped the horizontal stabilizer of Lieutenant Reid's aircraft on our left wing. It lost altitude rapidly and began a very steep dive. We watched in vain for blossoming parachutes. We led the second flight of the lead squadron and so were plagued by heavy contrails, which we encountered at 26,000ft. The mission route was from Lowestoft to Heligoland, Hamburg, Wittenberg, Target and return via Stettin, Rostock, Kiel and Heligoland. After we turned west at Stettin while approaching the islands in the Fehrmarn belt, we were alerted for 'Red Bandits.' Our fighter escort presently engaged large numbers of enemy fighters. About ten Messerschmitt 109s made a 12 o'clock level pass through the low group in our combat wing formation. A B-17 immediately dropped out of formation, heading for Sweden and cloud cover in that general direction. I watched a 109 cut out of the enemy squadron and begin his pursuit curve to attack a lone B-17 from 5 o'clock high. The enemy fighter pilot made the mistake of coming inside the range of their .50s before he was ready to shoot. Fire control from the B-17 was perfect - all .50s let go at once. The 109 passed the B-17, dived without pulling out and splashed into the Baltic. The B-17 continued on her way to Malmo. Two 109s approached our aircraft from 12 o'clock level but broke off their attack when Lieutenant Larrison[798] opened fire with his chin turret. Our #1 engine had been hit by flak over the target and it was leaking oil rather badly, so I worked a quick plot to Malmo, just in case. East of Kiel, we saw some of the red colored flak bursts with which the anti-aircraft batteries directed their fighters to our position. The oil pressure on #1 engine was sufficient to get us home without straggling."

On 20 May it was back to France again, when 367 B-17s and B-24s were sent to pound targets in France, while 271 B-24s and B-17s of the 3rd Bomb Division were despatched to bomb Liège and Brussels. Heavy cloud caused the 3rd Bomb Division to abandon its mission and part of the 2nd Bomb Division to be recalled. Bomb Groups were stood down on the 21st, but the following morning after bad weather had ruled out targets in France the heavies struck at Kiel and Siracourt. Five B-17s were lost.

With the good weather continuing the heavies made visual bombing attacks on several targets in France on 23, 24, and 25 May. On 23 May 804 B-17s and B-24s, including for the first time B-24s in the 34th Bomb Group at Mendlesham, commanded by Colonel Ernest J. Wackwitz, bombed several targets, including Hamburg, Saarbrücken, and French airfields for the loss of only one bomber.[799] The next day 447 B-17s bombed "Big-B," while 72 more attacked targets of opportunity and 400 Liberators bombed airfields at Orly, Melun, Creil, and Poix in France. John McClane, in the 44th Bomb Group, recalls:

"We were allowed to rest for 5 days after that frightening experience of Brunswick on Friday the 19th. Today turned out to be another 'fun day' as our target was an airfield 22 miles southeast of Paris and 5 miles North of Melun. Our course took us directly over the center of London. At briefing we had been told that the balloon barrage would be pulled down so we could make a low pass over the city to let the long suffering Londoners get a close look at the tremendous power of 'The Mighty 8th Air Force'. Take off was early at 0500 hours. Our group was divided into three separate squadrons [67th, 68th and 506th] of 12 planes each. We assembled over clouds with another 132 B-24s of the 2nd and 3rd Divisions making a total of 168 Liberators carrying 500 tons of bombs headed for the Melun airfield. After assembly we headed straight for London. There was no cloud cover over the city. It was a never to be forgotten sight as we traveled this huge city at approximately 1000 ft. The roar and vibration was something to behold. I doubt that in the foreseeable history of mankind that this sight will be repeated again. We continued on to the Channel then broke the coast of France in Normandy. From here we circled in around Paris from the west making our bomb run south of Paris to the target which lay between Paris and Melun. Our strike photo showed that the 68th Squadron's bombs landed squarely on target. Each plane carried 24 300lb bombs or approximately 3½ tons of high explosives. The flak was light and inaccurate inflicting no damage to our plane. Fighter support was so effective that we saw no sign of the Luftwaffe. Our outbound flight took us to the same old area between Dunkirk and Ostend where we crossed the Channel homeward bound. Generally we did not refer to a penetration of enemy territory as deep of a run around Paris as a 'Milk Run' but for all practical purposes this was a 'Milk Run'. We landed at 1115 hours after 6 hours and 15 minutes in the air."

Altogether 33 bombers were lost on 24 May. Cloud and thick contrails caused the 381st Bomb Group to lose contact with other groups in the 1st Wing, and fighters shot down eight B-17s. The "Bloody Hundredth" suffered even worse. 1st Lieutenant Francis "Frank" J. Malooly, pilot of *Powerhouse*[800] in the 350th Bomb Squadron, described the mission, his 27th, as "a complete disaster from beginning to end." His ground crew chief, Sgt George Pullar, who had given the Fortress its name, never had a crew finish their missions, and he was getting more nervous as his crew were closing in on 30. Malooly recalls:

"This was the period when the Air Force was moving flying officers from long stateside duly into Eighth Air Force combat groups. These people were Captains and field grade officers, some of whom were given positions of responsibility without, in my opinion, the required experience. My crew and I had already completed six or seven Berlin missions and our Squadron CO, Captain Jack Swartout had assured me that we had filled our quota of Berlin missions (more 'Big B's' than any other crew in the Group). However, a new and apparently inexperienced Major Maurice Fitzgerald who was going to be our new Squadron CO was scheduled to be Command Pilot for the Group and Swartout wanted his most experienced crews on the mission. I was a lead pilot and on this mission led the high squadron and was deputy group lead. The Group lead pilot was Captain James Geary[801] who had completed a tour with the 390th Bomb Group and then been assigned to the Hundredth."

After take-off the Hundredth had difficulty forming up with the Wing, and when the B-17s started across the North Sea they were badly strung out and behind the rest. They entered enemy territory in this same condition, and the low squadron was badly strung out and behind by several hundred feet. They were "meat on the table" for the *Luftwaffe*, and enemy fighters decimated the low squadron. *Powerhouse* had a bad fire in the right wing and was badly shot up, and Malooly's crew baled out. Geary's ship was "hit by a shower of lead" and flak and went down.[802] The plane flying on Malooly's left wing,[803] piloted by Lindley Williamson, burst into flames, and eight of the crew baled out to be taken prisoner. The co-pilot and radio operator were killed. The B-17[804] piloted by Lieutenant Delbert S. Pearson and Wilbert Lund was also knocked out by the fighters and disappeared into the clouds. Nine men baled out and were taken prisoner. The tenth man, a replacement ball turret gunner, was killed. By this time, eight of the 100th Bomb Group's Fortresses had turned for home, leaving the rest to release their bombs through a hole in the clouds with fairly good results, and to turn away in an attempt to avoid the heavy flak. The formation was then attacked by a succession of enemy fighters. *Nelson King*,[805] piloted by Lieutenant Emil J. Siewert, who was killed, was shot down. The bombardier and tail gunner also died. The rest of the crew baled out and were captured. Four more losses came from the 349th Squadron. The first was a B-17[806] piloted by Lieutenant Martin T. Hoskinson and Marvin Apking, who along with their crew were on their first or second mission. All ten men were killed. Next to go was the B-17[807] flown by Lieutenant Robert G. Roeder and Paul Lammers. Both men were killed, as were the navigator, engineer, radio operator, and toggelier. Although wounded, the two waist gunners managed to bale out with the ball turret gunner and tail gunner. *Times A Wastin*,[808] piloted by Lieutenant Henry F. Jespersen and Robert Atkins, was shot down. Both men and the engineer, waist gunner, and bombardier were taken prisoner after baling out. The rest of the crew were killed. The ninth and last B-17 lost[809] was piloted by 2nd Lieutenant Clarke T. Johnson and Raymond Lund, who along with their crew were on their first mission. Seven of the ten men aboard were killed, including the pilots and the navigator.[810] At the debriefing back at Thorpe Abbotts the only good news was that Colonel Ollen "Ollie" Turner and Captain Jack Swartout had finished their tours.

The 4th Fighter Group's Mustangs, led by Major "Goody" Goodson, were among those who flew a Penetration Support on the mission to Berlin. The P-51 pilots saw two B-17s hit by flak and explode over Berlin, and three others went down. No chutes were seen. The Mustangs had climbed to 30,000ft, and they saw 30-40 enemy aircraft at 35,000ft that headed for the Mustangs at 12 o'clock, and a fierce air battle ensued. A red-nosed P-51 was seen to overshoot a Bf 109 at 32,000ft, which then raked the P-51 with cannon fire, and the Mustang was last seen going down in smoke. 2nd Lieutenant Ralph K. Hofer, who had by now reached double figures, knocked down two more enemy fighters to take his score to twelve. He recalled:

> "I sighted four Bf 109s coming in below us. I attacked, but lost sight of them in the haze. I pulled up and sighted three FW 190s attacking a B-17 that was returning. We bounced them and I started shooting. We were trying to scare them off, but they didn't seem to see me. Finally I closed on one, getting strikes. The aircraft started smoking, the hood was jettisoned and the pilot baled. The other two broke up to the left. I then pulled up and saw Lieutenant Fraser, my wingman, behind the other two FW 190s. One of them made a split 'S' with Fraser following. I broke into the leader, preventing him from firing at Fraser. He did a split 'S' and I followed at 14,000ft. I got a few scattered hits. At 10,000ft, below the clouds, I got more strikes in a tight turn. He pulled sharply up into a cloud and jettisoned his hood. I did not see the pilot bale out, but the aircraft crashed in a field burning. It's ammo exploded at intervals. I took a picture of this."[811]

The next day, 25 May, crews correctly anticipated a "milk run" to the Low Countries. 2nd Lieutenant Dick Johnson in the 303rd Bomb Group flew his third mission of the war:

> "Target for today was the marshaling yards at Blainville, France. Since this would be a rather long mission, our take off time was a little earlier than usual. The first B-17 took off at 0547 and the last at 0558. The 303rd Bomb Group was to supply only twelve aircraft, with two spares, for the 41st Combat Wing, of which we were a part. London is 60 miles south of our field at Molesworth and our departure course took us straight south, past London. At that point we turned east and passed over a suburb of London, climbing to 19,000ft at 0731. From here we crossed the English Channel in a climb so that we penetrated the French coast at 23,000ft. Our penetration was at a point about half way between Le Havre and Boulogne as there were no flak guns nearby. Just out of range, we saw a few bursts of flak as we continued on a course, which took us within sight of Paris, which lay to our south. At the target we had taken an earlier lead, since the other combat wings had overshot the penetration course, which put us almost first to the target. We were low group on this mission and since the lead group overshot the IP we had a longer than usual bomb run. During the bomb run, the formation is most vulnerable to enemy action, as the bomb bay doors are open for the entire trip from IP to target. This alerts the German anti aircraft gunners that we will be flying a long, straight course to the target. This day, the bomb run was eleven minutes and we expected to have a great deal of flak come up. But nothing happened. Evidently the 88mm guns that we thought were there had been moved elsewhere. The weather was CAVU[812] therefore if there had been flak guns; we would have been 'Sitting Ducks.' This was the first time that I saw bombs exploding on the target. The extended bomb run allowed the lead bombardier to kill his drift to perfection and the Norden bombsight did its job flawlessly. There were no damaged aircraft and no aborts on this mission and all twelve returned to base just after noon. Total flight time, five and one half-hours. Over enemy territory, almost exactly three hours. We did our part to damage the German war machine for the upcoming invasion."

Despite perfect weather, some Fortresses in the 390th and 401st Bomb Groups bombed using radar. Command needed to know how successful PFF methods could be on D-Day if targets were obscured by cloud. It all served to increase speculation, at Framlingham and Deenthorpe at least, that the invasion of *Festung Europa* was imminent. "Invasion fever" was on everyone's lips. [813] GIs returning from 48 hour passes in London to their bases in East Anglia were full of vivid accounts of trucks, jeeps, transports, and staff cars jamming the English roads and narrow winding English country lanes, causing vast traffic snarl-ups. In Andover, Hampshire, office workers were given 15 minutes extra at lunchtime to cross the street! Passenger trains were being withdrawn, and trains out of the capital were crammed. For some weeks the headlines in the London press and *Stars and Stripes* had proclaimed that Operation *Overlord*, the invasion of the continent, was imminent. But where and when?

John Nargi, in the 384th Service Squadron, knew something "was up," because not only were all leaves cancelled, but also the mechanics were working night and day to prepare their fighter planes. In May all flight crewmen were ordered to carry their .45s at all times. Ground crews were issued carbines to have at the ready, in case enemy paratroops attempted to foul up any suspected plans. Wilbur Richardson, a B-17 gunner in the

94th Bomb Group at Bury St. Edmunds (Rougham), had grown up in Long Beach, California. With double summer time in effect in England darkness came very late, and the nights were much shorter than he was used to. So, in order to get some sleep before the usual crack-of-dawn (or earlier) briefing for a bombing mission he found it necessary to close the blackout curtains to darken the room by shutting out the later evening light. At Molesworth, Ben Smith Jr, radio operator-gunner in the 303rd Bomb Group, flew combat missions immediately. The first few short haul sorties were "milk runs," which gave the false impression that combat flying was "a piece of cake," but he and the rest of the crew knew that they would be involved in the long-awaited invasion of *Festung Europa*, and they expected all-out opposition. Ben Smith picked up the *Stars and Stripes* and read that American losses over Europe in the last five months were 1407 heavy bombers, 673 fighters, and 100 medium bombers. These figures did not include those killed or wounded when the planes returned to their home base or crashed in the United Kingdom. Over 14,000 men were lost in the heavies alone. The British, he read, had parallel losses.

At Shipdham, after 14 missions Charles Peritti's crew had become a seasoned crew. Peritti had already been advanced to 1st Lieutenant, and on 25 May the remaining three officers (co-pilot Burr W. Palmer, bombardier John F. Warga, and navigator John W. McClane, Jr.) were promoted to the rank of 1st Lieutenant. McClane had been awarded the Air Medal on 13 May after his 11th mission, and the first of three oak leaf clusters on 22 May, and he was beginning to feel "like a real vet":

> "Already we were being put in a lead position having worked our way up through the formation. Soon Peritti would be the 'A Flight' leader and I would be directing our course as a lead navigator. We no longer flew in low position. We were becoming leaders, not followers. The group had four squadrons of which three usually flew on any one mission. Each squadron had a lead navigator with a deputy on his wing. At this stage of the game, we were deputies but on D-Day and thereafter, we were leaders. We had been assigned a new NMF B-24H (42-95260), which Peritti selected the name of *Lili Marlene*.[814] How he came by this name I have no idea. He also arranged to have the picture of '*Lili*' painted on the right side of the nose of the plane. She was sitting on a bomb and, as one might expect, mostly nude. This plane had been especially equipped with a Gee Box. At this time only lead navigators had Gee Boxes. *Lili Marlene* was a beautiful plane - bright and unpainted with our squadron code letters of WQ in large letters on either side of the fuselage just aft on the side gunner windows. I was sure she would fly until old age sent her to the 'Great Haven in the Sky' where old bombers go. I know she is there now - even if she did meet with a premature death."

On 27 May the 8th switched to German targets when the rail network once again came in for a pounding by the Fortresses. Colonel James Luper, CO 457th Bomb Group, led the "Fireball Outfit" and the 1st Division to Ludwigshafen in *Rene III*.[815] The flak was heavy, and fighters made head-on attacks that verged on the suicidal. *Rene III* was badly shot up, but Luper managed to nurse her back to Glatton.[816] 2nd Lieutenant Dick Johnson in the 303rd Bomb Group, meanwhile, flew his fourth mission to Mannheim on 27 May:

> "We were assigned to position No.6 in the low squadron, known as 'Purple Heart Corner' because it is lowest in the squadron and farthest out. Mannheim was a heavily defended city on the Rhine River near Ludwigshafen, just a few miles northwest of Heidelberg. Mannheim was a bottleneck for transportation in that area. Our mission was to destroy the marshaling yards that would feed supplies to defend the coast during the D-Day invasion. We did not yet know when the invasion would be but knew it would be soon. Our assigned secondary target was the nearby city of Ludwigshafen. If overcast, PFF on Ludwigshafen. Target of opportunity Florennes/Juzaine airfield. Last resort, any military installation in Germany not adjacent to built up area(!) We were trying to spare German civilians. This phrase was usually reserved for use in occupied countries only. Thirty-seven of our B-17s were loaded with ten 500lb bombs each. Engines were started at 0815 and takeoff started at 0845. We assembled the group over Molesworth at 6000ft and departed base at 0945. We were two minutes late, due to keeping Division battle order. The logistics of forming up, joining your Wing and staying on course is almost mind-boggling. The Eighth Air Force put up almost a thousand bombers that day, using about two million gallons of gasoline. We departed the English coast at Beachy Head at 1039 and 16,000ft. We climbed as we crossed the English Channel and crossed the enemy coast in France at 1100 at 20,000ft. At the Initial Point we made a 30° turn to the target and opened bomb bay doors. Ten minutes before the target, the code word for visual bombing, 'Stud Horse' was given by radio. A six-minute bomb run was made on a straight line to the target and the flak started coming up. As we approached the city of Mannheim, the flak became intense and shell fragments struck many of our B-17s. The ceiling and visibility was unlimited, so the German flak gunners were aiming visually. The radar jamming *Chaff* that we dropped did little good. Only a few German fighter aircraft were seen in the distance, but didn't attack, as our escort kept them at bay. Our 35 B-17s dropped a total of 350 bombs on the target with good results. One B-17 jettisoned his bombs over Germany after they failed to release over the target. One B-17 received major damage and seven had minor damage. None were shot down. In my diary I have underlined the words, Very Lucky, as our plane escaped damage. Total flight time, seven hours. Time over enemy territory, three hours and 35 minutes."[817]

The 457th's tale of woe continued on 28 May. The group lost three more crews when a record 1341 heavies were despatched to seven oil targets in Germany. The *Luftwaffe* again concentrated their attacks, in this instance on the leading wings of the 1st and 3rd Bomb Divisions. The escorting fighters were overwhelmed, and over 300 fighters assailed the 94th Wing at the head of the 1st Division. Altogether 32 bombers were lost, including seven in the 401st Bomb Group.

Lieutenant John R. Shaffer, the bombardier in *Naughty Nan* in the 93rd Bomb Group, was flying his second mission to the synthetic oil refinery at Merseburg, the second largest of its type in Germany:

> "Flames reaching to 2000ft were proof enough that the Liberators had found their mark. Even 200 miles from the target, crews could still see a pall of smoke, which rose 12,000ft into the air."

Lieutenant William Bailey's crew in the 448th Bomb Group were flying their first mission. Ben C. Isgrig, the bombardier, recalls:

> "Our particular target was the ammonia section of the plant. We were carrying 48 100lb GP bombs and were in the first section over the target. I guess we were all pretty scared and nervous. I watched the lead plane's bombs begin to drop and started to toggle ours out, but, instead of falling clear, seven bombs in the right rear rack hung up. I went back into the bomb bay and was scared to see that the propellers on the fuses of three of the bombs were turning rapidly, which meant they were probably fused and liable to go off at the

slightest jolt. I got Kovalcheck, a gunner, to help me and were able to get them out by lifting them up one at a time and dropping them out It was a wonder that one or both of us didn't fall out of the bomb bay. It's no joke to stand on a foot-wide catwalk with no parachute at 22,000ft in a -20° breeze and no support and throw out bombs one at a time. Kovalcheck was using our one walkaround oxygen bottle; I had none. As we turned to leave the bomb bay I stumbled and nearly fell from the 'plane, but Kovalcheck caught me and pulled me through the door and to the nearest oxygen outlet. The trip home was uneventful."

John W. McClane flew his 15th mission in the 44th Bomb Group:

"On Sunday morning of 28 May I had the surprise of my life. When I went too early briefing (I was a lead navigator now) I could not believe what I heard. We were going to Zeitz again. The very same synthetic oil refinery 20 miles southwest of Leipzig, Germany that we had left wrecked and burning just 16 days before on our 10th mission of May 12th. My question was, 'What are we going back to Zeitz again for?' Well, little did we know of the German's ability to repair and even completely rebuild industrial plants that our intelligence people had considered destroyed. At this time of my limited knowledge, I thought we were going on a wild goose chase, which made no sense. We all knew better now and before the day was out, I was to once more look down on this refinery to see with my own eyes that it had been completely rebuilt and back in production.

"While rebuilding their oil refineries, the Germans also put around them some of the strongest concentration of anti-aircraft guns in all of Hitler's Europe. We no longer could expect just 4 gun ack-ack batteries to track and fire at us. These 'Grossbatteries' of 88mm as well as 105 and 128mm caliber were in groups of 12 to 24 guns that gave a 'shot gun' effect. The tighter our formation, the more effective they were. We dispersed *Chaff* to jam the radar, which aimed the flak guns. This was very effective except for the lead formation throwing out the first of the stuff. The first groups caught all hell, as I was to really find out on my 26th mission to St. Lô when we lead the Air Force. The mission was a major effort by the 8th Air Force. In all, over a thousand 4-engine bombers were sent to more than 30 different targets in Germany; 864 of these reached their objectives. Of all these planes, our 2nd Division Liberators made up the largest single force. The 44th Bomb Group's 26 planes were part of 187 to strike Zeitz with almost 450 tons of bombs whereas on 12 May we had only 250 tons. We were out to destroy this oil refinery once and for all.

"Take off was 1000 hours. Our fighter escort was so effective, we never saw an enemy on the way in or out. (However the 1st Division B-17s had 300 fighters attack them with rather severe consequences, especially the 401st Bomb Group which lost one-fourth of the 32 bombers MIA for the day from all three Air Divisions.) The AA gunners at Zeitz must have been low on ammunition or asleep because the flak was much less intense than we expected. However the flak that they did send up was accurate as our 506th Squadron lost one of its planes for the only loss of the day for the 44th Bomb Group. The 389th Bomb Group lost two more. Our bombing results were excellent. Visibility was unlimited. The black smoke was almost to our flight altitude before we were out of sight of the target. This time, 'we tore them up bad'.[818] We arrived back in Shipdham air base at 1730 hours, having been in flight some 7 hours and 30 minutes."

2nd Lieutenant Dick Johnson, in the 303rd Bomb Group in the 41st Wing, flew his 5th mission this day, to the Eifeltor marshaling yard at Cologne:

"The weather over Europe was predicted to be mostly clear and targets would include fuel and transportation systems. Our crew was assigned a special mission this day and would not participate in the regular effort to neutralize Nazi war materiel. In the night the armorers attached two strange bombs to the belly of each bomber, using special bomb shackles.[819] The bombs were side by side, with their wingtips only four inches apart. They had a 12ft wing span and were almost 12ft long.[820] The three groups in the 41st Combat Wing[821] were expected to put two battle formations in the air. The 303rd put 19 planes in the glide bomb formation, which left the base an hour earlier than the second element going to oil targets. Our take off time was about 0930, so that we could be out of the way of the next element. We crossed the French coast two miles south of Nieuport at 19,500ft and proceeded to Cologne. Our squadron, the 427th went in first. Starting at 140mph we started a dive until we reached 208mph. At this point, we leveled off for a few seconds and released the bombs nearly 18 miles from the target. Unfortunately, our bombs, as well as those of the other two groups following, mostly spun in and exploded in fields 15 miles from the target.[822] Upon our return to base, one engine on our '*Bet Jane*' had to be replaced due to flak damage on the way to the target. Later that evening on German radio, which we always listened to, William Joyce, or 'Lord Haw Haw,' as we called him, reported that Cologne had been bombed by allied bombers from an altitude of 40,000ft. We had quite a laugh about that, since the B-17 wasn't designed to fly quite that high."[823]

On 29 May 993 B-24s and B-17s were despatched to several targets, including the oil plants at Politz and the Junkers Ju 88 plant at Tutow, as well as three Focke Wulf 190 factories in the Reich. Some 888 of the heavies made visual attacks on aircraft plants and oil installations in Germany. Ben Isgrig had been assured that the bomb racks in their Liberator had been repaired, but eleven of the 32 100lb M47 incendiary bombs hung up and, wearing an oxygen mask this time, he salvoed them in the general area of Tutow. Thirty-four bombers were lost, including a 492nd Bomb Group Liberator piloted by Lieutenant William V. Prewitte, which was forced to ditch in the North Sea while returning from Politz. Prewitte's crew was rescued by an ASR launch from Gorleston. Lieutenant Elmer W. Clarey, co-pilot, become entangled in his parachute and was being dragged under before he was rescued by one of the members of the ASR launch who dived in to save him. The bombardier, Lieutenant Henry Muller, drowned after his parachute had failed to open.

Russell A. Grantham, 836th Bomb Squadron Operations Officer in the 487th Bomb Group at Lavenham, who was flying his fifth mission, flew the group lead:

"Being a staff officer, I did not have an assigned plane, but substituted with assigned lead crews and did not, therefore, have a regular assigned plane. We approached Politz with three squadrons of Liberators (approximately 38 planes). At the IP we were met by Me 410 twin engined fighters. They made repeated attacks into and past the target from a position of 11 o'clock high and aiming at my plane. The target was partially obscured by clouds and smoke from previous hit. However, we were able to place bombs on the target by a simple and effective device. We had developed a simple plastic sheet with elongated cross hairs that by over-laying the intelligence photos, we could select aiming points outside the obscured area, which lined up with the target and naturally, the cross hair intersection would automatically line up on the target. Our group received an 8th Air Force Commendation and I received the Distinguished Flying Cross."

2nd Lieutenant Dick Johnson flew his 6th mission this day, to Posen (Poznan)—"Slugging it out for ten hours":

"Part of our mission to prepare for *D-Day* was to decimate the German fighter force. Had this been accomplished earlier, the invasion would have been in early May. In order for the invasion to succeed, the Allies had to have mastery of the air and this had not yet occurred. We were to bomb a Focke Wulf assembly plant and airfield in Posen where the dreaded FW 190 was being built. We were assigned No.3 position, behind and to the left of the high squadron leader. Our group furnished 18 planes for the wing formation. We were in our aircraft at 0710 and started engines at 0800. We started taxi at 0810 and took off at 0825. It took one hour for all planes to get into formation at 8000ft over Molesworth. Climbing to 13,500ft we crossed the English coast at Cromer. Over the sea we climbed to 21,000ft, picking up friendly fighters. We crossed the enemy coast near the Dutch town of Ijmuiden, not far from Egmond, at 1044. Our course was due east, aimed directly at Berlin. While still out of range of their flak guns, we made a dogleg to the south. We then took a direct flight to Posen and drew a bead on the FW factory in the suburb of Erzesinki.

"The sky was cloudless and so our bomb run of 38 miles gave the lead bombardier plenty of time to kill the drift, which was 5° to the right of our track. This caused our true heading to be at a compass heading of 64° while our track over the ground was at 68° magnetic. The intervolometer was set at the Salvo position and when the bombs first appeared out of the lead plane, all the other planes dropped in unison. Despite considerable flak, the Norden bombsight did its job well on this mission. Much of the plant was destroyed, as were several buildings nearby. Coming off the target, we headed due north for 25 minutes, while letting down to 14,000ft from our bombing altitude of 22,000ft. This was done to conserve fuel, as this was a critical problem on such a long mission. At the lower altitude, the superchargers could be turned off and the engines leaned out for better fuel efficiency. After letting down to 14,000ft, we turned to the northwest and crossed into the Baltic Sea. At this point we crossed over an island that we thought was undefended. We were wrong. The island contained a four-gun battery of 88mm flak guns and we flew directly over them. Four bursts at a time were coming up every three or four seconds and the only thing that saved us was a quick turn to throw off their aiming lead. The second burst destroyed an engine on one of our planes and he started dropping back.

"We no sooner got over the open Baltic again than we noticed a small formation of planes off to our right, going in the same direction. They were German fighters trying to simulate our own P-51s. After they passed us a couple of miles, they made a turn to the left and their profiles gave them away as Me 109s and FW 190s. There were three of each and they made a diving left turn to attack us from the 1 o'clock high position. One Me 109 chose our plane as his target and came in firing his 20mm canon too soon, as they were exploding ahead of us. Beiser grabbed the yoke and pulled up a bit. I was convinced that the German pilot had drawn a mental Bullseye on the co-pilot's windshield, so I grabbed the yoke to assist Beiser. All our forward guns were firing at this point, but our gyrations prevented any serious damage to the Me 109. More importantly, it also prevented the German pilot from inflicting any damage on us. Our B-17 was very light at this time, having dropped our ten 500lb bombs and having burned most of our eight tons of gas. This Me 109 duplicated our every move, but was behind the curve, as he could not anticipate what we were going to do. At the last moment, I was sure that he was going to ram us, but he veered off our right wing tip so close that I could see his face and was startled to see that he was not wearing an oxygen mask. It was our rule to use oxygen above 10,000ft in daylight and from the ground up at night. He probably removed his mask at the start of his attack. Whether it affected his aim, I'll never know. We expected the fighters to come back, but they spotted our straggler and decided to finish him off. It didn't work, as two of the enemy planes were shot down and a third was damaged. On the way back to base we saw a B-17 go out of control and explode. Eight parachutes were counted. In the North Sea we saw another B-17 ditch, having run out of fuel. We saw one of the inflatable life rafts that had several men in it. Air sea rescue came and picked them up a couple of hours later. None of these downed bombers were from our base and we all got back safely, including our straggler who made it on three engines. Nine B-17s of our group sustained minor damage, while our straggler was listed as major. One aircraft was listed as damaged by friendly fire. This was our aircraft, as another B-17 firing at 'our' Me 109 fired a 50 caliber, armor piercing, incendiary bullet through our left wing. Fortunately for us, it missed our gas tank, which would likely have made us into a fireball. Guns on the B-17 cannot shoot parts off their own plane because of stops built into the mechanism, but it cannot prevent 'OOPS' from your neighbors. On this mission, the return flight took us very near neutral Sweden and from other groups, 8 bombers sought refuge from the war by landing at two fields there.[824] Total flight time for this mission was just over 10 hours. Time over enemy territory, 4 hours and 40 minutes."[825]

1st Lieutenant Ralph Golubock, pilot of B-24 *Princess*[826] in the 44th Bomb Group, flew his 27th mission on 29 May to Politz, following leave at the "Flak Shack" for a week:

"We were flying in the lead position in the low element of the low squadron, which put us pretty well back in the entire group formation. During the course of the mission I noted that my wingmen were having difficulty keeping up. They were both inexperienced pilots and had not done a great deal of formation flying. Without those two on my wing, I was in a rather exposed position. I don't remember an awful lot about the take off or the formation but I am sure that everything was rather normal until we got to the target and the target was deep, deep into Germany. Actually it was in Poland and in making our approach we came over the North Sea, made a feint to Berlin and then turned in a North easterly direction and went further on until we hit the target in Poland. It appeared that we hit the target well because upon leaving we saw a great deal of smoke arise. Up to the time that we hit the target I did not see any enemy airplanes.

"After leaving the target and making a left turn, we headed out over the Baltic. We were all feeling pretty good, like the mission was over, but in reality we were a long, long way from home. Shortly after breaking the coast and going over the Baltic, we were hit by a lone Me 410 or Me 210. It was very difficult to identify the aircraft because he came slashing through. I don't think he was aiming at my aircraft, I think he was just kind of spraying the formation and he hit me. When he hit, my No.1 engine was knocked out immediately and the fuel cells in the left wing were hit and fuel was flowing through the wing in huge amounts. Had any of this fuel hit the hot superchargers, I am sure we would have gone up immediately but for some reason it did not and the fuel siphoned off the wing, harmlessly, but we lost a good deal of fuel.

"The main problem we faced at this time is that when he hit our No.1 engine and knocked it out, I was unable to feather the No.1 engine because apparently he had knocked out the propeller feather motor also. We were almost on our back at this time. I was finally able to get the ship righted and into a somewhat normal position. Our wings were level but we were in a dive and the No.1 engine was winding up, we were still unable to feather it. This created a tremendous amount of drag on the port wing and it was extremely difficult to keep the ship flying straight and level. I then cranked in full trim tab on our rudder and full aileron tab. Even with the full trim tabs rolled in, I found it extremely difficult to plane in a straight position. I was forced to lock my right leg on the right rudder, holding it down as hard as I could in order to maintain any semblance of straight flight.

"Shortly after being hit, I rang the bell one time, which was to alert the crew to put on their parachutes and prepare to bale out. I did not ring the bell the second time because it appeared that the airplane was flyable and we would be able to get to somewhere. However, my tail gunner, S/Sgt Steven E. 'Zeke' Jones, having seen what happened, seeing the gasoline flowing off the port wing, decided it was time to part company and he baled out.[827] At this time I felt that the airplane was flyable and I called my navigator who, as I mentioned before, was inexperienced and asked for a heading either back to England or to Sweden. Unfortunately he did not have any charts that showed him how to go to Sweden. I also contacted Sgt Dunlop, our engineer; to determine our fuel situation and to transfer what fuel he could from the port wing to the starboard wing. We were able to salvage enough gasoline to where I felt that we could make it to Sweden. The chances of getting back to England were zero. Even without the charts I felt that I could find Sweden and I took a heading of approximately 340°, which I felt would bring us somewhere on the Swedish continent. I was totally unable to hold altitude with the No.1 engine windmilling and causing a tremendous amount of drag so I ordered the crew to dump everything that was available. All of the machine guns, all of the ammunition, of course the bombs were already gone, everything that was not held down in any manner was thrown overboard including the Norden bomb sight, which 1st Lieutenant William D. Fitzsimmons, bombardier took a great deal of pleasure in throwing overboard.

"With the lightened aircraft we were able to maintain altitude somewhere around 10,000ft. However, just at this time, a large formation of German fighters was approaching our position. When I saw them coming I thought that there was no way we could ever make land again, that they would shoot us down and that we were indeed dead people. Why they never attacked us I will never, ever know except, I assume, that they felt that we were gone already and there was no point in wasting ammunition or risking a crew to try to knock us down. They flew very close to us and as they went by I could only look and pray that one of them would not peel off and try to hit us because we had no defenses. Our guns were gone and we would be totally helpless. It has been one of the mysteries of my life as to why we were not attacked.

"After passing the enemy aircraft we proceeded on what we hoped was a heading to Sweden and as luck would have it we did hit land. However, we soon ran out of land and were back over the ocean and later on I discovered that we hit land at the island of Bornholm, which at that time was German occupied. They could have easily knocked us out of the sky. Why they didn't, again, I will never know. Shortly after passing the island of Bornholm we again hit land and this time it was Sweden. We were warned by Swedish anti-aircraft fire not to proceed beyond a certain point. I might add that we were briefed regarding the Swedes reaction to an incursion of an aircraft over their land. They would not try to shoot us down but they would attempt to steer us to the nearest airfield. This they did and in a very short time several Swedish fighters that were early American P-35s, picked us up. They were beautiful aircraft painted blue and yellow checkerboard and they formated on us and escorted us to Malmo.

"When we were hit our bomb bays were knocked open and we were unable to close them. This caused additional drag. One of the Swedish fighters tried to fly under us to look into the aircraft and when he did, he hit our left wing. It was only his radio antenna, which hit the wing but we did tear off his radio antenna. Again, why that wing didn't go, I will never know. We eventually found the airfield where they wanted us to land and we made an approach to the airfield in a right hand pattern because my No.1 was out and made an excellent landing on a grass field. When we landed we were immediately surrounded by Swedes in various trucks, all armed with sub-machine guns and were politely, but firmly, ushered into the headquarters building where their colonel interrogated us. The first thing the colonel asked me was why we had hit one of their fighters. I explained to him that in no way did we hit one of their fighters but their fighters hit us. When the colonel heard this he became enraged and had the Swedish pilot thrown in the brig. From that point we were sent to an intern camp and spent five months in Sweden, eventually returned to England in November of 1944 and shortly after I was returned to the States after flying either 26½ or 27½ missions."

Beginning on 30 May[828] American and RAF Bomber Command crews made all-out attacks on the invasion coast. Both were careful to place twice as many bombs on targets further afield as they did on the Normandy coast, for fear that the German defenders would learn where the assault would come. The enemy knew that invasion was imminent, but suspected that the first wave of troops would land in the Pas de Calais, further north. So, while the German defenders on the Atlantic Wall played their guessing game, the heavies continued their strikes on *Noball* sites in the Pas de Calais. Late on 29 May Mike Wysocki, who had flown his 29th and penultimate mission to Leipzig earlier in the day, was called to a special briefing. It revealed that the target for the morrow would be a rocket storage site at Warren, in the Pas de Calais. B-17s were to carry a special load of six 1600lb SAP (Semi Armor-Piercing) bombs to penetrate the roof. Only Wysocki and the other lead bombardiers in the 410th Squadron were privy to the information. On the morning of 30 May crews were called a little later than usual, had their breakfasts, and then went out to their Fortresses after briefing. While Wysocki's fellow crewmembers were getting ready to fly, the ground crew smuggled a couple of extra flare guns aboard in anticipation of the crew completing their tour. Wysocki dropped his bombs on the rocket site:

"I am very nosey - I like to see what happened so I put on my steel helmet and looked. All I could see was dust in the target area. I was disappointed to think on my last mission that all I dropped was a bunch of duds![829] When we came back our B-17 was like a Roman Candle with all the flares going. It looked like a good old fashioned 4th of July, only it happened to be Memorial Day!"[830]

Operation *Cover* called for raids on coastal defenses, mainly in the Pas de Calais, to deceive the Germans as to the area to be invaded by the Allied armies massing in Britain. On 31 May 1029 heavies, including for the first time B-24s in the 490th Bomb Group at Eye, Suffolk, led by the CO, Colonel Lloyd H. Watnee, were despatched, and only one bomber and three fighters were lost.[831]

2nd Lieutenant Dick Johnson in the 303rd Bomb Group flew his 7th mission this day:

"The weather briefing for today's mission indicated good weather over the target, but we soon found that towering cumulus clouds had built up while we were en route. Some topped out at 28,000ft, well above our planned altitude. The 303rd Bomb Group was to supply 14 aircraft for the wing formation and we were on our way by 0800. As we approached the enemy coast, Clouds appeared on our route and we had to deviate from the planned course. This took us almost over Brussels, Belgium, which was well defended. Almost immediately, the B-17 flown by Lieutenant Flick, who was flying off our right wing received a direct hit. One man in his crew was seriously wounded and they turned back to England, landing at an emergency strip at Chipping Ongar. Due to the clouds, we had to abandon our primary target at Colmar, France and the secondary, St. Dizier airdrome in France. Our target of opportunity became the airport at Gilze-Rijen in southern Holland because we could see it somewhat. Unfortunately, the weather caused us to only do a one-minute bomb run and our bombs fell between the runways into a wooded area. For some reason, two planes did not drop their bombs and returned them to base. We saw six enemy fighters but they did not attack, since they were being harassed by our P-51s. Two B-17s of our group sustained major damage and six had minor damage including our *'Bet Jane'*, which suffered a fist sized hole in her tail. Vertical stabilizer, that is. We were over enemy territory for an hour and 20 minutes on this mission."[832]

John W. McClane adds:

"Everyone knew the invasion was close at hand and we were going to the marshaling yards in Brussels as part of the pre-invasion offensive against the enemy transportation system. There had been a heated debate among the planners of our war strategy as to which would be the better use of our heavy bombers. One group thought the 'Transportation Offensive' was urgent to break the German's ability to supply their Western front once the invasion had taken place. Another equally vocal group said the Strategic Oil Offensive should take first priority. To me it seems now that we did both, we were knocking out Hitler's oil capacity and at the same time striking at any form of transportation.

"The 44th put up 26 planes and in all, the 2nd and 3rd Divisions assembled an Air Armada of 491 B-24s loaded with 8 1000-lb bombs to disrupt this vital rail facility. Take off was shortly before 0830 hours but we were back a little after noon having been in the air only 4 hours, the shortest combat flight time of all my 31 missions. The reason being clouds. They extended up to 26,000ft and there was no way we could see the target visually even though we came within 10 miles of it. It would have been far too dangerous to the Belgium population of this large city to take a chance of bombing by Pathfinder lead without being precisely sure of our aim. There was nothing to do but turn for home. We encountered no fighters and flak was very light and inaccurate. Of over 1000 bombers dispatched for the day, only one third were able to bomb their targets. The rest of us carried our bomb load back home.

"This was the thirteenth mission we had flown this month and we were tired. Fatigue was showing on everyone including the ground personnel who got less rest than the combat crews. They were up day and night keeping our bombers flying. Not enough can be said for these men. At the rate we were knocking off missions, it would have taken only another six weeks to complete our tour. Because we became a lead crew, we later only flew when it was our time to lead. Also we were due some rest leave sooner or later but as of now, the invasion was imminent and there was no rest for the weary."[833]

On 2 June the 8th Air Force mounted two strikes on V-weapons sites in the Pas de Calais. In the first raid, 776 B-17 and B 24s were involved. In the second raid, 293 bombers struck at airfields and railway targets in France. No bombers were lost.[834] On this date—his Mother's 44th birthday—2nd Lieutenant Dick Johnson in the 303rd Bomb Group flew his 8th mission to the large marshaling yards at Juvisy, in the southwestern suburbs of Paris. The aim of the mission was to delay German movement to the front lines during the upcoming invasion. Johnson's diary for that day reads:

"Paris, France (Marshaling yards) five tenths cloud cover. Moderate flak no damage. Saw hundreds of landing craft on English coast. Invasion soon maybe.

"Fourteen aircraft were furnished for the 41st Combat Wing from our group. The 427th Squadron was to lead our group. Our B-17s had been loaded with six 1000lb bombs and 1700 gallons of gas. Our time schedule for this mission was pretty tight, as we were to take off at around 1730 and arrive at the target before dark. The days were long at this time of year, so we were confident that we could make this schedule. We departed the English coast over Selsey Bill, at an altitude of 18,500ft. Selsey Bill is a point of land just east of Portsmouth. We crossed the English Channel, climbing to 22,000ft, hitting the French coast just across the harbor from Le Havre. We encountered a layer of clouds at our altitude and decided to drop down to 18,000ft. We made a feint toward Chartres and just before reaching their outer defenses, made a dogleg to the left and made a direct flight to our target. We bombed at 2032 just before the sun went down. We flew a circle around Paris at 21,000ft and headed toward Le Havre, where we departed the enemy coast a few miles north of that town. It was dark by then and no lights could be seen anywhere on the ground. Just before dark we saw a large group of British Lancasters heading out to do their nightly bombing.

"Our track to Molesworth took us about a mile west of London, which was so totally dark that it could not be seen. We landed at nearly 2300 and headed to the mess hall for a late snack, having eaten our box lunches on the way out. I was somewhat miffed to find that the mess hall personnel had gone to bed, leaving a large pot of coffee into which they had put too much cream and too much sugar. I was unable to drink it, since I always drank mine without sugar. This was my only gripe about food, since the Mess Sergeant had always done a great job."[835]

For the next three days hundreds of 8th Air Force bombers flew two missions a day to the Pas de Calais area. On 4 June *Sack Rat*, piloted by Lieutenant Clifford R. Galley in the 491st, developed a high speed stall while forming up and crashed near Sizewell, Suffolk, killing everyone on board. That evening the 361st Fighter Group accompanied five B-24s in the 753rd Bomb Squadron, 458th Bomb Group, making their second attempt to knock out a series of bridges on the Seine River with the radio-controlled *Azon* glide bombs. Though the 361st was able to claim one Bf 109 destroyed on the mission, Lieutenant Walter Kozicki in the 376th Squadron was shot down by a Bf 109 flown by Major Klaus Mietusch, CO III./JG 26, northwest of Romilly at 2015 hours, and he baled out.[836] On Monday, 5 June, 629 bombers attacked coastal defense installations in the Cherbourg-Caen and Pas de Calais areas, and three *Noball* sites and a railway bridge were also raided. 2nd Lieutenant Dick Johnson in the 303rd Bomb Group flew his 9th mission to the Cherbourg Peninsula and its heavy gun batteries. He wrote:

> "We made three bomb runs. Meager flak, no damage. Four tenths cloud cover on target. Saw hundreds of ships on English coast. Things may pop open very soon now. This was a short mission so we traded fuel for bombs. Each B-l7 was loaded with 16 500lb SAP bombs. We took off at 0615 with 12 B 17s and one spare. Since there were no aborts, the spare returned before reaching enemy territory. We departed England at Selsey Bill at 24,500ft and headed to our IP in the Channel, which was determined by LORAN.[837] Due to clouds, we tried three times to hit the primary target, each time returning to our IP, to no avail. Just ahead of our last attempt was a heavy gun emplacement next to a. landing strip. They received 144 semi-armor piercing, 500lb bombs of the nine aircraft in our part of the group just because the weather was bad elsewhere. After bombing, we let down over the Channel, through clouds and crossed the English coast at Portland Bill at 2700ft. We flew a direct course to Molesworth, arriving just before noon. Over the target area, there was moderate flak in several places but none close enough to damage any of the B-17s of our group. Only two fighter planes were seen and they were both ours. We were in the air four and half-hours with 35 minutes over enemy territory."

Abe Dolim in the 94th Bomb Group wrote:

> "We flew four hours on a mission to northern France but had to abort over Pas de Calais at 29,500ft because of severe stomach cramps among several crewmembers. Gas expansion is always a problem among crews at high altitude where air is thin and stagnant in a bomber. Odors of all sorts permeate the combined air-oxygen supply system and many are the complaint from crewmembers that have to put up with someone else's gas. I have learned to shave closely I or high altitude flying because facial hairs pressing into my skin under the oxygen mask cause a good deal of irritation. Condensation from moist breath forms a lump of ice on one's neck, so we wear mufflers to catch the moisture and to keep cold air out. We use silk inner gloves to keep our hands from sticking to the extremely cold metal parts of the aircraft. The flak suits we wear are made of laminated metal and weigh about 20lbs. They are cumbersome and cause one's shoulders to ache, but a buddy of mine has stopped three pieces of flak with his. We also wear flak helmets that are really infantrymen's helmets with the sides cut out to accommodate our large earphones. We are issued one box each of high carbohydrate ration candy, all we have to eat during the missions, some of which are nine to 10 hours in duration. However, the Group always has corned beef sandwiches and coffee or cocoa for us during interrogation."

Six B-24s, including *Missouri Sue* (a 44th Bomb Group PFF ship), which carried the 489th Bomb Group deputy Commander Lieutenant Colonel Leon R. Vance, were lost. A malfunction prevented bomb release on the target, a V-1 site near Wimereaux, and despite protests, Vance ordered the crew to go around again. This time the bomb drop was made by hand, but two bombs hung up. Now the flak had increased in intensity, and a 88mm salvo burst directly under the port wing. Captain Louis A. Mazure, the pilot, was killed instantly when he was hit in the temple, and Earl L. Gamer, the co-pilot, was seriously wounded. Three engines were put out of action, and *Missouri Sue* rose menacingly on the verge of a stall. The tall, rangy colonel, who was standing behind the pilots' seats, looked down to see that his right foot had been virtually severed from his leg, and was attached only by the Achilles tendon, which was jammed behind the co-pilot's seat. Despite his terrible injury, Vance managed to reach the panel and feather the three useless engines. Gamer cut all four engines and turned the B-24 towards England. When the shoreline came into view Lieutenant Bernard W. Bale, the radar navigator, ordered the crew to evacuate the B-24. Although he was suffering from shock, Bale managed to get the colonel down into his navigator's seat. He took off his belt and wound it around Vance's thigh to stop the blood spurting. His quick thinking undoubtedly saved Vance's life. Bale told him they would have to jump because there was no way they could land the B-24, especially since the two bombs were ready to go off on impact. The colonel shook his head and said he would not jump. Bale knew that he could not possibly drag Vance to the bomb bay and push him out, and he was also aware that the aircraft was rapidly losing altitude. There was little time left to save himself. Bale checked the tourniquet one last time, shook Vance's hand, and jumped from the open bomb bay. Vance managed to get into the cockpit and succeeded in ditching within reach of the English coast. The impact blew him clear of the aircraft, and ASR, who gave him immediate medical attention, quickly picked him up.[838]

That night Lieutenant Abe Dolim recorded in his diary "There have been all sorts of rumors about an imminent invasion of the enemy coast." At Molesworth, Ben Smith Jr. saw RAF aircraft and gliders going over, "wave after wave," and he knew that they would be going in the morning. He thought there would be "hell to pay," and did not sleep much that night. Many did not get much sleep that night. At Hethel, just outside Norwich, Lieutenant Duane A. Hall's nine-man crew in the 566th Squadron, 389th Bomb Group, which had been one of the replacement crews to arrive in May, had been assigned to a B-24H in good condition, called *The Little Gramper Jnr*. She had finished up one crew—a good sign—but the Hall crew were still waiting to fly her on a combat mission. On 5 June they were alerted to fly their first combat mission next day. That night the enlisted men in their hut listened alternately to the BBC and the enemy propaganda station. Both came in loud and clear. Lord Haw Haw, the traitor William Joyce, was in great form. "Shove it sideways," someone yelled. Each member of the hut had contributed a one-pound note to a pool to correctly guess the date for D-Day. S/Sgt Robert H. "Bob" Sherwood, the top turret gunner, had drawn 29 May, a date that came and soon passed by. Someone else would collect the £120.

16

The Great Crusade

"*Planes overhead will be ours.*"
General Dwight D. Eisenhower, Supreme Commander at SHAEF (Supreme Headquarters Allied Expeditionary Forces)

Planning the final date for the invasion involved a certain amount of guesswork, and it had kept the planners at SHEAF[839] awake for several nights. Only a select few knew that a stretch of the Normandy coastline from Quineville to just south of Caen had been selected for the long-awaited Second Front. The invasion had been due to take place in May 1944, but General Dwight D. Eisenhower, Supreme Commander at SHAEF, then postponed the date by a month to enable extra landing craft to be built. On 8 May he selected 5 June as D-Day, but the weather conditions had to be right. From early May onwards, 325th Wing aircraft and B-17s, B-24s, and de Havilland Mosquito PRXVIs in the 25th Bomb Group at Watton, Norfolk, made meteorological flights, gathering intelligence and weather data. A local storm front, forming suddenly east of Iceland and monitored by the *Bluestocking* Mosquitoes in the 653rd Squadron, 25th Bomb Group, forced Eisenhower to postpone the invasion for 24 hours. General Bernard L. Montgomery, C-in-C Land Forces, was prepared to go despite the weather, but ACM Sir Trafford Leigh-Mallory C-in-C AEAF[840] was not in favor, as so much depended upon air superiority. All convoys at sea had to reverse their courses, but two British midget submarines continued to their positions off the beaches to act as markers for the invasion army when it arrived. Group Captain J. M. Stagg, the Met Officer, predicted 36 hours of relatively clear weather with moderate winds, and on Monday, 5 June, Eisenhower turned to Montgomery and asked whether he could see any reason for not going on the morrow (Tuesday). Monty replied, "I would say 'Go!'" The other commanders agreed. "OK" said Eisenhower. "We'll go."[841]

A coded wireless message sent out by the BBC instructed the French Resistance to cut railway lines throughout France. Andre Heintz, 23, a French Resistance fighter, wrote, "I shall never forget that night or the thrill of knowing the Allies were coming to expel the *Nazis* at last."[842] Around midnight on 5 June S/Sgt Frank A. McKee at Watton could hear some of the early airborne invasion force flying overhead as he and his assistant finished getting PR Mosquito N5559 ready for an early D-Day mission. Since early that afternoon they had been painting on black and white invasion stripes, which came as a big surprise to them.[843]

It was late evening at Attlebridge airfield, just a few miles east of Norwich, when Lieutenant Claude V. Meconis, a B-24 co-pilot in the 785th Bomb Squadron in the 466th Bomb Group, began suspecting that "big doings" were in store:

> "Group operations ordered all lead crews to test-hop their airplanes before dark. While at our operations office, I chanced to glimpse an alert list labeled, 'D-Day Missions.' on it we were listed for the first and the third. We went up before dark and gave the A5 and bombsight the once over, then returned to the base just before 9pm to learn that we were alerted. Briefing was scheduled for 2330, breakfast for 2230 hours. That meant – well, we knew something big was up. We went to our barracks. Knots of us were gathered in our hut, swapping conjectures and growing more nervous all the time. Dike (our pilot) was like a burnt cat and Miller (the bombardier) ubiquitous, both wide-eyed at the prospect of big things. So was I. we three began worrying about the navigator, Brooks, who was still in town at 2230. He'd gone in that afternoon to get a blouse, having gotten out of camp just before an order restricted everyone. [He showed up]. All three of us dropped into our sacks for a few moments of relaxation prior to breakfast, but found it quite impossible to loosen up... I went into Tikey's room [pilot of another 785th Bomb Squadron crew] and listened to his co-pilot, Richard W. Smith tell me how rough the night assembly was going to be. He wished me luck with a grim face... After breakfast, which was really a late dinner of meat loaf, potatoes and oranges, we went to briefing room No.2 and began sweating out the big news. Hardly necessary to say, I felt about the same as back in High school just before going on the stage. Stage fright with me is a series of fever spells, fast pulse, yawns and gas on the stomach."[844]

At Deopham Green Gus Perna and Ralph Reese, tail gunner and left waist gunner, respectively, on *Smoky Liz*, were in the base theater when Norman Wright, the navigator, and James McLellan, the bombardier, were called to go to target study at the 452nd Group Headquarters. Reese recalls:

> "We suspected that something was in the air. We went back to our barracks and were told to report to briefing at once. During briefing, we were told this was 'It' and that our target for today would

be Le Havre. There would be wave after wave of planes to hit the coast. We could not drop any bombs after 0730, in case we hit our own troops. All planes after the bomb run were to turn to the right, so as to make one way traffic pattern because many planes were in the air. Every airfield in England had lights on at 0200. This was the first time since England had been at war. There was a solid overcast, so we had to bomb PFF. After we had landed at our base, the *Smoky Liz* would be loaded with 500 lbs for another mission."

It was common knowledge that the Allies were preparing to invade the Continent. Where? When? As a 21-year-old junior flying officer, it was not John W. McClane's concern:

"I knew when the orderly awakened me that morning that something unusual was afoot, as it was not our day to lead. At briefing I found the answer to my question. We were not going to fly the usual large squadron and group formation but rather small groups of six planes each. Every lead navigator that could be rounded up was required for this maximum effort. The rest of my crew were held in reserve for a later raid but for this early effort, I was assigned to another crew. I'm sure they were not pleased to have a strange navigator forced on them and I did not relish flying without my crew. A strong bond of trust developed among crewmembers, as it was a life or death situation on every mission.

"There was great excitement when the curtains concealing the route map were drawn back at briefing and we were informed that, 'This is It' - D-Day and that the landing was to be made in Normandy. Surprise? No, but fear of the unexpected? Yes. I fully expected the Wehrmacht and the Luftwaffe to resist with every ounce of strength available to them. My concern was fighter opposition to our bomber force. I was really fearful that this might be my last mission. Little did I know how overwhelming our air strength was and that the German defenders had no chance what so ever of inflicting any serious losses, much less of turning this aerial armada back. Take off was at 0300 hours. We were told in no uncertain terms that we were to fly a fixed and preset course to and from the target area. Once we broke the coast of England and passed over the Channel, there could be no alteration in course for any reason what so ever that would be tolerated. We were told that British fighters had instructions that any plane flying out side of the narrow prescribed corridor or any plane aborting and flying the wrong direction would be shot down without exception. The point was made so clear that I believed it 100% and so did everyone else. One thing that did please me was the fact that I was not going to miss out of the invasion. I really wanted to be a part of the show and would have been greatly disappointed had I not been selected to lead the flight."

At Horham, Suffolk, Henry Tarcza, a B-17 engineer-gunner in Mathew MeEntee's crew in the 95th Bomb Group, was awakened some hours before daylight. At first he thought that this was just another routine bombing mission over enemy-occupied Europe. Shortly after 0300 hours he enjoyed a breakfast of bacon and country fresh eggs, a wartime delicacy reserved only for the combat flying personnel. They entered the maximum security briefing room around 0400 hours, where the huge map on the wall was covered with yards of thick drapery. After all the noise of shifting chairs had ceased the briefing officer calmly pulled the covering material toward him, and a long moan from all the flying men echoed throughout the room, followed by a hoarse whisper, "*Invasion*."

The red streamers on the map ran from every air base in England and crossed the Channel, converging on one tiny spot near Cherbourg. The briefing Colonel pointed toward that area with what happened to be an old billiard cue and said, "Yes gentlemen. This is the day you've been waiting for and this is the spot that has been selected." It was a relatively short briefing because the navigators had already been given separate instructions. Before unlocking the exit doors the briefing officer smiled and said, "Good luck, gentlemen and give 'em Hell!"

At Molesworth, 2nd Lieutenant Dick Johnson went to briefing:

"'Today is D-Day,' the briefing officer announced. 'The invasion has already started and we are going to try to prevent the Germans from bringing up reinforcements. The weather is very bad and we may bomb by radar,' he said."

At Seething, Norfolk, 2nd Lieutenant Ben C. Isgrig, bombardier in 2nd Lieutenant William Bailey's crew in the 448th Bomb Group at Seething, went to briefing room at 2300 on 5 June. Bailey's crew had flown their first mission, to Merseburg, on 28 May, and by 6 June they had flown a total of five missions. At the briefing Colonel Jerry Mason, the CO, said, "This is it." Their target was *Omaha* Beach. The first mission was primarily concerned with the neutralizing of enemy coastal defenses and front line troops. Subsequent missions would be directed against lines of communication leading to the bridgehead. At a B-26 Marauder base in Essex Allen W. Stephens was awakened at 2 o'clock in the morning. This was his 21st mission, and take-off was at 0420. It was still dark. A steady rain was falling, and they could hardly see to taxi, much less fly. But there was no holding back, and they poured on the coals, taking off at 20-second intervals between shifts. By the time they cleared the end of the runway they could barely see the lights of the plane ahead of them. They climbed on instruments, and when they broke out on top of the cloudbank, they could see B-26s and all kinds of other planes circling around. Stephens recalled that it was "really a beautiful sight." By following prearranged signals, Stephen's B-26 tacked onto their squadron leader and subsequently were on their way across the Channel. He felt part of the spearhead of the invasion, entering the coast of France near Cherbourg over Utah Beach. His group's targets were coastal guns and blockhouses along the beach, which they were to hit in collaboration with shelling by naval vessels. His was among the very first aircraft to hit the invasion target.

Ralph Reese, in the 452nd Bomb Group at Deopham Green, recalls:

"At briefing at 1030 on 5 June we were told, 'This is it'. There would be wave after wave of planes hitting the coast. Our target was coastal defenses at Le Havre. We could not drop any bombs after 0730, the time the invasion was to start, for the danger of hitting our own troops. Every airfield in England had its lights on at 0200 - the first time since England had been at war. We carried 38 100lb demolition bombs but there was a solid overcast so we had to bomb using PFF. Bombs were away at 0659. We landed back at our base at 1030 and our *Smoky Liz* was then loaded with 500lb bombs for another mission within 24 hours."

The 8th was required to fly three missions. The first was primarily concerned with neutralizing enemy coastal defenses and front-line troops. Subsequent missions would be directed against lines of communication leading to the bridgehead. The bombers would be in good company, with no less than 36 squadrons of Mustangs and Thunderbolts patrolling the area. Initially, they would protect the "big friends," but would later break off and strafe ground targets. It was evident that there could be no delay, and that any stragglers would be left to their fate. Any aborts were to drop out of formation before leaving the English coast and then fly back to base at below 14,000ft. It was a one-way aerial corridor, and the traffic flow was intense. Aircraft would fly to and fro over the length of England dropping various colored flares to denote the aerial corridors. If a plane had to be ditched, only those ships returning to England from the bridgehead would stop to pick up crews. Crews were told that if they were shot down they were to wait in uniform until they could join their own troops in France. Finally, an "inspirational message to the departing troops" from General Eisenhower, the Supreme Allied Commander, was read out loud. Perhaps it was the tension brought on by the big occasion, but not all crewmen were impressed. Ben Smith at Molesworth thought that Churchill could have done it with a lot more class.

At briefings throughout East Anglia American fighter pilots and bomber crews tramped into the briefing rooms to be told what their mission on 6 June would be. At Rougham, Wilbur Richardson felt "this must be it for sure." Sure enough, at briefing it was. What a contrast there was. Usually it was groans when they learned of the target. Now there was animated talk and "yippie!" It would be off to the shoreline targets at dawn before the landings began about an hour later. At Kimbolton, Franklin L. Betz, navigator in *Ol' Gappy*,[845] flown by Captain Douglas H. Buskey in the 379th Bomb Group, groped sleepily for his clothes. He knew that to be awakened about 0400 for a mission was "pretty much routine," but to be "hauled out of the sack at about 0130 to report to briefing"—well, something unusual just had to be "up!" The atmosphere at briefing was invariably sombre. Sitting quietly on benches dozing or languidly puffing on cigarettes that glowed eerily in the soft light of the starkly furnished rooms, there was very little talk while the fliers, officers, and enlisted men waited for the CO, Colonel Preston, to arrive. "Tenshun!" someone up front bawled when the CO strode in. Everyone rose, standing erect, eyes straight ahead. "At ease," the Colonel said. The men sat down quietly, tensely awaiting roll call and the removal of the cover from the huge map of Europe on which the course to and from the target had been traced. If it showed a deep penetration of Germany that meant dangerous fighter attacks and flak encounters throughout the flight; a groan arose from the dry throats of the airmen that trailed off into excited whispers as briefing continued. But at 0230, when the briefing officer announced, "This is it - this is D-Day!" it was different; a lusty cheer shattered the quiet of a moment before. Whoops, whispers, and yells echoed from the gray walls. It was an unprecedented and ecstatic vocal demonstration by the fliers who had doggedly been carrying the war to Germany for many months with considerable losses of men and planes. It was the day they had awaited to share with the ground forces, and together they would assault the *Nazi* war machine, hopefully gaining a foothold on the mainland with the ultimate goal of driving the *Wehrmacht* back to the Fatherland and crushing it.

Briefings over, a line of trucks was assembled to take crews to their waiting aircraft. The pre-dawn calm of the countryside around the farmlands and in the towns and villages near the bomber bases was soon shattered by the roar of thousands of Wright Cyclones and Twin Wasps being pre-flighted at all points of the compass. Overhead the moon shone through a thick black undercast.

At Horham, McEntee's crew said little as they proceeded to their bomber in a canvas-covered truck. Tarcza was sure they all felt as he did. If the Germans shared his secret at that moment it could alter the destiny of mankind. They all did a good job of maintaining composure so that the ground crews might not suspect that D-Day had, in fact, arrived. Their B-17[846] bore none of the usual fancy paintings. On its nose were the simple words *El's Bells*, named by McEntee in honor of his girlfriend in New York City, and whom he later married. They waited in line on the runway for their turn to take-off. As they left the ground Tarcza had that very comforting feeling that he was coming back safely to England. They circled to gain altitude. It was early daylight, and the sight in the vast sky staggered Tarcza's wildest imagination. The air was thick with eastbound aircraft for as many miles as he could see in all directions. *El's Bells* joined in and headed toward France.

John Nargi, in the 384th Service Squadron, sensed something big was in the offing, because normally the B-17s were up and circling for hours before the fighters took off. But on this particular morning the sky was "just dark with planes. You would have thought it was a cloudy day." As the shadows passed over the field, it turned sunny then dark, sunny then dark. Nargi thought it was "unbelievable!" Eventually the bombers flew out towards the Channel and the fighters at his base took off. He marveled at what a sight it was!

Ol' Gappy lifted off from Kimbolton at 0445. Franklin L. Betz could see a "fluffy" layer of clouds below, which hampered visibility, but there were some breaks, and he could see the choppy dark waters of the English Channel. Droning steadily toward the continent, he gasped when a huge opening in the clouds revealed ships and boats of all sizes dotting the water as far as he could see. "Hundreds - no, there must be thousands," he thought. Although no one type of ship could be identified from nearly three miles high, he was to learn later practically the whole spectrum of powered vessels from battleships to motor launches made up the invasion fleet. Landing ships carrying thousands of troops, tanks, guns, vehicles, and ammunition were positioning for the dash to the Normandy beaches. Barrage balloons swayed lazily above the ships to which they were attached by stout cables. More holes appeared in the clouds, and the awesome spectacle continued to unfold. Betz rose from his seat in the navigator's cramped work area in the left rear of the B-17G's nose to get a better view from the right waist window. Fascinated, he saw puffs of white smoke from the huge guns of battleships and cruisers aimed toward the mainland, and a moment later massive explosions could be seen a short distance inland where the shells landed, kicking up a fountain of dirt and debris. That, he reflected, must be a mixture of "steel and stones, flesh and bones" when the targets were hit.

It was just getting light as Ben Isgrig's formation left the English coast, and the clouds broke enough for them to see the hundreds of ships in the Channel heading for France. He could plainly see the heavy warships shelling the coast, which was shrouded in smoke. Besides seeing more ships than he had ever seen before, there were also more heavy bombers in the air than he thought possible to put up in one area. The coast itself was covered in clouds, and he didn't see their target at all; neither did he see flak or fighters.

At Bury St. Edmunds, Joe Hamil's crew waited for take off. In the nose was Abe Dolim, and sitting beside Hamil in the cockpit of the Fortress was co-pilot Harvey T. Brown, who began taking notes:

> "It is 0600 - waiting for takeoff; lining up now. 0620 airborne. Have suspected for several days that it was coming off and last night when they called the first crews at 2300 and we heard so many planes in the air we guessed it, but when they told us in briefing we were very excited. The excitement has gotten into everyone's blood. Joe and everyone can hardly wait to get a view of 'it.' 0659 - Long just wrote Webster's and Yarborough's names on two of the bombs so they will be in on this anyway. One for Betty, too. 0820 - looked over London carefully with the binoculars - could not find Piccadilly Circus. English coast ahead. French coast approximately 0900. Could not see a thing. Undercast solid. I looked up and down the English coast carefully but saw only one boat in motion and quite a few landing craft anchored. We hit the French coast at the spot where the boys were making a beachhead. A few of the crew saw about a hundred landing craft through a break in the clouds. We went on in and bombed the target through the undercast from 14,000ft. Very little flak and inaccurate. We came around the islands of Guernsey

and Jersey. Saw a little flak there against a group of B-24's. Clouds cleared up near the English coast. Picked up two destroyers and several air sea rescue boats quite clearly with the binoculars.

"Joe and I listened to our assigned Channel for a while. Heard a Fortress calling in. At first, he was losing 700ft per minute, at 5000ft. Must have lost an engine. Then he called and said that he had lost all four, was at 2000ft and losing altitude rapidly. 'Should I use flaps?' he asked very excitedly. Then there was no more. Hope they ditched okay.

"A fighter kept jamming the channel talking to another fighter of ours. Had nine gallons of gas and was trying to get to an airfield. Saw an enormous air depot with more fighters than I've ever seen before. Must have been two or 300. Landed about noon. I slept until 1900. Ate and went back to bed. Slept until noon the next day, June 7. Ate again and when I came back to the hut had to go to Operations. Raining, cold and bad. Sat around for a while. Came back to pick up the mail. Two from Betty, two from mother, one from Sis, one from R. Baxter and this stationery."

Lieutenant Abe Dolim, who was flying his 18th mission, noted in his diary that there was "no flak," and that:

> "above the solid undercast at 10,000ft, we saw nothing but bombers and escorting fighters. We bombed a highway junction back of the invasion beaches flying at only 14,000ft and using radar for the drop. The word from Group HQ today is that there is no longer any limit to combat missions now that the invasion is on. We have been ordered to wear our .45s in case of enemy parachute troop attack."

As Lieutenant Claude V. Meconis, co-pilot to Lieutenant Dike on *SNAFU SNARK*[847] in the 466th Bomb Group, passed over the southern coast of England and headed south over the Channel he began straining his eyes to see some of the invasion fleet the briefing at Attlebridge had disclosed. A low undercast in patches obscured most of the water, but whenever open spaces permitted he could see landing craft and large ships moving south and southeast on a fairly rough sea. Also below, just above the clouds, he saw B-26 formations assembling.

As he moved in toward the beaches, Allen W. Stephens and the crew of the B-26 Marauder could see an armada of invasion vessels in the Channel below, their courses converging toward the several invasion beaches. Stephens had the surging feeling that he was sitting in on the greatest show ever staged—one that would make world history. As they flew nearer to the target, that feeling increased to exhilaration and excitement. He saw hundreds upon hundreds of ships moving toward the coast of France, and when he approached the target area, he could see their big naval guns shelling the coast. The Germans were not idle, however, as they threw heavy barrages at the landing craft. Stephens saw one large ship going down but still throwing shells at the coast. He saw hundreds of discarded parachutes that had been thrown off by paratroopers who had landed simultaneously with the other attacks. He saw one B-26 Marauder explode in mid-air near the target area. Stephens' group went through the heaviest concentration of anti-aircraft fire he had yet seen. Tracers and flak explosions were so thick that it looked impossible to get through without being hit, especially knowing that for every tracer there were six other rounds. The barrage literally filled the air all around, and the flak explosions made the air alive with fire. On the beachhead, there was a tremendous wall of smoke all along the shore where the bombs and the shells were exploding. The landing craft were moving up as the Marauders turned off the target area after dropping their bombs. Every move was timed to the split second. Stephens' B-26 went in at 4500ft on this first mission and their bombs went away at 0630, the precise time planned.

Meconis did not see a single friendly fighter, though 35 squadrons were expected as cover. He mused that they were probably at a low altitude, below the clouds, actively aiding the first assault on the coast. Anyway they did not need them. Meconis knew each man on the crew prayed for the success of whatever those in the landing barges below had to do. He knew that their job was infinitely the more dangerous of the two. His crew were scared a bit, because they did not know exactly what kind of air opposition the *Luftwaffe* would throw at them. Frankly, Meconis expected to see a sky "full of fighters and flak, all confusion," but he knew that the boys in the barges would meet "steel and concrete and a tough fight!"

In the 379th Bomb Group formation *Ol' Gappy*, swaying gently, throbbed on. There was still no sign of Bf 109s or FW 190s, but he could see that their "little friends" were out in force. The Lightnings, Thunderbolts, and Mustangs had invasion markings—black and white stripes on wings and fuselages—that were very prominent, providing an aerial umbrella for the landing forces. Strafing the enemy positions up and down the coast and for some miles inland, they were determined to help the GIs embarking on the great crusade. The white capped wake of hundreds of circling landing craft awaiting the order to head to the shore contributed to the drama of the scene. The cloud cover required a blind bombing technique using radar. According to Franklin Betz's log they were close to the target—gun positions near Arromanches roughly midway between the Cherbourg peninsula and Le Havre. The bombs dropped from the bellies of the bombers disappeared in the clouds to devastate and disrupt the enemy's fighting capabilities far below. Betz remembered the briefing officer's words, "There would be meager flak, if any at all." He was right. There was none. The German guns were busily exchanging fire with the mighty invasion fleet massed in the Bay of the Seine and stretching for miles into the Channel.

It was daylight, with the sun shining above the clouds in the east, as *SNAFU SNARK* turned right to head 270° for 90 miles until the 466th Bomb Group formation was west of the Cherbourg peninsula. Several bursts of flak came up. A group to their right passed too close to either Cherbourg or the islands just west of it. A ball of flak, like that Meconis had seen over Brunswick once, came up at them. Their let down over England was gradual. Clouds broke up, and when they arrived back at their base area, only small fair weather cumulus and haze existed. The sky was "a trifle overloaded," but the group managed to cut their way through the "snag" and land safely. An S-2 man, Hodges, met the crew at the plane for interrogation. They asked for news, but all Hodges could say was, "*The invasion is on.*" Meconis was so sleepy on the trip back that he contemplated taking a pill to keep awake. He was glad that he didn't, because the crews were allowed to go to bed immediately after landing. They were told that they would be called if they were needed.

At Hethel Lieutenant Robert A. Jacobs, a DR (Dead Reckoning) navigator in the 564th Bomb Squadron, 389th Bomb Group, was also having trouble with sleep, or the lack of it. Part of a lead crew, their mission was to lead the 446th Bomb Group from Bungay to bomb the invasion beaches of Normandy immediately prior to the ground assault. The 446th had been selected to be the first American heavy bomb group to cross the French coast on *the* day, but Jacobs' B-24 *Liberty Run* would be the first American bomber overhead the beaches. At 0220 *Liberty Run* took off, climbed to 10,000ft, and circled in their prescribed forming area, firing specific flares as the 446th aircraft assembled in formation behind them. The mission went precisely as planned except for an undercast, which necessitated bombing by radar. As *Liberty Run* approached the French coast, the radar navigator called Jacobs over to look at his PPI scope. It clearly showed the vast armada of the invasion fleet standing just off the coast of Normandy. It was a thrilling sight even on radar. Bombs were away at precisely 0600. *Liberty Run* led her aircraft back to Bungay via Portland Bill and returned to Hethel. Much to the crew's surprise, no flak or German fighters were observed, and their fighter cover was "everywhere." As they started to undress to get some rest, the lead crew was again told to get over to Bungay for another mission. During the course of the briefing the flight surgeon gave each aircrew member a pill with instruction to take it only "when you feel you can no longer keep awake." The crew had been up since 0230 5 June, and it was now the afternoon of 6 June, 36 hours later, and they were running on reserve energy.

There was little sign of *Luftwaffe* activity. The German pilots had been caught almost cold. In northern France *Leutnant* Wolfgang Fischer of 3/JG 2 finally received warning of the invasion in the early hours of 6 June at about 0500 hours, and his unit was ordered to Creil, just outside Paris. There in all haste their '*Dodels*' were prepared, and they took off at about 0930 hours for our first low-level attack on the landing fleet in the English sector of Caen-Bayeux, where the landing craft provided "excellent targets for our *1* and *3 Staffeln*." On board one of the LST landing craft was Gunner Len Woods of the 53rd Medium Regiment Royal Artillery, which arrived off *Sword* beach at 1000 on 6 June. They were unloading by driving onto pontoon rafts, which then ferried them to the beach. After the lower deck had been cleared a German fighter machine-gunned his craft and dropped a bomb that exploded under the bow doors. This distorted the bow doors and wrecked the lift. To finish unloading they had to pull away from the beach and tie up alongside another LST that had already unloaded and run their vehicles across from one ship to the other by means of wooden planks. Woods remarked, "It was a quirk of fate that with the thousands of ships in the area, one of the two German planes in the air managed to hit us." The only *Luftwaffe* presence over the invasion beaches that morning were two FW 190s flown by *Oberstleutnant* Josef "Pips" Priller, *Kommodore* JG 26 "*Schlageter*," and his regular *Kacmarek* (wingman), *Unteroffizier* Heinz Wodarczyk of the *Stab* flight at Priller's Lille-Nord command post. These were the only two fighters available to JG 26. [848] Near Le Havre the pair climbed into the solid cloudbank and emerged to see the invasion fleet spread out before them. Priller, in his usual FW 190A-8 "Black 13" *Jutta*, and Wodarczyk each made a full-throttle (400mph) 50ft low level strafing run over *Sword* beach with cannons and machine guns before landing at Creil.[849]

2nd Lieutenant Dick Johnson in the 303rd Bomb Group recalls:

> "Each B-17 was loaded with twelve 500lb and two 1000lb bombs and we were off at 0600 with 34 aircraft. Two aircraft aborted due to mechanical problems - Lieutenant Baleie of the 358th Squadron and Lieutenant Fackler of the 359th Squadron. This was my tenth mission with the 427th Squadron and Colonel Snyder, the commander, led the low flight. Walter Cronkite flew with Bob Sheets in "*Shoo Shoo Baby*" of our squadron on this mission. We were to bomb a bridge near the invasion coast, but the cloud cover at the target was total, so we were to bomb by PFF. Sixteen aircraft of the lead group dropped 192 500lb GP bombs and 30 1000lb GP bombs on the target, with unobserved results. Our flight had a radar failure and dropped no bombs. We flew our bombs back to base and made ready for our second mission of the day."[850]

Ben Smith, Jr, in the 303rd Bomb Group did not see a single German fighter, or even a burst of flak. "Amazing!" he noted, adding that he "could see a battleship – possibly the *Texas* out in the Channel, firing at shore targets." He saw a solid mass of ships offshore, beached landing crafts, and others streaking in with their precious burdens, and he knew that a beachhead had been made.[851] 2nd Lieutenant Dick Johnson in the 303rd Bomb Group flew his second mission that same afternoon:

> "Our target near the invasion coast was a bridge near Caen that we were unable to bomb because of an equipment failure on the lead aircraft. We saw flak again at a distance but we were not affected. The weather over the French coast was bad with 5/10ths cloud cover but we could see bits of the invasion activity. The number of wakes from ships and landing craft covered the entire English Channel for miles. We could see smoke on the French coast from all the artillery. To prevent being fired upon by our own gunners, the fighters and medium bombers had a wide, white stripe painted across one wing and around the fuselage. The heavies didn't bother with this, as we were too high to be seen. We had achieved the desired mastery of the air by this time and the Germans had a bitter joke amongst themselves: 'If you see a camouflaged airplane, it's British. If you see a shiny, unpainted airplane, it's American. If you don't see any airplane at all, it's German.' Much of our mission at this stage of the war was the attrition of experienced German fighter pilots. As they rose up to defend their country, our fighters shot them down. And so, on this day, the destruction of Hitler's Third Reich began in earnest and the outcome is in the history of Earth's greatest war."[852]

Bob Shaffer, lead bombardier aboard B-24 Liberator *Naughty Nan* piloted by Lieutenant Sneddon, in the 93rd Bomb Group at Hardwick, Norfolk, took off at 1400 hours. He noted that the flak was light and the mission successful. There was a full moon, and he had never seen as many ships of all descriptions as there were crossing the Channel. Shaffer saw battleships firing at gun emplacements and recalled "It was quite a sight - quite a show. The flak was light and the mission successful."[853] A fellow 93rd Bomb Group crewman was Ed "Cotton" Appleman, the engineer-gunner aboard *Duration Baby*, who was flying his 14th mission. He saw the Channel filled with Allied ships of all kinds, and he could see them just off the French coast making their landings. Though they had good fighter cover and the B-24s none he imagined they needed it. He saw no flak and no fighters. The group made two runs on the target, but *Duration Baby* did not get the bomb bay doors open in time. Appleman hoped that the "boys on the ground" had it as easy as they did. He still had 16 missions to go.

Flying their first combat mission of the war this day were the Liberators of the 493rd Bomb Group from Debach, near Ipswich. Altogether, 36 B-24s led by the CO, Colonel Helton, set out for Lisieux, but 10/10th cloud cover prevented the Group from bombing their target, and all 36 B-24s returned with their bomb loads intact. S/Sgt Richard Skinner in the 861st Squadron, in Captain Earl H. Johnson's crew, saw "more aeroplanes and more ships in the sea" than he would ever again see in one time. It was overwhelming to his senses. Then, at 1028 hours at 11,000ft *No Love- No Nothin* in the 863rd Squadron, piloted by Captain Jack Cooper, struck the tail of *Moby Dick* in the 862nd Squadron, which was being flown by Lieutenant Donald L. Russell. *No Love-No Nothin* was seen to disintegrate, and both Liberators disappeared into the overcast. There was only one survivor from Cooper's ship and none from Russell's.[854] Lieutenant Francis S. Milligan, who was to recall that the first raids the 493rd Bomb Group flew were "pretty easy with a few exceptions," but he says, "I guess we were too green to appreciate a 'milk run.' We did get an early taste of war however, when we saw the two ships collide in mid-air. The sight sobered most of us. (Getting pretty badly shot up later on at Orleans and again at Hanover did not raise our zest for battle either.)" Lieutenant Joe Gualano, a pilot in the 860th Squadron, adds. "It was said that 'Lord Haw-Haw' that evening, announced that Germany had nothing to fear from the new Group with the 'X' tail markings as they were killing themselves."

John W. McClane, who on D-Day flew two missions with two different crews, recalled:

"Our flight was to take us on a course west of our air base. We were to climb through the clouds until we got above them where we could assemble with the rest of our flight. All was going well, we were climbing on course through very dense clouds. There was no reason to suspect danger as every plane had its prescribed course to fly until we broke into the clear. As one might expect, I was busy at my desk doing dead reckoning. Visibility was at best only 50 to 100ft through the haze of clouds. Suddenly a loud and confusing shout of voices filled my earphones and about the same time I felt the tail of our aircraft go down sharply, perhaps as much as 30°, then almost as rapidly level out again. The babble of voices continued until the pilot calmed them down enough to find out what had happened. The men in the rear were almost in shock. They could hardly speak but finally the story came out. A British bomber had hit the right twin rudder of our plane. The waist gunners had seen it coming before the collision and assumed it was going to hit us broadside. I can only imagine what the RAF pilot thought when he saw a B-24 in his line of flight (if he saw us at all). We collided at right angles. The British bomber came from the north while we were going west. Why was a British bomber flying in the American Assembly Area? I mark it up to the SNAFU that goes with the best of planning.

"Finally the crew settled down. We were still flying on course and gaining altitude. Our pilot tried all the controls. They functioned perfectly. Being I was the only one that could see the rudders, being the upper gun turret gunner was not in place, the pilot asked me to look out of my astro-dome towards the rear. There was a foot position on each side of my navigation compartment that allowed me to stand up so my head was centered in the astro-dome. When I raised myself up and looked at the twin rudders, I saw a very unfamiliar sight. The right rudder had been knocked flat for at least 24 inches. The pilot asked me to watch the rudders while he tried the controls. Strange as it may seem, the damaged rudder did not effect the flying capability of the plane. We had every right to abort the mission and return to base. The pilot debated the idea with the crew and finally put it to a vote. The answer was a unanimous 'No.' Not a crewmember wanted to miss out of the excitement of the invasion. The plane continued to fly on course. I returned to my navigation duties. At long last we broke through the clouds into a brilliant blue sky.

"No one who has never experienced it can see in his mind the absolute beauty that the airman views when flying about a solid layer of white clouds with perfect visibility as far as the eye can see. We soon assembled with the other five planes of our flight. The 44th sent out 36 planes in flights of six planes each. We fell in line with dozens of similar flights on our way to the south of England. It was not until the mission was over and we had landed that it dawned on me that we were a strange sight flying in the formation. Radio silence forbid the other pilots from asking us what had happened to our right rudder. They later reported that their curiosity had almost gone wild trying to figure out what had happened to us. The other crews had six hours to look at our damaged plane before the morning mission was completed.

"As we flew south and west to the departure point to get in line with the rest of the Eighth Air Force bomber force headed for France, we had time to think about what would happen once we broke the English coast. What if the damage forced us to turn back? Should we reconsider committing ourselves to a 'no turn back' position? The pilot again made the decision to press on and again he had the full support of the crew.

"After several hours of assembly and flying on course, we did commit ourselves to the target. The clouds had cleared and we had a full view of the water. Our target was the shoreline of the western landing site near the town of Isigny. At this time, I do not know which beach we bombed. As we got closer to the French coast, the invasion fleet came into full view. I could see hundreds and hundreds of ships. The smoke of the guns from the battleships, cruisers and destroyers was very clearly visible to me. I could see hundreds of landing craft making large circles as they assembled to prepare for a run to the beaches. We passed directly over the fleet. I suppose I could say that I have personally seen with my own eyes the largest number of ships ever assembled in the history of mankind.

"Our 250lb fragmentation bombs hit the beach 28 minutes before the first landing craft went ashore. Not a German interceptor came near us. Even the flak was so light I wasn't concerned about it. The sky was full of Allied planes, single motor, two motors and four motor wherever I looked. The flight home was uneventful and we landed at 0900 hours. I went through debriefing and had lunch when I was notified that I was to fly a second mission that afternoon with my own crew in our own *'Lili Marlene.'* We followed the same course except this time we bombed the French town of Vire about 35 miles inland. I was in the air a total of 12 hours on D-Day."[855]

The "Sky Scorpions" flew four missions on 6 June: the first to *Omaha* beach, the second to St. Lô, and the third, Caen. The fourth was also to St. Lô. Lieutenant Duane Hall's crew were told that take off was 1555. Bob Sherwood translated that to 3:55. He never could get used to military time. The gunnery instructor met him at the plane, as he had promised. He moved along with Bob, joining him in the inspection of all the turrets, the gunsights, the bomb fuses, and bomb rack release boxes. Occasionally, he would offer a suggestion:

"Straighten the cotter pins safeties in the nose and the tail fuses before you take off. That way you won't have any trouble getting them out while you're climbing to altitude. You won't have enough light in the bomb bays with the doors closed and the racks full. The dim bulkhead lights aren't enough. Always carry a flashlight. Check the bomb shackles for chewed-up ears on the release levers. If necessary, get the shackle changed before take-off. Wipe the oil off the guns. Otherwise the bolt will freeze. You'll get a big temperature drop after 10,000ft. If the chamber is empty and the guns freeze, you'll have no guns for the whole mission. You won't be able to charge them. The gun heaters won't thaw them. Take off with a round in the chamber. When you test fire over the Channel, that first round will blow the bolt free and the ammo will feed. First three rounds will be slow and then the guns will take off at their regular rate of fire, 1000 rounds per minute. And don't forget to go to the tail turret and reach your hand up into the discharge chute. Sometimes a spent cartridge case will fall crossways in there. More cases will pile up on top of the jam. It will eventually stop the guns from firing. You won't be able to clear the stoppage in the air."

The take-off and climb to altitude went smoothly. They found their proper position in the formation. An hour and a half later they were leaving the coast and flying above the overcast Channel. As they neared the French coast they could see the intense activity opposite the landing beaches. Even at this day's operational altitude of 17,000ft, and despite the drifting cloud cover, they could see the approaches to the beaches crammed with ships. There were ship convoys strung out all the way back to England. It looked like you could walk back.

Every Allied plane that could fly was up this day. They converged on the landing area from every point of the compass. Some singly, some in ragged "vics" of three. Occasionally, Bob Sherwood would see proud, tight formations of 30 to 50 Spitfires or P-47s flashing their way in from the sea, going to unknown targets. Over 8500 Allied planes were aloft. No German aircraft were seen. The Sky Scorpions dropped their load on St. Lô and turned exultantly for home, shedding altitude rapidly.[856] A short mission, as they landed in just five and half-hours. They had slammed all twelve of the 500lb super demo bombs right into the rail junction. The RDX explosive was great stuff, more bang per ton than TNT. What a great mission. God bless that Canadian scientist for creating RDX. Bob Sherwood realized that he was now sweating. The plane was making its careful way along the perimeter track going to its hardstand. "Damn, I forgot to turn off my heated suit," he said. He found out later that no one had encountered much flak. The Group saw no fighters. The whole 8th Air Force had only lost very few planes. Hall's crew were not virgins anymore, and they had done well. "This whole thing is going to be a snap. Damn those lying Stateside instructors," thought Sherwood.

All told, four B-24 Liberators were lost on D-Day,[857] and one of them was from Sherwood's squadron, the 566th. *Shoot, Fritz, You've Had It* crashed and exploded at Northrepps, near Cromer, during assembly. The tail landed at Pond Farm, Sidestrand. Lieutenant Marcus V. Cowlney and all ten crew were killed. It was a sad blow for 11-year-old Norfolk schoolboy Fred Squires, who often walked the two miles from his home to the Hethel runway, creeping through the hedges and climbing into the aircraft. He did not like the olive green ones, so he picked *Shoot, Fritz, You've Had It*, a silver bomber, and he got in through the open bomb bays. He thought the smell was incredible. He didn't know then that it was from the aviation fuel and cordite. All he could see were what he thought were bombs, but were actually oxygen bottles, and he took it into his head it was going to blow up, so he got out as fast as he could and ran.

Henry Tarcza, aboard B-17G *El's Bells* in the 95th Bomb Group formation, "gazed with awe" at the hundreds of ships and boats off Omaha Beach. All were headed toward the beach, and it appeared from his altitude that one could almost step from one vessel to another and walk between England and France. His group of about 40 B-17s in close formation began to ease its way into the narrow corridor for the bomb run. At this time the bombardier instructed Tarcza to activate the bombs. He climbed out onto the catwalk, and after cautiously removing the safety pins from each bomb notified him that they were now "live." For the first time since take-off he now experienced a sense of fear. This was mostly of the unknown, because he began to wonder what the Germans had in store for them in that critical area. As they reached Omaha Beach the lead plane released a smoke bomb, which was a signal for all 40 aircraft to drop their bombs simultaneously. Thus, more than 100 tons of bombs exploded in a matter of a few seconds. This was the only mission over Europe when Tarcza actually felt the concussion of his own bombs. The explosions caused *El's Bells* to bounce and vibrate. He thought that, obviously, the long-planned invasion had remained a well-guarded secret. "We encountered no German aircraft in the target area and enemy gunfire was very light and inaccurate."

Air Forces Available in European Theater of Operations for Operation OVERLORD
Aircraft on Operational Stations 6 June 1944

A. Summary by Types:			
	Operational & Non-operational	Operational Strength	Effective
Heavy bombers-	3958	3455	3130
Medium and light bombers	1234	989	933
Fighters and lighter bombers	4709	3824	3711
TOTAL.	9901	8268	7774
B. Summary by Command:			
8th Air Force			
Heavy bombers	2578	2243	1947
Fighters	1147	961	961
Ninth Air Force			
Medium bombers	624	513	467
Light bombers	228	165	156
Fighters	1487	1132	1123
RAF BOMBER COMMAND			
Heavy bombers	1380	1212	1183
Light bombers	134	98	97
2ND TAF			
Medium bombers	88	67	67
Light bombers	160	146	146
Fighters	1006	856	831
ADGB			
Fighters	1072	875	796
TOTAL	9901	8268	7774

Eager RAF and USAAF fighter pilots were mainly disappointed that D-Day did not provide a rich hunting ground for *Luftwaffe* targets. USAAF P-38 Lockheed Lightnings were given the job of covering the ships in the Channel because not even the most trigger-happy ack-ack gunner on the ships could mistake the twin-tailed Lightning. Five squadrons of Lightnings flew cover all the time over the ships. Robert P. Tibor, a P-38 pilot in the 55th Fighter Group, was disappointed at first because the clouds were low and they could not see far. It did not look like "the show" was so big after all, but as the limited horizon unrolled he kept seeing ships, ships, and more ships. Big and little ships were spread from England to within 15 miles of the French coast, creeping under the cloud cover as darkness came. Out in front were the destroyers, cruisers, and battleships, and behind moved the concentration of troop and supply ships. In all Tibor was aloft on three occasions, and on the last one at 5 o'clock the weather had improved enough for him to see the water off the French coast. The coast was "black" with ships and landing craft, and he thought it looked like "the jam at Piccadilly Circus on a Saturday afternoon." Robert J. Rankin, a P-47 Thunderbolt pilot in the 61st Fighter Squadron, 56th Fighter Group, was one who "beat up everything" they could see, including an airfield where seven aircraft were lined up. The 56th Fighter Group had developed a new strafing technique, which entailed diving instead of coming in level. This made the P-47s harder to hit. When they got down to about 3000ft they started to pull out of the dive and opened up with their eight .50-caliber guns at the same time. As the noses of the P-47s swung in the pull out, the guns swept the field. The sitting planes were "plastered." Later Rankin and his colleagues ran into some Mustangs strafing a convoy of about 25 trucks and the P-47s joined in. Some of the trucks carried fuel and some munitions. When the thunderbolts made their first pass they had to circle around waiting for another. So many of the fighters were after the convoy that they had to queue up for a turn. The enemy crews ran for cover as the fuel went up and the munitions exploded. The flaming petrol spread over the ground under the trucks and a great column of black smoke billowed up.

On the evening of D-Day 3/JG 2 had just three serviceable FW 190s, but Herbert Hüppertz landed at about 2000 with eight FW 190s of his III *Gruppe*. Together with *Leutnant* Eickhoff, *Oberfähnrich* Heinz "Pritzel" Bär, and *Leutnant* Wolfgang Fischer of I *Gruppe* he was going to lead an attack on the beachhead and upon freight-carrying gliders. Eickhoff, Bär, and Fischer took off shortly after 2030 and approached at low level the great road bridge over Risle, west of Bernay, where they saw 12 Mustangs shooting up a German supply column. The FW 190s were too late to help, so Hüppertz led them away in a left turn at about 1200 meters. They headed for a light evening haze. It was then that they saw the other "Indians." The FW 190s dodged away from eight Mustangs and then caught four more. Fischer got his in a high reverse turn as he approached the bridge. The P-51 fell on fire into a wooded bank on the Risle and set a tree on fire. He then observed Hüppertz and his *Katschmarek* attack another aircraft. The fire was "devastating," and the Mustang disintegrated. Eickhoff and Bär each scored an *Abschuss* (victory).[858] Many in the *Wehrmacht* and the *Kriegsmarine* felt betrayed by the lack of German aircraft on D-Day. 22 year-old *Leutnant* Herbert Walther, in the 12th *Waffen-SS* Armored Division Hitler Youth (HJ), was one of them:

> "I know one thing; if the army had not been left by the Luftwaffe and the navy to fight alone, the invasion would have turned out very differently. But we had run out of planes."[859]

Robert P. Tibor of the 55th Fighter Group—in his P-38 Lightning—saw a Me 109 carrying bombs and dived for him, but somebody else got him. He didn't last long. The only other enemy plane he saw was another '109, which dived out of the clouds. Three Spitfires screamed into view after him. The 109 swooped down toward the water and up into the clouds again, the Spits right on his tail. Over the beachhead Tibor saw streams of tanks "crawling in" like "an invasion of beetles." He also saw gliders that had carried men in "lying all over the landscape." Some were broken. The ground was spotted with colored parachutes that had dropped guns and supplies. Like most others, he thought "Jerry" would throw up every plane that "would get a wheel off the ground," and it was just a milk run for the Allied fighters. Coming back he saw a big ship concentration moving out of the Thames estuary behind a smoke screen.

Wilbur Richardson flew two missions on D-Day, as did everyone else in the 94th Bomb Group. The few that didn't go on the early missions made theirs toward evening just after the others returned. Wilbur and his fellow crewmen stayed on the ramp between flights as their B-17s were refueled and re-armed. The press interviewed the young Californian as they waited. By the second sortie the cloud cover was broken up, and he could see even more of the action and the hundreds of vessels in the Channel. He saw the *Texas* firing her big guns, and watched the three 1400lb shells travel to the target. He told the pressman that the view from the ball turret was "an awe-inspiring sight." The crews were very tired due to the loss of sleep and so much time (15 hours total) in the air, but the events of the day left them keyed up and talkative.

At Horham, Henry Tarcza, returning in B-17 *El's Bells* in the 95th Bomb Group, was also interviewed by the press. He and his crew were a little apprehensive on their return to Horham because of a diminishing fuel supply. *El's Bells* landed at a RAF base in southern England, refueled, and flew on to Horham, where they gave an Associated Press reporter their views on the historic mission. Emotions varied. Many of their thoughts, feelings, and opinions they kept to themselves. Tarcza's pilot, Mathew McEntie, said, "Thank you men for your fine cooperation as a combat crew. It is doubtful if any of us will ever in our lifetime, participate in a historic undertaking of this magnitude." So far nobody has.

Franklin L. Betz's B-17 touched down at Kimbolton at 0926 hours, and he could sense an air of excitement on the base when he dropped to the ground from the Fortress after the pilot parked it in the dispersal area. "How was it Lieutenant?" asked the crew chief in charge of keeping the Fortress flying, an intense look on his leathery face weathered by the winds of his native Texas.

"What I saw through the breaks in clouds was an unforgettable sight," Betz replied. There was no time to say anything more. A truck pulled up to take the crew to interrogation, after which they had to get ready for the afternoon flight, his 30th mission. B-17s continued to peel off from the formation and land as the sun shone brightly through the cloud covering that was breaking up. Betz thought it a "good omen."

Throughout East Anglia crews rightly felt pleased with their contribution. However, as Allan Healy in the 467th Bomb Group, 2nd Bomb Division at Rackheath, near Norwich, Norfolk, says:

> "The D-Day missions were disappointing. No results of our action could be seen and we had not been able to do what we had in our potentiality to do to further the great undertaking. Nevertheless, the presence of nearly every flyable plane in England, the gigantic and continual roar of their engines and the bombs hurtling down through the overcast, must have given the Germans pause, aware of the destruction capable of being sent him from on high and given our own men a sense of security in the airpower overhead."[860]

An indication of the success of the operation was contained in a message from Lieutenant General Doolittle sent to all bomber bases:

"Today the greatest effective strength in the history of the 8th Air Force was reached; an overall effectiveness of approximately 75% of all crews and airplanes assigned. Please extend my congratulations to all members...for their untiring effort in achieving this impressive strength."

Bob Sherwood noted the sense of anticlimax after D-Day. There was a letdown after the thrill of D-Day. The 389th was alerted to fly every day after 6 June. Every day Hall's crew was slated to fly; each day there was a stand down. The weather was impossible. Fog and rain. Anything that was not paved turned into brown mud. The crews stayed in their damp, dark huts. They dashed out only to get meals. The humid mess hall smelled of powdered eggs, stale grease, and wet wool.

The intensity of weeks of pre-invasion missions and sorties on D-Day, and for long after, began to sap this strength, but replacements were on the way to the American fighter and bomber bases in East Anglia. Lieutenant Eugene Fletcher, soon to be the pilot of *Government Issue*, assigned to the 412th Bomb Squadron, 95th Bomb Group at Horham, arrived at RAF Valley, Wales, on D+1 via ATC. Upon deplaning, knowing the invasion was in progress and wanting some information about the war, he walked over to a Welsh farmer not far from the runway and asked if there was any news from the Continent. "Aye, 'tis a great contest going on over there. 'Tis a great contest." These were the first words to greet him in the ETO. Lieutenant Ed Wanner, another replacement who would soon pilot B-24 Liberator *Asbestos Alice* in the 700th Bomb Squadron, 445th Bomb Group, 2nd Bomb Division at Tibenham, Norfolk, was somewhat bemused. Wanner noted that here they were in a "foreign land" where they drove on the "wrong" side of the road, where "knocked up" meant they were busy that night, and where the great Normandy Invasion Landing was happening.

2nd Lieutenant Dick Johnson's diary for Wednesday, 7 June, reads:

"Cherbourg again. Invasion coast. Bombed German escape route. Target seven tenths covered. Used PFF method of bombing. No opposition from Nazis. Big operations: We are wholly supporting ground troops.

"Beiser and I were assigned to B-17 42-39875 named *'Buzz Blond'* and position No.3 in the 427th Squadron just behind and to the left of the lead plane of our squadron. I would ultimately fly 12 missions in this plane. Each of the 18 B-17s of our group was loaded with six 1000lb bombs to be delivered to a road junction near the invasion coast close to Conde Sur Neireau in western France. Eighteen other B-17s from our field were loaded with 500lb bombs, which were to be dropped on a road and railroad junction near Flers, France.[861] The planes bound for Flers took off starting at 0931 and ending ten minutes later with 19 aircraft in the air at 0941. Without a break, our 'A' group took off between 0941 and 0954. (Each group had a spare but since there were no aborts on this mission, they both returned before reaching enemy territory and thus got no credit for a mission). Two of our aircraft failed to bomb because of malfunctions. Due to overcast at the target, we bombed by radar from an average altitude of 21,000ft. Although the target area was totally clouded over except for very small holes, one crew reported bombs exploding in the target area, which could be seen during one of the brief openings. We were over enemy territory for 40 minutes but saw no flak or German fighters. We saw a few friendly fighters above the clouds that were our escorts. We could only get occasional glimpses of the invasion activity. Our route to the target took us due south, although we did a slight dogleg to the west of London and headed to France and arrived just out of flak range of Le Havre. As we approached the target at 21,300ft indicated (21,000 actual) the wind was 63mph from 340°, giving us a left drift of 18°. Our indicated air speed of 150mph gave us a true airspeed of 208mph and a ground speed of 207mph at the target. The outside air temperature was a relatively mild, minus 7° Fahrenheit. Bombs were away at 1208 and we returned to base, arriving at 1432 with all planes on the ground by 1503. Each aircraft had carried 1700 gallons of gasoline for this five hour and 20 minute mission."

Ralph Reese recalled:

"We headed for a railway bridge at Nantes. As we crossed the Channel at the beachhead we saw many landing barges up on the beach. I had never seen so many boats before in my life. There were many gliders on the ground near the beach. Our target was well hit and there were few bursts of flak. After the bomb run, we started across the Channel and were flying at 1000ft. We passed over 13 ships in a convoy on their return to England for more troops and supplies. We passed over a harbor in southern England, which was crowded with boats of every type."

Lieutenant Abel L. Dolim noted in his diary on 7 June:

"Mission #19. We crossed the invasion coast on the way to bomb a railway bridge over the Loire River at Nantes. The English Channel was positively jammed with ships and boats of all descriptions. Several landing craft were burning on the beaches. The fields near the coast were littered with Horsa and CG 4 gliders, all painted with black and white invasion striping. We took flak at Tours and then began our bomb run from the south of Nantes. Halfway down the bomb run, it became apparent we were on a collision course with a 3rd Bomb Division B-24 Group. The enemy was beginning to pound us with 88s so we elected to do a '360' and came up behind another B-24 group. The second bomb run was good. We hit the target just at the southern approach to the bridge and there was a very large ball of flame in the marshaling yard - -gasoline! We took more flak on the way out at Rennes and at Guernsey Island, where we were clobbered at only 11,000ft. It was quite late in the day (we had taken off at 1645) and there was a solid mass of dark clouds ahead, so we broke formation as we reached Portsmouth.

"We were on instruments at 8000ft altitude south of the London area when Hamil turned to a heading of 150°. I was puzzled, as it was not the heading I had given him earlier for Buncher-12. On the intercom, he told me that he had the 'Buncher' on radio direction finder (D/F). I tuned in on our frequency and it was the proper signal, but I knew our dead-reckoning position and it was next to impossible to receive Bury radio at that range. Also, with a bearing of 150° it had to be an enemy radio transmitter in France who was 'meaconing' the Bury beacon.[862] I gave Joe a new heading after convincing him that he had been tuned in on Jerry.

"North of London we broke out of the pea soup and chose to stay above the clouds in spite of the perfect bomber's moon. Joe [Hamil] received a radio report that enemy intruders were over our base so we were directed to clear the area and fly due west to Ireland for one-half hour and return. As I quickly dead reckoned for a change of course, Maybank suddenly opened fire with his chin turret. Unable to identify the visitor, we dropped into the safety of the clouds near Cambridge and began our turn to the west. The clouds opened up a little some minutes' later and we noted several fires on the ground to the north. Much later we approached Buncher 12 on an easterly heading, sweating out our low gas supply. Buncher 12 was on again and I was pleased to see the D/F needle line up very close to zero, which meant my DR course was good. I listened for the null (silence) then watched the needle swing around to 180° as we picked up the

Above left: A 305th Bomb Group B-17 returning to Chelveston at dusk. Some USAAF B-17s with flame dampers on the machine guns were used in night operations with the RAF late in 1943. (via Bill Donald) Above right: P-47C Thunderbolt in the 61st Fighter Squadron, 56th Fighter Group low over the sea during an escort mission. (USAF)

B-17G-15-DLs at Douglas Aircraft at Long Beach in September 1943. Rosie the Riveter has her hand on the chin turret of B-17G-15-DL 42-37846, which was assigned to the 331st Bomb Squadron, 94th Bomb Group at Rougham in October 1943 and named *Lucky 13*. Behind is B-17G-15-DL 42-37870, which was assigned to the 447th Bomb Group at Rattlesden in November 1943. It was reassigned on 3 November to the 333rd Bomb Squadron, 94th Bomb Group, and later joined the 364th Bomb Squadron, 305th Bomb Group at Chelveston on 23 November, where it was named *Palma II*. This Fortress and 2nd Lieutenant Robert P. Rippstein's crew FTR from the mission to Kiel on 22 May 1944. Seven men were KIA and three PoW. (Douglas)

B-17F-115-BO 42-30647 *Polly Ann* in the 366th Bomb Squadron, 305th Bomb Group en route to Stuttgart on 6 September 1943. The mission lasted seven hours, of which five hours were on oxygen. On 23 September 1943, while in the landing pattern over Chelveston, *Polly Ann* dropped from 2000ft and dived into the ground, striking two other B-17s on the way down (they managed to land safely). There were no survivors. Norman A. Drouin, the pilot, liked to sit in co-pilot Walter H. Menziel's seat during landing, and it is believed that while swapping positions, someone accidentally activated the autopilot. (USAF via Bill Donald)

Right: B-17F-85-BO 42-30057 *Raunchy* in the 351st Bomb Squadron, 100th Bomb Group, which Lieutenant Sam Turner flew to Switzerland on 6 September 1943 after being knocked out of formation. Turner crash-landed on Lake Constance, about 1¼ miles from land, and the B-17 remained afloat for about four minutes. The only man left in the Fortress as it sank was the ball turret gunner, S/Sgt Joseph F. Maloney, who had been killed by a 20mm shell. *Raunchy* was raised from the lake on 5 October and Maloney was buried with full military honors.

Above: B-24H-1-FO 42-7466 'N' *Ford's Folly*, a 578th Bomb Squadron, 392nd Bomb Group Liberator, was one of the first Hs to roll off the production line at Willow Run, and is being refueled at Wendling on 9 September 1943 for the Group's first combat mission. The Group was equipped with new B-24H and B-24J Liberators fitted with power-operated nose gun turrets. Three days earlier, on 6 September 69 Liberators, including those in the 392nd, flew a diversionary sweep over the North Sea for the Fortresses attacking Stuttgart. *Ford's Folly* was salvaged on 31 January 1944, repaired, and FTR on 11 September 1944. (USAF) Left: B-17F-15-VE 42-5763 *Bomb-Boogie* in the 401st Bomb Squadron, 91st Bomb Group, which was lost with Lieutenant Elwood D. Arp's crew on 6 September 1943. Four men evaded and six were captured. (USAF)

B-17F-100-BO 42-30362 The *Bonnie II* in the 561st Bomb Squadron, 388th Bomb Group releases its bomb load on target. *The Bonnie II* and Lieutenant Adalbert D. Porter's crew FTR on 9 September 1943 when a record 330 heavies were despatched to targets in France. Flak and a 20mm shell hit the B-17 on the bomb run over Paris, creating a large hole in the wing near the number one engine. Bombs were jettisoned and the crew baled out, the aircraft crashing at Houilles. Five crew evaded capture; the other six were captured and made prisoners of war. (USAF)

B-17F-75-BO 42-29923 *Lucky Strike* served in the 532nd Bomb Squadron, 381st Bomb Group at Ridgewell from 11 September 1943 after first equipping the 364th Bomb Squadron, 305th Bomb Group at Chelveston, where it was first named *Pappy's Hellions III* by the Varney Cline crew. *Lucky Strike* flew only two combat missions in the 381st Bomb Group in four months, and on the second of these on 4 January 1944 it was badly damaged over Kiel. *Lucky Strike's* pilot on this occasion was 2nd Lieutenant Rowland H. Evans, who nursed the bomber back to Norfolk, where he put it down at Cawston, north of Norwich. Two crewman were killed in the crash-landing, which wrote the B-17 off. Evans, who was a philosophy professor at Williams' College in Massachusetts before the war, survived the crash. He was listed as MIA on 22 February 1944 when he flew as part of 1st Lieutenant Lee W. Smith's crew in 42-39895 *Bermondsey Battler*, which was one of six B-17s that FTR after the raid on Bunde in Germany. (via Bill Donald)

B-17F-110-BO 42-30607 *Pat Hand* in the 337th Bomb Squadron, 96th Bomb Group, flown by Lieutenant Ken E. Murphy, takes a direct flak hit over Paris just after bombs away during the raid on the Hispano-Suiza aero-engine assembly plant on 15 September 1943. During the bomb run 42-3437, flown by Lieutenant James V. Richardson in the 339th Bomb Squadron, was sent spinning down and on fire after being hit by flak and his aircraft exploded. One crewmember survived and evaded capture, but the other nine men were killed. (USAF)

B-17F-70-BO 42-29750 *Rebel's Revenge* in the 323rd Bomb Squadron, 91st Bomb Group on a practice flight on 25 September 1943. *Rebel's Revenge* and 2nd Lieutenant John W. Perritt's crew FTR two days later (9 KIA 1 PoW). (USAF via Philip Kaplan)

B-17F-30-BO 42-5054 was assigned to the 306th Bomb Group on 7 August 1943, but it was transferred to the 360th Bomb Squadron, 303rd Bomb Group on 25 September and was named *Belle of San Joaquin*, which is seen here "supported" by a ground crewman. The Fortress returned to the ZOI on 7 May 1944 and was later scrapped at Kingman, Arizona, in November 1945. (Harry D. Gobrecht)

B-17Fs in the 570th Bomb Squadron, 390th Bomb Group escorted by high-flying P-47s and leaving contrails en route to Emden on 27 September 1943, was photographed by S/Sgt Stan Smith, a waist gunner on B-17F-120-BO 42-30783 *Stork Club* flown by Captain Keith Harris. In the foreground is B-17F-45-DL 42-3329 *Skippy*, whose pilot, 2nd Lieutenant George W. Harmon, was first to complete 25 missions in November 1943. *Stork Club* and 2nd Lieutenant Vincent F. DeMayo's crew FTR on 15 March 1943. On 5 February 1944 *Skippy* took off for a mission to bomb an airfield at Villacoublay, France, but whilst departing England the No.2 engine exploded. Lieutenant Thomas J. Sutters, pilot, was unable to feather the windmilling prop. He decided to return to base, but the engine set the wing on fire, and they only made it as far as the River Thames, where Sutters pointed the B-17 towards the Channel before all ten crew baled out safely. (USAF)

Oberleutnant Georg "Murr" Schott (left), *Staffelkapitan 1st Staffel* JG 1 and a veteran of the Spanish Civil War, was KIA on 27 September 1943 when his FW 190 "White 11" was hit by return fire during an attack on B-17s heading for Emden. Schott, who had 19 victories, was found dead in his dinghy three weeks later. His successor was *Oberleutnant* Robert Engleder (right).(via Eric Mombeek)

B-17F-25-DL 42-3111 *Local Girl* in the 324th BS, 91st Bomb Group was shot down at Geefsweer, northern Holland, by a Bf 109 after the raid on Emden on 27 September 1943. 2nd Lieutenant William G. Peagram, the pilot, remained at the controls while eight crew baled out over the coast of Ems. Peagram and Melvin Peters, waist gunner, who went on firing to the end, were found dead in the wreckage. Larson, engineer, and Cosgrove, navigator, drowned when the cords of their parachutes became entangled in the "botschuttings," or "flounder fences"; a device of twigs and branches to catch flat fish. Norman Eatinger, bombardier, was rescued by a Dutch fishing boat. (via Orlo Natvig)

One significant outcome of the XB-40 gunship was the adoption of the chin turret on B-17G models and also Douglas-built F models from -70-DL on. At Boeing, it was intended to fit chin turrets to B-17F-135-BO, but this block was redesignated B-17G-1-BO, and no Boeing-built Fs received chin turrets on the production line, although many Fs acquired them at modification centres in the U.S. and in the ETO. B-17F-75-DL 42-3522 *Gremlin's Delite* in the 533rd Bomb Squadron, 381st Bomb Group, was one such late model "F" with a chin turret. This aircraft, which at first was assigned to the 96th Bomb Group on 27 September 1943, finished her days at Walnut Ridge, Arkansas, in 1946. (USAF)

B-17F-25-DL 42-3082 *Double Trouble* in the 333rd Bomb Squadron, 94th Bomb Group. The pilot, Lieutenant Bill Winnesheik, aborted the mission to Bremen on 25 June 1943 after fighters knocked out two engines, and he landed in England despite a full bomb load. On 4 October 1943, during a mission to St. Dizier, France, fighters knocked out the No.3 engine and the propeller refused to feather, but the crew managed to crash-land at Margate. Vance Van Hooser, the assistant engineer-waist gunner, who was on his 23rd mission, was hit in the head by 20mm shell fragments and never flew again. (USAF via Peter Frost)

B-17F-110-BO 42-30604 *Badger's Beauty V* in the 350th Bomb Squadron, 100th Bomb Group, which was lost on 4 October 1943 with Captain Harold B. Helstrom's crew. (TAMM)

B-17F-110-BO 42-30604 *Badger's Beauty V* burning in a French field near Caen on 4 October 1943 after enemy action had knocked out the No.3 engine and damaged another. Joseph Shandor, one of the waist gunners, was hidden by the French Underground until January 1944, and he then walked over the Pyrenees into Spain and finally arrived in England. Three others in the crew also evaded successfully. The rest of the crew, including the pilot, Captain Harold Helstrom, were captured and taken prisoner. (TAMM)

B-17Fs in the 535th Bomb Squadron, 381st Bomb Group in formation. Nearest aircraft is 42-29941/R *TS Tarfu*, which FTR on 8 October 1943 when it crashed at Talge with the loss of six of Captain Edwin R. Manchester's crew. Four survived to be taken prisoner. Right is 42-30029/P *Chap's Flying Circus*, which FTR on 30 January 1944 when it crashed at Gravenage in The Netherlands with the loss of all ten of Lieutenant Carl O. Baer's crew. Furthest away is 42-30864/T, which FTR on 8 October 1943 when it crashed at Haupstedt, Germany. One crewman in Lieutenant William F. Cormany, Jr.'s crew was KIA and nine survived to be taken prisoner. (USAF via Philip Kaplan)

B-17F-120-BO 42-30758 *"Rosie's Riveters"* with Robert Rosenthal (kneeling, 2nd from left) and his crew with ground crew members. Rosie got the badly damaged *"Rosie's Riveters"* back to Thorpe Abbotts after the raid on Bremen on 8 October 1943 when the 100th Bomb Group lost seven B-17s. *"Rosie's Riveters"* was repaired, and Ross McPhee's crew took over the famous Fortress; in early February 1944 they renamed the aircraft *Satcha Lass*. The name lasted barely a week, because on 4 February *Satcha Lass* was heavily damaged on the mission to Frankfurt and McPhee crash-landed the plane near Mönchengladbach after trying to reach Holland. Pictured (kneeling) L-R: Lieutenant R. Bailey; Captain Robert "Rosie" Rosenthal; Lieutenant C. Milburn; and Lieutenant Winifred Lewis, co-pilot. Standing L-R: S/Sgt Loren Darling, waist gunner; U/k ground crewman; T/Sgt Michael Bocuzzi, radio operator; S/Sgt J. Mack; T/Sgt Clarence Hall, engineer-top turret gunner; u/k ground crewman; S/Sgt William DeBlasio, tail gunner; and S/Sgt R. Robinson. On 10 October Rosenthal and his crew flew *Royal Flush* to Münster and they were the only one of 13 crews to return to Thorpe Abbotts. (TAMM)

Robert Rosenthal at an awards ceremony at Thorpe Abbotts. (TAMM)

B-17s in the 388th Bomb Group crossing Bremen on 8 October 1943 at 23,000ft. The target below is obscured effectively by German smoke pots. None of the 23 Fortresses despatched by the Knettishall group were lost, but 21 were damaged by flak from the 260 AA guns at Bremen. (USAF)

B-17F-50-DL 42-3393 *Just A Snappin'* in the 418th Bomb Squadron, 100th Bomb Group lies wrecked beside a tree at RAF Ludham after returning from the raid on Bremen on 8 October 1943. (TAMM)

The wrecked top turret of B-17F-120-BO 42-30796 *Sunny II* flown by John Griffin in the 351st Bomb Squadron, 100th Bomb Group on the Bremen raid on 8 October 1943. An exploding 20mm shell blew away the top of the upper turret, hurling Sgt Harjo into the gangway leading into the bombardier's compartment. On landing the crew found bullet holes in all four propellers and one slug still lodged in the right arm of the tail gunner. (TAMM)

Major Gale "Bucky" Cleven (right), who went down over Bremen leading the 350th Squadron, 100th Bomb Group on 8 October 1943 flying with Captain Bernard DeMarco's crew in 42-3233 *Our Baby*. His good friend, Major John "Bucky" Egan, who had been on pass in London that day, joined Cleven in a PoW camp when he was shot down two days later when the 100th Bomb Group went to Münster. (TAMM)

B-17F-30-VE 42-5855 in the 423rd Bomb Squadron, 306th Bomb Group, which went missing with Lieutenant Dean C. Rodman's crew on 8 October 1943. The plane crashed at Golderstadt with the loss of five crew KIA and five taken prisoner. (USAF)

B-17F-50-DL 42-3352 *Virgin's Delight* in the 94th Bomb Group, piloted by Lieutenant Richard F. "Dick" LePore in the 410th Lead Squadron, and photographed by Captain Ray D. Miller, the squadron flight surgeon, leaving the burning Focke-Wulf factory at Marienburg on 9 October 1943. On the bomb run LePore was not using oxygen, and was in fact eating a Mars Bar from his PX rations! (USAF)

Smoke trails from B-17F-100-BO 42-30377 *Roger The Lodger II* in the 412th Bomb Squadron, 95th Bomb Group shortly before it went down in flames in Dutch territorial waters with Lieutenant Ralph W. Eherts' crew on the Marienburg mission, 9 October 1943. Fighters scored hits in the No.2 engine aboard *Roger The Lodger II* and put a rocket in the No.3 engine. Seven of Ehert's crew baled out, but two of the parachutes were on fire. The five survivors perished in the freezing waters of the North Sea. Robert Wing, the bombardier, had a premonition the night before that he would not return. (USAF)

B-17Gs in the 390th Bomb Group after bombing the target at Marienburg on 9 October 1943. Some 378 8th AF bombers were despatched to targets in East Prussia and Poland on the longest mission to date. On this day 378 heavies were despatched to three targets, with 115 aircraft in the 1st and 41st Combat Wings going to the Arado aircraft component plant at Anklam, near Peenemünde, as a diversion for 263 bombers attacking the port of Gydnia and the Focke Wulf plant at Marienburg. (The Anklam force lost 14 B-17s.) Anti-aircraft defences at Marienburg were limited, so the force bombed from 11,000-13,000ft, which resulted in 60% of the bombs dropped by the 96 Fortresses exploding within 1000ft of the MPI; 83% fell within 2000ft. Before the raid, the plant was producing almost half of all FW 190s for the *Luftwaffe*. Eaker called it "*A classic example of precision bombing*." (USAF)

B-17F-60-DL 42-3426 *Kemy II* (formerly *Spider* and *Kemy Jr.*) in the 571st Bomb Squadron, 390th Bomb Group. *Kemy II* and Lieutenant William W. Smith's crew was one of eight in the 390th Bomb Group, that FTR from Münster on Sunday, 10 October, where for the first time in the war the 8th Air Force bombed a residential area to deprive the Germans of its rail workers. Three of the crew were KIA; the other seven survived to be taken prisoner. It was a black day for the 13th Wing as a whole, which lost 25 of the 29 B-17s lost by the Third Division. Worst hit was the 100th Bomb Group, which lost 12 bombers. This brought its total loss to 19 in three days. In all, 88 bombers had been lost on three successive days, and the losses came at a time when intelligence sources revealed that *Luftwaffe* fighter strength was on the increase. (via Ian McLachlan)

Above left: B-17F-40-VE 42-5984 *Rusty Load* piloted by Robert Sabel in the 569th Bomb Squadron, 390th Bomb Group, which only just made it back from the mission to Münster on two engines, only two minutes of fuel remaining, and with over 750 holes in the fuselage. Sabel landed at Thorpe Abbotts after Framlingham was shrouded in mist and fog. (TAMM) Above right: B-17F-40-VE 42-5984 *Rusty Load* had huge holes in both wings, the rudder, and aileron, with both flaps shot away. Ground staff were amazed that the pilots could fly the plane, let alone land it, and they described their survival as "nothing short of a miracle." (TAMM)

B-17F-55-DL 42-3413 *Hard Luck!* in the 350th Bomb Squadron, 100th Bomb Group in formation. Above and behind the NMF ship is 42-31991 *Miss-Chief.* (TAMM)

Above left: B-17F-55-DL 42-3413 *Hard Luck!* in the 350th Bomb Squadron, 100th Bomb Group with Captain Loren Van Steenis ("The Flying Dutchman") and his crew. When Crew 13 had joined the Hundredth on 13 October 1943 they were told, "*You fellers are Crew 13. This is the 13th Wing. You're assigned to airplane #13. 'Oh yes, your airplane is named Hard Luck!*" (Its name derived from the date of its arrival - Friday, 13 August 1943 - and the last two digits of the serial number). Van Steenis' crew and ground crew L-R, standing: Crew chief, T/Sgt "Zip" Myers and S/Sgt Sokolosky (Ground Crew); S/Sgts Yarnell, Clothier, Schneider, Butchino, and Sgts Hill and Muzzinski (Ground Crew). Front: S/Sgt Robert Goodman, T/Sgt Halladay; Lieutenant Jack Ogg; Captain Van Steenis; Lieutenant Harold Becker; Captain Lester Torbett; and T/Sgt Earl Benham. Van Steenis' crew flew the plane for 17 consecutive missions. On 7 May 1944, while on the bomb run over Berlin, *Hard Luck!* was hit by a flak burst, that killed the navigator, Harold Becker, and wounded the bombardier, Lester Torbett. In the ensuing confusion, and with no navigator, Van Steenis and his co-pilot, Jack Ogg, lost the Group, but a P-47 rescued them and guided them home. Seven of the crew finished their tour. *Hard Luck!* held what must have been a record in the 8th AF, its first 50 missions being flown with original engines. "Zip" Myers was extremely proud of "his ship," and refused to allow inexperienced pilots to fly it - "that is if it could be avoided!" *Hard Luck* flew missions for a year and a day, being lost on its 62nd mission on 14 August 1944 when 2nd Lieutenant Donald E. Cielewich's crew baled out and all 9 men were taken prisoner. (via Michael P. Faley, 100th Bomb Group Historian)

B-17F-100-BO 42-30338 *Cabin in The Sky* in the 571st Bomb Squadron, 390th Bomb Group, which returned from the raid on Münster on 10 October, and Captain Robert Brown put in his gunners' claims of eleven fighters shot down. *Cabin in The Sky* was named from the Broadway musical, which featured the hit song, "Taking a chance on love." (TAMM)

Five of the crew of B-17F-100-BO 42-30338 *Cabin in The Sky* gather around the plane after a mission. The B-17 survived the war and was scrapped at Altus, Oklahoma, in August 1945. (TAMM)

B-17F-10-VE 42-5725 *Flapper* in the 365th Bomb Squadron, 305th Bomb Group at Chelveston on 13 October 1943. On 4 July 1943, when 192 Fortresses in the 1st Wing were assigned the Gnome and Rhône Aero engine factory at Le Mans and an aircraft factory at Nantes, the aircraft had to put down at RAF Portreath, but it returned to Chelveston two days later. On 22 August 1943 *Flapper* was transferred to the 532nd Bomb Squadron, 381st Bomb Group at Ridgewell and was renamed *This Is It!*. The B-17 returned to the ZOI in July 1944. (USAF via Bill Donald)

Contrails produced by fighter escorts and Fortresses dot the sky as the B-17s head for their target. (USAF)

B-24D 41-23667 *Ball of Fire*, a 328th Bomb Squadron Ploesti veteran, became the 93rd Bomb Group assembly ship, and was finally salvaged on 5 May 1945. (USAF)

B-24D 42-40506 *Fightin' Sam*, an original 389th B-24D in the 566th Squadron, and crew, commanded by Captain Tom Conroy, 566th Squadron CO, in his early combat days with the "Sky Scorpions." Left to right: T/Sgt Walter E. Taylor (KIA 5.12.43), waist gunner; Major Conroy (killed in the Korean War); Lieutenant Harley B. Mason (PoW 5.12.43), co-pilot; Al Ormsby, bombardier; Harold Roodman, navigator; and T/Sgt Robert W. McNair (KIA 5.12.43), radio operator. Kneeling: S/Sgt Doyle L. Kirkland (KIA 5.12.43), ball turret; Vic Scollin, waist gunner; and unknown. (Russ D. Hayes)

Crew of *The Eightball* in the 390th Bomb Group just before the second Schweinfurt mission. Lieutenant Richard "Dick" Perry is standing at the extreme right of the picture. (Perry)

B-17F-80-BO 42-29988 *The Uncouth Bastard* in the 364th Bomb Squadron, 305th Bomb Group at Chelveston on 13 October 1943, the day before this Fortress and 2nd Lieutenant Robert W. Holt's crew FTR from Schweinfurt. The aircraft crashed at Puffendrof, Germany. Six crew were killed, and four were made PoW. Prior to joining the 305th Bomb Group this B-17 was *Lucifer Jr* in the 535th Bomb Squadron, 381st Bomb Group at Ridgewell. (via Bill Donald)

B-17F-20-BO 41-24525 *What's Cookin Doc?* in the 547th Bomb Squadron, 384th Bomb Group on 13 October 1943. On 22 September 1943 this aircraft had been transferred from the 422nd Bomb Squadron, 305th Bomb Group at Chelveston. *What's Cookin Doc?* and 2nd Lieutenant Walter E. Garner's crew were lost on the 7 January 1944 mission to Ludwigshafen. (via Bill Donald)

The disintegrating remnants of a Bf 110 going down above Maastricht and the River Mass on the return from the mission to Schweinfurt on 17 August were caught on camera by a crewmember aboard *Wham Bam* in the 305th Bomb Group flown by Charley Sackerson. The enemy fighter was hit simultaneously by fire from two 56th Fighter Group P-47 Thunderbolts. (via Michael I. Gibson/Bill Donald)

B-17F-115-BO 42-30727 in the 367th "Clay Pigeons" Bomb Squadron, 306th Bomb Group taking off from Thurleigh. On 14 October 1943 42-30727 was piloted by Lieutenant William C. Bisson and was one of ten Fortresses the Thurleigh group lost when Brigadier General Orvil Anderson, commanding general of VIII Bomber Command, sent the bombers to Schweinfurt. Bad weather wrecked the timetable and losses were heavy. Flak knocked out two of Bisson's engines and fighters riddled the rear fuselage, killing S/Sgt Thompson E. Wilson, tail gunner. Only 2nd Lieutenant Charles R. Stafford, co-pilot, who exited through the side cockpit window, and four crewmen in the aft section escaped death. (Richards Collection)

B-17Fs in the 91st Bomb Group at Bombs Away. The B-17 bottom left is B-17F-5-VE 42-5714, which FTR with 2nd Lieutenant Robert M. Slane's crew on 14 October 1943. The aircraft crashed at Nancy, France, Eight men were taken prisoner, one evaded, and one was KIA. (USAF)

B-17Fs en route to their target. The nearest three aircraft are from the 305th Bomb Group. Left is 42-30807 WF-K *Katy*, which was lost with 2nd Lieutenant Gerald B. Eakle's crew on 14 October 1943 (1 Evd, 1 KIA, 8 PoW). Center is 42-3436 WF-R in the 364th Bomb Squadron, which had been assigned to the Group on 18 September 1943, and which was lost with 2nd Lieutenant Dennis J. McDarby's crew on the Schweinfurt raid on 14 October 1943 (5 KIA 5 PoW). Top is 42-30666 WF-M *Daisy Mae*, one of two Fortresses destroyed in the mid-air collision at Newton Browmswold on 15 November 1943. (USAF via Bill Donald)

Lieutenant David Williams, lead navigator in the 91st Bomb Group. (Williams)

Lieutenant Robert "Bob" Hughes, pilot of *Nine Little Yanks and A Jerk* in the 351st Bomb Squadron, 100th Bomb Group. (Hughes)

B-17 under fighter attack. (TAMM)

B-17F-40-DL 42-3271 *Nine Little Yanks and A Jerk* in the 351st Bomb Squadron, 100th Bomb Group, which was originally named by Lieutenant Robert "Bob" Hughes' crew. (Bob Hughes is standing, 2nd from right). They had picked up a brand new B-17 at Grand Island, Nebraska, in June 1943 and had named that aircraft *Nine Little Yanks and A Jerk*, but on arrival in England the plane was taken away for theater modifications and the crew never saw it again. At Thorpe Abbotts they were given 42-3271, which flew its first combat mission on 17 July 1943 to Hamburg, and a month later Hughes' crew named the plane *Nine Little Yanks and A Jerk*. Ground crew personnel painted the name, and the shapely nude pin up perched on a bomb was added by Frank Stevens. Bob Hughes flew *Nine Little Yanks and A Jerk* for the last time on 24 January 1944 when poor weather on the mission forced them to bring their bombs home. *Nine Little Yanks and A Jerk*, which had completed 28 missions, was salvaged on 7 March after another crew took the B-17 on a practice flight. On their return to Thorpe Abbotts the left main landing gear collapsed and the Fortress suffered severe rippling of the skin, which indicated irreparable twisting of the airframe. (TAMM)

A Messerschmitt Bf 110 *Zerstorer*, which was one of the fighter types defending Schweinfurt. (via Theo Boiten)

B-17F-120-BO 42-30799 *The Bigassbird II* in the 349th Bomb Squadron, 100th Bomb Group with ground crew and Owen "Cowboy" Roane's crew after their return from Schweinfurt on 14 October 1943. L-R: standing: Curtis Campbell, bombardier; "Cowboy" Roane; Omar Gonzales, navigator (PoW 5.11.43); Arthur Stipes; Pete Cook; and Ray Tomb. Front Row: Woodie Woodward, George Kennedy, Ray Morton (the Crew Chief), and J. Baggett. During phase training in the USA Roane's crew had flown a B-17 which they had named *Bigassbird*, and they had flown it to England in June 1943, where on arrival it was taken away from them for theater modifications and they never saw the plane again. In late June Roane's crew returned from their orientation course at Bovingdon to be one of the replacements for three crews in the 349th Bomb Squadron that had been lost on their first mission. After flying *Laden Maiden* Roane's crew were given a new B-17, which they promptly named *The Bigassbird II*, and in August 1943 ground man Ernest Lovato painted the distinctive artwork on the left-hand side of the fuselage. Roane's crew completed their tour on 29 November 1943. On 6 March 1944 *The Bigassbird II* FTR from the mission to Berlin. The pilot, Lieutenant William E. Murray, was killed instantly in the third fighter pass when he was struck in the head by a 20mm shell. Mahlon Hall, the tail gunner, who had also been hit in the head by a 20mm shell, had crawled up through the aircraft into the radio room, where he was attended to by the radioman, Fred Schillinger. Both men died in the crash. Seven men baled out and survived to be taken prisoner. (TAMM)

Lieutenant William "Bill" Rose (third from left back row) and his crew of *Sky Scrapper* in the 92nd Bomb Group. (Bill Rose)

B-17F-70-BO 42-29803 (seen here earlier in its career when it was assigned to the 365th Bomb Squadron, 305th Bomb Group and was named *Flat Foot Floogie*) was the only 381st Bomb Group aircraft that FTR from the Schweinfurt raid on 14 Ocotber 1943. Four of Lieutenant Bernarde M. Yorba, Jr.'s crew were KIA and six were taken prisoner. The plane crashed at Schweinfurt. (USAF via Bill Donald)

B-17F-70-BO 42-29784 *Smilin Thru* in the 545th Bomb Squadron, 384th Bomb Group, which crashed at Blaydon, Gloucestershire, on 14 October 1943 returning from the raid on Schweinfurt. This aircraft had previously served in both the 305th and 381st Bomb groups. (via Bill Donald)

Lieutenant Frederick B. Farrell's crew (Farrell is second from right) in the 366th Bomb Squadron, 305th Bomb Group beside their damaged B-17F-115-BO 42-30678 *Rigor Mortis* after returning to Chelveston from Schweinfurt on 14 October 1943. Lieutenant Frederick E. Helmick, bombardier, and Max Guber, navigator, had been taken away by ambulance to have their wounds treated in hospital. Guber had been hit in the face and chest by an exploding shell. Helmick, who needed 56 stitches to close wounds in his back and shoulder, returned home after hospitalization, having completed his 25 missions. *Rigor Mortis* was lost with Lieutenant Robert H. Safranek's crew on 25 February 1944. Three crewmembers were KIA and seven were taken prisoner. (via Bill Donald)

B-17F-15-DL 42-3037 was assigned overseas on 1 August 1943 and joined the 366th Bomb Squadron, 305th Bomb Group. It was christened *Windy City Avenger* in memory of *Windy City Challenger*, which was lost on the mission to Villacoublay on 14 July 1943. *Windy City Avenger* was transferred to the 384th Bomb Group on 20 September 1943 and was salvaged on 15 October 1943 after damage sustained on the Schweinfurt raid made it only fit for scrap. (via Bill Donald)

Colonel "Mo" Preston, CO 379th Bomb Group, listens to Major "Rip" Rohr on his return from Schweinfurt. Preston noted that Rohr "'ooked harassed, shaken and more agitated that I had ever seen him." (Preston)

The crew of *Lazy Baby* in the 364th Bomb Squadron, 305th Bomb Group. Front Row, L-R: Edward W. Deinhart, pilot; Brunson W. Bolin, co-pilot; Donald T. Rowley, navigator; and Carl A. Johnson, bombardier. Back Row L-R: George H. Blaylock Jr., engineer; Hurley D. Smith, radio; Raymond C. Baus, ball turret; Christy Zullo, right waist; Robert Cinibulk, left waist; and Bernard Segal, tail gunner. (USAF)

B-17F-F-120-BO 42-30831 *Lazy Baby* in the 364th Bomb Squadron, 305th Bomb Group, which 2nd Lieutenant Edward Dienhart crash-landed at Reinach-Aesch, Switzerland, on 14 October 1943 after bombing Schweinfurt. (USAF via Bill Donald)

B-17F-27-BO 41-24605 *Knock-Out Dropper*, which was flown on the Schweinfurt mission by Lieutenant John P. Manning, who led the low squadron in the 303rd Bomb Group formation. On 16 November 1943 the 359th Bomb Squadron Fortress set a new 8th Air Force record for a B-17 when Manning flew it on its 50th mission. *Knock-Out Dropper* was scrapped at Stillwater, Oklahoma, in late 1945. (via Harry Gobrecht)

The *Nazi* flag that fluttered over the Kugelfischer ball bearing plant, the largest of the four plants at Schweinfurt, was presented to the 305th Bomb Group at Chelveston by an Air Force journalist after the U.S. 42nd "Rainbow" Armored Division captured it on 11 April 1945. The 305th Bomb Group lost thirteen crews on the second raid on the plants on 14 October 1943. (via Bill Donald)

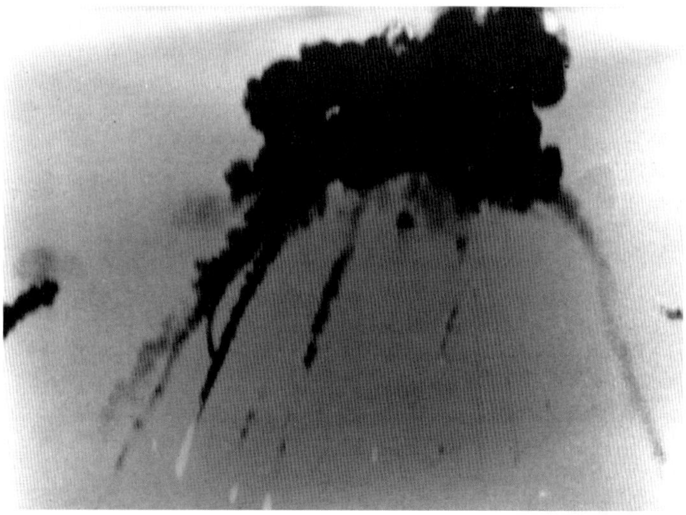

A 389th Bomb Group Liberator blows up. (USAF)

B-17F-115-BO 42-30666 *Daisy May* on fire on 15 November 1943 after a mid-air collision with B-17F-80-BO 42-29953 *Wolfess* while the two 364th Bomb Squadron B-17s were returning from gunnery practice near Newton Bromswold. *Wolfess*, piloted by 2nd Lieutenant Wetzel F. Mays, rose up in front of *Daisy May* and was chopped in half by the propellers. Both aircraft fell to the ground with no survivors. Varney Cline, pilot of *Daisy May*, who was flying with 2nd Lieutenant Denzel M. Smith and his crew, had only just finished his tour of missions the day before. *Wolfess* is in the field directly behind, just over the hedge. (USAF via Bill Donald)

The 91st Bomb Group began receiving their first Boeing built B-17G models late in 1943. (USAF)

Vega-built Fortresses at Burbank, California, in late 1943. B-17G-5-VE 42-39871, being hoisted above the others, served in the 8th Weather Squadron (P) and the 652nd Bomb Squadron, 25th Bomb Group at Watton, Norfolk, before being declared war-weary on 21 February 1945. B-17G-5-VE 42-39873 became *Stormy Weather* in the 615th Bomb Squadron, 401st Bomb Group and FTR on 1 August 1944. B-17G-5-VE 42-39869 (right) became *Heaven Can Wait* in the 412th Bomb Squadron, 95th Bomb Group at Horham, and FTR with Lieutenant Richard P. Bannerman and crew on 11 April 1944. B-17G-5-VE 42-39875 (off-centre) became *Buzz Blonde*, later *Helen Highwater*, and finally *Through Hel'en Hiwater* in the 303rd Bomb Group at Molesworth, and was lost on 15 January 1945. B-17G-5-VE 42-39876 (center) became *Gloria Anna* in the 569th Bomb Squadron, 390th Bomb Group. B-17G-5-VE 42-39892 was assigned to the 401st Bomb Group and was lost on a mission to Berlin in March 1944. Lockheed-Vega built 2750 B-17s in WWII. (Lockheed-California)

Bf 109G-6 26058, flown by 31 year old Major Kurt Brändle, CO of II./JG 3, when he was KIA on 3 November 1943 at Schiphol airfield only days before his death. A *Ritterkreuztrager*, Brändle was killed only moments after getting his final two kills, both P-47s, over the North Sea to the west of Amsterdam. At the time of his death, his score stood at 180 combat victories in over 700 operational sorties. *Feldwebel* Helmut Henning, Brändle's First Mechanic, is at the controls of the aircraft. Note the so-called clear-view *Erla-Haube* (or "Erla cockpit canopy") named after the Erla aircraft repair unit at Brussels. (Helmut Henning, via Rob de Visser)

B-17F-50-DL 42-3352 *Virgin's Delight* in the 410th Bomb Squadron, 94th Bomb Group. *Virgin's Delight* and 2nd Lieutenant Walter Chyle's crew FTR on 29 November 1943 when the aircraft was ditched in the North Sea with the loss of all the crew. (USAF)

B-17F-90-BO 42-30166 *You Cawn't Miss It* in the 332nd Bomb Squadron, 94th Bomb Group was lost with Lieutenant James K. Killlen's crew on 5 November 1943 when it was ditched in the North Sea. Eight crew perished and two survived to be taken prisoner. (USAF)

B-17F-45-DL 42-3301 *Cavalier* in the 367th Bomb Squadron, 306th Bomb Group, which bellied in at Thurleigh on 15 November 1943. This Fortress was repaired, renamed *Bouncin' Baby*, and was salvaged after a crash at Shipdham on 29 February 1944. (Joseph Minton via Larry Goldstein)

S/Sgt Forrest S. Clark, radio operator-gunner in Lieutenant Rockford C. Griffith's crew in the 67th Squadron, 44th Bomb Group at Shipdham. (Clark)

Lieutenant Benson in the 305th Bomb Group at Chelveston after returning from the mission to Gelsenkirchen on 5 November 1943. (USAF)

Colonel Turner and Lieutenant Colonel Henry G. MacDonald greet Captain Bennet at Chelveston on 5 November 1943 after the 305th Bomb Group returned from the mission to Gelsenkirchen. MacDonald commanded the Group for a time in late 1944-early 1945 and again in June 1945. (USAF)

B-17G-5-BO 42-31134 in the 569th Bomb Squadron, 390th Bomb Group, en route to the secret German heavy water plant situated near the little Norwegian town of Rjukan, about 75 miles from Oslo, on 16 November 1943. Intelligence sources had learned that this and the molybdenum mines at Knaben and a generating plant at Vermark, in the Rjukan Valley, were all connected with the German heavy water experiments, which would help give the *Nazis* the atomic bomb. In May 1944, 42-31134 was renamed *Gung Ho*, and on 10 September 1944 this aircraft and Lieutenant Charles F. McIntosh's crew FTR from a mission when it crashed at Nuremberg. Six crew were killed and three were taken prisoner. (USAF)

On 18 November 1943, while 127 B-17s raided Gelsenkirchen, the 2nd Bomb Division went to Norway to bomb the Ju 88 repair depot at Oslo-Kjeller and industrial targets in the capital, and wave after wave of enemy fighters pressed home their attacks on the Liberators. 1st Lieutenant Rockford C. "Rocky" Griffith's B-24H-1-CF 41-29161 in the 67th Bomb Squadron, 44th Bomb Group limped back across the North Sea with a badly wounded ball turret gunner aboard to Shipdham, where the landing gear failed to work. The flight engineer tried desperately to crank it down by hand but this failed too. Griffith ordered the seven members of the crew to bale out before he and the co-pilot, 1st Lieutenant L. W. Grone, successfully crash-landed the badly damaged B-24 on one wheel. Two hours later repair crews checking the wreckage found two unexploded German shells in the one "good" engine that had brought the crew home. (Urzal P. Harvel)

On 26 November 1943 the 56th Fighter Group claimed no fewer than 23 enemy fighters shot down. This famous photo shows sixteen pilots presumed to be the victors that day. Left to right: Captain Walter V Cook (two Bf 110s); Lieutenant Stanley Bixby "Fats" Morrill (Bf 109); Lieutenant John P Bryant (Bf 110); Lieutenant John H. Truluck (FW 190); Captain Walker H. Mahurin (three Bf 110s); Lieutenant Harold E. Comstock (Bf 110); Lieutenant Colonel Dave Schilling (two FW 190s); Major (later Colonel) Francis S. "Gabby" Gabreski (two Bf 110s); Captain Ralph Johnson (two Bf 110s); Major James C. Stewart, Group Operations Officer (Do 217); Lieutenant Frank W. Klibbe (Bf 109); Lieutenant Jack D. Brown (FW 190); Lieutenant Eugene O'Neil (half share Bf 110 with Lieutenant Mark K. Boyle); Lieutenant Raymond Petly (who did not score); Flight Officer Irvin E. Valenta (two Bf 110s); and Lieutenant Anthony Carcione (Me 210). Lieutenant Fred J. Christiansen, who destroyed a Bf 110, is absent from this picture, which may explain why Petly took his place in the line-up. Gabreski finished the war as the top-scoring fighter ace in Europe with 28 victories. On 29 March 1944 1st Lieutenant Stanley "Fats" Morrill was killed when bombs aboard a 93rd Bomb Group Liberator, one of two which collided at Henham near the 56th Fighter Group base at Raydon, exploded during the brave rescue attempt to save the crew. Morrill had nine confirmed victories at the time of his death, the last on 16 March when he shot down a FW 190 near St. Dizier. (56th Fighter Group WWII Association via Alan Hague)

Two ground crew in front of Ploesti veteran B-24D 42-40749 *Sack-Time Sally*, yet another example of Varga-inspired aircraft nose art, in the 565th Bomb Squadron, 389th Bomb Group at Hethel. This aircraft and Lieutenant Roy E. Braly's crew FTR on 26 November 1943 when the aircraft crashed at Drachten, in Holland. Six crew died and four became prisoners of war. (Hugh McLaren)

B-17F-75-DL 42-3540 *Bacta-th' Sac* in the 535th Bomb Squadron, 381st Bomb Group in formation. This aircraft, which was later renamed *Lucifer Jnr II*, was lost with 2nd Lieutenant Warren C. Hess' crew on 1 December 1943. Two crew evaded, one was KIA, and seven were taken prisoner. (USAF)

B-17G-1-VE 42-39839 in the 511th Bomb Squadron, 351st Bomb Group, which crashed at RAF Marham, Norfolk, on 26 November 1943. The Fortress was repaired by 2 SAD and was later used by 8th Air Force HQ, surviving to the end of hostilities, and returned to the ZOI in 1945. (Joseph Minton via Larry Goldstein)

Two B-17s trailing smoke going down during the Bremen mission on 29 November 1943. (USAF)

B-17F-75-DL 42-3520 in the 368th Bomb Squadron, 306th Bomb Group, which bellied in at Little Staughton on 29 November 1943 and was later salvaged. (Joseph Minton via Larry Goldstein)

B-17G-1-BO 42-31122 *Six Nights in Telergma* in the 568th Bomb Squadron, 390th Bomb Group, which was lost on 11 December 1943 when the heavies set out for Emden. Rocket-firing Me 110s and Me 210s made persistent attacks on the bomber formations and 17 heavies were shot down. *Six Nights in Telergma* was the lead ship piloted by Captain Hiram C. Skogmo. Of the eleven on board only three men survived. Among those lost was Major Ralph V. Hansell, the 390th Bomb Group Operations Officer and strike leader, who was flying in the co-pilot's seat. (TAMM)

B-17G-10-DL 42-37781 *Silver Dollar* in the 384th Bomb Group, which bellied in at Grafton Underwood on 26 December 1943. The aircraft was repaired and went MIA with Lieutenant Merlin H. Reed's crew on the mission to Berlin on 9 March 1944 (8 KIA, 2 PoW). (Joseph Minton via Larry Goldstein)

B-24D-160-CO 42-72856 *Nana* in the 567th Bomb Squadron, 389th Bomb Group at Hethel with 1st Lieutenant Rutledge "Rut" Laurens, Jr. (in cockpit window), and his crew. S/Sgt Hugh H. "Joe" Brewer, tail gunner, recalls. "The reason our ship was nose arted and named *Nana* was, at that time Emile Zola's book 'Nana' was a big hit with men. Nana was the best: French prostitute in history and since a lot of guys were fooling around in Ole London town, we thought we'd bust out with 'Nana.'" Lieutenant Rutledge Laurens and his crew and 41-28589 FTR from the raid on Bremen on 20 December 1943. All ten men were taken prisoner. On 1 December 1943 *Nana* was shot down by fighters near Julich, on the Dutch-German border. Five crew, including the pilot, 25-year old 1st Lieutenant Thomas P. Fravega, were KIA. Fravega's 31-year old brother, T/Sgt Anthony T. Fravega, radio operator-gunner, was among the five survivors. (Russ D. Hayes)

A P-51B in the 353rd Bomb Squadron, 354th Bomb Group is looked over by crewmen in the 401st Bomb Group at Deenthorpe in December 1943. (USAF)

B-17G-1-VE 42-39791 *Fletcher's Castoria* (a product name for a well-known brand of laxative) in the 350th Bomb Squadron, 100th Bomb Group, which crashed at Thorpe Abbotts on 4 December 1943 at the end of a local navigation and procedure check, with regular pilot 1st Lieutenant William Fletcher assigned to check out new pilot Lieutenant Martin Tashjian. The plane touched down and then took off again and climbed straight ahead to an altitude of 50 to 100ft before dropping down again, striking the left wing. Tashjian was seriously injured, the eight other crew suffered minor injuries, and the aircraft was destroyed. (TAMM)

Oberfeldwebel Anton-Rudolf "Toni" Piffer of JG 1, an Austrian, who on 16 December 1943 scored his 7th and 8th victories over B-17s. He is seen here shortly after landing at Dortmund. Piffer was awarded the *Deutsche Kreuz in Gold* (German Cross in Gold) on 29 March 1944, and was promoted to *Leutnant* on 1 May 1944. He was KIA on 17 June when P-47 Thunderbolts caught him unaware in his FW 190A-8 "White 3" near Argentan. He was posthumously awarded the *Ritterkreuz* on 20 October 1944 for his 26 victories in the west. His score included 20 *Viermots*. (via Eric Mombeek)

Having lost three engines over the target at Osnabrück on the 22 December 1943 mission, B-17F-30-DL 42-3184 PY-Q *USS Aliquippa*, 407th Bomb Squadron, 92nd Bomb Group, struggled westward on one engine before finally coming down near Azelo, Bornerbroek, in eastern Holland. Lieutenant Gene Wiley's crew and General Delmar T. Spivey were taken prisoner. Note that the two *Luftwaffe* soldiers guarding the Fort are wearing booty Irvin jackets. *USS Aliquippa* was dismantled and taken to the *Zerlegebetrieb* ("Dismantling Works") at Utrecht, where it was turned into scrap for recycling in the German war industry. (Coen Cornelissen)

For some, Christmas 1943 was the Americans' second in the European Theater of Operations. For many, like almost all of the men in this photo of 389th Bomb Group airmen at Hethel, it would be their last. For the survivors, there would be one more Christmas before final victory. (Russ D. Hayes)

Photo taken of a last night celebration in a night-club in Times Square in New York City in late October 1943, two days before these five enlisted men in 2nd Lieutenant Arthur W. Carlson's crew were among those who sailed for England aboard the *Queen Mary*. Only two of these men survived when B-17G-1-BO 42-31131 *Satan's Sister* in the 563rd Bomb Squadron, 388th Bomb Group was shot down over Ludwigshafen on 30 December 1943. L-R: S/Sgt Robert E. "Bob" Scalley, tail gunner (PoW); S/Sgt Charles H. Parizo, waist gunner (KIA); T/Sgt Harold L. Hawkins, engineer (KIA); S/Sgt James A. Neal, waist gunner (PoW); and T/Sgt Danny Letter, radio operator (KIA). (Scalley via Goldstein)

The Bloody Hundredth was well known for its high loss rate. On 27 December 1943, a wet, cold, gloomy and foggy day, three Forts piled up landing on the short runway at Thorpe Abbotts. 2nd Lieutenant Martin Tashjian was in the pilot's seat of B-17G-10-DL 42-37772 LN-S *Flyin' Jenny* in the 350th Bomb Squadron as the plane peeled off from the group formation aiming to land on runway 22. His touchdown occurred two thirds of the way down the 4200ft runway, and his speed was such that *Flyin' Jenny* ran off the end of the landing strip. Immediately in front of him was B-17F-65-DL 42-3474 EP-B *King Bee* in the 351st Bomb Squadron, which had preceded his landing and was now turning off onto the adjacent taxiway. The right wing of *Flyin' Jenny* struck the left wing of *King Bee*, swinging it around. Landing a few seconds after Tashjian, Lieutenant Ray Monrad in 42-6094 also overshot in the haze and crashed into the two interlocked Fortresses, causing irreparable damage to all three planes. *King Bee* was chopped in half. Amazingly there was no fire and no casualties. Tashjian had been seriously injured in the crash of *Fletcher's Castoria* at Thorpe Abbotts on 4 December. He was KIA on 15 March 1944 flying as formation control officer in the tail position of the lead ship (42-39934) over Brunswick. Herbert Devore aborted the squadron lead position after flares ignited in his cockpit, and only three men were able to bale out before the aircraft exploded. The mission would have completed Devore's tour of duty, and he had planned a celebration on their return to Thorpe Abbotts. (TAMM)

B-17F-120-BO 42-30796 *Sunny II* in the 351st Bomb Squadron, 100th Bomb Group was hit repeatedly by fighters on its 14th mission, to Ludwigshafen, on 30 December 1943, but George Brannan, the pilot, managed to reach England, and he bellied in at Starston, four miles short of Thorpe Abbotts. Salvage crews later cut the B-17 into sections and winched them on to low trailers for shipment to the breakers yard. (TAMM)

B-24D-15-CF 42-63960 *Dorothy* in the 564th Bomb Squadron, 389th Bomb Group over the North Sea. This aircraft crash-landed at Ash near Gravesend, Kent, on the return from the mission to Cognac-Chateaubernard on 31 December 1943, but it was repaired and returned to combat operations. It was salvaged on 25 February 1945. (USAF)

The crew of B-17F-65-BO 42-29656/S *Skunkface* in the 322nd Bomb Squadron, 91st Bomb Group inspect the damage to their Fortress after their return from a raid on Bremen in late 1943. This aircraft had originally been assigned to the 358th Bomb Squadron, 303rd Bomb Group at Molesworth in March 1943, and it was given the name *The Terrible Ten*. It was flown to Langford Lodge on 30 June to receive repairs to damage sustained on the 25 June mission to Bremen. *The Terrible Ten* returned on 5 July 1943 and was reassigned to the 322nd Bomb Squadron, 91st Bomb Group, who renamed the plane *Skunkface*. On 20 February 1944 *Skunkface* and 2nd Lieutenant Ernest B. Kidd's crew FTR from the mission to Oschersleben when the plane crashed at Malmedy, in Belgium. Two crew were KIA and eight taken prisoner. (USAF)

B-17s in the 306th Bomb Group in formation. B-17G-20-BO 42-31454 *St Anthony* was assigned to the 368th Bomb Squadron at Thurleigh on 30 December 1943, and it was retired on 9 November 1944, being transferred to the 29 TAC on 24 May 1945, and finally it was salvaged on 31 January 1946. (USAF)

B-17F-115-BO 42-30643 *Green Mountain Rambler* in the 364th Bomb Squadron, 305th Bomb Group at Chelveston on 6 January 1944. Lieutenant Edwin L. Little, who hailed from Vermont, home of the Green Mountains, christened the Fortress. After completing 19 missions the undercarriage collapsed while taxiing for a mission on 29 January 1944 when the co-pilot selected the "undercarriage up" instead of "flaps down" lever. Due to the proximity of the switches in the cockpit it was not uncommon on approach to landing to select "undercarriage up" instead of "flaps down." Eventually the "U/C Switch" was relocated to the base of the windshield. *Green Mountain Rambler* was scrapped. (via Bill Donald)

Captain (later Major) Don Gentile and his wife. Gentile scored 21.8333 victories in WWII, 16½ of them while flying the Mustang. He was KIFA on 28 January 1951 at Forestville, Maryland, while flying a T-33A. (USAF)

Major James A. "Goody" Goodson of the 336th Fighter Squadron, 4th Fighter Group, who scored 14 confirmed victories in WWII, including 9 flying P-51B/D aircraft 16 March -25 May 1944. He was shot down by flak flying P-51D 44-13303 on 20 June 1944 and was taken prisoner. (USAF)

FW 190A-7 of I./JG 1 taxiing at Dortmund early in 1944. (Seebrandt via Rob de Visser)

FW 190A-6s of *Sturmstaffel 1* lined up at Dortmund airfield, January 1944. Note the barrels of the four MG151 20mm cannon with which these aircraft were armed, the absence of the normal twin MG 131 nose-armament, and the variety in camouflage painting. Having been established in October 1943 with heavily-armored FW 190A-6s, this special bomber-destroyer unit conducted independent operations against the American combat boxes until April 1944 with FW 190A-6, A-7, and A-8 aircraft, when it was incorporated into IV. (*Sturm*)/JG 3 as 11./JG 3. Their special tactic was to attack the American bomber boxes in a tight, massive formation from behind, therefore the extra armament to the FW 190s. (Seebrandt via Rob de Visser)

Dortmund airfield, January 1944. Major Emil-Rudolf Schnoor, *Kommandeur* I./JG1 (second from right), looks on as his FW 190A-7 is serviced by his mechanics. The "Winged 1" painted on the engine cowling became the official emblem of JG 1 after the death of its *Kommodore*, Major Hans Philipp, on 8 October 1943 when he was shot down and killed by P-47s near Nordhorn. Philipp had 206 victories, including 177 on the Eastern Front. (Köhne, via Rob de Visser)

Mud-spattered FW 190A-7 WerkNo. 430352 *Schwarme 3* ("Black 3") of 2./JG 1 at Dortmund, January 1944. (Seebrandt via Rob de Visser)

B-17F-95-BO 42-30289 *The Dull Tool* (formerly *The Douche Bag*) in the 568th Bomb Squadron, 390th Bomb Group, which FTR on 4 January 1944. Four of 2nd Lieutenant James H. Prophett's crew were KIA and six were taken prisoner. (TAMM)

B-17G-20-BO 42-31444 was assigned overseas on 18 January 1944 and became "*Paper Doll*" in the 423rd Bomb Squadron, 306th Bomb Group. Note the flak damage in a sensitive spot, which might have been the reason the aircraft was renamed *Patches*. The Fortress was transferred to the RAF on 8 January 1945, returning on 5 March and being salvaged ten days later. (Russell J. Zorn)

B-17F-45-DL 42-3307 *Skipper* in the 351st Bomb Squadron, 100th Bomb Group, which crashed on 24 January 1944. Just after taking off for Frankfurt, a wayward B-24 rapidly converged on the B-17 on a collision course, and Arch Drummond instigated avoiding action. He dived and banked right, but *Skipper* plunged out of control, and the left wing struck the roof of a barn at Shelfanger, near Winfarthing, 15 miles from the base at Thorpe Abbotts. The full fuel tanks ignited, and the Fortress headed across fields towards a clump of trees, slicing the tops off before careening into a meadow beyond. The bombardier was hurled through the Plexiglas nose to his death on impact, but the surviving nine crew got out of the wreckage before the incendiary load exploded. (TAMM)

B-24D-125-CO 42-11013 *Trouble* in the 566th Bomb Squadron, 389th Bomb Group, flown by Captain David L. Wilhite (3rd from right, standing), was lost on 7 January 1944 when it was attacked by a rocket-firing FW 190 near Paris. A rocket exploded in the cockpit, and other hits signalled the end of *Trouble*. S/Sgt Robert H. Sweatt, the ball turret gunner (kneeling, right), was the only survivor. Back Row, L-R: T/Sgt Sam W. Flatter, radio operator; Lieutenant James J. McConnell, bombardier; Lieutenant Harry, navigator. Captain Wilhite; Rudy Salties, co-pilot; and T/Sgt Harold "Harry" Saunders, top turret gunner. Front Row, L-R: S/Sgt Charles O. "Denny" DeWitt, left waist gunner; S/Sgt Max J. Snyder, right waist gunner; S/Sgt George R. Caplinger, tail gunner; and Sweatt. All the crew pictured except Sweatt and the co-pilot (who was replaced by Lieutenant Wendell L. Dailey on the fateful 7 January mission) and Harry, who did not fly that day, were killed. So too was Major Kenneth M. Caldwell, CO 566th Squadron, who was flying as Command Pilot. Wilhite's crew had returned to combat duty after being released from internment in Portugal in the summer of 1943 after engine trouble prevented them from continuing to North Africa in July 1943

An American who was well known to the movie going public in the USA and Britain before the war was gangling 6ft 4in actor James Maitland Stewart. Born of Scottish-Irish parents on 20 May 1908 in Indiana, Pennsylvania, where his father was a hardware merchant, Stewart studied architecture at Princeton University, New Jersey, where he acted while a student. By 1940 he had appeared in over 20 movies and won an Academy Award for his role in *The Philadelphia Story*. In 1941 Stewart enlisted in the AAC (he owned his own aircraft, had logged over 200 hours of civilian flying, and possessed a commercial pilot's licence). In January 1942 Stewart received his commission and "wings," and on 7 July 1942 was promoted to 1st Lieutenant. Finally, in August 1943 Stewart was posted to the 445th Bomb Group, equipped with B-24 Liberators, at Sioux City, Iowa, as Operations Officer of the 703rd Bomb Squadron. After only three weeks, on 7 July 1943 he was promoted to captain and given command of the squadron on merit. In November 1943 the 445th left for Tibenham, Norfolk, England. (USAF)

B-17G-1-BO 42-31118 *Lady Millicent II* in the 338th Bomb Squadron, 96th Bomb Group, which bellied in at Snetterton Heath on 8 January 1944 and was salvaged five days later. (Joseph Minton via Larry Goldstein)

On 11 January 1944 the 303rd Bomb Group lost ten Fortresses on the mission to Oschersleben. B-17G-15-DL 42-37875 *Flying Bison* in the 427th Bomb Squadron sails past the cloud of smoke left by a disintegrating B-17. *Flying Bison* (formerly called *Express of 'D' Street*) was assigned overseas on 18 November 1943. It was salvaged in early August 1944. (USAF)

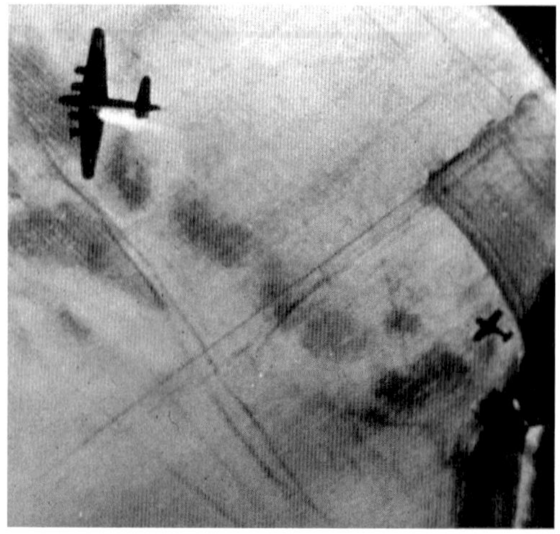

Above left: 1st Lieutenant William F. Cely, pilot, and 2nd Lieutenant Jabez I. Churchill, co-pilot, inspect the badly damaged B-17G-1-VE 42-39775/K *Frenesi* in the 333rd Bomb Squadron, 94th Bomb Group, which they brought home to Bury St Edmunds (Rougham) from Brunswick on 11 January 1944 with three wounded gunners after five crew and a cameraman had baled out over enemy territory. (The interphones were out and they did not hear Cely's exhortation "Poppa's gonna take you home.") Cely added the Silver Star to his DFC and Air Medal for bringing *Frenesi* back. The aircraft was so badly damaged that it was scrapped, but five of the crew fought another day in *Frenesi II* (43-388341). (via Ian McLachlan) Above right: A German fighter sets a B-17 on fire during the mission to Brunswick, 11 January 1944. (USAF)

On 11 January 1944 ten of the 15 pilots of II *Gruppe* JG 1, led by *Oberleutnant* Rudiger von Kirchmayr, claimed 11 Fortresses destroyed. L-R: *Leutnant* Fritz Wegner; *Oberfeldwebel* Leo Schuhmacher; *Oberleutnant* von Kirchmayr; *Oberfeldwebel* Rudolf Haninger; *Oberleutnant* Eberhard Burath; *Feldwebel* Max Sauer; *Stabsfeldwebel* Rudolf Martens (KIA 24 January 1944 by P-47 Thunderbolts near Tournai); and *Feldwebel* Schönrock. (via Eric Mombeek)

On 11 January 1944 the Mustang was still a well-kept secret, and the 354th Fighter Group 9th Air Force was the pioneer Mustang group in the ETO. Major James H. Howard, ex-Flying Tigers P-40 pilot in China and now CO of 356th Squadron, displayed "conspicuous gallantry and intrepidity above and beyond the call of duty" in action with the enemy near Oschersleben when he came to the rescue of some Fortresses. Howard was flying his usual P-51B *Ding Hao!* (Chinese for "very good") when the 354th provided support for a formation of B-17s on a long-range mission deep into enemy territory. As the P-51s met the bombers in the target area numerous rocket-firing Bf 110 *Zerstorer* fighters attacked the bomber force. The 354th engaged and Howard destroyed one of the 110s, but in the fight lost contact with the rest of his group. He immediately returned to the level of the bomber formation and saw that the B-17s of the 401st Bomb Group were being heavily attacked by German fighters, and that no "little friends" were on hand. Howard dived into the formation of more than 30 German fighters, and for 30 minutes single-handedly pressed home a series of determined attacks. He shot down two more fighters, and probably destroyed another and damaged one other. Toward the end of his action, Howard continued to fight on with one remaining machine-gun and his fuel supply dangerously low. Major Howard's brave single-handed action undoubtedly saved the formation. He was awarded the Medal of Honor. Howard's total score was 8.333 - all except two victories being scored flying the Mustang, 20 December 1943-8 April 1945. (USAF)

Major Emil-Rudolf Schnoor, *Kommandeur* I./JG 1, gets strapped into the cockpit of his FW 190A-7 at Dortmund airfield, January 1944. (Seebrandt via Rob de Visser)

Oberstleutnant Martin Drewes, *StaffelKapitän* 11/NJG 10, and his radio /radar operator, *Unteroffizier* Handke, claimed two B-17s shot down on 11 January 1944. Drewes had shot down two B-17s on 26 July 1943 (going down at Bremervörde and Leer) and B-17F-110-BO 42-30603 in the 423rd Bomb Squadron, 306th Bomb Group on 26 November 1943 (crashed between St. Nicolaasga and Doniaga). On 5 January 1944 he shot down a B-24 100km North of Nordeney, followed by two more B 17s destroyed on 11 January, his adversaries crashing at Nijverdal (42-30782 in the 369th Bomb Squadron, 306th Bomb Group) and into the sea 20 km NW of The Hague. These victories made *Oberleutnant* Drewes the top scoring *Nachtjagd* pilot in the daylight battles with the 8th Air Force 1943-44. Drewes, who was awarded the *RitterKreuz* (*RK* or Knight's Cross) on 27 July 1944 and *Eichenlaub* (*El*) on 17 April 1945, ended the war with the rank of Major and a score of 43 night and 6 day victories (including 4 claims for B-17s and B-24s) in ZG 76, NJG 3, and NJG 1. (via Theo Boiten)

B-24H-10-DT 41-28706 *Dream Boat* in the 753rd Bomb Squadron, 458th Bomb Group, which was assigned overseas in January 1944 and was salvaged on 5 May 1945. (USAF)

B-17F-45-DL-42-3329/F *Skippy* in the 570th Bomb Squadron, 390th Bomb Group taxies out at Framlingham with other Fortresses. *Skippy* was salvaged on 8 February 1944. (USAF)

B-24D-5-CO 41-23813 *Victory Ship* in the 44th Bomb Group, one of four Liberators in the 68th Bomb Squadron that were shot down b y JG 26 on 21 January 1944. (USAF)

A Messerschmitt Bf 110 attacks a formation of 91st Bomb Group B-l7s approaching their target on 22 January 1944. (USAF via Robert M. Foose)

B-17Gs under repair at the U.S. depot at RAF Honington in 1944. Nearest aircraft is 42-37972 *Gold Brick* XR-H in the 349th Bomb Squadron, 100th Bomb Group, with most of the left wing missing. This was the result of a mishap on the morning of 30 January 1944 when Lieutenant James R. Stout took off from Thorpe Abbotts for Brunswick and had to feather #1 engine, but as he prepared to land he found that the landing gear was inoperative. He circled the field to use up gas, jettisoned bombs and ball turret in the Channel, and crashed at Honington. *Gold Brick* resumed combat missions, but needed further work when it returned to Thorpe Abbotts with its right stabilizer missing as a result of the *Rammjäger* attack on a mission on 7 April 1945. Next is 42-31100 *The Gimp* in the 709th Bomb Squadron, 447th Bomb Group. Behind is 42-37716 BX-P in the 338th Bomb Squadron, 96th Bomb Group. (USAF via Philip Kaplan)

FW 190A-7 340283 "Gelbe (Yellow) 6" of 3./JG 1 was lost in combat with American *Viermots* on 8 February 1944. *Feldwebel* Gerhard Giese perished when his aircraft crashed near Charleville. It is seen here being topped-up at Dortmund airfield. (Seebrandt via Rob de Visser)

Left: M/Sgt Mike Barrett of Boston, Massachusetts, crew chief for a B-17, scrubs the ice off a wing of his plane, that took off from Framlingham for a raid over Germany on 10 February 1944 during a blizzard. (USAF via Philip Kaplan)

On the 10 February 1944 mission to Brunswick, 29 B-17s and eight escorting fighters were lost to the ferocious German defences. Five Fortresses came down in the Netherlands, including B-17G-20-DL 42-37950 *Dinah Mite*, 731st Bomb Squadron, 452nd Bomb Group, piloted by 2nd Lieutenant Thomas F. Sharpless, which force-landed northeast of Urk in the recently reclaimed land in the eastern Ijsselmeer (Zuider Zee), the Noordoostpolder. (Coen Cornelissen)

B-17F-100-BO 42-30337 *Flak Hack* in the 390th Bomb Group. From August 1943 to February 1944 *Flak Hack* served in the Framlingham Group's 570th Bomb Squadron before moving across to the 571st Bomb Squadron when the name was added to the Eightball. The aircraft served in the new squadron for only a few days before being lost with Lieutenant Grady E. Dover and crew on 10 February. Seven crew were KIA and three were taken prisoner. (TAMM)

B-17G-1-BO 42-31051 *Goin Jessies* in the 349th and 351st Bomb Squadrons, 100th Bomb Group, which flew its first combat mission on 7 November 1943 to Duren, and had flown 11 missions when this photo was taken at Thorpe Abbotts. *Goin Jessies* and 2nd Lieutenant Robert C. Koper's crew were lost on the mission to Berlin on 6 March 1944 when they were shot down by fighters about 60 miles short of "Big-B." Koper, who was on his fifth mission and his third attempt to bomb the German capital, was among the seven who were KIA. Three men survived and they were taken prisoner. (TAMM)

The jubilant crew of B-24D-90-CO 42-40722 *Little Gramper* taken the day they completed their final mission in February 1944. Top row, left to right: S/Sgt Russ Hayes, ball turret gunner; S/Sgt Leonard Boisclair, waist-gunner: Captain Howard "Ben" Walsh, pilot; S/Sgt Marcus DeCamp, engineer; and S/Sgt Charles G. Cavage, waist-gunner. Bottom row, left to right: Lieutenant Tom Campbell, navigator; Lieutenant Robert Schroeder, bombardier; S/Sgt Ernest "Jack" Cox, tail-gunner; and T/Sgt Arthur T. Marsh, radio operator. (That day the command pilot took the co-pilot's seat. Original co-pilot Lieutenant Sam "Bill" Blessing formed his own crew.) Soon after this photograph was taken Captain Tom Campbell was killed in a plane crash in Sweden. It was he who had originally called the reptiles in the African desert "grampers," from which the ship got its name. *Little Gramper* was retired in the summer of 1944 for conversion to the Group's assembly ship. The new NMF *Gramper Jnr* (44-40085) crashed at Hethel on 27 April 1944, plowing through a radio shack near No.2 Hangar. B-24J-10-FO 42-51665 was christened *The Little Gramper Junior 3rd* shortly after. (Russ D. Hayes)

B-24D 42-40604 *Satan's Angels* in the 328th Bomb Squadron, 93rd Bomb Group, which crashed in early February 1944 and was salvaged. (USAF)

Colonel Don Blakeslee, CO 4th Fighter Group, 1 January-19 November 1944. During December 1943 he was assigned to the 354th Fighter Group to help them enter combat, and he was so impressed with the Mustangs that they flew that when he returned to the 4th Fighter Group he argued forcefully to be equipped with the Mustang, which they were at the end of February 1944. Blakeslee's total victory score was 14.5, seven of which were scored flying P-51B/D aircraft. (USAF)

In February 1944 the 56th Fighter Group at Halesworth became the first 8th Air Force fighter group to use nose colors for identification. There is, however, no mistaking the wolf insignia on Lyle Adriense's "T-Bolt," which of course refers to Zemke's famous "Wolfpack." The 56th Fighter Group opted to retain its P-47 Thunderbolts throughout the war, the only fighter group to do so, and they even eclipsed all the Mustang groups by destroying more enemy aircraft in combat than any other. (56th Fighter Group WWII Association via Alan Hague)

B-17G-30-DL 42-38109 *Cabin In The Sky* in the 364th Bomb Squadron, 305th Bomb Group, which 1st Lieutenant William R. Lawley, Jr., helped by his bombardier, 1st Lieutenant Harry G. Mason, brought back from Brunswick on 20 February 1944 to crash-land at the Canadian fighter station at RAF Redhill. Two gunners were so badly wounded that they could not have baled out. Lawley's was one of three Medals of Honor awarded to B-17 crewmen, the only instance in the 8th's history that more than one was issued on one day. (via Bill Donald)

General Carl Spaatz shakes 1st Lieutenant William R. Lawley, Jr.'s hand after the pilot received the Medal of Honor. (via Bill Donald)

B-24H-5-DT 41-28654 *Spare Parts* in the 732nd Bomb Squadron, 453rd Bomb Group en route for Old Buckenham after a raid on a *Luftwaffe* airfield on 21 February 1944. This aircraft survived the war and returned to the ZOI, being scrapped in 1947. (USAF)

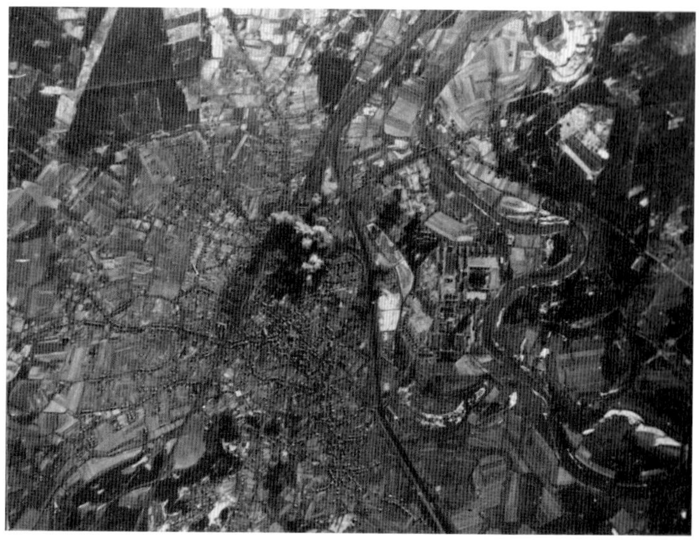

Above right: Bombs exploding on the target near Lingen on 21 February 1944. (USAF)

Loading the airmail addressed to Hitler. Ground crew prepare to load 500 lb bombs aboard B-17F-75-BO 42-29931 *Satan's Workshop* in the 360th Bomb Squadron, 303rd Bomb Group, for a raid on Germany. *Satan's Workshop* FTR on 22 February 1944. (Lieutenant Col Harry D. Gobrecht via Brian McGuire)

Left: *Oberfeldwebel* Adolf "Addi" Glunz, who as a *Staffelführer* (a probationary *Staffelkapitän*) led 5/JG 26 against the *Viermots* on 22 February 1944. In the first sortie of the day Glunz shot down a B-17 and forced two more out of formation. Later that same afternoon he claimed two more B-17s (who like his morning victims were in the 91st or 384th Bomb Groups) and a 78th Fighter Group P-47 Thunderbolt. Only two B-17 victories and the P-47 were confirmed, but these took his score to 57. Glunz, who is wearing the *Eichenlaub* (Knight's Cross with Oak Leaves), was assigned to JG 7 in February 1945 to fly the Me-262, but as far as is known, he never flew the jet fighter operationally. Glunz ended the war having flown 524 sorties and had 72 victories. Right: B-17G-15-VE 42-97474 *Homing Pigeon* in the 533rd Bomb Squadron, 381st Bomb Group FTR on 22 February 1944 with Lieutenant Francis N. Fridgen's crew. The Fortress crashed at Opherdicke, Germany, where this German policeman is searching the bodies (four were KIA) for their effects. Two men evaded and four were made PoW. (via Ron Mackay)

B-17F-I5-BO 41-24490 *Jack the Ripper* in the 324th Bomb Squadron, 91st Bomb Group, went MIA on 22 February 1944 with the loss of 1st Lieutenant James I. Considine's crew. It was the last of the original 91st Bomb Group aircraft to be lost. (USAF)

Final assembly line at Douglas, Long Beach, in December 1943. At the far end of the line is 42-38140, which was assigned overseas in February 1944 and joined the 335th Bomb Squadron, 95th Bomb Group, where it was alternately named *ETO Happy*, *The Princess Goose*, and *Dolly's Daughter*. This aircraft ended its days at Kingman, Arizona, in November 1945. Next is 42-38141, which was assigned to the 379th Bomb Group on 28 February 1944, where it was named *Pansy Yokum*. It FTR from the raid on French airfields on 9 July 1944 when 2nd Lieutenant Hugh E. Frye ditched in the North Sea. Next is 42-38142, which was assigned to the 463rd Bomb Group, 15th Air Force, and wrecked before leaving the USA. Next is 42-38143, which survived just over one month in the 15th Air Force, and then 42-38144, which was assigned to the 401st Bomb Squadron, 91st Bomb Group on 28 February 1944. It was given the name *Jezebel* and survived until 14 February 1945, when it FTRLOC and was salvaged a month later. Next is 42-38145, which was assigned to the 730th Bomb Squadron, 452nd Bomb Group, and was named *Rosalie Ann*. On 19 May 1944 during assembly in bad weather over Norfolk for the mission to Berlin, *Rosalie Ann* lost its tail in a mid-air collision with 42-31242 *Patty Jo* in the 563rd Bomb Squadron, 388th Bomb Group, and crash landed at Old Buckenham. Two of *Rosalie Ann's* crew were killed, while Lieutenant Salles crash landed 42-31242 at Watton with no casualties. Finally, with just the left tailplane and fin visible is 42-38146, which joined the 408th Bomb Squadron, 351st Bomb Group on 29 February 1944. This aircraft and 2nd Lieutenant John M. Morton's crew FTR on the Merseburg raid on 29 July 1944 when it was hit by flak and crashed at Beendorf, Germany, with the loss of all nine crew. (Douglas)

Major Pierce W. McKennon in the 335th Fighter Squadron, 4th Fighter Group. On 20 February 1944 at the start of "Big Week," Captain Henry L. Mills, Duane Beeson, and Lieutenant Pierce W. McKennon claimed a FW 190 apiece. On 28 august 1944 McKennon was shot down by flak near Strasbourg, and he evaded until 22 September. He returned to combat status, but was shot down by flak again on 18 March 1945 at Neubrandenburg air depot. He was rescued by Lieutenant George Green flying another Mustang, who landed and picked him up. McKennon was killed in a flying accident near San Antonio, Texas, on 18 June 1947 while flying an AT-6D. (USAF)

Above: Major Heinz "Pritzl" Bär, *Kommandeur* III/JG1, inspects B-17F-20-DL 42-3040 *Miss Quachita* in the 323rd Bomb Squadron, 91st Bomb Group at Bexten, near Saltzbergen, after he shot the Fortress down in a FW 190 on 22 February 1944 during a raid on Gütersloh, Germany, its 18th mission. Two of 2nd Lieutenant Spencer K. Osterberg's crew were KIA. The other eight survived to be taken prisoner. *Miss Quachita* was deemed repairable by a German salvage team, but she was strafed and destroyed by U.S. fighters before the Germans could retrieve the bomber. (USAF) Right: Major Heinz "Pritzl" Bär scored his 200th victory two months later on 22 April 1944. The top scoring NCO pilot in the Battle of Britain, Bär ended the war as the top scoring jet ace of WWII with 16 victories, and eighth overall on the list of *Experten* with 220 confirmed victories. Bär was killed in a light aircraft crash in 1957. (USAF)

A formation of B-24J Liberators in the 706th Bomb Squadron, 446th Bomb Group en route to the Messerschmitt Bf-110 plant at Gotha, 420 miles due east of the White Cliffs of Dover, on 24 February 1944. Intelligence described Gotha as "the most valuable single target in the enemy fighter complex." B-24J-95-CO 42-100360/B *Luck and Stuff* and Lieutenant Weems D. Jones' crew FTR on 29 April 1944. It crashed at Luckenwalde, Germany, killing three crew, while seven crew survived and were taken prisoner. (USAF)

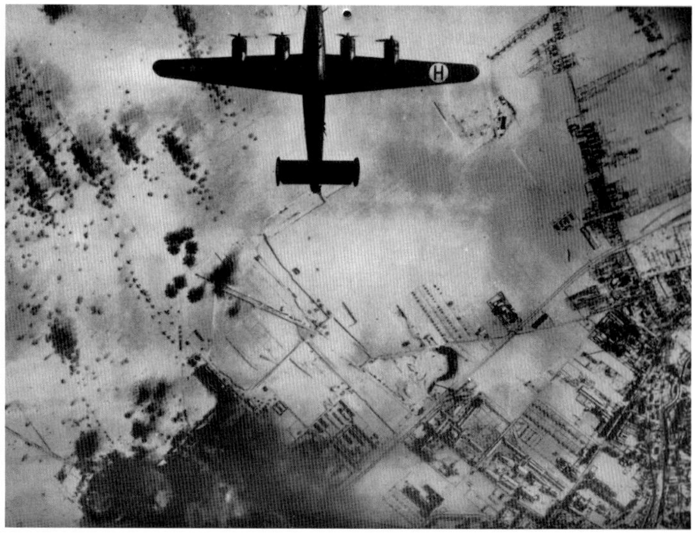

A 446th Bomb Group Liberator over the Gotha plant on 24 February 1944. (USAF)

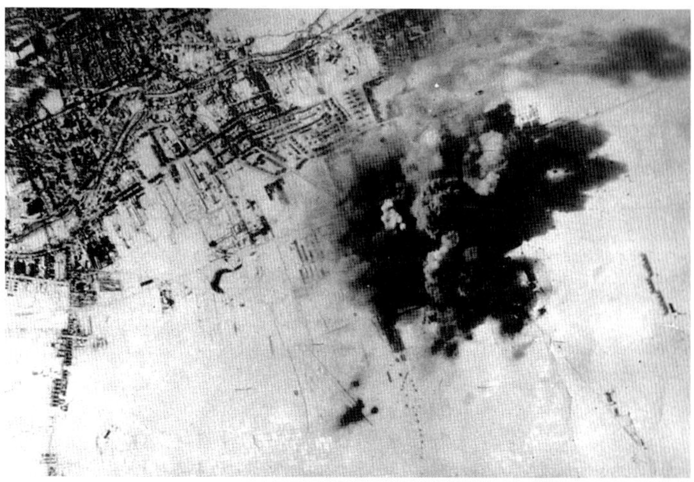

Bombs exploding on the Gotha plant on 24 February 1944. (Keilman)

Colonel Myron Keilman (right) in the 392nd Bomb Group receives the Distinguished Flying Cross from General Leon Johnson, CO 14th Combat Bombardment Wing. (Keilman)

Jim McGregor's lead crew in the 392nd Bomb Group at Wendling, who led the 14th Combat Bomb Wing over Gotha on 24 February 1944 in *Big Fat Mama*. (Keilman)

B-17s in the 457th Bomb Group flying through heavy flak on the mission to Schweinfurt on 24 February 1944. (USAF)

B-24D 41-24225 *Flak Alley* in the 506th Bomb Squadron, 44th Bomb Group, which was lost with 2nd Lieutenant Phillip W. Bell's crew on the mission to Gotha on 24 February 1944. Six members of the crew were KIA and four were taken prisoner. (USAF)

B-17F-120-BO 42-30788 *Mismalovin'* in the 350th Bomb Squadron, 100th, which FTR on 25 February 1944 when it crashed in the English Channel with the loss of eight of Lieutenant Stewart A. McClain's crew. Two men were rescued and were taken off into captivity. (TAMM)

March 1944, and at Chelveston Brian Gunderson (right) receives a copy of an interview he recorded for the BBC in London. Behind is B-17G-30-DL 42-38205 *Thundermug* in the 364th Bomb Squadron, 305th Bomb Group. This aircraft transferred to the 483rd Bomb Group in Italy at the end of the month and was renamed *Winged Fury*. It went MIA over Vienna on 16 July 1944. Gunderson, who flew one day and 50 night-leaflet dropping missions, retired in 1977 with the rank of Brigadier General. (via Bill Donald)

P-51s undergoing maintenance at Burtonwood. (USAF)

B-24J-90-CO 42-100295/V in the 68th Bomb Squadron, 44th Bomb Group, flown by Lieutenant Robert Rose and Jack B. Williams, which crashed at Thorpe Abbotts on 2 March 1944 after an engine fire. It was repaired, and was returned to airworthy condition only to be abandoned over England on 16 January 1945, returning from Dresden with Lieutenant Lindsay's crew. (TAMM)

Captain (later Major) Ray S. Wetmore in the 370th Fighter Squadron, 359th Fighter Group, who destroyed 21.25 e/a February 1944-March 1945 flying P-47s and P-51B/D Mustangs. (USAF)

Pilots in the 4th Fighter Group at Debden at briefing. (USAF)

Buncher signal again. Joe and I both knew we had just passed over our base. We landed at 0045 June 8 with hardly more than fumes in our gas tanks."

The co-pilot, Harvey T. Brown, wrote:

"Briefing at about 1530. Separate briefings for pilot, bombardier, navigator and radioman. Co-pilots picked up escape kits and went to ships. Really missed the briefing after getting used to it. We took off at 1700 and climbed up through 8000ft of clouds. Assembled at 13,000ft and at 1836 we hit the beachhead. About 5/10ths cloud coverage. Saw quite a few of the boats going forward and back. Hundreds anchored ashore. Too hazy to pick out and identify. Two heavy ships - probably battle wagons - shelling enemy positions. Went in to the primary (target) but clouds obscured it so closed the bomb bay and for half an hour or so took a cook's tour over France at 20,000ft with the doors open. Made one run at the secondary but did not drop - not much flak. Did a 360° turn and came in and dropped our bombs. Quite a bit of flak but we turned off before it got too close. Got my first glimpse of the target after bombs hit. Heavy gray smoke from the Nantes marshaling yard. Most of our bombs hit south of the river in fields. 'Very slow ground speed. Thought we'd never hit the coast out. About three hours over enemy territory.

"We let down to 13,000ft and skirted presumably Jersey and Guernsey but I saw the Isle of Guernsey coming and asked Abe if that was it. Pretty clear so I had a good view and watched it carefully. Saw some red gun flashes and told the boys to watch the flak. They really had our altitude and put it right in front of us. We made a sharp turn to the left and they tracked right along behind us. We hit the English coast about 2030 and on the way back we put on all of our lights. We were flying lead second element. Group leader started letting down through the clouds. We lost sight of him. He almost hit No.2 and us. No.5 aircraft came up on our right and almost hit us. I was really scared when I glanced back and saw that ship's belly above us with its lights and superchargers glowing. I grabbed the wheel from Joe and pushed it down. We left the bunch then and I breathed easier when we broke out of the clouds. We headed for the field and I picked up a 'Bandit' alert in the area of our field. We turned out our lights and headed west. We sailed around for about an hour skimming along the top of the clouds. The area we were in was clear so we could see planes landing below on the fields. I saw a group of lights after the planes and then the tracers as they threw up light flak. Really pretty. Very shortly Maybank fired a few rounds at a plane that came in at the nose. Caught a glimpse of it as it turned away. Think it was a P-47. Landed about 0045 and hit the sack about 0230. Slept until 1110, ate and came back. Order of the day, sleep this afternoon. Guess we shall have an early briefing tonight." [863]

Liberators in the 34th Bomb Group who were returning to Mendlesham after dark were hit by Me 410 night fighters right over their home field, and four B-24s were shot down in a matter of minutes.[864] Captain Oscar T. Hanson, who had flown his first mission on *D-Day* and was returning in his B-24, recalled:

"Several ships went down in flames. I heard a terrific explosion in the back of the ship and we were on fire. I gave the order to bale out and started climbing as we were only at 1000ft. I climbed to 7000ft and set the automatic pilot so I could head the ship out to sea. I expected to get hit again and everyone baled out except my engineer and myself. He noticed that the fire had gone out so he inspected the damage. I spotted a blacked-out airport in the moonlight so we decided to land. Our hydraulic system was shot so we had to crank the landing gear down mechanically and we had no brakes and no flaps. When the gear came down we could see that our wheel was so badly damaged it would collapse on landing. We made two passes at the field and them carne into land, skidding along the ground for a while and then turning sideways as the wingtip was dragging on the ground. Our landing speed without flaps was 120mph. Due to the danger of getting strafed by the enemy, the field was not lighted and I could just barely see the runways in the moonlight. They told us afterward that one of the fighters was looking for us but he was circling the field to the right and we were circling to the left and we passed each other twice over the field! We returned to our home field and the rest of the crew who had baled out straggled in one by one. None of the crew was killed. When we went back to look at our ship the next day we counted 14 holes from 20mm cannon. The ship was peppered with shrapnel and it was miraculous that no one was hit. The nose gunner broke his leg when he landed. The co-pilot jumped without his leg straps fastened and came very near to falling out of his chute. The tail gunner's chute failed to open so he fed it out with his hands. The radio operator pulled four times on the wrong handle before finding the ripcord and the bombardier landed right on our home field and was immediately surrounded by GIs who thought he was a German paratrooper. He said, 'Don't click them bolts at me, Ah'm from Texas!'"[865]

On Thursday, 8 June, 1135 8th Air Force bombers were despatched to communication targets in France, but bad weather prevented 400 heavies from bombing. A. J. Sinibubb, a navigator in the 323rd Bomb Squadron, 91st Bomb Group, flew his first mission when he flew as a spare aboard *Priority Gal*,[866] flown by Lieutenant Pryor, to the Hamburg oil refineries. This crew had almost finished their tour. Sinibubb wrote that he did not get a flak suit, and that fighter cover was "fair" and the flak "heavy but inaccurate," but that it hit the Plexiglas nose. He saw one plane in the wing ahead go down in flames:

"There was 10/10 undercast almost all the way but it cleared up over the Danish Peninsular. We had a visual run on the target. The weather cleared up over English coast on return. Flew at 300ft into base. Some Fun!"

2nd Lieutenant Dick Johnson in the 303rd Bomb Group flew his 13th mission to the marshaling yards at Orleans, south of Paris:

"The weather over the continent was still pretty bad but it seemed to be improving. We were to try to blow up the train tracks and the rolling stock carrying war goods to the front lines. We also hoped to drop a railroad bridge into the rubble. Beiser and I were again assigned to the '*Buzz Blond*' and our crew was complete. Sergeant Gorchesky, our radioman missed yesterday's mission with us because his radio expertise was needed in our squadron's lead plane. But he was back with us today. Our assembly was modified from plan because of two cloud layers. We finally assembled the group between these two layers. We flew 36 aircraft in three groups on this mission, taking off from 0431 to 0522 and were all back on the ground before noon, having largely wasted the mission because of a problem with the Norden bombsight in the lead plane. We did visual bombing with an 11-minute bomb run but in the last minute and a half the bombardier discovered that he needed two more degrees of drift correction. As he tried to crank in the correction, nothing happened, so he tried to crank in more turns with no results. He then decided to turn the mission over to the deputy lead, to do another bomb run. His decision was too late, however as the Norden sight released the bombs and all the other eleven planes dropped in unison. Our bombs struck even with the target but too far to the left by at least 500ft destroying some large, unknown buildings."[867]

In his diary entry for 8 June Abe Dolim wrote:

"Today we learned that the fires we saw last night were caused by several B-24s which were shot down during their landing approaches by Me 410s. Many of our bombers did not make it back to Bury last night but by afternoon they began to straggle in. Navigators took a ribbing from their more fortunate squadron mates. As I thought about yesterday's mission, it occurred to me that if we had gone in ahead of the two B-24 groups at target, the enemy would have been working us instead."

Next day the bad weather postponed any bomber strikes at all. It also severely curtailed operations on 10 June. Of the 873 bombers airborne, over 200 were forced to abort because of cloud conditions. 589 bombers, including 31 Pathfinders, attacked eight airfields in France and nine coastal installations in the Pas de Calais. A 448th Bomb Group Liberator shot down by flak just east of Evreux airfield, was the only bomber lost on 10 June. Ben Isgrig, in 2nd Lieutenant Bailey's crew in the 448th, who were flying their 8th mission, recalls:

"There were supposed to be some Me 410s down there and we were dropping 100lb GP bombs to make the 'field unusable. This was by far our worst mission. We were hit by flak before we got into the target area, several bursts hitting between the fuselage and the right wing tip. The ship directly behind us caught fire in the bomb bay and fell apart just as it dropped its bombs. Seven 'chutes were seen over the target - a hell of a place to have to bale out. Our left wing ship had its right waist window shot out and some men wounded. We dropped our bombs through clouds. The weather had been terrible since the invasion started."

On 10 June Field Marshal Wilhelm Keitel, head of Armed Forces High Command, rang Field Marshal Gerd von Rundstedt, Commander-in-Chief West from Paris, in a panic. "What shall we do?" he asked. Von Rundstedt replied, "Make peace you fool."[868]

17

The Bridge is Blown

"The bridge attributed to Belisarius
Is blown, and we cross the stream on foot
Towards the little town"

"*A Minor Front*," Robert Conquest

On 11 and 12 June bad weather ruled out targets in Germany and the 8th despatched its bombers to France again. On the 11th the 96th Wing was prepared for a strike on the highly important railway bridge at Blois-Saint-Denis on the Loire, about halfway between Tours and Orleans. After the briefings at Horsham St. Faith, Attlebridge, and Rackheath, crews were in no doubt as to what must be the final outcome of the attack on the bridge, which the Germans were using to supply troops attacking the Allied bridgehead. The Field Order called for the destruction of the bridge at all costs. There was to be no minimum altitude established for the bombing, which was to be made through the clouds in three-ship elements if overcast obscured the target. Lieutenant Colonel Harlan Oakes was one of those who flew in the 466th:

"I was not authorized to go on the raid," he says, "being in A-2 Section and working with British Intelligence. Warren K. Burt, pilot of the ship I flew in, agreed to say nothing of the matter. We proceeded to the hardstand after a briefing, which was short, being told that we would be more fully briefed when we were airborne. Had I known, coward that I am I would not have picked this mission for a 'joy ride'. I should have had an inkling that something was amiss as we were loading bombs at the hardstand in the darkness. One 2000lb GP bomb out of a total of three dropped on the hardstand: deathly silence and Burt's voice roared out: 'What the hell are you trying to do, kill us all?'[869] We were advised in the air that our rendezvous was with the 467th and were given a diversionary support unit, which faked a flight towards Paris. We were also advised to bomb visually, no matter how low we had to fly. Our cameras and intervalometers for photos were set for 20,000 to 25,000ft, the normal altitude. As a former photographer for the Air National Guard, I realized that the automatic cameras were going to leave a lot of blank spot on film and the results could not be ascertained. We maintained strict radio silence until we turned on the bomb run. By this time we were down to about 6000ft, as the cloud cover had lowered. On the actual drop the altimeter reading was approximately 5500ft according to Captain Burt. Our group lead navigator, Captain Leeds, had us dead on target and our lead bombardier, Captain Gerald Merket, had us dead on with bombsights. There was a lot of chatter on the intercoms during the run. Most of us were a little concerned over automatic flak at that altitude. We were certainly sitting ducks, lumbering along at about 155mph indicated airspeed. But the Lord takes care of fools and drunks and babies. Although no one had been drinking we certainly were thankful for his consideration of the other two categories.

"I had to open the escape hatch in the rear to get a shot of the run and was glad when Sgt 'Pop' Julian said he would hold on to my 'chute harness while I leaned out of the hatch to take the pictures. We had not one shot fired at us in anger, although we did see a convoy of Germans off to our right after the drop. Significantly, there were a couple of French farmwomen near the bridge, waving white cloths at us as we flew over. I should guess the most danger we were in on this raid was at the bombing time and when the lead pilot started to fly over a convoy in the Channel when we were returning to England. We bombed about 0900 hours and made landfall about 1000 hours in the West Country."[870]

John W. McClane flew his 19th mission on 11 June:

"The invasion of Normandy was only 5 days old. The 8th was out in full strength with tactical bombing support. Our targets were bridges, road junctions, rail transport, viaducts and airfields. The targets selected for the 44th Bomb Group were a bridge at Montfort and a viaduct at La Passonniere. My crew and myself were part of an 18 Liberator section sent to Montfort, a small French town 28 miles southeast of Le Havre, 22 miles southwest of Rouen and 82 miles down river from Paris. A bridge at Montfort spans the River Risle, a tributary joining the Seine near Le Havre. This bridge was our target for today. Take off was early at 0500 hours. As we penetrated enemy airspace, the Luftwaffe decided it was time to fight back. Four Me 109s made a diving attack and later twelve FW 190s struck us. Our gunners were too much for them, as we lost no planes due to these attacks. The enemy aircraft were up against great odds besides our defensive .50 caliber machine guns. Of 1055 B-17s and B-24s launched for this tactical offensive, 606 were effective over the 20 different selected targets. We were protected by 914 of our own fighters, which swamped anything the Germans could throw at us.

"Our bombardiers dropped as best they could through overcast. As a result, we never saw our bombs hit so we really do not know how effective they were. There was little flak. Being so close to the

Channel, we were soon out over the water again and on the way back to base. Landing was at 1100 hours having been in the air an even 6 hours. (The following day after this 19th mission, the Germans launched the first of their V-1 flying bombs against London from the very *Noball* sites the 8th Air Force had attempted to wipe out since December 1943. Hitler called these his 'Vengeance Weapons' (the German word being *Vergeltunsgwaffen*). During the summer until our ground forces overran the launching sites, the Fuhrer sent 2000 V-1s to England killing some 600 Londoners and wounding another 40,000)."

On 12 June 1278 B-17s and B-24s, including 25 pathfinder aircraft, dropped 3295 tons of bombs on 22 primary targets in northeastern France, and on secondary and targets of opportunity. Eight bombers were lost. One of these was *Crash Wagon III*[871] in the 551st Bomb Squadron, 385th Bomb Group at Great Ashfield, Suffolk, which was flown by Lieutenant Loren E. Jackson on his tenth mission when the 3rd Air Division bombed lines of communication around the Normandy bridgehead. The short mission across the Channel to the beachhead became even shorter when, approaching the target, flak disabled the No.2 engine, as Jackson recalls:

"Ross M. Blake, my co-pilot from Great Neck, Long Island and I were unable to feather the propeller. It kept windmilling and making a rather unsettling racket. We continued on course but began to lag behind the main formation. Shortly thereafter, a flak hit in our No.4 engine disabled it but we were able to feather the propeller. By now we were considerably behind the formation. When fire broke out and enveloped the entire left wing I rang the emergency bell and instructed the crew to bale out. I was eager to get out too, but hit a snag. I was wearing a parachute harness and had stowed my parachute under my seat. I reached over to get the 'chute but it was hooked on something under the seat and I was unable to free it. I wrestled with it and finally got it loose. As I was attaching it to the harness, I looked out the left window and saw that the fire was out. (I suspect that as I leaned forward with my shoulders pressed against the control column, I put the airplane into a shallow dive. Apparently, the increased air speed blew out the fire.) I called the crew on interphone to see if anyone was still aboard but I received no answer. I flew along alone for about ten minutes, following the formation in the distance. When the fire erupted again and had the No.2 engine and the left wing obscured by flames, I left my position in the left seat and went out the nose hatch.

"The smoking, flaming B-17 circled me twice resembling a huge wounded bird. As I was descending, I plotted my escape route. I was falling into a clear field and could see a thick cluster of trees not far away. I planned to head for the trees and hide until nightfall. I landed in tall grass and lay on my back to disengage my parachute harness. I got up and started walking casually toward the forest. Then I heard a shout. '*Halt!*' I pretended not to hear it and continued towards the trees. Again the command to halt. I turned around and saw a German soldier on one knee with his rifle pointed at me. I threw up my hands. He came toward me, still holding his rifle on me and said the words I dreaded to hear, 'For you the war is over.'"[872]

Also on 12 June, Lieutenant Joe Hamil's crew and the others in the 94th Bomb Group who were on combat status were roused at midnight, and they took off at about 0500 to bomb the airfield at Montdidier. Hamil's crew flew lead second element, and they left the English coast at approximately 0745. They hit the enemy coast very shortly thereafter near Ostend and there was no flak. Abe Dolim recalled:

"As usual we had checked our .50 caliber cartridge belts for 'short rounds' before takeoff (as soon as we attained altitude, we charged our .50s to keep one round in the chamber in case of icing. On the way to Montdidier a squadron of Me 109s passed us at 9 o'clock headed north for the invasion beaches. From now on they will have other fish to fry. Flak was light but extremely accurate and we took a number of hits. Our bombing was as accurate as their flak."

Hamil's co-pilot Harvey T. Brown adds:

"There was cloud coverage of about 2/10ths so I got some good views of France. Saw quite a few boats in the Channel coming and going. I spotted three major airdromes and picked them up quite clearly with the binoculars. Could not see any planes or signs of activity. May have been dummies. Also saw a grass field with one runway. Saw no fighters. Dolim thinks he saw some but I picked them up with binoculars and they were ours. May have been some others. Today was my halfway mark under the old standards. Hope they change it before long but would like to finish with this crew. There was not much flak today but it is the most accurate I have seen, bursting between the lead plane and us and No.2 and us. I thought sure we would catch it but we only had three holes, two in the tail, one behind Kelch and a dent in the leading edge. The boys said we really did a beautiful job on the target. One stick walking right down the runway. We landed about 1100. The Public Relations officer, C. Roy Babb, took pictures of Burnet Maybank with Abe, Joe, the engineer and me."

It was on 12 June that 2nd Lieutenant William Bailey's crew in the 448th Bomb Group flew their ninth mission when the 2nd Bomb Division despatched its Liberators to targets in France again. The 20th Combat Wing, of which the 448th Bomb Group was a part, was assigned a railway bridge about 12 miles south of Rennes. Durwood B. Stanley, the regular ball turret gunner, was withdrawn, and the crew reduced to nine members. It seemed as if the rest of the crew's ninth mission might have to wait when, just prior to take off, their B-24 developed electrical trouble. Leslie Fischer, the engineer, got the auxiliary generator running, and everything seemed fine until the crew got ready to swing onto the runway. Then the entire electrical system gave out. There was very little time to check the cause, so a ground crew was called for to tow the Liberator off the runway. Bailey's crew were given a replacement ship called *Squat 'N Droppit*. Aircrews are normally superstitious, and the change in aircraft brought mixed reactions from the nine men. George Cooksey exclaimed, "What a name for a B-24!" He thought it was a bad omen. The rest of the crew laughed at him. Ben Isgrig was undeterred; he thought the mission would be another "milk run."

Squat N' Droppit finally took off from Seething, but Bailey had a lot of catching up to do if they were to depart the coast of England in formation. *Squat N' Droppit* carried four 2000lb bombs in her belly, and when they finally reached altitude it became obvious they would not make it. Bailey had to tag onto the 446th Bomb Group from nearby Bungay as No.3 aircraft in the low lead element.

At the IP the mission turned into a disaster, as Ben Isgrig recalls:

"We started our bomb run but instead of dropping our bombs, the lead ship closed its bomb bay doors and headed towards England. Nearing the French coast we turned and headed towards the target again but once more we did not drop our bombs. By this time other groups in the same area had started home, leaving us on our own. We made a third run with the same results. Bailey said that we were getting low on gas and would have to leave formation and go home. He changed his mind and stayed with the 446th as it started its fourth and final bombing run. As we dropped our bombs we were flying on the right of the formation."

George Cooksey was also horrified by the actions of the lead ship:

"I'll never know what happened to the lead crew but they really screwed it up. Four times over the target! The turns caused the formation to spread. We were low on the inside and just barely able to remain above stalling speed during the left turns. By the fourth time over the target the Germans had our altitude and must have even had the serial number of our aircraft. The flak was everywhere. How demoralizing those black puffs were - getting closer and closer."

Ben Isgrig continues:

"We had been briefed to make a sharp left turn after crossing the target but instead of doing this, we waited too long and the lead ship led us directly over Rennes before beginning his turn. As we were flying on the right side of the formation we were in the position to catch the most flak, which we did. It was the most accurate flak I had ever seen, or hoped to see. The Germans had our airspeed and altitude exactly. We didn't have a chance. We cut sharply to the left and began doing individual evasive action. Over the interphone I guided Bailey away from where the flak was thickest as I had a good view of it from the nose turret; a much better view than anyone else on the ship. It seemed no matter which way we turned; the flak still hit us. To me it sounded like someone throwing gravel on a tin roof. There was an occasional shudder, as a larger piece would tear into the ship. I don't think I was scared; I don't know. I just wanted to get out of it as soon as possible. I wasn't wearing my flak suit as I hadn't thought I would need it, so I crouched down as far as possible in my turret and got as much protection as possible from my gun mounts and armor plating.

"After what seemed an eternity we were in clear air again and I breathed a sigh of relief. I relaxed and started looking for holes in my turret. Over the inter-phone I heard Bailey ask if everyone was all right but I don't remember hearing any replies. Our interphone was not working very well and my connection in my turret was not working at all. I had opened the turret doors and was plugged into a connection in the nose.

"After leaving the flak area we were slightly behind the formation but no further behind than we had been on several other occasions. We were gradually catching up when suddenly, I looked out and saw a stream of tracer bullets coming from the direction of the tail and crossing directly in front of me at about 100 yards. I don't believe the tracers were more than ten yards from me as they passed my turret. For a second I was so stunned I couldn't move, then I yelled, 'Enemy Fighters!' I don't know whether anyone heard me. At the same time I turned on my trigger switch and waited for the fighter to pass the nose but he evidently pulled off to the side because I never saw him. I heard the 20mm shells explode, four of them and our 'plane shuddered as they ripped into her guts. I don't know how many planes made passes at us, or how many times, but I believe it was three planes and I know that we were out on the first pass.

"A few jumbled words came over the interphone. I couldn't make them out. Then I heard Ken Zierdt, the radio operator, repeat over and over in a steady voice, 'Fire in the bomb bay, Fire in the bomb bay!' In a few more seconds someone said, "Get the hell out of here' and I saw Vic Fleishman, the navigator, take off his oxygen mask and put on his 'chute. I pulled my oxygen mask and interphone connection loose as the alarm bell rang and climbed out of the turret. Meanwhile, Vic opened the escape hatch. A thousand thoughts ran through my mind but I wasn't afraid; I didn't have time. By the time I had my parachute on, Vic was baling out and Fischer had crawled up the passageway and was waiting to jump. I don't know what Fischer was doing there; he was supposed to go out through the bomb bay."

George Cooksey was in turmoil. He thought, "We're hit!" Those next few seconds trying to assess the damage seemed endless. The oxygen was gone and so was the intercom:

"How were the guys in the waist and tail? No.3 engine gone. Right vertical stabilizer gone. Fire in the bomb bay. We were losing altitude. Bailey sounded the bale-out alarm. Where's Fischer? He's not on the flight deck Zierdt said Fischer had gone through the tunnel to the nose. Why didn't he open the bomb bay door? How about the guys in the nose and rear? Are they still there? Are they out? How long can we maintain control?"

Isgrig and Cooksey both wondered why Fischer had left through the nose. Fischer explains:

"A round had gone through the bomb bay and set the ship on fire and I did not want to open the bomb bay doors and fan the flames. My interphone was inoperative and I couldn't communicate with the rest of the crew. Zierdt was pulling my leg to come down out of the top turret above his radio compartment. I had a little jump seat so I pulled the release and fell out onto the flight deck. Zierdt handed me a fire extinguisher. It looked as if the hydraulic tank was on fire.

"Either the fire extinguisher was inoperative or Zierdt had already used it because it did not work. I stepped back onto the flight deck and I told Zierdt, 'Come on let's go!' Vic Fleishman was squatting over the escape hatch when I got there and as soon as he baled out I followed him."

Isgrig looked around and saw three fighter planes above him:

"I immediately thought they must be German. The nearest one, a Bf 109, turned and started diving at me. I thought he was going to machine-gun me and I prayed feverishly to God to help me. I pulled the shroud lines to start my body swinging; it was all I could do to help myself.[873] The other two planes were Mustangs. One of them circled lazily above me while the other followed the German down. The Bf 109 cut to the left; passing within 50 yards of me and began to climb. The P-51 was right on his tail and I never wanted anything in my life as much as I wanted him to kill the German who had shot us down. I was hysterical by this time and I screamed and cursed the German, waving and offering all my moral support to the American as he passed. The German didn't have a chance. Within ten seconds his ship began to fall apart and burn. The German baled out and he landed 300 yards from me."

The P-51 climbed toward Fischer after shooting down the Bf 109, circled him and waggled his wings before roaring away.[874] A young French girl, Margaret Lecotteley, had witnessed the shooting down of the Liberator and the subsequent fighter combat above her home in Romille. During the air battle, which had taken place at a relatively low altitude, the villagers had cursed as the German fired at the helpless American airmen, and then had cheered as the P-51 had finished off the German fighter. Margaret was the first to reach the German pilot, who landed in a yard in Romille. He handed her a knife and asked the young French girl to cut away the boot on his wounded leg. As Margaret stood over him with the knife German soldiers ran to the scene and prepared to shoot her. They thought she was attacking the pilot, but fortunately he stopped them from firing. The pilot was not seriously hurt and probably flew again.[875]

VIIIth Fighter Command provided support for the bomber missions on 12 June and attacked German communications and troop movements. For the 353rd Fighter Group, it was their most disastrous mission of the war. At Raydon at 0434 hours Colonel Glenn E. Duncan took off and led 48 P-47s, each aircraft armed with 3500 rounds of .50 caliber API ammunition and two 500lb bombs under the wings, but no external fuel, to the airfield at Evreux/Fauville. Hits were scored on freight cars parked in sidings and radar installations, and adjacent barracks were also bombed with three direct hits and two near misses. The P-47s descended below the cloud level at 3000ft and destroyed several trucks in a convoy in the vicinity of St. Saen before they were split up by light flak when they let down through the overcast. The remaining flight was forced to jettison their bombs as they were bounced by Bf 109s who flew out of the clouds and descended on the rear of the Thunderbolt formations in the vicinity of Dreux. The P-47 pilots dropped their bombs and belly tanks and went into a tight circle, but they were out-turned by the enemy. In the furious aerial battle that followed the 353rd Fighter Group pilots claimed six Bf 109s, but eight P-47s were shot down. Colonel Duncan claimed three 109s to take his overall score to 18.5 victories,[876] at one point calling for help over the radio, as he had six Bf 109s "surrounded!"[877]

On 13 June bad weather canceled large-scale bombing of high priority targets in Germany, and the bombers were instead dispatched to carry out bombing in overcast against airfields and other targets in northwestern France. On the first mission of the day cloud cover was less than anticipated, and visual runs were made by 128 B-17s against airfields at Dreux, St. Andre-de-L'Eure, and Evreux. 2nd Lieutenant Dick Johnson flew his 14th mission to Evreux airdrome:

> "The weather was finally clear over the target for today's mission. Opposition could nearly always be expected on clear days. We were to bomb the airdrome in order to harass the German fighter planes stationed there.[878] We were assigned the No.2 position behind and to the left of '*Miss Lace*', the lead plane flown by 1st Lieutenant P. E. Mitchell. Off our right wing, 2nd Lieutenant W. T. Means flew the deputy lead. Before we reached the French coast, the lead plane had to abort due to No.2 engine failure. Means moved up to the No.1 position and our spare flown by Lieutenant Lehman moved into the formation to complete the mission. Of the 40 planes we put up, only three aborted - '*Miss Lace*,' '*Old Glory*' in the 360th Squadron and '*Helen Heaven*' in the 358th Squadron. We flew to France after climbing up through a solid overcast and hit the coast headed toward the French town of Amiens, but turned south in a feint to Paris and finally to the target which was a few miles southwest of Paris. We each carried 18 250lb GP bombs and 1700 gallons of gasoline to hit the airfield. Just before we got to the target, the skies cleared and the visibility became unlimited. We could see the target from the initial point and the bombardier did a superb job, putting the pattern of bombs across the airfield, ruining both runways. The lead bombardier said that we bombed the target through the only hole in the clouds over Europe. We saw flak in the distance, but had no direct opposition. A real Milk Run. We were over enemy territory for an hour and ten minutes, on a 4 hour and 40 minute flight. We stayed close to the formation through the overcast and didn't get lost but two planes from other squadrons landed at another field."[879]

On the second mission of the day 208 heavy bombers, including 15 pathfinder aircraft, attacked airfields at Beauvais-Nivellers and Beaumont-sur-Oise, as well as bridges and scattered targets between Brittany and the assault area. Flak shot down two B-24s. VIII Fighter Command provided support for the bomber missions and carried out fighter-bomber and strafing missions against five bridges, three trains, 23 trucks, and four other vehicles. In all, the fighters flew 782 sorties and claimed six enemy aircraft shot down for the loss of four of their own.

John W. McClane flew his 20th misison on Wednesday, 14 June, when the 44th Bomb Group's target was Châteaudun, France:

> "On this date the greatest Bomber Force ever assembled by mankind was dispatched to interdict the transportation facilities of General Von Rundstedt's army. Our ground forces were still contained in the Normandy beachhead. The German soldiers were putting up a very stiff resistance in an effort to keep us from breaking out. The Air Force's job was to reduce his mobility and supply lines as well as his aerial defense capability. The 8th Air Force dispatched over 1500 Liberators and Fortresses. The 44th Bomb Group's 36 planes were part of 103 B-24s sent to bomb Châteaudun airfield. The city of Châteaudun lies 73 miles southwest of Paris and 53 miles east of Le Mans. Our bomb load was the maximum number of bombs our bomb bay racks could hold, i.e., 52 100lb bombs (but not our maximum weight of 8000lbs however). There was a way to allow a greater number of small bombs to be carried but there was much technical difficulty. This was a 'cluster attachment' but it often jammed the bomb bay shackles or broke loose completely, falling prematurely through the unopened bomb bay doors. We never used these devices that I'm aware of. This gave us a much better margin of safety on takeoff as we regularly flew with overload weights of fuel and bombs. Nothing made me more apprehensive than lift-off when we were at maximum load.
>
> "This was again another of these six hour missions we had been flying regularly in support of our invasion forces. Take off was very early in the morning at 0415 hours. This turned out to be a good day for the 44th as we saw almost no enemy opposition from the Luftwaffe and flak was very light over the target. Our bomb results were excellent with all tolled, 215 tons of high explosives being deposited by all groups on this important airfield. The flight back to base was uneventful and we landed just after 1000 hours."

On 15 June 1225 bombers attacked an oil refinery at Misburg, and the 1st Bomb Division struck mostly at airfield targets in northern France that could be used to launch *Luftwaffe* attacks on the Normandy bridgehead. In France, orders for *Oberstleutnant* Josef "Pips" Priller, *Kommodore Jagdgeschwader 26 "Schlageter,"* came through very early. He was to lead II./JG 26, III./JG 26, and III./JG 54 on an offensive sweep to an area to the northwest of Caen at 0625 hours. The weather forecast promised a fine day, and in no time at all the three *Gruppen* had taken off and were racing over the French countryside. Just after take off they were told to change course and fly towards five *Pulks* (big formations) of heavy bombers who were just inland of the French coast and heading east towards Paris. "Pips" Priller was among the first to spot the Americans flying at about 16,000ft. They were B-17s. Above the bombers were the escorting American fighters weaving to and fro searching for the German fighters that would surely come. "Pips" made the decision to attack the B-

17s before the escorting fighters lost altitude and dropped down to engage his formation. Priller was to recall in his subsequent combat report:

"I made an oblique attack on the first box from the side at the same altitude and obtained several strikes on one of the Boeings flying on the left side of the formation. After a battle at close range with the very strong escort, I attacked a formation of about 20 Liberators from the front. I fired at the Liberator flying the left outboard position in the first vee and I saw strikes in the cockpit and on the two left engines. After I dived away I saw the Liberator sheer away from the formation, bright flames coming from three engines and dive. I could not see it hit the ground because of the continuing air battle."[880]

The 492nd Bomb Group was not the only B-24 outfit to lose a Liberator to JG 26 on 15 June. Southwest of Chartres III./JG 26 caught the Liberators of the 392nd Bomb Group without escort, and the Bf 109 pilots made three attacks from the front and the rear. Major Klaus Mietusch, the CO, claimed one of the B-24s, while his wingman, *Unteroffizier* Erhard Tippe, claimed a *Herausschuss* after shooting a second B-24 from its formation. However, although very badly damaged, Lieutenant Harry A. White got the Liberator[881] back across the Channel and he crash-landed at Eye.[882] White recalls:

"We were attacked by fighters. John Wehunt, tail gunner, was killed. Glen Barnes, top turret gunner/flight engineer, suffered 32 wounds in his face and neck from splintered Plexiglas and flak when his turret was hit. He never returned to the crew. Our two waist gunners, Sergeants James Braceforte and Robert Dunbar baled out and later became PoW after our oxygen system was hit, exploded and caught fire. We went temporarily out of control and they thought we were going down. It was our 13th mission."[883]

2nd Lieutenant Dick Johnson flew his 15th mission on 15 June:

"We were assigned a massive railroad bridge across the Loire River at Tours, carrying two, 2000lb bombs on the belly of the planes, since a 2000lb bomb wouldn't fit into the bomb bay. We flew over a single flak battery at St. Martin and the flak gunners aimed visually. Our evasive turns were sufficient to ruin their aim and they only did minor damage to a few of the 12 planes in our squadron. Our bombs were fused at one tenth second at the nose and one hundredth at the tail. We did a 20-mile bomb run and all three squadrons hit the bridge with a good pattern. This was one of the longest bomb runs that I remember, being 14 minutes in a straight line. Lucky for us, there was very little defense at the target, as we would have been sitting ducks for a clear day, flying at 15,500ft. Usually, when the bomb bay doors opened on a clear day, the flak would come up in bunches, because the German gunners knew that we would not make any evasive turns. They could lead us by about one and a half kilometers so that the bursts would be right in our formation. As we approached the bridge with our bomb doors open, a train that was headed that direction suddenly stopped and started backing up. We were amazed that they were so desperate as to venture out in broad daylight. Since there were no enemy fighters to harass us, some of our escort planes went down to see what they could break. We were so busy getting into wing formation for our return home that we couldn't watch much of the ground activity. I sort of envied Charlie Lana, our ball turret gunner, as he had a ringside seat, as did some of the other gunners. At any rate, we had no failures that day, except that one aircraft Johnson aborted for mechanical reasons and our spare took his position in the formation. All 36 aircraft returned to Molesworth and were on the ground before noon. Total flight time was six hours and 15 minutes with two and a half hours over enemy territory."[884]

On 16 June 313 heavies, including four pathfinders, attacked four airfields and V-1 targets in France. Norman I. French, pilot of B-17 *Flack Rabbit*[885] in the 526th Bomb Squadron, 379th Bomb Group, recalls:

"We were awakened early for a bombing mission (it was to be my 30th) but, for some reason, the mission was called off. At noon we were called again. At the briefing session we were told that target, Laon/Couvern airfield near Paris, was a very important one, as it was believed that the Germans were trying to bring up reinforcements in an attempt to drive our invading forces back into the sea. Take-off was uneventful. We climbed though the cloud cover and joined our formation. Lieutenant George McHugh was leading our squadron[886] and I was on his right wing. This would have put us a little over 200ft apart. We had good cover from friendly fighters, but they were unnecessary, as there were no enemy fighters. As there was heavy cloud cover beneath us we were to bomb with the lead bombardier, who had electronic equipment, which would allow him to aim through the cloud and see the target.

"The bomb run, although the flak was thick and accurate, was uneventful but for one thing - the lead bombardier failed to drop his bombs! As we circled for a second run, my thoughts went back to my vow 'never to take a second run' but they also went back to the briefing that had stressed the grave importance of our mission. Although I felt sure a second run would be fatal, I hoped that if shot down, I might make it back beyond the lines of our ground forces before crashing. I looked ahead and saw a thick wall of black smoke and was sure we would be hit. I bent over to check my autopilot in the hope that it would hold the ship steady long enough for the crew to bale out, if necessary. I heard a loud explosion! There was a large hole in my windshield, right where I had been looking. A burst of flak had gone off just in front of my ship. That burst set McHugh's ship on fire! It also almost blew [Larson] my engineer's foot off. The squadron was scattered."

French's bombardier, Lieutenant William Braunsdorf, adds:

"We could only see three chutes. The next thing I knew we were hit. Kasper yelled, 'I'm hit!' Pappy called for Larson to check him out and give him first aid. I think Simmons, radioman, took over and Larson returned to position. We were on our bombing run at the time at 25,000ft. After 'bombs away' I turned to talk to Larson to see what our condition was and found him flat on his face. The first thing I thought 'God, he is dead too'. It was hard moving him but I got to him. No oxygen mask on his face so we shared mine as I kept pulling him. I worked on him and after a while, after he had oxygen, he started to come out of it. I was glad to see his eyes open. There was no oxygen bottle around so I couldn't get up on flight deck to see Kasper. I was told all was OK there - Simmons and the co-pilot were helping."

Norman French continues:

"I called for someone to aid my injured crewman, but to no avail. I turned control of my ship to my co-pilot and attempted to aid the injured gunner. The co-pilot, somehow, got the ship upside down! I grabbed the controls, righted the ship and called the squadron to form on me. To my complete amazement and surprise, I saw McHugh pull into position on my left wing! I could see that his ship was engulfed in flames, so I called him, on the radio (at least twice) and begged him to bale out. In a complete disregard for himself, he maintained his position until he had dropped his bombs on the target! He then put his ship in a steep dive in an obvious attempt to blow out the flames. One of my crewmen reported three chutes. We assumed the rest of the crew went down with the ship.[887] What McHugh did was more than brave. It was literally above and beyond the call of duty. He gave his life to do his part in accomplishing our mission. I have never before or since seen such a selfless act. I am proud to have known him. At the debriefing session I went to our group commander and orally recommended McHugh be awarded the Medal of Honor."

On 17 June 231 Fortresses, including 16 pathfinders, attacked 8 airfields in Northern France, but clouds and the malfunction of blind-bombing equipment caused nearly 100 aborts. Two B-17s were lost. A favorable break in the weather over Northern France permitted a second mission by 273 B-24s of the 2nd and 3rd Bomb Divisions against three airfields and two landing strips. Among the airfield targets were Cuissai-Lonrai, the base for I./JG 1, and Essay airfield near Alençon, the base for II./JG1. *Leutnant* Fritz Wegner, 5th *Staffel* JG 1, recounts:

"We put in a lot of effort to get our airfield into shape. Everything had not been finished when, on 17th June, a new attack caught us by surprise. The *Viermots* were flying due south. We thought they were heading for Paris. Suddenly someone shouted: 'Listen, the noise is increasing!' We then saw the enemy aircraft execute a turn and fly right over the airfield from the south. At this moment, sitting on a case of bombs, I was discussing our next mission. I shouted: 'Everyone head south off the airifield!' The men jumped into a wagon, which took off like a whirlwind! I was unable to catch it up. I was trapped and was soon joined by an old soldier. We had only a few seconds to get as far away as possible from our own bombs. We were going to receive enough of them! Hardly had we flattened ourselves on the ground when the heavens opened on us. An eternity later, we were still alive, but in a different world. Everything was in chaos. Our case of bombs had certainly vanished. An hour passed before the men returned. They did not think they would find us alive."[888]

2nd Lieutenant Dick Johnson's next mission on Monday, 19 June, was to the Pas de Calais, to bomb V-1 rocket installations. He recalls:

"After morning briefing, about half of the combat crews went to the chapel for prayers or last rites. Some of our crew did this, but I never did. I always relied on my own silent prayer: 'Thank You, God, for taking such good care of me.' This was a silent vow I had made as a 13 year old while living in Southern Illinois, never asking for anything in the future, but always thanking Him for keeping me alive and in good health. I had vowed to repeat this prayer every time I thought of it and still do to this day.

"For the morning mission we were loaded with 38 100lb GP bombs, which were to be dropped through the clouds to try to destroy a V-1 area using '*Gee H.*' navigation and identification equipment. The 40 aircraft of our group dropped 1513 bombs and were over enemy territory 30 minutes with a total flight time of four hours and 45 minutes.[889] In the afternoon the target was the same as the morning mission, a Buzz bomb station near Fiefs and Predefm in the Pas de Calais. Although it was considered a milk run, it was anything but that, as far as I was concerned. The lead plane in our group and others always carried a co-pilot in the tail gun position to check on formation. This was because a cockpit officer could name any ship by position to tell the lead pilot who might be out of formation. Today was my turn in the barrel. I was assigned to fly with Captain R. S. Harrison and Captain R. B. Dubell in the 359th Squadron's aircraft.[890] They were leading the group in this afternoon's mission. My diary reads: 'Pas De Calais, France. GH Robot Plane installations. Target 5/10ths covered. Same as this AM's mission. Temperature 26°C. Saw flak again but no damage.' This brief description shows a milk run all right, but when I got into the tail gun position with electrically heated suit and gloves I was out of my element. I made out OK during formation and departure but when I was about settled down after advising the pilot that everything seemed good about the formation, I noticed that the AFCE[891] or Autopilot, which we called 'George' was causing a good bit of movement at my new position. The swaying and yawing soon made me airsick. Not only that, I couldn't figure out how to fire the tail guns. I tried several times, finally giving up, as I figured that no enemy plane would attack from the rear, since all I could see behind me was hundreds of B-17s as far as the eye could see.

"I soon developed the dry heaves. It soon got so bad that I thought that I would barf my cookies with nothing to barf in. At that point I took off my flak helmet to use for that purpose, but managed to contain myself. It got to the point that I wouldn't have cared if I were shot down. I even contemplated taking off my oxygen mask for a while to see if that would ease the air sickness, but decided against it, since I knew that oxygen starvation was insidious, with no warning of any sort. We had periodic oxygen checks during all altitude flights and when someone didn't answer, the nearest crewmember took a walkaround oxygen bottle to check him out. Beiser and most of the crew didn't fly this mission and for a brief moment I was resentful for having been assigned this position. It gave me new respect for our tail gunner, Carroll H. Brackey. I guess it didn't help matters that gale force winds had arrived over the Channel, making flying even bumpier than usual. The winds were so strong the next few days that the Mulberry Harbor at *Omaha* Beach was destroyed and the British one was severely damaged. Parts of the American harbor were used to repair the one for the British at Arromanches. A large number of landing craft were also sunk during this stormy period."

On 20 June, when oil targets were pounded again, Dick Johnson went to Hamburg:[892]

"My diary read: 'Hamburg, (Yipe!). Bombed oil refinery and storage. Made good use of CAVU weather. Sure went up in flames. Flak so thick you couldn't see through it, but we flew through it. Got plenty of holes. Put our ship out for a few days. Sure earned that cluster. (To Air Medal).' The 303rd Bomb Group put up 39 B-17s for this mission to bomb the Rhenania Ossag Mineralolwerkes AG at Harburg, a suburb of Hamburg. We were to bomb from 25,000ft.[893] Each of our aircraft was loaded with 12 500lb GP bombs, fuzed at one tenth second at the nose and one fortieth second at the tail. Each B-17 was loaded with 2100 gallons of gasoline for the seven hour and two minute flight. Beiser and I were assigned to position No.4 in a composite squadron.[894]

"As we approached the city of Hamburg, the flak was unbelievable. The Germans were determined to protect their oil supplies at any cost. The flak explosions were constant and unrelenting, being so close that many could be heard to explode and throw fragments against the sides of the airplane. The angry, red center of some of the explosions meant that they were very close. To hear flak explode, it had to be within 50ft of our plane, otherwise the very loud engine noise would drown out the noise of an explosion farther away. Likewise, to feel a jolt from a flak explosion, it would have to be within 25ft or less from the plane. I saw plenty of red centers and heard several of them during our 41 mile (!) bomb run. Our ground speed against the wind was barely over two miles per minute, allowing the German defenders a good chance to track us in the straight and level flight from the Initial Point to the target.[895]

"We busted the target wide open. One group ahead of us had also hit the target and smoke was visible during the entire bomb run. There were many great explosions among the oil storage tanks and on the cracking plant itself. From our vantage point at 26,500ft we could see clearly that the target was completely covered by bomb bursts. We hadn't bothered to carry any incendiary bombs on this trip, but it seems that they would have been redundant. It was surprising that there would be a target of this importance still in existence in the city and suburbs of Hamburg, since it had already been razed by British night bombing, causing a firestorm of tornado intensity that covered most of the city. Only two of our B-17s escaped damage on this mission. Eleven suffered major damage, three crewmen were wounded by flak and the one plane was lost. It is remarkable that only one plane was shot down. Our plane suffered over 263 flak holes of various sizes and yet not a crewmember was hit and the airplane flew as if nothing had happened to it. Our bombardier, Ed Cooper almost lost it on this mission.[896] Flak was so thick that it fell like rain at times from explosions above the formation. One of these pieces of shrapnel came in the nose window and struck Ed on the breastbone and drove him six feet back into the navigator's compartment. There is no doubt that the flak suit saved his life, because when we returned to base we helped him cut the piece of flak from the suit. The flak suit is composed of small plates of tantalum steel that overlap each other like scales on a fish. There were always three thicknesses of these plates. The first layer had clasped the flak fragment so that it could not be removed. The second layer was bent sharply around the first and the third layer was only slightly bent. Ed sported a large bruise on his chest for several days, but was not injured enough to take him off flying status."[897]

Ralph Reese in the 452nd observed:

"The target was really flaming and smoking as we dropped our bombs and closed the bomb bay doors. Smoke reached as high as 5000ft. On the way back to the coast we saw many targets which had been bombed. They were burning and smoking and smoke reached as high as 10,000ft."

T/Sgt Ken Garwood also went to Magdeburg:

"This was our 15th mission and was part of the concentrated effort to destroy the German oil industry. It was our second trip to the oil refineries at Magdeburg. The first was on 28 May and was our third mission. We did sustain some flak damage but came back unharmed. We had no fighter escort flying with us, but we were told that there would be area escort that we could call in if needed. We flew over the North Sea and turned in to the enemy coast and about then our tail gunner, Tommy Rogers, started calling out fighters trailing behind us. Lieutenant DeBrandes told him to keep an eye on them and if they pointed their nose at us to start firing. We started our bomb run to the target through very heavy flak and about that time the fighters hit us. They were FW 190 and Me 109s. We dropped our bombs and the fighters came through their own flak to hit us. We were the last element in the group and were therefore prime targets. All of our gunners were firing and the ship was filled with smoke in the radio room.

"One FW 190 flew up along our right side and as I swung my gun around to shoot, a burst of 20mm flak came through the floor of the radio room and small pieces hit my leg. I dropped the gun for a moment and he was gone. He was so close I could see him clearly looking the damaged bomber over. By that time, our inboard engines were burning and because of the location of the fuel tanks, that was an automatic bale out signal. I reached for my chest pack chute, which I always kept at the base of the radio transmitter and when I picked it up, it was in shreds. The 20mm flak must have hit it when it came through the floor. I was prepared to jump while hanging on to one of the others but my ball turret gunner located a spare chute near the tail and snapped it on to my harness. Our tail gunner had been hit and he was helped from his position in to the waist where he baled out with the rest of us who were in the rear of the ship. We all were accounted for on the ground after we jumped, except for T/Sgt Lambrecht, our flight engineer. He was never found."[898]

R. D. Russell in the 702nd Bomb Squadron, 445th Bomb Group, and his crew in B-24J *King Kong* were flying their fourth mission on 20 June when the Liberators went to the Politz oil refinery:[899]

"What a day this was. Up at 0100, briefing at 0215, take off at 0520 with 10 250lb GPs. Formed in a rush and climbed on course. The 389th was high right ahead of us and after we had passed Kiel we saw two of their ships run together. One lost the tail and the other a wing tip. Both hit the water in a spin. We only saw five chutes.[900] Later we saw another ship hit the water and blow up. We saw nine chutes this time. It was part of a twelve-ship squadron of the 453rd lost to enemy fighters. We had a good tight formation so the Ju 88s didn't bother us.

"At the IP, nine minutes from the target, we could see other squadrons dropping and hitting the target. Also we could see a solid wall of flak and rockets. I was flying and didn't have a chance to put on my flak vest. We finally got over the target and through the flak. It was bursting all around and the 'frump and crump' sounded as though each burst was hitting us. Just as 'bombs away' came, so also a piece of flak. It hit our windshield and blew a hole in it about the size of a baseball. A piece of flak hit my throat mike, shattering it and lifted me right out of the seat and dropped me on the flight deck. The flak was so thick that the smoke filled the bomb bays and Jerry closed the doors to keep the sight away. Our bombs hit the MPI directly and so did the bombs from the twenty groups ahead of us. That's one target we won't have to go back to. Mission ended with all ships home safe. Flight time: 7:55 hours."

William C. Lawson, co-pilot on Ellis Woodward's crew in the 861st Bomb Squadron, 493rd Bomb Group, recalls:

"We shared a hut with Dave Conger's crew at Debach. Both crews were designed lead crews and each flew all their missions in either a lead or deputy lead position in the 493rd Bomb Group combat formations. My first mission was on 12 June. Our target was an airfield at Beauvais-Tille, France. This was the first mission in which the group was able to drop bombs; weather had precluded bomb drops ion those missions between 6 June and the 12th. Our crew flew the first group mission to Germany on 20 June. The target was an oil refinery at Misburg, a suburb of Hanover. This was my third mission and the first one where we really got shot-at. It was terrifyingly exciting and the B-24s put the refinery out of business for six weeks. Our crew flew 14 missions in the B-24s, the 14th mission being an attack on the railroad yard at Angouleme, a quiet town in southwest France. There was absolutely no enemy opposition. We flew at low altitude and actually saw German troop activity and the battle of Falaise Gap near Calais as we headed home. The next day we learned why such a benign target had to be destroyed. Allied troops had landed in southern France and Angouleme was a railhead between northern and southern France. After the Angouleme mission, the 493rd Bomb Group was stood down for the transition to B-17s. I don't believe we ever flew the same B-24 on more that one or two missions. The B-17 was a dream to fly after arm wrestling a B-24 for eight months. I respected the B-24 but the Fortress, I soon learned, could withstand a lot more abuse. Concurrent with the 3rd Division's conversion to B-17s only, 8th Air Force Fighter Groups equipped with P-38s and P-47s were converted to P-51s. Thus from September on, all but one of the 8th Fighter Groups flew P-51s."

Wednesday, 21 June, was notable for a raid on Berlin, and also for the second 8th Air Force shuttle mission of the war. The 4th Combat Wing and a composite from the 3rd Division led the 8th to Berlin with the 1st and 2nd Divisions behind. After the target 163 Fortresses of the 13th and 45th Combat Wings of the 3rd Division, each B-17 of which was equipped with a long-range bomb bay tank, would fly on to landing fields at Poltava and Mirgorod in Russia, while the rest of the force returned to East Anglia.[901]

S/Sgt James H. McMahon, a B-24 nose turret gunner on his 28th mission in the 409th Bomb Squadron, 93rd Bomb Group, was part of the mission to Politz (Stettin) on 21 June:

"It was very clear all the way in and out. We lost about 45 bombers and we were attacked in force by the GAF. Many of the bombers were hit very hard by flak over the target area and by fighter fire as we went in to the target and after we began our return to base. There were over 1000 heavy bombers attacking, supported by over 700 fighters. We were attacked in waves from head on. The enemy attacked in long lines abreast. They dove under the formations as they went through. I believe that I destroyed one FW 190 that almost crashed head on into our ship. I fired a very long burst at him and he exploded under the formation as he dove under our ship. I saw many B-24s blowing up during the fighter attacks and many spiraling down like falling leaves in flames, or out of control. Some of our ships received direct hits directly over the target and the fighters came through their own flak to get at us."[902]

The Berlin misison on 21 June was also John W. McClane's 21st mission of the war:

"After a lapse of 24 days, again we were scheduled to penetrate deep into *Nazi* Germany. In the meantime our crew had flown five tactical missions in support of the ground forces. But for today, it was back to "Big B" partly in retaliation for the V-1 attacks on London. Our target was the Daimler-Benz motor works at Genshagen, a suburb just south of the center of Berlin and east of the city of Potsdam. Our bomb load was 10 500lb bombs with take-off set for 0500 hours. A total of 1234 heavies were scheduled to bomb various targets in Berlin and its environs, a raid of epic proportions. Of these only 69 were to bomb Genshagen, of which 36 were to be 44th Bomb Group aircraft. The commander of Berlin's defenses had broadcast over Radio Berlin that it was impossible to prevent American daylight raids. He explained that the reason our bombs sometimes dropped before the *Achtung* warning system sent an alert was due to the speed of our raiders. He said, 'There can be no doubt about the fact that it is impossible for us to prevent an air attack. We can not do it.'

"Our Aerial Task Force took the North Sea route in order to skirt much of the hostile land area and to confuse the enemy as to our true destination. We could have easily turned south and back into western Germany but instead we broke the German coast near the great northern port of Hamburg. Our bomber stream was strung out for over 100 miles. It was spearheaded by B-24s of the 3rd Division, followed by B-17s of the 1st Division and then our B-24 Liberators of the 2nd Division with the 'back door' being made up of a large number of 3rd Division B-17s bringing up the rear. Use your imagination and try to visualize how this huge armada of four motor bombers must have looked and sounded like to an observer on the ground and to us actually flying in the formation.

"On the way in to Berlin I saw something I'll never forget. We passed a few miles away from Hamburg, the great port city on the North Sea. The RAF had been there the night before with their incendiaries and 'block busters' and as God is my witness, it appeared to me that every section of this huge city was on fire. An ugly pall of smoke was blowing to the southwest. It looked the way that one might imagine Hell to be.

"We never expected to attack Berlin anytime without Luftwaffe opposition and today was no exception. Even though we had excellent fighter escort, enemy interceptors slipped past our defenders with a number of Me 109 type fighters to strike at us. Our 506th Squadron took the most severe attack resulting in the loss of one of our planes. As one might expect, the anti-aircraft flak was severe. The Berlin area had 520 AA guns in a perimeter around the city. ('*Lili Marlene*' was hit a number of times with more extensive damage than we realized until we lowered our landing gear back at Shipdham. Of our 36 aircraft making this mission, 25 received flak damage, especially our 68th Squadron). It was reported that we received some rocket attacks also but I never saw them. I often missed out on seeing enemy fighter and rocket attacks, as I had a habit of pulling my flak helmet down low over my eyes so that all I could see was straight down in order to be better able to concentrate on my navigation. If I became too involved in watching the battle action I became too alarmed to think about my duties. I suppose one might call this the 'ostrich attitude'. I think we all had a little bit of a 'coward' in us but there was nowhere to run.

"We finally got back to England and home base after being in the air for 9 hours. The time was approximately 1800 hours when Peritti let our landing gear down only to find out that flak had damaged the hydraulic system to the nose wheel. Our flight engineer, Corlew, could not coax it down so we had no choice but to land with only the main gear and no nose wheel. All crewmembers prepared for a crash landing. My position was directly behind the pilot. There was a steel bulkhead that protected him from the rear. I had been trained to sit on the floor with my knees pulled up tight. I put my hands with fingers locked behind my head; elbows tucked in, with both my back and head tight against the steel plate so that when we hit, my head would not be slammed against the bulkhead. Peritti held the nose up as long as he could but finally it had to come down. As the nose began to grind along the runway, the flight cabin filled first then the aft fuselage with dust and smoke. The metal became red hot and melted the asphalt on the runway so that there was a terrible burned asphalt smell clogging our nostrils. We could not see beyond the one finger reach. There was also a loud grinding, scrapping and screeching noise. At long last, it seemed to me a long time, we came to a halt. All of us departed the plane as quickly as we could, choking for breath and trying to get our eyes clear. Luckily there was no fire and no crewmember had been injured either in combat or the crash landing. After we got our wits about us again, we began to survey the damage to '*Lili Marlene*'. She had been hurt but not mortally. The lower half of the nose had been ground off. The bombsight had been destroyed and my navigation desk and compartment was filled with melted asphalt. It was a mess.

"The 'strike photo' taken from our plane clearly showed the city. Warga had difficulty locating the exact target and bombs were dropped on the Pathfinder lead but I had no doubt that we were over our target and in the proper drop zone. I had many reference points on the ground in order to judge our location. Sure our bombardiers had trouble with the partial overcast but I knew where we were. The intelligence officer at post mission interrogation insisted that our strike photos showed that we had bombed Potsdam instead of Genshagen. No amount of reasoning would change his mind. It was made up and nothing I said would alter his decision. I was really aggravated over this, as we had been on a long, dangerous mission followed by a crash landing. I was in no mood for this nonsense but as far as I know the decision stood that we had bombed Potsdam. Needless to say, we got a poor rating for the day."

For Ken Weisl in the 384th at Grafton Underwood, the 21 June mission to Berlin was his 12th of the war:

"Flying time ten hours even. Altitude was supposed to be 26,000ft. Bomb load two incendiary and 8 GP. Target was the Friedrichstrasse Station in the city. Our own plane was down for repairs so we had to fly another plane. We were told that we were to fly the notorious 42-38013 *Nevada Avenger* or 'Old 013', as it was normally called. Its reputation was that it always came back but that it always brought back either a dead man or several badly wounded. Our pilot right away asked for a different plane but was told that 013 was the only one available and we had to take it. So we took the plane as ordered. When we got to the Channel and the spare ships turned back it wasn't long before we lost one of the engines and could not keep up with the rest of the formation. We dropped below some clouds so we were lost to the sight of the group. We dropped to about 1000ft. The pilot thought that at this low altitude any fighters just might not spot us, as they would be looking at the formation above! The pilot asked the crew if they thought we should turn back or go on in to the target? To a man the crew said, 'Go on in and bomb the station as briefed.' Not having a bombsight on board, when we got to the target area, we had to toggle our bombs along the tracks until we crossed over the station. We hit the station good. As we pulled off the target some fighters saw us and came after us. The tail gunner got one and I got another. The fighters only made the one pass at us. We then pulled in to a formation of cripples for better protection. We had lots of holes in the ship from the fighters but no one was hurt yet!"

2nd Lieutenant Dick Johnson in the 303rd Bomb Group was flying his 19th mission, and he wrote in his diary:

"'Big B' Berlin Germany. It's biggest raid of war so far. Flak intense and accurate. Several planes from this field did not return. Passed by Hamburg. It is still burning big and black from our yesterday's raid. We were lucky today. Only a few holes. 26,500ft. Over enemy territory 2 hours and 30 minutes. Carried eight 500lb GP and two 500lb incendiaries.[903]

"Beiser and I were assigned to the 'B' Group, which was in the low position and the No.4 position in the high squadron of six aircraft.[904] There were 18 planes in our group. We had our original crew together for this sortie, which would take 8 hours and 18 minutes from take off to landing. This was to be my second mission to Berlin where it is never considered to be a milk run but just after briefing a rumor came up that the British were going on this trip to Berlin at 14,000ft. We were all elated, knowing that the Germans would be after them instead of us. We figured that our part of the mission would surely be a milk run. We heard all kinds of rumors about this raid. That it would be to retaliate for the buzz bombs that were hitting London at about a hundred a day. We were to drop our bombs 'in train' at one every three seconds. These rumors didn't last very long and the mission went along just like any other large mission, although we did drop our bombs 'in train.' This was the only mission where we did this.

"The 303rd Bomb Group sent up 42 airplanes for this mission, 18 being in our low group. We assembled in position on the lead group over Molesworth and departed in combat wing formation. The weather over the target was fairly open and the city could be seen. We assumed that visual bombing would be the order, so our group began to take interval. Soon after the IP and opening bomb bay doors, the order came for PFF bombing, so our group pulled back into wing formation. Bombs were away at 1016 from 25,900ft. In the target area the flak appeared to be from at least two flak batteries. It was moderate, but very accurate, being continuously pointed. One three-gun battery was firing directly at our squadron. About a quarter mile to our left I noticed a triple burst and every three seconds there was another, only closer. Beiser was flying the plane during this bomb run and I could see burst after burst getting closer and closer, tracking our speed to perfection. Finally, a burst of three came just off the left wing tip and I could hear bits of metal strike our plane. I gritted my teeth, knowing that the next burst would be dead center on our aircraft. I had noticed that the bursts were showing elongated patterns, meaning that we were almost beyond their range and that final burst never came, as the German gunners moved their sights to another group following us. This was the most fear that I had encountered in combat, because I had time to think about it. Most of the time we were so busy that we didn't have time for fear. Usually, after we got into formation and headed for the enemy coast, the anticipation and fear would build until the first burst of flak was seen. I then settled down into a grim attention to duty and thought very little of it unless it got really rough.

"Three of our 18 planes were shot down over the target. One was the leader of our 427th Squadron and his No.4 and 5 planes. Beiser and I were often assigned to the No.4 position but today we were in that position in the high squadron of six planes. It was ironic that no plane was in the 'Purple Heart Corner' of that unfortunate squadron of five planes and still three of the five were shot down. Lieutenant Vermeer was scheduled to fly in that slot, but was unable to catch up with us, so he latched onto the 379th Group from Kimbolton and bombed with them. The 379th was part of our wing. Had he been able to reach his scheduled position, he might have been shot down with the other three. Allen's plane went down just after bombs away with the ball turret gunner still inside. All the others were made prisoners of war. Allen's left wing man, Lieutenant Oranges, was carrying bombs with long delay fuses. He survived the mission, returning home with the rest of us. The plane flown by Lieutenant H. G. Way went down about the same time. Both he and his co-pilot were killed, as were two others of his crew. His navigator, radio operator, ball turret gunner and tail gunner were all made PoWs. '*Mairzy Doats*' flown by Lieutenant Morningstar disappeared before the bomb run and was not seen to leave, since he was the lowest and farthest to the rear. The entire crew survived, being listed as prisoners of war. Morningstar's plane was equipped with a K21 camera and was scheduled to return early for photo processing.[905]

"Strike photos from other B-17s showed a startling scene. Directly below us in the path of our falling bombs was a B 17 out of position. Later pictures show a B-17 having his left stabilizer shorn off by a 500lb bomb dropped from above. That plane went out of control and was lost. As mentioned before, the bombs had to fall about 500ft or more before the protective vane spun off to leave the bomb armed. If this vane did not spin off in the air stream, the bomb could fall on solid concrete without exploding. If the bomb that struck the tail of that airplane had been armed, the plane would have disappeared in a cloud of fire and debris, perhaps destroying other B-17s as well.

"We had observed flak at five other places before Berlin, which was all black in color. Over Berlin the flak was mostly black from their regular 88mm flak guns but we also encountered white bursts from larger guns. Some fixed guns of larger caliber defended most large cities in Germany. Some were 105mm and some were 128mm, which we sometimes referred to as 155mm for some unknown reason. The German gunners sometimes signaled their fighter planes by using different colored bursts. Occasionally the German fighters would fly into their own flak bursts in the frenzy of battle, trying to press home an attack on a bomber. We had thrown out a lot of *Chaff* to disrupt the German radar, which they used when firing through clouds. The *Chaff* seemed to do a little good, as most bursts of flak were low, as evidenced by the loss of most of our low squadron. In our 41st Wing formation of two groups and one high squadron, our high squadron only had three planes with minor damage and none with major damage. Our lead group, which is at the middle altitude, had nine aircraft with major damage and eight with minor damage. The low group, in which I was flying, had two aircraft with major damage and eleven with minor damage and three shot down. Our plane was listed as 'Minor damage', since we only had a few holes to be repaired."[906]

Wilbur Richardson was in the ball turret of *Kismet* in the 94th Bomb Group formation in the leading 4th Wing. He recalls:

"The flak was extremely heavy at the target and we were bounced around by the flak bursts. Holes were appearing everywhere. Just before bomb release John Moser, who was concerned about damage, asked all of us to assess the situation. At that moment I saw fuel in a large stream coming from No.2 turbo. 'Feather No.2 quick,' I yelled anxiously. My heart was pounding. It was done. Moser then asked why because his instruments had given no hint of danger."[907]

Leo C. Riley, *Kismet*'s co-pilot, was far from happy. He wrote:

"Today we have just returned from a so-called retaliation raid on Berlin. It was very rough indeed and to my notion uncalled for. Our ship was shot practically into a sieve by flak. No.2 gas tank punctured but thank God it did not catch fire. No.3 pierced but kept running. We came home on three motors, but made it very nicely. Have quite a few flak frags I picked up in the ship. More scattered all over it. Left tire was blown out on landing, but we made it OK. Lead ship went down. Think the crew baled out. Fighters were there, but did not get to us. God has been kind to us again today. (On landing we found that No.2 motor had been on fire and for some unknown reason had gone out)."

Ken Weisl in the 384th Bomb Group in *Nevada Avenger* made it back to Grafton Underwood, as he recalls:

"At the base because we were lost from the rest of the formation, they never thought that we were crazy enough to go to the target by ourselves! So they tried to say that we dropped our bombs in the Channel and then just flew around to use up the gas. They would not give us credit for the mission. The fact that no one on the crew was hurt was not the way that old 013 brought its crews back! Well, the pilot remembered that we had a camera in the camera well and this camera started operating when the bomb bay doors opened. They got the pictures developed and they found that we hit the target but the main group missed it! All we got for the extra effort was credit for the mission. Of course this broke the jinx of the *Nevada Avenger* - 'Old 013'. Then we reported the two enemy planes that we shot down but the intelligence officer wanted confirmation from other crews and we pointed out that there were no other planes from our group around. He insisted that we had to have confirmation, so we told him to forget it. After that we never reported any planes that we had shot down or thought we had shot down."[908]

Meanwhile, the 163 Fortresses in the 13th and 45th Wings headed for their target, the Ruhland-Elsterwerda synthetic oil plant 50 miles south of Big-B. The shuttle force flew the northern route to Germany, climbing northeast to a point above the Friesian Islands, then heading due east as though to southern Denmark. When the Fortresses reached the German coast near Cuxhaven four B-17s in the 452nd Bomb Group were involved in a mid-air collision. Hank North, the tail gunner aboard *Ole Sal* in the Group formation, recalls:

"Ruhland was right near Berlin and they sent a diversionary group to Big B because they wanted us to arrive in Russia intact to impress the Russians. Me 109s hit us near Warsaw and knocked down Hernandez[909] flying right behind us. The gunners were the fellows that lived with us in the same hut at Deopham Green. When this occurred, I was watching it. It all happened real quick."

Lieutenant Alfred R. Lea, navigator of *BTO in the ETO*, adds:

"Our 75 B-17s had bombed what turned out to be the wrong target. We rejoined the other groups afterwards and headed for Poltava. While over Poland, those in command decided it would be good for the morale of the people in Warsaw if we went off course and flew far enough north to fly over the city. It caused riots in the streets; the first Allied planes to fly over since their own did it in 1939! Unfortunately, it gave the Luftwaffe time to rise up against us. Near Swory and Biala Podlaska we were attacked by 15 109s and, despite Lieutenant Sibbett, a valiant P-51 pilot who went down defending *BTO in the ETO*, we were shot down.[910] Three of our crew were so badly wounded they could not escape the German forces and were taken prisoner."[911]

During the trip to the target the most impressive sight was a glimpse of Berlin, and some of the B-17 crews saw a few B-24s go down as their turn came.[912] In the 94th Bomb Group formation, Abe Dolim waited for the bomb bay doors of the Fortress to open:

"Our bomb run was a straight 40 miles long at 90 knots ground speed due to a stiff headwind, instead of a tailwind as briefed. We unloaded our delayed action GPs and incendiaries over the Charlottenburg district while heavy flak from the 900-odd 88mm cannons around Berlin gave us the most accurate and sustained fire we had encountered to date. We watched one of our bombers drop out of formation and head for the deck. As we turned away from the target we saw many brightly blazing pinpoints of fire in the heavily built up residential area below. The demolition bombs used were fused to explode from one to 72 hours after impact. These, coupled with the incendiaries, created the maximum hazardous situation for the enemy fire fighting and UXB demolition crews. The 500lb incendiary canisters were designed to disintegrate after dropping about 1000ft and spew out approximately 200 2½lb thermite bombs, which literally rained death on the enemy. Some thermite bombs had anti-personnel fragmentation devices to discourage countermeasures. They exploded in contact with water and could only be put out by smothering with non-combustible material. Under no circumstances were we allowed to return and land with a load of delayed action bombs, as they were sensitive to shock. These are murderous weapons to use against civilians and there are many among us who are not proud of the day's accomplishment."

Over "Big-B" bombs fell from the bellies of the 388th and 452nd Bomb Group Fortressesl, and they were joined by those of the 100th Bomb Group. Captain Harry Crosby in the 100th Bomb Group formation recalls:

"The groups of our wing were in trail, the lead bombardiers synchronizing on the target. The corrections to course were rocky and the pilots found it difficult to keep our squadron in place. There was a tense order every once in a while like, 'More manifold pressure', or 'Watch No.3 engine, it's running high,' or a burst of exasperation as one of our wingmen overran us. Then, 'Bombs Away!'... The bombardier hit the switch. Lights on the instrument panel flashed. The plane jerked upward as the wings were suddenly released from their 6000lb burden. A sudden turn to the left. Eardrums cracked as we lost altitude to confuse the flak. Bomb bay doors closed. The flak, black, ugly and angry, grew worse. We'd been over these gunners for 20 minutes and many of the planes were racked by bursts."

Meanwhile, the shuttle force had touched down at Poltava. Hank North recalled that:

"they had Russian women on their AA guns. They also had Russian women serving us chow. Now we had some mechanics in there, preparing the field and getting it ready for us to come in there. I remember being in line and one of the guys said, 'I wonder what they are going to feed us?' Without blinking an eye, this Russian girl said 'Same old shit'. She had picked that up already."

A few hours after the 45th Wing had touched down at Poltava, while crews were attending debriefing sessions, Soviet anti-aircraft batteries were heard close by. Crews dismissed the barrage as a practice, but they were firing at an He 177 high-altitude reconnaissance aircraft, which had shadowed the formation about 400 miles into Russian territory. The Heinkel was too high even to be seen and flew off into the clouds to report its findings. The Fortress crews thought no more about it and went to bed. A few hours later 60 *Luftwaffe* bombers droned over Poltava and proceeded to drop flares. The Russian defenses offered little in the way of resistance, and the Germans were able to drop over 100 tons of bombs on the airfield at will. Hank North recalled that "the German bombing that evening was a massacre for us. The Germans came in about midnight and lit up the place like high noon." For two hours the German pilots made run after run, picking off aircraft one after the other, the heavy caliber shells of their machine-guns exploding and adding to the general chaos and noise. Ammunition dumps were blown up, and the fuel dump, containing 450,000 gallons of fuel, exploded in an angry orange mushroom of flame and debris. More bombs, more flares, and, as each wave completed its run, there was a series of three blinding flashes as they took photos of their bombing.[913]

In England, meanwhile, the 8th continued flying missions against V-1 sites in the Pas de Calais, and the Fortresses also made supply drops to gallant groups in the French Resistance movement. On 22 June 2nd Lieutenant Dick Johnson in the 303rd Bomb Group again flew two missions in one day. He recalls:

"Again we were doing tactical work to try to slow the rate of Buzz Bomb launches. My diary for the day reads: 'St. Omer, (Calais area) robot plane installations. Flew low squadron lead. Flak meager but VERY accurate. Three-tenths CAVU. Only 14 went out...Rough!' We carried 1700 gallons of gas for this four and a half-hour flight, being over enemy territory for 30 minutes. I have no idea why we were carrying two, 2000lb bombs on each airplane to bomb a small target, such as a launching site for buzz bombs. My own idea would have been to carry a bunch of smaller bombs inside the bomb bay. Of course I had no authority in the matter. And it didn't matter anyhow, since all we did was dig ponds for some farmer. We lost our leader, 1st Lieutenant R. W. Erickson who had Captain R. J. Lynch flying as mission commander in his aircraft named '*Mary Cary*'. They received a direct hit before bombs were away. Engines Nos.1 and 2 on the left wing were badly damaged and No.2 had a run away prop that couldn't be feathered.[914] The mission deputy, 1st Lieutenant J. T. Williams took over the lead and completed the bomb run but was himself hit by flak. He managed to get to Grafton Underwood.[915]

"Having dropped our two 2000lb bombs that morning in a feeble attempt to hit a Buzz Bomb site, our planes were loaded with 12 500lb bombs for an attempt that afternoon to bust a railroad marshaling yard at Lille. In my diary I wrote: '...We flew at 26,500ft and got only meager flak...My 6th raid in 4 days. That French flak is meager but plenty hot.' Beiser and I flew '*Tiny Angel*'.[916] We had a different bombardier again. He was 2nd Lieutenant G. A. Wellen, Jr.[917] Beiser and I were assigned to position No.8 for this mission, which made us leader of a three-plane element in the low squadron of the high group. Our 427th Commanding Officer, Colonel Snyder was leading this group, with our two newest crews flying positions No.2 and 3. Lieutenant Wardowski was to the right of the leader and Lieutenant Roy to the left. Both of these crews had flown only four or five missions. It is ironic that they were listed alone on the same page of the manifest and flew side by side on several missions. Yet they were lost on separate raids a few days later. Just after 'bombs away', the airplane in the 11th position of the 360th Squadron, flying in the high group, was hit by flak in the right wing behind the No.3 engine, causing a gasoline explosion.[918] Beiser and I had taken off at four minutes before four in the afternoon and landed at 2039 for a flight of four hours and 44 minutes. We were over enemy territory exactly one hour."

On 23 June two missions were again flown. At midday 211 bombers attacked 12 V-1 sites escorted by four Mustang groups, which broke away after the strikes and strafed transport targets in the Paris area. In the late afternoon 196 bombers attacked airfield targets in France. Henry A. DeKeyser, the 24-year-old left waist gunner in Lieutenant Bob Reese's crew in the 392nd Bomb Group, which was part of the B-24 force that bombed Leon-Athies airfield, recalls:

> "We were No.4 in the lead flight, flying in our B-24 in the 576th Bomb Squadron, directly behind the command ship.[919] Three ME's made a head-on attack and kept on going. They must have radioed our altitude because the flak guns opened up almost immediately. 2nd Lieutenant John Walters, the nose gunner, said on intercom: 'Oh my God!' He saw the command ship explode from a direct hit and No.2 and No.3 ships had also blown apart. I saw large pieces of B-24 going by and a body curled up in a ball and was gone. We watched for parachutes and saw none. Reese threw our 'plane into a dive. The rest of the 'planes were turning to one side or the other and diving. Four more black bursts of flak burst directly above us, just about in the place we had been in. Reese got on the radio and told the rest of the formation that had scattered to form on him. The flak was still coming up in four bursts in the track we would have been in if we had stayed on the same heading.
>
> "God was our co-pilot. It was solid cloud below, so the gunners on the ground could not see us without their radar. As we flew on we threw out *Chaff*. By the time Flight Officer Bill Minzenberg got us back on course we came off the French coast heading for London and flying over London was a no-no. We fired colors of the day and T/Sgt Ralph Buttzman, radio operator, was in touch with a ground station and we were cleared to fly over London as long as we stayed at about 20,000ft. The clouds were gone over England and we got a beautiful view of London and the countryside."[920]

On 24 June 2nd Lieutenant Dick Johnson in the 303rd Bomb Group flew his 22nd mission. Diary:

> "Bremen, Germany. Oil refinery. PFF. Target nine tenths cloudy. Flak moderate too intense. Few flak holes. Hate to go there on a clear day. Another 'Flak City'. We carried 18 bombs per plane. They were 250lb GP type. Our target if radar was the required method of aiming was Oslebshausen, a suburb of the industrial part of Bremen. We each carried 2100 gallons of gas for this trip. Beiser and I had the *'Buzz Blond'* again for this mission and were assigned the No.4 position in the high squadron of the low group. On this raid, Captain Bob Sheets, our operations officer was flying the lead and again, Wardowski and Roy were flying side by side behind him in positions No. 2 and 3. Sheets took off in a PFF plane and led 17 aircraft to fly low group of the 41st 'A' Combat Wing. We assembled over base at 4000ft and got into position with the lead group. We flew in Wing formation until the IP was reached. We overran the IP a small amount in order to take interval for bombing by groups. We came to the target behind the lead group and made a straight and level bomb run of seven minutes. Bombs were away at 1300 from 24,000ft on a magnetic heading of 211°. During the bomb run we encountered intense flak that didn't seem to be aimed at anyone in particular. After bombs away we immediately made a turn to avoid flak, at which time we rejoined the Wing until reaching the North Sea, where we fell into trail for the let down. After reaching friendly territory, the lead plane peeled off and returned to Chelveston where it was based.
>
> "Our use of *Chaff* probably helped in the flak avoidance, since the German gunners had to aim by radar, it being almost solid overcast at the target. We lost one B-17 from our group on this mission. Lieutenant Harold C. Farthing flying 42-37654 was straggling for quite a while and just before reaching the IP he had to leave the No.2 position of the low squadron. He was almost directly to our left in the formation; about a 100ft lower and gradually fell back, losing altitude until Charlie Latta, our ball turret operator, said that he had gone into the clouds. He never returned to base and we later learned that they all had to bale out. They all landed safely, but the bombardier, Flight Officer John D. Carson was reported to have been shot by the Germans when they learned that he was a Jew. On this six and a half-hour mission, we were over enemy territory for an hour and five minutes.
>
> "We finally got a pass to get away for a couple of days. We had missed only one day of missions in our absence. On 25 June our group flew two missions, both of which were fairly long.[921] On the morning mission to an airdrome at Toulouse/Francazal one of our B-17s ran out of gas over England. The crew baled out after the pilot headed the big glider, B-17 toward the sea. All the crew landed safely to become new members of the Caterpillar club. In the afternoon the group did bridge busting with mixed results. One group dropped 23 2000lb bombs with only one hitting the bridge, which remained standing. The other group had formation problems as well as personnel problems. The lead bombardier forgot to turn off the salvo switch and when he turned on the internal bomb rack switches, the bombs on his plane dropped at the IP. One other plane immediately dropped his bombs with the leader, but four other planes held on to their bombs, knowing that there was a malfunction. They dropped their eight bombs on a bridge at Sens, France with excellent results."

It was on 25 June that John W. McClane flew his 22nd mission to Amiens, France:

> "We departed Shipdham at 0930 hours and crossed enemy territory between Dunkirk and Ostend. Turning southwest for 85 miles we were at our IP outside of Amiens. The viability was excellent and we had no German fighter opposition. But the flak was very heavy and accurate at the target. We were at 25,000ft and there was no way that Warga could have seen this extremely small target. Flak was going off all around us. Warga aimed the best he could and released our bombs. Of course when our bombs left our plane, the others dropped on our lead. We were carrying 12 500lb bombs. I was looking out of the left bubble window of my navigation compartment as the bombs fell. One of my duties was to wait a few seconds and when I felt the last bomb leave our plane, to reach under my navigation desk with my right hand in order to push a red

salvo handle. The purpose of this was to mechanically release any bombs still hung up in the bomb bay that were not let go by their electrically operated shackles. We always took off with the bomb bay doors open. Water could be splashed onto the latches and would soon freeze as we gained altitude because the temperature was always far below zero. When the bombardier said, 'Bombs Away' I did watch the bombs fall. When I had waited the appropriate time, I bent over to push the salvo handle. Just a split second after I had moved my head from the bubble window a flak shell exploded just outside the left front of our plane. A large jagged hunk of metal tore through the window, passed over my head and neck and then tore a large ragged hole through my wooden navigation desk, splintering it all to pieces. The extremely cold air came rushing through the hole in the Plexiglas (not a scratch was on the metal window frame). This blast of air sucked up my maps and charts, throwing them through the maze of pipes and wires that separated my desk from the pilot and co-pilot's feet then tore them to bits. By the Grace of God I was spared. Had I moved one second later, my whole head would have been torn from by body. I sat up to survey the damage. When I saw I had nothing left with which to navigate, my desk was destroyed and I had been scared out of 10 years of growth, I became so angry that I guess I went into shock.

"The next thing I can remember was looking down at co-pilot 1st Lieutenant. Burr W. Palmer crawling through the tunnel at my left foot that connected the navigator and bombardier area to the flight deck. I watched him plug in his oxygen supply, his earphones and his electric flying suit cord. I wondered what he was doing. About this time Palmer took hold of the clothing on my left leg and shook it, I was sitting down in front of what used to be my desk. He said, 'Mac, are you all right?' I responded, 'Of course I'm all right. What are you doing down here?' Palmer went on to explain that Peritti, realizing we had been damaged badly, was checking out the crew to see if anyone was injured but that I would not respond even after a number of calls. So Peritti decided he had better send Palmer down to take a look being Warga was already back in the nose turret with the doors closed. I have no idea how long it took Peritti to make this decision nor how long it took co-pilot Palmer to disengage all his gear and crawl to my position but I guess it had to have been 6 or 7 minutes.

"We had to give up the lead to our deputy, as I had nothing with which to navigate. Three other planes in our squadron were also damaged by flak but fortunately no one was killed and the 44th lost no planes from any of the three squadrons. We landed back at Shipdham about 1430 hours after five hours of flight time. Yes, our bombs did destroy this Red Cross building. No, we did not hit the *Noball* target. Yes, we did get a poor rating for the day. This was the only mission that I went on that I was too upset to eat any supper. I wanted to believe that I was just plain mad at the AA gunners for what they did but I suspect the truth lies elsewhere."

On 25 June the "Yellowjackets" were also detailed to escort B-17s attacking transportation targets in France. At Bottisham, Lieutenant Vernon Richards in the 374th Squadron was hooked up in the cockpit of his Mustang by his crew chief, Robert Bland. As usual, Richards reached into his inside pocket and took out a combination cigarette case and lighter, removed a cameo ring, and asked if Bland would see to it that they were sent back to his parents if he didn't come back. This ritual had begun early in 1944 when on a particular mission he "expected to see great opposition." Ever since then, whenever great opposition was expected Richards would silently hand Bland his keepsakes. This gesture eventually came to be used to gauge the difficulty of missions by other ground crews. As soon as the P-51s were airborne, they would ask Bland if he had the items in his possession. Fortunately, he never had to follow up on Richards' request.

Lieutenant Colonel Joe Kruzel led the Group to the rendezvous point near Caen when he saw a running dog fight several thousand feet below. Kruzel took the 375th Squadron down from 21,000ft to investigate and encountered P-38s, 109s, 190s, and flak from 5000ft down to the deck. The Mustangs released their external tanks, split into flights, and joined the combat. Kruzel closed to within range of a FW 190 and fired a burst before his electric gun sight failed. He tried using his ring and bead, but in the P-51D it was set too low, and in lining up the ring and bead visibility over the nose of the plane was limited, making low flying on the treetops dangerous. Kruzel, however, stayed with the German through a series of evasive maneuvers, firing bursts from close range. Then the German pilot pulled up into a steep climbing turn and Kruzel was able to score several hits, and the fighter crashed and burned. In all, ten German fighters were claimed without loss during the 15-minute air battle. 2nd Lieutenant Jack S. Crandell claimed two Bf 109s destroyed after becoming separated from his flight.[922] Lieutenant Colonel Roy Webb, leading the 374th Squadron in *Sweet Thing IV*, his recently acquired P-51D, was credited with a FW 190. 2nd Lieutenant Urban L. Drew in the 375th scored the first of his six aerial victories in his tour after his leader, 1st Lieutenant Martin "Johnnie" Johnson, had fired several short bursts before three of his P-51B's four guns jammed. With a few well chosen four letter words Johnson said, "Drew, take it." Closing to 100 yards in each of two passes, Drew riddled the 109, which finally nosed into the ground and exploded. Captain Charles Cummings claimed a Bf 109 while piloting Lieutenant Colonel Thomas J. J. Christian's P-51D *Lou IV/Athlene*.[923] Captain Richard Durbin shot down a Bf 109, which during a four-minute pursuit and subsequent dogfight failed to jettison his belly tank. Captain Hugh D. Chapman also claimed a 109 destroyed, as well as one shared with a 363rd Fighter Group P-51. Finally, Vernon Richards shot down a FW 190 and a Bf 109 in rapid succession.

Edward R. Glotfelty, B-24 pilot 863rd Squadron, 493rd Bomb Group, recalls the 25 June mission to France:

> "After we dropped our bombs we had a runaway prop on [No.2] engine. I tried to feather but was unable to control it. The vibration was tremendous, shaking the whole plane. The noise was deafening. We lost speed and dropped out of the formation. The shortest return route took me over the Normandy beaches. My interest at the time was to hold altitude as much as possible but we were going down because of the great drag on the plane caused by the runaway prop. I started having trouble with the No.4 engine, the rpm surging, engine cutting out and the plane yawing because of the loss of power on the outboard engine. We were now down to 12,000ft and arriving over Normandy. I marveled at the panorama of ships and barrage balloons. With the second engine in trouble I didn't think we could make it back to England and I saw two airfields below me, one obviously new, one-runway fighter strip carved out of the countryside and one paved, mature field that was farther from the beaches. I decided to go down and chose the field closer to the coast. I circled over the field, saw fighters on the strip, guessed at the wind direction and had another engine lose power! We were out of position; no power and dropping like a rock. I ordered wheels up and decided to land on the wide dirt strip alongside of the runway. We hit perfectly. The left wingtip hit [a] second after the fuselage seemed to help cushion the crash. The fuselage split on the right side and the crew was able to get out through the crack. No one was injured, though Gene Croiner, the engineer, had some radio equipment fall on him. The force of the landing was so great that the No.1 engine was torn off completely

and the plane was a totally destroyed. The last I saw of the plane, a large crane was trying to drag the wreck out of the way so they could continue the war!

"We were checked out by a Canadian doctor, loaded on a truck going to the beach, put on a British LST and by the next day [were] back in England. The funny thing was that the only clothes we had were electric-heated flying suits. We spent the night in London and were treated like Poles or some foreign air force."

The next day, 26 June, the mission to the Munich area was scrubbed because of bad weather. The mission on 28 June to the Juvincourt airfield near Reims was Dick Johnson's first in four days:

"Beiser had just been promoted to 1st Lieutenant and we were in the *'Buzz Blond'* again. The mission was destined to be very rough on me. My diary for that day tells it all on one little bomb tag: 'Reims, France airfield south (Juvincourt) CAVU. Caught every flak gun in France. Led high squadron. Lost our left wing man who went down in flames (Lieutenant Wardowski)...Weather so bad on return we had to land at coast at B-24 base. 5 hours. Over enemy territory, two hours. Carried 38 X 100lb GP purpose bombs.' It was a bad day for me; having lost several new friends who had slept near my bunk in the 427th Officer's barracks.[924]

"I flew my 24th mission on 29 June; my last as co-pilot and it was a bad one. My diary for this day reads: 'Leipzig, Germany (Hot place) Aircraft plant for Me 109s. Flak was intense, accurate. Lost another wingman (Lieutenant Roy). Direct burst broke him in two at waist. No one was seen to get out. Saw other planes go down. Some in flames. No more like this for me, thanks.'

"Our 303rd Bomb Group furnished 36 planes for this mission, including a spare and one PFF plane from the 305th Bomb Group.[925] Our group started with 19 planes but we were down to 15 before we even got into enemy territory. As we approached the IP the message for visual bombing was received and we started taking interval for group bombing. It was about this time that a direct burst of flak tore 2nd Lieutenant Arnold K. Roy's *'My Yorkshire Dream'* in half at the waist. We saw no parachutes. Roy's crew were on about their sixth mission.[926] In two days, there were eight empty bunks in our barracks. This is what really brings it home to you. In the combat area when a plane went down, my reaction was, 'Thank God I wasn't over there.' It was later that it hit you that they were truly gone. After this past disastrous mission I finally got a three-day pass before going for check out in the left seat. A couple of us went to London to see the sights and took a bus to Trafalgar Square and then off to Piccadilly Circus. We went to a stage show just off the main square and afterwards we went into a small pub."

During the shuttle force's absence combat tours were raised from 30 to 35 missions. Headquarters also announced that deep penetration missions would rank equally with the short-haul raids in the table of missions per tour. Eventually, a fairer method was evolved when headquarters took into account the greater risks involved in flying deep into Germany. One of the more immediate ways of shortening a tour and earning a 30-day rest and recuperation leave was to "volunteer" for a second tour. On Tuesday, 11 July, Abe Dolim and the rest of his crew at Bury St. Edmunds were among many who were approached. Dolim had recently spent a week's "flak leave" at Aylesfield House and elected to take the 30 days' R&R and return to fly combat:

"To refuse meant flying eight more missions and I'd had my fill. My home was in Honolulu, Hawaii and I calculated what with slow convoys and Patton on his way to Paris, the war in Europe might be over before I had to return."[927]

Everyone was looking forward more in hope than anything else to the end of the war so that they could go home. Solon "Billy" Elliott, a radio-operator in the 491st Bomb Group, had written a letter to his aunt on 1 July saying that:

"After this war, I am going to spend the rest of my life resting. Remember how lazy we used to be - well, you haven't seen nothing yet."

Billy was a cousin of Ben Smith at Molesworth: "We had grown up together, lived across the street from each other when small, and later attended high school together." Late in July Ben Smith received a letter from his mother to say that "Billy had been killed on 13 July in a crash landing of a B-24."[928]

For all intents and purposes, the *Luftwaffe* failed to make any serious attempt in the first few days of July to challenge the awesome number of B-24s and B-17s being hurled against them. But finally on 7 July, when over 1000 heavy bombers attacked three synthetic oil plants, eight aircraft assembly plants, and engine works and other targets, *Sturmgruppe* JG 3 led by Wilhelm Moritz in the Leipzig area viciously attacked the 2nd Division B-24 Liberators again. For the second time the 492nd Bomb Group suffered severely, losing eleven of the 37 heavies lost that day.

On Wednesday, 12 July, John W. McClane flew his 23rd mission to Munich:

"We were assigned the deepest penetration of Hitler's Fortress Europe that our crew was ever to fly. The Group had gone to Munich the day before with the loss of one plane but the bombing results were so poor that the 8th Air Force was returned for a second try. Our target was the marshaling yards. Cloud cover the day before and again today was so complete that PFF led the group this time. We flew in three squadrons of 12 planes each carrying 6 500lb bombs and 4 500lb incendiary clusters. Take off was at 0900 hours. From the time we broke above the clouds over East Anglia until we returned, I never saw the ground again. Once above the clouds, there was a level layer of the most beautiful white clouds I'd ever seen. They were at perhaps 10,000ft where as we flew most of the way at 24,500. I had never seen such a solid flat 10/10ths cloud cover.

"The 44th Bomb Group was under the orders of Major Robert J. Lehnhausen as Command Pilot and we were deputy lead for the 68th Squadron.[929] I often pinpointed my position by observing the flak barrage thrown up by the enemy over the various cities as we passed by. It was a very unusual sight to see the beautiful white blanket of clouds with the sun shinning on then so brightly but with splashes of black flak smoke hanging in little balls above them. I don't know what the AA gunners thought they were shooting at, as our armada was often miles away. Maybe they were just frustrated and it made the population feel better. At any rate it was easy for me to know where their city was, as I certainly could not see it or anything else on the ground.

"Another beautiful sight was to watch the various Combat Wings (usually made up of three Bomb Groups) flying behind or in front of our position in the Bomber Stream. Sometimes they would be off to the side below us and we could look down to see dozens of four motor bombers flying in formation. But the planes of our own 68th Squadron as well as those of the other two nearby squadrons were the most fascinating to watch. Coming off of the wings of each plane was a set of snowy white, ribbon like streams of contrails (cloud like condensations due to the lift of the wing creating a rapid vacuum). I can't describe the grandeur of it all. The sight was breathtaking. It was difficult to realize we were at war except for the black flak. The Luftwaffe was absent. I saw no enemy planes the entire day even though we went the greatest distance over Germany and 50 miles further than Berlin from our base at Shipdham.

"It was the middle of the afternoon when our Group reached the IP to start our bomb run. Ahead of us lay Munich, hidden under a thick layer of clouds but we knew it was there as a tremendous flak barrage, with the typical black puffs of smoke, were everywhere. We were lucky, they could not see us from the ground and we had blinded their radar with our *Chaff.* I never became concerned about flak unless it was at our altitude. Today it was too low; not one shell came near enough to punch a hole in our fuselage for which we were mighty thankful. Flak could be much worse that enemy fighters and we all dreaded it.

"Warga released our bombs when the PFF lead radar bombardier dropped his. There was no way for us to judge where our bombs landed but we later found out that they hit right on target. Our H_2X radar proved itself on this day. We had another first on this mission to Munich. As we were passing over the city, we sighted B-24s of the 15th Air Force that had come up from Italy to join in the destruction. I don't know why but at the time two different air forces meeting over one German city sent a thrill all through me. I liked what I had just witnessed.

"The flight home was uneventful as the Luftwaffe refused to come up to meet us. I really had expected them to put on a show of force but it never materialized. I at least had something interesting to do being a navigator but almost 7 out of the 9 hours that this flight took; our gunners had to be on constant alert for any sudden attack. When it was all over, the gunners had an anticlimax let down. Again the beauty of the flight back to base at times mesmerized me. I wanted to forget the war. We arrived over our field about 1800 hours and spiraled through the overcast once more to be in touch with the real world."

At Rattlesden, Lieutenant Ernest "Bob" Rhode and his crew in the 709th Bomb Squadron, 447th Bomb Group considered themselves lucky enough to take part in one of the four missions to supply the French *Maquis* through the low-level dropping of supplies and arms. Alan S. Cook, co-pilot, recalls that:

> "Rhode, besides being a crack pilot selected for lead pilot crew training, had also been given probably the best navigator in the Group. Both the squadron and group navigators had recognized Lieutenant John Stockham's talents and Bob and John accordingly made a great team. In addition we were lucky to have Gordon Serrott as bombardier. We would have put money on him over any other bombardier in the Group. Gordon was a guy who enjoyed success because he knew how to relax and enjoy life without any real need for tobacco or alcohol and his second great skill was playing poker. We never saw Gordon miss a target or lose at poker!"

On 14 July (Bastille Day) Major Ed McRay led the 447th Bomb Group and the 4th Combat Wing on a supply mission code-named *Cadillac* to "Area 9" near Limoges, in the Charolles Mountains in the Savoy region, where the 8th had made its first drop only three weeks before. The *Maquis* had since gained control of an area 100 miles square; the equivalent of an entire French Department. They had succeeded in keeping the Limoges-Orleans railway closed since D-Day, and had been extremely successful in cutting communications. Now they needed replacement arms and ammunition to continue the fight. At the drop-zone Bob Rhode flew so close to the ground that the crew could wave at the men and women as they rushed from their hiding places in the woods and out onto the smoke-marked fields to gather the supply canisters. Gordon Serrott had a scare when one of the canisters "hung up" in the bomb bay. He tried to release it manually, but its parachute opened and was blown into the radio compartment, engulfing Sgt "Moose" Schwegel. Gordon quickly cut the shroud lines by leaning out from the catwalk while "Moose" opened his compartment hatch and pushed the parachute out into the slipstream. On the ground the women gathered in the nylon parachute, obviously intent on turning the material into clothing, such as lingerie!

The 14 July mission lasted 9 hours and 15 minutes, and fuel was critical. Since Rhode's B-17 was flying the "Tail end Charlie" slot they had much greater fuel consumption, and landed back at Rattlesden on only the vapor from the 100 Octane gas. Flying his first supply drop this day was Bob Maag, pilot of *Skinny*, in the 94th Bomb Group:

> "Our 18-plane formation split into three-plane elements to make the drop. The drop site was located in a valley at Valance and we took the big birds down to 3000ft. The guns, ammo, medical supplies and other essentials for guerrilla strikes, were packed into parachute canisters. As the 'chutes floated down we could see figures, pulling two-wheeled carts, dart out of the woods, retrieve the canisters and scurry back to cover. As we came out of the valley we were so low that I had to lift my left wingtip to clear the trees. My navigator pointed out Lake Geneva to us. The large body of water looked beautiful from the air. The mission was an enjoyable experience, made even better by the fact that we encountered no enemy action. However, not all missions that summer were as enjoyable. That familiar phrase, 'sweating it out' was no idle collection of words. When I was flying combat in the summer of '44 I literally had grainy salt deposits on the outside of my thick leather GI shoes! I'm not ashamed to admit that I was sweating every minute we were over enemy territory! When the flak bursts were thickest and closest I'd sing 'Home on the range' over the intercom (probably off key!) to relieve the tension."

Also during July the 8th flew missions to Germany in search of oil and other strategic targets in an ever-diminishing Reich. On 7 July Nick G. Plackis in the 390th Bomb Group flew his first deep penetration after making a few short haul sorties that proved to be milk runs, giving the crew the false impression that combat flying was a "piece of cake." But that was to change quickly on 7 July when they were exposed to their first "blood-bath" before ever getting near the target at Merseburg. Plackis says:

> "We had just crossed the English Channel and still over the Zuider Zee above Holland when our two wingmen on the right collided due to propwash turbulence while tightening up our formation, one directly on top of the other. It was like a slow motion movie. When the upper '17930 descended into the wings of the lower

one,[931] its props chewed into the aluminum while the lower '17's props were disintegrating the belly of the upper one. Gasoline was spewing everywhere and immediately ignited both aircraft into bright orange flaming torches. The No.2 prop of the upper plane broke off cleanly at the shaft in one piece and as it came off, it laid flat on the top of the wing as it slowly slid off into space. We watched in horror, as both flaming B-17s gently peeled off to the right, together, prior to going into a joined spin. We counted five chutes before both planes' separated. The lower one exploded in a tremendous blast with a full load of bombs, maximum long haul fuel and ten crew. The other Fortress blew up a short distance from the first, but we heard that some of the crew who baled out were captured and became PoWs."

Lieutenant Leo C. Riley, co-piloting a B-17 in the 94th Bomb Group, saw the two ships go down in flames over the Zuider Zee. He wrote:

"Such is fate again. Six chutes came clear, but 14 men burned to death. It all happened directly in front of us and we had to dodge the pieces to keep from getting hit."[932]

Nick G. Plackis again:

"As rough as the rest of the mission was, with fighters and flak, it all seemed anti-climatic after seeing our friends going down in flames. Though, as young and as impressionable as we were, our somewhat reckless and adventurous resilient spirit recovered us from this setback, anxiously giving us an optimistic attitude to eagerly look forward to boarding our Fortress for each subsequent mission and reaching our ultimate goal of 30."

For three successive days beginning 11 July, the heavies blasted industrial sections of Munich. The Bavarian city was important to the Germans at this stage of the war because the aircraft engineers and designers were building new weapons for the final aerial battles between the *Luftwaffe* and the Allied air forces. Jet aircraft and experimental works dotted the vicinity of Munich. The hub of the complex was the massive Allach aero engine works which, with assembly plants and *Luftwaffe* airfields close by, made Munich a top priority target. The Thursday, 13 July, mission to Munich was Wilbur Richardson's—and some of the rest of the crew of *Kismet* in the 94th—30th and final mission of their tour. Wilbur Richardson remembers the mission well:

"No. 30 would be remembered for just that, no matter what. Mine, again just a bit different. I was seriously wounded over the target by 155mm flak. There was one very small hole in the wing and a very large one in my turret and me. Just the two. *Kismet* - fate. I stayed in the turret to count the bombs away. I thought I could stick it out longer but I was losing too much blood. I reported to the pilot and he said to get out and the waist gunner could take my place as bandits were reported in the area. The radio operator, Bernard Jeffers and the right waist, Milo Johnson, stripped off my flight clothes and new pants and shirt I had just purchased. I was treated and placed in a survival electric blanket bag. A short time later fighters hit us. I jumped up at the sound of shooting and grabbed the radio gun. I didn't have any intercom so I wasn't sure what the action was. I saw only one that I could shoot at from that position. After a bit I realized I had nothing but a T-shirt and shorts on and I was getting awfully cold so I hit the blanket to get warm. It was three and-a-half hours back to the base and I was still losing precious blood. We left the formation to get back to base as soon as possible. Another ship joined us as a waist gunner had an arm wound. Upon landing I was strapped on a stretcher, placed in an ambulance for a ride to an Army hospital. I didn't get back to the base for over five weeks. A nurse tossed away the large piece of flak that hit me."[933]

Lieutenant Leo C. Riley, the co-pilot, wrote:

"Today has been quite a trying day for us. Briefed early to hit Munich. In three days over 3000 heavies have loosed their bombs on the fourth largest city in Germany and the House of Nazidom. Flak was heavy and intense. We were hit over the target. Richardson in the ball turret was hit badly in the leg by a piece of flak. Can't tell just how bad he is yet. The boy suffered immense pain as we were about three hours covering back and he lost quite a bit of blood. Just after the target, enemy fighters hit us, but God rode with us again and we did not get hit."[934]

On the 16 July mission to Munich, the 1st Scouting Force of Mustangs and Mosquitoes, developed and led by 42-year-old Colonel Budd J. Peaslee, was used for the first time. Peaslee's scouting force flew just ahead of the main bombing force, transmitting up-to-the-minute weather reports back to the task force commander to prevent him leading his bombers into heavy weather fronts that could disrupt the mission and, in some instances, lead to its cancellation.

On 17 July Dick Johnson flew his first mission as first pilot and a new crew on their first mission when the target was a railroad bridge at St. Quentin, France:

"1st Lieutenant H. C. Clark was the first new combat pilot to benefit from my status as a veteran combat pilot. His co-pilot, 2nd Lieutenant G. P. Vesy was left behind while I trained Clark in the fine art of forming up into a combat group and wing. The rest of Clark's crew was with me in 43-37666, a new B-17 named '*Full House*.' (Three sixes and two threes).[935] Each plane was carrying two, one ton bombs under the belly of our plane, as were all the others in our group. Our group dropped 71 of these big bombs aimed at a bridge near Peronne. One bomb from the plane I was flying refused to release and so we brought it back to base. It was just as well, since the other 71 bombs missed the bridge despite clear weather. Clark asked if it would be noticeable to land with two 1000lbs off to one side and I told him that they were so close to the center that they would never notice it if one was missing. You might notice it if it decided to release at touch down, however nothing happened."[936]

Peaslee's weather scouts again proved effective on the 18 July mission to the principal German research and development center at Peenemünde, on the Baltic coast, where German scientists were trying to create the atomic bomb.[937] The MPI was well covered with bomb hits, and smoke was reported rising to 12,000ft. The bomb pattern brought acclaim from General Spaatz, among others, who described it as, "one of the finest examples of precision bombing I have seen." General Williams added, "On this vital operation the 1st Division again demonstrated its ability to destroy the assigned objective regardless of its location or enemy opposition." Peenemünde was the furthest penetration into northeast Germany, and it was not until after the war that its importance was fully realized.[938]

Meanwhile, in France missions in support of the British and Canadian ground troops fighting near Caen were flown, as John W. McClane recalls:

"Caen is a town nine miles in from the English Channel and 32 miles southwest of Le Havre. On this effort we used 644 2nd and 3rd Division B-24s. The purpose of this mission was to blast a hole in the German front lines with a large scale tactical bombing, 300 yards, in front of the British and Canadian positions. Our bomb load was fragmentation bombs to kill enemy troops, not dig holes. After the bombing and before the Germans could recover, the British were to launch a large scale offensive trying for a major breakthrough. This had to be a visual bombing. Our specific drop zone was east of Caen by about ten miles called Troarns. It was carried out by 139 of our aircraft. The 44th Bomb Group supplied 38 of this number of which 13 were by my 68th Squadron. General Leon Johnson led the 14th Combat Wing consisting of the 44th, 392nd and 492nd Bomb Groups. The visibility at the target area was excellent, the flak intense. Our bombs landed exactly in the prescribed area as my strike photo indicated but in spite of this intense accurate tactical support bombing, the Wehrmacht's resistance was too great. The British and Canadians did cross the River Orne with some tanks and got onto more open land but the break out of the Allied Forces in Normandy did not materialize. There was no serious damage to any of the 44th Bomb Group planes nor any other of our Combat Wing. However one plane that went over our drop zone was shot down. After flying for 5 hours, we landed near lunchtime. Needless to say, we were all disappointed with the outcome of this battle."

On 20 July the 8th went to Leipzig. For Ben Smith in the 303rd Bomb Group, it was one of a series of missions into Germany that included Berlin and Dessau. He did was not able to recall much of the first two, but he has vivid recall of the "Leipzig affair," primarily because he was able to see more of what was going on:

"than I ever had before. At my station there was less visibility than anywhere else in the airplane but this time I stood up and watched. This was one of the big extravaganzas, where there was a maximum commitment on both sides: Total Armageddon. Over the target the sky looked like some surrealistic painting by Hieronymous Bosch. There was a pall of smoke as thick as a forest fire. With all the firing that was going on, it looked like the lights on the Los Angeles Freeway. Trailing long plumes of smoke, planes were falling, bombers and fighters alike. Parachutes dotted the weird landscape like random wildflowers.

"Once we got a frontal attack and an FW 190 came between us and the plane next to us, firing and rolling as he came. I got off a few bursts at him. I was firing point blank, I thought, but he kept going. The flak was unbelievable, barrage flak from one end of the sky to the other. Once we lurched sharply and I thought we had taken a direct hit. We had, but the shell failed to explode. It passed through our port wing, leaving a hole about two feet in diameter. Most of us didn't know about it until we got back. Dogfights were going on between our escort and their fighters among the bomber formations. The tail gunner and ball-turret gunner, having the best vantage points, kept calling out at intervals the falling aircraft, friend and foe. There was not even a brief lull in the fighting, not a single instant when some aircraft was not departing the conflict in flames. To make it an authentic Wagnerian apocalypse, the lurid sky-scape was lit up ever so often by spectacular rocket explosions. I couldn't see where they were coming from. Sometimes they were fired from the ground, but more often twin-engined German fighters launched these at the formations from a distance. Suddenly as I gazed out on this, a feeling of exaltation swept over me. It was magnificent. I had the sudden revelation: this would not be happening if men didn't love it. I realized there was a part of me that responded to this holocaust. It was the warrior instinct pure and simple. My battle blood was up. It is difficult to understand the paradox of men who are prouder than anything else of having participated in a pageant of total destruction such as this. I was no different - I was prouder of this than anything I ever did. Could it be that those who say 'Man is essentially a warrior-predator' are entirely correct?"

During July the 8th flew seven tactical missions in support of the Allied armies in northern France. On Monday, 24 July, Operation *Cobra* was scheduled to penetrate German defenses west of St. Lô and secure Coutances, but bad weather prevented all but 352 of the 1586 bombers from bombing the primary for fear of hitting their own troops. The 379th Bomb Group made three runs over the target before it found a gap in the clouds to bomb through. Accuracy was essential, and many bombers returned with their bomb loads intact, rather than risk dropping them on their own troops, as John W. McClane recalls:

"The mission of 24 July was a complete flop as to its intended purpose. It was to be a repeat of our effort at Caen on the 18th except at St. Lô, 34 miles west of Caen and with a much larger number of planes. We were to drop in advance of the US 1st Army in a carpet bombing tactical attack. 1586 B-24s and B-17s were dispatched of which 37 were from our 44th Bomb Group. Take off was early and we reached the drop zone in mid-morning. This type of tactical bombing, being only a few hundred yards in front of our own ground troops required absolutely clear visibility of the drop area. This was not in the cards for today as there was 10/10 cloud cover over the target area. Under no circumstance were we to drop our bombs under these conditions so we took our flak bursts and returned to base. For the 44th, it was a very uneventful day but little did we know what was in store for us tomorrow. This day affected the Germans very little but two mishaps turned this abortive mission into disaster for some of our own ground personnel. The first was an accidental tripping of the bomb release switch by a B-24 bombardier. When a large quantity of *Chaff* being thrown out by a forward plane hit his compartment, it startled him. His bombs fell on one of our own landing strips killing four men and wounding 14 others. In addition he destroyed two P-47 Thunderbolt fighters. The second unfortunate happening was even more disastrous. Another bombardier who was leading his squadron was trying to free a faulty release mechanism, which in turn salvoed his bombs accidentally. When they left the bomb bay, it was a signal for 12 following planes to drop their bombs, which they did. This incident killed 16 of our ground troops and wounded 60 more. After 5 hours and 45 minutes, we landed at Shipdham unaware of these tragic mistakes.

"An even worse accidental bombing of our own troops occurred the following day when we returned. It had been one week since our ineffectual carpet bombing in front of the British and Canadian troops at Caen. Only 24 hours had passed since our 'dry run' over the same target we were assigned to bomb today. This was to be a massive tactical carpet bombing in support of our armies fighting in the St. Lô area. Since the invasion six weeks before, our ground forces had not been strong enough to break out of the small beachhead area roughly extending from Caen on the east to St. Lô on the west and only 15 to 20 miles inland from the English Channel. General Eisenhower decided the time had come to make a major 'breakout' effort. He ordered the 8th Air Force to bomb just in front of his 1st and 3rd Armies.

"The weather had cleared considerably since the abortive attempt the day before. An even greater force of heavy bombers than before were scheduled for this mission. There would be 850 B-17 Flying Fortresses and 650 B-24 Liberators (1503 in all) carrying 3400 tons of bombs, destroying the enemy's ability to fight before this day was over. As lead navigator for the 68th squadron of this mission, I went too early briefing to prepare for this critical flight. After breakfast, all flying personnel assembled for the main briefing. We were instructed in great detail, as our target area was [the Marigny-St. Gilles region] a small rectangular section behind a road leading north and west from the city of St. Lô. The order to the pilots and bombardiers was to fly as low as necessary to keep below the clouds. This had to be a visual bombing as the target area was only a few hundred yards in advance of our troops who had pulled back behind this road. We were told to look for red smoke artillery shells to be fired by our forces into the drop zone.

"Our plane, '*Lili Marlene*', was the lead plane for the 68th Squadron. We had a Command Pilot on board as well as our own pilot and crew. All went well in the assembly and the flight to the English coast near Brighton south of London. There is approximately 100 miles of open water over the English Channel at this point to the French coast north of St. Lô and another 20 miles over land to St. Lô. The 2nd Air Division was leading the 8th Air Force, the 14th Combat Wing was leading the 2nd Division, the 44th Bomb Group was leading the Combat Wing and the 67th Squadron was leading the group. Our 68th Squadron of 12 ships was behind and to the right of the 67th. After we had broken the English coast and flown some distance over the Channel I became concerned, as I knew we were off course to reach out target and so advised the Command Pilot and Captain Peritti. It was an unforgivable sin to break formation, as this was part of our protection from enemy fighters but time and distance were running out the further we went. Everything depended upon the proper approach on the bomb run. Being a typical hypertensive navigator type, I began to stress over and over that we had to alter course if we were to reach the IP. I really do not know what I said or how I said it but my concern must have been convincing. I can only imagine the anguish the Command Pilot and my pilot must have gone through in wanting to keep formation on the one hand and my urging them to correct course on the other. It seemed like an eternity to me but finally I was asked for a new heading. I directed a change of about 20° to the right.

"After the change in flight direction, we began to pull away from the lead formation. They continued straight while we moved off to their right. After a few minutes it was obvious to anyone in either squadron that we would soon be far apart. What was going through the mind of the Lead Command Pilot and the lead navigator, I do not know. There must have been some soul searching. As for me, I was almost sick from concern that I had possibly made a mistake and had talked my pilot into committing an unforgivable disobedience of standing orders.

"The 68th Squadron kept to my course. The closer we got to the French coast, the more I realized my navigation was accurate. In the meantime, the lead squadron had pulled far off to our left but suddenly they realized the error in their course and made a large correction to parallel ours. Now the 68th Squadron was in the lead with the former lead behind us and to our left. We were now the lead for the entire 8th Air Force and naturally this would put us over the drop zone first.

"Now we had a new problem, the clouds were getting lower. Due to our orders to bomb visually Warga requested we follow the clouds down which we did. This put us at 14,000ft by the time we reached the drop zone. All hell broke loose. Every anti-aircraft gun the Germans could muster that could reach our low altitude was concentrated on us. Peritti had turned control of the plane over to Warga's bombsight. We had to fly straight and level. I pointed out to Warga the road from St. Lô and the red smoke shells, which were clearly visible. Like all bombardiers, he had nerves of iron, never became excited and had an excellent rating on most bombings. Today was no exception. I watched the bombs land squarely on target.

"Our job was done. Peritti now put the squadron into violent evasive action. Even over Berlin, the flak was neither as concentrated nor as intense as we were going through. Holes were being ripped through us at every explosion. I gave the order to correct course to the right and just as we made the turn and straightened out, a flak shell exploded directly under us. The concussion suddenly lifted '*Lili Marlene*' at least 20ft and just as quickly, we began to fall. I was thrown to the floor of my navigation compartment. Under my desk was a lever that opened the nose wheel doors, which was my escape hatch. I was not waiting around to assess the damage. I thought we had lost a wing and a combat flyer only has to see this happen to a nearby plane once to know there is no escape due to centrifugal force once the plane begins to spin and tumble. (This type of fear accounted for frequent premature bale-outs). I had my hand on the lever ready to jump. I did not take the time to disconnect my electric flying suit, the oxygen supply nor ear phone plug. Just as I was ready to go I heard Peritti say, 'Stay on board; the plane is still flying.' I stood up. We were still on the westerly course and beginning to leave the flak area. Our plane had been severely damaged. The flak shell had exploded directly under us spewing out steel in a cone shape. We had caught the concussion in the center of the cone and received over 400 flak holes from this shell and the AA barrage. We knew our two wingmen were hurt badly also but only after we landed did we know that the plane on the left of us had 600 holes and our deputy on the right had almost 1000. Believe it or not, not a man in any of the three aircraft received a scratch.

"Resuming my navigation duties, at the appropriate place, I ordered a turn to the right, which would put us on a northerly course up the Cherbourg Peninsula. At this point, something happened that I did not understand. Instead of turning as directed, Peritti asked, 'Mac, are you sure you want me to turn to the right?' Never had he ever questioned my navigation before. I was mystified and told him, 'Yes, turn as directed.' Peritti came back, 'But I see the English Channel ahead. We will fly back into the combat zone again.' I looked out. Sure enough there was water ahead but to my amusement it was the Atlantic and not the Channel. After assuring my pilot that it would take several minutes of flying up the peninsula before we could see the Channel, he made the turn to the right.

"Now we were flying north and could look to our right, easily seeing back into the battle area. There was a tremendous billow of dust up to several thousand feet being blown back over the American front lines by a south wind. I did not get the significance of this terrible turn of events until after we had landed. Our planes were loaded with 100lb fragmentation bombs set to explode on contact; the purpose being to kill enemy personnel, not to dig big holes that our tanks could not get past. This was the reason for this huge volume of dust being churned up.

"About this time I looked at the planes in the bomber stream when suddenly, one of the aircraft exploded falling into a nearby plane and into one or two more. It appeared that four planes came burning and exploding all at once in a jumble of wreckage falling through the sky. It looked terrible."

The two B-24s (*Miss Shirley* and 42-95026), both in the 567th Squadron, 389th Bomb Group, went down. S/Sgt Robert H. "Bob" Sherwood, the top turret gunner on *The Little Gramper*, saw the one above catch fire and pull up into a stall:

"The torching aircraft steepened her dive and slow-rolled to the right, just missing *Gramper*. Four men came out of the bomb bay and waist hatch. Then there was a pause. The next man jumped but opened his chute too soon. The blow torch flame kissed the nylon canopy for an instant and the parachute collapsed. The airman went into a clawing frenzy, his arms and legs thrashing, trying to gain purchase in the thin air. The plane stalled again and spun towards France. No one got out after that.[939] *The Little Gramper* was hit in the bomb bay by flak at the target. There was a hole in the wing between No.2 and No.3 engines. They missed the fuel tanks so it was not critical but the whole formation was busted open. As we dodged around the sky flying a constantly changing course *Gramper* groaned like an old horse."

John W. McClane continues:

"Finally we left the area and the English Channel did come into view. Needless to say, we were badly shaken up. We knew our plane had been severely damaged. There were holes all through my navigation compartment. I could see daylight through the fuselage as if it were a sieve. But thanks to the Grace of God, all our planes were flying and no one killed in our squadron. The 68th Squadron had paid the price for having taken the lead, 10 out of our 12 ships were damaged. As so often happened, the excitement of the battle caused me to perspire so greatly that the sweat run from under my helmet and froze into ice cakes on my forehead. We had about two hours of flying to return back to base. Our course took us around the city of London and we had time to think about the mission. a great concern gripped me. What was going to happen when we landed and were made to account for leaving the formation over the Channel?

"We reached our base and landed after 5 hours and 30 minutes in the air. Peritti was instructed to pull up in front of Group Headquarters rather than go to our usual hardstand. When I lowered myself out of the plane and looked up, the first thing I saw was Colonel John Gibson, Commanding Officer of the 44th Bomb Group. My heart sank. I could see a very serious look on his face. He stepped out of his Jeep and looked straight at us. With a wide rapid motion of his right hand starting at knee level swinging up over the top of his head, he demanded in a loud voice, 'YOU FOLLOW ME'. He also ordered that the camera be taken out of our plane and the pictures be developed at once.

"Needless to say, we did follow Colonel Gibson into the debriefing room. He spread a map in front of him and pointing to me said, 'WHERE WERE YOU?' In a stammering voice filled with trepidation, I began by explaining what had happened over the Channel and why we had changed course away from the lead squadron. Suddenly I was greatly relieved because Colonel Gibson said to forget about what happened on the way over the Channel. He wanted to know where we had dropped our bombs. All this time I thought we were in big trouble for having left the formation and now he did not give a hoot about that. I knew exactly where Warga had dropped our squadron bombs and pointed out the spot on the map, as did Warga. Intelligence came up with the pictures taken from our plane. They had even penciled lines over our designated strike area and almost every bomb was inside the lines. At this point Colonel Gibson's whole personality changed back to the usual good natured and likeable person he was. A smile broke over his face from ear to ear. The 44th was not at fault for a grievous error, word had filtered back that bombs had fallen short of the drop zone, crossing the road coming out of St. Lô and into the American lines, killing many of our men. Later I was told it was 260 men including General McNair.[940] Ours were the first bombs to drop so the target area was very visible. But the Groups following us could see nothing through the dense dust and dropped their bombs into the cloud until corrected by P-51s flying to indicate the correct drop area. History records that the Allied forces did break out of the beachhead as a result of this bombing. It was the greatest tactical bombing of the war."[941]

18

Battles of the Bridgehead and Beyond

"The plane blew to bits. The motors were torn from the wings and went tumbling through the sky with their props windmilling...The wings and the fuselage and the tail were torn to shreds. As the pieces of aluminum drifted and twisted while they fell, with each turn, the sun would be reflected off their surface back into my eyes as if they were mirrors. It was like watching a thousand suns turn on and off in a rapid random fashion. But the most spectacular sight was the gas tanks, which had been torn from the wings. They did not explode their gasoline but rather it burned in huge orange flames streaming out behind the tanks as they fell in a wavy fashion towards the earth below."

Lieutenant John W. McClane, navigator, 44th Bomb Group

On 28 July, 653 B-17s bombed the synthetic oil plant at Merseburg, while 57 others bombed Wiesbaden marshaling yards and an aircraft engine factory at Taucha. They were supported by 437 fighters, which later broke away to strafe ground targets. Seven B-17s and two P-51s were lost.[942] A. J. Sinibubb, navigator in Lieutenant Pullen's crew in the 323rd Bomb Squadron, 91st Bomb Group, which flew deputy lead, low squadron to Merseburg, was flying his 15th mission. Sinibubb wrote:

"Bomb load 10 500lb demolition. Route Base-Ampthill-St. Albans-Sp#7-Orfordness. Weather was poor, 8-9/10 coverage. On bomb run "Micky" operator screwed up. I missed target. (Light flak over actual target). We ran right into Leipzig and all hell broke loose. Flak bursts were so close that we could see the flash as they exploded. Six out of the 12 ships in our squadron came back on three engines. Our oxygen was shot out on the right side. (When we landed we found "fist" sized holes in #3 and 4 engines. Why they didn't go out on us I still don't know. They had to be taken off). Our regular toggelier was flying with another crew as we flew deputy and he was hit in the arm, flesh wound just below elbow. On the turn off from the target we ran into an experimental flak station and those Jerries really know how to shoot."

Dick Johnson, in the 303rd Bomb Group, flew his 26th mission to Merseburg:

"This mission would take us deep into Germany to the Leuna oil works where enemy resistance was always encountered. My second new crew was going with me in the B-17 named '*Betty Jane*' that I had flown several times before, including the glide bomb attack on Cologne. My new co-pilot for the day was J. A. Drewry with all his crew, except his co-pilot who was flying with yet another experienced pilot. This morning the 303rd Bomb Group put up 37 aircraft, taking off between the hours of 0550 and 0619 to make assembly over the Harrington Buncher at 9000ft. Each B-17 was carrying ten 500lb bombs. During assembly my aircraft was approached by another B-17, which caused me to fly a 360° turn to stay out of his way. By the time I returned to the assembly area the 303rd Group was too far ahead for me to catch up so I latched onto the 379th out of Kimbolton, which I knew, was going to the same target. Many pilots aborted when they couldn't find their group and I didn't want this stigma attached to me. Had I not known the destination of the 379th, I would have had no choice but to abort. During the mission the 303rd saw no enemy fighters but the 379th that I was flying with encountered a few. Our top turret gunner, Sgt E. H. Koch fired at a FW 190 that seemed to be trying to drag a bomb on a long wire through our formation. That bomb didn't explode and Koch didn't seem to hit the FW 190 who was about 3000ft above us flying in the same direction. The fighters were not pressing any attacks for some reason not clear to me since there were no P-51s in the immediate area. We encountered flak at seven different locations on this mission but the '*Betty Jane*' only suffered two minor wounds for this trip. We had been discharging *Chaff* to foil the German radar and it seemed to do some good. The target was overcast, so the German gunners could not sight visually, nor could we bomb visually. Most of the heavy concentration of flak seemed to always be behind us. Evidently we didn't do such a good job on the synthetic oil plant, as we later learned that we would go back tomorrow. Our flight time was 8 hours and 10 minutes, with 4 hours and 20 minutes over enemy territory."

Lieutenant George P. Fory, a pilot in the 100th Bomb Group, had his introduction to the Leuna flak on 28 July:

"Many times I had expressed that flak-wise, Merseburg was worse than Berlin. I suppose the worst condition for comparison was Berlin. There the flak was in curtains and of a barrage type where an area was filled with it, but Merseburg flak was mostly tracking type and always four bursts at a time. There was tracking type at Berlin too, but it wasn't so noticeable with all the other. The flak would come up in four bursts, generally 50-75 yards apart and usually staggered in elevation. If you saw three bursts, you wondered if you were in the fourth. The worst part of being in the lead was waiting for the flak to start. On one occasion we were in the lead and had passed the 'three minutes to go' point and no flak. About the time I asked the bombardier, 'Where's the flak?' A great big black, brown burst, seemingly big as the airplane, went off directly ahead of us on our level and immediately we were in it. For an instant I was in a pure 'puckering' state, as were the other crew who saw it Merseburg flak was brownish-black. Berlin flak was black. Munich flak was mixed brownish and pinkish centers. That was the way it looked to me anyway. The 28 July mission did not give me anything unusual to go on. I did not see any ships go down. Maybe I just didn't see them, or I was too busy. However, I saw black oily smoke above the undercast and by the time we passed the rally point it must have been at 20,000ft so I had assumed that we had hit it hard, but again, we went the next day."

Command Pilot Captain Herbert Howard, who flew with Lieutenant Austin Dunlap, led the 100 "A-Group," which filled in behind the leading 390th Bomb Group. The formation went over Leipzig by mistake, and the bombers flew towards Merseburg on a southerly course. At the target a very heavy flak barrage bracketed the B-17s. In the next few minutes the low squadron of 100 "A-Group" lost five out of the six B-17s. The first to go down was *Buffalo Gal*,[943] piloted by Lieutenant William T. "Buzz" Fitzroy. Of the nine men aboard five baled out and were taken prisoner, including the pilot. The rest were killed. *Sparky*,[944] flown by 2nd Lieutenant Jackson E. Phelps, was finished off by a fighter as it lagged behind. Of the nine men aboard only the tail gunner survived to be taken prisoner. The B-17 piloted by Lieutenant Eden C. Jones was next to go down.[945] The fourth loss was piloted by Lieutenant Carl C. Gustafson, Jr., whose crew were on their 22nd mission.[946] The Fortress piloted by 2nd Lieutenant Morris E. Clark, most of whose crew were on their first mission, was the fifth and final B-17 in the low squadron to be shot down.[947] *Regal Eagle*,[948] piloted by Lieutenant Gerald H. Steussy, the high squadron lead, also went down. All nine men baled out and were taken prisoner. In the meantime, the 100th "B-Group" led by Major Joe Zeller and Charles E. Harris had flown on course to Leuna.

George P. Fory recalls that the flak:

> "started sooner than the day before. Maybe the planes ahead had stirred them up, but they were there. The elevation was just on us and tracking was on our left and crossed over us before 'Bombs Away'. It stayed with us until we turned off the bomb run."

Charles E. Harris recalls:

> "The word Merseburg always brings back the memories of flak and more flak! To our crew, *Sack Artist* and I dare say most of the 100th; Merseburg was one of the worst targets, if not THE worst. Our crew hit that place three times. In each case, the missions were rough, primarily from the heavy concentration of 88mms. The 29 July mission is perhaps the most vivid in my memory as the flak that day was the worst ever. Until we hit the bomb run, it was pretty much like other missions. But as we started down the run I looked straight ahead and the sky was a continuous flak burst. Being the lead plane, there were no other planes to look at; the preceding Group was far ahead. I think that this was the only mission where I honestly thought to myself: 'We'll never make it through' and I said a quick prayer. Major Zeller was on the radio, in contact with the other groups and his apparent coolness helped settle me back into the routine of flying. The pilot of the lead plane was essentially on instruments. Maintaining exact altitude and speed was vital, also the heading provided by the navigator. Once the bombardier took control, the heading became his responsibility. After that one good look forward, I went back to the business of flying on instruments. For the pilot that was a blessing in a way, as it kept his eyes on the instruments and not on what was going on around but the Command Pilot, with no actual flying responsibility, got to see everything (poor guy). During the bomb run there were several 'bangs' that indicated flak bursts all too near but we didn't come home with any holes in the plane. At 'bombs away' I made a fast, descending turn to get out of the flak. At that time, getting away was primary and I left the instruments so that I could see where we were going so as to avoid conflict with any other groups in the area. Because of the evasive action, the group formation always loosened up a bit due to the maneuver. When a Command pilot was in the right hand seat, the normal crew co-pilot was 'promoted' to tail gunner. My navigator, Lloyd Coartney, said that the target was smoked out. He was leaning over John Dimel, bombardier, trying to point out where to hit, when he looked through the nose and saw all of those fighters headed right at us with tracers making it look like the 4th of July."[949]

Lieutenant George P. Fory again:

> "Being in 100B, we were not aware of what was going on with 100A at that time. About ten minutes after the Rally Point we saw a straggler below at about 10 o'clock, appearing to go very slow. As we came by him we could see two engines feathered and someone called, 'Bandits at 3 o'clock high'. The bandit was a Messerschmitt 262 jet. It peeled off and dove straight down on the straggler. The straggler blew up and the jet went on down out of sight. There were no parachutes seen by us.[950] I heard later that this was the first mission in which jets were used by the Germans to attack bombers. Many believed that the German fighter pilots were radioing our attitude to the flak guns and this may be true; it sounds feasible to me. They had some very accurate fire at Merseburg and there must be a reason for it. The best words I know of to describe Merseburg flak was that it was 'intense' and 'accurate.'"

Dick Johnson's diary entry for 29 July read:

> "Same target as yesterday. (Leuna Oil Works). Saw terrific dogfights over target between our P-51s and the enemy fighters. Target CAVU. And flak was terrific. Got several holes this time. Had third new crew. Carried 20 x 250lb GP bombs. Flight time, 8 hours and 35 minutes. Over enemy territory 4 hours and 20 minutes. I was flying the '*Bet Jane*' again today for an assault on Germany's most heavily defended city. My new crew for the day was that of Lieutenant P. F. Curetan, Jr[951]. The 303rd Bomb Group supplied 13 aircraft for the 41st 'C' Wing, High Group. We did a plan 'D' Group assembly over Harrington Buncher at 17,000ft and flew in Combat Wing formation while slowly climbing to 26,000ft. At the IP we took Group interval for visual bombing and dropped our bombs from a magnetic heading of 95°. At the target we saw about 15 Me 109s trying to attack the lead group but were being harassed by our P-51s. Just after bombs away, four of the fighters managed to elude the P-51s and made a single pass through the lead group without shooting any down. After we dropped our bombs we made a sharp right turn to avoid flak and at this time rejoined the wing formation for our return to Molesworth.

At the target there were no photographs of the actual bomb bursts as they were concealed in smoke and shadows in the target area. The Germans always tried to conceal their important targets with smoke screens but with limited success. The lead Group's bombs appeared to fall a little short of the MPI. They approached the target at 103° magnetic. The Low Group's bombs appeared to fall right on target. They flew to the target at 102° Magnetic. Our heading of 95° gave us a good separation from the prop wash of the other groups and our bombs were right on target. The lead group of the 'D' Wing following us headed to the target at 98°. Their lead bombardier didn't quite kill the drift and their bombs fell a couple hundred yards to the left of the MPI. Over England we dropped down to 1000ft and eventually had to fly at 300ft because of low clouds. Of the 51 aircraft furnished by our group for this mission, 32 sustained battle damage, but none were shot down, thanks largely to the effort by our P-51s over the target. Several of our B-17s had major damage from flak and many had flak holes, including my poor old '*Bet Jane*.'"

A. J. Sinibubb flew his 16th mission as navigator in *Nine-O-Nine*,[952] flown by Lieutenant Pullen, who flew low flight lead in the Hi Squadron in the 91st Bomb Group. Sinibubb wrote:

"Bomb-load 22 – 250lb GP. Route Base-Caxton Gibbet-Ely-Spalding-SP#4. Most of the trip was 10/10 undercast. We had fighters in the area and a dogfight commenced. Saw a couple go down in flames and hit the ground. Target was hit good. Flak was heavy and fairly accurate. On return trip across North Sea saw a ditched B-17. Crew were all out in dinghies. His coast and ceiling was 'O'. After going in for 50 over coast we decided to go back over North Sea, gain altitude, fly over precip and make instrument let down. As we made 180° we ran into a squadron flying behind us and we almost collided together. It was really scary. We saw a field and they shot up flares to guide us in. pilot made a wonderful emergency landing. We waited till the sky cleared before taking off again. Landed 1338."

In all, 569 B-17s in the 1st and 3rd Bomb Divisions attacked the Leuna plant, where they released 1410 tons of bombs. In the previous day's attack, 652 Fortresses dropped 1601 tons of bombs.

On 31 July Dick Johnson flew his 28th mission with a trip to Munich. His diary for this day reads:

"Munich, Germany (Rough). Carried incendiaries this trip. It looked like we made big fires too. The flak was really intense. Saw several B-17s go down. I carried quite a bit of flak back with me. Saw a few FWs but none attacked. Carried ten M17 Incendiaries of 500lb each. Over enemy territory 4 hours and 35 minutes."

Johnson recalls:

"The 303rd Bomb Group scheduled 38 planes to bomb the Aero Engine Works by radar. Two aircraft aborted and the mission was flown by 36 B 17s for an 8 hour and 10 minute flight. We had a late breakfast for this mission and finished briefing and were at the airplane at five minutes past eight. We started engines at 0855 and started taxi at 0905 with take off at 0915 behind the 358th Squadron, which was first and the 360th, which was just ahead of our 427th Squadron.[953] I was flying another new crew for this mission in 42-102569, which had no name. This was the first mission for 2nd Lieutenant T. A. Duncan and his crew, minus co-pilot, 2nd Lieutenant D.A. Singleton. We were loaded with 2700 gallons of gas and 10 M17 incendiaries of 500lb each. Beiser was leading us in the 41st 'B' Combat Wing, Low Group of 13 airplanes. We assembled over the Harrington Buncher at 7000ft and departed in Combat Wing formation. Since we were bombing by radar, we remained in Wing formation for the bomb run and dropped our bombs in the target area with the leader. We could see fighters through an occasional hole in the clouds. The flak was always bad at Munich and many B 17s were hit by fragments. Of the 38 planes of the group, 20 were damaged by flak, of which eleven were major. I was flying from the left seat on this mission and learned a little lesson on this date.

"Part of our protective gear was a 'skull cap' of flak resistant plates, which we wore under our '50 mission' caps. It was a heavy and uncomfortable thing and since I had never seen a hole in the top of a B-17, there were times that I would take it off and place it under the pilot seat with my parachute. Over Munich the flak was very bad but I still didn't get out my 'flak beanie' as I called it, until an 88mm flak shell passed just in front of No.2 engine, about five feet from my left elbow. The shell exploded about 30 or 40ft above our airplane and the base of the shell came back down on top of the No.2 engine. It went through the cowling and hit the collector ring hard enough to cut a half moon shaped hole. This caused an air leak in the intake manifold and the pressure dropped back a bit on that engine. Before I adjusted the manifold pressure, I reached under my seat and got my 'beanie.' I removed my hat, put the 'beanie' on my head and replaced my hat. Then I found time to adjust the manifold pressure. The damage to the engine was negligible but my ego suffered a bit in front of the new crew. I wore the beanie on all my remaining missions."[954]

On the mission to Ludwigshafen on 31 July B-24H *Hula Wahina II*, 704th Bomb Squadron, 446th Bomb Group, flown by 1st Lieutenant Emil Berry, was shot down by flak. 18-year-old S/Sgt Virgil R Huddleston, right waist gunner, recalls:

"We left the formation just a few minutes after dropping bombs. Rubenstein left through the nose wheel hatch, Monsulick and Sanders through the bomb bay, Carswell, Woods Kudlo and myself through the camera hatch in the rear. The remaining crewmembers I don't have any knowledge. Pulsipher was in the waist with parachute on, listening to interphone and uninjured. Berry and Good were at controls; both wore back type parachutes. Last conversation of the pilot 1st Lieutenant Berry, was interphone conversation and order for crew to bale out, he was last seen at the controls. German interrogator told me he was dead, but gave no reason but led me to believe that it may have been civilians. 2nd Lieutenant Good was talking to the pilot on intercom when last heard Germans told me he was dead but would not give the cause of death. But also led me to believe that it may have been the civilians. I thought that I had heard Pulsipher yell, 'Don't shoot' after he had landed. He was hiding in the bushes about 500 yards away…."[955]

Late in July the ball turrets were removed from many Liberators to improve stability and altitude performance. During the last week of July General Doolittle carried out the first stage of his plan to convert all Liberator groups in England to Fortresses.[956] At first crews resented the changeover, but they quickly grew to like the improved flying characteristics inherent in the B-17, and they praised the more spacious nose compartment and improved heating. There was also a downside, as Lieutenant Francis S. Milligan in the 493rd Bomb Group recalls:

"Changing over to Flying Fortresses was practically a guarantee from the 8th Air Force that from now on we would be visiting the Reichland - definitely the 'Big League'. Bremen, Merseburg, Magdeburg, Ludwigshafen, Münster and other German cities became our targets. Hitting the Hitler gang's back yard was a bit different than bombing V-1 launching sites in France. They really loved to shoot at us over the Fatherland. I think they must have given the school kids recess at Merseburg and each one had a flak gun. Flak and rocket trails were heavy over practically every one of the German targets. It was almost impossible to visualize how black the sky became when Jerry started to throw his stuff up at us. Flak always scared me but I think rockets made me just a bit shakier. Sitting there in the nose one saw a hell of a lot and watching those rocket trails start at the ground and head up towards me wasn't the most fun I've had in my life, yet never in all my missions did I see a plane hit by rocket."

By now Ben Smith, in the 303rd Bomb Group, was getting closer and closer to the day when his tour would be complete:

"Now that it looked as if I had a chance to finish, I began to sweat it out. I had finished 25 missions and had collected my DFC. Before I completed the required 30 missions, the limit was arbitrarily raised to 35, a fact which depressed me mightily.[957] After the Normandy invasion, the brass said we were going to fly unlimited missions, as did our friends, the RAF. This decision was so disastrous to morale that they finally relented. I actually had to fly 31 missions and was given credit for four I didn't fly. I don't know how they figured it; it made no sense to me.

"I was now an old combat veteran and though only 21 years old, I had seen enough for a lifetime. I had literally grown up in the war. More of my friends were dead than alive. A seemingly endless procession had come and gone out of our squadron. Only a handful of them had completed a tour of operations. I had seen them come and go, but always on my mind was the specter of Long's crew, who went down on their final sortie. The same thing happened to Holdcroft's crew. My 29th mission was to Germany. I had hoped not to go to Germany again, but there it was on the wall, Dessau - deep in the heartland of the *Third Reich*. I was dismayed but knew I had to go. We were bombing oil refineries in that area, which were top priority targets. These missions usually generated strong resistance. I sweated great drops of blood and was extremely edgy. I had not been like this before, but now I had a chance to win. As it turned out, my fears were groundless. Opposition was very light and all of our aircraft returned safely - just a long haul.

"My last two missions were to northern France. We did not get flak over the target on my last one and I began to think I had it made. Not so! As we droned ahead, suddenly a battery opened up on us and we were getting a lot of very accurate anti-aircraft fire. I am afraid that I panicked for the first time. Was I going to be snatched back into perdition after having come so far? It seemed so, but then it was over and we had come through.

"For the last time I saw the cliffs of Dover below and then we were peeling off and circling to land at Molesworth. We touched down, the brakes screeched and then we were taxiing toward the hardstand. My friends were waiting - Ward, Baldy, Chunk and Alvin. I could see a bucket of yellow paint. When I crawled out of the waist hatch, they grabbed me and painted '31' on my seat in huge numerals. I knelt and kissed the tarmac and it was over. Unbelievably, it was over. I was going to live."[958]

August followed the same operational pattern as July, with bombing raids on airfields in France and strategic targets in Germany. On 1 August, while bomb groups struck at airfields in France, 191 B-17s escorted by three P-51 groups again parachuted supplies to the French Resistance movement. Meanwhile, 75 B-17s escorted by a P-51 group bombed the airfield at Tours, and 387 B-17s escorted by another Mustang group attacked five airfields and a railway bridge in an area south and southwest of Paris. A fourth force of 320 B-17s was despatched to bomb targets in the environs of Paris itself. Bad weather caused over 100 aborts, but 219 planes bombed four airfields, five bridges, railway facilities, and a rail and highway junction. The fifth force of B-24s sent against eight V-weapon sites in northwestern France also ran into bad weather that caused multiple aborts, and only 34 Liberators managed to bomb their targets. Another force of 156 Liberators was despatched against seven V-weapon sites in the same area and an oil storage depot at Rouen. Bad weather again prevented raids on the V-weapon sites, but 85 B-24s bombed the oil depot and the railroad junction nearby. Four fighter groups strafed rail and ground vehicles during the course of the day, which cost five bombers and three fighters.

Next day the 2nd and 3rd Bomb Divisions flew two late afternoon missions against targets in France again. In all, 289 B-17s and B-24s attacked twelve targets, including oil dumps and depots and supply depots, railroad bridges, junctions, canal locks, airfields, and marshaling yards. Three P-51 groups flew escort for the bombers, two of them later strafing rail and highway traffic northeast of Paris. In the second mission over 390 bombers attacked 15 V-weapon sites, five bridges, an airfield, and a rail junction and bridge. Five Mustang groups flew escort, and three of them later strafed rail transportation targets. In total the day's losses numbered six bombers and six fighters, mostly to flak. No enemy aircraft were encountered. On 3 August, in the early afternoon nearly 400 B-17s and B-24s bombed marshaling yards in France and one in Germany, an oil refinery in Germany, as well as an airfield, road and rail junctions, bridges, and a few individual targets in France. Three of the six P-51 groups that provided escort later strafed transportation targets and airfields. 16 year old "Flak Boy" *Luftwaffenhelfer* Heinz Riediger, who helped to man heavy Home Flak Battery 230/VII in Friedrichshafen, recalls the 3 August raid:

"The daylight attack was to turn out to be even worse for the flak than the night attack of 27/28 April[959] for 23 flak auxiliaries in Schnetzenhausen were to lose their lives. In the morning it was drill as usual. Lie down, get up and line up, gunners' chain. Just as we are finishing the hooter sounded. We went to the guns, donned our steel helmets, put cotton wool in our ears. Ready. The shell was in the fuse-setting holder. At last the order 'scharfer Zielflug!' The first round thundered from the barrel. Command followed command: 'Group fire-group!' We had a new auxiliary from the Black Forest. His face showed a mixture of fear and laughter. Suddenly the bombs screamed down. It thundered and everything - the protective wall, the gun - shook. Instinctively everyone looked for what cover he could find. Clumps of earth struck my back. I felt, now you die the hero's death and an indescribable fear. I hoped it would soon be over. Then it was. At first it was like night all around. Dust hid everything. As it got lighter I climbed onto a bench in the gun revetment. What I saw outside was terrible. At '*Berta*' the gun lay outside its revetment, the carriage up in the air. No one survived there, I thought. Smoke rose up at '*Cäsar*', a bomb had torn open the revetment. A couple of powder-blackened and dirt-smeared figures, their clothes torn, were just rising up from the confusion. At '*Dora*' a demolished barrel stood sadly. Nothing moved. I was the first out from our revetment and hurried to *'Cäsar'* to give assistance. Groaning figures lay between the guns. An almost unbearable smell of powder and blood was everywhere. The *Obergefreiter* stared at us from maddened eyes. He kept moaning, 'Oh shit' and 'Oh God, I am ill, I want to die'. He was in a bad way, the poor fellow. Some had been flung out and lay there with amazingly contorted limbs. One man lay on the gun with a dusty and sunken face."[960]

On 4 August the 8th Air Force bombed several targets,[961] including a return to Peenemünde. For Dick Johnson it was his 29th mission:

"My diary reads: 'Peenemünde, Germany experimental station for V-2s: Lots of flak due to CAVU weather. Got only a few holes. Shot down a Me 110 on way back. Ball turret gunner got credit. Long, hard trip. Blasted it wide open. Won't have to go back!'

"At least I didn't have to go back. This was one of the most successful missions that I participated in. I was flying another new crew, that of 2nd Lieutenant L. M. Johnston in *'Jigger Rouche, Kraut Killer.'*[962] We each carried five 1000lb bombs and 2700 gallons of gasoline for this 9-hour trip. The 303rd furnished 37 aircraft for this mission and we had two radar ships from the 305th Bomb Group, which was a PFF Group that supplied these aircraft to many different groups. It later developed that we would not need to bomb by radar, as the weather had cleared at the target. We had made a plan 'D' assembly at 6000ft over Molesworth and took our 13 B-17s into the high group of the 41st Combat Wing formation to which we were assigned. We departed the English coast at Louth at about 11 o'clock and intended to fly at low altitude for a while to save gas. However, over the North Sea there was a cloud layer that caused us to start our climb to altitude a little early. We crossed the enemy coast at 22,000ft and maintained this altitude to the target, which was on the Baltic coast north of Berlin. Just before the IP we got a radio message that visual bombing would be done, so we took proper interval so that groups could bomb individually.

"We made a seven and a half minute bomb run from the IP to the target and bombs were away a few seconds after 1442 from 23,000ft, us being the high squadron for today's mission. The bombs from my airplane had delayed action, or 'Long Delay' fuses. This is how we added insult to injury. Some fuses of this type had a device built in, so that when the bomb struck the ground, a plunger broke a vial of acetone. The acetone slowly dissolved a celluloid diaphragm that was spring loaded. When the diaphragm was dissolved, a striker set off the bomb. The celluloid discs were of different thickness so that the thicker they were, the longer it took for them to dissolve. Thus there were no moving parts to the fuse and sound detectors could not hear anything except the final movement of the firing pin. By then, everybody within two miles could hear it.

"My bombs didn't explode with the others, but one was designed to explode three hours after impact. Each bomb had a different delay, so that the last bomb didn't explode until three days after the initial drop. My aircraft was in position 9, which is near the center of the formation. This same position in the other groups had the same fuses, so that there was a total of 15 delayed action bombs dropped onto the target. These were intended to harass the clean up crews and I have no doubt that they were quite unnerving. We had at least one aircraft carrying these bombs on most big industrial targets in Germany.

"We had taken off and climbed through a solid overcast in England, but over the target area the clouds were almost absent and visibility was 40 miles. The bombardiers flew the lead planes with the Norden bombsight, which was hooked to the autopilot and the bombs dropped automatically at the proper instant and position. The seven and a half-minute bomb run gave the bombardiers plenty of time to kill the drift.[963] As the bombs started falling, a speedboat on the canal turned and sped away in the opposite direction. It was just as well for him, because several of these 1000lb bombs hit the canal, damning it. We even thought that we might kill some of the big rocket scientists at the facility. We later learned that Werner Von Braun was at the facility that day. One non-operational Junkers 52 was seen near the west end of the east-west runway but the executive transports were nowhere to be seen.

"As we headed back home, going over the Baltic we flew over the Danish Island of Falster and immediately over the island of Lolland Maribo. At this point, the tail gunner of this new crew, S/Sgt E. S. Brown reported on the intercom: 'Tail to pilot, there's a Me 410 coming up behind us. No, I believe it's a 110.'

"'Are you sure it's not a B-25?' I asked.

"'No, it's definitely a 110 and he's closing.' The ball turret gunner, S/Sgt J. A. Czerwonka, confirmed that it was indeed a Me 110.

"'How far back?' I asked.

"'About two miles and closing' the tail gunner answered.

"'Well,' I said, 'we are on our way home and haven't fired a shot, so let him have it.' With this, the tail gunner and ball turret gunner started firing. After 30 or 40 seconds of almost continuous firing, the ball turret gunner yelled on the intercom, 'He's diving away! He's going straight down. He's picking up speed and still going straight down! He's crashed! He's crashed! I didn't see any parachute!'[964]

"After this action we got a little too close to Germany's northernmost city, Flensburg and flew within range of a battery of 88mm flak guns and a battery of larger guns that was fairly accurate. This after the target where the flak was fairly intense and accurate. Also at Eckernferde where a single battery of three guns peppered a few of us with fragments. Of the 39 B-17s that participated in this mission, 17 had battle damage, with eight major and nine minor. We were lucky that none of us was shot down. Even the Me 110 that we shot down had fired rockets at our group, but missed."[965]

On 5 August, the 8th returned to strategic targets with all-out raids on eleven separate centers in central Germany. Dick Johnson, who flew his 30th mission, recalls:

"The 303rd Bomb Group had been flying two missions per day for quite a while and today each squadron planned to put up ten B 17s each. Beiser was leading our squadron for this rush job and only six of us made formation with their assigned group. A few of the planes were so rushed that they were not fully loaded with bombs. We were to bomb six different targets in France in support of the ground troops. We were in the 'E' squadron of the 41st Combat Wing and we assembled over the Harrington Buncher at 3500ft. Since we were late in taking off, we took a short cut to Splasher 10 and then direct to Beachy Head at 20,000ft. As a result of this short cut, three of our planes couldn't catch up and tacked themselves onto another squadron. Our squadron's target was Crepieul, France where we did a ten-minute bomb run. We were not fired on by flak gunners as were some of the other squadrons and none of our squadron were damaged. The 'A' squadron lead ship was hit by flak, which knocked out the manual aileron controls and tumbled the gyros that operated the autopilot, just 45 seconds before bombs away. The bombardier recovered in time to do a fair job in his bombing attempt.

"The 'D' squadron was 20 minutes late to their target when they had to circle to avoid a large formation of British Lancasters in their path. At the target one plane was hit by flak, which disabled two engines. That squadron flew a direct course to England so that the disabled plane could land at Ford, near the White Cliffs of Dover.

"We saw two of the German rocket planes, the Me 163 *Komet* but with their five to six minute fuel supply, none could reach the 303rd formations. P-51s shot down several German fighters that day.

'Today was Beiser's last mission, as it was for most of our original crew. I had two more to go. I had the same co-pilot as yesterday's mission but was flying a mixed crew of enlisted men who were making up missed missions. My old favorite airplane, '*Bet Jane*' had to abort this mission when the pilot had to turn off both inverters due to an electrical short caused by a urine 'spill.' Many crewmen didn't like to use the relief tube that was located near the forward bulkhead of the bomb bay and simply relieved themselves on the bombs or in the bomb bay. Usually nothing happened, but this time the amplifiers were shorted out and no boost could be obtained for the superchargers. This practice was forbidden, but was often violated as in this case. The pilot brought the '*Bet Jane*' back to base with the wet bombs and the culprit was disciplined by having to fly an extra mission. The official report was softened to indicate that a urine can was accidentally knocked over instead of what actually happened. Thus, the culprit might have lost rank as well as having to fly another mission, if the whole truth were known."

August 5th marked John W. McClane's 27th mission, and it was back to Brunswick for his fourth time:

"We expected the worst anytime we headed to Brunswick. It was the second most feared target after Berlin due to flak but especially the excellent German fighter groups in the vicinity. Today's mission turned out to be an anticlimax to our fears. The 44th Bomb Group launched 34 aircraft for this mission. Twelve of the 68th Squadron planes made up the second section with the 67th in the lead and the 506th squadron in the third section. The group was led by PFF. In spite of the reputation of the German fighters they were notably absent on this day both flying into the target and back to base. All three Bomb Divisions dispatched a total of over 1200 planes to 15 different targets in Hitler's Germany. Just under 100 B-24s in the 14th Combat Wing were assigned to bomb an aircraft factory. Each plane was loaded with 13 100lb and 9 500lb bombs. We were protected the whole distance with very effective fighter escort. The clouds broke at the target so our bombardiers were able to drop their bombs visually. Our squadron achieved excellent results hitting squarely on target. The flak did not seem as intense as we had expected, our 68th Squadron receiving no serious damage.

"The flight home was uneventful except for one interesting thing. As we headed back towards the English Channel, a lone B-24 was flying perhaps 5000ft below us and off to our left. Its No.3 motor was on fire. The pilot put the plane on autopilot and we watched everyone bale out. (One of my jobs as navigator was to record how many and where men baled out.) The gunners were counting as they watched the crew abandon ship. The plane was now on its own without any crew when just like nothing had happened, the fire went out. All of us watched with fascination as the 'ghost ship' sailed merrily along. The course of the pilotless ship and ours paralleled each other for maybe 20 minutes when it came time for our formation to make a turn to the right. I'll forever see the image in my mind of this derelict flying off to eternity as our paths separated and we lost view of it. I wonder if it is still flying? It made me think of the song, *Ghost Riders in the Sky*."

Next day the B-17s struck at Berlin and oil and manufacturing centers in the *Reich*. On this occasion, 76 Fortresses in the 95th and 390th Bomb Groups hit the Focke-Wulf plant at Rahmel, in Poland.[966] Flight Lieutenant Edwin H. King, RAF, who was seconded to the 487th Fighter Squadron, 352nd Fighter Group, recalls;

"We were to escort the bombers to the target area (Magdeburg) joining up with them as they coasted in at Den Helder which meant getting to height over the UK. One could hear the bombers climbing whilst we were still at briefing and since the weather was poor we had to climb in sections through cloud from 600 to 18,000ft, joining up as a squadron and then a group on top. Over the continent the cloud began to break up and there was considerable opposition almost all the way in. I was again No.2 to Major Preddy and watched him get two Me 109s. I only got a squirt at one. After the target we were relieved and returned direct to UK with no further action, just the usual flak."[967]

Dick Johnson, in the 303rd Bomb Group, flew his 31st mission on 7 August with a trip to Paris, where the target was a large fuel storage area in an area inside the city limits, almost on the banks of the Seine in the St. Ouen section of the city. His diary reads:

"…Flak really rough. They tracked us all the way. I was luckier than most as I only got a few holes. Target CAVU except for haze. Carried 38 100lb bombs. Over enemy territory two hours and five minutes.

"I was flying in the No.2 position on the right wing of the lead plane. My new co-pilot for today was 2nd Lieutenant G. C. Lawrenson and we were flying 42-102569, which had no nose art. Thirteen airplanes were able to bomb this target while the rest went to Chartres to bomb the airfield there, as a target of opportunity. From our bombing altitude of 25,000ft the visibility was fair, with the target being obscured for a time with a thin layer of clouds. Another group from our wing turned in front of us at our altitude, giving us some violent prop wash, but twelve of our 13 aircraft bombed the primary target with only fair results. The new airplane being flown by Lieutenant Walker in the No.4 position failed to bomb because the bombardier failed to turn on the selector and salvo switches. They brought their 38 bombs back to base.

"We were in a ticklish situation where we had to be extremely careful not to bomb built up areas in occupied France. The bombs that we dropped had no nose fuses and had a one fortieth second fuse in the tail to give them instantaneous ignition. We were carrying 2000 gallons of gas for this 5 hour and 45 minute mission. There was intense flak throughout our seven-minute bomb run and just after bombs away it became very accurate until we took evasive turns. The German gunners were slow in getting our range while on the bomb run and by the time they got us in their sights the bombs dropped and we turned away to foil their two and a half kilometer sighting lead. Of the 13 planes in our low group, only three escaped damage. We had five planes with major damage and five, including mine, with minor damage."

On his 18th mission, navigator A. J. Sinibubb in the 323rd Bomb Squadron, 91st Bomb Group, flew in *Cheri*, piloted by Lieutenant Stunf, who flew Hi Flight lead, deputy squadron lead to an oil depot on a river.

They carried 20 250lb demolition bombs. Sinibubb recalled that the mission was:

"pretty easy. We went over battle lines at 20,000 but descended to 15,000 for bombing. A little flak was encountered over lines. Bombs fell short but hit a bridge. We flew over target. Rest of mission was uneventful. Large allied convoys were in Channel."[968]

On 8 August Dick Johnson, in the 303rd Bomb Group, flew his 32nd and final mission of his combat tour:

"We were to try a tactical attack on German ground troops in an area 11 miles south of Caen. Captain Bob Sheets was leading the raid with a ten-man crew. This used to be standard for the Flying Fortress but they had lately been reduced to a nine-man crew. Bob Sheets was in '*Shoo Shoo Baby*'[969] in our 427th Squadron. T/Sgt Frank X. Neuner was in Bob Sheets' top turret. He was a good buddy and roommate of my regular ball turret gunner, Charles W. Latta.[970] I was assigned to 'Tail End Charlie' for this raid, which was also 'Purple Heart Corner,' since there was nobody behind me. I had the same crew as on yesterday's raid, but with two different gunners on makeup missions. My erstwhile pilot, Theodore 'Bud' Beiser was 427th Operations officer, while Sheets flew the lead position. Beiser had just finished his tour of duty and was doing this office work while waiting transport to the States.

"This 41st 'B' Combat Wing, Lead Group with 12 B-l7s did an assembly at 5000ft over the Harrington Buncher Beacon and departed the English coast at Portland Bill at 14,000ft, which was to be our bombing altitude. The combat wing ahead of us didn't turn on the briefed IP and we had to follow them around to avoid flying a collision course. There were no clouds over the target, but the haze was so bad that we couldn't see the bright red and yellow markers that our ground troops had put out to identify the target that they wanted bombed. We made a bomb run, but the lead bombardier didn't drop because of this problem. The high group was the only one of our three groups to bomb the primary target and they missed it by over a half-mile. Luckily their bombs still fell in German occupied territory, destroying a lot of apple trees where a lot of vehicle tracks were visible.

"Our secondary target had a cloud bank over it at 12,000ft, so we finally picked a railroad siding and made a five minute bomb run and dropped 446 100lb bombs on that target with fairly good results, cutting the rail lines and a highway. According to the mission summary, flak was 'Moderate and inaccurate at the Primary.' This was written by Bob Sheets at the front of the formation while I was a quarter mile back and 500ft lower. My diary reads: 'Caen, France. German front line defenses. Flak was really rough as we were at 14,000ft. Didn't drop on primary and finally dropped on railway yard, but good. CAVU. I'd rather go to Berlin. Finis. DFC.' Only one B-17 received minor damage. Guess whose? At one time the flak was bursting all around our plane but several hundred feet away most of the time. I could see the angry, red center of these explosions several times. I often wondered if I was overly sensitive because it was my last mission and thought that they were determined to get me on this one last chance, but I thought at the time that one of those bursts might actually have my name on it.

"After we returned to Molesworth at 15 minutes past three, I did the necessary paper work and came out of the airplane, only to find the crew lined up in front of the airplane by the nose art, '*Miss Lace*,' to congratulate me. My co-pilot, 2nd Lieutenant George C. Lawrenson who just finished his second mission asked me.

"'How does it feel to finish your missions?'

"'Wait a minute and I'll show you.' I replied.

With this, I took off my 'Fifty Mission' hat, removed my 'Flak Beanie' and handed them to Lawrenson.

"'Hold these for me, will you?' I said. I untied and dropped my flak suit, which I picked up and handed to Lieutenant John P. Emmet our navigator who also acted as our bombardier. I removed my oxygen mask and throat mike and handed them to T/Sgt Leroy H. M. Foerster, our engineer-top turret. I unhooked and removed my parachute harness, which I gave to Sgt Robert H. Hitchcock, our radioman. I lifted my 'Mae West' life preserver over my head and handed it to S/Sgt Myron M. Musyka, the other waist gunner. I removed my leather A-2 jacket, which I handed to our ball turret gunner, Sgt Joseph A. Czerwonka who had shot down the Me 110. My flight gloves I handed to Sgt Donald L. Garlick, waist gunner who had just finished his first mission. I took off my flight coveralls with its escape kit and handed them to Sgt Wayne L. Rughe, our tail gunner, also on his first mission. This left me with my uniform pants, shirt and shoes. I walked to the middle of the line of crewmembers and faced them.

"'How does it feel to finish my missions, you ask?'

"With this, I did a standing back flip and landed on my feet. The crew applauded as I took a bow like a ham actor, the same as I did in my High School plays. The standing back flip was a standard with me that I learned, at McLeansboro, Illinois High School. I never told the crew how scared I was on this mission when the flak started bursting around us. But now it was over and I could actually look forward to going back home where instructors wouldn't yell at me and other people wouldn't shoot at me. Utopia, here I come! I lacked a month and two days of being 22 and a half years old, a combat instructor with 32 missions under my belt. They were giving me credit for three more missions, so that my official records would indicate that I actually flew 35 missions. I guess my job of flying new crews on their first missions made me earn it."[971]

Lieutenant John W. McClane, in the 44th Bomb Group, did not fly the mission to Le Perthe, France, on 8 August, but the Eightballs lost a Liberator on take off, as he recalls:

"As I stepped out of my barracks building at Shipdham I saw smoke rising beyond the perimeter of the field. I realized it could be nothing but one of our planes that had crashed. (I found out later the pilot had committed the ultimate sin in a four-motor bomber, he had banked into a dead engine, could not recover, rolled the plane onto its back where it fell straight down. On board was a full load of gas and bombs as well as nine other men). Later that afternoon, I decided to cycle to the site of the crash, which I found easily by following the back roads leading to the still plummeting smoke. When I came upon the scene, the utter destruction of a once proud bomber is difficult to describe; wreckage was scattered over a large area. I was the only person there except for the British Bomb Disposal Crew. The area was roped off, which I ignored. I proceeded to within a few feet of one of the craters caused by an exploding bomb. Not all bombs went off as I saw several scattered about, still unexploded. The bottom cone of the hole was filled with aluminium that had melted from the intense heat of the burning wreckage. Not too far away was a crew of three men, they had placed a rope around the trunk of the body of one of the pilots. Both of the unfortunate pilots were still sitting in their heavy metal bucket seals, their arms had been burned to stumps as were their legs. All their bodies including their heads were burned charcoal black. The clean-up crew gave a tug on the rope, expecting to extract the body but instead, the torso simply pulled apart like an overdone roast. I saw no other bodies, but on the way to my observation point, I saw an unburned electric flying glove. We always needed an extra glove so I was not above usurping this one for my emergency bag. When I picked it up, it took me no time to let it go again, as I noticed it still had a hand in it. One of the men pointed to my feet and said, 'Look what you are standing on, Governor'. I looked down; my left foot was on top of a man's skull, cut off at the hairline. Another man said I should move further away as they were going to defuse some bombs. By this time, I had seen more than I had bargained for, so I cycled back to the 68th Squadron area."[972]

On 9 August, the B-17 and B-24 crews were summoned to the usual daily briefing. At Lavenham, Norman K. Andrew, navigator in Jack Stanley's B-17 crew in the 837th Bomb Squadron, 487th Bomb Group, prepared to fly his first mission. Philosophically, he wrote in his diary:

"'1st mission today, 34 to go.' They woke us at 1.50am. Briefing time 3:00 am. So we knew it was pretty sure to be a long one. Had pineapple juice, fresh egg, hotcakes, sausage, cold cereal and coffee. Target Schmitt ball bearing works, Nurnberg. Took off 0715 -left England 0856. Over enemy coast 0921. Ran into overcast and cloudy weather. Turned back approx. 50 miles southeast of Aachen. Picked a target of opportunity - dropped on lead ship and leveled the town of St. Vith - in Belgium. Encountered flak at Liège -moderate. Landed 1220. Logged five and a quarter hours."

Bob Maag, in the 94th Bomb Group, was flying his 20th mission this day:

"We learned that our target was Stuttgart again, though it seemed highly unlikely to me that the mission would come off as planned. The weather officer informed us that the cloud cover over the target would extend to 40,000ft, at which altitude bombing would be impossible. Furthermore, they told us that, when we returned to base, all of England would be socked in from zero to 20,000ft, making landing impossible!

"We'd be taking our own *Skinny*. We didn't know at that time that she was something of a legend (the first B-17 in the 94th to complete 100 missions), but realized that she was a venerable veteran. We assumed she got her name from the fact that she was an anomaly - a B-17G with no chin turret. We sometimes speculated whether *Skinny* had lost her chin turret in an earlier battle, or had been built that way. We all felt at home on *Skinny* and liked having her for our missions because her missing chin turret gave us the advantage of lower fuel consumption.

"When we arrived at the hardstand we weren't surprised to learn that take-off had been delayed, first for one hour, then another. We were still dubious when we received orders for take-off and fully expected to be recalled. The forming and flight to the target area were routine and uneventful. When we approached Stuttgart we found that the cloud cover did indeed extend to 40,000ft. Since we could not bomb the target and no secondary target had been communicated to us, the formation turned for home. In Luxembourg we were led over some flak guns mounted on railroad cars and all hell broke loose. I don't know how many hits *Skinny* took but one that came through the Plexiglas caught me on the left side of the face and wounded George Bycxkowski, the top turret gunner, in the leg. I lost my left eye and the co-pilot, Ivan Walker, had to take over the controls. Lyle Haines and Smitty, the bombardier and navigator somehow managed to get me into the nose of the plane where they did what they could to keep me alive.

"During the trip back under these emergency conditions the crew performed magnificently. Since this was the sixth consecutive day we'd flown a combat mission with only two or three hours' sleep a night, it was all the more remarkable that everyone handled the emergency so well.[973] I know Ivan and I were so wiped out at that point that we had been alternating at the controls at the same time! I was conscious during that hairy trip home and remember lying in the nose and worrying about the weather over England and the fact that this would be Ivan's first attempt to land a B-17! I needn't have worried. Not only did Ivan get us down safely, he made sure that *Skinny* was the first to land, thus ensuring that George and I would get medical attention at the earliest possible moment. For their actions, Walker, Smith and Haines were awarded the DFC."[974]

On 11 August, 956 heavy bombers escorted by 578 fighters attacked transportation targets in France. T/Sgt Robert T. Marshall, radio operator/gunner in the 385th Bomb Group, who had flown his first mission on 21 June to Berlin, flew his seventh mission this day when the group went to Belfort, in southern France:

"This was not Channel hopping but it was a milk run. Variety, it's great. We were flying our first mission as the lead plane (in the B Group). Our target was a railroad yard at Belfort in the southeast corner of France near the Italy-Switzerland area. I studied the briefing map longer than usual. I made sure I knew where Switzerland was and allowed myself knowledge of what direction I would take off in should worse come to worse. I saw no flak on this trip and that defines a no ball to me. A milk run. How many more like this can we get? I rolled another seven today although in the front of the plane they said they saw flak in the distance.

"The bombs fell on the target on a beautiful summer day. We were at 14,000ft, low by our standard. The bombardier said he saw boxcars sail into space when the bombs exploded down there. I watched through the camera-well because there was no indication enemy fighters were in the area. First I saw a deserted little city come into view, picturesque, beautiful. It glistened in the sun; a peaceful scene that made me wonder if we were close to the Mediterranean. Roofs sparkled in the sun. Everything looked clean and was painted bright, pastel shades. It was 1155; almost high noon, when we sailed over and the bombs fell. It was a hellish sight. Eruption after eruption tore up the railyard as I watched. I did not want to see a stray bomb fall into that pretty town and none did while I watched. I continued to gawk through the camera-well after we pulled off and headed home. It wasn't long before I saw signs of war in Europe. As we moved into the general area of Paris I saw intersection after intersection where bombings and artillery shellings, apparently, left rubble. I saw bridges that were pulverized. Villages were rubble piles. We had P-51 escorts. I watched them dive down and strafe a train. It blew up as I watched. The train was all that I saw moving on the ground and soon it did not move. A wood came into view and smoke wafted out of it; perhaps a sign our fighter planes earlier had paid a call. It was simple to imagine German troops and tanks were in the woods. The smoke I saw was not like the smoke earlier over the target. At Belfort the smoke was created by the Germans. I saw their smudge pots burning around the field. The smoke was no more than a poor token. When our bomber stream went over the railyard it was completely uncovered: the smoke wafted away from a railyard.

"We were aloft 8 hours and 30 minutes and on oxygen for 5 hours. After we landed Brackett told me we had come within 10 miles of the Swiss border after I asked. He and Benton got Charlie into more hot water today. The command pilot overheard their discussion on the bomb run and told Charlie afterward they seemed to be more concerned about a bet with friends for a bottle of Scotch (whose bombing would be more accurate: keep the bombs in the railyard) than they were about bombing the target.

"Soldiering is a strange business. Maybe business is not the word for what I saw today. Nothing seemed heroic about it and I don't see heroic figures on this base, other than the Colonel. Epic characters where are you? These are ordinary people doing war work, like dropping bombs on a beautiful city on a bright summer day. War is not noble."

Villacoublay airfield, near Paris, meanwhile, was the target for the 13th Bomb Wing. The air raid sirens sounded over Paris as the 54-ship formation flew overhead, spreading as the pilots jockeyed for bombing position. At 1214 a furious anti-aircraft fire broke out as the Germans put up a box barrage of 88mm shells, which filled the airspace nearly 4000ft deep. Shortly after bombs away, while the last of the anti-personnel fragmentation bombs left the bomb bays, *Royal Flush* in the 100th Bomb Group formation was hit. The first shell hit the No.3 engine. The second and third shells hit: the second just behind the cockpit, and the third in the bomb bay. Fire broke out immediately. A massive smoke trail moderated to a steady black, sometimes gray plume as Alf Aske and his co-pilot, Lieutenant Charles S. "Chick" Barber, feathered the No.3 prop and cut off fuel to the engine. For a few seconds *Flush* held its position. A shudder went through the B-17 as the automatic pilot was put into operation. Then perceptibly, the ship began to lose altitude. As though under full control, *Flush* began a slow turn to the right. Down below 12-year-old Leon Croulebois, who was staying with his grandmother, saw an object fall from the *Flush*. It was the waist door. A second object hurtled down, then checked its descent as a white canopy of parachute opened above. Armanda Consorto was the first to leave the stricken aircraft. Now a second hatch door was seen to fall, followed by a body. Lieutenant Jim Magargee, the bombardier, left the ship. Then followed the tail gunner, Sgt Stuart Allison, Barber, and Sgt Chuck Nekvasil, the radio operator.[975]

R. D. Russell and his crew in the 702nd Bomb Squadron, 445th Bomb Group, flew their 23rd mission this day to Strassburg, Germany, where they were to bomb oil storage tanks. Russell wrote:

"Today 'we had it'. We slept late, got up at 0645 and went to breakfast. Returned to the hut we found a note telling us to be at briefing at 0845. We took off at 1130 with 24 250lb GPs in the '*Green Hornet*'. The formation was a mess and we had to use maximum power to stay up with them. The flak wasn't bad over the target but it was accurate! We had #4 engine shot out as the bombs were dropped and it caught fire. We had to feather it and couldn't keep up with the formation. We lost # 2 engine shortly after and started losing altitude immediately. I had the boys start throwing out anything that was loose. We kept dropping so they kept throwing out flak suits, guns, ammunition, radios and Whitey even threw the 'put-put' out, which was a shock to all of us when we needed it for the top turret (the only one with guns and ammo). No one was overly excited and all acted as though it was a routine flight. We determined to go home by way of Belgium rather than try for the beachhead. We were down to 7500ft and chugging along at 110mph. We dodged flak at Brussels, Antwerp and Ghent and then flew circles off the coast over a downed B-17 until Air Sea Rescue arrived. We made it home without further incident and even made a fair landing. Flight time 7:00 hours."[976]

On 13 August over 1300 heavy bombers escorted by six fighter groups attacked targets in France for the loss of 13 bombers. At Lavenham, Norman K. Andrew, navigator in Jack Stanley's crew in the 837th Bomb Squadron, 487th Bomb Group, flew the second mission of his tour. He wrote:

"Woke us up at 0545 for mission #2. On the way to breakfast we piled out of the truck and saw a buzz bomb. It was really moving along - stringing out flames behind it. It sounded a bit louder then an outboard motor. What a gliding angle! It hit about a mile and a half from the field. The briefing for the mission was the real Army stuff. Gave us series #3 charts and the '*Gee*' signals were series #2. Mission was three-ship element bombing behind the German lines about 25 miles west of Paris 1 mile south of the Seine. We went into France between Cherbourg and Bayeaux. We skirted the lines (on the Allied side). We were lead ship of our element. I was really sure that we stayed on course. Between St. Lô and Uire there was a 12-ship formation flying on our left about 8 miles. They plowed right over a flak battery at Falaise. I was looking right at them when one of the ships got a direct hit in the right wing. The wing broke off between #3 and #4. Wing fell in flames - the ship fell in flames, tight spin to the right. No parachutes observed. Three minutes later another one got a direct hit. All I could see was shiny bits of aluminum - just a ball of fire. No one had a chance. The formation did not try evasive action. As near as I could spot the flak it was close to Falaise. We turned on the IP and made a 15-minute bomb run. Hit a road -purpose of raid was to interrupt Jerry's supply lines. We dropped 36 100-lb GP bombs. About 20 miles SW of Rouen there were about 12 rocket bombs. They really leave a trail of smoke. Jack called out four planes down in flames before I saw what he meant. Van Nostrand called five parachutes - it was a high formation that the sun just hit at the right angle. After the rally point I called Jack to tack onto a formation. As usual Jack said, 'Hell, Andy, let's go home by ourselves - get there quicker.' So we drug into England with a formation on our tail. I can still see that B-17 in a tight right spin. I knew they couldn't get out - it was spinning too tight. I'd rather get a direct hit."

Over 800 fighter-bombers attacked marshaling yards and other transportation targets in a wide area northeast of the Seine. IXth Air Force fighters covered the ground forces and flew armed reconnaissance in the Alençon, Le Mans, Domfront, and Chartres areas. Major Robert C. McWherter in *Who Flung Dung* led eight P-51Ds of the 382nd Squadron, 363rd Fighter Group in the Alençon area from 0658 to 0915. Midway through the patrol at 0825, a dozen enemy fighters were engaged northeast of Le Mans, and the 382nd Fighter Squadron pilots claimed four kills.[977] Their victims were four FW 190A-7/8 pilots in the 3rd and 4th *Staffeln* in JG 26, while another pilot was WIA.[978] Among the other scorers in the group this day was Lieutenant James Jabara in the 382nd Fighter Squadron, who claimed a FW 190 and a Bf 109 damaged.

August 13th was John W. McClane's 28th mission, and he went to Rouen:

"After our tactical bombing at St. Lo three weeks before, our 1st and 3rd Armies had put General Von Kluge's Wehrmacht into disorganized retreat. The broken German Army was caught in a pincher trap near the small town of Falaise some 20 miles south of Caen. Their army was fleeing eastward towards this narrowing gap. All the time our 8th and 9th Air Force, especially the fighter-bombers were pounding anything that moved unmercifully. These savage attacks were creating pandemonium in the German Army. The job of the heavy bombers was to block any route of supply or escape surrounding the battle zone. Our Groups were dispatched as squadrons of 6 to 12 planes, each with some road junction, riverbridge, rail transport or communications center as its target. Today the 8th Air Force targets were to be transportation choke points between Le Havre and Paris. Specifically the target for the 44th was a road junction near the city of Rouen. This city lies astride the Seine River some 70 miles down stream from Paris and 45 miles east of Le Havre on the Channel. The 44th put forth 25 aircraft divided among three squadrons, the 67th, the 68th and the 506th. We were the lead for the eight planes of the 68th. For the life of me, I never did understand what our target was except a 'road junction'. If Warga our bombardier knew, he kept it a secret and judging by the strike photo taken from our plane, I'm not sure he knew. We flew for five hours just to bomb some miserable country road near the Seine River. But this was no 'milk run'.

"Our squadrons were lined up one in front of the other as we approached the Seine. The 506th Squadron was perhaps a half-mile or less ahead of us. As they approached the river, very heavy and accurate flak burst in their formation. I was looking directly at it when one of their planes started to burn. The plane fell out of formation and the crew baled out just before it exploded in front of us. There was a monstrous explosion, the plane literally disintegrated before my eyes. This was a bright cloudless day with unlimited visibility and the sun was shining bright. The plane blew to bits. The motors were torn from the wings and went tumbling through the sky with their props windmilling, as they fell in a large non-linear arc. The wings and the fuselage and the tail were torn to shreds. As the pieces of aluminum drifted and twisted while they fell, with each turn, the sun would be reflected off their surface back into my eyes as if they were mirrors. It was like watching a thousand suns turn on and off in a rapid random fashion. But the most spectacular sight was the gas tanks, which had been torn from the wings. They did not explode their gasoline but rather it burned in huge orange flames streaming out behind the tanks as they fell in a wavy fashion towards the earth below.[979]

"I was fascinated with the sight that I was witnessing until all of a sudden I realized that our squadron would be over the exact same spot in a minute or two. It sounds cowardly but I became obsessed with an uncontrollable fear. I got it in my mind that we would be the next 'plane to be literally blown out of the sky. As the flak began to reach us, I was paralyzed until we passed beyond their range. I never experienced such an intense emotion before or since."

On 15 August, when the Liberators went to bomb the hangar area at Vechta, Germany, south of Bremen and north of Dummer Lake, 2nd Lieutenant Ralph Elliott, a pilot in the 467th Bomb Group, flew the mission, his fourth:[980]

"We took off at 0900 loaded with four 1000lb GP bombs and 4 500lb incendiary clusters. At assembly time I counted hundreds of B-24s and B-17s in the air and on-course across the Channel they looked like flies. We crossed the North Sea and into Germany over the Friesian Islands and into the target, which the formation hit dead center. Only two of our bombs went out and the salvo handle wouldn't work at first so that we dumped six bombs on the town of Vechta itself I saw a large fire after the explosion so we must have hit an oil dump accidentally. We must have raised hell with 1500lbs of incendiaries in the town as well as 3000lbs of TNT and steel. There was no flak but the boys saw about 25 scare bombs near the target. They came up leaving a trail of white smoke and then exploded but didn't seem to do any damage. The fun began just as we came back out and were nearly to the Zuider Zee. FW 190s and Me 109s-hit the formation just behind us and my boys saw four B-24s go down. A couple blew up and the other two spun out of control. The P-51s began chasing them and got some. A P-51 came up alongside and made the bad mistake of pointing his nose at us. My nose gunner, top turret and waist gunner opened up on him as did some other ships and my boys hit him as we saw some smoke. Sorry, but he should know better than that. The Germans had some captured equipment and used our planes against us so we'd been told not to take any chances. The pursuit boys knew we'd shoot and knew better for the most part. Today was the biggest raid in history and between ourselves and the RAF we dumped between 6000 and 7000 tons of bombs on targets over enemy territory. Over Germany we could look out and see fires for miles after the bombing and there was smoke in all directions as far as I could see. I never again expected to see as many or as extensive fires as today."

On Friday, 18 August, T/Sgt Terry Parsons, a radio operator/gunner in the 862nd Squadron, 493rd Bomb Group, went to an airfield "Rue de Balcourt - or something like that" near Amiens.

"Rough! Wooee! Those ack-ack gunners have really been checked out. We lost two planes and the 34th Bomb Group, three. The Germans first shot blew our leader's tail clean off. He just went straight down - poor devils didn't have a chance. Washington got it too but I guess they all got out.[981] Hansen was really scared I guess, but so were we all. Our formation just split from hell to breakfast. 'A' Group didn't get much flak at all."

This same day, 2nd Lieutenant Philip G. Day flew his first mission as co-pilot in the 467th Bomb Group, which bombed an aircraft engine plant at Woippy, near Metz. Day recorded:

"No flak - no fighters - Excellent results...The 100-mission party of the Group was on 19 August and it was a wild, glorious, all night drunk out time. The Group had been stood down for 20 August; I am sure no one was fit or able to fly."

Meanwhile, in the 44th Bomb Group, John W. McClane flew his 29th mission to Nancy-Essey airdrome, 170 miles east of Paris and just south of Luxembourg:

"The weather was beautiful with unlimited visibility. This mission turned out to be my last for the month. The Luftwaffe had been forced to withdraw there after the capture of their field in northwest France. We had 23 aircraft make it to the target. We carried 52 100lb bombs each. We were the lead aircraft for the group and had been assigned an Intelligence Officer as an observer. This officer had been hanging around Group Headquarters for several days waiting for the right opportunity. It appears that in order for an intelligence officer to be allowed as an instructor at our training bases back home, he was required to fly at least one real combat mission in order to be qualified as an 'expert'. Common sense tells you that he would not pick a deep penetration into the heart of Germany as his first choice. This mission looked like an 'easy one' so he requested that he be allowed to fly with us. This guy was a real 'Eager Beaver'. He was all over us. At briefing, he asked a thousand questions and when we reached our plane and were preparing for the flight, again he was everywhere. I usually laid my charts out on the ground to study them or to go over the bomb run with the bombardier. I got a bit aggravated when he picked up my papers so he could 'study' them. Finally the flare came from the tower. It was time to board '*Lili Marlene*'. Peritti and the officer agreed in advance where he would be during the bomb run so he could get maximum visibility when the bombs were released and follow them down to the target. He was to lie on the 'catwalk' that ran the length of the bomb bays with his head to the rear of the plane and his body towards the flight deck.

"As lead navigator I had a great responsibility during the assembly. It was a complicated and exacting task. I really did not have time to fool with this 'observer' but that did not bother him. Again a thousand questions and he was taking notes. He wandered from one end of the aircraft to the other, asking each man about his duties. He almost ran us nuts but finally we reached the vicinity of Nancy and the IP and he took his pre-selected position. Nancy-Essey airdrome was well protected by anti-aircraft guns and they had us in sight as we were only at 15,000ft. The flak began to burst close by and before Warga was ready to release our bomb load a piece of flak came into the bomb bay striking one of the smoke bombs.[982] This bomb was only a short distance in front of the observer's head. Smoke began to pour out of the bomb and in short order our whole plane was filled with this white stuff. I could hardly see my navigation desk and I don't know how Peritti kept control of the plane.[983] Warga released our bombs when he was ready. He did not let little things bother him. (As our strike photo later showed, our bombs landed dead center of the airfield. He of course received an excellent rating for the day). The smoke finally blew clear of our plane. (The crews in our fellow squadron planes said later that we looked like nothing they had ever seen before with all the smoke streaming from us). On every mission Peritti made a check of the crew to see if anyone had been hurt. He received a negative response from all positions except the observer lying on the 'catwalk'. He did not respond. Peritti asked the radioman, John Schneider and our engineer, Paul Corlew to check on our passenger. He knew we had been hit in the bomb bay and feared the worst for our 'new crew member.' Schneider and Corlew got to the officer and reported back to Peritti that he was alive but would not talk nor let go of what he had been holding onto. They could not bring him back onto the flight deck as long as he held on. The bomb bay doors were closed so Peritti decided to leave our observer where he was.

"It was a long way back to base and we flew a total of eight hours, of which at least three hours were required to arrive back to Shipdham. This Intelligence Officer never said one word on the way back. I was busy navigating and did not have time to worry about him. I was glad not to have the aggravation that I had on the way to the target. Landing was late afternoon. When the plane finally rolled to a stop at our hardstand and the props stopped turning, I got out through the nose wheel door opening. I walked back to the open bomb bay and saw several of the fellows lifting our 'observer' out of the plane. A more pitiful sight, I've never seen. He could not stand up by himself and he was shaking all over. Boys will be boys, we began to razz him and ask if he would go with us on our next mission. In a very stammering, high pitched, quivering voice he said, 'I - I - I - I'll never-never-fly-fly-fly-fly again'. They put him in a jeep and we never saw him again."

From 19 to 24 August a low-pressure system gathered over the British Isles and Western Europe. During the stand-down it was announced that Paris had been liberated, and it was reported that the Romanians wished to seek peace.[984] On 24 August Norman K. Andrew, navigator in Jack Stanley's crew in the 837th Bomb Squadron, 487th Bomb Group, flew his third mission of his tour. He wrote:

"Was awakened at 0145 this morning by Dick Giles. They were on their way to briefing. I thought to myself 'Missed us this time' but the CQ woke me at 0200 for 0230 briefing. So after a breakfast of canned grapefruit, two eggs over easy, bologna (ugh!) and cereal and fresh oranges and coffee, I was well prepared for the shock of the rising curtain (on the mission route). Holy Smokes! Whoever planned this one should have given it to the Russians - it was sure a lot closer to them. Anyway, take-off was 0745. Target was a synthetic oil plant at Dresden. The secondary, an airplane assembly plant. Last resort, an airfield. It rained off and on until take-off. The apron to my flak suit was wet (really frozen stiff at 25,000 (-25C). We departed Splasher #7 at 0908, left England and headed for Heligoland at 0932. Just before Heligoland Dick lost his oxygen and aborted so the deputy lead took over. Saw a hell of a lot of flak all along the route but the nearest to us (except at the target) was approximately 300 yards. They used rockets. Not even close and saw one burst of red flak. The rest was black. Every town we went by was smoke screened but Bremen was getting quite a pasting. They were putting flak all the way up to 30,000 but I observed no hits.

"We made a very fancy bomb run - evasive action for all but about 3 minutes - then the bomb bay doors would not open electrically. So Rector cranked them open. Then on 'bombs away' only half the load dropped, 5 500lb GPs so Chuck hit both the salvo and the toggle switches. That did it, but it threw the other 5 500lb bombs about 3 sec over the target - approx. 1000ft. Hope we didn't kill any women or children with those wild bombs. Then Rector had to hand crank the doors shut while we were making just about a 180 and diving. There were 51 sure guns at the target. The ride home was just a ride. Some flak, but all of it wild. Logged 8½ hours - 5:05 on oxygen and traveled 1204 nautical miles not counting evasive action. On that oxygen - I had to move to the Bomb-Co-pilot line so Jack would have enough to get home - landed with the red light on and 75lbs on the gauge. We darn near ground-looped when we landed. The pin in the tail wheel sheared and we took off across the infield. To top it off it started raining like the devil and everybody got wet. There was one ship (B-17G) that landed at Lavenham that made it all the way back from Dresden on two motors. They had thrown everything they could out, including the parachutes."

Bishop E. Ingraham recalls the mission to Merseburg on 24 August:

"This was the first day that the 8th Air Force was hit by jet fighters. It was our sixth mission I believe and prior to that day our ball turret gunner had remained in his turret from takeoff until the return landing. However he had been talking to his buddies, other gunners and they had told them that once they arrived at the 'IP' they got out of the turret until after the bomb run because enemy fighters 'NEVER' flew through their own flak. Therefore on this day he was not in position. We were on our bomb run when the tail gunner announced, 'Something coming in on our tail!' Almost immediately after his announcement the turret gunner got into his turret. A few seconds later we sustained a direct hit in the bomb bay. We still had not arrived at the target so we still had full bomb load, 500lb bombs and the hit was partly under the floor of my radio room. The flak had knocked out some of the bombs but some were still in the bay and fusing. Several of us managed to release the rest. There was a fire in the cockpit and in the radio room, which we extinguished. Fortunately, we had dropped from about 35,000ft to approximately 12,000. I say fortunately, because our oxygen system had been punctured so we had no oxygen. Also one of the wing tanks had been hit and so it was another miracle that we did not have any problem there.

"Of course there was a radio check immediately after we were hit and the only crewmember not to respond was our turret gunner. A fragment had gone through his gunsight and critically injured him directly in his head. We had taken him out of the turret but even when the emergency oxygen mask was placed on him he did not revive. Later the Flight Surgeon told us that there was nothing more we could have done because of his injuries.

"All of the radios and navigation equipment with the exception of the 'Gibson Girl'[985] was destroyed. Fortunately I was able to run out the trailing wire antenna and attach it to the 'Gibson Girl'. I must have cranked on it for nearly 30 minutes and it was a welcome sight to see a P-51 just above us in, again I estimate about 30 minutes from the time I first began transmitting our SOS on the emergency radio equipment. Another miracle was the fact we never encountered another enemy fighter from the time we were hit. The P-51 guided us to a crash landing field on the coast, I believe was Woodbridge. I have not mentioned yet that many of our plane's controls were so damaged that it took both Captain Bosko and our co-pilot Curt Kohnert to maintain as level flight as possible. Consequently when we arrived over Woodbridge it was impossible for the pilot and co-pilot to bale out. Because of the damage to controls and possible brake damage the pilot ordered the rest of the crew to bale out. It turned out that he had neither flaps nor brakes but due to the field length they had no problem. We all were picked up at various points by the RAF and taken to their hospital where the injured were treated. A miracle for me personally was the fact I did not sustain even a scratch on this mission, even though my radio room was a shambles."[986]

At Knettishall, crews in the 388th Bomb Group who had been on a long, very tiring mission to Brux, Czechoslovakia, on 24 August awoke in the early hours of the 25th to be confronted with another shock. Richard Bing, the radio operator in Lieutenant Leon Sutton's crew in the 561st Squadron, recalls:

"At 6 am tired crewmembers assembled at squadron briefing. A white sheet covered the wall at the far end of the room. Behind its cleanness was a map of Europe and our dirty work for the day. Hopefully, we prayed, it was a short run to France. Allied armies were on the outskirts of Paris and, just maybe, they needed some help. After Brux, we needed a break. In strode the ever-confident Briefing Officer, an English riding crop tucked under one arm. (That was class.) 'Gentlemen', he announced dramatically, 'today you have the honor of destroying Germany's last remaining oil refinery.'

"'But Sir,' called a voice from the rear, 'we did that *yesterday!*' (Laughter)

"'All right, Gentlemen, let's get serious.'

"The sheet was ripped away. Crews whistled and groans filled the room. A thin red line arched high over the map of Europe. It spanned far out over the Baltic Sea...then dropped abruptly into the heart of the German Fatherland. (Oh my God, another deep strike.) With crop in hand the Briefing Officer traced the route. 'You'll assemble here.' he indicated 'and form here with the 3rd Division over the Channel. On the way in, Holland will be on your right. Your first land contact is Denmark. Enemy flak will be low and to your left. You'll continue over the Baltic (his short riding crop proved only partly utilitarian) then south into Germany. This will be your IP and here, gentlemen, is your target...Politz; 15 miles northwest of Stettin. Germany's last remaining oil...(All right, all ready.'). The route we've indicated,' he added, 'offers the least amount of fighter and flak opposition. In the target area itself our intelligence estimates about ninety 88mm flak guns. German fighter planes haven't been seen in weeks. Of course, the Krauts have been known to move both fighters and flak. They're quite mobile you know? (Boy doesn't that give you confidence?) I can give you this assurance. Allied fighters *control* the skies over Europe. The Luftwaffe is almost non-existent.' (Why didn't he mention flak I wondered? It was intense and accurate.) He hadn't finished. His next gem came straight out of a war movie. 'Gentlemen, I won't be able to join you today. The CO says I'm needed here on important matters. Of course, you know I'd rather be up there with you guys. I wish you all the best of luck.'

"I nearly called out, 'Come join us Mr. Briefing Officer. *We* have important matters over the skies of Europe'. I heard only murmurs. Wasn't anyone with me? How about a resounding 'boo' for this clod on stage?

"The General briefing became crucial. Crew's hurriedly scribbled notes, target information, bomb load, estimated time of arrival, enemy resistance, etc. Individual briefings followed: pilots and co-pilots; navigators, bombardiers and radio operators; engineers and pilots; engineers, radio operators and gunners; that's why they got us up so early.

"We were assigned *Cutie on Duty*, a fairly new B-17G, for the mission to Politz. She had 18 bombing raids to her credit and a welcome change to the clunkers we had been flying. The enlisted men were the last to arrive at the revetment area that housed *Cutie*. The officers were already on board. In the pilot's compartment his co-pilot, Lieutenant Harlan Thompson, a 25-year-old happy-go-lucky character from Athol, Massachusetts, joined Sutton. At 20 years of age Sutton was young for a bomber pilot but I had seen Lieutenant-Colonels who were still in their twenties. Sutton was the first member of the crew to fly a mission over Europe. On 4 August he went along as an observer on a raid on Hamburg. He was a changed man after that, becoming quiet and withdrawn.

'Tommy had just recently become the favorite of the enlisted men. At his insistence, we had all been promoted staff sergeants. Until then, I must have been one of the few flying corporals in the ETO. Before joining the crew, Tommy was a B-26 pilot in the States. He had it made but chose to volunteer for combat.

"In *Cutie*'s nose section Lieutenants Healy, the navigator and Harold Fisher, the bombardier got ready for the day's mission. Healy - 24 and the only other married man on the crew - was a serious, no-nonsense type. He was quiet and knew his job. Since we had made our peace over the Atlantic he had brought me more into the navigational side of flying. Fisher, 22, was our comic relief from Brooklyn, New York. He constantly reminded the crew of his Jewish heritage. 'If we're ever shot down, remember, my name is 'Fishetti!' 'Fish' had washed out of pilot training but was rapidly becoming a good bombardier."

S/Sgt W. "Midge" Midget joined Sutton and Tommy for *Cutie's* pre-flight check. When airborne, he manned the twin 50s in the top turret.

"In the radio room, the 'Chicago Gangster' (as I had been dubbed) busily tuned the Liaison and Command radio sets, checked the interphone communications and got the codebooks in order. In the waist, J. J. Camarda, E. Coleman and F. J. Bernjus helped the ground crew load the crates of ammunition aboard. They wouldn't load and check their .50 caliber machine-guns until we were over the English Channel.

"At 0805 hours *Cutie* and her crew waited patiently at the tail end of a long line of B-17s near the edge of the runway. It was still a gray, English morning and the ever-present fog threatened to scrub the mission. 'Skies over the target area are clearing,' advised tower control, 'you should be taking off shortly.' Pilots instinctively revved their engines. At 0820 hours the fog lifted briefly and a green flare pierced the murk. The mission was 'Go'. One by one 22 Forts of the 388th, which was flying lead and low groups in the 45th Combat Wing, roared down the runway and leapt skyward in search of their rendezvous with the 3rd Division over the Channel. One B-17 aborted for mechanical reasons. The sky cleared as we climbed steadily. 'Let's tighten up that formation', came a voice from Divisional Command. 'You're looking a little ragged.' Hundreds of B-17s snuggled closer and got to know each other. In the radio room I tuned into the BBC in London. The announcer spoke of an Allied success. 'The Paris radio announces that the French capital has been liberated, with the German commander ordering his men to cease fighting immediately. General Dietrich Von Cholitz, Chief of the Nazi garrison of about 10,000 men, signed the unconditional surrender order today in the presence of French Brigadier-General, Jacques-Phillippe Le Clerc and a US Corps Commander in the Montparnasse railway station.' I quickly switched to intercom. 'Hey it's official. They took Paris this morning.' 'Whee,' came the reply. From the crew's reaction you'd think the war was over.

"It was now 0830. England's fog was far behind. Europe's sun was rising. It was going to be a bombardier's sky. From the radio room I could see the coast of Holland. *Cutie* purred along. Her ground crew would be proud. Overnight, they had patched 32 flak holes in her tender body and replaced a two-foot piece of metal blown away from her tail. 'The young recuperate quickly,' I thought. We climbed past the 10,000ft level. The air was getting thin and the crew donned oxygen masks. Every air mile the weather improved. It would be a beautiful day. German flak greeted us over Denmark. It was low and to the left (one score for the Briefing Officer). My mind began to wander. I thought of something totally unrelated to the mission. Before take off a rigger had said, 'you guys better get back today 'cause Glenn Miller and his orchestra are gonna be here tonight for a concert. And according to one rumor, there would be 300 girls from Norwich and another 500 from London and Cambridge.' One officer had said, 'confidentially, they have to find their own quarters and absolutely be off the base in *three* days!' Musically, Miller was my favorite but what about the rigger's rumors? 'Hey skipper, we gotta get back today,' I said feebly on intercom.

"'OK. Let's knock off the idle chatter,' came the reply.

"Over the Baltic the 3rd Division swung right. Bomber Command broke radio silence. '10 minutes from IP.' Silently, I prayed this was Germany's last remaining oil refinery. Brux was a son-of a-bitch.

"'Waist gunner to pilot. Over.'

"'Go ahead Joe.'

"'Take a look to the left about 9 o'clock level.'

"'Looks like a '17? Probably lost and wants to join us?'

"'I don't think so. There's no markings on it.'

"'Keep an eye on it Joe. Could be a Kraut.'

"'No use skipper. She's leaving us right now.'

"The mystery B-17 peeled off and disappeared into cloud cover. It was a Kraut all right and by now German anti-aircraft was zeroed in on our altitude.

"'We've passed the IP,' called the Group Commander. 'We're committed to target.'

"In the nose, Fisher had the best view. He saw it first.

"'Oh my God! Look at that flak, its pattern and they're right on us!'

"Within minutes we were right in the middle of it.

"'I've seen three or four go down ahead of us,' said a dejected voice.

"'We're coming up on target,' said Sutton. 'Bombardier, you've got control; confirm!'

"'Roger, I've got control. Bomb bay doors open.'

"Thank God I couldn't see what was up front. Outside the radio window flak shells exploded in harmless looking black puffs. The rain of metal on *Cutie's* fuselage sounded like hailstones on a tin roof. Bang! *Cutie* took a hit in the right wing. She rolled a bit but held her course. Fragments of another shell ripped into the radio. The concussion knocked me down. From a prone position I surveyed the damage. The transmitter was smashed and the rudder cables severed. The cables got priority. Three or four were cut. I scooped them up, matched their thickness and held on for dear life. My hands moved with each rudder maneuver by the pilot. Was I helping or not? What did I know about flying a plane? 'I heard 'Bombs Away!' *Cutie* rose as she discharged her cargo of death. She took another hit in the waist. Why didn't somebody say something? Another explosion rocked the ship. We fell out of formation. It was a mortal wound. *Cutie* groaned and plunged earthward out of control. In the cockpit Leon and Tommy fought to right her.

"'Let's have an oxygen check,' said Tommy, breaking the silence. All the crewmembers responded. No apparent injuries. Coleman didn't answer. 'Get him out of the ball! Coleman, get out of that turret!'

"'Okay,' said Sutton, 'here's the situation. We've got her on automatic pilot and have some manual control. Make preparations to abandon ship.' (Hell, I had that in mind back on the runway.)

"'Ball turret to pilot. We've got a fire on the underside of the No 2 engine.'

"'Roger, hit the fire extinguisher. Feather No 2. Pilot to navigator, over.'

"'Navigator to pilot. Go ahead.'

"'How far to Sweden?'

"'I've been checking that, sir. I calculate about 30 minutes flying time.'

"'Let's give it a try.'

"*Cutie* swung north. The Baltic was clearly visible. The dark landmass of neutral Sweden loomed in the distance. (Come on girl, it was beautiful war over there!)

"'Waist gunner to pilot. Better keep her over land, skipper. We're trailing gas. Fire's hitting the tail section. Fish? Keep the bomb bay open. We can't get out back here.'

"The order is definite: 'This is Tommy to crew. Get the hell out of this plane!'

"I took off my flak suit, hooked the chest 'chute to the parachute harness and headed for the open bomb bay. None of us had jumped from a plane before but like the 'loose wires and jiggling tubes' of radio school, I remembered my Army training. 'If you ever have to jump,' said a sergeant, 'make sure your harness straps go underneath each testicle. 'Cause if they don't, when the 'chute opens, a baritone can quickly become a tenor.'

"'Midge' was the first to jump. I noticed a certain fear in his eyes but he didn't hesitate. Camarda was next. 'If my tough guy buddy can do it, so can I.' He straddled the bomb bay, dropped his GI shoes, brought his feet together and disappeared into space. I was up next. Gulp! I hesitated. I looked towards the pilot's compartment. Tommy was almost running towards the bomb bay. He had popped his 'chute and with his arms full of nylon I could see he wanted out in a hurry. Coleman and Bernjus crowded in behind.

"*Cutie's* wing fire was rapidly becoming *Cutie's* bomb bay fire. For some God-awful reason, the words of the Army Air Corps song came to mind. 'You live in fame or go down in flame 'cause nothing can stop the Army Air Corps.'

"'Bullshit! Geronimo!'"[987]

On 25 August over 1100 heavy bombers attacked four aircraft plants, three airfields, two experimental stations, and 15 targets of opportunity for the loss of 19 bombers. Fifteen fighter groups flew over 600 sorties in support of the bombers, and four of these later strafed ground targets, including numerous parked aircraft, of which 30 were claimed destroyed. In a follow up raid 92 heavy bombers attacked five liquid oxygen plants in Belgium and Northern France. Norman K. Andrew in the 487th Bomb Group at Lavenham was rudely awakened at 0430 hours for 0500 briefing for what would be his fourth mission. He wrote:

"Looked like a short one but it was sure longer than yesterday's. Left Great Yarmouth at 0932 and headed over the North Sea. Right through a stationary front. It really scattered the formation. We were reforming for 100 miles. Came over Germany at the Denmark peninsula about 5 miles left of course. Everything was smooth - solid undercast - when, with no warning the Flensburg flak batteries opened up. They must have tracked us for 10 minutes because the first bursts were right off our left wing in the formation. The plane would jump up about six inches every time a burst would let go underneath and there were several. One of the ships got his, jettisoned his bombs and headed home. We got the hell out of there. From Flensburg we cut across Kiel Bay to Nykobing on one of Denmark's islands. Angled across the Baltic Sea and hit Germany again near Stettin. Two flak batteries took shots at us going by but we were just out of range. We flew west of Stettin where the flak forced us to fly 4 miles off course. That flak wasn't very well figured out. Turned on a 6-minute bomb run and hit an experimental airfield (Rechlin, the Wright Field of Germany) on the SE shores of the Muritz Sea. Had about 15 flak guns at the target and they were good. One of the boys went down in flames - the stories vary from 3 to 9 chutes came out. It was the deputy lead - 6 officers and 5 enlisted men.[988] We had 71 holes from flak. Went north to Nykobing and home the same route as we flew out. Plane out for 4 days. Logged 9¾ hours but only 2¼-hours on oxygen. I'll dream of that bomb run - there were three bursts of three right across the nose. If that gunner had loaded just a little slower, he would have had us. Well, four down and 31 to go. Wasn't quite as scared today as yesterday - but that's not saying much. Better get some sleep - we're alerted for tomorrow - if we do 3 in a row is rough."

Eino V. Alve, a B-24 pilot in the 453rd Bomb Group, was one who went to a V-2 fuel dump in Belgium:

"Flying alone, we became sitting ducks for German fighter planes. An easy target, this crippled B-24. Indeed, a fighter plane did pick us up, but thank God, it was American and not German. He was flying a P-47 and came within eyeball range. He called over the radio, 'Hello Big Friend, this is your Little Friend. How much fuel to you have?' Just then a flak battery had our range again and began firing - hoping to finish us off. Our 'Little Friend' dove earthward, heading directly toward our enemy. His courage and skill put a stop to the German firing. We were saved. At this point, we could have headed for Sweden and internment for the rest of the war, but with the P-47 at our side as escort, I was determined to get our old B-24 safely back to Old Buck. The aircraft had stabilized by now; it was losing altitude steadily, due to the loss of the #3 and #4 engines but once we reached 10,000ft it leveled off and maintained level flight. We were confident now, that 'Big Friend' would return us even though the two right engines were inoperative. In the distance, I could see a sight that never looked better to those weary eyes: the White Cliffs of Dover. We were home! We landed without any problems but our faithful B-24 was full of holes. It had no brakes or flaps and was damaged beyond repair. She never flew again."

Hauptmann Heinz Knoke of III./JG 1 was aloft this day, and he wrote:

"Eventually we engaged about 60 Mustangs and Thunderbolts. My companions quickly disappeared and I found myself alone with my wingman, Unteroffizier Ickes, who stoically followed my desperate maneuvers to shake off a pursuing Mustang. With a risky move, I was able to surprise him and turn the situation to my advantage. He went down in flames. Then came a terrible shaking! Debris from my victim hit my aircraft. I had no other option but to bale out. On the ground, I was able to pass myself off as an American to four Maquisards and to eventually regain our lines. The Allies had broken through near Soissons. That night we had to retreat towards Cerfontaine in Belgium. I found out, sadly, that Ickes also had to bale out but was machine gunned on his parachute and was found dead on the ground."[989]

On 26 August 956 bombers escorted by 897 fighters attacked targets in France, Belgium, Holland, and Germany. Thirteen bombers and 13 fighters were lost, and 148 bombers and 15 fighters were damaged. Soon after take off from Framlingham, Suffolk *Ding Dong Daddy* flown by 1st Lieutenant George E. Smith and 42-102936 in the 390th Bomb Group collided over Hertfordshire, near Hitchin, and exploded, scattering pieces of aeroplane over a two and a half mile area. Everyone aboard *Ding Dong Daddy*, which crashed into woodland minus a wing and without its tail section, was killed, while five of the crew of 42-102936, which exploded in mid-air, including the pilot, 2nd Lieutenant Paul H. Bellamy, died. One of the crew on Bellamy's plane had managed to bale out safely, but as he was gathering up his parachute, a jagged piece of metal fell from the plane and pierced his chest, killing him instantly. 2nd Lieutenant Raymond A. Klausing, the navigator, survived after being blown clean through the Plexiglas nose.[990]

Norman K. Andrew, navigator in the 487th Bomb Group at Lavenham, flew his fifth mission in Jack Stanley's crew in the 837th Bomb Squadron. Andrew wrote:

"Up at 0400. Briefing at 0500. It sure looked good to look at the flak map and see Brest for the target. Not Brest itself, but a flak and coastal battery across the bay. Nice trip but there isn't such a thing as a milk run. We went over the target at 20,400. There were clouds about 9/10 but we had a beautiful hole and about a 1½-minute bomb run. The Air Leader had jumped the gun and decided to go under the clouds so we didn't drop. Damn it! So we circled around and came in at 17,400. I could see a battery in Brest winking at us. The ship jumped about a foot once but the only flak observed was at 7 o'clock level and close in. Found out later they were shooting gray flak and it blended with the clouds. Anyway I wish they would do that more often - it has its psychological advantages. Dropped 38 100lb GPs. I think we dumped them in the bay. However someone ahead of us has put a load on the target. I saw the smoke the first time over. Logged 7 hours. The best part of it was only three hours on oxygen and only 45 minutes carrying that flak suit. My shoulders are really sore from the last two long trips. So ends Mission #5. Traveled about 680 NM not counting the 2nd run. Make it 700 NM."

On 27 August Robert H. Tays flew his first B-24 mission in the 392nd Bomb Group to Hanover. He wrote:

"Aircraft are everywhere for the entire 8th Air Force is out this day...Upon arrival at the IP...a flak burst hit our No.3 engine. It stopped running almost immediately with just enough time to feather the prop. I added power to the remaining engines, stayed with the formation in position...Then it was bombs away. The sky was dark with flak bursts, some bursts close enough to hear over the roar of the engines and see the little orange flame in the center of the bursts."[991]

On 29 August 1st Lieutenant Walter J. Konantz in the 338th Fighter Squadron, 55th Fighter Group, which had just recently switched from P-38s to P-51s, flew his 12th mission after arriving at Wormingford. He had flown his first combat mission on 8 August when the group escorted the B-17s to Romilly-sur-Seine airfield south of Paris. The majority of Walt Konantz's 13 combat missions during August included some spectacular ground strafing and dive bombing of targets in France and Holland. On the 29th he was one of the 55th Fighter Group pilots who strafed train targets just over the French border into Germany. He recalled:

"I was 2nd or 3rd man on most of the train strafing. I shot up three trains, one of which was a long troop train. The train was moving fast when I raked it from the rear to the front and I saw soldiers jumping out of the windows while it was still moving at 30-40mph. When it finally stopped, I saw 50-60 people lying in the fields and ditches near the tracks. Another train made it safely into a tunnel and would not come out. Lieutenant Lanham shot down a Do 217 and I saw it crash."[992]

On 1 September Norman K. Andrew, navigator in the 487th Bomb Group at Lavenham, flew his sixth mission in Jack Stanley's crew in the 837th Bomb Squadron. Andrew wrote:

"Up at 0230 for 0345 briefing. However I've had so much sleep the last 3 days that I hardly slept at all. We are beginning to get some benefit from the occupation of France. We were scheduled to bomb Mainz, a supply depot. Going over we were behind the lines. However we ran into some pretty soupy weather. It went up to about 30,000. We circled around and over Paris trying to get through. Our position was #3 on the lead element; #1 and #2 were pathfinder ships. We milled around in the overcast for about 1½ hours. Ships and formations were everywhere. At one time one formation went right across over us and one went under. Really gave us a scare. The mission was finally recalled. Two ships, not from our field, had a mid-air collision - coming around a cumulus build-up from different directions. Some of our boys, on the way home, weren't quite on the ball and went over Le Havre. Got some flak but no damage. Logged 7 hours. Plus a few more gray hairs. Temperature went to -31C."[993]

On 3 September T/Sgt Robert T. Marshall flew his tenth mission when the 8th went to Brest, France:

"Briefing was 0230 this morning. I readied myself for a long haul, maybe to East Prussia. S-2 raised the curtain that covers the map and the route ribbon was short. Brest! Again! A coastal-battery target! S-2 said 19,000 *Nazis* are holed up at Brest and thereabout. Take-off was at 0515, a night take-off. Up we went into the dark for assembly. The whole 8th Air Force seemed to be up and milling around. My anticipation made the sweating-it-out begin early. Light, when it came, was eerie. A kind of golden light, not strong, not bright, just gold daylight. And then I witnessed something that made man, the bombers, the war, insignificant. It was an apparition bathed in soft, golden light. It was a peek into the unknown with the Supreme Being exposed. It was holy, majestic and awesome and it took me away from preparing myself to go into battle. On one side of the sky in half-light, a beautiful full moon set. At my left I saw a beautiful sun rising over the English Channel. Rays of color fired from the sun. In that light the sun, the moon and the shoreline were parts of an awesome painting. The rays gave the painting an effect that made me think of the times when I was a kid looking at pictures in the Bible. Angels wearing halos, the sky ablaze as it was when John baptized Jesus, like the picture when the dove flew in radiating light over Noah's Ark, like the scene when the angels sang above the manger in Bethlehem. Celestial, refracted light. It was all there with the sun and the moon. I watched and watched it. I had been searching the sky anxiously moments before, anticipating airplanes on a collision course as we went round and round assembling. Then this; a perfect full moon going down, awesome in itself in golden light, golden light giving the sun a supernatural appearance making it shout the power of the Creator.

"Daylight slowly increased in intensity. The shoreline below us - I suspect it was England - slowly etched into a hardness, as it came out of the shadow. The mysticism of the scene disappeared too quickly. Routine of assembly returned. We flew on, a mission unfolding and I pushed the moments out of my mind and returned to looking for enemy fighters. We flew toward Brest at 10,000ft and we were at that altitude when we went over the target at 0938, 4 hours after take-off. 'Bombs away!' I watched through the camera-well, looking between my boots. I saw the bombs fall and I saw the explosions. I heard the sound above the noise of the engines. The sequence of noise sounded like an ammunition dump might be exploding. The target was well camouflaged, one of many pillboxes back of the beach. Wrecked equipment littered the beach. I thought I could see barbed wire entanglements down there from 10,000ft. Later, Benton said his accuracy was excellent. The mission took 7 hours and 35 minutes to dump 38 100-pounders. It was a milk run except for the apparition."

Bad weather in September severely limited missions, and only 14 were flown during that month. On 8 September Lieutenant Norman E.

Freidman, a co-pilot in the 493rd Bomb Group at Debach, near Ipswich, flew his 17th mission, and his first in a B-17 since the group converted from Liberators:

"Our crew had been designated a lead crew. Therefore our navigator Lieutenant Billy McVicker from California, was back with us permanently. Briefing was held at 0300 for a mission to Mainz, west of the city of Frankfurt. We were always awakened early enough to be able to do our personal and get to the mess hall for breakfast. Our next stop was the main briefing room. All crews alerted for the mission assembled there for general and individual briefings. The very first thing that occurred always took our strict attention. The curtain was pulled back and a long string showed the route to and from the target area. The longer the string, the farther to the target, which meant more time in the air and more chances to get shot down. The operations officer briefed on the missions general facts, where we were going, what type of bombs we were carrying and what we were going to hit. He also briefed on the formation procedures to use and gave us the number and type of fighter groups, which would provide escort all the way in and out of enemy territory. He gave us the times they would appear. All of this of course was printed on forms for us to take along. All times, start engine, taxi, take-off, forming up etc were also noted on the briefing form. The next briefer was the intelligence officer. He gave us the target information, why we were hitting it, the amount of enemy flak and fighters we could expect on the route in and out and over the target He explained the latest in escape and evasion procedures for the area we were flying over. Our target was an ordnance depot. We climbed on course to 29,000ft flying deputy lead to Captain George Field. We here supposed to drop on PFF but the bombardier was able to drop visually. All the bombs landed well within the intended impact area. A good job. Light flak and no enemy fighters. Target destroyed.

"Next day there was no rest for our crew. We were briefed early in the morning for a mission to Düsseldorf, directly in the center of 'Happy Valley', so-called because of the concentration of flak guns. This area was the home of much of Germany's heavy machine industry. We were flying deputy lead in the low group off the wing of Captain George Bruck. He climbed on course to 29,000ft for our bomb run. The flak was very intense and accurate. Fortunately, our only casualty was the heel of Billy McVicker's shoe. A piece of flak entered the nose compartment and lodged in his shoe. There were no enemy fighters to harass us or our escort of P-51s. The bombing was fair and the target partially destroyed. Many planes had flak holes in them."

On 10 September over 1000 8th Air Force heavy bombers escorted by several hundred fighters attacked targets in Germany. The 96th Wing went off operations, and the 458th, 466th, and 467th began "Trucking" operations. Philip C. Day, co-pilot of *Lil' Peach* in the 467th Bomb Group, recalls:

"We hauled boxed goods and five-gallon Jerry cans of gasoline initially but soon we were hauling 80-octane gas only, in our 'plane's outer wing 'Tokyo' tanks, in tanks installed in the bomb bays and in fighter drop tanks carried in the waist area of the ship. These loads were about 2700 gallons, which were pumped off at the landing fields in Prance. In addition, we carried enough 100-octane in our wing tanks for the approximate five hours round trip. At the height of the operation there were 150 airplanes at Rackheath. All armament was taken from the 'planes except the Martin upper turret guns and ammunition and we flew at altitudes of 1000ft or less, ready to go 'on the deck' if attack by enemy fighters occurred."[994]

On 11 September over 650 heavies escorted by 14 fighter groups were sent to bomb six synthetic oil plants and other targets in the *Reich*. Lieutenant Norman E. Freidman in the 493rd Bomb Group at Debach, who was flying his 19th mission, recalled that the morning's briefing commenced at 0200:

"When we arrived at the briefing room, we stood there in awe at the length of string on the board. They must have unraveled two socks for this one. Our target was a synthetic oil refinery near the town of Brux, Czechoslovakia. Our instructions were to bomb only visually because of the proximity of the target area.

"The lead ship in our formation received an order over the radio to descend and make the drop at 11,500ft. He did not ask for authentication of the message from our operations! The flak was heavy and concentrated. At this low altitude, we here very vulnerable. On the first run over the target, the lead ship was shot down before he reached the drop point. We made a circle and came back over the target with the deputy lead in command. Just after bomb release, he was shot down. The bombs were dropped and hit as planned. A very good job. By this time the group was scattered all over the sky. Our crew took over as group lead and had to make two more runs near the target area to enable the planes to reform for the flight home. Most of the planes were shot up badly."[995]

Jack Sargeant, in the 92nd Bomb Group, recalls:

"I was in the low squadron on the mission to Merseburg. Our assembly departure from England and the run to the target was routine but then the fun began. If you could call it fun. Our run from the IP to target was on an easterly course at 29,000ft. While on the run for some reason the co pilot and I noticed the outside air temperature was minus 60°. This was probably the reason for the flight deck interior to be covered with about an inch of hoarfrost. The second surprise came just at bombs away when another outfit came towards us at the same altitude on a westerly course. This proved more than a little unnerving. Needless to say, the flak was going pretty good at this time. The third event happened at bombs away. Seems I remember hearing the bombardier say 'bombs...' at that precise moment we took a pretty good flak hit in the nose area. At the time the co pilot and I had on our steel helmets and when the hit occurred, we ducked toward the middle of the flight deck. So precise were we that we banged our heads together. The resulting clang was pronounced. Additionally, the hit in the nose caused a loosening of the hoarfrost in the cockpit. For a second it looked like a real winter snowstorm. Naturally, the first thing was to get a damage report from the crew. All reports from the rear were negative but we knew we had been hit. Finally, we located the damage, the glass dome used by the navigator, George Nobel, had been half swept away. Upon return to base some ground crewmembers took what was left of the glass dome and made an ideal wind wing out of it for a jeep. For several months thereafter whenever I saw that jeep it brought back memories of the Merseburg mission."

The missions were flown in the face of an estimated 525 enemy fighters. Some 52 heavies and 32 fighters were lost, and once again one of the worst hit was the 100th Bomb Group, which went to Ruhland.

The mission had begun badly for the "Bloody Hundredth" when, during assembly, B-17 43 37823 suffered an engine fire that forced Ferdinand Herres to abort. Unable to extinguish the blaze, the crew baled out over southern England while the bomber crashed on the Isle of Sheppey and burned itself out. 1st Lieutenant George Fory flew co-pilot to Major M. Young's PFF crew, which led the Group to Ruhland. Fory recalls:

"This was one of those one in a million experiences that had many things in it that were unforgettable. The first is that it was my sixth wedding anniversary. The next is that one of the lead crew pilots had briefed the new pilots that fighter opposition was a thing of the past. He was one of those shot down that day. Although fighter attacks had been few and I had not been under other than light activity, it was a surprise to many others and me when we got such an intense force that day. They came up out of the undercast. We had the figure of 40 pretty well established and while I could not see them as they came up, I had the running account on interphone. They came up, made their pass through the group and then went on back down. They did not hang around or make several passes as they usually had in the past. I had a slight case of 'Buck Fever' while the attack was going on, but I especially concentrated on flying straight and level, so as not to get distracted and I was a bit concerned. Later I remarked that the clouds were trying to give me vertigo, when someone remembered that there were no clouds up there, they were all beneath us. The "clouds" I saw were 20mm cannon bursts. There was a head-on pass made on us, but it was one pass and that was when I saw the 20mm bursts. The noise, extra excitement and wondering how the others had fared left something to be desired psychologically. The attack was 12 to 15 minutes before target time and we had to get busy on routine chores. The noise was deafening, while we were under attack and I remember how quiet I thought it was from there to bombs away!"

The attacks began at 1205 hours when, with no alarm on VHF, three waves of enemy fighters approached deceptively from out of the sun and completely overwhelmed the trailing and unprotected low group of the C formation in a frontal attack. They tore the 350th Squadron apart, shooting down nine Fortresses. With his wing tips burning and fuselage breaking up, Captain John Giles ordered his crew to bale out.[996] The B-17[997] flying off Giles' left wing simply exploded, killing the pilot 2nd Lieutenant Joseph H. Baine and four of his crew. The rest jumped clear of the plummeting wreckage and were taken prisoner. Lieutenant Albert E. Trommer's B-17 on Giles' right wing also went down.[998] 2nd Lieutenant Harold R. Taylor's aircraft,[999] which was flying directly behind Giles, did a wingover with fiery gas tanks and parts falling off, and then fell into the undercast. On regaining some control, the pilot and co-pilot tried to crash land, but all the crew except for one of the waist gunners were killed. The two Fortresses[1000] flying behind Taylor, although damaged, survived the initial onslaught and headed for home as the escort came in and scattered the enemy fighters. The first B-17 piloted by 2nd Lieutenant Paul E. Corley continued to be attacked, and all nine crew baled out and were taken prisoner. 2nd Lieutenant Harold R. Schulte, who was killed by a 20mm shell, piloted the second plane. His co-pilot, Richard Kiern, flew on for 20 minutes as the crew fought off the enemy fighters, only for the B-17 to be caught by the Leipzig flak. Six of the crew baled out and became prisoners of war.

The low element of the "C Group" was also badly hit, and it lost three of its number in quick succession. The first[1001] was piloted by Lieutenant Wesley R. Carlton. Of the nine men aboard only two survived when they were thrown clear when the ship exploded. The second plane,[1002] piloted by 2nd Lieutenant Hugh E. Holladay, on the left of Carlton's wing went down and five of the crew, who were on their fourth mission, were killed. The third plane[1003] was piloted by Lieutenant Lawrence W. Riegel who, along with his co-pilot, Joseph Johnson, and four of the crew were killed. Only the bombardier and navigator baled out, while the ball turret gunner was blown out of his turret but reached the ground safely. All three were taken prisoner.

Two Fortresses in the high element were also destroyed. The first of these[1004] was piloted by Lieutenant Orville C. Everitt. Six of the nine crew were killed, including Everitt. All three survivors survived to be taken prisoner, but one of the gunners died a few hours later in a prison hospital. The second B-17,[1005] piloted by 2nd Lieutenant Charles E. Baker, was badly damaged by a number of 20mm shells, two of which hit through a waist window, while another ignited a gas tank. Moments later the gas tank burst into flames, the wings shriveled, and the fuselage snapped in the middle. Only three men managed to bale out. Raymond Heironimus piloted the last of the Group's Fortresses to go down. After barely surviving the first attack, the B-17[1006] nosed up, stalled, and went down 6,000ft in a tight spiral, by which time the radio operator, William Terry, had baled out to become a prisoner of war. On recovering control, Heironimus called and informed Thorpe Abbotts that he was heading for Paris with 75 gallons of gas left in the severely damaged plane, which eventually crash-landed in a turnip patch hard by the front lines. Some French peasants arrived armed with a bottle of wine and horsemeat. The crew duly returned to Thorpe Abbotts while the plane was salvaged.[1007]

George Fory continues:

"The flak at Ruhland was moderate. Again, as at Merseburg, we had tracking and the usual four blasts together, but after the fighters, the flak seemed mild. I had expected the flak to be something like Merseburg and it certainly was no disappointment. About 45 minutes after target our No.4 engine quit. At the time I was watching a fighter plane circling, near what I thought to be a parachute. By this time we were homebound on a descending course and down to 18,000ft. We feathered and watched the Group move on when No.3 engine quit. So there we were 18,000ft, a fighter below and half our engines. We found the 'Tokyo' valves had malfunctioned, probably due to ice and had not given us fuel transfer. Also our gauges read 120 and 150 gallons in #3 and #4 tanks. After we had descended into warmer air the valves began working. We re-started the engines and came on home. Passing at a low altitude over the North Sea, we spotted a raft with some people in it, but the sea was too rough for identification."[1008]

T/Sgt Ernest M. Heidt, engineer-gunner in B-17 *Canvas Back IV*[1009] flown by 1st Lieutenant John E. Glasco in the 326th Bomb Squadron, 92nd Bomb Group, recalls:

"It was dark when we were called before breakfast for a mission to Merseburg. All went well as far as take off, rendezvous and heading over the Channel to the target. We were flying deputy lead in the high squadron. We encountered heavy flak (88mm) over the Rhine River. It was very accurate, except that it was about 50ft too high. Well, one burst popped over my head and I figured it had to go through our plane to get there but apparently no, or I wouldn't be writing this now! No enemy fighters were encountered on the way to the target. We had the ever-loving little brother fighter escort. We passed the IP and started the bomb run. The bomb bay doors were opened and approximately one minute from 'Bombs Away' at 29,000ft, we took a direct hit on the left wing tip, which blew off about 5ft of the tip and part of the aileron. We immediately drifted towards the lead ship on the pilot dove. Then we went into a flat spin. We salvoed our bombs. While in the flat spin we took a direct hit in the ball turret area. This hit blew T/Sgt Robert D. Heare, the radioman-gunner and S/Sgt Chester S. Hinds, the waist gunner, out of the plane. One of them opened his chute and the other one was opened by the concussion. I had pulled my oxygen hose and intercom chord off, dropped to the floor griping for my chest pack chute when I felt the terrific concussion against one leg that was against the bomb bay forward bulkhead. I actually looked and felt my leg to confirm that it was still attached. I found my chute and clipped it on to the harness and headed towards the forward escape hatch. Glasco was fighting the controls alone with his feet on the instruments. I shouted at him to ask if I could help. He shouted at me to 'Get the hell out!'

"After that I was hunched over the escape hatch and rolling out. (I was always afraid of baling out with the bomb bay doors open and the door was right in alignment to cut you in half). In all the excitement I forgot the part of training, which says to connect your mask to a portable walk-around oxygen bottle at high altitudes. Consequently, I passed out from anoxia. When I became conscious I was falling feet first in free fall. My chute harness had pulled loose from the slipstitching and was hanging overhead. I pulled one strap down to reach the ripcord, pulled it and the chute opened. It was very cold (I lost one of my gloves) and quiet, with a slight sound of the wind. I then had an uncomfortable feeling as I attempted to steer the chute. One of the keg straps was unhooked and the other was carrying my weight with my testicle. It hurt. I tried to dislodge it from this position until I got so weak I could hardly move. Then too, I could have accidentally unhooked the leg strap and gone into a real free-fall. Event though it was quiet, the Germans were still firing the 88 mm guns at the rest of the formation. Some of the flak bursts seemed to send me back up into the air. I counted five other chutes all higher than me. I didn't know an 88mm could fire so high and be so accurate. (First hit 29,000ft, second hit about 27,000ft). As we lost altitude and came closer to the ground small arms firing was evident by the pop and whistling. After the free fall it seemed at least ten minutes before I hit the ground. At about 50ft the ground came up damn fast. I hit the edge of an apple tree in an orchard. 1st Lieutenant Albert P. Knight, bombardier, landed about 100ft from me. I got out of my harness, ran over to him and there was an unwelcome committee consisting of five non-English speaking Germans with a pistol and two pitchforks. A few minutes later a soldier with a rifle showed up and took over. All this occurred at about 12 noon."[1010]

On 11 September 49 Mustangs in the 359th Fighter Group were assigned the task of providing penetration, target, and withdrawal support to bombardment forces attacking oil plants in the Merseburg area. They were to pick the B-17s up at 22,000ft in the Blankenheim area at 1030. Major Ben King and Major Bill Forehand were leaders. Rendezvous was perfect, and 25 minutes later battles raged that resulted in the Group's greatest day. The score: 35 enemy planes destroyed, four probably destroyed, and 18 damaged. It all began in the vicinity of Gissen, when 30 Bf 109s and FW 190s were sighted at 32,000ft preparing to attack the trailing bombardment formation. The 359th Fighter Group pilots immediately dispersed and drove the hostile fighters to the deck, destroying one and damaging two. Constantly on the alert for possible interception, a number of enemy aircraft were observed taking off from an airfield near Gotha at 1130 hours, and they aggressively dived to attack. The Mustang pilots outmaneuvered and destroyed five Bf 109s in the air, and then in the face of anti-aircraft fire strafed and destroyed four Ju 88s and Me-210s while damaging four others. Shortly thereafter an estimated 30 Bf 109s and FW 190s were sighted heading east at 30,000ft on the bomber track. Although outnumbered, an element of the 359th destroyed two and damaged another. At 1130 hours over 100 hostile fighters were seen at 30,000ft north of the bomber formation, and the 359th pilots immediately proceeded towards the enemy. They destroyed four, probably destroyed two, and damaged one, and then in individual dogfights destroyed four more enemy planes. Meanwhile, other pilots of the groups descended to a grass landing ground in the vicinity of Kelleda, Germany, and in dividing offensive tactics destroyed four and damaged nine parked aircraft. At 1203 hours, in the vicinity of Eisleben, after the target had been bombed 15 FW 190s executed vicious attacks on the bomber formation. The 359th destroyed six of the enemy aircraft, probably destroyed an additional two, and damaged one other. On the return to home base the P-51s destroyed seven locomotives.

The 11 September raids cost 45 B-17s and B-24s. It was also the biggest air battle of the war for the 55th Fighter Group, whose 52 Mustangs escorted the 3rd Air Division B-17s to Ruhland. 1st Lieutenant Walter J. Konantz, who was flying his 17th combat mission, recalls;

> "Just before rendezvous with our bombers we were climbing through 24,000ft and I had to get rid of my second cup of coffee. To use the relief tube in the P-51 it was necessary to undo the lap belt, unsnap the leg straps of the seat type parachute, then scoot well forward on the seat to use the relief tube, which was a plastic cone attached to a rubber tube which vents overboard out the belly of the plane. It was stowed on a clip under the seat. I was completely unbuckled, sitting on the front edge of my seat when a voice came over the radio, '109s, here they come'. About 50 Me 109s had bounced our squadron and about 50 more engaged our other two squadrons up ahead. Just a few seconds after the warning on the radio, a single Me 109 passed directly in front of me in a 45° dive. With a reflex action, I peeled off after him. He evidently saw me as he steepened his dive to the vertical. I firewalled the throttle and steepened my dive to match his. During this wide open vertical dive our speed increased to near compressibility, both airplanes were as skittish as a colt on a wooden bridge, As I was vertical and virtuously weightless, the slightest movement of the stick would cause me to leave the seat and be stuck against the canopy. A very slight pull on the stick would put me back down in the seat. I felt like a basketball being dribbled down the court as I bounced back and forth between the canopy and the seat. Just before I started a careful pullout at about 8000ft, I saw the airspeed needle bumping 600mph - 95mph over the redlined airspeed of 505mph. Holding a steady 4G pullout, I regained level flight at about 3000ft. Meanwhile, the 109 was bouncing around and appeared pretty unstable and hard to control at that speed. He started to pull out of his dive about the same time I did but was not successful. His right wing buckled through the wheel well area and he spun into the ground with a fiery explosion. The pilot had no time to get out. I claimed a 109 destroyed and what confirmed the claim was that after the massive 20 minute dogfight, one of the 55th Fighter Group pilots reported that he counted 30 fires on the ground, which would account for the 28 Me 109s claimed and the loss of two Mustangs. I never got close enough to the 109 to fire my guns and I was too excited to think to take gun camera pictures of the impact point. My plane had only a few popped rivets, which speaks well for our beloved P-51 and its equally dependable Merlin engine. I would also complement the sub contractor who made the sturdy canopy.

"The day after we were again on a bomber escort mission to central Germany.[1011] We had escorted our bombers to their target and were headed back toward England, cruising along at about 22,000ft, spread out in a comfortable formation. About the same time as they were called out on the radio I spotted two Me 109s headed north. Our entire squadron of 16 Mustangs made a 90° right turn and swung in behind the pair of 109s which were 3 or 4 miles ahead of us and at about the same altitude. As had been demonstrated many times in the past, the Mustang was a bit faster than the 109 and we slowly began to close on the two enemy planes. I figured that when the Mustangs got in range and the bullets started flying, the 109s would break right or left and certainly would not continue to fly straight and level at full throttle. I thought I might put myself in a good position if one of them turned right so. I moved far to the right of our main formation and waited. Sure enough, when the shooting started one broke to the left and one broke to the right and came my way. I was in perfect position to cut inside his turn and catch him in short order. I moved up to perhaps 100 yards behind him and with the vibration of my first few rounds fired; my gunsight bulb burned out. Being only 100 yards behind him, I started moving up to point blank range where I could just use the center of the windshield as a gun sight.

"I was about ready to try another burst from about 50 yards when I saw some tracers come close over my wings from behind. I looked behind and saw another Mustang firing right through my position at the Me-109 ahead. This guy seemed very determined to get this victory hoping he would not hit me. His stream of bullets were coming uncomfortably close so I moved out of his line of fire to the right and was flying formation with the 109 about 50ft off his right wing. I could see the pilot clearly; looking wildly behind as the bullets of the second Mustang began to pepper him. Then his canopy flew off and he stood up in the cockpit to bale out but the 280mph slipstream jerked him out of the cockpit and rolled him back down the top of the fuselage until he hit the vertical fin and rudder. He then bounced at least 10ft higher than his plane and fell away. I expected that he would have been killed or badly injured so I watched him fall until I could no longer see his body. Then I watched the area he was aimed at to see if I could see a puff of dust or perhaps his chute spilling when he struck the ground. However, at 600-800ft above the ground his chute opened and he survived the encounter. I know who was in the other Mustang but he denies it."

September 12th was the worst day in the brief history of the 493rd Bomb Group at Debach, which began the mission with 38 B-17s.[1012] It was a day that 1st Lieutenant (later Captain) Roy L. Holtman and his crew in the 861st Bomb Squadron, who flew deputy squadron lead on Captain Ellis Woodward's right wing, would never forget. It was Holtman's 24th birthday:

"What started out like any other mission, turned out to be the worst. The target – Magdeburg - a day to remember![1013] We took off and assembled at altitude, as was standard procedure and departed on course for our target. We arrived at our IP and established our track to the target, experiencing very heavy flak. As we left the target, we were jumped by Focke Wulf 190s, supported by Me-109s, which we subsequently learned were one of Hitler's elite *Luftwaffe* Storm Groups."[1014]

In the 860th Bomb Squadron, co-pilot Lieutenant Norman E. Freidman was flying his 20th mission and recalls:

"On the way to the initial point and on to the drop point we were attacked by Me 109s and FW 190s. They came from 6 o'clock and our low group received the brunt of the attack. More than half of the ships in this group were shot down including my friend, Lieutenant Al Goodman.[1015] The fighters left as we arrived in the target area and we started getting very intense and accurate flak. Lieutenant Ed Bisaro, our right wingman, was hit just back of engine No.2. The fuel caught fire immediately and the plane exploded. There was no time for the crew to bale out. All were lost.[1016] Captain Wesley E. Carter, leading the 3rd element of our squadron, was hit directly in the bomb bay. As he dropped out of formation, our tail gunner saw ten chutes. Our plane was struck in the nose by flak. The piece hit the only part of the nose that was made of double safety glass. Bombardier, Dale Reinhart, from Pennsylvania; was operating the bombsight at the time and was very lucky it didn't go through. Our fighter escort caught up with us as we came off the bomb run and the German fighters did not attack again This was a very rough mission."[1017]

It seemed to take forever for the Low Squadron to make it through the intense flak, since they were flying directly into a vicious headwind. Fortunately, all 12 aircraft emerged from the flak intact. But before the lead ship, Captain Woodward's aircraft, could close its bomb bay doors, which had been damaged by flak, a force of 20 or more FW 190s escorted by an equal number of Me 109s seemed to appear out of the flak and attacked the squadron from the rear. In moments seven B-17s were either spiraling down or descending on fire.[1018] The five remaining B-17s received varying degrees of damage, but remained under control. The Fortress gunners made a valiant effort from the five remaining aircraft, and claimed as many as four German fighters as they fended off their attackers. Continued German attacks succeeded in dispersing these remaining Fortresses and each sustained major damage.

"The Magdeburg raid," recalls Lieutenant Francis S. Milligan "was probably my roughest mission, even though we didn't get a single hole in the ship, But it made one sick at heart to sit there helplessly, watching planes explode in mid-air and remnants of men and machines fall to the ground."

Magdeburg was 1st Lieutenant Albert L. Tucker's crew's 13th mission flying in the 863rd Bomb Squadron.[1019] All the crew (except Edward J. Borowy, who had been taken off the crew when the ball turrets were removed from the B-24s, and then after conversion to B-17s the nose gunner went into the ball turret) were killed.[1020]

S/Sgt Hayward F. Deese, Jr., engineer-left waist gunner in Lieutenant George M. Durgin's crew in *Ulpy*,[1021] in the 863rd Bomb Squadron, recalls:

"After the bomb run FW 190s with 20mm cannons hit us from the rear. The first pass they shot down nine out of the 12 B-17s in the Squadron. Our B-17 and two wing crews were left. The fighters came after us, shot down the wing crews and shot us up with 20mm cannon and 13mm machine gun fire. I got three pieces of 20mm in my back and Don Gray, right waist gunner, had a 20mm explode in his face and 13mm slugs in each leg. (I was standing on two flak vests and when I picked them up to return them after the mission there was a hole about 8-inches diameter under them and a lot of 20mm shrapnel right where I had been standing. The flak vests were in shreds. They saved my legs and my life). Durgin called me to look at the left elevator for damage. I knew what was wrong because I put a burst of 50 caliber through it shooting at a Me 109."

The Low "C" Squadron[1022] was lead by crew pilot Captain Ellis M. Woodward and his co-pilot, 1st Lieutenant William C. Rawson, in *Ramp Happy Pappy*. Rawson recalls:

"In early September new B-17s were brought in to replace all of our B-24s and we were again assigned our own aircraft. Accordingly, on our first B-17 mission we were assigned *Ramp Happy Pappy,* someone else's aircraft. Well we showed them. We encountered what I consider was the most accurate flak of our entire tour; not the greatest quantity/volume of flak, but those German gunners were blowing aircraft out of the sky. Next, we were hit by fighters. The *Ramp Happy Pappy* took a jillion hits but kept on flying."

Ellis B. Woodward adds:

"After witnessing the explosion of the B-17, we dropped our bombs, cleared the flak area over the target, breathed a sigh of relief, turned left and headed for home. But our relief was to be short-lived. Over the intercom came the dreaded word, 'fighters.' We were leading a flight of 12 B-17s. Within 60 seconds, we could feel some of the hits from 20mm cannon shells ripping through the airplane. And within 90 seconds of the warning, we looked around and found that there was no one left in our squadron except us and our deputy lead - our right wingman -and us. All of the other 10 B-17s had disappeared, each with nine crewmen aboard. What a catastrophe! Arithmetically, that amounted to a loss of one human being per second...."

The arrival of P-51s finally forced the Germans to break off their engagements with the bombers. The dispersed, crippled Forts then set course for Allied occupied territory while tending to wounded crewmen and assessing their damage. Two of the five landed at Brussels to get aid for critically wounded crewmen, and to get their damaged aircraft on the ground.[1023] The other three elected to return the wounded to England, since their aircraft seemed airworthy for the flight across the Channel. One of them was 1st Lieutenant Roy L. Holtman's Fortress who, flying off Captain Woodward's right wing, had held his position throughout the attack, and stayed with his leader on the long lonely flight to England. Holtman recalls:

"Out of a squadron of 12 B-17s, Woody and I were the only two left in formation to return to England. We were able to make it back to Debach. On our way back from Magdeburg, we were only able to communicate with Woody's aircraft by Morse code with lamp flashes. His electrical and hydraulic systems had been shot out. I can remember Woody asking me to stay with him and I agreed with him totally. It was a very lonely and vulnerable feeling being deep in German air space, severely damaged and alone, except for each other. God was certainly with us on this mission as He was always. My 24th birthday was one to remember."

On reaching England, Captain Woodward elected to land at the emergency landing strip at Woodbridge because of damage that affected the flight controls of *Ramp Happy Pappy*. As soon as the crew made their exit *Ramp Happy Pappy* was towed off the landing strip and dumped in the junk heap. Apart from Holtman's B-17, the only aircraft from the low squadron that made it back to Debach was that flown by 1st Lieutenant G. Brown and crew in the 862nd Bomb Squadron.[1024] The remaining nine crews from the low squadron formation failed to return.[1025]

That night, in a Quonset at Debach, Ed Borowy spent his loneliest night in the Army, for apart from his old crew who shared his hut, the other crew in the hut had also gone down. Next morning Borowy was reassigned to Lieutenant Ed Glotfelty's new crew.[1026]

The legacy of Magdeburg extended to the German defenses guarding other cities in their homeland, and during 13 September-25 November 1944 they were responsible for the loss of eleven 493rd Bomb Group crews over Germany.[1027] Merseburg was another synthetic oil producing center guaranteed to send shivers down the spines of crews unfortunate to have to fly there. The most disastrous period in the 92nd Bomb Group's history occurred on 11 and 13 September when 12 B-17s were lost in consecutive missions to the city. On the first raid "Fame's Favored Few" were making a second run on the target when the Group encountered a terrific flak barrage and the formation became slightly scattered. Just at bombs away 15 FW 190s and Me 109s attacked the lead group. The attacks were savage, made in elements of three abreast firing 20mm shells. Eight B-17s in the 92nd were lost to the combined flak and fighter assault, as catastrophic a day as any in the Group's history.[1028] First reports placed the day's losses at 12, but four crews returned or were accounted for the next day, having either landed or abandoned aircraft in France or Belgium.[1029]

The mission to Ruhland on 12 September was a sad day for the 306th Bomb Group also, as Sgt Joe Hoffman, engineer-top turret gunner in 2nd Lieutenant Leon A. Risk's crew in the 368th Bomb Squadron, recalls:

"Our lead navigator took us too close to Berlin and we got the works. Me 109s and FW 190s came in on the formation 25 abreast and the first wave wiped out the lead ship and wingman. The second wave wiped out the rest of the box. They attacked from tail 6 o'clock and at the same level came in with firepower that was hard to match. My crew was flying high element, left hand wingman and we had a ringside seat. We were very busy putting out the firepower. The flak was heavy. Also, it was the first time I had seen parachutes and flak. The Germans would fire ahead and above the formation and it would float. If you hit it, it would explode. The German fighters just kept coming in, wave after wave. Tail gunner Caraaco had many hits on the German fighters. Same with ball turret Roco Ruso and waist R. A. Cooper. We could see other B-17 crews being cut down by bullets and 20mm from Me 109s and FW 190s. Gunners were standing in the waist windows ready to jump, but when the bullets hit them, they would fall head first and no chute would open. After many waves of Germans the final wave came in for the kill on the high element.[1030]

"We got 20mm in the radio room. Our rudder cable was almost through so we had to go on autopilot. Later, we repaired the cable with wire from the bomb rack. Also, No.3 engine had a direct hit to the oil tank and the #2 engine had a hit to the prop pitch line and lost it. Also, #4 engine was losing power from lack of fuel. But later we were able to keep it going by taking fuel from one of the dead engines and transferring it to #1 and #4 engines. When the last wave of FW 190s and Me 109s came in we returned fire and all made a peel off and went down OK but one FW `190 cut its speed and came in on us. He fired at us from 1000 yards and he was the one who caused most damage. But when he got in close he stopped firing and flew a close formation with us. He was so close we could not fire. Ball and waist and top turret waited because if we hit him and he exploded we would all be in trouble. We all waited for the right time. At one split second we dropped and he rose up. At this point I fired in the side of the FW 190 and got a direct hit on the pilot. His head went back against his headrest and blood was coming out of his oxygen mask.

The airplane rolled off on its left wing and went down. He exploded at about 1000 yards below. The ball turret gunner saw the plane go down.

"We joined two other planes from the group but could not hold formation with them so we dropped out and released the bomb load. We began the long way back to England. A P-47 picked us up and stayed with us till we were back over friendly territory. We went over the English Channel at about 500ft. We lost our radio so we could not identify ourselves and the British anti-aircraft fired on us but when we got close, I fired 'Red-Red' flares and they accepted it. They could see that we were in trouble."

Merseburg was the target on 13 September, and again the 92nd Bomb Group suffered severely. Four B-17s in the 327th Squadron were lost, including the lead plane, piloted by 1st Lieutenant Howard C. Donlon, which received a direct flak hit ten miles east of the target and exploded.[1031]

A. J. Sinibubb, navigator, also ventured to Merseburg on 13 September for his 27th mission in *Cheri* in the 323rd Bomb Squadron, 91st Bomb Group, flown by Lieutenant Basnight. Sinibubb wrote:

"Bomb load 10-500lbs. Total distance: 1033. Base-Caxton Gibbet-Newmarket-Lavenham-Orfordness. Take off 0641. Weather was fair. The engineer neglected to put more flak suits for bombardier and I up in nose. We took off without them but pilots gave us theirs. The bomb run was Snafued as someone on the crew called out 'Bombs Away' from the lead squadron and our bombardier salvoed his bombs. Since we were deputy lead the rest of the squadron dropped also. Bombardier later caught hell for his action. Flak over target was accurate and heavy. A couple of control cables were shot out and we had to make an emergency landing. Contrails formed at altitude. Occasionally we hit bad prop-wash. Flak was received over the Rhine also."

Meanwhile, the 8th Air Force fighter groups doled out punishment to targets in the *Reich*, while in mid-September Fortress pilots had to call upon all their experience to fly a mercy drop to beleaguered Poles in the ruins of Warsaw. The Polish capital was cut off from the outside world, with the Germans on one side and the Russians on the other. Russia had requested General Bor to rise against the German occupiers, but had then stood by while the gallant Polish Home Army was gradually being annihilated. Allied airmen in RAF squadrons operating from Italy supplied the Poles in August, but then operations ceased because of the danger to crews. Operations were restarted after Polish protests, but it was not until early September that the Russians finally agreed to cooperate and allow the B-17s to fly on to Russia after the drops. An attempt to reach Warsaw on 15 September was aborted because of bad weather. (It severely limited missions, and only 14 were flown in September.) On 11 and 18 September the 8th flew two final shuttle raids. On the first, 75 B-17s with 64 P-51 Mustang escorts attacked an armaments factory at Chemnitz and flew on to bases in Russia. On 13 September the Shuttle force took off and bombed the Diosgyoer steel works in Hungary before proceeding to 15th Air Force bases in Italy.[1032] The last 8th Air Force shuttle mission was flown on 18 September when 110 B-17s escorted by 150 Mustangs dropped supplies to the Polish Home Army in the ruins of Warsaw.[1033] Nick G. Plackis in the 390th Bomb Group at Framlingham, who was flying his 17th mission, recalls the shock at briefing:

"All gasped when the curtain was drawn back on the stage of the briefing room, revealing the map of Europe, with the longest ribbon from base to target, that we had ever seen. We were greatly relieved, however when we were informed that this was not going to be a turn-around but listed as Framingham with the target at Warsaw and landing at Poltava, Russia; since we would not have sufficient fuel to return to base. The purpose of the mission was to furnish the Polish underground with 12-500lb parachute canisters per plane from 107 B-17s that contained food, medical supplies, arms and ammunition to relieve the shortages needed for the Polish Resistance. Since the freedom fighters were non-communists and the Russians in their offensive had reached the outskirts of Warsaw, they refused to assist the Home Army since they wanted a Soviet dominated Poland. So they decided to sacrifice the resistors by letting the Germans do the job of slaughtering the Polish Home Army by not offering them any assistance."

Colonel Karl Truesdell, CO 95th Bomb Group, led the B-17s over Warsaw, and the supply drop was made from between 13,000 and 18,000ft amid limited but accurate flak. The strong American fighter escort was unable to prevent the *Luftwaffe* attacking the 390th Bomb Group, which was flying as the low group, during the dropping run. One Fortress was shot down, and another landed at Brest-Litovsk. Nick G. Plackis continues:

"On our approach to Warsaw from the south we followed the Vistula River northward, going over the target at an unheard of low altitude of 14,000ft for accuracy. The Poles in the meantime had marked the 'drop zone' with strips of white sheets. The Germans said that only 12% of the supplies bad fallen within the zone but according to an official statement made by Polish General Bor, he confirmed that the accuracy of the drop was 93%. During our 'bomb run' or 'supply run' a minimum of 140 heavy Nazi A/A 105mm guns were continuously firing at us, along with several hundred smaller 88mm A/A artillery. From the German side of the river, it looked like the finale of the 4th of July at Jones Beach, with guns flashing continuously. But if you looked at the other side of the river where our 'allies' were entrenched, you would also see plenty of flashing from the Russian AA guns. Amid the flak Me 109s were viciously attacking throughout our formation, knocking down one of our 17s, the *Till We Meet Again* over the target. Just moments after the drop, our plane, the *Kwitcherbitchin* took a flak hit off the right nose with a piece of shrapnel coming through the aluminum skin of our plane, hitting me in the right thigh to earn me the Purple Heart. After the target, we immediately turned due East while rapidly descending to treetop level, to head deep into Russia toward Poltava for our overnight layover, a bit over 1 hour away.[1034] During that hour while totally over Russia, we had four more B-17s shot down from 'friendly ground fire'. Our Commander, Colonel Moller, voiced his outrage with the Russian officials, who apologized profusely, but it was eventually suppressed. They were the most trigger-happy soldiers I ever saw. This was not a surprise mission to them and yet at treetop level where you could see the color of their eyes, you could see them shooting at us with pistols, rifles, machine guns, as if we were the enemy. God only knows why. So as not to cause an international 114 incident, we were forbidden to bring our twin 50 calibers into action.

"However, the peasants in Poltava were of a completely different nature, being gracious friendly, helpful and compassionate, with a wonderful open-air kitchen waiting for us, with excellent food for all crews. The medics took care of my injury, which was not too serious and I then rejoined my crew for the rest of the evening, who were celebrating while trying to forget the events of the day just past. The next day we were fueled and reloaded with bombs, briefed for our next target, the RR marshaling yards, at Szolnock, Hungary, on our way to our next layover station at Foggia, Italy, where we stayed for two days before ferrying back to our home station."[1035]

Meanwhile, missions from England continued.[1036] On 19 September Norman Friedman and the rest of the crew in the 493rd Bomb Group flew their 22nd mission when they were briefed to drop 500lb demolition bombs on an ordnance plant at Bielefeld, east of the Ruhr valley:

"We climbed to 29,000ft but a frontal weather area blocked our route to the target. The group leader turned the formation towards the secondary target, a warehouse area and railroad-marshaling yard at Darmstadt, Germany. The weather was clear and there has no flak or fighters in or near the drop area. We hit the target on the nose with much damage. En route home, we ran into very accurate tracking flak near the Rhine. Must be new guns, they were not noted on any of our maps. Captain Jacob H. Landerman, our right wing man was shot down by a direct hit in the waist area. We noted five chutes. Captain William C. Holman, Jr., who was leading the element below us, was also shot down. It looked as though all ten men got out OK. A piece of flak cut the gas line feeding our No.4 engine. We continued on course and when the gasoline tank feeding that engine ran out, we feathered it. We continued on with three engines but gradually fell behind the formation. Our course was to Brussels, Belgium, which was in allied hands. Due to bad weather, we could not land. We flew from Belgium back over the Channel to our home base at 4000ft in formation with a C-47 troop transport."[1037]

The noose was tightening around Germany's neck. In September *Market Garden*, one of the biggest operations of the war, went ahead using American and British airborne divisions to take the Eindhoven, Nijmegen, and Arnhem bridges on the Rhine with support provided by the Allied air forces. The operation has been described in an official report as "by far the biggest and most ambitious airborne operation ever carried out by any nation or nations." The aim was to cut the German-occupied Netherlands almost in half, and to prepare the way for an invasion of Germany that would bypass the northern flank of Germany's Westwall fortifications (The Siegfried line).[1038]

Market Garden was fraught with planning and logistical problems; not least a lack of transport aircraft (which necessitated the dropping of airborne troops over several days instead of en masse on one day), and bad weather made regular air reconnaissance difficult, and at times impossible. That is, except, for the Mosquito crews of 2 Group, 2nd TAF, and a few USAAF-crewed Mosquitoes in the 25th Bomb Group[1039] at Watton, Norfolk, who played their part in the build up and during the operation. On the night of 16 September three of the American crews were called in. They were told that they would go out early next day at staggered intervals, but no further details were given. Claude C. Moore, one of the Mosquito navigators in the 653rd Bomb Squadron,[1040] recalls:

"One plane was to take off at 2 am, one at 4 am and one at 6 am. Next morning, just before take-off, we were given the details - the Nijmegen-Arnhem area. Find the base of the clouds in the area. How thick and how low? Go down to the deck if necessary. Radio back that information. We were the last flight, at 6 am. Jimmy Spear was the pilot. The sky was already light when we left. It was only a matter of minutes from Watton to Holland. We skimmed across at 2000-3000ft. Soon we were at the target area, which, I learned later, was where the parachute drops were made and the glider-borne assault troops were landed. There were large clouds, intermittently broken, so we descended. At around 500ft we were finding the base of the clouds. Apparently High Command was not waiting for our information; there were planes everywhere. I had never seen so many fighters up close. Below us, above us, around us, on every side they were climbing, diving, milling like a swarm of angry bees. They were really beating the place up. We reported thick, low, occasionally broken, white clouds and smaller, gray puffs of clouds and gave the cloud base as approximately 400-500ft. The smaller, gray puffs of clouds were spaced all around. Only, I finally realized, they weren't small clouds. They were shell bursts. We were being shot at! I was startled to see a plane coming off the deck, climbing straight at us and closing - a snub-nosed, radial-engined plane. From the markings (cowling painted in a distinctive yellow-and-black checkerboard pattern) and the silhouette I took it to be from Hermann Goering's own elite group - 'Focke-Wulf 190' flashed through my mind. 'Damn,' I thought. 'This is it!' I'm sure that, mentally, I was frozen in space. But the next thing I knew, the snub-nose had zoomed past us. I did a double take. It was a P-47 Thunderbolt. We stayed in the area a little longer, made a few more weather reports, then headed back to Watton. At the base we were debriefed. We went over to the Combat Mess for breakfast and settled into the day's routine."

On 17 September 1113 medium and heavy bombers escorted by 330 fighter aircraft carried out bombing attacks to eliminate the opposition before the airborne forces of *Market Garden* went in later that day.[1041] Lieutenant Norman E. Freidman, a co-pilot in the 493rd Bomb Group who flew his 21st mission, recalls:

"We were briefed at 0400 to fly deputy lead in the low group on a history making mission. This was D-Day plus 103. We were to drop 260lb fragmentation bombs from 18,500ft on gun emplacements near Overflakee, Holland. C-47s towing gliders and dropping paratroopers would follow us in. The weather was clear [but] the attack itself proved unsuccessful after all attempts to make it go."

The 4th and 361st Fighter Groups were among those who tussled with JG 26 in the mid-afternoon on this momentous day. For four pilots killed in action JG 26 claimed three of the Yellowjackets in the Mönchengladbach and Nijmegen areas and two 4th Fighter Group P-51s in the Emmerich-Bocholt area. The 4th Fighter Group was being led by the CO, Lieutenant Colonel Kinnard, on Area Patrol from Harderwijk, Netherlands, to Wesel, Germany, from 1025 to 1545 hours when 15 Focke Wulfs bounced a few P-51s in the 335th Squadron.[1042] *Leutnant* Wilhelm Hofmann and *Oberfähnrich* Gerhard "Bubi" Schulwitz shot down two of the P-51s.[1043] Captain Louis H. "Red Dog" Norley, leading Caboose Squadron, got on the tail of one FW 190 and claimed it as destroyed, and 1st Lieutenant Ted E. Lines, leading Caboose Blue Section, claimed three FW 190s to put him on seven enemy aircraft destroyed in two missions. Lines' combat report gave the details:

"...when we were bounced from behind and above by 15 FW 190s...my Wingman hollered for me to break as I was trying to discard my right external wing tank. When I broke, I was head-on to five FW 190s and immediately started firing, causing one FW 190 to burst into flames. I turned starboard, still trying to drop my tank, as two FWs came under me, heading in the same direction as I was. I got on the tail of the one nearest me and started firing and the pilot baled out. At this point, a 190 closed on my tail and fired at me, hitting me in the tail and wing. My tank finally came off and I was able to maneuver onto the tail of the 190 that had been firing at me. After three orbits, he broke for the deck with me right on his tail. I fired from 500 yards down to about 100 yards and saw strikes on his engine, canopy, fuselage, wings and tail. He burst into flames and went into the ground and exploded."

In his combat report Captain Louis H. Norley stated:

"I was when Caboose Blue Section was bounced by 15 plus e/a from 6 o'clock high. Caboose Blue 3 called for a break but it was too late for one of the Sections, either 2 or 4 was already going down in flames. The bandits had been flying at the base of a layer of haze and with their light gray color were very difficult to see…I dropped my tanks. In a port break, I met an a/c head-on firing at me. These were supposedly Me 109s and this one, with an inline engine; looked like an e/a. I fired a short burst at long range. I then noticed two FW 190s on his tail; the closest one firing and getting strikes, as it became apparent that the plane I fired on was a P-51. I broke up, coming down on the tail of the FW 190 as he broke off his attack and turned to port. I dropped 20° of flaps and turned with him, the other 190 being attacked by my wingman. I fired. The 190 rolled and started to split-S, but leveled out and started to climb. I fired again with no results. He leveled off and did some skidding evasion efforts as I closed firing and skidding past him. He dove to port, allowing me to drop back on his tail. I fired, getting many strikes on his wings and fuselage. He flicked over on his back. The canopy and some pieces flew off and he went into a vertical dive, crashing into a farm yard where the plane blew up…I climbed up, found my Wingman, assembled the Squadron over Wesel and completed our mission."[1044]

JG 26's greatest loss was 25 year old Major Klaus Mietusch, CO III./JG 26, who was shot down and killed in the early afternoon while leading the Third Gruppe with about 15 Bf 109s to the landing zones. They climbed all the way through a continuous layer of thin cloud at 16,000ft and then, while over eastern Holland in the vicinity of the German border, Mietusch spotted a squadron of P-51s below them. Mietusch radioed that he was attacking and dived through the cloud. The 109s emerged through hazy overcast to bounce the 376th Squadron, which was flying as top cover for the Group. Mietusch's first burst of fire destroyed the No.4 plane of the cover flight (2nd Lieutenant Robert E. Geck in the 376th Squadron). *Oberleutnant* Heinrich "Jan" Schild hit the No.2 Mustang's (Lines) drop tank, and it dived away trailing a solid sheet of flame.[1045]

21-year-old 1st Lieutenant William R. Beyer in the 376th Fighter Squadron, 361st Fighter Group, who was leading Blue Flight,[1046] called for his flight to break while singling out a 109 for pursuit. It was Bf 109G-6/U4 Black 25 flown by Klaus Mietusch. Beyer later recalled:

"The Me 109 I followed used every evasive action to lose me, flying through clouds and doing several split-esses between 15,000ft and the deck. He chopped his throttle and threw down flaps at 1000ft and did another split-ess. I did the same and got on his tail on the deck. I began firing at 200 yards using about 40° deflection and got a few hits around the cockpit. He tried to continue his turn but went straight on into the ground, the pilot apparently dead."[1047]

On 18 September, when the Germans counterattacked and forestalled an American attempt to capture the bridge at Nijmegen, 252 Liberators, each loaded with about 6000lb of perishables and fuel supplies, set off to drop their loads over LZ.N Knapheide-*Klein Amerika* (Little America), near Groesbeek.[1048] Some Liberators and C-47s got in each other's way over the sea and were forced to abort, while others experienced navigational difficulties. The remaining Liberators dropped to 400ft over the drop zone. Just over 100 B-24 Liberators dropped supplies and ammunition to the American Airborne forces at Grosbeek, in the Nijmegen-Eindhoven area. "Dusty" Worthen, bombardier in Joe Rosacker's crew in the 93rd Bomb Group, recalls:

"The view along the route to the drop zone was incredible. Crashed C-47s, burned outlines of crashed gliders, gliders nosed up or on their back - a general mess. Our flight was over farming area. We could nearly see the flying feathers of the fluttering chickens; the cows were in full gallop - right through fences and bushes. The Dutch farmers were waving happily. It was certainly a different sight than we would see at our usual 22,000ft altitude. As we neared the target the small-arms fire became intense. We were hit several times. One slug stopped in the backpack parachute of our tail gunner."[1049]

Meanwhile, the 14th Wing dropped their supplies to the 101st American Airborne at Best. Ted Parker, a waist gunner in the 491st Bomb Group, recalls:

"At the target I opened the hatch in the floor and had to work quickly because we would be passing the dropping zone fast and at low altitude. In my haste my leg became entangled in the parachute straps attached to the ammunition track and I was pulled out of the hole when the last bundle went out. I just managed to cling to the track, but my legs were dangling out of the hatch. The Quartermaster [who had 'frozen' since take-off] ignored my calls for help. Finally the tail gunner, David Slade, heard me and came to my assistance."[1050]

In the 44th Bomb Group formation, Pete Henry[1051] received hits in the leading edge of his port wing. A .30-caliber shell cut the line supplying manifold pressure and also holed the fuel tank. Petrol began leaking into the bomb bays. Henry got his aircraft home, but one Liberator was forced to ditch in the North Sea. Only three crewmen were seen scrambling from the sinking bomber. Two groups of P-47s had failed to nullify the almost constant small-arms fire, and the 2nd Bomb Division lost 16 Liberators; 70 more were damaged, while 21 fighters were shot down.[1052]

The Allied and German air forces were grounded by bad weather on the 20th, and on 21 September only 90 P-47s of the 56th and 353rd Fighter Groups were able to provide escort and patrol support for the airborne forces.[1053] The 56th Fighter Group claimed 12 enemy fighters destroyed for the loss of one Thunderbolt, but they could not prevent the Ist *Gruppe* JG 26 from claiming 17-20 RAF C-47 Dakotas in 38 and 46 Groups.[1054] The P-47s of the 353rd Fighter Group reached the Nijmegen area in time to take on some of the attacking fighters of the IInd and IIIrd *Gruppen* JG 26, and the Wolfpack claimed 15 fighters shot down and one damaged. But the FW-190s, nevertheless, shot down three transports. The 353rd Fighter Group claimed three FW-190s destroyed, one probable, and one damaged for the loss of one Thunderbolt.[1055]

Reconnaissance over the Arnhem bridge was rendered almost impossible by the weather conditions, but the situation was so desperate that on 22 September five 25th Bomb Group Mosquitoes were despatched. Lieutenant "Paddy" Walker's navigator, Roy C. Conyers, recalls:

"We were to dip as low as possible to try to establish by visual observation who controlled the bridge, the Germans or the British. I thought that this regularity was crazy and mentioned it to Edwin R. Cerrutti, 654th navigator. His only comment was that the German Command wouldn't believe that we were that stupid."[1056]

As "Paddy" Walker flew over the north end of the bridge just below the fog at under 500ft, he and Roy Conyers could see Germans running for their anti-aircraft guns. Walker remembers:

> "Ground fire began almost immediately. This continued as we flew over and past the other end, on towards the coast. Tracer fire could be seen coming up around us and the plane was hit. I saw the left wing drop tank disintegrate and jettisoned both. The right engine was shut down and the propeller feathered. The fire went out, but the engine was inoperative. I was flying as low and as fast as possible to get out of range. As we crossed the coast additional fire was received, spurts of water coming up near the plane from the barrage; however, we were not hit. After we got out of range, I climbed up into the weather to gain enough altitude to make an emergency Mayday radio call, to get a 'steer' to the nearest base where the weather was suitable to land. We steered to Bournemouth. My Mayday call was answered by the sweetest girl's British accent – 'Tommy' Settle, a beautiful blonde WAAF at Tangmere. During the days that it took to repair the plane she and I became better acquainted."

On 23 September, during a support mission for *Market Garden*, the 352nd Fighter Group suffered their greatest single mission loss to date. The Bluenosers arrived in the area at 1530 hours and patrolled at an altitude of 800 to 4000ft until 1745 hours. German aircraft, which had been active during the previous few days, were nowhere to be seen, but intense and accurate flak was continuous in the area of the southern drop zone. Major Blanchard, in the 328th Squadron, was shot down when his P-51 was hit by flak near Gennep. He was seen to parachute safely from his burning P-51 and appeared to be unharmed. A disaster befell the 487th Squadron 45 minutes later when all four Mustangs in Red Flight, who were patrolling the Kleve (Cleves), Aachen, area, were shot down. Captain Clarence O. Johnson and Lieutenants Phanor Waters, Joe Ayers, and John Clark were last seen near Hengelo at 1700 hours, and last heard from on the radio giving their position at Amelo at 1730 hours. It was only when Clark returned from captivity that the story unfolded. Red Flight were flying the normal four-abreast combat formation at about 1500ft when they were bounced by a superior force of German fighters, and then they were fired at from the ground, so the P-51s dropped down to about 500ft. They started to circle and still had their drop tanks on. They were spotted just under the cloud cover, and eight to ten FW-190s opened fire. Clark pushed everything to the wall and started a sharp right turn and continued to turn, but the FW-190 continued to fire, and finally the German pilot got inside the Mustang, which Clark had pulled in almost to a stall. A burst of fire caught him near the pilot's seat and continued on into the engine, which caught fire. Clark pulled the canopy release, disconnected his harness, and just stood up until the wind pulled him out. The P-51 was at about 500 feet, and he was fortunate not to hit the tail.[1057]

On 25 September another *Bluestocking* mission was launched, as evacuation of the surviving paratroops from Arnhem began. 1st Lieutenant Clayborne O. Vinyard and his navigator, 1st Lieutenant John J. O'Mara, took off at 0126 hours in fog so thick they could only see 300 yards in front. They flew too deep into Germany, reaching the Frankfurt area before turning back. They descended to 18,000ft, but a nightfighter got on their tail and shot them down. Both men baled out and were later sent to *Stalag Luft I*.

Of over 10,200 British airborne troops landed in the Arnhem area, 1440 were killed or died of their wounds. 3000 were wounded and taken prisoner, and 400 medical personnel and chaplains remained behind with the wounded; about 2500 uninjured troops also became PoWs. There were also 225 prisoners from the 4th Battalion, the Dorsetshire Regiment. About 450 Dutch civilians were killed. The operation also cost 160 RAF and Dominion aircrew, 27 USAAF aircrew, and 79 Royal Army Service Corps despatchers killed and 127 taken prisoner. A total of 55 Albemarle, Stirling, Halifax, and Dakota aircraft from Nos. 38 and 46 Groups failed to return, and a further 320 were damaged by flak and seven by fighters, while 105 Allied fighter aircraft were lost.

John W. McClane, in the 44th Bomb Group, would be forever sorry that he missed the 18 September mission:

> "When the crews came back, they were ecstatic. One or two gunners from our crew were assigned to this mission. All they could talk about was how low they were. The Dutch people would line up along the route and wave handkerchiefs at them. One of our guys said they were so close that he aimed his machine guns at the people waving and tracked them as if he were going to fire. When the people saw the gun following them, they became frightened and made wild dashes to get out of the way. Our gunner would tell this story and laugh out loud. He thought it was a really funny joke to play on the people. The 44th lost no planes but every one of them had damage from small arms fire by the Krauts on the ground. The men who went on this mission had a ball. In some ways, it reminded the old timers of the famous Ploesti raid in Rumania. It would have been a fun navigational exercise for me even though the briefing documents and maps for the 14th and 20th Combat Wings were reversed.
>
> "Our crew got a chance to get in our licks against the Heinies on 26 September. Our target was the marshaling yards at Hamm, Germany. This railyard was one of the main networks east of Arnhem that the Germans used to send reinforcements to this sector of the front. We were not assigned to our own B-24H *'Lili Marlene'* for this mission. Instead we had been training in a B-24J PFF ship for the last three training flights. It had 'Mickey,' the H_2X radar, on board and a specially trained radar navigator was added to our crew to operate this device. The 44th Bomb Group was leading the 14th Combat Wing and we were the lead for the 44th. We had become a Pathfinder crew and I was the lead navigator for this mission. I did essentially the same type of navigation I did before and where I could not get visual checkpoints from the ground, the radar navigator fed information to me from his scope. We worked very well as a pair but at no time was there any doubt who was directing our course. I fed all the navigational instructions to our pilot, Peritti. I liked being a Pathfinder - it was fun. But this was my 30th mission and I would complete my tour on this day even though the rest of the crew would have only 29 missions.
>
> "Take off was 12.30 hours with 25 aircraft including our PFF plane and one other PFF in the formation. We were loaded with 6 1000lb bombs and two smoke bombs. We saw no enemy aircraft either going or returning but the flak was heavy as we approached the target area on the run from the IP. Our bomb bay doors were open and Warga was getting ready to release our bombs when from out of nowhere, a flight of B-17s passed under us about 500ft below and at about 30° to our line of flight. They had no business being there. No B-17s were scheduled to strike Hamm today but there they were directly under us. It must have scared the holy heck out of those guys when they looked straight up into our open bomb bays with our loads ready to drop any second. Flak was thick and heavy and we wanted to get rid of our bombs and go home but the order came to close the bomb bay doors. Peritti put the formation into evasive action and asked me to plot a return course to the IP so we could try again. Here I was on my last mission and we have to fly a second time through this anti-aircraft barrage. Oh! I was unhappy. I could

have rung the necks of that dumb bunch of B-17 guys. They were on their way home and here we had to do it again, I dreaded the thought. I directed the formation back to the Initial Point and we made the bomb run all over again through the flak. By the Grace of God, we all made it through with little damage to our planes. The flight home was without incident and we landed at 1815 hours after a five hour and 45 minute flight.

"The total loss for the day by the 8th Air Force was 9 planes out of 1159 dispatched. All in all, it was a good day except for those darn Fortresses. Now I could quit but I had already made up my mind that I would volunteer for one more so we could all go home together.'

Berlin! (USAF)

On 4 March 1944 B-17G-1-BO 42-*Superstitious Aloysius*, in the 350th Bomb Squadron, was one of eleven B-17s in the 100th Bomb Group that began the bomb run over Berlin. The plane, which had joined the Group in early 1943, had acquired the name courtesy of the ball turret gunner in Lieutenant Mark Cope's crew, although Frank Malooly and his crew flew the B-17 on the Berlin mission. Albert Freedman created the artwork image in 1942, and it appeared on a "Good Luck" card published in the USA and sent to thousands of GIs serving overseas. Aloysius carried a wishbone, a horseshoe, and a four-leaf clover, as well as a rabbit's foot. It brought good luck to ten or more crews in the 100th that flew the plane, and on 12 January 1945 it was flown back to the ZOI and scrapped at Altus, Oklahoma, in 1946. (TAMM)

B-17F-100-BO 42-30412 *Mischief-Maker II* in the 339th Bomb Squadron, 96th Bomb Group, which FTR on 4 March 1944 when it crashed in Belgium. Six of Lieutenant Paul Herring's crew evaded and five were taken prisoner. (USAF)

B-17G-30-BO 42-31735 *Lucky Lee* in the 351st Bomb Squadron, 100th Bomb Group, which flew its first combat mission on 3 February 1944 to Wilhelmshaven. Ten more missions followed until, on 6 March 1944, *Lucky Lee* and Lieutenant George Brannan's crew FTR from Berlin. Brannan ordered his crew out short of the target after the right wing and two engines caught fire. The co-pilot and navigator were killed, and the badly wounded radio operator later died in prison camp on 12 July. (TAMM)

B-17G-30-BO 42-31767 *Our Gal Sal* in the 351st Bomb Squadron, 100th Bomb Group, which went on to fly its 100th combat mission on 4 March 1945 and finish the war having completed 135 combat missions. (TAMM)

B-17G-30-BO 42-31767 *Our Gal Sal* flew its first mission on 1 February 1944 when Lieutenant Bob Shoens lifted off from Thorpe Abbotts for Frankfurt, but the mission was scrubbed. Shoens recalled that the name of the aircraft was chosen after the crew put names in a hat. The actual suggestion was "My Gal Sal," which was the famous song title from the 1942 Fox movie starring Rita Hayworth. They all agreed to change it to *Our Gal Sal*, and Frank Stevens duly applied the stunning artwork, which uniquely, was painted on canvas and then glued on to the side of the Fortress! On 6 March 1944 *Our Gal Sal* was badly damaged on the Berlin raid, but Bob Shoens brought her home after the rest of the Group had been decimated. He last flew the ship on 1 May 1944. *Our Gal Sal* is shown here after 17 missions, with its ground crew and "Uncle" Dune Shand and crew, who were one of at least 27 combat crews to fly this famous Fortress. (TAMM)

B-17G-1-VE 42-40056 *Holy Terror III* in the 351st Bomb Squadron, 100th Bomb Group, which FTR from the Berlin mission on 8 March 1944. All of Lieutenant Norman Chapman's crew survived after baling out of the doomed aircraft near Jüterborg. (TAMM)

Captain Don Gentile's crew chief John Ferra paints another victory symbol onto the nose of Gentile's P-51B 43-6913 *Shangri-La* in the 336th Fighter Squadron, 4th Fighter Group at Debden. Gentile scored 7 victories in this aircraft, and he was also awarded a half-share in a Bf 109 victory on 8 March 1944 when he was credited with three kills. He destroyed a FW 190 on 18 March and three more FW 190s on 8 April flying *Shangri-La* to take his final wartime score to 21.833. Gentile was killed in a flying accident in a T-33 on 28 January 1951 at Forestville, Maryland. (USAF)

88mm anti-aircraft guns on top of a flak tower in Berlin.

B-17G-5-BO 42-31227/0 *Dottie Jane* in the 447th Bomb Group, which 1st Lieutenant Arthur R. Socolofsky of Chicago nursed back to Rattlesden on 6 March 1944 following a direct flak hit under the floor of the radio room during a raid on Berlin. Cables, wires, and tubing hang limp and frayed out of the gaping underbelly of the aircraft. Through this battered mass of machinery, the Fort's radio operator vanished into thin air five miles above Germany. The aircraft was salvaged the following day. (USAF)

Far left: Former RAF Eagle pilot Major Henry L. "Hank" Mills, who joined the 334th Fighter Squadron, 4th Fighter Group at Debden on 23 October 1942. On 6 March 1944 Mills was shot down near Berlin and taken prisoner of war. He had scored six victories (USAF) Left: *Hauptmann* Peter Spoden, one of germany's leading nightfighter pilots with 24 night victories, who claimed a B-17 on 6 March 1944. Spoden survived the war and became a senior *Lufthansa* pilot. (Peter Spoden)

B-17G-70-DL 42-3491 *Chopstick G-George*, a PFF ship in the 812th Bomb Squadron, 482nd Bomb Group, on fire in the bomb bay on the mission to Berlin on 6 March 1944. The aircraft carried Brigadier-General Russell Wilson, 4th CBW CO, and was flown by Major Fred A. Rabbo. The mixed 385th Bomb Group and 482nd Bomb Group crew included 1st Lieutenant John C. "Red" Morgan, who received the Medal of Honor for his actions on 26 July 1943. (via Derek Smith)

1st Lieutenant John C. Morgan MoH ladles out soup in *Stalag Luft III* at Sagan, in Silesia. Morgan was shot down on the mission to Berlin on 6 March 1944 flying in *Chopstick G-George* in the 812th Bomb Squadron, 482nd Bomb Group, flown by Major Fred A. Rabbo. The Fortress was hit badly by flak and exploded, killing eight of the crew instantly and catapulting Morgan, who was carrying a back pack parachute under his arm, out of the aircraft. He managed to put it on after several attempts and was saved from possible injury when a tree broke his fall. (USAF)

Above left: Crew of *Blitzin' Betsy* in the 388th Bomb Group at Knettishall, Suffolk. Back Row L-R: 1st Lieutenant Lowell H. Watts, pilot; 2nd Lieutenant Robert M. Kennedy, co-pilot; 2nd Lieutenant Emmett J. Murphy, bombardier; and 2nd Lieutenant Edward J. Kelley, navigator. Crouching L-R: T/Sgt J. B. Ramsey, top turret; S/Sgt Ray E. Hess (KIA 6 April 1944), right waist; T/Sgt Ivan Finkle, radio operator; S/Sgt Robert H. Sweeney (KIA) ball gunner; S/Sgt Harold A. Brassfield (KIA), tail gunner; and S/Sgt Don W. Taylor (KIA), left waist gunner. (Watts) Above right: Bf 110G-4 night fighters of 5./NJG5 airborne during a daylight sortie against the U.S. 8th AF in early 1944. (Peter Spoden)

Erkner, a suburb of Berlin, seen from 21,000ft on 8 March 1944. The German defenders have made a spirited attempt to hinder American bombing with smoke pots. The first American bombs had fallen on "Big B" on 4 March, when 31 B-17s released bombs on the Kleinmachnow area southwest of the Reich capital. Two days later the 8th dispatched 730 heavies and almost 800 escort fighters to "Big-B"; 672 bombers dropped 1,600 tons of bombs on the city, and gunners claimed over 170 German fighters destroyed, but the 8th lost 75 bombers. On 8 March 623 bombers and 891 fighters hit Berlin again. The leading Third Division lost thirty-seven Fortresses. Next day nine more bombers were shot down by flak as the 8th tried to bomb Berlin through thick cloud. After a break in missions against the capital, on 27 March General Carl "Tooey" Spaatz sent his bombers to Berlin again. Altogether, the 8th Air Force dropped 4,800 tons of high explosive on Berlin during five raids in March 1944. (USAF)

B-17G-10-BO 42-31329 in the 334th Bomb Squadron, 95th Bomb Group, which crash landed at Oberriet-Kriessern, Switzerland, on the mission to Augsburg on 16 March 1944. Five of Lieutenant James W. Reed's crew were interned, and five who baled out over Germany were taken prisoner. (via Hans Heiri Stapfer)

Above left: A reporter interviews Ray L. Sears (later Lieutenant-Colonel, CO of the 735th Bomb Squadron, MIA 29 April 1944) and co-pilot Jim Kotapish in the 453rd Bomb Group at Old Buckenham, Norfolk, on their return from Berlin in the *Reluctant Dragon* on 8 March 1944. "On this clear day there were aircraft as far ahead and as far back as the eye could see. A mass of 1200 plus bombers and fighters that somehow made the sweating out of the bomb run a little more endurable." The 453rd lost four B-24s on the 6 March Berlin raid and one on 8 March. (Jim Kotapish Collection) Center: Colonel Joe Miller, 453rd Bomb Group CO, who was shot down on the 18 March mission to the Dornier Works at Friedrichshafen. Miller was flying Group Lead in the co-pilot's seat in B-24H 41-28649 *Little Bryan* in the 733rd Bomb Squadron, flown by Captain Stock, whose crew were taken prisoner. Colonel Miller landed in a French field, and he was soon in the hands of the French Resistance. Disguised as a priest, he made his way across France to Perpignan, but he was captured wearing civilian clothing by a German border patrol as he waited to cross into Spain and handed over to the *Gestapo*. While in his cell Miller thought back to 1938, when three German officers were attempting to set a new record flying from Berlin to Tokyo. Over the South China Sea their Heinkel developed engine trouble and they were forced to land in the Philippines. Their distress calls had already been picked up by the AAC in Manila, and a rescue mission led by Colonel Miller found them. Miller told his *Gestapo* interrogators of the incident. The *Gestapo* chief of the Paris region, T.T. Schmidt, conferred with Major Junge, the deputy commander at Oberusel who, as luck would have it, was the pilot of the record-attempt from Berlin to Tokyo. Junge recounted the rescue, and Schmidt casually remarked that he was holding an American colonel by the name of Joe Miller in Paris. Junge was convinced it was the man who had rescued him in 1938. He made a positive identification, and Miller was sent to *Stalag Luft III*. Meanwhile, Colonel Ramsey D. Potts assumed command of the 453rd Bomb Group. (Kotapish) Above right: *Leutnant* Dieter Gerhard of 2nd *Staffel* JG 1, with eight victories to his credit, was KIA on 18 March 1943 when 103 American bombers headed for Vegesack. Gerhard was piloting Bf 109G-1 "*Blue 8*" when his fighter was hit by return fire from a Fortress he was attacking from the rear, and he baled out into the North Sea. He managed to get himself clear of the parachute and into his rubber dinghy, which had inflated. *Leutnant* Heinz Knoke, who had been his friend since fighter school days and a colleague in Russia, flew low overhead and saw that he appeared to be either unconscious or in great pain, as it looked like he had been shot through the stomach. Knoke reported Gerhard's position by radio and crash-boat *Falke* was sent out to look for him. The crew found Gerhard dead in his dinghy late that night. Knoke was credited with the destruction of B-24 *Hot Freight* in the 93rd Bomb Group flown by Lieutenant Howard E. "Tarzan" Kleinsteuber. Sgt Louis A. Webb was the only survivor. (via Eric Mombeek)

B-17F-75-DL *Bastard's Bungalow* in the 418th Bomb Squadron, 100th Bomb Group was the second aircraft of this name, which originated with Charles "Crankshaft" Cruikshank's brand new Boeing built B-17F. (Subsequently this aircraft was reassigned to a newly arrived crew who renamed it *Terry 'n Ten*, which changed again to *Reilly's Racehorse* and was lost over Brunswick on 10 February 1944.) The second *Bastard's Bungalow*, meanwhile, was hit by flak over Dieppe on 18 March 1944, and the bursts damaged two engines and one prop refused to feather. Lieutenant Robert Horn nursed it as far as he could until more flak hit the Fort, and then a Bf 109 and FW 190 escorted him to a snow covered field on the edge of Darmstadt airfield, near Ulm, and the thumbs down signal indicated that they wanted Horn to belly land, which he did safely and without any casualties in the crew. The FW 190, which had circled, came in and tried to land beside the Fortress but nosed over on landing and crashed! Farmers with pitchforks rounded up the crew until the *Wehrmacht* arrived a half-hour later to escort them into captivity. (TAMM)

B-24J-65-CO 42-100073 *Sack Artists* in the 67th Bomb Squadron, 44th Bomb Group FTR on 18 March 1944 when it crashed at Fehraltdorf, Switzerland. Lieutenant Raymond J. Lacombe's crew were interned. (Bill Cameron Coll)

Extensive damage to the radio room area of B-17G-35-BO 42-31968 *Miss Irish* in the 350th Bomb Squadron, 100th Bomb Group on 19 March 1944 when the target was a *Noball* site at Marquise-Mimoyecques. Six minutes after crossing into France a 88mm flak shell detonated just below the nose of *Miss Irish*, piloted by John Gibbons. A second shell exploded near the tail. A third entered the left-hand side of the radio room and caused an exit blast on the right side, which seemed to raise the plane 100ft straight up. In the process the floor was torn away, and the radioman, Ed Walker, was blown out of the aircraft to his death. Several parachutes were rendered useless by flak, so Gibbons decided to fly the battered B-17 back to England. It was not until halfway across the Channel that the bombardier, Sterling Blackman, and the engineer, Ira Arnold, were able to jettison the bomb load in the bomb bay, where the bomb racks were twisted and bent. Gibbons and his co-pilot finally put the crippled Fortress down at RAF Raydon without brakes. The aircraft was later salvaged. (TAMM)

B-17G-45-BO 42-97328 *Heaven's Above* in the 561st Bomb Squadron, 388th Bomb Group, which was assigned overseas on 22 March 1944. It returned to the ZOI in June 1945 and was scrapped at Kingman, Arizona, in December 1945. (USAF)

Ground crew working on an overturned P-47 Thunderbolt. (USAF)

B-24J-90-CO 42 100306 *"War Goddess"* in the 446th Bomb Group, which landed at Visby, in Sweden, on 23 March 1944. All of Lieutenant Guy L. Schafer, Jr.'s crew were interned. (via Frank Thomas)

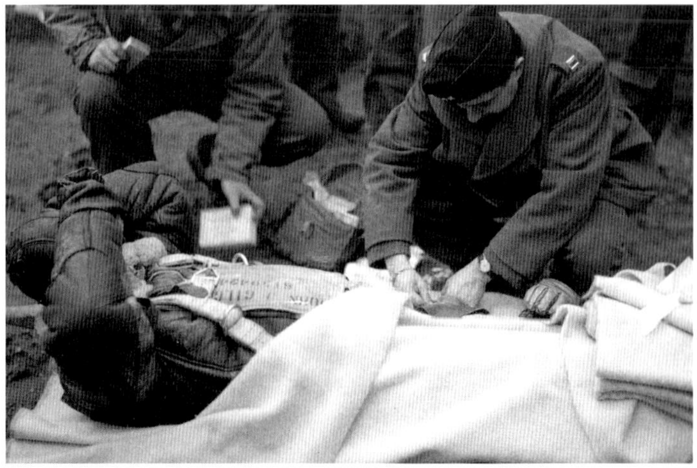

Above left: B-17F-70-BO 42-29751 *Miss Abortion* in the 534th Bomb Squadron, 381st Bomb Group at Ridgewell in formation with other of the Group's B-17s. This aircraft stalled on take off on 31 March 1944 and crashed. Originally assigned to the 338th Bomb Squadron, 96th Bomb Group at Grafton Underwood on 19 April 1943, this aircraft transferred to the Ridgewell-based 381st Bomb Group in December and was issued to the 534th Bomb Squadron. The bomber had been at its new base for just a matter of weeks when higher authority ordered that its unsatisfactory nickname be changed. 42-29751's crew duly obliged by re-christening the veteran B-17 *STUFF*. On 31 March 1944, after completing 21 combat missions, the bomber, with 1st Lieutenant Wayne G. Schomburg at the controls, crashed just short of the runway at Ridgewell following a routine practice flight. All six men in the scratch crew, including T/Sgt Donald B. Carr, who was a veteran of 20 combat missions, and Captain Paul H. Stull, Jr., the 534th Bomb Squadron's Engineering Officer, who was sitting in the co-pilot's seat, were killed. (USAF) Above right: A wounded crewman is treated back at base shortly after landing. (USAF)

Bombs away over Rheims-Campagne airfield on 28 March 1944. (USAF)

Lieutenant Abe Dolim, a Hawaiian born radio operator who flew two tours in the 94th Bomb Group at Bury St. Edmunds (Rougham). (Dolim)

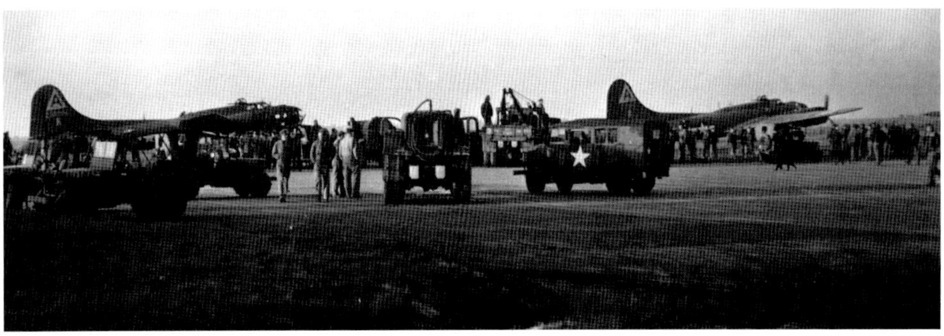

B-17G-10-VE 42-39996 LG-N *Boston Bombshell* in the 322nd Bomb Squadron (left), which was assigned overseas on 14 January 1944, and 42-39815 OR-N *Emeigh*, which was assigned overseas on 16 October 1943, in the 323rd Bomb Squadron, 91st Bomb Group at Bassingbourn. *Boston Bombshell* and 2nd Lieutenant John V. Dunlap's crew FTR on 16 August 1944 (7 KIA 2 PoW). *Emeigh* and Lieutenant Kenneth Sutherland's crew FTR from the mission to Münster on 22 February 1944 (7 KIA 3 PoW). (USAF)

Leutnant Karl "Charlie" Willius, *Staffelkapitän* 2./JG 26, climbs into the cockpit of his FW 190A-8 at Florennes, Belgium, in 1943. The national flags painted beneath his cockpit denote the countries over which Willius had seen action (Holland, Belgium, France, England, and Russia). After claiming a 44th Bomb Group B-24 on 8 April 1944 on his 371st combat mission (his 50th combat victory), "Charlie" was hit by a Thunderbolt in the 357th Fighter Squadron, 361st Fighter Group flown by 1st Lieutenant Alton B. Snyder. He was killed when his FW 190A-8 "Black 5" exploded near Genemuiden, Holland. His widow Lisette received a posthumous *Ritterkreuz* on 9 June 1944. (Lisette Arend-Willius)

B-24s in the Third Bomb Division leaving a burning target. (USAF)

P-51D 44-13887 *Little Joe* in the 357th Fighter Group at Leiston with ground crew. (USAF)

P-51D 44-14151 *Petie 2nd* in the 487th Fighter Squadron, 352nd Fighter Group at Bodney. (USAF)

B-24D-160-CO 42-72858 *Pistol Packin' Mama* lifts off from Shipdham. On 9 April 1944 Lieutenant Hiram C. Palmer was forced to land *Pistol Packin' Mama* at Bulltofta, Sweden, after sustaining damage on the Berlin-Marienburg mission and all ten crew were interned. The Fightballs' assembly aircraft, B-24D-1-CO 41-23699 *Lemon Drop*, a veteran of the Ploesti mission of 1 August 1943, can be seen in front of the hangar. (Bill Robertie)

B-17G-45-BO 42-97083 *Flatbush Floogie* in the 728th Bomb Squadron, 452nd Bomb Group crash-landed at Jadebusen, Germany, on the shore of the Baltic, on the mission to Rostock on 11 April 1944. Lieutenant Thomas L. Gardner's crew were taken prisoner. (via Hans-Heiri Stapfer)

Left: John L. Hurd, ball turret gunner in 2nd Lieutenant Francis L. Shaw's crew in the 614th Bomb Squadron, 401st Bomb Group, who were shot down on 11 April 1944 flying *Battlin' Betty*. All ten crew, including John L. Hurd, who was on his eleventh mission, were taken prisoner. (Hurd) Right: 1st Lieutenant Frank A. Cutler with S/Sgt Cy Hall on the wing of P-51B *Gig's Up* in the 486th Fighter Squadron, 352nd Fighter Group at Bodney. On 11 April 1944 Cutler, who was leading Blue Flight in *Soldier's Vote*, damaged a Ju 52 on the ground and claimed one destroyed in the air before shooting down two FW 190s of 4/JG 26 to take his score to 4½ (the Ju 52 kill was reduced to a half share). (via Bill Espie)

P-51B-7-NA 43-6578 *Soldier's Vote* in the 486th Fighter Squadron, 352nd Fighter Group, which 1st Lieutenant Frank A. Cutler was flying on 11 April when he destroyed two FW 190s. Cutler was KIA on 13 May 1944. (via Bill Espie)

On 11 April 1944 1st Lieutenant Edward S. Michael and 2nd Lieutenant Franklin Westberg in the 305th Bomb Group got B-17G-20-DL 42-37931 *Bertie Lee* home to England after it had been devastated by cannon fire and had plummeted into a 3000ft dive. Michael crash-landed at RAF Waltham, near Grimsby, despite his undercarriage and flaps having been put out of operation and the ball turret stuck in the lowered position with its guns pointing downwards. The airspeed indicator was not working, and the bomb doors were jammed fully open. Fighting off unconsciousness, Michael skillfully brought *Bertie Lee* down safely on its belly. His miraculous feat earned the second Medal of Honor awarded to a member of the 364th Bomb Squadron, 305th Bomb Group. (USAF)

B-17G-20-BO 42-31447 *Cookie* in the 338th Bomb Squadron, 96th Bomb Group, which was lost with Lieutenant Jack W. Splan's crew on 11 April when it was hit by fighters and crashed into the Baltic with no survivors. (USAF)

Left: 1st Lieutenant Edward S. Michael'd MoH. (via Bill Donald) Right: On 11 April 1944 General Dwight D. Eisenhower christened B-17G-40-BO 42-97061 *General Ike* with a bottle of Mississippi River water at Bassingbourn. Major James McPartlin in the 401st Bomb Squadron was responsible for the naming of *General Ike*, which flew its first operational mission on 13 April 1944, two days after it was christened. On 29 May 1944 *General Ike* led the 91st Bomb Group to Poznan, Poland, on the longest daylight raid of the war up to that time. *Ike* completed 75 combat missions, returned to the USA in June 1945, and was broken up for scrap. (USAF)

B-24J-90-CO 42-100330 in the 67th Bomb Squadron, 44th Bomb Group, which Lieutenant Rockford C. "Rocky" Griffith landed at Dubendorf, in Switzerland, on 13 April 1944 after losing their fuel supply in a fierce firefight over the target area at the Lechfeld jet airfield near Augsburg, in southern Germany. All the crew were interned. (USAF)

General Ike in the 91st Bomb Group at Bassingbourn. This Fortress flew its first operational mission on 13 April 1944, two days after General Dwight D. Eisenhower christened it. *Ike* completed 75 combat missions, returned to the USA in June 1945, and was broken up for scrap (USAF)

On 16 April 1944 Major Schnoor, *Kommandeur* I./JG 1, had a narrow escape when his FW 190A-7 "White 20" W. Nr. 340035 touched trees in low level flight and crashed as a result. Schnoor was badly injured. (Seebrandt via Rob de Visser)

B-17s in the 94th Bomb Group braving the flak en route to their target. B-17G-15-DL 42-37852 in the 410th Bomb Squadron, which was first named *Grand Old Lady* and was later renamed *The Payoff* and finally *Payoff, The Perry!!* was lost with 2nd Lieutenant Matthew L. Dillard's crew on 18 April 1944 when it was shot down by fighters near Friesach, Austria. One crewmember was KIA and nine were taken prisoner. (USAF)

A wounded gunner is led away to the medical dispensary after returning from a raid. (USAF)

Lieutenant Thomas H. Gunn, 323rd Bomb Squadron, 91st Bomb Group, flew B-17G-20-DL 42-37938 *Betty Lou's Buggy* safely back to Bassingbourn on 19 April 1944 after sustaining heavy damage from Bf 109s at the FW assembly plant at Eschwege, near Kassel. Fighters holed the left wing fuel tank, put a turbo out, damaged an engine, knocked out the elevators and left aileron, and exploded shells in the nose, cockpit, bomb bay, and fin, which severed the rudder controls. Robert D Smith, tail gunner, inspects the damage to the fin. Gunn could only control direction by using the engines, and had to apply full right aileron to keep the B-17 level. Only the co-pilot and navigator were wounded. *Betty Lou's Buggy* was repaired and survived the war, only to be cut up for scrap at Kingman, AZ, in December 1945. (USAF)

453rd Bomb Group crewmembers inspect the damage to their B-24 at Old Buckenham on 20 April 1944 after suffering a direct flak hit in the rear of the aircraft, which killed the tail gunner on the mission to Wizernes, in the Pas-de-Calais. L-R S/Sgt Bruce P. Prosser, gunner; 1st Lieutenant James S. Munsey, who was an instructor pilot flying with a new crew on its first combat mission; and S/Sgt Walter J. Thomas, waist gunner. Returning from Hamm on 22 April, Munsey was killed when B-24H-10-FO 42-52186 *Cee Gee II* (named after his daughter, Carole Geane) was shot down by a Me 110 intruder piloted by *Leutnant* Nommining of *II./KG51* at 2205 hours, 15 miles off the East coast. 2nd Lieutenant Robert O. Crall, co-pilot; T/Sgt William C. Grady, radio operator; T/Sgt Grover G. Conway, top turret gunner; and T/Sgt John F. McKinney, left waist gunner, also died. Munsey was posthumously awarded the DSC, which was later presented to his 2½-year-old daughter. (USAF)

B-17F-90-BO 42-30152 *Messie Bessie* in the 418th Bomb Squadron, 100th Bomb Group with Wallace Forsythe's crew. *Messie Bessie* had previously served with the 96th and 381st Bomb Groups and was salvaged on 28 April 1945. (via Michael P. Faley, 100th Bomb Group Historian)

Right: Burnt out remains of B-17F-85-BO 42-30091 *Blivit*, which crashed and burned on the perimeter track of Eye airfield on 20 April 1944 during a practice flight. Shortly after take off, Lieutenant Myron Richmond began a turn and attempted to join the formation with a "rather sharp angle" of approach. As a result, *Blivit* overshot and crossed into the slipstream of the formation at 7000ft and the B-17 stalled. Richmond did not have time or height to recover from the stall and the plane crashed, killing all ten crew. They had only joined the 100th Bomb Group ten days earlier. Blivit was reportedly one of General Dwight D. Eisenhower's favorite words, which he described as referring to "a one pound bag filled with 2lbs of horse manure." (TAMM)

Left: On 22 April 1944 15 Me 410s of *Second Gruppe* V./KG2 shadowed the 2nd Bomb Division returning to England and destroyed nine B-24s for the loss of two aircraft and crews, including the CO, 24-year old Major Dietrich Puttfarken, who remains missing. (via Ian McLachlan) Right: The crew of B-24J-50-CO 42-73497 *Vadie Raye*, in the 715th Bomb Squadron, 448th Bomb Group, April 1944. Standing, left to right: 2nd Lieutenant Andy H. Hau; 1st Lieutenant Elbert F. Lozes, bombardier; Captain Alvin D. Skaggs, pilot; 1st Lieutenant Donald C. Todt, navigator; and Lieutenant B. F. "Max" Baer, co-pilot. Kneeling: M/Sgt George Glevanik, top turret gunner; S/Sgt Ray K. Lee, left waist gunner; S/Sgt Francis "Frank" X. Sheehan, right waist gunner; T/Sgt Stanley C. Filopowicz, radio operator; S/Sgt Eugene Gaskins, nose gunner; and S/Sgt William F. Jackson, tail-gunner (KIA 5.9.44). (Sheehan)

On 22 April 1944 the Liberators were sent off late in the day to bomb the marshalling yards at Hamm, Germany. Their return, in darkness, was shadowed by Me 410s of *KG51* who succeeded in shooting down several B-24s in their circuits, and generally caused mayhem over the bases. One of the worst hit was Seething, where five 448th Bomb Group Liberators crashed at the end of the runway, including B-24H-1-DT 41-28595 *Ice Cold Katie* (lying between B-24H-5-CF 41-29240 *Tondelayo* flown by Lieutenant J. L. Barak and B-24H-15-CF 41-29575 *The Ruth E. K. Allah Hassid* (right)). In all, 13 Liberators crashed or crash-landed in east Norfolk on the night of 22 April. Two more were damaged on the ground. Over 60 men were killed and another 23 injured. The fires at Seething were not extinguished until 0330 hours the following morning. (Francis X. Sheehan)

Captain John Driscoll, 389th Bomb Group Gunnery Officer, receives the Airman's Medal from General James Doolittle after he had bravely pulled four airmen out of the burning wreckage of *The Little Gramper Jr.* (Driscoll)

Burnt out remains of B-24J-145-CO 44-40085 *The Little Gramper Jr* in the 565th Bomb Squadron, 389th Bomb Group at Hethel after it was shot down by a Me 410 intruder on 22 April 1944. Lieutenant Ed Foley landed with a flat tire and veered off the runway, narrowly missing the control tower, but the plane hit the signals hut and killed the occupants. (USAF)

2nd Lieutenant John W. McClane, Jr., navigator in 2nd Lieutenant Charles D. Peritti's crew in the 68th Bomb Squadron, 44th Bomb Group, and the ball turret gunner, S/Sgt Charles J. Alexander, who the crew called "Swoose" after "Alexander the Swoose," a popular song of the day. Peritti's crew flew their first combat mission on 22 April 1944. (John McClane Coll)

On 24 April 1944 2nd Lieutenant Raymond Hofmann in the 358th Bomb Squadron, 303rd Bomb Group put B-17G-25-BO 42-31669/J *Shoo Shoo Baby* down at Zurich, Switzerland, after suffering AA hits over the target. (USAF)

B-17G-35-BO 42-31981 in the 350th Bomb Squadron, 100th Bomb Group, which crashed at Thorpe Abbotts on 27 April 1944. On this date the Group flew a double mission for the first time in the war with a raid on a *Noball* site in France in the morning and an airfield at Thionville in the afternoon. (TAMM)

Left: S/Sgt John B. Palmquist, ball turret gunner in Lieutenant Ralph Wright's crew in the 349th Bomb Squadron, 100th Bomb Group, was awarded the Purple Heart for shrapnel wounds received on 28 April 1944. Palmquist was still hospitalised on 7 May when five of his crew were lost when approaching the East Coast; their Fortress (42-38053) was set on fire after flares carried in the top turret compartment ignited. The B-17 crashed in a wooded area at Herringfleet Hall, near Lowestoft, where it exploded, killing both pilots, the navigator, bombardier, and a replacement waist gunner. (John A. Miller) Right: 452nd Bomb Group Fortress over Berlin's Templehof airport on 29 April 1944. (USAF)

B-24H-1-FO 42-7546 *Alfred II* in the 577th Bomb Squadron, 392nd Bomb Group, which was badly damaged by fighters on the mission to Berlin on 29 April 1944. The crew struggled back across the North Sea, and when they reached the Norfolk coast they all baled out. (USAF)

B-24J-95-CO 42-100347 *Lil' Max* in the 707th Bomb Squadron, 446th Bomb Group carries out an experimental release of a formation cluster on 1 May 1944. *Lil' Max* and 2nd Lieutenant Thomas H. Gill's crew were lost on the mission to Holland on 26 September 1944. The Liberator crashed at Ahaus, Germany, and five crew evaded. Two were KIA and four were taken prisoner. (USAF)

B-24J-15-FO-42-52542 *Stinger* in the 791st Bomb Squadron, 467th Bomb Group, which Lieutenant Thomas Murphy successfully crash-landed at RAF Watton on 8 May 1944 following damage sustained on the mission to Brunswick. (Noble)

B-17G-35-DL 42-107091 *Forbidden Fruit* in the 728th Bomb Squadron, 452nd Bomb Group, which suffered flak damage on the mission on 8 May 1944. On 17 February 1945 *Forbidden Fruit* crashed after a mid-air collision while forming up. Joe Knoll and five of his crew were killed. (TAMM)

84th Fighter Squadron, 78th Fighter Group P-51D Mustangs in one of the First World War hangars at Duxford. The "Gauntlet Endurance" lettering refers to the 1930s when the RAF's Gloster Gauntlet biplane fighters of 19 Squadron were stationed there. The 78th, like their RAF predecessors, adopted bold markings, using a black and white checkerboard scheme. (via Ian McLachlan)

Oberleutnant Waldemar "Waldi" Radener in his FW 190A-8 "Brown 4" (W.Nr. 340001) leading 7./JG 26 from Coesfeld-Stevede on 4 May 1944. Note the rows of *Abschuss* victory bars on the rudder of Radener's aircraft, whose tally at that time stood at 20 kills. On 11 May he rammed a B-24 in air combat over France whilst flying "Brown 2" and was wounded. Barely recovered, he was shot down by a 339th Fighter Group Mustang on 15 June and was severely injured before baling out of FW 190A-8 "Brown 2." *Unteroffizier* Gerhard Langhammer of the 7th *Staffel* turned the newly-repaired FW 190A-8 "Brown 4" over when he hit a bomb crater while landing at Epinoy on 12 May and he suffered serious head injuries. (Werner Molge via Theo Boiten)

Left: *Oberleutnant* Waldemar "Waldi" Radener, who was decorated with the *Ritterkreuz* on 12 March 1945, finished the war as *Kommandeur* II./JG 300. His score of 37 *Abschüsse* in the *Reichsverteidigung* included 17 *Viermots*. (Walter Stumpf via Theo Boiten) Right: Major Walter "Gulle" Oesau (left), who claimed 10 aircraft in the Spanish Civil War, was the third German pilot to reach 100 victories. After a short spell on the Eastern Front he returned to the West to lead JG 2, then JG 1. Physically and mentally exhausted, he was shot down and killed in combat with P-51 Mustangs and P-38 Lightnings on 11 May 1944. He had 125 victories. On the right is *Oberleutnant* Hans Ehlers, who on 8 October 1943, flying a FW 190, collided with *Marie Helena* of the Bloody Hundredth. All ten men aboard the Fortress were KIA. Ehlers baled out with various facial injuries and a double fracture of the right thighbone. He was shot down and killed on 27 December 1944 by Mustangs of the 364th Fighter Group. At the time of his death Ehlers had at least 55 victories, including 23 *Viermots*. (via Eric Mombeek)

B-24H-10-DT 41-28738 *Meat Around The Corner* in the 754th Bomb Squadron, 458th Bomb Group, which had to put down at Jegenstorf, in Switzerland, on 11 May 1944 after bombing the marshalling yards at Epinal. Lieutenant Stuart Goldsmith and his crew were interned. (USAF)

Chick's Crew 360th Bomb Squadron, 303rd Bomb Group. Standing: Lieutenant Anthony "Chick" J. Cecchini, pilot (WIA 11.5.44); Lieutenant Stan Fisher, co-pilot; Edward "Jasper" Veigel, navigator (who, when asked by the pilot in the U.S. on the crew's first cross-country flight what town it was below, had replied Jasper, Texas. It was the port of Beaumont!); and Theodore McDevitt, bombardier. Kneeling: Cliff "Bachy" Bachman, flight engineer, who completed 52 combat missions; Clarence "Alvin" Cogdell; George Kepics, ball-turret gunner; Robert J. "Chunk" O'Hearn, waist gunner; Ben Smith, Jr., radio operator (WIA 11.5.44); and Ward Hudson, tail gunner (WIA 11.5.44). (Ben Smith)

Left: Ben Smith, Jr., radio operator in Lieutenant Anthony "Chick" J. Cecchini's crew in the 360th Bomb Squadron, 303rd Bomb Group. (Ben Smith) Right: Wilbur Richardson, a ball turret gunner in the 331st Bomb Squadron, 94th Bomb Group, who flew his 8th mission on 12 May 1944. (Richardson)

P-47 Thunderbolt 42-22468, which crashed on 12 May 1944. (via TAMM)

Left: Bullet holed B-17G-35-DL 42-107147 *Sweet Melody*, 360th Bomb Squadron, 303rd Bomb Group, which Lieutenant Anthony "Chick" J. Cecchini, a NY cop in peacetime, crash-landed at RAF Southend-on-Sea returning from Saarbrücken on 11 May 1944. (USAF via Robert M. Foose)

P-51B 43-24853 VF-U in the 336th Fighter Squadron, 4th Fighter Group in a stream with a bent prop after mishap. (USAF)

P-51Ds of the 374th Fighter Squadron, 361st Fighter Group overflying an airfield. Nearest aircraft is B7-W 44-14305. (via Steve Gotts)

B-17G-40-BO 42-97167 in the 339th Bomb Squadron, 96th Bomb Group at Snetterton Heath after extensive fuselage repairs. This aircraft and Captain Jack E. Link's crew FTR from the raid on Brux on 12 May 1944. Nine crew were KIA and one was taken prisoner. (USAF)

Personnel in the 93rd Bomb Group taking a break at Hardwick. (USAF)

B-17Gs in the 381st Bomb Group in formation. Nearest aircraft is B-17G-60-BO 42-102966 *Avengress II* in the 534th Bomb Squadron. This Fortress survived to the end of the war and was scrapped at Kingman, Arizona, in December 1945. (USAF)

Left: A 389th Bomb Group Liberator trails fire 300ft long and begins to break up after being hit in the fuel tanks during a mission to Münster. (USAF) Right: Colonel Beirne Lay, Jr., CO 487th Bomb Group. (via Philip Kaplan)

T/Sgt James W. Cannon was credited with five Japanese Zeros and 68 operational missions in the South Pacific on B-25s, B-26s, and B-17s, and 32 combat missions on B-17s in the 401st Bomb Group in the ETO. (via Walt Truax)

Above: 4th Fighter Group pilots attending prayers before a mission. (USAF) Right: 1st Lieutenant John W. McClane, Jr., receives the Air Medal on 13 May 1944 from Colonel John H. Gibson, 44th Bomb Group CO (John W. McClane Coll)

Lieutenant Charles D. Peritti's crew in the 68th Bomb Squadron, 44th Bomb Group in front of their B-24 *Lily Marlene* at Shipdham. Standing L-R: Lieutenant John McClane, navigator; Lieutenant Peritti; Lieutenant Burr W. Palmer, co-pilot; and Lieutenant John F. Warga, bombardier. Kneeling L-R: Cannetti, waist gunner; Stamper, tail gunner; S/Sgt Otho H. Freeman, waist gunner; S/Sgt Paul M. Corlew, engineer; and John Schneider, radioman. Not shown is S/Sgt Charles J. Alexander, ball turret gunner. (McClane)

B-17F-85-BO 42-30088 *Squawkin Hawk* in the 100th Bomb Group, the first B-17 in the Hundredth to complete 50 missions, which after being suitably adorned was flown back to the States on 16 May 1944 to take part in a War Bond tour. (TAMM)

Left: Ground crew at Snetterton Heath working on a fuel tank from B-17G-20-VE 42-97560 *Hang The Expense IV*, a PFF ship maintained by the 413th Bomb Squadron, 96th Bomb Group at the base. (TAMM) Right: B-17G-20-VE 42-97560 *Hang The Expense IV* ran off the end of the runway at Thorpe Abbotts on 19 May 1944 when Frank Valesh tried to land prior to leading the 100th Bomb Group on the mission to Berlin. Valesh, who had been a pilot in the 315th Bomb Squadron before becoming a PFF ship pilot, and his co-pilot, Lieutenant Booth, approached the base in the early hours. They requested landing lights as they approached, but this request was refused because of the possibility of intruders in the area. They circled for a time, and finally the runway lights were turned on but not the approach lights. Just as they approached the short runway someone on the ground fired a flare to assist their landing, but only succeeded in blinding the two pilots, and the bomber touched down too far along the runway and overshot. Four crew were injured and the plane was written off. (TAMM)

The crew of *Hang The Expense*. L-R, front: Frank Valesh; Maurice Zetlen; John Booth; and John "Dick" Johnson. Back Row: Sgts John Mytko; Roy Urick; Louis Black; Paul Carbone; Herschel Broyles; and Ernest Jordan. Legend has it that Valesh, who had a favorite saying "Hang the expense, give the canary another seed!" was supposed to have "lost" five B-17s before he completed his tour on 24 July 1944, but this is not quite true, and they were not all called *Hang The Expense*. The first loss was B-17G-1-BO 42-31035 *Hang The Expense* with its characteristic shapely red-headed gal on the nose which, with the tailwheel locked, careered off the runway at Thorpe Abbotts at the start of a "test flight" on 26 November 1943, hit two trees, and demolished Mr Draper's barn on the fringe of the base. The three-man crew of Valesh, co-pilot Russell "Pinky" Flack and 2nd Lieutenant Andrew Campion, and Miss Cook and Miss Yeager, their two American Red Cross girl passengers, did not suffer any serious injuries. Two months later at a Court Martial Valesh was fined $100. Valesh was at the controls of B-17G-5-VE 42-39867 on 24 January 1944 when the aircraft was crash-landed at RAF Eastchurch with the tail gunner's compartment blown away and the left elevator completely gone after it was hit by flak over Frankfurt. Roy Ulrick, the tail gunner, was blown out of his shattered turret, but incredibly he survived, mainly because he had packed his turret with flak vests and was wearing his parachute when he exited the aircraft. Though badly injured, he recovered, and he was sent to a PoW camp. The B-17, which the press release called *Hang The Expense Again*, though no name was ever painted on its nose, was repaired and assigned to another crew at Thorpe Abbotts, and later gained the name *Boeing Belle*. On 4 January 1944 Valesh was flying B-17F-40-DL 42-3271 *Nine Little Yanks and a Jerk* on the mission to Kiel when, soon after bombing, oil drained out of the No.2 engine and the prop ran away and refused to feather. It ran at 2500-3500 rpm all the way home, howling like a banshee, and Valesh put the plane down at RAF Leconfield with only 30 gallons of fuel remaining. Late in February 1944 Valesh transferred to the 482nd Bomb Group for specialist pathfinder training. After the loss of *Hang The Expense IV* Valesh was credited with "cracking up" a 95th Bomb Group PFF ship (42-97696) on 21 June 1944 when the Valesh crew led the 390th Bomb Group to the BMW works in Berlin. Flak knocked out two engines and a third quit over the North Sea, and Valesh crash-landed at the B-24 base at Seething with little fuel and no brakes. (TAMM)

B-17G-35-BO 42-32088, which was assigned to the 532nd Bomb Squadron, 381st Bomb Group as VE-M on 6 April 1944. Named *Dry Gulcher*, the aircraft went MIA with Lieutenant Harold C. Blog's crew on the Berlin mission on 19 May 1944. All nine crew survived and were taken prisoner. (USAF)

91st Bomb Group Fortresses en route to their target. B-17G-35-BO 42-32095 *Ack Ack Annie* in the 322nd Bomb Squadron joined the Group in 1944 after serving with the 457th Bomb Group from 16 March 1944. *Ack Ack Annie* completed 143 missions and flew the Group's last mission of the war on 25 April 1945 before returning home to be consigned to scrap at Kingman, Arizona, in December 1945. (USAF)

A stick of 1000lb bombs dropped from Lieutenant John Winslett's B-17G-30-VE 42-97791 *Trudy*, 332nd Bomb Squadron, 94th Bomb Group, over Berlin on 19 May 1944 knocked off the left horizontal stabilizer of Lieutenant Marion Ulysses Reid's B-17G-20-BO 42-31540 *Miss Donna Mae*, 331st Bomb Squadron, below. Reid's aircraft went into an uncontrollable spin, and at 13,000ft the wing broke off and the B-17 spun crazily to the ground. There were no survivors. (USAF via Abe Dolim)

Lieutenant John Keys flew B-17G-25-BO 42-31723/R *Sparky* in the 349th Bomb Squadron, 100th Bomb Group, home to Thorpe Abbotts on 19 May 1944 after a 20mm shell fired by FW 190s over Denmark on the return from Berlin had blown a large section of the tail fin away. *Sparky* was repaired and put back into service, flying again on 2 June when the B-17s bombed Boulogne. *Sparky* had been named by Clement Cowan's crew in honor of the radio operator "Sparky" Meyers, who was KIA on 18 March 1944 when he was hit in the back by 20mm shells as he stood on an ammunition box to reach the radio room gun during an attack by fighters. Sparky was buried three days later at Madingley Cemetery, Cambridge. On 29 July 1944 *Sparky* was hit by flak on the mission to the Leuna oil plant at Merseburg and was finished off by fighters. The only survivor in Jackson Phelps' crew was the tail gunner, although it was thought that several other crewmembers had baled out only to be murdered by German civilians. (TAMM)

B-17G-25-DL 42-38005 DS-G *Stormy Weather* in the 511th Bomb Squadron, 351st Bomb Group, which crashed at Sose Odde, near Osterholm, on 24 May 1944 after a mechanical failure on the raid on Berlin. Captain Robert B. Clay and crew were taken prisoner. (USAF)

Left: Captain Willard W. "Millie" Millikan in the 336th Fighter Squadron and other 4th Fighter Group pilots at Debden after a mission. On 22 May 1944 Millikan destroyed a Bf 109 northwest of Kiel to take his final score to 13 victories. Eight days later he was involved in a collision with another P-51B near Wittenburg and he became a PoW. (USAF)

Right: B-17G-25-BO 42-31698 and Lieutenant Clarence D. Wainwright's crew in the 533rd Bomb Squadron, 381st Bomb Group FTR from the mission to Berlin on 24 May 1944 after a mid-air collision. Near Gruental, two German women view the crashed aircraft in which seven crew were KIA. Two men survived and they were taken prisoner. (Ulrich Lange via Ron Mackay)

Above left: Captain Jack M. Ilfrey, who scored his 7th and final victory of the war on 24 May 1944 when he destroyed two Bf 109s at Elberswalde. All of "Happy Jack's" victories (he was also awarded a half share in a Bf 110 victory in 1942) were achieved flying P-38 Lightnings, six of his kills being achieved in the 94th Fighter Squadron, 1st Fighter Group in North Africa. Ilfrey, who had joined the 79th Fighter Squadron, 20th Fighter Group on 20 April 1944, was shot down on 13 June 1944 by flak NW of Lelion, but he evaded capture and returned. He became 79th Fighter Squadron CO on 28 September 1944, a post he held until 9 December that year. (USAF) Center: Captain Allen Bunte in the 4th Fighter Group. (USAF) Above right: A Bf 109 pilot bales out after his fighter is shot down by a USAAF fighter. (USAF)

Below left: P-51D Mustang LH-U in the 350th FS, 353rd Fighter Group passing beneath the wing of a Fortress. (via Ian McLachlan) Below right: On 28 May 1944 Fortresses attacked Cologne with GB-1 glide bombs. In this movie still B-17G PU-A in the 360th Bomb Squadron, 303rd Bomb Group releases two glide bombs on the target. (USAF)

1st Lieutenant Francis "Frank" J. Malooly and his crew in the 350th Bomb Squadron, 100th Bomb Group. L-R standing: T/Sgt Robert C. S. Barrie, radio operator; Malooly; 1st Lieutenant Charles H. Mauvais, navigator; 1st Lieutenant Robert W. Ballie, co-pilot; and 1st Ralph W. Guida, bombardier. Kneeling: S/Sgt Willard H. Miller, waist gunner; S/Sgt Nelson A. Pardee, ball turret gunner; S/Sgt Leonard W. Yeager, waist gunner; T/Sgt Arthur J. Perry, top turret gunner; and S/Sgt Lovenzo Genovese, tail gunner. On 24 May 1944 the crew were flying deputy group lead in B-17G-20-BO *"Powerhouse"* on the mission to Berlin when they were shot down and taken prisoner. (via Mike Faley)

Left: Ben C. Isgrig, bombardier in 2nd Lieutenant William J. Bailey's crew in the 712th Bomb Squadron, 448th Bomb Group, who flew their first mission on 28 May 1944. (Isgrig) A young Dutch family with a 108 gallon drop-tank, which was dropped by a P-47 over Zuid-Scharwoude, northern Holland, on 29 May 1944 when 187 Thunderbolts flew escort and support for the heavies attacking aircraft plants and oil installations. (Ab A. Jansen)

B-17G-35-BO 42-32076 *Shoo Shoo Baby* in the 401st Bomb Squadron, 91st Bomb Group was named by its crew after a popular song of the day. On 29 May 1944 it took Lieutenant Paul McDuffee's crew to Frankfurt on the first of 24 combat missions in which it was damaged by flak on seven occasions. Its last mission was to Poznan, Poland, on 29 May 1944, when engine problems forced Lieutenant Robert Guenther's crew to make a landing in neutral Sweden. The Swedish government was officially given seven B-17s as a gift, and in exchange American crews were repatriated. *Shoo Shoo Baby's* nose was lengthened by 3ft, and accommodation provided for fourteen passengers and 4400lb of cargo in the bomb bay. In 1955, after Swedish and Danish airline service and Danish military use, the aircraft was bought by a New York company and sold to the *Institute Geographique National* in Paris. In July 1978 *Shoo Shoo Baby* was flown by C-5 Galaxy to Dover Air Force Base, Delaware, and after a ten-year restoration to flying condition, was flown to the USAF Museum at Wright Patterson Air Force Base, Dayton, Ohio, on 13 October 1988, where *Shoo Shoo Baby* is now on permanent display. (via Frank Thomas)

Bombs fall from the bomb bays of B-17G-35-DL 42-107091 *Forbidden Fruit* in the 728th Bomb Squadron, 452nd Bomb Group over Schwerte, Germany, on 31 May 1944. Earlier that month Captain Edward Starka had put the B-17 down at Rattlesden on 8 May after flak had killed his rear gunner. *Forbidden Fruit* crash-landed on 17 February 1945 and was salvaged on 21 May 1945. (via Sam Young)

Exhausted 491st Bomb Group crewmembers at Metfield after returning from the group's first combat mission on 2 June 1944. (USAF)

On the evening of 4 June five B-24s in the 753rd Bomb Squadron, 458th Bomb Group made their second attempt to knock out a series of bridges on the Seine River with radio-controlled *Azon* glide bombs. (USAF)

P-51D 44-13808 D7-U in the 503rd Fighter Squadron, 339th Fighter Group. (USAF)

The 489th Bomb Group Deputy Commanding Officer, Lieutenant Colonel Leon Vance, with daughter Sharon. Vance received the Medal of Honor for his actions on 5 June 1944 when a flak burst hit the co-pilot and practically severed Vance's foot. Despite this, Vance flew on and bombed the target, later ditching his aircraft in the Channel; Vance was drowned in late July when the Douglas C-54 evacuating him stateside was lost without trace over the Atlantic. (Freudenthal)

Above: B-24J-40 1-CF 42-50466 *Ford's Folly* in the 578th Bomb Squadron, 392nd Bomb Group is loaded up with incendiary bombs at Wendling, Norfolk, for the Liberator's 100th mission on D-Day, 6 June 1944. On 11 September 1944 *Ford's Folly* was hit over Koblenz by fighters, which set the No.3 engine on fire. The aircraft was engulfed in flames, and was last seen spinning in and crashing with the loss of Lieutenant C. A. Rudd's entire crew. (USAF) Below: Swanner's crew in the 379th Bomb Group at Kimbolton, who flew the D-Day mission on 6 June 1944. Front row, L-R: Frank J. Bagdon, flight engineer; Frank Marsh, tail gunner; Al Tenenzaph, radio operator-gunner; Al Smith, waist gunner; Otis Creighton, waist gunner; and John Snyder, ball turret gunner. Standing, L-R: John L. Swanner, Jr., pilot; John East, co-pilot; Frank L. Betz, navigator; and Walter G. Collings, bombardier. (Frank L. Betz)

P-51B 43-7180/M and P-51D 44-13392/A *Fabasca V* in the 339th Fighter Group at Fowlmere, Cambridgeshire, in 1944. (via Ian McLachlan)

"Gentlemen. This is it!" The first indication for the majority of crews that 6 June was indeed *D-Day* came at a briefing at 0245 hours on that dramatic Tuesday morning, although at many bases that night wave after wave of RAF aircraft could be heard overhead. The mixture of shock, excitement, and enthusiasm on the faces of these combat crews in the 306th Bomb Group briefing room at Thurleigh was repeated at every base in eastern England. The 306th, like almost everyone else, flew three missions at 0430 hours, 0732 hours, and 1754 hours. (Richards)

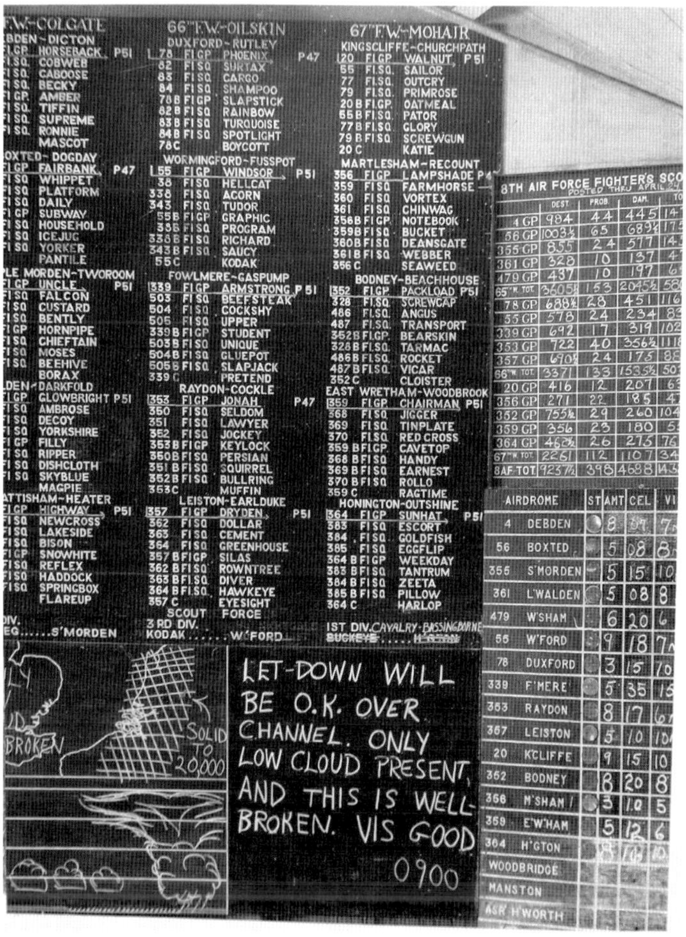

65th Fighter Wing Operations Block Wall. (USAF)

P-51Bs of the 376th Squadron, 361st Fighter Group taxi out. (via Steve Gotts)

In the early hours of 6 June the 446th Bomb Group at Bungay (Flixton) received Field Order No.328 over the teletype machine, informing them that the "Bungay Buckeroos" would be leading the 8th Air Force on the momentous day. Colonel Jacob J. Brogger, the CO and air commander, flew the mission in B-24H-25-FO 42-95203 *Red Ass* (which for public relations purposes was renamed *The Buckeroo* especially for the occasion!) However, the first of the formation to arrive in the assembly area to lead the group to the Normandy beaches was a PFF B-24 in the 564th Bomb Squadron, 389th Bomb Group flown by a 93rd Bomb Group crew. (USAF)

B-24 Liberators in the 487th Bomb Group, 3rd Bomb Division taxi out at Lavenham, Suffolk, while a formation of B-17s passes high overhead. In August the 3rd Division groups began converting from the B-24 to the Flying Fortress, and the Liberators were dispersed, chiefly among the Liberator groups of the 2nd Bomb Division. Lieutenant General Jimmy Doolittle intended to convert the 2nd Division to Fortresses as well, but was prevented from doing so because there simply were not enough Fortresses to spare. (USAF)

Right: 353rd Fighter Group pilots at briefing at Raydon. (USAF) Below: An 832nd Bomb Squadron, 486th Bomb Group B-24 Liberator passes over Allied shipping off the Normandy beachhead near Caen on *D-Day*, 6 June 1944. (USAF)

S/Sgt Hugh R. McLaren, ball turret gunner on B-24J-401-CF 42-50474 *D-Day Patches* in the 565th Bomb Squadron, 389th Bomb Group at Hethel. The Liberator was originally called *Patches*. On 6 June 1944 *Patches* was almost cut in half when a fragmentation bomb exploded prematurely. (Hugh McLaren)

P-47C Thunderbolt 44-19566 with D-Day markings in the 78th Fighter Group at Duxford. (via Andy Height)

B-24J-160-CO 44-40437 *Hairless Joe* in the 860th Bomb Squadron, 493rd Bomb Group with three P-51B Mustangs in the 363rd Fighter Squadron, 357th Fighter Group. *Hairless Joe* was named after the maker of "Kickapoo Joy Juice" in Al Capp's legendary satirical comic strip *Li'l Abner*, which had started in the Depression year of 1934. The Liberator was transferred to the 44th Bomb Group when the 3rd Bomb Division converted to Fortresses and it FTRLOC on 30 November 1944. (USAF)

Bob Shaffer sitting on a bomb in front of B-24J-401-CF 42-50505 in the 330th Bomb Squadron, 93rd Bomb Group at Hardwick. On *D-Day* Bob Shaffer was lead bombardier in B-24J-55-CO 42-99949 *Naughty Nan* piloted by Lieutenant Sneddon. *Naughty Nan* and Lieutenant Everett E. Johnson's crew were lost on 21 September 1944 when it was involved in a mid-air collision with another B-24 over Belgium. Five members of Johnson's crew were killed. 42-50505 was lost with Lieutenant Howard E. Jennings' crew on 6 February 1945. Two men were KIA and seven were taken prisoner. (Shaffer)

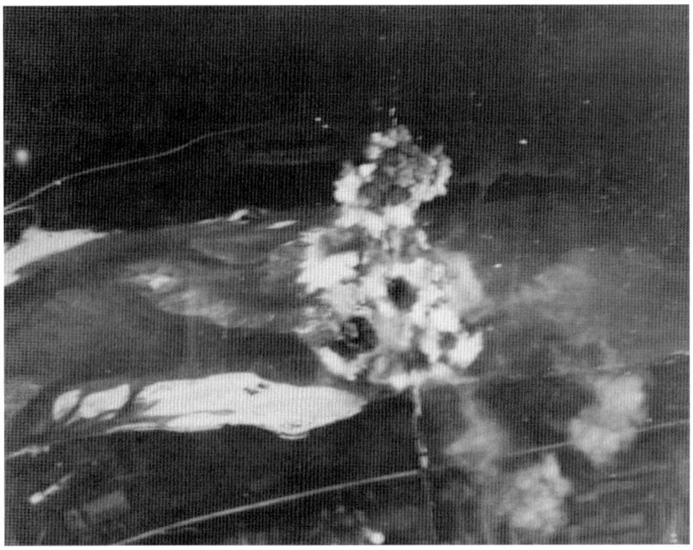

Bombs from Liberators in the 96th Wing hurtle down on the railway bridge at Blois-Saint-Denis in France on 11 June 1944, effectively preventing the flow of supplies to the beleaguered German Army in the Normandy bridgehead. This photograph was taken by Harlan Oakes in the 466th Bombardment Group at 5500ft while suspended half out of the camera hatch! (Oakes)

B-17G-65-BO 43-37516 *Tondalayo* in the 422nd Bomb Squadron, 305th Bomb Group at Chelveston in early June 1944. On 26 June 1944 it was transferred to the Night Leaflet Unit at Cheddington. *Tondalayo* was repainted matt black overall, but retained its distinctive artwork and 305th Bomb Group markings. On the night of 4 March 1945 *Tondalayo* was shot down in error off Clacton by British shore batteries that had opened fire on a German intruder detected in the same area. Lieutenant Colonel Earle Aber, CO 406th Bomb Squadron (which the unit had become on 11 August), was at the controls. After ordering the crew to bale out he and his co-pilot, 2nd Lieutenant Maurice Harper, remained at the controls in a desperate bid to reach the emergency field at Woodbridge. *Tondalayo* crashed into the sea in flames, killing both men. (via Bill Donald)

Above left: Joe Hamil's crew in the 94th Bomb Group celebrate the successful mission to Montdidier, France, on 12 June 1944. Front, standing, (left) is Abe Dolim. Back Row L-R: Hamil; Harvey Brown, co-pilot; Burnet R. Maybank, Jr., bombardier; Sgt Yarborough, engineer-gunner; and right, PRO C. Roy Babb. (C. Roy Babb) Center: Lieutenant Loren E. Jackson, who on 12 June flew *Crash Wagon III* in the 551st Bomb Squadron, 385th Bomb Group on his tenth mission when the 3rd Air Division bombed lines of communication around the Normandy bridgehead. (Jackson) Above right: A B-17 in the 100th Bomb Group over the French beaches. (TAMM)

P-51 44-14276 VF-A *Martha Jane* in the 336th Fighter Squadron, 4th Fighter Group. (USAF)

Green nosed P-51Bs and Ds of the 369th Fighter Squadron (IV) and 370th Fighter Squadron (CS), 359th Fighter Group from East Wretham, Norfolk, in formation. Each fighter group totalled 48 aircraft in three squadrons. After being relieved of escort duties, and if fuel reserves were adequate, fighter leaders were allowed to take their formations down to strafe airfields in the target area. (USAF)

Above left: Captain Robert W. "Father" Foy of the 357th Fighter Group, at Leiston, Suffolk. On 29 June 1944 Foy shot down two Bf 109s and a FW 190 to take his score of victories to 6 enemy destroyed. Foy, who finished the war with 15 victories, was killed on 25 March 1950 in a B-25 crash near Phoenix, Arizona. (USAF) Center: 2nd Lieutenant Ralph "Kid" Hofer in the cockpit of P-51B-15-NA 42-106924 QP-L *Salem Representative*. He scored 15 victories in WWII, all except two of them in the P-51. He was KIA on 2 July 1944 while supporting 15th AF bombers over the Balkans during an 8th AF Shuttle mission, flying P-51B-7 43-6746 in aerial combat at Mostar, Yugoslavia. His executioner was probably a pilot of JG 52. Probably the most colorful of all the aces, Hofer is the only one known to have been killed in combat with the *Luftwaffe*. (USAF) Above right: *Oberstleutnant* Josef "Pips" Priller, *Kommodore Jagdgeschwader 26 "Schlageter." Oberstleutnant* Priller's 100th victory came on 15 June 1944 when he shot down a B-24 while leading II./JG 26, III./JG 26, and III./JG 54 on an offensive sweep over northwestern France. His 101st and final victory came on 12 October when he shot down a P-51 Mustang of the 357th Fighter Group flown by Captain H.T. Pascoe, who survived to be taken prisoner. The majority of his victories scored in 307 combat sorties were fighter aircraft. Only 11 were heavy bombers. *Oberst* Priller's final sortie was leading I/JG 26 in a raid on Grimbergen in *Unternehmen Bodenplatte* on 1 January 1945. (via Theo Boiten)

B-24 Liberators in the 446th Bomb Group dropping bombs on Tours, France, on 15 June 1944; photographed by S/Sgt John K. L. Peterson, waist gunner in Captain Oliver W. Henderson's crew. (John Peterson)

B-17Gs taxi out at Bassingbourn, June-July 1944. Aircraft at right is PFF *Mickey* ship 42-97636/P in the 324th Bomb Squadron, which transferred to the 351st Bomb Group on 14 June 1944 and later served in the 615th Bomb Squadron, 401st Bomb Group and the 305th Bomb Group. The two olive drab B-17Gs are 42-97467/F and 42-31 883/Y *The Jub Jub Bird* in the 401st Bomb Squadron. 42-97467/F and Lieutenant Donald K. Bare's crew FTR on 18 July 1944 when they suffered a mechanical failure and they had to land at Bulltofta, Sweden. *The Jub Jub Bird* and Lieutenant Herbert W. Chouinard's crew FTR on 2 November 1944. Seven men were KIA and two were made PoW. The next two NMF B-17s in the line up are 42-107083/Q and 43-37610/Q *Zootie Cutie*. The latter and 2nd Lieutenant Carl M. Melton's crew force landed on the continent on 11 December 1944. The aircraft was repaired and returned to the ZOI in June 1945, and was scrapped at Kingman, AZ, in December 1945. B-17 43-37552/E *The Peacemaker* in the 401st Bomb Squadron is behind. *The Peacemaker* was written off in a crash-landing on 12 April 1945. The B-17G far right is 41-24460, which was assigned to the 423rd Bomb Squadron, 306th Bomb Group at Westover Field in August 1942. It was wrecked in a crash at RAF Sutton Bridge on 21 October 1942 after the life raft latch broke loose and the raft became entangled around the horizontal stabilizer. The aircraft was repaired, and was transferred to the 482nd Bomb Group on 22 August 1943. It went on to operate with the 379th Bomb Group before returning to the ZOI in October 1944 and was scrapped at Kingman, AZ. The OD B-17 below the NMF B-17 at the head of the column is a 379th Bomb Group Fortress, and to its right is 42-102449/R *Hale's Angels* in the 547th Bomb Squadron, 384th Bomb Group, which FTR when it was landed on the continent on 10 November 1944. It was repaired and was returned to the ZOI for scrapping in December 1945. In the same line are 43-37626/M and 44-4607/Q. 43-37626/M in the 322nd Bomb Squadron FTR with 2nd Lieutenant Joseph P. Paskvan's crew on 21 June 1944 with the loss of three men KIA and six made PoW. (USAF)

B-24H-25-FO 42-95132 in the 858th Bomb Squadron, 492nd Bomb Group, flown by 2nd Lieutenant David P. McMurray, burning in a field near the Normandy beachhead on 15 June 1944 after it was shot down by *Oberstleutnant* "Pips" Priller, his 100th victory of the war. (USAF)

B-24J-145-CO 44-40103 *Say When* in the 858th Bomb Squadron, 492nd Bomb Group at North Pickenham. On 20 June it was piloted by Lieutenant Malcolm M. Herber and was one of 14 Liberators that FTR from the mission to Politz and Ostermoor. Herber and four other Liberators landed at Bulltofta airfield near Malmo. Altogether, 18 Liberators landed in Sweden on that day. (Dan Winston)

B-17G-40-DL 44-6010/W in the 418th Bomb Squadron piloted by Dale McEwen and B-17G-70-BO 43-37686/G *Josephine* in the 350th Bomb Squadron, piloted by Henry Woodall, collided while taxiing prior to take off at Thorpe Abbotts on 21 June 1944 when the 100th Bomb Group set out to bomb Ruhland and fly to landing fields in Russia. The only officer who spoke Russian was on one of the crews, none of whom suffered any lasting injury. (TAMM)

On 21 June the 8th Air Force flew its second shuttle mission from England. The operation, code-named *Frantic*, involved 1311 bombers. Some 163 B-17s in the 13th and 45th Wings, each equipped with a long-range bomb bay tank, bombed the Ruhland-Elsterwerda synthetic oil plant 50 miles south of Berlin and then flew on to Russia, escorted all the way by 70 Mustangs in the 4th and 352nd Fighter Groups, some of whose pilots are shown heading for their planes. (USAF)

B-24J-155-CO 44-40299 in the 860th Bomb Squadron, 493rd Bomb Group was named *Purty Baby* by the crew and painted by Sgt Duane Bryers. It flew to England in April 1944. On 25 June, with two engines out, Lieutenant Daigle crash-landed the aircraft at the emergency airfield at Woodbridge after returning from St Avord, France. The aircraft was salvaged and repaired, and transferred to the 487th Bomb Group before being assigned to the MTO on 3 December 1944 by BAD2. (via Truett Woodall)

Below: The shuttle force touched down at Poltava, where later that night, 60 *Luftwaffe* bombers destroyed 44 of the 72 bombers, including Lieutenant Robert Wightman's B-17G-55-BO 42-102670 in the 96th Bomb Group, and severely damaged 26 more. (via Geoff Ward)

On 21 June 1944 a second formation, consisting of the rest of the 3rd Bomb Division, plus the 1st and 2nd Bomb Divisions, bombed Berlin and returned to England. Despite the intense fighter cover, 44 Fortresses and Liberators were shot down near the German capital. B-24H-25-FO 42-95089 *Dual Sack* in the 714th Bomb Squadron, 448th Bomb Group, piloted by 2nd Lieutenant Roland G. Fox, crash-landed at Bulltofta, Sweden. (via Frank Thomas)

B-17G in the 96th Bomb Group with the Alps on the horizon en route to the Ain and Haute Savoie on 25 June 1944 to drop supplies to the FFI (*Forces Françaises de l'Interiour*, or the "French Forces of the Interior") in Operation *Zebra*. The 96th Bomb Group contributed 14 aircraft to the operation, and 2088 supply containers were dropped by 176 B-17s in the Third Bomb Division, who were escorted by large formations of fighters, to five drop zones; two B-17s were lost, and two others aborted with mechanical problems. Further large-scale drops were made in July, on 1 August, and in September. (USAF)

The wing of B-24J-140-CO 42-110187 in the 467th Bomb Group breaks off after a direct hit in the fuel tanks over the target at Oschersleben on 29 June 1944. Pilot Lieutenant William H. Counts, who was blown out of the aircraft, was the only survivor. Eight other crew were killed. S/Sgt Thomas Hansbury, tail gunner, missed the mission. The night before he had been on guard duty at Rackheath, and Counts had decided that he would be in no fit shape for a mission, so he told him to stand down, but he would credit him with the mission. Hansbury was on his second combat tour, having flown 30 missions in a B-17 Group earlier in the war. The crew's engineer flew the tail turret position on the Oschersleben raid and the ball turret, unmanned, was retracted into the aircraft. (USAF)

B-17G-10-DL 42-37800 *Piccadilly Lilly II* in the 351st Bomb Squadron, 100th Bomb Group, which was salvaged on 27 June 1944. (TAMM)

B-17G-15-DL 42-37889 *Pride of Chehalis*, 336th Bomb Squadron, 95th Bomb Group, being inspected by locals after crashing in a potato field near Vroomshoop, the Netherlands, on 29 June 1944, when 1150 B-17s and B-24s were despatched to bomb the synthetic oil plant at Böhlen, a ball bearing works, and 11 aircraft assembly plants in the Leipzig area. 1st Lieutenant J. D. Cook and his crew baled out safely before the Fortress (one of 15 bombers lost) went down. Two men evaded capture. A total of 391 heavies returned with battle damage. (Coen Cornelissen)

On 4 July 1944 Captain Mayo R. Adams, Jr., in the 524th Bomb Squadron, 379th Bomb Group crash-landed B-17G-35-BO 42-32000 *Twentieth Century* in Miss Chaney's garden at Felpham, Sussex. The aircraft was salvaged by 2 SAD at Little Staughton on 10 July 1944. (via Paul Lincoln)

Left: *Little Warrior* of the 493rd Bomb Group was shot down over Fallersleben, Germany, on 29 June 1944. This dramatic photo was taken by S/Sgt Clifford Stocking, Jr., of the 862nd Bomb Squadron, a waist gunner in *The Green Hornet*. (via Truett Woodall) Right: On 5 July 1944 Lieutenant Colonel Francis S. "Gabby" Gabreski, CO 61st Fighter Squadron, 56th Fighter Group, scored his 28th fighter victory of the war. Gabby was shot down on 20 July by flak at Bassenheim airfield and he was captured. (USAF)

374th Fighter Squadron, 361st Fighter Group P-51B and D Mustangs from Bottisham photographed from a 91st Bomb Group B-17 on 11 July 1944. Nearest aircraft is P-51B 42-106839 B7-E *Bald Eagle* flown by Robert T. Eckfeldt. Next is P-51D 44-13357 B7-R *Tika IV* flown by Lieutenant Vernon Richards, then B7-O 44-13857 and P-51B B7-H. On 25 June 1944 Richards shot down a FW 190 and a Bf 109 in rapid succession. (via Tom Cushing)

P-51D 44-13926 E2-S being flown by 1st Lieutenant Urban Drew in the 375th Fighter Squadron. E2-S has been hastily sprayed with OD paint when VIIIth FC thought it would have to forward deploy fighters to France soon after D-Day, and it was almost brand new when this shot was taken on 11 July 1944. Later assigned to Lieutenant Abe P. Rosenberger, 44-13926 was written-off in a crash on 9 August whilst being flown by Lieutenant Don Dellinger, who was killed. (via Steve Gotts)

B-17G-45-BO 42-97272 BN-T *The Duchess' Daughter* in the 359th Bomb Squadron, 303rd Bomb Group suffered a taxi incident at Molesworth on 11 May when it was being flown by Lieutenant Sirany. It bellied in at the base on 5 July 1944 when 2nd Lieutenant I. J. Judy was at the controls. The aircraft was salvaged two days later, and the genre carried on at Molesworth with 44-6309 the *Duchess' Grand Daughter*, which was assigned overseas on 26 July and FTRLOC on 7 April 1945. (USAF)

During the 7 July 1944 raids against oil targets in Germany 28 Liberators and 9 Fortresses were lost, the majority to the heavily armored *Sturmjäger* FW 190A-8s of IV (*Sturm*)./JG 3 and II./JG 300. Two of the B-17Gs from the 390th Bomb Group were lost on the way in when 42-97983 FC-Z in the 570th Bomb Squadron flown by 2nd Lieutenant Larue F. Cribbs and 42-107070 *North Star* in the 571st Bomb Squadron flown by Lieutenant Lawrence J. Gregor collided over Hoorn, Holland. The smashed tail of *North Star* (seen here) plunged between the garage and the house occupied by the Sleutel family at the Westersingel. Thirteen of the 20 crewmembers from the two Fortresses and one of the inhabitants of Hoorn perished in the tragedy. (Jan de Groot via Ab A. Jansen)

Lieutenant Vernon D. Richards in the 374th Fighter Squadron, 361st Fighter Group. (USAF)

GIs of the 379th Bomb Group play ball at Kimbolton. In the background is B-17G-30-DL 42-38141 *Pansy Yokum* in the 524th Bomb Squadron, which ditched in the North Sea with Lieutenant Clarence E. Darnell's crew on 9 July 1944. (USAF)

375th Fighter Squadron, 361st Fighter Group P-51B and D Mustangs from Bottisham on 11 July 1944. The Group CO, Colonel Thomas J. J. Christian, is leading the four-ship in P-51D 44-13410 E2-C *Lou IV IV/Athlene*. Christian was shot down and killed on 12 August 1944 in this Mustang. The second P-51D in the formation is 44-13926 E2-S, being flown by the Group's third-ranking ace, 1st Lieutenant Urban Drew. Alongside Drew is Lieutenant Bruce Rowlett in his personal Mustang, 44-13568 E2-A *Sky Bouncer*, whilst occupying the No.4 slot, in soon to be retired P-51B 42-106811 E2-H *Suzy G* is Captain Francis Glanker. (via Steve Gotts)

Above left: B-17G-1-BO 42-31074 *Cahepit* in the 350th Bomb Squadron, 100th Bomb Group, which crash-landed in a meadow near Emmenbrucke, Switzerland, following the mission to Munich on 13 July 1944. The pilot, Donald Waters, his co-pilot, William Conselman, and the engineer were slightly injured. All ten crew were interned. (TAMM) Above right: B-17Gs in the 91st Bomb Group in formation. B-17G-50-BO 42-102509 *The Liberty Run* and Lieutenant Arthur F. Hultin's crew in the 401st Bomb Squadron FTR from the mission to Leipzig on 20 July 1944 when they were shot down by German fighters and all taken prisoner. Below this aircraft is the olive drab 42-31610/E *The Liberty Belle*, which FTR on 16 July 1944 when 2nd Lieutenant Don DaLisle's crew were forced to ditch in the Channel. All the crew was rescued. Below this Fortress is B-17G-35-DL 42-107027 DF-Y *Annie* in the 324th Bomb Squadron (formerly *Hikin' for Home* in the 401st Bomb Squadron). This Fortress, which was later renamed The *Bloody Bucket* in the 322nd Bomb Squadron, went to the 94th Bomb Group at Bury St Edmunds on 26 December 1944 and FTRLOC on 23 March 1945. Far right is B-17G-35-DL 42-107075/Q *Fancy Pants* (formerly *Champagne Girl*) in the 323rd Bomb Squadron, which 2nd Lieutenant Cyril J. Braund crash-landed at Obersaxen, Switzerland, on 19 July 1944 on the mission to Lechfeld after a mid-air collision with B-17G-20-BO 42-31542 *Bunky*, which was cut in half. All nine of 2nd Lieutenant Norman N. Burwick's crew were killed. (USAF)

Above left: During the evening of 15 July 1944 the bomb dump at Metfield, which contained 1200 tons of high explosive and incendiaries, exploded during unloading by the 882nd Chemical Company of a convoy of trucks carrying bombs. The bombs were not primed, but one exploded as the men kicked them off the truck and onto the ground. Five men were killed. In this photograph an airman points skywards at the truck's differential axle, which was discovered some time later in a village about a mile from the scene of the explosion, thrown there by the blast! Luckily, most of the men on the base were watching a movie at the time. The explosion was heard in Great Yarmouth, 25 miles away, where cinemagoers thought a V-2 had landed! The grass from the bomb dump to one of the hangars was scorched, and the bottom of the hangar ripped out. The 3rd SAD maintenance unit was notified of the blast at 2100 hours. An hour later a UC-64 landed at Metfield, bringing engineering officers to survey the damage to 491st Bomb Group B-24s near the centre of the blast. However, they soon returned to Griston because five unexploded bombs were still scattered about the dispersal area. By daylight the UXBs had been removed and the engineering officers returned. They found that seven B-24s could be repaired at the Sub Depot, while nine had to be transferred to the 3rd SAD for major repairs; six others were salvaged at Metfield. Missions were cancelled for three days while Headquarters held an inquiry. Lieutenant General James Doolittle, Major General James P. Hodges, and Major General Bill Kepner headed the investigation, which at first suspected sabotage. (Dan Winston) Center: Byron Cook (left) and F. Babisky (right) in Lieutenant Pohl's crew in the 560th Bomb Squadron, 388th Bomb Group are served a welcome cup of tea from the American Red Cross at Knettishall after baling out of their B-17 on 17 July 1944. Pohl landed 42-37849 *Red X Darling* safely after the entire crew except the co-pilot had baled out over the field. The ailerons of the aircraft had been shot away by flak on the mission to Houppeville, and Pohl gave his crew the choice of baling out or staying with the plane for an emergency landing. *Red X Darling* was salvaged on 31 May 1945. (USAF) Above right: 863rd Bomb Squadron crew interrogation on the hardstand at Debach following the 493rd Bomb Group's mission on 19 July 1944. L-R: Lieutenant Abraham "Hap" Galfunt, co pilot; Lieutenant Shelton, intelligence officer; Lieutenant P. B. Slawter, navigator; Lieutenant Chenard, intelligence officer; Captain Payne, intelligence officer; Lieutenant R. R. Harding, bombardier; and Lieutenant S. A. Abraham, pilot. (Galfunt)

Below left: On 11 July 1944 B-17G-10-BO *King Bee II* in the 351st Bomb Squadron, 100th Bomb Group remained at Thorpe Abbotts for patching and much needed maintenance while the Group flew the mission to Munich. Shortly after the return from the mission, *She-Hasta* took up position on its hardstand nearby. While its ball turret guns were being cleared and removed by the gunner one of the guns began firing, spinning the turret round and spraying more than 200 shells and tracer bullets around the airfield, and killing the unfortunate gunner instantly. One incendiary shell penetrated the wing of *King Bee II* and ignited the fuel tanks, which then exploded into a fireball. Two other B 17s parked nearby were also badly hit, but *King Bee II* was severely damaged despite fast action by fire crews to extinguish the blaze. During the incident, a firefighter was injured after he slipped and fell on the foam, which blanketed the wing of the blazing Fortress. When the flames were finally extinguished *King Bee II* was declared only fit for salvage. (TAMM) Below right: P-51 44-13947 5E of the 1st Scouting Force, 8th Air Force. On 16 July 1944, on the mission to Munich, the 1st Scouting Force of Mustangs and Mosquitoes, developed and led by Colonel Budd J. Peaslee, was used for the first time. Peaslee's scouting force flew just ahead of the main bombing force, transmitting up-to-the-minute weather reports back to the task force commander to prevent him leading his bombers into heavy weather fronts, which could disrupt the mission, and in some instances lead to its cancellation. Peaslee's weather scouts again proved effective on the 18 July mission to the principal German research and development centre at Peenemünde, on the Baltic coast. From the late summer of 1944 the black triangle was removed from the unit's aircraft, and the aircraft letter was applied to the fin in black with a red outline band. In March 1945 the 1st Scouting Force was renumbered the 857th Bomb Squadron and the 5E codes were replaced by 9H, the original 857th Bomb Squadron code letters. (USAF)

Belle of the Blue in the 423rd Bomb Squadron, 306th Bomb Group at Thurleigh on 20 July 1944 after a mission to Frankfurt. *Belle of the Blue* and 2nd Lieutenant Daniel W. Gates' crew FTR on the 12 September 1944 mission to Ruhland. The ball turret gunner was killed by fighters, but the rest of the crew managed to bale out safely. (via Richards)

B-17G-1-BO 42 31106 *Göering's Nightmare* in the 486th Bomb Group, which crashed on 23 July 1944 and was salvaged. Previously the aircraft had served in the 338th Bomb Squadron, 96th Bomb Group, and the 390th Bomb Group. Note the window defroster tube known as the "Elephant' Pecker," which provided heat for the bombsight, hanging down from the smashed Plexiglas nose. (USAF via Philip Kaplan)

B-17G-20-VE 42-97622 *Paper Dollie* in the 358th Bomb Squadron, 303rd Bomb Group, which crashed at Bishop's Waltham on 23 July 1944. Two of Flight Officer C. M. Miller's crew had been KIA. The other seven crew escaped injury. *Paper Dollie* was salvaged two days later by 2 SAD. (USAF)

Fortresses and Liberators at Dubendorf airfield in Switzerland after they had landed in the neutral country during hostilities. Nearest Fortress is flak-damaged B-17G-35-DL 42-107031 in the 550th Bomb Squadron, 385th Bomb Group, which Lieutenant Robert G. Turner force landed at Dubendorf on 13 July 1944 during the mission to Munich. The next Fortress in line is 42-37885 *Mrs F.D.R.* (formerly *Frostie* in the 545th Bomb Squadron) in the 545th Bomb Squadron, 384th Bomb Group, which 2nd Lieutenant Virgil R. Broyhill force landed at Dubendorf on 24 April 1944 during the mission to Erding. In each case the Swiss interned all ten crew. The third B-17 in line is 42-97138 in the 332nd Bomb Squadron, 94th Bomb Group, which Lieutenant R. A. McCullum landed at Dubendorf during the Friedrichshafen raid on 24 April 1944. Right is 42-31172 *Miss Patricia* in the 367th Bomb Squadron, 306th Bomb Group, which 2nd Lieutenant Irwin Schwedock landed at Dubendorf on 24 April 1944 during the mission to Oberpfaffenhofen after he had been hit repeatedly by fighters who put out the No.2 engine and caused the prop to windmill. (USAF)

Below left: B-24J-90-CO 42-100294, which was later named *Victory Belle*, and 42-100329/A in the 328th Bomb Squadron, 93rd Bomb Group en route to their target. *Victory Belle* and Captain Norman A. Roggenkamp's crew FTR on 24 June 1944 when the Liberator crashed at Treon, France. Four men evaded, five were KIA, and two were taken prisoner. 42-100329 crash landed on 18 September 1944 and was salvaged two days later. (USAF) Center: High flying B-17s leaving beautiful but deadly contrails. (USAF) Below right: B-17G-20-VE 42-97621 in the 350th Bomb Squadron, 100th Bomb Group, which was lost on 28 July 1944. Returning across the North Sea after bombing Merseburg, B-17G-35-BO 42-32009 *Black Cat 13* piloted by 2nd Lieutenant Albert S. Spear pulled up, climbed, and caught its fin on B-17G-20-VE 42-97621 flown by Wesley Stansbury. Spear's Fortress broke in two and Stansbury's went into a steep dive. Both crashed in the sea 26 miles from Lowestoft. The only survivor was waist gunner Robbie Gill, who baled out of the severed tail of Spear's B-17, and he was lucky to be rescued. (TAMM)

The Me 163B Komet, or *Kraftei* ("Power Egg") rocket-fighter had a maximum speed of 955 kph and was introduced into JG 400 early in 1944, but it never developed into an effective bomber-interceptor. Before the end of the war only 370 *Komets* had entered service. Many, including their pilots, were written off in landing accidents when the residual rocket propellants exploded. The top-scoring *Komet* pilot was *Feldwebel* Siegfried Schubert of I./JG 400 with three *Viermot* kills (including two B-17s on 24 August 1944) whilst operating from Brandis airfield. He was killed in a take-off accident on 7 October. (TAMM)

B-24J-60-CO 42-99990 *Short-Snorter* in the 579th Bomb Squadron, 392nd Bomb Group showing the Mobil flying horse logo. The name is derived from the tradition among early fliers that if a pilot landed in another country he would get someone to autograph and exchange a bill of that country's currency to prove that he had been there. Americans would embellish that, and at the first opportunity, generally at the bar, if the pilot could not produce a "short-snorter," as they were called, then the first round was on him, and then he would exchange the autographed currency. *Short Snorter* crashed on 3 August 1944. (USAF via Robert M. Foose)

On 28 July 1944 100th Bomb Group B-17G-45-BO 42-97393 *Pride of the Century* in the 349th Bomb Squadron and B-15G-55-BO 42-102598 *Super Rabbit* (pictured) in the 351st Bomb Squadron, which suffered an undercarriage failure on landing, were wrecked in runway crashes at Thorpe Abbotts. (TAMM)

A bemused S/Sgt Virgil R. Heddleston in the 704th Bomb Squadron, 446th Bomb Group is photographed shortly after his capture on Monday, 31 July 1944, after he baled out of his Liberator 42-52467 *Hula Wahina II* on the mission to Ludwigshafen. German civilians murdered Lieutenant Emil Berry, Jr., pilot, the co-pilot, and tail gunner. The other six crew survived and were taken prisoner. (Heddleston)

Victims of a Liberator crash at Shipdham. (USAF)

Above left: A B-24 Liberator in the 489th Bomb Group, 2nd Bomb Division over the Schulau oil refinery near Hamburg on 6 August 1944. August 1944 followed the same operational pattern as July, with bombing raids on airfields in France and strategic targets in Germany. On 6 August 953 bombers struck at Berlin, and at oil and manufacturing centres in the *Reich* for the loss of 25 bombers. (USAF) Center: 1st Lieutenant Walter J. Konantz in the 338th Fighter Squadron, 55th Fighter Group with his pet dog Scottie. (Konantz) Above right: Lieutenant Colonel Wallace E. Hopkins of the 361st Fighter Group on the wing of P-51D 44-13704 B7-H *Ferocious Frankie* at Bottisham, his second Mustang named for his wife. Hopkins was flying this aircraft when he shot down two FW 190s on 8 August 1944 to take his final wartime score to four. He was Group Operations Officer, and he flew 76 combat missions. (USAF)

The crew of B-17G-35-DL 42-107030 *Fifinella* in the 322nd Bomb Squadron, 91st Bomb Group receiving benediction before a mission. *Fifinella* was lost with Lieutenant Thomas P. Smith, Jr.'s crew on 13 August 1944 when the B-17crashed in France. Five men evaded, one was KIA, and three were taken prisoner. (USAF)

B-17G-40–VE 42-97991, seen here on a test flight in California, was assigned to the 366th Bomb Squadron, 305th Bomb Group at Chelveston on 9 August 1944, where it became a PFF aircraft. On 24 August 42-97991 went MIA with Lieutenant Roland B. Heusser, Jr., and crew, as well as Major Herbert A. Von Tungeln, on the mission to Merseburg. Beverly A. Hayes, radio operator, and Maurice F. Thomas, *Mickey* operator, were killed, and the rest were taken prisoner. (Lockheed)

Above left: B-17F-45-VE 42-6087 *Royal Flush* in the 418th Bomb Squadron, 100th Bomb Group was flying its 75th mission when it was hit by flak between the No.3 engine and the fuselage, causing the aircraft to spiral down and crash within sight of Villacoublay airfield. France, on 11 August 1944. Four of Lieutenant Alfred Aske's nine-man crew; who were all on their fifth mission, were killed, including one who is believed to have been machine-gunned by the Germans. Three of the crew were taken prisoner while Charles Nekvasil, radio operator, and Charles Barber, co-pilot, managed to escape and return to England. (via Chuck Nekvasil) Center: Lieutenant Colonel Thomas J. J. Christian, 361st Fighter Group CO, who was KIA on 12 August 1944 during a dive-bombing and strafing mission against rail targets at Arras, France. (via Steve Gotts) Above right: Captain John B. England, 362nd Fighter Squadron, 357th Fighter Group with his ground crew beside P-51D 44-13735 G4-H *U'Ve Had It!* at Leiston. England was awarded a half share in the shooting down of a Bf 109 in this aircraft on 18 August 1944. (Merle Olmsted via Ian McLachlan)

B-17Gs in the 369th Bomb Squadron, 306th Bomb Group over their target in 1944. B-17G-70-BO 43-37693, which was assigned overseas on 13 June 1944 and is dropping bombs, was lost with 1st Lieutenant Eldon L. Ralstin's crew on 16 August 1944 when it was last seen with one engine feathered and another on fire after taking flak hits. Ralstin and his radioman were killed. Seven men survived and were taken prisoner. The Fortress bottom left is B-17G-5-BO 42-31143/P *Satan's Lady*, which was assigned overseas on 19 October 1943, and which survived until the end of the war when it joined the 381st Bomb Group. (via Richards)

B-24 Liberators in the 446th Bomb Group in formation. B-24H-1-FO 42-7505/H *Old Faithful* was salvaged on 26 August 1944. The Liberator (top) is B-24H-1-FO 42-7609/D *Lazy Lou* in the 706th Bomb Squadron, which was salvaged after a non-operational accident on 18 December 1944. (USAF)

P-51Ds in the 368th Fighter Squadron, 359th Fighter Group in finger-four formation over Merseberg in 1944. 44-14652 *Betty Louise* CV-L is nearest the Brownie camera of Eugene F. Britton. 44-14500 *Griffin* (?) is next. Rudder markings were yellow and the cowlings bright green. (E. F. Britton via Ian McLachlan)

On 28 August 1944 the B-24 groups in the 20th Wing, 2nd Bomb Division were converted to a transportation role in support of the Allied ground forces in France, who were in urgent need of fuel and supplies. On 29 August the 93rd, 446th, and 448th Bomb Groups commenced "trucking" operations, as they were called. The 14th and 96th Wing went off operations on 11 September and were assigned to truck gasoline to the rapidly advancing American forces in France. At first Orleans-Bricy airfield south of Paris was used, but soon the base was changed to Clastres airfield near St. Quentin, which had been bombed by the Americans on 8 August when it was in German hands. Tents were set up on the field, and an interesting interlude began for the crews, like these men of the 791st Bomb Squadron, 467th Bomb Group loading up B-24H-15-FO 42-52303 U+ *Topper*. They spent some time here and collected various souvenirs, such as German war weapons and parts of wrecked aircraft. The Officers' Club at Rackheath was soon adorned with swastikas from *Luftwaffe* planes. Between 11 September and 3 October, when the B-24s returned to bombing missions, 646,000 gallons of gasoline were trucked to France. (Allan Healy)

Below: B-24H-25-FO 42-95189 *Weary* in the 66th Bomb Squadron, 44th Bomb Group, which crashed on 5 September 1944 and was salvaged the following day. (USAF)

B-17G-20-DL 43-37935 in the 418th Bomb Squadron, 100th Bomb Group, which suffered a taxi accident at Thorpe Abbotts on 1 September 1944 and was salvaged two days later. (TAMM)

Bottisham, 31 August 1944. P-51D *Gentle Annie* was flown in by Colonel Harold Rau, CO 20th Fighter Group; *Straw Boss 2* PE-X 44-14111 by Lieutenant Colonel James Mayden, CO 352nd Fighter Group; P-47D-25-RE 42-26641 LM-S *Hairless Joe* by Colonel Dave C. Schilling, CO 56th Fighter Group 12 August 1944-27 January 1945 (42-26641 was the aircraft in which Schilling destroyed 5 e/a on 23 December 1944); P-51D 44-14291 CL-P *Da Quake* by Colonel John L. "Jarring John" McGlinn, CO 55th Fighter Group; P-47 *Judy* by Colonel Phil Tukey, CO 356th Fighter Group; P-47D LH-E by Colonel Ben Rimmerman (KIFA 11 August 1945), CO 353rd Fighter Group; and P-38J (right) by Colonel Hub Zemke, CO 479th Fighter Group 12 August-30 October 1944, when he was taken prisoner. (USAF)

Left: B-17F-90-BO 42-30180 *Black Hawk* (formerly *Guzzlers*) in the 337th Bomb Squadron, 96th Bomb Group, which was assigned overseas on 6 July 1943 and was first assigned to the 384th Bomb Group. *Black Hawk* became an *Aphrodite* drone aircraft and was lost on the mission to Heligoland on 11 September 1944 when the pilot was killed baling out. (USAF)

On 11 September 1944, when the 100th Bomb Group lost eleven Fortresses on the mission to the Ruhland oil refineries, Lieutenant Harry Hempy flew B-17G-65-BO 43-37517 *Heaven Can Wait* back to Thorpe Abbotts with its tail compartment shot up and splashed with blood after S/Sgt Charles Emerson was badly wounded following an attack by a Bf 109 from 5 o'clock low. Emerson died a few days later in hospital. *Heaven Can Wait* was lost on 31 January 1945 when it was one of the Group's B-17s, that was recalled because of bad weather that curtailed the mission to Bremen. By the time the formations returned much of eastern England was covered in mist and low cloud, and several crews had difficulty finding the runway. Lieutenant William Appleton broke out of the cloud, roared low across the perimeter, and *Heaven Can Wait* headed directly for the control tower. To avoid crashing into it Appleton banked the B-17 to the right and crashed into two tents that housed 351st Bomb Squadron maintenance crews, who fortunately were at Squadron HQ for pay formation, as it was the last day of the month. *Heaven Can Wait* bellied in and caught fire, but all of Appelton's crew escaped largely unhurt. Twenty minutes later the bomb load, containing RDX bombs, exploded, leaving a crater several feet deep and sending one oif its engines 300ft into B-17G-90-BO 43-38610, which was instantly wrecked. Two other Fortresses nearby were damaged. (TAMM)

19

Home by Christmas?

We won't be home for Christmas,
Don't depend on us.
We'll have snow
But no mistletoe
Or presents on the tree.

Little had been seen of the *Sturmgruppen* since their successful attack on the 493rd Bomb Group on the mission to Magdeburg on 12 September, but all that was about to change on the 27th, when it was the Liberators of the 2nd Bomb Division that met with tragic results. While the B-17s headed for oil targets and engineering centers at Cologne, Ludwigshafen, and Mainz, 315 B-24s went to the Henschel engine and vehicle assembly plants at Kassel, in central Germany. For the 445th Bomb Group, it was a mission that would live forever as one of the most tragic, and probably the most disastrous raid for a single group in the history of American air warfare. The day began like many other days in England. Solid cloud overhead in the morning showed signs of probable rainfall, but groups put up a mission as scheduled. The 445th Bomb Group was used to days like this. However, in a few hours the combat crews were to learn that this was not just another day. Thirty-nine Liberators taxied out at Tibenham, but Lieutenant Rene J. Schneider's B-24 ran off the perimeter track and cut a tire, and took no further part in the mission. Crews sat impatiently in their cramped Liberators on the runway, waiting for a long time for better weather before they got the green light. Then, at 30-second intervals, each roared down the runway, lights on, slowly climbing into the pre-dawn darkness.

At 15,000ft the sun was shining brightly in the blue sky. Flares of red-green, at regular intervals, were fired from the Zebra ship—the gaudily painted, stripped-down old B-24 used as an assembly ship—as it continually circled to allow the 445th to form up on its tail. In the distance, other Zebras were firing green-green, green-red, or red-red, as they too circled in their patch of the sky. The group formed into a whole and took its place at the head of the 2nd Combat Wing. The wing joined the rest of the 2nd Bomb Division assembly line, which stretched for 60 miles and headed for Kassel. Lieutenant McLelland in *Tahelenbak*, Lieutenant Frost, and *Heavenly Body*, flown by Lieutenant Wilkins, aborted with various mechanical problems and returned to England. The remaining 33 Liberators flew on and made landfall at the Dutch coast before proceeding uneventfully towards Kassel. As they approached the IP the Liberator crews could see the Kassel flak coming up in a blanket and bursting at their altitude. At the group IP they were to turn downwind in a more easterly direction. Suddenly, before they got to the IP the lead plane in the lead squadron[1058] made a left turn and the whole group followed. Other navigators said that the Mickey man in the lead ship had screwed up. They knew they shouldn't have turned yet. By the time the lead pilot discovered the mistake it was too late to turn back on course, as all the other groups following were in the way as they proceeded to the correct IP. If the lead pilot had circled 360° and followed the last group in the 445th Bomb Group might have saved themselves, but they continued on an easterly course and headed for Göttingen, about 20 miles northeast of Kassel. Using PFF through solid cloud cover the bombs fell in open fields half a mile short of the town. Instead of leaving the area and making a beeline for England the lead ship followed the original plan for Kassel. This was to bomb downwind from the northwest, hit the target, turn south for about 50 miles, then turn west and cross the Rhine near Koblenz, and head for friendly territory in France before proceeding to England. The formation turned south from Göttingen with the intention of flying south to a line that would bring them back towards Koblenz. By this time the 445th Bomb Group were 100 miles behind everyone else without fighter escort.

The 445th flew into an area a few miles from Eisenach where II./JG4, IV./JG3 "*Udet*," and II./JG300 were forming for an attack. Each unit had a strength of around 30 specially equipped FW 190s with two heavy MG 131 30mm cannon and four MG 151/20 20mm machine-guns, as well as heavy armor plate that could deflect the American .50 caliber bullets with ease. In addition, three "cover" *gruppen* (I and III./JG4 and I./JG 300) were equipped with Bf 109s, and were to pick off any badly damaged stragglers left by the FW 190s. The fighters were directed by radio by the 1st Fighter Division at Doeberitz, but much to the chagrin of the ground commander, the *Luftwaffe* pilots at first failed to see any bombers. Then they did. The *Sturmgruppen* attacked at about 1003 hours in three waves, each one with fighters in line abreast from the rear, and with cannon and machine-guns blazing.[1059] The Liberators stood little chance, and the explosive effects of shells in the poorly armored bombers were devastating. In less than five minutes the *Luftwaffe* fighters decimated the 445th, shooting down no fewer than 22 Liberators in the space of just three minutes, and three more in the following three minutes. *Staffelkapitän* Oskar Romm of IV shot down three of the bombers in one single attack, and recalled:

> "The ground radio stations led the combat formation towards the enemy formation. After visual contact was established in the air, the

leader of the combat formation was given clearance to attack. As the squadron leader of the 15th Squadron, I had a good tactical position within the combat formation and attacked a flight of three bombers. Just like during my first downing of a *4-mot* over Oschersleben, 7 July 1944, my approach for the attack was divided into three actions, going off real quick, first to fire into the fuselage to hit the machine gun positions, then hit the pilot's compartment and finally to hit and set fire to two engines on one side of the aircraft. If two engines on one side were on fire, aeronautical control over the plane was almost immediately put out of action. I first attacked (as above) the bomber on the left position of the flight, then the one on the right and lastly the leading B-24 of the flight. I then pulled up in a steep turn and, while flying over them, observed them going down, spinning, burning and the breaking off of wings in the area of the burning engines. The film from my gun cameras showed the downing, demonstrating in an appalling way the location of the hits and the effect of the shots on the three aircraft. The two MK 108 39mm guns did the most devastating damage. I opened up aerial combat by first firing the two 13mm machine guns, then the two 20mm guns and between less than 400 meters and ramming distance, with all six guns firing off short bursts."[1060]

Attacks by *Unteroffizier* Ernst Schröder, a pilot in II JG/*Sturm* 300, were also successful, as he recalls:

"When we approached the bombers in a closed formation, suddenly some of these large aircraft started to catch fire, some even blew up. This led us to believe that other German fighter formations had attacked the Americans before us. But then it was very quickly our turn. My squadron leader and I had had a test gyro-sight installed in our aircraft. With the aid of this sighting mechanism I was able to down two B-24s within seconds. The [first] aircraft turned on its side and plunged. Also, the neighboring machine was already smoking from a previous attack. Both left engines were burning. I only needed to change aim to shoot again then this one stood in bright flames. The new aiming device was functioning astonishingly. I was so surprised and fascinated that I flew alongside my victim and stared at the meter-high flames, which were pouring out of this Liberator all the way back beyond the elevator. Then this great machine clumsily laid itself over on its back and went down."

B-24 pilots put out frantic calls for help on the fighter channel, and immediately, two Mustang groups covering the 3rd Division, 75 miles away near Frankfurt, and the 361st Fighter Group, escorting the 1st Division 100 miles distant, were speeding to the rescue. However, six precious minutes were to elapse before the 361st Fighter Group could reach the beleaguered 445th Bomb Group, and the other two P-51 groups arrived after the enemy had departed. 1st Lieutenant Victor Bocquin, who was leading the 376th Squadron, issued split-second orders to follow the bandits down as they dove toward the cloud layer below, while the remainder of the 361st continued the escort. During the fight that ensued, the pilots of the 376th Squadron operated singly or in groups of two or three in a frenzied pursuit of the enemy. Bocquin claimed three FW 190s destroyed, while 1st Lieutenant William "Bill" Rockafeller Beyer was credited with five FW 190s. One of the 361st fighter pilots intercepted Ernst Schröder's FW 190 at low altitude and dueled with the *Luftwaffe* pilot. Schröder wrote:

"After passing each other, we both turned our aircraft around and headed at each other with blazing guns During the first approach I received two hits in the tail unit. During the second approach, my guns failed. Evidently I had used up all my ammunition when firing at the two bombers, or my guns were jamming - I no longer know exactly what happened. We made about four or five more frontal passes at each other, but all that was left for me to do in order not to get hit again was to take evasive action. After the last frontal approach of the American I finally 'hugged' the ground and was lucky enough to escape - most likely because of the camouflage paint on my aircraft 'Red 19 – *'Kolle-alaaf!*'"[1061]

In all, the American fighters and bombers claimed 29 fighters (18 German pilots were killed). Credited with a total of 18 German aircraft destroyed in the air and another three on the ground, the 376th Squadron had set a temporary record among the fighter groups of the 8th Air Force for enemy aircraft destroyed by a single squadron on a single mission.[1062] One 361st pilot, 2nd Lieutenant Leo H. Lamb, died when he collided with a FW 190. The American fighters and bombers claimed to have shot down 29 fighters,[1063] but the 445th had lost 25 bombers shot down. Five more had crashed in France and England. Only five made it back to England. It proved to be the highest group loss in 8th Air Force history. There were 236 empty seats in the mess halls at Tibenham that evening. Altogether, the 445th lost 117 men killed and 45 officers, and 36 enlisted men had been made prisoners of war, some of them after they had been ordered by the Germans to collect the burned and charred remains of their colleagues from the crashed aircraft. In England, at 2nd Bomb Division HQ, a plan to bring in 28 crews from other groups was considered, but by nightfall it had been shelved, and the decision taken that all new replacement crews coming into the division would be diverted to the 445th. Ten crews were scraped together for the mission the following day, ironically, to Kassel again. *Patty Girl*, flown by another crew, was the only Liberator from the previous day's mission to fly. All ten crews returned safely to Tibenham on this occasion.[1064]

On Thursday, 28 September, 1049 aircraft took part in raids on two synthetic oil plants, a motor plant, and a city area all in or near Magdeburg, Kassel, and Merseburg. En route to the Fred Krupps Gruson Werke at Magdeburg the *Luftwaffe* succeeded in penetrating a strong force of American fighter escorts[1065] and they wreaked havoc. Ben Smith, who had earlier finished his tour of combat in the 303rd Bomb Group, lost many close friends:

"Take off from Molesworth was at 7:30 am. Twenty-eight aircraft and two PFF B-17s flew the mission. Everything seemed to promise another successful mission, as things had been sort of quiet for a while. The group was flying excellent formation. The crews were well trained and well led. Over continental Europe the weather turned bad. The target area was covered with high cumulus cloud formation reaching up to 18,000ft. They dropped their bombs on the railroad yards at Magdeburg, bombing through radar image. Only one plane was lost on the bomb run, '*Miss Umbriago*,'[1066] piloted by Lieutenant W. E. Miller. Four of the crew were able to parachute to safety.[1067]

"The German attack force were obviously veterans who knew their business. The 303rd Bomb Group had never taken such a pasting. One of the German leaders was an ace with 56 confirmed kills to his credit. He was the pilot who shot down '*Miss Umbriago*.' He was Oberleutnant Horst Haas and was later killed himself.

"Shortly after the formation turned off the target, they were assailed by a large group of about 40 to 50 FW 190s and Me 109s. This attack inaugurated the bloodiest aerial combat ever experienced by the 303rd Bomb Group. Nine of the low squadron B-17s were lost on the first pass. These aircraft were all from the 360th Squadron. The attacks were beam attacks from 5 to 7 o'clock and after a bomber was hit the fighters followed it down making sure of their kill. Up until that day the 360th Squadron had never had a really bad day such as other squadrons had experienced. This attack was a shocker.

"The 360th Squadron was very nearly wiped out. Many of the casualties were boys who were close friends of ours. Al Dennerle, who lived in our barracks, was one of these. He was best friend to Ward Hudson, our tail gunner. Al was of German lineage himself and had come to us from the 15th Air Force in Italy. He was a handsome, fun loving youngster who always wore a broad grin. Al was a radio-operator like myself. He had been on pass to London with us and seemed like one of our own crew. On that fatal day he was flying as a pick-up radio operator with the crew of Lieutenant Edward F. Shields. His bomber[1068] was badly hit by cannon fire. The flight engineer, Sgt Leland Nagel put on his chute pack and handed the pilot and co-pilot their parachutes. The aircraft exploded and went into a tight spin. Sergeant Nagel was blown out of the aircraft. When he came to he was free falling through space. He pulled the ripcord and his chute opened. Wilbur W. Lee, the bombardier, discovered the entire Plexiglas nose was blown away. He was able to escape through the opening and parachuted safely. Lieutenant Shields and the co-pilot Lieutenant Cooter were still belted to their seats after the fiery crash – 90% of the aircraft was destroyed by fire. All the crew were still in the wreckage except Lieutenant Lee and Sgt Nagel who parachuted safely. Al Dennerle, our buddy, perished with the others.

"Another B-17 was shot down on a second pass. The hard-fighting aerial gunners in the bomber formation were given credit for nine enemy fighters (confirmed). But that was hardly a fair exchange for the punishment they had taken. The formation that returned to Molesworth was but a remnant.[1069]

And so ended perhaps the saddest day ever experienced by Hell's Angels in combat. Ninety-nine crewmen were missing in action. The 303rd had fought a savage battle with the *Luftwaffe*, but that was only the beginning of their nightmare experience."[1070]

Meanwhile, other bomber crews fought their way through to the synthetic oil plant at Merseburg, where the Leuna plant manufactured the majority of synthetic fuel for Germany's rocket-powered fighters. The raid is recounted by Wayne E. Cose, the top turret gunner-engineer on David "Moon" Mullen's crew in the 486th Bomb Group at Sudbury:

"Our crew only had two missions under our belts and didn't realize what was ahead of us. The first one to Bremen on 26 September only involved a relatively few puffs of flak, which didn't seem to be close enough to register. Little did I realize the punch behind those puffs at the time. On the second mission, however, to Mainz on 27 September, I took back my thought, 'Is this all there is to it?' when a B-17 disappeared in front of us with a single direct hit burst of flak. Wow, nine men and a plane gone in one puff - those Germans are out to get us! On the Merseburg mission we soon found out that the Germans were really guarding their oil with walls of thick flak. The bursts were getting closer and closer. The thin aluminium skin was really taking a beating. In fact it was beginning to look like a sieve. There were huge holes in the wings where the flak pierced the self-sealing gas tanks. Some of the engines were taking hits and beginning to falter. A straggler joined our formation off our right wing during the confusion over the target and through the walls of flak. He was challenged by radio, IFF and color-of-the-day flare sometime before he joined us but he flunked them all. The fact that the straggler was OD colored wasn't all that unusual either, since this was common on all-out efforts. Reportedly, this was a German-manned captured B-17 sent up for the purpose of relaying the planes' altitude and heading to his anti-aircraft batteries. He had obviously accomplished his mission.[1071]

"Nilan 'Mac' Mack, the bombardier, called me on intercom so I'd be ready to fire the flare (other planes were to drop their bombs when they saw the flare). I then reached out of my turret toward the flare gun and found I'd have to get out of my top turret to reach it. Here we were at 28,000ft, 50° below, flak popping all over and I had to get out of the turret. Cussing to myself, I unbuckled my turret straps, unhooked my electrical heating suit cord, unhooked the oxygen line and stepped out to hook up a walkaround oxygen bottle. While I was waiting for Mac to zero in with his bombsight and to call me on the intercom (right after I stepped out), I heard a big 'Zing' and saw that about half of my top turret bubble was knocked out where my head would have been. I then got Mac's call and fired the flare. Up in the nose of the plane, Mac had his helmet and oxygen mask knocked off by flak and the nose compartment caught fire. Elliot Kolker, the navigator, put the fire out with a carbon tetrachloride fire extinguisher.[1072] Nos.2 and 3 engines were completely knocked out and No.2 was feathered to cut down wind resistance. Mullen said No.3 ran away so he pulled off power while trying to control the aircraft. Power was then applied slowly and the engine stabilized but if the throttle were moved it would run away. No.3 was not putting out full power, even though the props were turning, because of a big flak hole in the nacelle. Bob Atkinson, one of the waist gunners, was busy in the waist compartment mending severed control cables with electrical heating suit cords.

"Mullen told us to get ready to bale out. Salvatore 'Sal' Muscarella got out of his ball turret OK. We enlisted men in the back grabbed our chest pack parachutes, hooked them to our harnesses and stood by the waist compartment door, awaiting the actual bale-out order. Even though none of us had parachuted before, the possibility didn't look that bad now, considering the condition of the plane. We waited for what seemed like quite a while when 'Moon' called to say we seemed to be holding altitude pretty well and we might ride it out for a while. He told us to throw out anything that had any weight, which we could do without. We proceeded to throw out most of the guns and ammunition, extra flying suits; flak aprons and ripped non-essential radio equipment off the walls. We limped on and on this way. We hoped German fighters wouldn't jump us. Kolker was doing a bang-up job of navigating. 'Moon' and his co-pilot, Larry Iverson coaxed more out of the B-17 than the Boeing engineers ever planned or believed possible. Of course, we gradually lost altitude, but they actually brought our riddled plane over the continent and the English Channel to Sudbury."[1073]

Lieutenant George B. Reeves, pilot of *Rugged But Right* in the 851st Bomb Squadron, 490th Bomb Group at Eye (Brome), recalls:

"On this mission everything had gone smoothly until we had just finished the bomb run. Immediately after releasing our bombs there was a very close flak burst just to the right and behind us. The plane, *Rugged But Right,* lurched from the concussion and my first indications of the seriousness of the blow was the elevator control going limp and the plane starting on a gradual decline. About the same time the tail gunner, John Volin, yelled over the intercom 'Help! I'm hit.' I ordered the engineer, Doc Cagle, to take a walk-round bottle and go to his aid.

"We were at about 23,000ft. I soon found that with the stick pulled right back to my chest the plane would level out and with careful use of the trim tab we could maintain altitude. I also noticed, though, that the right rudder pedal had gone right the way down to the stop and was useless. In the meantime the other two planes in the lead flight abandoned us and returned to their squadron locations. Then one of the waist gunners reported that the oxygen supply had gone. Investigation showed that only the supply in the back half of the plane was damaged and so the crew devised a system with walk-round bottles so that everyone could use oxygen from the supply at the front of the plane. I realized that we would have to descend to a lower altitude, even though we were still deep in Germany and take our chances.

"A check with the navigator and the original flight plan indicated that in order to avoid flak we should continue to fly in an easterly direction for a short period before making a right turn to the south for a short distance and then head westward for home. The engineer had completed his check on the tail gunner and reported that he was unconscious and showed no sign of a pulse. We made the right turn and continued on the southerly track for the appropriate time, all the while flying through the heaviest flak I ever experienced. Finally we turned westward and eventually came out of the flak. I realized later that instead of avoiding the flak area, which was shaped like a triangle, by getting east of it we had actually gone down the upright leg and then turned west to come back along the bottom leg. However, God was with us and we did not suffer more damage.

"When time permitted the engineer and the other crew attempted to make repairs to the controls. The elevator of a B-17 is controlled by two cables of seven woven strands each, one down each side of the plane. One of the cables was completely severed and all but one strand in the other cable was gone. By using what we had on board, including heated suit cord the crew was able to restore fairly good positive elevator control. We were now flying back across Germany - alone and a sitting duck for any fighter that might come along. By now we had descended to 10,000ft to overcome the oxygen problem. All the way back across Germany we kept a very close and nervous eye out for any fighters but thankfully they seemed to be taking a nap that afternoon. We crossed the Low Countries and the Channel certainly did look good that day as we flew over it.

"As we got nearer to home I told the crew that because of the damaged controls and other unknown damage the landing could be hazardous, so I would fly over the base at sufficient altitude if anyone wanted to bale out. The whole crew wanted to know what I was going to do and I told them that I was going to take John Volin down. Everyone decided to stay with me. We were cleared for an emergency landing and but for the fact that the rudder pedal had been repaired sufficiently so that we had a brake but no rudder on the right side we would have spun out of control when we touched down. With left power and right brake, however, we were able to keep the plane straight and although we ran off the end of the runway no more serious damage occurred."[1074]

Lieutenant Cleaves' crew in the 850th Squadron, which also returned to Eye (Brome), was in difficulty too, as Jim Collins, one of the B-17 gunners, recalls:

"Flak was very heavy and we took about 20 hits in the tail wheel area. On approaching the base for landing the undercarriage had to be manually cranked down by the engineer, Glen Case. We did not know, however, that the tail wheel was broken and when we touched down the aircraft veered off the runway, plowing a deep furrow in the adjacent field. Smelling what we all thought was smoke, every man made a scramble for the exits when the plane came to rest, listing down on one side. Our waist gunner, Mike Lasprogato, dropped to the field from the waist exit and despite the fact that he weighed about 200lb and was normally much slower than I was, sprinted well ahead of me, shouting, '*Run, Rip, run!*' (The crew all called me Rip instead of Jim in those days, after the professional baseball player, Rip Collins). Fortunately the plane did not catch fire and no one was hurt."

At Eye, Lieutenant Rolland B. Peacock, Jr.'s crew in the 850th Bomb Squadron had become operational on 28 September. They awaited their first mission, as Lieutenant Jule F. Berndt, navigator, recalls:

"with a mixture of anxiety and excitement, fired-up as we were by the first-hand accounts of other crews and especially our hutmates, who had already completed 20-odd missions over enemy territory. Then on Saturday the 30th we were awakened at 0345 hours and told that briefing would be at 0500 hours. At briefing we learnt that we would be bombing the marshaling yards at Bielefeld, a target that was defended by 40 heavy anti-aircraft guns. Our position in the squadron was to be No.2 in the low element and our bomb load would be five 1000lb GP bombs."

More than 750 heavies took off to bomb three marshaling yards and an airfield at Bielefeld, Hamm, Handorf, and Münster, the last named being attacked by over 200 bombers. Meanwhile, over 100 B-24s hauled gasoline to battle areas on the Continent and thirteen fighter groups flew escort and two more flew support sweeps. Ten minutes after take off from Deopham Green *Melancholy Baby* in the 452nd Bomb Group, piloted by 28 year old Lieutenant Cliff Eccles, was in trouble. He recalled:

"I noticed that an engine was in flames. The trouble was far too close to our full load of gasoline for me to be very happy about it. For a quarter of an hour our fire extinguishers poured foam on the engine. We thought we could drown the fire or blow it out but it was hopeless. Turning back inland, I ordered the crew to bale out, headed the plane out to sea, set the automatic pilot and baled out myself, certain that the plane would crash in the drink. The crew thought that the loss of power on one side might have caused the plane to circle back."

The crew baled out near King's Lynn, Norfolk, and half an hour later *Melancholy Baby* was seen out of control over Derbyshire with flames coming from the fuselage. At 1057 it was spotted circling over the Merseyside area, and caused air raid sirens to be sounded for the first time since March 1943. By 1215 *Melancholy Baby* was heading towards the Irish Sea with the RAF in pursuit. Twenty minutes later the errant B-17 passed over Eire, and danger warnings were given before it was shot down twenty minutes later over the Atlantic.

At Eye, Lieutenant Rolland B. Peacock, Jr.'s crew in *Magnificent Obsession* had no such problems. Lieutenant Jule F. Berndt in the 490th Bomb Group continues:

"We took off at 0800 hours and climbed to 18,000ft to assemble. Then at 1000 hours, when Wing and Division assembly was complete the huge formation of planes headed over the Channel and toward Germany. Landfall had to be made at a definite point to avoid flak areas along the coast of enemy-held territory in France and Holland.

Everything seemed to be going satisfactorily until just a few minutes before the IP when the pilot made a crew check to determine who was depressing their push-to-talk button on the interphone (depressing this button causes a buzzing noise in the system). All crewmembers checked in except the bombardier, so the pilot instructed me to take a look at him. The bombardier was slumped back in his seat against the side of the ship. He was breathing heavily and his face was discolored and covered with sweat, even though our altitude was 25,000ft and the temperature was -35C. I grabbed an extra oxygen bottle and attached the stricken man's hose to it. After a few minutes of breathing on pure oxygen the bombardier was able to continue his duties although hindered by the after-effects of anoxia. At about the same time that this incident occurred, the ball turret gunner called and reported that his regulator had frozen up and then, a little while later that his mask had frozen. Each ship is furnished with an emergency kit that contains an oxygen mask, so the spare mask was passed down to him and his frozen one was taken to the radio room to be thawed out. This was a fortunate foresight, because some time later the waist gunner's mask also became useless when it filled up with ice; he was given the thawed-out mask.

"Near the end of the bomb run we saw our first enemy flak, a few scattered bursts well below and to the side of the formation. We were flying over a complete undercast and were bombing by instruments. The flak encountered over the target was meager and very inaccurate (later missions were to correct that first, but false, impression of this hazard). After leaving the target the remainder of the mission was quite uneventful for everyone except the waist gunner, who had the disconcerting experience of being air sick while still wearing his mask. We landed sometime after 1400 hours and when the guns and our equipment had been removed from the ship we were taken by trucks to the briefing building to be interrogated. We also received a double shot of whisky, followed by coffee and cookies, from the Red Cross. Then, tired but happy to have cleared our first big hurdle, we were taken to the mess hall and back to our hut."

On 30 September Norman K. Andrew, navigator in Jack Stanley's crew in the 487th Bomb Group at Lavenham, flew his seventh mission and their first as a lead crew. Andrew wrote:

"The mission today was a PFF but we still flew. No.2 in the high. Bombed the marshaling yards at Bielfeld. I think we dropped short. We had a pilotage bombardier getting his 25th mission in so he can go home. Pretty sharp boy. We had about 8/10 most of the way, 10/10ths the rest. We had no flak, no fighters. Some of the wings coming in behind us went too close to Münster. Osnabrück tried a few bursts - about ½ mile off our right wing. One of our boys flipped over on his back and tore the wing off of his left wing man (this was #037, the ship we flew over from the States). Both went down - must have been prop wash.[1075] One ship in the group behind us blew up. What a day!"

Andrew flew his 8th mission on 2 October when over 1100 heavies escorted by 17 fighter groups attacked four targets at the Bettenhausen ordnance depot, the Henschel plant, and other targets at Kassel. He wrote:

"The sergeant woke me up at 0215 for 0300 pre-briefing. For some reason they did not get me up for Target Study. Target: Primary - Airfield north of Kassel. Secondary - PFF on the marshaling yards in Kassel. For some reason I had a feeling of confidence all the way through. Slept soundly for two hours last night. After getting out to the hardstand and pre-flighting my stuff I lay down in the crew chief's tent and slept for 15 minutes. T/O 0645. We ran into some light inaccurate flak between Koblenz and Mainz as we crossed the Rhine. I was working like mad on my guns. Joe put the left hand gun on the right side and vice versa. I had to change the switches at 25,000ft and -40C. Was sweating when I finished - too busy to even watch the flak. The formation was really lousy - all over the sky. Supposed to come in on a mag. heading of 116 - came in on 176. Target about 8/10ths covered. Bombed from 27,400ft. On the turn from the target we were carried by an 80-knot wind over the flak area at Gorringen. Flak at target moderate - fairly accurate. At the RP I was watching one B-17 that was circling below us and losing altitude. Obviously hit. The right wing came off at #4 and the plane caught fire and disintegrated in not over 10 seconds. One chute observed. Not from our Group. Time of mission 7:45; 4:30 on oxygen. Maximum cold -44C. Easy trip home."[1076]

Lieutenant Ray E. Hann, Jr., a pilot in the 849th Squadron, 490th Bomb Group, celebrated the award of the DFC on 2 October:

"Unaware that flak had started a gasoline fire in the left wing of our B-17 during our run on the tank factories in Kassel, I flew back for more than 600 miles before the hidden flames burst into the open. None of my crew knew we had been hit until we were one mile from the field. Then Lieutenant McEwen my co-pilot saw that the wing was glowing-red from heat and smoke was streaming out of it. I called the field and told them we were coming in. The fire department had three trucks out to meet us and chopped holes in the wing with axes. Then they poured fire extinguisher on the gasoline. Flak must have hit us right over the target because there were holes all over the underside of the wing. For this 'extraordinary achievement,' as the citation put it, I was awarded the DFC."

Although John W. McClane had flown his 30th and last official mission of his tour on 26 September, he had decided to volunteer to fly a 31st so that he could finish up with the rest of his crew, who were on their 30th:

"I knew this was a foolish thing to do but I still felt it was my duty to stick by my crew. We had been through so much together in training, flying the South Atlantic and in combat that I could not turn my back on them. As a lead crew, they could not fly without a lead navigator. They let me know that they did not relish flying with an unknown navigator. Neither the crew nor the CO put pressure on me. It was my own personal decision; well knowing it could cost me my life. I did not regret the decision but before the day was out I had serious doubts concerning the wisdom of my rashness.

"We were to be part of approximately 300 assigned to bomb Hamm carrying well over 600 tons of high explosives. At first we were scheduled to go to Stuttgart, but it was decided that the rail transport through Hamm was the more urgent target. The importance of Hamm as a major rail route for the Germans to supply their Western Front was so important to the strategic offensive that our 44th Bomb Group was sent there four times during the war. It so happened that our crew went three of the four times, the first on our first mission of 22 April. We returned on my 30th mission, 26 September and the Group went again September 30th but we did not fly that day and now on 2 October we were once more off to Hamm. Again we were the lead in the same B-24J PFF ship that we flew on September 26th. We were flying very little now between missions but we did take this plane up once on 30 September for one and a half-hours of practice.

"The 8th Air Force dispatched about 1200 heavies to various targets in Germany. The 44th Bomb Group launched 25 aircraft and we were to lead the 14th Combat Wing, which led the whole 2nd Division. Again, my H_2X *Mickey* radar navigator and I were to be put to the test. Of the two positions, I had much the better job. I was the senior lead navigator working at my desk with full visibility out of the plane. The radar navigator sat in front of his Cathode ray tube in semi-darkness plotting our course by observing a very fuzzy gross reproduction of the ground below. But don't under estimate the value of his work. At times, we could see nothing on the ground in the target area. He then worked with our bombardier to determine when the bombs were to be dropped. When we were finally after two tries ready to drop the bombs, Warga was able to get a fair visual sighting but the H_2X equipment was a great aid to him. Our strike photo showed a 5/10ths cloud cover but some squadrons reported a 10/10ths. I clearly saw through the clouds where our bombs landed.

"But I'm getting ahead of my story. This, my last combat mission, was an almost exact repeat of our mission to the very same target just six days before. Once more we were on the bomb run with our bomb bay doors open when a group of planes crowded us to point where we had to fly through the tremendous flak barrage without dropping our bombs. Boy! Was I ever mad and scared? As on the previous mission, I once more had to plot our course back to the IP so we could make a second run over the target. All the way in to where we released our bombs and out the other side of the anti-aircraft fire, I kept praying to God to let us make it this one last time. We had survived all the flak the Germans could throw at us in 31 missions while sustaining hundreds and hundreds of holes. The Luftwaffe fighters came close several times but they failed also to shoot us down. After an easy flight back to base, we rolled to a stop after 6 hours and 30 minutes of our final combat mission. It was none too soon because in three days, the Nazis threw the first of their Me 163 rocket fighters against our bomber force. After landing, the whole crew gathered around the plane congratulating and slapping each other on the back. This was a happy day for us. But we all knew it was only by God's Will that we made it through without an injury among us. There is no way I can express in words the relief we felt. The strain of combat had taken its toll and it would be a full year before most of us would recover from this nightmare."[1077]

For others October marked the start of their combat career. On 3 October Lieutenant Bernie L. Iwanciow's crew in the 860th Bomb Squadron, 493rd Bomb Group, flew their first mission, to Nürnburg, one of the longest the group had flown. Lieutenant John O. "Rams" Ramsey, navigator, recalled:

> "The flak seemed to be to our right at the target. We had just taken off our flak vests at the Franco-German border, when a barge on the river between Metz and Nancy fired a four-gun battery at us. Our ship was the only one hit. A piece of flak came through the Plexiglas nose, missed Chuck [Charles H. Jeske, bombardier] and either glass or flak cut my pencil off in my hand."

The Thursday, 5 October, mission to Münster is described by Jule Berndt, navigator in Lieutenant Rolland B. Peacock, Jr.'s crew in *Magnificent Obsession* in the 850th Squadron, 490th Bomb Group, who flew their 3rd mission:

> "This was one of the most memorable of all our experiences. At briefing we were told the target was to be an airfield located on the outskirts of Münster. Our bomb load consisted of five 500lb GP bombs and two 500lb bomb clusters of incendiaries. Our position in the squadron was three in the lead, a truly honorable position for a crew with only two missions behind them. The trip over was made without incident, reinforcing the growing feeling that we were now becoming well accustomed to the tasks and responsibilities our positions called for. As we approached the target the clear skies told us that the raid would be under visual conditions, our first experience of this type of bombing.
>
> "Everything went according to plan as we turned on the bombing run from the IP but just a minute before it was time to release the bombs we ran into the most accurate flak we had ever experienced. Our squadron, in particular, was in the area of heaviest flak and it was quite evident that the German gunners were tracking us, for the flak was bursting right off the noses of the planes. Up at the front of our ship a piece of flak burst through the bottom of the Plexiglas nose and flung glass fragments all around. By the noises we could hear above the roar of the engines, we knew that our plane was taking hits. Just at the moment the bombardier announced bombs away, another flak burst hurled a second fragment through the bottom of the nose and broken glass struck the bombardier above the eye. Almost immediately a large piece of flak hit the glass port directly in front of the ball turret gunner, showering him with shattered glass. (After we had landed, one of the other crews told us that they had seen the shell burst directly below us and very close to the plane.)
>
> "I took a look at the bombardier and could find only a small scratch on his face. In the meantime the waist gunner had taken the ball turret operator from the ball and had put him onto oxygen in the radio room. When I got back to the radio room I found that the injured man had received lacerations about his eyes and it looked as though he had also particles of glass in the eyes themselves. It was impossible to make a proper examination because by that time the swelling had entirely closed both eyes. We placed him on a sleeping bed, which is standard equipment for planes and covered him with more blankets. I then applied boric acid ointment to his eyes and surrounding areas and placed compresses over them. The waist gunner then stayed on watch over him on the way back.
>
> "When I returned to my station I found that the oxygen on his system was almost down to zero, so I called the pilot, who is on the same system, to verify the reading. The pilot's gauge showed the same and later we found that part of our system had been pierced by flak. Fortunately the oxygen system in a plane is arranged in sections so that the failure of one supply will not leave the entire ship without oxygen. The only other damage we were aware of was a broken hydraulic line in our left wing.
>
> "To get back to the field and receive medical attention for our wounded gunner as quickly as possible, we broke away from the rest of the Group at the Dutch coast and came back alone. By increasing our air speed we beat the formation back by some time. As soon as we had taxied from the runway the wounded man was removed from the plane and taken to the hospital where about 400 fragments of glass were removed from his eyes and face. The fact that he did retain his sight is testimony to the remarkable skill of our army medics. Back on the ground we examined the plane and found many other

holes in it. One worth mentioning was in the horizontal stabilizer of the tail; it was almost six inches in diameter. If it had to hit, we were glad a flak fragment of that size had selected the least dangerous spot. We were more than grateful when our CO stood us down the next day to collect our ragged nerves."

William A. Johnson, a pilot of a replacement crew in the 493rd Bomb Group, which had arrived at Debach in September, also flew the 5 October mission. He filled in as co-pilot aboard a Fortress[1078] piloted by 1st Lieutenant Arthur A. Bisaro for the mission to an airfield near Münster. Johnson recalls:

"We took off just before dawn and as we climbed to our assembly altitude, we flew straight into sunlight. It was a beautiful day and finally, I was going to be part of the war! The climb and the assembly were routine and I soon found out that I needn't have worried about trying to remember a co-pilot's duties. Everything worked out well because I merely did whatever became necessary on my side of the cockpit. I had the responsibility to monitor 3rd Division radio frequency so I could relay any Division messages to the pilot. As we left the coast of England, we continued to climb until we reached our assigned bombing altitude, then we leveled off. As we turned to the southeast, we could see the coast of Holland and the Zuider Zee. We could also see many other groups of planes both ahead and behind us. All were headed east toward Germany. Our 'little Friends', the fighters, flying as our escorts were dodging in and out and crossing and re-crossing our path, but they also matched our progress to the east. We flew all the way to the target without seeing any flak bursts. I was quite disappointed at this, because I wanted to be able to tell my crew back in England what it felt like to be shot at. We dropped our bombs when the rest of our Group did. Then off to our right wing I spied about eight or nine flak bursts. I was about to ask the pilot if that was all there was to it, when I felt a jarring jolt to the plane. Looking in the direction the jolt seemed to come from, I saw that a 88mm shell had gone completely through our #1 engine without exploding. Dense black smoke came from the nacelle. I helped the pilot feather the #1 engine and trim the plane for 3-engined flight. By this time we had dropped out of our formation and had so reduced speed that the flak battery was tracking us. Again an unexploded shell that had its fuse set for a higher altitude hit us. This time the shell went completely through our right wing between the #3 and #4 engines. The #4 engine went dead and the #3 engine began to smoke fiercely. I feathered the #4 propeller. The hole in the wing allowed a steady stream of 100-octane gasoline to spew out like the stream from a fire hose. By this time, I was sure that we were doomed."[1079]

Nick G. Plackis, a bombardier in the 390th Bomb Group, flew his 22nd mission on 5 October to Münster:

"Just after 'Bombs Away' I had to free two jammed bombs in the bomb bay. Our load was six 1000lb bombs, three on each side of the compartment. The three in the right bay salvoed as programed. Of the three on the left, the bottom one went down fine. But the middle shackle malfunctioned and did not release its bomb, so when the upper bomb came off its shackle, it landed with a shuddering clunk, felt throughout our Fortress, as it smashed into the center hung up bomb, preventing the upper bomb from falling free. When the skipper, Phil Sheridan, sent me back to assess the situation, I realized what I was facing was not going to be a picnic. I saw that when the upper bomb released from its shackle, it also pulled out the wire retainers sometimes called "pins" that go into the front and rear bomb fuses. When these pins are pulled out, it frees the small propeller spinners on the fuses to rotate a certain number of turns in the windstream, supposedly on its way down to the target. After which a spring releases the spinner, activating a plunger to pop out, arming the bomb, so if the plunger is touched - BOOM. I knew I had to do something fast when I saw that spinner on the front of that 1000 pounder turning on its fuse in the windstream of the open bomb bay at 27,300ft altitude. The space between the front of the jammed bombs and the forward bomb bay bulkhead was too narrow for me to squeeze into while wearing my chest-pack chute, or carrying an oxygen walk around bottle. So, I had to squeeze down into the compartment and straddle the open bomb bay without those luxuries, while trying to release the jam. Just seconds prior to freeing the lower bomb, the spinner on the upper bomb popped off and I caught it in my hand as the plunger popped out, arming it. I had no choice now, since my only way out, was to desperately release the bombs, otherwise if I tried to climb out, either my shoulder, chest or back would touch and activate the fuse plunger, making us history. So, you can be sure I was quite relieved when both bombs gently left the compartment. Lucky too, that I was holding on, when the bombs dropped out since I was not prepared for the amount of suction they created. As groggy as I was from lack of oxygen, I scrambled up to the catwalk, assisted by our radioman Sid Levine, who shoved his oxygen mask onto my face saving my life, I guess this event could qualify for 'ABOVE AND BEYOND THE CALL OF NORMAL DUTY.'"

On 6 October, when the 8th went to Berlin at the IP near Nauen, the 3rd Division formation was forced to lose altitude to prevent flying through thick cloud. Unknown to the B-17 crews, in this layer of cloud lurked a strong force of enemy fighters. Using the cloud cover to excellent advantage, the German fighters were vectored by ground controllers right into the 385th Bomb Group formation, flying as the high group of the last combat wing. The surprise was total. To make matters worse, the 549th Bomb Squadron was in the process of turning on to the target and had become separated from the rest of the group. Most of the eleven B-17s shot down were from this squadron. Only the arrival of the P-51 escort prevented further carnage.

Despite mounting losses, there was increasing evidence that the 8th's bombing offensive—against oil targets in particular—was reaping rewards. During August 1944 German oil production had fallen to a paltry 16,000 tons, compared with 195,000 tons in May that year. The *Luftwaffe* was therefore forced to live off stocks accumulated during the winter and spring, and began to feel the bite as the fuel crisis grew.[1080] Doolittle continued to apply pressure on the German oil manufacturing industry, and on 7 October 1300 B-17s and B-24s bombed five synthetic oil refineries in Czechoslovakia and central and northeastern Germany.[1081] A. J. Sinibubb, in the 91st Bomb Group, flew his 32nd mission in *Cheri*, piloted by Lieutenant Basnight, who flew Hi Flight, Deputy lead in the Hi squadron lead with a bomb load of 10 500lb GP bombs. The target was the Brux oil plant in Czechoslovakia, a total distance of 1231 statute miles. Sinibubb wrote:

"Take off 0703. Base-Caxton Gibbet-Newmarket-Needham Market-Orfordness. Mission started off well but as we came in on the bomb run the target was covered over. The divisional commander gave the order to bomb the secondary target but the lead navigator screwed up and we almost had it. We made two runs on targets of opportunity. Frieburg and an airfield 10 NM of Leipzig were bombed.

Our squadron and lead hit the latter, the low squadron hitting the first. As we came off the target we headed NW and ran into Dessau. From there we turned and tried to get back on course. All this time we had been running into flak, very intense over Leipzig, Frieburg and Dessau, accurate. Luckily, in our squadron no one was hit. How that ever happened I don't know. We hit flak at Osnabrück and at Brux also. Over Brux it was pretty intense. Weather was pretty fair most of the way. We landed with no mishaps. Fighter support was excellent. Enemy fighters were reported in the area but did not attack us thank God. Our formation was bad and would have been easy prey for them. Krones, my buddy navigator, finished up on this mission."[1082]

S/Sgt Adolph J. Smetana, a tail gunner in the 351st Bomb Group at Polebrook, recalls the mission to Politz:

"Nearing the target I saw this 'boiling mass' of flak. We started to make a 360° turn and I thought, 'Thank God we don't have to fly through it'. However, I was soon to discover that another group had cut us off and we were only waiting our turn. God, it was awful. I could see 'planes falling from all over the sky. When the first flak burst was at our altitude I knew we had just 'bought the farm'. It was a hell of a ride through that stuff. Our group just simply dissolved. We finally got through after what seemed an eternity. We found ourselves flying in formation with only one other 'plane and that was all in flames. If it had exploded we would have gone up with it. I was so scared I couldn't even tell the pilot to get the hell out of here. (We were breaking in a new officer crew that day, flying their first mission.) Finally 'Pops', the top turret gunner, screamed over the interphone to get his bloody arse out of it or we would never see Polebrook again'. He shouted many other choice words over the interphone, but our pilot did what 'Pops' said and broke off. Out of the corner of my eye I saw cripples heading for Sweden, but mostly my eyes were focused on the flying coffin in front of us. It finally went out of control and started down. Tears welled up in my eyes and I prayed that nine spots would come out of that 'plane. One who didn't was our usual waist gunner, who had been with us since we had been grouped together at Ardmore AFB, Oklahoma. It was his very first mission in action."

T/Sgt Guy "Chuck" Chookoorian, radio-operator-gunner in Lieutenant Jay "Mac" McIntosh's crew in the 331st Bomb Squadron, 94th Bomb Group, who was on his 29th mission, went to Bohlen (Leipzig):

"That morning the 94th was split. Part of the group was designated to complement the 385th, which had suffered such tremendous losses (11 planes) over Berlin the previous day, that it was unable to put a full group in the air. Their destination was Merseburg. The 331st Squadron was assigned to the 95th Bomb Group with Bohlen its destination. Both targets were in the Leipzig area; however, Merseburg was the most dreaded target the 94th visited during my combat tour. Damage and losses sustained there were enormous. The flak was terrifying. The flak at Bohlen on the other hand was meager and though we had experienced Luftwaffe opposition on previous trips, it seemed a 'milk run' by comparison. So we of the 331st considered ourselves fortunate.

"Several of the crews on this mission were in the early stages of their tours. As we neared the initial point, Raymond "Speed" Spediacci, our tail gunner, made an observation about the looseness of our formation and commented that we'd surely be hit. The words were hardly out of his mouth when I heard machine gun fire and shouts of, 'Bandits' and 'We're being attacked' over the intercom. I left my radio and rushed back to my gun, the right waist, just as the Me 109s and FW 190s were passing through our formation. They were attacking us from the rear and coming in 6 or 7 abreast. The total number was later estimated at 60 or 70. The entire encounter didn't last 5 minutes. Then at 2 o'clock level I saw a Fortress with its left side afire from wing to rudder. And just to show how strangely-most certainly a defense mechanism - the mind works sometimes, all I could think of at that moment was the beauty and the brightness of the orange flame. I almost felt like a spectator. 'Mac' identified the plane as Major Lambert's. Then a helpless feeling came over me as I watched the pilot at the wheel trying to hold the craft on a straight course. I wished I had arms long enough to reach out and snatch these boys from their 'vehicle to eternity.' Then slowly it peeled away from us...back...back...back...and at 5 o'clock low it exploded. Mac's voice then came over the intercom asking how the formation was holding up. 'Speed' responded in a strained voice that no planes were behind us and he thought all were lost. I looked out the right waist and saw nothing. It was the same with Miltie Storm at the left waist. Then we just stared at one another. Obviously we were the only ones left. My eyes focused on the damage to our right wing. A large blackened hole was on top. It had apparently started to burn. Some of the boy's thought we took a 20mm burst there. A huge section of the bottom of the wing was ripped loose and flapping in the air. Gasoline was pouring out in a stream like a contrail. But we were still aloft.

"'Mac' tagged on to another squadron and we continued to the target. Reaching the IP I breathed more easily. A feeling of security actually came over me knowing we were over the target. Why, no German fighter would dare go through his own flak. Then Kenneth "Boots" Allmond, our co-pilot, ended our moment of respite by calling our attention to the 'squirt jobs' maneuvering around 2 and 3 o'clock. One of them mustered enough courage to make a pass. It was a Me 163 rocket propelled plane. To me it looked like something out of 'Buck Rogers.' It was at 1 o'clock and still out of range when I fired a short burst for the assurance that my gun was working. Boots said to save my ammunition and wait until it was within range. I didn't think it necessary to explain. I waited... I watched the plane as it drifted toward 3 o'clock. I felt my eyes were deceiving me; it was actually in a 'pursuit curve.' I saw the flashes in his wings and the bursts of the exploding 20mm shells nearing our plane. My initial reaction? I started to drop down behind the armor plate below my gun. Then just as suddenly came the realization that my eight crewmates and I, our plane - armor plate and all - were facing destruction. I started shooting. I continued firing until he was at about 4 o'clock. From my recollection, I sent 200, possibly 300, rounds in his direction. He stood there suspended for a moment. Then it seems the plane quivered, rolled over and started down. There was no fire, no parachute and no explosion. The last I saw of him, he was in a slow spiral heading earthward; and I could hear the boys yelling over the intercom, 'You got him, Chuck. You got him!'"[1083]

"Arny" Arneson, bombardier in the B-17 piloted by Jay D. McIntosh, 331st Squadron, 94th Bomb Group, who flew his 33rd mission on 7 October, recalls:

"Some targets were considered more difficult then other targets and all of the targets that were deep inside Germany were considered bad but the oil refineries being so concentrated in size were extremely heavily defended. The day we were being briefed to go to Merseburg and the intelligence officer said the flak would be very light and of course everyone knew that this was wrong. Some joker in the back of the briefing room sneezed a very loud '*horse shit*'. Everyone began to laugh and the tension was broken. Bohlen and Merseburg were about the two roughest targets that I can remember. The flak was always extremely heavy and extremely concentrated.

"The 331st Squadron put up the entire group of 12 airplanes that were flown on 7 October. There were supposed to have been 13 but the aircraft that was to have been flown by Robert Schumachur aborted for some reason and twelve airplanes continued on the mission. As we got deep into German territory our group got out of formation and we now realized that we were the prime target of this error. We were jumped by many FW 190s and Me 109s plus some Me 163s. We were involved with these enemy fighters for approximately 45 minutes. They were coming in at us and right on their tail were the P-47s and P-51s, which were flying after these German aircraft and flying through our own bullets in the attempt to knock them out. Guy Chookoorian, our radio operator, received credit for hits on one German fighter. It was really a mess with all of these aircraft going down and still being attacked by the fighters. Several of the airplanes went down in spins. The aircraft that flew group lead that seemed to be right in front of us was a cherry red all over the fuselage. I saw one man jump out of the rear door without a chute.

"After the fighter attack our airplane seemed to be alone. It was not until after the attack was over and we began to survey the damage that we realized that there had been a gas fire on the right wing from one of the hits, which we took. The top turret gunner-engineer, Richard Eiseman had seen this but did not have time to even comment during the attack as he was busy shooting at one of the attacking fighters. The next time he got around to survey damage the fire was out. We did not at that time drop our bombs but tacked on to one of the other groups that had not been attacked and we did drop our bombs on the target along with the group that we had joined. After the fighter attack was over and we had left the target area the rest of the mission was quite uneventful except that we were one sad bunch of people.

"Out of the 12 airplanes that were flying this mission there were two of us that managed to get back to our base at Bury St. Edmunds. Two of the airplanes landed on the continent because they could not make it back at that time. Our aircraft was shot up quite badly. There was a large hole in the left wing and numerous holes throughout the airplane. We were fortunate we had no wounded on this mission. The only damage to the other aircraft that made it back was one 50-caliber machine gun hole. When we returned to the base that night there were so many empty barracks that it was almost unreal. My bombardier instructor, L. J. Cooper, was flying in one of the airplanes that went down. He had joined our group about a month prior to being shot down. It took a few days before replacement crews were brought in and because I only had two missions left to fly I really never got to know any of those replacement crews."

Lieutenant Horace C. Waldorf, a pilot who flew 24½ missions in the 331st Squadron, 94thBomb Group, recalls:

"We were always hit by flak to some extent and were subjected to two minor fighter attacks by what appeared to be 'cadets' in training under the tutelage of one who seemed to be a skilled pilot. Neither of those times were bad and 7 October was the only time I was involved in a serious fighter attack with the exception of a very brief one when we dropped supplies to the Free French in the French Alps. On this mission to Merseburg I was leading the high squadron.[1084] We had a very quiet flight until the time, just short of the IP when FW 190s hit us seemingly from all directions. Several planes had been hit and some went down immediately but we were a little busy, too. The right wing was on fire and both props had to be feathered on that side. We determined that it was an oil fire and dove hard, up against the red line, to attempt to blow it out. We were somewhat successful, so we jettisoned the bomb load and headed west alone. The navigator, George Webb, worked out a position of some sort by estimates of time and speed of our evasive action and by visual observation of the ground. He warned me to turn to avoid a concentration of flak ahead. He also informed me that we were probably about 15 minutes from the front lines so we could bale out or crash land in friendly territory if the need arose. I was certain that it would be necessary to abandon the aircraft, as we had lost large pieces from the underside. (We couldn't see the damage but did see the pieces go) and it was difficult to maintain control and flying speed. I did not want to chance crossing the Channel since there were friendlies in France. He had just informed me of the proximity of the lines when the flight engineer, Stephen Stupak, informed me that the fire had broken out again in the wing and it was gasoline this time. We had a coded bale out statement for emergencies when no time was available to acknowledge the order to bale. I gave this command, set the autopilot as best I could, checked the ship to ascertain that all the crew was out, reached for my 'raunchy' cap, which I missed and jumped. After ten seconds I pulled the ripcord and the aircraft had already exploded. I could count eight other chutes, so I knew everyone had made it that far."[1085]

Lieutenant John O. "Rams" Ramsey, navigator in Lieutenant Bernie L. Iwanciow's B-17G[1086] in the 860th Bomb Squadron, 493rd Bomb Group, flew the second mission of his tour:

"There was almost a surly silence after the pandemonium that had taken place over the interphone system between the IP, the target area and the RP (rally point where the Group could sort of get things straightened out, reorganize what was left of the formation and head for home). The silence was a state of shock. Never before had we seen a 'mighty Fortress' fall from the sky like a game bird caught in the blast of a hunter's shotgun. Others were spiraling down, some trailing white smoke and some, black smoke. Our aircraft, 278, called by some '*The Jinx*' because of the number of wounded it had brought home and the amount of flak it seemed to attract, took its share this day. One shell exploded just above the fuselage between the nose and the No.3 engine. Fortunately most of the shell fragments had gone up. The right tire was ripped open. There were three large holes beneath the co-pilot's seat. Three pieces of flak that entered the right side of the nose compartment tore through the navigator's neatly folded flight jacket, which was on top of his parachute bag beside his seat and went straight out the left side. The radio operator's steel helmet had a one-inch deep groove in it. He insisted that someone examine him for a bloody wound, which fortunately he did not have, just a very big lump on his head. Our crew had never before seen shells explode so close that we could see the red burst of fire in the center of the exploding shells. Nor had we smelled cordite mixed with the air and oxygen that we breathed. Black gun smoke slid past our windows. We could hear the crack of the exploding enemy shells over the roar of the forty-eight hundred horsepower of the four engines. All this from an unseen enemy five miles below. No one to turn our 12 machine-guns on. No way to fight back. Their interphone discipline had always been good. Little idle chatter. Most comments were limited to responses to the bombardier's periodic oxygen check, info of value to the pilots or flight engineer, or observations to be logged by the navigator. When I announced that they were once again safely over friendly territory and they could remove the heavy flak vests if they so chose, there weren't the usual joyous responses. Eventually, one quiet voice said, 'If we don't fly tomorrow - Sunday - I'm going to church.' One after another, eight voices echoed 'Me too.' The next morning nine young Americans, four Catholics, a Jew and four Protestants attended a chapel service together. No one had ever given much thought to any denomination other than his own. After the service, as they stood outside the Nissen hut, which served as both chapel and theater, they were surprised by how much they thought alike."

Lieutenant Norman E. Freidman, a co-pilot in the 493rd Bomb Group, flew his 24th mission on 7 October:

"This was the first mission for our crew since returning from the 'flak shack'. Briefing was held at 0200. We were to lead the high element or 'B' group of the lead squadron. At take-off weather was clear, as it was the entire mission. We climbed on course over France in a southerly direction to 32,000ft. Our load was 500lb demolition bombs. The target was Merseburg, one of the largest synthetic oil refineries in Germany and not too far from Leipzig. No enemy fighters were seen; but the flak over the target was the most intense we have ever experienced. It looked like a solid black cloud. We dropped our bombs with no difficulty and hit the target. After turning 90° off the run-in heading, our plane was struck by a burst of flak near the No.3 engine. I was hit directly on the bridge of the nose between the eyes. The leather on my sunglasses was cut and each glass flew in a different direction without breaking. The flak missed my steel helmet and after hitting my nose, hit my flak suit near my lap and landed on the floor of the plane. The entry hole was above my head. Just then, No.3 engine quit running and the propeller was feathered. I slid out of my seat and tore the oxygen mask off my face. At 32,000ft it does not take long to pass out from the lack of oxygen. I dropped down between the two pilot seats and made my way to the nose compartment. Jim Rieck was alone on the flight deck. Mac immediately put the spare oxygen mask on me. I was starting to turn blue. Mac went to help Jim on the flight deck while Dale attended me. He gave me a shot of Novocaine to ease any pain. He then covered the nose area with Sulphur powder, which was new at the time, to prevent infections. The bleeding stopped because of the low temperature at that altitude, minus .68° Fahrenheit.

"After the engine quit we dropped out of formation. I passed out from the shot. A short while later I came to and noticed No.1 propeller was feathered. Dale told me the prop kept running away and could not be controlled. With only two engines we were losing altitude rapidly. Mac was on the radio calling for friendly fighters, as we were still deep in Germany. Finally a flight of four P-51s joined and stayed with us until we reached the English Channel. Jim and Mac decided we should drop the belly turret and all the guns and ammunition to lighten the plane. All this was done when we reached Belgium. We were then able to maintain an altitude of 4000ft for the rest of the mission. Jim landed the plane at the first base he was able to locate after descending through the undercast. It was the 445th Liberator Group at Tibenham near Norwich. Doctors at the hospital sewed the bridge of my nose and straightened it up. It was broken and lying over on the right side after twelve days in hospital! I returned to my home base and was presented the Purple Heart and another cluster to my air medal, which makes three. I was unable to fly combat missions because I could not wear an oxygen mask on the bridge of my nose. I returned to the States in January 1945."[1087]

Lieutenant Ernest "Bob" Rhode's and his crew's previous eleven missions in the 709th Bomb Squadron, 447th Bomb Group at Rattlesden had been a relative "piece of cake." A green crew, they had not seen a single German fighter, and had suffered only minor flak damage to their B-17. Since they still lacked true combat experience Rhode's crew soon acquired the well-known 8th Air Force "disease" of over-confidence. They had become cocky, and everyone shared a high level of confidence that they were near invincible. When 7 October came it was to prove an especially exciting day, as Alan S. Cook, co-pilot, recalls:

"The briefing officers did not provide any special insights into how dangerous the target at the Leuna synthetic oil refinery complex at Merseburg truly was. The plant was producing 60% of overall national output as well as nearly 40% of national oil resources. What also was not mentioned was that the flak battery defenders were the best, with many of the battalions there noted for their accuracy. Crews were told of the importance of a good strike, to maintain what was one of the highest bombing accuracy ratings' record for any Group in the 8th Air Force."

Rhode's crew were assigned to *Umbriago*, which although it was a B-17G, in its camouflage paint it looked like a beat-up B-17F. The crew wondered how such an ugly duckling could fall into the hands of a top crew. All the other Group B-17s were shiny in their polished aluminium, but *Umbriago* was a throwback to earlier years when bombers were camouflaged.

Umbriago took off into a beautiful sunny sky, avoiding the danger of mid-air collision as often occurred in bad weather. The Group crossed out over Orford Ness and the crew tested their guns. Rhode was flying Deputy Lead of what was the High Group in the Combat Wing, with Captain Don Harris and Lieutenant Mahl's crew leading. The 709th Squadron Operations Officer, Major George C. Smith, led the 4th Combat Wing in a PFF "Mickey Ship" in the 94th Bomb Group. Each assembly point was reached on time and in the correct position. The flak at the Dutch coast was avoided by crossing over the Zuider Zee, at which stage the fighter escort made connection. Known flak concentrations at Münster and Bielefeld were skirted around, as was a third concentration at Kassel. The weather was deteriorating, and German fighters were reported tailing the Group. As they reached the IP to commence the bomb run they shot down *T.N.T. Kate*[1088] in the 711th Squadron, which was being flown by Lieutenant Robert I. Harwood. His navigator was 20-year-old Karl W. Wendel, who was flying the second mission of his tour, having made his debut the day before when the 8th attacked Berlin. Wendel regarded Merseburg as being in the same class as "Big-B" when it came to flak, and knew that American crews gave it a healthy respect. *T.N.T. Kate* was going well when someone sang over the intercom that the flak was thick enough to land on. The group leader was shot down, and Karl Wendel found himself in the position of lead navigator; the youngest in the 8th Air Force, and on only his second mission! However, his new role was taken from his grasp as quickly as it had been thrust upon him. A direct hit knocked out *T.N.T. Kate's* oxygen system, and there was an almighty scramble to connect the masks to an alternative supply.

The intercom came alive with frantic calls for help. The ball turret gunner could not breathe. The radio gunner helped him. "Engineer to pilot, gas leaking like hell from the wing tanks!" Likewise, "There's a hole big enough to drive a Jeep through back here," reported the waist gunner. The heavy flak kept tracking them. No.3 engine was out, and No.2's propeller was out of control and windmilling frantically. Oil flowed like venomous bleeding. From his position in the nose Karl Wendel could see it congealing. *T.N.T. Kate* dropped out of formation, and the crew started throwing out all loose equipment to lighten the ship. On two engines they could not keep their altitude of 28,000ft. Then the bombardier salvoed the bomb load over the suburbs of Merseburg as the formation pulled away and proceeded to the alternative target because clouds obscured the primary. Wendel frantically began working out a new course. "Navigator to pilot, course two-nine-zero. Heading to nearest safety is 290°." He added, "If we can make it." "Roger," sounded above the noise of the engines and flak as *T.N.T. Kate* turned on the new course. Before the new course could be followed, No.4 engine was hit and caught fire. The stricken B-17 fell like a stone. Among all of this Wendel could hear the prosaic sound of a ringing bell, which added to the confusion and excitement. The navigator was first on the intercom.

"Are we baling?" he asked. His question went unanswered in the cockpit. The lonesome kid in the tail gun position was scared and yelled repeatedly, "Are we baling?" Karl Wendell waited no longer and shouted over the intercom, "Bale out! Bale out!" He had seen the bombardier beckon to him, then slip out of the navigator's hatch. Within seconds Wendel had followed him. Dropping through the hatch as he usually did when the crew landed, it felt odd to find that his feet did not touch the ground as he left the aircraft.[1089]

As the crew of *Umbriago* lined up on the bomb-run Rhode's crew were stunned by the sight ahead of them. Alan Cook recalls:

> "There was a solid black cloud of flak bursts in a number and precision that they had never before encountered. Their course was exactly bracketed and the crew stared at each other in silence. One of the crew recalled that 'it truly was *flak so thick you could get out and walk on it*.'"

Not only was it a wall of smoke—it was a box the length, width, and depth of the route into the target! Gordon Serrott, bombardier, was hunched over his bombsight in case the lead bombardier was knocked out of action. Clouds and smoke pots on the wound obscured the actual target. Lieutenant John Stockham, navigator, was also readying himself for a back-up role by carefully noting position and time and double-checking the course back to base. Then *Umbriago* flew into the flak bursts:

> "Instantly the crew felt the accuracy of the flak as they took a direct hit with a second close by. Stockham was hit in the thigh and another crewman felt a thump on his thigh. Looking down he saw a still warm piece of shrapnel nestling in his lap. Although *Umbriago* then lost the Nos.2 and 4 engines the crew were lucky that they were still left with power on both sides. No.4 was struck in the planetary gear system and the pilots could not feather the propeller. It vibrated, making for difficult flying. No.2 was struck in the gas lines, the main oil tank and the accessories section but they did manage to feather the propeller before losing all oil pressure.
>
> "After the bomb-run was completed Serrott found he could not close the bomb bay doors. After giving first aid treatment to John Stockham he found that the door motor controls had been shot out. Walter Hemhauser, engineer, climbed out of the top turret to hand-crank the doors shut, before helping Sgt Frank Wisnieuski out of the ball turret. Then, the ball turret was unbolted and jettisoned somewhere north of Kassel. *Umbriago* had lost altitude from 24000ft to around 10,000ft and they were all alone, flying at a near-stalling speed of 120mph and having run the remaining engines at maximum power settings well beyond the maximum recommended time. *Umbriago* mushed along like a badly wounded duck until it was were finally picked up by a friendly escort of seven P-47s that stuck with the B-17 us until they were clear of hostile territory. Rhode entered Holland north of the Ruhr but knowing that he could not cross the North Sea safely the pilot swung *Umbriago* left towards a recently captured RAF airstrip at Eindhoven. Bob Rhode set *Umbriago* down gently on the grass runway and taxied to a corner of the field. The crew duly expressed their gratitude at being safely back on planet Earth by kissing the ground."

Colonel James R. Luper, CO 457th Bomb Group, led the "Fireball Outfit" in *Rene III* with the Group Surgeon, Major Gordon Haggard, the Group Navigator, Captain Norman Kriehn, and the Group Bombardier, Captain Henry Loades, among others, as crew. The 457th crossed Politz and became enveloped in the heavy flak barrage. *Rene III* was hit in two engines, which caught fire. The bomb bay doors were closed, and Luper managed to keep the crippled bomber level for a moment, but the fires spread and engulfed the starboard wing, causing the outboard engine to fall away. Four men, including Luper, jumped from the nose of the doomed B-17, and another three went out through the waist windows. One man who baled out of the waist had his parachute on fire as it fluttered open and was soon engulfed in flames. The remaining sections of *Rene III* hit the water in Stettin Bay, and the fuselage, which still contained the bomb load, exploded on impact with the water.[1090]

Next day, 8 October, there was no mission for the B-17 and B-24 crews, but on the 9th over 1000 heavies struck at two marshaling yards and an engine plant at Mainz and bombed Koblenz, Gustavsburg, Schweinfurt, and two targets of opportunity in western Germany. Nineteen fighter groups, including two in the 9th Air Force, provided support. No missions were flown on 10 October. On the 11th, 130 B-17s supported by three P-47 groups bombed Wesseling synthetic oil plant and the marshaling yards at Koblenz. Next day over 500 heavies attacked marshaling yards at Osnabrück and aircraft industry targets at Bremen, as well as targets of opportunity, including Diepholz airfield. Eleven fighter groups escorted the bombers and claimed 18 enemy fighters shot down. Paschal H. Powell, a B-17 armorer-waist gunner in William J. "Bill" Miller's crew in the 728th Squadron, 452nd Bomb Group at Deopham Green, would never forget the morning of 12 October:

> "Checking the board the evening before, we had found the next day operational but our crew was not scheduled to fly. Early in the morning on 12 October a very rude fellow came in banging the blackout doors of our hut and proceeded to tell us that we were flying. 'The whole field is alerted. Everything that can fly will fly. The target has been changed. The bomb load had been changed and you guys are flying.' Sure enough, we were flying but not our '*Little Miss America*', which was being flown by another crew, but a plane by the name of '*Inside Curve*.' (We had trained together as a combat crew at Ardmore, Oklahoma and had brought '*Little Miss America*' from Kearney, Nebraska, brand new to the 452nd. We were so proud of her). Our target was Bremen. Pulling up to the hardstand where '*Inside Curve*' was the weather was so bad we could scarcely see the wet old B-17F for the fog, which drifted across. Water dripped off her wings and prop blades, adding to the ghostly effect in the semi-darkness. The Crew Chief met us (one of the greatest I had ever met).

I'm sure our faces registered our disappointment for his plane. He began to explain he had just installed four new engines on her and slow-timed her yesterday. 'She is the fastest plane on the field sir,' he said to Bill Miller. 'This is her 113th mission and nothing on the field can stay with her.' We started counting the painted bombs that represented the 112 missions flown and the swastikas numbering the fighters shot down. I had a very strange and eerie feeling about the mission - the weather, that old B-17F with 112 missions and now her 113th mission; the thought that we were not supposed to fly and we were flying. I couldn't shake that feeling off. Nothing seemed right. Even as we worked into position for take off, the brakes seemed to have a weird sound. However, once we were off the ground I felt better, although we were climbing in soup and at times I could barely see the ends of the wings. I took consolation in the fact that everyone had the same problems and all would be on the lookout for each other and stay on their heading. Our main objective was to get above the soup and make our formation. I pulled the pins on the bombs, arming them to explode when dropped. Over the English Channel we test fired our guns. Bill was edgy and asked, 'Do you all have to fire at once?' something he had never complained about. Then, that strange feeling came back; I couldn't get over it.

"At 13,000ft we had our oxygen check. I was eating a D-bar since I had had no desire for breakfast. The way we had found out that we were flying had ruined my appetite. Looking out the right waist window at the water running off the wing of '*Inside Curve*' it seemed that someone spoke to me and said. 'If you have to jump, you will be in a pretty fix.' I didn't even have my parachute harness on. I said, 'You're right' and I picked up the harness placing it on my shoulders like a coat and I continued to eat my D-bar. That same Voice came to me again saying, 'If you have to jump, you still won't be any better off.' I thought, 'That's strange,' so I fastened the leg straps and the chest strap on my parachute harness and noticed my parachute was behind the machine-gun mount where I always put it. All that done, I felt 'satisfied'. That had to be the Lord speaking to me. I didn't understand it but I believed it.

"Our ball turret gunner, Earl O. Bowen, was having trouble with one of his turret guns. It did not fire in the test, so he asked me to check his ammunition in the chute. I said, "Short Round' (his nickname), roll down and stay down until I tell you to come up; my throat mike cord is too short to reach and I'll have to unplug my mike in order to reach your turret.' 'Roger,' he said and down he went. After taking the top off his turret, I saw his ammunition had not caught on the feed pall when he thought he had loaded this gun on the ground. I was pulling the ammunition up in the turret chute when all of a sudden *Inside Curve* began to pitch and rock. One wing was going up and the other wing was going down with a fluttering motion. Never a word was said over intercom. I had only one thought in mind and that was to call 'Short Round' and tell him to roll up and get out of his turret for I knew we were in trouble. My thought was, we have hit the prop wash from another plane and then seemingly, we went all the way over on our back; twisting and whirling we began to spin down to the earth or sea - I was not sure. Oh! I felt so sick; I was so scared. 'Please, Someone, stop this thing from spinning.' I could not move; the force of gravity was so strong *Inside Curve* had quit spinning and had begun to dive from about 15,000ft, making the most horrifying sound I have ever heard in all my life. I screamed as loud as I could and I believe it was my death cry, 'Oh, God, have mercy on us.' As I screamed, it seemed I would go through the floor of the fuselage for the force was so great. *Inside Curve* blew up! When I had reached for the throat mike cord to call 'Short Round' to get out of his turret, I was flattened on the floor with my left arm stretched almost touching the cord with my fingers but unable to grasp it. I had remained in that position looking toward the tail not able to move until it blew up. At the time of the explosion, something hit me in the head very hard. Stars went everywhere; I felt faint. To my surprise, instead of passing out from the blow, I felt cold air rushing through the part of the plane I was in. I was in the waist that had broken off at the ball turret and at the tail door, just like a barrel with both ends open. As the cold wind rushed through that part, I realized I could move and it seemed I was being sucked out. I tried to catch hold of the ribs of the fuselage with my right hand when I noticed my parachute sliding right along beside of me. I grabbed it like a football under my left arm and looked and there was a snap on my parachute harness by a ring on the parachute. I just pushed down on the chute and I saw and heard the snap click as it fastened to the ring on my parachute. I do not remember fastening the other snap. I began to push with my feet and scoot as fast as I could in the direction I felt I was being sucked out previously. Almost to the broken edge where the tail had blown off, I pulled that red handle of my parachute and remember seeing the little pilot chute pop out as a kite in the wind, dragging the rest of the chute out and separating me from that part of the fuselage. It jerked me so hard that it raveled the chute around the top opening. One parachute packer told me it raveled because I was traveling so fast when it opened.

"My heart was beating so fast as I vowed I would serve God as long as I lived. As I looked up, I was so frightened to see my parachute acting as if it would collapse; but I know now since my second jump that that was because I was swinging. I did not see another chute anywhere as I was coming down and my heart could hardly stand it. One of the bombs blew loose and exploded to my left below me when it hit the ground, sending clods of earth the size of a piano up into the air and I just knew I would be hit. It was so hot and the air was so thin from the concussion of the bomb that breathing was very difficult momentarily. I heard another explosion further over to my left and flames licked high into the sky. That was what was left of *Inside Curve* with five of my crew still on board. I cried aloud. I felt my heart would literally come out of my body. I hit the ground in a one-wayed field. The wind was strong in that area and there was no fog. I was descending backward and hit on the side of a ditch that was in the field like an irrigation ditch. It's a wonder it didn't break my back. Instead it knocked me goofy for a moment; I thought I was in Germany. My chute started dragging me in that loose dirt before I was able to collapse it. I saw this lady running toward me and I gathered up my chute and ran from her. She said, 'Wait and let me help you.' As soon as she spoke, I realized I was in England. It was then she took my chute and wiped tears, blood and dirt on that beautiful silk. She kept saying, 'Oh, Laddie, you are hurt'. I was crying but I didn't realize I was bleeding. I said, 'Did you see any other chutes?' She said, 'Yes, one of your mates hit inside our yard fence. My husband kept hollering to him 'Pull it, mate, pull it, mate' and he pulled it and swung one time and hit in our yard.' That was Sidney Solomon, our navigator. He put on his parachute when we began to flutter. When *Inside Curve* blew up, he was blown through that plastic nose. He never remembered pulling his ripcord. Sid was really hurt bad but tried to hold up because of the loss we had just suffered. I felt no pain except in my heart. My nose was broken and I was bruised and skinned up; but all I could do was cry.

"Before we were rushed off to a British hospital nearby, the lady told us how she and her husband were eating breakfast when they heard that horrible sound of our bomber coming down. She said that they rushed out of the house just to see it come out of the clouds and it appeared as if the pilot had the engines wide open to try to pull it out of the dyke. 'He was able to pick the nose up just a little when those bloody wings folded and she blew up. The next thing we saw was you Yanks coming down.'

"I have always been grateful for that English couple and the staff at a British hospital were very kind. They and Intelligence asked us many questions and they also gave us as much information as they could. Naturally, Sid and I wanted to know about the rest of the boys. Several times Intelligence questioned us about the number on board, as they could only account for eight men. Finally we were told that the one who could not be found was Earl Bowen. I told them I knew he was in the ball turret, but they had not found the turret. As night came on word came they had found Earl. His turret had been blown off and it hit in a field and rolled into a thicket. They found Matt Ransom, the tail gunner, who had been blown out of the tail. The other five had gone down with the plane. A doctor told us they had to use a crowbar to pry the pilot's hands from the controls; his death grip never gave up. All the bodies of our crew were recovered. Sid and I were treated and kept several days. We were interviewed several times by American and British Intelligence. Was it sabotage, prop wash, or what? Only God knows. The 8th Air Force delayed the burial of our crew until Sid and I were able to leave the hospital and attend the funeral at the Military Cemetery outside Cambridge. All seven of their caskets were lined up in order according to rank; each covered with an American flag. We were asked to inspect each casket; as the Honor Guard saluted and folded the flag back, we could see and feel the dog tag of each member of our crew. We were representing their families. Sid and me were the only family they had in that part of the world. Did you ever bury seven of your own 'family?' This was the saddest day ever spent on this earth."[1091]

Two days later, on 14 October 1100 B-17s and B-24s bombed marshaling yards and targets in the Cologne area. *Jolly Roger*, piloted by 2nd Lieutenant William Klusmeyer in the 458th Bomb Group, took a direct flak hit in the nose. Lieutenant Robert L. Ferrell, the lead navigator, recalls:

"With his eye glued to the Norden sight, Ernest Sands, the bombardier, shouted, 'Bombs Aw…' The Plexiglas of the Emerson nose turret turned red with blood and the bombardier was blown from over the bombsight back into the nose wheel well. My left hand showed blood through my gloves from three shrapnel piercings and the smell of cordite seeped through my oxygen mask."

Ferrell went to the aid of the second navigator, Millard C. Miller:

"I slipped my hands under his armpits and pulled on him. His head fell back against my right shoulder. I looked at Miller and vomited into my oxygen mask and nearly drowned from it. I had never seen a human head hit by a shell. I laid him on the floor of the navigator's compartment. Sergeant Pohler, the engineer/upper turret gunner, dragged Miller through the tunnel and toward the flight deck, where he was thrown out the bomb strike camera hatch opening after Pohler secured a 25ft static line clip to his 'D' ring."

With a macabre touch, Ferrell made an entry into his navigation log using the blood lying on his table. Three rings on the bale-out bell ordered the crew to abandon the aircraft. A raging fire in the bomb bay forced the men back to the front compartment. Ferrell pulled the emergency handle on the nose wheel doors, but they failed to open:

"This was our only way out now," he continues. "Sands stooped over and jumped up and down on the nose wheel doors. They began to part and fly away. He dropped through the opening until his outstretched arms held him momentarily. He looked at me and shouted: 'This sure as hell pisses me off!' Then he dropped out and away." Ferrell quickly followed.[1092]

Lieutenant Wallace Johnson in the 490th recalls the mission of Tuesday, 17 October:

"I was flying our B-17 *Big Poison*[1093] on a mission to the marshaling yards at Cologne when we took an almost direct flak hit that severed all the oil lines on No.2 engine, including the one to the feathering pump. Consequently all attempts to feather that engine were futile; this caused extreme over-speeding of the prop and with no oil to the engine it soon seized, causing the crankshaft to shear. This left me with one prop running wild (windmilling), causing a huge amount of drag which I could not overcome, even with the other three engines at full power. As we dropped out of formation we were picked up and escorted by two little friends, P-51s. As pilot-in-command it was up to me at this point to make the decision to try and make the Channel crossing back home to Eye or attempt a landing on the Continent. I reasoned that there was a high risk of the runaway prop breaking away from its mount and slicing through the nose of the aircraft, with dire consequences. I also knew that there was a possibility I would have to ditch the plane in the Channel. Either way, concern for the safety of my crew made me decide to land at Brussels. Maintenance crews came out to meet us and their inspection revealed that the prop was ready to fall off with the touch of a finger. I was glad that I had made the right decision."

Many hoped that the war might be over by Christmas. During October 1944 many familiar personnel in the established groups returned to the States after completing their tours. Among the fresh, green replacements were a few veterans with a first tour in the ETO behind them. Abe Dolim, who on 17 October rejoined the 94th Bomb Group at Bury St. Edmunds, fell into this category. The young Hawaiian had left for his native island in July for 30 days R&R, hoping that the war would be over by the time his leave had expired. However, a second tour brought compensations: "It was good to be back among my comrades. People back home did not comprehend air warfare." One day a little bombardier "tough as nails," who was also on his second combat tour of duty, could be heard telling aircrew about air warfare, and in particular, the Marienburg mission a year earlier. Abe Dolim recalls:

"He had a cross-shaped scar above his left eye – a gift by way of a 20mm shell that exploded against his bombsight. After being slightly wounded three times, he still had not garnered a Purple Heart. It seemed you had to be out of commission for at least 24 hours for one of those. He told us how he was awarded a probable for a Me 110 because it went through the clouds and no one saw it crash. Feeling no pain after a few scotches he blurted out, 'I'd like to see the day a Me 110 flies with its fucking tail shot off.'"[1094]

For Harry W. Love, a B-17 bombardier in the 568th Squadron, 390th Bomb Group at Framlingham, 18 October was his "day of infamy," but it too was his 21st birthday…his "day of Rebirth":

"My story begins like so many other bomber crews, at 0400 hours As per schedule, the crews were awakened; the quick wash-up; off to the mess hail for the usual chow-down; back to barracks for completion of dress, storing of personal papers and finally, off to the briefing room. As rhetoric will have it, this was basically the routine for any bomber crew flying out of England. My attitude, no different from any other 21 year old; I was happy, had a great crew and festivities were planned for that evening when we returned from the bombing mission. At the briefing, we received our instructions. Our mission was to Kassel, Germany. (Considerably less difficult or dangerous we thought than Berlin, Regensburg, Augsburg or so many others.) During the briefing session, the members of the crew contemplated no unusually heavy problems. At the completion of the general briefing, the pilots, navigators and bombardiers parted ways for individual briefings. We then were driven to our assigned aircraft. The plane we originally had been assigned to was the *Silver Meteor*. It was however; taken out of service for this particular mission because of heavy damage it sustained two days prior, on a mission to Cologne.[1095] Therefore, we were reassigned to a brand new B-17G.[1096] *Bugs Bunny* was a truly magnificent looking craft as we approached it that morning. Inspection of armament loading procedures (which was my responsibility as bombardier) was conducted and before too long, it was take-off time. My pilot, Lieutenant Donald T. Drugan, was a masterful, highly prestigious, military man and competent in all aspects of his assigned field. Our co-pilot, John Mohn, was very astute, tolerant and somewhat more pacific than Drugan. Our navigator, Gerald Wasserman, a Brooklyn boy, was very dedicated to his job and an asset to our crew.

"Take off was uneventful. The weather was clear (although dark at the time of departure). We found our assigned positions at the prescribed altitude. Not too long thereafter, the British Coast was behind us. The order to 'check your guns and fire your guns' was given. The response traditionally heard was, 'All guns firing properly and in order.'

"We approached the coast of Europe at approximately 0830 hours. Our target was still an hour and a half away. We encountered no enemy fighters en route and the flak was light. The bomb run over the target was considered very successful. Upon making our turn off the bomb run after release of bombs, we headed in a northwesterly direction to meet up with the balance of the Wing, which could be seen 15-20 miles away. At this time it was quite apparent that we were five or six minutes behind schedule in our rendezvous with the Wing for our trip back to England. This necessitated our lead crew to change course some degrees further to the north, which brought us over a portion of the Ruhr Valley. On approaching this particular area, five or ten miles from our rendezvous, we began to pick up massive concentrations of flak fire. One of the first bursts came within 100 yards of the front of our plane. This was followed by 5 or 6 more immediately, thereafter, each one closer than the preceding one. It seemed that we were well tracked down below by the anti-aircraft crews. I announced to the crew that the bursts were directly in line. The pilot, in accord, confirmed my communication.

"Two or three seconds later we received a hit in the nose of the plane directly above the chin turret leaving a hole 15-20 inches in circumference. I immediately back tracked away from my chin gun position and took up a station to the right (which was the cheek gun). The cyclonic rush of air that came through was impossible to control. I recall vividly the navigator stating over the intercom, 'Nobody will know how close the bombardier came to buying it. The bursts of flak came through within inches of his right leg.' The anti-aircraft gunners on the ground weren't finished tracking our plane, for at that instant we received a direct hit in one engine (starboard side) with shocking impact. Massive vibrations developed and fumes and smoke filled the plane. Drugan, without hesitation, pulled out of formation and attempted to put out the flames within that particular engine by sideslipping the plane. Upon looking at the right wing it was obvious that the damage thereto, was extensive. The entire right wing was oscillating up and down 20-30°. On seeing this, I assisted the navigator Gerald Wasserman in putting on his chest pack. As bombardier, I always wore my backpack throughout the entire mission.

"I called to Drugan in the customary technique. 'Bombardier to pilot, do you have any instructions?' He replied, 'Bombardier, I hear you.' Looking back at the wing again I could clearly see the oscillation increasing. The engineer, Sgt Parker, dropped down from his position to our station with the navigator between us. I instructed the engineer to open the escape hatch located directly in front of him. He complied immediately. I again called to the pilot asking if there were any further instructions regarding possible bale out. The pilot, once again replied, 'Bombardier, I hear you' but no instructions followed. Looking out at the wing again (which was oscillating even more), it was obvious to me that the wing could not stay on much longer. At this point, firmly believing the alarm bell and intercom were no longer operating, I directed the engineer to bale out. Parker looked up to the pilot for some expression of guidance. He did not receive any. He then looked back at me and the navigator, who was directly in front of me. At this critical point (with little or no rime for conversation), a mandated determination had to be directed and carried out. The engineer would have to bale out of the plane first, the navigator second and then myself. I, in a loud tone (after removing my oxygen mask), ordered the engineer to bale out. Again he hesitated. I then began to physically push the navigator in that direction stating, 'We have to go; the wing is coming off.' The navigator looked at me with quite an acceptable (and understandable) look of doubt and shook his head. At that instance, the wing came off!

"It is apparent that with one of the wings off of a B-17 it will not fly. Our plane began to plummet down in a spiraling, leafy fashion to earth. At this point, I would assume we were in the neighborhood of 20-22,000ft. Quite instantaneously, all within the craft were seemingly welded to their specific positions. I was flung against the starboard cheek gun slamming my neck against it in a rigid fashion, unable to move a muscle due to the powerful centrifugal force exerted during the spiraling effect. At this moment, I vividly recall thinking of one thing and one thing only. 'What will Mom say or feel when she hears about me being killed in action?' There was no question or doubt in my mind that I was to meet 'my maker' in a matter of moments. There was no possible chance for anyone to successfully escape this situation.

"Two or three seconds later, there erupted a tremendous, all-encompassing explosion; I felt my entire body weight being lifted by an unknown force. I was literally catapulted through the air, head first and out the front Plexiglas nose of the aircraft. The gas tanks (I am assuming), from the other wing or in the body of the craft had been ignited by the flak we took. Luckily I did not black out. I was alert and fully cognizant of the entire situation. I knew instantly that I was free from the aircraft. I had the foresight, however, not to pull the ripcord immediately. As I began to fall to earth, I could clearly see burning debris from our aircraft. Far to the left, a chute opened: shortly thereafter on my right, another chute; and then a few seconds later, still another chute opened. This chute (the latter) perhaps opened too soon and as fate would have it, part of the burning debris struck his chute as it opened. Which crewmember it was, I could not identify. I held my ripcord with a firm grasp for what seemed to be hours but I'm sure it was only a second or two before making a move. I saw clear areas around me. I then pulled the cord and to my utter surprise, I felt no jerk, as anticipated. My most prevalent thought at this time was that, 'The parachute must have been torn from my back when I was blown from the front of the plane.' I looked up and there it was, blossoming beautifully above me. Perhaps the reason for not feeling the impact of the chute opening can be attributed to the mental trauma I had so recently experienced, i.e. being blown out of the aircraft. My thought at this time, 'My God, I'm going to he safe. I'm floating down to earth.'"[1097]

On Sunday, 22 October, more than 1000 heavies supported by 15 fighter groups attacked two military vehicle plants at Brunswick and Hanover, and two marshaling yards at Hamm and Münster. Norman K. Andrew, in the 487th Bomb Group, flew his 9th mission to Münster. He wrote:

"Target study 0545. It was what the uninitiated call a milk run - but I still sweat them all out to the target. We led the low squadron. The mission was strictly PFF - 10/10ths. Had one hole just east of the Zuider Zee. Something new was tried today. Two ships carried nothing but 1600lbs of *Chaff*. They flew above the high squadron and at the IP. They took off in a 200fpm dive with an eight P-51 escort. When we dropped the flak was bursting about 8000ft under us. I had a #27 set *Gee* box and was able to pick up the 'C' blip all the way. Load was 12 500-lb GPs. We put six on the target; three a half second over and three one second over."

Sergeant Francis W. "Frank" McKinley, a gunner in the 851st Squadron, 490th Bomb Group at Eye, Suffolk, recalls his 22 October mission:

"After many hours of ground school and flying time to familiarize us with the airfield and the surrounding area we were notified that on the next day we would be flying our first combat mission. We got our wake up call at 0230 hours and immediately the apprehension set in. After a breakfast of bacon and eggs came the very thorough briefing and we learnt that our target was to be the marshaling yards at Münster. We then went out to the aircraft, carried out the various routine checks and waited for take-off time. Eventually we got a green light from the tower and in the darkness roared down the runway blue flames shooting out of the turbos, to climb out. We broke out of the solid cloud cover at 10,000ft and the pilot gave the order to go on oxygen. There was a bright moon illuminating the silvery clouds below us as we looked for the red and yellow flares fired by the 851st lead ship to aid us in assembling into squadron formation. By the time the sun had risen the 490th was fully assembled and had entered the bomber stream at the precise time. Our crew, crew 100, was at last on its way to Germany for its first combat experience.

"We climbed slowly to our assigned altitude of 25,000ft and flew east into the sun towards Germany. There was solid cloud cover extending in all directions as far as the eye could see. The navigator informed us that we were crossing the Channel and the pilot ordered us to test fire our guns. By this time our fighter escort had joined us and they looked very impressive out there. When we reached the point of entering enemy territory the pilot ordered us to put on our flak helmets and flak vests; he also made one of the frequent oxygen checks, each of us reporting in turn on the intercom. We saw the group ahead of us dropping their bombs. The flak was light and there were no bandits in the target area. The order 'Rainy Day' came in from the lead ship and the radio operator started to dump the metallic *Chaff* that served to confuse the German radar-guided guns. By this time our bomb doors were open and we dropped our bombs on the signal of the lead plane, which was bombing by radar due to complete cloud cover. There was some moderate flak but it was inaccurate and no enemy fighters showed up; nevertheless we still kept searching for them just in case - we didn't want to be caught out as we made a sharp break away from the target and headed for home. As we touched down back at Eye everyone had that warm, relaxed feeling that follows what is called a 'milk run' - all planes back unharmed and nobody injured."

On 22 October Lieutenant Kenneth H. French, bombardier in Lieutenant Curtis R. McKinney's crew in the 490th Bomb Group, flew his 22nd mission:

"Today we had a fairly easy mission to Münster. We briefed at 0700 hours and took off at 1011 hours in a ground fog with 1000-yard visibility. We climbed to 18,000ft where we joined in formation with our squadron and then took a course across the North Sea. Our fighter support was good; they left us we were past the fighter danger zone and continued on with the boys who were going to Hanover and Brunswick. There were no enemy fighters seen or reported. After a flak-free run over Holland we reached the target area at about 1445 hours and as we flew past Osnabrück the flak really started. They were sending up a good box barrage and plenty of rockets but thank God we didn't get mixed up in it. We had a box barrage directly in front of us on the target (we had been briefed for 70 guns) but we turned off to the left to make the run. They sent up more flak but it was low and to the rear of us and we suffered no damage. About twelve rockets came up, right at our altitude and fairly accurate. I saw one explode at Osnabrück and it looked like a flash of lightning."

On 24 October, 415 P-47s and P-51s of the 8th Air Force carried out fighter-bomber raids in the Hanover-Kassel area. Nine aircraft were lost. Next day, Wednesday, 25 October, nearly 1200 heavies in five forces supported by eleven fighter groups attacked three oil refineries and several other targets. It was Lieutenant Kenneth H. French's 23rd mission, and he took off at 0853 hours for Hamburg, flying lead in the third element of the low squadron:

"We formed at 15,000ft with no trouble and left on time for a change, climbing to bombing altitude as we followed our course over the North Sea. Our fighter escort today was fair: we had four groups of P-51s pick us up at the German coast. Everything had gone well up to this point. We saw flak off Heligoland Island ahead of us just before we turned but no more until we were over our target at Hamburg. We were briefed for 250 anti-aircraft guns on the target and believe me they were all working. They also had 15 rocket guns in good working order. We went in on our bombing run at 25,700ft. We bombed by PFF through 10/10ths cloud cover. Those gunners certainly knew what they were doing; they used tracking and a barrage type flak and were quite accurate despite of all the *Chaff* we threw out. Fortunately for us, most of it was just off to our right. We were carrying 20 250lb GPs and spaced them over the target at 100ft intervals. Our ground speed was about 204mph and the temperature at flight altitude was about 28°C. The target was an oil storage depot and refinery just off a tributary of the Elbe 2 ½ miles south of the city of Hamburg and we think we hit it quite well because we saw four different columns of smoke come up through the undercast and spread out. We certainly hit something. Time of mission was 6 hours 40 minutes. We had no battle damage to our planes and all returned safely to base. But one aircraft from the 493rd Group was seen to go down over the target in a slow spin."

Next day, 26 October, Lieutenant Kenneth H. French flew his 24th mission, when over 1100 heavies attacked a synthetic oil plant at Bottrop and several other targets supported by 14 fighter groups:

"Today's mission got me my third Oak Leaf Cluster and the target was Hanover. After a delay due to bad weather we took off by instruments at 1053 hours in very poor visibility. Cloud coverage over the base was 10/10 and we had to climb to 8000ft before we got through the overcast. We were flying lead in the third element of the high squadron and formed at 16,000ft before climbing on course. Our formation today was very poor - we were all over the sky and we saw two planes from another Group collide while forming; pieces of both went down smoking and burning. Just as it had been at home, cloud cover at the target was 10/10ths. There had been a few breaks on the way but not many. We picked up our fighter escort of four groups of P-51s and two groups of P-47s just after we passed over the Zuider Zee but fortunately there were no enemy fighters seen or reported in the area. We had been briefed for 140 guns on the target but the flak was only moderate and inaccurate. They used a barrage and tracking method and also had about six rocket guns in action. We bombed ordnance depots; assembly plants and also tool factories. We carried five M17s and five 500lb GP bombs. Our gas load was 2500 gallons and our ground speed was 215mph; the intervolometer setting was 140ft. We bombed by PFF from an altitude of 26,300ft (temperature -36°C) and the results of bombing were unobserved. We had some flak just as we left the German border but it didn't last very long. The rockets on the target could be seen at least 60 miles away. We had no battle damage today and all the aircraft from our Group returned safely. Time of mission was 7 hours."

On Saturday, 28 October, over 350 B-17s escorted by four fighter groups bombed the marshaling yards at Hamm and Münster. Lieutenant Kenneth H. French, who went to Hamm, recalls:

"Using runway 21 we took off at 0830 hours, using instruments and climbed to 8000ft through overcast. We joined the formation at 23,000ft and crossed the English coast 9 minutes late. Only five Groups of the 3rd Division flew today; all the others were grounded. The weather was very bad and it almost caused a lot of accidents. We had dense and persistent contrails all the time - they were so thick over the target that we could hardly see each other on the way out and we strayed into flak near Dummer Lake. The flak over the target was a real problem. There were about 45 flak guns and 6 rocket guns on the target and they certainly weren't sleeping today. We had a couple of bursts just underneath us that lifted the plane right up. It was too close for comfort but luckily we didn't receive any damage at all. We also got over a flak area at Zwolle that wasn't supposed to be there, both going out and coming back. Our aircraft escaped but some of our planes suffered minor damage. We were carrying 20 250lb GP bombs with fuse settings of 1/10 and 1/40 and dropped them in train from 25,300ft at 100ft spacing. Our ground speed was about 165mph and the temperature recorded at our highest altitude was -44°C. Bombing was by PFF and the results were unobserved. No enemy planes were seen but Me 410s and Ju 88s were reported in the area. Time of mission was about 5 hours 45 minutes. Though everybody got through OK in the end, the bad weather and the flak made this a most uncomfortable mission and I never want to fly another like it again."

Two days later, on Monday, 30 October, over 600 heavies escorted by 15 fighter groups attacked oil refineries near Hamburg and eleven other targets, including the marshaling yards at Hamm and Münster again. Lieutenant Kenneth H. French, who was flying his 26th mission, went to Merseburg:

"We took off at 0815 hours with a full gas load, On our last four missions we had needed to use instruments to fly through the overcast but today it was clear for our SOP climb. We assembled at 16,000ft, left the English coast at 1030 hours and were joined by our P-47 and P-51 escorts. We were carrying ten 500lb GP bombs with 1/10 and 1/40 fuses but had to bring them all back with us because we only got as far as 060 40' E before turning back due to bad weather. There were clouds running up to 32,000ft and that was too high for our bombing. We encountered no flak, nor enemy fighters, though fighters were said to be in the area. We did however see four V-2 rockets going straight up to 40,000ft. Time of mission was 5hr 15 minutes. How I wish that all the missions could be as easy as this one."

By the autumn of 1944 oil targets had assumed top priority. The synthetic oil refineries at Merseburg, in Leuna, were attacked on at least 18 occasions in 1944.[1098] Bad weather throughout November slowed down the Allies' advance all along the western front and severely hampered missions. When they were flown they were usually against oil targets.

On 2 November, two forces of B-17s, 683 planes in all, attacked the vast *I.G. Farbenindustrie's* synthetic oil refinery at Leuna, three miles south of Merseburg, estimated to be producing 10% of all Germany's synthetic oil, and a third of all the enemy's ammonia and other chemicals. At briefing crews were warned that German fuel and replacement pilots were in such short supply that Hermann Göring, the *Luftwaffe* chief, was massing his forces to strike a telling blow on a single mission. All they needed was an opportunity. Norman K. Andrew, navigator in Jack Stanley's crew in the 487th Bomb Group at Lavenham, flew his 10th mission, their first as a lead crew. Andrew wrote:

"Up at 0330 for 0430 pre-briefing. Target: Merseburg, third highest priority target in Germany. Load 10 500lb GPs. Everything was fine until we hit the target area. Instead of a bomb run of 95 magnetic we finally dropped on 194 mag. Toured the Leipzig flak area from north to south (the long way). Four planes in our immediate vicinity went down in flames. Quite a rat race at the target - groups everywhere. Dick Giles, McDougall and Remaklus finished 30 today. Dick said that for the first time he was really scared and wanted to turn out. We were in flak for 12 minutes. It was classified as intense, accurate, barrage type. Evasive action was no good - it was everywhere and not just a few puffs. After landing the boys said Big B was a milk run compared to it. The Leipzig area has 450 guns and I think they had had a chance at us. My figures: 874 B-l7s over target. 4,370,000lbs of bombs. Our escort was 850 P-51s and P-38s. They tangled with the Luftwaffe at the IP at 1230. They hit the group behind us at the RP at 1330. 19 E/A were shot down over the target

- one P-51. We led the low squadron. What a day! Planes shot up - planes aborting - planes all over the deck coming home. Coming over the North Sea we saw a B-17 with no horizontal stabilizer. We had one small hole in our stabilizer."

Wayne Tex Frye, navigator in Jack O'Neil's crew in the 91st Bomb Group, recalls:

"This was one for the books! When we were awakened this morning, I felt that it would be a rough one. I had given Bill, our engineer the money to get a ring in town the night before and he had it over in his barracks in his locker. I told Wyatt that I didn't' think that I would be coming back from this one and I wanted him to get the ring and send it home to my wife. This was the third time I felt that I wouldn't make it. When I got to briefing, I was positive of it. The target was Merseburg; 473 flak guns and all of them big ones. Flying time 7:45. Time on oxygen 4:30. Bomb load-18 250lbs. We were to be the last group over the target. That is really being 'Tail End Charley'. We had had to change ships right at the last moment (normally we flew *The Witch*) and had '*General Ike*', an old timer named after Eisenhower.

"Flight altitude was 26,200ft where the temperature was -38°. As we neared the target the flak really started coming up. Some of the fellows said there was some 200mm flak. I don't doubt it at all. It was sure big. We could see enemy fighters ahead of us on the other side of the target and were afraid that we were going to get it from them. After we turned off the target we could see them preparing for attack. Bobbie, in the tail, was keeping us informed on their activities. About 400 Me 109s and FW 190s hit us. No words can describe how terrible this was. The 20mm started bursting all around us. Robbie and Bill and Mac were calling out the fighters all around the clock. I sure admired Robinson; he was back then shooting like mad and calling out every plane close to us. I heard him call up that he blew up one. A FW-190 came in and Bill really poured the lead to him. The pilot was either hurt or out of control or maybe neither, but he tried to ram into our right wing, just missing it as he was going down. Jack had to pull up the wing for him to miss it. A Me 109 did a slow half roll right over our plane and I called to Bill to get him. The top turret was so small that Bill couldn't sight straight up so he didn't get a shot it this one. Just then a FW-190 stalled out right in front of when my left cheek gun should have been but there was no such gun In my ship. I could have shot the pilot with a .45 pistol. I could see his face as easy as if in the same plane with him. Bill called up and said he just knocked down another fighter. A FW 190 came diving down in front of our nose and I started letting him have it with my right cheek gun. I could see the bullets going from his right wing tip right on into the cowling. Pieces of cowling starting flying off and his engine caught on fire and he started spiraling down. Before I was through shooting, my gun jammed and I had to try to fix it while watching everything and writing down observations in my log. Paul, the toggelier, damaged a fighter at this time. I kept wondering where the damned P-51s were.

"The two ships in our element were shot up and left the formation. Jack was really doing some wonderful evasive action. Then were four jet-propelled fighters around and one of the tail gunners in our squadron shot one down. The fighters kept coming back and attacking again. They were coming in with flaps down and their throttles back, just sitting back of us at 6 o'clock staggered, shooting at us. Bombers were going down all around us. Jim was riding in another ship and I did a lot of worrying about him. We had 16 separate attacks on our ship. After eight minutes of fighter attack, they finally stopped. I had seen one B-17 go down, apparently under control and two fighters followed him down and chopped him right in two.

"Our fighters finally showed up - two of them. I saw one '51 shoot down five German fighters in one sweep. It was a pretty sight but why in the hell weren't they there all the time? Bobbie called up and told us that we just had six planes in our squadron left out of twelve that started with us. Norman Passeger, my best friend and a fellow navigator had gone down. I kept looking for the ship that Jim was in. Finally it scooted up to join the rest of us. I was so thankful that he didn't go down that I shed a few tears right there and then. The flak was still coming up intense and accurate. It was really a pleasure to have flak instead of fighters. In the eight minutes of fighter attacks I made six entries in my log. I don't have any recollection of making any. The navigators were all messed up and did not quite know just where we were. I know I didn't. We did not come back the way we were supposed to, but we were on the way home even if the flak was still coming up.

"We finally got out over the North Sea but we could not relax, having been on such a nervous strain. I was still having a little trouble with my machine gun, it would shoot a few bursts and then jam, but I finally got it fixed. When we got to the coast of England, Bobbie came on the interphone and said, 'This is the first time I ever thought that I would be glad to see this damned country.' We all felt the same way. I smoked two packs of cigarettes after we could take our oxygen masks off. We had been under fighter attack for eight minutes and in flak for 45 minutes. We had been in the largest air battle ever since the war started.

"The German fighters were Hermann Göring's famed yellow nosed boys. We had 7.6mm machine gun holes all over the ship and a hole in the tail big enough to put a wash tub through from a 20mm cannon burst. When we got out of the ship every body was then waiting for us asking questions about everything. I was so sick at heart I just sat down on my equipment bag and couldn't say anything. I realized then that the crew of 'O'Neil and Company' were very lucky boys. I couldn't get over Passeger going down. On the lottery in the barracks the night before, he drew Merseburg (the winner), the lucky devil. There were sure lots of empty bunks in my room that night. Our group had lost 13 bombers. Mullins, pilot of the lead ship in our element, got back on two engines after we had counted him as Number 14. The next day we had to help sort out the fellows' clothes. They were to be packed and sent to their families. This was one job that I did not like. They had 13 new B-17s here now."

The 35 aircraft in the 457th Bomb Group formation, meanwhile, were blown 35 miles off course and away from the target by a 50-knot wind. They flew on alone and sought the secondary target at Bernberg. The "Fireballs" were out on a limb, and at the mercy of more than 400 fighters that were in the vicinity. At 1248 hours the "Fireballs" had still not joined the rest of the divisional bomber stream and came under attack from about 40 German fighters. Attacks were made on the low squadron from 6 to 8 o'clock low. The American gunners opened up on the 109s and 190s, and some fighters did go down. But then one by one the "Fireballs" fell out of formation and hurtled down. *Lady Margaret* had its fin severed by the wing of a passing FW 190, and several other hits sent it down in flames. It exploded shortly afterwards with only two men baling out in time. *Prop Wash* followed her down, and another seven B-17s exploded or crashed, with a further nine being badly damaged. Only the timely intervention by Mustangs saved the group from total annihilation.

John O. "Rams" Ramsey, navigator in *Lil Sergeant*, flown by Lieutenant Bernard Iwanciow, recalls:

"What a day! And we flew tail end Charlie position (the last ship in the Group - that gets all the prop wash) in the final three-plane element of the 'C' Squadron (Low). Only a great pilot like Bernard Iwanciow could hold a bomber in the 'tail end Charlie' position all the way to the target and back like he did at Merseburg. We were in intense flak for 18 minutes and heavy flak for 30 minutes. We had practically a visual run. Almost immediately after we dropped our bombs the 493rd was attacked by six Me 163s. Two of them made passes at our squadron, one at a time, from the rear. Our top turret and tail turret gunners got in good shots at them as they came in at 6 o'clock. One Me 163 went straight up ahead of us at about 500mph. He then went to our right wing (3 o'clock), turned and went high to 12 o'clock, then on around to 9 o'clock. He apparently thought we were going to fall behind and be separated from the Group. You can bet that was furthest from our minds. He must have decided that we were not about to become easy prey and he turned directly away from us at 7 o'clock. Phil Eannarino, the tail gunner and Gordon A. Nelsen, flight engineer-top turret gunner, were both putting a lot of lead at him. Phil's gun turret jammed. We saw Nelsen's tracers hit the Me 163 and it exploded immediately about 400 yards behind us. Nelsen was later awarded a cluster to the Air Medal for the first Me 163 downed by a bomber gunner - and apparently, one of the only two destroyed by bombers during the entire war. Sergeant Ward, our nose gunner, stopped a piece of flak in his flak suit. He wasn't hurt. Planes were exploding and going down everywhere. While we were under attack Lieutenant Colonel George Whitlock's plane[1099] received a direct flak hit between the #2 engine and the fuselage after leaving the target and before the Rally Point."

Henry B. Skeen, pilot of *Milk Run*,[1100] was flying his first mission with an experienced crew, and saw his leader's plane beside them blow up. "An absolutely terrifying trip":

"Whitlock's left wing was on fire, as well as the section from the radio compartment to the tail. The left elevator had been shot away, and the aircraft dropped off to the left, under control. After losing altitude slowly for almost a minute, it went into a steep dive and passed through the undercast out of sight. No chutes were seen."

John O. "Rams" Ramsey continues:

"A few minutes later a second plane [*Straighten Up and Fly Right - The Rock* flown by Lieutenant Robert I. Proudfit, Jr., in the 863rd Bomb Squadron] was shot out of formation by flak while leaving the target area. 'Red' Ivey was his navigator. The flak caused the #2 engine to begin smoking badly and the ship fell behind the rest of the formation and peeled off to one side under control. The B-17 crashed at Pogau."[1101]

Navigator 1st Lieutenant Lawrence W. Rasmussen, who was flying his 8th mission in the 493rd Bomb Group in *Sweet Sue*, wrote:

"I hardly can explain all that happened. Just after leaving the IP, a hunk of flak came through my compartment. It pierced the side of the ship, went through a walk around bottle, through part of a rubber life raft knocking it and my briefcase way across the compartment, hit me, before finally piercing the floor and lodging between the floor and under skin of the plane.

"After we dropped our bombs we kept on straight instead of turning. I've never seen so much flak in all my life. After we turned off the bomb run we were attacked by a Me 163, a very beautiful ship that can climb straight up. It went by so fast that I could only get a few shots at it. After the attack we saw Colonel Whitlock's ship catch fire and drop out of formation. Then we saw another flamer but it was earth bound out of control. We were in intense flak for over 30 minutes, entering the flak defense of Merseburg, Halle, Leipzig and Wiesbaden. The formation got screwed up when the Colonel went down - he was lead - so we crossed the wide flak area three times. When we got back we saw stragglers all the way damaged badly.

"We took stock of our *Sweet Sue*. The flak hole in my compartment, three gas tanks shot out, one motor about gone, a hole in the leading edge of wing [piercing the main spar just outside outboard starboard engine, a hole a foot away from ball gunner and several other perforations not worth mentioning. We were mighty thankful to be back off this one. We had been decoys to scare out the Luftwaffe and did. P-51s, P-47s and P-38s had a field day just north and east of us, knocking down almost 200 fighters. We lost 41 bombers and 30 some fighters. Dumped ten 500lb GPs somewhere near the target. (*Sweet Sue* was junked after this mission. Main spar was severed, which nearly took the wing off, the auxiliary spar brought the ship back)."

The 493rd Bomb Group flak officer, in his November report, stated that, including the two planes lost, 81% of the Group planes on the 2 November mission suffered flak damage. Altogether, the 8th lost 40 bombers and 28 fighters this day.[1102] Losses were so bad on this mission that groups were stood down on 3 November.

On 4 November more than 1000 heavies operating in six forces attacked synthetic oil plants, oil refineries, and a benzol plant at Bottrop, Gelsenkirchen, Hamburg, Harburg, Misburg, and Neunkirchen. Seventeen fighter groups, including a 9th Air Force group, provided support. Next day, Sunday, 5 November 1944, more than 1200 heavies attacked marshaling yards at Frankfurt/Main, Ludwigshafen, Karlsruhe, Hanau, and Kaiserlautern, and the synthetic oil plant at Ludwigshafen and rail facilities at Landau escorted by 15 fighter groups. Despite the escort, 37 heavies and fighters failed to return. Two of the B-17s that went missing were from the 490th Bomb Group. One was an 849th Squadron B-17G flown by 1st Lieutenant Robert L. Jackson. His tail turret gunner, Sgt Francis A. Malachowski, who at 23 was the oldest man on the crew, and thus nicknamed "Pops," recalls:

"On this mission, our 15th, the primary target was to have been Metz but when we got there it was covered in with 10/10 cloud so we flew on to our secondary target at Ludwigshafen. Over the target flak was intense and seconds after bombs-away we received two direct-hits, one near the waist and the other near the right wing. Our ship immediately fell out of formation and apparently collided with [*Penns-Belle*] Lieutenant [Clarence E.] Bridwell's ship below us in the [848th] low squadron. As I was to find out later, the sole survivor from the plane we hit was Paul Finot, tail gunner who survived because the tail section was separated from the rest of the aircraft enabling him to bale out.

"On the bomb run over the target the flak burst near the waist section mostly riddled my flak vest and not me, tearing it off my right shoulder and severing a 'chute riser so that only *one* was left to hook up to my 'chute pack. I was hit though by one fragment that lodged near the bridge of my nose and right eye and a few bits that pierced my helmet and lodged in my head. The impact pinned me against my guns for what seemed like an eternity. Bleeding profusely I finally managed to crawl towards the tail escape hatch and tried to kick it open. The release gear was jammed, so I semi-consciously crawled towards the waist hatch but found only blue sky. The tail was severed and I was coming down alone. It was almost a vertical dive and to this day I have no memory of getting out or pulling the ripcord."

Sergeant Francis W. "Frank" McKinley, a gunner in Lieutenant G. D. Lyon's crew in the 490thGroup, who had flown their first mission two weeks earlier, adds:

> "It is a very sobering sight to see your comrades shot out of the sky and no parachutes sighted coming down. We were all saddened on the way back, thinking about the loss of the two crews - 18 men who will not be with us in the mess hall tonight. At times like that you start to calculate the odds against completing your own 35 missions."

S/Sgt Richard Skinner, in Captain Earl H. Johnson's crew in the 861st Squadron, 493rd Bomb Group, were flying their 24th mission[1103] on 5 November. Since their first mission to Lisieux on *D-Day*, Skinner had flown 15 missions in a B-24 called *The Witch* before transferring to a B-17 when the Group re-equipped with Fortresses. Skinner recalled:

> "Captain Johnson's crew and my Squadron mates were some of the finest men I have ever known. We were now a lead crew. We had two extra men with us, a group bombardier and a group photographer to take pictures of the bomb strikes. I had become more frightened with each mission and I was grateful every night that we made it home to a clean bed and excellent meals. The bed and food were the two main reasons I did not want to be a member of the ground forces. On 5 November our plane was hit by anti-aircraft fire just after bombs away over a chemical plant at Ludwigshafen. Over the target the anti-aircraft fire was very heavy and we had just released the bombs when we got hit and lost our No.2 engine. We were flying at 27,000ft. We started dropping in altitude fast. We took another hit of anti-aircraft fire and with in one minute, maybe less than that, Captain Johnson gave the dreaded order to bale out. I was flying in the waist and I removed my oxygen mask to go to the escape door and pull the handle. It was supposed to salvo and fall off. It wouldn't and I couldn't be expending energy fast with no oxygen, but when your life is at stake you don't think and I was pushing and pulling it trying to get it to fall off. I passed out from lack of oxygen and woke up floating down with my parachute open. I knew the plane had blown up because there were pieces of aluminium floating around me like leaves. I was bleeding from the ears and nose, my hands and face were burned, my right shoulder was injured and I no longer had any boots on my feet. I had no idea how my parachute opened. I landed in a plowed field in broad daylight. It was windy, wet and cold. I could not get out of my parachute."[1104]

Despite the mauling of 5 November, the 8th was out again on the 6th when over 1000 heavies in six forces attacked oil and chemical installations, a canal aqueduct, and an aircraft repair plant, as well as three marshaling yards and several targets of opportunity in north and northwest Germany. Sixteen fighter groups provided support and later strafed ground targets in Northwest Germany and Holland. Wayne Tex Frye, navigator in Jack O'Neil's crew in *The Witch* in the 91st Bomb Group, went to the oil refinery at Harburg, on the southern edge of Hamburg. The day before when they had gone to the Frankfurt marshaling yards Frye had been "really jittery." They had flown spare, and as a consequence they had been put in the low squadron, which on that occasion had been a good thing, because the high "got hell shot out of them," although *The Witch* had several holes. On the 6th Frye noted:

> "Flying time - 7:45. Time on oxygen-5 hours. Bomb load: 6-1000# GP. Altitude, 25,000ft. The temperature, -39°. This was really a rough one. The flak had me scared plenty. It was awful close, intense and accurate. Major Taylor's ship, our lead ship, had a direct burst in the waist. We were flying right behind them. A piece of the plane came back and stuck in our No. 2 engine cowling. The ship buckled as it hit, but they kept going. They got the ship back to England but I'll never know how that ship flew. They couldn't get the bomb bay doors closed and that didn't help them any. The waist gunner and the radio-operator were killed and the radar operator was hit in the leg and later lost it. These targets all are rough now. We had 134 holes in the '*Witch*' today. She is getting quite 'patchy.'"

The 8th was stood down on 7 November, and then on the 8th over 2650 heavies attacked the synthetic oil plants at Merseburg-Leuna again, as well as the marshaling yard at Rheine and five targets of opportunity. Bad weather forced the recall of 350 other heavies. Eighteen fighter groups provided support and later strafed ground targets. 23 fighters failed to return. On Thursday, 9 November, the heavies returned to tactical missions in support of General George Patton's 3rd Army, currently halted at the fortress city of Metz. The bombers were called in to bomb German lines of communication at Saarbrücken, and also enemy gun emplacements to the east and south of Metz to enable the advance through Belgium to continue. The mission was deemed top priority, and at bases throughout East Anglia Fortresses taxied out in the mist and bad visibility. The conditions were instrumental in the loss of eight bombers during take-offs and landings, and further disasters befell some groups as the mission progressed. It was Lieutenant Kenneth H. French, bombardier in Lieutenant Curtis R. McKinney's crew in the 490th Bomb Group's 27th mission:

> "We took off this morning before dawn at 0730 hours, about an hour late. Two aircraft went off the end of the runway and though they weren't seriously damaged they did put that runway out of action and we had to change to the other one. We climbed up to bombing altitude, which was 18000ft. We only just managed to get into formation as the Group was leaving for Division assembly. Our primary target was to have been in support of our troops but we couldn't bomb there because of the overcast. We diverted to our secondary target, the marshaling yards at the north end of Saarbrücken, where we had been briefed for 175 guns. We did see a lot of flak and rockets but had none close to us at all. We carried six 1000lb GPs and the method of release was salvo for the primary and 150ft spacing for the secondary. This mission was all messed up - a 10/10 undercast at the target didn't help - and the official estimate of the bombing was 'missed the target'. I believe they hit a long way short. Air support was good and no enemy aircraft were sighted or reported. We got back just in time as bad weather, a mixture of snow and rain, closed in within 15 minutes of landing. Time of mission was 6 hours."

While on the bomb run over Saarbrücken, the 452nd Bomb Group encountered an extremely accurate and intense flak barrage. *Lady Janet*, flown by 1st Lieutenant Donald J. Gott and 2nd Lieutenant William E. Metzger, had three engines badly damaged and the No.1 engine set on fire. It began windmilling, and the No.2 engine was failing rapidly. No.4

showered flames back towards the tail assembly. Flares were ignited in the cockpit, and the flames were fueled by hydraulic fluid leaking from severed cables. The engineer was wounded in the leg, and a shell fragment had severed the radio operator's arm below his elbow. Metzger left his seat, stumbled back to the radio room, and applied a tourniquet to stop the bleeding. However, the radio operator was so weak from pain that he fell unconscious. The bombs were still aboard, and Gott was faced with the prospect of the aircraft exploding at any moment. He therefore decided to fly the stricken Fortress to Allied territory a few miles distant and attempt a crash landing. The bombs were salvoed over enemy territory, and all excess equipment was thrown overboard. Metzger unselfishly gave his parachute to one of the gunners after his had been damaged in the fire. As *Lady Janet* neared friendly territory, Metzger went to the rear of the Fortress and told everyone to bale out. S/Sgt Herman B. Krimminger, tail gunner, had died when his parachute had opened accidentally and snagged the blazing B-17's tailplane when he was pulled outside the bomber. Metzger then went back to his seat, and the two pilots prepared for a crash landing with only one engine still functioning and the other three on fire. An open field was spotted, and Gott brought *Lady Janet* in. At about 100ft the fire took hold of the fuel tanks and the bomber exploded, killing Gott, Metzger, and T/Sgt Robert A. Dunlap, the radio operator, instantly. Both pilots were awarded posthumous Medals of Honor.

Other crews came through unscathed, or so they thought. Flying his first mission this day was 19-year-old Lieutenant Bob Browne in the 487th Bomb Group at Lavenham:

> "The excitement of my first mission over enemy territory crowded out almost all thoughts except an expectation of seeing fiery Messerschmitt fighters flashing past with cannons blazing. But all my expectations were in vain. Nothing exciting happened. No fiery fighters, no flashing cannon, no exploding anti-aircraft shells nearby. Frankly, I was disappointed. At approximately 1500 hours I was swinging my B-17 about the circular concrete hardstand and the big ship halted in its sharp arc. As the engines were being cut, I could already see my crew chief, Sgt Jim Haley, racing down the taxi strip in a jeep, heading towards our Fort. I believe he got his jeep training at Le Mans! He stopped just short of the No.1 engine propeller arc, just as the props were coming to rest and was coming to meet me as I swung down through the bomber's forward escape door, seven feet to the concrete below.
>
> "'Boy,' I yelled at him, 'if all my missions are like this milk-run, I've got it made.'
>
> "Jim was a veteran. He had already wet-nursed six Fortress crews, efficiently keeping their ships running smoother than any in the group. I detected a rather incredulous look on his face as he said 'Lieutenant, let me show you something.' Then he methodically guided me on a tour around the Fort. Before we were finished, he had shown me no less than 27 jagged shrapnel holes in my ship, all from enemy anti-aircraft fire!"

Over 40 heavies and fighters were lost on 9 November when over 1100 heavies in conjunction with 9th Air Force aircraft hit targets in the Metz and Thionville area as the U.S. Third Army forces launched a full-scale attack on Metz. It was Norman K. Andrew's 11th mission. He wrote:

> "Up at 0200 for 0300 pre-briefing. Target: a honey right behind the lines. Some forts holding up General Patton. We were group deputy lead. For a while I thought we were going to lead. The primary was visual - secondary PFF. We couldn't see the primary until we were right over it - so we hit the secondary, the marshaling yards at Saarbrücken. We had flak in the high and low squadrons - one ship in the low caught on fire and blew up. Three chutes seen - 2 were on fire.[1105] Next day [when more than 600 B-17s and B-24s attacked airfields, marshaling yards and a chemical plant supported by 14 fighter groups] the CQ woke Bob and Chuck at 0350 for target study. Then he woke Jack and me at 0355 for 0430 pre-briefing. Target: marshaling yard just south of Koblenz, Germany (Oberlaunstein). We flew deputy group lead until just before the IP. We then took over the lead for a *Micro-H* bomb run.[1106] I called Whittnell just before the IP to see if he had it. He said yes, then, as we turned we slid into the Trier flak area. No damage. I got a *Gee* fix from the Ruhr chain at Bombs Away. We were right on course and 3½ miles from the target. Load 11 500-lb GPs."

On 11 November more than 400 heavies attacked Oberlaunstein, Koblenz, and Rheine marshaling yards, an oil plant at Schloven-Buer, and a synthetic oil plant at Bottrop supported by eleven fighter groups. Navigator Lieutenant Lawrence W. Rasmussen flew his 8th mission in the 493rd Bomb Group:

> "Today we were clay pigeons. We were one of the six *Chaff* ships, which carried special *Chaff* bombs, which were to explode five seconds after dropping. We went over Koblenz, our PFF target (marshaling yards) supposedly to aid the rest of the group. We went over, getting inaccurate flak 29,300ft at -45° C. However, Parker got a motor shot out. We saw a Me 163 on our way back - the jet plane attacked Parker, getting another of his engines and rumour says killed his waist gunner. Parker landed at Brussels. We got back OK, got special interrogation and I had the pleasure of telling Colonel Gerhard his *Chaff* bomb concoction was of no avail. Two holes picked up over target. The group was late and didn't even go over target so mission was just flak practice for Jerry."

No missions were flown until Thursday, 16 November, when the 8th returned to Western Europe to provide support for the advancing British and U.S. armies.[1107] The mission was very carefully planned to avoid bombing friendly troops near the targets just east of Aachen. After the "softening-up" bombardment by the heavies, the ground troops would advance on the enemy strongholds. The Allied artillery would fire red smoke shells every 500 yards along the front, and barrage balloons were also placed along the edge of the area. Other devices, such as radio signals on the SCS-51 sets normally used for instrument landings over England, were implemented. The use of the radio was especially worthwhile when 8/10ths cloud covered the front lines and helped ensure accurate bombing.

Sergeant Jim Collins, a gunner in Lieutenant Cleaves' crew in the 490th Bomb Group, recalls:

> "The mission today was to Düren, near the Siegfried Line where our ground troops were in tough combat with the Germans. It would have been uneventful had it not been for our experience on take-off. We were the 490th's lead ship and as we picked up speed along the runway in the wee, small hours of the morning the weather was very dismal to say the least. It was hard to see more than ten feet and as usual I was saying my prayers for the aircraft to get up safely. Suddenly, the end of the runway loomed up; the plane shuddered and I heard thudding sounds, as though clumps of earth were hitting us. Surprisingly, though, the aircraft roared on through the overcast darkness. Our intercom was deathly quiet. It was the policy of Lieutenant Cleaves, our pilot, not to use it unless there

was something really significant to report. The first sound I heard on the intercom was a whimpering noise like a small child ready to weep, then the skipper's voice said, 'Come in 'Judge'. What do we have down there?'[1108] There was no answer from the nose so Cleaves asked Glenn Case, the engineer, to go down there and see what was wrong. Casey later said that when he got into the nose there was blood on Huser's face and flight gear and that Huser was in shock. Jim Campbell, the bombardier, had become unplugged from the intercom and was also confused. Casey then saw feet, feathers and other body parts of large birds, about the size of crows, seemingly welded into the Plexiglas. After a few minutes of communications on the intercom between the forward crewmembers it was revealed that on take-off we had flushed a large flock of birds that were roosting on the grass off the end of the main runway. After we got above the overcast it was possible to see the bloody mess sticking out of the engine cowling and blood all over the wing. Although two of our engines heated up we led the low squadron to the Duren area and carried out the mission. On the way back orders came through that we were to land at RAF Carnaby because the weather had closed in at Eye.

"As we landed at Carnaby we were shocked to see all the fire and rescue units rush over to our ramp the minute we came to a halt. One medic dressed in a white coat ran up to me shouting 'Who got it?' Not understanding what he was talking about I said, 'Who got what?' to which he replied, 'Turn around and look at your ship.' It was then that we all discovered what a bloody sight the plane was. The crew then pieced all the story together. We enjoyed the hospitality of the RAF for two days before getting back to our base at Eye."

General Doolittle congratulated all groups, saying:

"... the 8th Air Force performed one of its most outstanding operations. The force took off under extremely adverse base weather conditions and successfully attacked targets on the immediate front of our ground troops almost exclusively by instrument technique with very good results. Ground commanders were highly pleased and report all bombs on or near the targets. Only one bomb fell wide but did no damage, with no injuries to friendly troops. It was a difficult task well done and I commend you for the capable and efficient manner in which it was conducted."

On Tuesday, 21 November, the 8th returned to Merseburg for the first of three more raids on the refineries in a week. Merseburg had become synonymous with flak, and crews hated all missions to the city. Herman L. Hager, radio operator in Lieutenant Frederick C. Wisner's crew in *Zoomeriago*,[1109] in the 603rd Bomb Squadron in the 398th Bomb Group, had already been there on two previous occasions, and he knew what to expect:

"To say the least, shivers always ran up and down our spines when we saw this mission on the map. Like Schweinfurt and others, this was one mission on which you could count your blessings if you returned unharmed."

The 398th Bomb Group dispatched 37 Fortresses this day, led by Major Templeman flying lead with the 602nd Bomb Squadron. Assembly and flight to the target were as briefed, but as the three squadrons started to take interval prior to the IP, dense and persistent contrails and a heavy layer of cirrus cloud were encountered. The group climbed through the cloud layers to 30,000ft, but the squadrons became separated in the process. The 602nd and 603rd Bomb Squadrons dropped their bombs on secondary targets using PFF, while the 601st bombed targets of opportunity. Shortly after the target, the 603rd Bomb Squadron began moving back into a defensive formation for the return home. About ten minutes after leaving the target at an altitude of 29,000ft the 603rd was still flying alone. Suddenly, ten Focke-Wulf 190s shot out from the clouds and made a frontal attack on the squadron, shooting down seven Fortresses. Among them was *Zoomeriago*. Herman Hager recalls:

"We received a direct hit in our left wing. The great amount of smoke seemed to fill up the entire aircraft. We didn't seem to be able to maintain the speed nor the altitude needed to stay with the formation so Fred Wisner left his position and tried to hang on at 'Purple Heart Corner.' Moments passed which seemed like hours. We hung on for dear life, at least hoping to make France. However, our luck ran out and six fighters took us on for a sure kill. We requested fighter support but not soon enough, I suppose. It was 1157 hours and *Zoomeriago* seemed to be burning everywhere. The magnesium alloy skin was actually on fire. I looked back towards the tail to see that Dave Labey, the tail gunner, had baled out. I left my position only to find the ball turret gunner, John Butler, without electric power to position the turret so he could get out. I immediately started hand cranking so he could exit and, after a brief signal of thanks, he lost no time in baling out. Marvin Clarke, the waist gunner, had released the emergency handle on the waist door and insisted I go first. By this time the ship was flat spinning. I sat at the threshold of the door and rolled into space. After pulling my ripcord the only other figure to come out of the waist must have been Marvin Clarke. His 'chute blossomed at approximately a quarter of a mile away at about 23,000ft. There was 10/10ths cloud cover so the earth was not visible. I found out later that the tops of the clouds were at about 10,000ft and the base at about 600ft."[1110]

It was on 21 November that Lieutenant Kenneth H. French, bombardier in Lieutenant Curtis R. McKinney's crew in the 490th Bomb Group, flew his 28th mission:

"Our briefed target for today was a synthetic oil refinery at Lutzkendorf, about 8 miles from Merseburg. We took off at 0810 hours and climbed in good weather to our assembly altitude of 17,000ft. Our aircraft had a fairly good position in the formation as we were flying deputy lead in the lead squadron. Bad weather had been forecast in front of us and even though we had climbed to 28,500ft to try to get over it we still ran into it when we reached about 8°E. The 1st Division also went to the same target today. They went in first at a bombing altitude believed to have been 21,000ft or less. Fighters hit them between the clouds and we were told that about 20 bombers were shot down. Our escort of P-51s took out 60 enemy fighters. Nearing the target, we received a call that there were fighters in the area but none attacked us. As we were approaching the IP we ran into more bad weather and were forced to turn around. The intention then was to attack our secondary target at Osnabrück but the PFF ship lost it so we diverted again to bomb factories at Lingen. In trying to find this target we flew over a lot of flak areas and our aircraft was holed in seven places. We took two hits in the right wing and one in the left, one in the Plexiglas nose just above my head, one just in front of the co-pilot, one in the horizontal stabilizer, another in the fuselage, just missing the ball turret and a final one in the pilot's oxygen bottle. Our ship suffered more damage on this one mission than it had in all the previous ones put together. There was no flak on the target, though.

"We carried twelve 500lb GPs with 1/10 and 1/40 fuses and dropped them from 28,000ft at an intervolometer setting of 150ft with the same ground speed. The bomb bay doors had to be manually cranked shut when the retracting motor froze up. The results of the bombing were later assessed as 'good to 'very good.' Weather over the Eye field was still clear when we landed. Time of mission was 6hr 20 min."

Leutnant Herbert Neuner, 2nd *Staffel*/JG1, recalls:

"On 21 November combats began again in dreadful weather: rain and fog. Our formation was directed due south towards a formation of *Viermots*. Suddenly, voices crackled over the intercom: '*Attention, Indianer behind us!*' Our Gruppe was split up. I dived but was hit several times. Having noticed that I was not being followed, I gained altitude and saw a large circle of aircraft. In the circle, aircraft, one behind the other, were weaving. I picked up speed, got behind a P-47 and shot it down. I broke away immediately and set course for home. By chance, the direction was good and I landed at Greifswald. If my memory is correct, only two or three of my companions joined me. We waited for further news. It was very bad: the absentees were posted missing and hour by hour their deaths were confirmed."[1111]

Major Edward F. "Ed" Blum of the 490th, formerly the 849th Squadron CO and now the Operations Officer, recalls the Saturday, 25 November, mission to Merseburg:

"Today I was scheduled to fly as the Command Pilot for the 490th Group lead on our mission to bomb the synthetic oil complex at Merseburg, one of the most heavily defended targets, with an estimated 120 anti-aircraft guns. We had our normal briefing and take-off and a beautiful day for a flight into Germany. The 490th was second group in the bombing stream for the 8th Air Force. As we came up to the IP, it became apparent that the lead group in front of us had picked up the wrong target and was going well north of the assigned one. We knew that we had located the right target so we decided not to follow them.

"By now the bombardier had taken over the aircraft and was controlling the Norden bombsight. As we bore down on the target, which was partially obscured by a large smoke screen (we were using radar to guide us), the bomb doors were opened and on the final approach, about half-a-mile before the release point, anti-aircraft fire hit us in the belly of the plane. The impact jolted loose our bomb load, including the signal flare that advised the rest of the ships in our 34-plane group to bomb at that point, with the result that we all dropped prematurely.

"As we turned off the target ground we now found ourselves leading the bomber stream because the real leader had gone well north of us. We had received a pretty good blow in the belly of the plane so we started checking around to see what damage had been done; fortunately there was nothing really serious. It soon became apparent, however, that the periodic compass, the main instrument for getting us home, wasn't functioning properly. I didn't feel we should be leading the entire Air Force with a damaged compass so I tried to communicate with the deputy lead to discuss what we should do. We were unable to make contact with our deputy lead, but we did manage to talk with the fighter escort, through whom I was able to get the next group in line, the third in the original bomber stream, to take over the lead as our group swung wide on the next turn to the west. After that turn we swung back in line behind the new leaders and followed them back to England without incident. Except for picking up some battle damage, we managed to get through that mission remarkably well, though we did have a ripped bomb cluster half-a-mile short of the target!"[1112]

Late in the morning of Sunday, 26 November, over 1000 Fortresses and Liberators, escorted by 15 fighter groups, headed for the hydrogenation synthetic oil plant at Misburg, near Hanover, a target partially destroyed three weeks before. Timing began to go awry, and the 1st Bomb Division formation was spread over 40 miles instead of 20 as briefed, and the three escorting groups could not hope to protect all the B-17s.[1113] Fifty FW 190s of III./JG 1 attacked the tightly packed boxes of bombers on a wide front between Uelzen and Perleberg. Three escorting groups of P-51s battled with the enemy for about 20 minutes.[1114]

1st Lieutenant Cy Broman, pilot of *Hubert*, 92nd Bomb Group, Hamburg, 26 November, recalls:

"We were well into Germany and at bombing altitude (27,500ft) when a tube in the turbo-supercharging system of #1 blew. The engineer, Matt Gravanic, looked at the equipment and said there was nothing he could do without a spare. At this altitude, without a supercharger, the engine had about as much power (or drag) as if it were feathered. Since we would be coming down later we left it running. We were about at the IP when #3 ran away from having too much applied power. Obviously we couldn't keep in formation so started to descend. No point in aborting at this time as we were so close to the target and we wouldn't have received credit for the mission. As a result we went over Hamburg at 20,000ft. Since we weren't flying formation I got a good look at the city and remember an impression of red roofs. We didn't have a bombsight but our navigator, Larry Moore, had been a bombardier before checking out on the 'G-Box', so at least we dropped bombs, a la RAF, on the city.

"At the time we were the only plane over Hamburg so the AA gunners used us for target practice. Each gun seemed to be aimed individually instead of sending up a box barrage. Larry stood up in the "astrodome" looking back and telling me which direction to turn depending on the last bursts of flak. We cost the Germans a lot of Reichsmarks that day. One burst was close enough to come through the right side behind the co-pilot, Walt Woodrow, knocking out his oxygen system and tearing a hole in Matt Cravanic's pants. The rest of the bomber stream had turned South to make a Cook's Tour of Germany (avoiding flak zones). I put the nose down to pick up speed and turned Northwest to get to the North Sea as quickly as possible. We went over Cuxhaven at 15,000ft and spent some more of Hitler's money. About this time I had the autopilot on, oxygen mask off, enjoying a cigarette, feet up on the rudder bars, when Walt picked up the mike and announced over the intercom, 'Don't shoot unless they shoot first'. I jumped up and said 'What?' He pointed off our right wing and there were four FW 190s almost flying formation with us. I got on the 'horn' and called our Group Leader (Foxhole) to get Fighter Control to send some '51s. Larry Moore, in his excitement, gave me the coordinates as being somewhere over Denmark (I heard about that later). He quickly changed them and I relayed the information to Foxhole. The 190s pulled ahead and made a pursuit curve approach from 12 o'clock, went under us so close you could almost reach out and touch them. To this day I have no idea why they didn't shoot. We were way off the main Bomber Stream, at a relatively low altitude with all four 'fans' going (we hadn't feathered #3 either, because even with it being pulled way back (the throttle) we were getting a little power from it), so perhaps they thought we were a German 'decoy'. Or perhaps they were on a training mission without ammo. Who knows? Somewhat later a couple of flights of '51s did show up. We were out over the North Sea by this time headed for home at 10,000ft. We had power again from #1. By coincidence we reformed on our Group as we reached the coast of England. Because of our experiences I had the 'honor' of landing first that day."

At this point the Liberators, now over Wittenberg, changed direction and headed south. Then they flew west past Stendal to cross the high ground at Gardelegen, and headed for the target from the east. All three *Gruppen* of JG 301 had taken off, and they converged on the bombers just as the leading elements were approaching Hanover. 150 enemy fighters broke through and carried out mass wave tail attacks on the Liberators out of the sun in waves of three and five. Mustang pilots and the B-24 gunners replied to the onslaught with heavy machine gun fire. Three FW 190s were shot down and their pilots killed, while over Rethen *Oberleutnant* Vollert, 5./JG 301 CO was intercepted by two Mustangs while hard on the tail of a Liberator and was downed after a tense dogfight.

Without fighter escort the 491st Bomb Group, which was the last over the target, was extremely vulnerable. The anti-aircraft guns ceased firing and over a hundred fighters bore in for the kill. Lieutenant Colonel Charles C. Parmele, CO of the 854th Bomb Squadron, flying as Air Commander in *Ragged But Right*, piloted by Captain Joseph R. Metcalf, decided to miss the flak ridden target area. He ordered a sudden left turn to the south and thence to the west to reach the original Rally Point with the rest of the bombers in formation. This may have been a mistake, as the fighter attacks from the south and east appeared to be on the increase. Parmele's decision effectively split the group, and placed the 854th Bomb Squadron about 1500 yards behind the leading 855th Bomb Squadron and off to the left by itself. At 1240, two minutes after bombs away, the 491st was attacked over the Teutoburger Wald and the Ems by about 75 single-engined fighters of III. and IV./JG 27 from Rheine, Hopsten, Achmer, and Hesepe, and IV./JG 54 from Vorden. The enemy fighters dived through the 854th, flying low-left, breaking up the squadron formation and attacking again, alone, or in pairs. They singled out stragglers and made their attack from 5 to 7 o'clock, a little high.

S/Sgt Al Oliveira, right waist gunner in Lieutenant Hal Fandell's crew in the 855th Bomb Squadron, recalls:

"Being the armourer gunner of our crew, I was required to remove the bomb fuse pins prior to approaching the target. On each of my 16 missions, I kept the pins and jotted information on each tag. On the Misburg raid, I noted we carried 12 500lb bombs. Also noted on the tag is that we encountered heavy flak to the point of being intense. News accounts at that time reflected that over 100 enemy fighters attacked us. Our Squadron was flying high right while the 853rd held the low left position. After leaving the target area, the 853rd developed a 'straggler' and assumed the high right position to allow the 'straggler' to maintain a position in the formation. The 855th then dropped to the low left position. I then had a remarkable view of what transpired. After leaving the target area enemy fighters came from high and to the rear of our formation. The 853rd flying high right was hit first and B-24s were exploding with engines falling in flames as well as bombers angling downward trailing smoke and flames. During this action I saw only three parachutes before the fighters turned their attention to the 855th.

"I clearly recall a FW 190 at my right waist position with cannon bursts exploding by the right wing of our B 24. I can also envision the German pilot with his oxygen mask appearing to be looking straight at me as I returned fire. On the left side of the 190 there was painted on the fuselage below the canopy, five American flag symbols reflecting his record of 'kills'. I continued firing and saw smoke coming from his engine cowl. Being excited, I fired thru our own vertical stabilizer. Between the stabilizer and the tail section, I saw the 190 spiral downward trailing smoke. There was no parachute. This action was confirmed by Lieutenant Jack Kolstad, navigator.

"Just about this time, a cannon shell exploded by the left waist window and S/Sgt Bill Meerdo, left waist gunner, fell against my machine gun and disengaged the 50 caliber from it's mount. I applied first aid and morphine to no avail. Bill had taken shrapnel in the neck and was killed instantly. Tail gunner S/Sgt Arzie Richardson could do nothing but watch as cannon fire hit his turret armour plate. His guns had frozen. Bomb bay doors were buckled and torn from flak. Control cables were severed and hanging in the waist section. Hal Fandell did an outstanding job of flying the plane back to England with the use of trim tabs. As for the 491st being singled out, I can only surmise it could have been the straggler, or to cover it briefly, a matter of being at the right place at the right time."

Wave after wave of fighters tore through the Low Squadron. Coming directly out of the sun at 10 o'clock high, the *Luftwaffe* attacked in waves of up to eight abreast, breaking away below the bombers. About ten waves attacked, followed by simultaneous attacks from 3 and 9 o'clock by German fighters four abreast or in echelon. When the attacks finally subsided, no less than 16 Liberators in the 491st had been blasted out of the sky in the space of just 15 minutes. Further bomber losses were prevented by the timely arrival over the Minden Canal of eight P-51 Weather Scouts led by Bob Whitlow, which held the FW 190s at bay until reinforcements could arrive to save the dozen remaining B-24s.[1115] Command acted quickly to replace the 491st Bomb Group losses. The control Tower log entries for 26 November said, '*Sixteen replacement B-24s arrived from Stansted, Shades of Dawn Patrol*."

Norman K. Andrew had flown his 13th mission in the 487th Bomb Group on 26 November to the marshaling yard at Hamm, when he had "never seen so many planes in his life." On the 27th he was "really surprised" to be awakened at 0445 for 0530 pre-briefing. He wrote:

"It was a *Micro-H* run on the marshaling yard at Bingen on the Rhine. Looked like a milk run but there was quite a bit of battle damage from flak. Kramer was leading the group. They had their bombsight, electrical system and oxygen shot out. Aborted at the target. We led home, but only got credit for a squadron lead. I was sure glad to get the lead - we were really skirting three flak areas. We are due to lead the low tomorrow if it's PFF. Saw two V-2s taking off for London - they were still within 10° of vertical when they passed out of sight at least 55 to 60,000ft. Traveling from 500 to 800mph."

On Thursday, 30 November, about 1200 heavies set out to bomb four synthetic-oil refineries in Germany: the leading 1st Division force were given the synthetic plant at Zeitz; the 3rd Division, Merseburg, 20 miles to the north; and the Liberators, Lutzkendorf. Wayne Tex Frye, navigator in Jack O'Neil's crew in the 91st Bomb Group, which went to Zeitz, recalls:

"We were in range of the Merseburg guns. Flying time 8 hours. Time on oxygen, 4 hours. Temperature, -35°. Bomb load – 20 250lb GP delayed action bombs. Flak was intense and accurate. We lost an engine but Jack flew better formation with just three engines than most pilots could with all four. Jack had a wonderful reputation for flying tight formation. There were lots of planes lost. I saw bombers go down all over the sky. We had a visual run on the target but did not hit it. I saw a P-51 hit by flak and go down on fire. We lost three ships. The Germans shot down 56 bombers today with flak."[1116]

1st Lieutenant Bob Voss, pilot of *The Dorothy V* in the 94th Bomb Group, which was assigned Lutzkendorf, recalls that:

"Oil targets were the absolute roughest. When the routes to targets would be uncovered at the early morning briefings and those red ribbons extended to Leipzig, Merseburg and Lutzkendorf an immediate feeling of dread was evident throughout the room. Those were always the targets with the most defensive guns and the most probability of German fighters. I know that those who ended their combat days while attacking marshaling yards, missile sites, airfields and aircraft manufacturing plants and whatever other type targets might offer opinions somewhat different but in my mind the oil targets were those where there was no doubt of intense opposition."

Bob Browne, in the 487th Bomb Group at Lavenham, had completed five missions, and he thought, "only 30 to go" as he prepared for his sixth during the early hours of 30 November:

"It was still dark at 0400 hours when the corporal shook me, saying, 'It's time to go sir, briefing is at 0500 hours.' I looked at my Air Corps issue watch, just one hour to dress, bike over to the mess hall a mile away, get breakfast (probably the usual powdered eggs and Spam), then race to the operations building for the mission briefing. Ice on the roads made the bike trips almost as hazardous as the combat missions. And there was always that cold, penetrating English fog that permitted about ten yards' visibility, at best. The large briefing room was quiet in anticipation, as Colonel Robert Taylor III, the CO walked up on to the platform. Without saying a word, he yanked repeatedly at cords at one side of the 30ft-wide curtains, parting them until the large map of Western Europe was completely unveiled. There was a sudden outburst of mixed moaning and profanity. There was a sinking feeling within as I traced the bright red wool yarn fixed with pins, showing the proposed route for the day's mission on the map. The red yarn started about 40 miles northeast of London, at our base and after several turns, aimed straight at the heart of Germany, to the city of Merseburg. The veteran pilot seated at my right turned to me and said, 'Serves us right, I guess, for goofing that last raid five days ago.' He was referring to the 25 November mission to the same target, when one of the poorest displays of 8th Air Force 'precision bombing' resulted in such minor damage that Germany's hottest target - the synthetic oil refinery at Merseburg - was in full production again only 12 hours later.

"The Colonel spoke. 'OK, your attention please. Now, you all realize the fiasco of the last attempt to destroy this target. I'm personally leading this one and we're going to give the Krauts their hardest blow today. It's been said before but, I repeat, destroy Merseburg and the German war machine will stop in its tracks. This plant is so important to the Germans that they rush in their repair crews and have always had the damage repaired before sun-up the next day.' He paused briefly, then added, 'Intelligence tells us the place is seething with activity, indicating a massive anti-aircraft effort. And we already know from experience that if you even look like you're headed for Merseburg, they put up a maximum effort with ack-ack and fighters too.

"An hour later, my crew and I were at our positions inside *Fearless Fosdick,* as our Fort was named. A four-foot-high vivid picture of 'Lil' Abner' with a four-leaf clover, wishbone, horseshoe and a rabbit's foot, was painted on each side of the fuselage, just aft of the Plexiglas nose. I, along with the other crewmembers, had completed all the required oxygen mask and electrically heated flight suit connections and we were waiting for the green flare from the control tower to start engines. Sergeant Haley and his ground crew had completed turning each propeller through several revolutions and were standing by with fire extinguishers. The armament specialists had long since loaded twelve 5001b demolition bombs in the bomb bay and thousands of .50 caliber machine-gun rounds for the 13 guns on board. Suddenly, there was the signal! It left a green trace gracefully arcing from the walk high up on the control tower and drifted towards the center of the runways. Almost as one, the 48 four-engined bombers of the 487th Bomb Group began starting engines. The same thing was happening at many airfields peppering the southeast English countryside. Soon, our bombers were working their way single file towards the take-off position. One by one, at about 30 second intervals, a bomber would take position at the end of the runway, hold hard brakes until all throttles were wide open and engines straining, then release brakes and take off, disappearing into the dark fog. After what seemed like hours, my turn came and, with engines wide open, the big craft accelerated to attain take-off speed. The 5000ft runway was really too short for a Fortress with a crew of nine, three tons of bombs and tanks topped off at 2850 gallons of gasoline. Through the fog the emergency steel matting could be seen just a few feet ahead. The end of the asphalt zipped past and the big tires vibrated as they rolled across the perforated steel matting. Just 300ft of runway left and a tug on the control column indicated that the big bird wasn't about to part with the runway. I reached down instinctively for the flap switch, holding it in the 'down' position until the indicator showed one-third flaps. I pulled back steadily on the control column and the Fort shuddered sickeningly off the runway.

"I quickly switched on the prop de-icers. This was always disconcerting. It sounded as though the fuselage was being peppered with a massive volley of shotgun pellets as the props threw ice particles at high velocity. Flipping the landing gear switch upward, I watched the indicator until it showed full retraction. There was a disturbing resonance in the drone of the four 1200hp Wright Cyclone engines. Adjusting the throttles returned the engines to a pleasing synchronous drone. Climbing eastward, red and yellow flares could be seen arcing southward. These came from the colonel's ship, which would maintain a spiraling climb, firing flares at five-minute intervals, until his bomb group had formed in four squadrons of twelve airplanes each echeloned behind him.

"An hour later we were crossing the Channel, headed southeast for the French coastal town of Calais. Our altitude now was 26,000ft. We would continue a southeast course to Verdun, where Patton's artillery and tanks at this very moment were probably pounding. At Verdun we climbed to our mission altitude of 28,000ft and leveled off, adjusting engines to cruising. Suddenly, the colonel's Fort began a long left turn. Several bursts of 88mm anti-aircraft rounds could be seen about half a mile ahead. That was the usual line flak from the dual-purpose guns below. Normally, it wasn't too accurate at altitude. However, the next bursts came uncomfortably close as the city of Metz passed under my right wing. We were now in enemy territory! All crewmembers were tense now and adrenaline was running fast. Messerschmitt 109s and Focke-Wulf 190s could be expected any moment. It was very comforting to see our fighters instead of German ones."

Both divisions had flown the route as briefed as far as Osnabrück, but the leading 1st Bomb Division formation flew on instead of turning for Zeitz. The 3rd Division wings were five to 15 miles south of the briefed route. The error placed the Division within range of 90 flak batteries at Zeitz, and the Fortresses were subjected to an intense and accurate barrage. A strong headwind reduced their speed and aided the German defenses.

1st Lieutenant Bob Voss, pilot of *The Dorothy V* in the 94th Bomb Group, recalls;

"This was certainly one of my roughest missions. The flak was horrendous and its effect on the bomber force was devastating. Its been a long time since that day but the memory of airplanes falling, exploding in mid-air, spinning down out of control some of their crews escaping by parachute will probably remain always. On the bomb run itself with the formations holding altitude, position and direction was the time of the great losses being inflicted. One could look in any direction and see the big planes going down. While on the bomb run our own aircraft took a hit, which became most obvious as we left the target. The engine instruments for Nos. 1 and 2 engines were indicating loss of oil pressure, erratic temperatures and manifold pressures with smoke trailing from the left engines. We were obviously losing power but it was impossible to identify the specific problem due to the instrument indications and we were a long way from home to think about making it on two engines."

Bob Browne in the 487th, meanwhile, was heading for Merseburg:

"Our escorts followed us to a point approximately 20 miles northwest of Merseburg. As we turned onto a southeast course at this point, it had become apparent where our target was. It was 18 miles straight ahead. The sky was so full of ugly black explosions that none of the blue sky could be seen through it! Watching the terrible sight ahead and knowing that he would be in the middle of it in less than three minutes, an almost hopeless feeling welled up inside of me. It occurred to me that only God could see me through it safely. In desperation I silently bargained with God. 'Lord, if you'll bring me through this alive, I'll serve you for the rest of my life.' This hasty communication brought much relief from the almost unbearable anxiety. Now, our bomb group was at the IP, the point where the ten-mile-run began in meticulous sighting and correcting for target alignment. Flak now was bursting all around us. Several bursts exploded right in front of the nose. More bursts right on top of the right wing. Another group burst straight ahead. Black puffs were everywhere. Forts were going down all around us. The colonel had already lost his right wing man. Didn't even see him go. There were two giant white balls of smoke about a mile ahead, showing where two Forts' gasoline tanks had exploded, probably taking other Forts with them. They were still falling. Even through the oxygen masks you could smell cordite. Enemy fighters were waiting outside the flak corridor, not daring to follow us through the seemingly impenetrable barrier of flying steel."

Russell A. Grantham, 836th Squadron Operations Officer in the 487th Bomb Group, adds:

"As we approached the IP, I noted the Group ahead of us had over shot the IP and in order to insure that we did not collide over the target, I held our turn for 30 seconds or so. The result was that our group approached the target right of the course of the other groups; therefore, we partially missed the 'box'. Our low squadron, which flew to the left and lower did however, have to go through the 'box' and sustained damage. Our group lost four planes out of the low squadron. I saw the No. 13 plane in the low squadron fall a few thousand feet and explode with no chutes sighted."

Bob Browne, in the 487th, continues:

"'Bombs Away!' There was the usual upsurge of the craft, bringing instinctive reflexes for forward control wheel, as the 6000lbs of bombs dropped free. What an awesome sight, as thousands of 500lb bombs fell in train simultaneously!"

Russell A. Grantham adds:

"Flames shot an estimated 12 to 15,000ft, with smoke above our altitude of 32,500ft."

Bob Browne concludes:

"Now the formation was in a steep bank to the right. The Colonel's voice could be heard over the airwaves, 'Let's get out of here!' The flight back was relatively uneventful. What a relief to park old *Fearless Fosdick.* But I dreaded having to inspect the old bird for battle damage. Sergeant Haley was always so obviously distressed when the Fort's skin was even scratched. How much more if she looked like the sieve I expected? As I left the forward escape door I could hear ambulances as they raced to pick up wounded and dead from other aircraft. Sergeant Haley was already at the nose of *Fearless Fosdick,* looking her all over. As I approached him, I could hear him muttering something. As he turned to me, I finally heard what he was saying. 'I can't believe it,' he muttered over and over. It was the sergeant's way of expressing the fact that he could not find a single scratch on *Fearless*. The old Fort sat there all shiny and spotless, as though she had never left the pad that day! It took about two weeks before the 487th could repair enough aircraft for another mission. The 8th and 9th Air Forces had just lost 29 Forts and Libs and over 40 fighter planes on this bleak day. But Merseburg had suffered its greatest damage too. And no doubt this helped considerably to bring the terrible conflict to an end."

The main oil production plants at Bohlen, Leuna, Lützkendorf, and Zeitz were severely damaged. The 8th Air Force lost 29 heavy bombers, the majority shot down by flak. Thirteen of the losses were from the 3rd Air Division. Others like *The Dorothy V* in the 94th Bomb Group made it back on a wing and a prayer, as Bob Voss recalls:

"I had elected to monitor the engines more by visual means of the engines and smoke rather than the instruments. I did shortly feather No.1 as the smoke increased but came to suspect that we had taken a hit somewhere in the instrument panel as well as the port engines, which proved the case after we made it back to base. Battle-damaged aircraft like ours were among the aircraft landing first and as a result we witnessed the disaster of the two B-17s colliding on final approach."[1117]

The losses affected men and morale. At Eye, Jule Berndt had remained on base with the copilot of the crew, even though they had been given a pass. The young navigator was deeply affected:

"When we learned during the afternoon that our boys had gone to Merseburg we went to the flight line to await their return. 'Sweating out' the return of the planes is quite some experience. Many of the crews and other personnel began to gather around the time that the formation was expected to return. At about 1630 hours we saw the first ships approaching from the east. They were the *Chaff* ships that precede the other formations over the target. As they landed we could see that all these planes were in good condition and we anxiously awaited the other bombers. It was with some anxiety that we counted the number of ships in the formation when it came into sight. Of the 36 that we knew had been despatched we could count only 24 and we wondered whether fighters had struck our group. The co-pilot and I were naturally keen to know if our ship, *Magnificent Obsession*, was one of the returning aircraft. It was then that we first saw the evidence of the great opposition our buddies had encountered. We could see four or five planes with engines feathered and there were a number that were shooting red flares indicating wounded on board or material damage to the plane. We were standing at the edge of the runway where the planes were landing and as each one roared by we would take a hurried look at the marking to see if it was ours.

"The landing did not pass without incident and there were a few anxious moments. One approaching plane struck prop wash caused by the preceding planes and suddenly dropped its wing dangerously close to the ground. It also lost its alignment with the runway and started to bear directly towards us. Thanks to the excellent control of the pilot, however, the plane was righted and came in for a nice landing. Another one landed and blew a tire but the pilot was able to move it off the runway. Yet another could not stop at the end of the runway and continued rolling out on to the grass. It is especially exciting to watch a plane with only three engines functioning come in and land but, happily, all the pilots who had feathered engines did neat jobs and landed their ships without damage.

"We were relieved when we saw *Magnificent Obsession*, showing no signs of any major damage, make its graceful descent. One becomes attached to a plane after it has served you so faithfully.[1118] When all the aircraft had landed we went to the hardstand where ours was parked to see what damage it had sustained. First of all we questioned the crew on the opposition they had encountered. The navigator told us that they had flown through 13 minutes of flak that was the most concentrated of any mission. Fortunately our plane had received only two hits. One of them had occurred on the bomb run just after three bombs had been released and had come through the left side of the nose, striking the bombardier's equipment panel and smashing it to a jumbled mass. The other hit had struck when the bomb bay doors were open, going through a substantial girder in that portion of the plane and then ricocheting out through the bottom of the wing.

"After talking that evening and the next day to a large number of the men who had gone on the raid I was able to piece together the events. The 490th had led the 8th Air Force over the target with our CO, Colonel [Frank P.] Bostrom, riding in the lead ship. Just before the target, the lead ship's pathfinding equipment became inoperative and another plane had to take over. Because of this, or perhaps due to faulty navigation, the formation missed the IP and ran into the flak areas beyond. Immediately a flak barrage was put up that many of the old crews termed as the heaviest they had ever witnessed... All the way into the target and for a time after bombs away, the planes were under constant fire of concentrated, accurate flak. The sky over the target was clear of clouds and the German gunners were tracking visually - the most dangerous of all conditions for the bombers. An idea of the opposition can be gathered from the headlines that appeared in the, *Stars and Stripes:* 'Terrific Flak Costs 56 Heavies. 30 Fighters Also lost.' The report revealed that it had been necessary to make a course correction near the target and this had brought the formation within range of 750 guns.

"Of the 36 planes that the 490th sent over, 31 of them received major battle damage but thankfully not a single one went down. Our Squadron CO, Major Lightner, had a rather tough time. He had two engines knocked out over the target and in order to keep altitude jettisoned a lot of equipment. Though the plane was severely crippled he did manage to land it at the emergency field in Brussels. A friend of mine in another squadron told me that a flak fragment came through the waist window. After knocking the safety mechanism from a gun it severed a whole group of wires on its way out, causing the tail wheel to lower, the alarm bell to ring and all the warning lights in the cockpit to flash. The pilot immediately notified the crew that the action of the alarm bell was accidental. Another flak fragment entered the bottom of the wing a few inches from the gas-tank broke up and came out through 21 holes in the top of the wing. In all, that plane was riddled with over 200 holes and there were some that had as many as 500. Another pilot said his astrodome, located on the nose of the plane in front of the pilot's compartment received a hit that almost sheared the entire structure from the plane.

"The result of the strain of such a mission on the nerves of the men was quite evident and next morning a lot of them were still talking excitedly about what they had been through. Another incident occurred at the dinner table when a member of the ground personnel made a few remarks to the effect that the missions now were not nearly as difficult as they had been. This brought forth a sharp retort from an Air Corps' man sitting next to him who said that he didn't see why combat crews couldn't have a mess hall for themselves!"

By the end of November more than 43 refineries, processing both crude and synthetic oil, had been destroyed.

20

The Ardennes Offensive

*"So here's to happy days ahead,
When you and I are free.
To look back on this interlude
And call it history."*

J. B. Boyle, written in POW camp

December brought the worst winter weather in England for 54 years. Water froze in the pipes, and a thin film of ice coated runways at bases throughout eastern England. The temperature dropped to as low as minus 18°C, but the worst feature of the weather was the lack of visibility during missions. The first 8th Air Force mission of the month went ahead on 2 December when about 275 heavies attacked marshaling yards in Germany, but over 150 bombers aborted because of heavy clouds. Eight fighter groups supported the missions and encountered over 100 enemy fighters, claiming 17 destroyed. Three more fighter groups flew sweeps over the Cologne-Kassel-Mannheim-Frankfurt/Main area and claimed 15 enemy machines destroyed. Eight Liberators were lost on the mission to Bingen. No missions were flown from England until 4 December, when over 1100 bombers bombed marshaling yards in Germany again. Most of the bombers and fighters that failed to return landed safely on the Continent. Navigator 1st Lieutenant Lawrence W. Rasmussen flew his 11th mission in the 493rd Bomb Group, flying his first combat mission with Bernard Iwanciow's crew and as lead of "B," or High Squadron:

> "We dropped 10 500 pounders and two M17 500lb incendiary clusters. I took a *Gee* fix at time of 'bombs away' and it fell right on course for target, marshaling yard round house at Giessen. Lead was a little messed, as we had to do a 180° and bomb on return. There was no flak over the target but on way we saw a ship in the 34th ahead of us fall out with No.1 engine burning. I saw three; possib1y four men bale out before the wing exploded. Then it started to spin but recovered into a steep dive. There was a hellatatious 150mph head wind on the way back. We were glad to be back though it was an easy one. Formation caught terrific prop wash. No.4 element leader Kolloff kept right over us. I shot a burst in front of him. If it ever happened that he flies 20ft over us again, I'll get him good, then. Going on pass tomorrow."

Next day more than 500 bombers attacked munitions and tank works at Berlin, the marshaling yard at Münster, and ten targets of opportunity. Fifteen escorting fighter groups met an estimated 285-300 fighters and claimed 90 destroyed. One of the kills was credited to Major Howard "Deacon" Hively, CO 334th Fighter Squadron in the 4th Fighter Group, who shot down a FW 190A-8 northwest of Nordhorn while the Group was escorting two *Aphrodite* B-17s. Hively's victim—his 12th and final victory of the war—was *Oberfeldwebel* Friedrich Buscheggar of 2./JG 26, who was killed when he attempted to land his badly shot up fighter at Marburg, northwest of Furstenau. Major Arthur F. Jeffrey in the 434th Fighter Squadron, 479th Fighter Group, claimed three FW 190s to take his score to nine.[1119] Lieutenant Charles J. Waggoner, pilot of a B-17 in the 729th Bomb Squadron, 452nd Bomb Group formation, struggled back towards England on one engine, but over Lohnerfeld the Fortress[1120] was shot down by Major Karl Borris of 1./JG 26.

Next day over 650 bombers supported by fighters flying over 750 sorties attacked the synthetic oil plant at Merseburg/Leuna and other targets in Germany. Sergeant Joe Hoffman, engineer-top turret gunner in 2nd Lieutenant Leon A. Risk's crew in the 368th Bomb Squadron, 306th Bomb Group, recalls:

> "On 6 December it was back to Merseburg. This time we came in to the target area and we could see nothing but a wall of black puffs. We were worried about going on the bomb run and we hoped it would let up, but the flak just filled the sky in our path. Leon Risk was flying lead ship. He pulled the group off the run and made a 360° turn with the twelve ships flying good formation. We made a circle and then re-entered the bomb run. At this time the flak let up and we made the bomb run and drop, on target, without too much flak damage. Back at de-briefing we were asked about the 360° turn and why, but when all crews were debriefed they all agreed that this was the only thing to do and saved heavy loss of life for the group."

After a two-day stand down missions resumed on the 9th, when almost 400 B-17s bombed two airfields and a marshaling yard in the Stuttgart area, while seven fighter groups escorted the bombers and strafed transportation targets. Next day, over 450 bombers attacked the marshaling yards at Bingen and Koblenz-Lutzel and several targets of opportunity supported by ten fighter groups. Two other fighter groups swept the area east of the target. There was no let up on the 11th, when over 1400 heavies attacked marshaling yards at Frankfurt/Main, Hanau, and Giessen, and road and rail bridges at Mannheim and Maximilliansau. Norman K. Andrew, in the 487th Bomb Group, flew his 16th mission, and it was a "Milk run - grade A all the way":

> "Our target was the marshaling yard at Giessen. We led the high. Had quite a time assembling - had to go higher to get out of the soup. On the bomb run we were briefed to go through the Koblenz and the Limburg flak. So, of course, the bomber stream overshot the IP. Went right over Limburg. They shot at the group ahead but not us. After the target we played along the edge of the Frankfurt flak, no shots close. We were supposed to go over Paris at 10,000ft on the way home - but weather didn't permit. Came over Belgium at 20,000 to top the clouds. Peeled off over Splasher #11 and came home. Visibility about 500 yards."

On 12 December almost 1200 heavies raided more marshaling yards and the Merseburg/Leuna synthetic oil plant, among other targets. Next day over 200 B-17s were recalled en route to their targets in Germany when the weather grounded the fighter escort. No missions were flown on the 14th, but on the 15th almost 650 heavies escorted by eleven fighter groups bombed the marshaling yards at Hanover and Kassel, as well as the tank factory in the town. On 16 December, when over 100 B-17s supported by three fighter groups bombed Stuttgart marshaling yard and other targets, Field Marshal Karl von Rundstedt and his panzer formations, using appalling weather conditions to his advantage, attacked American positions in the forests of the Ardennes on the French-Belgian border. They soon opened up a salient, or "bulge," in the Allied lines supported by an estimated 1400 fighters in twelve *Geschwader*. The Allied air forces were grounded by fog, and it was not until the 23rd that the fog lifted sufficiently to allow 400 B-17s and B-24s to be despatched to strike communication lines behind the Ardennes area and offer some hope to the hard-pressed infantry divisions in "The Bulge."[1121]

The dozen Eighth Air Force fighter groups that could safely get airborne supported the bombers. The *Luftwaffe* was up in force to support the *Wehrmacht* offensive, and nearly 80 enemy fighters were shot down. The 56th Fighter Group returned to Boxted, having claimed the lion's share with 37 destroyed (later reduced to 32 on the evidence of gun camera film), one probably destroyed, and 16 damaged. Eight of the 56 P-47s despatched had returned early with mechanical and equipment problems, leaving the remaining Thunderbolts to continue their sweep in the Bonn and Koblenz areas. Hostile forces were reported north of Bonn, but the enemy fighters disappeared among the clouds. Dave Schilling's formation was vectored towards two other formations of about 40-plus Bf 109s and 60-plus FW 190s. The 56th Fighter Group was flying at between 23,500 and 25,000ft, which gave them a 1000-2000ft height advantage over the enemy. Schilling directed his 62nd Squadron to spread out so that they might be mistaken for a *Luftwaffe* formation joining up, as their approach was being made from the rear. This tactic proved successful, and the Thunderbolt pilots gained complete surprise. In the air battle that ensued Schilling shot down five enemy aircraft,[1122] and the other pilots claimed 14. Major Harold E. "Bunny" Comstock, 63rd Fighter Squadron CO, who was nearing the end of his second tour, led his formation against the FW 190s, and they claimed 13 of the enemy.[1123] Comstock claimed two FW 190s destroyed and two FW 190s damaged SW of Bonn. His combat report was as follows:

> "...We came in from 25,000ft above, with the sun at 4 o'clock to us. I made one pass through the middle of the formation of 190s and damaged one in the left wing. Pulling up, I turned head-on into the circle and one FW 190 turned out of the orbit to fire at me. We both started firing at 1000 yards. His shots were below and when I hit him in the engine he stopped firing altogether. He broke to the left and down. When I turned to follow him his engine was going very slow and as I pulled in behind him, he jettisoned his canopy and jumped. The FW went into a shallow diving turn. I then pulled up and found myself underneath another FW 190 who could not see me. I stayed under him until he rolled out of the turn and then raised up right behind him. I opened fire, observing strikes all along the right side. Closing to 100 yards, there were more strikes on the tight side with pieces flying off. I then observed another FW 190 on the deck, so I pulled in behind him and fired from about 50 yards, observing very few strikes on the fuselage before I was out of ammunition."[1124]

Doolittle wanted to throw as much weight as he could against the German airfields to prevent any missions being flown by the *Luftwaffe* in support of the German land forces in the Ardennes. On Christmas Eve 1944, the Field Order at all bases called for a maximum effort, which most groups achieved by putting up all available aircraft, including war-wearies and even assembly ships. At Rackheath, a record 61 Liberators, including *Pete The POM Inspector* (the group's unarmed assembly ship), were airborne in only 30 minutes. Lieutenant Charles McMahon, a "Happy Warrior" pilot now on the Group Operations staff, who had decided to risk one last mission, flew *Pete*. He came through safely, though his aircraft was armed only with carbines in the waist positions. Controllers had to work overtime at some 3rd Bomb Division bases that were still congested with 1st Division Fortresses. Many had landed there after the mission of 23 December when their home bases had been "socked in." Visibility was still poor, and led to many accidents during take-off. At Podington, for instance, Lieutenant Robert K. Seeber's Fortress crashed into a wood about 200 yards to the left of the runway. The wood had not been visible during take-off because of the thick fog. About two minutes later Seeber's B-17 exploded, killing six of the crew. At Glatton, the 457th managed to get six aircraft off in reduced visibility, but the seventh crashed at the end of the runway and operations were brought to a halt for a time. Despite these setbacks, the 8th was able to mount its largest single attack in history with 2034 heavies participating. In addition, 500 RAF and 9th Air Force bombers participated in this, the greatest single aerial armada the world has ever seen. The 1st Division would be involved in a direct tactical assault on airfields in the Frankfurt area, and on lines of communication immediately behind the German "Bulge." Crews were told that their route was planned on purpose to go over the ground troops' positions for morale purposes.

Brigadier General Fred Castle, former CO of the 94th Bomb Group and now commander of the 4th Wing, drove to Lavenham airfield and elected to fly in the 487th formation to lead the 3rd Bomb Division on what was his 30th mission. In his pocket was a 30-day leave order. Soon Castle was in the air, flying with Lieutenant Robert W. Harriman and crew in *Treble Four*.[1125] All went well until 23,000ft over Belgium; about 35 miles from Liège, his right outboard engine burst into flame and the propeller had to be feathered. The deputy lead ship took over and Castle dropped down to 20,000ft. At this height *Treble Four* began vibrating badly, and he was forced to take it down another 3000ft before leveling out. The Fortress was now down to 180mph indicated air speed and being pursued by seven Bf 109s of IV./JG 3. They attacked and wounded the tail gunner, and left the radar navigator nursing bad wounds in his neck and shoulders. Castle could not carry out any evasive maneuvers with the full bomb load still aboard, and he could not salvo them for fear of hitting Allied troops on the ground. Successive attacks by the fighters put another two engines out of action, and the B-17 lost altitude. To reduce airspeed the wheels of the Fortress were lowered, and the crew ordered to bale out with the terse intercom message, "This is it boys." Castle managed to level out long enough for six of the crew to bale out, but at 12,000ft the bomber was hit in the right wing fuel tank and oxygen systems, which set the aircraft on fire, sending the B-17 into a plunging final spiral to the ground. Castle attempted to land the flaming bomber in an open field close to the Allied lines, but nearing the ground *Treble Four* went into a spin and exploded on impact.[1126]

Navigator 1st Lieutenant Lawrence W. "Ras" Rasmussen flew his 12th mission in the 493rd Bomb Group on this "the maximum effort of all maximum efforts." He noted that:

> "with the German push shielded by three days of fog - a CAVU day called for this. Our bomber stream left Felixstowe after tooling around England all morning - went south of Liège caught quite accurate flak over the lines - one burst enveloped the ship - caught flak all the way to the IP east of the target. We dropped 12 500lb Navy incendiary explosive bombs on an airfield southwest of Darmstadt - hangars and installations on north side of field - CAVU all the way, I saw the bombs hit the target through my B-3 driftmaster - what a sight! Returned through corridor south of St. Coar. It took us more than 9 hours - took off in dark and landed in dark - never seen so many airplanes in all my life - everything from heavies, mediums, lights and pursuits - gunners claimed they saw a P-51 shoot up a jet and another Me 109. Rest of group went to Frankfurt. We were complimented on the good work. This is Christmas Eve - very tired so hitting the sack."[1127]

Overall, the Christmas Eve raids were effective and severely hampered von Rundstedt's lines of communication. The cost in aircraft, though, was high. Many crashed during their return over England, as drizzle and overcast played havoc with landing patterns.[1128] Tired crews put down where they could. Any who felt like joining in the festive spirit on the bases were disappointed because another strike was ordered for Boxing Day, 26 December. Ground crews worked right around the clock, but it was all in vain. The weather and the widely dispersed groups resulted in only 150 aircraft being dispatched. The following day the wintry conditions were responsible for a succession of crashes during early morning take-offs. Max Stout, a co-pilot in the 453rd Bomb Group at Old Buckenham, recalls:

> "We were to be the first plane off. It was an instrument take-off. We were late to taxi and when we arrived, a new crew was lined up to take off. Being a new crew in the 733rd I suppose they were eager to show their mettle. The order of take-off wasn't all that important. Lieutenant Brown hurtled down the salt strewn, slippery runway. The B-24 refused to rise more than a few feet and crashed near the edge of the field. Three gunners scrambled clear before the bomb load exploded in three terrific explosions. The mission was scrubbed with no more planes taking off."

On 26 December 14 Mustangs in the 361st Fighter Group flew their first mission from St. Dizier with a sweep near Trier Göttingen at 17,000ft. A dozen FW 190D-9s led by *Oberleutnant* Hans Hartigs of the 4th *Staffel* JG 26 passed in front of the P-51s on a perpendicular course, momentarily unaware of the Americans. The 376th Fighter Squadron executed a diving turn to catch the German formation from behind.[1129] "We turned on them and they broke into us," reported 1st Lieutenant George R. Vanden Heuvel, who was flying tail end Charlie in *Mary Mine*.[1130] Vanden Heuvel took on a FW 190D-9 that was attacking his element leader, and he hit the Dora square on with a 20° deflection shot and it dived into the ground. The P-51D pilot then zoomed up looking for more enemy fighters, and he saw down below a FW 190D-9 chasing a P-51. The Dora was being flown by Hans Hartigs, and the formation leader, who was out of ammunition, was flying the P-51. Vanden Heuvel closed to 200 yards and gave Hartigs' 190D a burst of fire. The fighter half-rolled, and Hartigs baled out when his oil pressure dropped and his canopy filmed over with oil. Vanden Heuvel noticed that he was wearing a "beautiful leather outfit trimmed in white." When Hartigs hit the ground he could see the dead body of one of his 4th *Staffel* pilots lying on a parachute. A GI had shot *Unteroffizier* Hermann Grad at close range. Hartigs' life was spared and he was marched off to captivity.[1131] Vanden Heuvel was credited with one FW 190 destroyed to take his personal score to five and another shared with Captain Jay W. Ruch. In all, six Doras were claimed shot down (5 were actually lost) without loss; the 376th Fighter Squadron's pilots used the lead-calculating K-14 gun sight to good effect.[1132] 1st Lieutenant David Overholt, leading Yellow Flight, claimed one of the Focke-Wulf 190Ds at extreme range after latching onto the enemy fighter at 800 yards distance. Overholt recalled:

> "He made a sharp turn to the left and I closed my pippers on the gun sight down as small as they would go and fired ... I finished firing at about 600 yards and 65° deflection."

Seeing his bullets strike the German fighter repeatedly, he followed it visually as it went into a dive and struck the ground. 1st Lieutenant Homer Powell also used the K-14 to its full potential as he followed a FW 190D into a steep climbing turn:

> "I put the pipper on him at about 45° deflection and fired one long burst at 200 yards. He started smoking, burst into flame and spiraled aimlessly toward the ground."

Lieutenant Claire P. Chennault also claimed a FW 190D destroyed.

Meanwhile, Eighth Air Force HQ was only too aware of the problems confronting the bomber groups, but despite the dangerous conditions, the mission of 29 December had to go ahead. At 0840 a 390th Bomb Group Fortress crashed on take-off from Framlingham and plummeted into the center of nearby Parham village. The crew perished in the explosion, which shattered the windows of every home in the vicinity, but miraculously none of the inhabitants were harmed. At Rackheath, a ground fog came in over the base at take-off time and reduced visibility to a few feet. Lieutenant Colonel James J. Mahoney recalls the tragic events that followed:

> "Colonel Walter Smith called up Division headquarters and asked for permission to cancel or postpone the missions but Division refused. They said it was top priority and that the mission must be flown. Smitty woke me for advice and I called Division and told them it was impossible to take off. It was too foggy even to taxi and we had jeeps leading them out. But they told us to get airborne. I then woke Colonel Shower. The Division officer who was causing the trouble had been a classmate of his at West Point, so we hoped he could influence him. But the officer was adamant that the mission should go ahead, as it was in support of General Patton's forces near Metz. Colonel Shower decided to let the lead and deputy lead aircraft from each squadron go. These six 'planes would take off first and climb to form a skeleton formation and then fire flares. As the others came up it was hoped they would spot the flares and take up a prearranged position in the formation. Colonel Al Wallace, CO of the 791st Squadron, who thought it suicide to take off, flew in the right hand seat in the first B-24 [piloted by Lieutenant John F. Mottette] as

Command Pilot. It would be a take-off using instruments. We figured the lead crew pilots would be experienced enough to take off on instruments, but we had been having problems with faulty equipment sent by a subcontractor in the States. The first B-24 took off and within minutes Wallace called over the radio, warning us not to let anybody else take off. They had made it - but only just. The second B-24 taxied out. You couldn't see more than 20ft. We heard him go on emergency power. The engines really whined and it was obvious he was in trouble. We heard a crack, but nothing else happened and we kept waiting for explosions. The third B-24 really whacked the trees on take off. Colonel Shower told crews to turn off their engines and stay where they were. It was too foggy even to taxi and we had jeeps leading them out."

Mahoney and Smith climbed in a jeep and set off through the murky fog in search of the crashed Liberator. They could hear explosions rupturing bullet cases and the fierce crackling of flames consuming the aircraft, but the fog blacked out almost everything. Then they saw a reddish glow. The Liberators had been carrying eight 500lb bombs and the two officers heard six go off. Mahoney continues:

"We pulled over to the side of the road and climbed over fence. Suddenly, while in the middle of a field we heard the seventh bomb explode. We knew we were close and cautiously we waited until the eighth bomb went. Then the two of us started running towards the glow; but we were stopped by another explosion. Its force didn't knock us down but the air hit us. We had obviously miscounted. Then a tenth let go and it knocked us both down. [The two men heard fire-tenders and ambulances seeking the crashed plane and failing to find it. Mahoney told Smith to drive back to the guardhouse and tell them exactly where the aircraft lay. The heat was starting to lift the fog, and Mahoney was determined to get closer. He stood up, but yet another bomb exploded and momentarily knocked him out. No shrapnel hit him.] I was confused. I paused but no other bombs went off. I got up and walked towards the fire. People were yelling. Coming from the direction of the airfield were two gunners who were holding each other up. One looked in pretty good shape until I saw that he had a great big hole in the side of his head You could have stuck your fist into it. Both were shocked. What puzzled me was that they were coming from the wrong direction and quite a way from the blaze. There were no burn marks on their clothes. [The men told Mahoney later that when the bomber hit the trees they were thrown out.] By this time the heat from the fire had carved out of the still dense fog a dome of good visibility over the wreckage. We found another crewman who was just barely alive; before we could get him much farther from the fire, he 'checked out' on us. We worked our way around to the other side of the crash and found two more, both seriously hurt and burned. The medics put them on stretchers and took them away. Finding no more survivors, we were able to turn our attention to the wreck itself. The fire was starting to burn down and we could get a little closer. Our fire-fighting equipment couldn't get through the muddy field to the scene, but there was nothing left to save anyway, so it burned out.

"It was then that we got our first really good look at the scene as a whole and unearthed a very dramatic clue to explain the puzzling number of explosions. Sticking out of the very soft ground and twisted wreckage, I could count six propellers! We now realized we were looking at the charred carcasses of not one, but two airplanes. Further evidence then became apparent - the number of engines, turrets, some still unexploded bombs on the periphery and worst of all, bodies. In addition to the five who had come from the scene in varying states of injury, we counted eight bodies, leaving another five to be found deeper in the pyre. Some were burned so badly that we'd have to rely on Doc Mason's dental impressions for identification. There was one I was able to eventually identify.

"With my foot I rolled over what I thought might be a back pack parachute. Instead, it was the charred remains of the upper torso of Lieutenant Paul Kaminski. Paul was a fine young Polish-American boy from a coal mining region of western Pennsylvania. He had been with us for a couple of months and we were bringing him along in our lead crew training program. He was an excellent pilot, intelligent and eager. This day, as part of his training, he was riding as co-pilot in a squadron lead plane. An hour or so earlier that morning as I left the Briefing Room headed back to my quarters for what I had hoped would be half a night's sleep, I had said a few words to him as he and some of the crew were about to receive Holy Communion from Chaplain Sharbaugh before boarding a truck for a trip to their hardstand. Then, they were vibrant and impressive individuals. Now, in that terrible mess and carnage their individual features were obliterated and their remains shared the basest commonality - they all bled red."[1133]

On 30 December more than 1000 heavies again bombed lines of communication, and on the 31st the 1st Bomb Division kept up the attacks, while 3rd Division crews returned to oil production centers. S/Sgt Russell H. Thrift, a tail gunner in the 493rd Bomb Group, went to Misburg:

"As we approached the target, we found it to be a perfect day just as S-2 had briefed us. There was flak from 6 o'clock to 12 o'clock and just as thick as London fog. Rockets and flak - everything in the book. Jerry sure was trying to keep us away. The lead squadron went on in and we were right behind heading down that corridor of flak. Then 'bombs away.' All of the Forts, except those in our squadron had dropped their loads. I guess our squadron's lead bombardier didn't get the target where he wanted it in his crosshairs. When he said, 'we're going to take another run,' I thought right there that I couldn't have sold my life for a nickel! We banked around and headed back. Just before we got over the target there was a blinding flash and all hell broke loose right there in my lap! I was blind and groggy for about a minute, so I can't say exactly what happened. When the dust and splinters cleared, I could see out of one eye. One Fort was going down at 7 o'clock. As for ours, well, flak or a rocket had come up through the armor plating behind me, gone through the ammunition box, hit my right arm, smashed the Plexiglas in front of me, hit my tail sight and knocked it out through the tail window. Boy, that stuff really messes things up when it comes in like that!

"My guns wouldn't move and as far as the tail was concerned it was out of action. I remember calling the pilot over the interphone and telling his that I was hit. He sent T/Sgt Bronislov Sinkus, the radio-operator back with the first aid kit and he fixed me up. In the meantime flak had knocked out the oxygen on the right side of the plane and everybody was diving for emergency walk around bottles. When we finally got straightened out I found I was OK, except for a gash in my left arm and Plexiglas splinters in my eyes. Later, as we were on our way back and things were running smoothly again, I thanked God for keeping that stuff where it was, another inch or so and, oh well, here I am. I owe a lot to our radio operator the rest of my crew. They took care of things just as though they were participating in a training drill on the ground. The thing I do know; we sure gave 'Jerry' a headache! They told me that you could see smoke for more than 100 miles from the target."

Crews in the 4th and 13th Wings were assigned Hamburg. For Norman K. Andrew in the 487th Bomb Group, it was his and Jack Stanley's crew's 18th mission. Andrew wrote:

"A very rough day! Hamburg-visual. The CQ woke me at 0245. I thought it was Politz for sure. Target: oil refinery Hamburg. Took off and assembled in the dark. We had to switch planes at the last minute - late take-off. Went out over the North Sea. About 60 miles out I told Jack we were 8 miles right of course. 150 miles out I called the Air Leader - we were leading the low - and told him we were 20 miles right of course and about to run into the Friesian Islands. The lead claimed that he knew where we were - so - a few minutes later we had several flak bursts about 500ft off the right wing. As we passed Heligoland the clouds cleared off and we could see Hamburg 60 miles away. Went down the bomb run drifting over 30°. Chuck changed heading near the target so he would be able to kill the drift. He did - only 245°. We had a wind at 15°, 110 knots. Due to prop wash the fore and aft bubble was clear forward. We came the closest of our squadrons and we missed by 1500 yards. The flak was moderate to intense and accurate as hell. One of our ships had 60 holes in it. Tonight there are only eight ships available for tomorrow. After the rally point six FW 190s hit the group right behind us. They got three B-17s. Two flamers and one spinner. Our ground speed from Hamburg to the coast out was 74 knots. Boy! Did we sweat that out! The Cuxhaven corridor has been shut off but we had no flak. This one ran Merseburg a close second."

Clyde Crowley, a bombardier in the 95th Bomb Group in the 13th Wing at Horham, flew his 33rd combat mission as part of 2nd Lieutenant Charles H. O'Reilly's crew in *Queen Mary*:[1134]

"It was the turn of Sgt Bates, a togglelier in my squadron, to fly but he had gotten himself grounded because of a cold. I had a bit of a stuffy head myself but I was told that if I flew the mission my flight officer said he would see if he could get my tour of duty ended and send me home. This sounded like a good deal. When I went to briefing and learned that the target was to be Hamburg my spirits dropped. I snapped on my 'chute before take-off; something I rarely ever did. The day was a very cold and clear one. At the target area the flak was heavy. We started our bomb run. I opened the bomb bay doors after arming the bombs. When we reached the target I dropped the bombs. The radio operator, who could see into the bomb bay, called me on interphone and said one bomb, was hung in the rack. I tried again to unload the bomb but it wouldn't go so I asked O'Reilly to jettison racks and all. He did this and as soon as the radio operator announced the bay was clear I closed the doors. With a combined sigh of relief everyone seemed to be chatting at the same time. But not for long. The radio operator saw an enemy aircraft approaching. Our gunners fired but he got through and near enough to hit us with at least one 20mm shell. The ship was on fire. The pilot gave the order to abandon. Since I already had my chest pack on I probably was the first to get out. I kicked out the escape hatch and was gone. Four others managed to get out before the plane disintegrated.[1135] The rest of my tour overseas was spent in two Stalag Lufts."

Hamburg was the scene of another disaster for the 13th Wing's 100th Bomb Group, as William B. Sterret, navigator in Lieutenant Billy R. Blackman's crew,[1136] recalls:

"31st December 1944 is one day in my life I will never forget. When the map was uncovered in the briefing room we all gave a sigh because we knew that Hamburg was a rough target. For some unknown reason I believe that all of the crew had a feeling that this was going to be outlast one. We could not fly our own ship because an engine had been burnt up the day before so we flew a ship belonging to another squadron. When we had finished all of our last-minute checks, we gathered in the tent and waited by the fire until time came to start our engines. It was our usual procedure to kid one another and 'shoot the bull' but everyone was very quiet on this particular morning. We never told the ground crew where we were going because this was against security regulations, but they could guess just about what the target was by the way the crew acted. I am sure that they knew we were 'sweating this one out.' They were a swell bunch of fellows and would do anything they could to help you get back home.

"We took off at 0715 and went through the usual procedure of assembling over England. We left the English coast at 0900 and went up to the North Sea. The weatherman had told us that conditions were not so good, which was evident when we got in the air. The wind was supposed to be about 150 knots at altitude but it was actually much stronger than that. Consequently, we drifted about 30 miles south of our course that put us almost over Holland. The lead navigator began to correct our heading, which made us fly directly into the wind. This reduced our ground speed to about 100mph. We were supposed to come in above Heligoland Island but instead we came in below it and had to turn directly into the wind to reach our IP. We were all talking over the intercom and wondering what was going to happen next. Heligoland was our secondary target and even though we knew that the two islands were well defended we were wishing we could drop our bombs there.

"We finally got to our IP, turned on our rack switch, opened the bomb bay doors and started down the bomb run. At this point we all usually cut off our heated suits because the nervous energy was enough to keep you warm even though it was 50° below zero. Our turn to get on the bomb run was to the right and we were on the outside. This caused us to lag behind a little but finally we were able to get back into position. The target could be seen from our IP even though it took us about ten minutes to actually get over it. A group hit an airfield off to our right. We could also see the groups in front of us getting shot at and we knew that we would soon be in the middle of it. No one was saying a word. We were all just hoping and praying that we would come through without any trouble.

"Finally, we got into the flak, which was really accurate. We could hear the shells as they burst, which was too close for comfort. On our mission to Frankfurt I had told the boys that I could hear the pieces of shrapnel beating on the side of the ship and they had all said I was getting 'flak happy.' I knew they would agree with me this time. At 1133 the lead ship dropped his smoke bombs, which was a signal for all of the wing ships to drop their bombs. Andy hit the toggle switch and out went our bombs. You always felt better as soon as the bombs were gone because you felt like your job was done."

One by one all the Fortresses in the 100th Bomb Group formation began dropping their bombs. *Fools Rush In*, piloted by Lieutenant Floyd E. Henderson, was struck by flak while on the bomb run and dropped sharply, crashing into the B-17 flown by Lieutenant Clifton M. Williams, which was cleaved in two. Both aircraft fell to earth in flames.[1137] The sky over Hamburg was filled with accurate bursts of flak, and Lieutenant

Bill Blackman's Fortress was struck on the No.3 engine. Bill Sterret continues:

"We started for our rally point but had only flown about two minutes when Carson, the ball turret gunner, called Bill and said oil was pouring out of No.3 engine. The oil pressure gauge verified this fact so Bill feathered the engine. As soon as No.3 had stopped running Carson called again and said No.4 engine was also losing oil. Bill feathered this engine too. We were unable to keep up with the formation with only two engines but we could hold our altitude. Bill Blackman called us all and said, 'Stick with it boys. We'll get this thing home yet.' I told him to keep the same heading because it would bring us back out over the North Sea. Bill called for fighter escort but he couldn't contact any because they had been unable to get off the ground in England due to bad weather. He turned back on the intercom and said, 'Bandits in the area!' At this instant, Joe Pearl, the engineer, yelled, 'They're coming in at 6 o'clock!' I looked up through the astrodome and saw two FW 190s coming in on our tail. I turned around and grabbed my gun hoping I would get a shot in. No such luck. We could see tracers as they passed us. 20mm shells were also flying around. We all realized that our chances of getting through were really slim. A 20mm shell exploded in the cockpit and knocked all the insulation between the pilots' compartment and the nose into the section where I was. The ship was also on fire and started spinning. I realized that it was time to leave. When I got to the escape hatch Bob Fortney, the radio operator, was lying on his back on the catwalk. I thought he was hurt so I started to help him but he got up and told me to get out so I put one foot on the door and pushed it out. Then I jumped. As soon as I cleared the ship I took off my helmet, pulled my ripcord and looked back to see the ship blow up."[1138]

The rest of the 100th Bomb Group Fortresses were in the midst of a furious air battle. Lieutenant Wallace Wilson's B-17 was hit and started down. Lieutenant William Mayo had two engines knocked out and was last seen over Speikeroog Island. FW 190s and Bf 109s attacked in elements of two, three, and four, meeting the bombers 300 yards out before breaking off to reform and come in again. Gunners blazed away at the enemy fighters and scored a few kills, but without close fighter support, it was only a matter of time before they too were knocked out of formation. Lieutenant Paul Carroll's Fortress was hit and dived straight down. It temporarily recovered, and was last seen heading in a westerly direction. It did not return to Thorpe Abbotts. Lieutenant John F. Marin's B-17 headed for Holland with two wounded men aboard. *Faithful Forever*,[1139] piloted by Lieutenant Leo D. Ross, also got into trouble, as Raigh Mason, the copilot, recalls:

"We lost No.4 to flak on the bomb run and after leaving the target we lost No.2, also to flak. We were unable to hold speed and altitude and we dropped out of formation and headed for home plate. We were doing OK but losing altitude when Jim Wynn, tail gunner, reported that 20 bandits were at 6 o'clock low. The group included both Me 109s and FWs. Wynn had a hit on his fifties on the first pass. His .50 guns were inoperative and he was wounded. However, he stayed in the tail and faked firing. We got pretty well riddled. No.2 was on fire and we couldn't put it out. We called 'Little Brother' but received no response. I think we were at about 8000ft when we went into an uncontrollable vertical dive and lee said, 'Lets Go! Leo was a good pilot. Everyone got out although several were wounded and/or injured. I saw several flames and always felt that our gunners had six kills. We got credit for four."[1140]

Lieutenant Charles C. Webster's B-17 plummeted to earth in flames and exploded on impact. 2nd Lieutenant Ralph A. Whitcomb's right wing began to burn, and the bomber circled for two minutes under control before spinning down enveloped in flames.[1141] McNab and his co-pilot, Lieutenant Vaughan, were wounded, and their B-17 rose perilously close towards *The Little Skipper*,[1142] flown by Lieutenant Glenn Rojohn, who had moved in after Webster's B-17 had gone down. Collision was unavoidable, and there was a sickening thud as both aircraft shuddered and locked. McNab's engines were smoking, and Rojohn and his co-pilot, Lieutenant William Leek, frantically cut their engines to avoid a probable explosion. Still joined together, Rojohn and Leek made a superhuman effort and managed to steer the mass of aircraft towards the coast. Rojohn and Leek safely crash-landed their two aircraft pick-a-back in a German field. [1143] Altogether, the "Bloody Hundredth" lost 12 B-17s to JG 300 and to flak over the target—half the total borne by the entire 3rd Division.[1144]

On New Year's Eve Lieutenant Colonel Hank Orban of the 493rd Bomb Group led 38 B-17s to Misburg. *Day's Pay*,[1145] in the "B" Squadron, was forced to abort as Walter Faulkner, the co-pilot, who was on his last mission, recalls:

"Our last mission was supposed to be a milk run, but like all our milk runs, it turned out to be BAD. As we were climbing through clouds to make formation our #2 engine blew up and caught fire. Four crewmembers baled out before we got the plane under control; they perished in the Channel. We contacted ASR and searched ourselves but with no luck. We salvoed our load and landed at the emergency field on the coast."

Some 35 B-17s dropped 87.37 tons of bombs on Misburg. Lieutenant Henry B. Skeen, flying *Milk Run* for the last time, was leading the 4th element of three aircraft directly below and to the rear of the 3rd element. He recalls:

"For some reason the lead ship of the third element peeled out of formation, taking his element with him.[1146] We moved up into his position, but he decided to get back into formation, nearly ramming us in the process. We then resumed our position behind the lead ship. At the target there was extremely heavy flak and the lead ship's bombs hung up. The lead then did another bomb run and on release, his bombs blew up directly under him and directly in front of us.[1147] We flew through the blast with our bomb bay doors open, receiving over 100 holes and narrowly missing the lead as he went down with two engines on fire. Flak knocked out my tail gunner's window and knocked my co-pilot from his seat into my lap. Thanks to his flak vest he was not injured, but we were both blinded by Plexiglas particles. The engineer, who we had trained to fly the aircraft in such a situation, flew the aircraft from the aisle between the seats until we recovered our vision."

On 1 January 1st Lieutenant Walter J. Konantz in the 338th Fighter Squadron, 55th Fighter Group, flew his 48th combat mission when the Wormingford group escorted the B-17s to Derben oil refinery, near Stendal. Konantz recalled:

"Lieutenant Bodiford got hit by flak and baled out over France. He came back a few days later carrying his wadded up parachute. My girlfriend made Bodiford and me an aviators scarf out of it and a pair of panties for herself. On this mission we saw a couple of airfields with parked German planes but they laid a curtain of flak over them too thick to try to strafe."

Paul W. Pifer, radio-operator in B-24 *Battle Dragon* in the 446th Bomb Group, recalls the New Year's day mission:

"Pre-dawn New Year's Day 1945 was like any other winter day in England; cold, foggy and generally miserable. We were unceremoniously aroused at 0300 by an equally miserable Charge-Of-Quarters. Following the usual insipid breakfast of powdered eggs and Spam, we gathered in the briefing room for details of our impending mission over Germany. I had become 19 years old less than a month before. Our crew belonged to Lieutenant. Edward Markewitz; I say belonged because we worshipped the man - all of 28 years old. We nicknamed him 'Louie da Finger' after a prominent New York hood whom Eddie could mimic so well with his Bronx accent. This was to be our 10th mission. It was also to be a fateful day for us as well as many others. The designated target was the industrial town of Andernach, 10 miles NW of Koblenz. Good weather and minimal flak were predicted. We were flying the '*Battle Dragon*', a venerable craft of many missions. We were also assigned two extra crewmembers, James Tootell and Richard DuBois, who were flying their 34th make-up mission on order to fly No.35, the last, with their regular crew. Tootell was flight engineer. DuBois requested my regular position as radio operator; so I went to the waist as observer. The IP was Trier, Germany, a small medieval town just East of Luxembourg. For some reason the formation circled tiny Trier for a second directional bearing to our target. One of the three flak guns found our range on that second pass. No one was seriously concerned with three anti-aircraft guns until our ship shuddered from a sickening thud as No.3 engine was shot off its mounting. We could observe fuel being whisked back over the starboard wing - very frightening because of the great fire hazard.

"The pilot headed southwest and shortly thereafter our load was jettisoned over a forested area. With parachutes strapped on we awaited the inevitable bale out signal, which came when the fuel gauges revealed minimal gasoline remaining. At 22,000ft we jumped. When the others had gone out the floor hatch, I called Lieutenant. Markewitz on intercom to notify him that the waist was clear and I was jumping. He acknowledged by saying, 'Good luck, I'll see you down below, kid.'

"On leaving the aircraft, I righted myself, counted ten seconds because of the altitude and pulled the ripcord. Nothing happened! Probably instinct prompted me to clutch at the flap of my chest pack. After what seemed like an interminable lapse of time, the pilot chute blossomed forth past my face and then the main chute opened with a tremendous jerk on my body. I experienced exquisite right groin pain and nearly fainted. This was caused by carelessness on part, a loose harness strap. However it was good to be alive and I silently gave thanks to The Lord. I became aware of the B-24 spiraling around me in tight concentric circles, constantly losing altitude, its engines silent. A parachute opened several hundred yards above me. The aircraft continued to drop and finally crashed and exploded in flames on the side of a small wooded hill.

"I landed in a stubble cornfield, still in pain and had trouble spilling my parachute, which was dragging me over a swath of 8-inch corn stems. When the wind diminished, my chute folded and I was able to stand and free myself from the harness and sensed immediate relief from my pain. Markewitz landed about 100 yards away and we quickly made our rendezvous, lighted cigarettes and discussed what to do next. We didn't know whether we were in France or enemy-held territory. Our dilemma was solved when shortly we were completely surrounded by heavily armed civilians who turned out to be FFI (Free French). We had landed outside the village of St. Blin. Our nose-gunner, David Hensley was killed. His parachute never opened. Interestingly, four of us experienced 'failed parachute openings' upon pulling the ripcord. At our debriefing, it was presumed the chutes froze at altitude. The navigator sustained crushing fractures of his right heel upon landing. I had an incomplete fracture of the right pubic bone. He and I were conveyed to the 23rd General Hospital in Vittel at the foot of the Vosges Mountains. The hospital was a converted elegant hotel. There I met Lotsey Roney, a lifelong friend from my hometown in Punxsutawney, Pennsylvania. Lotsey was chief cook and somehow arranged for me to visit Mata Hari's former suite, which was sealed off, to the Army on the 8th floor.

"Shortly thereafter, following a very adequate assessment of our injuries, the navigator was returned to the U.S. for further treatment and I rejoined my crew. Jim Tootell and Richard DuBois flew mission No.35 with their own crew. They were hit over the target, losing two engines and finally crash-landed in France. What a finale for their last mission! 25 February 1945 we bombed Aschaffenburg from the '*Dragon Lady*", when we were hit by flak and had to feather No.2 engine. We made our way back to France and landed at a fighter base near Toul. There were no casualties but we were becoming leery of B-24s associated with the name '*Dragon*.'"

The USSTAF was clearly winning the battle of attrition in the war against the *Luftwaffe*, as trained fighter pilots at this stage of the war were impossible to replace.[1148] January 1945 marked the Eighth's third year of operations, and it seemed as if the end of the war was in sight. On 1 January the 1st Air Division (this day the prefix "Bomb" was officially changed to "Air") encountered enemy fighters in some strength during raids on the tank factory at Kassel, an oil refinery at Magdeburg, and marshaling yards at Dillenburg. The Magdeburg force came under heavy fighter attack, while the Kassel force was badly hit by flak. The *Luftwaffe*, however, was still far from defeated. The *Jagdverband* had made a few concerted attempts at turning back the bombers late in 1944, but on each occasion they had been beaten off with heavy losses inflicted by escorting P-51 Mustangs and P-47 Thunderbolts. On 2 November the Mustangs routed their German attackers, and the 352nd Fighter Group established a record 38 kills on that occasion. Despite losses on this scale, the *Luftwaffe* could still be relied upon to make a major effort against the heavies, and *Unternehmen Bodenplatte*, a desperate gamble to diminish the overwhelming Allied air superiority, was mounted at about 0900 hours on New Years Day 1945. The aim was to deliver a single, decisive blow against RAF and American aircraft on the ground in Holland, Belgium, and Northern France using 875 single-engined fighter aircraft, primarily in support of von Rundstedt's Ardennes offensive. The outcome, though, was far different. Though total Allied aircraft losses during *Bodenplatte* amounted to 424 destroyed or heavily damaged, the *Luftwaffe* losses were catastrophic.[1149]

The big gamble had turned into a disastrous defeat. The *Wehrmacht* advance in the Ardennes came to a halt and ultimately petered out. In the east, the Red Army prepared for the great winter offensive, which would see the capture of Warsaw and Krakow and take the Soviets across the German border. Germany had no reserves left. Hitler's last chance now lay in his so-called "wonder weapons," the V-1 and V-2.

21

Clarion Call

"This was the first time that I felt the concussion of our own bombs and also the first time I saw boxcars tumble through the air... I feel uneasy when a boxcar attains almost as much altitude as our bomber."

Lieutenant Abe Dolim, navigator, 94th Bomb Group

On 2 January 1945 the 8th once again pounded lines of communication, and raids of this nature continued for several days until the position in the Ardennes gradually swung in the Allies' favor. There was no respite, but for once the general "bitching" on the bases ceased when it was learned that General Ben Lear had been newly appointed to the ETO. Ground crews went about their daily chores with a new greeting, "Whattya hear from Lear?," connecting the appointment with an announcement that ground personnel would be drawn from the bomb groups as replacement infantry for invalided men who fought in "the Bulge." This added to the administrative problems on the bases, while the "ground pounders" began to realize that life in a bomb group was not so bad after all.

On 3 January Norman K. Andrew, in the 487th Bomb Group, flew his 19th mission of his tour when almost 1100 heavies escorted by eleven fighter groups bombed targets in western Germany. Eleven of the objectives were marshaling yards, and the 487th went to Aschaffenburg. Andrew wrote:

> "What a long day! Up at 0300. PFF. Our new CO, Colonel [William K.] Martin [who had taken command on 28 December] rode with us. We led the low. And finally, I really got some help from Lieutenant Wilkinson, pilotage navigator. It was solid 10/10ths all the way so he ran the *Gee* box. I plotted the fixes and had time to really navigate. I also gave Whit' a workout on his Mickey set when we ran out of range of the Rheims Chain. It was a long drawn-out mission - but an easy one. Entered France at Calais and skirted the Belgium-France border to the Rhine just north of Saarburg. Turned north to the target just 23 miles SE of Frankfurt. The only flak we had was 4 bursts from Stuttgart and that was about a mile off our right wing. The lead didn't drop on the primary but hit the secondary -marshaling yards at Pforzheim, Germany. They almost ran us into the Heidelberg flak. I took the low way to the left and rejoined them after they bombed. Milk run - only 11, maybe ten to go. (The Colonel told us it was nice navigating and the pilotage navigator (27 missions) told Jack that I was the best he had ever ridden with. Bashful, aren't I?)"

On 5 January the severe wintry weather over England was responsible for several fatal accidents during take-off for a mission to Frankfurt. Snow flurries swirled around the runways, and at Mendlesham a 34th Bomb Group Fortress came to grief while attempting take-off. The conditions were also responsible for a mid-air collision in the vicinity of Thorpe Abbotts. A period of fine weather beginning on 6 January, when more than 750 heavy bombers attacked marshaling yards and bridges and targets of opportunity, enabled the heavies to fly missions in support of the ground troops once more. Also on 6 January seven fighter groups flew escort, and one group strafed airfield and transportation targets. 1st Lieutenant Walter J. Konantz in the 338th Fighter Squadron, 55th Fighter Group, flew his 50th combat mission this day when the Wormingford group escorted the B-17s to Germerscheim. Konantz recalls:

> "We strafed Germerscheim airfield on the way out and the 338th Squadron got 13 aircraft destroyed. I got a Ju 88, which was slow catching fire, but when I looked back it was starting to burn. Captain Buskirk was hit by flak from the airfield and baled out. Lieutenant Ramm was badly damaged by flak but he made it back to base. He had to belly in at 200mph as battle damage made his plane uncontrollable below this speed."

For Norman K. Andrew, 7 January was "another day closer to home" when he completed his 20th mission when his crew led the 487th Bomb Group in the bombing of the Paderborn marshaling yards. They had to fly all the way home at 20,000ft because of clouds.

Missions were flown to tactical targets when the weather permitted, and when it turned bad the 8th mounted shallow penetration raids to *Noball* targets in France. Taking off in and flying in bad weather was bad enough, but a scrubbed mission, often called just after take-off, could cause more anxiety and morale to sag. Sergeant Arthur Dobias, a waist gunner in a 493rd Bomb Group B-17 flown by Lieutenant William H. Butler, recalls the mission at Debach on the morning of 13 January:

> "It was dark and it was snowing. Each man went about his job in the usual way - some not knowing it was his fatal flight. Our bomb load was four 1000lb. Bombs instead of the usual six, as we were the *Chaff* ship. We had just gotten airborne and were slowly gaining altitude. I was standing at my usual position at the right waist station looking out when suddenly the entire plane began to shudder like a live thing. The engines were roaring their all, it seemed, but we

were losing altitude fast. I felt the treetops of a hedge beat against the belly as we just cleared. The next instant we struck. I remember falling forward, - then nothing. The next thing I saw was flame, flame all over the waist. I was lying somewhere there where the lower ball turret had been. It was burning up - only one thing was in my mind - to get away and fast. I got up and ran back to the waist door. The ball gunner and the radioman were trying to get it open but it was jammed. Just how I do not know but somehow we got it opened and stumbled out into the snow. We had covered only a short distance when the gas tanks went up in one big 'whoosh' - shooting flame high into the air. After this I remember very little except that occasionally I remember that I wanted to return - my pals were in that plane - but the lower ball man would not let me. I reckon he saved me by so doing. Two of the bombs exploded when we were about half a mile or so from the wreckage. I faintly recall it, as it knocked us in the snow. After this I remembered nothing - till we walked into a farmhouse. The ball gunner bandaged my head, as I had a cut that was bleeding some. Butler and Sidney Jones co pilot, Ray H. Beeles, engineer and A. B. Muenzer, tail gunner, were killed. The bombardier and navigator were severely injured. It seemed like a dream but the empty bunks in our barracks proved it was not. We attended the funerals of our fellow crewmen whom we learned to love as brothers. And I feel it is only by the Grace of God that we escaped with our lives."

Walt Konantz had taken part in an uneventful P-51 escort for the B-17s to Bielefeld on 7 January, but 13 January, a freelance area support mission instead of its usual bomber escort missions, was a day he would remember for the rest of his life. He not only recorded his third kill, but it was the first claim for a Me 262 by the 55th Fighter Group. Konantz recalls:

"We were trimmed down from the usual 50 or so planes to just 37 P-51s. The 338th Squadron had three flights totaling 12 planes. The three squadrons spread out for a search for targets of opportunity. The 338th, having destroyed 14 planes on the ground at Giebelstadt airfield just a week before, headed for this field to see if there were any left. The dozen Mustangs were circling the field at about 5000ft, planning our strafing routes and picking out targets on the ground. At this point I saw a plane taxiing onto the runway and was surprised to see him take off. I would have thought we had been seen and the tower would have advised him to park the plane and seek shelter. I called out the now airborne plane but no one else saw him. He continued climbing; made a 180° turn and came back directly under me headed in the opposite direction. I did a tight 180 and ended up about 200 yards behind him. At this point, he had built up enough speed that I was no longer closing on him even though I was at full throttle and had made a diving turn behind him. The new K-14 gyroscopic gunsight had been installed in this plane only a week earlier and I had never fired the guns with this new sight before. It worked perfectly and the German plane, now identified as a Me-262, was saturated with nearly 40 hits. He made no evasive action whatsoever, possibly the pilot may have been hit. His left engine burst into flame and the Me 262 made a slow descending spiral and crashed on a railroad track about two miles from the airfield. The plane exploded on impact and probably cut the track.[1150]

"I still had some ammunition left so I headed back toward the field and picked out a twin engine plane as a strafing target and commenced my pass. The other eleven Mustangs had already strafed and all the flak gunners were alert and ready for me. Light flak was coming from all directions. I continued my pass until I got within range of my target and saw that it was a burned out hulk from last week. It could not have been strafed today as it was not smoking. I did not fire my guns but kept very low until I passed the boundary of the field. Somewhere on the pass, a single small caliber bullet, probably from a light machine gun, came into the cockpit from the left side, cut a six inch groove in my jacket sleeve and struck the radio control box on the right side of the cockpit. This put my radio out of commission.

"As I pulled up and started climbing there was not another Mustang in sight. With my radio gone I could not call to try and rejoin them. I headed west looking for any allied airplanes I could follow back to England. The weather was bad over England and I did not want to risk missing England entirely without the capability of getting DF steers to my home base or any other suitable landing field. I eventually spotted a 9th Air Force P-47, joined up with him and gave him hand signals that my radio was out and that I wanted to land with him. He got the message and took me to his home base at St. Trond, Belgium. I spent the night there, had my radio control box changed the next morning and returned to my home base at Wormingford about noon. My other squadron members all saw the fiery crash of the Me 262, heard not a word from me on the radio from that point on, then when I failed to return that night, they all assumed the worst. After landing, being debriefed on the previous day's activities and catching a ride back to the barracks, I walked in to find my barracks mates dividing up my personal belongings. They were very surprised to see me and happily gave back my belongings."

On Sunday, 14 January, the 8th Air Force despatched over 650 bombers supported by 15 fighter groups to mainly oil and other targets in central and northwestern Germany again. A smaller force of 187 Fortresses in the First Division escorted by 42 Mustangs and preceded by a sweep of the area by 62 Thunderbolts attacked the Rhine bridges at Cologne. Norman K. Andrew, who was flying his 21st mission as navigator in Jack Stanley's crew in the 487th Bomb Group, went to Magdeburg. Andrew wrote:

"Up at 0245 for pre-briefing. What a target! Route in feinted at Berlin, cut back between Berlin and Brandenburg - over Magdeburg synthetic oil refinery - by Hanover, Dummer Lake, Zuider Zee and out over the Hook of Holland. We were leading the low. Went over the North Sea route, in west of Neumünster, north of Hamburg and aimed at Berlin. About 50 miles past Hamburg I saw 4 P-51s drop their tanks and peel off. One strafed a railroad. Couldn't see the other three. About a minute after they went down the Luftwaffe jumped the 390th flying two minutes ahead of us. They got all eight of the low squadron [which was lagging 2000ft below and behind the rest of the group because of supercharger problems with the leading B-17] in about a 3-minute fight. Not 15 minutes after that scramble was over about 30 FW 190s queued up about a half-mile off our right wing. Before they could start in the P-51s hit them. Just before we turned north of Brandenburg they hit the 390th high squadron. I could see the 20mm shells bursting throughout the formation. Four B-17s went down. In the two attacks I saw about 12 fighters go down. Couldn't tell whether they were '51s or '190s. Our high lead lagged behind just before Brandenburg. He never came back - it is supposed that the fighters got him. When last seen he was behind us at about 18,000ft and in the target area.[1151] At the IP our lead bombardier lost himself and took off toward Leipzig instead of Magdeburg. I thought the Air Leader had decided to bomb the secondary but after making a 180 we lined out on about a nine-mile bomb run. Our group bombardier, Al Fillipane - riding with us - took the course as okay and killed his rate on the terrain. Result - we dropped east of the Elbe River. The high hit part of the target. The smoke screen was heavy.

"Meanwhile the high squadron, with the #3 man leading, hadn't caught up. So they avoided the flak and joined us at the RP. The flak was intense and accurate - hit our #2 engine, right outside my window. We also had 6 hits in the wings and tail. We had to feather #2 on the bomb run. About 15 minutes after, #4 started running rough and smoking. Our Air Leader thought it was about to catch on fire. Jack opened the cowl flaps and cut it back. We held the lead - otherwise we never would have kept up. I kept a course to Brussels available in case we needed it. The high squadron dropped on the marshaling yard at Osnabrück. At the Dutch coast we headed for home and had to feather #4."

The 467th Bomb Group went to the Hallendorf steelworks west of Berlin. For *Witchcraft*, one of the most famous of all Liberators, it was her 100th mission, all without once turning back. A newspaper reporter flew in *Witchcraft* to cover the unique event. The Liberator went on to fly 30 more missions, and no crewmembers were killed or wounded, and the aircraft never returned to Rackheath without first bombing its target. By the same token *Lassie Come Home*, a Liberator in the 458th Bomb Group at nearby Horsham St. Faith, was an unlucky ship. It returned from the 14 January mission to the Hermann Göring Works at Halle with one engine stopped and its landing gear down. The pilot, who was on only his third mission, banked into his dead engine. He lost a second engine and crashed upside down on a housing estate near the base, killing the crew and two children who had been playing in a garden.

The Fortresses were well protected by escorting Mustangs, including red- and yellow-nosed P-51s of the 357th Fighter Group commanded by Colonel Irwin H. Dregne and based at Leiston, Suffolk. In the past eleven months the veteran group had flown 252 missions (most of which were bomber escort), and its pilots had been credited with 517 victories. No less than 39 pilots had attained ace status. All told, the 357th shot down 60-and-a-half enemy aircraft, a record for any 8th Air Force fighter group that still stood by the end of hostilities in Europe, for the *Luftwaffe* never again met the American fighters on equal terms.[1152]

The 78th Fighter Group at Duxford also enjoyed some success on 14 January, with the Mustang pilots claiming six FW 190D-9s and half a dozen Bf 109G/Ks during a combat with II *Gruppe* JG 26. Major Anton "Toni" Hackl was leading the formation to their assigned patrol zone in the Cologne area when about halfway there they were bounced by seven P-47s in the alert flight in the 366th Fighter Group who had taken off from Asch, in Belgium. Despite having an initial advantage the 366th came off worse. East of Liège Hackl claimed a P-47, and west of Koblenz *Führer* Johann Spahn of 8th *Staffel* claimed another of the Group's Thunderbolts. The 366th Fighter Group claimed two Doras shot down, but none were in fact lost. Hackl's formation continued across Aachen, and west of Cologne he led them in a shallow left turn. Unbeknownst to Hackl, his fighters were being tracked by American radar on the continent, and 25 P-51s in the 78th Fighter Group were ordered to break off their bomber escort and make for the Cologne area.

Three miles southwest of Cologne Lieutenant Willard Warren in the 82nd Fighter Squadron, who was at 26,000ft, sighted 15 plus bogies down on the deck. Receiving permission to attack, he dropped tanks and took his wingman, William DeGain, down on a bounce. They barreled right through another 15 enemy aircraft they had failed to see and jumped the original formation. The Germans, who were in the process of assembling for an attack on the bombers, were taken completely by surprise. Pursuing three of the enemy fighters, Warren opened fire on a FW 190D with hits in the cockpit that killed its pilot and caused the Dora to flick into the ground. DeGain, traveling at 450mph and seeing that his leader was clear, moved up behind a Bf 109 and opened up with several short bursts, which caused the canopy to fly off and its right gear to drop. As he passed DeGain saw the pilot standing on his seat just before the Messerschmitt pulled up and its engine exploded, spinning it into the ground. Warren, meanwhile, caught a Dora positioning on DeGain, and he rolled over onto it, firing a deflection shot. His shells hit the 190D's cockpit canopy, causing the fighter to crash and explode.

When the bogies were called out at 1210 hours Robert Smith bounced a single FW 190D going north over Cologne. The two pilots played hide-and-seek from fog bank to fog bank, hopping over churches and tall buildings until Smith eventually got hits in the Dora's fuselage. At 50ft over northern Cologne the 190D's left wing went down, and it crashed and exploded in a three-gun heavy flak position.

Major Leonard Marshall, 84th Fighter Squadron, chased three fighters he thought were enemy aircraft, but he soon saw that one was a P-51 (Louis Hereford) pursuing two Bf 109s. One of the Messerschmitt pilots spotted Marshall behind him, and he broke left and tried to belly in. Hitting the ground at 300mph, the 109 disappeared in a huge cloud of snow and smoke. A wing came off and pieces flew in all directions. Turning his attention to the other 109, Marshall saw that Hereford was having trouble trying to get a bead on it. Marshall approached, and the 109 turned and fired a burst head-on. Both P-51s got in position behind the German and fired, Hereford from 400 yards, and Marshall from 800 yards. Marshall did not get any hits, but Hereford's attack caused the German pilot to bale out. Hereford quickly broke off because he thought Marshall represented another German on his tail. (Louis Hereford returned alone with a rough running engine, and he was finally forced to belly land at Merrillville, France.)

Richard Spooner, in the 83rd Squadron, got on the tail of another Bf 109. Closing to 200 yards, he fired and the German baled out as his fighter spun in. As Spooner was trying to film this kill, another enemy aircraft appeared and he gave chase. Closing to 400 yards on the deck, Spooner ran out of ammunition, so he decided to bluff the German. He closed to less than 100 yards, and the German broke right and hit some power lines before crashing in flames. Earl Stier got into a tight right-turning duel with one of the 109s hugging the ground heading east. When the German reversed his turn, Stier fired and caused a stream of coolant and oil. The German pulled up in a steep climb and baled out. Stier was just getting good strikes on another of six Bf 109s when 20mm went flashing over his canopy and he broke from three 109s on his tail. The last he saw of his second German the 109 was gliding down in trouble. Frank Oiler's leader and his wingman took out after two bandits going up a creek bed. A FW 190 went between them firing, so Oiler turned on his tail. He lost him over some woods, but picked up a Bf 109 and two FW 190s being chased by a lone P-51. Oiler called to the P-51 to take one and Oiler and his wingman took the other. The 190s broke opposite directions and the 109 went straight up. Oiler got into a Lufbery at 1100ft with the FW 190, and with the use of flaps got on his tail in two turns. Oiler fired a 3-second burst at about 35° deflection, and he observed many strikes in the cockpit, fuselage, and wing roots. Pieces flew off the 190, which did a half snap and went in upside down. Lieutenant Mark Wilson closed astern of a Bf 109 and had little trouble shooting off its left wing 3ft from the fuselage to send the German pilot spinning and snap rolling into the ground.

Having trouble dropping his right wing tank, Lieutenant Willis Lutz had been left above the fight by the rest of his flight. He tried to fire his guns to shake off the tank, but none of the guns would work. Deciding to go home, he saw three aircraft exit from the forest shading and, thinking they were P-51s, dived down to form on them. As he came closer he recognized them as FW 190s. Looking back he saw three more enemy fighters diving down on him from 5 o'clock. Lutz tried to get away, but they came in behind him. Pulling his left turn in tight, the four of them were in a Lufbery. Lutz pressed his gun-trigger as hard as he could and was delighted to find four .50s working. Gaining on the Germans in the turn, Lutz hit one and the pilot jettisoned his canopy and baled out. The American pilot gave another 190 a long burst, causing a fire in its right wing. The Dora flipped on its back at 100ft and crashed. Looking about, Lutz saw two FW 190s coming after him from the north. They all quickly got into another Lufbery, and again Lutz managed to outturn the enemy aircraft. After a couple of hits on a 190 he ran out of ammunition and the German pilot disengaged. Lutz ran a bluff on the remaining FW 190, which also turned tail and headed off to the east. Lutz resumed his course for England, but patchy ground fog forced him to hug the ground. He crossed Allied lines south of Aachen, and recognizing the area, he climbed to 350ft for a better view. As he leveled off, Allied AA guns opened up and hit his P-51 with their first burst. Lutz baled out and landed safely but injured near Hauset, Belgium.[1153]

On 16 January over 550 heavies supported by 13 fighter groups bombed two synthetic oil plants, two aircraft engine plants, and other targets in central Germany. At Lavenham, lead navigator Norman K. Andrew prepared to fly his 22nd mission. He wrote:

> "The CQ came in at 0300 but I was awake. Target: Dessau, Germany. Off the ground 0905. What a Cook's Tour it was. In over Holland and the Zuider Zee - north of Hanover and Magdeburg. Target: East of Leipzig - Schweinfurt. Over the Rhine River at Strasbourg. At this point we had our only flak - it was one gun (?) at the front lines. The bomber stream was about 5 miles wide and he had so many targets he couldn't make up his mind. Finally hit a ship, wounded two men. Returned to base - but was diverted to a RAF field at Finningley 120 miles north. We started running out of gas at Peterborough so we came down. Landed at Glatton. Traveled over 1400 miles over 5 countries."

On 17 January, more than 650 heavies supported by eight fighter groups flying close escort and three more flying area sweeps bombed three oil refineries and other targets in northwestern Germany. Next day only 100 B-17s supported by three fighter groups flew bomber sorties, attacking the marshaling yards at Kaiserlautern. After the bombing most of the Fortresses were diverted to bases on the continent because of heavy clouds. Norman K. Andrew flew his 23rd mission:

> "Was I surprised this morning! The CQ woke me at 0245 for target study. I had him check his list 3 times to be sure he was right. Target: Kaiserlautern, Germany. There were three groups of us in the 4th Wing going. They scrubbed the 1st, 2nd and all of the 3rd Divisions but us. At briefing they told us we would probably be diverted. At the target we (the low) and the high dropped first run. It was supposed to be cat and mouse - but the cat beacon did not have the code sheet delay. We dropped PFF and I had a Gee fix just 2½ miles short of the marshaling yards. The Air Leader with us wanted to circle the RP while the lead squadron made a second run. Bandits had been reported in the area and there was no flak at the target - so I said, Hell no - make a 2nd run with the high and lead. Then he told me the high had dropped so we went back over France and waited for them. On the way back we were diverted to Laon Couvron airfield, France. The soup was from 11,000 down to the ground. We made individual letdowns. What a nightmare! Couvron was full so we landed at Laon Athies A/F. The ground pounders were betting ever money that at least one B-17 would crash - but no one did."

Because of the weather the Liberators were prevented from flying a mission, but at Wendling the 392nd Bomb Group CO, Colonel Lorin L. Johnson, ordered a practice mission, "which," opined Quintin R. Wedgeworth, a navigator in the578th Bomb Squadron, "was in complete disregard for the weather." He added:

> "Lieutenant [J. C.] Decker and crew, from the 577th, disappeared during the snowstorm and were never heard from again. More victims of the North Sea, no doubt!"[1154]

No bomber missions were flown on 19 or 20 January, and missions only resumed on 21 January when about 750 heavies attacked targets at Aschaffenburg and marshaling yards, including one at Mannheim. At Lavenham, lead navigator Norman K. Andrew prepared to fly his 24th mission. He wrote:

> "Here we go again! Target: Primary, *Micro-H* on an armored vehicle works. Secondary, PFF on the marshaling yards - both in Mannheim, Germany. The 487th did not put up a group of our own. We led a squadron with Rattlesden (low). Formed at 12,000 and the weather caught us. Couldn't climb fast enough to keep out of it. So we took off on our own to avoid any planes in the clouds. Six of our wingmen went home when they became separated from us. We left England on our own and headed across France for Strasbourg. The contrails were dense, persistent - really hard to even see our own squadron. Our Air Leader really got worried about us being by ourselves. Jack and I had to argue like the devil before he saw the light on the bomb run. He wanted to bomb in group formation with just anyone. We wanted to take our seven-plane squadron in by ourselves. On account of Whitt is really an expert on PFF (couldn't bomb *Micro-H* - too far from the beacons). Then on the bomb run the bombsight froze up, due to lack of precautions by our visiting bombardier and Whitt dropped the bombs, aimed PFF at the center of Mannheim. Temperature at 27,000 was -65F and my left boot went out. Stamped my foot for five hours to keep it warm."

Quintin R. Wedgeworth, in the 392nd Bomb Group, was among those who went to the marshaling yards in Heilbron:

> "It was another blind drop with unobserved results. There was no enemy reaction on this 21st day of January. The weather really wasn't all that much better on the 28th either. We were still having snow squalls. But it was a double anniversary and tradition must be served. First of all, it marked the third birthday of the Eighth, having been activated at Savannah, Georgia on 28 January 1942. There were 74 officers, 81 enlisted men and no airplanes! Their mission: to pioneer strategic daylight precision bombing. Now, personnel and machines were numbered in the thousands and not many were questioning its mission any more.
>
> "I flew the Group mission as navigator in *Rebel Gal*.[1155] The assumed target was Dortmund, in the dreaded Ruhr Valley, or 'flak alley', as it was more normally referred to. Specifically, we were briefed to attack the Kaiserstuhl and Gneisenau benzol plants, three miles NE of the City. The Germans were mixing it with their gasoline to stretch their dwindling fuel supplies. The secondary was Münster.

Bomb Load: 12 500lb. The assembly was a botched-up affair from the word go! Take-off was scheduled for 0805 but the visibility, due to the swirling snow, strung us out so bad that we didn't get off until 0855 hours and the last eight ships couldn't make it at all! In addition to that, five more ships subsequently had to abort! The remaining 17 Liberators managed to form up at 17,000ft; departing beacon #21 at 0948 hours. Somewhat north of the planned course, we departed the English coastline NW of Happisburgh; heading out into the North Sea to check point A, where the climb commenced. Our ascent was a gradual one (less than 70 FPM) to the point of entry on the Dutch mainland; the coastal town of Den Hoorn. The climb continued all the way to Meppel, were we leveled off at 23,000ft. The time was 1125 hours and we were running 28 minutes late! The IP was a little Dutch village called Ootmarsum, so small that the lead navigators were unable to pick it up and thus caused us to overshoot the planed turning point. However, they quickly managed to correct the error near Schuttorf where I gave the orders to throw the *Chaff*. Instead of the code words 'Happy Day' they should have been 'Cold Day'; the temperature was a bitter 45 below!

"Up ahead there is a dirty looking cloud of ominous origin. In just moments, the faint smell of gunpowder began to ooze its way on board. The next salvo burst just ahead of us as we sailed thru the already dissipating puffs. Suddenly it was all around us; with some bursts close enough to jolt the airplane. I pulled my chest pack a little closer and climbed deeper into the flak helmet and vest. Miraculously, two full minutes went by without anyone being hit. It was as though the invisible projectiles had been launched with the intention of purposely coming as close as possible without actually hitting us! Such nonsense was abruptly terminated as several ships begin to evidence trouble; the tell-tale stream of black smoke spewing out the life blood of an impaired engine and ominously feathered props that now lay impaled and motionless on the bodies of their dead masters. Suddenly, one of our escorts (a P-51) exploded right overhead. The next volley rocked us and we too were hit; that metallic ring that had become all too familiar.

"The formation by now was a shambles and the lead ship was calling on the command frequency to fill in the holes and tighten up. The remaining aircraft strained to close the formation for the bomb drop. It had been three minutes since we entered the target area. Now, steady on the run, I didn't see how we could miss. With the German earth mantled in snow, the buildings, forests, roads, etc were all sharply contrasted. The twelve 500 pounders were finally discharged at 1202 hours and we started an agonizingly slow 180° turn to the left for Osnabrück. One of the 577th ships was now in real distress. Struggling to stay upright, it unavoidably collided with another, tearing off the latter's wing and sending them both plummeting earthward. Only four chutes were counted before the stricken vessels exploded into eternity.[1156]

"Our engines were running smoothly, apparently undamaged and no one had been injured. We began to breathe a little easier. To avoid the defenses at Osnabrück, we stayed well to the east thereof, utilizing the corridor between the city and the Dummer Lake. It was 1313 hours when we finally made landfall at Den Helder. We were 13 minutes behind schedule and 15 miles north of the planned route. The trip back across the lowlands had been mercifully uneventful! The water crossing took another 31 minutes and there was nothing very momentous about it either. The ETR at Wendling was 1356 hours. We were one minute late, which I thought was rather amazing considering that we were forty minutes off at the target! As the ships commenced peeling off into the landing pattern, I packed my junk into a briefcase and headed back for the flight deck; B-24s had a nasty history of nose gear failures. We touched down at 1415 hours, taxied to a revetment and climbed out. It was always good to feel the terra firma! As I stood there wondering what it was that made me feel unfamiliar with the surroundings, a ship with a *vertical* black-striped tail taxied by. I looked at Adsit; he returned a sheepish grin. We had landed at Shipdham, home of the 44th Group, our neighbors! They were only five miles SE of us, so the landing patterns almost overlapped. He had forgotten that we had been part of their formation today. We had to sit there, of course, until they were all down and parked. While waiting, we inspected the ship for flak damage. It didn't require too much looking. They had gotten only a piece of our tail feathers! There was just one hole thru the horizontal stabilizer. It hadn't seemed to bother anything, so we decided to fly her out of there. By the time we got back to the base, we were an hour late. The de-briefing guys were sure unhappy with us. They would be late for supper! They informed us that it had been a very successful strike, with 93% inside the 2000ft radius. But it had also been a costly one to us. Besides the two lost aircraft, the 576th had three wounded men and seven of the returning ships had battle damage."

Meanwhile, at Wormingford, 1st Lieutenant Walter J. Konantz flew his 53rd and 54th missions on 21 and 22 January when the 55th Fighter Group escorted the B-17s to Mannheim and Sterkrade. On the latter mission he and the rest of Red Flight closely escorted three crippled B-17s to the Dutch coast on the way home. On 29 January Walt Konantz notched his fourth aerial victory of the war when the 55th Fighter Group escorted the B-17s to Kassel. He wrote:

"Two flights (8 P-51s) left the bombers for a fighter sweep on the way out. Our flight ran into three Me 109s at about 5000ft, 100 miles northwest of Hamburg. I saw them first and led the flight to them. I picked the leader who was carrying an external belly tank. The other two were clean. I got a good burst into him, setting his belly tank on fire. He promptly dropped it and continued on, leading me over a small town that was throwing up 20mm flak. We ended up over the town at about 50ft, circling a brewery smokestack below its top. We were in a hard right turn pulling three or four Gs when I got a hit on his left aileron, blowing about a third of it off. The sudden loss of lift on that side caused him to violently snap to an inverted position. I left my gun camera running, expecting him to split ess into the middle of the town but he climbed inverted to a safe altitude and rolled upright. He then headed out into open country flying so low he was pulling up over fences and descending again on the other side. His prop tips were barely clearing the snow-covered ground and his prop wash was blowing up snow behind him like a car on a dusty road. After another good burst of hits, he simply pushed forward on the stick and bellied in at 280mph. He slid for more than a half mile, coming to rest in a grove of trees with his wings sheared off. When I passed over him, he was climbing out of the cockpit and saluted me as I went by. My wingman was close behind me and strafed the wreckage, setting it on fire. Whether or not the pilot escaped the strafing, neither my wingman nor me knew."[1157]

Quintin R. Wedgeworth, in the 578th Bomb Squadron, was one of those in the 392nd Bomb Group who visited the Altenbekin Viaduct near Paderborn:

"However, due to poor weather, the secondary (Hamm marshaling yards) was the target for this 29th day of January. The

29th was also the second anniversary of the first full-scale attack on the Reich when 806 bombers, together with 634 fighters for escort, bombed Frankfurt. We couldn't celebrate any anniversaries of our own, but we sure had a lot of 'firsts' going; first trip to the Ruhr Valley, first oil target and our first mission since baling out. The price we were paying to deny the Germans any oil was high, but it did not deter the High Command's determination for pressing home this campaign. The enemy, of course, was just as determined to protect their dwindling supplies. We would now test their resolve. The bombing had to be done with H_2X and the results were unobserved. Unlike yesterday's stormy venture, this mission turned out to be a milk run. The flak was moderate but inaccurate and all ships returned safely.

"Clouds continued to mask the British Isles and most of the Continent for much of the next two weeks. It cleared briefly on the 3rd of February, permitting the Group to accomplish mission #233. We had been assigned to the oil complex at Magdeburg but wound up bombing (by H_2X) the marshaling (secondary) yards. The flak was moderate and fairly accurate, with six ships being hit. The results were again unobserved but evidently considered poor since we were reassigned again on the 6th. (Mission #234 turned out to be a carbon copy of the previous effort. Plagued by bad weather, they were once again forced to use the H_2X system against the secondary.)

"We spent the next two days doing routine aircraft flight checkouts; an hour and 15 minutes on Wednesday and an hour and five minutes on Thursday. The Group was also active on these days, flying missions #247 and #248 against Siegen (east of Bonn) and Ingolstadt; south of Nurnberg. Both targets were marshaling yards. The weather prevented any visual sighting, so the bombing results went unobserved. All planes returned safely.

"The Germans had instituted elaborate defense measures to frustrate our oil offensive. The Luftwaffe conserved its fighters until it was certain that we would once again attack and then it would come up in force. Some 12,000 AA guns were moved into the areas ringing the targets. In some places, the gun concentrations were double of those around Berlin. Heavy smoke screens were used to obscure the targets and confuse the navigators and bombardiers. Huge labor battalions with great quantities of mechanical equipment and materials for immediate repair were stationed near the oilfields so that reconstruction could commence almost as soon as the last bomb had exploded. Even so, the Germans were losing this battle. Had our high command realized the real significance of their losses, we probably would have hit them even more."

By 3 February 1945, Marshal Zhukov's Red Army was only 35 miles from Berlin, and the capital was jammed with refugees fleeing from the advancing Russians; the strike against railroad stations and freight yards was designed to cause the German authorities as much havoc as possible. Major Robert "Rosie" Rosenthal, flying his 52nd mission, led the 100th Bomb Group and the 3rd Division, General Earle E. Partridge having approved the selection of a squadron commander to lead the division.[1158] The 8th lost 21 bombers over the capital and another six crash-landed inside the Russian lines. The B-17 flown by Major Rosenthal, flying with Captain John Ernst, was hit in the No.1 gas tank and the bomb bay a few seconds before bombs away, and the crew baled out after the bombs were dropped.[1159] Of the bombers that returned, 93 had suffered varying forms of major flak damage. Among the losses had been *Birmingham Jewel* in the 379th Bomb Group, which had set an 8th Air Force record of 128 missions.

Further German disruption in the face of the Russian advance occurred on 6 February, when 1300 heavies escorted by 15 groups of P-51 Mustangs bombed Chemnitz and Magdeburg, and the 8th resumed its oil offensive with raids on synthetic oil refineries at Lutzkendorf and Merseburg. Norman K. Andrew went to the latter target for his 25th mission. He wrote:

> "I wonder if there is any weather in which they don't fly in the ETO? Up at 0200 again this morning. Target: Hold your hat! The Bohlen synthetic oil refinery right in the center of the Merseburg-Lutzkendorf-Ziest areas. But - visual only. Dresden, secondary and Chemnitz, last resort. We led the high. Took off in the dark, as usual at 0705. Supposed to assemble at 17,500. Clouds finally forced us down to 7000. Went in over Holland. Toured over every flak area between here and the target. Bohlen was 10/10ths. Dresden had cover to about 30,000 so we hit Chemnitz PFF - two divisions - 1st and 3rd. The 2nd hit Magdeburg. After leaving the target we received word not to try to come home the northern way but to go south. About that time the lead's Mickey went out and our VHF was out. So the low took over and we went right over Schweinfurt (no flak). After wandering around near Stuttgart we took off across the Rhine between Karlsruhe and Mannheim. Got some meager inaccurate front line flak. Let down all the way across Luxembourg, Belgium and France. Crossed the Channel at 200ft. The base had no ceiling and we sort of felt our way in. After landing we watched the boys come in. They liked to scare us to death! Finally one went off the end of the runway. Three crews landed on the Continent and one crew baled out by Beachy Head. 10½ hours today. Flew over 7 countries - England, Holland, Germany, Czechoslovakia, France, Luxembourg and Belgium."

Bad weather forced all except one 1st Air Division Fortress to return to England while over the North Sea. Altogether, 22 bombers were lost in crash landings in England. The sole B-17 continued to Essen and dumped its load before returning home alone without meeting any opposition. Such an occurrence would have been unthinkable a few months before, but now the *Luftwaffe* had been all but swept from the skies.

Russell A. Grantham, in the 487th Bomb Group, recalls that:

> "Around 1 February I was called to Headquarters and told that I had been selected to lead the next raid on Leipzig oil refineries. I was also told that the same lead crew personnel would have to keep going back until it was 100% destroyed. At that time, the refineries in Leipzig had sustained heavy damage, but they would manage to partially recover after each raid. Air Force wanted them completely out of commission. It was somewhat disturbing to think that you may have to spend your last four missions going to Leipzig, but by that time we were veterans and you did what needed to be done. Our first of that series was relatively uneventful, except for concentrated flak in the target area. The cloud cover was intense and results not totally satisfactory. On our second mission on 6 February, the target was totally obscured by clouds and we went to the secondary target at Chemnitz. Our target was to be a large marshaling yard, which we hit smack on target. There was an enormous explosion and what we did not know then, but were later told, we had caught several ammunition trains assembled for shipment to the Russian Front. On the 3rd mission the sky was clearly visible and the balance of the oil industry in Leipzig was blown off the map. The mission was fairly routine with the heavy concentration of flak in the target area but no

fighters. On return to the base, I was advised there would be no need to return to Leipzig and I was relieved of duty and returned to the states for rest and recuperation. I was given credit for a full tour, but flew one mission less than the normally required number."

On 9 February 1200 heavies operating in six forces attacked Rothensee and Lutzkendorf synthetic oil plants and other targets supported by 15 fighter groups, six of which later strafed rail and road targets. Norman K. Andrew in the 487th Bomb Group, who flew his 26th mission this day, wrote:

"Looks like they are trying to finish us up on the rough ones. Today's primary was Bohlen, visual only. That's what is saving us lately, that visual only. Secondary: Wismar, PFF or visual. So we bombed Wismar marshaling yard and small arms plant. We really plastered it! We went in the Koblenz-Frankfurt corridor. No flak - surprise! Just north of Frankfurt six Me 262s jumped us but they didn't get a shot. One came across in front of us from 2 o'clock high to 8 o'clock low with a P-51 right on his tail. Rector had him in his sights but couldn't fire because of the P-51. That fellow was rugged - he circled around and tried again for a pass. Went right through the formation - but by then he had five P-51s after him and they weren't losing any ground either. I was too interested to be scared. At Hamburg and Magdeburg I was so scared I couldn't swallow but today I was wishing to hell I had my guns back in or at least my camera. We went on to the target, flying right over Wismar and didn't get any flak - it was 10/10ths. Today was about 5/10ths and they had a three-gun battery. What sharpshooters! Went in at 26,000ft and lost two ships. One went down at the target -lost a wing. The other one might have made France. Our pictures showed a perfect strike. One bomb went right in the building that was the MPI and we were dropping RDKs too."

On 10 February the heavies returned to the ever-diminishing Reich, now seriously threatened by the Russian armies converging from the east. Some 150 B-17s bombed the Dulmen oil depot, the town of Lingen, and the E-boat pens at Ijmuiden, in Holland, where the first raid using "Disney" bombs went ahead. The 45001b bomb invented by Captain Edward Terrell of the Royal Navy was powered by a rocket motor in the tail, and was designed to pierce 20ft of concrete before exploding. Their weight prevented carriage in the bomb bay of a B-17, so the nine B-17s in the 92nd Bomb Group dispatched to Ijmuiden carried two "Disneys" under each wing. Colonel James W. Wilson, the CO, led the raid, and strike photos were later to reveal a direct hit at the north end of the pens. Part of the E-boat shelters had also been hit where a final portion of the roof had not yet been laid, destroying a large section of the structure over three pens and damaging the north wall.[1160]

Operation *Thunderclap* should have begun on 13 February with a raid by the 8th Air Force on the old city of Dresden, in eastern Germany,[1161] but the weather prevented the strike going ahead. However, that night RAF Bomber Command carried out a two-fold attack on the city. So great were the conflagrations caused by the firestorms created in the great heat generated in the first attack that crews in the second attack reported the glow was visible 200 miles from the target.[1162] In a follow up raid shortly after 12 noon on 14 February the 8th Air Force despatched nearly 1300 bombers to attack marshaling yards at Dresden and other targets.[1163] From this total, 450 B-17s were sent to Dresden. Flying his first mission this day was William C. Stewart, a ball turret gunner in the 92nd Bomb Group at Podington:

"I got up, dressed, proceeded through the darkness to the combat mess and ate breakfast without much interest. The thought of flying the first mission was not conducive to having a good appetite. Walking into the enlisted men's briefing in a building near the flight line, I saw the room-size map of Europe on the front wall. There was a red ribbon on the map, held by pins, showing the route to be flown. The target on the map was Dresden. I had never heard of this German City before. We flew the dogleg route over the Zuider Zee and into Germany. The weather under us was completely cloud-covered and I could not see the ground. I turned the turret, keeping watch for enemy fighters all the way to Dresden. When we neared the IP I turned the turret facing forward and could see the black bursts of flak directly in front of us at our level. We flew to that place in the sky where the flak was heaviest and I heard the bombardier shout, 'Bombs Away!' The plane rose in the air and settled back. We had dropped our bombs on Dresden, which from published reports was still experiencing firestorms from the RAF bombing the night before. It was a long trip back to friendly territory and I finally got out of the turret when we were over France. By this time our fuel supply was growing short but we made it into AAF base right over the English coast. We landed and got sufficient gas to make it to Podington. However, the No.1 engine caught fire when started and had to be extinguished. We begged a ride back to the base with another 92nd crew who had also landed at the field. It was late in the evening when we finally reached our home base. Debriefing was held at the same time we were eating our evening meal. We were given one shot of whisky before eating and I felt a little light-headed afterwards. The debriefing officer asked his questions and it was then that I learned, when the other crewmembers answered, that the flak was 'meager.' I thought it was worse than that but this was only my first mission. The plane didn't get hit so this may have had something to do with it. I was to learn later on what 'intense' flak really was."[1164]

On 14 February almost 1300 heavy bombers attacked marshaling yards at Dresden, Chemnitz, Magdeburg, and Hof, as well as other targets at Wesel, Dulmen, and two airfields and ten town areas. Sixteen fighter groups escorted the bombers or flew area sweeps strafing ground targets. The Mustangs also engaged 75 enemy fighters and claimed 20 destroyed. Major Robin Olds, 434th Fighter Squadron CO,[1165] who was leading Newcross Green Flight in the 479th Fighter Group in a P-51K, claimed three of these. He recalled:

"Our squadron was between Magdeburg and Berlin at an altitude of 27,000ft and had started to make a 360° turn to the left when two bogies were called in at 6 o'clock low, passing from north to south. I glanced back and saw not two, but four bogies. As we made our turn, we lost altitude, going down to approximately 24,500ft. In the meantime, these four bogies made a 360° left turn also but they gained altitude during their turn. As we rolled out of the turn and headed about 90° again, the four bogies were an estimated 3000ft above and behind our formation. I thought that they were enemy but could not identify them positively. Then more bogies were called in at 12 o'clock high and passing 20° across our front, towards us. We turned right and started climbing after them. At this time, they split into three small groups, one continuing southwest, one heading west and the other, north. The squadron split up to go after them. I was closest to the six bogies that went southwest. They were flying in one flight of four, as in a regular P-51 formation, with two 'Tail-End-Charlies' lagging behind. As we climbed, I identified them positively as Me 109s. Before I drew into range on the last two, the flight of four,

A brand-new FW 190D-9 having just been flown in from the Focke-Wulf works to II./JG 26 at Reinsehler airfield, south of Hamburg, in September 1944. *Obergefreiter* Werner Molge is seen here checking out the controls of the aircraft. Note the tactical number "White 9" from the ferrying unit on the tail. (Werner Molge via Theo Boiten)

B-17G-35-BO 42-320237 *Betty Jane* in the 427th Bomb Squadron, 303rd Bomb Group, which went MIA with 2nd Lieutenant C.W. Heleen's crew on the mission to Gera oil installation on 13 September 1944. One crewman was KIA and eight survived to be made PoWs. (USAF)

Above left: B-17G-85-BO *Heaven Sent*, which joined the 350th Bomb Squadron, 100th Bomb Group on 1 September 1944 and flew its first mission on 18 September when the Group dropped supplies to the Polish Home Army in Warsaw before flying on to Mirgorod in Russia. *Heaven Sent's* Varga-style nose art was painted by S/Sgt Mike Garemko, engineer in Thomas Anderson's crew, who were the first to fly the B-17. On 6 February 1945 the crew were forced to leave the badly damaged Fort at the French fighter field at Dole, near Dijon. *Heaven Sent* was repaired, and it returned to Thorpe Abbotts to fly more combat missions before returning to the ZOI on 30 May 1945. (TAMM) Center: B-17G-40-DL 44-6009 *Flak Eater* with shark teeth adorning the chin turret, pictured with Flight Officer Jones and his crew in the 364th Bomb Squadron, 305th Bomb Group at Chelveston on 29 August 1944. This Fortress was forced to put down on the Continent on 4 December 1944. It was repaired, and *Flak Eater* returned to the ZOI on 23 May 1945 and was scrapped. (USAF) Above right: B-17G-15-BO 42-31412 *Mason and Dixon* in the 351st Bomb Squadron, 100th Bomb Group, which was assigned overseas in December 1943, pictured here with Ollie Turner and crew. The name and fabulous artwork was painted by Sgt Frank Stevens for pilot Captain Floyd H. "Buck" Mason and navigator William "Bill" Dishion, although the two men were assigned to the 349th Bomb Squadron and this Fort was never flown by Mason. On 28 July 1944 he was shot down piloting 42-97555 *Island F For Fox*, a 95th Bomb Group PFF radar ship, while leading the 100th Bomb Group on the mission to Merseburg. Two crewmen were KIA and nine survived to be taken prisoner. *Mason and Dixon* was flown on the second *Frantic* shuttle mission to Russia on 18 September 1944, and it sustained severe flak damage on the mission the following day. Left at Foggia as fit only for salvage, the B-17 was repaired, and it eventually returned to Thorpe Abbotts, where it resumed missions in mid-October 1944 and continued to fly combat until it was finally declared "war weary" and was returned to the ZOI. (TAMM)

Above left: B-17G-45-BO 42-97368 *Tailwind* in the 368th Bomb Squadron, 306th Bomb Group, which was lost with 1st Lieutenant John W. Sasser's crew on 12 September 1944 while leading the high group to Ruhland after being shot out of formation by flak. Two engines were immediately put out of action and several crewmembers were wounded, so it was decided not to bale out, but to try to reach a neutral country. Once out of formation the *Luftwaffe* spotted the cripple, and in a single pass they knocked out a third engine. With only No.1 still running the decision was made to crash land the plane, but the last engine failed on the final approach into a field. *Tailwind* dropped precipitately, clipped an oak tree, broke apart, and threw most of the crew out of the radio room, where they had assumed crash landing positions. Five men died in the crash. Sasser and three others survived, although they were all seriously injured. Sasser was the most critically injured, and he died on 20 March 1945 during surgery on his head wounds at Meinengen, Germany. (Richards) Center: B-17G-60-BO 42-102969 *Methuselah 969 Years* (so named for its last three digits of its serial number) was a 367th Bomb Squadron, 306th Bomb Group veteran. On 12 September 1944, when *Methuselah* was flown by 1st Lieutenant Earl R. Barr, fighters hit Nos.1 and 3 engines, the right wing, and the radio room, setting them on fire. Bale out was ordered, and most of the crew jumped, but T/Sgt Hector Chavez, engineer, and S/Sgt Nicholas Hoolko, ball turret, were still in the waist section when the Fortress exploded, but a section remained intact and they were able to bale out. Barr landed and stumbled around for several hours before police from a small town captured him. The only casualty was 2nd Lieutenant Mathew A. Meyerson, navigator, who either fell out of his chute or did not have it on when the plane exploded. (via Richards) Above right: *Unteroffizier* Ottomar Kruse, a FW 190A-8 pilot in 8./JG 26 during the summer of 1944. In his short spell of operations over the invasion front (8 combat sorties in four weeks) he shot down a 354th Fighter Group Mustang on 16 August at Rambouillet and a 474th Fighter Group P-38 Lightning on 25 August. On 16 September 1944 50th Fighter Group Thunderbolts shot down Kruse at Nutherveld and he became a PoW. (Ottomar Kruse via Theo Boiten)

Three Mustangs of the 359th Fighter Group at East Wretham, Norfolk. A new P-51D, 44-13669 "CV-I" *Pegelin* in the 368th Squadron, which accompanies two P-51Bs from the same unit, has yet to receive its fin fillet. (via Mike Bailey)

B-17G-70-BO 43-37715 GY-V *Lassie Come Home*, which was assigned overseas on 13 June 1944, and B-17G-55-BO 42-102578 GY-D *We Promised*, which was assigned overseas on 18 May 1944 (when it joined the 398th BG) in the 367th Bomb Squadron, 306th Bomb Group in flight. *Lassie Come Home* was salvaged on 8 January 1945. *We Promised* twice FTR when it was landed on the continent in March and April 1945 before being transferred to the 381st Bomb Group. It returned home in 1945 and was scrapped at South Plains, Texas, in June 1946. (USAF)

Above left: Captain (later Major) John A. Storch, CO 364th Fighter Squadron, 357th Fighter Group with Assistant Crew Chief Sgt Joe Kubarek and P-51D 44-13546 C5-R *The Shillelagh*, one of two Mustangs that had this name. Storch finished the war with 10½ victories. (Merle Olmsted via Ian McLachlan) Center: Major George E. Preddy, 352nd Fighter Group, whose final confirmed score of 26.833 (and 5 strafing) victories made him the second highest scoring American fighter ace in the ETO behind Gabby Gabreski. (USAF) Above right: Lieutenant Robert J. Bain and his ground crew in the 376th Fighter Squadron, 361st Fighter Group beside their P-51 Mustang *Blue Eyes*. (via Steve Gotts)

B-24 *Hard T' Find* in the 458th Bomb Group, which came from the 487th Bomb Group and was salvaged on 23 September 1944. (USAF)

On 18 September, when 252 supply-carrying B-24s headed for LZ.N Knapheide-Klein Amerika (Little America), near Groesbeek, in Holland, to drop supplies to the First Allied Army, this B-24 was photographed some miles west of Breda by Jaap Beynes, who risked his life taking this picture. The Dutchman was saving his precious film for the liberation, but felt compelled to take this remarkable photo. Some 80% of all the supplies dropped by the B-24s were recovered. (Jaap Beynes via Father G. Thuring)

P-51Ds of the 335th Fighter Squadron, 4th Fighter Group in September 1944. Nearest aircraft is WD-C 44-13779. (USAF)

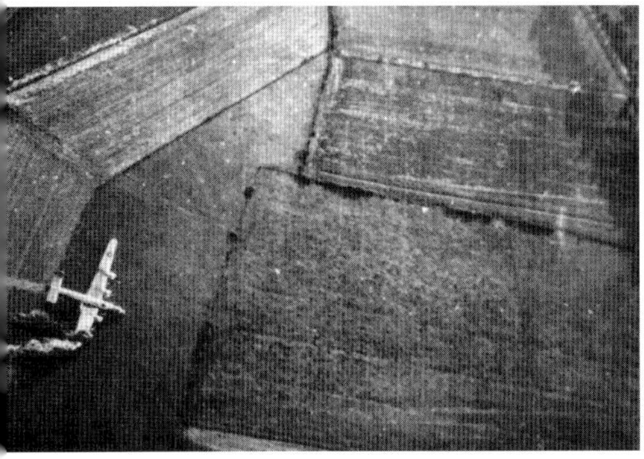

Above left: B-24J-140-CO 42-110164 *Blockbuster* in the 855th Bomb Squadron, 491st Bomb Group dropping supplies on 18 September. The 14th Wing dropped their supplies to the 101st American Airborne Division at Best, Holland. Several Allied gliders can be seen in fields in the right hand side of the picture. (Dan Winston) Left center: The 491st Bomb Group lost four Liberators on the 18 September mission, including B-24J-150-CO 44-40210 *I'll Be Seeing You*, the lead aircraft flown by Captain James K. "Jim" Hunter, and which also carried Captain Anthony Mitchell, the Air Commander. *I'll Be Seeing You* was shot down by small arms fire while flying at about 100ft. Only the tail gunner survived the crash. In all the 2nd Bomb Division lost 18 Liberators and 70 more were damaged, while 21 fighters were shot down. (Dan Winston) Below left: B-24 Liberators in the 44th Bomb Group dropping supplies on 18 September 1944. B-24H-20-DT 42-51101 WQ-E (left) is *Corky* in the 68th Bomb Squadron. WQ-V is B-24H-30-CF 42-50427 *Puritanical Bitch*. *Corky* was lost with Lieutenant Maurice D. Corwine's crew on 28 January 1945 on the mission to Dortmund. Four members of his crew were KISA and six were taken prisoner. *Puritanical Bitch* crashed at Shipdham on 22 March 1945. (USAF)

Above left: 1st Lieutenant William Rockafeller Beyer, known as "Bright Eyes" by his squadron buddies and well liked by everyone, had gained his first victory in the 376th Fighter Squadron, 361st Fighter Group on 17 September when he shot down and killed Major Klaus Mietusch, CO III./JG 26, a career officer who was a veteran of 452 combat sorties and had claimed 72 aerial victories. (via Steve Gotts) Above right: 1st Lieutenant William "Bill" Rockafeller Beyer (left) with 1st Lieutenant Victor Bocquin (right), who was leading the 376th Squadron, together accounted for 8 e/a destroyed and are writing up their encounter reports after their combat on 17 September 1944. After interrogation Intelligence personnel confirmed that the 376th Fighter Squadron's claim of 18 aerial victories plus three ground claims amounted to a record total for any 8th Air Force squadron in a single day's operations. (via Steve Gotts)

Left: 22-year-old pilot *Gefreiter* Ernst Schroeder, II.*Sturm*/JG 300 in the cockpit of his FW 190 *Red 19 "Kolle-alaaf!"* (Cologne-aloft - Schroeder was born in Cologne). On 27 September 1944 Schroeder destroyed one of the 25 Liberators in the 445th Bomb Group that FTR from a raid on Kassel. Five more crashed in France and England. Only five made it back to Tibenham. (Schroeder) Right: *Staffelkapitän* Oskar Romm of *Sturm* IV/JG 3 *"Udet,"* whose first downing of a *Viermot* was over Oschersleben on 7 July 1944. On 27 September 1944 he destroyed a B-24 of the 445th Bomb Group on the raid on the Henschel engine and vehicle assembly plants at Kassel, in central Germany, and the next day, he claimed two B-17 kills to take his tally to 85. (via Heinz Nowarra)

Below left and center: Eighteen *Luftwaffe* pilots were reported KIA on 17 September, including *Ofhr* Keim and *Oberfeldwebel* Weuack, with several others injured. (via Steve Gotts) Below right: 2nd Lieutenant William R. Beyer (left) posing for a PR photo with Captain Roy Webb. On 27 September Bill Beyer destroyed no less than five FW 190s in the vicinity of Eisenach. In total Beyer scored 9 confirmed wartime victories by 26 November 1944. (via Steve Gotts)

Above left: B-24 Liberators in the 445th Bomb Group en route to their target at Glinde, Germany, on 6 October 1944. (USAF) Center: B-17G-50-VE 44-8200 in the 861st Bomb Squadron, 493rd Bomb Group with its *H2X* radome extended, dropping bombs over the target. (USAF) Above right: B-17G-1-BO 42-31053 BX-W *Stingy* in the 338th Bomb Squadron, 96th Bomb Group, which was lost in a mid-air collision over Towcester, Northamptonshire, during a training flight on 9 October 1944. B-17F-75-DL 42-3510 AW-P piloted by 2nd Lieutenant Jack C. Core in the 337th Bomb Squadron rose straight up and hit B-17G-70-BO 43-37684 AW-E in the nose with its tail section, and 510 was sheared in two. Piloted by Lieutenant Nick Jorgenson, *Stingy* (which had been named for General Frederick Anderson, 8th AF Operations Commander's young son) hit 684 with its rudder and also broke in half. Core's crew of four were killed, as were all seven of Jorgensen's crew. (via Geoff Ward)

Above left: Lieutenant John O. "Rams" Ramsey, navigator in Lieutenant Bernie L. Iwanciow's crew in the 860th Bomb Squadron, 493rd Bomb Group, who on 3 October 1944 flew their first mission, to Nürnburg, one of the longest the group had flown. (Ramsey) Center: 1st Lieutenant (later Major) Urban L Drew, 375th Fighter Squadron, 361st Fighter Group, who finished his combat tour with 6 confirmed victories. On 7 October 1944, flying P-51D 44-14164 *Detroit Miss*, Drew shot down two Me 262s of *Kommando Nowotny* over Achmer airfield, the first Allied fighter pilot to down two of the jets in one sortie. Upon his return the American ace was recommended for the award of the DSC, but was turned down because of insufficient information. Drew's camera gun had jammed, and his wingman, Lieutenant Robert K. McCandliss, had broken away during the attack to avoid *Flak* and had not witnessed the actual shootdowns (McCandliss was shot down over Rheine airfield and became a PoW). In 1967 Drew received confirmation of the two victories from none other than Major Georg-Peter Eder, who witnessed everything from the ground after aborting his take-off with engine failure! In May 1983 Ben Drew was presented with the award of the Air Force Cross (modern equivalent of the DSC, and ranked second only to the MoH). He and Eder, two former adversaries, became firm friends. (via Steve Gotts) Above right: In October 1944 Major Joseph E. Broadhead returned to Leiston as the 357th Fighter Group Operations Officer. During the period from February to 28 May 1944 the 24-year-old pilot from Rupert, Idaho, had scored 6 victories in the 362nd Fighter Squadron, which he commanded from 10 March 1944. Broadhead added two more kills to his victory total before being promoted to Lieutenant Colonel in February 1945 and completing his second tour. (Merle C. Olmsted)

Above left: In Germany, three assault *Gruppen*, or *Sturmgruppen* (II./JG 4, IV./JG 3 *"Udet,"* and II./JG 300) had been formed to fly FW 190A-8/R2 fighters (also called *Rammbock* (Rammer) or *Sturmbock* (Battering Ram)) to ram American bombers. The fighter chosen was the heavy FW 190A 8/R2. Armored oil cooler, bullet-proof windshield, 6mm fireproof plates, and cabin sides, 9mm armor plate behind the pilot's seat, and standard 151/20, 2MK 108 3cm caliber weaponry led to double the fuel consumption. To guarantee three hours of flight, the fuel load was raised to 960 liters with a 300-liter ejectable auxiliary tank and a 110-liter auxiliary tank behind the pilot's seat. A tanked up and fully armed FW-190 A8/R2 had a flight weight of 7 to 8 tons. A 14-cylinder double star BMW 801 engine with a 2400hp maximum tried to make up for this additional weight, but the FW 190 was clearly inferior in dogfights with escort fighters. (Romm) Center: B-17G-15-VE 42-97442, which was assigned overseas on 21 February 1944 and joined the 532nd Bomb Squadron, 381st Bomb Group, crashed during a practice mission on 1 October 1944 and was later salvaged. (USAF) Above right: B-17G-90-BO 43-38452 *Undecided* in the 614th Bomb Squadron, 401st Bomb Group at Backs Torvmosse, Sweden, after suffering flak damage on the mission to Politz on 7 October 1944. 2nd Lieutenant Robert W. James' crew were interned. (via Frank Thomas)

Above left: B-17G-100-BO 43-38945/F *Duffy's Tuffys* in the 351st Bomb Squadron, 100th Bomb Group, and other Fortresses in the formation during Bombs Away. *Duffy's Tuffys* was later renamed *This Is It.* (USAF) Above right: B-17G-15-DL 43-37883 *Blue Streak* in the 834th Bomb Squadron, 486th Bomb Group, which was shot down over Merseburg on 2 November 1944. All nine members of 2nd Lieutenant David M. Paris' crew were killed. (USAF)

Above left: 2nd Lieutenant Robert L. Ferrell, 20 year old lead navigator on B-24J-5-FO 42-50864 *Jolly Roger* in the 755th Bomb Squadron, 458th Bomb Group, piloted by 2nd Lieutenant William Klusmeyer, Jr., which FTR from the mission to Cologne on 14 October 1944. All ten crew were taken prisoner. (Ferrell) Center: Belgian children playing in the wreckage of B-17G-40-DL 44-6083 *Betsy Ross* in the 603rd Bomb Squadron, 398th Bomb Group, which crash-landed near Berlare on 19 October 1944. (USAF) Above right: At Shipdham on 15 August 1944 Col. John H. Gibson relinquished command of the 44th Bomb Group to Colonel Eugene H. Snavely of the disbanded 492nd Bomb Group and an original member of the "Eightballs." The appointment was not popular, because the men of the 44th did not wish to be associated with the bad luck that had dogged the ill-fated 492nd Bomb Group. Snavely brought with him his deputy and his popular Operations Officer, Major John I. "Jack" Turnbull (pictured). Turnbull was a member of the United States lacrosse team that won gold at the 1936 Olympic Games held in Berlin, and he received his medal from Adolf Hitler. Lieutenant Colonel Turnbull was killed on 18 October 1944 on the mission to Leverkusen, Germany, when he was flying as Command pilot in the lead B-24H-20-DT 41-28944/D, *The Flying Ginny* in the 67th Bomb Squadron, which was flown by 1st Lieutenant Mike Bakalo. They collided with B-24H-25-CF 42-50381/D, flown by Lieutenant Julian H. Dayball during an electrical storm over Belgium. There were no survivors from Dayball's ship, and only the two waist gunners survived in Bakalo's aircraft. (James J. Mahoney)

Above left: B-17G-90-BO 43-38525 *Miss Conduct* in the 418th Bomb Squadron, 100th Bomb Group. The majority of Fred Schaffhausen's crew at Thorpe Abbotts chose the name when they began flying this B-17 in October 1944. *Miss Conduct* survived the war and was scrapped at Albuquerque, New Mexico, on 6 February 1946. (TAMM) Center: B-17G-45-BO 42-97234 *Bomber Dear* in the 322nd Bomb Squadron, 91st Bomb Group at Bassingbourn. This aircraft and Lieutenant Donald R. Sparkman's crew FTR on 2 November 1944. Six men were KIA and three were taken into captivity. (USAF) Above right: B-17G-40-VE 42-97976 *A Bit O' Lace* in the 709th Bomb Squadron, 447th Bomb Group. (USAF)

On 15 October 1944, just after bombs away and the start of the turn away from the target, a direct flak hit over Cologne literally tore off the nose of B-17G-30-VE 42-97746 piloted by 1st Lieutenant Lawrence M. deLancey in the 603rd Bomb Squadron, 398th Bomb Group, instantly killing the toggelier, Sgt George Abbott. Without instruments and maps, 2nd Lieutenant Raymond J. LeDoux, navigator, managed to navigate the bomber back, and deLancey and his co-pilot, 1st Lieutenant Phillip H. Stahlman, set the Fort down at Nuthampstead without further mishap. The Fortress was salvaged later by the 2nd SAD. (USAF)

Above left: B-24J-155-CO *Azon* Liberator 44-40275 *Shack Time* in the 753rd Bomb Squadron, 458th Bomb Group overflying its home base at Horsham St. Faith, near Norwich. This aircraft crash landed on 12 November 1944 and was salvaged. (USAF) Above right: B-24J-145-CO 44-40073 *Ark Angel* flown by Lieutenant David N. Bennett in the 853rd Bomb Squadron, 491st Bomb Group, one of nine Liberators in the Squadron that were shot down on the mission to Misburg on 26 November 1944. The Martin top turret was knocked out and a large hole put in the right wing before the B-24 went down. There were no survivors. (Dan Winston)

Above left: B-17G-45-BO 42-97330 *Chug-A-Lug*, which was assigned to the 535th Bomb Squadron, 381st Bomb Group on 24 April 1944, and which FTR with 2nd Lieutenant Julius Levitoff's crew on the mission to Hamburg on 6 November 1943. Hit by flak, *Chug-A-Lug* crashed at Rotenburg with two crew KIA and seven surviving to be taken prisoner. (USAF) Center: B-24H-15-FO 42-52571 *Snooper* in the 790th Bomb Squadron, 467th Bomb Group, which was lost with all nine men in 2nd Lieutenant Maynard M. Ungerer, Jr.'s crew on 10 November 1944. (Healy) Above right: B-24J 44-40271 *House of Rumor*, 854th Bomb Squadron, 491st Bomb Group, which was lost with Lieutenant George A. Meuse's crew at Misburg, 26 November 1944. Three gunners ignored the bale out bell and went down with the ship, firing their guns to the end. USAF

Above left: B-17G-50-VE 44-8183 LD-Q in the 418th Bomb Squadron, 100th Bomb Group at its snowy revetment at Thorpe Abbotts in early November 1944. A terrific snowstorm blanketed East Anglia on 9 November as the Group narrowly avoided colliding with other groups returning from the mission to support ground forces near Metz. 44-8183 suffered battled damage on the mission to Hamm on 26 November and force landed at St. Trond, Belgium. It was repaired and returned to Thorpe Abbotts before flying home to the ZOI for scrapping at Walnut Ridge. (TAMM) Center: B-17G-100-BO 43-38963/E in the 351st Bomb Squadron, 100th Bomb Group at Thorpe Abbotts in early November 1944. This Fortress and Lieutenant Lawrence L. Bazin's crew FTR on 10 April 1945 when they crash landed at Jemmeritz. One man evaded, five were KIA, and four were taken prisoner. (TAMM) Above right: A gunner in the 323rd Bomb Squadron, 91st Bomb Group tries to clear frost and snow off the tail gun position of B-17G-65-VE 44-8431. This Fortress was assigned to the Group at Bassingbourn on 4 November, and it flew 46 missions before returning to the USA in June 1945 before being broken up for scrap at Kingman, Arizona. (USAF)

Right: Major (later Major General) Donald J. Strait in the 361st Fighter Squadron, 356th Fighter Group on the wing of P-51D 44-15152 QI-T *Jersey Jerk*. Strait scored 10½ of his 13½ victories flying P-51s. (USAF)

Above left: P-51D-15-NA Mustangs *Develess 3rd* and 44-15016 *Heat Wave* of the 369th Fighter Squadron, 359th Fighter Group, 67th Fighter Wing at East Wretham. Near Merseberg on 21 November 1944, 1st Lieutenant Claude J. Crenshaw from Monroe, Louisiana, flying *Heat Wave*, shot down four FW 190s and claimed a probable to take his wartime score to 7 confirmed kills. This tally is even more impressive considering that only three of his guns were working, and he was also forced to open fire at deflection angles of up to 9 plus! Crenshaw had scored his first victories on 11 September when he shot down two Bf 109s, and he added a third seven days later. *Heat Wave* was just one of three Mustangs that Crenshaw was assigned during his seven-month tour with the 369th. Crenshaw, who also scored three ground-strafing kills, completed his tour with 270 combat hours. (via Tony Chardella) Center: B-17G-75-BO 43-37877 2G-E in the 836th Bomb Squadron, 487th Bomb Group on fire after a direct hit over Merseburg, Germany, on 30 November 1944. The aircraft crashed at Halle. Seven members of Lieutenant Lloyd W. Kersten's crew were KIA and two were made PoW. (USAF) Above right: On 30 November 1944, returning from a raid on Lutzkendorf, during landing peel-off at Rougham in rapidly deteriorating weather two 94th Bomb Group Fortresses were on short final, one directly above the other and converging when the tower advised the aircraft on final to go around. 42-97985, the lower aircraft, piloted by Lieutenant Owen W. Winter, 331st Bomb Squadron, responded immediately and pulled up into the aircraft above. It crashed and burned in a nearby field, and all except the tail gunner, who was critically injured, perished. The other aircraft crash-landed in a field without injury to the crew. (Abe Dolim)

Left: *Unteroffizier* Walter Stumpf of 7./JG 26 getting strapped into his seat of a FW 190A-8 in preparation for a sortie from Coesfeld airfield in the autumn of 1944. (Walter Stumpf) Right: Captain John B. England (22) (2nd from right) of the 362nd Fighter Squadron, 357th Fighter Group shot down four FW 190s flying P-51D-10 44-14709 G4-E *Missouri Armada* on 27 November 1944, to take his personal score to 16 confirmed victories in the ETO. His final total was 17½ kills. England was KIFA in an F-86F Sabre at Toul, France, on 17 November 1954. (via Merle C. Olmsted)

B-17G-75-BO 43-38011 *The Reluctant Dragon* in the 349th Bomb Squadron, 100th Bomb Group, which was named after the Walt Disney movie of 1941. *The Reluctant Dragon* suffered such severe battle damage on the mission to Merseburg on 30 November 1944 that it was deemed uneconomical to repair. (TAMM)

Below: P-51D *Mountaineer* in the 363rd Fighter Squadron, 357th Fighter Group after crashing at Bottisham. (USAF)

P-47 Thunderbolt *Squirt*, which was used as a hack aircraft by the 100th Bomb Group. Its YJ-G markings and nose cowl indicate that it had previously served in the 351st Fighter Squadron, 353rd Fighter Group. (TAMM)

Below: B-17G-35-BO 42-32099 *Fightin' Carbarn Hammer Slaw*, named for a comic strip character, in the 367th Bomb Squadron, 306th Bomb Group. This B-17 and 2nd Lieutenant Charles F. Manning's crew FTR from Berlin on 5 December 1944 when the plane ditched in the North Sea. All nine crew perished. (Richards)

The severed fuselage of B-17G-40-BO 42-97170 *Julie Mae* in the 527th Bomb Squadron, 379th Bomb Group falls to earth after a collision with 42-97833 *Silver Dollar* in the 525th Bomb Squadron on 9 December 1944. Seven of the men in Lieutenant Robert M. Kenniwick's crew in *Julie Mae* were KIA and only two men survived. All nine in Lieutenant Charles V. Faught's crew survived. (USAF)

B-17G-60-VE 44-8355, a PFF ship in the 710th Bomb Squadron, 447th Bomb Group, flown by 2nd Lieutenant Miles S. King, takes a direct flak hit on the bomb run on 24 December 1944. Eight crew were KIA and two made PoW. (via Derek Smith)

Above left: B-24s in the 458th Bomb Group from Horsham St. Faith, near Norwich, passing overhead Rackheath airfield en route to the North Sea. The Liberator top center is B-24H-10-DT 41-28709 J3-I *Lucky Strike* in the 755th Bomb Squadron, which was salvaged after a non-operational accident on 14 December 1944. (USAF) Center: B-17G-10-DL 43-37787 *Holy Smokes* in the 570th Bomb Squadron, 388th Bomb Group, which FTR on 5 December 1944 when it made an emergency landing on the Continent. All nine members of Lieutenant Burkheimer's crew returned and the Fortress was salvaged. (USAF) Above right: The wreckage of B-17G-65-VE 44-8444 *Treble Four* in the 836th Bomb Squadron, 487th Bomb Group, which was shot down and crashed in Belgium on Christmas Eve 1944, killing Brigadier General Frederick Castle, commander of the 4th Bomb Wing, who was leading the 3rd Bomb Division on his 30th mission. Lieutenant Robert W. Harriman and five of his crew were also KIA. Two crewmen survived to return to the Allied lines. Castle was posthumously awarded the Medal of Honor, the highest ranking officer in the 8th Air Force to receive the award. He and Harriman were buried in the American cemetery at Henri-Chattel. (Rougham Tower Assn.)

B-24 Liberators in the 458th Bomb Group taxi out at Horsham St. Faith on Christmas Eve 1944. (USAF)

Above left: Operating from St. Dizier, France, on 26 December 1944, 1st Lieutenant George R. Vanden Heuvel in the 376th Fighter Squadron, 361st Fighter Group, shot down a FW 190D-9 flown by *Oberleutnant* Hans Hartigs of the 4th *Staffel* JG 26. (via Steve Gotts) Above right: *Oberleutnant* Hans Hartigs of the 4th *Staffel* JG 26. (via Steve Gotts)

Ground crew working to clear the snow off of a 343rd Fighter Squadron, 55th Fighter Group P-51D Mustang at Wormingford. (TAMM)

B-17G-45-BO 42-97215/N in the 95th Bomb Group, which FTR on 31 December 1944. The plane crashed at Wesermünde, Germany, with the loss of four of 2nd Lieutenant Stewart D. Reed's crew. Five men survived and were taken prisoner. (TAMM)

B-17G-85-BO 43-38459/V *Cargo For Margo* in the 418th Bomb Squadron, 100th Bomb Group, which FTR with 2nd Lieutenant John F. Morin's crew on 31 December 1944 when the Bloody Hundredth lost twelve Fortresses on the mission to the Hamburg oil refinery. *Cargo For Margo* dropped back and lost altitude after the first fighter attack. Pilot was heard on VHF at 1250 hours saying he had two wounded men aboard but might be forced to ditch. Morin said he would try to reach Holland and had gasoline for one hour's flying. Morin had to crash land in a field near Emden, 4km North of Westerhusen. The crew was on their 15th Mission. (via Michael P. Faley, 100th Bomb Group Historian)

Above left: P-51 N2 *Shack Lassie* N2-O in the 383rd Fighter Squadron, 364th Fighter Group. This group was awarded a DUC for their action on 27 December 1944 when three of its squadrons claimed 29½ enemy fighters that were massing to attack the bombers bound for Frankfurt. Captain Ernest Bankey became an "ace in a day" with 5½ victories. (USAF) Center: On 26 December 1944 2nd Lieutenant Claire P. Chennault in the 376th Squadron, 361st Fighter Group, claimed a FW 190D of the 4th *Staffel* JG 26 destroyed. Chennault's father, the legendary Major General Claire Chennault, had led the famous American Volunteer Group ("The Flying Tigers") in China before the U.S. entered the war. (via Steve Gotts) Above right: B-17G-85-BO 43-38408 *Faithful Forever* in the 350th Bomb Squadron, 100th Bomb Group, which was shot down by fighters on 31 December 1944. All eight members of 1st Lieutenant Leo Ross' crew exited the aircraft as Ross held it steady, and he was later caught 20 km from the crash at Zeven. (TAMM)

Above left: B-17G-35-BO 42-31987 *The Little Skipper* in the 349th Bomb Squadron, 100th Bomb Group, which was also known as *Shilaylee*, and some say that the latter name was retained on the right hand side and the new name applied to the left side of the fuselage. 42-31987 and Lieutenant Glenn Rojohn's crew were lost on 31 December 1944 after the B-17 crashed in a field in Germany after a mid-air collision with William McNab's Fortress. (TAMM) Center: B-17G-1-BO 42-31066 *Fools Rush In* in the 351st Bomb Squadron, 100th Bomb Group, which was lost on 31 December 1944. (TAMM) Above right: B-17G-70-BO 43-37808 *Milk Run Mabel*, which served the 418th and 350th Bomb Squadrons in the 100th Bomb Group. *Mabel* was lost with Lieutenant Arthur R. Calder's crew on 10 January 1945. All the crew survived the bale out over the Allied side of the lines in Belgium. Calder, who was on his first mission, was KIA on 7 April 1945 flying in *Andy's Dandy's*. (TAMM)

In addition to the twelve B-17s in the 100th Bomb Group that FTR on 31 December 1944, B-17G-90-BO 43-38523 in the 351st Bomb Squadron, which was badly battle damaged, crashed at Thorpe Abbotts and caught fire. Altogether, 111 airmen in the Bloody Hundredth were killed or taken prisoner on 31 December. Red Bowman, writing in his squadron diary, wrote, "Today was another crucifixion for the Hundredth. We sent out 36 planes….12 were lost – mostly to fighters who bounced the Group near the Rally Point: Bombing was not so good. A sad New Year's Eve." (TAMM)

Having dispensed with his 75-gallon "teardrop" tanks to give him optimum maneuverability at low-level, Lieutenant Karl Dittmer of the 487th Fighter Squadron, 352nd Fighter Group taxies out at Asch (Y29), Belgium, in mid-January 1945 in *DOPEY OKIE* to commence yet another short-range patrol over the slowly advancing Allied frontline. Dittmer had claimed one kill up to this point in his career in the ETO. (via Bill Espie)

B-17Gs of the 401st Bomb Group at a wintry Deenthorpe on 12 January 1945. Nearest aircraft is B-17G-75-BO 43-38077 *Duke's Mixture* in the 615th Bomb Squadron. This aircraft was later reassigned to the 614th Bomb Squadron and renamed *Tag A Long*. It finished its days at Kingman, Arizona, in November 1945. (USAF)

Above left: On 14 January 1945 Captain Leonard K. "Kit" Carson in the 362nd Fighter Squadron, 357th Fighter Group at the controls of P-51K-5 44-11622 G4-C *Nooky Booky IV* shot down two FW 190s and a Bf 109. Carson finished the war with 18½ victories plus three Me 262s damaged. In the last year of the war the 357th Fighter Group had the highest scoring victory rate of all the groups and produced 46 aces. (Merle C. Olmsted) Center and above right: On 14 January 1945 161 enemy fighters were shot down. The 357th Fighter Group destroyed an incredible 60½ of them, a record which stood until the end of hostilities in Europe. The 20th Fighter Group claimed 19½ and the 353rd Fighter Group 9. The 357th Fighter Group CO, 27-year-old Lieutenant Colonel Irwin H. Dregne (seen here when he was Operations Officer in the 357th Fighter Group, and who commanded the group December 1944-July 1945), in P-51K-5 44-11678 *Ah Fung Goo/Bobby Jeanne* damaged one FW 190 and shot down a Bf 109 25 miles northwest of Brandenburg. Dregne recounts: "I told 'Greenhouse' Squadron to drop tanks and we turned into the 190s. They broke formation and scattered, some of them rolling some split-essing, but the majority broke right and then going into a Lufbery. I got my sights on a 190 and started firing observing strikes on the fuselage and tail. He broke left and then went into a spin. I broke left and continued turning finding myself in a Lufbery with 8 or 10 FW 190s. I started a tight climbing spiral, the 190s following but I was able to out-climb them. My flight was broken on initial attack by enemy aircraft flying through us." Dregne finished the war with five confirmed victories; he flew jets in the Korean War and died on active duty on 18 September 1967 at Selfridge AFB, Michigan. (Merle Olmsted via Ian McLachlan)

Above left: Returning from a raid on the Hermann Göring Works at Halle on Sunday, 14 January 1945, B-24J-155-CO 44-40283 *Lassie Come Home* in the 753rd Bomb Squadron, 458th Bomb Group, with one engine feathered and its landing gear down, crashed upside down in the back garden of No.14 Spynke Road, Norwich, on approach to the base at Horsham St. Faith. All except one of Lieutenant John J. Clayborn's crew were killed, and two children playing in the garden also died. (USAF) Center: Miss Elizabeth Shapley, a Bedford beauty queen honored as the "Squadron Sweetheart," was invited by the 423rd Bomb Squadron in the 306th Bomb Group at Thurleigh on 16 January 1945 to name one of their B-17s. Accompanied by her mother, Elizabeth christened a B-17G *Elizabeth's Own* and met the pilot, 1st Lieutenant Lorn A. Wilke, and members of his crew and the ground crew. On 15 December 1944 the weather was bad, and Wilke had a lucky escape when his plane was hit at about 2100ft over England by a 368th Bomb Squadron Fortress flown by 2nd Lieutenant Charles A. Crooks. Both bombers crashed at Greenham Common, killing all but Wilke and his co-pilot, 1st Lieutenant John A. Murphy, who both opened their chutes immediately. Wilke landed on the wing of a C-47 at the troop carrier base, injuring his leg. Elizabeth later married a pilot in the Group. (Richards Collection) Above right: 2nd Lieutenant Ralph K. Terry in the 863rd Bomb Squadron, 493rd Bomb Group was forced to put B-17G-60-VE- 44-8314 *Pair-A-Dice Kids* at Bulltofta, in Sweden, on 14 January 1945 on their seventh mission, to Derben. The crew had arrived at Debach as a B-24 trained crew, were converted to the B-17, and were originally assigned to the 100th Bomb Group before being reassigned to the 493rd Bomb Group. On 14 January 1945 *Pair-A-Dice Kids* had a runaway prop en route to Derben. It was feathered, but it caused them to drop out of formation and become easy prey for fighters in the area. 2nd Lieutenant Robert L. Preis, the bombardier, recalls: "We dropped our bombs and tried to get back to Debach. However, this was impossible because of the loss of power and the lack of gas that was lost from the disabled engine. We decided to head for Finland and as we were heading north we were hit by a 4-gun battery over Rostov, Germany and we lost another engine. At this time a Swedish fighter plane appeared and told us to follow him to an airfield, which was Malmo at the southern tip of Sweden. We were later told that if you flew across any part of Sweden you had to land or you would be shot down. We had one shot to land as we lost another engine on the final approach and could not go around again. A Swedish major entered the plane and recited the Geneva Convention on neutral countries and told us that we would be interned. He then asked us to hand over our guns. So ended our participation in the war." Terry and his "Pirates" (the name of a 1940s' comic strip) are pictured after arriving in Sweden. (L to R) Back Row: Aeosta, ball turret gunner; Lieutenant J. B. Merrill, co-pilot; D. W. Sheetz, waist gunner; R. H. Cogan, tail gunner; and P. F Butler, engineer. Front Row: D. K. Love, radio operator; Lieutenant R. K. Terry, pilot; Lieutenant R. L. Preis, bombardier; and Lieutenant R. Roth, navigator. (via Truett Woodall)

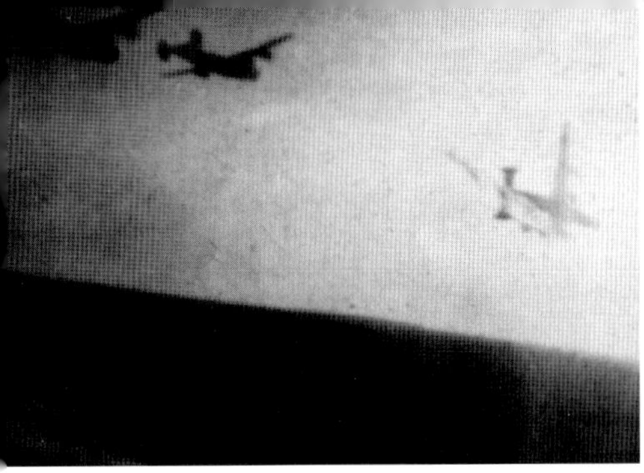

Above left: Captain Dean B. Strain, one of the last of the original pilots in the 491st Bomb Group still flying missions, was leading the 14th Wing to Hamburg, Germany, in B-24J-5-FO 42-51481 on 17 January 1945 when he took a direct hit between the third and fourth engines. All twelve men on board were lost. (Dan Winston Collection) Center: B-17G-50-VE 44-8151 *Princess Pat* in the 569th Bomb Squadron, 390th Bomb Group, which crash landed at Ettenheim, Germany, on 20 January 1945 after being hit by flak bombing Heilbron. One member of 2nd Lieutenant Earl D. Greenstreet's crew was KIA and nine returned. (TAMM) Right: On 22 January 1945 B-24H-20-FO 42-94811 Q2-S *Tommy Thumper II* in the 790th Bomb Squadron, 467th Bomb Group, piloted by Flight Officer John McArthur, crashed on a training flight from Rackheath at Old Catton, Norwich, while attempting to land at Horsham St. Faith. Having lost one engine, McArthur had then accidentally feathered the other engine on the same wing, causing the B-24 to spin in and crash in a large estate just off Church Street. (James J. Mahoney)

Above left: B-24J-1-FO 42-50558 *Miss America* in the 566th Bomb Squadron, 389th Bomb Group was shot down over Dortmund on 28 January 1945. The pilot, Lieutenant Alvin L. Berthelsen, and four crew survived, but five crew died. (USAF) Center: B-17G-65-DL 44-6814 *Choo-Z-Suzy* in the 368th Bomb Squadron, 306th Bomb Group at Thurleigh. This aircraft FTR from the mission to Fulda on 6 February 1945 when it landed on the continent. It was later flown back to the UK, and in May 1945 was transferred to the 381st Bomb Group at Ridgewell. (Richards) Above right: B-17G-70-BO 43-37815 EP L in the 351st Bomb Squadron, 100th Bomb Group in formation. This Fortress was assigned to the Group at Thorpe Abbotts on 28 June 1944 and was later transferred to the 482nd Bomb Group at Alconbury on 20 May 1945. It was broken up for scrap at Kingman, Arizona, in November 1945. (TAMM)

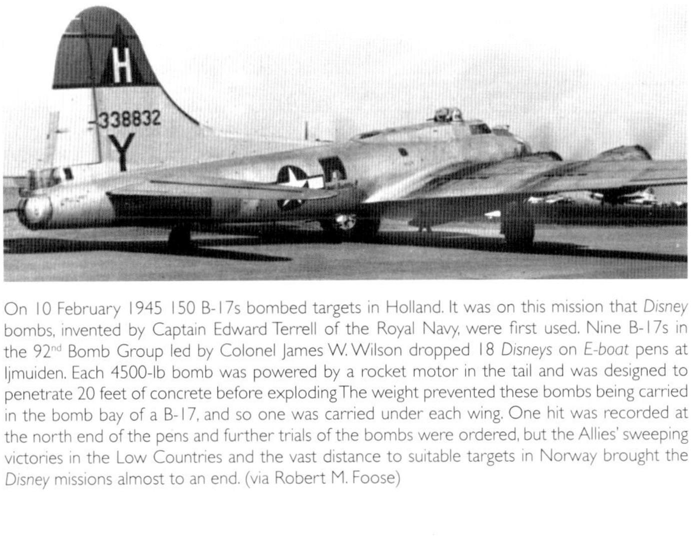

On 10 February 1945 150 B-17s bombed targets in Holland. It was on this mission that *Disney* bombs, invented by Captain Edward Terrell of the Royal Navy, were first used. Nine B-17s in the 92nd Bomb Group led by Colonel James W. Wilson dropped 18 *Disneys* on *E-boat* pens at Ijmuiden. Each 4500-lb bomb was powered by a rocket motor in the tail and was designed to penetrate 20 feet of concrete before exploding The weight prevented these bombs being carried in the bomb bay of a B-17, and so one was carried under each wing. One hit was recorded at the north end of the pens and further trials of the bombs were ordered, but the Allies' sweeping victories in the Low Countries and the vast distance to suitable targets in Norway brought the *Disney* missions almost to an end. (via Robert M. Foose)

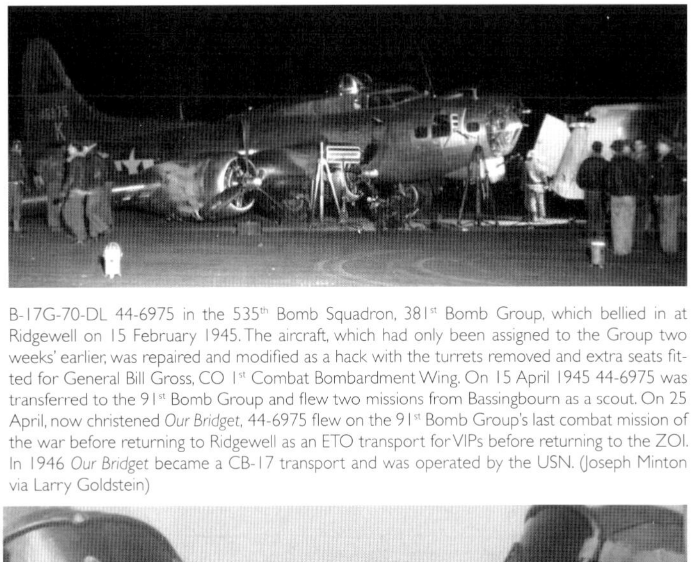

B-17G-70-DL 44-6975 in the 535th Bomb Squadron, 381st Bomb Group, which bellied in at Ridgewell on 15 February 1945. The aircraft, which had only been assigned to the Group two weeks' earlier, was repaired and modified as a hack with the turrets removed and extra seats fitted for General Bill Gross, CO 1st Combat Bombardment Wing. On 15 April 1945 44-6975 was transferred to the 91st Bomb Group and flew two missions from Bassingbourn as a scout. On 25 April, now christened *Our Bridget*, 44-6975 flew on the 91st Bomb Group's last combat mission of the war before returning to Ridgewell as an ETO transport for VIPs before returning to the ZOI. In 1946 *Our Bridget* became a CB-17 transport and was operated by the USN. (Joseph Minton via Larry Goldstein)

Lieutenant Walter Konantz and his younger brother, 2nd Lieutenant Harold Konantz, both of the 55th Fighter Group. Walt flew P-51D 44-72296 CL-P No.6, which Lieutenant Colonel John McGinn had named *Da Quake* (he downed four enemy aircraft in CL-P), and he flew it until his last mission on 6 October 1944. At this point the Mustang was taken over by Walt Konantz, who renamed it *Saturday Night*. It carried him through a full tour, flying over 60 combat missions without a mechanical abort. All four of Walt Konantz's kills were in this Mustang. Walt flew his last mission on 23 February 1945 and CL-P No.6 was taken over by Harold, who had just arrived as a replacement pilot. He left the name *Saturday Night* and had only to change the rank and first name on the canopy tail. On 7 April 1945 he was flying his 7th mission when he was hit by gunfire from the side turret of a B-17. He lost his coolant and the engine caught fire, forcing a bale out. He was a PoW for the remainder of the war. CL-P No.6 ended in a fiery crash 50 miles northwest of Berlin. (Walt Konantz Collection)

Above left: Due to the severe shortage of fuel, by early 1945 teams of oxen were used to tow tank wagons and other rolling stock on operational airfields. Here, a FW 190 of JG 105 is being serviced. (Karl-Heinz Jeismann) Center: Marker flares going down prior to the bomb run. (TAMM) Above right: 493rd Bomb Group B-17Gs in formation over Winter-Hasengr, Germany, on 22 February 1945. Nearest aircraft is B-17G-85-BO 43-38316 *Hank's Bottle*. (USAF)

Above left: B-17Gs in the 837th and 839th Bomb Squadrons, 487th Bomb Group in formation. Nearest aircraft is 44-8023, with 44-8039 behind. The latter was transferred to the 94th Bomb Group on 29 May 1945 and was salvaged on 3 April 1946. 44-8023 was scrapped at Kingman, Arizona, in December 1945. (TAMM) Center: Marvin Barnes, a gunner in the 452nd Bomb Group at Deopham Green, who on 17 February 1945 had to bale out of *Forbidden Fruit* after his B-17 hit severe prop wash forming for the mission and tipped over before crashing at Tibenham. (Barnes) Above right: B-17G-50-BO 42-102490 *Wicked Witch* in the 323rd Bomb Squadron, 91st Bomb Group, which was lost with Lieutenant Eddie R. McKnight's crew on 20 February 1945. Six members of the crew were KIA and three were taken prisoner. (USAF)

B-17G-70-DL 44-6968 *Sonof-A-Blitz* in the 83rd Bomb Squadron, 493rd Bomb Group at Debach in early 1945. (USAF)

P-51Ds in the 328th Fighter Squadron, 352nd Fighter Group undergoing maintenance outside a hangar on the continent when the Bluenosers (or The "Blue Nosed Bastards of Bodney," as they were known) were based at Asch and Chièvres in Belgium until 13 April 1945, when they returned to Bodney. Nearest aircraft with the cowling removed is PE-U 44-19533. (USAF)

B-24J-155-CO 44-40281 *A Dog's Life* in the 753rd *Azon* Squadron, 458th Bomb Group, which crashed at Spixworth Road, Norwich, near Horsham St. Faith airfield on 13 February 1944 with the loss of all the crew. (via George Reynolds)

B-17G-35-VE 42-97873/Y *Sack Happy* in the 563rd Bomb Squadron, 388th Bomb Group at Knettishall, which was salvaged on 25 February 1945. (via Larry Goldstein)

Above left: The pockmarked landscape at Pölitz, 3 March 1945, photographed by a Fortress in the 544th Bomb Squadron, 384th Bomb Group. (USAF) Center: A PFF Liberator in the 392nd Bomb Group overflys the smoking target at Braunkhale synthetic oil refinery on 3 March 1945. On this day the largest formation of German jets ever seen attacked the bomber formations heading for Dresden and the oil targets at Ruhland and shot down three bombers. (USAF) Above right: B-24J-60-CF 44-10552 in the 790th Bomb Squadron, 467th Bomb Group over Berlin on 18 March 1945. In the bottom left of the picture B-24H-15-FO 42-52546 *Southern Clipper* in the 788th Bomb Squadron has been hit by flak and is going down trailing smoke. Four of Lieutenant William E. Shinn's crew were KIA and six survived to be taken prisoner. (USAF)

B-17G-65-BO 43-37514 *My Son Bob* was assigned to the 381st Bomb Group at Ridgewell on 12 August 1944, and was twice forced to land on the Continent early in 1945, but was repaired each time, and it left for the ZOI in June 1945. *My Son Bob* was scrapped at Kingman, Arizona, in October 1945. (USAF)

B-17G-35-BO 42-32083 *Flatbush Floogie* in the 452nd Bomb Group, which on 26 February 1945 was shot down by fighters and flak and crashed at Zossen. All nine of 2nd Lieutenant Allan A. Marksian's crew survived and they returned. (TAMM)

Left: B-17Gs in the 324th Bomb Squadron, 91st Bomb Group drop their bombs on Berlin on 26 February 1945. Altogether 1102 bombers, escorted by fifteen fighter groups, struck at three railway stations in the German capital, as well as targets of opportunity, including Eberswalde. (USAF) Right: Liberators in the 409th Bomb Squadron, 93rd Bomb Group en route to Augsburg, Germany, on 1 March 1945. Both B-24J-5-DT 42-51305/W and B-24H-25-FO 42-95204/I *Down And Go* are fitted with *Carpet* "blinkers" to confuse German radar equipment. Only "W" has perspex covers over the apparatus. (USAF)

Below left: P-51 44-14923 *See Me Later*, 335th Fighter Squadron, 4th Fighter Group, flown by 2nd Lieutenant Kenneth Green, one of eight Mustangs lost from a force of 743 dispatched on 3 March 1945. *See Me Later* was hit by flak and crashed near Rotterdam. Green was taken prisoner. (Ab A. Jansen via Theo Boiten) Below right: P-51D 44-15074 *Big Noise* D7-J in the 503rd Fighter Squadron, 339th Fighter Group, piloted by 1st Lieutenant Dennis B. Rawls, which crashed on take off from Fowlmere on 15 March 1945. (Dennis B. Rawls via Ian McLachlan)

B-17G-30-DL 43-38179 in the 730th Bomb Squadron, 452nd Bomb Group crash-landed at Deopham Green on 21 March 1945 and burned out. (TAMM)

B-17G-35-VE 42-97880 *Little Miss Mischief* in the 324th Bomb Squadron, 91st Bomb Group, which crash-landed at Bassingbourn on 4 April 1945. Two months earlier the aircraft had FTR when it had to be put down on the Continent. (USAF)

Above left: 2nd Lieutenant Russell A. Goodspeed's crew in the 493rd Bomb Group at Debach, Suffolk. On 30 March 1945 the crew flew their first mission to the submarine docks in Hamburg when they were hit by flak. Returning, they crashed at Little Walden, where the right wing touched the ground and the plane broke in half at the trailing edge of the wing, killing five crew in the front of the Fortress. Goodspeed died six hours later. Only the flight engineer, the navigator, and Lieutenant Roger D. Laib, the co-pilot (2nd from left, front row), survived. (Roger Laib) Center: Father Keenam and the crew saying prayers by the nose of B-17G-100-BO 43-38887 *Perpetual Help* in the 751st Bomb Squadron, 457th Bomb Group at Glatton on 23 March 1945. This Fortress, whose name was changed from *Perpetual Hell*, survived the war and was scrapped at Kingman, Arizona, in November 1945. (USAF via Philip Kaplan) Above right: B-17G-90-B0 43-38594 *Lady B' Good* in the 457th Bomb Group having a wing change at the 2nd SAD Abbots Ripton on 30 March 1945. The aircraft, which was in for repairs from 18 March to 17 April, went on to survive the war before being scrapped at Kingman, Arizona, in November 1945. (USAF via Philip Kaplan)

Above left: On 4 April 1945 when Me 262s of III./JG 7 attacked the American formations, *Leutnant* Fritz Müller shot down *Trouble N Mind* in the 448th Bomb Group, flown by Captain John M. Ray, and *Leutnant* Rudolf Rademacher shot down 44-50838 piloted by Robert Mains. Only one man survived aboard Mains' ship, and six parachuted to safety from Ray's. The deadly R4M folding-fin air-to-air missiles were mounted on wooden racks beneath the outer wing of the Me 262. They could be fired in salvoes, or ripple-fired in waves. One hit was normally enough to destroy a four-engined bomber. Rademacher is reported to have destroyed 24 aircraft flying Me 262s and had a grand total of 126 victories. (USAF) Center: *Leutnant* Fritz R. G. Müller, one of the most successful Me 262 jet fighter pilots (six *Abschüsse* in III./JG 7 and the *Erprobungs Kommando 262*, November 1944-April 1945), playing with the *Staffel* dog whilst serving with III./JG 53 in Italy at the end of 1943. (Müller via Heilmut Detjens) Above right: B-17G-35-BO 42-32090 *Silver Dollar* in the 418th Bomb Squadron, 100th Bomb Group, which by mid April 1945 had completed 102 missions. On 18 April *Heavenly Angel* ran into *Silver Dollar* and flattened the tail fin, but the veteran bomber was given a new tail section and continued to be used as Colonel Jeffrey's "hack," and flew several *Chowhound* missions at the end of the war. When Colonel Jeffrey became the Deputy Director of Operations USAAFE he had the plane transferred to Wiesbaden, Germany, where he used it as his personal transport. *Silver Dollar* finally returned to the USA in 1950 and it was scrapped at Pyote, Texas. (TAMM)

B-17G-95-BO 43-38775, 602nd Bomb Squadron, 398th Bomb Group, dropping bombs early in 1945. This aircraft crash-landed on 21 April 1945, was repaired, and saw out the rest of the war. (via Frederick L. Carr)

Above left and center: B-17G-90-BO 43-38514 *E-Z Goin'* in the 349th Bomb Squadron, 100th Bomb Group, which was hit by a *Rammjäger* on 7 April 1945. Joe Martin got the badly damaged Fortress back to Thorpe Abbotts, where the damage was soon repaired by fitting a new rear half to the fuselage. (TAMM) Above right: Two of the crew of 42-37972 *Gold Brick* in the 100th Bomb Group beside their Fortress on 7 April 1945 after a flak burst had shattered the right stabilizer. Arthur Leader landed back at Thorpe Abbotts with a dead tail gunner. (TAMM)

Above left: B-17G-15-BO 42-31333 *Wee Willie* in the 322nd Bomb Squadron, 91st Bomb Group breaks in two and hurtles down near Stendal on 8 April 1945 after taking a direct flak hit in the wing. Eight members of 1st Lieutenant Robert Fuller's crew were killed and one man survived to be taken prisoner. (USAF) Center: B-17G-100-BO 43-38976 WE-J *She's A Honey* in the 364th Bomb Squadron, 305th Bomb Group at Chelveston on 10 April 1945 with her crew, led by Lieutenant George C. "Charlie" Kuhl, author of *Wrong Place, Wrong Time*. Front: Nichols "Nick" J. Paradiso, ball turret gunner, and Donald J. Seeley, tail gunner. Behind: Paul L. McGonabey, radio operator; Marion J. Stanley toggelier; John C. Jenkins, top turret/engineer; and Dale E. Remaly, waist gunner. Standing, L-R: Robert "Bob" V. Law, co-pilot; "Charlie" Kuhl; and Fred H. Tate, navigator. *She's A Honey* transferred to the 384th Bomb Group at Grafton Underwood on 9 May 1945. (via Bill Donald) Above right: On 14 and 15 April 1945 B-17s and Liberators bombed German troops manning 22 gun batteries along the Gironde estuary at Point de Grave in the Royan area, which was denying the Allies the use of the port of Bordeaux. On 15 April nearly 850 2nd and 3rd Air Division aircraft carried Napalm while the 1st Air Division carried 1000lb and 2000lb GP bombs. (USAF)

Above left: B-24J-5-FO 42-50882/B *Wolf Patrol* in the 705th Bomb Squadron, 446th Bomb Group unloads its bombs on a railway bridge over the River Salzach, near Salzburg, Austria, on 25 April 1945. In total, the 2nd Bomb Division B-24s, escorted by four fighter groups, bombed four rail complexes surrounding Hitler's mountain retreat at Berchtesgarten. Some 275 B-17s also escorted by four fighter groups bombed the Skoda armaments plants at Pilsen, in Czechoslovakia. One B-17 in the 92nd Bomb Group failed to return. This was the last combat mission flown by the 8th Air Force in the Second World War. (USAF) Center: B-17G-65-VE 44-8452 in the 493rd Bomb Group over Haarlem during *Chowhound* food drops to the starving Dutch population on 2 May 1945 when 40 B-17s led by Lieutenant Colonel Shepler W. Fitzgerald, deputy Group commander, dropped 3510 cases of food. (USAF via Truett Woodall) Above right: B-17G-70-DL 44-6954 in the 390th Bomb Group dropping supplies to the Dutch during the series of six *Chowhound* mercy missions, which ended on 7 May. During the winter of 1944-45 15,000 Dutch civilians died of starvation. (via Truett Woodall)

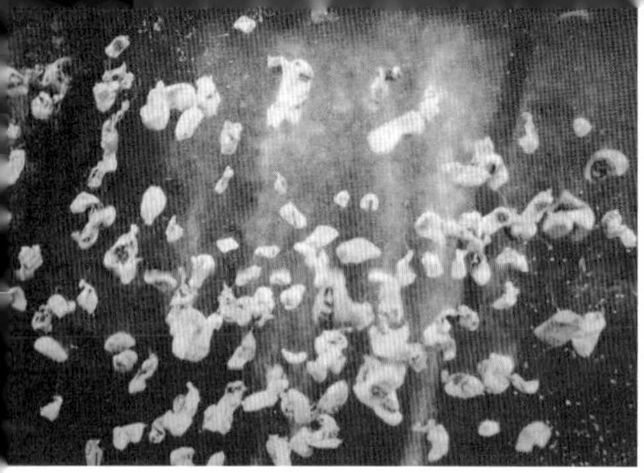

Above left: Sacks of flour being dropped over Haarlem, Holland, on 3 May 1945. Two days later the Germans in Holland surrendered. (via Truett Woodall) Center: The Dutch show their gratitude for the supply drops by cutting the words THANK YOU BOYS out of flowers growing in bulb fields, and the words MANY THANKS could be seen from the air in other fields. (via Truett Woodall) Above right: B-17G-55-DL 44-6507 *Lucky Patch* in the 526th Bomb Squadron, 379th Bomb Group, whose landing gear collapsed on landing at Kimbolton on 3 May 1945. The aircraft was salvaged three days later. (USAF)

Above left: At the end of hostilities in May 1945, hundreds of aircraft wrecks still littered the countryside on the continent. This Fortress, B-17G-30-VE 42-97781 *Eight Ball III* in the 359th Bomb Squadron, 303rd Bomb Group, came down on the edge of the Apeldoorn-Diemen Canal at Eerbeek, Holland, on 2 November 1944. Nine of Lieutenant Jack T. Davis' crew were taken prisoner, and one man was KIA. During the next year, souvenir hunters continued to strip the aircraft of parts. (Brouwer, via Ab A. Jansen) Above right: B-17G-95-BO 43-38757 *Peaselee's Payoff* in the 547th Bomb Squadron, 384th Bomb Group, which despite this mishap on 8 May 1945 was repaired and returned to the ZOI, where early in 1946 it was scrapped at Kingman, Arizona. (USAF)

Left: B-17G-55-DL 44-6585/K *Commando Chief* in the 423rd Bomb Squadron, 306th Bomb Group at Thurleigh was transferred to the 381st Bomb Group at Ridgewell in May 1945. *Commando Chief* returned to the ZOI in December 1945. (Richards Collection) Right: American servicemen were largely confined to their bases on VE Day, and memorable celebrations surpassed even the wildest Fourth of July parties. Here flares are being fired off at Seething. (via Pat Everson)

B-17G-70-DL 44-6888 AW-R *Sweet Chariot* in the 339th Bomb Squadron, 96th Bomb Group, flown by Lieutenant Harry Loveless, came to grief at Snetterton Heath on 11 May. (via Robert M. Foose)

B-17G-35-BO 42-31991 *Miss-Chief* in the 350th Bomb Squadron, 100th Bomb Group, which was involved in a taxi incident with B-17G-95-BO 43-38681 in the 349th Bomb Squadron on 14 May 1945. Both aircraft were salvaged. (TAMM)

B-17G-80-VE 44-8790 in the 418th Bomb Squadron, 100th Bomb Group, which overturned making a forced landing near Diss on 12 May 1945. (TAMM)

Above left: B-17G-100-BO 43-38933/G *Weary Wolf* (formerly *Dear Mom II*) in the 561st Bomb Squadron, 388th Bomb Group, in formation with B-17G-105-BO 43-39221/N, hit a hill near Lands End on 17 May 1945 during a navigational training exercise. The pilot, 2nd Lieutenant Henry J. Cole, his co-pilot, 2nd Lieutenant V. Ferguson, two navigators, and two groundcrew who flew as engineer and radio operator were all killed. (via Robert M. Foose) Center: Once victory in Europe was finally secured, the bomb groups were hastily re-tasked as transports and pressed into service shuffling former Allied PoWs home and airlifting displaced people from all over Europe. They also transported troops from the UK to Casablanca, where they continued on to the CBI Theater and helped move fighter groups to bases in Germany. Pictured is B-17G-40-DL 44-6097/D in the 390th Bomb Group. (TAMM) Above right: Mass formation of 100th Bomb Group B-17Gs with newly applied "Buzz Numbers" on the undersides of their left wings. Nearest two aircraft are LDY and 44-8156 LDU in the 418th Bomb Squadron. (TAMM)

Above left: Lieutenant Carl Thorkelson landed B-17G-85-VE 44-8834/G at Chartres airfield, in France, with a group of French workers as passengers during 100th Bomb Group repatriation missions in June 1945. (TAMM) Above right: Third Air Division B-17s lined up on the Continent at the end of the war during repatriation missions. (TAMM)

Above: 100th Bomb Group B-17G XRG newly applied to the underside of the left wing in close formation. (TAMM) Right: RAF airmen wave "cheerio" to a departing B-24 of the 44th Bomb Group at St. Mawgan, Wales, in May 1945. (USAF via Philip Kaplan)

B-17E *Yankee* on the line. When camouflage was adopted for bombers in February 1941, a star was added to each side of the fuselage and the rudder stripes were deleted, as was the star on the lower left and upper right wing. On 15 May 1942 the red centre of the star-in-circle insignia was deleted because of its similarity to the Japanese *hinomaru*, or "rising sun" marking, which Americans called the "meatball." (USAF)

Below: B-17F-10-BO 41-24487 *Eager Beaver* in the 368th "Eager Beavers" Bomb Squadron, 306th Bomb Group at Thurleigh, was the longest serving B-17F in VIIIth BC, September 1942-October 1943. It was transferred to AF Service Command on 1 May 1944 and returned to the ZOI in July 1944. It went to the Williamsport Technical Institute at Patterson Field, Ohio, on 20 June 1945. (USAF)

Above left: B-17F-60-BO 42-29536 *"Mary Ruth" Memories of Mobile*, 401st Bomb Squadron, 91st Bomb Group, which FTR with Lieutenant Kenneth L. Brown's crew on 22 June 1943. (USAF) Center: B-17F-55-BO 42-29524 was accepted by the AAF on the last day of 1942 and was assigned to the 423rd Bomb Squadron, 306th Bomb Group on 2 March 1943, where it was named *Meat Hound*. After completing a number of missions with this unit it moved to Molesworth on 30 July to join the 358th Bomb Squadron, 303rd Bomb Group. On 26 January 1944, whilst returning from the Focke Wulf plant at Oschersleben, this aircraft, crewed by 2nd Lieutenant Jack W. Watson's crew, was attacked by enemy fighters, who shot out two of its engines. Realizing the hopelessness of the situation, the pilot gave the bale out order and the men evacuated the doomed bomber in a series of delayed jumps over the Netherlands. Co-pilot 2nd Lieutenant C. C. David successfully evaded, three crewmen were killed, and six others captured. (USAF) Above right: In North Africa in 1943, S/Sgt Charles G. Cavage, waist-gunner, paints the letters spelling out the name *The Little Gramper* on the side of the 566th Bomb Squadron, 389th Bomb Group Liberator as T/Sgt Arthur J. Marsh, radio operator-gunner, looks on. (USAF)

Above left: B-24D-1-CO 41-23711 *Jerk's Natural* in the 93rd Bomb Group at Hardwick in August 1943 after returning from North Africa, where it was flown on the 1 August raid on Ploesti by Major John "The Jerk" Jerstad. *Jerk's Natural* was lost on 1 October 1943 flying from North Africa. (USAF) Above right: B-17F-27-BO 41-24592/G *Madame Betterfly* in the 366th Bomb Squadron, 305th Bomb Group, which 2nd Lieutenant Floyd E. McSpadden landed at Dubendorf, Switzerland, out of fuel on 6 September 1943 on the mission to Stuttgart. (via Bill Donald)

Above left: B-24D-90-CO 42-40738 *Fightin' Sam* in the 566th Bomb Squadron, 389th Bomb Group at Hethel. The ten Maltese (or Balkan) Crosses indicate the Ploesti mission and nine others flown against targets in the MTO during the "Sky Scorpions'" recent sojourn in North Africa, when they also attacked Wiener Neustadt in Austria. (John Driscoll) Center: B-17F-105-BO 42-30451 *V Mail Gets There Fastest* in the 368th Bomb Squadron, 306th Bomb Group, which was assigned overseas in September 1943. (USAF) Above right: B-17G-1-VE 42-39843, seen here on a test flight in California, joined the 364th Bomb Squadron, 305th Bomb Group at Chelveston in October 1943 and was named *Daley's Male*. This aircraft was salvaged on 11 December 1944. (Lockheed)

Below: Frank Walls poses in his co-pilot's window of *Shack Bunny*, 551st Bomb Squadron, 385th Bomb Group. This B-17F and Lieutenant Lyle V. Fryer's crew was lost over France on 20 October 1943 on the mission to Duren, Germany. All were taken prisoner. (William Nicholls)

On 11 April 1944 General Dwight D. Eisenhower christened B-17G-40-BO 42-97061 *General Ike* with a bottle of Mississippi River water at Bassingbourn. Major James McPartlin, 401st Bomb Squadron, was responsible for the naming of *General Ike*, which flew its first operational mission on 13 April 1944, two days after it was christened. On 29 May 1944 *General Ike* led the 91st Bomb Group to Poznan, Poland, on the longest daylight raid of the war up to that time. *Ike* completed 75 combat missions, returned to the USA in June 1945, and was broken up for scrap. (USAF)

Above left: B-17G-90-BO 43-38524 *Blonde Bomber II* in the 710th Bomb Squadron, 447th Bomb Group at Rattlesden finished her days at Kingman, Arizona, in 1945. (USAF) Above right: B-17G-75-BO 43-38067 *Big Chief Illiniwek* (later renamed *Joyride*) in the 412th Bomb Squadron, 95th Bomb Group, which was assigned overseas on 25 August 1944. The Fortress was landed on the Continent in February and March 1945, but it returned to the ZOI, where it was scrapped at Kingman, Arizona, in November 1945. (TAMM)

Left: B-24H-20-CF 42-50306 *Dragon Lady* in the 446th Bomb Group, which on 27 April 1944 was wrecked in a take off accident that killed all ten crew on 27 April 1944. (USAF) Right: B-17G-15-VE 42-97487 *Hangover Haven* in the 612th Bomb Squadron, 401st Bomb Group, which was assigned overseas on 12 January 1944. *Hangover Haven* crash-landed at Deenethorpe on 3 October 1944 and was salvaged. (USAF)

Above left: Lieutenant Colonel Francis S. "Gabby" Gabreski, CO 61st Fighter Squadron, 56th Fighter Group. (USAF) Center: B-24H-20-DT 41-28943 *Dumbo* and 735th Bomb Squadron, 453rd Bomb Group Engineering Officer Harry Godges at Old Buckenham, Norfolk. This aircraft was assigned overseas on 2 May 1944. Lieutenant Delbert Mann, whose wife Ann suggested the name after seeing a picture of the elephant made famous by Walt Disney, flew this Liberator to England. Mann and his crew were assigned to the 467th Bomb Group as replacements and never again saw *Dumbo*, which completed 77 missions in the 735th Bomb Squadron and was scrapped at Altus, Oklahoma, in October 1945. After flying a tour of 35 missions Mann was made 491st Bomb Group Intelligence Officer. Post-war he became an Oscar-winning Hollywood movie director. (USAF) Above right: Olive-drab B-17G-30-BO 42-31909 *Nine-O-Nine* in the 323rd Bomb Squadron leads other Fortresses in the 91st Bomb Group. *Nine-O-Nine* completed over 125 missions without a turnback. (USAF)

Left: Re-arming a P-47 Thunderbolt. (USAF) Right: Re-arming a P-51B Mustang in the 336th Fighter Squadron, 4th Fighter Group at Debden. (USAF)

Above left: P-51B and D Mustangs of the 487th Fighter Squadron, 352nd Fighter Group at Bodney, Norfolk. Nearest Mustang is 44-13530 *Millie*. A 12 inch blue cowling band was introduced in April 1944 and extended back covering the black anti-dazzle panel to the cockpit that same month. (via Bill Espie) Center: B-17G-50-VE 44-8158 *Bobby Sox*, which served in the 4th Bomb Squadron, 34th Bomb Group, 850th Bomb Squadron, 490th Bomb Group, and the 332nd Bomb Squadron, 94th Bomb Group before being scrapped at Walnut Ridge in December 1945. (USAF) Above right: P-47 Thunderbolt with its engine panels removed. (USAF)

B-17G-95-BO 43-38865 *Goin' My Way*, which flew its combat missions in the 349th Bomb Squadron, 100th Bomb Group before being transferred to the 490th Bomb Group, eventually being flown back to the USA soon after 6 July 1945 as part of Operation "Home Run." (TAMM)

Above left: B-17G-35-VE 42-97858 *Lady Fortune*, which arrived in England at the end of April 1944 and was assigned to the 95th Bomb Group at Horham, flying its first mission on 25 May. *Lady Fortune*, which owed its stunning nose art to the *Esquire* August 1944 calendar, flew 82 missions in the 95th Bomb Group before being lost on 10 January 1945. (TAMM) Above right: Lieutenant John W. McClane, navigator in the 68th Bomb Squadron, 44th Bomb Group at Shipdham. (McClane)

An 8th Air Force bomb dump. (USAF)

Left: Ground crew working on the Merlin engine of a P-51D Mustang. (USAF) Right: B-17G-65-BO 43-37544 *D-Day Doll* in the 710th Bomb Squadron, 447th Bomb Group at Lavenham, Suffolk. (USAF)

B-24H 42-94857 *Big Dealer* in the 493rd Bomb Group at Debach in 1944. (USAF)

Above left: B-24s in the 493rd Bomb Group taxiing out at Debach, Suffolk. (USAF) Above right: 100th Bomb Group airmen relaxing on the beach at Manfredonia on the Adriatic coast following the Russian shuttle mission. (TAMM)

Above left: Lieutenant Gerald H. "Gerry" Steussey's crew in the 350th Bomb Squadron, 100th Bomb Group with Russian officers in front of *"Black Cat 13"* 42-32009 after the first Russian Shuttle mission on 21 June 1944. Back Row L-R: Allan J. "Mac" MacAllister, bombardier; Carlos McCutcheon, flight engineer; Eddie Dumas, waist gunner; Tony Nocchiero, radio operator; Julius Greenwald, ball turret; Russian officer; and Howard J. "Bill" Leech, navigator. Front row: Joda Ticer, tail gunner; Frank C. "Pete" Petrdil, co-pilot; Gerald Steussey; and Russian officer. *"Black Cat 13"* went MIA with Wesley Stansbury's crew on 28 July 1944. (via Michael P. Faley, 100th Bomb Group Historian) Center: Russian soldier with Howard J. "Bill" Leech, navigator in Gerry Steussey's crew at Mirgorod in June 1944. (TAMM) Right: Russian soldiers dancing at Mirgorod in June 1944. (TAMM)

Above left: Russian soldiers and 100th Bomb Group crewmen at Mirgorod in June 1944 during the Russian shuttle mission. Americans are Frank C. "Pete" Petrdil, co pilot; Allan J. "Mac" MacAllister, bombardier; and Gerald H. "Gerry" Steussy, pilot. (TAMM) Center: B-17G-55-BO 42-102611 *Boss Lady* in the 350th Bomb Squadron, 100th Bomb Group at Thorpe Abbotts. This aircraft and 2nd Lieutenant John E. Donaldson's crew were lost on 27 June 1944 when the crew flew a practice mission with the 390th Bomb Group from Framlingham, and they were last seen about 5 miles off Great Yarmouth at 17,000ft. At the time towering cumulus clouds covered 8/10ths of the sky. The plane went into the North Sea and all ten crew, who had only joined the Hundredth a fortnight earlier, were drowned. (USAF) Above right: Ground crew working on the port inner engine of B-17G-55-BO 42-102611 *Boss Lady* in the 350th Bomb Squadron, 100th Bomb Group at Thorpe Abbotts. (TAMM)

B-17G-30-VE 42-97829 *Regal Eagle* in the 350th Bomb Squadron, 100th Bomb Group at Thorpe Abbotts, which was one of eight Group losses on the mission to the Leuna oil plant on 29 July 1944. All nine of Lieutenant Gerald H. Steussy's crew survived and they were taken prisoner. (TAMM)

B-24H 41-29177 *Ginger* in the 706th Bomb Squadron, 446th Bomb Group, which was lost with Lieutenant Ralph V. Shaffer's crew on 26 August 1944. Six crew were KIA and four were taken prisoner. (USAF)

Above left: B-17Gs in the 413th Bomb Squadron, 96th Bomb Group preparing to take off at Snetterton Heath. 43-37792/N was lost with Lieutenant Henry Chrismon's crew on the mission to Osnabrück on 21 November 1944. (USAF)

B-17Gs in the 96th Bomb Group taxi out at Snetterton Heath. On the runway, left, is 42-97775/L in the 413th Bomb Squadron, which crash-landed on 14 January 1945. Right, foreground, is 43-37794/T in the 337th Bomb Squadron, which was lost on 19 September 1944 with Lieutenant Raymond W. Bauman's crew (all PoW). Behind is 43-37687/Y in the 338th Bomb Squadron, which FTR when it landed on the Continent on 15 February 1945. (USAF)

B-17G-55-VE- 44-8256 *Yankee Girl* in the 359th Bomb Squadron, 303rd Bomb Group, which was assigned overseas in October 1944. (USAF)

On 6 July 1944 HM King George VI and the Royal party visited Thurleigh and HRH Princess Elizabeth christened B-17G-55-BO 42-102547, a lead ship in the 367th Bomb Squadron, *Rose of York*. Originally M/Sgt Edward S. Gregory, its crew chief, had named the Fortress *The Princess*. Later, the name was changed to *Princess Elizabeth*, and it was then that Gregory had the idea of having the plane christened by the Princess herself. The royal family agreed, but insisted that the name be changed, because if it were shot down, it would present the Germans with a propaganda coup. Sgt Malcolm B. Currie duly went ahead and painted the new insignia on the nose. At 1230 prompt, a 54-ship formation flew over the airfield in salute and, after the customary anthems and speeches, the Princess blessed the ship by breaking a bottle of English cider against a metal plate attached to the lowered guns of the chin turret. Captain Perry E. Raster's crew were presented to the royal family. *Rose of York*, flown by 1st Lieutenant Vernon E. Daley, Jr., was lost in the North Sea on 3 February 1945, returning from Berlin. All the crew perished. Also on board was Guy E. Byam, a war correspondent for the BBC who had covered the *D-Day* landings and had jumped with the British Airborne at Arnhem. S/Sgt George G. Roberts was in hospital having his appendix removed at the time of the loss. (Richards Coll)

B-17G-20-BO 42-31537 *Randie Lou* in the 350th Bomb Squadron, 100th Bomb Group, which originally was named *Buffalo Gal* by Lieutenant "Red" Harper. Lieutenant Chadwick's crew christened this plane *Randie Lou* in April 1944. Lieutenant William T. "Buzz" Fitzroy's crew and *Randie Lou* FTR from the mission to Leuna on 29 July 1944. Fitzroy and four others baled out and were taken prisoner. Four others were killed (three of them by civilians). (via Michael P. Faley, 100th Bomb Group Historian)

B-24H-1-CF 41-29137 *Dry Run* in the 705th Bomb Squadron, 446th Bomb Group, which was lost with 2nd Lieutenant James L. Cole's crew on 4 August 1944. Three men were KIA and seven were taken prisoner. (USAF)

B-24H-25-CF 42-50362 *Silver Eagle* in the 409th Bomb Squadron, 93rd Bomb Group at Hardwick. *Silver Eagle* FTR on 10 January 1945 when it was involved in a mid-air collision. (USAF)

B-24J-5-FO 42-50768 *Arise My Love and Come With Me* in the 754th Bomb Squadron, 458th Bomb Group at Horsham St. Faith, which survived to the end of hostilities and was salvaged at Altus, Oklahoma, in October 1945. (USAF)

B-24H-20-FO 42-94953 *Rugged But Right* (later *Misanthrope*), which served in the 490th Bomb Group and the 715th Bomb Squadron, 448th Bomb Group before being scrapped at Altus, Oklahoma, in late 1945. (USAF)

B-24H-20-FO 42-94940 *Nella* in the 701st Bomb Squadron, 445th Bomb Group, which was lost with 2nd Lieutenant William L. Boykin's crew on 26 November 1944. Six men were KIA and three were captured. Nella was a shortened form of Fifenella, the female equivalent of the Gremlin. (USAF)

B-24J-1-FO 42-95527 *"4-F,"* which served in the 327th Bomb Squadron, 93rd Bomb Group, and 448th Bomb Group, and was scrapped at Walnut Ridge, Arkansas, in 1946. (USAF)

B-17G-80-BO 43-38229 *Better Duck* in the 334th Bomb Squadron, 95th Bomb Group, survived the war and was broken up for scrap at Kingman, Arizona, in December 1945. (USAF)

The crew of B-17G-70-BO 43-37704 *Button Nose*, 535th Bomb Squadron, 381st Bomb Group, at Ridgewell studying their route for the target for today. *Button Nose* and Lieutenant Robert "Bob" G. Beackley's crew FTR on 8 August 1944 when they landed on the continent. *Button Nose* was salvaged on 14 November 1944. USAF. (USAF)

B-24J-155-CO 44-40286 *The Green Hornet*, which served in the 493rd Bomb Group and later the 491st Bomb Group. (USAF)

B-17G-80-VE 44-8731 *Knockout Dropper* in the 391st Bomb Squadron, 34th Bomb Group in 1945. (USAF)

B-24J-5-FO 42-50852 *Peg o' San Antone* in the 706th Bomb Squadron, 446th Bomb Group, which crash landed on 9 March 1945 and was salvaged. (USAF)

B-24H-25-FO 42-95058 *White Lit'Nin'* in the 705th Bomb Squadron, 446th Bomb Group.(USAF)

Left: B-24J-155-CO 44-40268 *Kentucky Belle* in the 706th Bomb Squadron, 446th Bomb Group, which previously served in the 493rd Bomb Group. The *Belle* was scrapped at Altus, Oklahoma, in late 1945. (USAF)

B-24H-10-FO 42-52154 *Male Call* in the 734th Bomb Squadron, 453rd Bomb Group, which survived the war and was scrapped at Altus, Oklahoma, in late 1945. (USAF)

B-24H-20-DT 41-28967 *Spotted Ape*, the 458th Bomb Group's second assembly ship, which was salvaged on 9 March 1945. (USAF)

B-17G-40-VE 42-97976 *A Bit O' Lace*, which was assigned overseas in June 1944 and joined the 709th Bomb Squadron, 447th Bomb Group at Lavenham. The aircraft was scrapped at Kingman, Arizona, in October 1945. (Charles E. Brown)

Left: B-17G-55-BO 42-102649 *Lady Geraldine*, which served in the 418th and 350th Bomb Squadrons in the 100th Bomb Group. (USAF) Right: Armorers moving bombs at the Horsham St. Faith bomb dump. (USAF)

B-17F-95-BO 42-30301 *Idiot's Delight* (formerly *Missy G*), which was assigned overseas in June 1943 and assigned to the 332nd Bomb Squadron, 94th Bomb Group at Bury St. Edmunds (Rougham). The aircraft was assigned to the 710th Bomb Squadron, 447th Bomb Group in 1944 and was lost on 19 June 1944 when it ditched in the English Channel. Nine of 2nd Lieutenant Theodore A. Milton's crew died, and one man survived to become a PoW. (USAF)

B-24J-1-FO 42-95527 GO-C *4-F* in the 328th Bomb Squadron, 93rd Bomb Group with PFF radome extended and the red-nosed PFF ship RE-Z in the 329th Bomb Squadron on Christmas Eve 1944. 42-95527 was scrapped at Walnut Ridge, Arkansas, in 1946. (USAF)

Left: B-17G-55-BO 42-102649 *Lady Geraldine* arrived at Thorpe Abbotts in early April 1944 and survived combat before being transferred to the 482nd Bomb Group on 25 May 1945 in exchange for a newer radar ship. *Lady Geraldine* was scrapped at Kingman, Arizona, in December 1945. *Lady Geraldine's* nose art shows three pairs of feet, two of whom are male and the middle set, female. Originally the middle set of feet were down-turned, but these were changed on the orders of the top brass! After flying 75 missions *Lady Geraldine*, which was transferred to the 482nd Bomb Group in exchange for a newer PFF ship, finished her days at Kingman, Arizona, in 1945. (USAF) Right: B-24H-25-FO 42-95167 *Never Mrs*, which joined the 734th Bomb Squadron, 453rd Bomb Group from the 34th Bomb Group after the latter group converted to the Fortress in August 1944. *Never Mrs* and 2nd Lieutenant John H. Friedhaber's crew FTR on 11 November 1944 when the aircraft crashed at Bottrop. Six crew were KIA and three survived to be taken prisoner. (Frank Thomas)

B-17G-50-DL 44-6483 was assigned overseas in September 1944 and was first used by the 1st Air Division before it was transferred to the 550th Bomb Squadron, 385th Bomb Group, where it was named *Ruby's Raiders* by Lieutenant Blackwell's crew after Ruby Newell, a WAC named by *Yank* magazine as the most beautiful WAC in the ETO. She was present at Great Ashfield when the nose art by Corporal Ploss was dedicated. *Ruby's Raiders* finished her days at Kingman, Arizona, in November 1945. (USAF)

Above: A FW 190 of the *Luftwaffe* taxies out. (Bundersarchiv) Left: B-17G-35-DL 42-107233 *Humpty Dumpty* was assigned to the 351st Bomb Squadron, 100th Bomb Group in May 1944. Sgt Frank "Steve" Stevens, whose workshop was close to hardstand #6 where ground crew chief M/Sgt Ray Christopher maintained the B-17, painted superb artwork based on "Forced Landing," one of the famous Gil Elvgren creations in the Brown & Bigelow calendar. On New Year's Eve 1944, on the mission to Hamburg, *Humpty Dumpty* was among the 12 B-17s in the 100th Bomb Group that FTR. All nine of Lieutenant Wallace Wilson's crew - on their 13th mission - survived, though Wilson suffered a badly injured leg and Herman Eckmeyer, the toggelier, hit the left side of the ship, injuring his ankle. *Humpty Dumpty* had flown more than 67 missions. (USAF)

A wounded gunner is removed from B-24H-15-CF 41-29393 *Liberty Lib* in the 752nd Bomb Squadron, 458th Bomb Group at Horsham St. Faith after the return from the raid on the Dornier factory at Lubeck on 25 August 1944. *Liberty Lib* transferred to the 467th Bomb Group at Rackheath late in October 1944 where it became the "Aggies'" second assembly ship, and was repainted and renamed *Pete The POM Inspector 2nd*. (USAF)

Lieutenant George D. Green, 4th Fighter Group, with his Mustang in mid-1944. When Pierce McKennon baled out of his P-51 near Berlin on 18 March 1945, Green set his P-51 down in a nearby field, threw the chute out, put McKennon in the seat, got on his lap, and took off. Sharing one oxygen mask, they made it all the way back to Debden. (USAF)

B-17G-55-DL 42-107230(?) *Yehudi* in the 349th Bomb Squadron, 100th Bomb Group at Thorpe Abbotts was salvaged on 2 December 1944. (USAF)

Below left: B-17G-30-VE 42-97834 *Mud in Yer Eye*, which was assigned to the 100th Bomb Group on 4 May 1944 and was lost when it exploded in mid-air over Kovarska on the mission to Ruhland on 8 September 1944. (USAF) Below right: B-17G-40-BO 42-97126 *The Latest Rumor*, which was assigned to the 351st Bomb Squadron, 100th Bomb Group on 2 March 1944, flying its first mission on 12 April. The undercarriage collapsed during evacuation of PoWs and displaced persons from Horsching, Austria, on 15 May 1945, and the Fortress was damaged beyond economical repair when an Army tank bulldozed the plane off the runway. (USAF)

381st Bomb Group B-17s over England. The nearest aircraft is 42-97503 *Princess Pat* in the 533rd Bomb Squadron, which crash-landed on 26 March 1945. Left is 43-37791, which FTRLOC on 18 December 1944. (USAF)

B-17G-35-BO 42-32090 *Silver Dollar* in the 418th Bomb Squadron, 100th Bomb Group showing the original artwork on the right hand side, which was repainted to incorporate a beautifully rendered dollar coin – the head on the port side and reverse on the starboard side. By mid-April 1945 *Silver Dollar* had completed 102 missions. (TAMM)

A Frosty day at Thorpe Abbotts. (TAMM)

Pegasus the Flying Horse, 784th Bomb Squadron, 466th Bomb Group, after the brakes failed and crewmembers tied their parachutes to the waist guns to slow B-24H-25-DT 42-51141 on landing at Attlebridge. (USAF)

B-17G-10-DL 42-37756 *Roarin' Bill* in the 335th Bomb Squadron, 95th Bomb Group, which was lost with 2nd Lieutenant Charles H. Mowers' crew on 24 January 1944 when it crashed at Waterloo, Belgium. Three crew evaded, one was KIA, and six were taken prisoner. The replacement *Roarin' Bill* in the 335th Bomb Squadron (B-17G-20-BO 42-31462) force landed on the Continent on 20 January 1945. Seven in Captain F. Beard's crew returned and two were taken prisoner. (via TAMM)

B-17G-15-BO 42-31412 *Mason and Dixon* in the 351st Bomb Squadron, 100th Bomb Group at Thorpe Abbotts with the airship sheds at Pulham St. Mary behind. (TAMM)

Below: B-24J-155-CO 44-40298 *The Shack* in the 861st Bomb Squadron, 493rd Bomb Group is a clever pun on the name of Ann Shackleford, who was the fiancée of Captain David L. "Doc" Conger, the pilot. This Liberator was one of several that were transferred to the 2nd Bomb Division in the summer of 1944 when the 3rd Bomb Division converted fully to the B-17, and *The Shack* joined the 458th Bomb Group. (USAF)

B-17G-15-BO 42-31347 *Billy Boy*, which was assigned to the 349th Bomb Squadron, 100th Bomb Group in mid-January 1944. After flying about 50 missions this Fortress was withdrawn from combat status by January 1945 and fitted with a new tail section for camera gunnery training. (TAMM)

B-17G-20-BO 42-31585 *Mount 'N Ride* in the 323rd Bomb Squadron, 91st Bomb Group was flown into Bassingbourn on 1 February 1944, and was quickly adorned with Starcer artwork in the form of that month's *Esquire* Varga calendar girl. This aircraft and Lieutenant Roman Maziarz's crew flew their first mission, to Avord, France, just four days after the bomber had been delivered to the 91st. On the 6th Lieutenant Doyle Bradford's crew took over the aircraft, and they continued to fly it without incident until 16 March, when it lost both inboard engines to flak during a raid on Lechfeld airfield. Bradford struggled over the Alps to Switzerland, where he put the bomber down safely at Dübendorf. Both the crew and its bomber were interned until the end of the war, *Mount 'N Ride* finally being flown back to Burtonwood on 8 October 1945, where it was scrapped. (USAF)

B-17G-1-VE 42-39791 *Fletcher's Castoria* in the 350th Bomb Squadron, 100th Bomb Group, which crashed at Thorpe Abbotts on 4 December 1943 and was destroyed. (TAMM)

B-17G-25-DL 42-38047 *Fever Beaver*, which was assigned to the 351st Bomb Squadron, 100th Bomb Group in January 1944, and which returned to the ZOI in May 1945 with 125 combat missions flown. (TAMM)

B-17F-90-BO *Messie Bessie* in the 418th Bomb Squadron, 100th Bomb Group, which was eventually salvaged at the end of April 1945. (TAMM)

B-17G-30-BO 42-31767 *Our Gal Sal* in the 351st Bomb Squadron, 100th Bomb Group, which arrived at Thorpe Abbotts in mid-January 1944 and flew 135 missions before returning to the USA at the end of the war. (TAMM)

B-17G-35-BO 42-31991 *Miss-Chief* in the 350th Bomb Squadron, 100th Bomb Group, which survived combat and a taxi-way collision at Thorpe Abbotts on 14 May 1945 before being flown home to the USA where it was scrapped. (TAMM)

P-47 Thunderbolts in the 56th Fighter Group line up for take off from Boxted. (USAF)

Above left: Tail gun position of a B-17G at Thorpe Abbotts with "Pudgy" and "Have a Heart" inscribed on the tail. (TAMM) Center: B-17G-35-BO 42-31987 *Shilaylee* in the 349th Bomb Squadron, 100th Bomb Group. In June 1944 this aircraft was given to J. D. Williams' crew after Mark Wilson's crew became a lead crew. It lost its famous white-walled tires and was renamed *The Little Skipper* for Williams' one year old son, although some say that the name only graced the left hand side, while the original name and winged Irish club were retained on the starboard side. *Shilaylee/The Little Skipper* was lost with Lieutenant Glenn Rojohn's crew on 31 December 1944 when it crashed pick-a-back in a German field after a collision with William McNab's 43-38457. (TAMM) Above right: B-17G-55-BO 42-102598 *Super Rabbit* in the 100th Bomb Group, which on 28 July 1944 suffered an undercarriage failure on landing at Thorpe Abbotts and was wrecked. (TAMM)

B-17G-20-BO 42-31530 *Quittin' Time* in the 351st Bomb Squadron, 100th Bomb Group, which was assigned overseas in January 1944 and was finally salvaged on 31 May 1945 when the Hundredth received new aircraft. (TAMM)

B-17G-20-DL 42-37936 *The All American girl* in the 351st Bomb Squadron, 100th Bomb Group, which was assigned overseas in mid-November 1943, was lost on its 99th combat mission on 10 January 1945. Every one of Lieutenant John Dodrill's crew were killed. (TAMM)

B-17G-65-BO 42-37521 *Skyway Chariot* in the 351st Bomb Squadron, 100th Bomb Group with the late war green nose-band. A black hammer and sickle indicates the Russian shuttle trip the plane made in June 1944. On 18 March 1945 this aircraft was one of four 351st Bomb Squadron B-17s that were shot down in an attack by four Me 262s on the final Berlin mission of the war. Six men in Lieutenant Rollie King's crew baled out before the ship exploded, killing all four gunners in the rear of the aircraft. (TAMM)

B-17G-40–VE 42-97991 on a test flight in California before it was assigned to the 366th Bomb Squadron, 305th Bomb Group at Chelveston on 9 August 1944. It was lost on 24 August 1944. (Lockheed)

Above: B-17F-95-BO 42-30235 *The Zoot Suiters* (formerly *Lonesome Polecat*), which was assigned overseas on 16 June 1943 when it was allocated to the 91st Bomb Group. It later transferred to the 412th Bomb Squadron, 95th Bomb Group, and in October 1945 was scrapped at Altus, Oklahoma. (via Michael Faley) Left: B-17G-25-BO 42-31723 *Sparky* in the 349th Bomb Squadron, 100th Bomb Group showing 26 missions on the bomb log. (TAMM)

B-17G-10-DL 42-37800 *Piccadilly Lilly II*, which was assigned to the 351st Bomb Squadron, 100th Bomb Group in late September 1943, and whose nose art was the work of the highly talented Frank Stevens. On 27 June 1944 *Piccadilly Lilly II* overran the runway at Thorpe Abbotts returning from a practice flight. A test flight subsequently revealed that the fuselage had been distorted in the accident, and reluctantly she was deemed beyond repair. (TAMM)

B-17G-25-VE 42-97696 XR-W *Terrible Termite* in the 349th Bomb Squadron, 100th Bomb Group, which was assigned overseas in May 1945. There were as many as six different B-17s in the 100th Bomb Group that Bill Terminello's crew flew, and all were named *Terrible Termite*, which was his nickname in New Jersey before the war. (TAMM)

Below left: B-17G-75-BO 43-37926 *Lotta Stern* (whose nose art was inspired by the Varga girl that adorned the back cover of the May 1944 Military Edition of *Esquire* magazine) was assigned overseas on 6 July 1944. *Lotta Stern* was assigned to the 490th Bomb Group, but spent most of its wartime career in the 100th Bomb Group before returning to the ZOI in July 1945. (TAMM) Below right: B-24J *Flamin' Mamie* was flown by Lieutenant Ambrose C. Shaw in the 862nd Bomb Squadron, 493rd Bomb Group while on TDY flying gas haul to the continent with the 27th Air Transport Group at Lyneham, near Salisbury, Wiltshire, in 1944. (USAF)

B-17G in the 569th Bomb Squadron, 390th Bomb Group at Framlingham. (USAF)

B-24H-25-DT 42-51114 *Whiskey Jingles* in the 733rd Bomb Squadron, 453rd Bomb Group survived the war and was scrapped at Altus, Oklahoma, in September 1945. (USAF)

B-17G-35-DL 42-107062 *Worry Bird* (formerly *Miss Bea Haven*) in the 562nd Bomb Squadron, 388th Bomb Group over Suffolk in 1944. This aircraft was scrapped at Kingman, Arizona, in November 1945. (USAF)

B-24J-160-CO 44-40439 *Shady Lady* served in the 493rd and 34th Bomb Groups in the 3rd Bomb Division until they converted to the Fortress and it was re-allocated to the 567th Bomb Squadron, 389th Bomb Group. *Shady Lady* and 2nd Lieutenant George S. Crock's crew FTR from the mission to Brunswick on 31 March 1945 when they were shot down by a pair of Me 262s. All nine crew were KIA. (USAF)

B-17G-85-VE 44-8810 *Target For Tonight* in the 349th Bomb Squadron, 100th Bomb Group, which flew in the 385th Bomb Group from January 1945 until the end of the war before transferring to the 100th Bomb Group at Thorpe Abbotts. S/Sgt Eddy Saville, a commercial artist before the war and the tail gunner in Captain Byron Allen's crew, painted the original nose art and title at Great Ashfield. The nose art was saved just before the aircraft was scrapped at Walnut Ridge in Ocotber 1945. (CAF)

B-24J-1-FO 42-50592 *Lady Marian* in the 701st Bomb Squadron, 445th Bomb Group, which returned to the USA in August 1945. (TAMM)

Two crewmembers inspect tail damage to B-17G-65-BO 43-37552/E *The Peacemaker* in the 401st Bomb Squadron, 91st Bomb Group. (USAF)

A FW 190A-8/R2 *Rammbock* (Rammer) or *Sturmbock* (Battering Ram). (Bundersarchiv)

The end of the line. B-17s surplus to requirements at a desert salvage depot shortly after the end of the war. (USAF)

B-17G-90-BO 43-38514 *E-Z Goin'* in the 349th Bomb Squadron, 100th Bomb Group, which returned to Thorpe Abbotts on 7 April 1945 after being hit by a *Rammjäger*. (TAMM)

B-17G in the 100th Bomb Group dropping supplies over Holland in May 1945. (TAMM)

B-17G-55-VE 44-8209 in the 100th Bomb Group discharging displaced persons during a repatriation mission at the end of the war. (TAMM)

B-17G-70-BO 43-37716 *5 Grand*, the 5000th Boeing-built Fortress, which was liberally autographed by Boeing factory workers, flew 78 combat missions, two food missions, and two PoW missions in the 338th Bomb Squadron, 96th Bomb Group. Allocated to the 560th Bomb Squadron, 388th Bomb Group to be flown home for a War Bond drive, the plane left for the USA on 9 June 1945, and it was broken up for scrap at Kingman, Arizona, in November that year. (USAF)

B-17G overflying Germany on a *Trolly* mission. (USAF)

well out in front, split-essed. The two bandits I was after continued at the same level. On reaching 30,000ft, I closed to extreme range. One of the bandits dropped his belly tank and headed down. Lieutenant Golden, Newcross Blue Four, took out after him. Fearing that the other Me 109 would do the same, I ranged him carefully with my K-14 gunsight and allowed a small amount of deflection above to take care of the sizable 450-yard distance between us. I squeezed off a very short burst and got hits, much to my surprise! The Jerry started a slow break to the right. Taking my time, I ranged him again, still allowing a little for the distance. Another short burst produced more hits. Having closed in to a better range by this time, I put the pipper right on his cockpit, let up a trifle on the graticules and gave him another burst. He received more strikes this time, right where my pipper rested. Black smoke poured out of his engine cowling and he snapped into a spin, recovered drunkenly and then went into a violent, uncontrolled spin from which he didn't recover. I started to follow, but realized that he had had it and broke off.

"Straightening up, I saw two more Me 109s ahead at 35,000ft and 16 to 18 FW 190s below them. All were heading southwest towards the B-17s attacking Chemnitz. I climbed again, figuring on bouncing the top cover first and then the main force. The same thing happened as before, one Jerry split-essed with Lieutenant Creighton hot after him and the other went straight. I fired at this one from slightly below and a dead astern range of 450 yards. As soon as I could see strikes, the 190 started right. Then with that beautiful K-14 sight, I got hits all over the right side of his fuselage. I obtained a few more hits as he rolled over into the inside of his turn, yawing and skidding. He must have been out of control because this yawing and skidding continued for a hit: sometimes he was upside down; sometimes he was falling sideways, but then he went straight down.

"This last bounce left me in perfect position to hit the FW 190s. Dropping my nose, I started down after them as they were making gentle left and right turns, in no apparent formation. I tacked onto the tail end man on the right side of the gaggle and closed into good range before firing. Just as I entered his contrail, I saw many strikes flashing and continued to fire for the next few seconds, placing my pipper midway between his wing tips, which were all that I could see. The 190 fell gently to the right and I realized too late that my closing speed was excessive. Even though I momentarily chopped my throttle, I glided on past him. I looked over and saw the German pilot slumped forward in his cockpit seat. His canopy was shattered and I went by slowly enough to note jagged holes in the left side of his fuselage. I blandly glided right on through the edge of the Jerry gaggle and out in front. As I had not the slightest intention to lead three Jerries anywhere, I did a half roll followed by a wing-low vertical 360 or loop. By the time I got three-fourths around in this maneuver, I looked through the top of my canopy and saw the 190s disappear into a thick cirrus formation that was between them and the bombers. I could still see my 190, because he was still in that steep diving turn to the right while the rest of his buddies turned left into the clouds. He disappeared momentarily, then reappeared underneath the cloud, going straight down. I watched him until he disappeared into a cumulus formation at 16,000ft. He never could have recovered from a dive like that at that altitude, even if he had been intact. I circled, looking for the rest of the FW 190s, but they had eluded me and I was all alone. I flew over to the last box of B-17s that hit Dresden and escorted a straggler halfway home."[1166]

On the 15th over 1000 heavies bombed the Magdeburg synthetic oil plant and marshaling yards at Dresden, Cottbus, and Rheine, and several targets of opportunity. Nine fighter groups flew escort for the bombers, and they later broke away and strafed transportation targets. Next day almost 1000 B-17s and B-24s hit benzol plants at Dortmund[1167] and Gelsenkirchen, and oil refineries at Dortmund and Saltzbergen, as well as marshaling yards at Osnabrück, Hamm, and Rheine. Wesel railroad bridge was also attacked, as were several secondaries and targets of opportunity. Norman K. Andrew, in the 487th Bomb Group, flew his 27th mission. He wrote:

> "Really surprised this morning. We were not up to fly at 1700 last night. But the CQ woke me at 0530. He tried at 0500 and I didn't wake up. 1030 take off. Target: Hamm marshaling yard. We flew the low on Rougham [94th Bomb Group]. Bombing was supposed to be visual - cat and mouse - *Micro-H*. Flak was moderate and accurate. No.3 ship in the lead blew up. We were bombing in 6-ship sections. Went in PFF and Al dropped visual at the last minute. Really hit the target, too - a beautiful hit. Just before bombs away we were spread all over Germany and bandits were reported in the area. To top it off I hadn't seen a P-51 all the way in. The section behind us told us later that the flak was tracking us all the way in and out - bursting right behind us. One went off right over the nose. It was between the sun and us and really blacked the nose out for a while. Came back to the field and couldn't see it until we were about 150ft over the runway."

The *Luftwaffe* was again noticeable by its virtual absence, but bomber losses continued to occur, mainly as a result of the bad weather, which often affected forming-up operations over England. Marvin Barnes, a gunner in the 452nd Bomb Group at Deopham Green, recalls:

> "It was 0600 hours on 17 February when the CO came in and awakened us for the mission. We dressed and went to chow and to briefing. After briefing and learning the target was Frankfurt, we went to the locker room and donned our flight suits. A brief Jeep ride took us to our plane, *Forbidden Fruit* and we installed our .50 calibers and checked out the oxygen equipment. Everything seemed in order except the ball turret gunner, S/Sgt Gibson, was having a problem installing his guns so I gave him a hand. Harry Cross, the tail gunner, asked me to help him adjust his parachute harness and then he helped me adjust mine.
>
> "Our pilot, Joe Knoll, started the engines and taxied out for take-off. The weather was terrible as usual for February and we had a pretty rough ride up through the overcast to 10,000ft. When we finally broke out on top we spotted our formation at about the same altitude and passing directly in front of us, making the long left-hand circle waiting for us to join them. Joe Knoll made a slow left turn to catch the formation on the other side of the circle and at this moment the left wing dipped to 90°, caused by severe prop wash. He pulled it back hard to the right and *Forbidden Fruit* did a barrel roll. Knoll pulled hard to the left and the plane did a slow roll and peeled off just like a fighter. It went into a flat spin and at this moment I kicked out the waist door. I had been pinned to the floor up to this point but the force that had me pinned gave up just long enough for me to jump. At that very second *Forbidden Fruit* couldn't take any more and she just disintegrated on her way down, spewing bits of silver metal everywhere.
>
> "My 'chute opened and I landed in a wheat field just outside the B-24 base at Tibenham. After being picked up by some fellows from the base I learned that Harry Cross and Sgt Hawkins had been thrown clear and were lucky enough to have had their 'chutes on and were OK. Gibson's 'chute did not open and he lost his life, as did Joe

Knoll. The navigator, toggelier, flight engineer and co-pilot also went down with *Forbidden Fruit* This incident qualified Cross, Hawkins and myself as members of the 'Caterpillar Club.'"

On 21 February more than 1200 heavies attacked military installations and communications targets at Nürnburg, and 13 other targets of opportunity in the area supported by ten fighter groups that later strafed ground targets, including Hitler's retreat at Berchetsgaden for the first time. On 22 February, George Washington's birthday, *Clarion*, the systematic destruction of the German communications network, was launched. More than 6000 Allied aircraft from seven different commands were airborne this day, and they struck at transportation targets throughout western Germany and northern Holland. All targets were selected with the object of preventing troops being transported to the Russian front, now only a few miles from Berlin. It was all part of the strategy worked out at Yalta by the "Big Three" earlier that same month. The strike was planned by Major General Orvil Anderson, 8th Air Force Chief of Operations, who said, "We could lose 300 planes today, but we won't." Despite the low altitudes flown, only five bombers were lost.[1168] Norman K. Andrew, who flew his 28th mission in the 487th Bomb Group, wrote:

> "Up at 0200. Target: Cheb, Czechoslovakia. Marshaling yards. Bombing to be from 12,000ft. Led the Group. Assembled and flew about halfway over Belgium at 6,000ft. Crossed the Rhine south of Strasbourg. Good view of the Alps - about 40 miles away. Descended to 12,000 and hit clouds. The bomber stream was all over southern Germany. We went to the TP. The primary and secondary were covered. So we wandered around Nurnberg. Jack wanted to bomb it from 16,000 but we bombed the last resort from 19,000 - PFF. Crossed into France. As soon as I got Jack on course for Ostend I went back to the waist and went to sleep. I really had a headache."

Abe Dolim in the 94th recorded the mission thusly;

> "The bombing was carried out at extremely low altitudes and our targets were secondary rail junctions and marshaling yards in smaller cities not previously bombed. Just east of Ansbach, our target, we passed an enemy airfield and I counted ten Me 109s and other types on the field. We were only 5500ft above the ground but they did not fire at us. This was the first time that I felt the concussion of our own bombs and also the first time I saw boxcars tumble through the air. I felt we were unnecessarily exposed to light flak, which can be murderous at low altitudes and slow speeds. I feel uneasy when a boxcar attains almost as much altitude as our bomber."

Clarion ripped the heart out of a crumbling *Reich*, and the following two months would witness its bitter conclusion. Even RAF Bomber Command could reduce its nocturnal role and join in the daylight war in harmony with the 8th Air Force. Teutonic legend tells of the Bavarian werewolf that can only be killed by a silver bullet. Now the all-metal finish B-17s and B-24s were poised like silver bullets to deliver the final blow against the German werewolves, while RAF Lancasters would overfly Hitler's mountain retreat at Berchetsgaden, in Bavaria itself. The legend had come full circle.

22

Path to Victory

"We were convinced that nothing could be changed about the outcome of the war. The war was completely lost ... On the other hand, we had the most advanced, far superior aircraft ... the first operational jet. We saw that the German population had to suffer under horrifying attacks without any hope day and night. Having the best fighters in the world ready to take off we couldn't sit down and tell the people, no ... we won't take off any more because the war is lost. It was a moral question for us. We had to go into combat."

Generalmajor Adolf Galland

On 23 February only four heavies failed to return from the 1274 dispatched. The flak batteries were being deprived of ammunition, and gunners had to conserve their meager reserves. Next day 1050 heavies attacked four oil refineries, three marshaling yards, shipyards, and two rail bridges, as well as an industrial area and a city area—all in Germany. Norman K. Andrew, who flew his 29th and penultimate mission in the 487th Bomb Group on 24 February, wrote:

"Up at 0130. Target: Sub pens at Bremen. Supposedly about as rough as Hamburg. We were leading the group with an Air Leader aboard. Take off was 0600 but was delayed 2 hours. I laid down on the cement floor at Engineering and really slept. Last night I 'sweated' this one out - only slept about a half-hour. Instead of a wing assembly line - we all hit Buncher 23 and on to Southwold. On across the North Sea to the Hook of Holland. I made it minute late. Finally, over the Zuider Zee we swung in the bomber stream. It turned out that it wasn't even our wing -but Task Force #2. By the time I convinced the Air Leader - we had overshot the pre-IP about 5 miles. So we cut across to the IP and hit it on the head. Made a PFF bomb run. Instead of 264 knots ground speed we went over Bremen at 190 knots 26,000ft. I only saw 2 bursts of flak just after bombs away. The flak was moderate to intense and accurate. It was bursting under and behind us. On the way home one ship from another group toggled on Quakenbrück. His 500lb GPs fell short - only one hit the marshaling yards and his hit in a field. Jack and Whitt finished up today so we buzzed the field shooting every kind of flare we had, except red-red. Damn near put one in the 72,000-gallon gasoline dump.

"Next day, 25 February was Graduation Day! I was almost ashamed to finish up on this one. Except that our primary was visual only. Munich - PFF and the weather was briefed to be 6/10ths plus. Also we were given a diversion base in France. What a trip! I rode the bomb aimer's seat. Clouds were 9/10ths to Strasbourg. Then 3/10 to 5/10. Had some light accurate front line flak. Twelve o'clock close in at Riegel. Had clouds over the bomb run but about 15 miles out I picked up the target, an underground oil depot on the south banks of the Danube just west of Neuburg. On the way in we wandered off course and nipped Switzerland and Austria. Finally Rusty saw the target. All 3 squadrons put their bombs right on the MPI. Results - good to excellent. I really had an easy day today."

The 8th put up 1141 heavies for the day's missions, and eleven fighter groups flew close escort. It was a similar scenario on 26 February, when 1102 B-17s and B-24s hit three railroad stations in Berlin supported by 15 fighter groups this time. Even the normally notorious flak defenses in Berlin could shoot down only three bombers over "Big B." Walter "Don" O'Hearn, tail gunner, 303rd Bomb Group, recalls:

"My time at Molesworth was from February to June 1945. We arrived at the base but had several weeks of waiting to be called into action. Our crew of gunners was assigned a barracks near the big hangar. We were assigned to the 427th Squadron, which was located just behind the bunker next to the main runway. On our first day at the barracks about twelve of us from two crews walked through the door. Someone's first remark was, 'When did the men in this empty barracks go home.' A voice called out, 'They didn't go home; they're visiting Germany as guests of the German PoW camp, or else they're dead. You rookies look around and pick out a bed.' It was a very quiet time after that remark was made to us. None of us 'new men' ever knew if the 'old timers' were pulling our leg and we didn't ask. Six of our crew finished 53 missions in 57 days, ending on 25 April 1945. This was as short a time for 53 missions as I have ever heard of. Our waist gunner was the first to be voted off the crew. He fell asleep on us on missions 2 and 3. Our co-pilot was hit by flak over Berlin and lost his foot from flak damage. He was a great pilot. We were members of Lieutenant Denison's and co-pilot Chuck Haynes' crew. Our plane was named *El Screamo*. Three trips to Berlin were plenty for all of us. We always had lots of 'black' flak. The third man to drop from our crew got drunk and tried to break into the Red Cross barracks. Of course, he was not welcomed with open arms."

On 28 February 1104 bombers escorted by 737 fighters attacked transportation targets in Germany. 2nd Lieutenant William W. Varnedoe,

Jr., navigator in 2nd Lieutenant George H. Crow, Jr.'s crew in the 550th Bomb Squadron, 385th Bomb Group, flew his first mission:

> "The target was a railroad marshaling yard of the Henschel Tank factory at Kassel. There was 10/10ths cloud at the target so we bombed by PFF. Over the target there was light flak, but no fighters. At this time, Jerry did not attack each raid, but would at random times, send up a massive fighter attack. The flak was inaccurate because of the clouds. We jammed the German's radar with *Chaff.* All the jamming seemed to work well. On this mission the 385th lost no planes. Although non-visual, the bombing results were unusually good and several of the day's targets were removed from the target list for good."

By March 1945 the systematic destruction of German oil production plants, airfields, and communications centers had virtually driven the *Luftwaffe* from German skies, and the *Third Reich* was on the brink of defeat. Despite fuel and pilot shortages, Me 262 jet fighters could still be expected to put in rare attacks, and during March almost all enemy fighter interceptions of American heavy bombers were made by Me 262s of JG 7 "*Hindenburg*," Adolph Galland's *Jagdverband* 44, EJG 2, led by *Oberleutnant* Bär, and I.KG(F) 54. However, the German jets and rockets had arrived too late and in too few numbers to prevent the inevitable.

On 1 March 2nd Lieutenant William W. Varnedoe, Jr., navigator in 2nd Lieutenant George H. Crow, Jr.'s crew in the 550th Bomb Squadron, 385th Bomb Group, flew his second mission:

> "It was our first mission as a full crew. This time the target was a railroad marshaling yard at Ulm, which caught 1300lbs of bombs this day. We flew left wing[1169] off Ruseki's crew who was in the lead of the Low Element of the Lead Flight of the Lead Squadron.[1170] Left Wing of the Lead Element was Chuck Armbruster's crew in *Mr. Lucky.*[1171] This put *Mr. Lucky* above and to the right of us. After assembly over England, we headed out over the Channel and began to climb to our cruising altitude en route. As we approached the Belgian coast, we also reached 10,000ft and went on oxygen. There was a cloud deck just below the Group. It was mostly flat and smooth on top, except that there were occasional humps of cloud here and there. Just as we reached the Belgian coast, the Low Element and Rusecki passed into one of these humps. Suddenly, Rusecki came up out of it in a steep climb. He came up just over us and into Armbruster's Fort. *Mr. Lucky* was contacted by Nos. 1 and 2 engines of Ruseki's B-17, which cut into *Mr. Lucky* about the rear of the radio room. Ruseki slid back chewing up the waist section of Armbruster's plane, which was now in two separate pieces. I lost sight of Ruseki's Fort and the tail of *Mr. Lucky*, as I focused on the front half, which was sliding to the left and dropping and was now mighty close to us on our level. I could clearly see Armbruster, looking back over his left shoulder trying to see what was happening. As he continued to slide toward us, Crow pulled us left, out of formation, or there would have been three planes in the collision. Armbruster's front half went into a flat spin and disappeared into the clouds, so near below. We then edged back into the lead slot, where Rusecki had been moments before. It was very eerie seeing all that metal ripping apart only yards away, but without making a sound as if in a silent movie. The constant, deafening roar of our own engines drowned out everything. Another lasting image was the sight of the radio operator falling out of Armbruster's plane - without his parachute. The whole thing was over in less than 15 seconds.
>
> "Crewmembers generally wore a parachute harness, but not the chute itself. These chest packs had clips, which could be quickly attached to our harnesses. However, after this incident and seeing that tumbling crewman, several of us wore our parachutes all the time while in the air, cumbersome or not. We later learned that there were only two survivors. The waist gunner of Ruseki's crew who baled out and the tail gunner of Armbruster's crew. Joe Jones was on his 22nd mission as tail gunner in *Mr. Lucky* with Armbruster's crew when he knew something was terribly wrong. The intercom was dead and there was no contact with the rest of the crew, but the aircraft was making some violent maneuvers. He tried to bale out his tail hatch, but it was jammed shut; he tried to go to the waist, but twisted metal blocked the way, so he sat back down in the tail. Joe remembered a new technique some airplanes were experimenting with, namely, using a drogue parachute as a brake. So he popped his chute and tried to stuff it out of a broken window, but the air rushing by was too strong and this came to naught. In the end, he says he just sat down and had a smoke, waiting. Six days later he woke up in a British hospital!"[1172]

On 2 March 1159 heavies were despatched to bomb synthetic oil plants at Bohlen, Ruhland, and Magdeburg, two oil refineries at Rositz and Schonebeck, and marshaling yards at Chemnitz, Dresden, and Magdeburg. Fifteen fighter groups flew 675 effective supporting sorties, and parts of some of three of these groups strafed airfields. Me 262s attacked near Dresden. Abe Dolim, who flew in the deputy lead ship in the 94th Bomb Group, saw them: "One of our bombers took hits from 30mm cannon fire. It all happened so quickly, only a few airmen saw the action." There appeared no immediate solution to the jet fighters of the dying *Luftwaffe*, but flak batteries had lost much of their effectiveness thanks to shell shortages and extensive ECM[1173] equipment. Abe Dolim explains:

> "On the Leipzig raid we had an extra crewmember, an NCO, who handled the ECM equipment called '*Panther*' designed to jam enemy radar transmissions."[1174]

Quintin R. Wedgeworth, in the 392nd Bomb Group at Wendling, flew as navigator aboard the *Wabash Cannon Ball* in the 578th Bomb Squadron, and they were assigned Magdeburg. Wedgeworth wrote:

> "It was time again and it was an ominous day for all who were overly superstitious. It was Friday, our 13th mission and we would be flying old number 313 (W)![1175] And can you believe, back to Magdeburg? During the first part of last month the Group went there five times out of six missions. (We wound up with 18 casualties and four ships destroyed). The briefing outlined the usual strategy employed for this target. The primary objective was the synthetic oil refinery north of the city, but it was stipulated that it must be a visual attack. Otherwise, the secondary was to be the marshaling yards in the center of the city. Only two squadrons from the 392nd were being committed to this effort. Our squadron would fly high right off the 44th Bomb Group and the 576th would fly high right off the 491st Bomb Group. Our bomb load was 10 500lb. The launch got underway on schedule. The wheels on our ship swung up and out at 0710 hours, just five minutes behind the lead ship. We climbed out over The Wash as usual and then circled back over beacon #21 to form up. The assembly had been planned for 12,000ft, but we were forced up another 2000ft in order to get on top. The proposed route went to King's Lynn, New Hunstanton and a point NW of Norwich and then departed the English coast at beacon #24. The lead navigator followed it closely on the first two legs but deviated somewhat from

there to the coast, eventually exiting just SE of Happisburgh, at 0844 hours.

"The climb to the enemy coast had been scheduled to commence at Checkpoint A. Since we were already at 15,000ft on arrival, it wouldn't be necessary to push it too hard. I guess I had been a little leery ever since we burned that one up on mission #6. We made landfall on the coast of the Netherlands just north of Bergen Aan Zee at 0922 hours; one minute ahead of schedule. The climb continued over Enkhuizen, the Zuider Zee, Meppel and the German frontier where we were supposed to level out at 22,500ft while rendezvousing with the P-51 fighter escort. However, we continued to push upward, reaching 23,000ft at checkpoint 3. The time was 0958 hours and we were precisely on schedule. In anticipation of some enemy reaction, we had been discharging *Chaff* for the last 14 miles but the Dummer Lake flak defenses were strangely quiet! Near the town of Celle, Lieutenant Down's crew[1176] broke away from the formation and headed back, but apparently under control. Although unusual, the ascent did not terminate until we had reached the IP, where we finally leveled off at 24,000ft. The point lay over the village of Wittingen. The *Chaff* screen was dispersed immediately and continued all the way into the target. We didn't have long to wait before the first bursts of flak began to appear; mostly below us. I pulled my helmet down (already had the vest on) around my chest and dragged the chute a little closer! Taylor was soon reporting that the lethal black puffs were climbing higher! Ahead of us and uncomfortably close, it was sure enough bursting at our level. Suddenly it was on all sides. The whole ship shuddered and bounced. Inevitably a loud metallic "clang" told us that we had been hit. The question was where? It wasn't visible from any of our stations. At 1037 hours I toggled the bombs loose in unison with the lead ship.

"As we circled left to withdraw, we (unknowingly) came close to becoming involved in a major air battle. Anticipating an attack against their dwindling oil supplies, the Luftwaffe had assembled a large force of Me-109s and FW 190s. However, the 353rd and 357th Fighter Groups intercepted them near Wittenberg. The Mustangs downed 30 of the e/a while losing eight of their own.

"The return trip was not the usual uneventful story, either. As before, we commenced discharging a screen of *Chaff* prior to reaching Dummer Lake. During this operation, someone accidentally fired their gun (or guns). Lieutenant Blakely's ship raked with the heavy .50 caliber ammo at close range tumbled from the 576th formation and was last seen spiralling down with only two chutes being observed.[1177] The flight back across the Netherlands was a sombre one. Because of some deep-rooted human emotion, accidental fatalities were always much harder to swallow than those which were the direct result of some enemy action. We arrived at Checkpoint 5 (Dutch Coast) at 1313 hours and commenced the letdown immediately. We were running a bit late as we descended across the North Sea...18 minutes to be exact. Our intended landfall was at Great Yarmouth, the usual point. However, for some inexplicable reason, while still 17 miles east thereof, we turned northeastward and came ashore over Happisburgh. We had made a similar deviation earlier this morning over the same area! Maybe the lead had a girl in Happisburgh? As we neared the base, I collected my briefcase and went aft to the flight deck, my normal station during landing. We touched down at 1420 hours and piled out as soon as Adsit had her parked. Except for one squadron, the effectiveness of this day's effort was poor. Although the target was partially obscured by clouds, our squadron bombardier got a visual sighting and put 74% within 2000ft of the MPI at the oil refinery. The other element (including the 576th) bombed the marshaling yards and wound up with poor results from the H_2X. Amazingly enough, our ship was the lone recipient of all that flak?!"[1178]

2nd Lieutenant William W. Varnedoe, Jr., navigator in 2nd Lieutenant George H. Crow, Jr.'s crew in the 385th Bomb Group, flew his third mission on 2 March:

"If my second mission sounded impressive, No.3 was also! The primary target was a Ruhland oil refinery but 10/10 clouds diverted the Group to the secondary target, a railroad marshaling yard on the outskirts of Dresden. The bomb load was 20 2501b GP bombs in each Fort. Intervolometer setting was minimum. Bombing altitude was 23,000ft. Colonel G. Y. Jumper, the 385th CO was leading the Group and our Group was leading the 93rd Wing and the entire 3rd Division. There was a shortage of navigators and radio operators so I flew as navigator for Lieutenant Thornton Audrain,[1179] whose regular navigator, who was filling in on Rusecki's crew on the mission the day before, was lost in that mid-air collision. On Audrain's right wing was 2nd Lieutenant Kenneth G. Tipton[1180] who was on his 3rd mission, his first with his crew. Dunlap in '*Sleepytime Gal*' filled left wing off Audrain.[1181] Leon E. Tripp, on his 14th mission, fitted in the diamond in the tail end Charlie spot.[1182] This made a total of 13 original planes for the Low Squadron. Dunlap aborted and dropped out of formation before getting to the IP. However, he bombed a target of opportunity, an airfield at Diepholz and made it back to Great Ashfield OK. As soon as Dunlap left the formation, Tripp pulled out of his Tail-End-Charlie spot and came in on the now vacant left wing of Audrain in the Low Flight. The lead navigator, R. E. Pittis, reported a wind shift near Hanover and the loss of his flux gate compass. However, he and the rest of the Group made the IP OK.

"Although not leading the 8th Air Force and not at the head of the bomber stream, our IP differed from the Group ahead, since we had a different target. The Lead Squadron and the High Squadron turned slightly short of the IP but the Low Squadron went on to the briefed IP over Oschatz. This left a gap in front of the Low Squadron. The official report says that the Low Squadron was 'straggling' 2 to 3 miles back of the group. Whatever the reason, Jerry was quick to take advantage in the break in the Fortress' covering firepower and attacked the Low Squadron 30 seconds before the IP.

"The Group Bombardier, E. J. Maloney, reported that the *Mickey* operator picked up the target and the rate checks were made from 14 to 5 miles. Bombs away at 1027 hours with results believed 'good'. The Low Squadron radar navigator, R. W. Law, also picked up the target 40 miles away but he then had difficulty with the *Mickey* set and no returns were obtainable. The 'C' Squadron bombed on the 'B' Squadron's smoke bombs. In any case, the Squadron Leader had ordered Group bombing when the fighters attacked. On the bomb run, I noticed what I thought was unusual flak bursts close by. Normal flak was a black smoke, elongated vertically. These were light gray, rather small and elongated horizontally. I had just started to describe them in the log when someone started firing his guns and I suddenly realized that fighters were attacking us. By then, numerous gunners were firing but no one had ever called out "bandits" on the intercom, as they should have. These 'odd flak' bursts were 20mm cannon shells fired by the fighters and fuse timed to go off in the formation.

"The first attack was by 12 Focke Wulfs and three Messerschmitt 109s coming in abreast and level from our rear (6 o'clock.) They fired those fused 20mm shells. Ground crews later reported flak damage to some of the Forts, but this was no doubt, shrapnel from these cannon shells. The Germans called this tactic their '*Sturm*' formation. We called it a 'company front' attack. They then made another similar pass from the front (12 o'clock.) Several then made pursuit curve passes, while most concentrated on the Forts dropping out of formation. Several crewmen sighted one of the new German jets, but it didn't join in the fight.

"During this fight a Me 109 seemed to pull up and stall at about 2 o'clock high. I lined up the right cheek gun, remembering the correct angle to aim and pushed the firing lever. Nothing. I recharged (cocked) the gun and tried again. Again nothing happened. I opened up the 50-caliber machine gun and found a crooked link in the ammo chain. I took it out and charged the gun but by now the fighters were gone and the fight was over. The chin turret had jammed also and Leverson, the bombardier, was manning the left cheek gun. Sometime during all of this, probably after most had dropped their bombs on the lead, Audrain had ordered the bombs salvoed and I did so because Leverson was quite occupied at the time. We have no idea where they landed. The official report states that most bombs felt in the middle of town and that everyone, including Audrain, released at 1027 hours but surely those from '481' were late and fell elsewhere.

"The escorting P-51s had also engaged the enemy and accounted for several Germans shot down. After I got the gun cleared and dropped the bombs, I had time to look about and assess the situation. We, in the Low Flight had lost half of our B-17s. Both of my wing Forts were gone as well as one just up ahead. Essentially, on each side of our B-17.

"On the bomb run, Tipton's B-17 was knocked out during the first attack. The co-pilot, Ed Craig, recalls that they were hit in the radio room and the tail section then sustained a burst in the main fuel tank. Nos.1 and 4 were on fire; the turbos out and the controls were half shot away. They began a split-S, but the autopilot held them level enough for alt to jump. The tail gunner was killed on impact with the ground, but all the others were captured and sent to a prisoner camp. On the way to interrogation the navigator was hit in the mouth by a brick thrown by a civilian and had a tooth knocked out. Craig and the bombardier were captured near Oschatz and then sent to Frankfurt for interrogation before being sent to a PoW camp. At the time, no one saw any parachutes and many reported that the plane had exploded."

Lieutenant Eugene J. Vaadi's aircraft[1183] was hit in the left wing tank at No.2, caught fire, and glided to cloud tops at 18,000ft when it exploded. Jesse Brown, Vaadi's co-pilot, remembered it this way:

"We were on fire and control was almost impossible due to control surface damage. The bale out order was given and no response was heard on the intercom. We saw the navigator Tom Conway, engineer, Ray Anthony and chin gunner, Neil Quell, bale out. I went back thru the bomb bay to see if everyone had left the rear of the aircraft and no one was seen. I came back up to the flight deck and told Gene that everyone was out. I then started toward the front escape hatch when Gene turned loose the controls; the aircraft started a descending slow roll. I had to pull myself thru the escape hatch as the aircraft was now upside down. The slipstream forced me against the wing and I was caught between the fuselage and engine and held tightly against the wing by the airstream. I then saw and heard an explosion. The next thing I knew I was floating down in my parachute with pieces of the plane falling all around me."

Neil Quell remembers:

"After we were on fire, I checked the waist and ball turret. Tony, the engineer and I both checked out the fire. The navigator had already left and we could see we were burning too bad to do anything about it. Tony motioned me to go, but I shook my head and motioned for him to go first. About then we were racked by more bullets. Tony climbed back into the upper turret and took out a FW that was riding on our wing. After this, Tony jumped and I followed. I free fell for what I guessed would take me to 10,000ft. By then the plane had blown up. I landed on a fighter field while the fighters were landing. The terrific wind caused me to be hurt when I hit the ground. I was completely paralyzed for about a month. The *Gestapo* questioned me for about two days before sending me to PoW camp. Our gunners were especially nervous after the Armbruster/Rusecki collision the day before and so when they heard 'bale out' they didn't tarry.[1184]

"After the turn off the target and the Germans had left, as I looked about to see who was left. In addition to Vaadi and Tipton, Tripp was also missing.[1185] Since both of Audrain's wingmen were gone and left wing up ahead. Audrain was now Tail-End-Charlie. But he pulled up into Vaadi's vacant left wing spot to finish the mission."

In the Lead Squadron, Lieutenant Robert A. Krahn, flying *Slick Chick*[1186] on his 30th mission, was shot down on the second attack. All crewmembers survived. Krahn remembers:

"We heard radio reports that the low Squadron, still in its spacing turn, had come under fighter attack. The next thing I noticed was that alt the P-51s of our Forward High cover had turned back to chase the enemy aircraft leaving us exposed. The first indication of trouble came shortly thereafter when top turret, Flem Williams, started firing almost directly into the sun. Within seconds, 15 FW 190s, three rows of five-abreast dived through the High Squadron and did a real number on us. One FW 190 passed just off my left wing tip. The pilot saluted me in passing and I returned his salute automatically. I thought his action was passing strange until I returned my attention to the cockpit to find my co-pilot, Oris Lundy, about to go into orbit yelling, 'We're on fire!' After a measure of calm returned to the cockpit, I was able to establish that we were dealing with a fire in #3 rather than a wing fire. Two 20mm shells in the accessory section had apparently ruptured all fluid lines and started a fierce fire, which had already burned off the tower inside quadrant of the nacelle. Three or four more 20mm shells had penetrated the wing area aft of #3 while 13mm bullets had made an absolute shambles of the right wing root and bomb bay area. Thank God we were not carrying RDX. Because of the hits in the wing root and bomb bay, our electrical power began to go immediately, so we were unable to activate the fluid shutoff valves to #3. Probably for lack of any better ideas, I elected to stay in formation. At bombs away, I again surveyed the situation and found the fire about to eat its way through the firewall and into the main wing area, which was surely swimming in fuel. I then decided to try for the Russian lines, which were not too far away. From our bombing altitude, I pulled out of formation and headed east in a diving sideslip, which I hoped would keep the fire out of the wing. At that time our landing gear and partial flaps came down because of electrical faults and no action on our part was helpful. I realized our position was hopeless, I then leveled and trimmed the aircraft and ordered a bale out. There were no objections! The 15 FW-190s, which hit the High Squadron, were not the usual blue-gray color. Some, if not all and particularly the FW 190 that passed off my wing tip, were still in desert tan and sported bright red engine cowls. Although our encounter was brief, I have sufficient reason to remember those birds vividly."

Sherry[1187] had his controls damaged in this second attack and had to drop out of formation. The tail gunner, James Bond, wrote in his diary at the time:

"...My oxygen system and interphone were shot out. I blazed away at the fighters and got a hit on a Focke Wulf 190. I tried to get something on my interphone but couldn't. I switched out my oxygen and got on another system. I blazed away again at the second attack and could hear their bullets whistle by. We were hit and out of formation. I didn't know where to expect fighters from next. I didn't know where we were headed or if we were supposed to bale out. After a while my waist gunner called me. Everyone was OK except he and Hatfield my RO were wounded when a 20mm shell exploded in the waist. The controls were shot out. Radio receiver out. Oxygen and interphone from waist back. Nos.1 and 2 props badly damaged. Hydraulic system was out." (Sherry nursed his B-17 to B-53, an emergency airfield in Melville, France, and landed OK.[1188])

On 3 March the largest formation of German jets ever seen made attacks on the bomber formations heading for Dresden and four separate oil targets at Ruhland. III./JG 7 despatched 29 Me 262s, whose pilots claimed six of the nine bombers, which failed to return in the area of Hanover-Braunschweig.[1189] 1st Lieutenant Donald J. Schmitt, a pilot in the 863rd Bomb Squadron, 493rd Bomb Group, flew the mission to Nienhagen industrial area at the controls of a B-17[1190] he had first flown on his 15th mission on 14 February when the target was marshaling yards at Chemnitz. As soon as he heard of the birth of his son on 27 March he had named his plane *Son Of A Blitz*. March 3rd was Donald Schmitt's 21st mission, and it was one he would never forget:

"Fighters had hit the Eighth Air Force the day before, so I didn't expect to see any today. We had a little flak upon entering Germany, otherwise there was none. But then things started to happen. We were flying in the low and just before the IP when our group formation got split up and the low Squadron was left behind. We had a visual target for our primary, but the low did not bomb it because a few scattered clouds covered it just before bombs away. On the way to the secondary, three jet planes hit our Squadron from 12 o'clock high. We were flying #3 element lead. We did not see them until they passed over our left wing because they came out of the sun. On that first pass, they got our left wing man.[1191] They made several other passes at us, but all the gunners were wide-awake and they never got in close enough after that first pass. They were twin nacelled jets and really a short looking ship. Their speed was really something. Three fighters hit the lead Squadron and knocked out two ships of which one returned.[1192] After all the damage was done, we finally caught the rest of our group. We returned on our brief course with all the ships well in formation. I was sure glad to hit the ground and hoped very much to see no more jet fighters. The fighter support was not too good. The day's mission was a total failure because the lead bombardiers missed both targets and they were visual. That night he wrote in his diary: 'BOY AM I GLAD THAT MISSION IS OVER.'"

The *Luftwaffe* seemed to have found a temporary new lease on life, for that night 30 Ju 88s attacked airfields in Norfolk and Suffolk. At Bury St. Edmunds the air raid warning siren was sounded at 2300. "Crash alarm, Red bandits, take cover." But the *Luftwaffe* had not dared to attack the bases for a year and no one took much notice, as Abe Dolim explains:

"Our air raid shelter was only about 50 yards away but no one rushed outside to freeze in the cold, enemy or no enemy. Inside Hut 28 we were welcoming a new crew. Soon we heard the unforgettable rapid beat of unsynchronized twin-engined enemy intruders. I told the newcomers the enemy was overhead and if he followed the usual procedure he would cut his engines and glide into position as soon as he identified his target. Several bombs exploded some distance from Bury. The new crew felt we were 'putting them on.' Suddenly, the raider cut his engines and seconds later all hell let loose as the sound of hostile cannon fire destroyed the absolute quiet of the station. The rookie navigator, sitting on the bed across from me, clad only in his underwear and flying boots, darted out the door. An hour later, he returned from the air raid shelter looking somewhat blue."[1193]

On 4 March the B-17s and B-24s headed singly to assembly points over France, adopting a new technique aimed at conserving fuel. The Fortresses formed up at Troyes, while the Liberator groups assembled near Nancy. In the 94th Bomb Group, Abe Dolim flew his 49th mission when his crew led a nine-bomber section to the assembly point at Troyes:

"The section leaders took off first and flew directly to 'Bunchers' in France where the assembly took place, instead of over 'Buncher 12' as usual. The enemy jammed hell out of the 'Buncher' at Troyes but I maintained position with the help of *Gee* fixes from advanced transmitters in France. We bombed Ingolstadt using *H_2X*. To date I'd flown with many bombardiers, most of whom usually said, 'Let's get the hell out of here' after 'Bombs Away' but one fellow I'll never forget said very quietly instead, 'Die, you bastards!' Like love, hate is a very personal emotion."[1194]

The 466th Bomb Group, led by Lieutenant Colonel John Jacobowitz, with Colonel Ligon flying deputy commander in the No.2 aircraft, led the 96th Wing to its target at Kitzingen after assembly, but thick cloud persisted over the continent and the bomb run was scrubbed. The secondary target at Aschaffenburg was also clouded over, so the call went out to switch to the marshaling yards at Stuttgart, about 80 miles from the Swiss border. Using *H_2X*, the 466th started a northerly bomb run on the target, but visibility was so poor that crews had difficulty seeing their wingmen. Suddenly, out of the murk roared a group of B-17s, also lost, sending the Liberators scattering wildly in an effort to avert a mid-air collision. The mission was abandoned when 20 B-24s became separated. The remaining eight B-24s, which had retained some semblance of formation, formed up on the lead aircraft and turned for home. In the lead was an *H_2X* ship, which spotted a town through a hole in the clouds. The lead crew navigator identified it as Frieburg, a town lying a few miles from the Rhine and southwest of Stuttgart. Some navigators suspected that the town might be Basle, in Switzerland, which was about 25 miles further south. Frieburg was a target of opportunity and a bomb run was ordered. Several minutes after the bomb run word came through that Basle had been bombed. The order went out for the formation to return to Attlebridge and crews, unaware that they had dropped their bombs on Swiss territory, were to remain in their aircraft until the base vehicles picked them up. News filtered through that the 392nd had also violated neutral territory.

At the turning point south of Stuttgart the 14th Wing received a recall message. The 44th started their turn home and the 392nd followed, although it soon lost the 44th from sight. The 392nd lead squadron, led by Colonel Myron Keilman, made a radar-bombing run on Pforzheim, but there was no sign of the second squadron. The 392nd lead squadron returned to England at 1320. Keilman wrote:

"Shortly after landing, our second squadron returned without apparent difficulty. At their debriefing, the lead crew explained how they got on the outside of the turn and lost us in the cirrus clouds and heavy contrails; that upon breaking out of the clouds they came upon what they believed to be Frieburg and bombed it as a target of opportunity. The debriefing was hardly finished when Colonel Lorin Johnson, the CO, was called to the telephone and a long conflab took place. Zurich, Switzerland, had been bombed."[1195]

On 8 March 2nd Lieutenant William W. Varnedoe, Jr., navigator in 1st Lieutenant George H. Crow, Jr.'s crew in the 385th Bomb Group, flew his 6th mission:

"The target this time was a Benzedrine synthetic oil plant at Dortmund. We flew as a crew in 43-39123, soon to be '*Possible Straight*.' A new hazard materialized on this mission. Due to some error, a whole Group of B-26s came over the target at the same time as the 385th, but headed in the opposite direction. We flew right through each other like cards being shuffled. Somehow there were no collisions. THAT must have confused the German anti-aircraft aimers tying to track us! It sure did nothing for our nerves. For a change, the weather was clear and we bombed visually. Flak was moderately heavy, but not very accurate, being of the barrage rather than an aimed variety. We sustained no hits."

On Friday, 9 March, Abe Dolim flew his 51st and final mission of the war when the 94th Bomb Group went to the marshaling yards at Frankfurt. He wrote of it later:

"My last mission was a wing-ding. We refused to drop our bombs eight miles short of the target where the rest of the group unloaded. Deputy group lead bombardier Lieutenant Cearley was mad as a wet hen because the lead aircraft did not turn the bomb run over to us when they began to experience mechanical difficulties. Captain Reed was reprimanded for returning to base with a full bomb load, thereby reducing the group's tonnage for today's mission. The whole mess is ridiculous! Nobody seems to give a damn whether or not we hit the target any more. What in blazes is tonnage worth if it does not hurt the enemy? Group is sore because we loused up their paper war - I'm glad. To hell with them - tonight I'll celebrate by getting plastered and forgetting the whole bloody war."[1196]

Abe Dolim, his second tour completed, returned home to Hawaii, while others continued accumulating missions in the hope that they too could soon go home.

On 10 March[1197] 2nd Lieutenant William W. Varnedoe, Jr., navigator in 1st Lieutenant George H. Crow, Jr.'s crew in the 385th Bomb Group, flew his 7th mission. Crow's crew was assigned to fly *Kentucky Winner*.[1198] Varnedoe recalls:

"I settled into the nose and readied everything for takeoff. The target was another Benzedrine plant, this time at Soest. Again we had a visual bomb run, but then we encountered fairly heavy tracking flak. We bombed with, as boasted by General Doolittle, 'customarily good results.' The Germans were getting really desperate for oil and fuel by this time. It was said that they pulled their fighters to the end of the runway with horses to save taxing gas and that even Goering had trouble getting gas for his car. On 11 March the target was an oil tank farm in Hamburg, fuel still being high on our target priority list. PFF bombing was planned due to a solid cloud cover and that is indeed what we did. However, these tanks were located on a peninsula sticking out into a harbor, which made their identification on the PFF scope very easy. Although the strike itself could not be seen, thick black smoke boiled up through the clouds to indicate that we hit the Bullseye."

Hank Wentland, a pilot in the 564th Bomb Squadron, 389th Bomb Group at Hethel, recalls the mission to Zossen on 13 March:[1199]

"During briefing, a large groan erupted when the map of our mission was uncovered and we saw a long red ribbon heading straight to Berlin! Our concerns were not assuaged when informed that we were not really going to Berlin but to a small town 5 miles south of 'Big B'. Wow, hope the Germans understand this! In closing we were told our Command Pilot for this mission would be Lieutenant Colonel Stewart, who was in the back of the room. We turned and saw him, a tall, lean figure, nonchalantly leaning against the doorjamb. Oh, we caught the wrath of every 88mm battery on the way in. And before we reached the Initial Point Stewart came on the radio and said, 'OK f-f-fellas…let's pull it in real t-t-tight!' Having heard the actor Jimmy Stewart stutter occasionally in pictures, I thought it was a cute affectation and now realized he had a real little verbal glitch. Anyhow, the German Officer Training groups in Zossen that were housed in tents, didn't enjoy their reveille call that morning consisting of 250lb bombs raining down and through their housing facilities."

On 15 March 1353 bombers escorted by 833 fighters hit the German Army HQ at Zossen, near Berlin, and a marshaling yard at Orienburg. Paul M. Montague, armorer-ball turret gunner in the *High Tailed Lass* in the 487th Bomb Group at Lavenham, flew his 17th mission to Oranienburg:

"This mission was another long haul into and out of Germany. Our crew had made it before. All went well until we approached the turning point toward the IP west of Berlin. We were flying at 24,000ft when, suddenly, an accurate burst of flak hit our ship. The pilot was seriously wounded, one engine quit, the intercom only functioned sporadically and all the control cables on the port side, except the rudder, were severed. This caused us to bank to starboard at about 30°. We dropped from formation, apparently unseen, lost altitude and turned toward Berlin. At only 12,000ft over Berlin a second flak burst smashed part of the Plexiglas nose, stopped a second engine, ruptured the oxygen system and started a fire in the bomb bay. Twelve 500 pounders stuck there would neither jettison nor toggle. Shrapnel hit several crewmembers. Our pilot gave us the alternative of baling out or staying while he attempted to ride the *Lass* down to a crash landing in Poland. As we gazed directly down at the Tiergarten, no one had the nerve to jump! The fire in the bomb bay was finally extinguished and we managed to jettison our bombs into a lake below. Thankfully, we were alone. No German fighters appeared. As we crossed the Oder River at only a few thousand feet, our Russian allies fired on us but no hits were sustained.

"Our pilot did a magnificent job of approach to what appeared to be a level field enclosed on three sides by woods. We had no flaps, gear, air speed indicator and many other vital instruments but all the crew survived the crash landing."[1200]

Although German jets continued to pose a very real threat, losses from collisions and accidents were often higher than those caused by fighter attacks. On 17 March, when 1328 B-17s and B-24s escorted by

820 fighters bombed targets in west and north-central Germany, the 490th Bomb Group was returning from a raid on Bittefeld when they encountered cirrus clouds that forced them to fly on instruments for 30 minutes. The Fortresses moved into tighter formation. Suddenly, a squadron in the 385th Bomb Group cut through the clouds into the 490th formation, causing one of the 490th ships[1201] flown by Lieutenant Arthur Stern to veer upwards. In no time at all it collided with another 490th B-17[1202] flown by Lieutenant Robert H. Tennenberg. The radio room in the lower Fortress took the full force of the collision and the aircraft broke in two. All nine of Stern's crew were killed. In Tennenberg's Fortress, Chester A. Deptula, the navigator, dragged the stunned nose gunner, John Gann, from the shattered nose to the radio operator's compartment. Despite a smashed engine, another partly disabled, a wing tip bent, the front of the nose knocked off, and the pilot's front view window broken, Tennenberg kept his B-17 airborne and managed to reach Belgium, where he made a successful crash-landing. The crewmen stepped out unhurt and surveyed the damage. Among the wreckage was the mutilated torso of a man later identified as the radio operator from the Fortress that had collided with them. He had been forced through the shattered Plexiglas nose of Tennenberg's aircraft on impact.

On 18 March a record 1327 bombers supported by 14 P-51 groups who flew 645 effective sorties went to Berlin, and 1251 of the B-17s and B-24s got their bombs away over two rail centers and two tank and armament plants in "Big B." 2nd Lieutenant William W. Varnedoe, Jr., navigator in 1st Lieutenant George H. Crow, Jr.'s crew in the 385th Bomb Group, flew his 11th mission:

> "When the briefing officer pulled the curtain back for this one we all 'Ooohed' and 'Aaaahed' for the black tape on the map led to Big B - Berlin. The target itself was a railroad yard in the heart of downtown Berlin. Weather was to be clear. (It was.) 1250 heavy bombers made this the largest raid of the war. On the climb to altitude our No.4 engine's supercharger[1203] refused to work. At low altitude it was a good engine but up where we were going, it would only draw 12 inches of vacuum, about the same as if it were feathered. But since we could keep up with the formation, we elected to go on. Fighters did not hit the 385th but they did attack other groups, some with their new jet fighters, the Me 262s. Overall, 24 bombers were lost, mainly to the jets. But flak was very heavy and quite accurate. The 385th lost Cock and Bloom's B-17s to the flak. Once I looked out to the left and saw a cluster of six flak bursts at our level. Shortly, there were six more, closer. The next six were very close and I could see the following six would intercept our flight path. But we were on the bomb run and could not take any action. I took a picture, but then I just tried to make myself as small a target as possible; hard to do when you're hiding behind 1/16th thick aluminum! The next six came on time and although, unlike in the movies, we never heard the actual explosion, the shrapnel hitting the B-17 sounded like someone throwing gravel on a tin roof. It did us no serious harm, however. A piece knocked the handle off the front exit hatch and other punctures hit nothing vital.
>
> "After 'bombs away' the Group made a sharp, diving turn to the left. This was normal to throw off that tracking flak after the straight bomb run. However, this evasive action turn was so tight, that with our right outboard engine not functioning, we could not turn that sharply to the left. (We were on right wing of our element.) We were literally slung out of the formation! However, the turn was sharp enough to carry the Group right back through the flak zone again. But, thanks to our bad supercharger, we missed that and finally caught up with the Group. Also, fortunately, there were no enemy fighters in the immediate area. Solo bombers were prime targets for them.
>
> "Ira, our ball gunner, wrote:
>
> "'I must confess that until Berlin I was confident that if some fate occurred in our Group it would affect the OTHER CREW. But now, and I don't want to sound too melodramatic, I suspected that misfortune could dial our number at any time and I think that conviction remained with me for the balance of our missions.'
>
> "Final assessment showed that half of all B-17s (of all groups) on that mission were damaged by flak. The appearance of the jet fighters caused quite a bit of concern, since they could out-fly anything we had. But apparently there simply weren't enough trained German pilots."

It was the second mission to the German capital for William C. Stewart in the 92nd Bomb Group:

> "The day was as bright and crisp as I have ever seen; more like a Technicolor movie than real life. There were a few small wisps of white cotton clouds interspersed through the picture but mostly it was clear. The sun glittered back from reflections of the shiny aluminium skin of the other ships in the formation. Before we reached the IP I could see the stretch of this great city. The streets were like a checkerboard beneath us and once in a while, an ant-like motor vehicle appeared on the streets. The movement of the scene below was unbearably slow and it seemed as though we were motionless. The black bursts of flak were also hanging ahead and right at our altitude the sky was completely peppered with the stuff. As I looked ahead I said to myself, 'And we're going to have to fly through that?'
>
> "I turned the ball turret to the right, at about the 3 o'clock position and could see the lumbering hulk of a Fortress, which was probably from another squadron, about 4000ft below us going in the opposite direction. Its nose was pointed downward with its tight wing toward my left. Its tight outboard engine was engulfed in red-orange flames streaking back about ten feet. There was no doubt that the plane was going down. I watched the scene transfixed and uttered silently to the crew of the plane, although really to myself, 'Get out. Get out!' As I watched one, two, three and then four small white blossoms appeared behind the craft. Some had made it out. I changed my gaze to one of the small white parachutes in the air with something hanging below; an airman, another American. As I watched small black puffs appeared around him as he slowly floated downward. The Germans were shooting at him with anti-aircraft fire. They could have used the 88mm ammunition better by going after the test of us still flying.
>
> "As we proceeded over Berlin the ship lurched and twisted from impacts but we kept going and finally unloaded our bombs onto a railroad station in the heart of the city. Once away from the city, the flight back was uneventful. When I turned my turret to about 2 o'clock I could see strips of aluminium skin peeled back from the right wing. When we landed we found we had taken what must have been a 105mm anti-aircraft shell through the wing. It left a hole that a man could put his head through near the inboard end of the 'Tokyo' gas tank. There were hundreds of smaller holes throughout the main body, wings and tail sections but no one was hit. I had learned what accurate and intense flak was."[1204]

On 19 March 1223 heavy bombers hit marshaling yards at Fulda and Plauen, and other targets at Jena and Zwickau, as well as airfields and jet aircraft plants. *Carpetbagger* aircraft dropped 82 agents into Germany. P-51 Mustangs flew 606 effective sorties in support of the bombers, and over 100 enemy fighters, including 36 jets in formation (the largest number yet seen in one formation), were encountered. U.S. fighters claimed 42 enemy fighters (including three jets) destroyed. Major Robin Olds in the 434th Fighter Squadron, 479th Fighter Group, who as Newcross Leader led the B group consisting of 16 P-51s in his P-51K, claimed a Bf 109 and a FW 190 to take his score to 12 victories.

Olds and his pilots made landfall between Knokke and Ostend at 14,000ft. They rendezvoused with the B-24s east of Strasbourg at 1408 hours at 21,500ft, and escorted them to, through, and from the target to Creilsheim, where the squadron broke from the bombers and swept the areas of Giebelstadt airfield, Kitzingen, Würzburg, Volkmarsen, Paderborn, and Münster. While in the Münster area, 25-plus FW 190D-9s of the Ist and IVth *Gruppen* JG 26 who were assigned a mission to provide airfield cover for the Me 262 photo reconnaissance jets at Münster-Handorf were sighted at 1615 hours at 8000ft. Bf 109s were also in the area. Having the advantage in the bounce after using the haze as cover during their approach, Olds led his Squadron in the attack on the FW 190s, though Yellow Flight became separated as the squadron closed. Olds' nine P-51s engaged the Focke-Wulf Doras, which immediately went into a Lufbery to the left, pulling contrails as they circled at 13,000ft in the haze. Olds' Squadron joined in the Lufbery, gaining altitude as the pilots waited for the Germans to break. The Dora pilots performed barrel rolls, shallow split-esses, and other maneuvers before pulling back up in an attempt to lure the P-51 pilots into following them down. Finally, as Olds reached the level of the enemy formation's leader the majority of the FW 190s broke downward and the Mustangs attacked. An eight-minute dogfight ensued in which JG 26 lost two FW 190D-9s and a Bf 109. One P-51 pilot took a 20mm shell in his wing from a burst of fire by *Leutnant* Friedrich Ramthun, but the American pilot made it home safely. 1st Lieutenant Richard G. Simpson confirmed the FW 190D-9 that Major Olds claimed:

> "Upon encountering the E/A we climbed to about 13,000ft and joined in their Lufbery to the left. Red Flight was directly behind White Flight and as the Lufbery got tighter, I saw a 109 roll over on his back, skid and then spin violently down. I did not see whether this 109 was under attack or not because of the haze and contrails. Nor did I see any strikes. The German leader was getting uncomfortably close in the turn, so I gave the word to break into them. Because of the contrails and haze, I continued the Lufbery, not knowing whether the Jerries were on our tails or not. A few moments later Major Olds ordered us to get below the contrail level; so I split-essed, pulling out at about 8000ft. As I leveled off I saw a FW 190 with two P-51s on his tail. The 190 was smoking badly and then he rolled over and went down in a steep dive, losing pieces of cowling and other parts as they flew off his aircraft. I broke to the right with my flight in order to investigate two bogies, which turned out to be a P-51 attacking another FW 190. The 190 pulled up sharply and I saw the P-51 firing and getting strikes all over the Jerry's fuselage. The 190 passed under my nose and after I completed my turn, I saw the E/A dive straight in and explode on impact. Because of the haze and thick contrails, it was impossible at the time to identify the pilots who had shot down the E/A described above; but at interrogation, it developed that Major Olds was the only one in the squadron who had attacked a Me 109. Additionally, the Me 109 that I saw was unquestionably out of control, spinning and skidding violently. The FW 190, which I saw crash and explode, was the one claimed by Major Olds."[1205]

On 21 March preparatory air operations for the forthcoming (23 March) crossing of the lower Rhine by Allied ground forces began. In morning raids 1254 bombers in conjunction with aircraft of the RAF and 9th Air Force attacking other targets, bombed ten airfields in NW Germany, a tank factory at Plauen, and a marshaling yard at Reichenbach.[1206] In the afternoon 90 B-24s bombed Mülheim an der Ruhr airfield. U.S. fighters flew almost 750 effective sorties in support of the two operations. Philip G. Day flew his 35th and final mission when the 467th Bomb Group made a visual bombing of an airfield near Osnabrück. Day wrote:

> "No flak or fighters. Excellent results. After passing over the target we started a left assembly turn and out of the cloudbank to our right, at our altitude and on collision course, popped a group of B-17s. There was grand confusion, a melee of aircraft and a bunch of fright, but all missed and both groups reformed. And so to Rackheath where I greased the B-24 in for the last time, then to debriefing, to critique and to get drunk. The great adventure was finished."

Included in the day's operations was a lone B-17, which was despatched to Oberusel to drop two tons as a *Micro-H* Mk II test. *Leutnant* Fritz R. G. Müller of III./JG 7 flying a Me 262 claimed the lone B-17.[1207] However, this B-17 does not appear in any loss listings. Müller recalled:

> "I took off with a section against a major attack in the area of Leipzig-Dresden. Our radio communications suffered particularly heavy interference on this day. At 7500 meters I came upon a Boeing flying on an easterly course south of Dresden, separated by about 10 kilometers from the rest of the formation at the same height and escorted by four Mustangs flying above and behind. I assumed that this aircraft had some special duty and decided to attack it. The radio interference was now so heavy that no communication was possible. I passed close below the Mustangs and although they followed my section trailing black smoke (full throttle); my airspeed indicator showed that I no longer had to bother myself about them. The Boeing was now ahead of me in a gentle turn to port and I was approaching it at an angle of about 10° from port and about 5° from above. At a range of about 1000 meters the rear gunner opened continuous fire. What now happened took only seconds. At about 300 meters my wingman and I gave a short burst with a little deflection. We observed about a dozen hits in the fuselage and between the engines of the Boeing -and then we had passed above it. Flying a wide turn (with the Mustangs behind us, trailing black smoke and getting ever smaller) we observed the end of the bomber. It spun for 2000 meters, several large parts broke away from the fuselage and wings and then it literally burst asunder. All of a sudden the radio interference had ceased. We had received no hits; set course for home and the Mustangs eased the strain on their engines as they realized the pointlessness of any further chase.
>
> "The effects of damage to the outer skinning at high speed were enormous. A dislodged, hand-sized piece of plywood from the undercarriage cover lost at 300 meters height and at a speed of 900 km/h made the Me 262 suddenly so nose heavy that I was only and using all my strength, able to pull out just before striking the ground. A strong rushing and rumbling noise made the background music. A harmless hit near the wingtip made a small hole in the slat and a flower-like hole at the exit. The effect: instant turning of the machine around the lateral and longitudinal axis and it seemed that the fuselage would break apart. Again hard work on the control

column and rudder pedals. Only after a considerable reduction of speed and trimming out did the machine again become reasonably controllable."[1208]

On 22 March 1301 B-17s and B-24s bombed targets east of Frankfurt and ten military encampments in the Ruhr in preparation for the forthcoming Allied amphibious crossing of the lower Rhine. The 8th bombed the Bottrop military barracks and hutted areas directly behind the German lines, while 136 B-17s of the 15th Air Force attacked Ruhland again and caused extensive damage to the plant. Twenty-seven Me 262s attacked the bomber formations and claimed 13 B-17s shot down, but only one Fortress was actually lost.[1209] Nine fighter groups strafed airfields, and P-51s claimed two of the jets destroyed.[1210] Next day 1244 heavies bombed rail targets as part of the rail interdiction program to isolate the Ruhr and cut off coal shipping. Since the loss of the Saar basin the Ruhr was the only remaining source of supply for the German war machine. On 23/24 March, under a 66 mile long smoke screen and aided by 1749 bombers of the 8th Air Force, Field Marshal Bernard Montgomery's 21st Army Group crossed the Rhine in the north, while further south simultaneous crossings were made by General Patton's 3rd Army. Groups flew two missions on 24 March, hitting jet aircraft bases in Holland and Germany, while 240 B-24s, each loaded with 600 tons of medical supplies, food, and weapons, followed in the wake of transports and gliders ferrying troops of the 1st Allied Airborne Army. The 446th, with Lieutenant Colonel William A. Schmidt (Bungay's Air Executive) flying as 20th Wing Commander, led the 93rd and 448th with 27 aircraft. Flying as low as 50ft, the Liberators droned over the dropping zone at Wesel at 145mph using 10-15° of flap to aid accuracy in the drop. Gray-white smoke shrouded the battlefields and engulfed the city of Wesel. Smoke canisters, which had blacked out over 60 miles of the front for more than two days, were still burning. The Liberators passed Wesel a mile to the south and continued to the dropping zone, which was strewn with wrecked and abandoned gliders, smoldering haystacks, and dead livestock.[1211]

One of the B-24s despatched from Shipdham was *Southern Comfort III*. In mythology the phoenix is "a bird which can only be reborn by dying in flames." So it was with *Southern Comfort*, which was lost over Foggia in August 1943. The ground crew had returned to England and were assigned to a fresh combat crew skippered by Lieutenant Waters. Their brand new B-24 was promptly named *Southern Comfort III*. Their luck held through 25 missions, the crew returning to the States to participate in a Bond-raising tour. Lieutenant Chandler and his crew, on their fourth mission, flew the "phoenix" on the supply mission. When the 44th arrived at the dropping zone a fierce battle was raging. The gunners of *Southern Comfort* strafed the German gun emplacements as Allied troops waded across the river with their guns above their heads. The B-24s had to drop their supplies on the opposite bank. *Southern Comfort III* was less than 100ft above the ground when, hit by German small-arms fire, it lost an engine. The aircraft rolled over and her belly struck the ground. She raised a cloud of dust, bounced into the air again to about 50ft, and then exploded. All the crew except the two waist gunners were killed. Sergeant Vance returned to Shipdham about three weeks later with both arms in plaster. He had been liberated when the British overran the German field hospital where he was being held captive.

Approximately 6000 aircraft, including Liberators, gliders, transports, and fighters, took part in the Wesel operation. Spasmodic and highly accurate small arms fire and 20mm cannon fire brought down 14 Liberators, and 103 B-24s returned with battle damage. Five of the 20 officers at 20th Wing Headquarters, including General Ted Timberlake, who flew in an escort aircraft, flew on the mission. Despite intense ground fire, the Wing hedgehopped to friendly territory and reformed in the Brussels area for the return flight to England. Some 104 B-24s returned to their bases with some degree of damage.[1212]

On 26 March 2nd Lieutenant William W. Varnedoe, Jr., navigator in Lieutenant George H. Crow, Jr.'s crew in the 385th Bomb Group, flew his 14th mission:

"After the success of operation *VARSITY-PLUNDER*, (the isolation of the Ruhr and the Rhine area) targets were dwindling. On this day the 385th returned to a target of the day before to hit a tank factory at Plauen, which put this works out of operation. Our ship was '*Possible Straight.*' We had in mind to paint some cards with Ace, duce, tray showing and two face down with a sexy female on back of the down cards, but it never got done. George Crow was promoted to 1st Lieutenant since our last mission. Although the mission itself went smoothly and successfully, the trip home got kind of hairy. Once out of Germany and over France we began to let down to stay under an ever lowering ceiling of clouds. A message came through giving us a whole new course with many new headings. Crow wanted to know how long the new course would take, so I began to plot and calculate all the new legs and their times. When done, George said that it would take too long and we'd better go straight home. I looked at the compass to see which leg we were on. We were on none of either the new or the old courses! Just at that moment, the clouds had us forced so low the formation completely split up and we were on our own. I had no idea where we had been going while I was doing all that figuring, so I tried to match us to something on the map. But we were too low. Everything just whizzed by. We were too low to see a pattern. In fact, we were really on the deck. Both Ira and I remember George lifting a wing to clear a church steeple! Well, no problem, I'd just head us to East Anglia and *G-Box* it home from there - except, and this was a big except, we didn't want to pass over Dunkirk, which was still in German hands. As low as we were, they couldn't miss us. But we avoided it and were soon over the English Channel. I did a 45° turn right, 90° turn left then another 45° right. This little dogleg let the English radar operators know we were not another German Buzz bomb to be shot down as soon as we got near the English coast. As we performed this maneuver we then discovered that there were 3 or 4 other red checkered tails following. I guess they were lost and thought we knew where we were going! Once over the Channel, sure enough, as I thought, G came in and the rest of the trip to Great Ashfield was uneventful."

The mission to submarine pens at Hamburg on 30 March was the 27th trip for 1st Lieutenant Donald J. Schmitt in the 493rd Bomb Group at Little Walden. It was one mission he wished he could have missed:

"We had a perfect day but it was also perfect for the Hun. It was uneventful until we hit the target and then things really happened. There were quite a few breaks in the clouds but not enough to allow a visual run. The flak was really rough. It was the most accurate flak I have been through so far. It reminded me of the flak in '*30 Seconds Over Tokyo*.'[1213] After the target, the Low Squadron leader made a turn right into another group. It was either breaking up the formation or cracking up a bunch of 17s, so everybody took off for themselves. We finally got back into formation after much difficulty. Weather on return was very bad. Very bad crack-up at field upon return."

The "very bad crack up" was the B-17 piloted by 2nd Lieutenant Russell A. Goodspeed in the 861st Bomb Squadron, whose crew were on their first mission [1214] Lieutenant Roger D. Laib, the co-pilot, recalls:

"After months of classes in gunnery school, weather prediction, aerodynamics and flight training, we hoped we were ready to do our part to help win the war. Out crew sat together in the ready room with the other flight crews to be briefed on the day's mission. We heard the moans from everyone when the cover was removed from the map of the target - the submarine docks in Hamburg with 271 flak guns protecting the city. After takeoff, we were to rendezvous with the 861st Squadron as we climbed toward the designated altitude of 29,000ft. After we passed 30,000ft the contrails from the planes obliterated a view of the land below. We were soon on our way - peering out the windows looking for enemy aircraft. Word was flashed to us to level out at 24,000ft because of clouds over the target. When we turned at the IP I looked toward my right and saw another squadron headed in the same direction to follow us over the target. On closer inspection, I noticed black smoke appearing beneath the planes - I realized it must be flak bursts I had seen in the newsreels. We immediately felt our plane start to bounce around and knowing we were not in turbulent air, knew flak was bursting beneath us. At that point, a big explosion shocked me into the realization that we were hit. I saw the windshield crack and, looking to our wing saw the prop of #4 engine slow to a halt and saw oil oozing from a hole in the wing.

"I switched my headphones from monitoring England, to the intercom and heard lots of yelling. Russell Goodspeed was trying to have me check for planes beneath us to salvo the bombs while he tried to feather the #4 propeller to reduce drag on the plane. The bombs were dropped but we were too late on the feathering procedure - the hydraulic oil had already frozen. Just then the crankshaft broke and the propeller cocked at an angle and started rotating slowly. We hoped it would not cartwheel across the flight deck. As we looked around now, our squadron was not in sight, having lost considerable altitude. We tried to maintain our altitude while Lieutenant Harold G. Teters, navigator, plotted our way back to England - alone.

"As we flew over the island of Heligoland in the North Sea, we wondered whether fighters from the five German airfields there would come by to shoot us down. Fortunately, our friendly P-47s and P-51s flew by the check us out periodically so we felt safer. As we passed by Holland on our left, we saw the other planes headed back but well below us. Apparently, we were fighting a strong head wind. I walked through the empty bomb bay to the radio room to check the condition of the crew. They were all smiles and excitedly told me how lucky we were to have flown through the barrage and were able to fly home. Several had holes in their flight suits but none were hit by the shrapnel.

"Debating whether or not to land at the emergency field at Woodbridge, the decision was made to try for our base at Little Walden. With the field in sight and all fuel warning lights blazing Sgt Harry N. Davis, engineer fired the rocket to inform the tower that the plane was damaged but no one was inured. Being so low on gas, we waited until well on the final approach before lowering the flaps. All the gunners were in the radio room in crash position so no one was up to check the flaps during extension. When the switch was activated, the right wing dropped and we thought that #3 engine had run out of gas but in reality the left flap moved into position and the right flap didn't. The wing tip touched the ground and the plane broke in half at the trailing edge of the wing. The tail section remained upright and the front half of the plane skidded to a halt in the farmer's field upside down.[1215] Later investigation found that the flak explosion had cut the right flap cable. The four airmen in the radio room – Sergeant's Frank E. Lee, radio operator, Robert Brewer, ball turret gunner, Haskell N. Newman, waist gunner and Clinton Halverson, tail gunner - were killed instantly as well as the toggelier, Sgt George Constandakis, in the nose. Russell Goodspeed died six hours later. Only the flight engineer, navigator and myself survived."

Bomber crews were now hard pressed to find worthwhile targets, and the planners switched attacks from inland targets to coastal areas. 2nd Lieutenant William W. Varnedoe, Jr., navigator in 1st Lieutenant George H. Crow, Jr.'s crew in the 385th Bomb Group, recalls:

"On 4 April, my 17th, we went back to Kiel again to mop up, I suppose. We flew in *Gypsy Princess*[1216] in the High Squadron. The flak, while still fairly heavy, was less accurate and there was no repeat of that 'Big Bang'. However, the 385th did lose two crews. On the return over the North Sea, Crimmins and Ritchie collided and both went down. They were Leads of the Low Flight of the Lead Squadron. Ira remembers that one of them was in a flat spin but the Group moved on out of sight before he hit the water; there were no chutes sighted. I gave Bill Kozosky, our radio operator, the location and he gave it to Air-Sea Rescue, but nothing was ever heard from them. A person could only survive a few minutes in the icy North Sea and this area was far from home."

On 5 April the 8th Air Force's superiority was such that the B-17s assembled over France before flying to targets in the Nürnburg area. 1st Lieutenant Donald J. Schmitt, pilot of *Son Of A Blitz* in the 493rd Bomb Group, flew his 30th mission when he went to the jet airfield at Unterschlauersbach near the city:

"We were briefed for bad weather but I never knew it could get as bad as it was today. We entered the soup after we took off and didn't get out of it till 20,000. We assembled over the Continent. We had to raise our assembly altitude to 26,000 because of high clouds and dense persistent contrails we left. We found our Squadron leader without much trouble and the more we flew around, the worse the contrails became. When assembly time was up, we had only a few ships in formation. We flew all the way to the IP in contrails. At IP we let down to 23,500 and found an opening. We bombed the field visually with good results. The lead and high Squadron bombed Nuremberg itself and really laid their bombs in the heart of the city. They were ahead of us so I got a very good view. Fires and smoke covered the whole city. By bombing the airfield, we missed all the flak, which was over the town of Nuremberg itself. It was intense and accurate. After bombs away, we started to let down to 1000ft because of clouds. We crossed the Rhine at this altitude and really saw the sights. Near Brussels we had to let down to about 500ft because of a low front. The weather was pretty bad with quite a bit of rain. We crossed the Channel at about 100 to 200ft above the water. It was a very tiring mission but very interesting. Only 5 more to go and then I go Home To My Dear Wife and Son."

Everywhere the Allies were victorious, but while the Germans kept on fighting, missions continued almost daily. In Germany, the now desperate situation called for desperate measures to be taken against the all-powerful bomber streams, and last ditch attempts were made by the *Luftwaffe* to try to stem the tide.[1217] A plan conceived late in 1944 was the deliberate ramming of American bombers by converted Bf 109 fighters called *Rammjäger*, flown by pilots of *Sonderkommando Elbe*. On 7 April around 130 Bf 109s and their escort fighters took off from their airfields around Stendal and Gardelegen to ram bombers heading for underground oil refineries in central Germany, but only an estimated 25 Messerschmitts and a few Me 262s managed to break through the American fighter screen. Diving from a height of 33,000ft, 22 bombers were rammed, of which 14 were B-17s and eight were B-24s, but *Rammkommando Elbe* lost 31 Bf 109s.[1218] Despite the losses to ramming attacks in the previous September, American aircrew were still largely unaware of the nature of the attacks, and most crewmen thought that the aircraft lost when the *Rammjäger* dived into the bomber formations were the result of collisions. The 389th Bomb Group was leading the 2nd Air Division to Duneberg when the *Rammjäger* struck. One victim was the 389th lead aircraft, *The Palace of Dallas*, flown by Lieutenant Bob C. Dallas with the Group Commander, Colonel John Herboth, aboard.[1219] Earl L. Zimmerman, radio operator, recalled:

> "Colonel Herboth's plane headed for the ground and I don't think anyone baled out. The deputy lead was hit in exactly the same area, right in the cockpit. The plane stayed level for a few moments then pulled up about 100ft above the formation and plunged toward the ground without spinning. I do not recall seeing any chutes from this plane either but as it was not spinning there is a chance that some of them got out."[1220]

The Bf 109 bounced off the lead ship and hit the deputy lead ship flown by 1st Lieutenant Walter R. Kunkel in the 566th Bomb Squadron, and this also went down.[1221] The left waist gunner on the lead plane, S/Sgt Kratoska, recalls:

> "When the German attack started, there was a fighter encounter at 9 o'clock high about 1000ft above us. Dallas, our pilot, cautioned us to be sure of our target before shooting. Almost simultaneously [S/Sgt Mark] Strauss, the tail gunner, started firing very heavy, so I - leaned back to look through his turret to see what he was shooting at. I picked up the German fighter coming straight and level and firing at us. He broke off to his left outside the No.3 aircraft in our formation. He was in such a position that I could not shoot at him without hitting No.3 and he continued to turn at about our same altitude. I did not see any other fighter American or German, in the immediate area. The German was now heading at us from about 11 o'clock slightly above us on his right side perpendicular to our plane off flight He could have missed us if he had leveled out, but there wasn't time because of our closing speed. I instinctively ducked and he hit in the pilot's lap shearing off the front of our plane. Three of us survived – Strauss, S/Sgt Bob Gilloon, the right waist and me. Gilloon and I bounced off the top of the fuselage as we went into a spin. I cannot remember who opened the escape hatch, but I do remember my chute was next to it and I caught the chute before it fell out. Because of the spin it was difficult to get out We were at 22,000ft when we collided and I would guess we got out at about 5000ft."

1st Lieutenant Walter E. Kunkel, pilot, flying deputy lead, wrote later:

> "A Me 109 dove on the lead aircraft, bounced off and struck my ship. The Me 109 hit behind the pilot cockpit at approximately the top turret position. The top turret tore off making a large hole in the top of the aircraft. S/Sgt Albert W. Pfarr was in the top turret at the time without his chest pack attached. The radio operator's section immediate/v caught fire. The rudder and elevator controls were completely jammed. The airplane then went into a steep dive finally turning over on its back. During this time, an effort was made to use the AFCE, throttle and ailerons to right the aircraft: I gave the bale out order during the dive, but I don't think the interphone was working. I then yelled the order out to the personnel on the flight deck. It was impossible for the crew to move on the aircraft because of the centrifugal force. Consequently no one was able to bale out at this time.
>
> "When the aircraft was on its back, violent motions were noticed and the aircraft began to break up. The engineer, S/Sgt Edward Moniak, was thrown onto the instrument panel and was observed not to have his chest pack on. I do not know for sure if Moniak was injured or not. I think he was unconscious and we were still at high altitude at the time and he was not wearing an oxygen mask. Another crewmember, I am not sure who, was on the flight deck and had a premature opening of his chute in the cockpit. The chute was on fire. As the plane was breaking up, my command pilot, Major James Tolleson and myself were thrown clear of the aircraft. I am not sure where we left the ship possibly through the hole in the top of the cockpit. After baling out could see one other chute. I saw nothing of the major part of the aircraft. However I did notice pieces of debris in the air. I did not see the aircraft hit the ground."[1222]

Ross D. Woods, nose gunner on the B-24 directly behind the Deputy lead, recalls:

> "After the Lead and Deputy Lead were taken down by the 109 our pilot, 19 year old 1st Lieutenant Jeff Piercy ordered the firing of the flares and then took over the lead position. Piercy lifted our plane slightly to avoid being the next victim of the havoc being thrown our way. While re-forming the squadron we ended up under the high right and were on the bomb run when I saw their bomb doors open. I alerted our pilot and we then ended up under the low left also with their doors open. The bombs of the high right came so close to our wing that we could read the fine print. Almost at the same time the left low dropped their load close to our left wing All this time we were able to stay out of the way and send our own bombs to the target area. Our tail gunner, Bernard 'Bernie' Dispenza, kept a sparking plug from the 109 which had penetrated our plane near the tail section, hit the bulkhead and landed just behind him on the walkway."

1st Lieutenant Donald J. Schmitt, in the 863rd Bomb Squadron, flew his 31st mission when the 493rd Bomb Group went to Gustrow ordnance plant:

> "Well, here is one for the books. Another exciting mission. Take-off and assembly were normal. We climbed to bombing altitude, which was 15,000. Everything went smooth until we came near Hanover and then things really happened. The thing we dreaded most hit us. That's right – we were hit by fighters. We were flying in the high squadron and for some unknown reason we were their target. They succeeded in making several attacks on us. They knocked out one ship. Our Squadron accounted for two Me 109s. One of them went down right over our nose. Our upper gunner had a hand in shooting him down. Another came up from underneath chased by three P-51s. He pulled up but that was where he made his mistake, because all three of the 51s let go and down went the Hun. Another Me-109 damaged tried to run one of our ships. He didn't succeed, but did take part of the horizontal stabilizer off. The ship returned safely. We were under fighter attack for about 1½ hour and it sure was no picnic.

They finally let us alone at the IP and we went on to the target. We made a visual run and laid our bombs right on the MPI. Great fires and large columns of smoke rose from the whole area. The bombing results were excellent. The return trip was over the same route as we had come in on, but with out the fighters. I guess they had enough the first time. The formation flying today was really excellent. The ships were locked wingtip to wingtip. Our group accounted for two kills and 4 possibilities. We are getting close to the end of our time, but things are starting to get rough."

Lieutenant Robert L. Miller, another pilot in the 863rd Squadron, 493rd Bomb Group, wrote in his diary:

"Got hit by fighters today for the first time. Emo gets a confirmed one who came in on us and damned near rammed us. Nick Teodosio and Pete Gamoian each got a Me 109. 'Twas a perfect day for it (fighters) and we were only at 15,000ft. Had about 6/10 cumulus, which made it swell for them. Had mighty fine fighter cover and they saved our necks. I saw them shoot down three myself but not before four Me 109s nailed three B-17s from the group ahead of us. I've never felt so sick in my life before as when I saw them blow up. We lost one ship over the target. Seemed under control but they baled out. Our P-51 escort was cruising up and down the bomber stream when the alert, 'Red Bandits in the area!' was given. Our whole crew really perked up. I looked out. In the distance was a plane that resembled a P-51. Something was hanging below the wings, like a belly tank. Our fighters had already dropped their belly tanks on the bandit alert! And this 'plane was flying alone, something our fighters never did. I called the waist gunners to alert them and they had already seen the same thing. This Me 109 turned toward us on a pursuit curve and our right waist gunner opened up. The German flew past our tail where Pete began firing and he came on around to our left side where Nick got him. In a short time they got another Me 109 I never saw but which was confirmed. We began to relax a bit when suddenly the engineer's guns behind me started shooting. I looked out my cockpit window to see a FW 190 shooting at the lead plane, just to our right and us. He appeared to be trying to ram the lead plane if he wasn't successful in shooting him down. His wheels fell down and he began to wobble from side to side. Had he wobbled to his right he would have rammed the lead plane and we would have gone too in the explosion but he passed in front of us, wobbling to his left. I could see his head slumped down. I'm sure he must have been dead."[1223]

2nd Lieutenant William W. Varnedoe, Jr., navigator in 1st Lieutenant George H. Crow, Jr.'s crew in the 385th Bomb Group, wrote:

"Although we hit the target visually, there was no flak. However, we did draw fighters this time. Three Me 109s attacked and then a single Me 109 came straight at the formation from the rear. Lanny in the tail and Charles Stewart, the tail gunner on Burich's plane, which was filling in the low diamond, opened up on him. We speculate that one of them must have killed the pilot since the 109 kept straight on and rammed Burich. Whatever else the Germans were, they weren't suicidal. Both the B-17 and the 109 went down."[1224]

The *Rammjäger* also attacked the 100th Bomb Group formation en route to an underground oil storage depot at Buchen, on a canal near Hamburg, as Griswold Smith, one of the pilots, recalls;

"Radios came to life with shouts of "Bandits in the area'. This had been called several times on other missions and we had begun to look upon it as 'crying wolf but I called the gunners on the intercom and told them to be on the alert anyhow. Then I heard the groups in front of us calling for P-51s as they were being hit by Me 109s. Earl Baugh, the tail gunner, was the first on our crew to see an enemy fighter. He reported them attacking and shooting down a straggler. The first pass was made from 7 o'clock low, up through 'C' Squadron and then on to us. Baugh, the tail gunner and Anthony Russo, the ball turret gunner, were the first in the squadron to open fire. This Bf 109 put a couple of slugs into us. One went through the nose and almost got Paul Wilkerson, the bombardier and Wilson Turnipseed, the navigator. When this happened 'Wilk' said he looked at 'Turnip' and could see it dawn on 'Turnip's' face that this was the 'real McCoy'. 'Turnip' started unlatching the nose guns and firing like hell. 'Wilk' said that he started shooting at our P-51 escort and 'Turnip' maintained he was 'keeping the area clear'. The fighter went past us and turned back down at us. 'Wilk' and Stanley Szalwinski, the engineer, were pouring .50s into him from their two turrets and John O'Leary got a few from the waist. I think he was diving directly for us, but he came just in front and knocked the left horizontal stabilizer off Lieutenant Martin's ship[1225] in front of us. That Bf 109 diving into the formation spurting flames all over presented such a vivid picture that I shall never forget it. When he hit Martin's ship there must have been some sort of explosion, as the nose and cockpit of our ship were filled with black smoke and dust. The Bf 109's wing flew off and went over my wing, knocking Lieutenant Joe King's ship[1226] in the 'horizontal diamond.'[1227]

"Another Bf 109 came in from 5 o'clock high. Everyone said he was coming directly at us, but our gunners put out so much lead that he diverted and crashed into a ship in the lead squadron. We saw both ships explode.[1228]

'The reason we got so many fighter attacks directed at us was because we were the top ship and the corner ship in the group and therefore around us was the least possible concentration of friendly fire. Ordinarily, fighters made their passes in a dive to get greater speed. The enemy fighters stayed with us for about an hour. We were at 15,000ft as no flak was expected. However, there was plenty of accurate flak at the target. I never thought I would be glad to see flak, but I was this day because it meant the fighters wouldn't come in. We started out with ten ships in our squadron and on "bombs away" there were six ships. We were glad to return from this one. There were so many holes in the nose that 'Wilk' nearly froze sitting up there on the way home. There was plenty of close support by the P-51s all the way back across the North Sea. I guess they finally found us. And to think, I met plenty of boys in London who completed an entire tour without seeing a single enemy fighter."[1229]

The determined onslaught by the *Rammjäger* and the Me 262 pilots did not stop 1261 heavies dropping almost 3500 tons of bombs on 16 targets in Germany, but many crewmen at debriefings were apprehensive that the *Luftwaffe* might be resorting to *Kamikaze* tactics. In reality, *Rammjäger* pilots were not suicidal. They were only expected to disable a bomber before baling out. At least seven, but probably more, *Elbe* pilots survived their ramming attacks to report their successful mission, although most of them were seriously injured in the process. One of them, *Obergefreiter* Heinrich Rossner, was reported to have brought down two B-24s near Visselhövede/Soltau by ramming. He too was injured, but managed to bale out. Intelligence officers offered the opinion that German fighter pilots must have been dead at the controls before colliding with the bombers. At the interrogation at Hethel, it was assumed that the Bf 109 pilot had been dead when he hit the lead ship. Earl L. Zimmerman recalled. "It was certainly a suicidal way to attack a B-24 formation with fighter escort." "Jimmy" Stewart, the Deputy Wing Commander, told the 389th Bomb Group crews what a fine job they had done of destroying the target when the lead plane and the deputy lead plane were both lost at the IP. John B. "Buff" Maguire, a pilot in the 566th Squadron, recalled that his remarks were "just as impressive as any movie I have seen him in."

The following day, 8 April, the 8th was again out in considerable force, putting up nine groups in the 1st Division together with six groups of Mustangs. The 2nd Air Division put up nine B-24 groups with four groups of escorting fighters, and the 3rd Air Division put up 14 groups of B-17s with four groups of Mustangs. In all, more than 1150 B-17s and B-24s were to bomb targets in the Leipzig, Nuremberg, and Chemnitz areas. Sergeant Byron Schlag, 711th Bomb Squadron, 447th Bomb Group, who was flying his ninth mission as tail gunner in *Ol' Scrapiron*,[1230] the mission was nearly his last day on earth, as he recalls:

> "We were off to bomb the marshaling yards at Holzwickede, northeast of Koblenz, Germany. It was supposed to be a 'milk run' with meager flak and no enemy fighter action anticipated. We had to make a second bomb run because the lead bombardier had sighted on the wrong target at the IP. After we had circled, we dropped our load from 23,000ft and turned to begin the trip home. It had been a quiet mission and I hadn't noticed anything unusual until the navigator reported that we were nearing Koblenz and the Rhine River. Suddenly, out of the corner of my eye, I saw pieces of aluminum flying by, including a large panel of engine cowling. Just as I pressed the intercom button to notify the pilot, I heard our engineer say, 'Pilot, look out…!'
>
> "At that instant I experienced a horrifying crash as we were hit. Just before losing consciousness, I remember crying out, 'Lord, help me!' Then, total oblivion set in. Some time and several thousand feet later, I awoke. Although quite disoriented and dazed, I knew I was alive and falling. I had to get out! As I collected my thoughts, I discovered a belt of .50-caliber ammo around my neck. We must have rolled over for the belt to come out of the box beside me: I then realized that I was falling, right side up in the tail of the bomber. I pulled off my helmet and flak suit, untangled myself from the ammo belt and started for the escape hatch in the tail. It appeared jammed and wouldn't open. I turned towards the waist door and saw only a circle of sky! The rest of the plane was gone! I now realized that I was floating down alone in the severed tail. (Another B-17[1231] had lost a wing from a direct hit by flak and it had collided with our plane, cutting it in two just behind me.) I always kept my parachute buckled on one side and I quickly attached the loose ring to my harness, then crawled back to the edge of the opening and hung my legs over the side. Below me, I saw what was left of our plane going down in a flat spin ahead of me. It soon crashed into a wooded area where the large trees stripped the wings as it impacted. At that moment, I was sure my entire crew had perished, including my best friend, Eddie Shibble, who had enlisted with me.
>
> "As I had reservations about my chute's opening, I decided to pull the ripcord while I sat there on the edge of the tail section. If it popped open, it would pull me free of the fuselage. If it malfunctioned, I'd take my chances and ride the tail down. When I yanked the ripcord, the chute did open and pulled me out, but I was already so low that I swung up and back…just once…and quickly hit the ground. Our training and briefings had conditioned us to believe it was our duty to escape, so I immediately got out of my harness and started to run away from the small valley where I had landed. As I ran to the top of a knoll, I was shot at by the *Wehrmacht*, who were in the area. Clearing the hilltop, I was confronted by a German soldier riding a bike. I'm probably lucky he was there. Otherwise the irate civilians from a nearby village might have killed me. (Intelligence had briefed us about known killings of parachuting airmen.) After I had surrendered myself to him, the screaming civilians surrounding us began beating me. The soldier pushed me to the ground and lay over me, taking much of the beating himself. This hysteria abruptly halted with the arrival of a German officer. The officer and several soldiers escorted me to the town. While en route, they took me past the plane's tail section, sitting upright and undamaged with the rudder and stabilizer intact. It had floated down like a leaf and may have offered as much safety as my chute.
>
> "What followed was the first of several intense PoW interrogations at diverse locations, while I, in turn, obsessed about escape. During one such episode, an officer and two enlisted men in a black Mercedes from a small village to Giessen were transporting me. As we approached the city, we heard an air raid siren. After the driver and officer looked through the windshield, they made several excited exchanges, pulled the car to the roadside and stopped. He and his men jumped out of the car and into a deep ditch on the right, leaving me alone in the rear seat. I immediately jumped into a gully on the other side and spotted a P-51 bearing down on the Mercedes. It made two strafing passes and peeled off. Shaking the several inches of dirt off me, I crawled on my stomach past the burning car to the other side of the road. Looking into the ditch, I saw the officer and both soldiers lying dead. I immediately got up and ran towards the nearest wooded area to hide.
>
> "I was soon recaptured by the *Volkstrum* and given my worst interrogation, being beaten with a rifle butt until I was unconscious. When I finally awoke I was in a solitary cell at a Luftwaffe base outside Giessen. As bad as I felt after being beaten, being an Air Force sergeant somehow earned me better treatment on this base in the days to come, especially from one 70-year old solider. He had to serve or be interned or killed. One morning as I was praying for my safety, I heard shellfire sounds, different from those I was used to hearing. I suspected the Americans were coming. My guard at first denied it, but later, he admitted the Americans were shelling Giessen. The next morning, my friendly German came to take me away. He said he had been ordered to kill me but, instead, would take me to a nearby village where I would be safe. He took me up some stairs from what turned out to be a basement cellblock and on through a long hall. There was an Air Operations room on the left and a pilot's dormitory with bunks on the right. As we left the buildings where I had been held, we observed total chaos on the main road to the right. Civilians and soldiers on bikes, in trucks and on foot, were retreating from the city. I looked down the field towards a landing strip with hangars to one side. I could hear the sounds of artillery whistling overhead and exploding at the end of the base. As my guard and I were about to crawl under the arc of cannon fire to a small village across the strip, we heard the popping of a motorcycle behind us. A *Waffen SS* officer rode double with a driver. He called my guard to attention, saluted and proceeded to question him as to whom he was, my identity and what he was doing with me. After much excited conversation directed my way, the officer motioned for the guard to take me to the wooded area alongside the building where I had been held and to shoot me. As we walked to the trees, the old man was

muttering, 'Ach, mien Got, please forgive me,' he whispered. He told me he would be shot if he didn't follow the *SS* officer's orders. We stopped. He got out his pistol and with the *SS* man screaming at him to hurry, placed the muzzle at my right temple. At that point, we were both praying fervently. I felt as if my entire body had gravitated to my feet and had left only an empty skeleton standing there. My feet felt like two concrete blocks. I remember thinking, 'God, after all this, why now?' At the very moment I was to be shot, an artillery shell fell short and exploded near the officer, knocking both him and his driver to the ground. With that they hurriedly picked up the motorcycle and sped off into the retreating crowd on the road. My guard and I collapsed together, both of us totally drained. After about 40 minutes we had regained our strength and were able to crawl beneath the shellfire to nearby village. I never learned the old man's name. He took me to the home of Albert Abedd and other friendly Germans who took care of me until I was liberated by Patton's 7th Armored Division."[1232]

Meanwhile, on 9 April about 1200 bombers supported by 15 fighter groups hit ten jet airfields and other targets in south central Germany. The day before Griswold Smith, in the 100th Bomb Group, had flown a long, long mission to Eger, Czechoslovakia, his crew's Air Medal mission. Smith recalled that "we'd really had our fill of combat now":

"On 9 April we hit Reim airfield five miles east of Munich. German jets were using it. The day was very clear and one could see many other airfields being hit by other groups. The object was to destroy airfields that could be used by jet planes in southern Germany. Jet airplanes required an exceptionally long runway. We could see where they were using their autobahns for that purpose. We let down to about 3,000ft on the way home and could plainly see where the ground forces had been creating havoc. Passing over the Rhine we saw several destroyed bridges and two pontoon bridges."

1st Lieutenant Donald J. Schmitt in the 863rd Bomb Squadron, 493rd Bomb Group, flew his 32nd mission when the Group added its bombs to the airfield at Munich. He wrote in his diary:

"Let me tell you, combat is still rough. This should have been a Milk Run and for us (Lead Squadron) it was, but for others it was rough. The weather was just fair. Up until target time it was perfect, but clouds over target forced us to bomb from 22,000 instead of 25,000. We had a visual run and really laid our bombs on the MPI. Just before bombs away, a ship in the Group ahead of us blew up from a flak hit and after bombs away a ship out of our high squadron blew up.[1233] The trip home was uneventful. Visibility back at the base was excellent."

Griswold Smith, in the 100th Bomb Group, was part of the formation who on 10 April flew a mission to Burg airfield, near Magdeburg:

"It was just about the worst of all. Again our target was jet aircraft. We were flying in the low squadron of the 100th Bomb Group, which was the worst place to be when the jets attacked. The jets usually made their attacks in twos and threes from 6 o'clock low or level, because from that angle they looked like P-51s with wingtip tanks and the gunners were afraid to shoot until they got in teal close. They would coast in on a formation from the rear with their jets off, open fire, turn on their jets and vanish with terrific speed. They were armed with 30mm cannon. They made several passes at us from 6 o'clock low. I distinctly remember two ships going down in flames. I believe a couple of others were crippled and knocked out of formation; one or two aborted earlier. Anyway, there were damned few left when we went over the target. Lieutenant Reeve, who was on his first mission, was flying in my squadron in front of me and a little higher. He burst into flames and a wing ripped off on one of the first jet passes.[1234] They put a few holes in us too but no one was hurt. I credited my life to Earl Baugh and Anthony Russo the tail and ball turret gunners, for putting out so much accurate fire that the jets diverted their attacks when they came in close. We were in the best position for them to attack.

"We had a toggelier flying with us this day who missed an excellent chance to destroy a jet. 'Turnip' said the toggelier 'just sat there and looked at it.' That happened to a lot of people when fighters came in unexpectedly close. It is very astonishing and interesting: not to mention deadly. The papers said this was the biggest day yet for the 8th Air Force as it destroyed 205 enemy fighters. They also said that if the Germans had developed jets just a little earlier, the 8th would never have succeeded. I heartily agreed with this opinion. Out conventional fighters, the P-51 and the P-47 didn't have a chance of catching a jet in the air. When they shot one down it was because they were lucky enough to sneak up on one with his jets off and shoot him down before he knew what had happened, or if they came out of a cloud directly on top of one. Ordinarily, they would see one floating around with jets off and would start chasing him. He would sit around 'til they were almost in range, then he would turn on his jets and make them look as though they were sitting still."[1235]

2nd Lieutenant William W. Varnedoe, Jr., navigator in 1st Lieutenant George H. Crow, Jr.'s crew in the 385th Bomb Group, wrote:

"10 April. My No. 22. Another airfield was the target, this time at Nurippin. We bombed visually in '*Sleepytime Gal*.'[1236] There was no flak at Nurippin, but there was some light but accurate flak at Wittenberg on the way back. A piece of flak struck my headset control box and bent it all out of shape so I couldn't change the settings, however, I had it set on intercom and it still worked there. This flak was not marked on our flak maps so we supposed it was railroad flak moved in overnight. In fact, the Group was letting down to get off oxygen, this area being briefed as free of flak zones. Yet, we could see the other groups, up ahead, getting heavy flak. We wondered why our fearless leader didn't stay higher a little longer, rather than take us through it at that low altitude. On this one, *Rum Dum* dropped out of formation. Howard A. Muchow had a 'pick up' crew and was flying *Rum Dum* on this mission. [1237]

"#378 had already completed 105 missions without an abort, and the CO, as well as the ground crew, were out to capture the all time record for the Group. They knew the flak would be as thick as pea soup over and around the Berlin area, and they knew the German fighters would be making a determined stand against their reaching the target. Germany might be coming to its knees, but the war was still very real. These thoughts seemed jumbled as we climbed for altitude over the Channel. And how right they seemed going into the target, with the black and gray puffs of flak raining against our old girl. It was like someone throwing gravel, only this metallic gravel was blasting through the airplane. The thought passed through my mind that the gals down below were doing a good job today. Immediately after 'Bombs Away', the No.1 engine took a direct hit and then No.3 was hit. As we feathered No.3, I saw that No.1 was on fire and we feathered it. We started loosing altitude and falling out of formation, when over the airways we heard bandits being called out by another squadron.

"A frantic call was sent out on the fighter channel for help and protection from our little friends. And there they came- three beautiful P-51s to help us down and stay with us-one high, one low, with the third dropping his flaps and gear to come alongside and give us the thumbs up and 'V' sign. Then he saw the fire in No.1 engine and up came his flaps and gear and he moved away out. I gave the order to bale out, but the crew wanted to stay with 378 and ride it down, hopefully too friendly territory. Who wanted to check out, first hand, the stories of captured airmen?

"We were losing altitude rapidly, when suddenly ahead I saw an open field and thought I would try my luck. It was downwind and I recall thinking we could not make it. If only we could hang on a little longer and swing the old girl around and set it down. It was like a dream. We were on the ground and rolling, when suddenly we saw troops coming out of the woods toward us. Were they Germans? No, thank God, they were English... and they were just arriving to take over the open field for front line fighter support! We had made it and no one was hurt. Only Heaven knows why. Upon our return to Great Ashfield, the FIRST question asked was, 'Can *Rum Dum* fly?' The SECOND question was, 'How's the crew?' ... But I will always remember the old girl and how she got us back into friendly territory. (Poor old *Rum Dum* never made it back to Great Ashfield, although it did get flown to France, then later crash landed in England, only to be salvaged)."[1238]

As a result of the bombing of the jet airfields about all Me 262 units were forced to withdraw to the Prague area. The continual pounding of German airfields reduced the threat posed by the jets. However, other hazards sometimes caused casualties in the B-17 groups, as they did on 13 April when the 398th Bomb Group from Nuthampstead flew its 188th mission of the war to Neumünster. Over the target a leading aircraft salvoed his RDX bombs in error. Two of them touched about 400ft below, exploded, and brought down six Fortresses in the 601st Bomb Squadron, five of which had to be abandoned on the Continent. RDX bombs were fitted with close proximity fuses, and were most unstable at all times unless handled with great care. Bombing results were later described as "excellent," but at a high price indeed.

Walter "Don" O'Hearn, tail gunner in *El Screamo* in the 427th Bomb Squadron, 303rd Bomb Group, recalls:

"Our 26th mission was the most frightening of all. It was to Oranienburg, Germany, almost within sight of Berlin, 40 miles to the south on 13 April. Six to eight Me 262 jet fighters hit our group. *Henn's Revenge*[1239] in the 555th Squadron flown by 2nd Lieutenant Robert I. Murray was shot down in this air battle. Eight men were killed and the flight engineer got out of the aircraft. During this time, a Me 262 dove past me so fast I couldn't turn my two .50 machine guns on him. This 262 dropped down about 5000 to 6000ft in a wide turn and then came up directly behind our B-17. We were flying "tail end Charlie" so I had this aircraft all to myself. I made the very most of this situation; I started firing at him from a long distance and never let up but kept hitting his right engine. I continued to score hits on the engine until he was about 120ft from me. At that time the engine and wing tip blew off. The 262's momentum carried it to within 55 to 45ft from me. We were both looking at each other. Just as suddenly he began his fall from about 25,000ft, approximately 43-63 miles from Oranienburg, Germany. The 303rd Bomb Group interrogation officer really had no interest in a buck Sergeant's report on a 262, which may have been the last Me 262 shot down by an enlisted man in World War II. Lieutenant Denison put me in for a DFC but it was not even considered. The flak was what really startled a B-17 tail gunner to get jumpy. They called us 'flak happy' and that we were."

On 14 April 1161 B-17s and Liberators carried out a specialist task. Their target was a pocket of German resistance (some estimates put the force at 122,000 men) manning 22 gun batteries along the Gironde estuary at Point de Grave, in the Royan area, which was denying the Allies the use of the port of Bordeaux. The bombers were called upon to help dislodge them after all appeals to surrender had proved in vain. Conditions were perfect, and crews at briefing believed it would be a "milk run," as the defenses were negligible, and the flak was unlikely to reach the high-flying bombers. However, almost from take-off things began to go wrong. At Horsham St. Faith, *Hookem Cow* and another B-24 in 754th Squadron crashed shortly after take-off within minutes of each other. Altogether 1161 heavies hit 22 defensive installations along the Gironde estuary. The 467th successfully dropped all their 2000lb bombs within 1000ft of the MPI, with half the bombs falling within 500ft. This was a bombing pattern unsurpassed in 8th Air Force history. The 389th Bomb Group lost two Liberators when 3rd Air Division B-17s, making a second run over the target, released their fragmentation bombs through the "Sky Scorpions" formation. Two more crash-landed in France, and a fifth limped back to England.

The next day nearly 850 2nd and 3rd Air Division aircraft returned to the area, and for the first time carried Napalm—460,000 gallons of it. The 1st Air Division carried 1000lb and 2000lb GP bombs, while three fighter groups snuffed out any gun emplacements that opened fire on the bombers. Mosquitoes were also called in to sow a cloud of *Chaff* to snow radar screens that might be used to direct the radar-controlled flak guns. These precautions were the only protection the bombers had to prevent their lethal cargoes being exploded by German gun batteries. The bombers released their 75-85 gallon liquid-fire tanks, along with conventional incendiaries, on the east bank of the Gironde estuary. Captain Ralph Elliott, flying his 25th mission in the 467th Bomb Group, flew group lead, with Major Seiler as command pilot for the raid. Elliott recalled:

"Each napalm tank was about 8ft long and one and a half feet in diameter and when it exploded it covered am area of 60 square yards, taking the oxygen out of the air and destroying everything there. What a show it was. At 15,000ft the smoke was so thick we couldn't see our wingmen. A few puffs of flak about 100 yards out. Just before bombs-away, No.1 engine started to smoke and oil pressure began to fluctuate. When the engine began to shake, I feathered it. I increased power on the other three engines to maintain our usual 160mph on the bomb run and held the formation together so Archie bombed with no difficulty. We weren't worried about bombing accuracy - just hitting the general area. The napalm containers had no ballistic characteristics whatsoever. They were made of heavy cardboard and at altitude some of the detonators popped out like loose corks, so the bomb bay smelled of raw gasoline most of the way to the target. We all sort of held our breath and hoped no wayward spark would set the whole thing off. For once I didn't have to mention NO SMOKING to the crew. I held the lead till the rally and then left to come home on our own. We headed toward the main emergency field at Merville at 800ft and for 300 miles and two hours had a birds-eye view of all France. Landed OK and left our ship for an engine change."[1240]

On 16 April Orders of the Day No.2 from General Spaatz ended the strategic mission of the 8th Air Force, and only some tactical missions remained.[1241] Men such as 1st Lieutenant Donald J. Schmitt in the 493rd Bomb Group, who were coming to the end of their tours, were sweating out each and every mission, any one of which could be their last. The *Son Of A Blitz* pilot had flown his 33rd mission, to Royan, on the 14th, when his navigator had finished up. Schmitt noted in his diary "I'm really starting to sweat now." His 34th mission had followed on 15 April, which again was to Royan. He recorded that both missions were "Milk Runs in a run," and he was "sure am glad." The day after was the day he had anxiously been waiting for, and he "sure hoped to fly." He did. His 35th mission on 16 April was to Rochefort, France, where a German pocket was holding out. Schmitt need not have worried. It was an "easy" mission. He was so happy he could not even write anything on the mission except "Visual bombing. Good results."

On 17 April more than 950 B-17s and B-24s attacked eight railway centers, junctions, stations, and marshaling yards, as well as an oil depot in east Germany and western Czechoslovakia. Eighteen U.S. fighter groups flew support, encountering about 50 fighters—mostly jets—and claimed 13 destroyed, including four jets. The American fighters strafed numerous airfields and claimed over 250 aircraft destroyed on the ground. Eight B-17s and 17 fighters were shot down, including six B-17s by Me 262s of JG 7. One of the victims was *Towering Titan* in the 305th Bomb Group, flown by Lieutenant Brainard H. Harris, which appeared to be rammed by a Me 262. The collision tore off a wing panel from the left wing of the B-17G; the jet exploded, and *Towering Titan* went into a gradual dive, disappearing through the clouds. One parachute was seen.[1242]

The German corridor was shrinking rapidly, and the American and Russian bomb lines now crossed at several points on briefing maps. On 18 April 2nd Lieutenant William W. Varnedoe, Jr., navigator in 1st Lieutenant George H. Crow, Jr.'s crew in the 385th Bomb Group, flew his 25th mission:

> "We went to yet another railroad marshaling yard. However, this one was at Kolin, Czechoslovakia, near Prague. We flew as a crew but with Lee N. Withrow as a bombardier and without Mac in our old standby, '*Possible Straight*.' We were to bomb visually, but some scattered clouds messed up the bomb run and we, in the high squadron, were forced to go around and make another pass. This was a very, very long trip, but there was no flak. Perhaps the Germans thought we couldn't go that far and I too had my doubts but we did."

During the week 18 to 25 April, missions were briefed and scrubbed almost simultaneously. General Patton's advance was so rapid that at least on one occasion crews were lining up for take-off when a message was received to say that General Patton's forces had captured the target the B-17s were to bomb! The last major air battles between fighter groups of the 8th Air Force and the *Luftwaffe* took place on 18 April when 1211 heavies escorted by more than 1200 fighters were sent to attack Berlin. Forty Me 262s of *Jagdgeschwader* 7 shot down 25 bombers with rockets. It was the final challenge by a dying enemy. The *Luftwaffe* was finished, destroyed in the air and starved of fuel on the ground.

Jim Boehling, a navigator in the 731st Bomb Squadron, 452nd Bombardment Group (H), recalls the last wartime loss of the 452nd Bomb Group:

> "On 20 April we checked the crew list for the next day's mission and there we were, the crew of 2nd Lieutenant Frank B. Bell scheduled to fly our first combat mission. Our co-pilot, Lieutenant Murphree's name, however, had been replaced by 1st Lieutenant George V. Pringle, a veteran of 29 missions. That was as usual so that we would have some with experience in the cockpit. So it was early to bed to try for some sleep after flying a practice mission that day and because of an early briefing in the morning. Crews returning from recent missions were reporting them as milk runs. However, thoughts of the 7 April mission when the 452nd was hit hard and lost four B-17s to the new German jet fighters and the rumors that the Germans were setting up a strong redoubt in Southern Germany kept going through my mind. Would tomorrow be another one of those days when anything could happen? I did manage to get a couple hours of sleep that was fitful at best when the Charge of Quarters woke us at 0230 for briefing at 0345. After a quick, bleary-eyed fresh up and slipping into uniform, I hopped onto my bike and headed for the chapel where the Catholic boys received communion before the mission. I thought that it was a good way to start the day that could very well be one's last but the chaplain didn't show up so my good intentions were to no avail, but I felt better for having made the effort just the same. Breakfast was a bit hurried but I made it to briefing on time all right.
>
> "At the general briefing for the whole crew it was announced that the target would be Munich and the alternate Ingolstadt, which was about 50 miles north of Munich, both being deep in southeastern Germany and portending a long day ahead. The weather was predicted to be poor most of the way and a cold front located along and just west of the Rhine River had to be crossed. The other aspects of the mission - ordnance, take-off time, expected flak and that the Group would assemble on the continent over Rheims about 80 miles east-northeast of Paris, were all covered. The time hack was given to synchronize our watches and we were dismissed to our special briefings.
>
> "I joined the navigators to pick up my charts and logs, plot the route to and from the target and alternate target, the estimated time of arrival at assembly points, turning points, initial points and the predicted winds and weather along the way. I felt pressed for time and became a bit anxious when some of the experienced navigators began packing their equipment and leaving the room. I finally got everything plotted and double checked that I had packed everything in my briefcase - charts and flight plan, E-6B computer (manually operated and nothing like modern electronics), protractor and dividers, weather card, code flimsy and, by all means, several sharpened pencils. (We didn't carry celestial navigation equipment on combat missions, thank heaven). I was just about the last navigator to leave the briefing room and still had to go to my locker and get into flight clothing, all the way down to the inner electric suit. I was careful to leave my personal belongings and wallet, which we were not allowed to take along. When I finally had it all done, I checked that I had everything with me - briefcase, parachute and harness, inflatable life jacket, electric and leather gloves, helmet, oxygen mask and throat microphone. I was the last to climb aboard the truck that took the crews out to the revetments and the waiting airplanes, relieved that I hadn't held them all up to any extent.
>
> "It was still dark when we arrived at the airplane we would be using. Before boarding we all pulled the propellers through to clear the bottom cylinders of any accumulated oil. Then, we who flew up front tossed our equipment into the forward hatch and swung ourselves up into '*Slienthe Je Vahr*', which is Gaelic for 'a long and happy life'. Her number was 43-38356 K+ and it had the code name of 'Broomstick Charlie'. The auxiliary battery was plugged in, inverters activated, lights turned on and the big silver fortress was coming to life. The thought struck me that I had never been on a B-17 so heavily loaded - fuel tanks full, 22 250lb bombs in the bomb-bay, boxes of .50 caliber ammunition at all the guns and turrets and heavy

steel-ribbed flak vests at each station. The nose compartment was so filled that there was hardly room to move about. I wondered how so much weight could be lifted off the ground. It had been said that the 452nd had lost only one B-17 on take-off and, unfortunate as that was, it was reassuring that there hadn't been more. I unpacked my equipment, spread my charts and flight log on the navigator's table and laid my parachute on it to my left. Following training advice at Deopham, I had clipped the strings, which tacked up the left riser of my parachute, extended the riser and snapped the clip to the left chest-buckle of my harness, still leaving the pack out of my way so that I had room to work.

"Dawn was just breaking when the green flares went up and the sound of the first engines starting could be heard in the distance. It was sometime before our turn came, but then one by one the four Wright-Cyclone engines puffed blue smoke and roared to life. After the run-up of the engines to check magnetos, oil and manifold pressures, we moved out and took our place in line on the perimeter track. After most of the planes had taken off and the B-17 in front of us had started down runway 225, we moved out and lined ourselves up. With the brakes held firm, the throttles were moved forward until the four engines were revving at full power. About 30 seconds after the plane in front of us had started its roll and had left the runway; our pilot released the brakes. We lurched forward and slowly began our take-off run. Through the Plexiglas nose, I watched the runway lights as they passed to the rear, slowly at first, then ever faster. A glance at the airspeed indicator on my table showed the needle turning 40, 50, 60. As the runway rushed beneath us ever faster and the needle showed 70, 80, 90, *Slienthe Je Vahr* lightened up and finally, for what I had no way of knowing at the time, was airborne for the last time. We had used up practically all the runway, but cleared the fence by a far margin. I entered the time of take-off in my log as 0705, which was double summer time. The wheels came up and we made a shallow climbing turn to the left and the town of Attleborough came into view off to the left beneath the early dawn haze.

"I called the pilot on the intercom and asked for a heading of something like 150°. As we came over to that course, we continued our shallow climb and were soon in overcast. I began making the routine entries in my log - time, heading, indicated and true airspeed, altitude and outside temperature and, when possible, position coordinates and wind-direction and velocity. We broke out above the clouds and coasted out over the North Sea near Felixstowe, although the undercast obscured the town.

"We climbed to 8 or 9000ft and leveled off. The clouds cleared for a while and I could see the Thames Estuary far off to the right, so I estimated our position by visual relative bearings to points of land around it and recorded the coordinates and other data in my log. The clouds closed in beneath us again before we reached the continent near the French and Belgian border. The waist gunners either side of the compartment fired off a few bursts from each machine gun and I felt the airplane quiver as the others did the same.

"Soon we could see the cold weather front far ahead of us which briefing had told us about. Pringle called me to say that Group lead had instructed that because of the weather we would be going to the alternate target of Ingolstadt instead of Munich. Also a planned turn to the south at the little town of Homburg would not be made. About 40 minutes after leaving the Buncher we reached our assigned altitude of 21,000 or 22,000ft. Pringle called to say that the Group would continue climbing in an effort to get above the front, or at least to reach a saddleback (as he called it) in the clouds, so that we wouldn't have to fly into the clouds of the front. We passed over the city of Metz, which was visible briefly through a break in the undercast. We continued climbing and as Lieutenant Delmar Hallet, the element lead, on whose right wing we were flying in tight formation told me after so many years, we reached more than 29,000ft and the controls became mushy because of the thin air and heavy load at that altitude. As we approached the front. Pringle called me again to say that it was likely that we would not clear the cloud tops now and the gap was not wide enough for all the planes in the Group to pass through visually. Because it appeared we would be forced to fly on instruments, he wanted to be able to talk with Bell on intercom and he asked me to listen to the Group Lead on the VHF radio channel and relay any instructions to him that they ought to know about. I answered, 'Roger-Willco' and turned the selector switch on my radio jackbox to the command channel. That was my last communication with Pringle and the rest of the crew on the intercom.

"After a minute or so of not hearing anything of consequence on the radio *Slienthe Je Vahr* went into a cloud. I looked out my navigator's window and could not see Hallet's plane, which was no more than 50ft away. I was sure that the pilot had also lost sight of it. Almost immediately, I perceived a turn to the right, which I took to be the proper procedure to put some distance between the element lead and us. Although I never saw the formation again, we must have come out of the first cloud before going into another.[1243] After our turn to the right and in solid overcast, I felt the plane pull into a rather steep climb. I took that to be wrong and before having time to think about it, the plane was pulled up sharply again and this time I suspected that whoever was on the controls had not made a good transition to instrument flying. The engines were running normally but the climb could not be sustained because the airspeed dropped. The nose dropped and the left wing fell. Without visual reference, I had a strong sensation of falling and believed we had stalled out and had begun a steep spiral down. I was not on intercom and I thought that I shouldn't disturb the pilots who would be intensely preoccupied in so dangerous a situation but I was anxious to know what was happening in the cockpit. I thought of the flight engineer, Seth Wagner and threw off my oxygen mask and crawled through the bulkhead opening with my parachute under my arm because I had attached it to my harness earlier. I tapped Wagner, who was standing behind the pilots, on the leg, but he gave me no response. I returned to my navigator's table and noticed that the altimeter was winding down rapidly. The toggelier, George Grubbs, was watching me, so I pointed to the altimeter for his benefit, in case he had not perceived that we were falling. At the time I believe we were in a near vertical dive and spinning slowly. I had heard that fully loaded B-17s didn't recover from spins. I thought that time was fast running out. I caught the attention of the toggelier and pointed to my parachute and gestured downward to suggest that maybe we should bale out. He only looked at me expressionless. By this time I believe we had lost several thousand feet and the spiral had become a near vertical spin. I consciously considered that the airplane would be righted and able to rejoin the formation but I thought the odds were against it so I decided to leave although the bale out alarm had not been sounded. I believed, too, that my leaving would convey to the toggelier and engineer how serious I thought the situation was in hopes that they, too, might feel the same way and follow me. I motioned to Grubbs that I was leaving. With my parachute under my left arm I crawled to the hatch below the flight deck, turned the handle on the door, which I decided not to jettison, shouldered the door open against the rush of the slipstream and rolled out head first. The ice crystals buffeted my face and skinned my cheekbones. I looked at my watch to time my free fall but after about 15 seconds my parachute popped open, probably from the grip of my hand on the D-ring, because I don't remember consciously pulling it. I felt relieved although I was hanging from only the left riser, having forgotten to fasten the right one to my harness. After a while, which didn't seem very long, I heard a shattering crash, which I thought at first was thunder and then I thought maybe it came from a mid-air collision because it sounded so near. Being in solid overcast, I never saw *Slienthe Je Vahr* after leaving, but I could not escape the thought that what I had heard had involved her.

"I continued to fall for perhaps ten minutes or more. My mind was so preoccupied that I didn't think to look at my watch again. At length I broke out below the overcast at what I estimated to be a thousand or 1500ft above the ground. Right away I saw a pall of black smoke and pieces of metal fluttering down at my altitude just below the cloud base at what appeared to be a hundred yards or so though it must have been further. Unharmed I landed in a field being plowed by an elderly farmer behind a pair of oxen. A light rain was falling and the wind dragged me a little ways before I collapsed the chute. The farmer paid no attention. I was fairly sure that I was in Allied occupied Germany so I did not worry about being mistreated. I never loaded the clip into my .45 pistol, which we all carried in our right knee pockets. As I pondered what to do, about ten German youths approached and I told them in the little German that I learned in high school that I was an American. They put a canvas over me to shield me from the rain and offered me a bicycle ride into the nearest town, which turned out to be Landau, about ten miles west of the Rhine River and a mile or so to the west of where I landed. Along the way two French soldiers turned me over to a couple of American soldiers in a jeep who took me to their quarters in a railroad car. Within 15 or 20 minutes, an American officer came in and took me to the military headquarters in the City Hall in Landau. After some questioning, I was turned over to the 64th Fighter Control Wing at Edenkoben, about six miles to the north. It was there that I learned that *Slienthe Je Vahr* had dived into the ground and that none of the others had survived the crash. Along with the pilot, co-pilot, engineer and toggelier were the radio operator, Guy Fitts, ball turret gunner, David Adams, right waist gunner, Albert Devoto and tail gunner Paul Head. During its dive the airplane had broken in two at the waist and the tail section, virtually intact, landed some distance from the crater of the crash. Paul Head had been in the tail gunner's position and Devoto's parachute had opened and snagged on or been snagged by the tail, which carried him down with it. Although requested to help with identification, I chose not to and did not visit the site."[1244]

On 20 April 2nd Lieutenant William W. Varnedoe, Jr., navigator in 1st Lieutenant George H. Crow, Jr.'s crew in the 385th Bomb Group, flew his 26th mission:

> "I flew with 1st Lieutenant W. J. Karls' crew as navigator in '*Miss Fortune*'[1245] in the 549th Squadron on what was to be my last combat mission. I wound up with more missions than the rest of my crew, as I occasionally flew with other crews, like this one. Navigators were in short supply it seems. Enemy opposition to the bombing raids had virtually disappeared by the end of April. On my final mission, the 385th hit some more railroad marshaling yards at Wustermark. There was no flak or other opposition on this visual run which had very good bombing results."[1246]

The end came on 25 April 1945, when 306 B-17s of the 1st Air Division bombed the Skoda armaments factory at Pilsen, in Czechoslovakia, while 282 B-24s, escorted by four fighter groups, bombed four rail complexes surrounding Hitler's mountain retreat at Berchtesgarden. To 40 aircraft in the 92nd Bomb Group went the honor of leading the strike force.[1247] The 303rd Bomb Group at Molesworth chalked up the command record this day, flying its 364th mission, while other groups came close to equaling it. Unfortunately, with victory so close, losses were experienced. Lieutenant Lewis B. Fisher's crew became the last in the 92nd to be shot down, struck by a flak burst. Their B-17 was last seen over Pilsen going into the clouds in a spin, trailing flame and black smoke. No parachutes were seen. Bombing was made visually, but several runs were necessary because of the cloudy conditions in the target area.[1248] The following day the American and Russian armies met at Torgau, and the world waited for the inevitable unconditional surrender. Further bombing missions were cancelled and the bomb groups were stood down.

At Podington, on 29 April the long-awaited, once-postponed 300th mission (flown on 7 April) party got into full swing. After a formal program in the morning in which the CO, Lieutenant Colonel James W. Wilson, and the guest of honor, Brigadier General Bartlett Beaman, Chief of Staff of the 1st Air Division, delivered speeches, the base was entertained by Mustangs of the 364th Fighter Group. The "Divisionaires" band of the 1st Air Division provided the music, and celebrations continued late into the evening. At Kimbolton, the 379th Bomb Group had good cause to celebrate. This group had flown more sorties than any other bombardment group in the 8th Air Force, had dropped more bombs on the enemy than any other group, and had the lowest abort rate of all groups in combat since 1943.

Starting on 1 May, before the Germans surrendered, Fortress crews[1249] flew mercy missions called *Chowhound* to starving Dutch civilians in Holland until the end of hostilities. During the winter of 1944-45 15,000 Dutch civilians had died of starvation. Some of the deaths had been caused by the Germans in revenge for the help that Dutch railway workers had given the Allies at the time of the Arnhem operation. Agricultural land had been flooded as an anti-invasion measure, and the invasion of Germany from the west had also left 3½-million Dutch in western Holland living in a virtual island fortress. The food drops were possibly the greatest post-combat contributions made by the bomber crews. Jim French, a B-17 tail gunner in the 452nd Bomb Group, recalls:

> "A truce was arranged. We were ordered to reconstruct and strengthen the huge bomb bay doors in order that each bomber could carry 4500lb of canned 'C' rations in 50lb cases. They were to be dropped in a free-fall from an altitude of 300ft on a bomb-scarred airstrip west of Amsterdam. Armaments were not to be carried. As the B-17s crossed the coast of the Netherlands, the 900 combat veterans were scared. Was it a trick? Was this to be where the propaganda machine of Herr Goebbels would bolster the Third Reich by the destruction of 100 bombers in one blow? The Allies had blown the dykes a few days before to bog down a possible land invasion. At dawn this bright sunshiny morning a Flying Fortress named *Not Today-Cleo* lumbered with an unusual cargo - would its bomb bay doors hold the shifting weights of the canned delights? There was to be radio silence. As the B-17s approached the European coast, the planes were low enough that rolls of barbed wire could be seen, strung for miles along the beaches. Uniformed German soldiers were patrolling, but only glanced up at the aluminium birds. The airmen began to rest easier at no sign of the deadly ack-ack guns. All of a sudden the intercoms were alive with laughter and joy.

"'Look at 3 o'clock!' someone hollered. The bombers were flying over thousands of tulips in full bloom. Some Dutchmen, or maybe lots of them, had removed part of the tulips in a huge field. Plainly spelled out so it could be clearly read from the air, but not on the ground, were special words, which said, '*Thanks Yanks.*' The crews were exultant. As the four engines roared at full throttle over the airstrip, hundreds - no thousands - of what looked like little matchboxes tumbled from the planes ahead. They were the boxes of 'C' rations. As they hit, broken open and scattered wildly, cheers could be heard. Thousands of people lined the roads outside the airstrip barriers; they were not to collect the food gifts until the drop was complete.

"A native was riding a bicycle on a dyke. He looked up, the cycle turned; he rode into a canal.

"In Europe, cows were staked on a chain 20-30ft long to graze. One ran in fright. As she came to the end of the chain, she went tumbling head over heels. In England's eastern counties cows were accustomed to low-flying planes, either landing or taking off. The noise would not have caused a stir. As the planes thundered over the city of Amsterdam, again the Germans were noticed, some on foot, some in tanks or other war vehicles. On the roof of a 10-storey building stood people waving and holding the 'Stars and Stripes' all unseen by the enemy in the streets. What a glorious way for the Dutch to express their gratitude to a handful of Yanks. The planes turned northwards across the Zuider Zee, the North Sea and back to base at Deopham Green in East Anglia. In a few days Churchill announced to the world victory in Europe was at hand."

Griswold Smith, who had flown his final combat mission in the 100th on 18 April, adds:

"We flew three or four mercy missions to Holland until the end of hostilities, carrying food. One of them was before the Germans surrendered. They had promised us a corridor to fly across the country unmolested at low level. We could see German troops in uniform marching around with swastikas flying. Our second mercy mission was on the day the Germans in Holland surrendered. We taxied out in the usual manner when the hydraulic system on the ship stopped working. The ship in front of us stopped and it looked as if we couldn't avoid running into her. Aneinolli, bombardier and Robascowitz, navigator, were having a fit trying to get out of the nose. The co-pilot was madly stamping on the brakes and I was frantically teaching around trying to throw all the switches in the cockpit. Several gunners standing behind my seat were sweating blood. We finally restored the hydraulic system and stopped the ship in the last possible fraction of a second. Erwin Jones, a college classmate from my home town and a lieutenant in an air defense company at Thorpe Abbotts, was riding in the very front of the ship in the glass nose, oblivious to all out troubles. After we had finally stopped, he calmly turned around and innocently asked the navigator if we weren't awfully close. The navigator couldn't answer; he wasn't able to breathe yet!

"We went in at 200ft, buzzing a small sail boat on the Zuider Zee and blowing it over. We had orders not to drop unless we saw crowds of civilians but the Dutch were lined up around the edges of the field, waving and cheering. They had really turned out. Flags were flying everywhere and the streets were packed with people. It was a great day for the Dutch. We dropped our 4000lb of food after trouble with the improvised 'drop doors' in the bomb bay. We buzzed Amsterdam a couple of times. O'Leary, who was riding up front in the nose where he could get a better view of the town, called over the interphone, 'Church steeple coming in at 12 o'clock high!'"

Bill Carleton was another in the 100th Bomb Group who went across Amsterdam at rooftop height:

"I remember a little Dutch boy looking up and trying to race us on his bicycle. As we approached the target area, the Dutch had arranged stones to say 'Thank You' in large letters just as we crossed the field. There were planes ahead of us who made their drops and people were running across the target area to get the food, unmindful of the fact that they could be knocked to kingdom come with a can of Spam. Planes all around us were starting to drop their food but our plane flew across the field without any salvo. The bombardier had gone to sleep! He awoke with a jerk and made the drop into the Zuider Zee. Such folly, but how typical. The best of intentions, the worst in execution. I hoped the forthcoming peace would be better than that!"[1250]

23

The Breaking of Nations

"There was never a good war or a bad peace."
Benjamin Franklin

During the first week of May the German armies surrendered one by one to Montgomery at Lüneberg Heath, to Devers at Munich, and to Alexander at Casserta. And finally, at 0241 on 7 May, at a little red schoolhouse in Reims that was SHAEF headquarters, General Dwight D. Eisenhower accepted the German surrender, which brought the war in Europe to a formal end. A simple cable announced the end to "five years, eight months and six days of bloodshed and destruction" in Europe: "The mission of this Allied Force was fulfilled at 3 am, local time, 7 May 1945. Eisenhower."

Sixteen war correspondents witnessed the German surrender. All except one of them agreed to a press embargo until an official announcement of the war's end could be made simultaneously by all combatants, including the Soviet Union, who were planning a surrender ceremony of their own in Berlin. Edward Kennedy of Associated Press, "a hard-nosed wire service correspondent," decided to telephone his report to his Paris office, which relayed it to New York via London, and within the hour news of the surrender broke, but the only official announcement, ironically, was made by Hamburg Radio. In Britain people were, in the words of the song, looking forward to "getting lit up when the lights go on in London," but now nobody knew whether it really was time for celebrations to begin. In America, officialdom appeared to do everything to stifle celebrations before they began. All bars were closed for 24 hours, and flags were kept at half-mast in deference to the late President Roosevelt, who had died in office in April. On 7 May Mayor La Guardia urged all the people of the City of New York who had "thoughtlessly left their jobs" to go home and to be patient. In London, King George VI noted "a terrible anti-climax!" Prime Minister Winston Churchill used the "secret line" to the White House, asking President Truman that he bring forward the official announcement. Truman refused to do so without the approval of Joseph Stalin, but Churchill knew that the Soviet dictator was playing power politics, and he felt he could delay no longer. The British Ministry of Information announced that Tuesday, 8 May, would be VE (Victory in Europe) Day, and a holiday in Britain. The announcement went on to say that the Prime Minister would make a statement at 3 pm. The King would broadcast at 9 pm, and Wednesday, 9 May, would also be a national holiday. Stalin, meanwhile, wanted to postpone the announcement until "he had given further consideration to the surrender terms." Washington finally lost patience with Soviet procrastination, and in the early hours of 8 May President Truman held a news conference to announce the German surrender on all fronts to American, British, and Soviet forces. Up to 30,000 New Yorkers gathered in Times Square, but Truman's victory proclamation went largely unheard, because no one had thought to have it relayed over loudspeakers.

There was a phrase for the early days of May 1945. It was as Thomas Hardy had said of an end to an earlier war, "a time of the breaking of nations." In Germany, VE Day found many of the occupying forces still in a somber, reflective mood. Censorship delayed word to the public, and as a result there were no scenes of wild elation among the American troops. For the majority of American soldiers in Germany it was "just another routine day," but for the British, well, at least one unit received a rum ration and also set up a Bren gun to allow gunners to take turns in loosing off tracer! Some troops captured a flock of German sheep and cut "V" signs on their backs. It appeared to one officer when he stepped out into the night as if all the troops in Rhineland were hell-bent on lighting up the heavens. "Very lights swished into space, sizzled, and burst, draping the sky in flamboyant baubles of reds and greens. Searchlights mounted beside the Rhine performed evolutions too fantastic even for an Einstein to chart...." The pyrotechnics and the singing, shouting, and endless drinking were accompanied by "rifle shots, the rat-tat-tat of machine-gun fire and heavier explosions from mortars, detonations from mines and some louder bangs." At least ordinary Germans could now walk the streets without fear of being fired at, but that was about the limit of their emotional response to VE Day. Those who had lost homes and businesses were to be seen wandering dreamily across the bombsites, "as if hoping to awake to a new reality." In the cities there was a desperate shortage of accommodation, and in spring 1945 hundreds of thousands of Germans were living rough: water from the tap was no longer fit to drink, sewers overflowed, and food was scarce except on the black market. One soldier wrote:

> "What have these people to live for? Their dear ones killed, their houses destroyed, tragedy everywhere... They thought to rule the world - all the agony, the tears and the suffering have recoiled on them a hundred fold."

In France, German army garrisons were still ensconced at St. Nazaire and Lorient, on the Atlantic coast, and at the Channel port of Dunkirk, and it was not until 9 and 10 May that Dunkirk, St. Nazaire, and Lorient were finally returned to Allied control. In war-torn and battle-scarred Paris "the bells pealed and cannons roared," and the Parisian streets were fully lit for the first time since 1939. A victory V shone over *les Invalides* and another in red, white, and blue above the *Arc de Triomphe*. Everywhere the streets disappeared under a surge of humanity. At 3 o'clock General Charles de Gaulle spoke over the street loudspeaker system. In the sunshine thousands shouting and singing snatches of the *Marseillaise* marched down the Champs-Elysées and along the city's avenues and boulevards and on into the night. They were still marching at dawn the next morning. Pistols were fired into the air from moving cars, aircraft overhead dropped multi-colored flares, and fireworks boomed in all directions. "Paris was Bedlam" wrote a *Herald Tribune* correspondent.

Bill Carleton, in the 100th Bomb Group, sums up possibly the feelings of many at the war's end:

> "All wars are senseless and yet World War Two was unavoidable. We had gained victory not necessarily though superior intellect but rather through the belief that we were in the right. Like all human endeavors, we were fraught with frustration and at times, saddled with stupidity but the love of man and the love of our country brought forth accomplishments and sacrifices beyond man's own comprehension. The 100th Bomb Group was known throughout the land not because we were superhuman but rather because we were human. Our fame and notoriety spread not just because of Regensburg or Berlin or the Russian mission, but also because of our losses and yes, even because of our 'faux pas.' We were famous and to some of the new flyers, infamous, both for what we did and what we gave. Mighty as we were with our 70 to 80 bombers and our 4000 men, we were but a small fraction of the total force ultimately applied against the Axis powers. We contributed our part and it was our knowledge and belief that others were making an even greater sacrifice that assured us of ultimate victory."

When victory came the B-17 groups were assigned many tasks, such as flying Allied prisoners of war home from their camps in eastern Europe to France and airlifting displaced persons from Linz, Austria, to their homes in France, Holland, Denmark, and all other recently occupied countries. The B-17 crews airlifted troops from the United Kingdom to Casablanca, where they continued on to the China-Burma-India Theater and also acted as "moving vans" for fighter groups going to Germany as part of the occupation forces. In addition, "Trolley' or "Revival" missions were flown to bombed out cities, the aircraft crammed with ground personnel to show them what destruction their aircraft had wrought. The flights ranged from 1000 to 3000ft, and the routes took passengers on what they described as a "Cook's Tour" of specially selected towns and cities that had been bombed over the past four years.

VE (Victory in Europe) Day took place on 8 May. At Debach, Robert "Gus" Gaustad, navigator in the Munday crew, recalls:

> "in front of a neat and flower-bordered farmhouse not far from my hut a small American flag was displayed, along with a large sign which read, 'Thank You America!' I was moved to tears."

Walt Cranson was "really glad to be flying [a *Trolley* mission] on such a day and to see so many miles of celebration. "VE DAY! Hurray!!" He wrote:

> "Took along three rolls of toilet paper for my celebration...really makes confetti when unwound and thrown out in bunches. Had the boys in tail turret watch it! We flew high - sorta scaring the guys... still saw lots! Circled Brussels three times...shooting flares and me kicking off the toilet paper like mad. Everybody celebrating below... Flags everywhere and people waved like mad!' Ralph Elliott wrote to his wife Vonny in the US:' VE DAY it says in the papers. I read it on the way to Germany...we went to Mannheim, Hanau, up the Rhine again, across to Antwerp, Walcheren and home. The Belgians sure knew it was VE DAY. We saw flags in every town we went over including Bruges, Brussels, Ghent, Antwerp and others. They had English, French, Dutch, American and Belgian flags on all the houses, stores, factory chimneys, cathedrals-and outhouses to boot. We came back over some little town and saw the town square full of people; all celebrating-so we buzzed the place and shot a mass of flares. At Antwerp there were thousands of people on the streets so we did a circle and fired more flares. We saw prisoner of war camps full of thousands of men between Frankfurt and Koblenz. So many bridges were down that we could hardly remember the pictures. We've been loafing today but as usual our 'Dear Colonel' has taken care of us by restricting us to the post. Just his idea of seeing we don't celebrate too much. NUTS!"

American servicemen everywhere were restricted to base. One wrote that:

> "No reason was given. Possibly the rationale was that until Japan was defeated, we in the military had no business celebrating; or since the war in the Pacific was going so well, perhaps the big brass thought that we could wait and do all our celebrating at once when Japan surrendered."

At Thurleigh, Bedfordshire, the 306th Bomb Group was ready to celebrate, but the final arrival of VE Day left the men:

> "somewhat subdued, as there had been so many premature declarations of peace. Each time spirits had risen, only to drop again, so on the official day there was not quite as much levity as one might have imagined earlier. According to one diarist, 'a 'brown haze' settled over Thurleigh, only to be lifted after supper when kegs of beer were rolled out on the baseball diamond."

However, some American servicemen were able to celebrate off base. T/Sgt Wiley S. Noble, an ordnanceman, was one of only four personnel to leave their base at Watton, Norfolk, on VE Day because the CO had directed them to get suitable fireworks:

> "The road was filled with men and women celebrating and the girls dashed up to our Jeep to kiss us. You'd never believe the offers we had and I am not talking about the fine wine and Scotch they so generously supplied!"

Walt Cranson, meanwhile, had landed after his flight to Belgium, disgorged his "passengers," and had then set off again with his crew because:

> "we wanted to see another big Capital celebrating, Yes, London! We found it - circled down to 400ft...and I really dumped a lot out over Piccadilly...Man, were the streets packed, flags and bonfires everywhere. So low - could see the mob waving and climbing up on the lions of Trafalgar Square."

In London crowds gathered early, encouraged by a change in the weather from storm clouds the night before to warm sunshine. Bells pealed. Flags flew from all the buildings. Shop windows were filled with red, white, and blue clothes, flowers, and materials. Mollie Panter-Downes noted that:

> "every member of every family, from the smallest babies, with their hair done up in red-white-and-blue ribbons, to beaming elderly couples who, utterly without self-consciousness, strolled up and down the streets arm in arm in red-white-and-blue paper hats. Even the dogs wore immense tricolored bows. Rosettes sprouted from the slabs of pork in the butcher shops…."

Girls in thin, bright dresses with cornflowers and poppies in their hair and with red-white-and-blue ribbons around their waists, and some with their uniformed boyfriends, streamed out of offices and buildings and into the parks and streets.

Aircraft flew overhead and streamers, ticker tape, and paper poured out of every window and balcony. Hermione, Countess of Ranfurly, on the fourth floor at the Air Ministry in Adastral House, Kingsway, thought that it was "a brilliant time" to throw some of Air Marshal Slessor's "more boring papers" out. She peeled the canvas off one window and emptied the contents of five waste paper baskets onto Kingsway. The countess "longed to be more generous but did not dare." There was no traffic, because the people of London and their children and thousands of visitors filled the streets and pavements and parks to celebrate victory in Europe. She eased her way into the Strand and progressed at "snail's pace" towards Trafalgar Square:

> "It was a good-natured multitude and except for the sounds of feet and voices there was a silence over London - a silence loaded with emotion. A few people were crying and a few were laughing but the majority trudged forward silently."

In Trafalgar Square the steps, lions, and lampposts were "coated with people." Whitehall appeared to be paved with heads. "This is it - and we are all going nuts," wrote a *Daily Mirror* reporter:

> "There are thousands of us in Piccadilly Circus. The police say more than 10,000 - and that's a conservative estimate. We are dancing the Conga and the jig and '*Knees Up Mother Brown*' and we are singing and whistling and blowing paper trumpets. The idea is to make a noise. We are. Even above the roar of the motors of low-flying bombers 'shooting up' the city…."

From a vantage-point on the steps of the silent and boarded National Gallery Ben Foote, in the 392nd Bomb Group, absorbed the euphoria of more than one million people gathered in Trafalgar Square, spilling toward the gates of Buckingham Palace:

> "The happy throng, bursting with the enthusiasm and good feeling brought on by the end of almost six years of war and sacrifice, staged a gigantic community songfest, interrupted only by cheers for the celebrities that were making their way to the Palace to pay their respects to King George VI. They chanted everything from '*God Save the King*' to '*White Cliffs of Dover*.'"

Around 5 o'clock the Royal Family, Winston Churchill, and Clement Atlee, his deputy, came out on the balcony of Buckingham Palace. Churchill drew a "deep, full-throated, almost reverent roar," and the crowds cheered themselves hoarse as the Royal Family disappeared and reappeared on the balcony like stage performers at the Palladium. They appeared eight times in all.

In Piccadilly Circus a black bereted soldier in the Tank Corps climbed the little pyramidal Angkor Vat of scaffolding and sandbags that was erected early in the war to protect the pedestal of the Eros statue after the figure had been removed for safekeeping. At the top he took a tiptoe Eros pose aiming an imaginary bow while the crowd roared. A paratrooper in maroon beret followed, and once on top reached down and hauled up a blonde in a very tight pair of green slacks. The Tank Corps soldier promptly grabbed her in his arms and, encouraged by ecstatic cheers from the whole Circus, for a moment seemed about to enact the classic role of Eros right on the top of the monument. GIs joined them, and before long the pyramid was covered with servicemen and young girls. The *Daily Mirror* reported:

> "We are dancing around Eros in the blackout but there is a glow from a bonfire up Shaftesbury Avenue and a newsreel cinema has lit its canopy lights for the first time in getting on for six years. A huge V sign glares down over Leicester Square. And gangs of girls and soldiers are waving rattles and shouting and climbing lampposts and swarming over cars that have become bogged down in this struggling, swirling mass of celebrating Londoners."

Captain Robert H. Tays was on leave in London when VE Day occurred:

> "Lights came on and thankful prayers were said.[1251] London went wild and we partied for several days and nights."

Earlier that afternoon the base restriction at Thurleigh was lifted, and most of the 306th Bomb Group personnel headed for Bedford:

> "What they saw," recalled one diarist, "amazed every man. The English had dragged every 'bloody' light bulb in town and strung it up outdoors. The streets were filled with a blaze of lights that hurt your eyes. The people, old and young, filled the streets and danced and sang *Roll Me Over And Do it Again* at the tops of their lungs. There had been great fear for the conduct of the Yanks but the spectacle of the staid and reserved English letting their hair down, as it had never been down before so startled the Yanks that they were left without a leg to stand on. For once the British 'out-hollered' and 'out drank' the Americans."

On the American bases in East Anglia, the average GI mirrored the confusion of the world outside. Pearl Harbor had yet to be avenged, and rumors of redeployment to the Pacific and arguments about the merits and demerits of the newly announced point system for discharge abounded. It was "Two Down and One to Go." Italy and Germany had been "licked," and while Japan was heading for defeat, nobody was certain how long it would take. Redeployment of 8th Air Force personnel, which numbered 300,000 men and women, had already begun. At Seething, Norfolk, Pat Everson, a 12-year old schoolgirl, sat at the bedroom window crying, as she did not want the Americans to leave:

> "They had brought color and excitement to the children around the base. They fired flares and rockets to celebrate VE Day. I could not remember fireworks. Usually if any light were seen in the sky or

bangs heard it was something to do with searchlights or guns. My mother explained that the war was over and that they were celebrating this and also that they were so happy to be going home to America."

Many people were sad to see the bomb groups go, and a few Americans, married to their English wives, have remained ever since. The young, sometimes brash, Americans had become a part of everyday life, and their departure was greeted with a mixture of great sadness and joy. Almost all left their youth behind in a land they had come to love and respect. Many hundreds lie buried at Madingley, where each year a memorial service is held for those who died flying from these shores.[1252]

On Sunday, 13 May, a Victory Flypast was made over "Widewing," the 8th Air Force headquarters where Lieutenant General James H. Doolittle and his staff were housed. About 1400 bombers and fighters took part, and Captain Ralph Elliott's crew in the 467th Bomb Group, with Colonel Albert J. Shower as command pilot in the right hand seat, led the heavies.[1253] Elliott recalled:

> "Colonel Shower and I had the 467th in formation at about 6000ft and were ready to head south at the head of the column, on course to High Wycombe, when the clouds moved in. We knew we had to get back on the ground shortly or we'd have to make an instrument approach coming in over the North Sea. I saw a hole, tapped the Colonel on the shoulder and pointed to it and he said, 'Go'. We took the formation down under the cloud layer and followed the usual formation landing procedure to get back on the ground. We were quite disappointed, because we had flown 3 hours 15 minutes the day before, making a dry run of the route - just like a bomb run - to identify all the checkpoints and the 'target'. Of course, nowhere in the history books is this part of the mission mentioned. But I think at least one true account should be left to posterity; none of which detracts from the honor of the day and the record of the 467th as having done the most accurate bombing of WW II."

Final honors, therefore, went to more than 700 American fighters. Wave after wave flew over the old abbey, which before the war had been a school for girls. In the summer of 1942, when Eaker had chosen "Pinetree" to plan the future of his embryonic and untried bombing force, some of the bedrooms still displayed a prim little card that said, "*Ring twice for mistress.*"

The B-17s then began airlifting troops from the United Kingdom to Casablanca, where they continued on to the China-Burma-India (CBI) Theater, and also acted as "moving vans" for fighter groups going to Germany as part of the occupation forces there. The bomb groups returned allied PoWs to England and France, and airlifted displaced persons from all over Europe. Then *Trolley* or *Revival* missions in bombers crammed with ground personnel were flown at heights ranging from 1000 to 3000ft over bombed out cities to show them the outcome of Allied bombing over the past four years. The middle of May saw the bomb groups leaving the east of England for America or Germany. People thronged the streets of the towns and villages as the "Yanks" marched to waiting trucks and railway stations en route to ports of embarkation. Bombers with 20-man crews left almost daily. Liberators in the 467th circled Rackheath in a farewell gesture. Lieutenant Fred Jansen flew *Witchcraft* home with crew chief Joe Ramirez aboard, having completed 130 missions without a turn back.

Captain Ralph Elliott wrote home to his wife Vonny:

> "...you asked about coming over after the war is over...I don't think I'll ever want to come back. I've seen a lot and of course wartime England isn't at its best, but there's no place like home and I do mean it. So I think your idea of Bermuda sounds OK...or just a cabin up among the pines and lakes...."

Goodbye G.I. Bud. Now you know the way
Come back and see us in a brighter day.
When England's free and the
Scotch is cheap but strong
And you can bring your pretty wives along.

Goodbye G.I. don't leave us quite alone.
Somewhere in England we must write in stone
How Britain was invaded by the Yanks
And under that 'a big and hearty thanks'

A. P. Herbert, a famous English historian, for the opening of the American Red Cross Club in London in 1945

Glossary

Abschuss	Confirmed victory in air combat
Abshüsse	confirmed victories in air combat
Abschussteiligung	Contribution to a confirmed air-combat victory
AI	Airborne Intercept (radar)
Alarmstart	Scramble
BG	Bomb Group
CBO	Combined Bomber Offensive
Deutsche Kreuz im Gold (DKG)	German Cross in gold
Dicke Autos	'Fat Cars' (B-17s and B-24s)
E/A	enemy aircraft
Eichenlaub (El)	Knight's Cross with Oak Leaves
Eisernes Kreuz 1, II (EK I, EK II)	Iron Cross (1st and 2nd Class)
Einsatz	Operational flight
Erganzungsgruppe (EGr)	Replacement or complement wing
ETO	European Theater of Operations
Express-Express	R/T code for 'hurry up'
Flak (*Flieger Abwehr Kanonen*)	Anti-Aircraft Artillery
Feindberuhrung	Contact with an enemy aircraft
FG	Fighter Group
FS	Fighter Squadron
Führer	Leader
Geschwader	Roughly equivalent to three RAF wings. Comprises three or four *Gruppen*
Gruppe	Group containing three or four *Staffeln,* designated by Roman figures eg. IV./JG26
Gruppenkommandeur	Commander or Captain, a Gruppe command position rather than a rank
Herausschuss	Claim for a bomber shot out of formation
Horrido!	Tallyho!
Jäger	Fighter
Jagdbomber (Jabo)	Fighter-bomber
Jagdgeschwader (JG)	Fighter wing, includes three or four *Gruppen*
Jagdwaffe	Fighter Arm or Fighter Force
Kacmarek	wingman
Kommandeur	Commanding officer of a *Gruppe*
Kommodore	Commodore or Captain, a *Geschwader* command position rather than a rank
Kurier	R/T code for 'Allied heavy bomber'
Luftwaffe (LW)	Air Force
Lufbery	A Lufbery, or "Luftberry," as it was sometimes known in its corrupted form by American fighter pilots, was named for the World War I American fighter ace Major Gervais Raoul Lufbery who scored 17 victories. The Lufbery Circle was a defensive tactic, in which a group of aircraft flew in a tight circle, making it difficult for enemy aircraft to break into and attack without themselves being attacked.
Maschinen Gewehr (MG)	Machine gun
Maschinen Kanone (MK)	Machine cannon
Pauke-Pauke	R/T code for going into attack'
PTO	Pacific Theater of Operations
Reflex Visier (Revi)	Gunsight
Reichsluftfahrtministerium (RLM)	German Air Ministry
Reichsverteidigung	Air Defense of Germany
RitterKreuz (*träger*) (RK/RKT)	Knight's Cross (holder)
Rotte	Tactical element of two aircraft
Rottenflieger	Wingman, the second man in the *Rotte*
R/T	radio telephony
Schlachtgeschwader (SG)	Ground attack wing
Schwarm	Flight of four aircraft
Schwarmführer	Flight leader
Schwarzemänner	ground crews or 'black men', so-called because of the color of their tunics
Schwerten (S)	Knight's Cross with Oak Leaves and Swords
Stab	Staff flight
Staffel	Roughly equivalent to a squadron, designated sequentially within the *Geschwader* by Arabic figures, e.g.: 4./JG1
Staffelkapitän (Stk)	Captain, a *Staffel* command position rather than a rank
USSTAF	United States Strategic Air Forces (8th and 15th AFs)
Viktor	R/T code for have received and understood message'
Viermot	Four-engined bomber
Zerstörer	'Destroyer', Bf 110 fighter aircraft
Zerstörergeschwader (ZG)	Heavy fighter wing (Bf 110 or Me 410 twin-engined fighter)
ZOI	Zone of the Interior (USA)
Zweimot	Twin-engined bomber

German Ranks and Their Abbreviations

German Ranks	U.S. equivalent
Reischmarschall	no equivalent
Generalfeldmarschall	General (5- Star)
Generaloberst	General (4-Star)
General der Flieger	Lieutenant General
Generaileutnant	Major or General
Generaimajor	Brigadier General
Oberst	Colonel
Oberstleutnant (Obstlt)	Lieutenant Colonel
Major	Major
Hauptmann (Hptm)	Captain
Oberleutnant (Oblt)	1st Lieutenant
Leutnant (Lieutenant)	2nd Lieutenant
Stabsfeldwebel (StFw)	Flight Officer
Oberfähnrich (Ofhr)	no equivalent
Oberfeldwebel (Ofw)	Master Sergeant
Fähnrich (Fhr)	Officer candidate
Feldwebel (Fw)	Sergeant
Unteroffizier (Uffz)	S/Sgt
Obergefreiter (Ogfr)	Corporal
Gefreiter (Gefr)	Private First Class
Flieger (Flg)	Private Second Class

Endnotes

Chapter 1:

1 Red, a navigator, was lost on one of the early missions over Bremer.

2 Ben Smith, Jr., is a grandson of one of Stonewall Jackson's 'toot cavalry' and a keen student of Civil War history. Long after the war he came upon a small volume written about his grandfather's brigade by a private soldier. In this way, he was enabled to gain a remarkable insight into the daily lives of the common soldiers of that era. He resolved to do the same thing with his own experiences in WWII. *Chick's Crew: A Tale of the Eighth Air Force,* first published in 1978, is a direct result of his chance encounter with the journal of the private soldier who cared enough to leave his story for posterity.

3 Born Gladwyne, PA, 25 June 1886. Graduated from USMA and commissioned in the infantry, 14 June 1907. After service in the Philippines was assigned to the SC in April 1911, where he became one of the U.S. Army's first qualified pilots having received instruction at Dayton, Ohio in June that year. He later became a flying instructor in the Aviation School set up in the SC. Arnold saw no service in Europe during WWI, his administrative ability gaining him the post of Chief of Information Service, Aviation Division, SC in 1917 and later Assistant Director, Office of Military Aeronautics. Commanded Rockwell Field, CA in 1919. A friend and admirer of Mitchell, Arnold took a more cautious path to achieve similar ideals. In 1925 his flair for the written and spoken word gained him position of Chief, information Division, Office C of AC. Entered CGSS and graduated in June 1929. Commanded 1st Wing at March Field, CA, November 1933-March 1936 and while holding this command led a flight of B-10 bombers to Alaska gaining the Mackay Trophy award. Promoted Brigadier General (temporary) in February 1935 and appointed Assistant Chief of AC. With the death of Major General Westover, Arnold became C of AC in September 1938. Became the Army's Deputy C of S for Air in October 1940 and given the overall command of the Army's air arm in June 1941 with the creation of the AAF, first U.S. Chief of the AAF and with the reorganization of Army command he became CG, AAF on 9 March 1942. Promoted Lieutenant General (temporary) December 1941 and General (temporary), March 1943. Received a 5th star in December 1944, first air officer to achieve this rank. A notable writer, his book *Global Mission* (1949) reflects his receptive approach to the various aspects of airpower and an intense determination to succeed. Died 15 January 1950.

4 Also on 2 January the War Department in Washington announced that United States ground forces were to be sent to Northern Ireland. On 8 January the activation of USAFBI (U.S. Forces in the British Isles) was announced. A third announcement stated that a bomber command was to be established in England.

5 Born 13 April 1896 at Llano, Texas. School teacher before obtaining a commission in the infantry in August 1917. Detached for flying training November 1917. Pilot and Assistant Adjutant, Rockwell Field CA 1918-19. Served with 2nd and 3rd AS, Philippines 1919-22 and on return to U.S. became CO of 5th AS at Mitchel Field, NY 1922-23. Two university courses followed and up until 1932 Captain Eaker held Executive Officer assignments in Washington. During this period he was also associated with technical evaluation and experimentation. In 1927 he participated in a goodwill Pan American flight and was decorated by three governments. Acted as chief pilot 1-7 January 1929 during record endurance flight over Los Angeles where air-to-air refueling was successfully employed. In 1933 he made the first 'blind' Trans-continental flight of USA. Commanded 34th PS, 17th PG in the mid-1930s and staff appointments in Washington 1938-40. Collaborated with General Arnold in writing *Winged Warfare, This Flying Game*. Executive Officer to Chief of Air Corps in 1940. Commanded 20th Fighter Group at Hamilton Field, CA January-September 1941 and then spent a month in the UK as a special observer. Joined 1st Air Force HQ at Mitchel Field late 1941 and chosen to head an expeditionary bomber command destined for the UK. In December 1942 became the CG of 8th Air Force. Directed the 8th Air Force campaign until January 1944 when he was transferred to the MTO to command the new MAAF. Flew on the first 15th Air Force 'shuttle' mission to Russia in June 1944. Remained overall Allied air commander in the MTO until the end of hostilities. Deputy CG of the AAF after returning to the USA, April 1945 holding this office until his own retirement in June 1947. Died

6 The red headed Yale-educated pilot and writer had penned the classic *I Wanted Wings,* which, in 1941, had been made into a successful movie by Paramount and will be remembered as the movie that made Veronica Lake famous. It was written originally to tell what happens inside a boy who "just has to fly."

7 Operations and Training.

8 Supply.

9 Intelligence.

10 The first of the B-17 groups activated was the 34th - at Langley Field, Virginia, on 15 January 1942 - but the group was used to train other groups and remained in America until late March 1944.

11 On 15 February, the fourth and final bomb squadron, the 342nd, joined the already activated 340th, 341st and 414th Bomb Squadrons. Fortunately, many of the personnel in the 342nd Bomb Squadron were drawn from the Overseas Training Unit and were well acquainted with the B-17E, the latest model of the Flying Fortress. At the end of March the 97th Bomb Group moved to Bradenton-Sarasota AAB, Florida. The airfield was not vet completed and was located in what looked like a swamp in which palmettos abounded. Tents were pitched and all personnel were confined to base as the training program got under way. In order to meet the required 125 hours flying, aircrews did some flying at night. Jeeps were parked near the runway so their headlights could he used to mark the end of the tarmac.

12 12,500 men of the 97th Bomb Group, 1st Fighter Group and the 31st Fighter Group plus their service echelons stumbled up the gangplanks under masses of equipment to be greeted by a member of the ship's crew who thrust into their open mouths, since their arms were full, a sheet of paper directing each man to his bunk and mess hall. All personnel were ordered below decks where, before the war, passengers had wallowed in sumptuous luxury. There was little luxury now for the cramped soldiers and it was rumored that, officially, the *Queen Elizabeth* was returning to Britain empty. Tasks were allotted during the voyage and some 97th Bomb Group personnel were assigned to gun crews on the 50 caliber machine-guns stationed along the top deck in case of air attack.

13 There was sublime irony in its selection as the reception base for the first B-17 group in the European Theater of Operations (ETO). In May 1941 the RAF had taken possession of Polebrook airfield for the purpose of training crews for manning 90 Squadron, which was to be equipped with the B-17C, or Fortress I as the British referred to it. During June 1941 5 Fortress Is were delivered to Polebrook and 90 Squadron began operations on 8 July when three took part in a daylight raid on Wilhelmshaven. The RAF flew 24 operations during the summer of 1941. By September it was decided that the Fortress was unsuitable for further bombing operations. Although it was an extremely well built aircraft its defensive firepower of 5 manually operated 5-inch machine-guns and one '303-inch machine-gun was totally inadequate for daylight operations over such heavily defended targets on the Continent. Bombing, too, was inaccurate but then the top secret Norden bombsight was deleted from all 20 models delivered to the RAF. As a result of the RAF's abortive trial period, modifications were made to the B-17 and Boeing evolved the B-17E, which incorporated power-operated gun turrets and a tail position. It was this aircraft, which now equipped the 97th Bomb Group.

14 The *Luftwaffe* did its best to welcome the Americans to Northamptonshire, scattering incendiary clusters over the Polebrook base on the night of 25 June, in a raid lasting 15 minutes. Damage was negligible and 4 nights later, flares were dropped, making the night sky as bright as day, but no bombs fell. Perhaps the *Luftwaffe* was checking to see if the Fortresses had arrived. In fact they were en route. The 340th and 341st air echelons had taken off for Dow Field, Maine and those of the 342nd and 414th, for Grenier Field, New Hampshire. Flying north, the 342nd Squadron encountered bad weather and was forced to put down at Mitchel Field, New York. From there they joined the 414th Squadron at Grenier Field. Meanwhile, the 340th and 341st Squadrons had arrived at Dow Field and complained that the ball turrets were malfunctioning. Repair crews were called in and, by the end of May, the B-17s and their crews were assembled at Presque Isle, awaiting orders. An attack on June 1 by the Japanese on the Aleutians changed plans dramatically and, next day, the 97th Bomb Group and P-38s of the 1st Fighter Group were scheduled for detached duty with Western Defense Command. All four squadrons in the 97th Bomb Group arrived at their destinations on 5 June and immediately began flying coastal patrol missions. On 23 June the danger over, the 97th Bomb Group returned to Presque Isle for the flight to Prestwick via Goose Bay, Labrador, Greenland and Reykjavik, Iceland. Crews had a choice of routes, either via Bluie West 1 (Narsarssuak) on the south coast of Greenland or Bluie 8 (Sondre Stromfjord) on the west coast. On 26 June the B-17s left Presque Isle and reached Goose Bay. Three hours and 10 minutes later the formation was airborne for Bluie West 1, arriving there to discover that the weather had changed for the worse, making it impossible to land. Next morning 11 of the B-17s returned to Goose Bay, having been in the air for over 13 hours. Four crews ran into trouble in a snowstorm and had to land on a Greenland icecap and were later rescued. After having resolved some communication problems and having received reports of improving weather conditions moving in, the 97th Bomb Group was soon heading out over the 'Great Circle' route on regular schedule. This first proving flight led to many innovations for which thousands of airmen using the Northern Ferry Route in the months to come would be most grateful. Experience was an excellent instructor and one recommendation that all crewmen should be issued with sunglasses became standard operating procedure.

15 On 4 July 12 US-built Boston (A-20) medium bombers thundered low across the North Sea to four airfield targets in Holland. 6 of the aircraft carried RAF crews while 15th Bomb Squadron personnel manned the other half dozen. At Bergen Alkmaar the Boston flown by Lieutenant Stan G. Lynn USAAF and his American crew was hit by flak after bombing and crashed on the airfield killing all on board. A RAF Boston was shot down by a Bf 109 of *Jagdgeschwader 1* off the Dutch coast. The formation attacking De Kooy airfield were forced to fly through 3 miles of flak, which prevented all three Bostons from bombing. Lieutenant Jack Loehrl's Boston was hit by flak north of the airfield. Apparently, Loehrl made the fatal mistake

of making a normal turn, allowing the flak gunners to anticipate his course. Loehrl crashed on the beach. He and his two gunners, Sergeants Wright and Whitham, were killed. Lieutenant Marshall Draper, the bombardier, survived and was taken prisoner. The other wing ship, with Captain Kegelman at the controls was also badly hit. The starboard engine took a direct hit and burst into flames and the propeller flew off. Kegleman's right wing tip struck the ground and the fuselage actually bounced on the surface of the airdrome, tearing a hole in the belly of the bomber. Kegelman lifted the Boston back into the air on one engine and got the aircraft home. In the middle of Ambassador John C. Winant's Fourth of July party at the Court of St. James in London, Captain Harry C. Butcher, General Eisenhower's Naval aide, was called to a side room in the J. Pierpoint Morgan mansion to take a 'phone call from General Charles L. Bolte. He passed the results of the first American raid to General Eisenhower. Of the four airfield targets, only one had been attacked successfully. Of the six American crews taking part, only one had engaged the *Luftwaffe* with good results.

16 Carl A. Spaatz born 28 June 1891 at Boyertown, Pa. Graduated from USMA West Point and commissioned in the infantry June 1914. Stationed a year in Hawaii from October 1914. On return to USA received pilot training at San Diego, CA. Assigned to 1st AS as pilot on Mexican border during 1916. Promoted Captain May 1917 and sent to France where he commanded the AS training base at Issoudon. In 1918 spent a period with 2nd PG and shot down three enemy a/c. Promoted Major 1920 and commanded Kelly Field, Texas October 1920-February 1921. Became Air Officer 8th Corps Area and in November 1921 he assumed command of 1st PG, holding this command at Ellington Field, Texas and Selfridge Field, Mich, until September 1924. Major Spaatz then entered the ASTS at Langley, VA and after graduating in June 1925 went to Washington for staff duties in the Office of C of the AS. In January 1929 Spaatz and his crew accomplished an air-refueled flight lasting 6 days. The following May he was assigned to command the 7th Bomb Group at Rockwell Field, CA and in October 1931 became CO of the controlling 1st Wing at March Field. In June 1933 he returned to Washington as C of AC, Training and Operations Division, following which he attended the CGSS. Promoted Lieutenant Colonel early in 1936 and in June assigned to GHQ Air Force, Langley Field. Early in 1939 he returned to Washington to take up the appointment of Assistant Executive Officer to the C of AC. Promoted Colonel that November he was sent to the UK in the spring of 1940 as a special military observer. On return, in October, he became Arnold's assistant and was promoted Brigadier General. During 1941 Spaatz was head of the Plans Division and later became Chief of Air Staff. With war he was made CO of AAFCC and promoted Major General in January 1942. Detailed to organize forces for a European campaign he then assumed command of the 8th Air Force in the UK in July. In November 1942 he went to North Africa, commanding the 12th Air Force and the NAAF with promotion to Lieutenant General in March 1943. Later in 1943 he became Deputy Commander of the MAAF, returning to the UK in January 1944 to become first commander of USSTAF. Promoted General in March 1945 he returned to Washington in June and was then despatched to Guam to form U.S. Strategic Air Forces Pacific. Spaatz was present at all three WWII unconditional surrender signings. Post-war he became commander of the AAF in February 1946 and the first C of S of the new USAF when founded in September 1947. Retired 30 June 1948. Died 14 June 1974.

17 Tibbets was to fly an even more historic mission three years later when he piloted the B-29, *Enola Gay* - named after his mother - over Hiroshima. Van Kirk and Ferebee flew the same positions that day.

18 Though Eaker initially could call upon only a few B-17 Flying and in Fortress and B-24D Liberator bomb groups their presence had an immediate effect on the *Luftwaffe*. German day fighters now had to drive the heavily armed and armored American bombers from the skies by co-ordination of fighter formations and closed formation attacks, particularly since the standard 8.8cm flak promised no great results at altitudes above 8000 meters. In 1976, Albert Speer, Hitler's minister of armaments production, admitted that the combined efforts of VIII Bomber Command and RAF Bomber Command tied down 900,000 men who could have been used to put Russia out of the war before the Allied invasion of France.

19 Early trials with the FW 190 were undertaken at *Erprobungsstelle Rechlin* and in March 1941 a team from JG 26 headed by Oberleutnant Karl Borris, *Staffelkapitän* of 6./JG 26 with Oberleutnant Otto Behrens as technical officer began the task of introducing the FW 190A-1 into *Luftwaffe* service. In August 1941 the first of the new aircraft were delivered to 6./JG 26 at Le Bourget and on 27 September Spitfires and FW 190s clashed for the first time. Following the attack on the Soviet Union in summer 1941 the *Luftwaffe* fighter force in the west consisted of about three full fighter regiments - JG 1 in north-west Germany, JG 26 in the Pas de Calais and the Low Countries and JG 2 defending the Atlantic coast ports of France. JG 2 and 26 had 9 *Staffeln* each, a *Staffel* being a squadron with a strength of about 12 fighters, organized into three *Gruppen* each; in total about 200 fighters. Periodically *Gruppen* or *Staffeln* in JG 2 and JG 26 would be sent to other fronts and their place taken by units from other *Jagdgeschwadern* so that a strength of about 200 fighters was maintained. In November 1941 the first FW 190A-1s were delivered to the *Geschwader-Stab* of JG 26 under Oberstleutnant Adolf Galland. By January 1942 both II./JG 26 under *Hauptmann* Joachim Müncheberg and III./JG 26 under *Hauptmann* Josef Priller were operational with the FW 190A-2, I. *Gruppe* receiving their first aircraft in March. In March 1942 II./JG 26 was re-equipped with the FW 190A-3. In April the whole of JG 2 commanded by Oberst Walter Oesau was equipped with the FW 190A-3. It quickly became apparent that the FW 190A was more maneuverable in every respect than the Spitfire V, apart from in a turning climbing fight. The German fighter also had a higher maximum speed and was able to break off combat at will. The Spitfire V gave its best performance at around 20,000ft but the German fighters, particularly the Bf 109, had superior performance at high altitude and both the 109 and 190 could out dive the Spitfire. *Luftwaffe* fighters normally chose to make their attacks from higher altitudes and more often than not from out of the sun when they would open fire and then dive away to lower altitude before climbing to reform. In summer 1942 the Spitfire IX with its excellent high altitude performance appeared and this fighter altered the balance of what had been an unfavorable situation for the RAF though the *Luftwaffe* fighters retained the advantage of being faster in the dive. During the late summer of 1942, the FW 190A-4 entered service. This version was powered by the BMW 801D-2 engine, which, with the addition of MW-SO water-methanol injection could provide 2100hp for short periods. On 23 June 1942 the first FW 190A-3 fell into British hands. The machine was piloted by Oberleutnant Armin Faber, an Austrian and adjutant of III./JG 2, who landed by mistake at Pembrey, South Wales after a raid extending up the Bristol Channel. On the way home he had become lost and believed he was over France when he landed on British soil. The mistake provided the Allies with valuable information on the fighter. Faber successfully deceived the British authorities into believing that he was an epileptic and he was repatriated in 1944, so that he was flying again in combat until the end of the war.

20 The three *Gruppen* of JG 26 flew no less than 377 sorties, both against the Allied aircraft and against sea and ground targets. For 6 FW 190s lost, the *Geschwader* claimed 38 aircraft shot down, plus another 11 probables.

21 Brigadier General Newton Longfellow was one of Eaker's closest friends since they had served in the 3rd Aero Squadron in the Philippines in 1919. At the end of July 1942, Eaker put the newly arrived Colonel Longfellow forward for promotion to brigadier general. On 21 August Eaker placed General Longfellow in command of the 1st Bomb Wing. Colonel Charles T. Phillips, with whom Eaker and Longfellow had gone to the Philippines in July 1919, was given the 4th Bomb Wing. (Phillips was KIA in North Africa on 15 December 1942). Longfellow, who was given command of VIIIth Bomber Command on 2 December 1942, when Eaker moved to command 8th Air Force HQ, was, according to Geoffrey Perret in his book *Winged Victory*: "Perpetually overwrought, (he) struggled to overcome its (VIIIth Bomber Command's) difficulties by shouting himself hoarse... (His) nonstop ranting had earned him the nickname 'Screaming Eagle.' At the end of June (1943) he was sent home, a burned out wreck." (General Arnold held the opinion that Eaker's Bomber Commander was "especially weak.") Eaker replaced his oldest friend as commanding general of the VIII Bomber Command on 1 July with Major General Frederick L. Anderson. In turn Eaker recommended Longfellow to the commander of 2nd Air Force, a training command, in the U.S. Eaker added: "He is a tireless worker and despite the fact that we almost killed him off here working, or carrying the responsibility for 24 hours a day, 7 days a week, I believe he will spring back after a few weeks' rest and do a tremendous job..." Longfellow got the job but was reduced to his regular rank as colonel.

22 Lay uses this incident in his novel, *Twelve O'Clock High,* where "Captain Reynolds, Public Relations. Bomber Command." has the same run-in, not with Tibbets, but rather Lieutenant Jesse Bishop, after the latter's actions in The blood soaked cockpit of his B-17 after The back of his pilot's head had been blown off; an action which earns Bishop the award of the Medal of Honor.) Lay and Tibbets later became great friends and collaborated on an MGM movie about his Hiroshima experience called *Above and Beyond.*

23 The B-17F was supposed to be an improvement on the B-17E. However, it was equipped with only two 30 caliber machine-gun mountings in the nose although it had additional .5 sockets modified later in the field. Externally, the B-17F differed little from the B-17E, its most noticeable feature being a frameless Plexiglas nose. Inwardly, however, it incorporated over 400 major design modifications, which, although making it 1000 lb heavier than the B-17E, made it more suitable for combat. The 92nd Bomb Group personnel were disappointed to receive the 97th's battered B-17Es in return but their time would come when they flew combat missions and became known as "Fame's Favored Few."

24 Over Cayeux Captain Frank G. Ward of the 92nd Bomb Group was attacked by 6 FW 190s and one fired into the tail, killing Corporal John E. Bungard, the tail gunner, mortally wounding Corporal Hubert W. Crowell and severely wounding Sgt Robert C. Smith. John F. Segrest, the navigator, was slightly wounded. One 97th Bomb Group gunner, Sgt Julius L. Kleiman, was killed and three others wounded. One died of his wounds three days later in hospital.

25 On 17 October 1942 the Red Cross reported that Lipsky and five of the crew were PoWs.

Chapter 2:

26 Born 14 December 1896 at Alameda, CA. Attended the University of California and enlisted as a flying cadet in the SC Reserve in October 1917. Commissioned 2nd Lieutenant in March 1918. In September 1922 made the first Trans-continental flight in the USA. Entered MIT in 1923 and received Master's and Doctor's degree in 1924 and 1925. In October 1925 won a Schneider Trophy contest. Resigned regular Army commission in February 1930 but remained on the reserve as a major. Made a number of record flights during the 1930s chiefly in racing aircraft. Member of Baker Board Enquiry into the AC in 1934 and only civilian to advocate separation of AC from Army. Ordered to active duty in July 1940. Organized special strike force to bomb Tokyo during early 1942, carrying out the operation with B-25 bombers from carriers in the Pacific on 18 April 1942. Awarded the MoH for this action. Commanded 4th Bomb Wing from June-August 1942 then sent to Europe as Commander 12th Air Force, taking this force to North Africa in November. At the end of February 1943 assumed command of XII Bomber Command, which he relinquished in November 1943, moving to the UK to command of 8th Air Force. Remained CG 8th Air Force in UK until July 1945 and then in Pacific until September 1945. After retirement headed USAF Scientific Advisory Board for a number of years.

27 17 Liberators of the 93rd Bomb Group arrived in the UK and in October were joined by the 44th Bomb Group.

28 Born 15 November 1906 at Columbus, Ohio. Graduated from Ohio State University with a degree in civil engineering. Accepted as a flying cadet in 1928, completing training in October 1929 at Kelly Field, Texas and assigned to the 27th PS, 1st PG at Selfridge Field, Michigan in 1930 and received fighter assignments until 1937 when he went to the 2nd Bomb Group at Langley, Virginia as Operations Officer, 49th Bomb Squadron. Took part in two record breaking flights by YB-17 Flying Fortress to South America acting as lead navigator. Navigator of XB-15 on 2839-mile flight to the Galapagos Islands on 9 May 1940. In January 1941 organized 7th Bomb Squadron, 34th Bomb Group when activated at Langley but in June was seconded to Ferrying Command to undertake pioneering flights to Africa in B-24s where he served as command navigator. Returned 34th Bomb Group in October 1941 and became Group Operations Officer. In April 1942 he became Group Executive of 306th Bomb Group and in July he took command of the 305th Bomb Group at Muroc, CA from Ernest H. Lawson (who returned to command the 305th Bomb Group in November 1943 and was KIA leading the Group over Hamburg on 18 June 1944). He took the 305th to England and entered combat in November 1942. His efforts to improve bombing technique, notably the idea of lead crews, brought him promotion to Brigadier General and command of 4th Bomb Wing (later 3rd Bomb Division) in July 1943, a post he held until June 1944. LeMay's drive and dynamism was such that both in Europe and the Pacific he almost single-handedly changed the concept of long range bombing forever.

29 For administrative and accommodation reasons each bomb group would base all its 4 squadrons on one airfield. This resulted in the 97th Bomb Group's 342nd and 414th Bomb Squadrons having to vacate Grafton-Underwood and move to nearby Polebrook to rejoin the 340th and 341st Squadrons.

30 Life remained miserable for 800 men who had to live in tents until the end of November 1942 when more suitable accommodation was finally made available.

31 The origins of the English-based B-24 Liberator force began with the activation of the 44th Bombardment Group on 15 January 1941, almost 12 months the United States declared war on Japan. Although at the time the U.S. was still officially neutral it had already become involved in the protection of Atlantic convoys. In April 1941 the first U.S. overseas air base was established in Greenland with the agreement of the Danish Government and by May the Germans had begun U-boat attacks on American shipping. These attacks remained fairly sporadic until the end of August when an increase in their activity prompted President Roosevelt to warn Germany and Italy that if their vessels of war entered waters whose protection was deemed vital to America's security then they would do so at their peril. The last pretence of American neutrality was finally abandoned in November 1941 when Congress repealed the remaining neutrality statutes. On 7 December 1941 Japan, with her attack on Pearl Harbor, resolved the position. During late 1941 the 44th began receiving its first B-24Bs and B-24Cs. In February the following year the Group moved to Barkesdale Field, Louisiana, where it embarked on anti-submarine patrols in the Gulf of Mexico. By this time the 44th had become so proficient that its movement overseas was delayed and instead it was used to train other urgently needed units. Like a gigantic game of pool the 44th was broken up and pocketed round the world, leaving only a nucleus of the original personnel who called themselves the "Eightballs." The 93rd Bomb Group was created from 44th personnel and was activated at Barkesdale Field on 1 March 1942. Later two further splits formed "Killer" Kane's 98th Bomb Group, which was dispatched to North Africa, and the 90th Bomb Group, which went to the South West Pacific, where it became famous as the "Jolly Rogers." The 93rd Bomb Group under the command of Colonel (later Brigadier-General) Ted Timberlake completed its first phase of training on 15 May 1942 when it moved to Fort Myers, Florida. There it remained for almost three months while Staff secured supplies and organized the men into combat crews. The 93rd - and the 44th – flew anti-submarine patrols over the Gulf of Mexico and along the coast of Cuba. In all, three U-boat kills were credited to the 93rd, one of which went to Lieutenant John Jerstad. On 2 August the 93rd began leaving Fort Myers for Fort Dix and the journey on slow troop trains took about 13 days. The ground echelon's stay was a short one and they soon embarked for Great Britain. The air echelon, however, did not follow overseas immediately but was transferred to Grenier Field, New Hampshire, where it was to make its final preparations for overseas duty and to receive its brand-new B-24Ds. The 404th Squadron had been re-deployed during training and it was not until March 1943 that the 506th Squadron was to join the Group.

32 At Grenier Field, New Hampshire on 17 August Murphy's crew spent a restless and expectant morning sitting around the operations-room awaiting the arrival of their new aircraft. It was eventually ferried in about midday and Murphy and his men went out to inspect it. They were not told that the ferry pilot had been glad to get out of it, claiming that it was jinxed - which was perhaps just as well. Having completed their inspection they were confronted with the problem of finding a name for it. It so happened that a current pursuit of the men on the base was that of rolling dice and this was often accompanied by the expression, "Shoot Luke, you're faded." After some discussion one member of the crew offered this phrase as a name and eventually, abbreviated to "Shoot Luke', it was adopted; a typically informal beginning for one of the most famous B-24s in the ETO.

33 The 93rd Bomb Group ground echelon in the *Queen Elizabeth* docked at Greenock on the night of 4 September. Unloading commenced the following day and by 1630 hours the last of the men had arrived at Greenock railway station where they were piped aboard their train by a Scottish band. Alconbury airfield was only partially completed on their arrival and afforded little luxury with only a few billets having been erected. This caused widespread problems, not least for the two Squadrons, which had to sleep under canvas in a field of mud. Shortly after their arrival the men attended various lectures and received briefings on English social customs, mail security and RAF operational procedures. Amid rumors of yet another "split" on 26 July 1942 the 'Eightballs' were suddenly ordered to move to Will Rogers Field, Oklahoma and pick up some LB-30 Liberators to begin training for overseas duty. On 30 August the air echelon moved to Grenier Field while the ground echelon prepared to move to Fort Dix two days later. While still at Grenier Field, the 44th CO, Colonel Frank H. Robinson decided that the Eightballs should have their own insignia and a winged Eightball was painted on the nose of each aircraft. When the 44th began flying in England the Group became "The Flying Eightballs." In August an echelon of the 66th Squadron left for Cheddington. It remained there until it was reunited with the 67th and 68th Squadrons at Shipdham in early October that same year.

34 At Shipdham the 44th replaced Marauders of the 319th Medium Bomb Group who had been in Norfolk since September. During mid November the Marauders began to leave for Operation *Torch* in North Africa. The 44th was confined to base for 5 weeks before being permitted to visit Norwich and the surrounding villages although the RAF liaison officer on the base did invite some WAAFs over for a party from near-by Swanton Morley in an attempt to alleviate the boredom of such confinement. Crews were separated from their Liberators for 6 weeks while modifications were made at Langford Lodge in Northern Ireland. Armament underwent several field modifications. Machine guns on the early B-24Ds had to be reloaded by hand with drums containing only 36 rounds of ammunition. These were changed to automatic belt feed systems, which increased the rate of automatic fire to several hundred rounds. New 0.50 caliber machine guns were installed in the vulnerable nose section and even "twin fifties" fitted in the field were made to protrude from the glasshouse. Either the bombardier or the navigator had to lie on his stomach to fire them. However they had the advantage of offering very little wind resistance and were much lighter than the later nose turrets which were installed to combat head-on attacks. Bill Cameron viewed the makeshift gun installations with some skepticism but they proved effective and the *Luftwaffe* soon learned the lesson they taught and reverted to conventional pursuit tactics.

35 The 92nd Bomb Group flew a diversionary feint along the French coast while 6 B-17s in the 97th attacked St. Omer- Longuenesse airfield. In all, 49 B-17s were despatched this day.

36 B-17 41-24397 *Phyllis* was salvaged for scrap.

37 Late in 1942 the 8th Air Force lost all its P-38 Lightnings when they went to North Africa with the 12th Air Force. The decision must have been bitterly regretted for it was not until 15 October 1943, the day following the Schweinfurt disaster, that the Lightning re-entered combat in England when the 55th Fighter Group at Nuthampstead became operational on the P-38H. The "H" had a combat radius of 400 miles. During early November 1943 individual squadrons of the 20th Fighter Group, which had been busy working up on the P-38H at King's Cliffe since August, flew missions as a fourth squadron in the 55th. They would not fly their first full Group mission until 28 December 1943.

38 T/Sgt Erwin Wissenbeck, who was knocked out of his top turret, came to and found Olsen was leaning far out of his seat, bleeding profusely and Joseph N. Gates was slumped over his wheel. Also dead were T/Sgt Thomas W Dynan, radioman, S/Sgt Bruce Nicholson, waist gunner, Wilder and Kaylor. ' Wissenbeck was the only other crewman to bale out.

39 *Luftwaffe* slang for "ship."

40 Slang for very large aircraft.

41 Stammberger's victim was either *Snoozy II* or 41-9018 of the 327th Bomb Squadron, 92nd Bomb Group flown by Lieutenant Francis H. Chorak, which went down in the Channel. 1 crewman evaded, 5 KIA and three taken prisoner

42 A second 93rd Bomb Group B-24 crash-landed at Northolt.

43 Mietusch's Stirling/B-17 victim may have been 41-24362 flown by Lieutenant Donald M. Swenson in the 419th Bomb Squadron, 301st Bomb Group. Swenson ditched in the Channel and ASR rescued the crew. Or it may have been 1st Lieutenant James M. Stewart's *Man O'War* in the 92nd Bomb Group, which lost the No.2 engine then both outboard engines began to overheat and lose power. Stewart nursed the ailing ship to the Channel and was also prepared to ditch until a lone Spitfire flown by Flight Lieutenant A. J. Andrews of 91 Squadron turned up and guided him safely to Manston.

44 Officially, 41-23678 *Bathtub Bessie/Big Eagle* in the 330th Bomb Squadron flown by Captain Alexander Simpson was shot down by flak and crashed near Lille but this may be the kill claimed by Priller. Simpson and two others survived and were made PoW while one crewman evaded and 6 were KIA. Or it may have been the 93rd Bomb Group B-24, which actually crash-landed at Northolt.

45 With so many gunners firing at the same targets it was inevitable that "scores" would be duplicated. When the heat of the Lille battle had died away the American gunner's scores were whittled down to 25-38-44 and finally 21-21-15. The Germans actually lost only one fighter.

46 83 B-17s and 24 B-24s of the 93rd were despatched, while 17 B-17s of the 11th CCRC were to bomb Cherbourg.

47 Pens were poor targets, small in area and protected by reinforced concrete roofs, 16ft thick. A drop from 16,000ft gave a 1600lb armor-piercing bomb impact velocity enough, about 860ft per second, to penetrate almost 8 inches of armor.

48 *Francis X*, flown by Lieutenant Francis X. Schwarzenbeck in the 342nd Bomb Squadron, *Johnny Reb*, piloted by Lieutenant Milton M. Stenstrom and 41-24344 flown by Captain John M. Bennett, both in the 414th Bomb Squadron.

49 On 25 October 1942 the 93rd Bomb Group's 330th Squadron was transferred to Holmsley South, Hampshire, for anti-submarine duties with RAF Coastal Command over the Bay of Biscay. Similarly, the 409th operated from St. Eval in Cornwall and both Squadrons provided long-range convoy protection duties for the Operation *Torch* invasion fleet, scouring the Bay of Biscay for up to 12 hours at a time looking for elusive U-boats. Despite a handful of sightings no attacks were made but two *Luftwaffe* incursions were countered in November. The most memorable clash occurred on the 21st when Major Ramsay D. Potts in the 330th was

faced with an onslaught of 5 Junkers Ju 88s. Undaunted, the Liberator gunners, aided by the Germans' cumbersome approach, dispatched two and damaged a third. The two Squadrons returned to Alconbury in late November. Sandwiched between the 409th's arrival on the 26th and the 330th's on the 28th, the 329th Squadron was transferred to Hardwick, Norfolk, to operate in conjunction with the 44th. Until the Squadron's move to Norfolk, the 93rd had not suffered any further operational losses in its 8 missions following the first to Lille. However an entire crew perished on 30 October when their Liberator crashed on an internal flight in Somerset. During November the 2nd Bombardment Wing, with its HQ at Old Catton, Norwich was charged with training air units for eventual posting to North Africa. However it was soon selected to control all B-24 Groups and in early November it was announced that the 93rd would soon transfer to that Wing.

50 41-24388.

51 On 17 November Major John Knox, the 341st Bomb Squadron CO, took off from Predannack in 42-2969 with General Duncan aboard. Duncan was part of Major General Carl Spaatz's party who were flying to Gibraltar to talk to General Eisenhower about creating a unified air command. Duncan's B-17 flew seperately from the others and he carried a duplicate set of papers. About 75 miles off the French coast, Knox's Fortress experienced engine failure, caught fire and was ditched. It broke up in the rough seas and everyone on board perished. The 409th Bomb Squadron participated in a fruitless search for the Fortress. Tibbets remembers that Duncan was "a fine airman and a real gentleman who had been chosen to play a major part in the air war in Africa."

Chapter 3:

52 For three months the 97th Bomb Group and to a lesser extent the 301st Bomb Group, had pioneered American daylight bombing from England. Thanks to their sacrifices, immediate changes were made in air policy and subsequent arrivals in England would come to thank them for it. The 8th also lost 4 fighter groups in the transfer to the 12th Air Force.

53 The Eightballs got their first opportunity to prove themselves when 8 B-24s, each displaying the characteristic Flying Eightball emblem, flew a diversionary sweep for the Fortresses, attacking positions at Cap de la Hague in Holland. The B-24 Group's introduction to combat would probably have been sooner had it not been for the unserviceability of some of their Liberators and the transfer of several machines to anti-submarine duties.

54 Major William Wyler, the famous Hollywood director who had produced *Mrs Miniver* in 1941, was sent to England late in 1942 to make a documentary about 8th Air Force operations, principally for American cinema audiences. Wyler was given a great deal of help by General Eaker and his subordinate staff, not least Lieutenant Colonel Beirne Lay, Jr., a Hollywood screen writer with *I Wanted Wings* among his list of credits. Wyler headed for Bassingbourn and was given more help by Colonel Stanley T. Wray, CO of the 91st Bomb Group, affectionately known as "Wray's Wragged Irregulars." Filming for the morale-boosting documentary began early in 1943 after bad weather had delayed its start. On occasion additional scenes were shot at other bases and ground shots were interspliced with real live action over the continent. Five combat photographers were MIA aboard planes, which FTR from raids over the continent. By the spring of 1943 several B-17s at Bassingbourn were running neck and neck for the honor of being the first to complete 25 missions. One Fortress, which caught Wyler's lens more than most, probably because of its emotive and eye catching name, was the *Memphis Belle,* which was piloted by Captain Robert K. Morgan of Asheville, North Carolina. During crew training at Walla Walla, Washington, he had met Miss Margaret Polk of Memphis, Tennessee who was visiting her sister in Walla Walla. The romance between the pilot and the Memphis girl flourished for a time and Morgan flew over the French sub pens and German dockyards in a sweater knitted by Margaret. A Hollywood scriptwriter would have had them married and flying off into the sunset but war was no respecter of tradition and Morgan and Margaret later married other partners. The legendary artwork, though, remained indelibly painted on the nose of the B-17 through thick and thin.

55 5 men were killed aboard 41-24472. Adams successfully evaded and later returned to England on 24 April.

56 The 44th and 93rd Bomb Groups between them despatched 12 B-24Ds on the St. Nazaire raid.

57 Hartin evaded and spent 5 days at large in France before being rescued by the Underground and he was eventually escorted to Spain and safety.

58 Check was KIA on 26.6.43 while on his 25th and final mission.

59 B-24D 41-23745 *Katy Bug* crashed at Alconbury killing 4 of the crew.

60 Nine of Lieutenant Ralph J. Gaston's crew survived and they were taken prisoner. Later, the German fighter pilots that had shot them down visited them in hospital. The B-17 flown by Lieutenant Robert W. Seelos also came in for heavy attention by enemy fighters and flak. Fragments from a 88mm shell hit his navigator Lieutenant Charles G. Grimes in the small of his back. "Pappy," as he was affectionately known because he was older than most, managed to call on intercom to his pilot, "Seelos, I'm hit bad,' before he died. John King the co pilot was wounded by the same burst of flak. Robert Dresp, the co pilot in another ship, was severely injured in the buttock and he also suffered massive internal injuries but despite his wounds he tried to help his pilot James M. Ferguson handle the plane on the way home. After landing Dresp was taken to the 2nd General Hospital at Oxford where he died several weeks later. The return home of the bodies of good friends like "Pappy" Grimes had a greater impact on crews and ground personnel than the loss of a plane and crew and his death hit the group hard.

61 The B-17E was equipped with four .30 caliber flexible machine-gun mountings but they had to be operated by the bombardier who was already over-committed. Whichever mounting he used, it only offered a very poor field of fire. Navigators could also operate a flexible mounted 5 Browning machine-gun from enlarged windows (often called "cheek" guns) either side of the nose but these suffered from the same problems as the bombardier's position. In each case a blind spot was left in front which neither the ball turret or upper turret could cover. The 91st lost two bombers to head-on attacks and the commanders of the 322nd and 323rd Squadrons, the group navigator, bombardier and gunnery officers, were among the casualties. Two other B-17s were badly hit, one of which crashed near Leavesden, Hertfordshire while trying to make it home to Bassingbourn and three of the crew were killed. *Quitchurbitchin'* was the only 91st B-17 to return. The 303rd Bomb Group suffered its first loss when 41-24568 *Lady Fairweather* in the 358th Bomb Squadron was shot down in flames near the target to crash in the sea with the loss of all 10 crew. Lieutenant Clay Isbell's B-17 in the 306th Bomb Group was shot down on the bomb run. Isbell and 6 of his crew were trapped when the Fortress exploded. Because of the head-on attacks enterprising armament chiefs experimented with tail guns in the nose but the problem would only be solved when chin turrets were fitted during assembly. By the end of 1942, Fortresses arriving in England needed well in excess of 100 urgent modifications before they were considered combat-worthy.

62 Eder had joined JG 51 on the Channel coast in December 1940 but he did not achieve and kills. Transferred to the East for Barbarossa, he destroyed 10 Soviet aircraft before being badly wounded on 24.7.41. In 1942 he returned to operations with 7/JG 2.

63 Early in December the 305th Bomb Group moved from Grafton "Undermud" to the mud at Chelveston, late home of the 301st Bomb Group.

64 On 27 November 8 Liberators and crews in the 329th Bomb Squadron, 93rd Bomb Group had transferred to Hardwick 11 miles south of Norwich, in order to evaluate the *Gee* navigational device for USAAF use to fly "intruder" or "moling" flights over Germany. These were an attempt to disrupt working schedules in German factories by causing air-raid warnings to sound, upsetting civilian morale and impairing industrial output. After only a week at Hardwick the 329th moved to Flixton airfield just outside Bungay. Flixton was still in the throes of development when the 329th arrived. The first intruder or 'moling' mission was undertaken on 2 January 1943 when 4 *Gee*-equipped B-24s took off for various parts of the Ruhr. Radio transmitters spaced at intervals throughout Great Britain beamed out given radio signals, which were picked up by the *Gee*-carrying bombers. The time lag between the signals received, after certain calculations, indicated the B-24s' exact position. Operating singly, because of the flight's experimental nature, the 329th lost the concentrated firepower that formation flying afforded it. However diminishing cloud on this first "moling" mission forced the Liberators to return to Flixton. Six more attempts were made - the last on 28 March. The project was subsequently abandoned and the 329th supplemented the 44th Bomb Group on conventional missions after its secret equipment had been removed. The experience had been rewarding, however and some crews later formed the nucleus of the USAAF Pathfinder units set up to perfect blind-bombing techniques.

65 On the morning of 6 December 24 Liberators in the 328th, 330th and 409th Squadrons took off from Alconbury for Portreath in Cornwall where they were refueled for the long oversea flight to Oran. A few ground crews had been carried with them for this purpose while those that remained at Alconbury prepared to travel to Hardwick. On the morning of 7 December the formation droned over the sea and headed south. Crews stripped off their heavy combat clothes as they flew through bright sunny skies. The 328th and 409th Squadrons broke off and headed for Tafaroui airfield but the 330th experienced difficulties. Three Liberators deviated from their course heading and were fired upon by Spanish Moroccan coastal batteries. One of the 330th Bomb Squadron B-24Ds crashed into a mountain south of Tafaroui and all on board were killed. The '10-day' detachment extended to almost three months. Finally, on the night of 25 February the 93rd took off from Gambut and headed back to England. The flight was marred by the loss of the 8th B-24D of their campaign.

66 *Cherry* in the 422nd Squadron, flown by William A Prentice was possibly the victim of *Unteroffizier* Heinrich Schnell of 3./JG 26, who claimed a bomber west of Etaples, or Major Gerhard "Gerd" Schöpfel commanding II./JG 26, who also claimed a bomber shot down. All except Lieutenants Henry J. Webber and Harry O. Williams, who both parachuted to safety, were killed. Williams died a few days later of infection in a wound to his thigh. Eyewitnesses credited the tail gunner, Sgt Leaham Bryant, with shooting down the fighter as *Cherry* hurtled down. Sgt Norman E. Olson was also given credit for a "probable". Schnell was KIA in Russia on 17 February 1943.

67 It was Ehler's 17th confirmed kill, Wloschinski's first.

68 On 6 December.1./JG 26 lost one of its most promising pilots in the air combats near Etaples when *Leutnant* Graf Uiberacker did not return from his 169th "*Feindflug*." Two days previously he had claimed his seventh victim in air combat.

69 On 8 December a VIII Bomber Command study of air attacks on U-boat opens indicated that available U.S. bombs were incapable of penetrating roofs of the pens from any bombing level low enough to maintain accuracy. Next day a special report on the first 1100 bombers dispatched by VIII Bomber Command 17 August-23 November, justified high-level daylight precision bombing.

70 The 306th returned to combat status, putting up 18 Fortresses for no loss.

71 On this mission 41-24585 *Wulf Hound,* became the second aircraft lost by the 303rd Bomb Group when it was force-landed on the continent and the *Luftwaffe* later put it into service.

72 Only the 303rd had bombed the marshaling yards, losing two B-17s in the attempt, so a return was ordered. However, the weather intervened again and for 8 days Eaker used the time to build up his aircraft strength.

73 80 B-17s of the 91st, 303rd, 305th and 306th Bomb Groups.

74 Schöpfel, who had scored 22 victories in 1940 including 4 Hurricanes on 18 August 1940, was credited with a B-17 kill to take his score to 46. He left the *Geschwader* on 10 January 1943 to become Operations Officer of *Jafü* Brittany, the fighter control unit defending

the U boat bases and survived the war with 40 victories. "Pips" Priller, who at the time had 81 victories, replaced Schöpfel as JG 26 Kommodore.

75 41-24452.

76 41-24432 *Danellen* flown by Lieutenant Dan W. Carson.

77 Tomek baled out and landed in a French garden. He was in no condition to make good his escape because he had been wounded in the hand by a 20mm shell and had broken his ankle in the landing. Tomek was taken to hospital in Paris, treated for his wounds and later sent to PoW camp where he remained for the rest of the war.

78 41-24512 in the 32nd Bomb Squadron. *Rose O' Day* and Lieutenant Ralph A. Felton, Jr.'s crew FTR on 4 March 1943 when it ditched in the Zuider Zee (7 KIA. 3 PoW).

79 At the end of 1942 the P-47 was the only readily available American produced high performance fighter. 200 were sent to Britain in December 1942 and January 1943. At Bovingdon airfield near Bushey Hall, VIII Fighter Command HQ, test pilot Major Cass Hough flew a number of flight tests in a P-47C. In a power dive he experienced compressibility, the vice-like action of air as the speed of sound is approached. Comparison tests by other pilots against captured *Luftwaffe* fighters operated by the RAF revealed the following: At altitudes up to 15,000ft the Bf 109G and FW 190A had all-round better performance than the P-47C, most notably in rate of climb. The P-47's performance progressively improved above 15,000ft and between 25,000 to 30,000ft it surpassed those of the enemy fighters except for rate of climb and acceleration but then the P-47 was double the weight of a Bf 109 and half as much again as the FW 190. Under full power in level flight the Thunderbolt was faster than both enemy machines above 15,000ft, the advantage rising to as much as 20-30mph at 30,000ft. Although the 109 and 190 could initially accelerate well in a dive, the P-47C soon overhauled them and easily out-dived both from high altitudes. The P-47C could turn with the 109 and 190 provided its speed kept above 200 mph. P-47 pilots were advised to avoid combats at low altitudes and slow speeds and never to try climbing away from an enemy unless having gained good momentum in a dive. A Bf 109G averaged 11 minutes to climb from near ground level to 30,000ft and FW 190 14 minutes, while a P-47 needed 20 minutes.

80 B-17 42-3288 *Green Fury II* in the 338th Bomb Squadron, 96th Bomb Group piloted by 1st Lieutenant Stanley P. Budleski. *Green Fury II* dived out of control, crashing on Nordeney Island with the loss of 6 crew. 4 men were made PoW. Swoboda baled out and reached the ground uninjured.

81 Their nickname originated from an American war correspondent who writing in *The Saturday Evening Post,* said that the squadron reminded him of a bunch of clay pigeons. The name stuck! (During October 1942-August 1943 the 367th suffered the heaviest losses in VIIIth Bomber Command).

82 B-17F 42-5071.

83 Nygaard was burned on the face and arms. He went out of the nose hatch, followed by the bombardier, Lieutenant John S. Trost. The only other survivor was Lieutenant Frank Leasman, navigator, who was caught under debris until the engineer freed him. With the B-17 still upside down and at about 4000ft, Leasman climbed out of the nose hatch and then jumped up as the Fortress passed under him. For a time Leasman evaded capture after being rescued by a French girl in the Resistance but he was captured later. Trost successfully evaded and on 9 February he crossed the Pyrenees on foot into Spain. He eventually reached Gibraltar on 21 April and was back in London within three days.

84 41-24495.

85 McKee evaded capture and was back in England on 26 January 1943. The 8 men in his crew who baled out were captured.

86 41-24489 in the 367th Bomb Squadron.

87 McKesson and 6 of his crew survived. The *Clay Pigeons* Squadron's original complement of 9 crews now numbered just three. American gunners claimed 53 enemy fighters shot down. These claims were later reduced to 21 confirmed but in fact JG 26 lost 1 fighter and its pilot, while III./JG two lost two pilots killed. As far as the bombing went, just 72 of the heavies were effective over the target at Romilly 1 of the bombs dropped had hit a German mess hall killing 200 of the enemy.

88 In October 1940 after being rejected by the RCAF because he was one inch too short, Gordon had joined the 7th Bombardment Group. When the Group departed for Salt Lake City, prior to going overseas, Shorty was left behind to do three months' hard labor for being improperly dressed. On 7 December 1941, his sentence completed, he intended to join the "Flying Tigers" as a ground man. But the Japanese attack on Pearl Harbor changed all that and he threw up his job as armorer to take up aerial gunnery. In England Shorty's disciplinary record while on the ground did not improve and LeMay was forced repeatedly to "bust" him to Private. However, the 305th needed men like Gordon. Experienced gunners were few and far between and already cooks, clerks, medical orderlies and truck drivers, *et al,* were being used as crew replacements. To get around the problem, when Shorty went on a mission he had his stripes returned to him but, on the ground once more, he became a Private again.

89 B-17 42-29664 in the 358th Bomb Squadron.

90 Two other 303rd Bomb Group Fortresses were MIA with 9 men KIA and a further 11 PoW.

91 *Little Beaver*'s supercharger failures would plague her crew for some time to come. Major Donald MacDonald treated his Squadron's malfunctions with skepticism and recriminations followed. The crew of *Little Beaver* were not credited with the mission because of their abort. Bill Cameron wrote: "I began to realize that the price of a ticket back to the ZI might be pretty high." Inexperience was the main problem, as he remembers: "Fortresses had a larger wing area than the B-24s and were somewhat easier to fly in formation, especially at high altitude. Straight and level, as on a bomb run, both were good platforms, but in formation there was probably more jockeying of controls and throttles in the B-24s. We often had one pilot on the controls and the other on the throttles for this reason. We had problems to begin with on the superchargers because we made heavy corrections, pulling off power while flying formation to keep from overrunning the aircraft. However the superchargers continued to rain air into the closed carburetors and the engines would then cut out completely. We later overcame the problem to some extent by trying to fly using the supercharger controls rather than the throttles for such speed adjustments. This was difficult and not always successful. All this was necessary when the Group was flying a tight formation but if the lead ship started evasive action, then we had problems. Later when we had power controls (usually referred to as the 'formation stick') and the superchargers were changed from levers to rheostatic-type controls, these problems were eliminated. But they were real at the time and many aircraft turned back because their superchargers had been blown out trying to stay in formation. We were untrained in formation flying at high altitude until we arrived in England but with experience the problem was eventually solved after a few months." Because of the high rate of ammunition expended the 44th began carrying boxes of additional ammunition on the catwalk of the bomb bays. They had to wait two weeks before their adoption was complete. There then followed an unbroken series of scrubbed missions for the Group. Bad weather was a prime cause and morale began to slump. Over the next few months the 44th remained in the wings of the European Theater while Fortress units attacked in strength. Any aspirations the 44th had of doing the same were thwarted by requests for diversionary sweeps and then by attrition meted out by the *Luftwaffe*. Spares were slow getting through and the 67th Bomb Squadron felt the squeeze most in the coming weeks.

92 Major Algene Key, CO of the 66th Squadron was awarded the Distinguished Service Cross for his leadership on the raid.

93 The 303rd Bomb Group had put up 21 Fortresses for the raid and B-17F 41-24566 *Zombie* was shot down by enemy fighters with the loss of all the crew. B-17F 41-24581 *The 8 Ball* in the 358th Bomb Squadron was badly damaged and made an emergency landing and was written off at Bovingdon after 8 members of the crew had baled out.

94 Born 28 May 1905 at Rockford, Ill. Graduated from USMA, West Point and commissioned in the artillery June 1927. Detailed for flying training in July 1929, graduating from Brooks and Kelly Fields, Texas. In June 1930 assigned to Langley Field, VA, as Operations Officer 49th Bomb Squadron and of the parent 2nd Bomb Group in July 1933. February-June 1934 he was involved in the Army Air Mail operation in the eastern USA, thereafter entering the ACTS at Maxwell Field where, after graduating in spring 1935, he remained as a bombardment instructor. Promoted Captain, June 1937. In July 1939 assigned to the Operations and Training Division of the WD/GS in Washington. While in this he contributed to a number of Air Corps documents including the influential AWPD-l. Promoted Major (temporary) in December 1940. In November 1941 he was made Assistant Secretary WD/GS and received temporary promotion to Lieutenant Colonel in January 1942 and less than a month later, to Brigadier General. In March he became Deputy C of S, HQ AAF. Assigned to the 8th Air Force in October 1942 commanding the 1st Bomb Wing until the end of the year. In January 1943 Brigadier General Kuter went to North Africa serving on Eisenhower's staff and becoming Deputy Commander, NAAF in April. Recalled to Washington in May 1943 he was designated Assistant Chief of AS for Plans. For two years he prepared the studies for and determined the means to implement operations against major objectives in all theaters; as Arnold's senior planning member he attended the JCS conferences at Quebec, Cairo and London and represented Arnold at Malta and Yalta. Promoted to Major General (temporary) in February 1944. In May 1945 sent to the Mariana's as Deputy Commander, AAF, POA, to organize the U.S. Strategic Air Forces in the Pacific.

95 Born 1903. Flying training in the early 1920s. Member of the Air Corps aerobatic and demonstration team 1931-35. Instructor at ACTS in Air Force Section, 1935-1938. Graduated Army C & GS School, 1939. Chief, Strategic Intelligence Section, Office of Chief of AC, 1940. Chief, European Branch, Air War Plans Division, HQ AAF in 1941 being a member of the team that produced AWPD-1. Member of the Joint Strategic Committee, JCS, 1942. In summer 1942 promoted Brigadier General and sent to UK as Deputy Theater Air Officer, ETO. Headed team producing AWPD-42. Commanded 3rd Bomb Wing from early December 1942 and the following month assumed command of the 1st Bomb Wing, directing operations of B-17 groups until June 1943. Assigned as Deputy to C in C, AEAF, returning to Washington later in the year to serve on Joint Plans Committee, JCS. In April 1944 he became Deputy CS AAF and CS, 20th Air Force, directing B-29 operations. Assigned as CG, XXI Bomber Command in August 1944 and moved to Mariana's with the B-29 force. Recalled to USA in January 1945 to direct B-29 training operations.

96 All ten members of Lieutenant Love's crew in 42-5078 in the 366th Bomb Squadron were killed.

97 Captain Tribbett, his crew and a lead navigator were KIA on the 26 February 1943 mission to Wilhelmshaven in *Arkie*.

98 Of the survivors, a gunner, S/Sgt Alan E. Magee of the 360th Bomb Squadron, had an incredible escape. Flying in 41-24260 *Snap! Crackle! Pop!* Magee received at least 28 wounds and was tossed out of the burning B-17 without a parachute. As he was falling he blacked out and crashed through the roof of St. Nazaire railway station. A German doctor saved his arm, which was almost torn off and he treated him for injuries to teeth, leg, knee and ankles. Magee was well cared for by the Germans in hospital and survived as a PoW. 2nd Lieutenant G. M. Herrington, the navigator of the same aircraft, lost a leg due to enemy gunfire. He became one of the first USAAF men to be repatriated and later married the nurse who treated him in a Washington hospital.

99 Major William Lanford, 368th Squadron, 306th Bomb Group CO, led the Group's remaining ships back to England where bad weather forced them to seek shelter in Cornwall.

Three days later they set off for Thurleigh but the formation strayed south, over the Channel Islands and they were bracketed by flak. One Fort piloted by Lieutenant Robert E. Brandon was lost and the crew were lost without trace. It was not until 8 January that the formation finally made it back to Thurleigh. By then the Group had a new CO. The irrepressible Colonel Frank Armstrong, Jr., took command of the battle-weary 306th Bomb Group at Thurleigh in succession to Colonel Overacker. On 17 January Lanford was summoned to Eaker's HQ. The RAF had "raised hell" because it lost two planes in the search for Brandon's aircraft. Eaker told Lanford, "I haven't seen you since I pinned that medal on you. You've been an outstanding commander in this theater but you made a mistake and you are going to pay for it. Chip tells me you want to go home. [Lanford had a new son born since leaving for England.] If you stay in England I assure you I'll give you your rank back and probably one more promotion." Lanford thus became the second of the original squadron commanders to leave Thurleigh. See *First Over Germany; A History of the 306th Bomb Group* by Russell A. Strong.

100 Eventually, all elements returned to Shipdham on 8 January.

101 III./JG 2 claimed 15 victories, all of which were confirmed. *The JG 26 War Diary Vol.2* by Donald Caldwell. Grub Street, London. 1998.

102 Bill Cameron recalls: "The St. Nazaire debacle was the official reason given for Colonel Robinson's dismissal. 8th Air Force HQ blamed him for not ensuring that the aircraft had enough fuel for the mission. However some believed Headquarters used the incident to relieve Robinson of his command because he continually complained of the lack of sufficient replacements in the light of increasing losses. He could not always send out the Group on missions although ordered to do so by HQ because at the time the 44th was losing aircraft and crews faster than they could be replaced. Six months later Colonel Leon Johnson said much the same thing but by then the arguments were much better understood and he was respected for them rather than sacked."

103 Eaker's aide James Parton confirms in *Air Force Spoken Here,* his biography of Eaker that he was unimpressed with Overacker's outfit, which unlike the other two groups appeared slovenly and undisciplined. Parton indicated as much to Overacker and the Royal visit then went "pretty much like the others, but there was a notable absence of spit and polish." Eaker told "Tooey" Spaatz that he had better relieve Overacker, but the general waited 6 more weeks, by which time the 306th's bombing and loss record was the worst in VIIIth Bomber Command, Something had to be done.

104 In 1946, while many people's thoughts turned to peace, others were still thinking of war. Beirne Lay, Jr., who was working for MGM on *Above and Beyond,* another aviation film, received an interesting approach from Sy Bartlett, who as a major had been General Spaatz's aide. Bartlett was now working as a screenwriter at 20th Century-Fox Studios and he wanted Lay to co-write a book and screenplay about the air war called *Twelve O'Clock High.* The central character was "General Frank Savage" who was modeled on none other than Brigadier General Frank Armstrong, with whom he had struck up a close friendship in WWII. It was Lay who came up with the fictionalized 918th Bomb Group commanded by Savage, which he arrived at by taking the 306th Bomb Group and multiplying it by three. The leading players featured in *Twelve O'Clock High* are based on men such as Generals Eaker and Armstrong, as well as group commanders and their crews generally, who not only shaped the future of the 8th Air Force, but who affected the evolution of the 306th Bomb Group also. The actual incident (the morning of 4 January when Eaker, Armstrong and Beirne Lay arrived at Thurleigh from HQ in the wake of the St. Nazaire debacle the day before) where General Eaker arrives at the guard post only to be waved through without the necessary military courtesies is re-enacted for the cameras. Eaker is portrayed as "Major General Patrick Pritchard.' Likable, decent, Colonel Keith Davenport, aka Chip Overacker, played by Gary Merrill, is popular with his crews, but he cannot prevent the high losses, delegate, nor impose the strong discipline needed to change things. He is replaced by resolute hard taskmaster and West Pointer Frank Savage, aka Gregory Peck. Savage uncompromisingly sweeps info office not so much a new broom, but like a whirlwind. Gradually, he earns his crew's grudging respect, but not their devotion. He does not seek it. He requires only their obedience instilled by military discipline, both in the air and on the ground. Training, training and more training follow, until the 918th's poor formation flying is improved. Savage knows that wallowing in self-pity and calling themselves the "Hard Luck Group" is not going to help the air crews, least of all place bombs squarely on target, the reason for their entire being. In what is arguably the most memorable scene in the movie, in the briefing room Savage finally brings the crews to the reality of their situation with swift, sharp, shock treatment. He stuns his new charges (and the audience) with a well-directed bucket of ice-cold water more accurate than a bomb strike. It chills every spine in the room and in every theater across the country. Savage fires from the hip and tells them straight - "You're not going home. You're going to die. In fact, consider yourselves already dead!" In the case of Frank Savage we witness his steady mental decline as battle fatigue overtakes and finally engulfs this remarkable leader of men. Ultimately, Savage allows the full weight of responsibility to fall squarely on his shoulders and his alone, much in the same way that events had overtaken Davenport. Savage continues to fly missions when it is not essential or required of him to do so. He insists on leading from the front as if he still has something to prove to his men, He begins to crack and then suffers the final painful mental breakdown at planeside prior to a mission. He is so wracked with mental fatigue that he cannot summon strength in his arms to lift himself up and into the nose of his B-17. This final part of Frank Savage's persona is not based on General Armstrong at all, but the incident, as Lay confirmed did happen to "a very fine commander." It seems that this "very fine commander' was another regular officer, Brigadier General Newton L. Longfellow. In 1948 with the novel nearing publication Fox became very interested in the possibility of a screenplay of the same name and studio head Darryl F. Zanuck promptly purchased the movie rights. The central theme in the movie version would be the gradual and ultimate destruction of General Savage, played superbly by Gregory Peck. *Twelve O'Clock High* draws upon the 306th Group's troubled early combat history and its effect on the combat crews.

105 41-24601 in the 365th Bomb Squadron crashed at Lille with the loss of all 10 crew. Two B-17s in the 369th Bomb Squadron, 306th Bomb Group were lost over Marq en Baroeul at Lille, France. 41-24498 flown by 1st Lieutenant Jack A. Spaulding, returning to flying after illness, was killed, along with 5 of his crew (4 PoW) and 41-24471 *Four of A Kind* flown by Captain James A. Johnston who was killed along with 2 other crew (7 PoW) were involved in a mid-air collision. Ten Fortresses were damaged. Gunners claimed 6 fighters destroyed and 13 probably destroyed.

106 On 20 December the *Luftwaffe* had made its attacks from dead ahead, or 12 o'clock level. Closing speeds of around 550mph made it difficult to keep targets in effective firing range for more than a split second and there was always the fear of collision at the back of the German pilots' minds. Larger attacking formations and simultaneous attacks by fighters rather than in trail were to be used. While they would still use the head-on approach, the angle of attack would be from 10 degrees above the horizontal - otherwise known as 12 o'clock high, which in experiments were found to be more effective. As before, the best chance of knocking a bomber out of formation was to kill the pilots in the cockpit.

107 Five bombers were shot down and many returned badly damaged by flak and enemy fighters. The 303rd, which flew its 11th mission, had despatched 21 B-17s from Molesworth but only 12 returned to base. Of these 5 were damaged, three of them extensively. 41-24606 *Werewolf* in the 358th Bomb Squadron limped back on one engine. Lieutenant Oxrider ordered his crew of 9 to bale out over the south coast and he then landed *Werewolf* in the grounds of a mental hospital in Dawlish, South Devon. Later, the aircraft was fitted with three new engines and in order to make a runway 2500ft long so that *Werewolf* could be flown out to Honington Air Depot for major repairs, trees, walls and hedges were cleared away. 41-24565 *Idaho Potato Peeler* in the 359th Bomb Squadron, flown by Lieutenant Bales made a safe crash-landing at Chipping Warden airfield with no injuries to the crew. 41-24579 *Thumper* in the 360th Bomb Squadron, flown by Lieutenant John Castle and Lieutenant Fitzimmons belly-landed at Lulsgate Bottom after 8 crewmen had baled out. S/Sgt Billie L. Stainer was killed when his parachute failed to open and 5 others were injured. 41-24587 *Bad Check* in the 417th Bomb Squadron with Captain Southworth at the controls landed at Exeter after the starboard inner engine had failed when badly damaged by flak and the wings were damaged by cannon shells from FW 190s and Bf 109s. Five aircraft were missing with the loss of 20 lives. 22 men survived and were taken prisoner and the others evaded capture. *Leutnant* Otto Stammberger's *9th Staffel*, flying from Vannes with III./JG 2, were officially credited with two of the B-17 losses while 7./JG 2 claimed four.

Chapter 4:

108 The Liberators were tasked to fly a diversionary raid on Wilhelmshaven where an earlier photo reconnaissance had revealed the pocket battleship, the *Admiral Scheer* to be in dry dock and also that considerable construction was being carried out to the docks.

109 At Molesworth Walter Cronkite of United Press and Homer Bigart of the New York *Herald* had arrived to report on the 303rd's activities. Cronkite flew the Wilhelmshaven mission on board 41-24635/S piloted by Captain Hagenbuch. Andy Rooney of Stars *and Stripes* flew in Captain William J. Casey's plane in the 306th Bomb Group.

110 Oberleutnant Hugo Frey, *Leutnant* Dieter Gerhard and *Unteroffiziers* Herbert Hanel and Lohr, the last two sharing the spoils were the claimants. (Hanel was killed just three days later, while shooting down a RAF Wellington, 35km northwest of Terschelling on 30 January. His FW 190A-4 was hit by debris and plunged into the North Sea). JG 1 lost 7 fighters and 4 pilots killed.

111 41-24637 in the 366th Bomb Squadron. 5 men survived. 5 KIA. In the 91st Bomb Group Charles "Red" Cliburn got *The Bad Penny* back to Bassingbourn with all the control cables shot away except one elevator and the ailerons. Having lost their way over the North Sea the Liberator crews wrongly identified Lemmer in Holland as Wilhelmshaven and they dropped their bombs to the north of the harbor town. Howard Adams, who had to abort the mission at 17,000ft with a clogged line to the supercharger on No.3 engine, went down to watch the others return to Shipdham after dinner and noticed that two Liberators were missing. He later found out that they were his friend and West Point classmate, 1st Lieutenant Maxwell W. Sullivan [flying *Spirit of 76*] and Lieutenant [Nolan B.] Cargile [flying 41-23690]. Both were in the 68th Bomb Squadron. "On talking with the others, I learned what had happened. As they neared the German border around 30 enemy fighters came up to meet them - mostly FW 190s and Me 109s. For around half an hour they were under attack and not being able to find their target, they dropped their bombs on a [Dutch] coastal town [at Lemmer]. During one of the numerous frontal attacks, the Huns scored a hit on Sully's No.3 engine, setting it on fire, which soon grew in fury as he dropped out of formation. Soon the fire had burnt a large section of the wing away and in no time the right wing folded back along the fuselage and Sully plummeted down [into Terschelling harbor] for his last landing. The crews in the other planes watched helplessly as his plane disintegrated in the air and fell into the sea like a burning rag. Two men were seen to jump out and float towards the sea in their parachutes. A third man jumped but his chute trailed out behind him, never seeming to open fully. Their fate is still unknown [Lieutenant Albert W. Glass was the only survivor but he had to have a leg amputated after being rescued.] A little while later another FW 190 came in on a head-on attack aiming at Cargile's plane. Either through accident or design, as he went to turn away, his wing clipped the wing and then the right tail fin of Cargile's B-24, knocking both off. The FW 190 [possibly Feldwebel Fritz Koch of 12th *Staffel* JG 1, who was apparently killed by fire from a 68th Squadron Liberator] seemed to fold up and then go into its last dive. With part of his wing gone the big B-24 dropped away like a fluttering leaf, finally going into a tight spin, its fate sealed. None of the

crew was seen to jump. Captain Wilkinson, a very swell fellow and friend, was the navigator in Sullivan's ship. As the attack continued many of our ships were shot up, but no more were knocked down. Captain James E. O'Brien had a waist gunner and bombardier killed and his navigator wounded. [O'Brien barely made it home. His bombardier, Lieutenant Reg Grant and his assistant radio operator, S/Sgt M. Deal had both been killed and his navigator, 2nd Lieutenant Leroy Perlowin, was severely wounded by a 20mm shell, which also slightly injured one of his gunners, Sgt Guilford]. Nearly every ship had a hole in it somewhere; Billings having a shell come through the cabin between him and his co-pilot. Everyone was sobered up by this raid and we're beginning to realize that war is no picnic."

112 American gunners claimed 22-14-13 enemy fighters. Again the figures were inflated: JG 1, for instance, lost just 7 FW 190A-4s and Bf 109G-ls with 4 pilots killed. It was not an especially well executed mission. Next morning at a 1st Wing meeting at his Brampton Grange HQ General Hansell, his group commanders and staff felt that the combat formations did not keep close enough together to give shielding protection, one to the other. 54 aircraft was not enough aircraft to be able to defend themselves and it was deemed that poor formation flying resulted in aircraft becoming separated and an easy prey to fighters. Poor visibility at the target made the bombing very difficult and a target as small as this should only be assigned when the weather was very clear and visibility good. Many things that later became standard operating procedures were discussed. Despite the criticisms the raid caused disquiet in Germany. In February German night fighters would be put into action against the American day formations whenever they flew without escort. The first use of night fighters of NJG 1 against American formations took place on 4 February, when 86 bombers attacked Emden, Hamm and Osnabrück. It was believed that the heavily armed Bf 110 night fighters would bolster the day fighter arm and prove effective against American day bombers but it was a false notion.

113 Having received a credit for two combat missions and a letter of commendation from General Eaker for his flight to and from North Africa.

114 41-24575 in the 365th Bomb Squadron.

115 Jabs was a seasoned combat veteran who had his first taste of action during the Battles of France and Britain when he served as a Bf 110 *Zerstörer* ("Destroyer") pilot in ZG 76. He quickly became one of the leading fighter pilots in the Bf 110 day-fighter force with 7 a/c shot down during the Battle of France and another 12 Spitfires and Hurricanes over England during the summer of 1940. Decorated with the *RitterKreuz* (*RK* or Knight's Cross) October 1940 and thereupon successfully led his 6./ZG 76 during the campaign in Crete. His *Staffel* became 9./NJG 3 in November 1941 and on completion of night fighter training Jabs became an operational night fighter pilot. He went on to claim his 1st night kill (a Stirling) on 25/26 June 1942 and was appointed *Staffelkapitän* of the elite 11./NJG 1 at Leeuwarden in November 1942. By the end of 1942 he had shot down 4 RAF night bombers. Jabs survived the war with 50 (28 night and 22 day) victories.

116 Jenkins and five of his crew were killed and 4 survived to be taken prisoner.

117 Völlkopf, a 22-year-old *Experte* with 6 confirmed *Abshüsse* in 5./NJG 2 and 9./NJG 1 was killed when his Bf 110G-4 G9+GT crashed whilst flying at low level near Rheine/Wesfalen airfield on 21 June 1943. His *Funker Unteroffizier* Heinz Huhn survived his three pilots - Oberleutnant Gildner (KIA 24/25.February 1943), *Leutnant* Oskar Köstler (killed, 9/10 April.1943) and Völlkopf - but after Völlkopf was KIA Huhn decided he had had enough and he never flew again. For the remaining years of the war he served as Operations Officer at Bergen/Alkmaar and St. Trond airfields.

118 Alfred Naumann, whose gunner was *Unteroffizier* Bärwolf, was credited with his first daylight *Abschüsse*.

119 Ground Control Interception (radar).

120 Feldwebel Erich Handke had joined 12./NJG 1 with his pilot, Feldwebel Georg "Schorsch" Kraft, in October 1942 and they were amongst the *Nachtjagd* crews ordered to fly against the American combat boxes in early 1943.

121 Apart from the two 110s that made belly landings on Ameland and near Leeuwarden 6 more Bf 110s of IV./NJG 1 were badly damaged and none of these aircraft would be serviceable to combat the RAF night bombers that night. *Leutnant* Heinz Grimm of IV./NJG 1 died on 13 October 1943 from wounds sustained over Bremen from his own flak defenses. He was awarded the *RitterKreuz* (*RK* or Knight's Cross) posthumously on 5 February 1944 for his 26 night kills and 1 B-17 on 4 February 1943.

122 Despite successfully ditching off the Dutch coast at Waddenzee all the crew were killed. Davidson had previously been the co-pilot in Cliff Pyle's crew before being made a first pilot and given his own crew. Three more B-17s, two from the 91st Bomb Group and one from the 303rd were lost on the mission. FW 190s of JG 1 claimed 10 B-17s shot down for the loss of two pilots, Oberleutnant Walter Leonhardt (*Staffelkapitän* 6./JG 1) and *Unteroffizier* Rudolf Mayer (12./JG 1).

123 B-17F-25-BO 41-24575 XK-G *Sunrise Serenader* managed to put down safely at Chelveston but it was so badly damaged it could not be taxied off the runway. The aircraft was repaired and it was later transferred to the 384th Bomb Group in September 1943. On 13 November *Sunrise Serenader* entered severe turbulence and crashed at Wargrave, Berkshire, killing 2nd Lieutenant Ralph J. Connell and 8 crewmembers. See *"John Burn One-Zero-Five...": The Story of Chelveston Airifled and the 305th Bomb Group in pictures* by William Donald. (GMS, 2005).

124 1st Lieutenant Rufus A. Oliphant and crew in *Railway Express* were shot down by enemy fighters and all the crew were killed. Captain Thomas Cramer, pilot of *Captain And His Kids* had three engines shot out in the attack but still managed to cross the Channel and put the Liberator down on a beach at Sandwich. Despite all the "Eightballs" endeavors the *Togo* remained afloat.

125 In all, 71 B-17s and 18 B-24s were despatched.

126 All ten men in Lieutenant John B. Long's crew were killed while one man survived from Billings' aircraft.

127 I./JG 2 and 9./JG 26 made aggressive attacks on the B-17 formations and 6 - two each in the 303rd, 305th and 306th Bomb Groups - were shot down. *Leutnant* Otto "Stotto" Stammberger led 9./JG 26 and hit one Fortress in the cockpit. He saw it fall from formation but was then hit in the hand and he had to dive away. He was credited with a *HSS* (*Herausschuss* or separation). From the same Staffel Feldwebel Edgar Dorre claimed a B-17 2.5km SW of Pleuradeur and *Unteroffizier* Erich Swartz claimed another Fortress 6-10km West of Ploermal. In the 303rd Bomb Group 41-24541 *Spook* in the 358th Bomb Squadron flown by Captain Lawrence G. Dunnica (6 KIA. 4 PoW) and 42-2967 *Shack Hack* in the 360th Bomb Squadron flown by Captain William H. Breed (9 KIA. 1 PoW) both crashed in the English Channel. (Bf 109s of 2/NAGr 13, a reconnaissance Staffel, claimed two B-17s over the English Channel). In the 305th Bomb Group 42-5058 *The Hun Hunter* flown by Lieutenant Henry M. Burman in the 364th Bomb Squadron crashed at Redon, France (7 KIA. 3 PoW) and 41-24611 *Boomerang* in the 422nd Bomb Squadron flown by Captain Charles J. Steenbarger crashed at Malestroit, France. (2 Evd. 1 KIA. 8 PoW). In the 306th Bomb Group 42-5175 flown by 1st Lieutenant Joseph A. Downing in the 367th Bomb Squadron and 42-5717 flown by 1st Lieutenant William H. Warner in the 423rd Bomb Squadron FTR. Downing's B-17 was heavily damaged by flak immediately after bombs away and repeated hits from FW 190s knocked out a third engine. Downing left the shelter of another Fortress, which had tried to give him protective cover, and he put the B-17 into a dive from 10,000 to 4000ft where he found some desperately need clouds in which to hide. Then he ordered the crew to bale out. 42-25175 went down in the Bay of Biscay. One man was KIA. Downing and 6 of his crew were taken prisoner. Another two evaded successfully and got to Gibraltar and Spain. (Lieutenant Howard W. Kelly, co-pilot, at one time even sat in a FW 190 at St. Brieuc airfield intending to fly it out but after an hour studying the instruments he finally concluded that he would be caught before he could get the fighter started. Kelly reached Gibraltar on 21 April and was back in England three days later). During the first attack by FW 190s, William Warner was mortally wounded by a bullet, which hit him between the eyes. His Fortress was then blasted by 6 more FW 190s in a frontal attack. T/Sgt Claiborne Wilson, engineer had to get out of his turret to help the co-pilot, Lieutenant Arnold Carlson pull back Warner's body, which was slumped forward jamming the controls. As Carlson put the B-17 into a rapid descent Wilson went through the bomb bay and into the radio compartment to alert the crew to bale out (2 Evd. 6 KIA. 2 PoW). See *First Over Germany; A History of the 306th Bomb Group* by Russell A. Strong. JG 26 claimed two of the B-17s and I/JG 2, six.

128 The 305th formation failed totally because of a bombsight malfunction in the lead aircraft.

129 The 44th's continuing losses had increased doubts in certain circles as to the value of the Liberator in the ETO. The Group itself and its ability to continue operations also lay in the balance. Lack of adequate numbers was a prime consideration and could be largely attributed to maintenance and replacement problems. The B-17 crews however, saw the Liberators in a completely different light, claiming with some justification that with them along the *Luftwaffe* had completely forsaken the Fortresses. However, the number of Liberators was about to be increased by the return of the "Traveling Circus." On the night of 25 February 1943 the 93rd took off from Gambut and headed back to England. Only Major K. K. Compton the Group's Operational Officer remained behind. He was promoted to full Colonel and assumed command of the 9th Air Force's 376th Bomb Group in Egypt. Most of the crews were not sorry to leave because the original 10-day detachment had extended to almost three months. The homeward flight was marred by the loss of the 8th Liberator of the campaign. The men of the 93rd went to Hardwick - their new base - to be greeted by a blaze of publicity; their African exploits having preceded them.

130 The day before the 66th Squadron had lost the popular pilot Captain "Wild Bill" McCoy and his crew when their Liberator lost its tail assembly at 4000ft during a training flight. Immediately after, the Liberator went into a flat spin and dived into the ground, killing everyone on impact.

131 Becker had scored his first kill on 16 October 1940 when he downed a Wellington of 311 Squadron RAF and in 1941-42 he had developed into one of the leading "*Experten*" in the *Luftwaffe* night fighter arm. He not only shot down 40 bombers in 1942 but also taught the new and young crews from his experiences. To them Becker was an inspiring fatherly figure. The "Night Fighting Professor," as he was dubbed, was instrumental in introducing the *Lichtenstein* AI radar into the night fighter arm in 1941. Most of the night fighter aircrew were sceptical about this new device – they liked to rely on the "Mk.1 Eyeball" - but Becker took the lead and had one of the still experimental sets installed in his Do 217Z night fighter at Leeuwarden aerodrome. Guided by the revolutionary radar, he shot down no less than 6 RAF night bombers between 8/9 August and 29/30 September 1941. Most of his colleagues and the *Luftwaffe* High Command were now convinced that the AI radar was an invaluable new asset in the night battle against the British bombers and the *Lichtenstein* went into mass production shortly after. In the course of 1942, most of the *Luftwaffe* night fighters were equipped with the AI.

132 Knoke, like the Pied Piper who was followed by the children who were never to return, hailed from Hamelin, an industrial town in Lower Saxony on the Weser River and he lived on the same road, which was known as the Koppenstrasse. The son of a policeman, who had served as an infantry sergeant, young Knoke joined the Hitler Youth in 1935. In August 1939 he took command of about 4000 boys of the Jungbann in the Hamelin District (Kreis). By 1940 he was under training as a fighter pilot and on 18 December 1940 he was one of 3000 officers of all services who heard Goring and Hitler speak at the Berlin Sportpalast. Next day Knoke was posted to JG 52. In June-July 1941 he flew combat sorties in Russia during

Barbarossa but did not score any victories before being posted to JG 1. He scored his first combat victory, a Spitfire on 5 March 1942.

133 41-24623 in the 365th Bomb Squadron.

134 B-17F 41-24604 in the 366th Bomb Squadron (10 PoW).

135 B-17F 42-5056 in the 364th Bomb Squadron (10 KIA).

136 I./JG 1 claimed 13 victories including two Fortresses in the 91st Bomb Group (*Kickapoo* flown by Captain John Swais and *Short Snorter II,* piloted by Lieutenant Beman E. Smith) and three in the 305th Bomb Group. Altogether, 7 Fortresses were lost. The Germans probably came to regret capturing Shorty Gordon because he would cause them more trouble than he had Colonel LeMay! Shorty escaped from PoW camp three times. Once the 5ft 2in American, disguised in Lederhosen and with hair oiled flat and chin well shaven had little difficulty passing himself off as a Bavarian youth. He obtained a bicycle and intended riding all the way to the Swiss border. He was caught but his third attempt was a success and in February 1944 he reached England via France. Gordon became the first American airman to receive the Silver Star for escaping.

137 The B-17 landed with a gaping hole where the rudder should have been, a shattered nose section, a wing spotted with ragged shrapnel wounds and its fuselage riddled from nose to tail with flak and cannon-shell holes. One shell had crashed through the fuselage directly behind the tail gunner's position, leaving a gash the size of a grapefruit. One by one, the crew climbed out - uninjured. They reported they'd made a pretty good bombing run.

138 The mounting losses in VIII Bomber Command meant that, by the end of January 1943, casualties had exceeded replacements with only 24 bomber crews arriving in England to replace 67 lost on missions that month. February was little better with 22 aircraft losses.

139 B-17F 42-5139.

140 The 303rd and 305th Bomb Groups turned south and successfully bombed the Wilton Feyenoord shipyards near Rotterdam. 21 B-17s in the 306th Bomb Group aborted the mission and 20 returned to Thurleigh with bombs on board. 42-5129, Captain William E. Friend, Jr.'s B-17 in the 368th Bomb Squadron was badly damaged and set on fire by Feldwebel Reinhold Flecks and *Unteroffizier* Hans Meissner, both of 6./JG 1 at 1025 hours and fell out of formation. The fire took hold and Friend gave the order to bale out over the sea. Seven parachutes were counted yet no survivors were ever reported. The crew probably jettisoned the bomb load while under tighter attack: 9 bombs hit two schools and two houses at Den Briel near the Hook. Four Dutchmen were killed and between 60 and 70 children were dead or missing.

141 These were probably 42-5370 flown by Lieutenant Harold H. Henderson (9 KIA. 1 PoW) and 41-24512 *Rose 0'Day* captained by Lieutenant Ralph A. Felton, Jr. (7 KIA. 3 PoW). These B-17s crashed in the sea west of Texel and Den Helder respectively, at 1128 and 1134 hours.

142 41-24464 in the 324th Bomb Squadron.

143 Although the American gunners claimed 13-3-4, III. and IV./NJG 1 lost only a Bf 110 each. FW 190s of II./JG 1 and JG 26 suffered no loss. Four B-17s were shot down and 34 casualties caused during a strike on Hamm. Losses might have been higher than for the introduction of new, armored flak vests, developed by Colonel Malcolm C. Grow, Chief Surgeon of the 8th Air Force, in association with the Wilkinson Sword Company of Great Britain and worn by 10 crews in the 91st Bomb Group this day. They certainly saved the life of a radio-operator aboard one ship when a 20mm shell fragment struck his vest just above the hip. The armored vest, consisting of heavy canvas covered with overlapping plates of manganese steel protecting the chest and back from low velocity shrapnel and ricocheting missiles, was only dented. The whole suit weighed 20lb and was cumbersome in the aircraft but the suit on a later raid at least saved one other life when a 20mm shell exploded just 2ft from a bombardier's chest. It peppered the vest but the bombardier was unhurt. In all, 300 suits, each with a quick-release mechanism, were ordered from Wilkinsons. The *New York Times* was quick to report in September 1943 that "A London firm, specializing since 1772 in the manufacture of swords, is now beating its products into something much more useful at the moment. It is making suits of mail for American airmen…Thus the cycle rolls around again, the American fighters, like the Yankee at King Arthur's Court, find themselves back in medieval armor..."

144 Most pilots of the 4th Fighter Group at Debden had some combat experience and a few had extensive experience, having been formed from the RAF Eagle Squadrons on 12 September 1942 when 71, 121 and 133 Squadrons were transferred to the USAAF. The 4th Fighter Group retained its nimble Spitfires until March 1943 when it converted to the P-47C. 40-year old Colonel E. W. Edward Anderson the CO was given the task of bringing the 4th Fighter Group into line with USAAF procedures but his task proved difficult. His pilots were reluctant to change the lessons learned in the RAF and most pilots were unhappy about converting from the Spitfire to the Thunderbolt. Likewise, the 78th Fighter Group, who had flown P-38s until most of the Lightnings and their pilots were transferred to the 12th AF in North Africa - were not enamored with the P-47 either. Thunderbolt-trained replacement pilots arrived from the States while its flight and squadron leaders who remained after the P-38s were sent to Africa had to retrain locally on the P-47. The 78th Fighter Group would fly its first P-47 mission on 13 April 1943. The 56th Fighter Group, which had begun receiving P-47s in June 1942, was also placed on operational status on 13 April 1943.

145 Devars and Wyer were captured a day or two later.

146 *Emmy Lou* crashed at Maromme at 1405. There was just one survivor.

147 On 11 May Roth was awarded the *Deutsche Kreuz im Gold* (*DKG* or German Cross in Gold) for 18 *Abschüsse*.

148 Jackson Hall had been grounded for medical reasons leaving only the crews of *Suzy Q, Little Beaver* and that of Captain Gideon W. Bucky' Warne's of the original 9 crews.

149 Automatic Flight Control Equipment.

150 This automatically controlled the aircraft in straight and level flight, or maneuvred it in response to the fingertip control of the pilot or bombardier. The autopilot's vertical flight gyro could detect any flight deviations of an aircraft from level flight the instant they occurred and just as instantaneously, operate the controls to correct them. The autopilot control panel was located in the pilot's compartment and contained the switches, lights and knobs used to operate and adjust the autopilot.

151 *Leutnant* Dieter Gerhardt had thought of this idea late in February 1943. In the early morning of 18 March, Gerhardt and Knoke made a practice flight off Heligoland with each dropping 4 100lb bombs on a sack, which was towed by a Ju 88. Gerhardt's third bomb scored a direct hit and the idea became a reality.

152 *Hot Freight* fell into the sea 10km southeast of Heligoland. It was Knoke's 5th victory.

153 In fact, he claimed it at 1537 hours off Heligoland. Possibly *Eager Beaver,* a 93rd Bomb Group B-24D, which although badly hit and was seen to drop from formation with a smoking engine, made it back to England.

154 *Shoot Luke* with a patched-up crew was out in the lead again on 31 March on a mission to Rotterdam and again on 5 April to Antwerp. The 93rd flew a diversionary mission on 4 April and the mission to Brest on the 6th was one of the worst Murphy's crew ever experienced. *Liberty Limited* flown by Frank Lown was shot down over the target and *a 20mm shell, which missed the tail gunner by a few inches, hit Shoot Luke*. Almost a month later a postcard from Lown arrived at Hardwick via the Red Cross - he was a PoW in Germany.

155 Four days later Colonel Ted Timberlake assumed command of the 201st Provisional Combat Bomb Wing. The 44th and 93rd were joined later by the 389th Bomb Group in June 1943 and the 2nd Bomb Wing was reorganized into provisional Combat Wings. Colonel Addison T. Baker assumed command of the Traveling Circus' on 17 May 1943.

156 "We were coming home from Wilhelmshaven when the ship was badly shot up by German fighters. Shortly after several attacks on us, the ship was shot up so badly that we all had to bale out, in spite of the fact that we were out a bit over the North Sea. We all came down in the vicinity of Alte Mellum Island, but into the water. Sgt Klug, the left waist gunner and I were the first two picked up by a ship headed for Heligoland. Apparently, all others drowned, or died of exposure in that frigid water before rescuers found them." *Maggie* was shot down by *Oberleutnant* Sommer of I./JG 1 (his 2nd victory.) *Cactus* was shot down into the sea off the coast of Holland by *Leutnant* Pancritius of 8./JG 1 for his third "kill."

157 42-29537 of the 324th Bomb Squadron, 91st Bomb Group flown by Lieutenant John A Coen, was shot down by *Leutnant* Georg-Peter Eder of 12./JG 2. Eder was injured by return fire from the B-17s but was able to force land his badly damaged Bf 109 at Beaumont-Le-Roger. Eder had joined JG 51 on the Channel coast in December 1940 but he did not achieve and kills. Transferred to the East for Barbarossa, he destroyed 10 Soviet aircraft before being badly wounded on 24.7.41. In 1942 he returned to operations with 7/JG 2.

158 At Molesworth 20 B-17s had lifted off beginning at 0935 hours. Several minutes later, flying in close formation in heavy cloud over Wellingborough 41-24559 *Ooold Soljer* and *Two Beauts* in the 303rd Bomb Group were lost in a mid-air collision. *Ooold Soljer* was completely demolished with the loss of 8 lives and 42-29573 *Two Beauts* crashed with the loss of 7 lives. A memorial marks the crash site in the village of Mears Ashby.

159 Williams crashed into the sea shortly after 1245 hours, 60 miles off Ostend. There were no survivors.

160 Before the war the Renault works had been the largest producer of vehicles in France and now the Germans were using it to turn out military trucks and tanks. Their output was estimated at 1000 trucks, tanks and armored cars a month. On the night of 3/4 March 1942 the RAF had destroyed the plant but the Germans had rebuilt it in 9 months by using slave labor. The Germans had even managed to increase production to 1500 vehicles a month.

161 Oesau, who claimed 10 aircraft in the Spanish Civil War, was the third German pilot to reach 100 victories, on 16 October 1941. After a short spell on the Eastern Front he had returned to the West to lead JG 2, then JG 1.

162 During late summer 1942 the FW 190A-4 powered by the BMW 80lD-2 engine appeared. Water-methanol injection provided 2100hp for short periods and the aircraft. Although the FW 190A proved an extremely effective fighter, operational experience revealed that the power of the BMW 801 engine tended to drop off at altitudes of 22,967ft and above. Attempts were therefore made to improve the high altitude performance of the aircraft with FW 190A B and C versions.

163 Investigation later showed that the right main wing-spar had been all but shot through. Incredibly, not only did *Dry Martini III* make it home to Chelveston, with 160 cannon and bullet holes, the 305th Bomb Group gunners claimed 25 enemy fighters destroyed, 6 probables and 5 damaged. *Dry Martini III*'s gunners alone were credited with the destruction of 10 enemy fighters, a record for a bomber crew on a single mission. Pronounced beyond repair *Dry Martini III* never flew again and instead was used as a "hangar queen". Lieutenant Herschel B. Ellis and his crew in the 422nd Bomb Squadron went down in their flaming Fortress. Ellis and 7 others of his crew baled out and were captured but the bombardier and ball-turret gunner were killed aboard the aircraft. *Available Jones,* flown by Lieutenant Morris M. Jones of the 364th Bomb Squadron was also shot down. Lieutenant Harold P. O'Neill in the 366th Bomb Squadron flew the third 305th Bomb Group B-17 lost. Two of the crew were killed, the rest were made PoWs. *Holy Mackeral!* flown by Lieutenant Ercil F. Eyster in the 359th Bomb Squadron, 303rd Bomb Group was the fourth B-17 lost. Six of the crew were KIA and 4 were taken prisoner. Two of the B-17s lost were claimed by *Hauptmann* "Wutz" Galland of II./JG 26, while Oberleutnant Karl Borris of 8th *Staffel* claimed a third. A fourth was awarded to Major Walter Oesau of JG 2. In all, American gunners claimed 47 German fighters destroyed. The real losses were two JG 26 pilots killed and 1 wounded.

164 During the war, 4000 Bf 109s were repaired at this factory.
165 He was able to make a wheels-up landing in his FW 190A-4 on the airfield at Ghent at 1515 hours but died from loss of blood early the following morning. Geisshardt had been decorated with the *RitterKreuz und Eichenlaub* (*RK* or Knight's Cross with Oak Leaves (*El*)) for his 75 victories on the Eastern Front. His total victory score was 102 confirmed victories. *Luftwaffe Fighter Aces* by Mike Spick, Ivy Books, 1996.
166 It was Priller's 84th victory.
167 The B-17, which crashed 4kms NW of Zandvliet, Belgium, was Galland's 38th victory. On 18 May at Vitry Generalfeldmarschall Hugo Sperrle presented the *Deutsche Kreuz im Gold* (*DKG* or German Cross in Gold) to *Hauptmann* Wutz Galland.
168 Only 3 crew baled out before the crippled bomber spun in near Adinteloord, 50kms north of Antwerp.
169 It was his 5th victory. Seelos came down on the edge of the town of Wuustwezel, Belgium and he was captured. He eventually ended up at *Stalag Luft III*. Seven of his crew managed to evacuate the doomed ship but the top turret gunner; a waist gunner and Lieutenant Murray were killed. In an outfit reputed for its high turnover rate, Murray had the shortest tour of all in the 306th Bomb Group - a matter of hours only. Kramarinko and S/Sgt William E. Baker evaded capture and together reached Spain, only to be caught and handed over to the Germans. On 13 May Oberleutnant Otto Stammberger, *Staffelkapitän*, 4./JG 26 was shot down by a 331 Squadron Spitfire. He had to exit his FW 190 when the fuel tank exploded, but his parachute failed to open fully and he was seriously injured on landing. He would not return until October.
170 Code name for several squadrons carrying out a high-speed sweep over the enemy occupied territory to entice enemy fighters to combat.
171 After washing out of U.S. flight training in January 1940 Peterson had joined the RAF in July and earned his wings on 15 Ocotber that same year. He joined 71 Squadron in November and became its CO in November the following year. After scoring a probable on 6 July flying a Hurricane he scored his first victory on 7 September when he shot down a Bf 109F flying a Spitfire Vb. By the time he transferred to the USAAF as a Major on 16 September 1942 he had scored 6 victories and 3 probables with 6 more damaged. Peterson was promoted Lieutenant Colonel on 21 October 1942. He served as the 4th Fighter Group Executive and Operations Officer from 16 September 1942-19 May 1943 when he was taken off operations after 200 sorties total. After a spell as Assistant A-3, Operations and Training at 8th FC he returned to the 4th Fighter Group as its CO on 20 August 1943 and He was promoted to full colonel on 22 October 1943. Peterson remained in command of the 4th Fighter Group until 1 January 1944.
172 On 17 April another *Rodeo* aimed at diverting enemy fighters away from a B-17 mission was unsuccessful and for the 56th Fighter Group uneventful when a sweep along the Dutch coast a week later was similarly devoid of any contact with the enemy. Hub Zemke tried out a new formation staggering the squadrons and flights so that the group formation was like a giant V when viewed in plan. There was no edict on how formations should be flown and the P-47 groups experimented to find the most desirable for control and deployment against the elusive enemy. In France meanwhile, changes in German fighter tactics and the disposition of units were afoot. It was announced in *Luftwaffe* circles that one of the Americans' greatest adversaries, the pilots of JG 26, were to transfer to the Russian Front where it would trade places with the Green Hearts *Geschwader*, JG 54. However, the transfer was only partially complete when in the spring of 1943 the growing strength of VIIIth Bomber Command increased pressure on the *Jagdgeschwaders* in the west and the transfer of the remaining *Gruppen* and *Staffeln* was first postponed and then cancelled by Generalmajor Adolf Galland.
173 Hodges and Lown were captured and sent to *Stalag Luft III*.
174 Eight of the crew were captured. George and T/Sgt Warren A MacGregor, engineer, were KIA.
175 See *First Over Germany; A History of the 306th Bomb Group* by Russell A. Strong.
176 39 B-17s suffered battle damage, two men killed and 4 WIA. Gunners claimed 63 enemy fighters shot down.
177 Youree completed his combat tour on 29 June 1943, the Thurleigh group's 50th mission.
178 *First Over Germany; A History of the 306th Bomb Group* by Russell A. Strong.

Chapter 5:

179 During April 1943 some important visitors arrived in Norfolk. Lord Trenchard, the "Father of the Royal Air Force," visited Station 104 on 6 April and personally congratulated the aircrews. Lieutenant General Frank Maxwell Andrews, Commanding General of the ETO, visited Hardwick on 27 April. One week later, on 4 May, General Andrews was killed along with the first crew at Hardwick to complete its tour. Lieutenant Shannon and his crew in *Hot* Stuff crashed into a bleak Icelandic mountain on their way home to America. Only Sgt George Eisel, the tail gunner, who had escaped two similar disasters, survived after being trapped in the wreckage for 14 hours. Andrews Field in Essex was named in honor of the late Commanding General on 17 May 1943.
180 Having led every mission the 56th Fighter Group had flown to date Hub Zemke felt someone else should be given the opportunity.
181 See *Zemke's Wolfpack* by Roger A. Freeman.
182 *First Over Germany; A History of the 306th Bomb Group* by Russell A. Strong.
183 The co-pilot; navigator; radio operator and the two waist gunners were killed.
184 42-29649.
185 On 15 July when Secretary of War, Mr. Stimson flew in to Thurleigh to confer the Medal of Honor on "Snuffy" Smith, as his plane rolled down the perimeter track, he looked out and saw a Fortress with a chewed-up tail. He said to a General: "I would like to meet the tail gunner of that Fortress." The gunner's name was Sgt Harris Benjamin Goldberg, born in Boston - Brookline, Massachusetts, who went to Canada to join the RCAF and put in for flying but washed out because of depth perception so he took a gunnery because it would get him to England most quickly. He landed in Scotland in October 1941 and later became a gunner in a RAF twin-engined Wellington crew. He flew the 1/2 June 1942 *Millenium* raid on Essen and the 25/26 June 1942 1000-bomber raid on Bremen, which was attacked by 1006 RAF aircraft. "That was bad. We lost 52 on that raid. Went in at 12,000ft, got hit and damn near fell to pieces. We went down to 2000ft and sort of stumbled home at about 90mph. Don't really know how we got home. All my crew were English. We used to have some pretty wild arguments about the States staying out of the war. After that night over Bremen we argued but never really got mad any more. Going through something like that brings you pretty close." After flying 42 missions in RAF bombers, completing 273 operational hours and surviving a crash in a 'Wimpy' in the Sinai desert in November 1942, Goldberg transferred to the 8th Air Force and flew 17 missions in Fortresses. ("Snuffy" now insisted on being saluted by officers (as is the right of an enlisted MoH recipient) and he adopted the British fashion of having his award printed after his name. He flew only 4 more missions before being transferred to a ground job.) See *First of the Many* by Captain John R. "Tex" McCrary and David E. Scherman. 1944.
186 *First Over Germany; A History of the 306th Bomb Group* by Russell A. Strong. The 91st lost one aircraft when 41-24547 *Vertigo* piloted by Lieutenant Robert D. Rand ditched in the English Channel with the loss of 5 crew KIA and 5 PoW. The 303rd lost two aircraft on this mission. 42-5780 *Black Swann* and 41-24610 *Joe Btfsplk* went down with the loss of 13 lives. Cliff Pyle and the crew of *We The People* came through safely. Within 10 days of this mission he was attached to the 1st Bomb Wing with the title of "President, Tactical Advisory Board." The Board's primary function was to advise the commanding general about combat tactics and to monitor the preparation of the Tactical Doctrine. This eventually turned into the well known "Standard Operations Procedures."
187 During the summer of 1943 Major Clark Gable the Hollywood movie star who had won an Oscar for his role in *It Happened One Night* in 1934 was in England to make a different kind of movie. Although he was 42 years of age, on 12 August 1942, following he death of his actress wife Carole Lombard, who was killed in an air crash while on a Bond tour, Gable voluntarily, enlisted in the USAAF. In October 1942 he graduated from the Officers Candidate School in Miami as a 2nd lieutenant and attended aerial gunnery school. On the personal insistence of General Hap Arnold, he was assigned to the 351st Bomb Group to make a motion picture of gunners in action. Gable's first flight was made from Molesworth in *Eight Ball Mk II* on a mission to Antwerp. Two more flights followed, to Villacoublay on 10 July and Gelsenkirchen on 12 August, much of the air-to-air film being taken by Gable and an MGM cameraman, Andrew J. McIntyre. On the next flight the Fortress *Ain't I Gruesome?* came under heavy attack and was hit 15 times. Gable's last flight was on 23 September to Nantes. In October 1943, having accumulated more than 50,000ft of 16mm film, Gable returned to the States. "*Combat America*" finally appeared in October 1944..
188 Major General Frederick L. Anderson, Jr., was born 4 October 1905 at Kingston, NY. Graduated from USMA and commissioned 2nd Lieutenant in the Cavalry June 1928. Undertook flying instruction the following year, graduating at Kelly Field, Texas, in September. Served with air units in the Philippines 1930-1934. Entered the ACTS and in July 1940 became Director of Bombardment Instruction. In January 1942 became Deputy Director of Bombardment at AAF HQ. Promoted Brigadier General and sent to the UK, commanding 3rd Bomb Wing February-April 1943. Became CO 4th Bomb Wing in April 1943 and CG VIII Bomber Command in June. With the inactivation of VIII Bomber Command in January 1944 he became Deputy Commander for Operations at USSTAF.
189 In the mid-afternoon, 97 B-17s of the 1st Bomb Wing attacked the Avions Potez aircraft factory at Meaulte. The straggling 351st Bomb Group formation of 14 B-17s abandoned the mission in mid-Channel. Three B-17s in the 1st Bomb Wing FTR. A 305th Bomb Group ship captained by Lieutenant Harold C. Pierce of the 365th Bomb Squadron was shot down by flak with the loss of 5 crew killed. Major Pips Priller JG 26 CO and *Leutnant* Hoppe of 8th *Staffel* put in claims for the two 91st Bomb Group B-17s shot down. Both came from the 323rd Squadron. *Vulgar Virgin*, flown by Lieutenant Lawrence J Stark, crashed and exploded at Abbeville with the loss of 8 crew. 42-5406, flown by Lieutenant Homer C. Biggs, Jr., was lost with 7 crew. Six men were taken prisoner from the two Fortresses. Eleven B-17s, including one badly damaged by a bomb dropped by a JG 26 FW 190, returned with battle damage.
190 *NUMBER ONE PRIORITY*, from *Skyways to Berlin*, Major John M. Redding & Captain Harold Leyshon. Bobbs Merrill, 1943.
191 In addition to the regular bombing sorties, in March and April 1943 the 44th flew some night-training missions over England for possible night-bombing assignments with the RAF. Several B-24s were also seconded to RAF Coastal Command for raids on German shipping and naval forces.
192 Thanks to the addition of the 4th Wing Groups and the 351st Bomb Group at Polebrook the total number of bombers available meant Eaker could diversify his attacks with a multiplicity of options, further improved by the debut of twelve B-26 Marauders. Altogether, 196 bombers would make simultaneous attacks on 4 targets, the principal attack by 115 B-17s of the 1st Bomb Wing and 21 B-24s of the 44th Bomb Group on the Germania and Deutsche Werke shipyards at Kiel. Meanwhile, 15 B-17s of the 96th and 351st Bomb Groups would bomb Wevelgem airfield and 42 Fortresses of the 94th and 95th Bomb Groups, the Ford and General Motors plant and locks nearby at Antwerp. The fourth raid was to be made on a power station at Ijmuiden, Holland by 12 B-26 Marauders of the 322nd Bomb Group at Rougham, near Bury St. Edmunds. Large numbers of Spitfires and P-47s were to escort the bombers. At around 1035 hours the Marauders swooped in low over the Dutch coast and continued over the outskirts of Amsterdam

at rooftop height. They bombed a generating station at Ijmuiden with delayed action mines and then departed as quickly as they came. It was a curtain raiser for a vast armada of aircraft, the like of which had never before been seen on German radar screens during daylight hours.

193 Ernst had flown to England with the 68th Bomb Squadron in September 1942. On 3 January 1943 the "Flying Eightballs" had bombed St. Nazaire and on the homeward journey the group was forced to land in Wales after running low on fuel. Ernst flew the mission in 41-23771 *Bat Out of Hell*, piloted by 1st Lieutenant Ray I. Hilliard, which crash-landed at Haverfordwest and was destroyed. The crew were taken to a Catholic hospital where that night the co-pilot, 2nd Lieutenant Dale K. Canfield, died of his injuries. After a few weeks in hospital the survivors were returned to Shipdham where Ernst and the others were used as replacements for crewmembers lost on missions.

194 The interphone on board *The Rugged Buggy* was put out of action in the blast and all communication with the 5 men in the rear of the ship was lost. Unbeknown to O'Brien, flak had also blown a hole in the tail, knocking Sgt Castillo out of his rear turret and almost amputating his foot in the process. Three crewmembers in the tail came to his aid and quickly realizing the extent of his injuries, pushed him out of the aircraft, pulling the ripcord on his parachute pack for him and then they too baled out. One of the three men, Sgt Van Owen, the assistant radio-operator/waist gunner baled out over the sea but he was drowned in Kiel Bay despite wearing a Mae West. Ironically, he had always had a fear of drowning even when wearing a life preserver. A German ship picked up his body and brought him ashore.

195 Originally, flak helmets were M-1 infantry steel helmets, which were subsequently standardized for use and later put into production, with refinements such as elongated hinged ear flaps which permitted the user to wear his leather helmet with its built in headphones on missions. To enable the headset to be worn over a cap in flight the "fifty mission crush" cap was created by removing the "front spring stiffening" (or grommet). This effect was further enhanced by soaking the cap overnight and subjecting it to as much abuse as possible and it then became known as the "fifty mission crush," which was considered *de rigueur* in some combat theaters.

196 Ernst wasted no time and baled out of the doomed aircraft. On the way down he could see thick smoke coming from the Kiel shipyards. He landed on dry land, in a farmyard not far from a Danish village near the German border where German soldiers captured him immediately. Ernst had been held in a farmhouse where a housewife washed his hair and face blackened by the fire in the aircraft. The *Gestapo* and two *Luftwaffe* officers arrived and took him away in a patrol car. Castillo was lying on a stretcher with his foot and leg bandaged and bleeding.

197 Reed nursed the B-24 back to Shipdham where the crew baled out after he and his co-pilot, 1st Lieutenant George W. Winger set course on autopilot for the North Sea before they too baled out. *Scrappy* had to be shot down by RAF Spitfires. Wygonik had landed in the target area and German soldiers soon picked him up. Later, his right eye was removed at hospital in Vienna before he was eventually repatriated. Eight other 44th Bomb Group B-24s were damaged and 12 men were WIA. *Margaret Ann* returned to base with 1 gunner mortally wounded and three seriously wounded. *Ruth-less,* piloted by Lieutenant Frank Slough in the 506th was very badly damaged but made it back, although Slough finally had to crash-land in Northern Ireland because Shipdham was so congested that it could not take any more aircraft in trouble. III./JG 54 lost 7 Bf 109s by return fire. Next day, 15 May, this *Gruppe* was further decimated during B-17 raids against targets in the German Bight, losing 8 aircraft. Two very experienced *Ritterkreuzträger, Hauptmann* Fink and *Leutnant* Rupp were among those KIA.

198 The following day the survivors from the Kiel raid were put on a train for *Dulag Luft I,* the German interrogation camp at Oberusel near Frankfurt in southwest Germany. The journey provided an opportunity for the men to admire the beautiful countryside and witness the results of Allied bombing at close quarters as the train steamed through the hard-hit cities of Hamburg, Hanover and Kassel. At Hamburg station O'Brien and his fellow "Eightballers" were transferred to another train while a heavy bombing raid was in progress. Their train got away safely and there were many opportunities to escape but everyone felt uncertain and lost. The train finally pulled into Frankfurt railway station at the end of their tiring journey. The prisoners were forced to spend the night sleeping on the overcrowded and very cold station platforms. At around 11 o' clock on the morning of 16 May Jim O'Brien and his fellow prisoners arrived at the little railway station near *Dulag Luft*. They disembarked and were made to walk to the camp itself. They enjoyed the walk because it was the first opportunity they had had to stretch their legs after the cramped confines of the train and sleeping rough in railway stations. They were admitted into the camp compound and immediately put into the "cooler" where they were searched. They were issued with wooden clogs and old Polish uniforms. Jim O'Brien reflected ruefully that this was to be his permanent fate as a "Kriegie." However, that evening he was given back his combat clothes and some food was issued. It consisted of two slices of black bread for lunch and 5 cooked potatoes in jackets for supper plus a kind of soup made from grains of barley, oats and potatoes. O'Brien was later moved to the regular "cooler," really a tight shut cell with bars. Despite the hard bunk he slept well that night. He spent all next day in the cooler under constant questioning by his captors. O'Brien saw a "V" marked on one of the walls and he began re-marking it. This did not please the guard, who immediately turned on the electric heater until the prisoner was almost roasted. Despite this and the constant intrusions for questioning O'Brien now had time to collect his thoughts, reflect on his shooting down from start to finish and review his life up to then. He wondered if his predicament would be permanent and his thoughts turned to escape. On 18 May O'Brien awoke from a good night's sleep too more questioning. Reaction was beginning to set in and the American Major complained about his treatment. However, he received no sympathy from his German captors, who moved him and some other prisoners to the camp lager that evening. Everyone was suspicious of everyone else, especially towards the British officers who were administering the lager. However the move meant better food and the internees tasted the best of Red Cross cuisine including *mashed potatoes,* carrots, *Spam, cheese* and tea. They slept well that night with the improved food inside them. On 19 May the officers were separated from the enlisted men. Next day O'Brien, Bishop, Brown, Westbrook and their fellow officers were ordered into railway boxcars for the journey to their permanent camp at *Stammenlager* (*Stalag*) *'der Luftwaffe" (Luft III)* at Sagan near Breslau in occupied Poland where they would be 'guests of the *Luftwaffe*' until May 1945.

199 Martinek was taken prisoner. McTaggart lost 25lbs in weight while evading capture. He worked his way southward across the Pyrenees into Spain. Adamina rode his T-bolt down to the water and ditched successfully.

200 II./JG 26 shot down two B-17s of the 351st Bomb Group. Both *The Annihilator*, piloted by Captain William P. Forsythe in the 510th Squadron and Lieutenant Clifford J. McCoy's B-17 in the 508th Bomb Squadron, crashed at Courtrai.

201 42-3115 spun out of formation at only 2500ft and crashed on North Beveland Island at 1315, near Kats village. All the crew were killed. Oberleutnant Sternberg of JG 26 claimed a second (possibly a 94th Bomb Group) B-17 over the Scheldt estuary. A 78th Fighter Group P-47 (one of three Thunderbolts lost) and a Spitfire were also shot down by pilots of JG 26 but the German unit lost two pilots to return fire from the bombers. *Hauptmann* Karl Borris, Kapitän of 8th *Staffel,* who was forced to bale out at 22,000ft after coming off worse against a bomber, was fortunate to survive when his parachute failed to open properly. A fourth FW 190 was shot down by the 78th Fighter Group.

202 Altogether, 193 B-17s bombed targets at Emden, Heligoland and Wilhelmshaven.

203 Victory.

204 Short for Juggernaut because of the aircraft's ability to out-dive any other fighter.

205 Philipp was KIA on 8 October 1943 during air combat with B-17s and escorting fighters over Nordhorn, Germany, after having claimed a B-17 for his 206th and final victory.

206 *Luftwaffe* pilots were on a points system, which converted to various awards. An *Abschuss* or shoot down of a *Viermot*, or *4-mot* (4-engined bomber) earned three points, while a *Herausschuss*, or separation, was worth two. A pilot, who finished off an already shot up 4-engine bomber, was awarded one point for *endgültige Vernichtung*, or final destruction. Decorations were awarded after points' totals were reached. For instance, one point earned the recipient the Iron Cross 2nd Class and 3, the Iron Cross 1st Class. 40 points were needed for the *RitterKreuz* (*RK* or Knight's Cross) although this varied in practice.

207 In reality it was the gasholder in the suburbs of Amsterdam.

208 Williams and Sgt Jesse Lewis, tail gunner, scrambled to safety out of the camera hatch, climbed into a life raft and watched the Marauder sink in about 45 seconds. The time was 1224 hours and they were 80 miles from England. They spent 5 days in the raft before being rescued and returned to England and to the 322nd Bomb Group. Lieutenant Matthews' plane was shot into the sea at 1230. There were no survivors. Feldwebel Niederreichholz of *Stab* II./JG 1 and *Oberfeldwebel* Winkler of 4./JG 3 were the victorious *Jagdflieger* on this occasion.

209 Of the 60 airmen shot down in enemy territory, 22 survived as PoWs. Whilst a PoW, Colonel Stillman surmised that the mission was a disaster and one factor had contributed to its failure. When Captain Stephens aborted at the start of the mission, he climbed to 1000ft. Stillman did not blame him for this, as it was standard operating procedure for the B-26 in order to allow the crew to bale out if necessary. However, Stillman was convinced that in so doing Stephens had unwittingly exposed his aircraft to enemy radar, thus alerting the Germans to the presence of the rest of the force. As a result of the 17 May disaster, the 322nd Bomb Group was stood down and the Marauder program was put on hold temporarily. It was deemed suicidal to fly the B-26 at low level, so tactics were rethought and the B-26 was used at medium level. The 322nd Bomb Group moved to Andrews Field near Braintree, Essex as a part of this strategy and resumed operations on 31 July 1943. Colonel Glen C. Nye, the man who had nursed the 322nd Bomb Group in the early days of its existence, before Colonel Stillman, took command.

210 Contrary to popular belief, *Memphis Belle* was not the first to complete an 8th Air Force tour, but its 25th mission on 17 May was duly recorded (using a "stand-in" B-17F) in 16mm color and used with great effect in the documentary. On 26 May the crew were introduced to HRH King George VI and Queen Elizabeth at Bassingbourn and on 9 June General Eaker paid them a visit and then bade them a stateside farewell to take part in a bond tour of U.S. cities. What finally emerged in April 1945 was a colorful and exciting 38-minute masterpiece, which gave American moviegoers a timely reminder of the grim reality of the war, which was being fought at high altitude in the skies over Europe. Britons saw the film for the first time in the winter of 1944-45.

211 *Avenger II*, a B-24 of the 44th Bomb Group developed engine trouble on the Bordeaux raid and crash-landed in Gijon, Spain. It brought the total losses for the day to 17. Ed Mikolowski, lead navigator, *Suzy Q,* 44th Bomb Group, Bordeaux mission, 17 May 1943. "Gentleman" Jim DeVinney flew lead bombardier, recalls: "Suddenly through the haze and mist we saw a break in the coastline. Although it wasn't very plain, it stood out well enough to be recognised as the estuary that curves crazily from the Bay of Biscay to Bordeaux, 30 miles inland. When we reached the IP on the bombing run a few minutes later, it was the bombardier's baby. He took over. It was the finest piece of precision bombing I ever hope to see. The locks collapsed, water gushed out of the basin into the river; there were hits on the bottleneck of the railroad yards, strikes on the aero-engine factory. It was beautiful!"

212 8th AF now had the authorization to proceed with daylight strategic bombing within the type of combined offensive it had long sought. CBO plan listed the destruction of German fighters as the immediate primary objective. Primary objectives in order of importance were 1. U-boat yards and bases. 2. The German aircraft industry. 3. Ball bearings and oil. Secondary objectives were 1. Synthetic rubber and tires and military motor transport.

213 *Leutnant* Kestel was one of three 9th *Staffel* pilots who were killed while intercepting 8th AF bombers over the North Sea on 25 June 1943.
214 Earlier that day, at 1312 hours, Priller had claimed a 78th Fighter Group P-47 in the Scheldt Estuary. See *The JG 26 War Diary Vol.2* by Donald Caldwell. Grub Street, London. 1998.
215 KIA by P-47 Thunderbolts on 6 August 1944.
216 30 year old Oberleutnant Hans Munz, *Staffelkapitän*, 1./JG 1, was washed ashore on 27 June 1943 and buried at Westerland. Burath's B-17 claim of 21 May 1943 has not been identified as several of the 12 B 17s that were shot down by 2./JG 27 (5 *abshüsse*) and I./JG 1, whilst returning from raids on Emden and Wilhelmshaven crashed into the North Sea.
217 The 95th Bomb Group was also due to move, from Alconbury to Framlingham, Suffolk, but its departure was marred by a tragic accident. At 2030 hours on 27 May a tremendous explosion shook the countryside for miles around Alconbury when a 95th Bomb Group B-17 exploded while in the process of being loaded up with 10 5001b bombs. 19 officers and enlisted men were killed and 20 severely injured, one of whom died later. Four B-17s parked in the vicinity of the explosion were destroyed and 11 others were damaged in the blast. Because no one in the actual proximity of the explosion survived, the cause of the disaster is unknown although an investigation board later attributed the probable cause to a defective fuse detonating from causes unknown. The 351st Bomb Group meanwhile, remained at Polebrook.
218 On 27 May only 11 bombers hit St. Nazaire.
219 Seven YB-40s also made their debut this day. In January 1943 Major Robert B. Keck in the 92nd Bomb Group had left Bovingdon for the United States to lead back a flight of new and secret Fortresses for use with the group. Called YB-40s and fitted with 16 machine-guns, including two top turrets, they were intended to be used as "Destroyer escorts" for conventional Fortresses. Thirteen YB-40s were assigned to the 327th Bomb Squadron and Major Keck became its CO. Their arrival also meant a resumption in combat missions for the 92nd Bomb Group.
220 Situation Normal All Fucked Up.
221 168 B-17s bombed Wilhelmshaven while 30 bombed the secondary target at Cuxhaven. About 20 fighters attacked the low groups in the 4th Bomb Wing.
222 B-17, 42-5430 *Pappy*.
223 The 1st Bomb Wing lost 8 B-17s in all and the 4th Bomb Wing, 1 Fortress. 62 B-17s returned damaged. three of the missing Fortresses went down over the North Sea. The 379th Bomb Group lost 5 to enemy action and a 6th crash-landed at RAF Coltishall, Norfolk on the return. The American gunners claimed to have shot down 85 enemy fighters. Only 7 German fighters were destroyed or damaged and two pilots injured. Fighters for attacked the 1st Bomb Wing over an hour. The units involved were 6./JG 11 (5 *Abschüsse*) based at Leeuwarden and III./JG 26, from Nordholz, flying new Bf 109G-4/R6 and –6/R6 "gunboats" with MG 151/20 cannon in large underwing gondolas.
224 During those early missions, there had been several crew changes and replacements. Lieutenant George Hendershot, co-pilot, had been promoted to skipper of his own Fort and was replaced by Lieutenant Jack Amphlett. Bombardier Lieutenant Martin Stanford had been transferred. Only Captain Harrison and Lieutenant Robert Schaefer, navigator remained from the original commissioned crew. Sgt Joe Langford had broken his hand in a training accident and had been replaced as flight engineer/top turret gunner by Sgt Jim Curtis of Red Wing, Minnesota. Our 5-man rear gunnery crew - all sergeants - was still together - radio operator/ gunner, Charlie McNemar, Weston, West Virginia; ball turret gunner, Jeff Davis Polk, Tulsa, Oklahoma; left waist Gunner, Earl Porath, Nebraska; tail gunner, Eino "Ossie" Asiala, Freda, Michigan and me.
225 On the evening of 12 June Loren McCollom had taken the 56th Fighter Group on another sweep over the Pas de Calais. They went in at 20,000ft, far below their usual altitude. McCollom figured that the *Luftwaffe* always expected us to be up around 30,000ft and might be caught off guard at a lower level). A *Staffel* of FW 190s was seen about 5000ft below while over Belgium. Schilling's flight went down to attack and McCollom took a long deflection shot at an FW 190 as they broke and dived. Captain Walter Cook of the 62nd went down on some Focke-Wulfs that were trying to circle round and coming up behind the last man he held his fire until around 300 yards away and then let fly. His first shots struck the fuselage and then as prop wash caused his plane to veer slightly his fire began going into the enemy's left wing. A large puff of black smoke indicated he had hit the ammo compartment and a large piece of wing came off. Cook broke off the attack and pulled away. The FW 190 was seen going straight down in an uncontrolled spin. As the enemy pilot took no evasive action it seems likely Cook's opening burst killed him. Zemke recorded in his memoirs, "At last the 56th had made its first confirmed kill! At the same time I couldn't help speculating that at the current rate of attrition it would take a hundred years to decimate the *Luftwaffe*."
226 Lieutenant Robert Johnson also claimed a FW 190 but only one FW 190 was lost when Obergefreiter Heinrich Zenker was killed in the P-47 attack. And *Oberfeldwebel* Karl-Heinz Bocher was wounded. In the afternoon 44 Thunderbolts of the 78th Fighter Group flew their sweep over Ypres and St. Pol. II./JG 26 shot down two of the P-47s for no loss.
227 Early in 1943 the FW 190A-5, essentially similar to the A-4 appeared, though it differed in having a revised engine mounting to allow the BMW 801D-2 to be fitted 15cm (5.9 inches) further forward. This arrangement was designed to eliminate the problems of engine overheating, which had plagued the early aircraft.
228 All 13 men aboard baled out but only Lieutenant Willard Brown, group navigator, survived. A strong offshore wind carried Forrest and the 11 other crewmen to their deaths in the cold Baltic Sea. Forrest was the first American general to be lost in combat in Europe.
229 At the time of his death Ruppert had 21 kills.

Chapter 6:

230 In 1941 RAF Bomber Command carried out three attacks on Hüls, sending 11 Halifaxes and 7 Stirlings to bomb the chemical works on 12/13 June, followed by 86 aircraft on 6/7 September, 90 bombers on 12/13 October and 81 aircraft on 28/29 December. The last raid on this target was by 167 Lancasters on 17 March 1945.
231 Of all the bombardment groups in the 8th Air Force the 100th Bomb Group at Thorpe Abbotts is perhaps the best known. Often referred to as the "Bloody Hundredth", in the less than two years the 100th was in action in Europe, the group lost 229 Fortresses -177 "MIA" and 52 from "other operational losses." It is the third highest total among 8th Air Force units: More precisely, the 100th had the highest loss rate among its sister groups for the 22 months it was operational. When it left England in 1945 the "Bloody Hundredth" had become perhaps the most famous, albeit "jinxed" Bomb Group in the Eighth Air Force.
232 B-17F 42-30016 crashed near Terneuzen.
233 42-29984 in the 533rd Bomb Squadron.
234 42-30021 in the 533rd Bomb Squadron.
235 However, Lieutenant Jobe in the 381st Bomb Group brought the crippled *Little Chuck* back and he crash-landed at North Foreland. Two 384th Bomb Group B-17s FTR. *Salvage Queen*, flown by Lieutenant Fred G. Disney ditched in the Channel with the loss of 7 crew and the other crashed at Goes in Holland. Four of 2nd Lieutenant Robert J. Oblinski's crew were killed.
236 The first weeks of YB-40 operations indicated that the idea of multi-gunned B-17s flying in bomber formations would not work. The additional machine-guns on each YB-40 did not add materially to the combined firepower a group formation could provide. The *Luftwaffe* regularly attacked only stragglers and the YB-40s were unable to protect these from concentrated attacks. Howard Hernan had an opportunity to look over one of the three multi-gunned B-17s assigned to the 303rd shortly before the Hüls raid and concluded later, "With all the armor plating around the tail and waist gun positions, the Martin turret over the radio room and all the extra ammunition, the YB-40 just had to be tail heavy. Of course, it weighed the same when it got off the target as it did when it got there. When we dropped our bombs we were somewhat lighter and it made a lot of difference. I believe it was mistake to spread the YB-40s around the group. My opinion was that they should have been left fly as a squadron and then if they wanted to attract any fighters, to bear out a little and let them in. The YB-40s had a tremendous amount of 6 power but if they lost an engine they were trouble." (Losses were not made good although YB-40s continued flying missions until the end July 1943.)
237 61 B-17s were damaged. I./JG 1 at Schiphol; III./JG 1 at Leeuwarden; III./JG 26 from Nordholz; III./JG 11 at Oldenburg and 12./JG 54, were other units involved in the air battle of 25 June. JG 1 shot down three B-17s. *Gruppenadjutant*, Oberleutnant Hardt of III./JG 1 was KIA bringing down a B-17, three pilots were wounded and another was MIA. The American gunners claimed 62 enemy fighters shot down though the real score was 12 lost and 6 damaged. Five pilots in III./JG 1 were KIA or WIA. 9./JG 26 had three pilots MIA. 12./JG 54 lost another pilot KIA near Wesermünde.
238 Two 63rd Fighter Squadron pilots had to abort due to mechanical trouble before the group made landfall over the enemy coast at Dieppe at between 24,000 and 26,000ft, 35 minutes after take-off.
239 *Jafü* or *Jagdfliegerführer*, fighter command/control unit(s) or its commander.
240 *Leutnant* Götz Schmidt flying a Bf 109G-3 was shot down and WIA.
241 Seven pilots in JG 26 claimed 10 P-47s in the 56th Fighter Group of which 7 were confirmed. The 61st Fighter Squadron aircraft flown by 2nd Lieutenant Justus Foster limped back to Hawkinge with extensive battle damage caused by 20mm cannon shells. 2nd Lieutenant Eaves in the 62nd Fighter Squadron and Lieutenant Clamp in the 63rd Fighter Squadron also landed at Manston with 20mm battle damage, Clamp with a metal fragment lodged in his left arm. 1st Lieutenant Ralph Johnson's P-47, also hit by 20mm shells, had the hydraulic system holed, causing one wheel to come down. The pilot made for his home station, from where Colonel Zemke took off to fly alongside and offer radioed advice on maneuvers to try and shake down the other main wheel leg, which refused to budge. A one-wheel landing would most likely precipitate a fatal crash, and as this leg could not be retracted, Zemke advised Johnson to fly to the coast and bailout over the water. Successfully vacating the cockpit, Johnson's parachute deposited him in the sea just north of Great Yarmouth, where a RAF ASR launch quickly rescued him. Four pilots never returned; three from the 61st and one from the 63rd, all later notified as KIA.
242 57 B-17s in the St. Nazaire force returned with damage and three dead crewmen.
243 On 6 May Operation *Husky* - the invasion of Sicily – began. Early in June Brereton was informed that three 8th Air Force Liberator groups would join his two B-24D groups – the 98th "Pyramiders" and the 376th "Liberandos" - for a second attack on Ploesti. Ploesti was the center of an important of strategic oilfield producing 60% of all Germany's needs. By increasing the Liberator's fuel capacity to 3100 gallons they could just about make it to the target from North Africa. In June 1942 a detachment of 23 B-24Ds under the command of Colonel Harry H. Halverson, codenamed "HALPRO," which was en route to join the 10th Air Force in China had bombed Ploesti with limited results. No further raids were made on Ploesti and then on 6 March 1943 Field Marshal Erwin Rommel launched what proved to be his last offensive. It failed and he was recalled to Berlin. The path was now clear for another strike on the Ploesti oilfields. In April 1943 bomber chiefs in London pressed General Lewis Brereton, CG 9th Bomber Command, for another attack, but he was anxious to contain his bombing force for the Tunisian and Sicilian battles that lay ahead.
244 For the 93rd Bomb Group the long overseas flight meant a return to the African desert they had forsaken on 25 February 1943. The Liberators flew to Libya where they came under

9th Air Force control. The 93rd and 389th were based near Benghazi while the *Eightballs* were based at Benina Main, one of Mussolini's former airfields, 15 miles from Benghazi. A few days' later operations began in earnest, with missions in support of the Allied invasion of Sicily. The airfield at Lecce in Italy was bombed and on 5 July the 93rd took off on the first of 10 missions in support of the Italian campaign. Most of the missions were flown without escort and soon losses began to assume the proportions sustained at the height of the raids on the U-boat pens in France. On 19 July the Liberators made the first U.S. bombing attack on Rome. Although the Italian capital had been declared an open city, its railway yards had nevertheless remained the chief center of supply for the Axis forces in Italy. Because of the city's cultural and religious significance the briefing for the raid was the most detailed and concise the combat crews had ever received. More than 100 B-24Ds bombed the Littoria yards and the raid was declared an unprecedented success. Only one bomb "got away" and slightly damaged a basilica. It was precision bombing at its best, but the conditions had been kind.

245 On 6 July Brereton had told his 5 group commanders that a low-level daylight attack would be made on Ploesti to achieve maximum surprise and ensure the heaviest possible damage in the first raid. Brereton had studied target folders for two weeks before making his decision. Most of the crews were apprehensive. This was no ordinary mission and morale was not improved when Brereton told them that losses were expected to be as high as 50 %

246 Malfunctions and accidents en route reduced the effectiveness of the Liberator force and navigational errors caused severe problems in the target area, forcing some groups to bomb each other's assigned targets. 167 B-24Ds actually attacked their targets, dropping 311 tons of bombs on the Ploesti refineries. 44 B-24Ds were lost. Three B-24s crashed into the sea. 8 B-24Ds were interned in Turkey, while 19 landed in Cyprus, Sicily and Malta. Of the 92 that returned to North Africa, 55 were battle damaged). At least 33 Liberators were downed by flak and 10 by fighters (I./JG 4, IV./JG 27) and Bulgarian and Rumanian units for the loss of 10 German and 15 Rumanian fighters. Five Medals of Honor were awarded to personnel, 4 of them to 8th Air Force personnel. Following a well-earned leave the Liberator groups resumed raids on Axis targets in Austria and Italy. On 13 and 14 August they bombed the Messerschmitt factor at Wiener Neustadt in Austria. On 16 August they bombed Foggia in southern Italy. Three B-24s in the 67th Bomb Squadron, 44th Bomb Group were lost, including *Buzzin' Bear* and *Suzy Q*. After the bombing of Cancello on 21 August the three 8th Air Force groups were ordered back to East Anglia to continue the war against Germany.

247 This Fortress crashed at Elbent with 6 crew dead. 2 crew evaded. 2 were captured.

248 Aboard B-17F 42-3190, 332nd Bomb Squadron, 94th Bomb Group.

249 42-3190.

250 First produced in 1921, the Browning M2 was basically an enlarged version of the .30 inch M1917A1. The M2 weighed 65lb, had a muzzle velocity of 2900ft per second and was produced in greater numbers than any other U.S. machine-gun in WWII though it was generally accepted that a flexible .50 caliber was inaccurate beyond 1000 yards. All enlisted men in an aircrew were aerial gunners. Various attempts were made to eliminate the defensive blind spot below the belly of the Fortress by fitting cumbersome looking contraptions to house a pair of .50 calibers. When the combat worthy B-17E appeared late in 1941 a Bendix twin .50 caliber machine gun turret just aft of the bomb bay replaced the tub-like belly machine gun position. It was aimed and fired by a gunner sighting through a bubble just aft of the turret but in combat sighting proved difficult and firing became haphazard at best. Midway through production it was replaced by the Briggs/Sperry retractable ball turret. The Sperry was hydraulically suspended from the inside the aft fuselage and it could be raised and lowered externally while in flight. The ball turret could only be entered from inside the Fortress after becoming airborne by rotating the guns straight down, which brought the entry door inside the aircraft. Each gun had an ammunition box with a chute for feeding the guns and leading away the links and fired shells. The top box (maximum capacity 505 rounds) fed the left gun; the lower box (maximum capacity 425 rounds) fed the right gun. Controlled power drives gave tracing rates from 0° to 45° per second in azimuth and 0° to 30° per second in elevation. The gunner's hand controls and elevation limit stop were in a unit which regulated the amount of turret movement in azimuth or elevation. When the handgrips were released they returned to their center position. The gunner sighted his twin fifties through a Sperry gunsight located between his knees. Gun firing switches in parallel were at the end of each handgrip. Either switch fired the guns. The gunner operated the range control with his foot. Foot pressure in the support increased the range up to 1000 yards. Behind the flight deck the electrically operated Sperry top turret was fired by the flight engineer who stood on a steel platform inside the turret which was a completely independent unit turned in azimuth and elevation by hand controls. The location was positioned well forward so that it could augment the nose guns in forward defense. The twin .50 Brownings could be rotated 360° horizontally and upwards of 85° and could be brought quickly to bear on any attacking fighters approaching from any direction. When not occupying the turret the gunner stood or sometimes sat in a small jump seat between the two pilots assisting them in monitoring the numerous gauges on the instrument panel and calling out airspeeds during take offs and landings. Also, from his two positions, the engineer could easily observe the engines and both wings that contained the self-sealing fuel tanks. The B-17F and G retained the conventional tail gun installation but when the United Air Lines Modification Centre at Cheyenne, Wyoming completely redesigned the tail gunners' enclosure, a modified tail-gun arrangement gave the twin fifties greatly increased elevation and azimuth range. The "Cheyenne" or "Pumpkin" installation as it was named also improved all-round visibility by using larger windows and the ring and bead sight outside the window for sighting purposes was replaced with a new reflector sight. Large wooden trays to hold 500 rounds per gun were situated on each side of the gunner. The new turret was installed during various stages of production at all three B-17G plants. The waist gunners' K-5 post-mounted.50 caliber machine guns were replaced later by K-6 gun mounts, which allowed them to swivel the machine gun inside and outside rectangular window openings, which improved visibility and increased the field of fire. The cumbersome metal ammunition boxes were replaced by belt feeds and plywood ammunition boxes containing 600 rounds of .50 caliber shells were mounted on the inside of the plane. Later, all .50s were power-operated, armor plate was installed and beginning with the Boeing B-17G-50-BO, the directly opposite waist-gun positions were staggered to allow the gunners more freedom of movement in combat.

251 Oberstleutnant Egon Mayer, Kommandeur, III./JG 2 shot down 42-3190. The 94th Bomb Group lost 4 B-17s, the total losses for the Le Bourget strike. Harrison elected to crash-land the Fortress to save the engineer, whose parachute had been burned in the fire aboard the aircraft. Harrison, his co-pilot and the engineer, managed to escape with the help of the French Underground. They walked across the Pyrenees into Spain.

252 A Lufbery (or "Luftberry" as it was sometimes known in its corrupted form by American fighter pilots) was named for the WWI American fighter ace Major Gervais Raoul Lufbery of *Escadrille SPA. 124 - the Escadrille Lafayette*. The Lufbery Circle was a defensive tactic, in which a group of aircraft flew in a tight circle, making it difficult for enemy aircraft to break into and attack without themselves being attacked. Lufbery, born in France of French parents who later emigrated to America, was third in the roll of American aces with 17 confirmed victories. When WWI began Lufbery joined the French Foreign Legion and obtained a quick transfer to the *Service Aéronautique*. In December 1914 Lufbery successfully applied for pilot training and he was posted to *Escadrille VB.106*. In May 1916 he was transferred to the *Escadrille Lafayette* and he had scored 5 victories by early October. His subsequent career brought him promotion and many decorations, including the first award of the British Military Cross to an American. With America's entry into the war Lufbery was transferred, with the rank of Major to the U.S. Air Service and he was subsequently given command of the famous 94th Aero Squadron. He was killed on 19 May 1918 while attacking an Albatros two-seater reconnaissance aircraft over the 95th Squadron's base at Tool when his Nieuport 28 burst into flames. Lufbery fell from the burning aircraft at an altitude of 6000ft, whether deliberately or accidentally, will never be known.

253 Eder's bomber victim was *Windy City Challenger* of the 422nd Bomb Squadron, 305th Bomb Group (which crashed at Lieuesant, south of Paris), part of the force of 116 B-17s of the 1st Bomb Wing attacking Villacoublay Air Depot between 0811-0815 hours. Seven of Lieutenant John E Perkins, Jr.'s crew were killed and 3 were taken prisoner. (The other 1st Bomb Wing force of 64 B-17s, which attacked Amiens/Glisy airfield at 0742 hours, was the only one of the three forces sent out early this day to have escorts. Bf 109Gs of 3./JG 27 and II./JG 2 attacked shortly before the target was reached and a 3./JG 27 Bf 109 shot down *Widget* in the 535th Bomb Squadron, 381st Bomb Group flown by Lieutenant Robert J. Holdem, the only loss to the Amiens force). Three P-47s were lost - one in the 4th Fighter Group and two in the 78th Fighter Group and one battle-damaged Thunderbolt was abandoned off Newhaven - pilot saved. (Major Wutz Galland, II Gruppe CO claimed 3 P-47s this day). The Villacoublay air depot strike force lost three B-17s, bringing total bomber losses for 14 July to 8. At Villacoublay the hangars housing the FW 190 repair facility of *Luftflotte* 3 were destroyed, along with 70 FW 190s.

254 The 78th Fighter Group had lost its first CO, Colonel Arman Peterson on 1 July when he was shot down and KIA near Ouddorp, Holland. Pete Peterson was 28 years old; he came from Flagstaff, Arizona and he called his Thunderbolt *"Flagari"* because he did not want people to forget his old home town. Lieutenant Colonel Melvin F. McNickle took Peterson's place.

255 *Unteroffizier* Harry Kubon of the 5th *Staffel* JG 26 was WIA. He baled out of his FW 190A-4 into the Somme Estuary and was rescued.

256 The *"Little Old Lady"*

257 Later in hospital DeGenero was awarded the DSC for valor and sent home to recover from his wounds Major "Wutz" Galland's second P-47 that he claimed also made it back to England where the pilot baled out into the Channel. And he was rescued.

Chapter 7:

258 B-17 42-30206 *Happy Daze*, 410th Bomb Squadron, 94th Bomb Group

259 One crewmember was KIA. On 26 July an airborne lifeboat dropped by a 279 Squadron Warwick from Bircham Newton near to the ditched crew who steering westward, sailed it for 120 miles, at which point they were picked up by a Danish fishing boat. The Danes agreed to take the crew to England and instead of returning to Denmark decided to join the Free Danish Navy operating from the British Isles.

260 In the 306th Bomb Group 2nd Lieutenant Wesley E. Courson's B-17 and *Unbearable II* flown by Flight Officer Norman A. Armbrust were shot down after the bomb run. *Dixie Demo II* flown by Lieutenant Alphonse H. Maresh made it back to England but had to make a dead stick landing in the sea off Cromer. All 10 crew were rescued.

261 In *Twelve O' Clock High* Lay use the incident in a scene where Lieutenant Jesse Bishop, the 918th Bomb Group co-pilot awarded the his Medal of Honor for doggedly getting battered ship back to Archbury, staying at the controls for 1½ hours after Lieutenant McKesson, his pilot had been killed. In the script, McKesson, "a beefy six-footer" is mortally wounded by a burst of enemy gunfire from fighters out of the sun from 12 o'clock high which blows off the back of his head, exposing the brain. In the same attack, the top turret gunner slips through the flight deck hatch and falls to the floor, his right arm blown off at the shoulder and is spouting blood all over himself and against the inside of the aircraft. Lieutenant, Heinz Zimmerman, Bishop's navigator, "his coveralls spattered with the drying, dark stains of another man's blood" tries to give him a shot of morphine, but it is 40 below at 25,000ft and he bends the needle and cannot get it in. Next Zimmerman tries a tourniquet, but the arm is off to close to the shoulder and he can only bandage him as best he can. Finally, Zimmerman, who knows

that critically wounded gunner will not survive the two hours back to base, puts a parachute on him and places the ripcord in his hand before dumping him out of the nose hatch, praying that the French or the Germans will get him to hospital and save his life.

262 II./JG 1 alone claimed 7 *viermots* destroyed for the loss of two aircraft (both pilots safe).

263 At Debden and Duxford a large number of big crates arrived yielding the new 200-gallon unpressurized auxiliary gas tanks, which were being debuted by 8th Fighter Command. The P-47C/Ds were rapidly modified to accept the tanks, which would permit a round trip range 30 miles deeper into enemy airspace than the 8th's fighters had previously gone.

264 All except the 94th and some in the 96th Bomb Groups had turned back.

265 Burath's victim was *Spook III*, flown by 2nd Lieutenant Francis J. Reagen in the 336th Bomb Squadron, which was finished off by *Gruppenkommandeur Hauptmann* Emil-Rudolf Schnoor, his 3rd victory. *Spook III* ditched in the North Sea with the loss of all 10 crew. It brought the 95th Bomb Group's losses for the day to three. Lieutenant James F. Rivers' B-17 in the 334th Bomb Squadron crashed at Hoehausen and all the crew were taken prisoner. *Exterminator* flown by 2nd Lieutenant Fred D Hughes in the 412th Bomb Squadron crashed at Lathen, Germany and all the crew were made PoW. Pilots of JG 1 claimed five other B-17 victories.

266 15 Fortresses in the 4th Wing were shot down on the Oschersleben raid, including one crippled B-17, which crashed into two others, bringing all three down.

267 B-17 42-3116 in the 407th Bomb Squadron flown by 2nd Lieutenant Harold W. Porter crashed at Wageningen. 2 KIA. 8 PoW. B-17 42-29798 in the 326th Bomb Squadron flown by 1st Lieutenant Benjamin Smotherman crashed at Schelluinen. 10 PoW. Earlier that morning at 0916-0920 hours three B-1Fs were claimed north of Sylt and NW of Heligoland by JG 26 and at 1015 *Unteroffizier* Heinrich "Jan" Schild of 2nd *Staffel* claimed a B-17 NW of Hertogenbosch. See *The JG 26 War Diary Vol.2* by Donald Caldwell. Grub Street, London. 1998.

268 Lieutenant Duane W. Beeson claimed a Bf 109 at Westhooft-Emmerich. Lieutenant Raymond C. Care, a FW 190. Captain Roy Evans a Bf 109 15miles W of Arnhem. Lieutenant Frank Boyles a FW 190 10 miles SE of Utrecht. Lieutenant Leon Blanding a FW 190 10 miles SE of Utrecht. Captain Lee Gover a FW 190 25 miles E of Rotterdam. Colonel Edward W. Anderson, two FW 190s E of Rotterdam and Captain Carl H. Miley, a 109 E of Rotterdam. In fact, 1 and 11 *Jagdgeschwadern* lost 20 FW 190s and Bf 109s with three pilots killed and 8 injured, I./JG 26 another 3 FW 190A-5s, two of which were shot down by return fire from the bombers and the other to a P-47. All three German pilots were WIA, one of whom broke his neck when he crash-landed but he survived to fly again in 1944. See *The JG 26 War Diary Vol.2* by Donald Caldwell. Grub Street, London. 1998.

269 Flying P-47C 41-6238.

270 39 B-26 Marauders attacked targets in Holland and France.

271 All 10 crew were reported to have baled out but two men were later reported KIA.

272 *Oberfeldwebel* Heinz Kemethmüller of 7./JG 26 was credited with this victory.

273 *Hauptmann* Hermann Staiger, CO 12./JG 26 was credited with the destruction of both bombers. Two of Berryman H. Brown's crew, Harry W. Lofgren the ball turret gunner and 20-year old S/Sgt Eric G Newhouse, waist gunner were KIA. Eric Neuhaus had left his native Austria in 1938 as a boy of 15 to escape the *Nazi* persecution of the Jews, finally arriving in the USA. On 7 December 1941, the day the Japanese bombed Pearl Harbor, Newhouse though he was not yet an American citizen, tried to enlist in the AAF. He was rejected but he turned up at his enlistment at Wausau, Wisonsin for 120 consecutive days until they finally accepted him. He became a gunner in the AAF and went to England. The 29 July mission was his 7th combat sortie. Officially, the 306th Bomb Group was credited with the destruction of three Bf 110s and three FW 190s. JG 26 lost 1 Bf 109G-6 and three were damaged). JG 11 claimed 8 Fortresses.

274 Early P-47 missions without belly tanks averaged 1 hour and 45 minutes to the maximum of 2 hours and 5 minutes. With the 75-gallon pressurized tanks, missions were from 2 hours 30 minutes to 2 hours and 50 minutes. The 165-gallon tanks gave another 45-50 minutes range and with two 108-gallon wing tanks the P-47 Groups flew shows up to 5 hours and 30 minutes but the tanks were metal and in short supply. The treated pressed-paper 108-gallon wing tanks gave further range but they also caused some problems. The grass field at Duxford for instance was uneven and it was not unusual to punch a hole in the tank on takeoff. The paper tanks were sometimes difficult to drop in combat, because they occasionally froze at high altitude. One of the tricks used to jettison a recalcitrant tank was to have a wingman slip his wingtip between the tank and the wing and knock it off the pylon. Late in 1943 P-47 Groups were using up to 480 tanks a month and tried to keep a 6 to 8 mission back stock on hand. Fighter units were assigned their escort relay points by the size of the tanks they carried on the show, which dictated their range.

275 Lieutenant Colonel McNickle, the CO, would be leading the show in WZ-M 42-7961, the same aircraft in which Lieutenant Maxwell had experienced a compressibility dive.

276 Just as *The Old Squaw* finally reached the coast of England, No.4 engine quit, out of fuel. Campbell was forced to put the B-17 into a glide. He managed to reach an airfield just before the No.2 began to splutter. Other aircraft were not so fortunate, some ditching in the Channel and others having to make crash landings all along the coast as one by one they ran low on fuel.

277 An attack on Courtrai-Wevelgham was abandoned.

278 A 388th Bomb Group B-17, 42-30208, flown by Fight Officer E. Pickard, south of Antwerp and Feldwebel Ernst Christof of 1./JG 26, over Flanders, at 0825 and 0835, respectively. The latter's claim, his 9th victory, was B-17F 42-30290 *Lucky Lady II*, flown by 2nd Lieutenant Carmelo P. Pelusi, of the 338th Bomb Squadron, 96th Bomb Group, which had jettisoned its bomb load and had two engines knocked out by flak over Belgium. It exploded and came down near Tielrode. Five crew were killed and 5 baled out and were taken prisoner. Christof was KIA just over two hours later, when 1st Lieutenant Kenneth G. Smith of the 335th Fighter Squadron, 4th Fighter Group shot him down over Schouwen.

279 42-3100.

280 Three engines were put out of action and 4 crewmen baled out before the doomed B-17 descended into cloud near Ascheberg. One of the men was almost certainly killed when he hit the tail. Six men remained aboard as Humason brought the aircraft in for a crash landing at Deelen, where it was strafed by at least one of the FW 190s. Post suffered a broken leg and lost an eye as a result of the strafing and he was repatriated in 1944.

281 His victim 5kms SE of Est was 41-24399 *Man O'War* flown by 2nd Lieutenant Keene C. McCammon in the 323rd Bomb Squadron, which crashed at Opjne. 8 of McCammon's crew were killed and two were taken prisoner. Naumann's *Staffel* lost three FW 190s and 1 pilot KIA to return fire from the B-17s. Feldwebel Peter Crump claimed a YB-40 near Arnhem but no B-17 "gun ships" were lost this day.

282 The group lost three B-17s this day, including one Fortress, which crash-landed at Alconbury.

283 The 9-man crew and photographer Sgt Bruce, who called themselves *The Miracle Tribe,* lived up to this name, 2nd Lieutenant Miracle putting the crippled bomber down in the North Sea where all 10 men were picked up by ASR.

284 After radioing England for directions the resistance turned him over to the Germans for medical treatment and he was made PoW near Ravestein in Holland. At least 24 *Luftwaffe* fighters were lost over Holland. JG 1 lost 8 FW 190A-4s and A-5s destroyed with another three severely damaged when their pilots crash-landed their Bf 109G-6s after being damaged in air combat. JG 2 lost 7 destroyed; JG 11 one Bf 109G-6 destroyed with another 5 G-1s and G-6s between 15 and 80% damaged. JG 26 had 4 write-offs and JG 54 lost another 4. In all 8 Bf 109s and 16 FW 190s were destroyed. Ten Jagdflieger were killed and two were MIA. Another 9 fighter pilots were injured. Spitfires escorting the B-26s in the early morning attack on Woensdrecht airfield shot down two of these fighters, both of JG 26. The remaining 22 *Luftwaffe* fighters lost were all victims of the fierce dogfights with P-47s and in attacks with the B-17s.

285 As Roberts was dispatching his target's wingman, Flight Officer Glenn Koontz set fire to another, which went into a death dive.

286 No JG 26 fighters were lost so the victories probably were at the expense of JG 1 and JG 11.

287 335th Fighter Squadron pilot, Captain Donald A. Young, FW 190 at 1130 hours, 15 miles SE of Rotterdam; Lieutenant. Pierce W. McKennon, FW 190, 1135 hours, Zalt Boomel, Holland; Lieutenant. Frank Boyles, FW 190 at 1135 hours, Zalt Boomel; Lieutenant. Aubrey C. Stanhope, FW 190, 1135 hours, south of Arnhem; and Lieutenant Kenneth C. Smith, the FW 190 flown by Feldwebel Ernst Christof of 1st *Staffel* JG 26 at 1140 hours, over Schouwen Island.

288 Lieutenant Frederick D. Merritt, 335th Fighter Squadron, flying P-47C 41-6248. He was either hit by B-17 fire or followed a Bf 109 down, which his leader, Don Young, had shot at. Merritt was not seen after the attack on the 109. *Hauptmann* Rolf Hermichen of I./JG 26 claimed a P-47 destroyed at 1015 hours in the Dordrecht area.

289 When Intelligence finished debriefings, they knew this near three-hour mission was one for the record books. The 78th Fighter Group's string of pioneer "Firsts" included the first Group belly' tank show; first Group penetration of Germany; first 8th Air Force Fighter Ace, Captain Charles P. London; first 8th Fighter Command strafing attack, Lieutenant Quince L. Brown; first 8th Air Force Triple Victory, Major Eugene P. Roberts; highest 8th Air Force mission victory score to date (16) and the first 8th Fighter Command Group to score in double figures. Major Roberts was shortly awarded the DSC for valor during this mission. The statistics for July showed the increased pace of combat with 19 missions, 21 victories, 5 MIA, 1 WIA, 2 crash landings and 2 air-sea-rescues.

290 And Lieutenant Buster Peek.

291 B-17F 42-29797 *Old Ironsides* ditched in the North Sea with the tail gunner dead. 9 men returned. Peek was KIA on 31 August flying *Eager Beaver,* when he was again forced to ditch in the sea. This time only the tail gunner survived.

292 Hernan learned later that Pentz had crash-landed his B-17, one of 25 lost this day, and that 9 of the crew, including Dougherty were taken prisoner. JG 1 claimed ten of the losses when all three *Gruppen* made contact with a formation of about 300 B-17s over the Ruhr area after intense flak over Solingen had disrupted the formation. II./JG 1 lost one pilot killed and 12 fighters were damaged by return fire. Eleven other bombers lost were claimed by I. (6) and II./JG 26 (5). *Leutnant* Jorg Kiefner of 3./JG 26 shot down 42-5807 of the 327th Bomb Squadron, 92nd Bomb Group. This Fortress crash-landed at 1020 hours near Azelo, Bornerbroek, eastern Holland. Eight of the crew were taken prisoner. B-17F 42-30081 *USS Aliquippa*, of the 407th Bomb Squadron, 92nd Bomb Group flown by Lieutenant Gene Wiley, was credited to *Unteroffizier* Hein Heuser of 2./JG 26 east of Arnhem. On board was Colonel (later General) Delmar T Spivey of Training Command, who was on only the first of his 5 scheduled missions as part of an inspection tour. Spivey's first - and last - of his planned 5-mission tour, a "milk-run" over the Ruhr, ended with his capture. All the crew survived and they too were taken prisoner. The 92nd Bomb Group had started out for the marshaling yards at Gelsenkirchen but bad weather forced them to bomb a target of opportunity at Bochum.

293 On 15 August the air echelon of the 392nd Bomb Group flew their Liberators into Wendling their new base 8 miles northeast of Swaffham, Norfolk from the USA. The Group had been activated on 26 January 1943 at Davis-Monthan Field, Arizona and placed under the command of Colonel Irvine R. Rendle. On 18 July, its training completed, the ground echelon sailed from New York, its port of embarkation. It was on 1 August while other Liberator Groups

from England were attacking the Ploesti oilfields that the ground echelon began arriving at Wendling. The Group's B-24Hs and B-24Js were fitted with a power-operated gun turret in the nose, which replaced the Perspex-domed nose that had been a feature of the B-24Ds. However their installation posed an immediate problem for the ground crews because the Group had begun receiving the B-24Hs while the ground echelon was still at sea. When the ground crews were at last able to familiarize themselves with the new aircraft, the aircrews were attending mandatory lectures on RAF flying control procedures, aircraft recognition and the *Gee* navigational device.

294 The prime target was the Kugelfischer Werke. Subsidiary targets were the Vereingte Kugellager Fabriken Works I and II, the Deutsche Star Kugelhalter and the factories of Fichtel & Sachs, all located along the winding Regnitz River.

295 Crews were told that production at Regensburg was estimated at 200 Bf 109s a month, or approximately 25 to 30% of Germany's single-engine aircraft production. Few doubted the importance of mounting a mission against the plants, but hitherto, the campaign against the German aircraft industry had been waged within reasonable striking distance from the British mainland. The original plan to bomb all three plants on one day, 7 August, had been disrupted by bad weather, so the plan had been modified to bomb each target when the opportunity arose. On 13 August Wiener Neustadt was bombed by B-24s of VIII Bomber Command and on 14 August by B-24s of the 9th Air Force, both forces flying from North Africa.

296 The early morning ground mist turned into a summer fog when the day dawned and plans had to be hastily changed. Timings were crucial and the 4th Wing needed daylight to land in North Africa so they could only be delayed an hour. The 1st Wing would have to wait 3½ hours for the Regensburg escorts to return, refuel and rearm. Four escort groups were briefed to go out with the Regensburg force in the morning and meet the Schweinfurt bombers coming back in the afternoon. The original plan would have given fighter controllers about 2½ hours to turn their P-47Ds around but the changes caused by the weather gave them an hour less than was required. It just was not possible to refuel the Thunderbolts with the few tankers they had on their bases in that time. As a result only the 56th and the 353rd of the four escort groups would fly the second mission and the latter had only flown its first group combat mission on 12 August. (On 9 August the 353rd Fighter Group had provided 16 P-47Ds to fly as a fourth squadron with the 56th Fighter Group). The 200-gallon flush ferry tank provided for early P-47C/D models was unsuitable for combat and there were not enough 75-gallon drop tanks available. A British-made 108-gallon tank made of pressed paper could be used under the fuselage or two could be fitted beneath the wings, increasing radius of action to 350 miles and 445 miles respectively. While they gave an extra half-hour over enemy territory the bathtub-shaped tanks, first used on 12 August, were only suitable for low and medium altitude operation because they lacked a means of pressurization. Fuel could not be drawn much over 20,000ft, which meant that the tanks had to be released before reaching the Thunderbolt's usual operational altitude. Moreover, the tanks were difficult to install, tended to leak, affected the center of gravity of the P-47 and sometimes failed to release. If fuel were left in the tanks too long it started to dissolve and weaken the sealing material. They also had a habit of banging against the underside of the P-47 when released or not coming away at all, forcing an abort. Their use on 12 August had at least enabled the 56th Fighter Group to remain airborne for 2 hours 12 minutes, giving 20 minutes of extra cover for B-17s bound for the Ruhr. No successful contact was made on this mission, or on the next two occasions when use was made of the troublesome tanks.

297 Thomas E. Murphy a commercial airline pilot from Waltham, Massachusetts was an original pilot in the 100th Bomb Group who flew B-17F-30-VE 42-5864 *Piccadilly Lily*. 100th Bomb Group Historian Michael P. Faley says, "Lieutenant Colonel Beirne Lay, Jr., was supposed to fly in *Alice From Dallas* on the Regensburg mission but Major Gale 'Buck' Cleven, upon seeing that the 350th was flying 'tail end Charlie' had him moved to the high squadron in Lieutenant Thomas Murphy's *"Piccadilly Lily."* Who knows, *Twelve O' Clock High* may have never been written or made into a movie if it were not for that one small decision!"

298 Over 300 fighters drawn from JG 1, JG 2, JG 3, JG 11, JGr 25, JG 26, 11./JG 27, 11./JG 51, III/JG 54, JG 300 and ZG 26 were ranged against the B-17 formations.

299 P-47s of the 56th Fighter Group had taken off from Halesworth and they cleared the clouds at around 5,000ft. They were able to make formation with little trouble and the "Wolfpack" picked up the rear box of bombers near Antwerp and stuck with them to Eupen before having to turn back. Although some interceptions of enemy aircraft took place no conclusive results were obtained. 1st Lieutenant Gerald W. Johnson fired at a Bf 109 before it eluded him. The P-47s returned after another disappointing flight.

300 This was credited to his wingman *Leutnant* Georg Kiefner after it was found that Hermichen's guns had not been fired. However, as this claim was for the final destruction of an already-separated aircraft it was never submitted to the RLM and was not added to Kiefner's claims total. Hermichen's total victories by the end of hostilities stood at 64 *Abschüsse*, 8 of which, were on the Eastern Front and 45, including 26 *Viermots*, were on the Western Front. He had been decorated with the *RitterKreuz und Eichenlaub* (*RK* or Knight's Cross with Oak Leaves (*El*). *Luftwaffe Fighter Aces* by Mike Spick, Ivy Books, 1996.

301 Brigadier General Frank O'D "Monk" Hunter, chief of VIII Fighter Command, insisted the 353rd's operational advancement would be accelerated under an experienced leader and that neither the 4th or 78th Groups had anyone he rated as highly as McCollom. Next morning Zemke had orders cut for Mac's transfer to the 353rd permanently. On 25 November 1943 McCollom was shot down and taken prisoner. (See *Zemke's Wolfpack* by Roger Freeman).

302 The first Fort to go down was 42-30389 *Dear Mom* of the 331st Bomb Squadron, 94th Bomb Group, which went down after a frontal attack by Major Karl Borris, *Kommandeur*, I./JG 26, crashing at Lummen, Belgium, with the loss of 6 of the crew.

303 *Alice From Dallas*, piloted by Lieutenant Roy F. Claytor, who was leading the second element of the low squadron, was shot down by flak bursts at 1020 hours while over eastern Belgium. The B-17 erupted in flames and 8 men managed to bale out safely. Edward Musante's - the right waist gunner - parachute fouled the horizontal stabilizer and he was killed when the aircraft exploded. The ball turret gunner was also killed after failing to get clear in time. For most of the crew it was only their tenth mission. Both Claytor's wingmen, 2nd Lieutenant Thomas D. Hummel flying 42-30311 and Lieutenant Ronald W. Braley flying 42-30070 *Tweedle O' Twill*, were shot down by a combination of flak and fighters. Bf 109s attacked 42-30311 from head-on about 10 minutes from Nuremberg. The first shell went through the nose. Another hit the prop on No.2 engine and damaged the mechanism. As the B-17 dropped out of formation the fighters attacked again and hit the Tokyo tank in the left wing starting a fire. Hummel ordered the crew out. Seconds later the oxygen tanks ignited and the plane exploded blowing three of the 4 men in the waist clear. S/Sgt Richard Bowler, replacement waist gunner, later died of his injuries. The B-17 crashed at Schornsheim, 15km south of Mainz. Nine of Braley's crew baled out near Tauberbischofsheim, a suburb of Würzburg about 125 miles before the target and they were captured and their wounds treated. Braley's radio operator, James Blair, had been wounded earlier over Holland when the first wave of fighters struck but he was still firing his guns when struck in the chest by a 20mm and instantly killed. (See *Century Bombers; The Story of the Bloody Hundredth* by Richard Le Strange, 100th Bomb Group Memorial Museum, 1989). A B-17 in the 95th Bomb Group was also shot down. In addition, B-17F 42-30063 *Picklepuss*, which formed part of Major Kidd's lead squadron, was knocked out of formation soon after crossing the Moselle. As Captain Robert M. Knox pilot, tried to climb back into position, the fighters came in again and hit a second engine. *Picklepuss* became separated from the rest of the group and with all hope of catching them up gone the crew was faced with the daunting decision as to whether they should try and get back to England or head for Switzerland. 2nd Lieutenant Ernest Warsaw, navigator opted for England and after a brief discussion, they all readily agreed. On reaching the German border however, just south of Aachen, the plane was confronted by three Bf 110 nightfighters of NJG 1, which had taken off from St. Trond with orders to hunt down any returning cripples. Two of the fighters promptly attacked from the rear and were shot down, although both pilots landed safely. The third attacked from the front and after firing a burst of 20mm cannon, the bomber's right wing snapped off and both wing and fuselage spiraled down in a dive. Warsaw, Sgt Walter Paulsen, radio operator and T/Sgt Glover Barney, engineer, were able to bale out. 2nd Lieutenant Edwin Tobin, bombardier was probably thrown out after climbing into the cockpit to help where he found Knox and the co-pilot 2nd Lieutenant John O. "Bob" Whitaker fastening their parachutes. What happened next remains uncertain but *"Picklepuss"* is believed to have exploded. Knox, Whitaker and the four gunners in the rear of the plane were killed. Tobin remembered nothing about his descent and remained in a deep coma for the next two days and came round in a German hospital. *Hauptmann* Von Bonin, *Kommandeur*, II./ NJG 1, who was leading the vic of three Bf 110s is credited with the destruction of *Picklepuss*, which crashed at Schmalgraf near Kelmis at 1140 hours.

304 Nine of 2nd Lieutenant Henry P. Shotland's crew, who were on their first mission, baled out before the B-17 exploded and they were taken prisoner.

305 T/Sgt Lawrence E. Godbey, engineer, died from wounds sustained by a 20mm shell, which hit him in the shoulder and hip. 1st Lieutenant Dan Mckay, bombardier and 2nd Lieutenant John C. Dennis, navigator, badly burned, survived the bale-out and they were treated in Frankfurt hospital for several weeks before being sent to a PoW camp. Pilot, 1st Lieutenant Curtis R. Biddick and T/Sgt Robert D. DeKay, radio operator, were also killed. Flight Officer Richard L. Snyder's remains were discovered months later hanging from his parachute in a tree.

306 Lieutenant Norris Norman, bombardier, who was hit by shell splinters including the rider ring from the shell, which had wrapped itself around the bone in his upper arm) maintained that there was no panic aboard *Phartzac*: "If anyone lost control I cannot believe that over two people were involved. It is also believed that anything of this nature was of very short duration and did not affect the outcome of the mission in any way. Norman Smith, radio operator, was killed at his station. The bombardier and James parks, top turret gunner remained at their duty positions and continued to perform after being wounded. A projectile had hit Parks' leg and traveled upwards at an angle and came out the other side making a hole 6 or 7 inches long. During the battle I called Paddy [Blazier] in the ball turret and said, 'Paddy here come two at 11 o'clock low.' Paddy replied, 'Let the sons of bastards come…' that didn't sound like a panicked airman to me. I believe very strongly that all the airmen in the back of the aircraft performed in an outstanding manner. They were the best. This crew completed the mission; two-thirds of the squadron did not return. Norman Smith was buried at Constantine, Algeria." See *Century Bombers:The Story of the Bloody Hundredth* by Richard Le Strange. 100th Bomb Group Memorial Museum, 1989.

307 42-30042 *Oh Nausea* flown by Lieutenant Glen S. Van Noy had such a long history of malfunctions it was reputed to have never completed a mission or to have dropped a bomb on its objective. Soon after crossing the enemy coast a fighter pass knocked out one engine and at the target a 2nd engine was lost. Under almost constant attack, William Crabb, radio operator who was manning the ball turret this day, ran out of ammunition before reaching Regensburg although he had started the mission with 1100 rounds for one gun and 900 for the other. Realizing that they probably could not reach Africa, the decision was made to try for Sicily, which, according to the morning briefing would fall to the Allies that day. One bomb had hung up over the target and bombardier William Couch tried to release it over a small airfield near the Brenner Pass but without success. Later it was released manually over the Mediterranean. Van Noy went down to about 500ft and the crew began to throw out everything detachable to lighten the ship - even shoes were discarded. Such efforts were in vain as a 3rd engine went out about 90 miles north of Sicily and Van Noy and co-pilot James Evans made a perfect landing on the sea. *Oh Nausea* floated for an hour and a half before finally sinking, allowing the 10 crew time to get into two 5-man dinghies and a smaller one with rations and a radio. After cranking

out emergency signals all night they were picked up the following morning by Germans in a flying boat. Also taken prisoner was Colonel William Kennedy, the commander of a gunnery school in the States, who was on a tour of British bases and who volunteered to fly a mission to get some first hand experience as to what problems the gunners were facing in combat. Ironically, S/Sgt George Gineikis, who Kennedy replaced in the tail gun position, was obliged to return to gunnery school when, after a later raid he failed to clear his gun and accidentally shot his own aircraft's tail. On completion of a refresher course, he continued with his tour. See *Century Bombers; The Story of the Bloody Hundredth* by Richard Le Strange. 100th Bomb Group Memorial Museum, 1989.

308 Despite the fire and an oxygen failure, *Torchy 2nd* successfully bombed the target and the crew extinguished the fire and managed to reach North Africa safely.

309 The 390th had placed 58% of its bombs within 1000ft of the MPI and 94% within 2000ft. *Rick O'Shay* flown by Captain Gerald F. Ritcher, circled Regensburg after the bombing and the crew could see smoke towering up to almost 10,000ft. It was a sight to cheer all the crews in the surviving 128 ships in the 4th Wing as LeMay led them off the target. The 2nd Combat Wing was forced to swing around in a 360° turn and make another bomb run after the target had been obscured by smoke from the leading wing's bombs. Then it was the turn of the last two groups over the target, the 95th and 100th to add their incendiary clusters to the conflagration.

310 All ten members of 2nd Lieutenant Ashbrooke W. Tyson's crew in 42-30017 *All Shot to Hell* in the 568th Bomb Squadron were taken prisoner. 42-30316 *Madie* in the 568th Bomb Squadron, crashed at Bellheim, Germany. One member of 2nd Lieutenant James R. Regan's crew was KIA. The other nine crewmembers were taken prisoner.

311 All ten members of 2nd Lieutenant Wade H. Sneed's crew in 42-3310 *Blood Guts & Rust* in the 568th Bomb Squadron survived and they returned. Three members of 2nd Lieutenant Raymond A. Becker's crew in 42-3333 *Purgatory Pete* in the 569th Bomb Squadron were KIA. Seven survived to be taken prisoner.

312 B-17F 42-30315 in the 569th Bomb Squadron.

313 Fries and his *Bordfunker*, *Unteroffizier* Alfred Staffa had claimed their first kill, a Lancaster III SE of Charleroi on 11 August 1943.

314 Fries had just shot down B-17G 42-30017 *All Shot To Hell* of the 568th Bomb Squadron, 390th Bomb Group, the exploded remains of which, came down at Bringen on the western banks of the River Rhine. All 10 of 2nd Lieutenant Ashbrooke W. Tyson's crew survived and were taken prisoner.

315 Fries landed at precisely 1300 and taxied immediately to the hangars where armorers found that one cannon and two machine guns had been jammed by burst cartridge cases. In all, 15 II./NJG 1 crews were scrambled from St. Trond on 17 August 1943 to combat the American formations heading for Schweinfurt and Regensburg. Although 7 B-17s were shot down by II./NJG 1 during the day 4 Bf 110s and one pilot were lost through return fire and in combat with Thunderbolts of the 56th Fighter Group. Almost all the other Messerschmitts returned with such severe battle damage that they could not be sent off to hunt for Bomber Command aircraft raiding Peenemünde the next night. Otto Fries finished the war with 14 confirmed and four unconfirmed *Abschüsse*.He was shot down three times, by a Stirling on 28/29 August 1942 and he and *Unteroffizier* Alfred Staffa were shot down a second and third time later in the war while flying He 219s and they ejected to safety on both occasions. On 19/20 May 1944 they were the second aircrew ever to eject under combat conditions after their He 219 *Owl* suffered an in-flight engine fire. On 16/17 January 1945 a RAF Mosquito shot down Fries and Staffa). They were credited with ten confirmed night kills August 1943-April 1944, plus two unconfirmed *Abschüsse* in daylight, a B-17 on 17 August and a P-47 on 14 October 1943. After being posted to 2./NJG 1 in early July 1944 Fries and Staffa flew the He 219 from Venlo airfield and added another 6 victory claims (4 of which were subsequently confirmed) to their score before the end of the war.

316 The 100th Bomb Group's total loss of 9 B-17s was the highest loss in the 4th Wing, which lost 24 bombers in total.

317 London's *Piccadilly Circus* had the reputation of being a major haunt for those seeking pleasures of the night and the capital was a great attraction for Allied servicemen on leave. Prostitutes or *Piccadilly Commandoes* as they were better known were always on hand to relieve GIs of their money. The notorious females inspired decorations and associated names on at least 50 USAAF planes. *Piccadilly Lily* became even more famous when Lay chose to use it as General Frank Savage's ship in his and Sy Bartlett's early post-war novel *Twelve O' Clock High!* and cinemagoers saw it in the movie of the same name. Twelve B-17s were used in the making of *Twelve O' Clock High,* which was filmed largely at Eglin AFB, Florida and Ozark, Alabama, from February to 1 July 1949. All the Fortresses are in 91st Bomb Group markings, easily distinguished by the white Triangle A on the tail fins. Chief Technical Advisor Colonel John H. deRussy USAF, formerly Operations Officer of the 305th Bomb Group personally led the formation flights, group landings and takeoffs featured in the movie and filmed at Ozark. DeRussy's superiors forbade him from also making the memorable belly-landing sequence and this was performed by veteran Hollywood stunt pilot Paul Mantz at Ozark early in May. *Twelve O' Clock High* was finally complete on 1 July 1949 and, when edited, ran for 133 minutes. This most famous of black and white aviation movies was premiered at Grauman's Chinese Theater in Hollywood on Christmas Day 1949. Lead actor Gregory Peck, who played General Frank Savage, summed up the movie perfectly when he said; "It is gratifying to be part of a movie that is still being shown 25 years after we made it, I think the picture still has meaning for audiences because of its integrity. We managed to dramatize a true story without resorting to false theatrics and sentimentality."

318 Galland's remains were discovered two months later, buried with the wreckage of his FW 190A-5 530125 12ft deep in earth at Hees-Vlijtingen 5km west of Maastricht. At the time of his death "Wutz" Galland had flown 186 combat sorties, during which he had scored 55 day victories, including 8 American *Viermots* and 37 Spitfires. He may have been the victim of an attack by Captain Walker 'Bud' Mahurin, who was credited with two FW 190s. These were the first of 20.75 victories Mahurin would score before he was shot down on 27 March 1944. He returned to Allied control on 7 May but he was not allowed to fly combat in Europe. Flying F-86E Sabres in the Korean War Mahurin destroyed three MiG-15s and he was also credited with a half share in a MiG kill as well as one "probably" destroyed.

319 Oberleutnant Konrad von Donner's FW 190 was damaged on the same pass and he landed at Brussels-Evere. Gomann was given three weeks' home leave to recover from his injuries.

320 42-7877 HV-D one of several P-47s received by the 56th carrying acknowledgements to communities or organizations that had raised the fighter's purchase price in war bonds.

321 Two days later when the 56th Fighter Group used similar tactics to claim another 9 fighters Gerald Johnson notched a single kill making him the 56th Fighter Group's first ace. Schiltz ended the war with 8 victories. Johnson eventually scored a total of 16½ aerial victories and he was detached to fly with the 356th Fighter Group in November 1943 before being shot down on 27 March 1944 by ground fire and taken prisoner. In later years he rose to the rank of lieutenant -general in the USAF and commanded the 8th Air Force during the Vietnam War.

322 In all the 56th Fighter Group claimed 17 fighters plus 1 probable and 9 damaged. Their losses were three, a 63rd element leader shot down by a FW 190 and two 62nd Squadron pilots who were last seen chasing a Bf 110 during the initial bounce. The Group could only speculate that single engined fighters had jumped them.

323 Later he complained that the III/JG 1 pilots were *Leichenfledderei* (corpse-looters) for failing to make a single concerted attack. See *The JG 26 War Diary Vol.2* by Donald Caldwell. Grub Street, London. 1998.

324 41-24564 XK-W in the 365th Bomb Squadron. three of 2nd Lieutenant Douglas L. Mutschler's crew were KIA. 7 PoW.

325 42-29735 in the 532nd Bomb Squadron flown by George R. Darrow was ditched in the North Sea and all 10 crew were rescued. Zeschke was KIA exactly a year later, on 17 August 1944, when his FW 190A-8 was hit by light flak over Caen. See *The JG 26 War Diary Vol.2* by Donald Caldwell. Grub Street, London. 1998.

326 27 B-17s in the 1st Wing were so badly damaged that they never flew again.

Chapter 8:

327 32 out of a formation of 36 386th Bomb Group Marauders successfully bombed Woensdrecht at 1032 hours without loss. This forward fighter base was largely destroyed in another B-26 raid by the 386th and 387th Bomb Groups, on 3 October 1943 and again by the 387th Bomb Group on 9 October. Persistent Allied raids against coastal fighter bases like Woensdrecht, Schiphol and airfields in Belgium and France forced the *Luftwaffe* to abandon the use of these forward fields by the end of 1943. This lost them the ability to respond early to incoming Allied bombers bound for the *Reich*.

328 B-17F 42-30068, flown by 2nd Lieutenant B. Howe in the 561st Bomb Squadron, 388th Bomb Group was hit by flak, which set his #4 engine on fire and he dropped out of formation. He was then attacked by enemy fighters near Haamstede and went down. *Unteroffizier* Erich Schwartz of 8./JG 26 claimed a B-17 in the 388th Bomb Group but it was not confirmed. Howe and 7 of his crew were KIA. 2 others became PoWs.

329 Four 1st Bomb Wing B-17s were lost. Three of these were claimed by JG 26, which had a tough time fending off Spitfires (10 squadrons of Spitfires were airborne this day) and Typhoons which were airborne to protect B-25s and B-26s attacking Amiens and Poix and, later, the Fortress formations attacking the Dutch airfields. In addition, the B-17s were also supported by a force of 175 Thunderbolts, the P-47s of the 4th and 78th Fighter Groups being used as penetration support and the Thunderbolts of the 56th and 353rd Fighter Groups, serving as the withdrawal support.

330 38 B-17s bombed Gilze-Rijen between 1802 and 1814 hours, while 55 Fortresses bombed Flushing at 1756 hours.

331 42-29807 *Lady Liberty*, flown by Lieutenant Ralph R. Miller in the 364th Bomb Squadron, with 8 crew KIA and 2 taken prisoner. Three of the 4 B-17s lost were claimed by JG 26, which had a tough time fending off Spitfires (10 squadrons were airborne) and Typhoons, which were to protect B-25s and B-26s attacking Amiens and Poix and later the Fortress formations attacking the Dutch airfields. Over Woensdrecht one B-17 was lost. P-47s and Spitfires shot down three of JG 26's fighters, while 1 FW 190A-4 crashed, out of fuel and two Bf 109Gs were shot down by return fire from the B-17s. Grunlinger was KIA on 4 September 1943 when a 127 Wing Spitfire shot him down west of Norrent-Fontes.

332 The 303rd Bomb Group lost two B-17s on the mission. 42-3192 *City of Albuquerque*, flown by Lieutenant James Nix in the 358th Bomb Squadron, crashed at Raamsdonkveer in Holland with the loss of 4 crew. 42-5392 *Stric Nine* in the 427th Bomb Squadron, flown by 2nd Lieutenant Lauren H Quillen, crashed into the North Sea with the loss of 6 crew.

333 *Miss Billie Jnr* in the 327th Squadron, 92nd Bomb Group was damaged by flak over the target and 1st Lieutenant Winston J. Tucker ditched in the Channel. ASR rescued all 10 crew. The 303rd and 305th Bomb Groups each lost one B-17 apiece, while *Fast Woman*, a 508th Bomb Squadron, 351st Bomb Group Fortress piloted by Lieutenant William A Suit, was shot down by Oberleutnant Walter Matoni CO, 5th *Staffel*, JG 3km NW of Dunkirk. *Fast Woman* crashed at St. Omer. *Oberfeldwebel* Addi Glunz of 4./JG 26 was credited with shooting down *Augerhead*, piloted by Lieutenant William Monahan in the 303rd Bomb Group, 4 days later during the raid on Amiens-Glisy airfield. two other B-17s in the 91st Bomb Group also FTR.

334 *Air War Europa: America's Air War Against Germany in Europe and North Africa. Chronology 1942-45*. Eric Hammel. (Pacifica Press 1994).

335 Only part of one force was able to attack a target. 16 B-17s bombed Denain/Prouvy airfield and 18, Mardyck airfield.

336 A 20mm shell had hit the turbo-supercharger under the rear fuselage, which starved his engine of air at the higher altitude. Zemke got back to England without incident. Victory claims by Naumann and Feldwebels Karl Ehret and Wilhelm Mayer of 6./JG 26, were sent to Berlin but only Ehret received confirmation of a victory over the Thunderbolts because the other crashes had not been witnessed.

337 Johnnie Vogt had scored his first victory on 19 August when he was credited with a Bf 109 near Walcheren Island. He scored seven more victories flying P-47s in the 56th and 356th Fighter Groups and finished the war with the rank of major. General Vogt retired from the Air Force on 1 September 1975. Kehl was KIA on 25 February 1944 in combat with a 4th Fighter Group P-47 near Metz.

338 42-29725. Four crew were captured while 6 evaded.

339 Their victims were either 381st Bomb Group or 384th Bomb Group machines. In all, 9 B-17s FTR to England. Mayer also claimed a 56th Fighter Group P-47 near Creil but his claim was not confirmed.

340 The 392nd Bomb Group flew its first mission on 6 September when its Liberators made a diversionary sweep to aid the Fortresses attacking Stuttgart.

341 1st Lieutenant W. P. Beecham's crew in *Impatient Virgin II* were interned in Switzerland and *Sky Shy,* flown by Flight Officer M. Bowen, tried to join him but the aircraft was on fire and the tail gunner had been killed in his turret. Nine men baled out and German civilians murdered the radioman.

342 The 389th Bomb Group now back to full strength, flew its first mission from England to Leeuwarden in the company of the 44th. However, thick cloud obscured the target and they were forced to seek "targets of opportunity." Four days later the 202nd Combat Bombardment Wing (Provisional) was redesignated the 14th Combat Wing with all the 4 B-24 Groups under its control. Its HQ was located at Shipdham and Colonel Leon Johnson moved from the 44th Bomb Group to command it. Lieutenant Colonel James L. Posey was promoted to command the "Eightballs." The new Wing hierarchy heralded a new era for the Liberators. Johnson addressed the many new arrivals, telling them they were joining B-24 Groups which would be further increased and their squadrons strengthened.

343 On 15 September a motor convoy took personnel to their new base at Podington where they were to remain for the remainder of the war. The hardstands at Alconbury were filled with the B-17s and B-24s of the 482nd Bomb Group, which was to become part of the "Pathfinder Force", attached to the 8th Air Force, equipped with radar bombing aids. Eaker and his staff had professed interest in British radar bombing aids, which could be used to defeat the cloudy conditions, which always seemed to obscure American targets, and by October 1943 the British *Gee* system was being installed in B-17s and B-24s. *Gee* was the first of several blind bombing and navigational aids developed by the British and utilized signals received from two ground stations to give an aircraft its exact position. The second type, *H_2S*, an airborne radar scanner, gave a crude impression of the terrain below on a cathode ray tube in the aircraft. *H_2S* was a British navigational radar developed by Dr. Lovell at the TRE (Telecommunications Research Establishment) at Malvern, Worcestershire, which produced a map-like image on a CRT (cathode ray tube or radar scope screen) of a 360° arc of the ground below the equipped aircraft. *H_2S* equipment was difficult to install because the revolving scanner antenna had to be extended clear beneath the aircraft. The scanner was covered with a large plastic bubble, which gave *H_2S* equipped B-17s the appearance of having a bathtub slung under their nose. City areas on coastlines or estuaries were chosen as targets when using *H_2S* because of the clear distinction between water and land on radar screens. This technique allowed a large increase in raids during the test period in late 1943 and early 1944. About 80% of 8th Air Force missions in the last quarter of 1944 used some type of radar bombing devices, either for navigation or targeting. About half of all blind bombing missions were "near failures" or worse. When using non-visual techniques in total overcast conditions, just 39.8% of all bombs dropped by the 8th Air Force landed within 3 miles, and 58.5% within 5 miles. Only 0.2% landed within 1000 ft in total overcast. In 4/10 to 5/10 cloud cover, 48.5% landed within 1 mile and 4.4% within 1,000ft; in 6/10 to 7/10 overcast conditions, 36.5% fell within 1 mile and 2% within 1000ft; with 8/10 to 9/10 cloud cover. 22.5% fell within 1 mile, and 1% within 1000ft.

344 The changes did not stop there. At Chelveston, the 305th Bomb Group lost its 422nd Bomb Squadron, which became a night leaflet squadron, dropping propaganda literature over Germany. Ten months earlier the squadron had been earmarked for such a task, but daylight operations had continued to take precedence over night operations. The 422nd was not the only outfit to begin practicing nocturnal missions.

345 369 RAF heavy bombers attacked the factory on the night of 15/16 September for the loss of three aircraft. This was a moonlit raid on the factory and Pathfinders marked the target accurately and the Master Bomber brought the Main Force in well to carry out some accurate bombing. Every building in the factory was hit and a large fire was started.

346 Late in the afternoon of 15 September the 389th Sky Scorpions took off from Hethel for a raid on the airfield at Chartres as part of the *Starkey* deception raids on airfields in northern France, which had begun on 9 September. Their return to Norfolk was made in darkness and the crews, who were inexperienced in night landings, in their haste to get down quickly, abandoned all landing-pattern disciplines.

347 B-24 42-40938 AG-D *D-Cup* in the 330thBomb Squadron piloted by 2nd Lieutenant William Loveday crashed at Yvetoit, France.

348 B-24 41-23810 *Tarfu* was lost with Lieutenant Andrew M. Reynolds' crew on 4 January 1944. 6 KIA.3 PoW. It was 2nd Lieutenant Tommy Atkinson's last mission with his crew as he flew the next mission with T. U. Collins' crew and was forced to land at Hogsby, Sweden in B-24 41-24111 RE-P *Piccadilly Filly.* The crew were interned. Butler flew his 4th mission of his tour in North Africa and now without a regular crew he had to "beg to go on missions."

349 At the end of September 1943, apart from the single-engined Bf 109 and FW 190 day fighters, B-17 and B-24 crews now faced over 150 Bf 110Gs and Me 410A-1/B-1s in 5 *Zerstörergruppen.*

350 One B-17 ditched in the sea off the Northumberland coast after 13 hours of flight, culminating in a vain search for an airfield. *Ascend Charlie* in the 390th Bomb Group suffered a similar fate when it crashed at Abergavenny, Wales. All of Lieutenant Herbert I. Turner's crew were killed. In the 388th Bomb Group *Sandra Kay,* flown by 1st Lieutenant H. O. Cox, Jr., crashed just south of RAF Shobden and all 10 crewmembers were killed. 2nd Lieutenant Henry J. Nagorka's *Old Ironsides* ditched in the sea just north of The Wash. The two waist gunners drowned and the tail gunner lost a leg. The third 388th B-17 that got into difficulty was *Gremlin Gus,* flown by Lieutenant Jarrendt. It crashed into the side of a hill at North Moulton, killing Ed Baliff, the cameraman and seriously injuring the navigator and bombardier. Three others in the crew were slightly injured. The luckiest man on board must have been James F. Jones, the tail gunner. Shortly before *Gremlin Gus* crashed, it touched a hilltop and Jones was thrown violently against the tail gunner's door, which gave way, throwing him out into space as he pulled the ripcord. He spun through the air as his parachute released, the billowing silk helping to cushion his body as he hit the ground at around 200mph. Jones was knocked unconscious and rolled almost 100 yards before stopping. About two hours later he remembered awaking and seeing a red flare in the sky. Incredibly, his only injuries consisted of a badly sprained leg and several bruises and contusions. When he arrived back at Knettishall, fellow group members listened to his story in utter amazement.

351 The 44th, 93rd and 389th Bomb Groups returned to Norfolk in the first week of October having bombed the Messerschmitt plant at Wiener Neustadt in Austria on 1 October when 8 Liberators were lost and 8 more were written off in crash landings in Africa on their return. Soon after, the main part of the 44th returned to England but was stood down for the mission to Vegesack on 8 October in order to lick its wounds. These hardly had time to heal when on the following day the Eightballs joined in the raid on Gydnia on the Baltic coast. German smokescreens proved so effective that they completely missed the target. During the latter part of October insurmountable cloud barriers blunted long-range operations over the Continent.

352 On 3 March 1944 Lieutenant Gossage and his new crew were flying B-17G-25-DL 42-38017 when they were hit by flak and suffered a damaged No.1 engine and the engineer was seriously wounded. Gossage headed for Sweden but five Ju 88s intercepted them and Gossage lowered the undercarriage and the lead Ju 88 escorted the Fortress to Schleswig-Holstein airfield in Denmark, which was used by NJG 3. All the crew were taken prisoner and the relatively intact B-17 was to have been put to use by the *Luftwaffe* but it was reported that Allied fighters later strafed and destroyed it on the ground. (See *Plane Names & Bloody Noses; The 100th Bomb Group (Heavy)* by Ray Bowden. Design Oracle Partnership, Dorset, England. 2000). It was reported that parts were subsequently used on B-17 41-21585, which was operated by the top-secret *Kampfgeschwader 200* as A3+BB, one of at least ten B-17s used on long range *Kommando Olga* clandestine agent-dropping and sabotage-missions over Allied territory, some lasting up to 13 hours, mainly on the Eastern Front. A3+BB is reputed to have been used in this role over England and Russia from late 1943 until it was shot down by American AA fire at Luvigny, France on the night of 2/3 March 1945 whilst on its way back from an agent-dropping mission to Belgium and France. See *Battles With the Luftwaffe: The Bomber Campaign Against Germany 1942-45*, Theo Boiten and Martin W. Bowman. Janes, 2001.

353 *Local Girl* was shot down at Geefsweer, northern Holland by a Bf 109. 2nd Lieutenant William G. Peagram, pilot, remained at the controls while 8 crew baled out over the coast of Ems. Peagram and Melvin Peters, waist gunner, who went on firing to the end, were found dead in the wreckage. Larson, engineer and Cosgrove, navigator drowned when the cords of their parachutes became entangled in the "botschuttings" or "flounder fences"; a device of twigs and branches to catch flat fish. The Germans would not allow Dutch fishermen to go out and save them. Only later were they allowed to retrieve the bodies. Pegram, the pilot, stuck to his post and it cost him his life. His body was found near the wreckage. Peters kept firing at the German fighters to the end and also went down with *Local Girl.* The other 6 crewmembers were safe and were sent to PoW camps. Norman Eatinger, bombardier, was rescued by a Dutch fishing boat.

354 Two had flown in each of the 1st and 3rd Division formations; the inclusion of a second *H_2S*-equipped aircraft per formation was a necessary precaution because the intricate *H_2S* sets often failed to function properly. On arrival at Emden, only one set in each formation was still working. Despite some confusion in maneuvering above the overcast at the approach to the target, the leading combat wing in the 1st Division successfully dropped in with the pathfinder aircraft from 22,000ft. The 2nd Combat Wing dropped on the smoke markers while the 3rd Combat Wing found no sign of the markers and was forced to seek alternative targets. One of the three combat wings in the 3rd Division managed to bomb visually after exploiting a gap in the clouds. Subsequent photographic reconnaissance however, proved that only the *H_2S* assisted formations had achieved a fair concentration of bombs on Emden, while other bomb patterns ranged as far as 5 miles away from the city.

355 Further radar bombing was delayed because the 482nd Bomb Group had insufficient aircraft and crews to participate in a major mission and there were several days on which conditions were suitable for visual attacks in western Germany.

356 Seay and his crew had fallen to what the RAF knew as a "Wild Boar" tactic where day fighters were used in conjunction with searchlights. It was highly successful. Five crew were KIA, 5 PoW. B-17F 41-24616 *Sam's Little Helper* survived the war and was flown home to the USA in 1945.

357 The P-47D, with the installation of a 108-gallon belly tank, could escort the bombers as far as Duren on 4 October when 282 bombers hit Frankfurt, Wiesbaden and Saarbrücken. Among the 56 fighters claimed shot down on the raid was a confirmed FW 190 kill, which went to S/Sgt Donald W. Crossley, a tail gunner in the 95th Bomb Group. He established a new record of 12 confirmed kills, which was unsurpassed by the end of hostilities.

358 Despite the improved firepower forward the heavy nose turrets reduced the Liberators' speed. They also made the bomber a very cold aircraft to fly in at altitude because icy drafts entered the aircraft through a gap between the nose section and the turret.

359 The 445th had been activated at Gowen Field, Idaho and the 446th at Davis-Monthan Field, Arizona. Lieutenant Colonel Robert E. Terrill, a West Pointer, was named CO of the 445th and training began at Orlando, Florida, nicknamed "Snafu U" by the freshman outfit, for combat initiation. During early June 1943 the 445th, now 1800 strong moved to the salt-flats at Wendover Field, Utah. During the first week of July the 445th moved to Sioux City, Iowa. During August early September 1943 three crashes occurred during training flights killing 27 men in the 445th. Crews became unsettled, resigning themselves to being part of a jinxed outfit. However there were no further accidents. In early September new B-24Hs began arriving at Sioux City and the 700th, 701st and 702nd Squadrons were moved with their bombers to neighboring fields. Meanwhile, on 6 June 1943 the 446th Bomb Group had moved to Alamogordo, New Mexico, but was almost immediately moved again to Lowery, Colorado, to complete training. On 18-19 October the 446th ground echelon departed for Camp Shanks, New York and was joined by the 445th ground echelon, which had begun leaving Sioux City on 20 October. On 27 October they both sailed for England aboard the *Queen Mary,* which docked at Clydeside on 22 November. Men were confined to the ship until the following day when they boarded a troop train, which carried them to Norfolk. The 445th detrained at Tivetshall Station near Tibenham in the early hours of 4 November. On 18 October the 445th air echelon was inspected by the POMs. 62 crews were now ready for the flight on the Southern Ferry route to England and they left Sioux City in late October 1943. Simultaneously, the 446th, which had departed for Lincoln, Nebraska, on 20-26 October, traveled by the same route. One 445th Liberator was lost between Puerto Rico and Brazil and a 446th B-24 veered off course over France and was shot down. The 446th touched down at Bungay (Flixton) on 4 November.

360 On 8 October more than 350 bombers in the 1st and 3rd Bomb Divisions would attack the port at Bremen and Vegesack again. The area was noted for its flak defenses and much of northwestern Germany's fighter strength was concentrated nearby so several attempts were made to reduce the effectiveness of the *Jagdgruppen.* In order to split the enemy fighter force, plans called for the 1st Division to approach the target from Holland while the 3rd Division crossed the North Sea and approached the target from the northwest. 55 B-24s of the 2nd Bomb Division, living up to their nickname, the "2nd Bomb Diversion" would fly a long, curving route over the North Sea to attack Vegesack.

361 Thayer manned one of the waist guns in *Our Baby.*

362 *Gee* was a British navigational device involved a special aircraft radio receiver working on pulsed signals received from three ground stations. It was limited to a range of about 400 miles. By late 1942 *Gee* had been rendered almost ineffective by German jamming, and it was replaced by *Oboe*. *Gee-H* was a development of *Gee*, giving more precise fixes to aircraft and *Micro-H* was a further development of the *Gee* system using ground stations' signals, but combined with H_2X for bombing.

363 After the P-47 escort had withdrawn, low on fuel, the B-17s, which approached Bremen from two different directions in an attempt to fool the German controllers, were met in strength. The ruses and feints and the use of airborne *Carpet* radar jammers aboard some of the B-17s for the first time, were not enough to prevent the loss of 27 B-17s and three B-24s. P-47s, before they had to return, low on fuel, took on Geschwaderstab JG 1 over Nordhorn and accounted for Geschwaderkommodore Major Hans Philipp, a 206-victory ace. Oberst Walter Oesau, previously Jagdfliegerführer 4 Brittany and forbidden to fly operationally assumed command two days later. Physically and mentally exhausted, he was shot down and killed in combat with P-51 Mustangs and P-38 Lightnings on 11 May 1944. He had 125 victories.

364 FW 190 A-6, Werke number 530715, Black 5, flown by 29 year old *Leutnant* Hans Ehlers, *Staffelführer* of 2./JG 1, collided with 42-3386 *Marie Helena,* piloted by 2nd Lieutenant Raymond J. Gormley, in the low squadron of the 100th Bomb Group. All 10 men, including Gormley were KIA. Ehlers survived the mid-air collision and baled out with various facial injuries and a double fracture of the right thighbone. His aircraft crashed near the village of Neuenhaus, Hentheim, 9km from the Dutch border. On 11 November 1943 Ehlers was promoted to *Staffelkapitän* of 3/JG 1 and became *Kommandeur* of 1/JG 1 in May 1944. In July 1944, when Ehlers received the Knights Cross, he had been shot down no less than 12 times and was credited with the destruction of 20 *Viermots.* Robert J. Cupp, manning one of the nose guns on 42-30235, *The Zoot Suiters,* the lead aircraft in the 95th Bomb Group's low squadron, saw Ehlers and a second FW 190 pass through the 100th Bomb Group formation. This second FW 190 passed over the formation and crossed his path. The pilot, probably Johannes Kreimeyer of 1/JG 1 was killed when his FW 190 A-6, Werke Nr.550729, exploded after receiving several short bursts from Cupp's 50 caliber. His aircraft crashed 2km NW of Vroomshoop, Holland. Following the collision between Gormley and Ehlers 1st Lieutenant Frank H. Meadows' *Phartzac* was torn apart from what appeared to have been an explosion in the bomb bay area (8 KIA 2 PoW). Minutes later 2nd Lieutenant Arthur H. Becktoft's *War Eagle* was observed by Owen "Cowboy" Roane and Robert N. Lohof leaving the formation under control with its No.3 engine on fire. It crashed with the loss of 1 KIA and 9 PoW. (Radio operator T/Sgt Floyd A. Lowe was hit between the shoulder blades by a 20mm shell and probably died instantly). The encounter reports from the 95th and 390th Bomb Groups reveal that between the European coast and the beginning of the bomb run (a period of about 30 minutes) these two groups were attacked by no less that 42 fighters, of which all but 8 were FW 190s or Bf 109s. Also, from the perspective of the 3rd Division's surviving crews, the level of German fighter interception was more prominent than had been the situation throughout most of September and early October, but did not match the vigor endured by those who survived the 17 August "double strike" mission.

365 Incredibly, almost all the crew *of Salvo Sal* managed to bale out of the doomed aircraft. All six enlisted men were captured by German patrols shortly after landing. 2nd Lieutenant John J. James, co-pilot, had jumped with a parachute that had been holed by a cannon shell and broke his leg in a bumpy landing. He was taken prisoner by German soldiers and hospitalized. 2nd Lieutenant Carl L. Spicer evaded capture and made it home to England via France and Spain. MacDonald and McGlinchey also evaded capture and traveled along the evasion lines through Holland and France into Spain, only to be caught at a crossing point on the Pyrenees. They were sent to *Stalag Luft 1,* Barth.

366 The 100th Bomb Group had lost 7 B-17s. Three of these were 42-30840 (Herbert Nash, pilot and 2 crew KIA), Bill MacDonald's *Salvo Sal* (1 Evd 1 KIA 8 PoW) and *Our Baby,* flown by Captain Bernard "Benny" A. DeMarco with Major Gale "Bucky" Cleven CO of the 350th Bomb Squadron, who together with the other 10 in the crew were later reported to be PoWs. A fourth was Captain Thomas Murphy, flying *Piccadilly Lily.* Murphy, Captain Alvin L. Barker, 351st Bomb Squadron Operations Officer, co-pilot 2nd Lieutenant Marshall F. Lee, who was riding in the ball turret, Derrell Piel, Elder Dickerson and S/Sgt Aaron A. David, tail gunner, were KIA. The five other members of the crew survived and they were taken prisoner. The 390th Bomb Group had lost three B-17s including *Devil's Daughter* and *Blood, Guts and Rust II.* The 96th contributed three B-17s to the division's loss. Altogether, the 8th lost 26 bombers, including 14 in the 3rd Division. The unfortunate 381st Bomb Group, flying as low group in the 1st Division formation, lost 7 of its 18 bombers, including the lead ship. If it had not been for the installation of *Carpet* blinkers aboard some 96th and 388th Bomb Group B-17s, losses might well have been much higher. *Carpet* was another British invention, which used radio signals to interfere with radar-directed flak guns. Over the next two months *Carpet* devices were fitted to all Fortresses. Experienced crews could not be totally replaced, but new crews were now passing through the Combat Crew Replacement Center at Bovingdon daily. Since 1 March 1943 the 398th Bomb Group had assumed the duties of the CCRC and by December that year would have trained over 300 B-17 crews.

367 The Anklam force lost 14 B-17s, all from the 1st Combat Wing.

368 42-3554 ditched in the North Sea. 5 of Lieutenant William F. Whelan's crew were KIA. 5 PoW.

369 Colonel Harding was a graduate of West Point and a famed football coach for the Army.

370 The B-17s' direct route was planned so that the 216 P-47s could escort the bombers all the way to the target. However, when the 352nd Fighter Group turned back as planned at 1148, their place, which should have been taken by the 355th Fighter Group, went unfilled, as the latter group remained fog-bound in England.

371 At 1453 hours, just 9 minutes from the target, the fighter attacks began. First to attack were the single-engined fighters, which paused only when the flak opened up at the approach to the target. They resumed their attacks again after the *Zerstören* waded in with rocket attacks to add to the carnage.

372 Justice evaded capture. Two members of his crew were KIA and seven were taken prisoner.

373 Worst hit was the unlucky 13th Wing comprising the 95th, 100th and 390th Bomb Group. It took just 7 minutes to tear the "Bloody Hundredth" formation apart, losing a dozen B-17s, while the 390th lost 8 out of 18 despatched and 5 out of the 20 95th Bomb Group B-17s despatched also FTR. Twelve B-17s were claimed by JG 26, 7 of which were confirmed. Only the intervention of the 56th Fighter Group prevented further losses. Lieutenant Robert Johnson destroyed two fighters to become an ace and was joined by Major David Schilling and by Captain Walter Beckham of the 353rd, both of whom downed their 5th fighters on this mission. In all, 30 B-17s were either shot down or written off in crashes. Fourteen were claimed shot down by JG 1 and 11, with another 8 *Herausschüsse and* two P-47s shot down, one by Oberleutnant Knoke - his 18th victory. The Americans claimed 180 fighters shot down, 105 claims being submitted by the 13th Wing alone. The *Luftwaffe* actually lost 25 fighters, including three JG 26 fighters and 9 Bf 110s and Me 410s and 7 FW 190s and Bf 109s of JG 1 with 4 pilots killed in this *Geschwader.*

374 Nine members of 2nd Lieutenant George E. Starnes' crew in 42-3415 *Miss Behavin* in the 571st Bomb Squadron were KIA and one man was taken prisoner. Six members of Lieutenant Wade H. Sneed, Jr.'s crew in 42-3328 *Miss Fortune* in the 568th Bomb Squadron were KIA and four were taken prisoner.

375 The armored Flak vests consisted of heavy canvas covered with overlapping two-inch square plates of 20-gauge manganese steel and it protected the chest and back from low velocity shrapnel and ricocheting missiles. Five main U.S. types of various weights became available and were appropriate for each crew position. The M-1 had armored front and back panels while the M-2 was armored in the front only. M-3 Tapered Sporrans could be attached to the front of the flak vests. The Tapered Sporran was usually worn by crewmen in a sitting position where the lower part of the body was unprotected. Full Sporrans, which protected all frontal area of the body and were usually worn by the gunners. Flak vests were not personal issue but were delivered to the aircraft before the flight and picked up afterwards for inspection.

376 Winant was among the six men who were taken prisoner.

377 Vance was later awarded the DSC.

378 A 100th Bomb Group Fortress.

Chapter 9:

379 On 1 October 1943 British Intelligence sources had estimated that despite round-the-clock bombing of aircraft factories and component plants, the *Luftwaffe* had a first line strength of 1525 single and twin-engined fighters for the defense of the western approaches to Germany. American sources put the figure at around 1100 operational fighters. In reality, the *Luftwaffe* could call upon 1646 single and twin-engined fighters for the defense of the Reich; 400 more than before the issue of the *Pointblank* directive, although only about a third of this force was ready for immediate use, the remainder being reserves or temporarily unserviceable. The Allies' figures confirmed their worst fears.

380 *In My Book You're All Heroes* by Robert E. O'Hearn. Privately Published 1984.

381 *Wrong Place! Wrong Time! The 305th Bomb Group and the 2nd Schweinfurt Raid October 14 1943.* George C. Kuhl. Schiffer 1993.

382 USAF Historical Research Agency, *History of the 381st Bombardment Group,* Maxwell AFB, Montgomery, Alabama.

383 42-29952 in the 366th Bomb Squadron.

384 *Sizzle* was the last B-17 off the ground at Chelveston.

385 *Wrong Place! Wrong Time! The 305th Bomb Group and the 2nd Schweinfurt Raid October 14 1943.* George C. Kuhl. Schiffer 1993.

386 *First of the Many* by Captain John R. "Tex" McCrary and David E. Scherman. 1944.

387 *The Fall of the Fortresses* by Elmer Bendiner. Souvenir Press 1980.

388 2nd Lieutenant Bohn E. Fawkes' crew were given a brand new B-17G for the mission, which no one else wanted because the chin turret caused drag. The crew had been flying *Duffy's Tavern* on recent missions since losing "*Tondelayo*" on the mission to Stuttgart on 6 September when they were forced to ditch in the Channel.

389 1st Lieutenant Joseph W. Lukens was flying with Lieutenant William C. Bisson and crew.

390 1st Lieutenant Richard Butler was Thomas' replacement.

391 *In My Book You're All Heroes* by Robert E. O'Hearn. Privately Published 1984.

392 Roy Davidson's engineer, Fred Krueger, declined the B-17 assigned to the crew (this ship, 42-3453, was flown on the first Schweinfurt raid by Lieutenant Silas Nettles' crew in the 96th Bomb Group and a windmilling engine contributed to their demise near the IP) and Davidson was allocated *Wolf Pack* instead. Nettles' crew meanwhile, flew the mission in the 100th Bomb Group formation.

393 The 333rd Bomb Squadron was used at Rougham as a fill-in squadron. This meant that crews were usually given the tail-end positions.

394 General Anderson hoped to send 460 B-17s and B-24s into Germany in three task forces; the 1st and 3rd Bomb Divisions flying 30 miles apart while 60 Liberators of the 2nd Bomb Division brought up the rear, flying to the south on a parallel course to the B-17s. Unfortunately for Davidson and the mission as a whole, unpredictable weather would intervene before take-off and effectively end the Liberators' participation in the mission.

395 *In My Book You're All Heroes* by Robert E. O'Hearn. Privately Published 1984.

396 William "Bill" Allen flew 103 missions including some on a second tour in the 350th Bomb Squadron, 100th Bomb Group.

397 These two groups would fly in the 13th Wing, the last wing in the 3rd Division task force.

398 In 1943 30 Mosquitoes were diverted from British production after the Canadian allocation of 120 for the Americans had been reduced to just 60 B.XXs because of RAF demands. These, plus 11 Canadian-built F-8 models, were delivered to the 802nd (later, 25th) Bomb Group at Watton, Norfolk. However, these were not as popular with the pilots and navigators as the British-built Mosquitoes and they were soon reassigned to a bomb group in Italy. The 802nd, with the 7th Photographic Group became part of the 325th Photographic Wing, commanded, after August 1944, by Colonel Elliott Roosevelt, the President's son. The 652nd Bomb Squadron was equipped with the B-17 and B-24 while the 653rd Bomb Squadron used Mosquito T.III and PR.XVI aircraft on meteorological flights, known as *Bluestockings,* gathering weather information from over the continent. The 654th, or the "Special Squadron," flew day and night *Joker* photo missions and scouting sorties just ahead of the main bombing force, transmitting up-to-the-minute weather reports back to the task force commander to prevent him leading his bombers into heavy weather fronts. The *D-Day* invasion was determined by intelligence gathered on *Dillies* (night photography missions of coastal defenses). A local storm front, forming suddenly east of Iceland on 5 June and monitored by the *Bluestockings,* postponed the invasion for one day until 6 June. On *Joker* missions the Mosquitoes dropped 1,000,000-candlepower-type M-46 flash bombs to illuminate and obtain evidence of enemy troop movements and bridge construction conducted under the cover of darkness. American Mosquitoes accompanied Project *Aphrodite* and *Anvil* pilotless drone operations using war-weary B-17s and PB4Y-1 Liberators respectively. Each aircraft was packed with 18,000lb of Torpex, a nitroglycerine compound and was flown to a point over the English coast or North Sea. There the pilot and co-pilot baled out, leaving the drone to fly on and be directed onto its target (normally a V-1 or V-2 site) by remote control via a Ventura "mother ship." Strike analysis depended upon the films brought back by the accompanying Mosquitoes to determine the success, or failure, of the mission. Each *Aphrodite* and *Anvil* mission was preceded by a *Bluestocking* weather reconnaissance flight over the target by a 653rd Bomb Squadron Mosquito. After the drone was airborne, a Mosquito in the 654th Bomb Squadron joined the mission carrying an 8th Combat Camera Unit (CCU) crewman. The mission was to fly close to the drone and to photograph its flight and its effects.

399 The 60 Liberators in the 2nd Air Division took-off from their airfields in Norfolk and Suffolk but only 24 arrived at the rendezvous point. The remaining 25 managed to link up with 53 P-47s of the 352nd Fighter Group but such a small force would have been decimated by the *Luftwaffe* and the flak guns, so both fighters and bombers aborted after circling for half-an-hour. The B-24s and their P-47 escort were redirected on a diversionary sweep over the North Sea as far as the Friesian Islands to aid the Fortress formations.

400 *In My Book You're All Heroes* by Robert E. O'Hearn. Privately Published 1984.

401 *In My Book You're All Heroes* by Robert E. O'Hearn. Privately Published 1984.

402 Seventeen B-17s in the 305th Bomb Group led by Major Charles G. Y. Normand had taken off from Chelveston 6 minutes late and, after completing assembly, had been unable to find either the 92nd or 306th Groups. Normand led his group first to Daventry and then to Spalding without sighting the rest of the 40th Wing. He tried in vain to contact Peaslee by radio, but about 30 miles short of the enemy coast the 305th caught sight of the 351st and 91st Bomb Groups of the 1st Combat Wing. Normand's B-17s filled the still vacant low group spot provided by the absence of the 381st Bomb Group, which had taken longer to assemble than anticipated due to a 10,000ft overcast which hung over Ridgewell. Eventually, Major George Shacklady's 16 aircraft finally caught up with the 1st Combat wing over the Channel and moved in next to the 351st Bomb Group in the high position.

403 *In My Book You're All Heroes* by Robert E. O'Hearn. Privately Published 1984.

404 Though Sam Mehaffey did not get to Schweinfurt, he had his share of the excitement and fright. In the following months, he flew many more missions with several crews in Just about every position in the formations, from tail-end-Charlies to lead crews and finished a tour of 32 missions on 23 July 1944.

405 *In My Book You're All Heroes* by Robert E. O'Hearn. Privately Published 1984.

406 This, the only U.S. fighter lost on the mission was shot down by Addi Glunz of 5th *Staffel* JG 26 near Budel at 1400 hours. See *The JG 26 War Diary Vol.2* by Donald Caldwell. Grub Street, London. 1998.

407 Bf 110s of the *Zerstörergruppen* and FW 190A-5/R6s and Bf 109Gs of JG 1, JG 3, JG 26 and JG 27 carried two underwing *Wurfgranaten* WGr 210mm rocket tubes for the unguided W Gr. 21 *Dodel* missile. II./JG 26 were the first to test these in battle but they were too cumbersome for single-engined fighter aircraft and it was decided to equip the *Zerstörer,* or heavy twin-engined fighter units, with the rocket devices instead. FW 190s and Bf 109Gs carried a streamlined and jettisonable under-belly *Rüstsatz R3* or auxiliary 66-gallon (300 liter) drop tank for long-range missions.

408 *In My Book You're All Heroes* by Robert E. O'Hearn. Privately Published 1984.

409 McCallum and his co-pilot, 2nd Lieutenant Homer D. Fitzer who was flying his first mission and three others were KIA. 5 men were taken prisoner.

410 The radio operator and ball turret gunner were both killed by rocket fragments. One of the waist gunners failed to bale out and Cole, who elected to remain in the aircraft to allow the others to bale out, was blown out in the subsequent explosion and his body was found later, hanging in his parachute from a tree.

411 42-30710 in the 423rd Bomb Squadron. Jackson went down with his aircraft and Bernard Bernstein; navigator was killed as he baled out. Two gunners were also KIA. The rest of the crew landed safely.

412 42-30199. 1 Evd. 1 KIA. 8 PoW.

413 *Piccadilly Commando* had lost its No.4 engine in one of the first attacks, but it had been feathered successfully and Holmstrom managed to maintain formation. Just past Frankfurt a large hole appeared in the left wing and fuel began streaming out. The pilot asked Flight Officer Philip D. Anderson, his navigator, for a heading to Switzerland, but just as Holmstrom pulled out of formation a German fighter followed and opened fire. *Piccadilly Commando* went into a climb and Holmstrom ordered the crew to bale out. Anderson and 1st Lieutenant Jack A. Kelly, the bombardier, went out through the nose hatch and were never found. Holmstrom and 5 of the crew survived.

414 *In My Book You're All Heroes* by Robert E. O'Hearn. Privately Published 1984.

415 The B-17 had been hit on the bomb run between Würzburg and Schweinfurt, three engines were hit and one was on fire when Butler pushed the bale-out alarm button. All the crew baled out safely before the aircraft exploded and were captured. Jim Harris concludes. "I was picked up by a farmer and was soon joined by our navigator, Ken McCaleb who had landed near me. We were taken to a military post of some sort. Later that night we were transported to a fighter base where we were kept for a few days. Many of us at the fighter base were wounded, some seriously. I had a minor shrapnel wound in my shoulder and had injured my back when my chute opened. We were given no medical treatment. As a point of interest, I had learned to respect the German fighter pilot for his skill and courage. However, while confined at the fighter base I learned that our regular bombardier, Joe Lukens [who flew with 1st Lieutenant William C. Bisson], was strafed and killed in his chute. I also learned that others had been hanged and shot by civilians. German pilots came to the room where we were held. The younger pilots were very arrogant and boastful. The older pilots were altogether different. They apologized for the actions of their younger cohorts when we complained."

In the lead ship, one of Schoolfield's waist gunners, T/Sgt Robert J. Conley, was seriously wounded in the left hand by an exploding 20mm cannon shell. S/Sgt Bert Perlmutter, the other waist gunner, applied a tourniquet and Conley returned to his guns, shooting down a FW 190 at 150 yards. Conley passed out and after recovering returned to man his guns again. He later received the DFC for his action.

416 While leading his lone group across the North Sea Major Normand had attempted several long turns to try to join the wing following. He finally elected to speed up and try to join the wing in front, which he thought was the 40th but which turned out to be the 1st Wing. Normand slowed to this wing's speed and took over the vacant low group position left by the absent 381st Bomb Group, which when it did arrive, took a high position on the right of the

351st Bomb Group. The 305th's epitaph is contained in the 1st CBW history which recorded, "Fortunately for us, the 305th, which as unable to find its own gang, came along with us and flew low box on our incomplete wing formation. This they did at their own expense…"

417 S/Sgt John E. Miller and Lieutenant John C. Manahan, respectively.

418 *Sizzle* was much lower than the other bombers and had come under attack from three FW 190s led by Major Johannes Seifert of the 3rd *Staffel* JG 26. They came in from the tail and S/Sgt William B. Menzies the 17-year old tail gunner claimed a hit on one of them (*Unteroffizier* Horst Richter of 3rd *Staffel* in FW 190A-4 5807 "Yellow 9" was KIA), as they went by. As *Sizzle* passed over the northern outskirts of Maastricht, Seifert broke off the engagement as *Sizzle* rolled over on its left wing and began to spin. At 1340 it crashed near Limmel, a small Dutch village north of Maastricht and several miles east of the Belgian border.' Shortly after the crash, the bomb load exploded. Murdock, if not already dead as a result of enemy gunfire, died in the crash of his plane near Maastricht Smith, Menzies and Sgt John W. Lloyd, ball turret gunner, all landed safely. They were captured within 15 minutes of each other in the vicinity of Maastricht. T/Sgt Thelma B. Wiggins, radio operator, had been wounded in the right heel by shell fragments just prior to bailing out through the waist exit. He landed right beside a canal nearly 16 miles southwest of his crewmates at Tongeren, well inside the Belgian border. He now went into hiding with some newfound friends. Sgt Lester J. Levy, right waist gunner hit the ground. He was captured immediately and spent several weeks in the hospital Later that day, T/Sgt Russell Kiggens, engineer and waist gunner, S/Sgt Tony E. Dienes were found dead in the wreckage. Kiggens was last seen stepping down from the top turret and seemed okay but for some reason he never made it out of the B-17. The severely wounded and unconscious Dienes was last seen lying on the floor by the left waist and had no chance to jump. John C. Manahan's parachute failed to open and he fell on the dike of a canal. He was discovered lying with his unopened chute later that day by two civilian workers. It was rumored that after baling out John E. Miller joined the Dutch Underground and was active with them until his death on 26 March 1945.

419 Flying 42-3436 in the 364th Bomb Squadron.

420 *In My Book You're All Heroes* by Robert E. O'Hearn. Privately Published 1984.

421 One of the attackers, 23 year old Feldwebel Helmut F. Brinkmann of 7./JG 1 flying a Bf 109 was shot down by fire from several of McDarby's gunners. The 109 went into a steep dive and crashed near Haanrade, Holland. The pilot's remains were never found. *Wrong Place! Wrong Time! The 305th Bomb Group and the 2nd Schweinfurt Raid October 14 1943*. George C. Kuhl. Schiffer 1993.

422 McDarby's Fortress went down and crashed at Maastricht. Linrud, tail gunner Dominic Lepore, ball turret gunner Ben Roberts; radio operator Hosea Crawford and McDarby survived and were captured. Five others were KIA.

423 *Legacy of Lazy Baby* by Jean-Pierre Wilhelm, *Reader's Digest*, October 1993. Jean-Pierre Wilhelm and his friends were among those who arrived at the crash scene only minutes after the crash. "…[We were] tingling with excitement at the prospect of seeing our heroes up close. But when I dropped my bike and ran to where a small crowd of locals had gathered what I saw was horrifying. My heroes were there all right but the 'invulnerable' Flying Fortress was nothing more than a smoking shrapnel-riddled wreck splattered with gore and reeking of aviation fuel. The crew's uniforms were stained with blood; their faces lined with tension. They looked suspiciously like ordinary human beings." Donald Rowley's young widow Jerrie would later receive her husband's Silver Star.

424 42-30242.

425 Kenyon's radio operator was killed and the other nine survived to become PoW. Later that evening as the four officers of the Kenyon crew sat in their adjacent prison cells, they were visited by a 21 or 22 year old German officer who claimed to be the FW 190 pilot who shot them down. He offered to take them to dinner but the Americans declined.

426 B-17 42-30814 crashed about 220 yards short of the village of Adendorf, about 40 miles east of the Belgian border and about 8 miles southwest of Bonn 1 KIA. 8 men including Skerry were taken prisoner.

427 See *Wrong Place! Wrong Time! The 305th Bomb Group and the 2nd Schweinfurt Raid October 14 1943*. George C. Kuhl. Schiffer 1993.

428 Phil Taylor and his crew survived and finished their 25 missions. On his second tour he completed 15 more missions as a bombardier.

429 *In My Book You're All Heroes* by Robert E. O'Hearn. Privately Published 1984.

430 Jim Bradley completed his 25 missions on 7 November 1943.

431 See *Wrong Place! Wrong Time! The 305th Bomb Group and the 2nd Schweinfurt Raid October 14 1943*. George C. Kuhl. Schiffer 1993. Major Normand was promoted to the rank of Lieutenant Colonel on 27 October 1943. He was shot down on 24 August 1944, survived and was taken prisoner.

432 *In My Book You're All Heroes* by Robert E. O'Hearn. Privately Published 1984.

433 Vaughter evaded for two days before being caught. The rest of the crew were also taken prisoner.

434 *In My Book You're All Heroes* by Robert E. O'Hearn. Privately Published 1984.

435 1st Lieutenant Ralph T. Peters' B-17 had arrived over the target with its No.2 engine out but had completed the bomb run. After bombs away the group went into a climb from the 22,500ft bombing altitude and Peters' Fortress, suffering from the strain imposed on its damaged wings, gave up the ghost and he ordered the crew to bale out. All 10 made it before the B-17 exploded. About 20 minutes after the target, 1st Lieutenant William C. Bissom's B-17 in the 367th Bomb Squadron was brought down by flak - which scored two direct hits on the engines - and fighters. S/Sgt Thompson E. Wilson, the tail gunner, was killed. Charles R. Stafford, the co-pilot and 4 others managed to bale out safely. When the heat of battle eased a little the tail gunner and formation observer, Lieutenant Curtis L. Dunlap, who had tried to keep abreast of what was happening, could only tell a shocked Schoolfield that just 5 ships were left. Schoolfield and his co-pilot, Captain Charles Flannagan nursed their ailing bomber home despite a fire in the No.3 engine and a failed attempt to bale out when the bale-out button refused to work.

436 See *In My Book You're All Heroes* by Robert E. O'Hearn. Privately Published 1984. One by one all of Nettles' crew were rounded up. Eugene Sebeck recalls: "Later that night we were brought together in a dingy prison. Sitting on a cold floor, feeling pretty miserable with German guards all around apparently willing to shoot us at the slightest move, I had forgotten about my letter and hopes of becoming a pilot. Nettles leaned over and said, 'Hey Sebeck, why don't you tell them you re supposed to go home (to the States).' That brought a laugh, one of the few I would have for the next 19 months as a PoW." All of Scarborough's crew who were flying Nettles' old ship *V-Packet* were captured after they baled out when their engines had quit too.

437 Davidson's crew continued fighting the wheels but two engines were gone (one refused to feather and began windmilling) and they were on fire. Another bomb group was sighted and Davidson pulled up under them but he was unable to keep up with them. The oxygen supply was exhausted and Carl Gibson had a bad bullet wound in his knee. Louis W. Koth, the radio operator, had lost an arm. Both the waist gunners and Louis Koth baled out. With no oxygen for the wounded, Davidson hit the deck and flew just above a layer of thick haze.

438 Davidson recalls: "We hit some cows with a little thud but it did not slow the plane up. (The French were pleased because they had more beef on the black market the following day than since the war started!) We skidded along the field and we were still going quite fast when we hit the trees on the other side and came to an abrupt halt. Everyone was all right because most of the crew had time to put their seats back and get into their crash positions. 'We scrambled out and the two Bf 109s made a couple of victory rolls on their passes over us. One of the German pilots delighted in making a couple of strafing runs. Fortunately, none of the crew was hit. We got the wounded out and gave Gibson a shot of morphine since he couldn't walk. The crew scattered in groups of twos and threes and started walking. Krueger, Mungenast and Davidson headed in one direction while Charlie Breuer, the bombardier, and Stan Chochester headed in another. Al Faudie took off alone. It was the last they all saw one another." (Faudie made contact with the French Underground and lived with them for almost a year and-a-half until liberation. Louis Koth, Claude Page, Arthur Howell and Carl Gibson were all captured and though they spent some time in German Lazarets [PoW hospitals], all survived the war). Chochester and Breuer made contact with the French Underground and a few weeks later were flown back to England aboard a RAF Lysander. Both men were back in England about 35 days from the time they were shot down. Davidson and Krueger also made contact with the French Underground but were later captured during an unsuccessful attempt to cross the Channel and were sent to *Stalag Luft III*.

439 Early in December 1943 Wilbur Klint checked out as a pilot and he finished his tour with his own crew. His 25th mission on 20 February 1944 was an 8-hour round trip to Bernberg. Klint adds, "That was the only time that the base at Molesworth looked beautiful."

440 One of these landed in East Anglia while the other remained in formation.

441 *In My Book You're All Heroes* by Robert E. O'Hearn. Privately Published 1984.

442 "The next morning our plane was brought to the ramp to assess the damage. It looked like a sieve. Still, the control wires and all four engines had not been damaged. Gay had not been kidding about his turret guns being broken. One was bent a full 90°. Spent shells from the radio gun had jammed his turret. We learned our lesson. Never again did we run out of oxygen, ammunition, or have a stuck turret. The plane as declared unsafe for flying. A general visited us while we were clearing out our personal gear. He had been in the tower the night before and he was going to write a letter of commendation for each man of the crew. (We never received it.) When a B-17 from our base picked us up, everybody was ready except our radio operator, Frank Cline, who was lecturing the replacements about the 'big picture.' The day's mail had been deposited on my bunk. One letter was from a stranger named Margaret Cline. She had written at the request of her mother who wanted the pilot to know she was praying for the safety of the crew and especially for the pilot who had so much responsibility. Her mother suggested that Frank not be told of this letter, as he might resent the intrusion. Margaret added that she, too, was praying for our safety. We had prayed throughout the mission for our lives. None of us was injured on the raid. A bullet spent itself in Frank Cline's clothes. We survived our first seven missions and went on to complete our full tour of duty. Five of the six gunners flew the same 25 missions with me. Did we see God?"

Bill Rose began a second combat tour in 1945 and he returned home to the USA in November. At Pyote, Texas in June 1943 as he had walked over to meet his crew, Rose had wondered; "which of these guys has a sister that I'm going to marry?" Frank Cline was the "guy" whose sister Rose would marry. They married in December 1945 with Frank Cline as best man. They lived happily ever after. Their seven children can attest to that.

443 *In My Book You're All Heroes* by Robert E. O'Hearn. Privately Published 1984.

444 One of the 379th Bomb Group B-17s (42-29776) that FTR was piloted by 2nd Lieutenant Samuel A. Gaffield, Jr., which split in half when a German fighter crashed into it (9 KIA. 1 PoW). Another was *The Iron Maiden* in the 525th Bomb Squadron flown by 2nd Lieutenant Roland H. Martin, Jr., which was hit by flak, which blew the nose off just after bombs away. Irving Rittenberg, the bombardier, recalls. The pilot ordered us to bale out. The navigator, Dan Maher, threw my chest chute to me and started to go out the nose hatch. The plane went into a spin. The centrifugal force pinned us both against the side of the plane. I could not snap on my chute. Fortunately, about 500ft above the ground, the pilots were able to pull out of the spin and dropped the landing gear so the Germans would stop shooting at us. We were able to crash-land onto a plowed field with a Me 109 buzzing us. Linden Price, the co-pilot and I took off into the

woods. Roland Martin and the engineer went in the opposite direction. I never saw them again. The other 6 crewmen baled out. We hid in the woods for hours but as soon as we stuck our noses out, some farmers captured us. Nearly all the 525th Bomb Squadron was wiped out that day. I met a few guys from my squadron in the PoW camp.' *In My Book You're All Heroes* by Robert E. O'Hearn. Privately Published 1984.

445 *In My Book You're All Heroes* by Robert E. O'Hearn. Privately Published 1984.

446 "The two Schweinfurt raids are etched indelibly in my mind. The challenge and responsibility of being lead navigator of the first aircraft over the target on both missions made me sweat the navigation more than the flak and fighters. I was too busy to dwell long on what was happening to us those days. Most of us non-pilot crewmembers were not decorated for our efforts: I shall always be proud of the words "Navigation was Suberb." which appeared in official narratives.' David Williams was shot down near Cologne on 4 February 1944. After two nights in a civilian jail and about three weeks in solitary confinement at *Dulag Luft*, he had a five-day trip in a cattle car to *Stalag Luft III* and saw the effects of a bombing raid from another perspective - the target. One was in the middle of a marshaling yard in Frankfurt during an 8th Air Force day bombing and another in Berlin, during a RAF attack. He spent the rest of the war digging tunnels and adapting to the life of a *Kriegsgerfangener* until liberated by the Russians in April 1944. In prison camp he taught navigation to pilots, using his imagination to produce gear to simulate the E-6B computer, Mercator charts and a star compass - tools of the navigator's art. He also became determined to seek a regular commission and become a pilot. He accomplished both goals. After the war he completed pilot training as a major and accrued 23 years of Air Force service time. He flew generations of bombers from the B-29s through the B-52s. Continuing flying after retirement, he earned FAA ratings of ATP, CFII, ASMEL, SES and Commercial Helicopter.

447 *The Fall of the Fortresses* by Elmer Bendiner. Souvenir Press 1980.

448 All 10 of 2nd Lieutenant Matthew A. Zack's crew in 42-3056 were KIA.

449 *In My Book You're All Heroes* by Robert E. O'Hearn. Privately Published 1984.

450 4 evaded. 6 PoW.

451 *In My Book You're All Heroes* by Robert E. O'Hearn. Privately Published 1984.

452 LeMay retained command of the 3rd Division until June 1944 when he returned to the USA and was promoted to major general before being sent to take command of XX Bomber Command in India. He earned a transfer to XXI Bomber Command in January 1945. His successful direction of the strategic bombing campaign against Japan saw him take command of 20th Air Force in July 1945 and he became Chief of Staff, Strategic Air Forces, Pacific early in August. His post-war service included Deputy Commander of Research and Development at AAF HQ December 1945-October 1947 and C in C United States Air Forces Europe (USAFE) in Germany October 1947-October 1948. Lieutenant General Curtis E. LeMay assumed command of SAC (CINCSAC) on 19 October 1948. During his 9-year tenure (19 October 1948-30 June 1957) SAC became the world's most powerful military force operating on a global basis. On arrival at SAC headquarters LeMay had demanded to see the war plan. There was no war plan he was informed. Within weeks of taking over LeMay had replaced SAC's deputy commander, chief of staff, director of operations and director of plans and replaced them with generals who were all veterans of the Pacific strategic bombing campaign. As he said in his memoirs: "My determination was to put everyone in SAC into this frame of mind: *We are at war now.* So that, if actually we did go to war the very next morning or even that night, we would stumble through no period in which preliminary motions would be wasted. We had to be ready to go then..." At the outset of the Korean War in 1950 he urged the Pentagon to "*turn SAC loose with incendiaries on some North Korean towns.*" In the 1960s he advocated an all-out strategic bombing offensive against selected targets in North Vietnam too. Single-minded and methodical in his purpose LeMay's credo was unchanged from WWII - "*If you destroy the* [enemy's] *capability to win war, then the will to wage war disappears also.*" LeMay's suggestions fell on stony ground and he retired as Air Force Chief of Staff in 1965 but he was proved right. Interviewed in 1988 he said, "...*It wasn't until the last* two *weeks of the war that we even approached [a strategic air campaign]. When we turned the B-52s loose up north – that started what would have been a strategic campaign and it would have been completely over in a few more days if we had just continued it....*" The 11-day LINEBACKER II campaign undoubtedly was instrumental in forcing the North Vietnamese back to the peace table. Peace talks were resumed on 8 January 1973 and on 27 January a cease-fire agreement came into effect.

453 Schweinfurt soaked up 482.8 tons of high explosives and incendiaries but losses were high. The 1st Division lost 45 B-17s and the 3rd Division lost 15 Fortresses. Worst hit of all the groups was the 305th Bomb Group, which lost 13 of 18 despatched. Major Johannes Seifert, Kommandeur, II./JG 26, shot down 42-29952 at Limmel, Maastricht, with the loss of 5 of the crew. FW 190s of I./JG 1 shot down at least 6 other 305th Bomb Group B-17s over the Dutch-German border and by Bf 109s and FW 190s of II. and III./JG 1. Next highest loss was the 306th Bomb Group with 10. The 92nd Bomb Group lost 6 and a 7th was written off in a crash landing at Aldermaston. The 379th and 384th Bomb Groups each lost 6 B-17s in combat and three crews from the latter group had to abandon their aircraft over England, making 9 in all. The 303rd Bomb Group lost two aircraft. 42-29477 *Joan of Arc* was shot down just after leaving the target area. 9 crew were taken prisoner and two were KIA. 42-5482 *The Cat o' Nine Tails* arrived over Molesworth, which was shrouded in fog but as the B-17 had been badly shot up and was low on fuel the pilot, 2nd Lieutenant A. G. Grant, ordered the crew to bale out. The B-17 crashed in the back yard of a house in Riseley, Bedfordshire about 10 miles S of Molesworth. The 91st, 351st and 381st Bomb Groups each lost one B-17. In the 3rd Bomb Division the 96th Bomb Group lost 7, the 94th 6 and the 95th and 390th, 1 apiece. The 100th, 385th and 388th Bomb Groups suffered no loss. Of the bombers that returned to England, 142 in both divisions were damaged as a result of fighter attacks and holed by flak.

454 Only 88 out of the 1222 bombs dropped actually fell on the plants. Production at the Kugelfischer plant - largest of the 5 plants - was interrupted for only 6 weeks and the German war machine never lacked for ball bearings throughout the remainder of the war. As in many other German industries, dispersal of factories ensured survival for the German ball-bearings industry and careful husbanding of resources meant that some forms of machinery needed less or no ball-bearings at all.

455 It was only when the city was finally overrun by U.S. armored divisions that America could at last confirm that it had "got Schweinfurt." In recognition of the 8th's heavy losses and the 305th's in particular the "Rainbow Division" presented the German flag captured flying over the Kugelfischer plant to the group at Chelveston shortly before it returned Stateside.

456 Four were claimed by JG 26. Oberstleutnant "Pips" Priller claimed a 96th Bomb Group B-17 southeast of Arras-Cambrai and *Leutnant* Erich Burkert of 9./JG 26 claimed a second 96th Bomb Group B-17. B-17F 42-3439 piloted by 2nd Lieutenant Charles F. Gerger in the 413th Bomb Squadron crashed 3km SE of Utrecht, Holland, in the village of De Bilt with the loss of 5 crew. Gerger and three others were captured while 1 man evaded. (This was Burkett's 2nd victory. On 17 August he shot down a B-17 on the Schweinfurt raid. Oberleutnant Burkert was KIA on 21 January 1944 when he was shot down b y a 353rd Fighter Group P-47 east of Laon-Sissonne). 42-30372 *Shack Rabbit II*, flown by 2nd Lieutenant Robert E. Grimes and crew in the 339th Bomb Squadron, on only their 5th mission, crashed 3km S of Venray, southern Holland, with the loss of 4 of the crew. Grimes and the bombardier evaded, while 4 men were captured. *Hauptmann* Peter-Paul Steindl and *Hauptmann* Klaus Mietusch CO III./JG 26, each claimed a 358th Bomb Squadron, 303rd Bomb Group B-17. 42-29571 *Charlie Horse* flown by 2nd Lieutenant William R. Hartigan and 41-24629, flown by Lieutenant John W. Hendry, Jr., both crashed at Cambrai. Three men in Hartigan's crew evaded, 6 were captured and 1 was KIA. In Hendry's crew, 8 men were captured and 2 KIA.

457 The first Mustang fighter-escort mission for the bombers was not flown until 5 December.

458 Originally assigned to the 9th Air Force and equipped with P-5lBs, the 357th was transferred to the 8th AF in exchange for the P-47-equipped 358th, for urgent long-range escort duty.

Chapter 10:

459 AN/APS-15, usually known as H_2X, or "*Mickey Mouse*" (later shortened to just *Mickey*) was a U.S.-developed version of H_2S. The first use of H_2X was made on the mission to Wilhelmshaven in October 1943. Sets were available in sufficient numbers by late 1943 to mount the first major raids to test its effectiveness, and it became the standard device for bombing through overcast conditions. Using H_2X on D-Day 1365 8th Air Force bombers dropped 2798 tons of bombs through cloud behind the beachheads 30 minutes before the landing.

460 Seven bombers were lost in a fierce air battle with elements of JG 1, JG 11, JG 26 and ZG 26 over the German Bight. German losses were relatively high; III./JG 1 alone lost 8 Bf 109s, including two *Staffelkapitäne*, to escorting P-47s and P-38s.

461 *Oboe* was a British technique adopted by the AAFs got its name from a radar pulse, which sounded like a musical instrument. Two ground stations were used, but in contrast to *Gee*, an aircraft's position was assessed at the ground stations, which operated on re-radiation of radar signals directed at the aircraft. Its range was 280 miles.

462 Nicknamed the "Blue Bunny" suit. Electrically heated one-piece flying suits developed by the General Electric Co. were standardized in 1941. The two-piece F-3A suit appeared in October 1944 and was designed to be worn over long underwear and underneath the A-15/B-11 suit. The F-3 would protect in temperatures as low as minus 60°F.

463 Three B-24s and 8 B-17s were lost, including 1 in the 92nd Bomb Group and two in the 388th Bomb Group. Near Gelsenkirchen the I./JG 26 made a pass at the 1st Bomb Division formation during which Feldwebel Peter Aherns of 3./JG 26 claimed the 92nd Bomb Group machine, which had been hit by flak just past the target. It was 42-30007, the lead aircraft, piloted by Captain John O. Booker in the 327th Bomb Squadron with Major Wilson P Todd, who had just assumed command of the Squadron. The B-17 crashed at Wesel (1 Evd. 9 PoW). Intervention by P-47s then scattered the enemy fighters, shooting one FW 190 down and forcing two others to crash land. (The 56th Fighter Group became the first 8th Air Force fighter groups credited with 100 enemy aircraft destroyed). The IIIrd *Gruppe* of JG 26 meanwhile, mixed it with the 3rd Bomb Division Fortresses and their P-47 escorts in the 353rd Fighter Group. The 353rd shot down two Bf 109G-6s and two other 109s force-landed with combat damage. JG 26 claimed a 353rd Fighter Group P-47 and *Hauptmann* Hermann Staiger, CO 12th *Staffel* JG 26, claimed a 388th B-17 at Dortmund. The Knettishall Group lost two B-17s to enemy action (Group records contend that all three losses this day were attributable to flak - a third crashed in England after receiving battle damage over enemy territory). B-17 42-30789, flown by 2nd Lieutenant W. J. Bramwell, was hit in the #1 engine just before the target and pulled out of formation and dropped its bombs. When last seen the #1 propeller was feathered and the engine was on fire. 42-30142 *Pistol Packin' Mama* flown by 2nd Lieutenant R. M. Walker, whose crew were on only their 3rd mission, fell behind just after bombs away with the bomb bay doors still open. Walker left the formation from 27,000ft with the #2 propeller feathered and #3 engine smoking. While the crew was baling out, S/Sgt R. B. Feese, the ball-gunner's chute caught on the tail section of the B-17 and he was carried down with the aircraft. B-17 *Lucille Ball* in the 351st Bomb Group returned over England and was on autopilot when it suddenly dived steeply into the cloud over Suffolk. The pilot, 1st Lieutenant Donald Gaylord, managed to pull the B-17 out of the dive and make an emergency landing at Ipswich Airport.

464 A failure of PFF aircraft caused the 95th, 96th, 100th and 388th Bomb Groups to turn back before the enemy coast, leaving just the 61 unescorted B-17s of the 94th, 385th and 390th in the 4th and 13th CBWs to continue to the target.

465 42-230795 *The Wild Hare* in the 548th Bomb Squadron, flown by Lieutenant John P. McGowan, which crashed at Druner. (1 Evd. 1 KIA. 8 PoW)

466 42-39812 *Casey Jones* in the 322nd Bomb Squadron, flown by Lieutenant Richard W. Ralls, which crashed at Tilburg, Holland (9 KIA. 1 PoW). 42-39855 *Ole Bassar* in the 331st Bomb Squadron, flown by Lieutenant Paul J. Kane, which crashed at Fijnaart, Holland (3 KIA. 7 PoW). 42-39868 in the 331st Bomb Squadron, flown by Lieutenant Robert B. O'Hara, which crashed at Numansdorp, Holland (7 KIA. 3 PoW).

467 Glunz's other claim on 11 November for a B-17 of the 94th Bomb Group southwest of Dordrecht was confirmed. A second 94th Bomb Group B-17 fell to the guns of *Hauptmann* Johannes "Hans" Naumann, 7th *Staffel* CO, who had a B-17 confirmed NNW of Breda. These two B-17s were 42-39812 *Casey Jones*, flown by Lieutenant Richard W. Ralls in the 332nd Bomb Squadron, which crashed at Tilburg, Holland killing 9 of the crew and 42-39855 *Ole Bassar*, piloted by Lieutenant Paul J. Kane in the 331st Squadron, which crashed at Fijnaart, Holland with the loss of three crewmen. The seven others were taken prisoner. Oberleutnant Rudolf "Rudi" Leuschel, 8th *Staffel* CO's victim, which he hit southeast of Numansdorp and crashed near this location, was also confirmed. It was 42-39868, flown by Lieutenant Robert B O'Hara in the 331st Bomb Squadron. Seven crew were KIA and three taken prisoner.

468 Oberleutnant Wolfgang Neu, 4./JG 26 CO, was credited with shooting down a 96th Bomb Group B-17 northeast of Arnhem. B-17 42-37830 in the 413th Bomb Squadron, piloted by 2nd Lieutenant Henry E. Marks, Jr., crashed with the loss of seven crew.

469 B-24H 42-7540 *Crew Chief*, in the 576th Bomb Squadron, piloted by Lieutenant John Harris, took off in heavy overcast, became lost and failed to find the formation. When the B-24 let down through the overcast on the return it was hit by flak and the crew evacuated the ship while Harris and co-pilot Louis Kearns put the bomber down south of Rotterdam. B-24 42-7561 *Mac's Sack II* piloted by Lieutenant Ralph Lamma in the 579th Bomb Squadron encountered flak and fighters, which left Nos.1 and 2 engines burning. Lamma had no alternative but to order his crew out before the B-24 went into a spin near Oldenburg, 25 miles west of Bremen. Lamma and four of the crew were lost. B-24H 42-7503 *Miss America* in the 577th Bomb Squadron, which was flown by Lieutenant Frank Marfia, is believed to have been damaged by enemy action and went down in the North Sea on return after running out of fuel. All ten crew perished. B-24H 42-7483 *Big Dog*, flown by Lieutenant Isaac Marx in the 578th Bomb Squadron, was hit by flak just before the target and made its way back over Holland. It was attacked north of Zwolle by *Oberfeldwebel* Hans Heitmann of 4./JG 26 who sent it crashing to earth. As the doomed B-24 hurtled down all the crew baled out successfully. Feldwebel Wiegand of 4th *Staffel* JG 26 was also credited with a 355th Fighter Group P-47 destroyed SE of Zwolle. Lieutenant Lanphier flying P-47D 42-8626 was KIA. JG 11 lost 4 fighters on 13 November, II./JG 26 another 4 Me 410s.

470 The raid, comprising approximately 155 bombers, destroyed the power station in addition to other parts of the facility, resulting in a complete stoppage of the entire manufacturing process. The Germans later decided to ship their remaining heavy water stockpile to Germany. However, all 546 tons of the heavy water was sent to the bottom of Lake Timm when the ferry boat being used to transport it was blown up by SOE agents over the deepest part of the lake.

471 B-17 423542 *Shady Lady II* was assigned to the 487th Bomb Group on 16 July 1944.

472 41-29161 in the 67th Bomb Squadron.

473 *Innocence and Death In Enemy Skies; A True Story of WWII Adventure and Romance* by Forrest S. Clark. Jawbone Publishing Corp. 2004.

474 41-29164 in the 67th Bomb Squadron.

475 Griffith and his co-pilot, 1st Lieutenant L. G. Grone got the Liberator back to Shipdham where the one landing gear failed to drop. Sgt Earl J. Parrish, the flight engineer, tried in vain to crank it down by hand. Griffith called off the crash landing in favor of a belly landing but the stubborn undercarriage leg failed to respond when Parrish tried to retract the "down" leg. Griffith refused to panic and ordered everyone except Grone and Kuban to bale out. Forrest Clark baled out, fell to the ground and gripped it with both hands in a gesture of relief and thanksgiving. He was certain he had landed in Holland, but a Norfolk farmer holding a pitchfork soon reassured him. Two hours later repair crews checking the wreckage found two unexploded German shells in the one good engine that had brought the crew home. Griffith won the Silver Star for bringing the bomber back and saving the lives of his crew. He went on to complete 20 missions.

476 *Vagabond King* in the 389th Bomb Group piloted by Captain John B. McCormick was shot down into the Skagerrak with no survivors. B-24D-30-CO 42-40128 *War Baby* flown by Lieutenant Frank Kilcheski in the 328th Bomb Squadron, 93rd Bomb Group landed at Orebro, as did B-24H-1-FO 42-7502 *Bakadori* flown by 2nd Lieutenant Davis M. Fogerty in the 578th Bomb Squadron, 392nd Bomb Group. B-24D-15-CF 42-6391 *Corky* in the 68th Bomb Squadron, 44th Bomb Group piloted by Captain Baxter W. Weant circled the airfield at Trollhattan, firing signal flares to inform the Swedes that it was about to land. Policy at that time called for the burning of any aircraft that landed in neutral territory and the crew set fire to their B-24 shortly after landing.

477 Forrest Clark gradually recovered and was "trying desperately" to get back on flying status when on 21 December he flew as a waist gunner aboard *Emmy Lou II*, a Liberator with a distinguished combat record, in a 44th four-plane practice formation from Shipdham to the Wash. The flight was a combination of test hop (because the B-24 had been in for repairs after severe battle damage on a mission to Bremen) and group practice formation. *Emmy Lou II's* largely regular crew was captained by one of the most experienced pilots in the group, Captain Richard Butler, a Ploesti mission pilot with an outstanding record of combat. The bomber was named in honor of his daughter. He had crash-landed *Miss Emmy Lou* at Catania, Sicily, on the return from Wiener Neustadt. T/Sgt Donald Eslocker, who was banned from flying above 10,000ft after suffering frostbite to his face and hands on a bombing mission, was aboard as engineer to qualify for his monthly flight pay. He stood on the flight deck behind Butler and co-pilot, Jerry Grell on take-off. Nick Garcia, from armament, was along for the ride while Kooken, Chamberlain and Boulanger, were gunners to be. Butler recalls, "The flight was routine enough until the formation break up. We were at 800ft, in the pattern for landing, when there was an explosion in the No.2 engine. With the explosion, the other three engines also quit!" Clark adds, "Before we could take any crash positions we hit with a great jar and wreckage went flying. Roy Neeper, who was also a Ploesti veteran, was standing near me in the waist position. The wings clipped off trees and plowed into the soft farm field, sending showers of earth over us. This was the closest I ever came to dying, even more so than Norway. It is my firm belief that in the split seconds before the crash Butler managed, in some miraculous way, to soften the impact to such an extent as to save lives; our lives. He narrowly missed a farmhouse. We could have lost the entire crew and the pilot, a great loss of manpower, to the 44th. I do not to this day understand how anyone got out?' *Emmy Lou II* crashed at 1830 hours in farmer Percy Kiddle's field at Wood Farm now part of the Bradenham Hall estate. Clark sustained back injuries jumping out of the B-24 from the waist gun position. Butler was seriously injured. Grell, Nicholson and Mason wound up in a Yorkshire hospital. Mason and Nicholson got out in a few days. Some time in January 1944, Grell and Butler got back to the 44th where it was decided that they would be sent home as hospital patients as it would take so long for their broken bones to heal in the English climate.

478 Air Marshal Sir Arthur Harris was in the midst of a campaign of area bombing German cities at night using Lancasters and Halifaxes, while B-24 Liberators and B-17 Flying Fortresses of the 8th and 12th Air Forces stoked the fires by day. From 18/19 November 1943 to 24/25 March 1944 Berlin was subjected to 16 major raids, which have gone into history as the Battle of Berlin. On 22/23 November 764 RAF bombers raided Berlin. *See Battles With the Nachtjagd* by Theo Boiten and Martin W. Bowman. (Schiffer Publishing, 2006).

479 29 B-17s and 5 fighters were lost. Almost all the heavies lost came from the main raid on Bremen. German claimants came from II./JG 27, IV./NJG 1 (attacking stragglers over northern Holland) and ZG 26 *Zerstören*. 86 enemy fighters were claimed destroyed, 26 of them by B-17 gunners.

480 42-37821. Cliff Hatcher, Adolph Delzoppo and Erwin Smith were not flying with Pyles this day. They had been replaced by three other crewmembers for combat indoctrination. The FW 190A-6 was probably the one flown by Oberleutnant Fritz Falke of 8./JG 26, who was most likely already dead when he hit the B-17. The only survivor was the tail gunner, Harold E. Norris. The tail broke free during the impact explosion and Norris managed to bale out before it fluttered like a leaf to the ground. He evaded capture and was passed along the French Underground to Spain, where he recovered from frostbite and was returned to England. Two other 94th Bomb Group B-17s were also lost - 42-3185 *Queen Bee* and 42-37815 *Miss Lace*. Oberleutnant Wolfgang Neu, the 4th *Staffel* CO, claimed a 94th Bomb Group B-17 West of Nantes at 1045 hours, *Oberfeldwebel* Hans Heitmann of the 4th *Staffel* another SSE of Creil at the same time and Feldwebel Ernst Zirngibl of the 8th *Staffel* a 94th Bomb Group B-17 near Paris at 1040. On 29 March 1944 Heitmann, who had 11 victories was awarded the *Deutsche Kreuz im Gold* (*DKG* or German Cross in Gold).

481 *Unteroffizier* Franz Vandeveerd of the 3rd *Staffel* JG 26 also claimed a 78th Fighter Group P-47 NW of Paris at 1100 hours. Three of the 78th Fighter Group's pilots were missing over France. 2nd Lieutenants John Herrick and Wayne Dougherty were shot down in the air fight and became PoWs. 1st Lieutenant Ralph E. Cormier was KIA. A small measure of revenge for these losses was gained on 30 November when Major Jack Oberhansly led the 78th Fighter Group to cover withdrawing bombers near Aachen, Germany. They finally rendezvoused with the late bombers at Eupen, Belgium, where Oberhansly came in behind a FW 190 trying to finish off a straggling B-17. Someone called out the enemy aircraft as a P-47 and Jack had to pull up from his attack to correctly identify the plane, then did some flick rolls with the FW 190, firing down to 200 yards before he overshot the plane, then in a smoking dive. On 30 November JG 26 lost 4 Bf 109G-6s in combat, two of which, were credited to the 78th Fighter Group. It is therefore possible that Oberhansly's victim was Feldwebel Ludwig Pötter of 10./JG 26 who was one of three pilots in the Gruppe who died in combat that day. *Unteroffizier* Hans-Gerhard Fieguth was WIA after a fight with a 78th Fighter Group P-47 and he landed safely at Rheine. 30 November ended a rather fruitless weather plagued month of 11 missions, 6 victories and three combat losses for the 78th Fighter Group.

482 Eight of the crew baled out. Five including the pilot were taken prisoner. Co pilot Jean Pitner, navigator Arno Plischke and engineer Andrew Hathaway evaded. Max Newman, radio operator and George Jones, ball turret gunner, were killed. Waist gunner Carl Glasmeier was WIA. See *Century Bombers; The Story of the Bloody Hundredth* by Richard Le Strange. 100th Bomb Group Memorial Museum, 1989.

483 "On Christmas Eve three guards came and said I was wanted by the camp kommandant. I was escorted to the Officers Club, which was decorated accordingly. The Commandant greeted me, shook hands, asked me to sit and offered me some wine. I hesitated, thinking the wine might be drugged, but I did take a few sips on being assured it was good German Rhine wine. I was told the man seated across from the Kommandant wanted to question me. From his treatment by the latter I assumed he was of General status although he was wearing a sweater with no badges of rank, military riding pants and boots. He asked me a range of questions about home and my family before showing me a copy of a Berlin newspaper with its front page displaying my picture with the '*Murder Inc*' artwork. He said he had been sent from Berlin to ascertain if I really were a gangster but thought it was obvious to him that this was not so and concluded by stating that I would probably hear no more about the incident. He wanted W to know why we had named the aircraft so and I replied we had not in fact done so and indeed did not even know why it was so named. He gave me the newspaper and said he thought I might want to keep it as a souvenir.

"On 28 December I was thrown in the 'cooler' from where the next morning at 0530 I was extracted and taken out the Camp main gate towards Barth. When I asked one of the two guards where we were going he said 'Berlin'. We arrived there about noon. While on the train I surmised the Germans were taking me there to conduct a fake trial and then hang me in the public square to gain even more propaganda value out of '*Murder Inc*'. I was held in a PoW camp housing Italian and Russians inmates for two days. On the 30th a 6ft guard who spoke good English took me to a large building in the city center, which he said, was the Foreign Office. A Major then escorted me to the 4th or 5th floor. The office I now entered had a desk and several chairs. One man sat behind the former with a second beside him and, standing up, they asked me to sit down. The first man announced himself as Dr. Paul Schmidt, Hitler's interpreter and said the other man's wife had been killed in an air raid. I was not then impressed because I simply did not believe either his claimed status or what had supposedly happened to the woman. I did think they were testing my reactions. I had never heard of Schmidt but I now believe his claim to be who he said he was. He justified German's invasion actions by saying the German minorities in the lands bordering Germany had been maltreated. He asked me for my opinion of his country's position. I told him when Hitler came to power during the Depression he had improved the economy, put the people back to work and generally got things rolling once more. This was the same as Roosevelt had done for America, but when Hitler started invading neighboring countries that was bad. I further said they might have succeeded in their plans had they not taken on England. Russia and Africa in their overall pattern of conquest. Their worst mistake was in persuading the Japs to attack Pearl Harbor. Then I said, 'Could it be you did not know the Japanese were going to attack Pearl Harbor?' There was no response but their re-action suggested this to be the case as far as I was concerned. They simply said something about the Japanese being great people.

"Schmidt retorted that all Americans were overly optimistic. This was after I had said America's entry into the War guaranteed Germany's ultimate defeat. They asked if I thought the American soldier was superior to which I said 'No, it is the production power of the United States that would overwhelm you'.

"Dr. Schmidt said all Americans were overly optimistic and set out to convince me Germany would win the War. He must have thought he had succeeded because he said all PoWs did not live in camps: some live in Berlin apartments with all social facilities. He suggested he had the influence to make the necessary arrangements and ended by inquiring, 'Is there anything you would like me to do for you?' I said 'Yes', he said 'What?' and I responded 'Take me back to the POW camp and leave me alone'. Having said he could do almost anything for me, he now seemed apologetic that he could not do so because there were other people in Berlin who wanted to see me and wasn't sure how long I would be kept in the capital. I was then returned to the Berlin camp from which I was summoned…Subsequently I was taken back to Barth. I did see cartoons and pictures about '*Murder Inc.*' in German magazines. One day a fellow PoW showed me a magazine in which he claimed my story was being serialized. I was reputedly described as one of Al Capone's gangsters who was in Alcatraz when war broke out. President Roosevelt supposedly asked the prison Governor for his 'meanest man' who could be sent over to kill German women and children: the Governor said Kenneth Williams was the best man for the job. Roosevelt accordingly ordered my release for me to then organize the effort, entitled '*Murder Inc*'!" "*Murder Inc*" crashed on take-off on 21 February 1944 after an engine failed and an attempted low-level circuit for landing ended in Lieutenant Evans bellying - in ½ mile E of Oundle. The bomber did blow up but only after the crew were safely extracted.

484 Only 80 heavies got their bombs away when cloud prevented the 1st and 2nd Bomb Divisions from continuing to the target.

485 Four were from the 384th Bomb Group and 5 came from the 91st Bomb Group. Four B-17s were claimed by JG 26 and two were confirmed as 384th Bomb Group machines.

486 B-24 42-40769 RE-S *Iron Ass* in the 329th Bomb Squadron was being flown by Lieutenant Horace R. Ketchum. 1 KIA. 9 PoW.

487 B-24 42-63987 in the 409thBomb Squadron crashed at Herresbach. Six of 2nd Lieutenant Joseph M. Wurzer's crew were KIA. 4 PoW.

488 The Liberators were escorted by along the route to Solingen by P-38 Lightnings of the 20th Fighter Group. *Hauptmann* Klaus Mietusch CO III *Gruppe* JG 26 carried out a single bounce on one of the Lightnings and it went down spinning. Three 56th Fighter Group Thunderbolts were shot down, two of them claimed by JG 26 pilots. (See *The JG 26 War Diary Vol.2* by Donald Caldwell. Grub Street, London. 1998). Two of the 355th Fighter Group's Thunderbolts were also lost. P-47D 42-22545 (Williamson) was lost to flak. P-47D 42-8006 (J. Hull) was shot down over Liège and the pilot was killed.

489 The ship that Butler saw blow into a million pieces was B-24D 42-40807 *The Oklahoman* piloted by Lieutenant Harley B. Mason in the 567th Bomb Squadron. Due to overcast obscuring their view of the target, orders were received to cancel the bomb drop and for the squadron to return to base with their bombs still aboard. During the time the Liberators circled waiting for the order to return, the lead navigator made a navigational error, which brought the Group over land instead of sea. St. Nazaire was France's only deep-water port and also home port of a U-boat base and the area was therefore heavily protected by 88mm anti-aircraft batteries. Thinking they were over the sea the B-24s descended to about 14,000ft whereupon they were bracketed by heavy flak. The next thing Mason remembered was that he was unconscious for a few moments, and then as he regained consciousness he recalled his body tumbling through the sky. He reached for his ripcord just as his body tumbled into the cloud deck below. The very next instant he remembered being in the water, the wind was blowing and that it was a very cold winter day. A German boat picked up Mason and taken to hospital, from where, in the next day or so, he was shipped by train to a PoW camp on the Baltic. The bodies of his nine crewmen were also recovered.

490 *Q-for Queenie*, otherwise known as 41-24105 *Tupelo Lass* YM-Q in the 409th Bomb Squadron, was salvaged.

491 Lamb's triple victory 5 miles N of Langeoog Island on 11 December 1943 raised his total to 4. He scored three more victories in 1944 to take his final wartime score to 7. Lieutenant Paul A. Conger of Piedmont, CA also of the 61st Fighter Squadron, destroyed three enemy aircraft and damaged another. He finished the war with 11 confirmed victories.

492 42-63968.

493 Strips of tin foil cut to the exact length of the German radar signal.

494 B-24 42-40983 *Judith Lynn* FTR on 1 April 1944 with Lieutenant Joseph M. Soznoz crew. 9 KIA.

495 The 93rd Bomb Group lost 5 B-24s. 42-63969 flown by Lieutenant Grady C. Hunt. 9 KIA. 42-41015 flown by Captain Herrell E. Ford. 9 KIA. 42-41002 flown by Lieutenant Richard B. Mays. 9 KIA. 42-63982 *Jack Frost* flown by Lieutenant Luther S. Bird. 3 KIA. 6 PoW. 42-46974 *Boomerang II* flown by Lieutenant Harry A. Daywalt. 1 Evd. 5 KIA. 3 PoW.

496 officer candidate.

497 Godfrey had scored his victory on 1 December when he destroyed a Bf 109 over the Ruhr Valley. By the end of the war his total victories stood at 16.333. Two other JG 26 pilots were KIA on 22 December by P-47s of the 56th and 78th Fighter Groups and a 6th Bf 109 pilot was KIA as a result of return fire from the B-17s. See *The JG 26 War Diary Vol.2* by Donald Caldwell. Grub Street, London. 1998.

498 Odom had already been credited with one destroyed and another damaged. For this he had been noticed by Lieutenant Colonel Glenn E. Duncan and recently promoted to flight leader. He had extensive flying experience as a civilian and the rest of the Squadron regarded him as an excellent flyer. His fellow pilots described Dub as "about five eight, as most of us were, but slight. His white hair and clear, albino like, skin, made him look fragile and delicate, but it was only an illusion. I always felt under that skin there were wires and rubber bands. He stood out in a crowd, not just because of his light hair, but because of his good looks. Without his too wide nose he could have been considered pretty. He was normally quiet. With his ever-present cigarette going, he'd settle back, fasten his eyes on yours and listen eagerly, but when it came to talking about himself he didn't volunteer much. He took his time when he talked and gave thoughtful answers to questions. He seemed always just a little far away - somewhere else- like he was maybe thinking of home and wishing he was there." Lieutenant Tom "Pinky" Lorance, his best friend, was also flying in Red flight. (See *Jonah's Feet are Dry - The Experience of the 353rd Fighter Group during World War* II).

499 42-39795 in the 360th Bomb Squadron.

500 Five of Osborn's crew were captured, 3 were KIA and 2 evaded.

501 1st Lieutenant Jesse W. Gonnam was awarded a 109 "probable," a 109 "destroyed" (shared with Lieutenant Gordon L. Willits) and a 109 "damaged." He voiced his frustration at the incendiary ammunition his aircraft was carrying by saying that if he had had his usual ammunition he would have claimed 3 destroyed. 1st Lieutenant Wilton W. Johnson was awarded a FW 190 destroyed. (See *Jonah's Feet are Dry - The Experience of the 353rd Fighter Group during World War* II).

502 Only navigator 2nd Lieutenant Leonard D. McChesney and bombardier 2nd Lieutenant Charles W. Compton survived. Both evaded capture and returned to England by 17 April 1944. The 8 crew who died were buried in a common grave near the small hamlet of Liry, 5 miles east of Cernay Durmois, where *Laden Maiden* crashed.

503 42-39759.

504 Eight of Brigman's crew evaded capture and two survived to be taken prisoner.

505 All 10 men baled out. *Heaven Can Wait* crashed just north of Les Rosiers, 3kms southeast of Monthois. The pilot, 2nd Lieutenant Francis P. Smith and the co-pilot, 2nd Lieutenant James P. Law, were taken prisoner. The rest of the crew, who were on their 5th mission, successfully evaded, spending some comfortable time in Paris.

506 Bob Scalley concludes: "The tail section of our B-17 had crashed onto the farmhouse. Frank Brincat was recovering and wanted to retrieve a first aid kit from the aircraft. The farmer said '*Nicht boom boom*,' thinking the yellow oxygen bottles were bombs. Frank eventually got a kit and gave me a shot of morphine. I only became fully conscious 6 days later in a hospital in Heppenheim about 20km from Ludwigshafen. Frank and I had really 'lucked out' because the tail section from '*Satan's Sister*' had killed a woman and child in the farmhouse. How come those Germans did not execute Frank and me?"

507 II./JG 26 and some fighters in JG 2 attacked the Liberators at once but they had to break off when they ran low on fuel. At 1150 hours 15 km NW of Soissons Oberleutnant Walter Matoni claimed one of the six B-24s that FTR. See *The JG 26 War Diary Vol.2* by Donald Caldwell. Grub Street, London. 1998.

508 At 1330 hours Feldwebel Wilhelm Mayer of 7./JG 26 claimed a P-47 4km N of Soissons before he broke away to land at Laon to refuel to return to Grevillers At 1400 hours 12 km SE of Beauvais *Leutnant* Waldemar "Waldi" Radener of 7./JG 26 shot down a P-47 and 36 minutes later he destroyed a B-17 32km WNW of Arras. See *The JG 26 War Diary Vol.2* by Donald Caldwell. Grub Street, London. 1998

509 They had dropped their belly tanks early in the mission when a Bf 109 was sighted and the additional drain on their fuel with the escort assignment lasting nearly 10 minutes longer than scheduled. This left them little choice when they were bounced but to try to evade the 190s by diving away.

510 Dilling evaded and eventually returned to England via Spain. Flak batteries at Dunkirk claimed Captains Hayes Button and Winfield McIntyre but they too had run out of fuel and they came down in enemy territory. At 1300 hours Feldwebel Kurt Schmidtke of the 4th *Staffel* JG 26 claimed a straggling B-17 but the claim was not filed. Feldwebel Wilhelm Mayer flew a

third combat sortie at 1515 and he was vectored toward a crippled B-17 flying alone which he quickly shot down at 1540 hours 22 km NW of Arras. (See *The JG 26 War Diary Vol.2* by Donald Caldwell. Grub Street, London. 1998). Altogether, 17 B-17s were lost this day. 23 German fighters were claimed destroyed.

511 (Radkte eventually recovered from his wounds and he and his crew flew the mission to Berlin on 6 March 1944 in *Ronnie R.* when they were hit by fighters and finished off by *Oberfeldwebel* Reinthaler of JG 11. Radkte and eight of his crew, including Pinner and Agnetti, survived and they were taken prisoner. The ball turret gunner was KIA. Reinthaler's Bf 109G was shot down soon after his attack on the B-17 by Lieutenant Robert Wise in the 78th Fighter Group and the German pulled his ripcord on his parachute only moments before he hit the ground and he was badly injured but he survived.) 42-30796 "*Sunny II*" piloted by Lieutenant George W. Brannan failed to reach Thorpe Abbotts and crash-landed at Starston, near Harleston not far from base. One man was severely wounded and two were slightly wounded. After an inspection, the plane was salvaged. After being hit by fighters and losing two engines Frank Valesh put 42-39867 down at the first airfield the crew could find, a grass field at Lympne in Kent, a Spitfire base. Navigator John "Dick" Johnson recalled: "The mess was some lord's manor house, with a hidden stairway to the master suite and a sunken black marble tub in the bath. They were very hospitable and loaned us civilian clothes so we could be 'presentable in the mess' and they let us sign for drinks. We never did find out who paid the tab but we did hang one on. Right after we did get to bed, a little WAAF knocked on the door and inquired as to what hour we wished to be 'knocked up in the morning.' …The CO was not too happy with the ruts our B-17 had made in his airfield but he did thank us for being 'considerate enough to land along one edge.'" 42-39867 was soon repaired and flown back to Thorpe Abbotts. On 24 January 1944 42-39867 had its tail shredded by flak over Ostend as the crew flew home and Valesh nursed the ailing B-17 to RAF Eastchurch where he put down safely. 42-39867 needed a complete tail section before the plane was airworthy again. The B-17 was later named *Boeing Belle* and it survived to the end of the war flying between 100-135 combat missions. It was finally scrapped at Kingman, Arizona in late 1945.

Chapter 11:

512 Blaylock and one other crewmember were killed. Colonel William A. Hatcher, Jr., and 8 others were later reported to be prisoners.

513 Altogether, the 351st lost 9 B-17s.

514 On the other side of the Channel JG 26 enjoyed mixed fortunes too. Two of its pilots were killed and three were wounded. *Leutnant* Kurt Vavken of 7./JG 26 added to JG 26's overall score with a confirmed victory over a 96th Bomb Group B-17 5 km north of Ault. His victim was 42-31121 flown by 1st Lieutenant Ralph A Woodward in the 338th Bomb Squadron, one of the Fortresses attacking ball bearing factories outside Paris. Three of Woodward's crew were killed. Also, *Oberfeldwebel* Addi Glunz of 5./JG 26 was credited with the destruction of a B-17 between Lorient and Auringes.

515 B-24 42-40990 *On The Ball* was lost three days later, on 7 January 1944, when it and Lieutenant Charles W. Walters crew FTR. 6 Evd. 3 KIA.

516 *Belle of Maryland* made it back to Bury St. Edmunds but 4 other B-17s in the 94th, including *Lil Butch,* did not.

517 42-31212.

518 McGough, Patton, Johnson and Milton L. Church and Kenneth O. Blye, two of the gunners, evaded and all were later returned to England by the French Resistance escape lines. Ralph Hall, the engineer, crossed the Pyrenees into Spain and returned to England in August 1944.

519 General Carl "Tooey" Spaatz returned to England to command the new organization while Doolittle assumed command of the 8th Air Force with its headquarters moving to High Wycombe. Lieutenant General Ira C. Eaker was transferred to the Mediterranean Theater. Eaker had built up the 8th Air Force from nothing and Churchill told him in January 1944, "The predictions you made to me at Casablanca last February about our combined bomber missions, including 'round the clock bombing' are now being verified. I no longer have any doubt that they will prove completely valid." Jimmy Doolittle, the famed Tokyo leader and former air racer, was well known to American airmen. His directive was simple: "Win the air war and isolate the battlefield."

520 James Maitland Stewart, better known as Jimmy, was born of Scottish-Irish parents on 20 May 1908 in Indiana, Pennsylvania, where his father was a hardware merchant, Stewart studied architecture at Princeton University, New Jersey, where he acted while a student. After summer stock in Falmouth, Massachusetts he made his professional debut in *Goodbye Again* and went with it to Broadway. By 1940, when he appeared on Broadway again, in *Harvey,* he had appeared in over 20 movies and had won an Oscar for best actor for his role in *The Philadelphia Story.* In 1941, to everyone's amazement, he gave up his $16,000 (£3,250) a month salary in the movie industry and at 32 years of age, tried to enlist in the AAC. Stewart owned his own aircraft, had logged over 200 hours of civilian flying and possessed a commercial pilot's licence. However, he weighed only 147lb, 10lb too light for the gangling 6ft 4in actor and he was rejected. In less than a month he had reached the prescribed weight but before he could enlist, his draft number came up. Stewart reported to Moffett Field, California on 21 March 1941 where he completed his basic training. Publicity-conscious officers tried to make sure Stewart remained a public relations figure for the AAC while he did little or no flying. Stewart shunned the publicity and logged another 100 hours' flying at his own expense during weekend passes. All he wanted was to fly, preferably in combat. However, it was not until January 1942 that he received his commission as a 2nd Lieutenant and "wings." On 7 July 1942 he was promoted to 1st Lieutenant He flew Curtiss AT-9 Jeep advanced trainers at Mather Field. It was thought that his constant desire for combat was too much in the Hollywood tradition and for 6 months he was restricted to checking out bombardiers at the Bombardier Training School, Kirkland Field, Albuquerque, New Mexico. Stewart took a heavy bomber course at Hobbs Field, New Mexico, where he checked out as first pilot, or aircraft commander, before being sent to Gowen Field, Idaho for 9 months as a B-17 instructor. He became Operations Officer and checked out 4-engine bomber pilots in emergency procedures at 2nd Air Force HQ at Salt Lake City. Finally, in the summer of 1943, after countless requests for a transfer, Stewart was posted to the 445th Bomb Group, equipped with B-24 Liberators, at Sioux City, Iowa, as Operations Officer of the 703rd Bomb Squadron. After only 19 days, on 9 July 1943, he was promoted to captain and given command of the squadron on merit. In November 1943 the 445th left for Tibenham on the Southern Ferry Route and Stewart went with them. His first mission was on 13 December 1943 when he led the high squadron to bomb the naval docks at Kiel. On Bremen three days later and a mission to Calais on the coast of France on Christmas Eve, Stewart showed his mettle, demonstrating a high degree of training and leadership ability.

521 South of Paris 35 FW 190s and Bf 109s made vicious attacks and the lead aircraft, 42-41013 *Trouble* in the 566th Bomb Squadron flown by Captain David L. Wilhite went down after a direct rocket hit in the cockpit. S/Sgt Robert H. Sweatt, the top turret gunner, was the only survivor. Sweatt recalled. "The FW 190 knocked our right wing off at about 21,000ft and by the time I got my 'chute on the 'plane was spinning and burning. I was halfway out of the waist window when the B-24 exploded and I was blown out. Wendell Dailey, my co-pilot managed to get out, but the Germans killed him when he landed on the ground. [The rest of the crew were never found.] I fell about a mile before I could get the 'chute open. My jugular vein was punctured and I had to pinch my neck to stop the flow of blood. Later, when I landed, I filled the hole with mud." When the French found him Sweatt was unconscious and seriously ill from wounds and fever. The French hid him in a secret medical facility for several weeks until he recovered. While he was in hospital his watch, which had been attached to his steel helmet when he baled out, was found, still running and returned to him. Sweatt was later transferred to Paris; sent along the French *Bonaparte* underground line, he finally reached England on 23 March 1944.

522 Even so, the 389th lost 4 B-24s. Apart from *Trouble,* also lost were 42-7593 *Blunder Bus* in the 565th Bomb Squadron flown by 2nd Lieutenant Royce F. Smith (2 EVD 1 MA 7 PoW) while 42-40747 *Heavy Date* flown by Lieutenant Carl A. Mattson (4 EVD 5 MA 1 PoW) and 42-63977 *Los Angeles City Limits* piloted by Lieutenant Earl P. Cooper (3 EVD, 6 MA I PoW) came from the 567th Bomb Squadron. Altogether, the 8th lost 12 bombers and 7 fighters on the 7 January raids but considerable damage was caused to various chemical and substitute war material plants. The twin city of Mannheim was also heavily hit and damage was caused to the engineering and transport industries. Colonel Milton Arnold wrote a letter of commendation to the 445th Bomb Group and James Stewart in particular. One statement from the letter commends the group on the splendid display of superb air discipline. It further states that "the good judgement of Major Stewart…in maintaining an excellent group formation, yet making every attempt to hold his position in the Combat Wing formation, is to be commended:'

523 Spoden started his night fighting career with 4 RAF heavies shot down in August and November 1943. Spoden flew several missions in daylight during the first months of 1944. "Only crews with few night victories were selected for these sorties, as the aces were too valuable for the powers that be. We youngsters usually just came into readiness at night, as in the *Himmelbett* night fighting system; the most successful crews were scrambled in the first waves. Nevertheless, those daylight missions were quite exhausting, as we were also at readiness at night. What's more, we were too slow in daylight with our 110 equipped with *Lichtenstein* and flame-dampers and tactically we were at a disadvantage due to our approach from behind. When we came into firing range of the heavy defensive fire of the American bombers, it was like flying into a shower! The 109 and 190 on the other hand attacked the *Pulks* from head-on and out of the sun. Consequently, the losses among our night fighters were horrendous."

524 5 B-17s and 7 B-24s were lost.

525 *Leutnant* Rolf Saligmann of 5th *Staffel*, Fähnenjunker-Feldwebel Hellmuth Wirth of 6th *Staffel* and *Leutnant* Kurt Vavken of 7th *Staffel* JG 26 were KIA flying FW 190A-6s while *Unteroffizier* Gerhard Falkner of 5th *Staffel* baled out of his FW 190A-6 with mild burns. Falkner was KIA on 27 April 1944 when a 356th Fighter Group P-47 shot him down. See *The JG 26 War Diary Vol.2* by Donald Caldwell. Grub Street, London. 1998.

526 *Oberfeldwebel* Addi Glunz of 5th *Staffel* also claimed a 4th Fighter Group P-47 near Boulogne. Three B-17s were claimed shot down by *Leutnant* Wilhelm Hoffmann and *Unteroffizier* Gerhard "Bubi" Schulwitz both of the 8th *Staffel* and Oberleutnant Otto Hummel of the 6th *Staffel. Hauptmann* Karl Borris CO I Gruppe, Oberleutnant Kurt Kranefeld and *Leutnant* Georg Kiefner each claimed a 358th Fighter Group P-47. Hummel was KIA on 8 February 1944 when a 20th Fighter Group P-38 shot him down. See *The JG 26 War Diary Vol.2* by Donald Caldwell. Grub Street, London. 1998.

527 B-24 41-24192 *Dogpatch Raider* was lost on 3 February 1944 when it crashed on take off from Hardwick.

528 VIII Fighter Command had dire need for the long-range escort fighter which could fly as far on its internal fuel as the P-47 could with drop tanks, but the first 8th Air Force unit to receive the P-51B was the 357th Fighter Group at Raydon, Essex. It did not fly its first escort mission until 11 February 1944. However, the weapon the 8th had needed so badly ultimately equipped all but the 56th Fighter Group in the command and literally proved a war winner.

529 Only 49 Mustangs remained to provide support over the target area for the two groups that were left. A squadron of Lightnings managed to rendezvous with the bomber stream but had to turn back before the bombers reached the outskirts of Brunswick.

530 The 385th and 447th bombed the target with devastating results, the former group placing 73% of its bombs within 1000ft of the MPI. Then it was the turn of the 94th. 19 B-

17s placed 73% of their 100lb incendiaries within 1000ft of the MPI to cause widespread damage to the Waggum plant. The bombing of the Junkers plant at Halberstadt was described as "good" and the results at Oschersleben were even better. (Lieutenant Colonel Louis G. Thorup commanded the 447th Bomb Group 31 March-30 June 1945).

531 The 94th Bomb lost 8 B-17s, one of which was flying with the 447th, which lost two B-17s.

532 Altogether, 42 Fortresses and two fighters were lost. In August 1944 all the 1st Division groups that took part in the raid received the Presidential Unit Citation.

533 42-31175.

534 42-39758. All 10 crew were captured after baling out.

535 Two aborted. The composite group, led by Captain Dennis Sharkey flying with a high squadron from the 92nd Bomb Group, had 14 more B-17s from Thurleigh.

536 42-3486 in the 812th Bomb Squadron flown by Lieutenant James J. McGinnis crashed at Hallendorf. 8 KIA. 2 PoW.

537 42-30782.

538 42-29993.

539 in 42-31451.

540 42-31236.

541 aboard 42-31538.

542 The *Luftwaffe* lost 39 aircraft on 11 January 1944. Voight was KIA on 11 April 1944 when he was shot down by 1st Lieutenant Frank A. Cutler in the 352nd Fighter Group flying a P-51.

543 This Fortress was most probably claimed as "destroyed" by Oberstleutnant Martin Drewes, StaffelKapitän, 11/NJG 10 and his radio /radar operator, *Unteroffizier* Handke who claimed two B-17s shot down on 11 January 1944. Drewes had shot down two B-17s on 26 July 1943 (going down at Bremervörde and Leer) and B-17 42-30603 in the 423rd Bomb Squadron, 306th Bomb Group on 26 November 1943 (crashed between St. Nicolaasga and Doniaga). On 5 January 1944 he shot down a B-24 100km North of Nordeney, followed by two more B-17s destroyed on 11 January, his adversaries crashing at Nijverdal (42-30782 in the 369th Bomb Squadron, 306th Bomb Group) and into the sea 20 km NW of The Hague. These victories made Oberleutnant Drewes the top scoring *Nachtjagd* pilot in the daylight battles with the 8th Air Force 1943-44. Drewes, who was awarded the *RitterKreuz* (*RK* or Knight's Cross) on 27 July.1944 and *Eichenlaub* (*El*) on 17 April 1945, ended the war with the rank of Major and a score of 43 night and 6 day victories (including 4 claims for B-17s and B-24s) in ZG 76, NJG 3 and NJG 1.

544 A former Eagle pilot with 5 victories flying Spitfire Vbs.

545 Whalen ended the war with 6 victories and a probable.

546 1st Lieutenant Duane W. Beeson claimed a FW 190 in the Soissons-Cambrai area, as did Lieutenant Gerald Montgomery and Lieutenant Hipolitus Thomas "Tom" Biel. His and Beeson's victories were confirmed and they took Beeson's score to 7. It was the first of Biel's 5 outright victories. He was KIA at Worms on 24 April 1944 in aerial combat in a Mustang. Captain Don S. Gentile claimed two FW 190s. Flight Officer Robert H. Richards claimed a FW-190 while 1st Lieutenant Vermont Garrison received credit for two FW 190s, which crashed in the Compiègne Woods. 1st Lieutenant Louis H. "Red Dog" Norley was awarded a half share in a FW 190 kill, which was later credited to him as a "damaged." (See *Stars & Bars: A Tribute to the American Fighter Ace 1920-1973*. Frank Olynyk. Grub Street 1995) JG 26 suffered three casualties dueling with the 4th Fighter Group that afternoon. *Hauptmann* Johann Aistleitner 5th *Staffel* CO and *Unteroffizier* Werner Kaiser were killed and Major Wilhelm Gath was WIA. See *The JG 26 War Diary Vol.2* by Donald Caldwell. Grub Street, London. 1998.

547 These strikes were no longer regarded as milk runs because the Germans, having realized their vulnerability to air attack moved in additional flak batteries and the bombing altitude was raised to 20,000ft.

548 The 66th Bomb Squadron lost *Queen Marlene* piloted by 2nd Lieutenant Martin E. Spelts in the position known to all as Purple Heart corner. At 1514 hours this aircraft was seen to wing over and dive down with no chutes. It hit the ground and exploded. This loss occurred during the first attack by I./JG 26 and the pilot is believed to have been hit, because the aircraft was not visibly damaged. S/Sgt Richard A. Mayhew, tail turret gunner and the sole survivor successfully evaded capture and returned on 29 May 1944. He was sent back to the U.S. for skin grafts and treatment. In the 68th Bomb Squadron *Ram It-Dam It/Aries*, flown by Lieutenant Hartwell R. Howington (KIA) went down. Sgt Archie Barlow, engineer and three others evaded and eventually returned to England. B-24 42-7514/O flown by 1st Lieutenant Gary M. Mathisen also went down to fighter attacks. No one reported seeing any parachutes but three men did survive, though one of these, probably Sgt Leo M. Tyler, ball turret gunner, was seriously injured. He died later. When 2nd Lieutenant Donald R. Hoeltke, the bombardier, hit the ground, he was immediately surrounded by troops with about 18 bayonets shoved at him. There was no possibility of him evading capture. Hoeltke was later sent to *Stalag Luft I* Barth and he remained there until the end of the war. JG 26 also hit B-24 42-7501/P piloted by 1st Lieutenant Frank W. Sobotka and the bombs were dropped immediately. The stricken B-24 was observed to circle off to the left and to begin burning, apparently under control. Lieutenant Milton L. Rosenblatt, co-pilot baled out and came into contact with the Underground about three days after landing. The only information they could give him about his crew was that Abe Teitel, bombardier was alive and that Frank Sobotka's dog tags were found in the wreckage of the plane. Teitel and Rosenblatt evaded and subsequently returned to England. 1st Lieutenant Fred Butler, navigator, S/Sgt Charles W. Shockley, left waist gunner, S/Sgt August F. Smanietto and S/Sgt Ross J. Andrew, right waist gunner were made PoW. *Victory Ship* (so called because of its code letter "V") piloted by 1st Lieutenant Alfred A. Starring was hit by JG 26 and Nos.1 and 2 engines were set on fire but the pilots managed to keep in formation. When the enemy made following attacks, this B-24 went down in flames. Seven parachutes were seen to open. JG 26 pilots claimed 5 B-24s: Oberleutnant Artur Beese (2), *Leutnant* Leberecht Altmann, *Leutnant* Georg Kiefner and *Unteroffizier* Hans Ruppert. (See *The JG 26 War Diary Vol.2* by Donald Caldwell. Grub Street, London. 1998). *Liberty Belle*, flown by 1st Lieutenant Keith Cookus in the 67th Bomb Squadron, who was leading the formation attack on Agathe D'Aliermont, was hit severely by flak. Cookus managed to nurse the shattered Liberator back across the Channel where it was written off in a crash at Manston. Two of the 13 men aboard were killed. Three men who baled out over France were taken prisoner.

549 See *The JG 26 War Diary Vol.2* by Donald Caldwell. Grub Street, London. 1998. Beckham's wingman, 1st Lieutenant Hassell D Stump was close behind but failed to score though 1st Lieutenant William Thistlethwaite, flying White three was credited with a 109 destroyed. Lieutenant Colonel Duncan, Lieutenants Sperry and Johnson shared a Do 217 destroyed. Walt Beckham scored his 18th and final aerial victory on 8 February 1944. He was shot down by flak 14 days later and taken prisoner.

550 B-17 42-40009 in the 324th Bomb Squadron, 91st Bomb Group flown by Lieutenant Marco DeMara.

551 Feldwebel Kurt Schmidtke of the 4th *Staffel* JG 26 claimed a B-17 at Calais and it was confirmed. 42-30181 *Lover Boy* piloted by 2nd Lieutenant Clay A. Burnett was shot down at Brussels with the loss of 4 men KIA. 6 men survived and were taken prisoner. 42-37756 *Roarin' Bill* flown by 2nd Lieutenant Charles H. Mowers went down at Waterloo (3 evaded, 1 KIA, 6 PoW). Feldwebel Gerhard Wiegand of the 4th *Staffel* shot down a 55th Fighter Group P-38 but as no one witnessed the kill he did not file a claim. However, the P-38 had crashed south of Terneuzen. Kurt Schmidtke was KIA on 7 July 1944 when his FW 190A-8 was shot down by a P-51 6 km SE of Nantes. See *The JG 26 War Diary Vol.2* by Donald Caldwell. Grub Street, London. 1998.

552 42-7547/X.

553 Oberleutnant Kurt Kranefeld of I./JG 26 shot down a 385th Bomb Group B-17 south of Maubeuge at 1245 hours and Oberleutnant Wolfgang Neu CO, 4./JG 26, did likewise. (*Hauptmann* Neu, Kapitän of the 4th *Staffel*, was KIA with American fighters on 22 April 1944. He had 12 victories including 7 *Viermots* gained in 111 combat sorties). Five minutes later, 8km SSW of Le Cateau Feldwebel Heinz Gomann was credited with shooting down a 388th Bomb Group B-17. It was *Mary Ellen*, piloted by 1st Lieutenant F. P. Hennessey, which had been hit by flak over the target and was trying to make it back flying on the deck. (Hennessey and navigator, 2nd Lieutenant C. Richardson, baled out and evaded capture, returning to England on 22 March 1944. Four of the crew were captured and three crewmembers were KIA. Gomann also received confirmation for the shooting down of a 389th Bomb Group Liberator into the sea west of Calais at 1348 hours. It was *LA City Limits* flown by Lieutenant Boyd L. Dout. All 10 crew perished. *Hauptmann* Karl Borris's claim for a B-17 east of Bonn and Feldwebel Josef Zirngibl's claim for another B-17 were also confirmed but 3 other claims by JG 26 pilots for two more B-17s were not. A claim by *Leutnant* Wilhelm Hoffman of 8./JG 26 for a 95th Bomb Group B-17 shot down 2km north of Lutrebois at 1330 hours was confirmed. The 95th Bomb Group lost two B-17s this day - 42-3545 in the 334th Bomb Squadron, which was flown by 2nd Lieutenant Andrew Rozentinsky, crashed at Brussels and *Spook #5*, flown by 2nd Lieutenant James D. Higgins in the 336th Bomb Squadron, crashed at Ziegfeld. JG 26 were also credited with the destruction of 4 fighters.

554 Stahnke had reported to JG 26 from pilot training in October 1943. Pinder's B-24, which crashed into a pine forest a few miles outside Wibrin near Liège, was his first victory. On 26 February 1944 Stahnke landed at Florennes to refuel. As he took off, the Focke Wulf's engine seized and he made an immediate forced landing, damaging the aircraft and suffering minor injuries. Stahnke was KIA on 15 March 1944 when he was one of three pilots shot down while circling Rheine airfield by a Spitfire of 401 Squadron RCAF, which was escorting some B-26 Marauders. See *The JG 26 War Diary Vol.2* by Donald Caldwell. Grub Street, London. 1998.

555 Grono was later repatriated to the USA but died from TB in August 1944. Pinder and T/Sgt Abe Sofferman, radio operator, baled out and the latter landed near the tiny farming village of Wibrin and Pinder not far away. A Belgian farmer and a postal worker saw the parachutes of Pinder and Sofferman. They took both men to the *Armee Blanche* (Belgian White Army) that was centered around Houfallize and in the wooded mountainous countryside of the Ardennes. The partisans were blowing up bridges and other strategic facilities to hamper the German Army. Pinder and Sofferman were captured on or about 26 February after a 4-day battle, ending in the surrender of those in hiding. Only Sofferman would not allow himself to be taken prisoner. He took his gun and made a run for it and was shot and killed by the Germans while trying to avoid capture. Pinder was taken prisoner and transported to prison in Liège and later to a *Stalag* in Germany. Forrest S. Clark recalled in his book *Innocence and Death In Enemy Skies; A True Story of WWII Adventure and Romance* (Jawbone Publishing Corp. 2004): "Abe Sofferman had a deeply felt hatred of the Germans for what they did to the Jews and he carried this into combat missions. Even then the word was beginning to filter out of Europe about atrocities committed against the Jews and other minorities. That was what the war was all about to him. He had a tragic air about him and a form of personal crusade against the Nazis. He was imbued with a savvy sense about the bullies of the world. He had used it against the neighborhood bullies of his youth. In the war he saw the Nazis as the greatest bullies of his time and went after them just as he would have at home in the city. He was the first to be ready for missions, volunteering if necessary and eager to strike his individual blow against the *Nazis*. He felt fear like we did. He sweated out missions like we did. And he did not like the killing anymore than we did. But he was a man of convictions that ran deep. Abe knew what would be in store for him if he were captured. More than once he told me he would never allow himself to be taken prisoner. One day in the barracks, I saw him polishing his .45 GI pistol. I asked

him what he was doing. He said he was merely getting ready. To him it was getting ready for the confrontation when he would have to fight the gang, the *Nazis*. 'If I come down in enemy territory I will not be taken,' he told me."

556 D 24 11 29157.

557 Seven of the crew, including Maynard and his co-pilot John E. Norquist, perished, while the navigator, ball turret gunner and Nichols, baled out and were taken prisoner.

558 See *The JG 26 War Diary Vol.2* by Donald Caldwell. Grub Street, London. 1998.

559 *Leutnant* Klaus Kunze was KIA on 16 March 1944 when a 78th Fighter Group P-47 shot him down.

560 (See *The JG 26 War Diary Vol.2* by Donald Caldwell. Grub Street, London. 1998). In all the 355th Fighter Group lost 4 P-47s on 29 January. P-47D 42-8610 (Martin) was shot down near Limburg and the pilot evaded. P-47D 42-75455 (McCurdy) was shot down and he also evaded and later fought with the French Underground. P-47D 42-8504 (Rankin) was shot down near Koblenz and the pilot killed. P-47D (42-????) (Fischer) was shot down by FW 190s near Limburg and the pilot was taken prisoner.

561 Fifteen fighter groups escorted the bombers. Frankfurt was almost within P-47 range, although target support could only be carried out by the few long range P-38 Lightning and Mustang groups while 8 Spitfire squadrons covered the final stages of the return flight.

562 *Leutnant* Waldemar "Waldi" Radener of the 7th *Staffel* claimed a B-24 destroyed 10km SE of Albert at 1200 hours. His victim was 42-7542 *Black Widow* in the 707th Bomb Squadron, 446th Bomb Group that ditched in the English Channel with Lieutenant Marvin W. Garber's crew. *Oberfeldwebel* Erich Scheyda of 3./JG 26 claimed a B-17 3km NE of Brussels at 1320 hours. 30 minutes later *Leutnant* "Charlie" Willius, 2 *Staffel* CO claimed a B-17 1km East of Cousoire. *Oberfeldwebel* Alfred "Fred" Heckmann, 3rd *Staffel* CO shot down a B-17 10km ESE of Rotterdam at 1430 hours. His victim was 42-31292 in the 569th Bomb Squadron, 390th Bomb Group. All 10 of Lieutenant Clarence B. Strait's crew survived and were taken prisoner. A claim by *Feldwebel* Gerhard Wiegand of 4./JG 26 for a B-17 S of Toureui at 1300 hours was not upheld.

563 A 56th Fighter Group pilot shot down Gefreiter Werner Pietruschka of the 5th Staffel, who put his FW 190A-6 down in a field with only moderate damage to the aircraft and slight injuries to himself. Another P-47 pilot shot down and killed Obergefreiter Wilhelm Peukert. See The JG 26 War Diary Vol.2 by Donald Caldwell. Grub Street, London. 1998.

564 Probably the FW 190A-6/7s flown by *Leutnant* Gottfried Dietze east of Hasselt and *Feldwebel* Heinrich "Jan" Schild near Ath. Both pilots were WIA. See *The JG 26 War Diary Vol.2* by Donald Caldwell. Grub Street, London. 1998.

565 Lieutenant Virgil Meroney fired at a FW 190 at 200 yards and watched as the E/A burst into flames but two P-47s and their pilots were killed in the vicinity of Emden. Lieutenant Ray Cornick in the 328th Bomb Squadron was reported to have been shot down and Flight Officer Joseph Sweeney in the 487th ran out of fuel on the return trip and is believed to have crashed in the Channel.

566 On 5 February the ranks of the B-17 formations were swelled by the addition of the 452nd Bomb Group.

567 B-24 42-99939 AG-E in the 330thBomb Squadron was lost on 3 March 1944 when it crashed on take-off from Hardwick.

568 41-28626 YM-P *Thunderbird*. Nine of 2nd Lieutenant Albert B. Austin's crew KIA. 1 Evd.

569 *Unteroffizier* Rolf Simmank was KIA northeast of Paris. *Oberfeldwebel* Hans Erbskorn and *Unteroffizier* Otto Salewski were WIA, both pilots making belly landings. Erbskorn was KIA on 28 October 1944 when a Spitfire of 412 RCAF Squadron shot his Bf 109G-14 down. Salewski was KIA on 14 January 1945 when a 78th Fighter Group P-51 Mustang shot him down at Uckerath-Bonn. See *The JG 26 War Diary Vol.2* by Donald Caldwell. Grub Street, London. 1998.

570 *Leutnant* Charlie Willius 2/JG 26 CO shot down 42-38015 in the 338th Bomb Squadron, 96th Bomb Group, which was in the low squadron in the 45th CBW formation. Willius hit 42-38015 in the gas tank. The bomber exploded and the wing came off as the B-17 fell into the undercast to crash at Pisseleux. Nine of 2nd Lieutenant Jacob Kurfberg's crew were KIA. One waist gunner survived to become a PoW.

571 The latter claim was discounted. In fact the only P-47 lost this day fell to the guns of JG 2 *Kommodore* Major Egon Mayer.

572 Two were in the 326th Bomb Squadron: 42-37984 piloted by 1st Lieutenant Milton V. Shevchik, which crashed at Amiens, France (9 Evd. 1 PoW) and 42-31387 flown by 1st Lieutenant Warren E. McMurray, which crashed at Châteauroux (4 KIA. 6 PoW). 42-40032 in the 327th Bomb Squadron flown by 2nd Lieutenant Robert D. Lehner, crashed at Vailly, France (1 Evd. 6 KIA. 3 PoW) FTR. *Unteroffizier* Gerhard Guttmann of 8./JG 26 was ultimately credited with the destruction of one of the 92nd Bomb Group Fortresses at Catheux, 17 km SE of Poix.

573 See *The Route As Briefed; the History of the 92nd Bomb Group 1942-45* by John S. Sloan. Argus Press, Cleveland, Ohio. 1946.

574 Oberst Walter Oesau of JG 1 destroyed an American fighter also. The 358th Fighter Group claimed two Bf 109s shot down and one damaged.

575 On 16 April 1945 Ellenrieder was injured while test flying a FW 190D-9 and he was removed from flying status having scored 13 aerial victories in 175 combat sorties.

576 All three of these pilots were killed in the attack, but Lieutenant Raymond Phillips noted in his report that Lieutenant Nussman, as his last act, tried desperately to warn him. "The first I knew of the bounce was when Lieutenant Nussman, Red Leader, pulled up with an Me-109 on his tail. He was still wiggling his wings to warn me even when the E/A had perfect deflection on him. At that time my ship was hit by enemy fire turning me away from Nussman and I lost sight of him. Being alone and failing to find Nussman, I joined with Yellow Flight (328th) and returned, landing my damaged A/C at Lympne." Lieutenant Fieg also managed to get his riddled fighter back.

577 Bär was a strong personality known for his straight talking, who had arrived at JG 1 on 21 January 1944 from the fighter training school at Orange in France. At the end of 1940 Bär had been the top-scoring NCO pilot with 13 *Abschüsse*. His score increased to 17 before his *Gruppe* was transferred east for *Barbarossa*. Bär shot down 96 Soviet aircraft despite being hospitalized with spinal injuries for a time. Then, as Kommandeur, he led I/JG 77 in Sicily against Malta and went on to North Africa. After the fall of Tunisia in spring 1943 he was withdrawn from operations with malaria and a stomach ulcer, his score 158. He returned to combat late that year as *Kommandeur* of II/JG 1 on home defense, flying the FW 190 for the first time against American bombers and claiming at least 21 victories.

578 In all, 29 Fortresses and 9 U.S. fighters were lost on 10 February. JG1 lost 5 pilots - two of them KIA - as a result of combats with American fighters. *Leutnant* Rudolf Kasischke and *Unteroffizier* Hans Hitter both died in their fighters. Oberleutnant Eberhard Burath's FW 190 was hit and he baled out, landing in a snow-covered field, on all fours with the parachute silk wrapped all round him looking like "a pig trying to find a truffle." *Unteroffiziers* Harald Feist and the promising Helmut Stiegler belly landed their FW 190s and also lived to fight another day. Feist was KIA on 21 February 1944, when Steigler was wounded. On 12 May 1944 Steigler was one of 7 of the unit's pilots KIA when he was shot down in combat.

579 B-24 42-63978 *Lonesome Polecat* flown by Lieutenant Omar A. Turner in the 330th Bomb Squadron crashed at Rouxnesnil. All 10 KIA. B-24 42-100428 GO-M *Willie's Worry* in the 328thBomb Squadron was salvaged on 29 May 1945.

580 Two 78th Fighter Group pilots were killed. It was thought that 2nd Lieutenant Donald R. Morsch and 1st Lieutenant William S. Swanson might have been killed in a mid-air collision. What is certain is that *Feldwebel* Gerhard Wiegand of 4./JG 26 claims for two 78th Fighter Group P-47s south of Arras was upheld. JG 26 also claimed 4 P-38 Lightnings in the 20th Fighter Group, three of which were confirmed. On 29 March 1944 *Fähnenjunker-Feldwebel* Gerhard Wiegand, who had 21 victories was awarded the *Deutsche Kreuz im Gold* (*DKG* or German Cross in Gold).

581 42-31388 crashed at Inval. DiBetta and his crew had been one of 7 replacement crews that had arrived at Thurleigh on 16 October two days after the costly Schweinfurt mission. The engineer, radio operator and left waist gunner were all hit in the fusillade of 20mm fire and the B-17 was well on fire by the time DiBetta reached the clouds at 8000ft. One of the officers helped T/Sgt Fortunato V. Chiccarelli whose arm had been almost severed by gunfire. Chiccarelli was taken to the nose and pushed out with his parachute ripcord handle snapped to a static line to pull it open 25ft from the plane. Chiccarelli was picked up by the Germans immediately, hospitalized and his arm was amputated. He eventually recovered and was liberated at the end of the war. One of the rear gunners fought his way forward through the flames to tell the pilots that the fire in the back could not be extinguished: DiBetta ordered bale out. About this time 4 or 5 holes also appeared in the right wing. With the plane on autopilot, the crew baled out. When Wolf got ready to leave, the plane abruptly nosed over to the right. He returned to the flight deck, leveled the wings and then jumped; he was probably the last one to leave. When Wolf came out of the clouds he was alone and did not see any other chutes. He did see the plane break through the clouds and finally blew up in the air. The only crewmember lost was S/Sgt James H. Coleman, ball turret gunner. Wolf landed in a woods north and west of Saarbrücken and was later taken in by the French Underground. He and S/Sgt Leonard F. Bergeron, left waist gunner, who had been the first out of the plane and had opened his parachute immediately; were eventually returned to Portsmouth, England by boat. Bergeron was of French-Canadian origin and could speak French, By 3 April they were in London. DiBetta; T/Sgt Clyde E. Hewitt, Jr., radio; S/Sgt Guy H. Golden, Jr., waist and S/Sgt Eldo C. Weseloh, tail gunner, all avoided capture and were hidden by a Underground unit until General George S. Patton's Third Army overran the area and liberated them. They were returned to England on 13 August 1944 where their whereabouts had been unknown from the time of the raid. Two other crewmembers, 1st Lieutenant Raymond F. Feilbach, navigator and 1st Lieutenant Jerroll E. Sanders, bombardier, were captured. (In February combat claimed 17 crews in the 306th Bomb Group). See *First Over Germany; A History of the 306th Bomb Group* by Russell A. Strong. Oberfähnrich Erich Scheyda was KIA on 7 May 1944 in his FW 190A-8 at Athies-Laon by a Spitfire of 411 RCA Squadron. Scheyda had been with the Geschwader since August 1941 and had been credited with 20 *Abschüsse* in 188 combat sorties. He was posthumously awarded the *Deutsche Kreuz im Gold* (*DKG* or German Cross in Gold) at the end of May. See *The JG 26 War Diary Vol.2* by Donald Caldwell. Grub Street, London. 1998.

582 42-29863 (formerly *Kentucky Babe*) in the 509th Bomb Squadron (4 Evd.1 KIA, 5 PoW).

583 42-31099, which crashed at Lauz near Amiens. 7 in 2nd Lieutenant Robert V. Laux's crew evaded. 3 PoW.

584 Guttmann was KIA on 27 March 1944 when his FW 190A-7 was shot down at Chartres by a 359th Fighter Group P-47. See *The JG 26 War Diary Vol.2* by Donald Caldwell. Grub Street, London. 1998.

585 B-24 41-23721 *Ready Teddy* was salvaged on 6 August 1944 and again on 11 June 1945.

586 John Butler had flown 139 hours and 25 minutes of combat time with eight different pilots in 17 different Liberators. On 15 February 51 B-24s again bombed the V-weapon site at St. Pol/Siracourt while 34 P-47s bombed targets of opportunity.

Chapter 12:

587 On 20 February, after 10 days pause in combat, the three Gruppen of JG 1were in action against an armada of 1003 bombers escorted by 17 squadrons of American fighters

and 16 RAF. Twenty FW 190A-6s and A-7s made three passes against the bombers. The third, at about 1300 hours in the region of Mulhouse, was the most effective: three B-17s and two P-38s were claimed (*Oberfeldwebel* Reinhold Flecks claiming a B-17 and a P-38). I. Gruppe were also engaged, *Oberfeldwebel* Rudolf Hübl claiming a B-17 but 2nd *Staffel* lost their *Staffelkapitän, Hauptmann* Harald Römer, killed. His place was taken by a veteran of JG 54, Oberleutnant Helmut Biederbick who had served on the Eastern Front with JG 54 when victories were still relatively easy... "Loudspeakers blared out military marches. We would gather near our aircraft, accompanied by the music, which was sometimes interrupted by news concerning the advance of the We followed their progress on a map. Each Squadron Leader had a telephone on the wing of his aircraft and linked to the Stab section. The music was interrupted: "*Sitzbereitsschaft*" - cockpit readiness. At any moment we could be taking off. A green flare over the airfield was the signal; engines would be started and we would take off. "When the "*Dicke Autos*" or "*Indianer*" were sighted, we flew for several seconds parallel to the formation in order to evaluate its strength and direction. We were aware of the escort fighters, but often they did not attack at this moment. We picked up speed, swept wide of our target and carried out a 180° turn. We were then head-on and opened fire while traversing through the bomber stream. During this move, our formation lost cohesion and that was what the enemy fighters were waiting for. They then picked us off at the rear of the "*Viermots*". From *Defending the Reich; The History of Jagdgeschwader 1 "Oesau"* by Eric Mombeek.

588 Major Jimmy Stewart led 28 Liberators of the 445th in the leading 2nd Combat Wing to Brunswick. On this raid visual bombing was impossible so Stewart assumed the lead position an in spite of aggressive fighter attacks and later heavy anti aircraft fire, held the formation together and directed an accurate bombing run over the target. The 445th lost three Liberators to flak. Stewart's actions earned him the award of the DFC. On 22 March he led the wing again, this time to Berlin. This was his first trip to Big-B and, when asked by newsmen if it was any more unusual than his others, Stewart sad, "Unusual? We hit Berlin, didn't we?' By now the Top Brass considered that Stewart had been flying too many missions and he was moved on 30 March to the 453rd Bomb Group at Old Buckenham, as Operations Officer to replace Major Curtis H. Cofield who had been KIA only three days before. Over the next few weeks Stewart took his turn as Air Commander of bombing missions. On 13 April he flew 2nd Combat Wing lead against German aircraft manufacturing installations near Munich. All but one of the 453rd Bomb Group Liberators returned to Old Buckenham. On 3 June 1944 Stewart was promoted to lieutenant colonel and on 1 July he moved to 2nd Combat Wing Headquarters at Hethel as chief of staff to Brigadier General Ted Timberlake. By July 1944 apart from being awarded the DFC for "exceptional achievement in combat while leading an attack on aircraft factories at Brunswick," he had also earned an Oak Leaf Cluster to the DFC, the Air Medal (February 1944) with one Oak-Leaf Cluster (March 1944). (A second OLC would follow in March 1945). On 29 March 1945 Stewart was promoted full colonel. He served at 2nd Wing Headquarters as executive officer, chief of staff and finally wing commander, until 14 June 1945. James Stewart died at his home in Beverly Hills on 2 July 1997 aged 89.

589 The 15th did not take part because it was committed to supporting the Anzio operation.

590 Direct hits were achieved on the principal assembly shop at the Erla Maschinenwerk Messerschmitt production factory and its other large assembly building was observed to be on fire as the bombers left the target area.

591 B-17 42-29656 in the 322nd Bomb Squadron flown by 2nd Lieutenant Ernest B. Kidd was hit in three engines and the pilot ordered the crew to bale out. Two men were KIA. 8 who landed near the Chièvres airfield were captured.

592 42-31763.

593 B-17G 42-30499.

594 The bomber stream was swelled by 36 B-17s of the 457th Bomb Group, which was making its debut and principal targets were the aircraft factories at Brunswick. The 15th Air Force was grounded by bad weather.

595 5./JG 1 was withdrawn from the action for 6 weeks on 15 March 1944. On 28 April Knoke was promoted *Hauptmann* and given command of 5./JG 5.

596 His final assignments were as commander of the jet fighter school at Lechfeld from January 1945, where he flew the He 162 and finally with JV 44, which he commanded after Galland was wounded and Günther Lutzow (108 victories) was killed. Bär's 220 confirmed victories made him 8th in the overall list of *Experten*. He accounted for more Western-flown aircraft (124) than any other German pilot except Marseille and whereas almost all Marseille's victories were scored in Africa, Bär scored at least 75 of his against British and American-flown aircraft in Europe. Of these, 16 were scored with the Me 262, making him the leading jet ace of all nations until about 1973, a handful being scored with a special aircraft fitted with a rocket motor, so adapted to intercept high-flying Mosquitoes. Bar had to bale out 4our times and make many force-landings. He survived the war but he died in a light aircraft accident in April 1957.

597 Two of the B-17s lost were from the 95th Bomb Group, which succumbed to fighters of JG 26. 42-30634 *Liberty Belle* piloted by Lieutenant John P. McGuigan in the 412th Bomb Squadron crashed into the Zuider Zee with the loss of 6 crew. The rest were captured after baling out. 42-3462 *San Antonio Rose* piloted by 2nd Lieutenant Morris R. Marks in the 336th Bomb Squadron crashed into these waters with the loss of 8 of the crew. Two men were captured and made PoW. *Oberfeldwebel* Addi Glunz, 5th *Staffel* CO and *Unteroffizier* Gerhard Loschinksi of 7./JG 26 shot down these two B-17s. Three days later Loschinksi was shot down and killed in combat with a 357th Fighter Group Mustang.

598 The 1st Bomb Division scored a notable success at the Junkers works at Oschersleben and Bernberg but lost 39 Fortresses in the day's raids, including 7 in the 306th Bomb Group. Enemy fighter interceptions were high despite the hope that a simultaneous attack on Regensburg by the 15th Air Force would split the German fighter force. 118 bombers of the 15th Air Force bombed the Messerschmitt assembly plant Regensburg for the loss of 14 aircraft.

599 42-38041.

600 42-5052 *Mizpah* with pilot 2nd Lieutenant J. Moffat; 42-31399, piloted by 1st Lieutenant C. D. Crook; 42-5788 *Pluto's Avenger*, pilot 2nd Lieutenant J. R. Morris and 42-29931 *Devils Workshop*, piloted by G. E. Underwood. 18 men were lost in the aircraft, the rest becoming prisoners.

601 42-5081.

602 42-39785 captained by 2nd Lieutenant D. C. Headlee with co-pilot 1st Lieutenant G. H. Shupe at the controls.

603 42-31239 piloted by 1st Lieutenant M. L. Smith and 42-31562, 8 men being killed and 12 taken prisoner. In all 41 bombers were lost. Hardest hit was the 1st Bomb Division, which lost 38 B-17s (the 2nd Bomb Division lost the three other bombers this day). JG 26 pilots claimed 7 B-17s shot down and all came from the 91st or 384th Bomb Groups, which lost 5 and 4 B-17s respectively. *Oberfeldwebel* Addi Glunz claimed two B-17s shot out of formation in the first combat sortie of the day. That same afternoon he claimed two Fortresses in the 91st or 384th Bomb Group and a 78th Fighter Group Thunderbolt shot down. Glunz received confirmation for two B-17s and the P-47 to take his tally to 58 victories. A 353rd Fighter Group P-47 was claimed shot down by *Hauptmann* Hermann Staiger, CO 12th *Staffel* at Mönchengladbach. His victim was Captain Orsinger, on attachment to the 352nd Fighter Squadron, 353rd Fighter Group from the 366th Fighter Group who was last seen in a spin. *Unteroffizier* Paul Gross of the 5th *Staffel* JG 26 and *Hauptmann* Horst Sternberg CO 6th *Staffel* JG 26 were KIA when their FW 190A fighters were shot down by 4th Fighter Group Thunderbolts. Lieutenant Colonel Don Blakeslee had led a Withdrawal Support to Aachen-Schweinfurt from 1313 to 1700 hours and the Group split up due to weather. The 334th and 336th Squadrons joined up on the Rhine between Koblenz and Bonn with 24 1st Division B-17s at 1503 hours. At 1517 hours when 8 FW 190s attacked a circling B-17 at 9,000ft and the 335th Fighter Squadron, 4th Fighter Group engaged, Major George Carpenter, Lieutenant Bernard J. McGrattan and Lieutenant Albert I. Schlegel each claimed a FW 190 destroyed Lieutenant Pierce W. "Mac" McKennon claimed a Bf 109. The 4th Fighter Group left the bombers at 1535 south of Brussels. Feldwebel Peter Crump of 6th *Staffel* JG 26 was WIA when near Mönchengladbach his FW 190A-7 was hit by a 78th Fighter Group P-47 and he was forced to bale out. He hit the ground hard and damaged ligaments in one knee. *Obergefreiter* Leo Przybyl of 5th *Staffel* JG 26 was WIA by return fire from a B-17. (See *The JG 26 War Diary Vol.2* by Donald Caldwell. Grub Street, London. 1998). Other victorious German pilots included Major Heinz "Pritzel" Bär and *Hauptmann* Hermann Segatz who claimed two B-17s. *Oberfeldwebel* Rudolf Hübl also claimed his 13th victory, a Fortress. Hübl destroyed two Liberators on 24 February 1944 and he scored his 19th and last victory with JG 1 on 23 June 1944. Segatz was KIA on 8 March 1944. He had at least 34 victories.

604 114 B-17s and B-24s of the 15th Air Force returned to Steyr. 17 bombers FTR.

605 A ninth, the newly operational 458th, flew a diversionary sweep over the North Sea.

606 On 22 February 27 B-24s had taken off from Tibenham for Gotha and for 25 of them the recall was merely a stay of execution for the tragic return to the German city on the 24th. Two aircraft, which did not receive the recall, went on to Gotha and bombed the target.

607 Divisional Assembly Line.

608 The 392nd was extremely accurate, dropping 98% of its bombs within 2000ft of the aiming-point. The average percentage of bombs dropped by the 2nd Bomb Division, which fell within 2000ft on visual missions under good to fair visibility in February 1944, was only 49%. In comparison the 1st Fortress Division achieved 76% and the 3rd 77%. The 44th had also achieved a highly accurate bomb run. Intelligence later estimated that 6 to 7 weeks' Bf 110 production was lost. American Intelligence described Gotha as "the most valuable single target in the enemy twin-engine fighter complex." Its destruction was well received by the Eighth Bomber Command who later awarded the 392nd and the 445th Presidential Unit Citations for their part in the raid.

609 B-24 42-40619/N *Nana* and Lieutenant Freeman A. Carlton's crew, 567th Bomb Squadron (3 KIA. 7 PoW). 42-100280 *Lil Audrey* and Lieutenant Marion B. Brown's crew, 565th Bomb Squadron (1Evd. 9 PoW). Lieutenant James O. McMullen, Jr., (1KIA. 9 PoW). Lieutenant Alton C. Belanger (8 KIA. 3 PoW). 2nd Lieutenant Claude E. White (8 KIA. 2 PoW) and Lieutenant Donald R. Nowak (5 KIA. 6 PoW).

610 Feldwebel Wiegand and Oberleutnant Nau both had claims for a 4th Fighter Group P-47 confirmed.

611 Turley was KIA on 6 March 1944.

612 At least 4 of the Bf 109Gs were from JG 26. Obergefreiter Helmut Greim, Fähnenjunker-Feldwebel Kurt-Heinz Dylewski, Fuhrer Burghardt Wölke and Oberleutnant Karl Wunschelmeyer were all KIA. Wunschelmeyer had earlier destroyed a 92nd or 306th Bomb Group B-17 at Hasselünne. Two other JG 26 FW 190A-4/6 pilots were shot down by P-47s in the 56th Fighter Group. *Unteroffizier* Gerhard Mohr was KIA and Feldwebel Franz Vanderveerd was WIA. *Hauptmann* Karl Borris, *Staffelkapitän* 1st Gruppe JG 26, claimed a 56th Fighter Group P-47 north of Rheine. See *The JG 26 War Diary Vol.2* by Donald Caldwell. Grub Street, London. 1998.

613 The 92nd Bomb Group lost two B-17s on the Stuttgart-Augsburg mission. 42-37755 *Dotty G* flown by 2nd Lieutenant Clifford P. Beach landed in Switzerland and all 10 crew were interned. 42-30623 flown by 2nd Lieutenant Charles G. Nashold. (1 Evd. 2 KIA. 7 PoW)

614 42-31245 and 42-30728 respectively.

615 42-31979.

616 See *First Over Germany; A History of the 306th Bomb Group* by Russell A. Strong.

617 See *The JG 26 War Diary Vol.2* by Donald Caldwell. Grub Street, London. 1998.

618 6 KIA. 4 PoW. 42-37880 crashed at Poix Terron, France.

619 42-31142 crashed at St. Martin, Belgium (2 Evd. 8 PoW).
620 42-39841 crashed at Saarbrücken (5 Evd. 5 PoW). Zirngible was KIA on 22 June 1944 when his FW 190A-6 was shot down NE of St. Cyr by a P-38 in the 474th Fighter Group. Two other 96th Bomb Group losses were B-17 42-30123 *Big Dick* in the 338th Bomb Squadron flown by 2nd Lieutenant David D. Jarrett crashed at Regensburg (5 Evd. 5 PoW) and 42-38043 in the 413th Bomb Squadron flown by Lieutenant George A. Smiley, which crashed at Stuttgart (2 KIA. 8 PoW).
621 Edner was shot down on 8 March 1944 NE of Berlin and he was taken prisoner.
622 Garrison, who was from Mount Victory, Kentucky, was shot down on 3 March 1944 by flak near Boulogne flying a P-51B.his total score stood at 7 victories. Flying F-86F Sabres in Korea in 1952-53 he added a further 10 and 2 probables to his wartime score.
623 JG 26 lost four FW 190A-6/7s to the 336th Fighter Squadron, 4th Fighter Group and two pilots KIA including *Hauptmann* Rudolf "Rudi" Leuschel, 8th Staffel Kapitän, who was shot down 16km South of Metz.
624 Mayer had been awarded the *Schwerten* (*S*) or Knight's Cross with Oak Leaves and Swords. His total score was102 victories, which included 25 *Viermots*.
625 42-37932.

Chapter 13:

626 42-38075. All 10 crew were killed.
627 All 10 men aboard Ahlwardt's ship (42-38075) were killed in the explosion.
628 In all, 11 bombers FTR. 79 of the 748 heavies despatched attacked targets of opportunity including Wilhelmshaven and Heligoland.
629 42-38016 in the 350th Bomb Squadron.
630 42-31627 and 42-31595 respectively.
631 The leading 385th Bomb Group at the head of the 4th Combat Wing came in for persistent fighter attacks. Brigadier General Russell Wilson was flying in a 482nd Bomb Group H_2X-equipped Fortress and his crew included Medal of Honor recipient John C. Morgan, now a 1st Lieutenant. Just as the formation approached the Berlin area the flak guns opened up and bracketed the group. Wilson's aircraft was badly hit but continued on the bomb run with one engine on fire. Major Fred A. Rabbo, the pilot, gave the order to bale out after the bomber began losing altitude, but before they could take to their parachutes the aircraft exploded killing 6 of the 10-man crew. Incredibly, Morgan survived, being somersaulted out of the aircraft with his parachute pack under his arm. He managed to put it on after several attempts and was saved from injury when a tree broke his fall. Morgan was captured and sent to *Stalag Luft III*.
632 Comprising the 95th, 100th and 390th Bomb Groups.
633 B-17 42-38059 in the 418th Bomb Squadron.
634 B-17 42-30278 in the 418th Bomb Squadron.
635 B-17 42-31800 in the 418th Bomb Squadron.
636 B-17 42-97491 in the 418th Bomb Squadron.
637 B-17 42-97482 in the 418th Bomb Squadron.
638 B-17 42-39994 in the 418th Bomb Squadron.
639 All 10 crew were interned and they were repatriated by 19 November.
640 B-17 42-31735 in the 351st Bomb Squadron.
641 The radio operator was badly wounded and he died later, on 12 July, in a prison camp. After exploding, the Fortress crashed near Hausstette.
642 B-17 42-38044 in the 351st Bomb Squadron.
643 Rish and co-pilot Frank Smith were killed, as was the tail gunner and the ball turret gunner. The rest of the crew were taken prisoner. The wreckage came down in the vicinity of Quakenbrück.
644 B-17 42-30170 in the 349th Bomb Squadron. "Just about the oldest on the field at Thorpe Abbotts" and "definitely a wreck, of two crash landings" and which had previously flown under 3 other names - *Torchy 2nd*, *Hot Spit*, and *Miss Carriage*.
645 B-17 42-31051.
646 *Nelson King* had been named in honor of the former radio operator on the Lauro's crew who on a mission on 29 November 1943 having removed his gloves at over 20,000ft where the temperature was close to -50° to replace an iced up oxygen mask on the ball turret gunner, his hands had turned purple and swelled to three times their normal size. King's walk-around oxygen bottle froze and in the efforts to save the ball turret gunner, he lost the tips of several fingers to frostbite and he never flew again. *Nelson King* was lost with Lieutenant Emil J. Siewart's crew on 24 May 1944. (1 KIA. 9 PoW).
647 B-17 42-38011 in the 350th Bomb Squadron.
648 B-17 42-38197 in the 350th Bomb Squadron.
649 B-17 42-31731 in the 349th Bomb Squadron.
650 B-17 42-30799 in the 349th Bomb Squadron.
651 B-17 42-39872 in the 350th Bomb Squadron.
652 See *Century Bombers; The Story of the Bloody Hundredth* by Richard Le Strange. 100th Bomb Group Memorial Museum, 1989.
653 The American Army liberated Willis and Gladys 6 months later.
654 B-24 42-64460, which crashed at Plantlünne. The 453rd lost three other B-24s on the raid: 42-52226, which crashed at Edam in the Netherlands; 42-64457 and 42-52191 *Litle Joe*, both of which went down in the North Sea.
655 B-17 42-38022 *Lil Opportunity* that crashed at Plantlünne was flown by Lieutenant C. E. Johnson (2 KIA.8 PoW).
656 Possibly B-24 41-29299, which crashed at Nijkerk, Holland. All 10 of 2nd Lieutenant Thayer Hopkins' crew survived and were taken prisoner. The Group lost 4 other B-24s. Oberleutnant Greiner of IV./NJG 1 shot down 42-52306 and it crashed at Münsterlager. (Greiner is also credited with shooting down B-17 42-38118 in the 91st Bomb Group). B-24s 41-29286 and 42-52450 were brought down by flak and crashed in Holland. 42-52515 *Ford's Follies* was hit by flak and crashed at Petzow, Germany.
657 B-17 42-31448 crashed at Etzweiler. All 10 crew survived and were made prisoners of war. The 381st Bomb Group also lost B-17F 42-3215 *Linda Mary* flown by 2nd Lieutenant Richard W. "Slick" Coyle in the 532nd Bomb Squadron, which crashed at Magdeburg 30 minutes short of Berlin (9 PoW. 1 KIA). And B-17G 42-31553 *Myer's Flaw*, flown by Lieutenant Edward E. Haushalter in the 534th Bomb Squadron, which crashed at Wernsdorf after being hit by head-on fighter attacks on the bomb run. (5 KIA. 5 PoW).
658 U.S. fighters claimed 81 enemy fighters shot down and the bomber gunners claimed 97 destroyed; the *Luftwaffe* actually lost 64 fighters destroyed and two damaged beyond repair. This was a loss rate of 12.5% of those committed to action.
659 Including *Hello Natural* in the 448th Bomb Group whose crew was forced to seek refuge at Bulltofta airfield in Sweden to become the first of 19 of the group's B-24s, which would be forced to land in Sweden during the war, the highest total of all the Liberator groups. Other B-24s lost included B-24J 42-109832 *De Icer* and B-24J *Balls of Fire* in the 93rd Bomb Group and B-24H 42-7586 *God Bless Our Ship* in the 445th Bomb Group.
660 100 FW 190s and Bf 109s of JG 1, JG 11 and III./JG 54 were the first to attack the incoming bombers, between 1200 and 1230 and between Osnabrück and Hanover. JG 3, the *Schwarmstaffel*, I./JG 302, II. and III./ZG 26, the *Einsartzstaffel Erla*, ZG26 and even 16 night fighters of NJG 5 and IV./NJG 1, totaling at least 134 aircraft, unleashed their might north of Magdeburg at 1235 and attacking for over one hour without a pause. *Leutnant* Iffland in JG 3 shot down 42-31079 in the 91st Bomb Group. Major Heinz Bär of JG 1 shot down 42-31680 in the 92nd Bomb Group. On the way back, elements of JG 1, JG 2, JG 11, JG 26, JG 300 and IV./NJG 1 - 85 fighters in all - intercepted the badly battered bomber formations just to the east of the Dutch-German border, at around 1430 hours. Among the German losses on 6 March was *Hauptmann* Hugo Frey, the 28-year-old St.Kpt, 7./JG 11, who was shot down and killed in his FW 190A-6 "White 1" at Erm-Sleen, Holland. Frey was one of the *Jagdwaffe*'s foremost "*Viermot* killers"; among his 32 victories were 26 B-17s and B-24s. In the hour before he was killed, probably by return fire, Frey claimed his final 4 B-17s destroyed.
661 Colonel Neil "Chick" Harding was suffering from gallstones but had refused to report to the medics. Over the past few days his health had deteriorated and preparations were being put in hand to send him back to the United States for an operation. Colonel Robert H. Kelly became 100th Bomb Group CO on 19 April.
662 The Bloody Hundredth's only casualty was 42-3271, *Nine Little Yanks and a Jerk*, which was salvaged with a badly wrinkled skin.
663 The E-6B computer was designed to be used for nearly all computations in navigation and bombing. The Automatic Bombing Computer, which was used with the M-Series bombsight, enabled bombardiers to allow for wind and automatically indicated the drift angle and dropping angle for any heading of the aircraft. The C-2 computer or the AN computer was used to allow for bombing altitude. The G-1 computer enabled bombardiers to find the true airspeed. The J-1 Sighting Angle Computer gave a sighting angle for a 30 or 50 second bombing run.
664 1st Lieutenant Earl H. Bond was killed in P-47 42-8652 PZ-O *The Bid*, which crashed near Mergate Hall at Bracon Ash. The other 5 486th Fighter Squadron pilots escaped serious injury. See, *USAAF Fighter Stories; A New Selection*, by Ian MacLachlan. (Sutton Publishing, 2005).
665 The fighter groups, which accompanied the 1st Task Force bombers through the penetration and target portions of the mission claimed 37-4-8.
666 P-51B 43-7022 PZ-W.
667 The Second and Third *Gruppen* JG 26 plus the 4th *Staffel* had rendezvoused with the 6 *Jagdgruppen* of JG 1 and JG 11. Attacking in in trail in closely spaced strings of 10 to 12 aircraft, they singled out the rearmost B-17s in the 45th Combat Wing, which was leading the 3rd Bomb Division. They succeeded for once in overwhelming the escorts, which on this part of the route were the P-47s of the 56th and 353rd Fighter Groups. Sixteen B-17s in the leading 45th CBW (6 in the 96th Bomb Group and 5 each in the 388th and 452nd Bomb Group formations) were lost. Eight of these crashed between Steinhuder Lake and Braunschweig, 6 of them the victims of the IInd *Gruppe* JG 26. *Hauptmann* Hermann Staiger, CO, 12./JG 26 claimed a 388th Bomb Group B-17 north of Hanover and another Fortress at Potsdam. Fähnrich-Feldwebel (officer candidate) Gerd Wiegand shot down a 353rd Fighter Group P-47 at 1325 hours and was then was WIA when his FW 190A-6 was shot down by a 56th Fighter Group P-47 at Damme at 1325 hours. Wiegand suffered injuries that kept him out of combat for three months. Some of the German fighters followed the B-17s to the outskirts of Berlin where *Leutnant* Wilhelm Hofmann 8th *Staffel* CO, shot down a 363rd Fighter Group P-51 of the target escort at 1325 hours. Oberleutnant Walter Matoni CO, 5th *Staffel* JG 26 was credited with the destruction of a B-17 at the Mittelland Canal at 1330 hours and a 452nd Bomb Group B-17 shot out of formation 10 minutes later. Feldwebel Gerhard Guttmann was credited with the destruction of a B-17 in either the 96th or 388th Bomb Group at 1400 hours. Feldwebel Hans Prager of 5/JG 26 was credited with the destruction of a 388th Bomb Group B-17 at 1335 hours. Feldwebel Gerhard Vogt of 7/JG 26 was credited with the destruction of a B-17 in either the 96th or 388th Bomb Group and a 452nd Bomb Group B-17 at 1330 hours. (See *The JG 26 War Diary Vol.2* by Donald Caldwell. Grub Street, London. 1998). The 388th Bomb Group's 5 losses were as follows: 2nd Lieutenant M. J. Moran flying 42-30829 "*Princess Pat*" was hit by fighters near Celle. The FW 190 caused the left wing to come off and the plane flipped on its back and no chutes were seen at this time. 8 men got out and were taken prisoner. 2nd Lieutenant A. O. Amann flying 42-30340 "*Screaming Red Ass*" was hit by Bf 109s. When last seen, the No.3 engine was feathered and both wings were badly shot-up. The plane crashed west of Magdeburg. Only one

man survived. 1st Lieutenant W. W. Lentz flying 42-38138 was hit by fighters just inside the Dutch coast. One of the enemy a/c with his cockpit in flames hit this a/c on the left elevator and rudder sending the plane into a dive. Five crew were thrown out when the plane exploded in the vicinity of Celle. One of the survivors, 2nd Lieutenant J. D. Pond, bombardier who was flying with a makeup crew as his regular crew had finished their missions a few days previously was taken prisoner and incarcerated at *Stalag Luft I*, Barth. 2nd Lieutenant H. B. Pou flying 42-31214 "*Return Engagement*" was hit by fighters and the crew baled out near Hanover. Seven survived to be taken prisoner. 1st Lieutenant L. T. Tobias flying 42-37819 was hit by enemy a/c and dived out of the formation. Six crew baled out and the plane blew-up at the radio room before crashing near Helmstedt airfield. On the bomb run another Combat Wing crossed in front, making the 388th Bomb Group attack impossible so a target of opportunity was sought. A 20mm shell from an enemy fighter killed a bombardier in a B-17, which returned to Knettishall and in another two waist gunners were wounded. (See *The 388th At War* by Edward J. Huntzinger). Bomber gunners claimed to have shot down 63 enemy fighters while the escorts claimed a further 79 for the loss of 18 of their own. In fact, 27 *Luftwaffe* fighters were lost on 8 March.

668 Klaus Mietusch, CO III/JG 26 and two pilots made a beam attack on the rear bombers of a combat wing and rolled away. Mietusch claimed a B-17 shot out of formation south of Zwolle-Braunschweig at 1325 hours.

669 P-47D 42-8473. When he was assigned this Thunderbolt he told his ground crew chief that the left side of the plane was his to name and the right side was theirs. Al Giesting, Meroney's Crew Chief named the right side *Josephine Hedy*.

670 Bf 109G-6 410743 White 5 1st Lieutenant Duncan R. Donahue flying 42-8754 claimed a 109 "damaged" at 1545 hours.

671 Bf 109G-6 Werke Nummer 162032 "Black 21" which was shot down North of Meppen at 1600 hours. Meroney's 8th victory firmly established him as the Bluenosers' scoring leader and foremost P-47 Ace. At this point in the war, Meroney had outscored the entire 486th Squadron 8 to 7 and many were already seeing him as the Group's Ace of Aces. Meroney scored a 9th and final victory on 16 March before he was shot down by flak and taken prisoner on 8 April 1944. All 9 of his victories were scored flying P-47D 42-8473. Virgil Meroney flew F-84s in the Korean War and flew 141 combat missions in F-4s in SE Asia, 81 of them over North Vietnam. His son, Virgil Kersh Meroney III was MIA in Laos on 1 March 1969 in an F-4D. (See *Stars & Bars: A Tribute to the American Fighter Ace 1920-1973*. Frank Olynyk. Grub Street 1995).

672 Mietusch has been described by Donald Caldwell as "a wild man in the air" who "paid no apparent heed to his own personal safety or that of his pilots, who were under his orders to keep up the attack until forced by damage, low fuel, or low ammunition to break off." Mietusch received the *RitterKreuz* (*RK* or Knight's Cross) on 26 March after his 60th victory and he was promoted *Hauptmann*.

673 Curtis E. LeMay, 3rd Division Commander singled out the 45th Combat Wing for special praise in the Daily Bulletin No 69 dated March 9 1944. "The crews of the 45th Combat Wing delivered a punishing blow today to the morale of all Germany. In successfully putting bombs on the enemy's capital and his vital plants they furthered the war effort more than any of us can adequately evaluate. At the present writing, the major part of the hurt to the 3rd Division forces fell on the gallant crews of the 96th, 388th and 452nd Bomb Groups. The spirit and fight these units displayed made it easier on the other wings who wanted to share the brunt of the battle with them. Convey to all officers and men who participated, my deep admiration for the courage and determination with which they pushed the air attack into the heart of the enemy territory and blasted Berlin."

674 In the first American operation to Berlin on 4 March the "Bloody Hundredth" had won through to the target with the 95th while all the others had turned back. It had lost one B-17 that day but successive raids on the capital that week cost the group another 16 aircraft. It was for its "outstanding performance of duty in action against the enemy in connection with the initial series of successful attacks against Berlin, 4, 6 and 8 March 1944 that the 100th was awarded its second Presidential Unit Citation on 3 March 1945." Altogether, the 8th Air Force attacked Berlin on 5 occasions in March 1944.

675 Life expectancy was put on average at 11 missions at this stage of the war. Hatcher was one of the lucky ones. As if to confirm his good fortune on April 18, during yet another raid on Berlin, the *Grand Old Lady* was one of 8 B-17s taken from the 94th. Of the 11 aircraft Cliff Hatcher flew during his tour, 9 had gone down with other crews. Hatcher wrote later, "Lady Luck has certainly been with me. Of the 54 crews in the original Snow Provisional Group, only 4 survived their missions."

676 "Everybody wanted to see our crew make it. We waited for a 'milk-run' to complete our tour. On 19 March we went to Frankfurt and we made it. As we entered the flight pattern over Podington, we broke away to buzz the field. There was a definite pattern for this. We went 90° to the landing runway and right at the tower where we pulled up went around and landed. Of course, we had to be last in the formation to do this and have no wounded on board. On an earlier mission we carried a bombardier who was on his 25th. Now, on *our* 25th, there were 6 of us who were flying their last mission together. It was a great day and we duly buzzed the tower. Then we partied until our papers came through. What we didn't realize was that we were war weary. My weight going into combat was about 160lb but I was now down to 140lb." Bill Rose and 5 fellow crewmembers had completed their tours just in time because 4 days later the 92nd lost 5 crews to heavy flak and fighter attacks during a raid on Herben-Hamm. Four of the crews were from Rose's squadron, the 326th. In 1945 Rose returned to the 92nd Bomb Group and flew part of a second tour.

677 It was *My Ass'am Dragon* in the 44th Bomb Group, flown by 1st Lieutenant David R. Talbott. The other Liberator lost was *Pocatello Chief* in the 392nd Bomb Group, piloted by Lieutenant Bert D Miller, which crashed at Hiddenhausen, Germany. *Leutnant* Karl "Charlie" Willius, CO of 2./JG 26, claims to have pursued a damaged 392nd Bomb Group B-24 out over the North Sea and shot it down 50 miles east of Great Yarmouth, Norfolk, at 1630 hours. However, the only other loss this day was a 100th Bomb Group B-17, which exploded at the target.

678 42-7643 in the 700th Bomb Squadron.

679 Staiger, a *RitterKreuzträger* (*RKT*) or Knight's Cross holder, scored a total of 63 *Abschüsse* including 50 on the Western Front 26 of which, were *4-mots*. *Fighter Aces* by Mike Spick, Ivy Books, 1996.

680 Quince Brown was awarded the Silver Star for this 4-kill mission. In April he was promoted Captain and further promotion to major followed. He went on leave to the U.S. after his first tour, returning to the 84th Fighter Squadron on 28 August 1944. On 1 September he scored his 12th and final victory. Five days later he was shot down by flak 2km west of Schleiden. He baled out and was murdered by a Schutzstaffel *SS* officer. See *Stars & Bars: A Tribute to the American Fighter Ace 1920-1973*. Frank Olynyk. Grub Street. 1995.

681 41-29174 in the 577th Bomb Squadron. 1 Evd. 9 KIA.

682 42-109824 in the 577th Bomb Squadron. 7 KIA. 3 PoW.

683 B-24 41-28742.

684 The 392nd suffered its heaviest single mission loss, losing 15 aircraft and crews and 9 other ships damaged by fighters and flak, all totaling 154 casualties. Strickler, who became a PoW, was the only survivor on Books' crew. He died aged 85.

685 Altogether, 43 bombers and 13 escorting fighters were lost on the 18 March raids.

686 Captain Stock's crew were taken prisoner and although Colonel Miller evaded he was caught trying to cross the Pyrenees into Spain. After being interrigated by the *Gestapo* he was finally sent to *Stalag Luft III*. Meanwhile, Colonel Ramsey D. Potts assumed command of the 453rd Bomb Group. In all, 43 bombers and 13 of the 925 fighters dispatched were lost. USAAF fighters claimed 13 victories, while the bomber gunners put in claims for 45-10-17.

687 Thereafter, each of the three bomb divisions operated one pathfinder squadron apiece. The 1st Division assigned the task to the pioneer 305th Bomb Group at Chelveston while PFF responsibilities in the 3rd Division were allocated to the 96th Bomb Group at Snetterton Heath.

688 Two days later the weather was responsible for the loss of two more 466th Bomb Group ships which were involved in a second mid-air collision, near Osterburg. On 27 March two more collided, shortly after take-off from Attlebridge.

689 The Ploesti strike was Don Chase's 7th mission. Lieutenant Charles Whitlock was forced to abort 125 miles short of the target with fuel transfer problems and oiling difficulties, which forced them to shut down No.1 engine and feather the propeller before No.4 lost power also and they put down safely on Cyprus. While he and 3 other members were grounded with respiratory and ear infections on 16 August six of their fellow crew and four replacements FTR when *Timb-a-a-ah* was shot down over Foggia. Chase wrote: "Long after the last ships returned and the sun had set we mournfully trekked back to our tent area. It was a night of anguish. Eight of our Group's aircraft had failed to return. If I had been older, instead of 22, perhaps I might not have searched for a symbolic reason, which governs fateful events. But regardless, I picked up my Gurkha Kukri that I had been the custodian of since our crew were presented with it in Cyprus, walked into the desert and threw the curved 10-inch blade across the sand into the darkness. It had brought only bad luck. More than half my crew were gone, probably dead. I cried." (Whitlock and the navigator were taken prisoner by Italian troops, 3 gunners were KIA and of the 4 replacement crewmembers, 2 were KIA and 2 PoW). For the next 3 months, in England, Chase flew no combat missions but in mid-December he took the place a radio man on Lieutenant James Hill's crew who had fallen, or was blown, from the foot-wide bomb bay catwalk during the bomb run and had parachuted into France. He flew his next 10 missions with Lieutenant. Hill and his battle-experienced crew, who completed their tour on 25 February 1944. Prior to landing Hill buzzed the base perimeter strip at Shipdham "with full power at an altitude too low to estimate." He then climbed at a steep angle, rocked the wing and put the B-24 through a modified chandelle, "the resultant G-force of which made my body feel as if it were filled with cement instead of thin, scared blood." At that time Chase still had 8 missions to fly before ending his tour.

690 "I flew my 21st mission on 24 March, to St. Dizier. Squadron Operations passed along the news that each crewman must now fly 30 missions, not 25, before his tour of combat was over. Instead of four I now had nine missions to go. It was disturbing news. I didn't think I had enough luck to take me through nine. Operations called me in and said I'd only be required to fly a total of 28, based on the number of missions I'd already flown. Okay, fine, but that still meant three extra missions."

691 By 19 May 1944 John A. Miller in the 100th Bomb Group would complete 6 missions to the German capital; the greatest number of Berlin missions in one tour by any 8th Air Force member. "Altogether, we started out for Berlin 7 times. Twice our co-pilot went nuts and tried to crash us into the sea. These times the crew fought him off the wheel and we aborted. After the second time he didn't return to our crew. He wasn't a coward; he just couldn't go back to Berlin."

Chapter 14:

692 *Judith Lynn* (42-40983) crashed at Bougemeron. All 9 crew were KIA.

693 See *The JG 26 War Diary Vol.2* by Donald Caldwell. Grub Street, London. 1998.

694 Captain C. H. Koch.

695 It later transpired that 26 B-24s in the 392nd had dropped 1184 100lb bombs on a forested area 3 miles southeast of the Swiss town of Schauffhausen over 120 miles from Ludwigshafen and the CO, Colonel "Bull" Rendle, had some explaining to do. The mistake led to America paying the Swiss thousands of dollars in reparations. Koch was rebuked and never again allowed to perform the function of lead navigator. Keilman concludes. "As a personal

friend, I felt sorry for Captain Koch. He had flown as my navigator on numerous 8- and 10-hour ocean patrol missions between Ecuador and the Galapagos islands in 1942…When the radar set malfunctioned, the odds were against precision navigation and the command pilot should have recalled (aborted) the mission." The 1 April mission cost the 2nd Division 10 B-24s.

696 42-110087 in the 713th Bomb Squadron piloted by Lieutenant Harrison C. Mellor ran low on fuel and 50 miles north of Paris he gave the order for the crew to bale out. 9 of the crew landed safely and evaded. Sgt William Warren was killed when his parachute failed to open. (Mellor only finally got his chute to open when 400ft from the ground). 4 of the crew successfully evaded and were returned to Seething. B-24 42-52098 *Crud Wagon* flown by Lieutenant Charles Knor, left formation in order to conserve fuel but all 10 crew baled out when it was realised that they would not make England. Lieutenant Charles McBride, bombardier, watched from the catwalk of the bomb bay, as the navigator, Lieutenant Stanley Baranofsky, baled out feet first through the open bomb bay. McBride continued to watch him fall until he heard a loud staccato noise above the whine of the engines and realised it was a fighter firing at them. Straight away he jumped out head first with his eyes shut! McBride and two others evaded. The 7 others were captured and taken prisoner. *Eastern Queen* flown by Lieutenant Kenneth Weaver, was evacuated by the crew at just after 1330 hours over France rather than risk a ditching of the aircraft. 9 men landed safely but the 10th, Sgt Harvey Dickey, died after his parachute failed to open. The rest of the crew were captured immediately. B-24 41-28763, one of two PFF ships from the 564th Bomb Squadron, 389th Bomb Group flown by Lieutenant Alan J. Teague and which carried the 448th Bomb Group CO, Colonel James Thompson who was flying as command pilot, lacked enough fuel to reach England and fell out of formation. The B-24 slowly drifted behind the others but three P-47s provided escort. On reaching France Teague ordered everyone to bale out. Colonel Thompson was killed when his parachute failed to open. (Colonel Jerry Mason, an ex-fighter pilot in the CBI Theater, took over the 448th Bomb Group at Seething two weeks later). Teague successfully crash-landed the bomber in an open field. He scrambled away and was captured when he returned to try and destroy the Liberator. Three of the crew who evaded capture returned two days after the crash with French Underground members and overpowered two German sentries before destroying the PFF equipment on board. See *The 448th Bomb Group (H): Liberators over Germany in WWII* by Jeffrey E. Brett (Schiffer 2002). *Unteroffizier* Heinz Gehrke suffered second and third degree burns and various splinter and bullet wounds on 22 February 1945 when his FW 190D-9 was hit and set on fire by a Tempest flown by Squadron Leader D. C. "Foob" Fairbanks of 274 Squadron, 2nd TAF. Moments earlier the American pilot had shot down and killed another JG 26 pilot. Gehrke got caught on the tail of his fighter but he finally broke free and his parachute opened just before he hit the ground. He remained hospitalized until November 1945. See *The JG 26 War Diary Vol.2* by Donald Caldwell. Grub Street, London. 1998.

697 42-100356. Schwartz was one of three pilots who shot down a Soviet Yak-3 fighter north of Spandau on 24 April 1945. See *The JG 26 War Diary Vol.2* by Donald Caldwell. Grub Street, London. 1998.

698 Altogether the 4th Fighter Group claimed 33 destroyed and 9 damaged. Four to 6 B-24s were seen going down in flames with 15 to 20 chutes seen in the air at one time. Two P-51s collided in the air west of Wittengen and one chute was seen to open. 2nd Lieutenant Robert P. Claus and Captain Frank Boyles were KIA. One red-nosed P-51, believed to have been piloted by 2nd Lieutenant Howard N. Moulton, Jr., was shot down west of Wittengen. He and 1st Lieutenant Robert Hughes, who was also shot down, became PoWs. Seven pilots in the 334th Squadron combined to claim 7 Bf 109s and FW 190s and a Ju 52 destroyed. They also damaged 7 Bf 109s and FW 190s and one Ju 52. The 336th Squadron destroyed 13 and the 335 Squadron destroyed 12. See *Debden Warbirds*.

699 The majority of the losses came down in the area of Brunswick due to persistent fighter attacks. The 445th lead ship, with Lieutenant Colonel Robert Terrill, the CO, aboard, had two engines knocked out by flak over the target. Despite this, Terrill succeeded in bringing his bomber home on the two remaining engines and was later awarded the DFC by Colonel Ted Timberlake.

700 In P-47 42-75558 E2-N.

701 See *Yellowjackets! The 361st Fighter Group in World War II*. Paul B. Cora, (Schiffer 2002)

702 *Leutnant* Karl "Charlie" Willius, *Staffelkapitän*, 2./JG 26 who was flying his 371st combat sortie claimed a 44th Bomb Group B-24 as his 11th *Viermot* and his 50th combat victory.

703 Snyder had pumped 750 rounds into the FW 190 flown by Willius who was killed His FW 190A-8 "Black 5" exploded near Genemuiden, Holland. His widow Lisette received a posthumous *RitterKreuz* (*RK* or Knight's Cross) on 9 June 1944. Willius' body was not recovered until 1967, buried in his FW 190 15ft deep in a Dutch polder. Near Benthein the 361st Fighter Group also shot down the FW 190A-8 flown by Fähnenjunker-*Oberfeldwebel* (Senior officer candidate) Emil Babenz of 2./JG 26, who was killed. Babenz had scored 24 *Abschüsse* in 325 combat sorties. See *The JG 26 War Diary Vol.2* by Donald Caldwell. Grub Street, London. 1998.

704 *Leutnant* Heinrich "Jan" Schild of 2./JG 26 claimed a 361st Fighter Group P-47 at Gelsenkirchen at 1600 hours but the claim was not confirmed. See *The JG 26 War Diary Vol.2* by Donald Caldwell. Grub Street, London. 1998.

705 *Feldwebel* Walter Gocksch of 10./JG 26 claimed a 353rd Fighter Group P-47. South of Assen at 1510 hours. Gocksch was KIA on 21 June 1944 by a P-47 pilot in the 406th Fighter Group southwest of Paris-north of Boissy. *Feldwebel* Walter "Poldy" Polster of 11./JG 26 claimed a 355th Fighter Group P-51 east of Zwolle At 1515 hours. In all, the 355th Fighter Group lost three P-47s. Lieutenant Reedy flying P-51B 42-106463 was shot down near Brunswick. He survived and was taken prisoner. Lieutenant Dickson was KIA flying P-51B 43-7147 *Miss Aberdeen*. Lieutenant Olson was killed by flak near Celle while flying P-51B 43-6589 See *The JG 26 War Diary Vol.2* by Donald Caldwell. Grub Street, London. 1998.

706 Nine men in the 392nd Liberator were killed and 7 men in the forward section of *Might of the Eighth* were killed instantly when 5 500lb bombs and the full fuel load exploded. The forward section disintegrated and wreckage flew through the air. Incredibly, two men, including Captain (later Colonel) John Driscoll, the Group Gunnery Officer in the 566th Squadron, who was in the waist position to take strike photographs of the target, survived. Driscoll and two others were trapped in the still-intact tail section, which spiraled to earth like a falling leaf. The three men grabbed their chest packs and tried to escape through the hatches but the tail gunner failed to open his hatch and he was killed in the crash. Driscoll opened his hatch with some difficulty and baled out at 1000ft, pulling his parachute shroud as he drifted to avoid hitting the now-burning tail section. Although there was no fuel in the tail section, a combination of hydraulic fluid and oxygen from the bottles quickly started a fire. Driscoll landed in the back garden of the Bailey's farm near Foulsham, which housed a family of 5 daughters. Three bombs, which failed to explode, fell near the bomb dump at RAF Foulsham, which contained some RDX (high-explosive) bombs.

707 58 Liberators had originally arrived at Rackheath but one had crashed on a training flight trying to land downwind on the shortest runway on the field. The pilot was demoted to co-pilot. "In which ignominious state," wrote Colonel Shower, "he flew several missions. After taking the bump in a graceful manner, I was happy to give him a crew and he turned out a very good aircraft commander." Fortunately none of the crew had been injured in the crash. Five other Liberators had been reassigned to other Groups as replacements and now all but three Liberators were serviceable for the Group's first mission.

708 Hurd landed, injuring his ankle and was captured immediately. He finished the war at *Stalag Luft XVII*, Krems, Austria.

709 In November 1944 Michael was proposed for a Medal of Honor but Major General Emory S Adams, President of the War Department Decorations Board turned the proposal down but he was later overruled. Adams considered Michael's efforts simply not heroic enough and he stated that "... when the pilot learned that the bombardier's parachute was unserviable, there was nothing to prevent him giving him his own parachute to Lieutenant Leiber and order the latter to bale out. Therefore Lieutenant Mitchael's decision to endeavor to land his plane, either in France or England, was not 'above or beyond the call of duty."' Ed Michael knew nothing of this until December 1983, when during a reception in New York for Medal of Honor recipients hosted by President Regan, he was discussing the incident with *Washington Times* reporter John Sherwood.

710 These ships were piloted by 1st Lieutenants Charles D. Easley and John R. Weaver, Jr., and 2nd Lieutenants Ernest L. Portson, Charles E. Mikesell, Robert J. Rasmussen and Donald H. Shufeldt. This disaster was the greatest yet suffered by any one squadron in any one mission. (On 23 March the 326th Squadron had lost 4 aircraft over Berlin; the 327th Squadron lost three at Schweinfurt, 14 October 1943.) Other aircraft lost on the Stettin mission were piloted by 2nd Lieutenant Richard W. Donaher in the 326th Squadron and 2nd Lieutenant John E. Harris in the 327th Squadron. S/Sgt John R. Kindred in the 327th Squadron, tail gunner on 1st Lieutenant Virgil W. Hill's aircraft, was killed by enemy fighter fire.

711 P-51B-7-NA 43-6578 PZ-P.

712 FW 190A-7 170038 Black 4 and FW 190A-7 170042 Black 7 respectively.

713 Cutler's claim for the Ju 52 destroyed in the air was reduced to a half share after gun-camera film showed that Anderson had also fired on the fighter and scored hits. Cutler received credit for the destruction of the two FW 190s as well as one Ju-88 destroyed and one Ju 52 damaged on the ground and one locomotive destroyed. Cutler destroyed two Bf 109s in the vicinity of Gifhorn on 8 May and he destroyed another Bf 109 on 13 may to take his score to 7.5. He was killed in a collision south of Grimmen flying P-51B42-106483 on 13 May.

714 42-31156 *Big Stoop* crash-landed on Bornholm. 6 Evd. 4 PoW. Torretta adds: "About three weeks later we heard they had landed on the small island which was occupied by the Germans. About one month later they came back to the field all dressed in civilian clothes. Six of them had escaped to Sweden and they were returned to us."

715 Wroblewski flew his 30th and final mission on 14 May 1944.

716 384th Bomb Group.

717 41-29118 *Nine Yanks and a Jerk* in the 703rd Bomb Squadron crashed at Pewez, Belgium. 5 of Lieutenant Samuel G. Scheichkorn's crew evaded. 2 KIA, 3 PoW. 42-7601 *Sin Ship* in the 702nd Bomb Squadron crashed at Liège. 4 of Lieutenant Joseph Pavelka's crew evaded. 6 KIA. 42-100203 in the 700th Bomb Squadron crashed at Tohogne, Belgium with the loss of 9 of 2nd Lieutenant Benjamin L. Love's crew. The 1 survivor evaded. 42-109807 *Tennessee Dottie* in the 701st Bomb Squadron piloted by Lieutenant John B. Anderson crashed at Roquefort, France (4 Evaded, 1 KIA and 5 PoW). 42-110021 in the 700th Bomb Squadron piloted by Lieutenant Herbert W. Schultz crashed at Widemont (4 evaded, 6 KIA). In the JG 26 formation Oberleutnant Walter Matoni's claims for two 445th Bomb Group B-24s shot out of formation near Liège at 1305 and 1328 hours were confirmed, as was one by *Leutnant* Wilhelm Hofmann, 8th *Staffel* CO, 52 km east of Charleville at 1340 hours. Feldwebel W. Busch's claim for a 445th Bomb Group B-24 12 km NE of Namur at 1338 was also upheld. *Leutnant* Radener, 7th *Staffel* CO claimed a B-24 shot out of formation 18-km north of Namur at 1310 hours. See *The JG 26 War Diary Vol.2* by Donald Caldwell. Grub Street, London. 1998.

718 Two of JG 26's FW 190s were destroyed by the 352nd Fighter Group and three more were shot down either by the 78th or 366th Fighter Group pilots.

719 *Unteroffizier* Karl Gathof of 6th *Staffel*, JG 26 was KIA 5km south of Malmedy at 1330 hours in his FW 190A-7. *Leutnant* Wolfgang Grimm of the same unit was also KIA in his FW 190A-6 at Malmedy. *Unteroffizier* Karl Willand of 8th *Staffel* JG 26 who was flying a FW

190A-5 was KIA at 1315 hours north of Dinant by a P-47 pilot in the 78th Fighter Group. See *The JG 26 War Diary Vol.2* by Donald Caldwell. Grub Street, London. 1998.

720 Edmonds went on a mission with the crew of 2nd Lieutenant John I. Scarborough in the 67th Squadron to Friedrichshafen on 16 March 1944. He was killed when 42-7549 *Shark Face* returning form the mission on two engines, crashed at Kingsnorth near Woodchurch, Kent. *Shark Face* had lost an engine just before the target and the crew could see Switzerland across the other side of the lake but Scarborough had said, "Let's go home." Six of the crew were killed and Scarborough, Edmonds and Loren M. Bean, co-pilot were laid to rest at Cambridge. *See Innocence and Death In Enemy Skies; A True Story of WWII Adventure and Romance* by Forrest S. Clark. Jawbone Publishing Corp. 2004.

721 In B-24 42-100330.

722 In December 1944, Forrest Clark escaped from Switzerland with the aid of the U.S. agents in Berne and the French Resistance, making his way to Lyons, France, just before Christmas 1944 during the Battle of the Ardennes.

723 *Chick's Crew: A Tale of the Eighth Air Force* by Ben Smith, Jr., 1978, 1983, 2006.

724 On 9 April Mission 132 was to the airfield and Focke Wulf assembly plant at Marienburg, which was hit by 98 B-17s of the 1st Bomb Division. Forty 303rd B-17s took off but 42-31616 *Spirit of Flak Wolf* crashed shortly after take-off when failing to gain sufficient altitude it hit a tree, which tore off part of its stabilizer. Still unable to climb it crashed to the ground near Winwick and burst into flames killing the pilot, 1st Lieutenant J. J. McGarry, Jr., and 5 of his crew. The rest of the crew were badly injured. Eight other aircraft returned early from this mission with various problems. The remaining 31 aircraft from the 303rd Bomb Group successfully dropped their bombs on the target with no loss. This mission lasted 11 hours 38 minutes, the longest flown thus far. Captain Robert Lynch was lost on 23 July 1944 piloting B-17G 42-102960. Lieutenant William D. Morghan and his crew survived and were picked up. Ben Smith was to recall. "We flew a number of short raids to France in July, none of them very eventful, except one. We were bombing V-I sites at Lille in northern France. The resistance was surprisingly brisk. We lost one aircraft over the target and the lead plane piloted by Captain Robert J. Lynch was set on fire by flak. Although burning, he stayed with us until Bombs Away. Out over the Channel headed for home, the burning engine exploded. The men had no choice but to jump over the English Channel. They all got out but Lynch. He set the automatic pilot and then jumped himself. We watched the stricken bomber spiral down and finally strike the water, sending up a huge geyser. This was the only time I ever saw an aircraft go into the drink. We could see all of the 'chutes in the water and saw rescue boats speeding to the scene. Although they appeared to be very close, three of the fellows were never found. They were our buddies and lived in the barracks next door to us. Captain Lynch was decorated for this brave feat."

725 76 prisoners escaped from the North Compound of *Stalag Luft III* on the night of 24/25 March 1944 before "*Harry*" (the name of the tunnel) was discovered. ("*Tom*" had been discovered in the summer of 1943 and was blown up by the Germans. "*Dick*" was used subsequently to store tools and equipment for *Harry*.) 50 of the escapers were captured. They included Squadron Leader Roger Bushell SAAF, who as "Big X" organised the successful escape and Brettell, who was caught together with Flight Lieutenants R. Marcinus, H. A. Pickard and G. W. Walenn near Danzig. The *Gestapo* took them to remote spots and shot in the back of the head. Only Bram van der Stok, Royal Netherlands Navy; Flight Lieutenant Jens Einar Mueller, Royal Norwegian Air Force and Flight Lieutenant Peter Rockland RAF made "home runs."

726 "*First Mission*" by Bert Stiles from his classic book, *Serenade to the Big Bird*, which he wrote while flying a 35-mission tour 19 April-20 July 1944.

727 "La French" is 1st Lieutenant John E. LaFontin, pilot of one of three B-17s in the 91st BG that were lost flying as part of the high squadron in the 381st Bomb Group's "B" Group on the mission to Eschwege. Stiles called him "La French" because he "could never remember the last part." Altogether, five 1st Bomb Division B-17s were lost bombing Eschwege airdrome and aircraft industry targets at Kassel. *The Keystone Mama* failed to return with Lieutenant Robert S. Wylie's crew on 19 May 1944. Eight crew were KIA. One became a PoW. Bert Stiles flew co-pilot to Sam Newton on 17 missions up until 12 June 1944 and then flew his last five missions as co-pilot to W. R. Langford (1) and Lieutenant W. Green to complete his bomber tour. Instead of returning to America on leave now due to him, Stiles asked to be transferred to fighters, and he moved to the 339th Fighter Group and to P-51s. At age 23, he was shot down and killed on 26 November 1944 while escorting bombers to Hanover.

728 Eight men were KIA and two taken prisoner.

729 On 15 April the crew had left the replacement and indoctrination center in North Ireland for Tibenham in an old war weary B-24D which had been stripped down and made into a transport. Fifty men and their entire B-4 bags etc were thrown in the belly of the plane and they were ordered to sit wherever they could find space to squat. They all knew that the plane was badly overloaded and there was great relief when they finally touched the runway late in the afternoon at Tibenham, the home field of the 445th Bomb Group, 15 miles south of Norwich. They were fed and given a place to spend the night. Peritti's crew were to be assigned to a squadron the next day. However in the morning, word came for four crews to transfer to another Bomb Group, 15 miles west of Norwich, which had just suffered severe losses and needed replacement. On 8 April the 44th Bomb Group had lost 11 out of 27 planes due to flak and fighters. In short order the 44th was decimated. Peritti's crew were not too happy to be a replacement under these circumstances but as it turned out, they would be eternally grateful that they were assigned to the 44th Bomb Group.

730 Later, when the ball turrets were removed from our Liberators we hated to lose "Swoose" Alexander. He was the "character" of our crew and a fun person to know. Swoose was assigned to another crew and soon completed the required 30 missions. What happened to Alexander, I do not know as he volunteered for a second tour.

731 *Yesterday's Dragons: The B-17 Flying Fortress over Europe during WWII* by Abel L. Dolim.

732 Ceiling and Visibility Unlimited.

733 Seven B-17s including *Thru Hel'en Hiwater* and *Nero* in the 303rd Bomb Group and *Just Nothing* in the 91st Bomb Group FTR. Five B-17s in the 3rd Bomb Division and 4 B-24s were lost to flak and fighters although the U.S. fighters claimed 22 *Luftwaffe* fighters for the loss of 15 of their own. The *Luftwaffe* had been on the look out for stragglers hit and damaged by flak at the target. One was the aptly named B-24 *Flak Magnet* in the 753rd Bomb Squadron, 458th Bomb Group flown by 1st Lieutenant George N. Spaven, Jr. At the target an AA burst had peeled back a large section of top-fuselage and it's skinning now flapped wildly in the slipstream while inside, fuel spewed from three ruptured main fuel cells. The crew worked feverishly to stem the fuel leaks, jettison the 500lb bombs still aboard and keep *Flak Magnet* airborne, but they could not prevent the crippled Liberator from dropping out of formation. They were now completely alone and a target for any *Luftwaffe* fighters. At Stormede Major Heinz "Pritzel" Bär, CO, II./JG 1, with *Oberfeldwebel* Schumacher flying wingman, took off in their FW 190s to intercept the badly damaged Liberator. Bar was a veteran with 199 victories. *Flak Magnet* would be his 200th. Bär saw the bombs fall from the Liberator and dived on the B-24 from 5 o'clock. He expected return fire from the Liberator's tail turret but Herman Peacher had baled out when fuel had engulfed his turret. In fact by now none of the guns aboard *Flak Magnet* were manned. Bär looked through his Revi reflector sight and blasted the bomber with cannon and machine gun fire and the No.2 engine burst into flames. Spaven tried doggedly to keep the B-24 airborne but the odds were just too great. From the shattered cockpit, Spaven and his co-pilot Lieutenant Robert L. Zedeker could see Bär's FW 190 peeling off to the right, as he swept round for a frontal attack. Releasing his seat harness, Zedeker hoisted himself clear, yelling at Spaven, "Let's get the hell outta here!" Bär's next burst shattered the instrument panel, killing Spaven in the process. The back of his armored seat saved Zedeker and he scrambled out of the doomed bomber. 2nd Lieutenant Peter Kowal, navigator, followed. *Flak Magnet* dived steeply, exploded and crashed near Hoetmar. The victorious Bär landed at Stormede to a rapturous welcome. He climbed out of his FW 190, "Red 23" and was helped from his flying suit to celebrate his 200th victory.

734 A few days earlier, in the early hours of 12 April, 10 intruders had penetrated airspace over East Anglia and a Me 410A-1 of KG 51 had shot down a B-17 flown by Lieutenant Donald M MacGregor in the 413th Bomb Squadron, 96th Bomb Group while on approach to the 390th Bomb Group base at Framlingham.

735 They share a common headstone at Cambridge Madingley cemetery. Munsey was posthumously awarded the DSC on 13 July 1944.

736 1st Lieutenant Melvin L. Alspaugh.

737 Blum was KIA on 9 September 1944.

738 In all the confusion, 12 Liberators crashed or crash-landed in Norfolk and Suffolk as a result of KG 51's actions. 38 American crewmen were killed and another 23 injured. *Hauptmann* Viner of the 4th *Staffel* and *Leutnant* Loness of the 5th *Staffel* were credited with a B-24 apiece. Feldwebel Zorn of 6./KG 51 was credited with a Liberator and a B-17 (sic) and *Unteroffizier* Leonim, also of the 6th *Staffel,* was credited with three B-24s, one of them west of Orfordness. Feldwebel Volg of 6./KG 51 shot down a B-24 south of Norwich. Ten miles southeast of Norwich at 6000ft two 458th Bomb Group Liberators, one piloted by 1st Lieutenant Teague G. Harris, Jr., which crashed near its base at Horsham St. Faith and the other, flown by 2nd Lieutenant Charles W. "Red" Stilson, which crashed on the Southwestern side of Norwich, were reported hit by fire from the intruders. Harris and three of his crew survived but the 6 others died. Stilson and 6 of his crew survived. It is believed that Stilson's B-24 was brought down by "friendly" AA fire. Two other victories were credited to *Unteroffizier* Drongal and Feldwebel Dormsten. KG 51 lost two Me 410A-1s and their crews. Oberleutnant Klaus Kruger and Feldwebel Michael Reichardt, his Bordfunker (radio operator) gunner, in 9K+HP and *Hauptmann* Dietrich Puttfarken and his radio-operator-gunner, *Oberfeldwebel* Willi Lux in 9K+MN, were lost. Just who shot the two Me 410A-1s down is open to conjecture. One Me 410A-1 was claimed shot down by S/Sgt Raymond G. Chartier, the tail gunner aboard *Peggy Jo* (before the *Hornisse* shot down the B-24). S/Sgt Lewis Brumble, left waist gunner aboard *Last Card Louie* of the 458th Bomb Group flown by Lieutenant H. W. Wells was credited with the destruction of a Me 410 at 6000ft at 2230 hours southeast of Rackheath airfield near Norwich. This Me 410 was reported to have fell on its right wing and dived straight into the ground on fire followed by a large explosion when he hit the ground. The nose gunner and a waist gunner aboard a 389th Bomb Group Liberator flown by Lieutenant P. T. Wilkerson also claimed the destruction of a Me 410 in the same area. Local eyewitnesses say the Me 410A-1 broke away, racing seawards as Wilkerson's B-24, its engines and fuel tanks riddled, caught fire and spiraled out of formation from about 3000ft. Six of the Liberator crew perished. The Me 410 flown by Oberleutnant Klaus Kruger and his radio operator, Feldwebel Michael Reichardt, crashed and exploded in a field at Ashby St. Mary. Uncertainty surrounds the disappearance of Puttfarken and *Oberfeldwebel* Lux's Me 410, because no trace of it has ever been found. Quite possibly it is the one seen by eyewitnesses and it probably crashed into the North Sea.

739 Overall command of the Combined Bomber Offensive and the 8th Air Force officially passed on 13 April to General Dwight D. Eisenhower the newly appointed Supreme Allied Commander.

740 On 22 April the Fortress crews in the air echelon of the 398th Bomb Group led by its CO, Colonel Frank P. Hunter, landed at Nuthampstead to join the 1st Combat Wing in the 1st Bomb Division. April is not one of England's better months and the squally showers and cold damp days soon turned Nuthampstead into "Mudhampstead." Fortresses began arriving 10 a day until the group was up to full complement. After the system of deploying aircraft in long straight lines at their Rapid City base in the heart of the Black Hills of Dakota, the

system of dispersal in England made life very difficult. During April the first of three new B-24 Groups arrived to join the 2nd Bomb Division. On 18 April North Pickenham laid out its black carpet of runways for the Liberators of the 492nd Bomb Group and then on 25 April there arrived at Metfield in Suffolk, the wound echelon of the 491st Heavy Bombardment Group. The latter's ground echelon had been selected from the 4 B-24 Groups already stationed in England. The 491st had begun life at Davis-Monthan Field, Arizona, in October 1943 but when the Group moved to Biggs Field, Texas, in early November that same year, its wound echelon was transferred to B-29 Groups. The 492nd, which was in a more advanced state of preparation for movement overseas, took the 491st's place and had sailed to England before them. Colonel Eugene Snavely had been posted from the 44th to command the 492nd on 26 January 1944. He and his crew flew into North Pickenham via the Southern Ferry route to be greeted with slashing rain. It had turned the runway into a skidpan and some crews experienced difficulty in landing. Meanwhile, further south, at Metfield was also awaiting another B-24 Group, the 491st. In early August 1943 the 353rd Fighter Group commanded by Lieutenant Colonel Joe Morris, equipped with P-47 Thunderbolts, flew into the base. The 353rd stayed at Metfield until early 1944. Early in April 1944 plans for the forthcoming invasion of Europe involved redeployment of both 8th and 9th Air Force Groups. All 5 of the 9th Air Force's fighter groups in the Colchester area were required for the operation and the airfields at Metfield and Halesworth were now needed for the 491st and 489th Bomb Groups. On 12 April therefore, the 353rd vacated Metfield for Raydon, Suffolk and on 18 April the 56th Fighter Group left Halesworth for Boxted.

741 Also in April 1944, Generalmajor Adolf Galland, the *Luftwaffe* fighter commander, revealed to his superiors that since January that year the day fighter arm had lost mote than 1000 pilots. He estimated that each enemy raid was costing Germany about 50 aircrew and at that rate the time was fast approaching when the *Luftwaffe* would lose air control over Germany.

742 These aircraft were piloted by 2nd Lieutenants Richard P. Anthony and Bernard Rosenfeld in the 326th Bomb Squadron, 1st Lieutenant William W. Parramore and 2nd Lieutenants Earl Howard, Jr., and James E. King, all in the 407th Squadron. *Lil'Brat,* King's aircraft, exploded over Baltenswil, Switzerland. Funeral services were held for the crew in Berne on 27 April and the bodies were interred at Munsingen, where U.S. military authorities some time before had acquired a cemetery. 1st Lieutenant Gordon E. Clubb of the 325th Squadron had the dubious distinction and near-tragic experience of being struck by the bomb salvo of a higher group. In violent evasive action to avoid the heavy flak at Oberpfaffenhofen, Clubb's ship was struck by two 500lb GP bombs, one shearing away the horizontal stabilizer and the other knocking out the No.3 engine. The latter bomb landed on the wing back of the dinghy, bouncing into the engine. By even more violent evasive action, Clubb managed to dislodge the bomb, but not until after he and his crew had undergone a very tense 60 minutes. Upon landing away, at Bradwell Bay, the bomb fuse was discovered in the stricken engine.

743 JG 26 claimed 12 B-17 *Abschüsse* and two pilots received 2 points towards their *RitterKreuz* (*RK* or Knight's Cross) for a *HSS* (*Herausschuss* or separation) and two others 1 point for a *endgultige* (*eV* or final destruction). Two pilots claimed a 355th Fighter Group Mustang each. See *The JG 26 War Diary Vol.2* by Donald Caldwell. Grub Street, London. 1998. The group lost 4 P-51s: Hillman KIA flying P-51B 43-7103 *Miss Doris;* Sturm flying P-51B 43-7140 *Arkansas Traveler* who survived and was taken prisoner; Norman who was KIA flying P-51B 42-106433 and Demers who was KIA by flak while flying P-51B 42-106723 *Moon.*

744 "It was not until September when word and pictures finally convinced my crew that I had not dreamed my wild story. A confidential report published by the 2nd Bombardment Division entitled '*Target Victory*' came to group operations. As squadron navigator of the 68th Squadron I was in a position to obtain a copy, which described in great detail the destruction that I had witnessed. Not a train moved through the Chalons marshaling yard for two months. By this time, the invasion was three weeks old and this important rail community was denied the German defenders. At long last I was vindicated." McClane was appointed Squadron Navigator on 30 August 1944. He adds: "The position of Squadron Navigator called for the rank of Captain and I was recommended for promotion to this grade on 4 October but I was not given my Captaincy. The 'Table of Organization' called for only one Captain Squadron Navigator. The dates reported could not overlap even one day, which it did in my case. I never let it bother me. I was so young and looked like a kid; I never expected it to happen anyway. It would have been almost embarrassing to have been a Captain in my training after I returned home to the ZOI and besides, I was happy just to be alive."

745 Eighth Air Force heavy bomber losses from all missions this day were four planes. 254 others were damaged, two beyond repair. Three airmen were KIA, 16 WIA and 40 MIA.

746 "Colonel Kelly had only been in command for 9 days but in that short time we had learned to dislike him. Of course none of the regular aircrews even knew the man but Kelly had come to the group with the idea of straightening it out. The worst part of this for us was that we would fly a combat mission and when we returned he would have us take off again on a practice mission! We also noted that Kelly had not yet flown a mission with us. This was for our own good, of course and we did start flying the tightest formations you ever saw (anything to stop those practice missions), but at the time we were really angry.'

747 Palmquist was still in hospital on 7 May when we started out for Berlin. Just as we were leaving England I watched the old "17 his crew were flying dive out of formation. Somehow the flares, carried in the passageway to the nose, had exploded. All of Palmquist's officers were burned to death. The gunners baled out after much trouble.'

748 B-17 42-37866 crashed at Abbenrode. 2 KIA. 8 PoW.

749 42-31144 crashed at Destedt. 9 KIA. 1 PoW.

750 42-102421 crashed at Weferlingen. 9 KIA. 1 PoW.

751 The 447th Bomb Group's 11 losses took its monthly total to 21 aircraft lost. The 94th and 96th Bomb Groups losses for April 1944 were also 21 bombers apiece; the 8th's heaviest of the war.

752 Sgt Falk, flying his first mission with the crew as waist gunner, was killed instantly by a shot through the head. Two of the crew evaded for the rest of the war. Cotner was sent to *Stalag Luft III.*

753 He and the crew were later reported to be prisoners of war. Lieutenant John L. Low, the Group Bombardier, evaded capture for 296 days in enemy-occupied Holland and was liberated on 29 April 1945. 25 Liberators were lost, including a 458th Bomb Group B-24, which was forced to land in Sweden. In all, 579 bombers hit Berlin while 38 other heavies attacked targets of opportunity in the area, including Magdeburg.

754 "I had the same type chest pack parachute harness on. My parachute was on the floor by my feet. We had been instructed that if for some reason you did not have time to snap the chest pack on the nipples of the harness, then just grab your chute, jump out with it in your hand and snap it on as you fell through the air. After my experience of seeing the man come out of the plane without a parachute I had immediately reached down and snapped on my chest pack even though it was considerably in my way to work at my desk. When I turned in my parachute after the mission I asked to be issued a back-pack chute. The orderly behind the desk asked what position flew. When I responded that I was a navigator, he said that navigators wore chest packs. I had news for him and he issued me a back pack without an argument. Never again did I ever take off without my parachute on my back. I even would flip up the corners to be sure the nylon was in place as rumors had it that some men had baled out only to find an army blanket stuffed in the nylon's place. The story had it that some guys found it would influence their girl friends if they gave them the nylon. I don't know how much truth was in the rumor but you can be sure I was not going to take the chance. I for one would never forget that day and like every mission I ever had in combat, I flew it twice: once in reality and again that night in my dreams. I relived in vivid detail every event and emotion that I had experienced. One of our enlisted men actually 'baled out' of his top bunk several times while dreaming."

755 The same fighter that missed Peritti's ship hit the B-24, which was not from the 44th Bomb Group. 2nd Lieutenant Keith C. Schuyler, pilot of 42-100279 (one of three 44th Bomb Group B-24s lost this day – the others being 41-29471/X piloted by 2nd Lieutenant Glenn H. Sweigart (3 men survived to become PoWs) and 2nd Lieutenant Richard J. Hruby who ditched 41-29513 off the English coast) describes the incident in his autobiography, *Elusive Horizons* (Avon Books 1992): "A B-24 that had been lagging at 7 o'clock drew in close at 5 o'clock just as a German came through. The fighter smashed head-on into the big one right at the nose turret and both planes exploded in a ball of flame…Then it was over. Just like that." (Schuyler's ship was badly hit by flak and was unable to keep formation. Jumped by fighters they dove for cover in clouds at about 5000ft before all ten men baled out to become prisoners).

756 Of the 679 B-17s and B-24s dispatched, 618 were effective. They dropped 1498 tons of bombs. 63 bombers were MIA. Two planes were interned and 432 damaged. 18 men were KIA, 38 WIA and 606 MIA. Of 814 fighters dispatched, 13 were MIA. (*Luftflotte Reich* had put up probably what was the best-coordinated defensive effort of the war for the loss of 12 pilots killed and 5 injured and 21 fighters destroyed. *The JG 26 War Diary Vol.2* by Donald Caldwell. Grub Street, London. 1998.)

757 "They raised it to 30 missions before I completed my tour just to be sure none of us made it and then I volunteered for a 31st against all current wisdom to never volunteer for anything. I did survive the 31 missions and 'GOD WAS WITH ME!"

758 42-31498 *Passionate Witch II* flown by 2nd Lieutenant Kenneth L. Chism crashed at Hassenberg with the loss of 1 KIA and 9 PoW.

759 Six Bf 109s of IIIrd *Gruppe* JG 26 bounced a flight of 355th Fighter Group P-51Bs escorting the bombers to Metz from out of the sun and *Leutnant* Peter Reischer CO II *Gruppe* shot down and killed Lieutenant Kaminski at 1845 hours.

760 These two groups, commanded by Colonel Glendon P. Overing and Lieutenant Colonel Beirne Lay (who had been one of Eaker's original staff officers in 1942) at Sudbury (Acton) and Lavenham respectively, had arrived in England in April to join the 92nd Bomb Wing. Lay had taken command of his Group on 28 February 1944.

761 In the afternoon 81 B-17s bombed *Noball* sites, while 56 B-24s bombed marshaling yards at Brussels.

762 "A strange thing happened on this mission. The 96th Bomb Group B-17s stationed at Snetterton Heath about 20 miles south of Shipdham were scheduled to go to Berlin along with the rest of the B-17s but they became lost. They fell in with the B-24s going to Brunswick. The enemy fighters attacked them savagely shooting down 10 of their number. We were called the Eightballs because we were a jinxed outfit suffering losses out of proportion until the jinx was broken after the ill fated mission of 8 April. Then the 492nd Bomb Group took over our misfortune and even the 100th Bomb Group was called the Bloody 100th. The prize for the worst hard luck goes to the same 96th that followed us to Brunswick this day. They had the unenviable title of having the greatest loss rate of any bomber group in the USAAF." (In additon to the 36 bombers shot down on the morning raids five more were lost in the afternoon).

763 42-100287.

764 9 of Lambertson's crew were captured and 1 was KIA. Kramer was hidden by some Belgian farmers, given a civilian suit and, accompanied by a Belgian who was presumably an underground agent, struck out for France. En route two German soldiers examined the Belgian's papers, but they were not in order and he was later shot. Kramer was taken to *Luftwaffe* headquarters in Brussels, where he was threatened with execution before being sent to *Stalag Luft III.* Altogether, two B-17s and 4 Liberators FTR; one each in the 389th, 448th, 453rd and 466th Bomb Groups. JG 26 claimed two Liberators and two of the 7 USAAF fighters

lost this day. *Leutnant* Addi Glunz, CO, 6./JG 26, destroyed B-24 42-52186 *Sunshine* in the 735th Bomb Squadron, 453rd Bomb Group 7km E of Turnhout and B-24 42-52584 *Worry Bird II* in the 787th Bomb Squadron, 466th Bomb Group piloted by Lieutenant Allender, 7 kms SSW of the town in the space of 6 minutes. Three chutes were seen from *Worry Bird II* before the doomed Liberator stalled and spun down. Crews said that the fighter, which hit the B-24, was reported shot down. In fact it was Glunz's wingman, *Leutnant* Peter Rober who was brought down. Rober was able to force-land his FW 190A-8 near Keel and he suffered only slight injuries. Bob Shaw, *Worry Bird II's* navigator recalled. "When our plane was hit the front end was nothing but a mass of flames. I had no choice but to abandon the plane. I grabbed my chest chute like a football and went out the nose wheel door. On the way down I attached it to my harness. It wasn't easy, because I had to remove my oxygen mask to see where it should be attached! Then after pulling the ripcord, the pilot chute didn't pop – it had been burned off (that is my guess). I reached in and pulled a hand full of silk out and the resultant jerk was most welcome. I judged myself to be about 3000ft off the ground and soon landed on top of a fence. I was taken to St. Giles Hospital in Brussels for 10 days, then a series of stops before arriving at *Stalag Luft III* near Sagan. I was reunited with our co-pilot, H. F. Hall, in jail in Brussels. Neither of us knew the fate of all crewmembers until the war was over. Five of us baled out (the bombardier, DiDomenico was never heard of). Four survived the war." *Sunshine* piloted by 2nd Lieutenant Edward J. Perro crashed at Arendonok, Belgium, with the loss of 5 crew.

765 B-24 42-94999, 506th Bomb Squadron.

766 Most of the evadees were liberated by the U.S. 3rd Army on 13 August 1944.

767 Lay, who returned safely to England and who later adapted *Twelve O' Clock High* for the TV series of the same name, died on 26 May 1982. Meanwhile, the 92nd Bomb Wing had become badly disorganized after losing its leader and deputy leader. *Leutnant* Wilhelm Hofmann led his 8th *Staffel Schwarm* so close to the B-24s in their head-on pass that his wingman, Fähnrich Waldemar Busch, rammed a 487th Bomb Group Liberator, causing it to crash. Busch's propeller was knocked off, but he was able to force-land his FW 190A-7 and suffered only slight wounds. 44 km west of Chartres, Oberleutnant Waldemar "Waldi" Radener, CO, 7./JG 26, made a successful attack on a 487th Bomb Group B-24 and then accidentally rammed a second. Radener baled out of his FW 190A-8 with minor injuries. Both of these B-24s made it back to England, where the crew of one baled out. *Lazy Lady* piloted by Lieutenant Lorin D. McCleary crashed at Varize, France. 9 KIA. 1 PoW. *Peg-O-'My Heart* flown by Lieutenant Frank Vratny, crashed at Bretonelles, France (4 Evd. 7 PoW). 42-52763 *Mean Widdle Kid* flown by Captain Edward J. Brodsky crashed at Orgeres, France. 7 KIA. 3 PoW.

768 *Chick's Crew: A Tale of the Eighth Air Force,* by Ben Smith, Jr., 1978, 1983, 2006.

769 "I think we went on pass after our fifth mission. We had been decorated with Air Medals. The plumage of a warrior was just as important to us as it was to Caesar's legionnaires. We were inordinately proud of our silver wings, Presidential Unit Citations and Air Medals. Men will endure much bizarre and varied punishment for the trinkets that declare them valorous. We were no different. Before we parted, there would not be one of us who was not tested to the limits of his endurance, but these trinkets were important to us as though they were the symbols of what we experienced."

770 Lieutenant John A Long's crew flying B-17 42-97260 *Bow-Ur-Neck-Stevens,* 360th Bomb Squadron, crashed. 7 KIA, 4 PoW.

771 Eight B-17s and 8 Liberators were lost???

772 "Jasper never came back. An explosive shell had destroyed his eyesight in one eye and he would never fly again. Ward showed up one day and started flying missions again. We flew together sometimes, but he flew a lot with other crews also. He still had some missions to fly when I left the 303rd."

773 Cechinni returned to the 303rd after Ben Smith left but never flew any more combat missions. He remained in the Air Force after the war.

774 Two composite 4th Wing formations meanwhile, went to a FW 190 repair depot at Zwickau. Also, 823 B-17s and B-24s were despatched to bomb marshaling yards and airfields in France, Luxembourg and Belgium escorted by 668 fighters.

775 42-110042 in the 67th Bomb Squadron flown by 2nd Lieutenant Lewis I. Vance (1 KIA 9 PoW).

776 By JG 1 (two B-24s); JG 3 (10 B-127s); JG 26 (one B-17) and JG 27 (21 B-17s). The remaining 12 were probably shot down by flak. U.S. fighters claimed 61 enemy machines shot down for the loss of 7 of their own. 28 German pilots perished, 26 others being injured.

777 Over 200 enemy fighters attacked the two composite formations for half an hour and the 4th Wing lost 11 bombers, including 7 in the 447th Bomb Group. The Fortresses that won through to the target achieved a highly effective bomb drop. Pride of place went to the 385th led by Colonel Vandevanter, the CO. He slowed down his own formation so that other, disoriented, groups could re-form on them before commencing the bomb run. The 385th stole the bombing honors, placing 97% of its bombs within 2000ft of the MPI. This feat earned the group a Distinguished Unit Citation.

778 42-39941.

779 Jones and tail gunner Lewis Lanham were the sole survivors. Incidentally, the area Jones went down in on that fateful day, was Bad Camburg, about 28 miles NNW of Frankfurt, Germany.

780 The crewman who hit the Plexiglas nose was Lieutenant Fred L Myren, riding as Formation Officer in the tail turret of the lead ship flown by Lieutenant Boris Slanin (3 KIA/7 PoW). Myren bounced off into *Lady Stardust II*'s right wing.

781 *Lady Stardust II* got as far as the Channel, where it was ditched, becoming one of the 14 B-17s the 452nd Bomb Group lost this day. Total 8th Air Force heavy bomber losses were 46 B-17s and B-24s and a staggering 412 bombers damaged. As a result of this raid, oil production at the Sudetendeutsche plant was 100% inactive during June 1944.

782 "The fighters stayed with the string of chutes. They flew among us (I cannot bring myself to believe that they were trying to spill the chutes - a close pass and bank creates a vacuum and down like a string). A couple of the crew were down in a lush meadow. They made a couple of passes at them but did not fire a shot. They stayed with us until all members were on the ground. I was picked up at once by the under ground on landing, (The aircraft pancaked In on a hillside at Namur, Belgium. It did not burn). Eventually, I was taken to Liège where I was issued forged work papers and passport and I stayed with the resistance fighters until I was captured. I had no military proof that I was an American. I was taken to Liège Prison and later turned over to the *Gestapo*. I remained in prison solitary for 14 weeks. Had my head bashed in, all my teeth knocked out, my toes and fingers broken, beaten to a pulp at least once a day and some days twice or three times. My testicles were the size of indoor baseballs, they kept me no shoes and naked throughout my stay, a 4 by 6 solitary cell with a handful of straw and a bucket. From Liège we made 5 more stops. At the sixth stop I was placed in *Stalag Luft IV* at Gross Tychow Poland."

783 "We made it alone without any fighter cover all the way to a point a few miles east of the Rhine before 6 Me 109s hit us from the rear. We got two of them for sure and had a probable, a third that was streaking for the ground with heavy smoke pouring out. The 109s plastered us good, knocking out the controls and who knows what else. We baled out and got out OK, were buzzed, but not fired upon in our 'chutes by the remaining 109s. We were captured immediately a few miles east of St. Goarshausen on the Rhine. Our tail gunner sustained the only serious injury, a bad laceration of his knee and calf; a really nasty and painful wound. Farmers with pitchforks and soldiers were literally waiting beneath for me to land. We spent almost a year in *Stalag Luft III* and I think almost all of us were picking flak fragments from our hides for weeks to come. My pilot and I managed to escape in April 1945 and make our way to contact with the 45th Division.'

784 Worst hit was the 45th CBW. The 452nd Bomb Group lost 14 B-17s, the 96th 12, including two which collided whilst under attack and the 388th, one.

785 Finally, Don Chase could not resist anymore. He just had to do something positive. As an enemy aircraft came barrelling through the formation he pulled the trigger of his Verey Pistol and fired a signal flare at him. Useless? Foolish? Certainly. But he did get to fire one futile "shot" at the enemy.

Chapter 15:

786 Twelve B-17s and B-24s were lost. The fighters claimed 47 enemy fighters shot down for the loss of 5 of their own.

787 "My pilot, Lieutenant Beiser was to fly with the rest of our crew while he flew co-pilot for an experienced pilot, Steven Bastean, who finished his tour in mid-June. All crews were thus flown on their first mission. This policy of flying experienced pilots with new crews was necessary in order to teach the 'green' crews how to get into formation. After this first mission, the new crew was reunited for subsequent missions. Little did I know at that time, that on my last 8 missions I would be flying 7 or 8 new crews on their first mission, using their pilot as my co-pilot."

788 "Most are aware of the V-1 'Buzz Bomb' and the V-2 suborbital rocket. What most people don't realize is that Hitler had under way, a V-3. This was the so-called 'London Gun' being installed in western France, at Mimoycques. It was to consist of two batteries of 25 guns each; the barrels of which were each 416ft long. Installed along a steep incline, they would be capable of firing a 55lb shell into the city of London. If the Allies had allowed this weapon to be completed, it would have eclipsed the damage done by the V-1. The explosive propellant would have altered the range and direction so that the entire city of London could be targeted. Unfortunately for the Germans, the earth removal scars caught the attention of Allied reconnaissance planes and the site was periodically bombed." On 15 May 166 B-17s and B-24s bombed V-weapon sites in France. No bombers were lost and 128 of the heavies dropped 485 of tons on the *Noball* sites.

789 "'Tail End Charlie' is one of the most vulnerable positions in the formation. 'Purple Heart Corner' is the next plane on the outside of the formation. There was an undercast at the target and we bombed by radar. The lead plane was equipped with this system and all following planes dropped at first appearance of bombs from the lead plane."

790 As a matter of fact, on 12 June 1944, when we first heard that these pilotless "Flying Bombs" were being launched by the Germans, we thought it was an act of desperation on their part, that they had no more pilots or planes to strike back with. In other words, it was very funny to us but later we changed our tune when we went to London on rest leave only to be brought back to reality by five of them exploding close by.

791 "On 11 May, the 492nd Bomb Group, a new addition to the 14th Combat Wing, flew its first mission. They were stationed at North Pickenham, 12 miles to our west. These guys had come to England as the first group ever to have the new all silver Liberators. These 'Hot Pilots' prided themselves as being unusually good at formation flying. Before their combat began, we were told to watch a 'fly over' by this new group so our pilots could see how it was done by 'experts.' Needless to say, they resented this display and said so in no uncertain terms but not loud enough for General Johnson, head of the 14th Combat Wing, to hear them."

792 "Each B-17 was loaded with 2700 gallons of gas and 12 500lb bombs. At 6lbs per gallon the weight of fuel for each plane was 16,200lbs and bombs weighed 12,000lbs for a total of over 14 tons. The B-17G carried over 5000 rounds of ammunition for its 13 machine guns. The weight of these .50 caliber machine guns, plus oil for the engines and oxygen for the crew often brought the take-off weight of these aircraft to over 65,000lbs. Empty, they weighed about 35,000lbs."

793 "Berlin had large numbers of 88mm flak guns all around the city. Also, many fixed guns of larger caliber were deployed in the area. Many of these were 105mm and some were

128mm. They were not as accurate as the 88s but made a larger explosion. When the target aircraft couldn't be seen, these guns fired a burst that would explode at or above our altitude, thus forcing us to fly through a rain of shell fragments, or 'flak.'"

794 42-31386

795 Eder was flying FW 190A-8 "Red 24." Amount of ammunition used (against B-24): MG 131, 120 rounds and MG151/20, 80 rounds. The 2nd Bomb Division encountered 150-200 enemy fighters between Dummer Lake and the IP and again after leaving the target area. At Waggum airfield 30 FW 190s and Bf 109s attacked from 12 o'clock skidding through the formation head-on. At Steinhuder Lake, more then 220 enemy fighters were encountered. A total of 12 B-24s and 4 P-47s were lost. Of Eder's 78 victories, 36 were 4-engined bombers.

796 "Although we had to abort twice on our first scheduled run to the 'Big City' on 29 April. First, *Luscious Duchess* had developed turbo problems and then the second ship had a runaway prop at altitude. 2nd Lieutenant Kenneth L. Chisum's crew that took our place were shot down."

797 There were no survivors from Lieutenant Marion Ulysses Reid's B-17G-20-BO 42-31540 *Miss Donna Mae* in the 331st Bomb Squadron.

798 KIA, August 1944.

799 B-24 *Sweet Lorraine* in the 458th Bomb Group collided with a Fortress over Eye, Suffolk, while forming up for the mission to Bourges. All 10 crew aboard the Liberator were killed.

800 42-31534, formerly *Shilayee* in the 349th Bomb Squadron.

801 in 42-97845.

802 All 10 men survived and they were taken prisoner.

803 42-31941.

804 42-97095.

805 42-31306.

806 42-102635.

807 42-102648.

808 42-102528.

809 42-102624.

810 See *Century Bombers; The Story of the Bloody Hundredth* by Richard Le Strange, 100th Bomb Group Memorial Museum, 1989.

811 Captains "Deacon" Hively and Willard Millikan and Lieutenants Gillette, Lang, Fraser, Jones, Russel, and Speer combined to claim 8 other e/a destroyed. See *The Debden Warbirds*. Ralph Hofer scored his 15th and final victory when he downed a Bf 109 in the Magdeburg area on 28 May. He was KIA on 2 July 1944 while supporting 15th AF bombers over the Balkans during an 8th AF Shuttle mission, flying P-51B-7 43-6746 in aerial combat at Mostar, Yugoslavia. His executioner was probably a pilot of JG 52. Probably the most colorful of all the aces, Hofer is the only one known to have been killed in combat with the *Luftwaffe*.

812 Ceiling And Visibility Unlimited.

813 18 Allied air forces began the pre-invasion bombing of France. The 9th Air Force began bombing targets in the Pas de Calais, railway marshaling yards and important bridges. RAF Air Chief Marshal Sir Trafford Leigh-Mallory remarked that the 9th Air Force was by far the most effective force in knocking out these types of target. From the beginning of May the 9th dispatched more than a thousand aircraft each day, weather permitting, against targets in Normandy and the Pas de Calais. The part played by the Allied Expeditionary Air Force during the build up to the Invasion was crucial to its ultimate success. By day the RAF's 2nd TAF (which had been formed in Norfolk on 1 June 1943 under AVM Basil Embry) and the 8th and 9th Air Forces, which comprised 6080 tactical and strategic aircraft, blasted enemy targets in Northern France and Belgium. At night the "heavies" of RAF Bomber Command added the weight of its bombs to marshaling yards and enemy positions.

814 The song *Lili Marlene* was based on a German poem of 1915 and it became a favorite of German and British troops during WWII. The lyrics began: *Underneath the lantern by the barrack gate, Darling I remember the way you used to wait, 'Twas there that you whispered tenderly, That you loved me, You'd always be, My Lili of the lamplight, My own Lili Marlene…* American troops particularly liked *Lili Marlene* as sung by the German-born actress and singer, Marlene Dietrich. Maria Magdalene Dietrich was born on 27 December 1901, the second child of *Leutnant* Louis Erich Otto Dietrich and Wilhelmina Elisabeth Josephine Felsing. In 1935 Adolf Hitler demanded that the famous German actress return to the Fatherland. Dietrich, who was an ardent anti-*Nazi*, refused and all her movies were banned in Germany. Dietrich became a naturalized U.S. citizen and she devoted most of her energy during WWII to entertaining Allied troops. Her major claim to fame was her work with the USO. During the Africa and Italy campaigns she withstood much privation in order to stay with the troops at the front, where she not only entertained but also helped coordinate hospital and mess details. In the French andGerman campaigns she often rode with Patton at the front. Her vehement denouncement of the *Nazi* regime and her participation in radio broadcasts aimed at Germany got the desired result - she got under the skin of the *Nazis*. For her work, the US, French and (eventually) Israeli governments awarded her medals.

815 The 1000th B-17 built by Douglas and named after Luper's wife.

816 During final approach, however, only one undercarriage leg would extend despite repeated attempts to lower it. Finally, Luper had to land *Rene III* on only the one wheel, skillfully keeping her straight and level for as long as possible before the left wing began to sag. The Colonel killed his ignition switches just before the Fortress dipped and plowed an arc across the airfield. The entire crew was unhurt and was able to walk away unscathed. *Rene III* was repaired and flew again but three other B-17s in the 457th FTR and 19 were severely mauled.

817 In all 923 B-17s and B-24s pounded the German rail network on 27 May. 24 bombers were lost, including B-24 42-95159 in the 755th Squadron, 458th Bomb Group, which collided with *Briney Marlin*, another 755th Squadron B-24 north of Cromer in undercast during assembly. 42-95159 went into a spin and only 1 crewman, who left by the waist window, was seen to escape. Two men aboard *Briney Marlin* baled out but those who remained with the aircraft managed to bring it home safely to Horsham St. Faith.

818 "Anyone who has read Albert Speer's *Inside The Third Reich* will recall that he said that as long as we struck at his factories, he could keep production going by repair, dispersal and going underground. But on May 12th, the day we started bombing the oil refineries, he knew the war was lost. Production of gasoline and oil dropped from 182000 tons in March 1944 to 39000 tons in July to 12000 tons in August and less than 5000 tons by September 1944. After the war, many German leaders said that no single thing greater than the 8th Air Forces attacks on their oil resources was responsible for the collapse of the Nazi war machine."

819 Experimental GB-1 "*Grapefruit*" glide bombs, developed by fitting small wings and empennage to a 2000lb GP M34 bomb.

820 "When our crew arrived in early May, a strange sight greeted us. The barracks for the 427th Squadron, to which we were assigned, were the only billets on the airdrome and all along the armament roads, were stacked row upon row of some strange flying machines. They consisted of wings and a double boom tail mounted on a 2000lb bomb. This strange device was supposed to be mounted in pairs under the belly of a B-17 and dropped on the enemy from a distance, thus sparing the aircrews from the intense flak that was encountered over many targets. The idea had merit, but there were many problems. The visibility at the target had to be 50 miles, which is rare in Europe. This caused a couple of other attempts to be scrubbed in the past. The bombs depended on inertial guidance for directional control after release. This consisted of a series of gyroscopes driven by a battery. This was a special project that 8th Air Force commanding general, Hap Arnold, had adopted, so it had to be tried. This day the predicted 50-mile visibility arrived over Europe and the mission was on."

821 303rd, 384th, and 379th Bomb Groups.

822 "59 B-17s in the 41st Combat Wing released 116 GB-1 glide bombs but not one bomb came within a mile of the yards. However 42 hits were scattered throughout Cologne, killing 82 people and injuring over 1500 others. Many of the bombs fell into sections of the city already bombed out by night missions of the RAF. Unfortunately for the Germans, the bombs arrived before their air raid sirens had sounded."

823 "Three nights later they had figured what really happened and Lord Haw Haw said that any airman shot down during such a mission, would be executed the same day. He said that it was a terrorist raid, which it turned out to be, but this was not our intent. This was not the reason that the attempt was never repeated, however. The failure of the system was evident from the results. The 11-second delay in the fuse meant that this 2000lb bomb would possibly skip through town for 11 seconds before exploding. The glide ratio of these bombs was an amazing 5 to 1, which meant that if we dropped them from 4 miles high, they would travel 20 miles before striking the ground. An interesting aside on this mission concerns the batteries that ran the gyroscopes in the guidance system of these 'Grapefruit' bombs. The stacks of bombs sat on the ground for so long that many of the batteries failed to hold charge and so the 41st Combat Wing ordered a new supply from the States. The battery company said that they no longer made this type of battery and that they would have to set up a complete assembly line and therefore could produce no less than several thousand batteries. After all the hassle back and forth, the batteries arrived at Molesworth after the mission was over. After it was decided to not fly any more glide bomb missions, the mechanics of the 427th Squadron used these batteries in an innovative lighting system for the barracks." The other mission of 28 May to oil and transportation targets throughout Germany was met by fierce resistance. Upward of 300 German fighters flew up to intercept the bombers and in some cases USAAF fighters were out of range. The results were generally excellent but 32 bombers and 14 fighters were lost. From the 303rd Bomb Group, 2nd Lieutenant Alvin C. Determan was shot down. VIIIth FC claimed 27 enemy machines destroyed for the loss of 9 of their own while IXth FC, which dispatched 527 fighters under VIIIth FC control, claimed 38 enemy fighters for the loss of just 5 of their own. 26 Fortresses that FTR were from the 1st and 3rd Bomb Divisions. Three B-24s of the 3rd Bomb Division force that attacked Lutzkendorf/Halle and Wetzlar were lost. The three other Liberators lost came from the 2nd Bomb Division. By 24 May the first-line German fighter strength had declined to 246 single-engined fighters and 35 twin-engined *Zerstörer*. On 28 May at least 40 *Luftwaffe* aircraft (15% of the fighters that engaged the Americans on 28 May) FTR, 18 pilots being KIA and 13 more injured. For these losses, they claimed 36 heavies and 11 fighters shot down.

824 One was the now famous "*Shoo Shoo Baby*" which was restored at Dover Air Force base in Delaware and is now on permanent display at Wright Field in Dayton, Ohio.

825 For the second day running strong enemy fighter formations opposed the bombers, whose gunners claimed 62 of them shot down. 673 U.S. fighters were airborne and they claimed 39 enemy fighters destroyed for the loss of 10 of their own. Actual *Luftwaffe* losses on 29 May amounted to more than 50 aircraft shot down, 44 aircrew KIA (including two leading aces) and 19 others being injured in air combat. II./ZG 1 flying the obsolete Bf 110G-2 was decimated to the SE of Vienna, 8 *Zerstören* being lost and 17 aircrew killed, 7 others wounded. The *Gruppe* was unable to score any victories on this fateful day. Even so, 17 Liberators were lost and 17 B-17s also FTR. However, the Leuna works suffered a 50% drop in production after the raids in May; the Pölitz works was even worse hit on 29 May.

826 42-63962 in the 506th Bomb Squadron.

827 "'Zeke' had earlier made the headlines in the *Stars & Stripes* when he got two Me 109s with one burst. It seems that he hit the top Me 109 and that one crashed into another one that was coming in from low. He got them both!"

828 On the morning of 30 May 911 heavies, including, for the first time, the B-24s of the 489th Bomb Group at Halesworth, were despatched in 6 forces to attack aircraft targets in Germany, marshaling yards in Belgium and France and *Noball* sites in the Pas de Calais.
829 A couple of months later Major Stevenson, the 410th Bomb Squadron CO called me over and told me those damn Navy bombs went through the roof right down to the cellar and blew the joint out of operation!
830 928 heavies in 6 forces escorted by 672 fighters continued its pounding of aircraft industry targets in Germany, marshaling yards in France and Belgium and *Noball* sites in the Pas de Calais. Twelve bombers and 9 fighters were lost.
831 Four specially equipped Liberators in the 753rd Bomb Squadron, 458th Bomb Group attempted to bomb 5 bridges at Beaumont-sur-Oise, Melun and Meulan in France with the revolutionary *Azon* glider bomb. The device could be released by an aircraft at a distance and then directed on to the target. Basically, it was a conventional 1000lb bomb fitted with radio-controlled moveable tail fins. Visibility had to be good to enable the operator in the B-24 to see it right to the target. For this purpose a smoke canister was attached. Each bomber could carry three such bombs, but had to circle the target as many times to release them, which was an obvious disadvantage. The 30 May raid ended in failure with none of the bombs hitting the target. Experimental raids continued in June, with, at most, 15 Liberators being used on any one mission but results did not improve and General Doolittle abandoned the project. Later versions of the radio-guided bomb included the *Razon* and the 12,000lb *Tarzon* used by B-29s in Korea.
832 "My wife Marjorie and I visited this airfield in May 1992 with Dutch author, Ivo M. De Jong. Our bombs that had fallen into the wooded area destroyed a large store of fuel that the Germans had hidden there. Our bombs nearly struck the fire station and one fell into the pond that supplied water to the fire fighting equipment. This 500lb bomb struck the pond so centered that it blew all the water out of the pond without changing its contour. This left very little water for the fire fighters to put out the gasoline fire that our bombs caused. German headquarters at the field in 1944 were built next to a Dutch school, so that the Allies would not bomb it. It worked, as their HQ never was hit in the half dozen times that the field was bombed. On one mission to this field, the bombs from another group in our wing fell short and landed in the Dutch village, killing 21 civilians. This was one of the unfortunate aspects of high altitude bombardment."
833 "I had another problem other than fatigue. I don't know where the idea originated but for some crazy reason, when I laid down to go to sleep, if a plane flew low over our squadron area, I had this inordinate fear that it was going to crash into our barracks. I know this sounds silly but it was not funny to me. I carried this fear back to the USA with me and it pestered me all during my pilot training as a student officer. For years after the war, I could not shake this morbid idea from my mind."
834 In the afternoon mission, 319 B-17s and B-24s including for the first time, B-24s of the 489th and 491st Bomb Groups flying the first full 95th Wing mission, were despatched to bomb airfields and railway targets in France. The two 95th Wing groups bombed Bretigny, Creil and Villeneuve airfields near Paris for the loss of one 491st Bomb Group Liberator and 4 489th B-24s. Flak also caused varying degrees of damage to 59 other machines. 35 491st Liberators approached their home base at Metfield, Suffolk in gathering darkness and landed safely but at Halesworth three of the returning 37 489th Liberators crashed and had to be written off.
835 Recon photos the next day showed that we had done a good job on the railroad marshaling yards. Our total flight time was 5 and half-hours, with one hour and 40 minutes over enemy territory.
836 After successfully evading capture and making contact with the French Resistance, Kozicki returned to England in August 1944.
837 This was a less sophisticated version of modern LORAN (Long-Range Navigation), which could take crews within a quarter mile or so of their destination.
838 Vance was awarded the Medal of Honor. He was the fifth and final airman in the 2nd Bomb Division to receive the award (the other four awards were for Ploesti on 1 August 1943). He underwent amputation of his right foot and was later invalided home in a C-54. Somewhere between Iceland and Newfoundland the Skymaster with its crew and patients disappeared without trace. Bale was later shot down, on a mission to Stuttgart, his 25th operation and made a PoW.

Chapter 16:
839 Supreme Headquarters Allied Expeditionary Forces, whose HQ since 28 May 1944 was at Southwick House near Portsmouth.
840 Allied Expeditionary Air Forces.
841 2nd Lieutenant Dick Johnson in the 303rd Bomb Group says. "We learned later that the invasion of France was scheduled for 5 June after having been cancelled from its original schedule of early May. Of course we didn't know the exact day until being briefed for the actual D-Day invasion. In retrospect, it might have been better in May except for logistic problems in getting poised along the English coast. Also, it was not considered prudent for May since we had not yet achieved mastery of the air. It is incredible that the Germans were not expected to know the exact place of the invasion, since the thousands of ships were easily seen from the air and the sea."
842 SHAEF estimated that about 16,000 Frenchmen were under arms and their participation was crucial. So too were the RAF Special Duty squadrons and the American *Carpetbaggers*. Just prior to and shortly after D-Day an increased number of OSS *Joes* (agents), SOE operatives and three-man *Jedburgh* sabotage teams were dropped into France by specially modified B-24 blacked painted Liberators from Harrington and RAF Special Duty units at Tempsford. On the night of 3/4 June 23 *Carpetbagger* B-24s were dispatched. On 4/5 June a *Carpetbagger* B-24 taxied out at Tempsford carrying 4 agents who were to be dropped into the Limoges area. Among them was 22 year-old SOE agent Violette Szabo, known to the Resistance as "Corrine." The B-24 pilot received word that the weather up ahead was bad and aborted the mission right there on the runway. The *Joes* returned to Hassell's Hall, the lovely Georgian house at Sandy concealed in woods, which was used as a club house and dormitory by the agents. On the night of 5/6 June 11 Liberators were dispatched to drop zones and the *Carpetbagger* Liberator carrying Violette Szabo passed over the invasion fleet heading for Normandy. At the drop area the *Maquis* failed to flash their reception lights and caused the mission to be aborted. (Finally, on the night of 7/8 June Violette and her three companions were successfully dropped in France but on 10 June she was captured and in January 1945 she was executed in Ravensbrück concentration camp). British, French and American nationalities were all represented and they added greatly to the successful D-Day assaults. Four Hudsons of 161 Squadron at Tempsford flew 22 sorties making radio contact with Resistance groups on D-Day.
843 D-Day arrived early at RAF night bomber stations in the first few hours of the night of 5/6 June, because the British heavies were assigned to softening up targets such as enemy gun positions covering the invasion beaches. On 5 June Operation *Glimmer* simulated a naval attack on the Pas de Calais area in order to deceive the Germans into believing that the D-Day landings were there and not Normandy. This was achieved by flying a progressive square search pattern between Newhaven and Boulogne, dropping *Window* continuously. The plan was successful. Five Fortresses of 214 Squadron in 100 Group RAF also operated in support of the D-Day operation in an *ABC* (*Airborne Cigar*) jamming role. A protective patrol lasting over 5 hours was flown at 27,000ft stating just north and east of Dieppe and running almost perpendicular to the coastline carrying out jamming and *Window* dropping in conjunction with 24 Lancasters of 101 Squadron of 1 Group.
An assault behind enemy lines was also made, by more than 23,000 airborne troops, 15,500 of them American. Departing from Portland Bill on the English Coast, 6600 paratroopers of the 101st Division in 490 C-47s and 6396 paratroopers of the 82nd Division were dropped over the neck of the Cotentin peninsula. Two parachute regiments of the 101st Division were to drop just west of the lagoon, silence a heavy battery and seize the western exits of the causeways leading from *Utah* beach and head off an eastern German advance. One parachute regiment was to drop north of Carentan, destroy the rail and road bridges over the Douve and hold the line of that river and the Carentan canal so as to protect the southern flank of the Corps. The 82nd Division, landing farther inland, was to drop astride the Merderet River south and west of Ste. Mere Eglise, block the Carentan-Cherbourg road and extend the flank protection westward by destroying two more bridges over the Douve and secure the Merderet crossings. Heavy fog and German guns meant that the pilots ware unable to drop the paratroopers precisely as planned. Only one sixth of the men in the 101st Division reached their destination points. The first regiment of the 82nd Division fared better but the second suffered heavy supply losses and much of the division was left without sufficient arms. Don McKeage of F Company, 505th Parachute Infantry Regiment noted that, "All went well until arriving near the DZ 'O,' the C-47s did not slow up for the drop. Everyone in the 2nd Battalion agreed that it was the highest, fastest jump ever made. Eyeballs had to be screwed back into their sockets. The 2nd Battalion landed on or near the DZ. Except for one stick from F Company and they headed for the center of Ste-Mere-Eglise." Both Divisions formed smaller improvised squads and by 0430 the 82nd had captured Ste. Mere-Eglise. The 101st Division casualties totaled 1240, of whom 182 were killed. The 82nd Division suffered 1259 casualties of whom 156 were killed. Of the 6396 paratroopers of the 82nd who jumped, 272 or 4.24% were killed or injured as a result of the drop. Of the 6600 paratroopers of the 101st Division, only about 2500 had assembled by the end of the first day.
844 *Stories of the Eighth; An anthology of the 8th Air Force in World War Two*, John H. Woolnough (The 8th AF News, 1983).
845 42-40003, which in 1945 was re-assigned to the 490th Bomb Group.
846 42-102447 in the 334th Bomb Squadron. *El's Bells* put down at RAF Ludham on 21 March 1945 and was salvaged.
847 B-24 41-29387, which FTRLOC on 11 November 1944 and was salvaged.
848 The 1st *Gruppe* was heading for Reims while the 3rd was en route to Nancy-Essey in SE France. *Hauptmann* Johannes "Hans" Naumann's 2nd *Gruppe* at Mont de Marsan and Biarritz had taken off at 0700 and flew as far as Vrox, where they waited for further orders. The 3rd *Gruppe* reached the JG 2 airfields at Creil and Cormeilles by 0930 but did not begin flying sorties until noon, while the 2nd *Gruppe* flew from Vrox to Guyancourt near Paris and took no further part in the momentous day's events.
849 Wodarczyk was KIA on 1 January 1945.
850 "Since we tried to bomb and went over enemy territory for 30 minutes, we got credit for a mission, which was number 10 for me. By bringing our bombs back, we avoided 'Americide' which is the accidental killing of our own troops, such as the one during the invasion of Sicily, on 11 July 1943. On that night, the paratroops and infantrymen of the 504th Regiment, boarded C-47s and headed for Gela. Even though warned in advance, anti aircraft gunners on ships and ashore, shot down 23 of the 144 troop transports, killing 93 paratroopers and wounding over 400. On 24 July 1944 bombs fell short and killed 16 American soldiers and wounded nearly 100 others. Worse yet, the next day Lieutenant General Leslie J. McNair was killed along with 101 other infantrymen when bombs fell short. 308 others were wounded in that mishap. General McNair received a direct hit and his only identifiable remains was a portion of a finger with his West Point ring attached."
851 On the first day of the invasion, 150,000 Allied troops landed on the beaches. A week later the total was a half million men. Six weeks later the total had reached 2 million men and a quarter million vehicles.

852 "In the years since D-Day, much has been said about this historic event. It was the greatest invasion in the history of man. It ultimately established the United States as the premier super power that it has remained. I feel that my own participation was important, but both of my missions on that day were milk runs, as it was for most of the heavy bombers crews who flew that day. Penetrating the thick overcast over England and the Continent was a much greater danger than the Germans had to offer that day. The ground troops who did the fighting on that day deserve the bulk of the credit. Our mission to neutralize the German Air Force had worked very well, but there would be resurgence in the missions to come."

853 B-24 42-99949 GO-I *Naughty Nan* in the 328th Bomb Squadron was lost on 21 September 1944 when it was involved in a mid-air collision with 42-94969 *Big Noise II* over Belgium. Five of Lieutenant Everett E. Johnson's crew were KIA. 4 returned. All 8 of 2nd Lieutenant Carl F. Mullin's crew were KIA.

854 The death toll could have been higher - a piece of flak went through the steel helmet worn by Sam Hale, the 861st Bomb Squadron commander, through the cloth helmet and lodged on top of his head. Two inches taller he would not have gone on to finish the 26 missions he flew.

855 "D-Day set me one mission ahead of the rest of my crew. This put my life in great jeopardy when I later volunteered for my 31st mission. I could have stopped at 30 but my crew being a lead crew could not fly without a lead navigator."

856 The Sky Scorpions' earlier mission to St. Lô had been cloud covered and the lack of PFF B-24s resulted in the Group bringing their bombs home.

857 As well as the two 493rd Bomb Group B-24s lost in the collision; a 487th Bomb Group Liberator from Lavenham was shot down.

858 Alter landing at Senlis, two reporters sent in confirmation of their victories, for they had seen the whole battle. Fischer's combat career ended abruptly on 7 June, when his FW 190 was shot down by AA gunfire while attacking shipping off the British beaches. He survived to become a prisoner. His commander, Herbert Hüppertz was credited with 5 Mustangs destroyed on 6 June. Two days later Hüppertz was KIA at Caen. He had 68 *Abschüsse* including 35 in the Battle of Britain and Western Front and 33 on the Eastern Front. He was decorated with the *RitterKreuz und Eichenlaub* (*RK* or Knight's Cross with Oak Leaves (*El*). *Luftwaffe Fighter Aces* by Mike Spick, Ivy Books, 1996.

859 The front was rapidly reinforced and, by 20 June, the following FW 190 equipped fighter units were operational: I. and II./JG 1, I. and III./JG 2, IV.(*Sturm*)/JG 3, IV./JG *5,* I./JG 11, I., II. and III./JG 26, I., II. and III./JG 54, JGr 200 and II./JG 300. *German Aircraft of the Second World War.* J. R. Smith & Antony Kay. (Putnam 1972).

860 Altogether 2362 American bomber sorties involving 1729 B-17s and B-24s were flown on D-Day, dropping 3596 tons of bombs for the loss of only three bombers. VIII Fighter Command flew 1880 sorties and claimed 28 enemy fighters shot down. In the period 6 June-31 August the RAF flew 224,889 sorties, losing 2036 aircraft (983 of which were from Bomber Command and 224 from Coastal Command). Aircrew KIA/MIA totalled 1035 from 2nd TAF and ADGB (Air Defense of Great Britain), 6761 from Bomber Command and 382 from Coastal Command.

861 Our group was capable of putting 40 B 17s in the air at any given mission but since a group of that size would be cumbersome, we always made two groups which we called the 41st Combat Wing "A" group and 41st Combat Wing "B" group.

862 Meaconing is the technique of duplicating a true D/F signal with a similar signal indicating a false bearing designed to confuse enemy airmen.

863 On the night of 6/7 June no less than 1012 RAF aircraft were sent to bomb French coastal batteries and 946 aircraft got their bombs away on target. Three aircraft were lost, two of them Halifaxes of 4 Group on the Mont Fleury raid and one Lancaster of 6 Group on the Longues raid. Only two of the targets - La Pernelle and Ouistreham - were free of cloud; all other bombing was entirely based on *Oboe* marking. At least 5000 tons of bombs were dropped, the greatest tonnage in one night so far in the war.

864 41-29572 *Glamor Girl.* 42-52696 *Cookie's Wailing Wall.* 42-52738 *Wilson.* 42-94911 *Piccadilly Tilly.*

865 Captain Oscar T. Hanson, who received the DFC, was KIA on the mission to Merseburg on 30 November 1944 when he was piloting B-17G 43-38059 (1 Evd. 4 KIA. 4 PoW). On 7 June two B-24s in the 490th Bomb Group were wrecked in a runway collision at RAF Feltwell. A night fighter shot down one of the intruders and near Colchester a B-24 gunner shot down a RAF Beaufighter in error.

866 B-17G 42-97304 OR-C *Priority Gal* was finally lost on 31 July 1944 when she FTR with Lieutenant Henry W. Supchak and crew. All 9 men PoW.

867 We later learned that something was against the drift knob with enough pressure to prevent the corrections from being made. It was probably the bombardier's parachute harness that caused the malfunction, since the sight checked out fine at the repair shop. Lieutenant Hogan was the hero of the day. The 359th Squadron, which held the high group position, rescued the mission when the 11 planes of that group laid a perfect pattern on the railroad bridge. Hogan was the bombardier of the day for that feat. The low group did just as badly as our group's effort. They had to make a second pass at the target and had a short bomb run. Some aircraft were still jockeying into their positions when bombs were away. Some of the planes were in slight banking positions, which tossed their bombs to one side, making a poor pattern. Some days it just doesn't pay to get up. The lead plane in our squadron, the 427th, was called "*Shoo Shoo Baby*" after the song by the Andrews Sisters. The 360th Squadron's lead plane was named "*Sack Time*" after our favorite indoor sport in those days. Lead plane of the 358th Squadron was "*Princess Pat*" with the usual seductive nose art. Hogan's hero was "*Heller's Angels,*" flying lead in the other 360th formation.'

868 By the end of June, excluding an emergency landing strip, 10 airfields had been built in the beachhead area.

Chapter 17:

869 The 458th Bomb Group, with 12 Liberators from the special 753rd *Azon* Squadron, led the mission with 15 Liberators of the 467th and 19 B-24s of the 466th.

870 This was the first low-altitude bombing ever performed by heavy bombers operating from England and the result was decisive. The bridge was completely destroyed in the hail of bombs dropped by the 96th Wing and the 458th received a 2nd Bomb Division citation.

871 *Crash Wagon III* had been named "rather retroactively" because Jackson's first B-17 had crash-landed in Northern Ireland at the end of the flight from the USA when the landing gear refused to function. His second B-17 was lost on his crew's first mission two weeks later when they were forced to ditch in the English Channel.

872 Navigator, Gerald Shaffer was killed when his parachute failed to open. Loren Jackson saw the Germans bury his body near Beauvais. Some French women onlookers tossed flowers on his grave. The Germans showed Jackson his dog tags and asked him if he knew him. He said, "No." They said, "You should; he was on your crew. Fred Martini assistant flight engineer/gunner, evaded capture for some time, masquerading as a Catholic priest in France. He was finally betrayed and sold out to the Germans. He was incarcerated in the concentration camp at Buchenwald for some time until he was able to convince the authorities that he was an American military man. Sam Pennell, one of the waist-gunners, also did a stint in Buchenwald with Martini. They evaded together, were captured together and spent time together in that infamous camp. Felipe E. Muzquiz, Jackson's Mexican ball-turret-gunner, Ted Dubenic, the tail-gunner, Ervin Pickerel, radio operator, Blake and Armando Marsilii, flight engineer, all survived the war. Jackson and Haught were taken to Brussels where they spent a week in solitary confinement before a prison train took them to *Dulag Luft.* After a few days they boarded another prison train and went to *Stalag Luft III* at Sagan via Cologne and Frankfurt. They were imprisoned at *Stalag Luft III* until the end of January 1945. Jackson had been promoted to 1st Lieutenant the day before he was shot down but he did not know this until after he returned to Allied control but the added pay was welcome.

873 Kenneth Zierdt, radio operator, was hit by machine-gun fire from the Bf 109 as he descended by parachute. Zierdt landed in a plowed field and was alive for some time. Two Germans stood over him and would not allow the French to attend to him. After he died, the Germans cut out his zippers and took his watch and wedding ring.

874 Long after the war Isgrig and Fischer discovered that their savior had been Major George Preddy of the 352nd Fighter Group. Preddy, who was killed on Christmas Day 1944, was the second highest scoring American air ace of WWII in Europe.

875 *Squat N' Droppit* had come down at about 1000 hours. Vladimir Kovalchek, one of the waist-gunners, was wounded and captured but before the day was out most of the crew avoided capture and were safely in the hands of the French Resistance. At the end of July Bailey's crew were returned to England after linking up with American tank columns. At Omaha Beach Isgrig, Fleishman, Van Horssen, Cooksey, Bailey and Buck were put on a LST with a boatload of prisoners for Southampton. Leslie Fischer, who had been hidden separately, made contact with American columns in Rennes and was returned to the beachhead in a Jeep with two Intelligence officers and was interrogated officially at a PoW cage full of German prisoners. In September 1944 the crew flew home to the USA via the Azores arriving in Maine because of a hurricane along the mid-Atlantic states. The crew traveled to New York by train for more interrogation and were home for Christmas 1944.

876 Colonel Duncan scored his 19th victory on 5 July and two days later he was shot down by flak NE of Nienburg in P-47D-22-RE 42-25971 LH-X *Dove of Peace VII.* He evaded and made his way to Holland where he remained with the Dutch underground until liberated on 14 April 1945 in Arnhem.

877 1st Lieutenant Earl Carlisle Main who was leading Red flight in 42-26313 was pulling up from a strafing run on a convoy when he saw at least 20 fighters coming towards them at about 2 o'clock to the convoy. He called them in as Bogies and soon, someone yelled "109s, 109s" and "Drop your tanks and bombs." The P-47s met the 109s head on, firing but they had a speed advantage as they were descending slightly and the P-47s were climbing. Immediately after meeting head on Carlisle broke hard to the left and went after a 109 in a right turn. While trying to close on him he checked his tail and found a 109 trying to close on him. Carlisle led his all he could and then fired a short burst. The Bf 109 climbed into the cloud layer where the two adversaries did exactly the same thing and Carlisle had to take cover in the clouds. Breaking out below he found himself directly in front of three 109s at very close range. Carlisle quickly took two 20mm hits, which peppered his legs with fragments. He baled out glancing off the tail but without further injury. Upon hitting the ground Carlisle's left leg broke badly just above the ankle, where the fragment entered. German troops promptly picked him up and late that afternoon he was in hospital. Flight Officer John Joseph Phelan was hit and crashed with his aircraft (42-22779) at Villes Sous Bailleul. Major Dewey Ernest Newhart in 42-26402 was hit in the target area and he was later heard on the radio trying to make landfall out. Before he could reach safety he was bounced by a further two enemy aircraft. Badly hit, he was unable to either evade or engage the aircraft. Alone, he was shot down with his aircraft. An additional 30-35 Bf 109s flying in groups of 9 attacked the remainder of the Squadron. 2nd Lieutenant Goffredo Moretto flying 43-2551 fought off 10 109s but he was hit and forced to bale out near the village of Moisville, suffering burns to his hands and face. He was taken in by a local farmer and made it back through Allied lines on 28 August. 1st Lieutenant Richard Bedford shot at one of the 109s and got a few strikes before he was attacked by two more that scored a number of strikes and his P-47 (42-25768) caught fire. Bedford baled out and was able to evade for some

time before being captured by the Germans in Paris. 2nd Lieutenant Edwin D. Peters P-47 (42-25768) was hit and caught fire. He left the dogfight, put out the fire and headed home. Over the Channel the P-47 caught fire again and he baled out but hit the tail, which cut his leg off below the knee. He was afraid he'd bleed to death, so on the way down he took off his belt and made a tourniquet with it. He lost his dinghy and had to struggle for an hour and a quarter in the water until an ASR launch pulled him out. The salt water had coagulated the blood. Lieutenant Richard V. Keywan destroyed a 109, which went down in flames and got hits on two more before two 109s got on his tail as he was heading for the cloud layer. He was hit and forced to bale out but he was too low and he hit the ground before his chute opened. 2nd Lieutenant John Gabriel was unable to avoid the enemy fighters in the tail bounce and a German fighter blew his whole empennage off of 42-26011. Gabriel parachuted to safety and three days later he met the French people who had buried Keywan. The Resistance hid Gabriel until liberated by advancing American infantry. 1st Lieutenant James O. Ruscitto claimed one Bf 109 destroyed and one damaged. 2nd Lieutenant Harold O. Miller claimed his first aerial kill. 2nd Lieutenant Swift T. Benjamin claimed one Bf 109 damaged. See *Jonah's Feet are Dry - The Experience of the 353rd Fighter Group during World War II.*

SE of Rouen *Leutnant* Peter Crump of 6th *Staffel* JG 26, *Leutnant* Wilhelm Hofmann 8th *Staffel* CO and their two wingmen came across two climbing P-47s which were starting their attack on a Bf 109. Using the dawn haze and the terrain to their advantage Crump and Hofmann approached the P-47s and they opened fire before the Thunderbolt pilots knew what had hit them. Crump's salvo hit the left-hand side of his P-47's engine and fuselage and the fighter immediately burst into flames and dived away to the left. Hofmann attacked the pilot of the other P-47 in the same manner and he baled out. Crump filed a claim for a P-47 15-20km SE of Rouen at 0623 hours. Hofmann put in a claim for a P-47 40km SE of Rouen at 0625. *Leutnant* Karl-Heinz Kempf of 9th *Staffel* claimed a P-47 at Lisieux at 0614 hours. See *The JG 26 War Diary Vol.2* by Donald Caldwell. Grub Street, London. 1998.

878 We had missed a mission on 12 June because of maintenance problems with our *"Buzz Blond."* A B-17 with no name was shot down on the 12th when it was hit by a direct flak burst at the left wing root and another directly in the bomb bay, while the bomb bay doors were open for a drop one minute later. The aircraft burst into flames and disintegrated. Only the tail gunner survived.

879 On 13 June the first V-1 started arriving in the London area. Of 4 "Buzz Bombs" fired only one inflicted any damage, killing 6 and injuring 9 others.

880 Priller had just achieved his 100th victory. It was B-24H 42-95132 of the 858th Bomb Squadron, 492nd Bomb Group flown by 2nd Lieutenant David P. McMurray, one of 26 B-24s of the 492nd Bomb Group, part of the force directed to bomb the railway bridge across the Loire River near Tours at La Frilliere. In this one head-on pass, Priller had hit the Liberator's right wing, damaging Nos.3 and 4 engines. McMurray recalled: "I couldn't feather #4 and it dragged along. We salvoed our bombs, but 15 minutes later #3 supercharger went out and we had to drop out of formation. I got a heading for the beachhead and we made a run for it. When our #2 prop governor went out I told the guys to stand by. We were at 7000 and could see the French coast about 30 miles ahead. The navigator (2nd Lieutenant John F. Ferrell) signaled we were over friendly territory (they weren't) and then baled out. He was captured. We then lost #1 - out of gas and in 15 seconds the whole crew baled out. But every time I let go the ship started to tip over. So I put down full flaps, put power on #2 and #3 and trimmed the plane for a glide. I left the seat at 1800ft, detonated the IFF equipment and made a delayed jump. When I saw cows in a pasture, I pulled the cord." Ferrell landed in enemy territory and was taken prisoner. The rest of the crew landed in Allied hands and 48 hours later all 9 men were back at North Pickenham. Ferrell's mistake saved his life, when on 7 July, now a PoW in Germany, the rest of the McMurray crew were killed when they were shot down over Bernberg in their B-24. *Oberst* Priller survived the war with 101 victories.

881 B-24 42-95025 in the 579th Bomb Squadron.

882 Mietusch was KIA on 17 September 1944.

883 392nd Bomb Group gunners claimed two victories but in actuality return fire from the B-24 gunners brought down only one Bf 109G, flown by 9th *Staffelkapitän*, Oberleutnant Victor Hilgendorff, who had an artificial right leg as a result of injuries sustained in 1942 when he was shot down. Hilgendorff jumped from his stricken Bf 109 and landed in a French field carrying his false leg under his arm! Two P-38s in the 55th Fighter Group shot down two Bf 109Gs of JG 26 and two P-51 Mustangs of the 339th Fighter Group destroyed two FW 190As.

884 On the crew's next mission, on 16 June, to Juvincourt airdrome, Beiser's crew had to abort when 42-39875 *Buzz Blond's* No.3 engine gave trouble. This supposed "Milk Run" resulted in damage to 14 planes in the 303rd Bomb Group, causing one plane to land at Nuthampstead with a wounded crewman.

885 42-38057.

886 in 42-31648.

887 2 EVD, 2 KIA, 5 PoW.

888 Cuissai-Lonrai was bombed by 25 Liberators, which dropped 60.8 tons of bombs on the airfield. Essay was badly damaged by 38 B-24s, which dropped 98.2 tons of bombs on the airfield. As a result, *II Gruppe/JG 1* had to move to Semallé several kilometers distant, where, on 25 June, many of its FW 190s were destroyed by P-47 Thunderbolt fighter-bombers and the German pilots had to return to Germany to re-equip. From *Defending the Reich; The History of Jagdgeschwader 1 "Oesau"* by Eric Mombeek.

889 "This type of mission was called a '*No Ball*' target, which is tactical rather than the usual strategic missions that we were trained to do. We were still trying to support the invasion forces and stop the V-1 assault at the same time. I suspect that this mission scared a lot of people, but did little damage." Only the day before, a V-1 flying bomb killed and wounded nearly 200 guardsmen in Wellington Barracks in London when it struck their barracks. The V-1 missiles were now arriving at about 100 per day. Our attempts to destroy the launching sites were largely failures, since the sites were small and easily hidden. Nearly 2000 Allied airmen died in the 80 days of these assaults. Also, these bombs killed over 6000 civilians and nearly 18,000 were injured. Flying bombs traveled at 400 mph and only the British Meteor, a jet-propelled fighter could catch one. Yet, with over 2000 anti-aircraft guns, some with proximity fuzes, nearly 2500 of these weapons fell on London and the same amount on Antwerp, Belgium after its capture by Allied ground troops.

890 42-97291.

891 Automatic Flight Control Equipment.

892 In 42-39875.

893 The Eighth Air Force put up 853 B-17s and 695 B-24s for a total of 1548 heavy bombers.

894 "The first three aircraft were from the 360th Squadron, with us leading our element of 4 aircraft of the 427th Squadron, the 41st Wing 'A,' High Group that we were part of consisted of 9 aircraft of the 360th and 11 of our 427th. This put us in position No.10 in the group. The lead aircraft carried a K17 camera and two of our planes carried K21 cameras. These two aircraft left the formation after reaching friendly territory and landed first for photo work. The 358th and 359th Squadrons carried out the same system. In all, 12 cameras were carried by planes of the 303rd Bomb Group but *Banshee* in the 360th Squadron carrying a camera had to abort when he suffered an engine failure. Another of our aircraft in the 360th Squadron had a delayed takeoff and was not able to find the formation and so returned to base."

895 "Just before the IP, the B-17 flown by 1st Lieutenant J. T. Parker, nearly dead ahead of us, suffered a double engine failure due to flak damage. He was able to keep up for a short while and dropped his bombs with the formation. He could not keep up with the homeward bound formation but lost altitude while still under control. When we last saw him he was down near the ground, still under control, but he never made it back to base and all 9 crewmembers became guests of the German Government for the rest of the war."

896 Cooper was again flying with another crew and we had a new man to replace him for the day. Ed was flying with 1st Lieutenant G. T. Savage, Jr., in 42-107099 *"Old Ninety Nine."* Lieutenant C. F. Eisel was our temporary bombardier.

897 Several crewmembers each received an extra DFC for this mission. For my part, I lived through the mission and received an Oak Leaf Cluster to my previously awarded Air Medal. The Air Medal was given to each airman upon completion of 6 missions and an oak leaf cluster is given to signify another of the same. This was my third Air Medal. Our 7 hour and 2 minute flight had us over enemy territory 1 hour and 50 minutes.

898 "When we hit the ground, the German civilians were waiting for us and I had a few bruises and a black eye for a few days. Our bombardier was also badly beaten but none of us except the tail gunner had to be sent to a hospital, as a result of his wounds from the enemy planes. When we baled out, we were at about 21,000ft and I delayed my chute opening until the ground looked close. I must have free fallen about 15,000ft. We had been told to do this to avoid flak and fighters. I spent the rest of the war as a PoW and returned home in June 1945." The 8th lost 12 B-17s and 37 B-24s. 17 were shot down by fighters, 19 by flak, while 19 heavies force-landed in Sweden. 12 escorting fighters were also lost. JG 300 lost 9 pilots KIA and 5 WIA while the Me 410-equipped ZG 26 and ZG 76 lost 17 crew KIA and 14 injured. After the 20 June raids, German oil production was just 24,250 tons, down from 214,000 tons in March 1944.

899 The main 2nd bomb Division thrust was a 9½-hour round trip to Politz and Ostermoor, while 130 Liberators bombed V-1 sites in France. The *Luftwaffe* intercepted the Division en route to Politz and Ostermoor while it was temporarily without adequate fighter cover. The 355th Fighter Group had been delayed by its new type drop tanks, which failed to jettison, leaving only the 339th Fighter Group to protect the entire 2nd Bomb Division. Bf 110s and Me 410s ripped through the formation over the Baltic with rockets firing and cannons blazing.

900 42-100351 flown by Lieutenant William Powers and 42-95144 piloted by Lieutenant Herschell K. Campbell. 17 KIA. 3 PoW. Three of the 389th Bomb Group's B-24s were forced to land in neutral Sweden.

901 The shuttle mission, code-named *Frantic*, involved bombing a synthetic oil refinery just south of Berlin before continuing to Russian airfields at Poltava, Piryatin and Mirgorod, all east of Kiev. The Italian-based 15th Air Force had already flown a shuttle mission to Russia on 2 June but the 8th was forced to wait until 21 June because of the demands made upon it by the Normandy invasion. Five of the groups (the 452nd formed the sixth) had flown the first shuttle mission, to Africa, in August 1943. The Regensburg shuttle leader, General Curtis E. LeMay (as he now was), had been transferred to the Pacific early in June 1944 and Major General Earl E. Partridge, under whose direction the second shuttle was to be flown, took his place at 3rd Bomb Division HQ. The 4th Combat Wing and a composite from the 3rd Bomb Division would lead the 8th Air Force to Berlin with the 1st Bomb Division next in line, then the 2nd Bomb Division, with the rest of the 3rd Division bringing up the rear. After Berlin they would return to England, leaving the 13th and 45th Wings to fly on to Russia escorted all the way by 70 Mustangs of the 4th and 352nd Fighter Groups. The 388th Bomb Group with the task force commander, Colonel Archie Old, at the helm, provided an "A" Group, which led the 45th Combat Wing, plus the low and high squadrons of a composite group, which was low group in the 13th "B" Wing led by the 452nd Bomb Group. It was hoped that the RAF would join in the massive daylight strike on Berlin in retaliation for the V-1 attacks on London but lack of fighter support for the slower Lancasters with their limited firepower would prevent their participation. Even so, the 8th was able to assemble 1311 bombers for the momentous mission. The return to England would be made in July via Italy and bombing a target in France en route home. On 22 July the 15th Air Force made the first all-fighter shuttle raid on Europe, attacking *Luftwaffe* airfields in Romania and then landing at Russian bases.

902 "The mission lasted 8 hours. I talked to the Chaplain and told him that I felt that the 'law of averages' was catching up on me and I felt that I was going to 'go in.' I flew the next day however and nearly bought it. I was interned in Sweden the next day after taking a hit in the gas tanks over Berlin. I met some of the men who had also been on the Politz raid who had made it to Sweden the day before I got there and we talked about the mission. We all felt very good about destroying the target."

903 "When going to Berlin, each B-17 carried 2700 gallons of gasoline and 5 tons of bombs. Gasoline weighs 6lbs per gallon, giving us a take off weight of 65,000lbs. The empty B 17 weighs about 36,000lbs."

904 In 42-102411 because 42-39875 was under repair due to the extensive damage it had received on the Hamburg raid the day before.

905 "We usually lived in a day-to-day existence, knowing that the next mission could be our last. Many men reacted differently to the stress of almost daily combat. When Allen was shot down my thoughts were not about 'Poor Lieutenant Allen' but 'My God, I'm glad I wasn't over there.' When I returned from the mission I went into the barracks before I went to debriefing where I met another pilot. 'Hey,' I said, 'Lieutenant Allen got shot down today.' 'No shit,' he said, "I wonder if his pants will fit me.' I was shocked but said nothing more. I couldn't imagine anybody being so callous about a friend or acquaintance being shot down and possibly killed. I figured that his attitude might have just been his defense strategy."

906 "At debriefing there is always a gripe sheet that is later printed and given to headquarters. On this mission to Berlin, the sheet was a little longer than usual. Out of 19 complaints, one was for placement of camera switch. One was for radio buncher and two were for equipment placement. One gripe was about our crossing over Kimbolton's traffic pattern as we arrived at our base. Three gripes were about need for more passes or space between missions. ('I haven't had a pass for 11 missions in three months.') One gripe was for short supply of ammunition and 6 gripes for not enough sleep. ('Why do we have such early missions? Why couldn't we have them a little later so we can get more sleep?') (In answer to this latest question: The target should be encountered as early in the day as possible before afternoon cumulus clouds obscure too much of the area.) There were two complaints about the sandwiches that we carried on a mission. ('More meat or peanut butter instead of jelly.') Today our liquor allowance after missions was absent and there were three complaints about that. ('Need whiskey, especially after Berlin raid.') ('What happened to the whiskey today?') ('How about liquor?') Our crew flew this mission with a plane whose guns hadn't been cleaned and Beiser complained about that. ('Crews should have clean guns for next mission. Guns on this A/C were not cleaned today.') I suspect that the harried ground crews were very busy repairing airplanes from our mission to Hamburg yesterday. The plane that we flew to Hamburg yesterday was not on this Berlin mission, due to extensive damage that had not been repaired as yet."

907 "*Kismet* made it back to Bury St. Edmunds but was out of action for two days for repairs. One of the spars had received a direct hit. As we left the ship on the taxiway with a flat tire, I picked up my 'chute and found it riddled with holes."

908 "In the mid-Sixties I was working at a chemical plant that used some German-made BASF machines and so they had several maintenance men that were from Germany who worked in the factory that built them. One day at lunch in the cafeteria one of the German workers noticed that my belt buckle had a B-17 on it. He asked if I flew during the war. I told him 'Yes' and with that he told me of an occasion when he was about 10 years old. He said that he lived near the Friedrichstrasse railroad station and while he was in the railyard picking up coal for his mother's stove at home, this B-17 bombed along the tracks and that it scared him but good. While he was telling me his story I asked him if he could see any markings on the tail of the plane and he said, '*Yes*' and that he would always remember it. I had been sketching under the table our 'triangle P' that was on all our group tails and then I said, '*Was it like this?*' For a second he just sat there and looked. Finally he said, '*How do you know what it was?*' I told him of our little flight and that it probably was the plane that I was in!"

909 2nd Lieutenant Louis R. Hernandez flying 42-38202 *BTO In the ETO* and 6 others evaded. 3 PoW.

910 The Poles gave Sibbett a hero's burial and made a wooden cross marker with an emblem depicting wings and a propeller.

911 Hernandez, Lea and the other 5, including Sgt Robert Gilbert, a P-51 crew chief who was flying with them, evaded capture. They were picked up by Polish partisans of the 34th Regiment and served as infantrymen for 40 days, attacking German forces and pillaging Russians preying on Polish civilians. Our adventures were all under extremely adverse circumstances as the 34th was limited to rifles, machine-guns, pistols, grenades and plastic explosives. The Germans had unlimited resources and personnel but were unable to restrain the 200- 300 man unit. Lea recalls that, "Our opponents included the *Gestapo*, *Wehrmacht* and the *Luftwaffe*. At one time plans were being laid to take over a *Luftwaffe* base long enough for the 7 of us to commandeer a Ju 88 and fly it to England! We had captive pilots' manuals to study but we called it off because it would have been too costly in partisans' lives for just 7 of us to get away. The planes looked very tempting as we surveyed them from our hiding places in the adjacent forest! We finally made our way, with the 34th Regiment Commandant 'Zenon's' help, into Russian-held territory, thence with the Red Air Force from base to base to Poltava. We were awarded the '*Kryx Walxyuch*' (Cross of Valor) by the Poles for our infantry service. Later we were also awarded the '*Memorial Medal of Armia Krajowa*' by the Poles for our services in the AK (Resistance Forces). When we got back to England we lectured on evasion tactics for a month before being sent home to the States."

912 Despite intense fighter cover the *Luftwaffe* made a few attacks on the Berlin force. Near the capital, Me 410s swooped on the rear of the 1st Division formation and made several attacks on the B-17s. Altogether, 44 Fortresses and Liberators were shot down on the raid.

913 David M. Nichol, former Moscow correspondent of the "*Chicago Daily News*" wrote: "Until the raid began the operation could only have been described as a milk run" or routine flight. The big fleet of American heavies took off from their British bases and flew almost without incident across most of Europe. Only one man in the formation was injured over the target near Berlin. Earlier in the day, with other Allied and Soviet newspapermen, I had flown from Moscow to watch their arrival. They came in like the veterans they are, filling the sky with their wheeling traffic patterns and the thunder of their motors. They put their planes down so expertly and rapidly that at one time there were five of the big bombers on the single runway. Cameras ground out a record of their welcome, which was genuine. A woman officer handed a bouquet to one of the visitors. The field was functioning well, for the 15th Air Force, flying from Italy, had already marked the way. But the first suggestion of trouble came while the crews were still telling their stories to Intelligence officers. Off in the distance, an anti-aircraft battery opened up. Too high even to be seen, a German reconnaissance plane had followed the bombers about 400 miles into Soviet territory. Shell bursts like puffs of cotton in the sky traced its course. Some of the officers dismissed the firing as practice, however, and the weary crews tumbled into tent cots, some of them not waiting to eat.

"Most of the correspondents were billeted in a railroad sleeping car on a nearby siding, but William L. White of '*Readers' Digest*,' Eddy Gilmore of the "Associated Press" and I headed for the hospital area where we had friends. We sat and talked until late in the soft summer night. There was no moon but the sky was filled with stars. We went to bed. A few minutes' later sentries with whistles alerted the camp. We listened, then slept some more, until suddenly the guns were firing from every direction. Tracers ripped the sky. We could hear motors in the blackness above. The Germans came on, methodically, purposefully. They swept over the field, leaving a trail of parachute flares like million-candlepower Japanese lanterns.

Back they came on their bombing run. Gilmore was dressed, but White and I were in pajamas. With the hospital staff and some of the fliers, we stumbled into the trench at the end of the tent row. The next two hours were a hideous nightmare. Back and back came the Nazi bombers, picking out targets they had missed on earlier runs. The light and medium anti-aircraft that hammered continually seemed not to disturb them' a bit. When one wave had exhausted its bombs, another took its place. To the best of our knowledge none was shot down.

"Very early a fuel dump went up in an angry orange mushroom of flame and smoke. Out near the runway a fortress caught fire, then another, and another, and another. The heavy caliber cartridges of their machine guns began to explode, adding to the general din and danger. More bombs, more flares, and as each wave completed its job, a series of three blinding flashes as they took pictures of their handiwork. It was on the basis of these that Berlin first announced the destruction of 20, then 45 of the grounded planes.

"American causalities were amazingly light, especially since fliers and groundcrew alike were housed in tents and the only shelters were slit trenches. One was killed instantly by a stick of bombs that fell squarely in the hospital area and a second died of wounds. About 20 received lesser injuries. The heaviest losses occurred among the Red Army men and women stationed at the base. Disregarding the rain of bombs, the guards stayed on the field, attempting to put out the fires and to move aircraft. Several were killed, but no figures ever were made available. Several Red Army girls died when another bomb fell on the anti-aircraft battery they were manning. The same blast killed three Soviet newspaper correspondents who had left the dubious security of a shallow ditch and were running across the field.

"Casualties began to come in. They were treated in the trenches. The body of a boy was found dying in a tent. A second was given an emergency injection of plasma. The trenches filled up with each new blast as sleepy, barefooted fliers in various stages of undress found their way to them. A Russian girl panicked, and started out. White pulled her back. By this time he had found a blanket and was wrapped up like an Indian chief. One of the American nurses was jittery until she was given a job. An orderly wondered if the four-foot deep trenches shouldn't have been zigzag instead of straight. 'No' said the Virginia major in a slow, soft voice. 'They should have been deeper.'

"Long after the last of the bombers left, the planes on the field continued to burn. Each man began to take stock, first of himself and then of the general havoc. Our tents had been cut into ribbons. Gilmore's bed was on fire. White's uniform, left hanging over a camp chair, was in tatters. My metal-cased typewriter had been struck by a spent bullet and sealed shut. I never did find my cap.

"The early morning light disclosed a sickening sight. We walked out into the field, surrounded by the broken, sagging skeletons of B-17s. Only a cluster of motors and twisted propellers marked where some had been. Even the planes that looked untouched had been shot full of holes. The oil lines on our Liberator had to be repaired. We met a group of Russian officers, also checking the damage. It included major general Alexander Perminov, commander of the field. We expected to be ordered away. Instead, he carefully showed us one of the hundreds of 'butterfly mines' - anti-personnel bombs about the size of tomato cans - and cautioned us against even approaching them. Soviet sappers were exploding them with long poles, but it was later in the afternoon before a runway could be cleared even at the side of the field sufficiently to permit us to take off for Moscow. Among the men there was resentment and anger, but there was something new. Veterans of scores of missions over Europe, some of them had experienced bombing for the first time from the receiving end. 'I never thought it was anything like this,' one of them said soberly.

"The raid produced immediate charges that the field was insufficiently protected. For a time it threatened to become a serious disagreement between the Americans and the Russians. Apparently there were no night fighters, no radar. Cooler heads pointed out that what there were of these previous weapons were at the distant front."

The heaviest loss in personnel occurred among the Red Army men and women stationed on the base. They completely disregarded the bombing and attempted to extinguish fires and move aircraft. 25 Russian soldiers were killed, including several Red Army women, some of whom were manning an AA battery, which received a direct hit. American casualties were incredibly light, considering that combat and ground crews were billeted in tents and their only protection was slit trenches. A stick of bombs that fell squarely in the hospital area killed one American instantly and another died later as a result of his injuries. About 20 others received minor injuries. The early morning light revealed hundreds of butterfly bombs littering the airfield. American and Russian personnel were told not even to approach them and Russian sappers exploded them with long poles. Major General Alexander Perminov, commander of the airfield, was among those who inspected the damage. Skeletal remains of the Fortresses were clustered around the airfield like carcasses. Some were only a collection of engines and twisted propellers that marked the spot where once bombers had stood. Altogether, 44 of the 72 bombers that landed at Poltava were completely destroyed and another 26 riddled with machine-gun bullets and bomb fragments. 15 other American and Russian aircraft were also destroyed during the raid. Further losses to the 13th Wing Fortresses at Mirgorod and to the Mustangs at Piryatin were, however, avoided because shortly before dark they took off and flew, low enough to escape the German radar screen, 150 miles further south to Zaporpozhe, distant enough to be safe. That night raiders dropped a flare over the deserted field and bombed under that chandelier for an hour and 50 minutes. The German raids led to serious disagreements at high level between the Americans and Russians. The Americans complained about the lack of fighter support, radar and searchlight facilities at the bases. The Soviets pointed out that they were all badly needed at the Front. General Carl Spaatz was to concede later that the Poltava raid was the "best attack the *Luftwaffe* ever made on the AAF. At around 1215 hours on 26 June, the surviving Fortresses took off on the next stage of the shuttle to Foggia, Italy, with a raid on a Romanian oil refinery en route. Crews reported seeing a large column of smoke and flames shooting skywards after the attack. At Foggia Main, repairs were carried out to aircraft damaged in Russia and during the raid on the oil refinery. Some aircraft were too badly damaged for further combat and were sent back to England by the much-coveted ATC route via Cairo and Casablanca. The appropriately named, *Belle of the Brawl* in the 388th Bomb Group touched down at Payne Field, Cairo, with over 100 linen patches glued over holes in her fuselage. Hank North in the 452nd Bomb Group recalled that, 'We were given little packets and told not to open this unless something serious occurred and we will need it. In there was a compass about the size of your fingernail, $30 and a map. The $30 I spent in Cairo or someplace but the map was made of silk and we could use it to wash our face, or use it for bowl movement. All you then had to do was stick it in water and it would clean up.' On 5 July the 13th and 45th Wings took off from Foggia on the final leg of their shuttle. Crews flew quite low over Rome and then headed for the marshaling yards at Beziers, in France. (Hank North flew his last mission, to Berlin, on.27 August).

914 'The lead plane was last seen headed for the English coast at Beachy Head. They never made it, as the airplane was vibrating very badly and finally the runaway No.2 engine exploded. The crew was ordered to bale out over the Channel, but before they could all get out, the airplane exploded and half the crewmembers were killed. Naval vessels rescued 5, including the mission commander, Captain Lynch, but the pilot; Roger W. Erickson was killed, as were the other officers in the front of the plane. There were two navigators on the lead plane for this mission, 1st Lieutenant Emilio M. Sbrolla and 1st Lieutenant Lawrence D. Ross; both killed. Bombardier 1st Lieutenant Dick W. Merz was also killed, as was the right waist gunner, S/Sgt Elwood Schoonmaker."

915 "Our 427th Squadron supplied the weather plane for this mission. This was our old 'F' Model that had been stripped and sealed. The ground crews had installed 21 high intensity lights on the airplane, which flashed the letter 'C' in Morse code while it was acting as formation ship. It was painted with red and white stripes that were 10ft wide in a diagonal pattern. As a combat bomber it had been named '*Vicious Virgin*.' This was changed to '*Scarlet Harlot*' after the paint job and I sometimes referred to her as '*The Virgin Harlot*.' Mostly we referred to the plane as '*The Barber Pole*,' which we dearly loved to fly. It was so fast that I had said at the time, that if you gave me a 5 minute start, a P-51 couldn't catch me before it ran out of gas."

916 42-102432, which would be shot down on the tragic raid of 15 August with the loss of the pilot, 1st Lieutenant H. S. Cook, his engineer, Sgt Slight and a waist gunner, Sgt Joyce.

917 Our regular bombardier, Ed Cooper was to fly with Lieutenant Savage in our old "*Buzz Blond*" as was David Glass, our erstwhile waist gunner. The poor old "*Buzz Blond*" couldn't get enough air speed to keep up and had to abort. Lieutenant Langford was flying as a spare and filled Lieutenant Savage's empty slot.

918 Only one parachute was seen to come from the stricken plane. This was the radio operator, T/Sgt R. H. Johnson, who evaded capture and was returned to American control. The rest of the crew were killed.

919 Piloted by Lieutenant W. T. Whittemore with Captain M. H. Graper, Operations Officer of the 577th Squadron.

920 Bob Reese; Joe Tonnata, the co-pilot; Bill Minzenberg; Gus Thornton, the top turret gunner and Ralph Buttzman, were all killed over the village of Foxly, Norfolk, on 5 July 1944 on a practice mission.

921 On 25 June over 1100 heavies were despatched to targets in France on two missions, 1 in the morning and 1 in the afternoon. In the morning, 258 Liberators of the 2nd Bomb Division, 137 B-24s of the 3rd Bomb Division and 263 B-17s of the 1st Bomb Division bombed airfields, power and transformer stations and an oil dump. During the afternoon, 274 B-24s of the 2nd Bomb Division attacked airfields at Bretigny and Buc and an air depot at Villacoublay near Paris. The day's two missions cost 13 bombers and two fighters. Two of the B-24 losses were from the 489th Bomb Group, one of which, 42-95249 *Teaser*, flown by 2nd Lieutenant J. D. Coffman, was shot down by *Unteroffizier* Hermann Grad of 4./JG 26, who had taken off from Boissy-Le-Bois with Oberleutnant Heinz Kemethmüller, CO, 4th *Staffel*, an *Experten* with 89 victories and a *Ritterkreuzträger*. The two pilots had no trouble in catching the ailing Liberator, which had flown over their base on two engines after being damaged by flak at Villacoublay. Kemethmüller presented Grad, who had yet to score a victory, with the invitation to shoot the B-24 down. He dispatched his victim at 14,000ft from 11 o'clock high, knocking out a third engine while the crew was otherwise occupied watching the wing and who failed to notice the approaching FW 190s. Everyone aboard survived and they went into hiding with the Resistance but only two of crew made it to the Allied lines. The pilot and the rest of the crew were betrayed to the *Gestapo*. On 5 August they were captured and as they were in civilian clothing, they were transported to Buchenwalde concentration camp on the last train out of Paris before the U.S. Army retook it. In October 1944 a list containing the names of the Allied airmen at Buchenwalde was smuggled out of the concentration camp to a *Luftwaffe* base nearby and the OKL demanded that the airmen be turned over to the *Luftwaffe*. It was only just in time for they were due to be executed a week later. Coffman and his crew spent the rest of the war as PoWs. *Unteroffizier* Hermann Grad, who did not score any more victories, was shot and killed by American troops on 26 December 1944 after he was shot down flying a FW 190D.

922 Crandell was killed on 26 August 1944 while strafing ground targets.

923 Lieutenant Colonel Thomas J. J. Christian, CO 361st Fighter Group was KIA on 12 August 1944 during a dive-bombing and strafing mission against rail targets at Arras, France.

924 A flak battery at Laon scored a direct hit near the right wing root of "*Old Crow*" flown by my recent friend, P. S. Wardowski. The plane immediately became a ball of fire and rolled over in a 180° turn to the left. I soon lost sight of it, but Charlie Latta in the ball and Carroll Brackey in the tail counted 6 parachutes. After diving 3 or 4000ft, the airplane exceeded its limit and disintegrated into thousands of pieces. Wardowski was not able to get out. Neither was the navigator, W.C. Bimbaurn or the tail gunner, D. G. Wagner. This was their 5th or 6th mission. Remarkably, the co-pilot, N. E. Hainlin was able to team up with the two waist gunners, Sgt A. Willard and Sgt J. I. Snede and they all evaded capture with the help of the French underground. Bombardier, 2nd Lieutenant C. F. Eisel became a PoW, as did the engineer, Sgt R. J. Kowatch and the ball turret gunner, Sgt B. L. Hope. Of our 26 B-17s, only 6 escaped damage. Six had major damage and 14 had minor damage, one being lost. Since the German gunners were aiming visually, the chaff that we dropped to jam their radar did little good. When we found our destination of Debach we were flying so low to avoid clouds that we had to make shallow turns to avoid hitting trees with our left wing tip, Amazingly, all our group landed safely and after a little red tape for landing away from base, we all returned to Molesworth before dark. Nine of us landed at Debach, 10 at Hardwick, two at Seething, one at Lavenham one at Downham Market and one made it to Bradwell Bay on 3 engines, Literally. This B-17 flown by Lieutenant Mac Connell had been hit by flak, which destroyed an engine, which fell from the plane. It is to his credit that he didn't bale his crew out over enemy territory. When Lieutenant E. C. "Al" Lehmann landed at Downham Market in 42-107099 "*Old 99*" after the tail number, he had two wounded crewmen aboard. He had been flying below and behind Lieutenant Wardowski. Our old friend "*Betty Jane*" flown by Lieutenant Gallagher was the only one who managed to land at Molesworth.

925 "Incredibly, there were 7 aborts, including two from our 427th Squadron. '*Buzz Blond*' had a fuel pump failure on No.4 engine and '*Pogue Ma Hone*' had high oil pressure and high oil temperature in one engine. '*Duchess Daughter*' of the 359th Squadron had a supercharger go out. Lieutenant Carpenter in '*Bad Penny*' in the 359th Squadron had a bad ear problem at altitude and had to return. '*Lonesome Polecat*' of the 359th had a fuel shortage. '*Fearless Fosdick*' of the 358th Squadron didn't hear the change in assembly altitude and couldn't form up. '*Clover Leaf*' couldn't find our group and so latched onto the 379th Group out of Kimbolton. During our crossing of the North Sea we received a recall order and the 379th returned to base along with our '*Clover Leaf*.' Our leader was not able to identify the sender of the recall order, even though it was given in authentic language, so we continued on the mission. It was a favorite trick of the Germans to send phony messages to try to disrupt our missions. It seldom worked, but today it was partially successful."

926 "We found out later that the ball turret gunner, Sgt L. K. Black, had managed to get out of his turret and snap on his chute while the plane was in its death dive. He later said that the bombardier managed to get out also, but his chute didn't open properly. Black said that 1st Lieutenant L. E. Weiss went past him with a 'streamer' and was never able to open the chute properly. Black was the only survivor of this ill-fated B-17. Roy's co-pilot, R. E. Quint had told me that he was going to be a father in just a few months. This baby girl was born on 4 January 1945 and was named Tawny. She is now Tawny Quint Young, living in Nevada City, California."

927 The Hawaiian gambled and had lost. He was given an A-4 air travel priority and Patton slowed down after he got to Paris. It was good however to be back among his comrades. "People at home did not seem to comprehend air warfare." Victor Bonomo, who also returned to the Group, finished his second combat tour, a total of 50 missions, in March 1945 and was possibly the first in his group to be twice nominated for the "Lucky Bastard Club." Abe Dolim was the second "two times winner," having amassed a total of 410.25 combat hours on 51 combat missions. "The last weeks and days were an agony. [When] finally it was all over, I was FREE, home safe and I didn't give a damn if I ever laid eyes on the old whore [B-17] again."

928 Billy Elliott was killed when *Delirious Dolores*, flown by 2nd Lieutenant Max R. Shea, was lost returning from a mission to Saarbrücken. The B-24 Liberator, which had two engines feathered, clipped the tops of trees and crashed in a field at Morningthorpe near Hardwick airfield and caught fire. Elliott, Shea and three others died in the crash. "They had been flying continuously… Billy and his friends were buried in the beautiful American Cemetery at Cambridge where 3800 Americans, almost all of them airmen, sleep the sleep of heroes."

929 Major Robert J. Lehnhausen's brother, Lieutenant Edward C. Lehnhausen, a pilot in the 68th Bomb Squadron at Shipdham, was KIA on 18 October 1944. flying 42-50596 *Flak Magnet*. All the crew were KIA.

930 42-97983 in the 570th Bomb Squadron flown by 2nd Lieutenant Larue F. Cribbs.
931 42-107070 *North Star* in the 571st Bomb Squadron, flown by Lieutenant Lawrence J. Gregor.
932 Eight of Gregor's crew were KIA and two survived to be taken prisoner. Five of Cribbs' crew were KIA. 5 survived to be taken prisoner. Both Fortresses crashed at Hoorn, Holland.
933 The 8th lost 9 aircraft on 13 July.
934 Leo C. Riley completed his tour in August. He almost did not come back from the mission on 14 July when enemy fighters hit them and they fought them for about 20 minutes. Riley flew co-pilot for Lieutenant Gette. The Mission was 11 hours long and Riley had to do most of the flying because Gette had the bends. On 28 July it was Leipzig. "What a flak alley. It was heavy and intense, but fortunately did not come too close to our wing. One piece busted the window just about a foot in front of my face. Gave me quite a start. In another words, scared the dickens out of me. Three more to go. Hope they are all easy ones. Will I be glad to get back to the States. These last ones are the hardest. Sweat, sweat, sweat." Next day he started for Leipzig again, but just off the Friesian Islands his B-17 developed trouble in No.3 engine and had to turn back. Riley wrote: "The rest of the boys went on. Flak shot most of them up pretty bad. Quite a few wounded and one co-pilot killed. Was quite glad to turn back as Leipzig is a rough place to go. The crew has two missions to go and I have three. Hope they are nice easy ones, but I have my doubts as there is no such thing as an easy mission in the ETO any more." On 31 July he once again "visited the little German city of Munchen better known as Munich. The place where Nazism was born. Mission was quite a long run. Flew through clouds and also clouds of flak, which was very accurate. Several holes in ship. One hunk of flak was headed in my direction, but thank goodness it was deflected by armor plate. No fighters, although they were very active in the vicinity. We lost two ships and crews. One crew ditched in the North Sea, two more to go." On 6 August Riley started the mission to Hamburg. Just inside Cuxhaven he and the crew "were practically shot to pieces by flak. Four ships fell out at once. Then we had trouble getting out of Germany. Every time we would start out, they shot at us. Finally we made it through a very narrow channel and passed Heligoland Island and out to the very welcome North Sea. The air was very clear and we were very close to the Jerry fighters. Finally made it though and what a long trip on three engines. Many wounded returned and two ships have not been heard of yet. One more to go. God be with us again."
935 This airplane would be involved in a mid-air collision with another, unnamed 427th Squadron B-17 on 9 November 1944 killing 17 men in the two airplanes with only one survivor. The tail gunner in the other plane escaped when the tail was severed from the fuselage.
936 "Just after I finished my 'New Crew' duty in less than a month Clark was shot down with 8 others when 20 or 30 enemy fighters attacked our group. Clark was killed, as was his co-pilot, 2nd Lieutenant G. P. Vesy. Also killed were the other two officers on the crew, 2nd Lieutenant R. J. Davies, navigator and Flight Officer E. E. Brosius, bombardier. Two of the 5 enlisted crew were also killed on this 15 August mission. They were the engineer-top turret gunner S/Sgt H. P. Scott and radio operator-waist gunner; S/Sgt F. Roswall, Sgts C. A. Sikora, Jr., C. S. Cruttenden and E.W. Bjorn became prisoners of war. On the mission that Clark and his crew were lost there were a total of 9 B 17s lost to enemy fire, mostly by fighters. The 303rd Bomb Group lost almost a fourth of its B-17s on that raid to an airfield in Wiesbaden, Germany. 39 were sent out and 30 returned. 23 men were killed, 22 in crashed bombers and one in the '*Flying Bison*.' I was there when it returned to Molesworth on this, its last flight, being so badly shot up that no attempt was ever made to repair it. I was saddened that my new friends were killed for such a small return on their bombing investment. The airfield was damaged but not to the extent that the Germans couldn't repair it quickly."
937 On the night of 17/18 August 1943 596 heavies of RAF Bomber Command had devastated the V-2 rocket site complex at Peenemünde, destroying 27 buildings in the northern manufacturing area and flattening 40 huts in the living and sleeping quarters. The foreign labor camp to the south suffered worst of all and 500-600 foreign workers, mostly Polish, were killed. The whole target area was covered in craters. Of the total of 606 aircraft assigned, 44-engined bombers and one Mosquito were lost (6.7%) and 32 suffered damage. The raid is adjudged to have set back the V-2 experimental program by at least two months and to have reduced the scale of the eventual rocket attack on Britain. *See Battles With The Nachtjagd* by Theo Boiten & Martin W. Bowman, Schiffer Publishing, 2006.
938 On 19 July 1200 bombers attacked targets in south-central Germany again and two days later the 8th went to Schweinfurt. Peaslee's weather scouts were instrumental in preventing the 1st Bomb Division entering a cloud belt that towered to 28,000ft. The 2nd Bomb Division did not receive the radio signal put out on the fighter-bomber frequency and 26 Liberators FTR as a result of collisions and enemy action. In sharp contrast, the 1st Division lost only three bombers and the 2nd and 3rd Divisions wasted no further time in forming their own scouting units.
939 In all, 20 men parachuted out of the two Liberators. Aboard 42-50478 *Miss Shirley* piloted by Lieutenant Frank J. Schwermin 6 survived to be taken prisoner while three evaded and 1 was KIA. Aboard 42-95026 flown by 2nd Lieutenant William D. Roe, 1 was KIA, 5 evaded and 6 were taken prisoner. 41-23683 *Jo Jo's Special Delivery* was among the others damaged in the collision and crash-landed at Manston.
940 Bombs from the last few B-24s in the 2nd Bomb Division hurtled into American forward positions, killing 101 men and wounding 308 others. Among the dead was Lieutenant General Leslie J. McNair. Five bombers were shot down
941 Operation *Cobra* the breakout of the American forces from Normandy was heralded by air attacks by 3000 Allied aircraft, which paved the way for the breakout and several days later Allied and German troops clashed in the Battle of Brittany. John McClane adds: "Yet the bombing of 25 July is consistently given little notice in any history book I ever read, even those devoted to the 8th Air Force. I never understood why this fantastic event that broke the German front only rates at most one line in the history of WWII. Years later when I was an eye specialist Mr. Physter, a patient of mine, told me that when the bombs began to fall short, he dove into his foxhole but that the concussion rolled him around like a toy doll. Another friend, Chester Rotter was a Captain with the infantry. He said that where as his company was not able to advance one hedgerow the day before that after this tremendous carpet bombing, he led his men 5000 meters before they found a German who could stand up and fight. All the others were either dead or near dead with blood coming out of their nose, mouth and ears. Dr. Rotter said the one thing he most remembered was that all the cattle were laying on their backs with all four legs up in the air."

Chapter 18:

942 111 B-24s sent to bomb targets at Brussels and an escorting fighter group were recalled because of cloud cover at the targets and another 180 Liberators dispatched to bomb targets in France also failed because of heavy cloud. Fighters flew 237 sorties supporting the B-24s and strafing ground targets. No aircraft were lost on these missions.
943 B-17G 42-31537.
944 B-17G 42-31723.
945 Five of the crew of 42-31903 including both pilots were killed while four baled out and they were taken prisoner.
946 Of the nine men aboard B-17G 42-107211, only the engineer survived to be taken prisoner.
947 B-17G 43-37655. Five of the crew, including both pilots, were killed and four were taken prisoner. Some of those who died were killed on the ground by the Germans and one crewman who was taken prisoner was beaten with clubs and rifle butts.
948 B-17G 42-97829.
949 Charles E. Harris adds: "Our crew had a real rough beginning; badly mauled on two missions and in the Red Cross flak shack after only 6 missions. But soon after that we were designated a lead crew and were only touched on one mission after that, when my Command Pilot got shot up."
950 Just after bombs away B-17 42-102667 piloted by Captain Robert Schomp, who led the low squadron, was struck in its right Tokyo tank. With flames streaming from the wing to the tail the crew baled out and they were all taken prisoner. The ship exploded seconds after the pilot jumped. The B-group also lost B-17 42-107007 "*She Hasta*" piloted by Lieutenant William "Grind-'em-out" Greiner, who was flying to break in a new crew. (James Coccia's who had joined the Group on 17 July). With an engine out and other damage, the plane dropped out of formation and was then attacked by a Me 262, forcing the pilot to ditch in the North Sea off the coast of Ameland. Eight of the crew made it to the shore where they were captured immediately. Waist gunner Bernard Baumgarten was severely wounded and he went down with the aircraft. The rest of Greiner's crew had recently completed their tours.
951 He was to be KIA on 21 November at this same target. The only survivor of this 9-man crew would be radio operator, T/Sgt J. A. Ellis. Civilians would murder some of the others.
952 B-17G 42-231909 whose last three digits suggested the Fortress's name.
953 "My former pilot, Theodore R. 'Bud' Beiser was the lead pilot for our squadron with J. E. Fletcher as his co-pilot and J. B. Coffey as navigator and C. M. Webster as bombardier. All 4 men were 1st Lieutenants. T/Sgt Lennie J Buchanan was top turret, S/Sgt Charles W. Latta was ball turret; T/Sgt Benny J. Gorchesky was radio man-waist gunner, while the other waist gunner was S/Sgt James W. Haines. S/Sgt Carroll H. Brackey was the tail gunner. All these sergeants were from our original crew and had all been promoted since arriving at Molesworth."
954 "My airplane was listed as having major damage, although it was nothing compared to what would happen to it later. On 8 January 1945, this aircraft would be involved in a bad landing after a mission to Koblenz. The pilot would land long on a short runway and go off the end of the runway, across a road and into a farmer's field, doing major structural damage to the right wing and engines. All systems on the B 17 are run by electricity with the exception of cowl flaps and brakes, which require hydraulic pressure supplied by an electric motor. On this date the engineer had to drain fluid from the system when he found a switch missing to the electric motor that supplied pressure for the brakes. Upon return to base the engineer refilled the reservoir, but air got into the brake line, thus negating the hydraulic pressure to operate the synthetic rubber expander tube which forces the brake pucks to push against the brake drum. Thus, no brakes."
955 The *Volksturmer* murdered Berry, 2nd Lieutenant John B Good, co pilot and S/Sgt Lewis E Pulsipher, tail gunner. The accused were tried at Dachau, Germany during the period 30 June-15 July 1947 before a General Military Government Court. Police President Fritz Dietrich, Karl Hunsicker and Wilhelm Stemmler, received death by hanging. Three others were indicted and tried. Two received sentences of life imprisonment and one received 4 years in jail. Huddleston was found by a dachshund and captured by a forester. Dozens of people crowded around him, some taking pictures. The *SS* police showed up and took him to St. Wendel for holding. He and the other 6 crew were sent to PoW camps. The remains of the Liberator came down near Dudweiler in the district Saarbrücken. The Heavy Flak Battery 631 claimed it.
956 The 486th Bomb Group at Sudbury and the 487th Bomb Group at Lavenham, which formed the 92nd Wing, were taken off operations and by the end of the month, were ready to begin combat missions in Fortresses. During the period end of August-mid-September the three B-24 groups of the 93rd Wing (the 34th, 490th and 493rd), also changed over to the B-17. The 95th Wing, which had begun with only two groups, ceased to exist on 14 August, when the 489th was transferred to the 20th Wing as a fourth group.
957 In August the combat tour was extended to 35 missions on the grounds that individual missions appeared less hazardous.

958 "I had become cynical, irreligious and hard as nails. Moreover, I was inflicted with a dangerous fatalism, so much so that when I was back in the States, I volunteered for another tour of combat. But that's another story."

959 Friedrichshafen was bombed by 322 Lancasters and a Mosquito in moonlight and 1234 tons of bombs were dropped in an extremely successful attack using good PFF marking. RAF Bomber Command later estimated that 99 acres of Friedrichshafen, 67% of the town's built-up area, were devastated. When the American bombing survey team investigated this raid after the war German officials said that this was the most damaging raid on tank production of the war. A civil report stated that 136 people were killed and 375 injured in Friedrichshafen and that 656 houses were destroyed and 421 severely damaged. *Source, "The Bomber Command War Diaries: An Operational reference book 1939-45"* Martin Middlebrook and Chris Everitt. Midland 1985.

960 On 3 August 12 aircraft were claimed destroyed. Six bombers and 6 Mustangs FTR. Later in the afternoon 515 bombers attacked 20 V-weapon sites, two airfields and a railroad bridge and a junction all in France and two oil refineries and a storage depot in Belgium. Four oil facilities in France and a road and rail bridge in the Netherlands and marshaling yards in Belgium were also bombed. Six fighter groups provided uneventful escort and only one bomber was lost.

961 In the late morning and mid-afternoon raids, over 1250 bombers attacked 4 oil refineries, 4 aircraft factories, 4 A/Fs, the Peenemünde experimental establishment and torpedo plants in Germany, two coastal batteries in Pas de Calais area and two Weapon sites, two A/Fs, a M/Y, a railroad crossing and a bridge in NW France. All the Eighth's 15 fighter groups supported the operations, flying 782 sorties.

962 42-31432.

963 Of the three groups doing individual bombing on this mission, our high group had the best score, having 100% of our bombs fall within 2000ft of the MPI. 95% fell within 1000ft and 60% fell within 500ft. The low group did nearly as well with 95% of their bombs falling within 1000ft of the MPI and 30% within 500ft. The lead didn't do quite as well, with 93% within 2000ft and 25% within 1000ft. They only got 5% within the 500ft circle. Our High group also had the most concentrated bomb pattern, it being 1230ft by 900ft, which indicated that we were flying a tight formation at bombs away. The Lead group's pattern was 1800ft by 1150ft. The low group's pattern was 1700ft by 1350ft.

964 It seems evident that some one in the group got a lucky hit on the pilot from nearly one mile away and after we landed I put in a claim for Czerwonka, only to find that several claims were made for this same airplane. I thought Czerwonka should have gotten credit, since we started firing first and the plane was hit while still a mile away. However, the powers that be finally awarded the "Kill" to S/Sgt Richard L. Smith who was tail gunner for 1st Lieutenant Bob Moreman flying Low Lead in the 359th Squadron. I've never been able to figure out how the tail gunner on the lead plane could shoot down an enemy fighter coming in from the rear of the formation with all the 20 or so other tail gunners firing at the same plane from positions further to the ream and hundreds of feet closer to the action. But, he was on the lead plane. The Me 110, 210 and 410 were all very similar and could only be identified by close scrutiny. No matter, they were all enemy planes. They had a twin rudder rather like a B-25 Mitchell Bomber, but other than that, the resemblance was superficial. These twin engine fighter bombers were no match for our P-51s and usually hung back to wait for a gap in the fighter support, at which time they flew behind a formation of bombers and fired rockets into the formation from behind. They had to get within a half mile of the formation to be effective and this posed a dire threat to them.'

965 The bombers claimed three airplanes destroyed and fighters, 39 destroyed in the air and 15 on the ground. Strafing claims included numerous items of rolling stock. 14 bombers and 15 fighters were lost during the day.

966 After the bombing the two groups flew on to their shuttle base at Mirgorod in Russia, scene of such devastation two months before. During their stay they flew a raid to the Trzebinia synthetic oil refinery and returned to Russia before flying to Italy on 8 August, bombing two Romanian airfields en route. Four days later they flew back to Britain on the last stage of their shuttle. Toulouse-Francaal airfield was bombed on the flight back over France. This third shuttle by the 8th Air Force proved more successful than the disastrous shuttle of June 1944 with not a single Fortress being lost.

967 *"Ramrod 483"*, 5 August 1944. Preddy was awarded confirmation of 1 Bf 109 destroyed and 1 probable. Next day he shot down 6 confirmed Bf 109s before going on leave until October 1944. He returned as CO, 328th Fighter Squadron. On 25 December 1944 Preddy scored his two final victories to take his score to 26.8333. Preddy was killed by friendly fire the same day.

968 On 7 August also the 492nd Bomb Group, 2nd Bomb Division was withdrawn from combat having lost 54 aircraft in May-July 1944. This was the heaviest loss for any B-24 group for a three-month period. The 491st Bomb Group moved from the 45th Combat Wing to take the place of the 492nd in the 14th Combat Wing.

969 42-97311.

970 We knew Frank from his experience of swimming in the English Channel on 1 December 1943. His aircraft, piloted by Lieutenant A. Eckhart, ran out of gas after a mission to Solingen, Germany. They had to ditch in the Channel, but were all saved by ASR.

971 "My last mission on 8 August lasted 4 hours and 40 minutes with an hour and 15 minutes over enemy territory. That was to be my last flight in Europe. Once a person's tour of duty was over, they got in a hurry to get rid of you in order to make room for the replacement crews that were coming every few days. Of course they would allow one to sign up for another 35 missions, but few ever did. During my 32 missions I flew 12 different B-17s in combat, not including the two trips in the '*Barber Pole*,' '*Scarlet Harlot*' weatherplane of our 427th Squadron. I flew combat in the '*Buzz Blond*' 12 times. '*Bet Jane*' 5 times, '*Rosie O'Grady*' twice, '*Tiny Angel*' twice, '*Miss Lace*' twice, '*Queenie*' twice, '*Jigger Rouche, Kraut Killer*' one time, '*Full House*' one time. The other 5 had no nose art. The first and third of my students that I took on their first missions were KIA 4-5 weeks after my tour was over. I took H. C. Clark on his first mission on 17 July and he and three other officers and two EM were KIA on 14 August in the '*Jigger Rouche*' when German fighters shot them down over Wiesbaden. '*Tiny Angel*' that I flew on my 24th and 30th missions was shot down at the same time with the pilot, engineer and one waist gunner killed. On 10 January 1945 '*Buzz Blond*' collided with '*Iza Vailable II*' over Bonn, Germany, destroying the tail gun position, killing the gunner, Sgt M. M. Mooney. The nose of '*Buzz Blonde*' was badly damaged, causing the bombardier and navigator to bale out, thinking they were out of control. They became PoWs, while the others regained control and made emergency landings at friendly airfields. The pilot and co-pilot of '*Iza Vailable II*' received the DFC for keeping their aircraft from crashing, with much of the tail missing. The '*Bet Jane*' that I flew 5 times, including the glide bomb attack on Cologne was shot down on 13 September with the pilot being the only one killed when his parachute failed to open. '*Full House*,' the only 'new' B-17 that I flew in combat was in a midair collision with another 427th aircraft. 17 men were killed in the two aircraft, with only one survivor. On 21 November my third 'student' was killed with all but the radio operator. They were flying one of the 'newer' planes built in 1943. Some B-l7s built in 1944 were starting to show up during these months. '*Miss Lace*' was hit by flak on a mission near the Russian lines and landed in Poland where it was left behind. '*Queenie*' later made a crash landing in England, but was salvageable. During my 32 missions the 303rd Bomb Group lost 20 B-17s to enemy action. One of these may have gone to Sweden. One of our B l7s made an emergency landing in Switzerland with 60 holes in the airplane, some disabling. I was able to see many B-17s of other groups shot down as well.

"As a result of these 20 losses during my tenure, 80 crewmen lost their lives, some being murdered by German civilians. One was evidently shot because he was a Jew. The pilot and co-pilot of one downed bomber were hung in small trees and pitchforked to death by civilians. This had always presented a dilemma to combat crews who had heard rumors of such murders. I had carried my .45 pistol on my early missions, but later abandoned this practice. If caught by civilians, you might fend them off until a military man arrived, but on the other hand, this might give a military man an excuse to shoot you, claiming that he had been threatened. Catch 22.

"During the course of the war, starting with their first mission on 17 November 1942, our 'Hell's Angels,' 303rd Bomb Group, flew 364 missions, ending at Pilsen, Czechoslovakia on 25 April 1945, just 13 days before Germany surrendered. Unfortunately, German flak gunners got the last of our 181 lost B-17s, killing three of the 8 man crew in our 427th Squadron's 'new' B-17, 44-83447 that had no nose art."

972 The Liberator was B-24H-20-CF 42-50328/D *Pregnant Peg*, flown by 2nd Lieutenant Myron G. Jacobs, which crashed and exploded on the Yaxham Road near the base shortly after take-off. Two months earlier, returning from the mission to Politz on 29 May, Lieutenant Conrad "Connie" Menzel successfully crash-landed *Pregnant Peg* in a field near Shipdham. The left landing gear collapsed and the aircraft was extensively damaged. The temporary installation of a telegraph pole in the bomb bay enabled the Liberator to be flown out of the field on 10 June by a recovery crew to the 3rd SAD at Watton-Griston for repairs.

973 Between 6 July and 9 August we'd logged 167.55 hours.

974 "After our mission of 9 August, *Skinny* was sent to the hangar to be used for parts - but a changed decision saw her repaired for combat. She flew her 109th mission in December 1944 to January 1945. It was then decided to send her out one more time to make it an even 110 and on that mission three of her engines failed and the pilot put her down somewhere in Belgium. I don't know whether those miracle men of the ground crew were ever able to get *Skinny* airborne again. I do know I'll always have a warm spot in my heart for her and my wonderful crew.'

975 Leon Croulebois did not see Sgt Robert F. Williams leave the ship. Flak had killed him instantly and he plunged from his upper turret into the flaming bomb bay. He did not see Lieutenant Gordon "Bud" F. Davis, the navigator. His body was shredded by the first flak hit. Lifeless, it rode in *Flush* to the ground. The aircraft crashed at Bois de Clamart, a Paris suburb. He did see Allison leave the ship, shortly after jettisoning the tail gunner's escape hatch. Leon watched as ground fire danced his body around on the shroud lines of his 'chute, leaving him hanging nearly lifeless. Allison died minutes after reaching the ground. Leon watched as Aske hurtled out the waist door. The ship was now low. The same ground fire tore through his body. He died hanging in his parachute. A tricky wind caught ball turret gunner Norman Fernaays as he left the ship. It raced him toward Meudon where, still at speed, he bounced off the tile roof of Madame Braconnier' s home, landing heavily in the garden of the home next door. He lived, was sheltered by Madame Braconnier and was the first to return to military service soon after Paris was liberated. Chick Barber and Chuck Nekvasil crashed down in their 'chutes near the Orphelinat Lazaret (hospital). The *SS* captured Nekvasil and Chick was taken only minutes later. Consorto eluded capture for 24 hours but was captured and he and Magargee were taken to Germany. Barber was marched to a German barracks. Nekvasil, his pelvis and his coccyx fractured in the impact of his parachute landing and shoeless (the force of his 'chute opening had snapped his flying boots off, was marched to Lazaret. Late in the afternoon he was taken on a stretcher to an ambulance, which picked up Barber and took them on a long ride through Paris to the Beaujon hospital at Clichy. After a week and-a-half of minimal care both men made a night escape, with the aid of the FFI and finally linked up with the French 2nd Armored Division.

976 R. D. Russell's crew completed their 35 missions on 28 September 1944. The day after their B-24J, *King Kong* was lost over Kassel.

977 Lieutenant Lee E. Webster, two FW 190s and a Bf 109 destroyed; Lieutenant Warren .C. Littlefield, one FW 190 destroyed; Lieutenant Donald E. Frye, one FW 190 probably destroyed and one Bf -109 damaged. See *The 363rd Fighter Group in WWII In Action over Europe with the P-51 Mustang*. Kent D. Miller. Schiffer. 2002.

978 *Unteroffizier* Wilhelm Schäfer 3./JG 26 was KIA when his FW 190A-8 was shot down 50km West of Boulogne. *Unteroffizier* Erich Burmeister was KIA when his FW 190A-8 was shot down Northeast of Le Mans. Feldwebel Robert Hager was KIA when his FW 190A-8 was also shot down North east of Le Mans as was *Leutnant* Wolfgang Mars. *Unteroffizier* Hans Kukla was WIA. At Alençon at 0811 hours Lieutenant George J. Brooks who was on his 5th mission, was shot down by *Leutnant* Joachim Günther of 3./JG 26. (Brooks evaded capture and shortly returned).

979 The plane was B-24 42-95150 *Passion Pit* flown by Lieutenant John L. Millikin, who evaded. All of his crew survived and they were taken prisoner. It was their 30th and last mission of their tour of combat.

980 In 42-52590/H. Elliott made 1st Lieutenant on 9 September, with a raise in pay... almost $400. He made captain on 25 March 1945.

981 The leader's aircraft was B-24H-15-FO 42-94745 *The Bold Sea Rover* flown by Lieutenant James L. Glaze with Major R. J. Sirks in the right hand seat. There were no survivors. Eight men aboard 41-29473 *Bolicat* including the pilot, Lieutenant George H. Washington were KIA. John Doyle, the nose gunner, was severely wounded and was helped by Norman C. Grant the navigator. A chute was put on Doyle just as a second explosion rocked the B-24. He was to follow Grant out the nose wheel door opening and the navigator presumed that he did, but after opening his chute and looking around Grant could not see any other chutes. Five of the crew were found in the wreckage, two were never found and Doyle's body was discovered some distance from the crash. Grant was captured. See *Helton's Hellcats: A Pictorial History of the 493rd Bomb Group* by Martin W. Bowman and Truett Lee Woodall, Jr. Turner 1998)

982 "Aboard all lead planes the first two bombs held by the bomb bay shackles were 'smoke bombs.' The purpose of this was to mark the bomb path as they left our plane. They were known as 'Skymarkers' or 'Smoke Streamers.' When they were released, they started immediately to emit a very dense pure white smoke. The other bombardiers in the squadron would release their bombs on this signal."

983 "Flak had become our number one concern. I later found out that during the month the 8th Air Force lost 131 aircraft to anti-aircraft fire compared with only 39 shot down by fighters. On 10 September 1944, between my 29th and 30th missions, orders were cut for our crew to take official combat leave. The enlisted men were ordered to Pangbourne rest home in Berkshire. The four officers were to proceed to Roke Manor near Ramsey, Hants AAF Station #503. These were official 8th Air Force Rest Homes established to let the combat personnel wind down. All of our crew traveled together to London. There we separated for the respective rest homes."

984 On 20 August the 20th Wing Liberators were converted for 'trucking' fuel and supplies to the Allied ground forces in France. On 25 August Paris was liberated.

985 A radio for the life raft. It was so named because the distinctive curved yellow hand-crank generator, which provided power for the distress radio signal, was shaped like a Gibson Girl's waspish waist. The "hour-glass" figure was attributed to the personification of the feminine ideal in the satirical pen and ink illustrated stories created by Charles Dana Gibson, during more than 15 years spanning the late 19th and early 20th century. This unit with accessories was for use in case of forced landings on water. It contained in a yellow waterproof bag, which had buoyant qualities. Originally carried on the flight deck, to be either released on the small tethered parachute provided just before impacting the water or thrown out by a crewmember after ditching, the pack was soon repositioned in the dinghy escape hatch and made accessible from outside the aircraft. The set automatically transmitted a coded signal. The aerial wire was carried aloft by either a fold up/down metal fame box kite or balloon provided and inflated by a hydrogen generator.

986 25 B-17s and B-24s were lost during raids on oil and industrial targets on 24 August 1944.

987 "After the world's fastest l-to-l0 count I pulled the ripcord. The pilot 'chute rushed past my face. Then, WOMP! I looked up and oh, what a sight. A beautiful white canopy held firm at the 9000ft level over one scared Chicago staff sergeant. The descent seemed slow. The silence was eerie. I missed the roar of *Cutie's* engines. I saw her die in a burst of glory as she plowed into a German farmhouse. It all seemed so unreal. I couldn't believe I had just jumped from a burning airplane. I looked for the 388th but they were long gone. The Baltic was clearly visible. My now elusive Swedish dream faded in the distance. I began to relax and even started singing and waving to the other guys. Hell, there was nothing to this baling out of the plane. With a little more practice I could join the 101st Airborne. 'Screamin' Eagle Bing.' What was I saying?' [Dick Bing landed but could only count 7 other parachutes. Two were missing. Bing teamed up with Tommy Thompson and together they evaded capture for two hours. Then two shots range out]. Instinctively, Tommy drew a .32 caliber pistol from his flight jacket. I didn't know he had it. Enlisted men were told not to carry sidearms. That could get us killed. Maybe the officers had other instructions but I wasn't about to find out. 'Tommy, if you plan to use that,' I said, 'then get away from me. I'm unarmed.' Before a decision was made, we both saw the biggest of all Germans grinning and pointing a pistol at us. He was huge and must have been 8ft 10in at least. And that pistol he was holding was easily an 88mm flak gun. 'Tommy discretely slipped his .32 back into his flight jacket. 'Raus' screamed King Kong. We didn't know what 'Raus' meant but we believed his command. 'Kong' introduced some friends; a more belligerent band of civilians. Their hate was understandable. We had just bombed out their town and here was an enemy they could reach. One, an elderly farmer, charged like an angry bull. He telegraphed a right hand all the way from Berlin. I sidestepped and the blow grazed my head. This infuriated him. He began pounding on my chest. 'Luft Gangster! Terror Flieger,' he shouted. I could see he didn't like me one bit. Tommy had walked a few steps ahead. I saw it coming but I couldn't warn him. Another farmer slammed a rifle butt into the back of his head. He fell but got up quickly. The crowd moved in for the kill. BANG! A shot rang out and they stopped. Four *Luftwaffe* regulars arrived to claim their prisoners. As they tied our hands, 'Kong' got into a heated argument with one of his friends. He had Tommy's pistol; the friend had the box of shells. I'll never know how it ended but my money was on the big guy. The guards led us to Midge's body. He'd caught a bullet in the back of the head, almost execution style. His body was stripped of shoes, watch and wedding ring. A young teenager, waving a pistol, was boasting how he had killed the enemy. The guards motioned us to pick up Midge. We carried him to a clearing 200 yards away. A short time later, a truck drove up carrying Camarda, Fisher and Coleman. Sutton, Healy and Bernjus were missing. Tommy and I climbed on the truck." Leon Sutton and Healy never showed up. Sutton had gone down with *Cutie* and Healy's parachute failed to open. Bing and the surviving enlisted men were sent to Stalag I and 17B PoW camps while Tommy Thompson and Fisher were sent to *Stalag Luft III*, Sagan. *Cutie* was the only loss in the 388th although 19 out of the returning 20 aircraft at Knettishall showed marked signs of minor flak damage. The oil campaign had claimed yet another victim while for the victors, the spoils. That night the Glenn Miller Orchestra played to a packed house in a Knettishall hangar.

988 B-17 43-37980 in the 839th Bomb Squadron flown by Lieutenant Joseph A. Duncan. 9 KIA. 2 PoW.

989 Friedrich Ickes of 11./JG 1 was flying Bf 109G-6 412171, "Black 6" when he was shot down. Knoke returned to his base at Vailly with his parachute under his arm. See *Defending the Reich; The History of Jagdgeschwader 1 "Oesau"* by Eric Mombeek. On 9 October 1944 *Hauptmann* Heinz Knoke suffered a shattered left knee and right pelvis when his car was blown up by a limpet mine in Czechoslovakia while en route to Anklam and he never returned to combat. He had 44 victories. He was awarded the *RitterKreuz* (*RK* or Knight's Cross) on 27 April 1945.

990 *Silvered Wings High in the Blue Heavens*, Julian Evan Hart, (Treasure Hunting November 2000).

991 Tays made the decision to drop out of formation and make it home alone. They landed 30 minutes behind the rest of the group.

992 On 29 August the 93rd, 446th and 448th Bomb Groups in the 20th Wing began 'trucking' missions to the troops in France, who were in urgent need of fuel and supplies. The bulk of the operation was completed using Liberators, whose cavernous fuselages were ideal for the task. Crew chiefs stopped painting bomb symbols on the Liberators and instead stenciled flour sacks and freight cars. The aircraft flew empty to the depot in southern England, where Royal Artillerymen loaded them with urgently needed foodstuffs and medical supplies and they then flew over the Channel, dropping down to tree-top level to Orleans-Bricy airfield, about 70 miles south of Paris.

993 Following this mission Stanley's crew had a break of almost a month as they were designated a lead crew and they took some appropriate training. It meant that they now had only 30 missions to fly instead of 35.

994 On 12 September the 458th Bomb Group alone delivered just over 13,000 gallons of fuel to units in France.

995 Our ball turret gunner, Sgt Matthew Palese, from Maryland, was hit in the buttocks by a piece of flak. The radio operator and the waist gunner gave him immediate first aid. This would be his last mission. He was sent home to the States to recuperate. The planes of Lieutenant Brewer and Lieutenant Addy were last seen heading east in a distressed condition shot up and smoking. Reports told us they crash landed somewhere in France and ended up in allied hands. After we returned to base, we discovered the order to descend had come from German radio and the flak crews were waiting for us. We were easy targets.'

996 B-17 43-37863. All 9 men reached the ground safely and were taken prisoner. Bombardier Harris "Red" Skelton later discovered "a chunk of cannon shell" lodged in his posterior.

997 43-38047.

998 42-102657. Only 4 men baled out to be taken prisoner while the rest, including the pilot, were killed.

999 43-38076.

1000 43-37880 and 43-38043.

1001 42-97154.

1002 42-102695.

1003 44-6089.

1004 42-97834.

1005 42-97806.

1006 43-38161.

1007 For a complete account of the raid see *Century Bombers; The Story of the Bloody Hundredth* by Richard Le Strange. 100th Bomb Group Memorial Museum, 1989.

1008 A postscript to the Ruhland raid came in 1949 while on the Berlin Airlift at Rhein-Main. My Link instructor there, an ex-*Luftwaffe* pilot, told me that he was on that raid and that they had taken off with just enough fuel for one pass and power off to base. He said most of them had landed on the autobahns after the raid. They were using synthetic fuels and oils then, but what proportions he didn't say." George Fory completed his tour on 12 October 1944 having flown 23 leads, but, because he was at odds with Colonel Jeffrey, he went home a first lieutenant.

1009 43-38290.

1010 All the crew, except 1st Lieutenant Aaron O. Karvonen, navigator, S/Sgt Charles J. Wild, ball gunner, and S/Sgt Glenn E. Edwards, tail gunner, survived. *Canvas Back IV* crashed at Groet in Holland. Hiedt adds. Our plane was the first B-17 to go down over the target. German fighters hit the remainder of the group after passing the target. They made one pass and knocked out the whole low squadron'. In all, 8 B-17s in the 92nd Bomb Group were lost on this raid and 4 more either landed or were abandoned on the continent.

1011 The 1st Division hit oil targets at Brux in Czechoslovakia while the 3rd Division bombed marshaling yards at Fulda. 217 B-17s bombed the Brabag synthetic oil refinery at Rothensee and the ordnance depot at Friedrichstadt in the old Hanse town of Magdeburg again. The Brabag synthetic oil plant, built in 1936, the Junkers aero engine factory at Magdeburg/Neustadt, the Krupp tank works at Buckau and an ordnance depot at Friedrichstadt, were among the main producers of war materials for Hitler's Germany.

1012 Two aircraft aborted, leaving 36 to bomb the target.

1013 Magdeburg was defended by 13 flak batteries each comprising 6, later 8, 88 or 105mm guns and two railway mounted flak batteries comprising 4 105mm guns. Despite the continual loss of young personnel to the fronts, Germany found it possible to double the numbers of *Grossbatterien* personnel, principally by decreasing the personnel per battery and using about 75,000 *Luftwaffenhelfer* (schoolboys). All schoolboys in Germany at age 16 had to enter the flak school in their neighborhood. In addition, approximately 15,000 women and girls, 45,000 volunteer Russian PoWs and 12,000 Croatian soldiers, were drafted in to the air defense of the *Reich*.

1014 In Germany three assault *Gruppen*, or *Sturmgruppen* (II./JG 4, IV./JG 3 "*Udet*" and II./JG 300) had been formed to fly FW 190A-8/R2 fighters (also called *Rammbock* (Rammer) or *Sturmbock* (Battering Ram) to ram American bombers. *Hauptmann* Werner Vorberg, II.*Sturm*/JG 4, explains: "JG 4 was created in August 1944 in Salzwedel to break up bomber groups with tightly formed *Sturm* fighter attack Gruppes flown by volunteer pilots who had pledged their allegiance by shaking the hand of their commander, Oberstleutnant von Kornatzki. They were a) to look only for a fight with *Viermots* and whenever possible to avoid engagement with a fighter. b) To not open fire on the bombers until 150 to 200 meters, when the 4 engines appeared in the target circle of the Revi gunsight. c) To ram the bomber if weapons failed or the gunfire was ineffective. In retrospect, the chance of surviving a ramming and jumping out with a parachute sounds like heroic suicide. It had however, an ulterior motive: The closed rank of the attacking fighters was designed to disperse and waste the defensive fire of the bomber formation. Everyone would open fire at the closest distance possible so they had to be motivated. The *Sturmgruppen* were considered elite units and there was no lack of volunteers. German airmen knew about the escalating, brutal and unrelenting bombing of residential districts, the shooting at everything below by the host of superior escort fighters - at farmers behind the plow, at bicycle riders, pedestrians and Red Cross ambulances. They also knew that if a peace treaty was sought, not the slightest mercy was to be expected (that also caused hatred) and that the German people had to expect the complete and final annihilation of the German Empire. This knowledge motivated the *Sturm* fighter for his tasks. He was supposed to break through the attacking formation of heavily armed bombers with no consideration of the hail of fire and destroy them. The fighter chosen was the heavy FW 190A 8/R2. Armored oil cooler, bullet-proof windshield, 6mm fireproof plates and cabin sides, 9mm armor plate behind the pilot's seat and standard 151/20, 2MK 108 3cm caliber weaponry led to double the fuel consumption. To guarantee three hours of flight, the fuel load was raised to 960 liters with a 300-liter ejectable auxiliary tank and a 110-liter auxiliary tank behind the pilot's seat. A tanked up and fully armed FW-190 A8/R2 had a flight weight of 7 to 8 tons. A 14-cylinder double star BMW 801 engine with a 2400hp maximum tried to make up for this additional weight but the FW 190 was clearly inferior in dogfights with escort fighters. Therefore, the *Sturm* units were sent against the bomber squadrons under the protective cover of lighter Me 109s. The first missions were flown in August 1944 with 4 squadrons of 11 machines each. In spite of noteworthy success against B-17 units, the newly established *Sturmgruppen* already had 8 wounded and 30 killed on 11 and 12 September 1944."

1015 1st Lieutenant Alfred L. Goodman and crew in the 861st Bomb Squadron were flying in B-17G 43-38214.

1016 Lieutenant Edwin Bisaro and his twin brother 1st Lieutenant Arthur A. Bisaro both served as pilots in the 860th Bomb Squadron at Debach. Arthur saw Edwin's plane go down and following his loss, he was sent home within days for a brief leave. Eight of Ed Bisaro's crew were killed and only 1 man survived to be taken prisoner. Arthur Bisaro returned to the squadron after his brief leave and on 5 October 1944 he too was shot down. His B-17 43-38546/S crashed at Ludenscheid. All the crew survived, two were taken prisoner and the other 7 returned to duty.

1017 Lieutenant Brown returned to the field with his plane so shot up, no one could determine now he made it. Evidently the fighter escort timing was off and they were not in position to fend off the initial fighter attack. Al Goodman became a prisoner and returned home OK.

1018 1st Lieutenant Alfred L. Goodman in the 861st Bomb Squadron and in the 863rd Bomb Squadron; 1st Lieutenant Edwin F. Cockerham, 2nd Lieutenant James P. Kitteson, Lieutenant John H. Oates, 2nd Lieutenant George W. Owen, 1st Lieutenant Charles W. Spencer and 1st Lieutenant Albert L. Tucker.

1019 in B-17G 43-38261.

1020 Borowy had arrived in England on D-Day aboard the Cunard liner *Queen Elizabeth*.

1021 43-38264.

1022 861st Bomb Squadron.

1023 Lieutenant George M. Durgin, Jr.'s crew and Lieutenant Crick's crew, both in the 863rd Bomb Squadron. Hayward F. Deese, Jr., concludes, "We landed at Brussels and put Gray, Ray H. Higginbotham, Jr., tail gunner and myself in the Canadian 1st Army Field Hospital. Gray died that night. When we flew back to Debach the next day we were the only crew out of 12 from the Low Squadron to make it back and we were two men short."

1024 Brown returned with 4 wounded crewmen and his B-17, like Captain Woodward's, was so badly shot up, that it was salvaged.

1025 William C. Rawson recalls: "Our crew's remaining 15 missions were to Germany. The missions were all long and tough. There was always flak, often intense, but lacking the accuracy we saw at Magdeburg. Our fighter escorts were successful in keeping German fighters at bay and even though we saw German fighters many times, they never again cut through our formations the way they did at Magdeburg. We flew our last mission on 13 January 1945, bombing a factory on the outskirts of Mainz, Germany. After Magdeburg we did fly our own aircraft, '*Ole Rambler*.' We were able to fly it on every mission as far as I can remember, thanks to the work of a superb ground crew lead by T/Sgt Frye."

1026 When his new crew finished their 35 missions, even though Ed had only 21 missions both as a B-24 and B-17 ball turret gunner he followed them to Southampton and sailed home with them on 30 January 1945! Borowy was awarded the Air Medal with two Oak Leaf Clusters

1027 About 450 fighters attacked the formations and 45 heavies were shot down. Merseburg proved a particularly dangerous destination for the 493rd Bomb Group with three crews lost during November on the 2nd, 21st and 25th. Henry B. Skeen, pilot of B-17G 43-38340 *Milk Run* in the 862nd Bomb Squadron, 493rd Bomb Group wrote in his diary: "Now we make believers of the crew. Over Merseburg with terrific flak, we lost an engine and ran low on fuel. My navigator, Lieutenant Leake, gave me a heading from the Merseburg area that took us directly across to Debach. This was important because of our fuel situation and because we were separated from our Group, flying single ship across most of Germany. A non habit forming practice."

1028 These aircraft were piloted by 1st Lieutenant John E. Glasco and 2nd Lieutenant Max W. Cook of the 326th and 327th Squadrons respectively and 2nd Lieutenants Thomas A. Andrew, Harold Wallace, William B. Kannapin, Horace S. Potter, William J. Mcllonie and Leonard L. Smith, all of the 407th Squadron. Additionally, T/Sgt Leonard D. Kennedy, radio operator of 2nd Lieutenant Russell J. Bundeson's crew, baled out over the target, apparently misinterpreting an order to stand-by. Sgt Kennedy was a member of the 327th Squadron.

1029 Among these was Major Jack S. Griffin, CO of the 327th Squadron, who flew in the lead aircraft piloted by 1st Lieutenant Neil S. Holbrook of the 407th Squadron. Griffin was hospitalized for a few days on the Continent after crash-landing near Paris.

1030 The entire attack did not last longer than 5 or 6 minutes but in that time the *Luftwaffe* accounted for 8 B-17s in the 306th Bomb Group. The first was *Belle of the Brawl*, the high squadron lead, flown by Major Robert Farwell. 9 men baled out safely. The 10th man, 2nd Lieutenant William D. Markle, flying his 25th mission as co-pilot, was KIA when he fell out of his parachute harness. *Tailwind*, flown by 1st Lieutenant John W. Sasser, *Methuselah*, flown by 1st Lieutenant Earl R, Barr, *Umbriago*, flown by 1st Lieutenant Charles C. Wegener, *Belle of the Blue*, piloted by 2nd Lieutenant Daniel W. Gates, *Lady Luck*, flown by 2nd Lieutenant Lewis H. White, Jr., and the B-17s flown by 1st Lieutenant Paul F. Bailey and 2nd Lieutenant Marvin W. Freeman. Hoffman got credit for a FW 190, which came in from 7 o'clock high and exploded after two bursts from Hoffman's guns.

1031 Other missing aircraft were piloted by 1st Lieutenants Harry W. Eck and Jack A. Peck and 2nd Lieutenant Warren D. Stallings. Nor was this the extent of the day's bad news: the plane piloted by 1st Lieutenant Elvan E. Hendrickson, also in the 327th, crashed at Woodbridge, Suffolk, killing T/Sgt William B. Post and S/Sgts Robert L. Shackelford and Frank Wililewski, radio operator, ball turret gunner and waist gunner, respectively. Of the 14 aircraft crews lost in action during September, the 407th and 327th Squadrons were hardest hit with 6 and 5 followed by the 326th with two and the 325th with one.

1032 On 17 September the shuttle mission was completed as 72 B-17s and 59 Mustangs flew without bombs from Italy to England. Two B-17s and a P-51 aborted and a P-51 crash-landed SW of Paris. 70 B-17s and 57 Mustangs landed safely in the UK.

1033 The Polish capital was cut off from the outside world, with the Germans on one side and the Russians on the other. Russia had asked General Bor to rise against the German occupiers, but had then stood by while the gallant Poles were gradually annihilated. Some RAF flights operating from Italy supplied the Poles in August, but then ceased because of the danger to crews. It was not until early September that the Russians finally agreed to co-operate and allow the B-17s to fly on to Russia after the drops and an attempt to reach Warsaw was made on 15 September. Captain Pete Hardiman, a P-51 pilot in the 354th Squadron, 355th Fighter Group, recalls: "On 15 September the 8th Air Force attempted a shuttle operation, named, 'Frantic 7' to help relieve Polish freedom fighters in Warsaw. We were to rendezvous with three bomb groups but after one and-a-half hours flying, we received a recall." *Frantic 7* was aborted because of bad weather and it was not until the 18th that the 13th Wing was able to fly all the way. Captain Pete Hardiman continues: "On 18 September Field Order 577 'Frantic 7' Dash One was started. The 95th, 100th and 390th Bomb Groups were to be escorted to Warsaw by the 4th, 355th and 361st Fighter Groups. Rendezvous was to be 1145 at Koszalin on the Baltic Coast; the actual meet was between Stettin and Torun. Heavy flak damage was received by the B-17s near Stettin but 107 of them made it to Warsaw and dropped food and medical supplies. Unfortunately, most of the supplies fell into German hands. One of the damaged B-17s was escorted to land at Brzese [and one 390th Bomb Group B-17 was shot down]. The remaining B-17s made it to Poltava and Mirgorod. Our fighter base was Piryatin, where we were all landed by 1520. On 19 September most of the fighters left Piryatin to rendezvous with the B-17s at 1330 hr near Horodenka, Poland and crossed over Czechoslovakia, Rumania and Hungary and bombed their target near Brod, Yugoslavia. There was much heavy flak but we all made it to Italy, landing at Foggia at 1600. After a short rest we left Foggia at 0959 on 22 September to rendezvous with the B-17s near Marseilles at 1325. All 355th aircraft were down at Steeple Morden by 1700 hr. This was the most awe-inspiring mission I ever took part in."

1034 105 B-17s and the 64 Mustangs succeeded in reaching their shuttle bases at Mirgorod and Poltava.

1035 "Upon our return to base in England, my skipper put me in for the Purple Heart and the Flight Surgeon insisted I must be grounded for 8 more days, since 5 had already passed. I tried to convince him that this might cause me to miss my next mission with my crew and that the injury was not an impediment to performance of my duties. As I predicted, when my crew finished with 30 missions, I had completed only 29, so that in a few days, on 2 November 1944, I picked up an open spot with a green crew for my 30th, to Merseburg, Germany."

1036 To maintain the Allied push through France during late August and early September the 8th began "trucking" supplies to the troops. The bulk of the operation was completed using Liberators, whose cavernous fuselages were ideal for the task, but some Fortresses were also used. 3rd Bomb Division groups also dropped supplies to the *Maquis*.

1037 "We had to wait until 25 September to fly our 23rd mission, a relatively easy one. We briefed at 0300 for a raid on Ludwigshafen. We climbed on course to 29,000ft for the bomb run. At the initial point, a complete cloud cover obstructed the target area. We dropped our 7800lbs of incendiary bombs through the undercast using PFF. All the flak in the area was about 3000ft below the entire formation. The only fighters we saw were friendly. The next 8 days were spent by our crew out in the country at a home given over to the Americans to be used for rest and relaxation. It was called a "flak shack" and we enjoyed it."

1038 The Allied plan was to capture bridges on the Rhine in Holland at Veghel, Grave, Nijmegen and Arnhem, using Britain's 1st and the American 82nd and 101st Airborne Divisions, cut off the Germany Army in the Belgian sector and save the bridges and the port of Antwerp for the American army units and British XXX Corps advancing north from the Dutch border.

1039 Part of the 325th Photographic Wing, commanded, since August 1944, by Colonel Elliott Roosevelt, the President's son.

1040 The 653rd Bomb Squadron was one of three in the 25th Bomb Group and was equipped with Mosquito TIII and PRXVI aircraft for meteorological flights, known as *Bluestockings*, gathering weather information from over the continent. A local storm front, forming suddenly east of Iceland on 5 June 1944 and monitored by the *Bluestockings* had postponed the *D-Day* invasion for one day until 6 June.

1041 The first airlift alone involved 360 British and 1174 American transport aircraft and 491 gliders, accompanied by 910 fighter escorts. During the course of the operation 20,190 parachutists, 13,781 glider-borne troops, 5230 tons of equipment and stores, 1927 vehicles and 568 pieces of artillery were landed behind the German lines.

1042 JG 26 also claimed three Spitfires and three RAF Mustangs on 17 September. 8th Air Force fighters and ADGB flew 1037 escort and patrol sorties in support of the operation. One of the JG 26 pilots was shot down and killed by a RAF Mustang while two more died when 4th Fighter Group P-51s shot them down. See *The JG 26 War Diary Vol.2* by Donald Caldwell. Grub Street, London. 1998.

1043 1st Lieutenant Clifford E. Holske and Lieutenant Nicholas W. Vozzy, 335th Fighter Squadron FTR. Vozzy was killed at 1345 hours in the Bocholt area flying P-51B 43-6841 and Holske's P-51D 44-14054 was shot down. He burned both hands badly when he baled out and received no treatment until two days after his capture. Oberleutnant Hofmann the 5th *Staffelkapitän* was KIA on 26 March 1945 after shooting down a RAF Tempest for his 44th victory. Schulwitz was KIFA 25 March 1945 in a take off collision in his FW 190D-9 at Nordhorn.

1044 *See The Debden Warbirds: The 4th Fighter Group in WWII* by Frank E. Speer (Schiffer, 1999). Although the 4th Fighter Group was credited with 6 FW 190s (Lieutenant Davis also claimed 1 destroyed and a possible second one) only two were lost. Louis H. Norley's victim was his 8th outright victory of the war. On 2 November Norley destroyed a Me 163 SE of Leipzig. He returned for a 2nd tour in 1945 when he was promoted Major and given command of the 334th Fighter Squadron. On 19 March Norley was leading A Flight as they cleared the skies ahead of the bombers. Nothing much was seen on the outward leg, but on the return "Red Dog" sent a Bf 109 down SE of Frankfurt to take his final total to 10.333.

1045 Of the three Mustangs claimed shot down by JG 26, only 2nd Lieutenant. Robert E. Geck FTR to Bottisham.

1046 Beyer was a native of Danville, Pennsylvania where he had worked in a local factory until enlisting in the Army just over a month after Pearl Harbor. After an initial stint as a glider pilot, he completed regular flight training in late 1943 and arrived at Bottisham as a replacement in April 1944.

1047 A career officer, Mietusch had joined the Geschwader in 1938 and he was a veteran of 452 combat sorties. He had claimed 72 aerial victories. He was shot down 10 times and was wounded at least four times. He had 75 victories and was posthumously awarded the *Eichenlaub* (*El or* Oak Leaves) to his *RitterKreuz* (*RK* or Knight's Cross) two months after his death. In all, the pilots of the 375th and 376th Squadrons claimed 14 enemy aircraft destroyed, giving the 361st the day's highest total of planes shot down in the 8th Air Force. Among those who recorded aerial victories was 2nd Lieutenant. Claire P. Chennault in the 376th Squadron, whose father, the legendary Major General Claire Chennault, had led the famous American Volunteer Group ("The Flying Tigers") in China before the U.S. entered the war. 1st Lieutenant Dale Spencer claimed 1½ Me 109s destroyed raising his total to 9½ aerial victories, just three days before he departed for the States at the close of his tour. Spencer's record would stand as the top score on the 361st Group victory list.

1048 The day before some of the Liberators had flown practice trucking missions over Norfolk and on the 18th 6 specially modified B-24s in the 458th Bomb Group delivered over 9000 gallons of fuel to General Patton's forces in France.

1049 The 1st Allied Airborne Army recovered 80% of all supplies dropped by the 20th Wing at Groesbeek.

1050 The 14th Wing Liberators flew over a small town and came under small-arms fire from some Germans who could quite easily be seen in the streets. One bullet, well spent by the time it reached the B-24, hit Ted Parker in the cheek. He watched helplessly as the lead aircraft, flown by Captain Jim Hunter and carrying Captain Anthony Mitchell, the air commander, was shot down. "She took one bounce and struck some haystacks, exploding in a large orange flame," he says. "Our altitude was about a hundred feet at the time. The tail gunner was the only survivor. Some Dutch monks hid him until liberated." The 491st lost 4 B-24s on the mission.

1051 Flying deputy lead of the third squadron in an ex-490th Bomb Group B-24J, later named *Henry* after the King Features cartoon character.

1052 On 19 September, the 458th despatched 24 Liberators to France, carrying 38,016 gallons of fuel for the troops. Colonel Albert J. Shower's 467th Bomb Group was also involved in the "trucking" operations. He recalls: "From 19 September until 3 October the 96th Wing flew no combat missions, but established a forward base at the airfield at Clastres, near St. Quentin. We ferried gasoline for Patton's tanks and motorized units." During its 14 days of "trucking" the 467th delivered 646,070 gallons of 80-octane fuel to the Allied armies. In 13 days of "trucking" missions the 458th also delivered 727,160 gal of fuel to the tank units

1053 The situation of the British 1st Airborne Division in Arnhem was now desperate and despite poor weather the Polish 1st Parachute Brigade was at last dropped in the area to the south of Arnhem. 16 Stirling glider tugs and 13 Dakotas crashed in the Arnhem-Nijmegen area out of 114 transports despatched. JG 26 claimed 20 C-47s. The Polish Airborne Brigade failed to break through and the survivors mainly covered the return of the remnants of the 1st Airborne Division across the Rhine on the night of 24/25 September.

1054 *Oberleutnant* Alfred "Fred" Heckmann claimed 4 of the transports for his 66th-69th victories. *The JG 26 War Diary Vol.2* by Donald Caldwell. Grub Street, London. 1998. Heckmann, a *RitterKreuz* (*RK* or Knight's Cross-) holder scored a total of 71 *Abschüsse*, which included 54 on the Eastern Front). *Luftwaffe Fighter Aces* by Mike Spick, Ivy Books, 1996.

1055 The 350th Fighter Squadron led by Lieutenant Colonel Gallup spotted 30-40 FW 190s and Bf 109s and engaged them from 9000ft to the deck just south of Nijmegen. 1st Lieutenant Ralph T Allison claimed a FW 190 destroyed but was awarded a probable. 1st Lieutenant John L Schilt was credited with a FW 190 damaged. 1st Lieutenant Vernon G. Rafferty was credited with a FW 190 destroyed shared with his wingman, 1st Lieutenant Robert Hedler, who went on to destroy a second. 1st Lieutenant Bayard C. Auchincloss claimed a FW 190 destroyed, which was later reduced to "damaged." Near Arnhem a FW 190 was spotted by Captain Lloyd G. Hally Leader of White flight flying YJ-D (42-22523) who went after it and was last seen going down through overcast. Hally FTR. His wingman, 2nd Lieutenant Richard F. Vomaske, lost him while evading an initial burst of flak and went on to claim a Bf 109. Oberfähnrich Otto Fussi of 6./JG 26 was killed at Nijmegen when his FW 190A-8 was shot down by a P-47 pilot. *Oberfähnrich* Günther Patzke of 9./JG 26 was KIA when a 353rd Fighter Group P-47 pilot shot down his Bf 109G-6 at Groesbeek. Two other JG 26 pilots who were flying FW 190A-8s were WIA by 353rd Fighter Group P-47 pilots. *Leutnant* Wilhelm Hofmann CO of the 8th *Staffel* JG 26 claimed a P-47 at Zwolle at 1733 hours. 13 minutes earlier he had claimed a C-47 at Deelen. See *Jonah's Feet are Dry - The Experience of the 353rd Fighter Group during World War II* and *The JG 26 War Diary Vol.2* by Donald Caldwell. Grub Street, London. 1998.

1056 1st Lieutenant Robert Tunnel and his navigator-cameraman, S/Sgt John G. Cunney FTR. Both men are now interred in the American War Cemetery at Neuville en Condroz, Belgium.

1057 A German Army unit captured Clark. He had a hole in his right thigh about 8 inches in diameter all the way to the bone and immediately after capture he was taken to a small hospital where doctors operated on his leg. At the Interrogation Center at Frankfurt about Thanksgiving 1944. He was told that the other pilots were killed in the fight. After about two weeks Clark was sent to Wetzlar before being moved by train to *Stalag Luft III* at Sagan. *Leutnant* Gerhard Vogt 5/JG 26 CO who was lading, claimed two P-51s at Goch (KN) at 1733 and 1735 for his 41st and 42nd *Abschüsse*. *Oberfeldwebel* Wilhelm Mayer 5/JG 26 claimed a P-51 at 1734 at Goch (KN), his 21st victory. (Mayer was KIA on 4 January 1945 at Lohnerbruch by a Spitfire of 442 Squadron RCAF. He had 27 victories and in March 1945 he was awarded a posthumous *RitterKreuz* (*RK* or Knight's Cross). Feldwebel Arthur Paul of 6/JG 26 claimed a P-51 at Goch (KN) at 1735 for his first victory. (Paul was KIA at Liège -Bastogne on Christmas Eve 1944 by a P-47 in the 36th Fighter Group. Führer Maximillian Busch of 6/JG 26 flying FW 190A-8 171576 Black 12 collided with one of the three Mustangs lost at 1700 hours 30 km NNW of Wesel and both planes crashed and burned. All three Americans were buried near Calcar, Germany. Capt Clarence O. Johnson had destroyed 4 and claimed three probables flying P-38s in the MTO and claimed three in the air and 6 more on the ground during his tour with the 487th, giving him a grand total of 13-3-1 enemy aircraft destroyed. At the time of his death Johnson was among the top 10 in 352nd scoring and was 13th at war's end. Lieutenant Elmer Smith took an 88mm shell, which only missed the ammo tray in his right wing by less than an inch. Smith still managed to get the P-51 back to Bodney even though it had a 3ft hole in the wing. See *The Blue Nosed Bastards of Bodney* and *The JG 26 War Diary Vol.2* by Donald Caldwell. Grub Street, London. 1998.

Chapter 19:

1058 Flown by Captain John H. Chilton with Major Donald W. McCoy, the 700th Squadron CO. aboard.

1059 *Hauptmann* Werner Vorberg, II.*Sturm*/JG 4 was to recall. Rarely reinforced, the II./JG 4 flew on 27 September 1944, the first mission against about 30 B-24s. After taking off from Welzow (south of Berlin) under the protection of two groups of Bf 109 escort fighters and after repeated course changes and coming undisturbed by enemy fighters, the unit reached the Liberators and flew from behind into the stream of bombers that were numerically superior to us. We divided up and flew toward individual ships. Whoever was not shot down by the bombers had success or had to ram. After passage from the back of the formation to the front, shot down ships were observed. Crews from *4-mots*, flying further ahead, were bailing out in rows before they were even attacked. Ten or 12 bombers exploded in the air, although they had already dropped their bombs. That also led to collision losses on our side due to the closeness when opening fire. After the march through the entire stream of bombers, we distanced ourselves quickly by swinging down from the place where the battle took place, in order not to be caught by enemy fighters. Our losses included 10 machines, one squadron captain and 6 other pilots. Three pilots were wounded; one of whom had rammed and survived and whom after the war lived in Mannheim. I do not know how many of our *Sturmgruppe* were lost on that day as the gun camera films were confiscated by the victorious powers. The Sturm Gruppe continued attacks on *Viermots* until the end of 1944. After that they were called to action in defense of the Fatherland.'

1060 On 28 September 1944 Romm again took off against bombers en route to Kassel and he shot down two B-17s.

1061 Literally translated, "*Up With Cologne!*" (Schröder was born in Cologne). One 361st Fighter Group pilot, 2nd Lieutenant Leo H. Lamb, died when he collided with a FW 190. Altogether, 29 enemy fighters were claimed shot down by the American fighters and bombers and 18 German pilots were killed.

1062 JG 3, 4 and 300 claimed 39 bombers shot down on 27 September and another 23 were claimed destroyed by the *Luftwaffe* on the 28th but the *Jagdwaffe* had again suffered serious losses. Within 48 hours, 63 pilots were posted killed or missing, 26 others being injured in air combat over mid- and western Germany.

1063 18 German pilots were killed. At a meeting of the Fighter Pilots' Association on 7 September 1988 in Geisenheim, Germany, *Hauptmann* Werner Vorberg of II.*Sturm*/JG 4 met a number of comrades who had participated in the air battle of 27 September 1944. In long conversations they attempted to recall the events of 44 years earlier. "The *Sturm Gruppe* JG 4 had suffered devastating losses during their first engagements of the 11 and 13 September 1944 with the more than 30-fold superiority of the Americans. We had already lost 38 of the original 44 pilots, including the *Kommandeur*. The 6th and 8th *Staffeln* were out of commission for the engagement because only two pilots were available. The 5th was again at full strength thanks to replacements; the 7th then had the remaining pilots of the 6th and the 8th *Staffeln* added to their wretched number of 5 pilots. Thus with great effort, we finally scraped together 20 fighters that took off in two *Staffeln* from Welzow. The 1st and 3rd *Gruppen*, equipped with Bf 109G-10s commanded by Major Michalski took over the duty of protecting the clumsy *Rammbock* FW 190A8/R2s from above. They also led the Gruppe through the cloud cover, with repeated course changes to combat altitude of 23,000-26,000ft. It is without doubt to the credit of the fighter officers of the 1st Fighter Division, that they knew how to set our course, so that we did not run into the Mustangs and Thunderbolts accompanying the stream of bombers. We reached our targets unharmed because we were well prepared by the information sent at intervals by radio. The two units formed two spearheads with the flight captain in the middle. This way, all members of the unit got a bomber in his sights. For us in the fight, there was no 'half life insurance' of being covered by the unit leaders or by a watchdog, as we had learned and practiced at fighter pilot school. Every individual carried the same risk but also had the same chance for success. There was only the spearhead - a *Sturm* attack according to the model of the infantry. The defensive fire of the *4-mots* - a seemingly impenetrable barrage - was broken through recklessly and, as ordered, only from the attack distance of 650-1000ft. Only after the 4 motors of the bomber filled the target circle of the reflex sight did we open fire with our 6 weapons, in which the 3cm ammunition of the machine guns had the most effective results. Missing the giant monster was almost impossible at this short distance from which one could recognize clearly the faces of the gunners in their firing positions aboard the bombers. Within minutes the terrifying, weapon-filled bombers stood in bright flame, ablaze, burning, bursting apart, losing wings, debris and entire engines, with which some attackers collided.

"In hordes, crew abandoned their bombers. In a few minutes, the two units had swept the massive stream of bomber from the sky and by diving away cleared themselves from the area of the battle. Then the P-51 escort fighters appeared. Our unit failed in the attempt to reform. We flew home alone. On my return to Welzow, a wheel along with its shot-up support fell off when I let down my landing gear. I had to land on my belly. More than half of those who had started out were missing. The 7th *Staffel*, with its borrowed crews, was wiped out. The 5th *Staffel* came away much better off. They must have broken off before the Mustangs and Thunderbolts appeared. As far as one can draw conclusions from the crash sites of the downed planes, the greater part of the loss storm fighter were probably due to the defensive fire of the bombers, which also the numerous engine hits on the returning machines proved. Only individual pilots were wiped out by the American escort fighters on the flight home. In an air battle with them, the awkward FW 190A8/R2 was unequivocally inferior."

1064 On 27 September also the 92nd Bomb Group completed its 200th mission with a raid on the marshaling yards at Cologne and Lieutenant Colonel James W. Wilson assumed command from Colonel Reid, who was still suffering from a flak wound sustained on a mission to Gelsenkirchen on 26 August.

1065 15 fighter groups took part in the day's missions and they claimed 26 fighters destroyed.

1066 42-97187, in the 360th Bomb Squadron.

1067 "Six of the crew of were able to bale out safely. 2nd Lieutenants Conn and Swill made successful bale-outs but were killed on the ground. Sgt Leo Waldron baled out unhurt. Sgt Calvin Zenio had baled out also but his legs were injured. Waldron gave first aid to his friend. They stayed together in a German farmhouse for an hour. Zenio was sent to a hospital, but Waldron was dragged away by a group of German farmers and murdered. A German soldier captured Lieutenant Miller. German civilians tried to kill Miller but were prevented from doing so by his captor. Long after the war Miller was able to obtain the gun camera footage of the FW 190 shooting down *Miss Umbriago* by Oberleutnant Haas. Other airmen from some of the other missing aircraft were known to have baled out successfully but were reported as killed by the Germans. Sgt Claude McGraw, a survivor, saw the personal effects of Sgt Shep Kerman. He knew that Kerman had pushed Sgt Jack Timmus out of their stricken aircraft. He knew that he was conscious and only slightly wounded when he baled out. Yet McGraw was advised by German soldiers, that Sgt Kerman had bled to death." *Chick's Crew: A Tale of the Eighth Air Force* by Ben Smith, Jr. Third edition. 2006.

1068 44-8330.

1069 Altogether, 11 Fortresses in the 303rd Bomb Group were shot down.

1070 *Chick's Crew: A Tale of the Eighth Air Force* by Ben Smith, Jr. Third edition. 2006.

1071 "Our straggling plane was initially suspected by our 'little friends,' the P-51 Mustangs, of being the German-manned B-17 because our radio equipment was malfunctioning and prevented Verdan 'Buzz' Wiedel, our radio operator, from identifying us as friendly. But he flashed the code outside the waist compartment with a light and properly identified us. The P-51 found the straggler and shot him down."

1072 "Little did anyone know at this time but experts later determined that carbon tet' on hot metal creates poisonous phosgene gas. Mac got quite a dose of this while he was without his mask. He is probably the only air crewman to receive a chemical warfare wound."

1073 "My flight records showed this mission to be 8hr 15min long; longer than usual. After we deplaned, Major Rex, the 833rd Operations Officer proceeded to chew out Mullen for disobeying his instructions to leave the plane on the taxiway. Instead, he pulled it into a hardstand to avoid blocking other planes. After looking at the plane it was easy to see Major Rex's viewpoint. The ground crew later commented there were about 300 holes in the plane."

1074 "John Volin was removed from the plane and it was determined that a piece of flak had severed a main artery below the heart and he had died almost instantly. That piece of flak, the size of the end of your thumb, had gone through armor plate, a rack of .50-caliber ammunition and lodged in John's chest. The plane had about 30 holes in it so *Rugged But Right* was truly rugged. Co-pilot I believe was Chuck Connors. Members of the original crew that day were Charles Felt, radio operator, Donald Reynolds, ball turret gunner, Doc Cagle, engineer, Doyle Burkett, waist gunner and John Volin, tail gunner."

1075 43-38037 flown by Lieutenant Raymond F. Jackson. 7 KIA. 2 PoW. 43-38154 flown by Lieutenant Harold E. Oesch. 8 KIA 1 PoW. Both Fortresses were from the 836th Bomb Squadron.

1076 The Cologne motor works and the Hamm marshaling yards were also attacked. 15 heavies and 11 fighters FTR.

1077 John McClane returned to the USA and he trained as a pilot but the war ended before he could be posted overseas.

1078 B-17G 43-38546 "S"

1079 A short while thereafter, over Holland, Bisaro's crew baled out. All the crew survived 2 to be taken PoW, the other 7 including Johnson, returning to duty.

1080 During September 1944 German oil production plummeted to only 7000 tons and draconian measures were called for. Reich-minister Albert Speer was given 7,000 engineers from the army and an unlimited number of slave laborers to reconstruct the synthetic oil-producing plants. Hundreds of additional flak guns were erected around the "*Hydriesfestungen*," as the plants became known and workers, who now came under the direct supervision of the *SS*, built deep shelters in which to take cover during air raids. Plants quickly demonstrated a remarkable ability to regain full production quotas and between bombing raids were able to produce 19,000 tons during October (39,000 tons in November).

1081 By this time the *Luftwaffe* had only 360 fighters and pilots available for combat duty in *I./Jagdkorps*, 90 of which were in action against the U.S. air forces, 7 October. 52 bombers and 15 fighters were destroyed for the loss of 20 pilots KIA and 4 injured.

1082 B-17G 43-37625 OR-W *Cheri* and Lieutenant Robert W. Harris' crew FTR on 2 November 1944 (2 KIA. 7 PoW).

1083 "When we reached base, we learned that Lieutenant Brown and his crew had returned from the mission. Probably assuming that the entire squadron was lost, they turned around after the first fighter attack. A third plane, piloted by Lieutenant Schumacher, I believe, aborted about midway during the mission because of a mechanical malfunction."

1084 In B-17 43-37566 QE-O *Fortress Joker,* which was alternatively named, *A Little Behind; The Joker* and finally, *Fortress Joker*.

1085 "No one was injured or wounded with the exception of the co-pilot, Lieutenant Ward, who was on his first indoctrination ride with me that day. He had his chute catch in the top of a tall tree and fell hard, injuring a leg. I went through the usual solitary, interrogation and travel to a 'permanent camp' where I was 'rescued' by the Russians in May of 1945. None of the other crewmembers were in the same *Stalag* I was in. I did see 3 or 4 of the enlisted men in a truck, which moved us at one time. Conversation was forbidden, so we did not exchange much information. I did see George Webb, navigator, Lyle DeRousse, bombardier and Lieutenant Ward in France before coming back to the USA." Eugene V. Beggs, flight engineer in Lieutenant Delbert B. Main's crew, whom Horace C. Waldorf had been co-pilot, prior to forming his own crew, recalls: "We were all deeply shocked to learnt that Waldorf and crew had been shot down. We were all very close to him but never had the opportunity to get acquainted with his new crew. The enemy fighters I saw were highly respectful of a tight formation and quite often further discouraged by our own fighter escort. I think some of the most severe attacks against a formation were in sheer desperation. These were usually head-on attacks with several fighters hitting the formation in a one pass, mass attack. They quite often took out most of the 13-plane formation and suffered heavy loss themselves. This was quite true on 24 December 1944 when General Castle was shot down. We were a short distance behind, at a lower altitude and passed through much of the debris."

1086 43-38278.

1087 Our crew make-up was; pilot, James Rieck from Texas; navigator, Billy McVicker from California; bombardier, Dale Reinhart from Pennsylvania; engineer and top turret gunner Elton Fritz from Washington; radio operator and gunner, Giuseppe Amore from Massachusetts: waist gunner Roy Krick from Minnesota; ball turret gunner, Matthew Palese from Maryland; nose turret gunner John Boyce from Illinois; tail gunner Richard Bronn from Massachusetts and of course myself.

1088 42-102441.

1089 Wendel struck the roof of a house on landing and bounced off it into a back yard. He was soon captured after being surrounded by an angry mob that wanted to beat him. Being able to speak German was probably the only thing that saved him from being beaten to death. He learned later that two of the crew had been murdered in this way. All except the bombardier, ball turret gunner and the engineer, were put on a train for Frankfurt and finally PoW camp.

1090 Altogether 4 bombers in the 457th Bomb Group were lost over the target, including Luper's wingman and the deputy lead ship piloted by Lieutenant Moland. Luper and Captain Kriehn survived and were taken to *Dulag Luft* for interrogation and eventual shipment to *Stalag Luft IIIA*. Politz was a disastrous raid for the 457th. The 38 aircraft that returned to base were badly damaged and 16 required sub-depot repairs. Only 4 ships came through unscathed. A short time later Colonel Harris E. Rogner assumed command of the "Fireball Outfit."

1091 "Our crew had been together since Lincoln, Nebraska and were very close. The other members of the crew were Joseph A. Kayatta, co-pilot; Robert H. Brucks, bombardier; Charles A. Bacharach, engineer and Johnny J. Wilson, radio operator. Solomon was sent back to the States to a hospital. I was sent to the 15th Air Force in Italy and assigned to the 815th Bomb Squadron, 483rd Bomb Group where I started flying again. Later with my new crew in Italy we were shot down over Ruhland, Germany on 22 March 1945 and those of us that survived were taken prisoner."

1092 Klusmeyer, co-pilot Fred Wright and Ferrell landed in Boppard, Germany, near the same farmhouse and they were taken prisoner. Miller also survived but although one or two of the enlisted men initially managed to avoid capture, they were eventually caught.

1093 43-37894.

1094 *Yesterday's Dragons: The B-17 Flying Fortress over Europe during WWII* by Abel L. Dolim.

1095 *Silver Meteor* was finally lost, on 15 March 1945, when it was involved in a taxi-ing accident and salvaged.

1096 43-38189.

1097 Love was captured at 0900 hours on 19 October. Some weeks later he had the heartwarming pleasure of seeing three of the EM of his crew. The tail gunner Conwell was blown out of the tail section. Raymond Hutt was blown out of the waist gunner's compartment and the radio operator, Ledford, was blown out of the top section of the craft's radio compartment. The ball gunner, Stevens, had not emerged from the ball nor did he have his chest pack on at the time the wing disengaged itself from the aircraft. Out of a crew of 9 only 4 survived. After spending about 8 months in *Stalag Luft III*, Sagan and Moosburg, Harry Love was liberated by Patton's 3rd Army on 29 April 1945 and he returned home in May of that year.

1098 On the final raid, on 30 November, 29 American bombers and 40 fighters were shot down. Between 8 October-2 November 1944, the *Luftwaffe*, in an effort to regroup and to conserve forces for Adolf Galland's proposed *Gorse Schlag*, largely avoided combat with the bomber formations. Only on 2 November, fighter forces were again hurled en masse against the 8th Air Force attacking oil plants in central Germany, notably Leuna. However, of the 490 fighters in action that day, 120 were shot down, 780 pilots surviving. 40 bombers FTR, 30 of which were destroyed by FW 190s of *Sturm Gruppen* IV./JG 3 and II./JG 4 who lost 30 of the 61 aircraft dispatched - almost a 50% loss rate. While raids on oil centers did not noticeably diminish the *Luftwaffe's* fighter capacity, it seriously hampered He 177 bombing operations in the east, so although Doolittle's oil raids were not directly aiding the 8th, they were helping to shorten the war. Ironically, the only units not greatly affected by the oil campaign were the Me 262 *Jagdverbande*, which used the low-grade petrol still in abundance. During September Hitler had reconsidered the Me 262's role as a fighter rather than the fighter-bomber he had once envisaged. Forty were immediately formed into a fighter unit, commanded by the Austrian fighter ace, Major Walter Nowotny. "Kommando Nowotny," as it was known, became operational in October 1944 and, during the first month of operations, shot down an estimated 22 American bombers.

1099 Whitlock was flying as Command Pilot in 44-3246, a 34th Bomb Group B-17G, piloted by Captain Vernon G. Alexander.

1100 43-38340.

1101 One crewman was made PoW; the other 8 men aboard evaded with help from the Dutch Underground and were hidden until May 1945.

1102 The 91st lost 12 Fortresses. It was for his actions this day that 2nd Lieutenant Robert E. Femoyer, a navigator in the 447th Bomb Group, was posthumously awarded the Medal of Honor. Femoyer's B-17 was rocked by three flak bursts, which showered the aircraft with shrapnel. Femoyer was hit in the back and the side of his body but refused all aid despite his terrible wounds so that he might navigate the Fortress back to Rattlesden. He was propped up in his seat to enable him to read his charts and the crew did what they could for him. It was not until they reached the North Sea that Femoyer agreed to an injection of morphia. He died shortly after the aircraft landed.

1103 in 43-38359.

1104 6 KIA.5 PoW. "Lieutenant James 'Jim' Muise, navigator landed just prior to me unhurt except he was also bleeding from the nose and ears because of the explosion and ran over and spilled the air out of my chute and got me unbuckled from it. Sgt Alfred Atkins, tail gunner managed to jump out of the plane but the rest were blown-out. Five of the 11-man crew survived the explosion but all landed far apart with the exception of Muise and me. The last I saw of my three crewmembers was when I was put in jail that night in a small town called Hemsbach."

1105 B-17 44-6290 in the 836th Bomb Squadron flown by 2nd Lieutenant Joseph I. Herring. 2 KIA. 7 PoW.

1106 A beacon combination with H_2X.

1107 It was the largest air and ground cooperative effort to date when over 4,000 Allied aircraft dropped more than 10,000 tons of bombs on enemy targets.

1108 Paul Husar, the navigator, was called Judge because he held a law degree. Later, in civilian life, he became a real judge down in Texas.

1109 42-102600.

1110 Hager enjoyed only the briefest of freedom before being captured in the Leipzig area by an *SS* trooper on a motorcycle. Later, he was marched through a throng of about 300 irate villagers and had a tooth knocked out by a rifle butt after turning to look at a Bf 109. He was taken to a jail in Erfurt run by *Gestapo* before being sent to *Dulag Luft* for interrogation. He subsequently became a guest of the German Government at *Stalag Luft IVA*, Keifheyde, in Pomerania.

1111 His victim was a 78th Fighter Group P-47 Thunderbolt from Duxford; the only P-47 lost this day when the fighter group was part of the escort for 366 B-24s of the 2nd Bomb Division attacking oil refineries at Hamburg. In all, the 8th lost 4 B-24s and 15 fighters on the Hamburg raid. JG 1 lost 20 fighters (including 8 in 2 minutes over Erfurt) and 14 pilots killed in combat with the American fighters on 21 November. Four were wounded. Two victories were recorded over B-17s, one each to *Leutnant* Demuth and *Unteroffizier* Enderle. *Feldwebel* Oswald was credited with a *Herausschuss*. *Defending the Reich; The History of Jagdgeschwader 1 "Oesau"* by Eric Mombeek.

1112 The 490th Bomb Group lost 1 aircraft, *Pennsy Belle*, flown by 2nd Lieutenant Frank Delmerico. 9 PoW, 1 KIA.

1113 *Jagdkorps* I prepared to launch 550 fighters, although in the event, just over 400 would make contact with the enemy formations. As the heavies passed Oldenburg in the north and headed southeast towards the Elbe, FW 190A-8/-9s of I and II./JG 1 and Bf 109G-14s of III./JG 6 were sent off from Mecklenburg and JG 301 were brought to a state of readiness on its airfields at Stendal, Sachau, Solpke and Salzwedel.

1114 II./JG 1 alone lost 5 fighters to the P-51s in as many minutes. JG 6 lost three pilots near Salzwedel and the 9th *Staffel* lost 4 fighters. II./JG 1 alone lost 5 fighters to the P-51s in as many minutes. JG 6 lost three pilots near Salzwedel and the 9th *Staffel* lost 4 fighters.

1115 The Weather Scouts claimed 5 enemy fighters shot down and one damaged. Escorting Mustangs accounted for 7 fighters of III and IV./JG 27. Oberleutnant Heinrich Sterr, 16th *Staffel* CO, IV./JG 54 was shot down by a P-51 over Vorden whilst coming into land. Sterr had 130 victories, 127 of them on the Eastern Front. *Hauptmann* Haase, CO I./JG 3 "Udet" was killed in a crash on take off after he collided with his wingman. Total B-24 losses this day were 21 while 53 returned battle damaged and with 15 crew aboard these KIA. The B-24 gunners claimed 12 fighters shot down while the escort fighters claimed 42 kills, of which the 361st Fighter Group claimed 23 enemy aircraft shot down. The *Luftwaffe* had suffered very heavily: losing 122 fighters, with 57 pilots killed and 30 wounded. JG 301 alone lost 39 fighters and 26 pilots KIA or MIA and 13 wounded. JG 1 lost 11 pilots KIA or MIA. P-51s of the 364th Fighter Group, one of the groups protecting the 1st Bomb Division, shot down two Bf 109G-14s of JG 26. *Leutnant* Erich Ahrens of 3./JG 26 shot down Lieutenant Jack Gaston of the 364th Fighter Group. (9 P-47s and P-51s and 13 B-17s were lost this day). Next day, 27 November, the ranks of the *Tagjagd* were further depleted with another 51 fighters and 31 pilots KIA, to Mustangs. By December 1944, *I. Jagdkorps* had only just over 1000 fighter pilots left alive, two-thirds of them hastily trained and very green replacements.

1116 "Bill Meyer inherited the *Witch* from us and early in January 1945, they caught a direct burst and exploded in the air with no survivors. The *Witch* must have done close to 80 missions when it went down."

1117 Lieutenant Owen W. Winters (who shared the same hut as Voss) and the entire crew of 42-97985 except for the tail gunner, who was seriously hurt, were killed. The crew of 44-8177 crash-landed and were uninjured.

1118 *Magnificent Obsession* was lost with 2nd Lieutenant Carl J. Faust, Jr.'s crew on 9 March 1945 when it was shot down by AA and crashed at Mülheim, Germany. Two men were KIA and 7 survived to be taken prisoner.

Chapter 20:

1119 He would increase his score to 12 with a triple kill on 23 December and another victory followed on 25 December when he destroyed a Bf 109 SW of Bonn. With another Bf 109 destroyed on 14 February 1945 his final score reached 14 confirmed victories.

1120 44-8518. Only one man in the 9-man crew survived to be taken prisoner of war.

1121 The 1st Bomb Division's attack on the marshaling yards at Ehrang, Germany, earned a commendation from Brigadier General Howard M. Turner. "I wish to extend to you and all officers and men of the bombardment groups which participated in the mission of 23rd December 1944 my congratulations for the excellent manner in which the mission was executed. Operating in extremely adverse weather conditions, these units exhibited a high degree of determination and skill in clearing the Division area, attacking the marshaling yards at Ehrang and landing in weather conditions equally as adverse, without the loss of a single aircraft. Excellent bombing results were obtained. Convey to participating officers and men my appreciation of a job well done…'

1122 Schilling was awarded a DSC (his second) for his leadership on the mission. He was now the leading 8th Air Force fighter ace in combined air and ground victories.

1123 One 63rd Squadron P-47 went down during the mêlée, whilst another with serious battle damage managed to regain Allied-held territory before the pilot had to bale out.

1124 During the combat Comstock fired 1229 rounds of API. His attacks were made with only the left guns firing, as the armorer had not cocked those in the right wing. His two victories took his score to five. (Promoted to lieutenant colonel in 1954 and to colonel on 15 January 1966, he flew two tours in Vietnam, the first as CO of the 481st TFS, for a total of 170 missions in SE Asia). The 61st Fighter Squadron, which provided top cover, claimed five e/a. JG 26 lost 4 FW 190A-8/9s (*Unteroffizier* Hermann Bischoff, Obergefreiter Erhard Schmidt of 2nd *Staffel* and *Unteroffiziers* Edwin Zubiako and Franz Wering of 3rd *Staffel* were KIA) and 5 others crash-landed, injuring two of the pilots. 364th Fighter Group Mustangs shot down two FW 190 Doras. (Feldwebel Werner Frass was KIA. *Leutnant* Helmut Wirth, who was WIA landed and ran from his 190D before it exploded. (Wirth was KIA on 4 March 1945 when a 391st Fighter Squadron, 366th Fighter Group P-47, shot him down). Major Anton "Toni" Hackl, CO II *Gruppe*, claimed one of the 364th Fighter Group Mustangs before he led 5 fighters off towards an unescorted heavy bomber formation near Cologne. These turned out to be 30 RAF Lancasters and an *Oboe*-equipped 8 Group Mosquito flying a daylight operation against the marshaling yards in the city. (See *The JG 26 War Diary Vol.2* by Donald Caldwell. Grub Street, London. 1998). Hackl claimed one Lancaster and the Mosquito. Six more Lancasters were claimed by 5 other pilots. One of the Lancasters that FTR was flown by Squadron Leader R. A. M. Palmer DFC who was leading the formation-attack. His Lancaster was hit by flak and set on fire but Palmer got his bombs away before his aircraft went down out of control. He was awarded a posthumous Victoria Cross. See *Battles With the Nachtjagd* by Theo Boiten and Martin W. Bowman (Schiffer Publishing. 2006).

1125 44-8444.

1126 Brigadier General Castle was posthumously awarded the Medal of Honor; the highest ranking officer in the 8th Air Force to receive the award. General Henry H. Arnold, Chief of the U.S. Air Forces, later dedicated Castle AFB in his honor. His loss was felt greatly by many in the 94th Bomb Group at Bury St. Edmunds where he had taken over a demoralized outfit after relinquishing a staff job and had knocked it back into shape. At the end of the war one of the prisoners held in a PoW camp near his former base at Bury St. Edmunds was, ironically, Field Marshal von Rundstedt.

1127 Rasmussen flew 23 missions; his last on 8 April 1945 and three food drop missions.

1128 For 4 B-17s destroyed, IV./JG 3 lost two pilots MIA and 5 PoW on 24 December. The *Luftwaffe* suffered the loss of 85 pilots KIA/MIA, plus another 21 wounded or taken prisoner.

1129 The FW 190's most glaring weakness throughout its service life was its poor high-altitude performance, and to correct this late in 1944 the FW 190D-9, more popularly known as "long-nosed Dora" or Dora-9, entered service, first with JG 54 and later 1./JG 26. Some pilots warmed to the Dora while others were not so enthusiastic. A liquid-cooled Jumo 213A engine, not Kurt Tank's first choice but the only option available at this stage of the war powered the new model. In front of it the annular radiator gave the impression of a radial. The long in-line engine had to be balanced by a lengthened rear fuselage to maintain the correct center of gravity, which resulted in the FW 190D being 4ft longer than the FW 190A. The Dora lacked the high turn rate and incredible rate of roll of its close-coupled radial-engine predecessor though it was slightly faster, having a maximum speed of up to 422mph at 21,650ft. The new fighter was also faster in the climb and dive than the FW 190A but at low altitude, the top speed and acceleration were inferior to those of Allied fighters. Methanol-water injection produced excellent acceleration when it was required in combat but this was in very short supply and most Doras had a top speed of around 360mph. It was planned to introduce engine-mounted cannon but the war situation resulted in the standard D-9 being armed only with two 13mm MG 131 machine guns above the engine and two 20mm MG 151/20 machine cannon in the wing roots.

1130 P-51D 44-14685.

1131 See *The JG 26 War Diary Vol.2* by Donald Caldwell. Grub Street, London. 1998

1132 Introduced in the spring of 1944, the K-14 gun sight was fairly advanced for its time. The sight had a 100mm fixed reticle instead of the P-51Bs optical sight with a 70mm reticle, which was too small for any angle-off shooting. The new sight made deflection shots and range estimation somewhat easier. It consisted principally of a piece of slanted, clear glass centered above the instrument panel directly in the pilot's line of sight. Onto the glass was projected a center dot of yellow light, known as a "pipper," which was surrounded by a circle formed of 8 diamond shaped dots. Once the pilot set the known wingspan of an enemy plane using a knob on the sight itself, he then centered the pipper on his target and, using the control knob mounted on the throttle handle, expanded or contracted the diamonds so that they continually bracketed the target. The K-14 automatically calculated the amount of lead needed for the range of the target and so long as the pilot kept the pipper centered on the enemy aircraft and enclosed it tightly within the diamonds; he had an excellent chance of scoring hits.

1133 The second B-24 (42-51572 flown by Lieutenant David W. Foster) had taken off and hit the trees and had made a wheels-up belly landing in the field near the base. The third Liberator (42-95115 *Topper II* piloted by Lieutenant Karl F. Schellhas) had done exactly the same and had landed almost on top of the crashed aircraft. Fire crews found only the charred remains of the 10 crew in *Topper II* and five men were killed and 4 injured in Foster's B-24. The crew of the first B-24 to take off (42-94881) piloted by Lieutenant John F. Moffette with Lieutenant Colonel Albert L. Wallace the Command Pilot in the right hand seat, baled out over Suffolk after heading the bomber towards the North Sea. The fourth B-24 to take off was 42-95032 *Silver Chief* flown by Lieutenant Donald E. Reab. The fifth ship off crash-landed at Attlebridge airfield. See *The 467th Bomb Group History* by Perry Watts (Schiffer) and *Reluctant Witness: Memoirs from the last year of the European Airwar 1944-45*, James J. Mahoney and Brian H. Mahoney.

1134 44-6528 in the 334th Bomb Squadron.

1135 4 KIA. 5 PoW.

1136 43-38215. Blackman's 418th Bomb Squadron crew were on their 13th mission.

1137 Only three men in each crew aboard 42-31066 *Fools Rush In* and 43-38124 flown by Lieutenant Williams survived.

1138 "Bill said that he reached behind his head to fire the Verey pistol to call for help and a 20mm shell exploded and knocked him out. When he came to he rang the bell and then managed to get his 'chute on. When he got down to the nose the ship blew up. He came to falling through the air and pulled his ripcord. The next thing he remembered he was on the ground and Krauts were standing around him. They told him that another boy (Bob Freshour) had been found with his 'chute open but he was dead." Basil Numack, one of the waist gunners and Joe Pearl were killed by fighters. Carson was unable to get out of the ball turret and Fortney did not have his 'chute on. Andy Herbert, the tail gunner and Tom Pace survived and were made PoW. Tom Pace was blown out of the ship. The last thing he remembered he was lying on the floor in the waist and could not move. When he recovered consciousness he reached for his ripcord but the concussion had broken his shroud and his parachute was dangling above his head. He finally gathered his senses and pulled the ripcord. "I landed in the middle of a field surrounded by woods. I took off my 'chute and started into the woods but the Krauts were coming from all directions with rifles. This was enough to make me stop. There was also about 6 inches of snow on the ground. They searched me and said, 'For you the war is over.' I did not realize the significance of this statement until later. At Frankfurt (Oberusel) we were put in solitary confinement, interrogated and accused of being spies unless we gave the information our interrogators needed. I said my dog tags were proof enough and refused to answer any questions. Finally, I was handed a piece of paper with answers to most of the questions and told to sign it. I refused and was taken back to my 8ft by 13ft cell. The truth was they knew more about what was going on than I did."

1139 43-38408.

1140 Raigh Mason adds: "I must have popped my chute too soon because I passed out, came to once, quite close to the ground, and passed out again. I had a compressed fracture of the 4th and 5th lumbar region and a broken collarbone (clavicle). When I came to four or five farmers surrounded me and I could not get up. I knew my collarbone was gone but I did not know about my back except that it was very painful. The farmers got me up and took me to a nearby farmhouse where they gave me some soup and relieved me of my GI watch, wallet, cigarettes and my escape kit. In a short while a German soldier arrived on a motorcycle sidecar and they loaded me in and took me to a big room filled with 8th Air Force personnel that had been shot down that day. Some of my crew were there and we made believe that we did not know each other. I ended up that night at a *Luftwaffe* base. Nurses set the shoulder but it didn't hold. They didn't have the proper bandages. A flying officer in the bunk above mine who had lost a leg died that night. Next morning I left for *Dulag Luft*. When I left in the morning I saw what appeared to be a flyable B-17 sitting on the ramp. At Obermasfeld (Lazaret) my collarbone was reset and I was then sent to *Stalag XIIID* at Nürnburg. The camp was pretty grim."

1141 43-38436, piloted by Lieutenant Charles C. Webster went down with 4 men KIA including the two pilots (5 PoW). 43-38535 piloted by 2nd Lieutenant Ralph A. Whitcomb was hit after the target and went spinning down in flames (5 KIA. 4 PoW).

1142 B-17G-35-BO 42-31987 had two names during its time in the 100th Bomb Group. The original name was *Shilaylee* but in June 1944 when the plane was taken over by J. D. Williams's crew it was renamed *The Little Skipper* for the pilot's one-year-old son. Some say that the aircraft had this name on the left-hand side of the fuselage while the original name and winged Irish club was retained on the left.

1143 Of the 6 men in Rojohn's crew who baled out, 4 survived. S/Sgts Little and Chase were KIA. 4 of the McNab crew also survived.

1144 42-107233 flown by Lieutenant Wallace G. Wilson went down and all 9 crew survived. 43-38381 piloted by 2nd Lieutenant William Mayo went down with the loss of all 9 crew. 42-31895 flown by 2nd Lieutenant Paul L. Carroll was shot down (9 PoW). 43-38459, flown by John F. Marin, was crash-landed near Emden (1 KIA. 8 PoW). *Luftwaffe* units lost 37 pilots KIA/MIA, including one *gruppen Kommandeur* and three *StaffelKapitäne* and a further 12 pilots injured.

1145 43-38223.

1146 The lead ship (B-17G 44-8352) was piloted by Captain David B. Whitlock and Lieutenant R. B. Malone, 862nd Bomb Squadron.

1147 Following the bombs' blast the aircraft went into wide spirals, but was under control. #1 and #3 engines were on fire. One crew reported that Malone waved his hand as the aircraft left the formation. When the aircraft was at 15,000ft one of the crew was seen to bale out. It is believed that there was an explosion in the plane at 5000ft, at which point the aircraft fell off in a tight spin and crashed. All 10 crew were KIA. Lieutenant Henry B. Skeen's crew at this point became a lead crew and gave up *Milk Run* to a new crew. Skeen flew 26 missions and later became a command pilot.

1148 German production of fighter aircraft actually increased through 1944 into 1945. It had peaked in September 1944, when 1874 Bf 109s and 1002 FW 190s were completed. (Though that same month, an average of three German fighters – and two pilots KIA - were lost for every B-17 or B-24 shot down). The dispersed manufacturing plants were beyond the power of the 8th Air Force to seriously damage. Therefore, some postwar surveys concluded that the

8th Air Force bombing offensive was a failure. But the bombing was just good enough that the *Luftwaffe* fighters had to keep rising to attack and then the P-51s and P-47s mostly destroyed them.
1149 300 aircraft were lost, 235 pilots were killed and 65 pilots were taken prisoner.

Chapter 21:
1150 Following correspondence with Lorenz Rasse and Herr Boehme in 1986 Walt Konantz learned that the pilot of the Me 262 (Werke Nu. 110601 9K+EH) was *Unteroffizier* Alfred Färber of 1./KG 51 another former bomber unit that was converting to the jet aircraft at Giebelstadt. Färber was on an acceptance flight following maintenance and repair work on his Me 262.
1151 44-8563 flown by Lieutenant Omar D. Stemple, which crashed at Gutenpaaren after being hit by flak and fighters. 2 KIA. 9 PoW.
1152 The 20th Fighter Group claimed 19-and-a half victories and the 353rd Fighter Group claimed 9 enemy aircraft shot down. In all, 161 enemy aircraft were destroyed. Only 13 P-51s and three Thunderbolts were lost during the great air battle of 14 January. JG 300 reported 27 pilots killed and 6 wounded and JG 301 had 22 pilots killed and 8 wounded. General Jimmy Doolittle sent a message of congratulations to Colonel Dregne. In part it read: "You gave the Hun the most humiliating beating he has ever taken in the air. Extend my personal admiration and congratulations to each member of your command, both ground and air, for a superb victory." The 357th Fighter Group, which was to finish the war with no less than 38 aces, was awarded a Distinguished Unit Citation for its impressive part in the battle.
1153 In all JG 26 lost 7 FW 190D-9s and 4 Bf 109G/Ks in the Cologne area. Among the dead and missing was *Ritterkreuzträger Oberleutnant* Gerhard Vogt CO 5th *Staffel* who had 48 victories was another 78th Fighter Group victim. His FW 190D-9 was shot down SE of Cologne after he tried to escape in cloud near the ground. Major Anton "Toni" Hackl returned to receive confirmation of a 78th Fighter Group P-51, his 175th victory and another downed 78th Fighter Group Mustang was awarded to Gefreiter Mittag for his first kill. A second mission flown by the 78th Fighter Group later in the day ran the kill tally to 14-0-14 when the 83rd Squadron's red flight bounced 4 FW 190s in the traffic pattern of an airdrome north of Diepholz, Germany. See *The JG 26 War Diary Vol.2* by Donald Caldwell. Grub Street, London. 1998. Anton "Toni" Hackl scored 192 *Abschüsse*, 105 of which were on the Eastern Front and 87, which included 32 *4-mots*, were on the Western Front. He was awarded the *Schwerten* (S) or Knight's Cross with Oak Leaves and Swords). *Luftwaffe Fighter Aces* by Mike Spick, Ivy Books, 1996.
1154 B-24 42-95223 *Little Lulu* and the 5 crew aboard were lost.
1155 42-94838.
1156 42-95164 *Lady Eve* flown by 2nd Lieutenant James R. Dodd (8 KIA. 2 PoW) and 42-50868 flown by 2nd Lieutenant William N. Schuster (5 KIA. 4 PoW).
1157 49 years later Walt Konantz learned that the fighter was Bf 109G-14 WerkeNummer 464493 "Blue 32" and that it was being flown by Oberleutnant Waldemar Balasus II./JG 27. On 28 January a flight of 5 Bf 109s had taken off from Liegnitz near Breslau in Silesia (eastern Germany). Their destination was Boyens-Haderslev airfield in Denmark about 400 miles northwest. The flight leader was Feldwebel Horst Petzschler. No.2 was *Hauptmann* Post; No.3 Oberleutnant Balasus; No.4 Oberleutnant Mielke and tail end Charlie, Oberleutnant Müller. This mid point refueling stop was Stendal, a city about 60 miles west of Berlin. Feldwebel Petzschler had his orders to take these student officers, all former Ju 88 bomber pilots, to the Danish airfield to join EJG-1 a training school to check out bomber pilots, transport pilots and even glider pilots, on the Bf 109. After returning to Stendal the officers pulled rank on Petzscler and all 4 flew to Hamburg to spend the night with relatives. Petzscler flew on to their destination alone on 29 January. That day the three student pilots took off from Hamburg at about 1300 hours for Denmark. It is knot known why the 4th plane did not take off with the others. Waldemar Balasus led the 3-ship flight. He was carrying an external fuel tank under his fuselage while his two wingmen were not carrying external tanks. About 30 minutes after take off, they were cruising northwest at 5000ft when they spotted 4 Mustangs at 5 o'clock level. The P-51s were about 5 miles behind but were slowly closing on the flight of Bf 109s. When the Bf 109s broke Lieutenant Roy D. Miller leading Acorn Yellow flight went after one and Lieutenant Thomas Kiernan the other. The two 109s pursued by Miller and Kiernan also bellied in after being damaged by gunfire and both pilots survived. Petzschler meanwhile, had landed at Voyens-Hhadersley at about the same time as his comrades were being shot down. Balasus arrived two days later by train and the other two downed pilots who had been more seriously injured, arrived a week later in an ambulance. Petzschler, who flew 297 combat sorties in FW 190s and Bf 109s, with 26 confirmed victories (22 of them Soviet, a B-17 and one B-24 and two P-51s) was shot down 13 times with 11 crash-landings and two bale outs. All his shootdowns were due to flak except one when a P-51 shot him down on 28 May 1944 near Magdeburg. His wingman was killed that day. On 4 may 1945 Petzschler flew his Bf 109G-10 (Yellow 5) to Sweden Where he was interned until January 1946, at which time he was turned over to the Soviets. He spent almost 4 years as a prisoner as all German pilots were considered war criminal by the Russian authorities. After the war many captured German pilots were put on trial in Russia and executed, while others were interned for up to 10 years. Petzschler emigrated to Canada in 1953 and later entered the USA where he worked at several aircraft manufacturing plants as a toolmaker. He retired to Wichita after his last job with Beechcraft. Waldemar Balasus survived the war and he died on 18 September 1989. Walt Konantz flew 64 missions 8 August 1944-3 February 1945. He shot down two Bf 109s, one Ju 88 and one Me 262, the first one claimed by the 55th Fighter Group. He was also credited with 21 locomotives destroyed, one staff car, one truck and one German soldier on a motorcycle on 21 February 1945 without firing a shot! He also "spread a little misery" in a German occupied French town by riddling the municipal water tower. His missions after 6 October 1944 to the end of the war were flown in 44-72296 CL-P No.6. Lieutenant Colonel John McGinn had named it "*DA QUAKE*" and flew it until his last mission on 6 October. He also downed 4 enemy aircraft in CL-P and he and CL-P were over Berlin on 7 occasions. At this point, CL-P No.6 was taken over by Walt Konantz who renamed the fighter "*Saturday Night.*" It carried him through a full tour, flying over 60 combat missions without a mechanical abort. All 4 of Walt Konantz's kills were in this Mustang. "*Saturday Night*" and its pilot were over Berlin three times and participated in the longest round-trip escort mission of the war when they escorted B-17s to Gdynia, Poland and returned. "*Saturday Night*" landed at Wormingford with 5 gallons of fuel remaining after logging 7 hours and 30 minutes flying time. Less than half the others made it back home, landing at closer airfields due to low fuel. Another pilot, Lieutenant Colonel Elwyn Righetti, flying CL-P in Walt's absence, downed one more Bf 109. Walt Konantz flew his last mission on 23 February 1945 and CL-P No.6 was taken over by his younger brother, 2nd Lieutenant Harold Konantz, who had just arrived as a replacement pilot. He left the name "*Saturday Night*" and had only to change the rank and first name on the canopy tail. On 7 April 1945 he was flying his 7th mission when he was hit by gunfire from the side turret of a B-17. He lost his coolant and the engine caught fire forcing a bailout. He was a PoW for the remainder of the war and CL-P No.6 ended in a fiery crash 50 miles northwest of Berlin.
1158 Accompanied by 900 fighters, 1200 B-17s and B-24s dropped 2267 tons of bombs into the "Mitte," or central district of Berlin, killing an estimated 25,000 inhabitants and destroying 360 industrial firms, heavily damaging another 170. Photo-Reconnaissance revealed that an area 1½ miles square, stretching across the southern half of the "Mitte" had been devastated. The German Air Ministry sustained considerable damage, the Chancellery was hard hit and the Potsdamer and Anhalter rail yards were also badly hit.
1159 Ten of the crew of 44-8379 reached the ground safely. Rosenthal landed in Soviet territory and he was later reported to be in Moscow. The bombardier was KIA. Ernst caught his leg on a jagged edge of the bomb bay while baling out and he later had the leg amputated. Four other B-17s in the 100th Bomb Group FTR. (See *Century Bombers; The Story of the Bloody Hundredth* by Richard Le Strange, 100th Bomb Group Memorial Museum, 1989).
1160 Colonel Anthony Q. Mustoe, CO of the 40th Combat Wing, Captain Edward Terrell, Lieutenant Commander John B. Murray RN and the First Sea Lord were at Podington when the bombers returned and later examined the strike photos. Both Terrell and Murray had worked closely in the development of the explosive. Although only one hit had been scored, the officers were shown what the "Disney" bomb was capable of and further trials were ordered. On 4 April the 92nd Bomb Group dropped "Disney" bombs on U-boat pens at Hamburg However, the Allies' sweeping victories in the Low Countries and the vast distance to suitable targets in Norway, brought the "Disney" missions almost to an end.
1161 Dresden was targeted as part of a series of particualy heavy raids on German cities in Operation *Thunderclap* with a view to causing as much destruction, confusion and mayhem as possible to support of the Russian armies converging from the east.. The other cities were Berlin, Chemnitz and Leipzig, which like Dresden, were vital communications and supply centers for the Eastern Front. *Thunderclap* had been under consideration for several months and was to be implemented only when the military situation in Germany was critical. At the Yalta Conference early in February 1945 Josef Stalin the Russian leader and his army chiefs, asked that the RAF and 8th Air Force paralyze Berlin and Leipzig and prevent troops moving from the west to the eastern front. British Prime Minister Winston Churchill and American President, Franklin D. Roosevelt agreed on a policy of massive air attacks on the German capital and other cities such as Dresden and Chemnitz. These cities were not only administrative centers controlling military and civilian movements but were also the main communication centers through which the bulk of the enemy's war traffic flowed. Spaatz had set the wheels in motion with a raid on Berlin on 3 February. Magdeburg and Chemnitz were bombed three days later but the most devastating raids of all fell upon Dresden starting with an 800-bomber raid by the RAF on the night of 13/14 February.
1162 For most of the participating aircrew the Dresden raid of 13/14 February was another well executed and very efficient area bombing attack. Dresden was bombed in two RAF assaults three hours apart, the first by 244 Lancasters and the second by another 529 Lancasters. Calculations were that a delay of three hours would allow the fires to get a grip on the sector (provided the first attack was successful) and fire brigades from other cities would concentrate fighting the fires. See *Battles With the Nachtjagd* by Theo Boiten and Martin W. Bowman, Schiffer Publishing. 2006.
1163 Marshaling yards at Chemnitz, Magdeburg and Hof were also bombed as were a road bridge at Wesel, an oil depot at Dulmen, two airfields and 10 town areas and numerous targets of opportunity. 16 fighter groups escorted the bombers or flew area sweeps, strafing ground targets.
1164 316 B-17s actually attacked Dresden. The 8th Air Force was to return to the city of Dresden again in March and April 1945 on similar raids but the Allied air forces' top priority remained the oil-producing centers.
1165 Olds had scored 5 kills flying P-38 Lightnings in August 1944 before the 479th Fighter Group had converted to the P-51 that September. His first P-51 victory came on 6 October 1944 when he shot down a FW 190.
1166 Major Olds' claims for two Bf 109s and the FW 190 destroyed were confirmed and they took his score to 10. 1st Lieutenant Gail E. Jacobson, Newcross Green 2, wingman for Major Olds, recalled: "After the bounce we were at 6 o'clock high to the FW 190s so we dropped our noses and went down on them. The 190s dropped their tanks and went into a left turn, then cut back to the same heading. Major Olds closed on the E/A to the far right, so I slipped over to the left and tacked onto the middle one. Major Olds opened fire around 200 yards and dead astern of his 190. He got lots of good strikes all over the 190. I was within range of my own Jerry, so I opened fire, but hit propwash and was thrown off. Major Olds' FW

190 went off to the right and I didn't see him after that because I overshot and had to split-ess. I confirm Major Robin Olds' claim of two 109s destroyed and I also confirm that he scored many good strikes all over the FW 190." Major Olds only fired 407 rounds of .50 caliber API ammunition during the whole of three successful encounters, which speaks well of his skill and experience. It also complements the functionality of the K-14 gunsight he was using. That little beauty was a gyroscopically actuated, lead-computing optical system, which when properly used in circumstances of battle, assuming the pilot using it was the attacker, was called an "Ace-Maker." It computed the correct lead angle for target crossing speed at ranges from 200 to 800 yards. It contained two optical systems, one fixed, that projected a cross, surrounded by a 70-mil ring on a reflector glass. The other was the gyro system, which projected a circle of 6 diamonds that surrounded a central dot called the "pipper" on the reflector glass. The systems could be switched between or used simultaneously. The diameter of the diamonds could be changed by setting the span scale lever on the face of the sight or by rotating the throttle twist grip. This was called "ranging the diamonds". Once the target aircraft was engaged, properly framed and tracked for a minimum of one second, the sight computed the correct gunnery lead so that the pilot just had to keep what he wanted to hit "under the pipper." In actual usage, the sequence of operation was: 1. Identify the target and set the span adjustment lever to correspond with the span of the airplane. 2. Fly the airplane so that the target appears within the gyro reticule circle and rotate the throttle twist grip until the diameter of the gyro reticule corresponds to the target size. 3. Frame the target with the gyro reticule circle by rotating the twist grip as range changes. Track the target smoothly for one second and then fire. 4. Continue ranging and tracking while firing. While all this was occurring, when firing, the pilot was releasing 6 streams of armor piercing incendiary ammunition at the rate of 550 rpm per gun. The rounds were constructed so that when they struck an object such as an aircraft's skin they gave off a bright flash to indicate where they had struck. See *The 479th Fighter Group in WW2 in Action over Europe with the P-38 & P-51*. Terry A. Fairfield (Schiffer 2004).

1167 The Hoesch coking plant at Dortmund was estimated to be producing 1000 tons of benzol a month.

1168 including two B-17s to a Me 262 jet fighter of III./JG 7 flown by Gefreiter Notter.

Chapter 22:

1169 in 42-31922.

1170 in 43-38273.

1171 43-38035.

1172 "The tail of *Mr. Lucky* had landed in a cow pasture on a farm near Slijpe, Belgium. A local ferryboat steward, beached by the war, named Gilbert Deschepper, found him, cut him out of the tail with an axe, and evading German sympathizers took him to that British hospital. He fully recovered. No one knows to this day why that Fortress came up abruptly like that. It is speculated that the cloud hump may have had an updraft, or perhaps Rusecki flying formation, concentrating on the plane he was flying off of didn't see the cloud coming, then, suddenly loosing visibility, got vertigo. We'll never know. Some of the debris struck the Fort in the low diamond and it dove straight down to nearly the water. But, although there were oxygen leaks, two guns out of commission and the rudder jammed, it rejoined the formation and finished the mission."

1173 Electronic Counter Measures.

1174 This equipment reduced the effectiveness of radar-controlled flak guns.

1175 42-50313.

1176 44-40436. "We learned later that Lieutenant Down's crew had bombed a target of opportunity and then were subsequently hit by AA fire while attempting to leave the French coast near Calais. One of the waist gunners was injured and died before they could reach Manston."

1177 42-51302 flown by 2nd Lieutenant Willis G. Blakely crashed at Detmold, Germany. 5 KIA. 5 PoW.

1178 "The same oil refinery at Magdeburg was once again scheduled for attack on the 3rd of March. Our crew had the day off. For the first time in the last 7 strikes, the weather permitted all three squadrons to bomb visually. Even so, the 576th made a poor drop; they were 3800ft short. Our squadron was leading and although they didn't exactly put it right down the barrel, they managed to squeeze 54% into the 2,000ft mark. Several close sightings of Me 262s probably interrupted their train of thought to some degree. The flak didn't help either. It was intense and moderately accurate; causing extensive damage to ten of the ships. On the following day, a tank depot in the city of Aschaffenburg (SE of Frankfurt) was scheduled for mission #251. We were fortunate to be absent again! Due to bad weather over East Anglia, the Division formed up east of Paris. It should be said that they attempted to assemble, because it was poorly executed, leaving many stragglers who were then forced to latch onto other groups. The situation went from bad to worse with the deteriorating weather, and our Group (what there was of it), eventually attacked Pforzheim, a city SE of Karlsruhe and some 80 (?) miles south of the assigned target. Some of the wanderers straggled too far south and several B-24s (including some of ours) bombed the Swiss border towns of Zurich and Basle!'

1179 in 42 102481, later to be named "*Kentucky Winner*".

1180 in 44-8417.

1181 42-102636.

1182 in 43-38148.

1183 42-97979 *Leading Lady*.

1184 "All of Vaadi's crew did jump OK before their Fort blew up, although at the time only 5 parachutes were seen by the rest of us. Jino broke an ankle on landing. Oddly enough, this same Oschatz was the IP for the mission."

1185 In Tripp's crew both of the Leon's and Ed, Dan, Francis Henry and Robert were killed. Only Ed Batz and Richard were listed as missing. The co-pilot of Tripp's crew has said: "There were several fires on the ship and the controls were evidently shot out because the ship would not respond. The bale out order was given both by bell and interphone. After the crew had ample time to get out, I went down to the nose escape hatch, finding the engineer sifting beside it because it was jammed. I reached over to pull the emergency release handle when the ship rolled over and blew up. The explosion knocked me unconscious. When I recovered I was falling free. I waited and pulled my chute. I was taken prisoner two hours later." "Francis Aires, navigator in Platt's crew, but in the Low Flight Lead on this raid, was shot four times and badly wounded, yet continued to navigate back to Great Ashfield. He was awarded the Silver Star."

1186 43-37871.

1187 in 44-8415.

1188 After the target, the low squadron was even further behind and therefore it headed for a different Rendezvous Point (RP), cutting a corner, and joined the 34th Group. But all then made it back to Great Ashfield without further losses. The only incident being that Bensing of the Lead (548th) Squadron in 4415 on his 26th mission, also had to land at B-53 in France to refuel.

1189 *Ritterkreuzträger Hauptmann* Gutmann of 9./JG 7 was killed during this action.

1190 B-17G-70-DL 44-6968.

1191 B-17G 43-39050 in the 863rd BS, piloted by 2nd Lieutenant George Graff, which crashed near Hildesheim, Germany. 3 KIA. 6 PoW.

1192 B-17G 43-38297 in the 860th BS, piloted by Lieutenant Charles A. White, Jr., was shot down by Me-262s and crashed near Apelem, Germany after the 9 man crew had baled out. The crew were taken PoW.

1193 Six of the attackers were shot down, two of them by RAF Mosquitoes. The attack on Bury St. Edmunds damaged the control tower. Great Ashfield was bombed and strafed and Rattlesden, Lavenham and Sudbury were also attacked. The intruders returned again on the night of 4 March but damage to the bases was insignificant.

1194 On 8 March Dolim flew as navigator of a B-17 transport, which hauled 27 officers and men from the 385th Bomb Group at Great Ashfield to Paris-Orly for 48-hour passes. "After a couple of hours in Paris we picked up a return load of 'happy warriors' from the 100th Bomb Group and deposited them at Thorpe Abbotts. Major Harry H. Crosby, the group navigator helped me navigate on the way back. It was good to see him again. We had first met on the *New Amsterdam* on our return to England in September."

1195 Stringent interrogations by Intelligence officers followed the debacle and some crews had their return to the States blocked because of the 6 weeks' investigation into the incident. The U.S. Ambassador had only recently attended a memorial service and visited reconstruction projects resulting from the previous bombing of Zurich on 18 September 1944. General Marshall urged Spaatz to visit Switzerland secretly and reparations involving many millions of dollars were made to the Swiss Government. A court martial was held with Colonel James M. Stewart appointed president of the court. Jackson W. Granholm, a 458th Bomb Group navigator at Horsham St. Faith and defense counsel, recalls, "I had the unpleasant honor to be the defense counsel for the pilot and navigator of a lead squadron crew who put a beautiful bomb pattern on the railroad yards in Basle. They thought they had bombed Freiburg, Germany and were tried in a general court for culpable negligence in the performance of duty. Because the questions were those of navigation, I was named to the defense board. The court was held at our group base at Horsham St. Faith…We achieved an acquittal after a week-long court, longest in history of the 8th Air Force.' No further action was taken though at least one lead crew was restricted to base until April 1945.

1196 "Two days later my photograph was taken for the group records. One look at it and I saw the same look that I have seen so many times on others. A sort of weariness is apparent but most of all the expression is one of emptiness, features completely drained of emotion. I have lost 15lb since I started combat flying but none of my shirts fit me around the neck - it has expanded almost one inch within the last year. My nerves are not what they should be; I've become tense, irritable and unfit to fly or live with. Today I feel a sense of pride in having played a small part in the great drama of those days that truly belong to history. I formed friendships, which have endured throughout the passing years with some of the finest men I have ever met. Many of our squadron mates suffered long imprisonment or gave their lives for our cause. As for the B-17, I am not ashamed to say that in 1944-45 I regarded her as a slow, flammable old lady who was really out of sorts among fast young friends and who became my potential enemy every time I flew a combat mission. Had it not been for the long-range escort fighter, the *Luftwaffe* would have driven us from the skies over Germany."

1197 Trier became operational as the first tactical American airfield in Germany having been overrun by the 3rd U.S. Army and a member of the 36th Fighter Squadron landed a P-47 on an airstrip near Aachen, Germany, the first American combat plane to voluntarily land in Germany since the start of the war.

1198 42-102481.

1199 On 1 March Wentland had flown his first mission, to the marshaling yards at Ingolstadt. "Immediately after the debriefing session of our first mission (and while the jigger of medical libation still addled my brain), I thought to visit the CO of the 564th and ask for a transfer back to stateside. My reason was that Mission #1 had made me as expert on aerial warfare as I ever would be. Consequently, I felt I would be of more value to the war effort back home at some Advanced Training Center preparing new crews for the realities of aerial warfare. However, the bike ride back to the 564th area must have cleared my brain somewhat because I didn't stop at Squadron HQ after all. You see with a clearer head I reasoned that our CO just wouldn't have grasped the significance of my request."

1200 The co-pilot and the engineer were later placed in a hospital for Russian wounded and the 7 remaining crew were "looked after" by their Russian Army hosts. The crew was disrobed by some Russian Army women who then proceeded to wash them with cloths and basins of water. Their uniforms were taken away and replaced with 'pyjamas' (the type worn in concentration and prison camps). Montague continues: "Little did we 7 suspect that everything would be pantomime for two ensuing weeks and these pyjamas would be our clothes. We were under constant guard. We were prisoners - not guests of our 'allies.' Just as we were falling asleep several of us heard the unmistakable click of the lock in our door. Next morning we had our first breakfast. I recall being very thirsty and I spotted a large cut-glass container of water in the center of the oval breakfast table. After pouring a glass-full, I took a large swallow and my breath was whisked away! Pure vodka at 0530! I tried to warn the crewmembers but was speechless. A few others made the same error. The Russians roared with laughter. For the next two weeks we used vodka in our cigarette lighters; it worked marvelously like an acetylene torch!" Montague and his fellow crewmembers were finally transported to Poznan and on through Poland to Lodz where they continued to Kiev. They finally reached a Russian fighter base near Poltava where a Lend-Lease C-46 flew them nearer freedom. Montague recalls: "After flying for quite a time we noticed the co-pilot coming back to the area where the wing joins the fuselage. He unscrewed a cap of some sort, removed a rubber siphon from his jacket and proceeded to drink something. Could this possibly be de-icer fluid? Our pilot, his head still bandaged from our crash, remarked, 'My God! I may have to end up flying this plane.' After flying some hours at high altitude over some mountain ranges, we began out descent and finally made a very rough landing in Tehran, Persia. This was the last we were to see of any Russians. After spending a few days at the American base in Tehran we were flown on to Abadan by an American pilot in a C-47 transport. From then on it was shuttle hops by American pilots to Cairo, a nearly deserted base in the Libyan desert, on to Athens, Paris and finally to Lavenham. Since we were due for R&R about this time, we were granted a week's leave and spent a most pleasant time in Girvan, Scotland before returning to base to fly two more missions."

1201 43-38046.

1202 43-38071 in the 849th Bomb Squadron.

1203 in 43-38549.

1204 12 B-17s and a B-24 were shot down and 16 bombers were forced to land inside Russian territory. Although flak was particularly hazardous on this mission the defensive honors went to 37 Me 262s of the Geschwaderstab and III./JG 7 who claimed 12 B-17s shot down and 6 *Herausschüsse* (HSS) as well as one fighter for the loss of only two jets. The "Bloody Hundredth" lost 4 bombers this day, including one ship, which was cleaved in two by Me 262 gunfire. By the end of the month the 8th was to lose 30 bombers to the German twin-engined jets.

1205 1st Lieutenants Gail F. Jacobson and Frank M. Taylor shared the other FW 190. See *The 479th Fighter Group in WW2 in Action over Europe with the P-38 & P-51*. Terry A. Fairfield (Schiffer 2004). *Unteroffizier* Wilhelm Düsing and Feldwebel Karl Hofmann in the 2nd *Staffel* flew the two FW 190s claimed by Major Olds and Jacobson/Taylor. Both German pilots were shot down at 1620 hours and they baled out but Hofmann's parachute failed to open and Düsing hit his head when he landed and his injuries ended his operational career. See *The JG 26 War Diary Vol.2* by Donald Caldwell. Grub Street, London. 1998. Olds destroyed a Bf 109 over the Dummer Lake on 7 April and he also damaged a Me 262, to take his wartime score to 13 victories. He was credited with 4 MiG-21s shot down in combat during the Vietnam War January-May 1967. See *Stars & Bars: A Tribute to the American Fighter Ace 1920-1973*. Frank Olynyk. Grub Street. 1995.

1206 The 21 March missions were the start of a massive 4-day assault on the *Luftwaffe*, with 42,000 sorties being made over German airspace.

1207 At 0950 at 7500m, S of Dresden.

1208 Müller was credited with 16 *Abschüsse* whilst serving with III./JG 53 1943-44 and 6 (one RAF Mosquito and 5 U.S. aircraft) flying the Me 262. On 25 March 1945 he shot down a Liberator in flames at 1025 at 7000m S of Lüneberg. No parachutes were observed. (The left turbine of Müller's 262 was hit by return fire and he force-landed at Stendal, where he rammed into a Ju 88 parked in Hangar No.5. He managed to douse the fire before it got out of control). On 4 April 1945, he shot down a Liberator at 0945 at 7000 meters in the Bremen area. On 9 April 1945 Müller destroyed a Thunderbolt at 8000m W of Berlin. On 17 April he shot down a B-17 at 7000m in the Elbschleife N of Prague.

1209 Captain Robert B. Grettum s crew in the 392nd Bomb Group returned to Wendling in their PFF Liberator, firing flares at 2000ft in celebration of completing their final mission. Somebody fired a flare from a gun that was probably not locked. The flare-gun probably spun round, because the aircraft caught fire. Grettum and 7 others perished in the ensuing crash.

1210 *Oberfeldwebel* Lübking with 38 *Abschüsse and* Feldwebel Eichner, both KIA.

1211 Eight of the 9 20th Wing squadrons loosed their wicker loads with attached multi-colored parachutes in the dropping zone. They encountered spasmodic and highly accurate small-arms fire. This and heavy 20mm cannon fire caused the loss of 6 20th Wing Liberators - three in the 446th Bomb Group and three in the 448th Bomb Group. 17 of the Bungay Buckeroos' B-24s sustained battle damage, while the 448th's lead ship, carrying Colonel Charles B. Westover, the CO, crash-landed in England with two men wounded. The deputy lead crew was forced to bale out over England. 20mm fire pierced the armor plating and struck the control column of one of the 93rd Bomb Group Liberators but the two pilots escaped injury in the subsequent explosion.

1212 On 24 March, the 15th Air Force bombed Berlin for the first time when more than 150 B-17s hit the Daimler-Benz tank works in the city. Meanwhile, 271 B-24s finished off the Neuburg jet plant bombed on 21 March. On 27 March, 12th Air Force P-47 Thunderbolt fighter-bombers strafed Lechfeld airfield in Bavaria and destroyed large numbers of German jet aircraft.

1213 B-17G-85-BO 43-38311 in the 860th BS, piloted by Lieutenant Lewis B. Hoagland was hit by flak and crashed near Buchholz, Germany. 1 KIA 9 PoW. B-17G-105-BO 43-39226, in the 861st BS, piloted by Lieutenant Martin Dwyer, Jr., was also hit by flak and crashed near Pinneberg, Germany. 1 KIA, 9 PoW.

1214 B-17G-105-BO 43-39078.

1215 near Bartlow. The aircraft was salvaged on 26 April.

1216 43-39088.

1217 One plan, in the autumn of 1944, had been Adolf Galland's "*Grosser Sclag*" ("Big Stick"). The *general der Jagdflieger* had worked out detailed plans to launch a mass-attack by 3700 fighters in 18 *Geschwaders* against a large-scale Allied daylight bombing raid in order to deliver a knock-out blow. His assembled force however, bled to death during the Ardennes offensive and *Bodenplatte* and during raids like 26-27 November 1944.

1218 Mustangs and P-47s shot twelve down, three by flak, 5 were lost in crash landings and 11 were lost to unknown causes. 18 of the *Elbe* pilots were KIA or MIA, with 7 others wounded. Total German fighter losses on the day were 133 aircraft destroyed.

1219 B-24 44-49254.

1220 11 KIA, 2 PoW.

1221 B-24 44-49533.

1222 It was not the first time Kunkel, who evaded and returned to England had survived a shooting down. On 25 December 1944 during the Battle of the Bulge the 389th were bombing crossroads when they were attacked by a single German, fighter, which caught Kunkle's plane and the crew all baled out. The crew were coming down in their chutes between the lines and could see both the Americans and the Germans coming after them. As soon as he touched down Kunkle ran towards the American troops who thought they might be German spies. They asked, "Who won the World Series?" Kunkle said, "How the hell do I know. I was on the boat coming over at the time. Probably the Dodgers." The GIs got them to the rear and they were eventually sent back to Hethel.

1223 B-17G 43-39070 in the 860th Bomb Squadron, piloted by 2nd Lieutenant Warren P. Whitson, Jr., was attacked by enemy fighters and crashed near Warin, Germany (10 PoW).

1224 All 10 in 2nd Lieutenant George E. Burich, Jr.'s crew were KIA. 44-8744 crashed at Gifhorn.

1225 B-17 43-38514. As well as severing the left stabilizer it knocked off a large part of the rudder and the fighter's propeller sliced into the fuselage cutting the control cables to the tail surfaces. With very little control left Martin and his co-pilot made it back to Thorpe Abbotts with the help of the crew who moved to the rear of the B017 to raise the nose and the front. The Fortress was soon repaired by fitting a new rear half to the fuselage.

1226 B-17 42-37972 *Gold Brick*.

1227 "Martin and King managed to make it back to England and they were each awarded the DFC. 'Wilk' and our crew got credit for the '109.'"

1228 B-17 42-97071 flown by Lieutenant Arthur R. Calder. Both fighter and bomber were last seen in the vicinity of Steinhuder Lake, spinning down in flames. All 9 KIA.

1229 "Lieutenant William 'Bill' Howard [B-17 44-8334] went down on this mission. A FW 190 got him on one pass, a diving fly-through attack. His navigator, Douglas Jones, had gone to navigation school with Turnip. The three of us had gone to Norwich the night before on pass. He was taken prisoner and was released after VE Day – the civilians who captured him had knocked his front teeth out. [6 PoW. 3 KIA]. After this mission the mental and physical strain was so much that I was too tired to keep up the log of my missions. Missions were coming every day with no rest in between. I would land from a mission and the pilots' truck would be waiting to carry me to the mission critique. From there I would stagger over to the mess hall and gorge myself After that I would waddle over to my barrack and fall in bed until the Alert Sergeant woke me the next morning for briefing. Following that schedule I didn't have much time to write notes on my missions. I planned to catch up on them in a couple of days while they were still fresh in my mind but somehow I never got around to it."

1230 B-17G 42-31582.

1231 43-38971 in the 34th Bomb Group, whose pilot, 2nd Lieutenant Myron A. Boiser and 9-crew, were KIA.

1232 "I was removed from that location, put through several more interrogations by the forward American Military Police and, finally, moved to the 90th General American Hospital in Verdun, France. There, during an inquiry by an American Intelligence officer, I learned that beside myself, there was only one other survivor from my crew. My best friend, Eddie Shibble, was miraculously still alive. Without a parachute, he had fallen 23,000ft in the other half of the plane and was still sitting in the ball turret as it crashed through the trees! While I was recuperating at Coral Gables Hospital in Florida I went home on leave and found Eddie in the Deshon Army Hospital at Butler, Pennsylvania. It was, to say the least, an emotional reunion. 'Since Eddie was Catholic and I was Protestant, we had often visited each other's churches, as well as having attended Jewish services together. I said to Eddie, 'When you found out your chute was gone, what did you do?' 'I stayed in the ball turret and prayed,' he replied. 'To whom?' I asked. 'To anyone who would listen.' It was only by the Lord's grace that both Eddie and I survived, when both of us could have died so easily, so many times."

1233 B-17G 44-6513 "*Boisie Bell*" in the 860th Bomb Squadron, piloted by Lieutenant John E. Silverman was hit by flak and crashed near Munich. 10 KIA.

1234 B-17 43-38840 crashed at Zobbenitz. 8 of 2nd Lieutenant Delbert D. Reeve's crew were KIA. Only the bombardier baled out and he evaded.

1235 On 10 April German jet aircraft shot down 10 American bombers but 297 German aircraft were destroyed on the ground.

1236 42-102636.
1237 The crew of Jim Staber had settled on the name of *Smokey Stover* after a cartoon character for their Fort [42-31378] but hadn't painted anything yet. But listen to David Farmer tell it: "It was getting close to take-off time and Charles Guffy, our ball gunner, had been in town the night before drinking limey beer and was feeling a trifle woozy. We gave him a little oxygen and poured him into the turret. A short while into the flight when we started having all our oxygen checks, someone called Guffey a 'Rum Dum.' He in turn called someone else a 'Rum Dum.' On the next oxygen check, when the pilot called for a report, without realising it, the reports were coming back from all stations as 'Rum Dum 1,' 'Rum Dum 2,' 'Rum Dum 3,' etc. After the mission was over, and we had landed safely, our pilot, Jim Staber, told the crew chief, Keen, that we had changed the name of the plane to '*Rum Dum*.'"
1238 On 11 April Varnedoe flew his 23 mission when he was assigned to 2nd Lieutenant Harold A. Lovegreen's crew in 6569: "By now there were no more oil targets and German factories were no longer a menace. Only tactical bombing in behalf of the onrushing ground forces remained. That is why we again went to a railroad marshaling yard, this time at Ingolstadt. We bombed it visually with no flak at the target. Bombs away with excellent results. A real 'milk run.'" On 14 April 1945 Varnedoe flew his 24th mission when he and the rest of the crew were back on "*Possible Straight*" on the mission to Royan. On 16 April the crew had another pass and they went on what was their last trip to London while in the Army Air Force.
1239 B-17G 44-48427.
1240 One 458th Liberator left the formation after bomb release and headed inland with one engine feathered. A total of 180 heavies, supported by the French ground troops of the 6th Army Group, bombed 16 defensive installations. French forces later captured the port. "*The Stars And Stripes* Monday 26 April announced. "Heavies Throw Fire To Free Bordeaux; Using a new type of fire bomb for the first time, as well as thousands of high explosives, 8th Air Force Fortresses and Liberators flew more than 2450 sorties Saturday and Sunday in a drive to wipe out German pockets of resistance in the Gironde area and free the big French port of Bordeaux... Many of the 1300 bombers taking part in yesterday's clear weather assault were loaded with tanks which explode on impact, ignite incendiary material and splash the flaming contents over an area of approximately 60 square yards. Tanks containing more than 460,000 gallons of this liquid were showered on the target areas in the vicinity of Royan on the east side of the Gironde estuary in an assault co-ordinated with movements of French ground forces. In addition to the new fire bomb, more than 6,000 100 lb incendiaries were dropped in the same area- There was no enemy opposition,-and the bombers were unescorted." Ralph Elliott concludes: "As a result of the Royan mission the French awarded a batch of *Croix de Guerre* medals to the crews who led the mission. At least, that was the intent, as we knew it at the time. Unfortunately, the French didn't make that designation clear and the medals were awarded in the 8th Air Force in order of rank (RHIP -Rank Has It's Privileges), so the furthest down the medal got was to 467th CO, Colonel. Shower plus several 2nd Air Division officers - none of whom flew on the mission."
1241 On 16 April over 700 aircraft were destroyed.
1242 Post-war enquiries revealed that the parachute was that of Major Georg-Peter "Schorch" Eder who was the pilot of the Me 262 that rammed *Towering Titan*. There were no survivors aboard the Fortress. Eder's Me 262 had been damaged by gunfire and the pilot, who chivalrously allowed opponents to escape the final lethal burst when they were obviously finished, baled out for the 17th time in the war, and having been wounded 14 times in the process! *Towering Titan* was Eder's 78th and final confirmed kill. See "*John Burn One-Zero-Five...": The Story of Chelveston Airifled and the 305th Bomb Group in pictures* by William Donald. (GMS, 2005).
1243 "Later I was told that we peeled off to the right before disappearing into the cloudbank. Delmar Hallet said that the gap was just not wide enough for our plane, which was on the far right of the formation and that our plane could not have been brought in any closer."
1244 "I traded my parachute, flight pants and boots for a uniform shirt, pants and shoes, but kept my flight jacket and asked that a message be sent to Deopham in hopes of stopping an MIA telegram's being sent to my parents which, as it turned out, they were spared. I spent the night with the 64th, which was under curfew because of German snipers in the area. The next day, a Sunday, I caught a ride on a truck convoy going to Nancy, France and the same evening took the night train to Paris and was told to report to the Francia Hotel, 100 Rue Lafayette, which the Air Force had taken over for billeting transient Airmen. The following day I flew to London where I reported to the 8th Air Force HQ after which, I caught the train for Deopham Green, where I surprised the few people I knew there when I walked in that evening. Personal Effects Section had gathered up my belongings, so I had to reclaim them. I was given a week's leave for rehabilitation at Moulsford Manor near Reading and returned to base on 4 May. The War ended on the 7th and I was transferred to the 728th Squadron on the 8th. I flew two prisoner haul missions and quite a few practice flights with several different crews mostly for celestial navigation practice in preparation for the flight back to the USA in late June."
1245 43-38118.
1246 "The 385th only flew one more mission in the war, to Utrecht on 2 May 1945, and I was not on it. The 385th sustained the last shot fired in the war against the 8th Air Force. It slightly damaged one B-17. The tactical mission of the 8th was also declared at an end after 2 May and no more combat missions were flown. On 7 May Germany unconditionally surrendered. We shot Verey pistols (flares) in lieu of fireworks and felt very, very happy. We had survived! It was a doubly good day for me as well, for my promotion to 1st Lieutenant came through!"
1247 "Fame's Favored Few" was the oldest group in the 8th and this was its 310th and final mission. The total would have been greater had it not been for the group's role as a training outfit during the early part of the war, so other groups surpassed the mission total.
1248 Ten Me 262s of I./JG 7, fighting to the last, claimed 7 B-17s shot down.
1249 RAF *Manna* operations had begun on 29 April.
1250 On 7 May the heavies flew their sixth and final supply drop to Holland. The supply drops had already claimed two B-17s, when they collided soon after take-off. Tragically, the war was to claim its final heavy bomber victims on the 7 May mission. A 95th Bomb Group B-17 with 8 crew and 6 passengers (from the Horham photographic section), piloted by Lieutenant Lionel N. "Spider" Sceurman, got into difficulties over the North Sea after a food drop near Hilversum. At 1500ft oil was seen spurting on to the No.2 engine nacelle. Oil pressure dropped to zero and thick, acrid smoke filled the fuselage. The engine was shut down, but the fire extinguishers failed to put out the fire. Sceurman, who put the Fortress into a controlled dive to "blow" the fire out, knew the engine was in danger of exploding, so he ordered the crew to bale out. Incredibly, 6 of the crew and one of the photographers got out before the engine exploded at 600ft. The bomber's wingtip hit the surface of the sea and the aircraft cartwheeled and sank immediately. All this happened just 5 miles east of Benacre Ness on the Suffolk coast. A Lancaster of 550 Squadron diverted the nearest ship to the scene and the RAF crew even dropped their own Mae Wests to crewmembers seen in the water. An ASR OA-10A Catalina of the 5th ERS at Halesworth picked up Lieutenant James R. Schwarz, the co-pilot and S/Sgt David C. Condon, the togglier. Lieutenant Russell J. Cook, the navigator, was rescued by a RAF Walrus but died before reaching hospital. The bodies of "Spider" Sceurman and Norbert Kuper, the armorer-gunner and one of the 6 passengers, were recovered and, together with those of Cook and S/Sgt John J. Keller, the ball turret gunner, whose body was washed ashore, were interred in the U.S. Military Cemetery at Madingley, near Cambridge. Sceurman had wanted to celebrate the final day of the war with the same crew he had trained with in Florida and at the flight line had asked Tony Braidic, his original bombardier, if he would change places with Dave Condon. Braidic declined and flew the last mission with Lieutenant Paul Crider instead.

Chapter 23:

1251 The blackout had officially ended on 24 April but the lights-out after dark rule remained in force until 10 May. *Country Boy Combat Bomber Pilot*, by Robert H. Tays. 1990.
1252 A few miles away bomber, fighter and transport wings of the U.S. 3rd Air Force, established in England on 7 August 1948 under the command of Major General Leon W. Johnson, continue to maintain the peace and freedom won by units of the 8th Air Force operating from "Little America" alongside their RAF comrades in 1942-45.
1253 Colonel Albert Shower was the only bomb group commander in the 8th Air Force to bring his group to England and retain command of it until the end of hostilities.

Bibliography

Air Ministry, *The Rise and Fall of the German Air Force 1933-1945* (London 1948).
Bekker, Cajus, *The Luftwaffe War Diaries* (London 1967).
Boiten, Theo and Bowman, Martin W., *Raiders of the Reich. Air Battle Western Europe. 1942-1945* (Airlife 1996).
Boiten, Theo and Bowman, Martin W., *Battles With the Luftwaffe.* (Janes 2001)
Bowman, Martin W., *Great American Air Battles of WW2* (Airlife, 1994)
Bowman, Martin W., *Four Miles High* (PSL 1992)
Brown, Captain Eric, *Four of the Finest,* RAF Yearbook (1975)
Cora, Paul B. *Yellowjackets! The 361st Fighter Group in World War II* (Schiffer 2002)
Donald, William, *John Burn One-Zero-Five...'* (GMS Enterprises 2005)
Gotts, Steve *Little Friends: A Pictorial History of the 361st FG in WW2* (Taylor Publishing 1993)
Held, Werner *Fighter! Luftwaffe Fighter Planes and Pilots* (New York 1979)
Caldwell, Donald J. *JG26. Top Guns of the Luftwaffe* (New York 1991)
Caldwell, Donald J., *The JG 26 War Diary Vol.2.* (Grub Street, London. 1998)
J. Campbell, *Focke Wulf FW 190 In Action,* (Squadron Signal, Carrolton, TX 1975)
Davis, Larry *P-51 Mustang In Action.* (Squadron Signal 1981)
Duxford Diary 1942-45 (W. Heffer & Sons 1945)
Fairfield, Terry A. *The 479th Fighter Group in WW2 in Action over Europe with the P-38 & P-51.* (Schiffer 2004)
Goebel, Robert J. *Mustang Ace,* (Zenith Press 1991)
Green, William *Warplanes of the Third Reich.* (Doubleday New York 1972)
Gruenhagen, Robert W. *Mustang, the story of the P-51 fighter.* (Arco 1976)
Hall, Grover C. *One Thousand Destroyed.* (Morgan Aviation Books Dallas 1946)
Jarrett, Philip *Aircraft of the Second World War.* (Putnam 1997)
Johnson, Air Vice Marshal J. E. 'Johnnie', CBE DSO DFC *Full Circle: The Story of Air Fighting.* (Pan 1964)
Long, Eric F. *At The Controls.* (Airlife 2001)
Morris, Danny, *Aces and Wingmen.* (London: Neville Spearman, 1972)
McLachlan, Ian, *USAAF Fighter Stories.* (Sparkford. Haynes Publishing, 1997).
McLachlan, Ian, *USAAF Fighter Stories; A New Selection.* (Sutton Publishing, 2005).
Miller, Kent D. *The 363rd Fighter Group in WWII In Action over Europe with the P-51 Mustang.* (Schiffer. 2002)
Mombeek, Eric *Defending The Reich; The History of JG1 "Oesau"* (JAC Publications 1992)
Morgan, Len *P-51 Mustang. Famous Aircraft Series.* (Morgan Aviation Books 1963)
Nowarra, Heinz J. *The Focke Wulf 190; A Famous German Fighter.* (Harleyford 1965)
Nijboer, Donald, *Cockpit: An Illustrated History.* (Airlife 1998)
Olynyk, Frank *Stars & Bars: A Tribute to the American Fighter Ace 1920-1973.* (Grub Street 1995)
Powell, R. H. *The Blue Nosed Bastards of Bodney.* (Privately Published Dallas 1990)
Price, Dr. Alfred *Luftwaffe Handbook 1939-1945* (London 1986).
Priller, Josef *JG26. Geschichte eines Jagdgeschwaders. Das JG26 (Schlageter) 1937-1945* (Stuttgart 1980)
Smith, J. R. and Kay Antony, *German Aircraft of the Second World War.* (Putnam London 1972)
Speer Frank E., *The Debden Warbirds: The 4th Fighter Group in WWII.* (Schiffer 1999)
Spick, Mike, *Luftwaffe Fighter Aces* (Ivy Books 1996)
Scutts, Jerry, *Mustang Aces of the Eighth Air Force.* (Osprey 1994)
Swanborough, G. & Green, William, *The Focke Wulf 190.* (Arco New York 1986)
Wagner, Ray, *American Combat Planes.* (Doubleday & Co. Garden City, New York. 1982)
Wells, Ken, *Steeple Morden Strafers 1943-45.* (East Anglian Books 1994)
Wood, Tony & Gunston, Bill *Hitler's Luftwaffe* (London 1979)

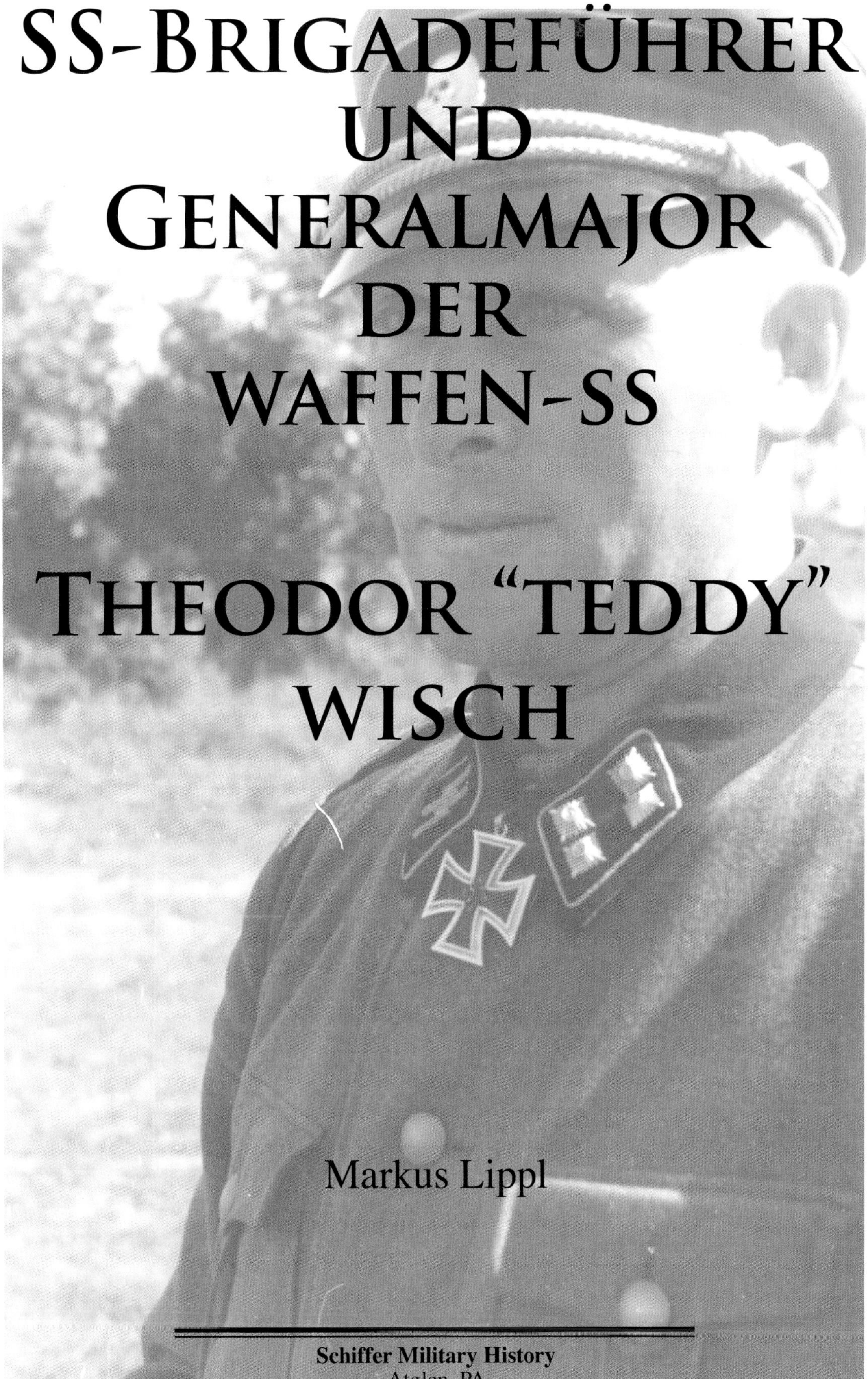

SS-Brigadeführer und Generalmajor der Waffen-SS

Theodor "Teddy" Wisch

Markus Lippl

Schiffer Military History
Atglen, PA

To
Lennart and Tamiris

Book Design by Ian Robertson.

Library of Congress Control Number: 20122931292

Printed in China.
ISBN: 978-0-7643-4046-8

We are interested in hearing from authors with book ideas on related topics.

Published by Schiffer Publishing Ltd.
4880 Lower Valley Road
Atglen, PA 19310
Phone: (610) 593-1777
FAX: (610) 593-2002
E-mail: Info@schifferbooks.com.
Visit our web site at: www.schifferbooks.com
Please write for a free catalog.
This book may be purchased from the publisher.
Try your bookstore first.

In Europe, Schiffer books are distributed by:
Bushwood Books
6 Marksbury Avenue
Kew Gardens
Surrey TW9 4JF, England
Phone: 44 (0) 20 8392-8585
FAX: 44 (0) 20 8392-9876
E-mail: Info@bushwoodbooks.co.uk.
Visit our website at: www.bushwoodbooks.co.uk
Try your bookstore first.